Communications
in Computer and Information Science

1754

More information about this series at https://link.springer.com/bookseries/7899

Ana I. Pereira · Andrej Košir ·
Florbela P. Fernandes · Maria F. Pacheco ·
João P. Teixeira · Rui P. Lopes (Eds.)

Optimization, Learning Algorithms and Applications

Second International Conference, OL2A 2022
Póvoa de Varzim, Portugal, October 24–25, 2022
Proceedings

 Springer

Editors
Ana I. Pereira ⓘ
Instituto Politécnico de Bragança
Bragança, Portugal

Florbela P. Fernandes ⓘ
Instituto Politécnico de Bragança
Bragança, Portugal

João P. Teixeira ⓘ
Instituto Politécnico de Bragança
Bragança, Portugal

Andrej Košir ⓘ
University of Ljubljana
Ljubljana, Slovenia

Maria F. Pacheco ⓘ
Instituto Politécnico de Bragança
Bragança, Portugal

Rui P. Lopes ⓘ
Instituto Politécnico de Bragança
Bragança, Portugal

ISSN 1865-0929   ISSN 1865-0937 (electronic)
Communications in Computer and Information Science
ISBN 978-3-031-23235-0   ISBN 978-3-031-23236-7 (eBook)
https://doi.org/10.1007/978-3-031-23236-7

This Springer imprint is published by the registered company Springer Nature Switzerland AG
The registered company address is: Gewerbestrasse 11, 6330 Cham, Switzerland

Preface

This CCIS volume 1754 contains the refereed proceedings of the Second International Conference on Optimization, Learning Algorithms and Applications (OL2A 2022), a hybrid event held during October 24–25, 2022.

OL2A 2022 provided a space for the research community on optimization and learning to get together and share the latest developments, trends, and techniques, as well as to develop new paths and collaborations. The conference had more than three hundred participants in an online and face-to-face environment throughout two days, discussing topics associated with optimization and learning, such as state-of-the-art applications related to multi-objective optimization, optimization for machine learning, robotics, health informatics, data analysis, optimization and learning under uncertainty, and Industry 4.0.

Five special sessions were organized under the following topics: Trends in Engineering Education, Optimization in Control Systems Design, Measurements with the Internet of Things, Advances and Optimization in Cyber-Physical Systems, and Computer Vision Based on Learning Algorithms. The OL2A 2022 program included presentations of 56 accepted papers. All papers were carefully reviewed and selected from 145 submissions in an single-blind process. All the reviews were carefully carried out by a scientific committee of 102 qualified researchers from 21 countries, with each submission receiving at least 3 reviews.

We would like to thank everyone who helped to make OL2A 2022 a success and hope that you enjoy reading this volume.

October 2022

Ana I. Pereira
Andrej Košir
Florbela P. Fernandes
Maria F. Pacheco
João P. Teixeira
Rui P. Lopes

Organization

General Chairs

Ana I. Pereira   Polytechnic Institute of Bragança, Portugal
Andrej Košir   University of Ljubljana, Slovenia

Program Committee Chairs

Florbela P. Fernandes   Polytechnic Institute of Bragança, Portugal
Maria F. Pacheco   Polytechnic Institute of Bragança, Portugal
João P. Teixeira   Polytechnic Institute of Bragança, Portugal
Rui P. Lopes   Polytechnic Institute of Bragança, Portugal

Special Session Chairs

João P. Coelho   Polytechnic Institute of Bragança, Portugal
Luca Oneto   University of Genoa, Italy

Technology Chairs

Alexandre Douplik   Ryerson University, Canada
Paulo Alves   Polytechnic Institute of Bragança, Portugal

Local Organizing Chairs

José Lima   Polytechnic Institute of Bragança, Portugal

Program Committee

Ana I. Pereira   Polytechnic Institute of Bragança, Portugal
Abeer Alsadoon   Charles Sturt University, Australia
Ala' Khalifeh   German Jordanian University, Jordan
Alexandre Douplik   Ryerson University, Canada
Ana Maria A. C. Rocha   University of Minho, Portugal
Ana Paula Teixeira   University of Trás-os-Montes and Alto Douro,
                                       Portugal
André Pinz Borges   Federal University of Technology – Paraná, Brazil
André R. da Cruz   Federal Center for Technological Education of
                                       Minas Gerais, Brazil

Joseane Pontes	Federal University of Technology – Ponta Grossa, Brazil
Juan Alberto G. Esteban	Universidad de Salamanca, Spain
Juan A. Méndez Pérez	University of Laguna, Spain
Juani Lopéz Redondo	University of Almeria, Spain
Julio Cesar Nievola	Pontifícia Universidade Católica do Paraná, Brazil
João Paulo Coelho	Polytechnic Institute of Bragança, Portugal
Jorge Ribeiro	Polytechnic Institute of Viana do Castelo, Portugal
José Ramos	NOVA University Lisbon, Portugal
Kristina Sutiene	Kaunas University of Technology, Lithuania
Lidia Sánchez	University of León, Spain
Lino Costa	University of Minho, Portugal
Luis A. De Santa-Eulalia	Université de Sherbrooke, Canada
Luís Coelho	Polytecnhic Institute of Porto, Portugal
Luca Oneto	University of Genoa, Italy
Luca Spalazzi	Marche Polytechnical University, Italy
Maria F. Pacheco	Polytechnic Institute of Bragança, Portugal
Manuel Castejón Limas	University of León, Spain
Marc Jungers	Université de Lorraine, France
Marco A. S. Teixeira	Universidade Tecnológica Federal do Paraná, Brazil
Maria do R. de Pinho	University of Porto, Portugal
Marco A. Wehrmeister	Federal University of Technology – Paraná, Brazil
Markus Vincze	TU Wien, Austria
Martin Hering-Bertram	Hochschule Bremen, Germany
Mikulas Huba	Slovak University of Technology in Bratislava, Slovakia
Michał Podpora	Opole University of Technology, Poland
Miguel Ángel Prada	University of León, Spain
Nicolae Cleju	Technical University of Iasi, Romania
Paulo Lopes dos Santos	University of Porto, Portugal
Paulo Alves	Polytechnic Institute of Bragança, Portugal
Paulo Leitão	Polytechnic Institute of Bragança, Portugal
Paulo Moura Oliveira	University of Trás-os-Montes and Alto Douro, Portugal
Pavel Pakshin	Nizhny Novgorod State Technical University, Russia
Pedro Luiz de P. Filho	Federal University – Paraná, Brazil
Pedro Miguel Rodrigues	Catholic University of Portugal, Portugal
Pedro Morais	Polytechnic Institute of Cávado e Ave, Portugal
Pedro Pinto	Polytechnic Institute of Viana do Castelo, Portugal

Contents

Optimization

Artificial Intelligence

Optimization in Control Systems Design

Measurements with the Internet of Things

Computer Vision Based on Learning Algorithms

Machine and Deep Learning

Machine and Deep Learning

Techniques to Reject Atypical Patterns

Júlio Castro Lopes[1]([✉])[ID] and Pedro João Soares Rodrigues[2][ID]

[1] Research Center in Digitalization and Intelligent Robotics (CeDRI),
Instituto Politécnico de Bragança, Bragança, Portugal
`juliolopes@ipb.pt`
[2] Instituto Politécnico de Bragança, Bragança, Portugal
`pjsr@ipb.pt`

Abstract. Supervised Classification algorithms are only trained to recognize and classify certain patterns, those contained in the training group. Therefore, these will by default, classify the unknown patterns incorrectly, causing unwanted results. This work proposes several solutions, to make the referred algorithms capable of detecting unknown patterns. The main approach for the development of models capable of recognizing these patterns, was the use of three different models of Autoencoders: Simple Autoencoder (SAE), Convolutional Autoencoder (CAE) and Variational Autoencoder (VAE), that are a specific type of Neural Networks. After carrying out several tests on each of the three models of Autoencoders, it was possible to determine which one performed best the task of detecting/rejecting atypical patterns. Afterwards, the performance of the best Autoencoder was compared to the performance of a Convolutional Neural Network (CNN) in the execution of the referred task. The conclusion was that the VAE effectively detected atypical patterns better than the CNN. Some conventional Machine Learning techniques (Support Vector Machine (SVM), Random Forest (RF), Logistic Regression (LR)) were also tested. The one that presented the best performance was the RF classifier, achieving an accuracy of 75% in the detection of atypical/typical patterns. Thus, regarding the classification balance between atypical and typical patterns, Machine Learning techniques were not enough to surpass the Deep Learning methods, where the best accuracy reached 88% for the VAE.

Keywords: Autoencoder · Deep learning · Convolutional neural networks · Atypical patterns · Machine learning

1 Introduction

Artificial Intelligence (AI) has been one of the areas in Computer Science that have gained more importance in recent years [1]. This increase in significance is due to its ability to perform tasks that historically only humans could perform and, in most cases, can execute them even faster and more efficiently than the human being himself/herself.

Within the area of AI, Neural Networks (NNs), a vast set of algorithms that work in analogy to human neurons, allow the recognition of the most diverse data patterns. Due to its recognition capability, the NNs, specifically the Supervised Classification Neural Networks (SCNNs), were a critical tool in developing the current work because they allow the grouping and classification of images using Deep Learning (DL). To be able to carry out the described task, SCCNs are subjected to a training process through which they learn to recognize specific patterns. These patterns are defined as belonging to a particular category/class. However, as SCNNs are only trained to recognize and classify specific patterns, those contained in the training dataset, when they find an atypical pattern comparing to the training dataset (i.e., a pattern that does not belong to any of the classes known to them), they will automatically classify the unknown pattern as belonging to one of the dataset classes, resulting in undesirable results.

This work entails creating a neural network (NN) strategy capable of correctly classifying patterns in the training dataset, as well as identifying and rejecting unknown patterns, which are classified as atypical and not belonging to one of the classes. Although this work is more focused on DL methods, several conventional Machine Learning (ML) algorithms have been tested.

Despite being a difficult task, developing a system capable of detecting/rejecting atypical patterns is critical because there is a massive amount of information that is constantly increasing in the real world. So, these algorithms must react appropriately to the new information, just as a human being would be able to. The capacity of NNs to recognize and classify patterns is advantageous and has many applications in the real world [2], such as image processing; segmentation and analysis; voice recognition; fingerprint identification; computer vision; seismic analysis; medical diagnosis.

In order to solve the proposed problem, three distinct models of AutoEncoders (AEs) (algorithms specialized in the reconstruction of the information through its learning) were used: Simple AutoEncoder (SAE), Convolutional AutoEncoder (CAE), and Variational AutoEncoder (VAE). After performing several tests on the mentioned models of AEs, it was determined which one performed better the task of detecting/rejecting atypical patterns to the training dataset. Subsequently, a Convolutional Neural Network (CNN) for classification, was also developed to compare its performance with the performance of the best AE, thus determining the model that best performs the detection/rejection of atypical patterns. Additionally, with the CNN model previously trained, the training features from this model were extracted, to test the ML algorithms' ability to detect atypical patterns. The present work was totally programmed using Pytorch.

2   Related Work

Since this paper aims to solve a well-known problem in DL and ML classification, several approaches have already been proposed.

Zero-Shot Learning: Zero-shot learning is a novel concept and learning technique without accessing any exemplars of the unseen categories during training. Yet, it is able to build recognition models with the help of transferring knowledge from previously seen categories and auxiliary information [3–7]. This Zero-shot Learning approach, aims to solve different classification problems. In these approaches, the objective is to learn the unseen objects and not detect/discard them. These papers propose an identification system that detects/rejects atypical patterns without direct learning, when faced with these unknown patterns.

Selective Net: At the time that Selective Net was published (2017), the rejection option had rarely been discussed in the context of NNs and had not been considered for deep NNs (DNNs). Existing NN works consider a cost-based rejection model [8,9], whereby the costs of miss classification and abstaining must be specified, and a rejection mechanism is then optimized for these costs [10]. The proposed mechanism for classification is based on applying a carefully selected threshold on the maximal neuronal response of the softmax layer (softmax response).

The work that most closely resembles the current work is Selective Net. However, the formulation of Selective Net is very different from our approach, since they have considered Monte Carlo - dropout and softmax response to be able to reject undesired patterns. The purpose of Selective Net is the same as ours, however they follow a different approach. In this work, we have used AE's, CNN for classification, and also ML techniques to be able to perform the rejection procedure.

3   Methodology

The present section describes the two types of NNs and all the ML techniques used in this work to solve the proposed problem.

3.1   Deep Learning Methods

The first proposal was made to detect/reject atypical patterns, taking into account DL concepts such as AE's and CNN's.

Autoencoder is a neural network composed of two components: an encoder and a decoder. The first, the encoder, is responsible for encoding the information contained in the input; the second, the decoder, is in charge of converting the encoded information back to its original format [11]. This procedure aims not to obtain an exact copy of the information contained in the input. The real purpose of this mechanism is to reconstruct information through its learning instead of its memorization. The reconstructed information has certain useful properties that have different natures depending on the type of AE used in the decoding process. In this project, the AE used was the VAE, since it was the one that had the best performance out of all the models of AE's used in Sect. 4.1. A VAE, like traditional AE's, consists of an encoder and a decoder, whose purpose is to reconstruct the information contained in the input in the best way possible. However, VAE's, unlike the others, allow the transformation of information and the production of new patterns from it. The production of new patterns by VAE's is possible if the training process is regularised accordingly. A slight modification was made to introduce that regularisation in the encoding/decoding process. Instead of encoding an input as a single point, it was encoded as a distribution over the latent space [12].

Convolutional Neural Network(s) make it possible to recognize data in many formats. However, due to the focus of this project being the processing of data in a specific type of format (image), it becomes relevant to specify that the type of NN used for this purpose is called CNN. Although this type of NN is not only used in image recognition, that is its main application [13]. Since pattern processing is a CNN's specialty, this NN will be beneficial in analyzing, classifying and grouping the patterns. The CNN will work as a classifier, so its output will be the standard one-hot code (10 units), which encodes the class to which each image belongs. After the training of the CNN, the values saved in the ten positions of the output vector will be numerically analyzed and compared to AE to conclude which one performs the best in the classification of atypical patterns.

3.2   Machine Learning Methods

Classification and regression tasks are both types of supervised learning, but the output variables of the two tasks is different. In a regression task, the output variable is a numerical value that exists on a continuous scale. In contrast, in a classification task, the output of an algorithm, fall into one of the various pre-chosen categories. The classification model attempts to predict the output value when given several input variables, placing the example into the correct category [14]. In this paper, supervised machine learning methods were used to perform the classification task. For a matter of comparison, some ML techniques such as Logistic Regression (LR), Support Vector Machine (SVM), Linear discriminant analysis (LDA), Random Forest (RF) and ADA-Boost were taking into account in this work.

Logistic Regression. LR is a classification algorithm used when the value of the target variable is categorical. Logistic regression is most commonly used in binary problems when the data in question has binary output, so when it belongs to one class or another, or is either a 0 or 1 [14]. LR has many applications in real programs such as, spam detection [15], credit card fraud [16] or even tumour prediction [17]. Multi-class LR classification extends standard LR by allowing the variable to predict, to have three or more values. The implementation of LR multi-class classification follows the same ideas as binary classification. When we have more than two classes, the true class is denoted by one, and the rest of the classes becomes zero. For prediction on given data, LR multi-class classification returns probabilities for each class in the dataset and whichever class has the highest probability is our prediction [18].

Support Vector Machine. For years, an enormous amount of research has been carried out on SVMs and their application in several fields of science. SVMs are one of the most powerful and robust classification and regression algorithms in multiple fields of application. The SVM has been playing a significant role in pattern recognition which is an extensively popular and active research area among the researchers [19]. SVM originally separates the binary classes with a maximized margin criterion. However, real-world problems often require discrimination for more than two categories. The multi-class classification problems are most commonly decomposed into a series of binary problems such that the standard SVM can be directly applied [20].

Linear Discriminant Analysis. Linear discriminant analysis (LDA) is generally used to classify patterns between two classes. However, it can be extended to classify multiple patterns. LDA assumes that all classes are linearly separable, and according to this, multiple linear discrimination function representing several hyperplanes in the feature space are created to distinguish the classes [21].

Random Forest. RF classifiers fall under the broad umbrella of ensemble-based learning methods. They are simple to implement, fast in operation and have proven to be highly successful in various domains [22]. The RF approach comprises many "simple" decision trees in the training stage and the majority vote across them in the classification stage. Among other benefits, this voting strategy can correct the undesirable property of decision trees to overfit training data. In the training stage, random forests apply the general technique known as bagging to individual trees in the ensemble. Bagging repeatedly selects a random sample with replacement from the training set and fits the trees to these samples. Each tree is grown without any pruning. The number of trees in the ensemble is a free parameter that is readily learned automatically using the so-called out-of-bag error [23].

Ada-Boost. The AdaBoost method, proposed by Freund and Schapire [24], utilizes boosting to obtain strong classifiers by combining the weak classifiers. The model is re-trained with the erratic predicted samples of the previous runs. This process is repeated several times [25].

4   Evaluation

This section presents several tests performed on the three distinct models of AEs used, in order to determine the model that best suits the detection of atypical patterns. Once determined the best AE model in the referred task, a mathematical formula will be built to determine a value (threshold) from which it will be possible for the network to classify this pattern as typical or atypical. Regarding CNN, the rejection procedure will consist of the determination of two threshold values. It will be possible to define conditions to classify the pattern introduced in the network as typical or atypical. For the ML algorithms, the process will be identical to the CNN, since we also have an output of 10 classes, but this time with probabilities and not with class activations.

4.1   Best Autoencoder Selection

Three distinct AE models were used in this work:

- Simple Autoencoder (SAE) - This model used four linear layers in the input, followed by ReLu activation functions. The following sequence of neurons was used in the SAE model: 784, 128, 64, 12 and 3. In order to improve the reconstruction capability, a neural addition variant was also added, being the number of neurons: 784, 128, 64, 12 and 12.
- Convolutional Autoencoder (CAE) - This model used two convolutional layers in the encoder, followed by ReLu activation functions and also MaxPool2D. The first convolutional layer used an input of 1 channels and output of 16, being the kernel size = 3, the stride = 2 and the padding = 1. The second convolutional layer used an input of 16 channels and the output of 12, the kernel size was 3, stride = 2, padding = 1. On the other hand, the decoder used 3 convolutional layers followed by ReLu activation functions. The first layer used an input of 12 channels and an output of 16, the kernel size = 3, the stride = 2 and the padding = 1. The second layer used an input of 16 channels and an output of 8, the kernel size = 5, the stride = 3 and the padding = 1. The third convolutional layer used 8 channels in the input, 1 in the output, the kernel size = 2, the stride = 2 and the padding as 1. For this model the neural addition variant was also added, in this variant the kernel size, the stride and padding were kept the same, the number of channels was modified. In the input, the first layer was modified to 1 in the input and 32 in the output, the second layer was then modified to 32 channels in the input and 24 in the output. In the output, the first layer was modified to 24 channels in the input and 32 in the output, the second layer was modified to 32 channels in the input and 16 channels in the output and finally the third one, used 16 channels in the input and 1 in the output.
- Variational Autoencoder (VAE) - This model is composed by 4 fully connected layers. The first layer is composed by a linear layer, which has 784 neurons in the input and 400 in the output. The second layer is composed by two identical linear layers, which one with 400 neurons in the input and 20 in the output. The third layer is composed by a linear layer with 20 neurons in the input and 400 neurons in the output. The fourth layer is composed by a linear layer, with 400 neurons in the input and 784 neurons in the output. Note that is this model, the encode process is done with the first and seconds fully

connected layers and the decode process, with the third and fourth layers. In the neural addition variant, only the layers with 20 neurons, were increased to 40.

All AE models were trained using the MNIST dataset [26]. With the AE trained, it was necessary to load each trained model, to be able to perform the calculation of the Euclidean Distance (ED) between the input and output vectors, thus allowing the estimation of the difference between two images (input and reconstructed image). Then, a program was developed to scroll through all the images (input and reconstructed) used in the AE training (the same set of images, were used to train all models), which allows the calculation of the mean and standard deviation of the ED between the input and the output vector of this set of images. Equation (1) shows the ED formula, where u stands for input vector and v for the output vector.

$$ED = ||u - v||_2 \tag{1}$$

The next step consisted in the development of a program that enabled the loading of atypical patterns with the purpose of evaluating the behaviour of the machine in that situation. In order to determine the best AE model, three atypical patterns were used Fig. 1.

(a)   (b)   (c)

Fig. 1. Atypical Patterns: (a) Pattern 1; (b) Pattern 2; (c) Pattern 3.

The other patterns used were the typical patterns derived from MNIST's handwritten digits. Note that the AE's have three variants, the original model, a new model with more neurons and a model with more neurons and a slight change in the Weight Decay (parameter of optimizer Adam). The weight decay reduces the weights of each neuron in the network by a factor proportional to the learning rate. When using a very high value in the learning rate (in this case, the value that is used for learning rate = 1e-3 (0.001)), the weights will be reduced by that factor. It was then experienced the reduction on the weight updates changing the Weight Decay parameter from 1e-5 (0.00001) to 0. Table 1 presents the value of the ED calculated for the AES and its variants. Also, in all tables, there is a "Neural Addition" section in which the number of neurons in the intermediate and final layers has been increased.

By the analysis of Table 1, we can verify that there is a difference relatively significant compared to the network response at typical and atypical patterns.

The Table 2, shows the results obtained using the CAE.

Table 1. Euclidean distances simple autoencoder

Euclidean distance	Variants of SAE		
	Initial model	Neural addition	Weight decay = 0
Mean (typical)	4.8107	4.0399	4.1778
Deviation (typical)	1.6105	1.1775	0.8859
Pattern 1	15.2141	15.522	15.469
Pattern 2	14.3357	13.4492	14.4248
Pattern 3	10.0456	7.4656	7.607

Table 2. Euclidean distances convolutional autoencoder

Euclidean distance	Variants of CAE		
	Initial model	Neural addition	Weight decay = 0
Mean (typical)	4.2344	2.9627	2.6983
Deviation (typical)	0.6686	1.0253	0.803
Pattern 1	12.6383	11.6515	12.7347
Pattern 2	11.1279	10.2543	10.8106
Pattern 3	4.6726	4.0556	4.7197

The results presented by the CAE were satisfactory in relation to the calculated mean, but in relation to atypical patterns, the results show that this model will be ineffective in their rejection. As we can see in Table 2, regarding pattern 3 in all variants, the network has a wrong tendency to classify this pattern as typical. This erroneous trend in classification is because this pattern has certain characteristics similar to the digits of the digit 0 class.

The Table 3, presents the performance of VAE.

Table 3. Euclidean distances variational autoencoder

Euclidean distance	Variants of VAE		
	Initial model	Neural addition	Weight decay = 0
Mean (typical)	3.933	4.056	4.2161
Deviation (typical)	0.8086	1.0413	0.9916
Pattern 1	15.3003	14.8616	14.3432
Pattern 2	14.256	14.6451	14.7369
Pattern 3	7.1152	8.1099	8.2469

By analyzing the Table 3, we were able to verify that the AEV obtains a good response concerning typical and atypical patterns. After performing all the tests, it was possible to determine the model that best suits the rejection of atypical patterns. To determine the best AE, the Eq. (2) was used, where the solution presenting the highest value will correspond to the ideal AE solution.

$$Threshold = \frac{Pattern3}{Mean + 3 * StandardDeviation} \tag{2}$$

In the formula previously presented (Eq. (2)), Pattern 3 was used as a reference, since it is the pattern that the network tends to miss the classification as typical. It was also considered 3*Standard Deviation to maintain the classification error on typical patterns at a superficial level (0.3%). After using this formula in all models and variants of AE, it was then possible to determine that the best AE to reject atypical patterns is the variant with the number of neurons increased and weight decay = 0 in the VAE. It is now possible to affirm that the AE will identify a pattern as atypical when the ED between the input and output vector is greater than 7.1909 (value determined from Mean+3*Standard Deviation). The AE will classify a pattern as typical when the ED value between the input and output vector is less than 7.1909.

4.2   CNN Threshold Determination

In this work, we have used a CNN with two convolutional layers and one fully connected. The first convolutional layer received 1 channel in the input and 16 in the output, using a kernel size of 5, a stride of 1, padding of 2. The second convolutional layer received 16 in the input and 32 channels in the output, the kernel size was 5, the stride 1 and padding 2. The fully connected layer received a total of 1568 activations which returned in 10 (the number of classes).

After the train of the CNN, a program was developed to load the CNN model (already trained on the MNIST dataset), upload an image, and reproduce the classes' activations in the output. This will allow us to verify the classification ability of this model. It was then necessary to make the network able to classify typical and atypical patterns, defining two thresholds (point from which it will be verified, or not, a certain condition). To define the threshold values, ten typical patterns (one sample of each class) were designed. Both threshold values were obtained using these ten typical patterns.

For the calculation of threshold 1, the mean and the standard deviation of the highest activations were calculated (one activation in the set of ten outputs). The threshold 1 allows to know the threshold value that establishes one of two classification boundaries of a typical-atypical pattern. For the calculation of threshold 2, the mean and the standard deviation of the differences between the two highest activations were calculated. The threshold 2 allows to know the threshold value that establishes the boundary of classification of a pattern as typical-atypical. Note that the same equation (Eq. 3 was used for the calculation of both thresholds.

$$Threshold = Mean - 3 * StandardDeviation \tag{3}$$

Threshold values, three deviations below or above the mean, were considered to keep the error below 0.3% for typical patterns (such as in AE). After the use of both formulas, it was possible to determine the values of the thresholds. Threshold 1 = −893.9464, threshold 2 = −139.0475. On threshold 2 it was considered the module of the number −139.0475, since the ED can never be a negative value. Once defined the thresholds, it has been determined that an atypical pattern will be identified when:

– The maximum activation value (highest neuron) is below Threshold 1.

or

– The Euclidean difference between the two highest activations is less than the Threshold 2.

It has also been determined that a typical pattern will be identified when:

– The maximum activation value is greater than Threshold 1.

and

– The euclidean difference between the two highest activations is greater than Threshold 2.

4.3   Machine Learning Methods

After training the CNN, a program was developed to load the model (already trained on the MNIST dataset) and then extract the training features from the layer previous to the last one. This process will allow the application of ML techniques over this data and then make predictions in new observations. The output of all ML methods used is the probability given by the prediction for each class. The definition of the thresholds was very identical to the threshold defined in the CNN. To be able to make comparisons, the same ten typical patterns were used as well. The classification process is exactly the same, but this time, since we are dealing with probabilities, the threshold formula will be slightly different. Note that both threshold 1 and 2 are calculated using the same formula (Eq. 4).

$$Threshold2 = Mean - \frac{3}{StandardDeviation} \qquad (4)$$

5   Tests and Results

This section presents the tests carried out, using the different methods described in the previous section, in order to determine the most effective model in the detection of atypical patterns. A test dataset was built that consisted of 30 typical patterns (three of each class) and 30 atypical patterns to evaluate the performances. Ten of the typical patterns were the patterns used to determine the thresholds. Confusion Tables (CT) were used to compare the performances of the models. CTs are used as measures of performance for classification problems using ML and DL, where the output can be two or more classes. In this case, it consists of a table with four different values that correspond in different combinations of predicted and actual values. Figure 2, presents the general form of a CT that will be used to expose the performance of the models.

Actual Values

		Typical	Atypical
Predicted Values	Typical	True typical (TT)	False typical (FT)
	Atypical	False atypical (FA)	True atypical (TA)

Fig. 2. Confusion matrix illustration

5.1 Autoencoder Tests

Regarding the classification of typical patterns, the VAE failed in the classification of digits that belong to classes 0, 5, 6, 8 and 9, classifying one pattern of each class incorrectly as atypical. In these errors the majority of them was due to the fact that the VAE is reconstructing the digits of this classes wrongly as a digit that looks very similar to digits of class 3 (digits 5, 8 and 9). The digits that belong to classes 0 and 6, were incorrectly classified due to some blur in the reconstructed image.

The Fig. 3 shows the performance of the VAE, illustrated in a CT.

Actual Values

		Typical	Atypical
Predicted Values	Typical	24	1
	Atypical	6	29

Fig. 3. Confusion table autoencoder

5.2 CNN Tests

Regarding the classification of typical patterns, the CNN has failed in the classification of digits that belong to classes 0, 1, 6, 7 and 9 (in digit 9 class, two digits). In all digits, the activation of the digit itself is the highest activation (that is, the network correctly associates each digit as belonging to its class), but in all these digits, the condition defined by threshold 2 does not occur. This means that the activation of another class is close enough to the real class. In other words, the network classifies these digits with some difficulty.

In the classification of atypical patterns, the CNN incorrectly classified two of the patterns. In both miss classifications, the CNN classifies this patterns as a digit that belong to class 4.

In Fig. 4, it's possible to see the performance of the CNN illustrated by a CT.

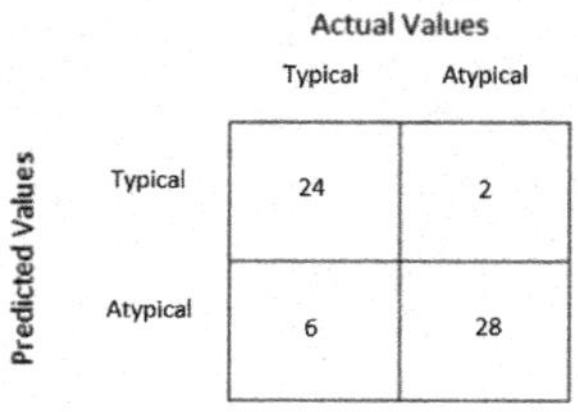

Fig. 4. Confusion table CNN

5.3   Machine Learning Techniques

All the different techniques have performed differently in the classification process. In order to compare ML methods with methods totally based on DL and NNs, first of all, it will be chosen for this comparison, the techniques that best performs this task. In Table 4, it's possible to see the results obtained by all ML techniques in the classification procedure.

Table 4. Machine learning methods performance

ML methods	Correct		
	Typical	Atypical	Total
LR	25	16	41
SVM	19	26	45
LDA	22	16	38
RF	15	30	45
ADA-Boost	4	25	29

The results were considered reasonable, excluding ADA-Boost, which have a performance lower than 50% (29 correct classifications in 60).

Since we have two tied methods, both should be included to make comparisons. LR should also be included because it is the technique that better performs the classification of typical patterns, in comparison to all methods (the performance of this classifier is not very good, but it keeps most of the typical patterns, and it's also capable of detecting some atypical).

Most of the typical patterns incorrectly classified by these classifiers belong to classes 7, 8 and 9. To better represent the performance of these techniques, CTs were also built, Fig. 5.

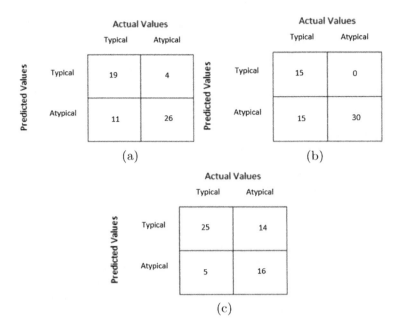

Fig. 5. (a) Confusion Table SVM; (b) Confusion Table RF; (c) Confusion Table LR.

Table 5. Performance metrics

Model	Metrics		
	Accuracy	Sensitivity	Specificity
VAE	0.8833	0.9600	0.8286
CNN	0.8667	0.9231	0.8235
SVM	0.7500	0.8261	0.7027
RF	0.7500	1.0000	0.6667
LR	0.6833	0.6410	0.7619

5.4   Performance Comparison

The Table 5, shows the values obtained for the performance measures of the chosen tested methods.

After the analysis of Table 5, it is possible to verify that the percentage of success when almost all models claim that a certain pattern is typical (Sensitivity) is higher than the overall percentage. However, when the models claim that a certain pattern is atypical (Specificity), the hit rate is less than the overall percentage (Accuracy). LR classifier is an exception here because, in this classifier, the hit rate in atypical patterns (Specificity) is higher than the overall accuracy. It can also be seen that in the detection of atypical patterns, the model that has better performance is the RF classifier. Although by introducing this detection capability to the classifier, we have 50% of miss classifications in typical patterns, which is a very high percentage. Overall, the stronger model that would be the recommended one to perform this detection is the VAE. This model just misses, classifies one atypical pattern, and we also just lose 6 typical patterns.

6   Conclusions

This paper has presented some methods to detect/reject atypical patterns in ML and DL classification problems. This work has consisted in the development of various models of AEs (algorithms specialized in information reconstruction); additionally, a CNN was also developed (Convolutional Neural Network that had a function of a classifier), as an intention to compare its performance with the best AE model. This work also proves that ML techniques (using the information extracted from the CNN model) are also able to detect and reject some of the atypical patterns. Through the analysis of the work carried out, it can be concluded that almost all models and classifiers proved to be acceptably effective in the detection/rejection of atypical patterns, with an error rate of 12% for the VAE, 13% for the CNN, 25% for SVM and RF classifiers and 32% for the LR classifier. It is also possible to conclude that there is a higher accuracy rate by almost all techniques used when they found an atypical pattern than when they found a typical pattern. This is due to the fact that, when we introduce the rejection capability, the models and classifiers will sometimes wrongly reject some typical patterns that should be accepted, thus causing unwanted results. Despite this error in the classification of typical patterns that sometimes happens, it is possible to conclude that almost all techniques can perform, with moderate to good confidence, the task that was the fundamental objective of this work, the rejection of atypical patterns. However, according to the values presented at the beginning of the paragraph relating to the error rate of the best techniques used, the VAE has a lower error rate than CNN and all ML methods, which confirms that the use of AEs should be the main approach to perform this task. In any case, it should be noticed that the evaluation of patterns always has a certain subjectivity index, depending on the training performed by the models and classifiers. In short, after the completion of the work, it was considered that the objective initially defined was successfully completed, with an acceptable error rate.

In order to improve the classification rate, future work can be performed.

- Implement the models and classifiers on usable platforms in order to evaluate the performance of each of them in real situations.

- Improve the calculation of decision thresholds, taking into consideration not only the distribution of typical data but also the distribution of atypical data.

- Combine the two models in order to able to extract better features to use in the train of the ML classifiers.

References

1. Holzinger, A., Kieseberg, P., Weippl, E., Tjoa, A.M.: Current advances, trends and challenges of machine learning and knowledge extraction: from machine learning to explainable AI. In: Holzinger, A., Kieseberg, P., Tjoa, A.M., Weippl, E. (eds.) CD-MAKE 2018. LNCS, vol. 11015, pp. 1–8. Springer, Cham (2018). https://doi.org/10.1007/978-3-319-99740-7_1
2. Abiodun, O.I., Jantan, A., Omolara, A.E., Dada, K.V., Mohamed, N.A., Arshad, H.: State-of-the-art in artificial neural network applications: a survey. Heliyon **4**(11), e00938 (2018)
3. Rezaei, M., Shahidi, M.: Zero-shot learning and its applications from autonomous vehicles to COVID-19 diagnosis: a review. Intell.-Based Med. **3–4**, 100005 (2020). https://doi.org/10.1016%2Fj.ibmed.2020.100005
4. Lampert, C.H., Nickisch, H., Harmeling, S.: Attribute-based classification for zero-shot visual object categorization. IEEE Trans. Pattern Anal. Mach. Intell. **36**(3), 453–465 (2014)
5. Larochelle, H., Erhan, D., Bengio, Y.: Zero-data learning of new tasks. In: Proceedings of the 23rd National Conference on Artificial Intelligence - Volume 2, ser. AAAI 2008, pp. 646–651. AAAI Press (2008)
6. Rohrbach, M., Stark, M., Schiele, B.: Evaluating knowledge transfer and zero-shot learning in a large-scale setting. In: CVPR 2011, pp. 1641–1648 (2011)
7. Yu, X., Aloimonos, Y.: Attribute-based transfer learning for object categorization with zero/one training example. In: Daniilidis, K., Maragos, P., Paragios, N. (eds.) ECCV 2010. LNCS, vol. 6315, pp. 127–140. Springer, Heidelberg (2010). https://doi.org/10.1007/978-3-642-15555-0_10
8. Cordella, L., De Stefano, C., Tortorella, F., Vento, M.: A method for improving classification reliability of multilayer perceptrons. IEEE Trans. Neural Networks **6**(5), 1140–1147 (1995)
9. De Stefano, C., Sansone, C., Vento, M.: To reject or not to reject: that is the question-an answer in case of neural classifiers. IEEE Trans. Syst. Man Cybern. Part C (Appl. Rev.) **30**(1), 84–94 (2000)
10. Geifman, Y., El-Yaniv, R.: Selective classification for deep neural networks (2017). https://arxiv.org/abs/1705.08500
11. Baldi, P.: Autoencoders, unsupervised learning, and deep architectures. In: Guyon, I., Dror, G., Lemaire, V., Taylor, G., Silver, D. (eds.) Proceedings of ICML Workshop on Unsupervised and Transfer Learning, ser. Proceedings of Machine Learning Research, vol. 27, Bellevue, Washington, USA: PMLR, 02 Jul 2012, pp. 37–49. https://proceedings.mlr.press/v27/baldi12a.html
12. An, J., Cho, S.: Variational autoencoder based anomaly detection using reconstruction probability. Spec. Lect. IE **2**(1), 1–18 (2015)
13. Bhandare, A., Bhide, M., Gokhale, P., Chandavarkar, R.: Applications of convolutional neural networks. Int. J. Comput. Sci. Inf. Technol. **7**(5), 2206–2215 (2016)
14. Cheng, W., Hüllermeier, E.: Combining instance-based learning and logistic regression for multilabel classification. Mach. Learn. **76**(2), 211–225 (2009)
15. Wijaya, A., Bisri, A.: Hybrid decision tree and logistic regression classifier for email spam detection. In: 2016 8th International Conference on Information Technology and Electrical Engineering (ICITEE), pp. 1–4 (2016)
16. Sahin, Y., Duman, E.: Detecting credit card fraud by ann and logistic regression. In: International Symposium on Innovations in Intelligent Systems and Applications 2011, pp. 315–319 (2011)

17. H.-L. Hwa, et al.: Prediction of breast cancer and lymph node metastatic status with tumour markers using logistic regression models. J. Eval. Clin. Pract. **14**(2), 275–280 (2008). https://onlinelibrary.wiley.com/doi/abs/10.1111/j.1365-2753.2007.00849.x
18. Bisong, E.: Logistic regression. In: Bisong, E. (ed.) Building Machine Learning and Deep Learning Models on Google Cloud Platform, pp. 243–250. Apress, Berkeley (2019). https://doi.org/10.1007/978-1-4842-4470-8_20
19. Cervantes, J., Garcia-Lamont, F., Rodríguez-Mazahua, L., Lopez, A.: A comprehensive survey on support vector machine classification: applications, challenges and trends. Neurocomputing **408**, 189–215 (2020). https://www.sciencedirect.com/science/article/pii/S0925231220307153
20. Wang, Z., Xue, X.: Multi-class support vector machine. In: Ma, Y., Guo, G. (eds.) Support Vector Machines Applications, pp. 23–48. Springer, Cham (2014). https://doi.org/10.1007/978-3-319-02300-7_2
21. Vaibhaw, Sarraf, J., Pattnaik, P.: Brain-computer interfaces and their applications. In: Balas, V.E., Solanki, V.K., Kumar, R. (eds.) An Industrial IoT Approach for Pharmaceutical Industry Growth, pp. 31–54. Academic Press (2020). https://www.sciencedirect.com/science/article/pii/B9780128213261000024
22. Belgiu, M., Drăguţ, L.: Random forest in remote sensing: a review of applications and future directions. ISPRS J. Photogramm. Remote. Sens. **114**, 24–31 (2016)
23. Caie, P.D., Dimitriou, N., Arandjelović, O.: Artificial intelligence and deep learning in pathology. Elsevier **114**, 149–173 (2021)
24. Freund, Y., Schapire, R.E.: A short introduction to boosting. J. Jpn. Soc. Artif. Intell. **14**, 771–780 (1999)
25. Kaya, A., Keceli, A.S., Catal, C., Tekinerdogan, B.: Model analytics for defect prediction based on design-level metrics and sampling techniques. In: Model Management and Analytics for Large Scale Systems, pp. 125–139 (2020)
26. LeCun, Y.: The MNIST database of handwritten digits (1998). http://yann.lecun.com/exdb/mnist/

Development of a Analog Acquisition and Conditioning Circuit of Surface Electromyogram and Electrocardiogram Signals

Luiz E. Luiz[1,2]([✉])[iD], João Paulo Teixeira[1][iD], and Fábio R. Coutinho[2][iD]

[1] Research Centre in Digitalization and Intelligent Robotics (CeDRI) Instituto Politécnico de Bragança, Campus de Santa Apolónia, 5300-253 Bragança, Portugal
a52482@alunos.ipb.pt, lluiz@alunos.utfpr.edu.br, joaopt@ipb.pt
[2] Universidade Técnologica Federal do Paraná,
Campus Toledo, 85902-490 Paraná, Brazil
fabiocoutinho@utfpr.edu.br

Abstract. The use of wearable devices to monitor vital signs has become something usual, at the same time, here are an increasing demand in improving signal accuracy with a low power consumption. This work presents a conditioning circuit for electrocardiogram and surface electromyogram signals in a reliable way alongside filter and gain modules developed on the area of interest of such signals. At the end, the results obtained are presented, showing the conditioning capability of the circuit, leaving the proof of behaviour in real-life situations to be proven.

Keywords: Surface electromyogram · Electrocardiogram · Signal conditioning · Biosignals

1 Introduction

The characteristics that allows something to be treated as a biosignal are vast, since it can be defined as the representation of a physiological phenomenon, which are practically unlimited [1]. Despite this, some mechanisms of vital importance for the survival of living beings have a greater importance within this group, such as the behaviour of the heart, brain or muscles.

The heart is the central organ in blood circulation of the human body, it has four propulsion chambers, two upper ones, the left and right atria, and two inferior ones, the ventricles, also left and right. To perform the circulation, it executes two movements: systole, contraction of the chambers, and diastole, their relaxation [2].

The electrocardiogram (ECG), graphically represents the behaviour of the heart, displaying the differences in electrical potential during cardiac functioning cycles [3]. In the mid-1960s, ambulatory electrocardiogram devices appeared,

A. I. Pereira et al. (Eds.): OL2A 2022, CCIS 1754, pp. 19–34, 2022.
https://doi.org/10.1007/978-3-031-23236-7_2

which were called Holter, allowing the monitoring of the heart behaviour for hours, making it possible to detect cardiac dysfunctions during the patients daily behaviour [4].

Within the surface electrocardiogram method there are several configurations in the positioning of the electrodes. In this work it will be adopted the acquisition with 3 electrodes, two of them of potential connected in a horizontal line at the height of the heart and a third one of reference connected to the left floating rib [5–7].

The graphic representation of the Holter's device has certain divisions defined in such a way that, in a cycle without any anomaly, the signal should be similar to that represented in Fig. 1.

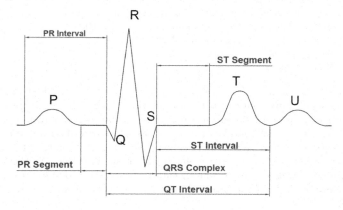

Fig. 1. Expected signal of an ECG.

The "P" wave occurs at the beginning of the atria contraction, while the "QRS" complex symbolises the beginning of the contraction of the ventricles, which remain contracted until the end of the "T" wave, where re-polarisation occurs [8].

The characteristic amplitudes of each parameter depend on factors external to the heart, such as the material of the electrode or where it is positioned, however, with regard to the duration of the partial cycles in normal situations, the following behaviour can be expected: the "P" wave should remain below 110 ms, the "PR" interval between 120 and 200 ms, the "QRS" complex less than 120 ms and the "QT" interval less than 450 ms for men and 470 ms for women [9,10].

Furthermore, in relation to the electromyogram (EMG), the objective is to identify and possibly quantify muscle movements, allowing applications that go beyond medical diagnosis, such as in the control of electrical devices, through gestures, or even body prostheses [11].

The less invasive way of obtaining this signal is through the surface electromyogram (sEMG), where electrodes are placed on the skin, above the muscle, and another on a nearby bone region, as a reference [11,12].

The graphic representation of sEMG signal has two main states, the level when the muscle is in contraction, presenting higher amplitudes, and the level with it at rest, where the signal is practically null [13].

These different human body biosignals have their own behaviour in terms of amplitude and frequency bandwidth, because of that, each scenario must have its own circuits, designed for the desired case. The Fig. 2 shows the difference in magnitude and frequency between sEMG [5] and ECG [6], as well as the operating ranges of each.

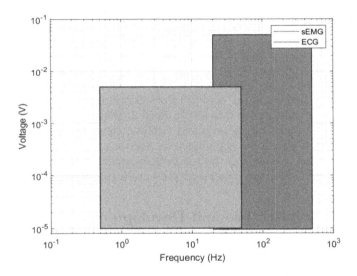

Fig. 2. Bandwidth of interest sEMG and ECG.

Moreover, with the advancements in miniaturisation of electronic components, their use in the health field has become more significant, allowing the capture of various biological signals that assist in the detection and diagnosis of diseases [14].

As defined by Constantine and Fotiadis [15], a wearable medical device is a non-invasive and autonomous system that performs a function, such as patient monitoring. As it is a wearable equipment, it must be put directly on the skin, or through an accessory, as is the case of smartwatches, so these devices must be designed aiming at a minimization in size, weight and consumption, as they must be practical and non-intrusive in prolonged uses.

Besides the use of such wearable devices in practical equipment where the interest is to allow the user to monitor their vital signs, there are more accurate devices that aim to generate data to assist health professionals in the diagnosis of specific conditions, where the quality of the collected information comes to a higher preference in opposition to the miniaturized characteristic and easy handling present in the wearable systems mentioned previously [16].

Among the priorities given to these equipment that prioritise the fidelity of the final signal are the definition of the digital signal and also the initial analog conditioning of it, so that this definition is the least polluted with noise possible.

Considering these needs, it is possible to make a comparison with the relative state-of-art, where part of the proposals of those circuits are made with 12 or 14 bits converters [17–19], the analog conditioning is made with different frequency values of the presented area of interest [19,20], or even conditioning without the presence of attenuation in the network frequency range [20]. In addition, the circuit presented in this work aims to work in blocks, making it possible to increase the amount of sEMG in a single patient, without the need to add another AD converter.

In order to combine the qualities of each technique, this article will address the development of a modulated system capable of acquisition and conditioning the ECG and sEMG signals without harming the reliability of the acquired signal, but aiming at the future implementation in wearable devices, creating the need for miniaturization [21] and low power consumption [22] in the process.

The paper is structured as follows. In Sect. 2, the systems block diagram is defined in order to establish the required circuits, then the components are calculated and defined to achieve the objective. Section 3 presents the final circuits and their behaviour, comparing the theoretical results with the expected ones. Finally, Sect. 4 concludes the paper and presents future work.

2   System Architecture and Development

Briefly, the circuit blocks of both ECG and sEMG are basically the same, the signal is obtained with the help of three electrodes, these are then led to the conditioning blocks. First, the signals from the electrodes are combined into a single signal. Thereafter, this single signal is amplified to be adjusted to a desired voltage range, then the signal goes through a set of filters, which have their respective frequency responses, where their combination forms a passing zone of the desired frequencies, making it easier to visualise and eliminate noise. Finally, these analog signals must be converted to digital, where they can be stored or sent to portable devices, such as a smartphone. The block diagram of this system can be seen in Fig. 3.

2.1   Signal Acquisition and Amplification

The first stage of conditioning, as mentioned before, is the unification of the signals obtained through the electrodes, for this, as both ECG and sEMG use the potential difference between two points, the signal of such electrodes must be subtracted, while the third electrode serves as a common mode filter. In the case of sEMG, its third electrode signal must be connected to the system reference,

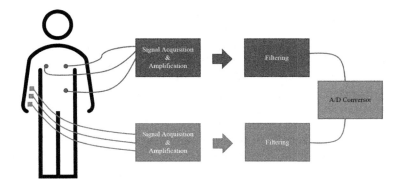

Fig. 3. Systems block diagram.

however, for ECG, the third electrode is called right-leg drive (RLD), that is, during the subtraction process of the two potential electrodes, the average of them is collected, its polarity is inverted, amplified and conducted to the patient body, where, as it is negative, it compensate the common noise level present in the body.

To combine the signals, an instrumentation amplifier is used, which works similarly to the difference amplifier, but with a better common mode rejection ratio (CMRR), besides a higher precision in the matching of the internal components, which would be a problematic factor to achieve if the circuit was assembled in a discrete way. In general, the use of this integrated circuit has some similarities with a normal operational amplifier, having both inverting and non-inverting input and positive and negative power supply, however, there is also a point to define an internal reference and a pair of pins that serves for gain control.

In order to achieve values as close as possible to those expected, the integrated circuit INA128 (Texas Instruments) was chosen, because, in addition to its low power consumption, it has a CMRR capable of being higher than 120 dB and adjustable gain configuration through external resistors. These characteristics will be essential in the ECG conditioning circuit, given the need to obtain the average of the inputs.

With the main potential electrodes circuit done, all that is now required is to adjust the behaviour of the third electrode. In the sEMG, as shown in the Fig. 5a the electrode is connected to the reference, as the common mode signal present in the third electrode will be shifted to zero, the common effect present in the other two electrodes will also be zero, cancelling its effect, as a second signal subtraction.

Furthermore, another action adopted to help noise attenuation of the INA128 is to shift the DC level of its reference, in order to do this, a pair of resistors of the same nominal value will be connected from the circuit 5 V supply, dividing the voltage to approximately 2.5 V, after which a voltage follower will be put in place to conduct this shift to the integrated circuit reference without interfering in the division. To filter oscillations of the source, a capacitor was placed in parallel with the second resistor.

For the ECG circuit, as it is intended to reduce the CMRR in a more controlled way, an average of the subtraction of the signals is collected through the gain control resistor, this one being divided in two of the same value, in the connection between them, a voltage follower amplifier is placed in order to not interfere in the gain value, from this, the signal is amplified and inverted using an integrator amplifier, as shown in Fig. 5b.

This amplifier has a variable negative amplification ratio based on frequency, with greater magnitude in the components close to the DC level. Due to this effect, and in order to avoid an infinite theoretical gain, which in practice would lead the operational amplifier to saturation, a resistor is placed in parallel with the feedback capacitor, thus limiting the gain in continuous current.

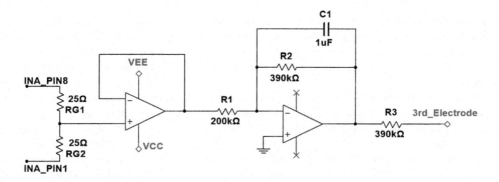

Fig. 4. Third electrode circuit of the ECG

The output of the latter amplifier is then inserted into the patient body through the third electrode (Fig. 4), closing the mesh, this potential acts contrary to the common mode present, reducing its effect. Regarding the INA128 reference of the ECG circuit, the same voltage divider applied in the sEMG will be implemented.

Subsequently, the amplification of the signals is treated. As seen in the Fig. 2, the sEMG signal has a normal amplitude ranging from 10 μV to 50 mV, while the ECG signal ranges from 10 μV to 5 mV. Considering that at the end of the circuit, an analog-to-digital conversion will be performed on the output signal and the converter is set for a voltage range from 0 to 5 V, the maximum peak of these signals should be close to but less than 5 V. The required gain in V/V is calculated by:

$$G = \frac{V_{max_{ADC}}}{V_{pk}}, \tag{1}$$

resulting in a necessary gain of 100 V/V to the sEMG circuit and 1000 V/V to ECG.

Although it is possible to insert this gain in any modules of the circuit, its application in the INA128 is again beneficial in the common mode rejection ratio, since, as can be seen in the Table 1, the greater the gain configured in the IC, the greater the magnitude of CMRR.

Therefore, the gain will be entirely provided to the signal in the differential amplification, being defined through the existing resistance between the pins R_G through the relation given by:

$$G_{INA128} = 1 + \frac{50 \ k\Omega}{R_G}. \tag{2}$$

Table 1. CMRR x Gain ratio in INA128 (adapted from the INA128 datasheet).

Parameter	Test conditions		MIN	TYP	UNIT
CMRR	G = 1	INA12x(P/U)	80	60	dB
		INA12x(PA/UA)	73		
	G = 10	INA12x(P/U)	100	106	
		INA12x(PA/UA)	93		
	G = 100	INA12x(P/U)	120	130	
		INA12x(PA/UA)	110		
	G = 1k	INA12x(P/U)	120	130	
		INA12x(PA/UA)	110		

In this way, the required resistance for the sEMG and ECG is calculated, obtaining 505 Ω and 50.5 Ω respectively. As for the ECG circuit, two resistors must be placed in series, the closest possible commercial value is 25 Ω, while for the sEMG, a resistor of 499 Ω will be used. Thus, the first block of the conditioning circuits is complete (Fig. 5).

2.2   Filtering

After acquiring the electrode signals and turning into a single output, the signal will be filtered in order to eliminate noises. Again, each signal must have its own filtering blocks, configured according to each need, but in short, each one will have a high-pass, a low-pass and a notch filter, to serve as an additional to CMRR to prevent the occurrence of noise from the electrical power line.

As shown in Fig. 2, the sEMG signal has an operating range of frequencies 20 Hz 500 Hz, while the ECG signal operates between 0.5 Hz 50 Hz. A Sallen-Key topology, active filters with two conjugate complex poles (i.e., second order filter),using one operational amplifier, two resistors and two capacitors per filter was designed to meet requirements.

Analyzing the complete target, it can be noticed that at the end of the filtering, the circuit must be shifted in a positive DC level, since the AD conversion

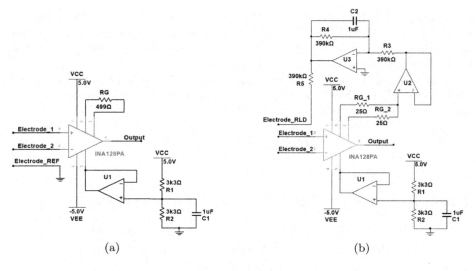

Fig. 5. First stage of conditioning. (a) sEMG circuit. (b) ECG circuit.

will be done in the 0–5 V range and the graphical representations has a negative part. Considering this detail, its adopted a 2.5 V shifted reference in the filters, this comes from the same reference used in the INA128. Furthermore, the filters blocks are sorted into: low-pass, notch and high-pass.

Thus, starting with the design of low-pass filters, following the standard model shown in Fig. 6, it is necessary to calculate the value of the passive components, using the filter cutoff frequency in

$$f_c = \frac{1}{2\pi\sqrt{R_1 R_2 C_1 C_2}} \tag{3}$$

and the quality factor

$$Q = \frac{1}{2\pi f_c C_1 (R_1 + R_2)}. \tag{4}$$

Considering a Butterworth, or maximally flat, response format, the quality factor should be as close as possible to 0.707 [23].

To simplify the calculations, in the case of the low-pass filters, the value of the resistances will be considered 2.2 kΩ both, starting with the sEMG low-pass filter calculations, at an expected cutoff frequency 500 Hz, using the Eq. 4, the value of the capacitor connected to the non-inverting input can be defined as:

$$0.707 = \frac{1}{2 * \pi * 500 * C_1 * (2200 + 2200)}$$

$$C_1 \approx 100 \ nF.$$

After, using the Eq. 3, the value of the feedback capacitor can be set as

$$500 = \frac{1}{2 * \pi * \sqrt{2200 * 2200 * 100n * C_2}}$$

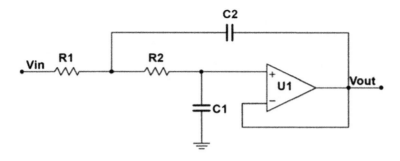

Fig. 6. A second order sallen-key low-pass filter topology

$$C_2 \approx 200\ nF.$$

Regarding the ECG filter, the adopted cutoff frequency will 50 Hz. Therefore, the capacitors are calculated as follows:

$$0.707 = \frac{1}{2 * \pi * 50 * C_1 * (2200 + 2200)}$$

$$C_1 \approx 1\ \mu F$$

and

$$50 = \frac{1}{2 * \pi * \sqrt{2200 * 2200 * 1.1\mu * C_2}}$$

$$C_2 \approx 2\ \mu F.$$

Thus, as commercial value should be adopted, the actual frequencies and quality factors are recalculated and set out in Table 2.

Table 2. Designed values for resistors and capacitors in the low-pass filter

Low-pass filters						
Circuit	R_1	R_2	C_1	C_2	Q	f_c
EMG	2200 Ω	2200 Ω	100 nF	200 nF	0.707	511 Hz
ECG	2200 Ω	2200 Ω	1 μF	2 μF	0.707	51 Hz

Regarding the notch filter, this model has a frequency response similar to a common band-rejector, but with a very narrow blocked bandwidth and a sharp magnitude drop, so that it is possible to reject only desired values. To do this, 50 Hz twin-T filter is inserted into the circuit, the standard model can be seen in Fig. 7. First, two conditions must be adopted:

$$R_1 = R_2 = 2 * R_3$$

and
$$C_1 = C_2 = \frac{C_3}{2}.$$

As the notch filter of the two circuits must have the same cutoff frequency, 50 Hz, the passive components will have the same value and are calculated from:

$$f_c = \frac{1}{2\pi * R * C}. \tag{5}$$

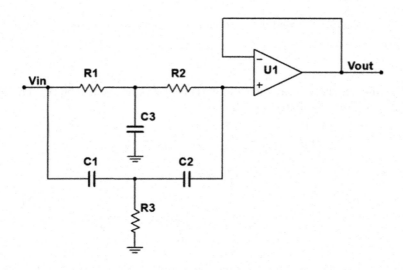

Fig. 7. Notch filter topology model

Adopting as the value of the capacitors,

$$C_1 = C_2 = 1 \ \mu F$$

and

$$C_3 = 2 \ \mu F,$$

the value of the resistances can be calculated as follows:

$$50 = \frac{1}{2 * \pi * R * 2\mu}$$

$$R \approx 2.1 \ k\Omega.$$

After adjusting the component values within those commercially available, the cutoff frequency is calculated again, obtaining the results expressed in Table 3.

Table 3. Designed values for resistors and capacitors for the Notch Filter

Notch filter						
R_1	R_2	R_3	C_1	C_2	C_3	f_c
2100 Ω	2100 Ω	1070 Ω	1.5 μF	1.5 μF	3 μF	50.52 Hz

For the high-pass filters calculation, the resistors and capacitors from the low-pass model are swapped, as can be seen in Fig. 8, in the same way, the quality factor equation receives some changes, being calculated by:

$$Q = \frac{1}{2\pi f_c R_1 (C_1 + C_2)}, \tag{6}$$

therefore, the parameters used to simplify the calculations must occur in the capacitors, this being:

$$C_1 = C_2 = 1.5 \ \mu F.$$

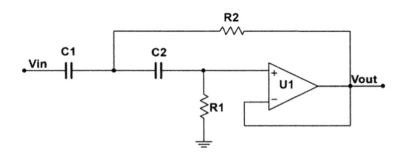

Fig. 8. A second order sallen-key high-pass filter topology

Starting with the calculation of the filter 20 Hz cut-off frequency of the EMG, using the Eq. 6 and the parameterised values, it is found that:

$$0.707 = \frac{1}{2\pi * 20 * R_1 (1.5\mu + 1.5\mu)}$$

$$R_1 \approx 7870 \ \Omega.$$

Then, using the Eq. 3 to calculate the value of the feedback resistor:

$$20 = \frac{1}{2\pi \sqrt{7870 * R_2 * 1.5\mu * 1.5\mu}}$$

$$R_2 \approx 3920 \ \Omega.$$

Similarly, the resistance calculations are made for the ECG filter with a cutoff frequency of 0.5 Hz:

$$0.707 = \frac{1}{2\pi * 0.5 * R_1(1.5\mu + 1.5\mu)}$$

$$R_1 \approx 301 \ k\Omega$$

and

$$20 = \frac{1}{2\pi\sqrt{301k * R_2 * 1.5\mu * 1.5\mu}}$$

$$R_2 \approx 147 \ k\Omega.$$

Calculating the cutoff frequency and the quality factor corrected for rounding based on the commercial value of the components, the values expressed in the Table 4 are obtained.

Table 4. Designed values for resistors and capacitors for the high-pass filter

High-pass filters						
Circuit	C_1	C_2	R_1	R_2	Q	f_c
EMG	1.5 μF	1.5 μF	7870 Ω	3920 Ω	0.708	19.1 Hz
ECG	1.5 μF	1.5 μF	301 kΩ	147 kΩ	0.715	0.5 Hz

Finally, with all filters configured, it is necessary to couple these to an analog-to-digital converter compatible with the expected definition, for this reason the integrated circuit ADS1296 is chosen, where, besides being able to make conversions with up to 24 bits of definition, this chip has a high level of rejection of the electrical network noise. In addition, the chip has 6 channels, so it is able to convert one ECG module and 5 sEMG modules.

3   Results

Once all the parameters of the acquisition and conditioning systems are defined, the frequency response of the concatenated filters can be obtained, as well as the gain implemented by the instrumentation amplifier. Firstly, the blocks are connected in series, as can be seen in Fig. 9, obtaining the final circuit, both for the electromyogram Fig. 9a, and for the electrocardiogram Fig. 9b.

After, a source of alternating current will be connected, in both circuits, in the position of the electrode 1 and the electrode 2 will be connected in the reference, with this, analyzing the output of the systems, it is possible to quantify the effect of the system for each frequency applied in the source. Considering a test frequency from 100 mHz to 5 kHz and overlapping the responses in their respective areas of interest shown in Fig. 2, the result expressed in Fig. 10 is obtained, with the right Y-axis being to the filter attenuation magnitude in dB.

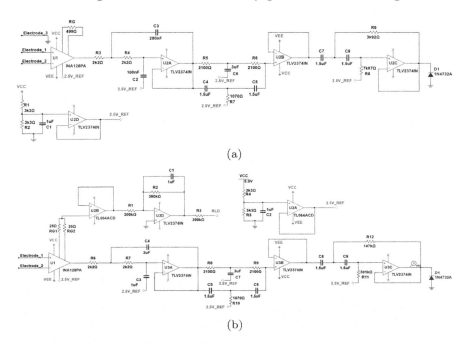

(a)

(b)

Fig. 9. Final circuits. (a) sEMG. (b) ECG.

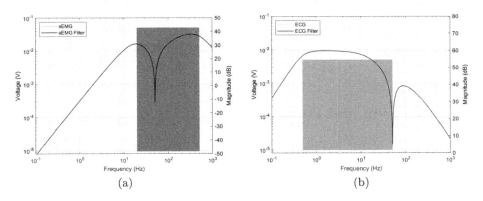

(a)   (b)

Fig. 10. Frequency response overlaid in the interest area. (a) sEMG. (b) ECG.

As it is possible to identify, the response of the filters meet the expectation, attenuating frequencies outside the area of interest. And in relation to gain, it is noted that the values in the pass bandwidth of the sEMG filter varies between 30 and 40 dB, converting to V/V using the equation

$$G(V/V) = 10^{\frac{G(dB)}{20}}, \tag{7}$$

is noticed a gain between 31 and 100 V/V. As for the gain of the ECG, it is stabilized at 60 dB, or, using the Eq. 7, 1000 V/V until the start of the notch filter decay.

The 50 Hz attenuation in both circuits, considering the final signal, is around 52 dB, considering a power line noise with the same amplitude as obtained signal, there is a signal to noise ratio of approximately 400.

Due to the implementation of a low-pass filter with a frequency close to a notch in the sEMG, the expected gain of 40 dB in the low-pass bandwidth ends up being attenuated due to the beginning of the abrupt decay of the notch. For this reason the first part of the sEMG and the end of EMG areas of interest have a lower gain than expected.

Assembling the circuit in a breadboard and connecting the electrodes to a body, the results shown in Fig. 11 are obtained, exhibiting the capabilities of the developed circuit.

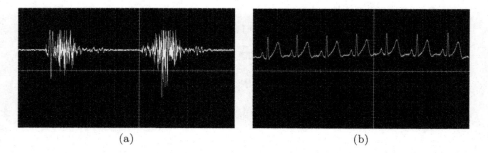

(a)   (b)

Fig. 11. Circuit response connected to a body. (a) sEMG. (b) ECG. (2 V/div and 500 ms/div)

4   Conclusion and Further Work

The need for a higher quality in obtaining vital signals together with the constant miniaturization of the devices capable of accomplishing such goals, makes mandatory the design of low power consumption systems and precise filters, always aiming at an increase in the quality of the final signal. In this paper, it was presented a possible way to achieve these results in a modular way and with low power consumption. In future studies, this system can be implemented, allowing long-term tests and some circuit adjustments such as the possibility of excluding the N50 Hz filter for being a battery powered device and the attenuation characteristic for such frequency by the ADS1296 chip.

Acknowledgment. The authors are grateful to the Foundation for Science and Technology (FCT, Portugal) for financial support through national funds FCT/MCTES (PIDDAC) to CeDRI (UIDB/05757/2020 and UIDP/05757/2020) and SusTEC (LA/P/0007/2021).

References

1. Kaniusas, E.: Fundamentals of biosignals. In: Kaniusas, E. (ed.) Biomedical Signals and Sensors I, pp. 1–26. Springer, Heidelberg (2012). https://doi.org/10.1007/978-3-642-24843-6_1
2. Dutra, A.F., Nicola, A.L.P., Sousa, L.A., Yamaguti, S.T.F., da Silva, A.P.L.: Anatomia e fisiologia cardiovascular. In: da Silva, A.P.L., França, A.A.F., de F. A. Benetti, C. (eds.) Enfermagem em Cardiologia Intervencionista. Editora dos Editores (2019)
3. Giffoni, R.T., Torres, R.M.: Breve história da eletrocardiografia. Revista Médica de Minas Gerais **20**(2), 263–270 (2010)
4. Mittal, S., Movsowitz, C., Steinberg, J.S.: Ambulatory external electrocardiographic monitoring: focus on atrial fibrillation. J. Am. Coll. Cardiol. **58**(17), 1741–1749 (2011). https://doi.org/10.1016/j.jacc.2011.07.026
5. Sestrem, L., et al.: Data acquisition, conditioning and processing system for a wearable-based biostimulation. In: Proceedings of the 15th International Joint Conference on Biomedical Engineering Systems and Technologies. SCITEPRESS - Science and Technology Publications (2022). https://doi.org/10.5220/0011002300003123
6. Teixeira, J.P., Ferreira, A.: Ambulatory electrocardiogram prototype. Procedia Comput. Sci. **64**, 800–807 (2015)
7. Borghi, P.H., Kuhn, E., Teixeira, J.P., Lazaretti, G.S.: Android-based ECG monitoring system for atrial fibrillation detection using a bitalino® ECG sensor. In: Proceedings of the 15th International Joint Conference on Biomedical Engineering Systems and Technologies. SCITEPRESS (2022)
8. Carrillo-Esper, R., Carrillo-Córdova, L.D., Carrillo-Córdova, D.M., Carrillo-Córdova, C.A.: The u wave in the electrocardiogram. more than an academic curiosity. Médica Sur **22**(1), 27–29 (2015)
9. Reis, H.J.L., Guimarães, H.P., Zazula, A.D., Vasque, R.G., Lopes, R.D.: ECG manual prático de eletrocardiograma. In: ECG manual prático de eletrocardiograma, pp. 121–121. Editora Atheneu (2013)
10. Varella, A.C., et al.: Avaliação eletrocardiograma - guia rápido para enfermeiros. UTS: Instituto Nacional de Cardiologia (2021)
11. Lopes, V.H.S., Baccarini, L.M.R., Pereira, E.B., Santos, T.M.d.O., Galo, D.P.V.: Projeto e desenvolvimento de um sistema portátil de condicionamento e aquisiçao de sinais emg. In: Congresso Brasileiro de Automática-CBA, vol. 1 (2019)
12. Hermens, H.J., Freriks, B., Disselhorst-Klug, C., Rau, G.: Development of recommendations for SEMG sensors and sensor placement procedures. J. Electromyogr. Kinesiol. **10**(5), 361–374 (2000). https://doi.org/10.1016/S1050-6411(00)00027-4. https://www.sciencedirect.com/science/article/pii/S1050641100000274
13. Fu, Z., Hashim, A.B., Jamaludin, Z., Mohamad, I., Nasir, N.: Optimizing surface electromyography acquisition without right leg drive circuit. Int. J. Eng. Sci. Technol. **1**(1), 13–19 (2017)
14. Arney, D., Venkatasubramanian, K.K., Sokolsky, O., Lee, I.: Biomedical devices and systems security. In: 2011 Annual International Conference of the IEEE Engineering in Medicine and Biology Society, pp. 2376–2379. IEEE (2011). https://doi.org/10.1109/IEMBS.2011.6090663
15. Glaros, C., Fotiadis, D.I.: Wearable devices in healthcare. In: Silverman, B., Jain, A., Ichalkaranje, A., Jain, L. (eds.) Intelligent Paradigms for Healthcare Enterprises, pp. 237–264. Springer, Heidelberg (2005). https://doi.org/10.1007/11311966_8

16. Cheol Jeong, I., Bychkov, D., Searson, P.C.: Wearable devices for precision medicine and health state monitoring. IEEE Trans. Biomed. Eng. **66**(5), 1242–1258 (2018). https://doi.org/10.1109/TBME.2018.2871638
17. Sobya, D., Muruganandham, S., Nallusamy, S., Chakraborty, P.: Wireless ECG monitoring system using IoT based signal conditioning module for real time signal acquisition. Indian J. Public Health Res. Dev **9**, 294–299 (2018)
18. Morales, D., Garcia, A., Castillo, E., Carvajal, M., Banqueri, J., Palma, A.: Flexible ECG acquisition system based on analog and digital reconfigurable devices. Sens. Actuators A **165**(2), 261–270 (2011)
19. Merletti, R., Botter, A., Troiano, A., Merlo, E., Minetto, M.A.: Technology and instrumentation for detection and conditioning of the surface electromyographic signal: state of the art. Clin. Biomech. **24**(2), 122–134 (2009)
20. Shobaki, M.M., et al.: High quality acquisition of surface electromyography-conditioning circuit design. In: IOP Conference Series: Materials Science and Engineering, vol. 53, p. 012027. IOP Publishing (2013)
21. Scheffler, M., Hirt, E.: Wearable devices for emerging healthcare applications. In: The 26th Annual International Conference of the IEEE Engineering in Medicine and Biology Society, vol. 2, pp. 3301–3304 (2004). https://doi.org/10.1109/IEMBS.2004.1403928
22. Seneviratne, S., et al.: A survey of wearable devices and challenges. IEEE Commun. Surv. Tutor. **19**(4), 2573–2620 (2017). https://doi.org/10.1109/COMST.2017.2731979
23. Karki, J.: Active low-pass filter design. Texas Instruments application report (2000)

Sensor Architecture Model for Unmanned Aerial Vehicles Dedicated to Electrical Tower Inspections

Guido S. Berger[1,2,3(✉)], João Braun[1,2,4,9], Alexandre O. Júnior[1,2],
José Lima[1,2,4], Milena F. Pinto[7], Ana I. Pereira[1,2], António Valente[3,4],
Salviano F. P. Soares[3,4], Lucas C. Rech[5], Álvaro R. Cantieri[6],
and Marco A. Wehrmeister[5,8]

[1] Research Centre in Digitalization and Intelligent Robotics (CeDRI),
Instituto Politécnico de Bragança, Bragança, Portugal
{guido.berger,jbneto,alexandrejunior,jllima,apereira}@ipb.pt
[2] Laboratório para a Sustentabilidade e Tecnologia em Regiões de Montanha
(SusTEC), Instituto Politécnico de Bragança, Bragança, Portugal
[3] Universidade de Trás-os-Montes e Alto Douro, Vila Real, Portugal
avalente@utad.pt
[4] INESC Technology and Science, Porto, Portugal
[5] Federal University of Technology, Paraná, Curitiba, Brazil
wehrmeister@utfpr.edu.br
[6] Federal Institute of Paraná, Curitiba, Brazil
alvaro.cantieri@ifpr.edu.br
[7] Centro Federal Tecnológica Celso Suckow da Fonseca, Rio de Janeiro, Brazil
milena.pinto@cefet-rj.br
[8] University of Münster, Münster, Germany
wehrmeister@uni-muenster.de
[9] Faculty of Engineering, University of Porto, Porto, Portugal

Abstract. This research proposes positioning obstacle detection sensors by multirotor unmanned aerial vehicles (UAVs) dedicated to detailed inspections in high voltage towers. Different obstacle detection sensors are analyzed to compose a multisensory architecture in a multirotor UAV. The representation of the beam pattern of the sensors is modeled in the CoppeliaSim simulator to analyze the sensors' coverage and detection performance in simulation. A multirotor UAV is designed to carry the same sensor architecture modeled in the simulation. The aircraft is used to perform flights over a deactivated electrical tower, aiming to evaluate the detection performance of the sensory architecture embedded in the aircraft. The results obtained in the simulation were compared with those obtained in a real scenario of electrical inspections. The proposed method achieved its goals as a mechanism to early evaluate the detection capability of different previously characterized sensor architectures used in multirotor UAV for electrical inspections.

Keywords: Unmanned aerial vehicles · Sensor modelling · Robotic simulator · Electrical inspections

A. I. Pereira et al. (Eds.): OL2A 2022, CCIS 1754, pp. 35–50, 2022.
https://doi.org/10.1007/978-3-031-23236-7_3

1   Introduction

The use of multirotor unmanned aerial vehicles (UAVs) in most electrical inspection operations carried out nowadays is done through manual commands executed by a ground operator, which determines the distance and positioning of the aircraft concerning the set of electrical cables or the electrical tower infrastructure visually. A second operator on the ground is responsible for analyzing the images of the inspected site in a base station [1].

Although operators on the ground currently conduct the methods of electrical inspections by multirotor UAVs, technological trends indicate that increasingly high-risk operations must rely less on human action and progressively more on the autonomous capabilities of multirotor UAVs. These autonomous capabilities must be dictated by a reliable sensory detection system that senses the UAV's operating environment and automatically avoids potential collisions between the aircraft and obstacles in the inspection environment [2].

With this, the problems generated around visual perspective uncertainties, which generally occur during operations in which the UAV is far from the visual contact of the operator on the ground, would no longer occur through the detection of obstacles by different combinations of sensors positioned strategically over the body of the multirotor UAV [3].

To ensure the detection of multiple obstacles in electrical inspection environments, it is necessary to know the operation of different technologies, seeking to identify which sensors are capable of being applied in this environment. This means that not only the detection capabilities of obstacles belonging to the electrical towers must be evaluated, but also the correct coupling of multiple sensors in the UAV structure, evaluating the regions that can interfere with the detection performance when installed on the aircraft body [4].

This research presents a sensor distribution method for UAVs to detect multiple obstacles in detailed inspection scenarios in high voltage towers. This research is a continuation of the work presented by [5], adding new results that advance the previously proposed theme linked to electrical inspections by multirotor UAVs.

The methodology applied for this research initially evaluates the detection performance of different sensors in front of objects used in high voltage towers. Then, a sensor architecture is modelled in the CoppeliaSim simulator, whose objective is to identify multiple obstacles in a scenario of electrical inspections by UAVs. This sensor architecture is modelled from the beam pattern of the sensors that obtained the best results based on the considerations pointed out by the first set of evaluations.

A sensor architecture, identified as suitable during the simulation, is embedded in a real multirotor UAV designed to fly over a decommissioned electrical tower. Detection data are collected by the sensor architecture in the real environment and compared with the sensory detection data in the simulated environment. The remaining of this work is organized as follows. Section 2 presents the related works and the background of this work. The materials and methodology are presented in Sect. 3. In Sect. 4, the results observed by the experiments are presented, and finally, in Sect. 5, the conclusion and future directions for the work presented are addressed.

2   Related Works

One of the main challenges within the context of autonomous navigation by multirotor UAVs is to be able to autonomously and adaptively avoid the different types of obstacles belonging to the scenario inspected by the aircraft. In this sense, it is vital to understand the working dynamics of different types of sensors when used in multirotor UAVs in multiple obstacle detection tasks [6]. This happens because several factors, such as those related to the exposure environment of the sensors, that can be an element that compromises the detection performance of certain sensory technologies [7].

LASER detection sensors, for example, present great difficulties to be used outdoors because, in conditions of high exposure to sunlight, fog and snow, this type of sensor can present unreliable distance measurements [8]. Most of the works found in the literature use LASER sensors with Time of Flight (ToF) technology in a controlled environment, where there is little or no interference to the sensor. In this way, many works involving applications of LASER sensors in UAVs are used in indoor environments, employing these sensors to perform tasks of multiple obstacle detection and altitude control [1]. LASER measurement sensors based on Time of Flight (ToF) technology emit a pulsating LASER beam, calculating the distance from the obstacle through the time between sending the signal and receiving it. Due to the ability of the LASER pulse to travel roughly at the speed of light in the atmosphere medium, a large number of detection samples per second are obtained, making this type of sensor more accurate compared to ultrasonic sensors [9].

Unlike LASER sensors, ultrasonic sensors (also known as sonar) can detect obstacles even in foggy environments, under direct or indirect sunlight exposure, and are widely used in multirotor UAVs for indoors or outdoors operations [10]. Like LASER sensors, ultrasonic sensors work using the Time Of Flight method, measuring the time taken by sending and receiving a high-frequency sound wave that operates at the speed of sound. When this sound wave hits an obstacle, it returns to the ultrasonic sensor, which converts it into an electrical signal, interpreting this signal as a measure of distance [9].

However, ultrasonic sensors in outdoor environments are also affected, where there is no local temperature control, where the speed of sound increases by approximately 0.6 m/s for every 1°C rise. This increase in the propagation speed of the sound wave can induce inaccuracies in the distance measurements obtained by the ultrasonic sensor, generating detection uncertainties about the target obstacle. To permanently establish the same propagation speed of sound waves, temperature sensors are incorporated into the sonar control system to analyze the ambient temperature variation. Through this feedback, the ultrasonic sensor control system can maintain the same speed of sending the sound wave [11].

Typically, ultrasonic and LASER sensors are used together on the structure of the multirotor UAV because they present distinct advantages in obstacle detection [10]. However, certain regions in the multirotor structure can be noise sources for certain types of sensors, minimizing or nullifying their obstacle detection capabilities. In regions located on the extremities of multirotor UAVs, sonars can present unreliable distance measurements due to the constant vibrations generated by the engines or the gust of wind caused by the rotation of the propellers [12].

LASER scanner sensors with LiDAR technology can also fail if attached to regions of the UAV that experience constant vibrations, especially when fitted over the ends of the multirotor. In this case, the vibration can cause discontinuity on the point cloud produced by the sensor on the target objects [13]. Other strategies found in the literature adopt multiple ultrasonic sensors grouped around the UAV to create a vast obstacle detection region. However, this sensory arrangement allows the emergence of the crosstalk effect. The crosstalk effect occurs when multiple sonars are very close to each other, causing the beam pattern of the sensors to overlap, and with that, the signal sent by a given sensor ends up being received by the adjacent sensor, which can lead to failures in the detection of obstacles [14]. Figure 1 illustrates the ultrasonic sensor's beam pattern and how the lobes' overlapping between sonars is represented, causing the crosstalk effect.

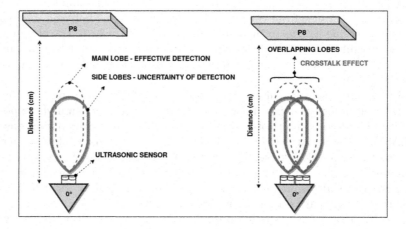

Fig. 1. Crosstalk effect by overlapping the lobes of ultrasonic sensors.

In other cases, few ultrasonic sensors are used on the structure of the UAV to detect multiple obstacles. In this case, objects that are not perpendicular to the acoustic axis of the ultrasonic sensor, where the effective detection by the sensor occurs, may not be correctly detected, generating unreliable distance measurements and thus characterizing problems related to angular uncertainty [6].

3   Materials and Methods

This chapter presents the methodology adopted for the development of this research. The first step is centred on the characterization of different types of sensory devices, evaluating detection performance issues based on their techno-logical characteristics and data extracted from their manufacturing manuals. A set of components belonging to a high voltage tower is used as a target to deter-mine which sensors have the best detection performance. The characteristics of the sensors, such as the maximum and minimum detection ranges, conditions of use in indoor and outdoor environments and capabilities to identify obstacles of different properties and geometries, are raised and discussed. The adversities in the sensor application environment, such as high sun exposure, vibration and temperature change, are explored to select sensors that are unaffected by this. At the end of the first step, it will be possible to determine the best sensors to be applied in the electrical inspection environment.

These sensors are then modelled in a second step in the CoppeliaSim simu-lator, representing their beam pattern based on the data collected by the sen-sory characterization and the data contained in their manufacturing manuals. A sensor architecture is modelled on a multirotor UAV, considering the sensory coverage over the aircraft body and positioning the sensors so that they are not affected by crosstalk and angular uncertainty-related issues. In this virtual scenario, the sensor architecture is used to identify the base of a high voltage tower and the set of electrical cables. Finally, in the third step, an actual mul-tirotor UAV is developed containing the same sensor architecture modelled in the CoppeliaSim simulator. This UAV is then used to fly over a deactivated actual electrical tower, collecting information from the sensory architecture of the electrical tower base and electrical cable assembly. Figure 2 illustrates the methodological steps adopted in this research.

3.1   Characterization of Sensors in a Controlled Environment

The objective of the evaluation in a controlled environment is to find the sensors that present detection results from at least 2 m away. This distance was cho-sen considering the minimum safety distance of a UAV when used in electrical inspections. These sensors were chosen because they are small, easy to integrate into multirotor UAVs, and energy-efficient. The detection sensors used in this research are shown in Table 1.

The components used in the experiment are parts used in high voltage towers with a non-uniform geometry. Unlike the other components, the metal plate (P8) was used because it presents a geometry that is easy to detect by the sensors, allowing the comparison of the response curves of an object that is easy to perceive compared to other objects that have complex geometries for perception. The components used in this step are shown in Fig. 3.

To conduct the experiments in a controlled environment, the following pro-cedures were adopted:

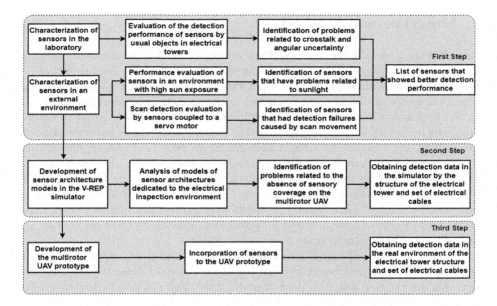

Fig. 2. Task flow adopted the methodology.

Table 1. Maximum and minimum detection capabilities of the sensors.

Sensor	Range(cm)	Resolution (mm)	Current (mA)	Price ($)
HC-SR04	2-400	3	15	1
RCW-0001	1-450	1	2.8	1
US-15	2-400	0.5	2.2	2
US-16	2-300	3	3.8	2
VL53L0X	0-200	1	19	5
VL53L1X	0-400	1	16	15
YDLiDAR X4	0-1000	1	380	99
LiDARLite V3	0-4000	10	135	130

- All objects used as targets have their orientation always in front of the sensors. The positioning of objects is done manually and guided by a tape measure with a precision of 1 mm.
- All ultrasonic sensors used a temperature and humidity sensor (DHT11) to correct variations in environmental conditions.
- All objects used in the experiments were manually positioned in front of the sensors every 10 cm until they reached a distance of 450 cm. For every 10 cm of distance between the object and the sensor, 45 detection samples are collected.
- The sweep angle of the YDLiDAR X4 sensor was set to 10°.

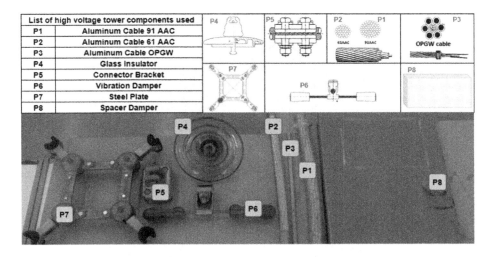

Fig. 3. Components of a high voltage tower used in the research.

– Data from all sensors, except for YDLidar, were obtained from a data acquisition system implemented in an Arduino Mega 2560 controller board. YDLidar data were obtained from a data acquisition system implemented in Raspberry Pi.

With the dataset extracted in this first evaluation, the simple arithmetic mean and variance of the detection values of the sensors were stored. Then, tests were performed only with the ultrasonic sensors to identify the range of detections used in different angular positions. This evaluation sought to determine the limit angle for the detection of ultrasonic sensors when used individually or grouped without problems related to the crosstalk effect and angular uncertainty. For this, each ultrasonic sensor was tested individually at $0°$ and subsequently at angles of $15°$, $25°$ and $35°$ over the P8 (metal plate) object, storing an amount of 45 samples for every 10 cm traveled, until reaching the maximum detection distance of the sensors on the target object.

Then, angular detection assessments were performed using ultrasonic sensors in pairs, following the same methodological procedures adopted for the individual evaluation. For this, an 8BYJ-48 stepper motor was coupled to each ultrasonic sensor, aiming at precision and synchronization between the positions of $15°$, $25°$ and $35°$ as illustrated in Fig. 4.

3.2 Characterization of Sensors in an External Environment

The tests conducted outdoors were carried out during times of high solar incidence, during the early afternoon. The main objective of this evaluation was to analyze whether LASER sensors have detection capabilities even under strong sunlight. Initially, LASER sensors with a longer detection range were used, i.e.,

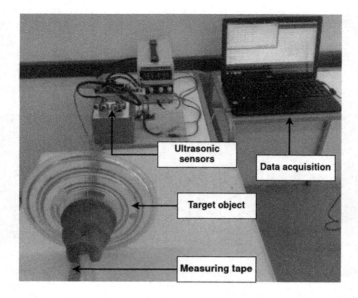

Fig. 4. Evaluation of angular detection by ultrasonic sensors.

the YDLiDAR X4 and LiDAR Lite V3 sensors, to detect a wall at a maximum distance of up to 10 m. A measuring tape was used to guide the sensors at each 1-m displacement in front of the target. For each meter travelled, 400 detection samples were acquired.

In the second sequence of tests involving ultrasonic and LASER sensors with lower detection capacity, tests were carried out to analyze the performance of the sensors when used in constant motion. For this, a servo motor was used as a base to couple each sensor, providing a scan detection range of 180°, detecting a wall that was used as a target. A tape measure was used to guide the positioning of the sensors on the target. The scanning detection evaluation generated an amount of 400 samples for each 1 m of distance travelled between the sensors and the mark, reaching a maximum distance of 4 m.

3.3 Multirotor UAV Prototype

The multirotor UAV was developed with the purpose of validating a sensor distribution model that detects obstacles in an electrical tower. For this, a small aircraft was developed with the ability to perform controlled and stable flights.

3.4 Model of Sensor Architecture

By the CoppeliaSim simulator, different beam patterns are modelled, representing the detection performance of the sensors integrated with a multirotor UAV. The beam pattern model is built by correlating the results presented by the sensory characterization versus the detection distances informed in the sensor manufacturing manual. From this information, the size of the sensor beam pattern is modeled, as illustrated in Fig. 5.

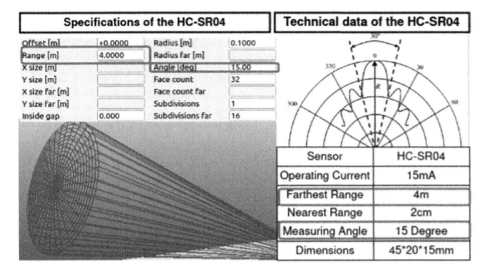

Fig. 5. Beam pattern of the HC-SR04 sensor modeled on the simulator.

4   Results

This section presents the results obtained by the methodology proposed in this research.

4.1   Result of the Characteristics of the Sensors in a Controlled Environment

The responses generated by the laboratory tests helped identify the types of sensors with the greatest detection range on the different types of components existing in high voltage towers. Among all the components evaluated in this first experiment, the object P3 (OPGW cable) was not properly detected by most sensors, which is the object of greater detection complexity evaluated in this experiment. In an overview, it is possible to observe in Fig. 6 the sensor detection relationship between object P8 (metal plate) and object P3. As it is a thin object, the OPGW cable presented great difficulties in being detected by most sensors in this evaluation. Unlike object P3, the metal plate proved easy to detect due to its simple and uniform geometry, making it possible to analyze the maximum detection performance of the sensors involved in this research.

The HC-SR04 sensor presented the best detection performance over the set of electrical cables (P1, P2 and P3), perceiving obstacles at a range greater

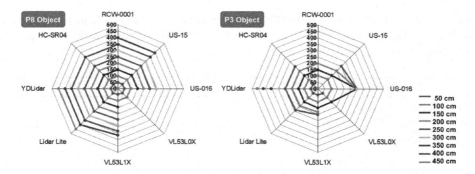

Fig. 6. Preliminary results obtained during tests in a controlled environment.

than 2 m away, as shown in Fig. 7. Based on these responses, it was possible to estimate that in the face of a scenario of detection of power transmission lines, a multirotor UAV developed for this application may have the ability to detect objects of thin thickness at a distance considered safe, taking into account that the detection will occur at a distance of at least 2 m.

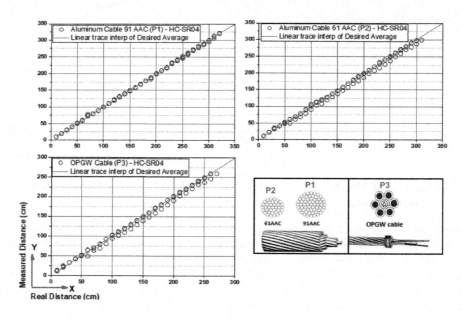

Fig. 7. Detection results of the HC-SR04 sensor on electrical cables.

The results generated from the comparison between the individual detection and the pairs of the ultrasonic sensors on the P8 object show that before the positioning between 0° and 15°, problems related to the crosstalk effect introduced errors of detection on the P8 (metal plate) object. The intensification of the crosstalk effect occurred when positioned at 0°, with the total superposition of the lobes of the ultrasonic sensors. It was identified that with the positioning of 25°, detection results were produced between ultrasonic sensors with greater proximity to the desired average distance. Problems related to angular uncertainty were generated from the positioning of 35°. Overall, the HC-SR04 sensor presented the best detection performance, identifying obstacles at a distance range of more than 2 m.

4.2   Sensory Results in External Environment

The results presented in this evaluation helped to identify which sensors are not affected by sunlight, temperature variation and vibration generated by a servo motor. Figure 8 shows the results obtained by the sensors evaluated in the external environment, indicating that the YDLiDAR X4 sensor has a null detection range under high sunlight. Unlike the YDLiDAR X4 sensor, the LiDARLite V3 LASER sensor could identify the target even under high sunlight, presenting characteristics that allow it to detect targets regardless of lighting conditions. Among the shortest range sensors, represented by the HC-SR04, US16, and VL53L1X, the HC-SR04 sensor presented the best detection results.

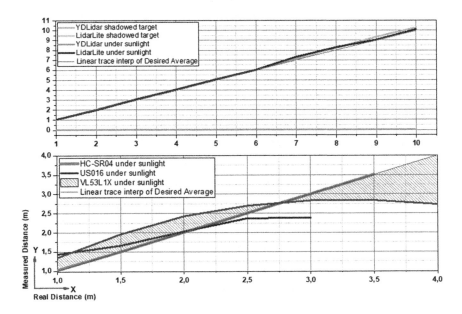

Fig. 8. Results of sensory detection obtained in the external environment.

4.3   Sensor Achitecture for the UAV Prototype

It was identified by the results obtained in Sect. 4.2 that the HC-SR04 and LiDARLite V3 sensors have the characteristics required to compose the different models of sensor architectures together with the CoppeliaSim simulator. Other sensors used in the experiments did not meet the expected requirements, these being (I): detection capacity greater than 2 m away, (II): identification of multiplThe results presented show a relationship between the values obtained in the simulation and the real environment, indicating similarity between the detection ranges of the sensors applied in the electrical inspection environment. In future works, the objective is to integrate artificial intelligence systems applied to autonomous navigation based on the sensory architecture used in this research. In addition, it will be possible to add new sensors in other regions of the UAV aiming for omnidirectional detection systems obstacles, (III): identification of thin obstacles such as electrical cables, (VI): be able to identify obstacles even under high sunlight, (V): be able to identify obstacles even in constant vibration.

The sensory architecture model developed in the simulator is composed of 4 HC-SR04 ultrasonic sensors that are positioned on the front end of the UAV and a LASER LiDAR Lite V3 sensor. The ultrasonic sensors are separated from each other in an angular position of 25°, a configuration that presented the best results during the sensory characterization steps. In this architectural model developed, both the HC-SR04 and LiDARLite V3 sensors perform a sweeping horizontal movement at 180°, making it possible to carry out detections both in the frontal and lateral regions of the multirotor. Figure 9 presents (a) the architectural model defined as ideal and used in the simulated environment; (b) the architectural model defined as ideal coupled to the actual UAV.

Fig. 9. Sensor architecture model defined.

For data acquisition in the simulated environment, the UAV was positioned just in front of an electrical tower, collecting a set of 400 samples of the tower structure and moving every one meter of distance until it covered the range of 10 m. It also evaluated in the simulator the ability to detect the set of electrical cables by the UAV, collecting detection information within the range of 1 to 4 m away.

4.4   Comparison of Simulated Data to Actual Data

Following the same procedures adopted in the simulation, the actual UAV was used to fly, remotely controlled, over a set of high voltage towers, obtaining detection data from the infrastructure of the electrical tower and the group of transmission lines. In this test environment, a tape measure was used to mark the actual positioning in relation to the aircraft. Three LASER indicators are attached to the UAV to point out the approximate location of the aircraft in relation to the tape measure. Figure 10 illustrates in (a) system to assist in viewing the positioning of the UAV; (b) test environment; (c) acquisition of tower infrastructure data; (d) data acquisition of the electrical cable assembly.

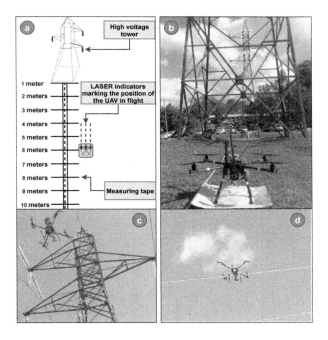

Fig. 10. Procedures and tests performed on a real electrical tower.

The results presented by the sensory detection in a simulated environment were closely related to the actual detection values. During the simulation, all four sensors could adequately identify the base of the electrical tower within the determined distance range, from 100 cm to 400 cm. When comparing with the values of sensory detection obtained in a real environment, it can be seen that, in general, there were detection variations around 50 cm, except for HC-SR04 (2) which indicated a variation around 100 cm. The detection variation of the ultrasonic sensors was because the structure of the actual electric tower has a complex geometry, being hollow and not uniform. Figure 11 presents the results obtained by the sensory detection of the HC-SR04 sensor on the structure of the

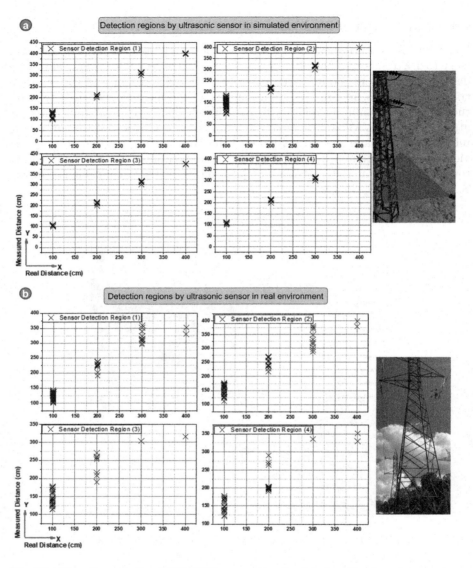

Fig. 11. Detection results of HC-SR04 sensors in simulated and real environments.

electrical tower, wherein (a) the results obtained in the simulation are presented; (b) results obtained in a real environment.

As with the HC-SR04 ultrasonic sensors, the LASER LiDAR lite V3 sensor presented detection results close to the desired distance ranges, accurately detecting the structure of the electrical tower up to the 10-m distance mark in high sunlight. For the acquisition of detection data from the set of electrical cables, the UAV initially remained positioned in front of the electrical lines at approximately 1 m away, collecting detection information by performing smooth movements away from the transmission lines. The values obtained by the sensors were filtered so that only detection data within the range of 100 cm to 400 cm were kept.

The results show that the HC-SR04 sensor can detect the set of electrical cables, which are constituted in the real scenario by the 91 AAC cable, that is, the P1 object. The number of detection points obtained by the set of ultrasonic sensors, identifying the set of electrical cables at distances greater than 300 cm, shows the ability to detect thin objects at a safe distance by the UAV. In the simulated scenario, the detection results by the set of sensors HC-SR04 presented capacities similar to those obtained by the real environment.

5   Conclusions and Future Work

The main objective of this research was to propose a sensor distribution method based on geometric representations. With this, it is possible to preliminarily visualize the detection and performance behaviour of different types of sensor architectures in multirotor UAVs. Based on the technical characteristics of the sensors that presented the best results in this study, namely HC-SR04 and LiDAR Lite V3, a sensor architecture modelled through the CoppeliaSim simulator was proposed, with the ability to identify the base and sets of electrical cables of a high tower voltage at distances greater than 2 m.

The results of this research show that multiple ultrasonic sensors, which operate 25° apart, do not present problems related to the *crosstalk* effect due to the distance between the beam pattern of each ultrasonic sensor. Problems related to angular uncertainty were generated from the positioning of 35° between ultrasonic sensors and less than 25° when causing the crosstalk effect. Sensor detection evaluations in outdoor environments showed that low-power LASER sensors, such as the YDLiDAR X4 sensor, cannot detect obstacles in the face of high sun exposure.

The results presented show a relationship between the values obtained in the simulation and the real environment, indicating similarity between the detection ranges of the sensors applied in the electrical inspection environment. In future works, the objective is to integrate artificial intelligence systems applied to autonomous navigation based on the sensory architecture used in this research. In addition, it will be possible to add new sensors in other regions of the UAV aiming for omnidirectional detection systems.

Acknowledgment. The authors are grateful to the Foundation for Science and Technology (FCT, Portugal) for financial support through national funds FCT/MCTES (PIDDAC) to CeDRI (UIDB/05757/2020 and UIDP/05757/2020), SusTEC (LA/P/0007/2021), Oleachain "Skills for sustainability and innovation in the value chain of traditional olive groves in the Northern Interior of Portugal" (Norte06-3559-FSE-000188) and Centro Federal de Educação Tecnológica Celso Suckow da Fonseca (CEFET/RJ). The project that gave rise to these results received the support

of a fellowship from "la Caixa" Foundation (ID 100010434). The fellowship code is
LCF/BQ/DI20/11780028.

References

1. Tsuji, S., Kohama, T.: Omnidirectional proximity sensor system for drones using optical time-of-flight sensors. IEEJ Trans. Electr. Electron. Eng. **17**(1), 19–25 (2022)
2. Aswini, N., Krishna Kumar, E., Uma, S.V.: UAV and obstacle sensing techniques - a perspective (2018)
3. Yasin, J.N., Mohamed, S.A., Haghbayan, M.H., Heikkonen, J., Tenhunen, H., Plosila, J.: Unmanned aerial vehicles (UAVs): collision avoidance systems and approaches. IEEE Access **8**, 105139–105155 (2020)
4. Mahjri, I., Dhraief, A., Belghith, A.: A review on collision avoidance systems for unmanned aerial vehicles. In: International Conference on Information and Communication Technology Convergence (2021)
5. Berger, G.S., Wehrmeister, M.A., Ferraz, M.F., Cantieri, A.R.: Analysis of low cost sensors applied to the detection of obstacles in high voltage towers. In: Proceedings of International Embedded Systems Symposium (IESS 2019) (2019)
6. Niwa, K., Watanabe, K., Nagai, I.: A detection method using ultrasonic sensors for avoiding a wall collision of quadrotors. In: 2017 IEEE International Conference on Mechatronics and Automation (ICMA), pp. 1438–1443 (2017)
7. Jordan, S., et al.: State-of-the-art technologies for UAV inspections. IET Radar Sonar Navig. **12**(2), 151–164 (2018)
8. Gupta, N., Makkar, J.S., Pandey, P.: Obstacle detection and collision avoidance using ultrasonic sensors for RC multirotors. In: 2015 International Conference on Signal Processing and Communication (ICSC) (2015)
9. Ben-Ari, M., Mondada, F.: Sensors. In: Ben-Ari, M., Mondada, F. (eds.) Elements of Robotics, pp. 21–37. Springer, Cham (2018). https://doi.org/10.1007/978-3-319-62533-1_2
10. Nieuwenhuisen, M., Droeschel, D., Beul, M., Behnke, S.: Obstacle detection and navigation planning for autonomous micro aerial vehicles. In: International Conference on Unmanned Aircraft Systems (2014)
11. Papa, U., Ponte, S.: Preliminary design of an unmanned aircraft system for aircraft general visual inspection. Electronics **7**, 435 (2018)
12. Suherman, S., et al.: Ultrasonic sensor assessment for obstacle avoidance in quadcopter-based drone system. In: International Conference on Mechanical, Electronics, Computer, and Industrial Technology (2020)
13. Deng, C., Liu, J.Y., Liu, B.Y., Tan, Y.Y.: Real time autonomous transmission line following system for quadrotor helicopters (2016)
14. Shoval, S., Borenstein, J.: Using coded signals to benefit from ultrasonic sensor crosstalk in mobile robot obstacle avoidance. In: Proceedings 2001 ICRA. IEEE International Conference on Robotics and Automation (Cat. No. 01CH37164) (2001)

Is Diabetic Retinopathy Grading Biased by Imbalanced Datasets?

Fernando C. Monteiro$^{(\boxtimes)}$ and José Rufino

Research Centre in Digitalization and Intelligent Robotics (CeDRI), Laboratório para a Sustentabilidade e Tecnologia em Regiões de Montanha (SusTEC), Instituto Politécnico de Bragança, Campus de Santa Apolónia, 5300-253 Bragança, Portugal
{monteiro,rufino}@ipb.pt

Abstract. Diabetic retinopathy (DR) is one of the most severe complications of diabetes and the leading cause of vision loss and even blindness. Retinal screening contributes to early detection and treatment of diabetic retinopathy. This eye disease has five stages, namely normal, mild, moderate, severe and proliferative diabetic retinopathy. Usually, highly trained ophthalmologists are capable of manually identifying the presence or absence of retinopathy in retinal images. Several automated deep learning (DL) based approaches have been proposed and they have been proven to be a powerful tool for DR detection and classification. However, these approaches are usually biased by the cardinality of each grade set, as the overall accuracy benefits the largest sets in detriment of smaller ones. In this paper, we applied several state-of-the-art DL approaches, using a 5-fold cross-validation technique. The experiments were conducted on a balanced DDR dataset containing 31330 retina fundus images by completing the small grade sets with samples from other well known datasets. This balanced dataset increases robustness of training and testing tasks as they used samples from several origins and obtained with different equipment. The results confirm the bias introduced by using imbalanced datasets in automatic diabetic retinopathy grading.

Keywords: Diabetic retinopathy grading · Deep learning network · Retinal fundus images · Diabetic retinopathy dataset · Imbalanced dataset

1 Introduction

Diabetic Retinopathy is a serious and common health condition, caused by diabetes mellitus, that affects the human retina, causing damage to blood vessels which become leaky or blocked, generating microaneurysms, soft and hard exhudates and haemorrhages [29] (see Fig. 1). Blood vessels grow and swelling in the central part of the retina can lead to vision loss or even blindness.

Although there is no knowledge of the total number of people affected with moderate and severe forms of glaucoma or diabetic retinopathy, it is estimated

A. I. Pereira et al. (Eds.): OL2A 2022, CCIS 1754, pp. 51–64, 2022.
https://doi.org/10.1007/978-3-031-23236-7_4

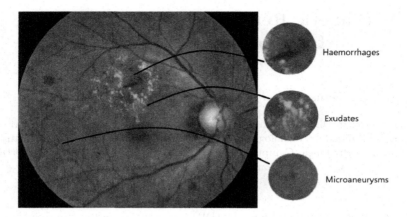

Fig. 1. DR lesions in a retina fundus image.

that several million cases of eye diseases could have been avoided if there had been a timely diagnosis [34]. It is known that screening, early detection and prompt treatment of DR allow prevention of visual impairment. With the rising incidence and prevalence of DR, public health systems in both developing and developed countries should implement and maintain a DR screening program for people with diabetes [30].

Accordingly with the International Clinical Diabetic Retinopathy Disease Severity Scale [33] (ICDRDSS), there are five severity levels of DR depending on the presence of retina lesions, namely: *normal* (grade 0) - no abnormalities; *mild DR* (grade 1) - tiny bulges develop in the blood vessels, which may bleed slightly but do not usually affect vision; *moderate DR* (grade 2) - swelling and distortion of blood vessels; *severe DR* (grade 3) - widespread changes affect the blood vessels, blocking them, including more significant bleeding into the eye and prominent microvascular abnormalities; *proliferative DR* (grade 4) - neovascularization or vitreous/preretinal hemorrhage which can result in loss of vision. This grading is important to determine the exact stage of DR to begin a suitable treatment process and to prevent the retina deterioration and the possible blindness.

A worldwide problem associated with DR is the reduced number of specialists to follow the patients: e.g., in China there is a ratio of one ophthalmologist for 3000 diabetes patients [8]. To overcome this problem, several computer aided diagnosis techniques, mainly based on deep learning schemes, have been proposed to automatically detect DR and its different stages from retina fundus images.

Deep learning models are designed to automatically learn feature hierarchies through back-propagation by using multiple layer blocks from low to high level patterns [4]. The automatic extraction of the most discriminant features from a set of training images, suppressing the need for preliminary feature extraction, became the main strength of deep learning approaches.

There still remain some concerns associated with the automated DR classification approaches proposed in the literature that are preventing their use in clinical applications. Although such methods have achieved high performance in a specific imbalanced dataset, more studies are need to known how they may perform on other datasets. Here, the major issue at stake is the reduced model reliability. An important underlying factor is the fact that the majority of published approaches used imbalanced datasets in their studies. Using a dataset where more than 70% of the samples are healthy retina images and only 2% for one of DR grades will introduce bias in the results. Alyoubi et al. in their review paper [2] discuss the existing DR grading techniques and have shown that even when doing multi-level classification, the available DL based approaches provide only a DR grading result.

Deep learning networks (DLN) automatically extract the most discriminative features from training images. Nevertheless, which features are extracted to make a classification decision remains somehow unknown. Since experts usually evaluate the DR grade based on the presence of lesions in the retina, we believe that while automated techniques do not demonstrate that their results are based on the lesions, such techniques will not be accepted as a reliable substitute of human ophthalmologists. To sum up, more and thorough investigations about the usage of deep learning methods work for DR grading are needed.

In this paper we introduce a deep learning-based method for the problem of classifying DR in fundus imagery. To avoid over-fitting produced by imbalanced datasets in one DLN, our approach applies several of the best known DLN models that were trained and tested in a balanced dataset. This balanced dataset increases the robustness of the model, allowing it to produce more reliable predictive results than those obtained by using imbalanced datasets.

The remainder of this paper is organized as follows: in Sect. 2, previous related works are presented and reviewed; in Sect. 3, we describe the used materials and the proposed method; Sect. 4 presents the results and some discussion on the findings; finally, in Sect. 5, some conclusions are drawn.

2   Related Works

Automatic systems for DR recognition based on image features have been proposed for a long time. In general terms, those approaches extract some feature characteristics to identify retina lesions [5]. The majority of these classification techniques are binary classifiers that classify data only into two classes: normal and DR affected [13]. The problem with these methods is that they do not allow to identify the disease severity even when it is known that a patient has DR.

Recent increasing of computational resources and capabilities have created the opportunity to develop deep learning models for DR detection and grading. This section reviews the studies in which the DR datasets (EyePACS, APTOS or DDR) were classified into five classes accordingly with the ICDRDSS scale. The majority of published DR grading studies used imbalanced datasets.

Pratt et al. [21] presented one of the first studies employing a DLN for classifying DR samples in five classes. They obtained an accuracy of 0.75 but could not classify the mild class accurately. An important limitation is that they trained the network with limited number of images from a skewed EyePACS dataset, which could prevent the DLN from learning more features.

Wan et al. [32] studied the performance of four available pretrained networks to detect the five stages in the EyePACS dataset. During the preprocessing stage, the images were filtered with a NonLocal Means Denoising function. Transfer learning was done by fine tuning the last fully connected layer. They reported the best accuracy of 0.957 for the VGG16 architecture. However, they have used the biased imbalanced EyePACS dataset.

Bodapati et al. [6] presented an approach where features extracted from multiple pre-trained DLN are blended using a multi-modal fusion module. These final weights are used to train a DLN employed in DR grading prediction. Experiments were conducted in the APTOS dataset using 80% for training and 20% for validation. The authors did not used a test dataset. They achieved an accuracy of 0.81 over the validation dataset. Unfortunately, they have used the imbalanced version of the APTOS dataset.

Li et al. [17] classified DR levels in their dataset (DDR) by fine-tuning five available pretrained networks. They identified a new DR grade for images without quality for being classified. The SE-BN-Inception network [15] obtained the best accuracy of 0.828, including grade 5 samples, and 0.751, removing grade 5 samples. The work highlights the difficulty in classifying mild DR, and the frequency with which severe DR is misclassified as moderate. Still, they have used an imbalanced version of the DDR dataset, that produces biased results.

Majumder and Kehtarnavaz [19] proposed a multitasking deep learning model for DR grading in five levels. They used a Multitasking Squeeze Excitation Densely Connected Network that consists of a SEDenseNet classification model, a SEDenseNet regression model, and a MLP classifier. They achieved an accuracy of 0.82 for the EyePACS dataset and 0.85 for the APTOS dataset. Unfortunately, they have used the imbalanced version of the datasets.

Alyoubi et al. [1] proposed a deep learning model (CNN512) to classify retina fundus images into one of the five DR stages. To overcome the different levels of light in the samples, the retina images were normalised. For the normalization, they subtract the mean and then divide the variance of the images. This achieved an accuracy of 0.886 and 0.841 on the DDR and the APTOS public datasets, respectively. Again, the imbalanced version of the datasets were used.

Some studies [22,24] identified the problem associated with imbalanced datasets and achieved balance among grade sets by replicating a small number of images to a large number by data augmentation. In spite of that, the variability of features trained and tested will be very low, introducing bias in the results.

Qummar et al. [22] ensembled five DLN models to encode the best features and improve the classification for different stages of DR. They used stacking to combine the results of all different models and generate a unified output. They obtained an overall accuracy of 0.648. To overcome the bias created by the imbalanced EyePACS dataset they balanced it via data augmentation. However, this process used only the original images in each grade set. For example, in the grade 4 set they obtained 4119 images from just 113 original images. The variability of features in such augmented images is, of course, very small.

In a recent work, Rocha et al. [24] applied the VGG16 network to classify the diabetic retinopathy in five and six levels in the DDR, EyePACS and IDRiD databases. They balanced the three datasets by using data augmentation over the original images as in [22], thus with the same variability issue. The number of samples per class was 800 (DDR), 3000 (EyePACS) and 140 (IDRiD). The accuracy for five levels in each dataset was 0.854, 0.779 and 0.898, for the DDR, EyePACS and IDRiD datasets, respectively.

For comprehensive details of research in the field of DR detection readers are encouraged to see the excellent reviews of Alyoubi et al. [2] and Tsiknakis et al. [31]. In these works the authors discuss the advantages and disadvantages of current DR classification techniques and analyse public DR datasets available.

3   Proposed Method

In this section we introduce the details of our framework. First, we introduce the DR datasets, then the preprocessing methods and, finally, the DL approach to classify the samples in the five DR stages.

3.1   Diabetic Retinopathy Dataset

The automation of DR recognition and grading depends on large image datasets with many samples categorized by ophthalmologists. The results depend on the number of samples and their acquisition conditions. A small number of images may result in poor learning models, that are not sufficient to adequately train the deep learning architecture.

Another factor to consider in DL approaches is the size and quality of datasets used for training and testing datasets. Over-fitting is a major issue in DLN, as imbalanced datasets make the network to over-fit to the most prominent class in the dataset [31].

Most of the publicly available datasets contain less than 2000 images, like the Indian Diabetic Retinopathy Image dataset (IDRiD) [20], with 516 images, or Messidor 2 [9], with 1748 images. The Asia Pacific Tele-Ophthalmology Society (*Kaggle* APTOS) [3] dataset contains 5590 images (3662 samples for training and 1928 samples for testing) collected by the Aravind Eye Hospital in India; however, only the ground truths of the training images are publicly available.

Kaggle EyePACS [12] is the largest DR dataset with 88702 images (35126 samples for training and 53576 for testing) classified into five DR levels. This dataset was classified by only one ophthalmologist, which can potentially lead to annotation bias. It consists of a large number of images which were obtained under a variety of imaging conditions by different devices at several primary care sites throughout California [12]. Maybe due to such variability, there is a large number of images where the eye's features are indistinguishable due to the presence of noise, artifacts produced by lenses, chromatic distortions or low light.

In fact, accordingly with the dataset curators, the presence of these extraneous features was an intended goal, in order to better simulate a real world scenario.

The DDR dataset [17] is the second largest dataset, consisting of 13673 images divided in 6835 for training, 2733 for validation and 4105 for testing. Retina fundus images were collected between 2016 and 2018 across 147 hospitals in China, and annotated by several ophthalmologists according to the ICDRDSS scale, using a majority voting approach.

DR screening produces some low quality images that are meaningless to analyze and grade due to the lack of information. In this way, a new class (Grade 5) was created to include these ungradable images, as showed in Fig. 2.

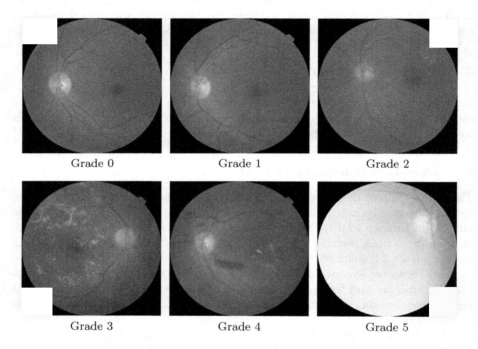

Fig. 2. The DR grades: normal retina (Grade 0), mild DR (Grade 1), moderate DR (Grade 2), severe DR (Grade 3), proliferative DR (Grade 4), ungradable (Grade 5).

Table 1 shows the distribution of training, validation and test images per class, for DR grading in the two largest publicly available datasets (EyePACS and DDR). The training set of the EyePACS dataset is usually split in 80% for training and 20% for validation [21].

The class labels of the datasets are highly imbalanced, specially in the *Kaggle* EyePACS dataset, with more than 73% of the samples annotated as normal, whereas severe and proliferative DR samples only account for less than 3% each.

To reduce the classification bias, Li et al. [17] and Qummar et al. [22] have augmented existing samples from the 1, 2, 3, and 4 classes, to produce new

Table 1. Number of samples per class in the training, validation and test sets of largest publicly available DR datasets.

Dataset	DR class	Training	Validation	Test	Total	Percentage
EyePACS	Grade 0	25810	–	39533	65343	73.6%
	Grade 1	2443	–	3763	2329	7.0%
	Grade 2	5292	–	7860	13152	14.8%
	Grade 3	873	–	1214	2087	2.4%
	Grade 4	708	–	1206	1914	2.2%
	Total	35126	–	53576	88702	
DDR	Grade 0	3133	1253	1880	6266	45.8%
	Grade 1	315	126	189	630	4.6%
	Grade 2	2238	895	1344	4477	32.8%
	Grade 3	118	47	71	236	1.7%
	Grade 4	456	182	275	913	6.6%
	Grade 5	575	230	346	1151	8.5%
	Total	6835	2733	4105	13673	

samples. Although augmenting the dataset does not make it totally balanced, it does help to lessen the biases. Nevertheless, as this augmentation process, in some classes, is based only in a very small number of images, the variability of features learned by the DLN does not increase.

To overcome this problem, in our experiment we have balanced the DDR classes in all the sets, using random samples of the same class, from the Eye-PACS, APTOS and IDRiD datasets, thus obtaining the balanced DDR dataset (BDDR) with a total of 31330 samples. Usually, the works that have used the DDR dataset have removed the class 5 set. In order to do a fair comparative study, we also removed this class.

Table 2 shows the distribution of training, validation and test sets per class for the balanced DDR dataset. Only a small number of samples from grades 3 and 4 of the training set have been obtained by rotation, though even when joining all the five datasets we cannot obtain the number of samples we need.

Using several datasets, that were collected on different resolution, equipment, and geographies, allow to incorporate this variability into our model, which increases the generalization by reducing sensitivity to the image acquisition system. Using only one imbalanced dataset oversimplifies the identification process, making it impractical to be used for recognizing DR in images obtained worldwide in different conditions [31].

3.2   Image Preprocessing

As the used DR datasets were obtained from different locations with different types of equipment, they may contain images that vary in terms of resolution

Table 2. Number of samples in each grade set for training, validation and test sets of the balanced DDR dataset.

DR class	Training	Validation	Test	Total	Percentage
Grade 0	3133	1253	1880	6266	20.0%
Grade 1	3133	1253	1880	6266	20.0%
Grade 2	3133	1253	1880	6266	20.0%
Grade 3	3133	1253	1880	6266	20.0%
Grade 4	3133	1253	1880	6266	20.0%
Total	15665	6265	9400	31330	

and aspect ratio. The images could also contain uninformative black space areas that may induce some bias in the training and test processes.

Image preprocessing is thus a necessary step to enhance image features and to ensure the consistency of images. In order to reduce the black space areas, the images were cropped to a circle that limits the retina. The image resolution was also adapted to each deep learning architecture, e.g. 224×224 for ResNet and 299×299 for Inception architectures.

In some works only the green channel of images was extracted due to its high contrast in blood vessels and red lesions [18]. However, these approaches loose the colour information. Contrast enhancement is a common preprocessing approach used to highlight the image features like blood vessels or retina lesions. A technique often used is image normalization based on the min-pooling filtering [13,35]. In our experiments we adopted the Contrast Limited Adaptive Histogram Equalization (CLAHE), applying it to each colour channel. Figure 3 shows one original image and the outcome of the preprocessing techniques employed in it.

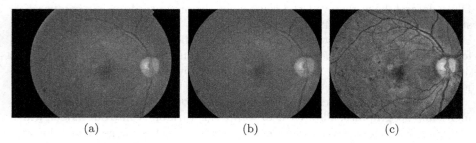

(a)   (b)   (c)

Fig. 3. Preprocessing steps: (a) original image, (b) cropped image, (c) CLAHE image.

3.3   Deep Learning Architectures

In our approach, ten state-of-the-art DLNs were used: VGG 16/19 [25], ResNet 50/101 [14], Inception-V3 [27], Inception-ResNet [26], Xception [7], DenseNet201 [16], DarkNet53 [23] and EfficientNetB0 [28].

Training a deep learning network is very demanding in terms of computational resources and data required. Unlike images of everyday objects, as those in the ImageNet dataset [11], large medical images datasets are very hard to obtain due to the necessary annotation time and legal issues involved [31].

Transfer learning is a commonly used technique that transfers the knowledge from a pretrained network on a large dataset and it is used to solve a recognition or classification task in which limited training data are available. All the ten deep learning architectures were fine-tuned by initialising their weights with ImageNet values and re-training all of their layers with the BDDR dataset.

We used the fine-tuning strategy, as well as the stochastic gradient descent with momentum optimizer (SGDM) at their default values, dropout rate set at 0.5 and early-stopping to prevent over-fitting, and the learning rate at 0.0001. SGDM is used to accelerate gradients vectors in the correct directions, as we do not need to check all the training examples to have knowledge of the direction of the decreasing slope, thus leading to faster converging. Additionally, to balance the memory consumption and the performance of the network, we used a batch size of 32 to update the network weights more often, and trained them in 30 epochs.

To preprocess images further, all samples go through a heavy data augmentation process which includes flipping, 180° random rotation, rescaling factor between 70% and 130%, and horizontal and vertical translations between -20 and $+20$ pixels. The networks were trained using the ONNX package for Matlab® on a computing node of the CeDRI cluster equipped with a NVIDIA A100 GPU.

We used 5-Fold Cross-Validation, where in each set the images were split on five folds, allowing the networks to be independently trained and validated on different sets. Since each testing set is built with images not seen by the training model, this allows us to anticipate the network behaviour against new images.

4   Results and Discussion

All the proposed approaches available in the literature that applied deep learning techniques to classify the *Kaggle* EyePACS, APTOS or DDR datasets used the imbalanced version of the datasets. Table 3 summarizes the accuracy for each class and the overall accuracy (OA) for the three DR datasets. In the approaches that used the DDR dataset we have removed grade 5 samples.

When using imbalanced datasets, the accuracy tends to bias towards majority classes [22]. Analysing Table 1 and Table 3 we can see that these results correlate well with the number of samples used in each class. If we use a balanced dataset with the samples in the classes equally distributed then the DLN can learn the features properly, but in the situation of unequal distribution, DLN over-fits for the highly sampled class. The OA is obtained as a weighted average of the accuracy grades and, as the weight of grade 0 is very high, the importance of an accuracy of 0.0 for grade 1 in the work [21] does not change the OA value (e.g., in the EyePACS dataset an accuracy of 0.95 for grade 0 contributes with a minimum value of 0.70 for the overall accuracy).

Table 3. DR grading classification on the test set for *Kaggle* EyePACS, APTOS and DDR datasets in terms of accuracy.

Dataset	Grade 0	Grade 1	Grade 2	Grade 3	Grade 4	OA
EyePACS [21][a]	0.950	0.000	0.233	0.085	0.443	0.738
EyePACS [22][b]	0.973	0.546	0.509	0.617	0.596	0.648
APTOS [10]	0.986	0.476	0.727	0.250	0.083	0.766
APTOS [1]	0.978	0.729	0.860	0.000	0.644	0.842
DDR [17]	0.945	0.048	0.646	0.127	0.582	0.751
DDR [1]	0.988	0.254	0.926	0.234	0.648	0.890

[a] Pratt et al. [21] have used only a subset of 5000 samples from EyePACS.
[b] Qummar et al. [22] have used a balanced EyePACS using data augmentation.

In our experiments we used a balanced version of the DRR dataset, by completing the grade sets with samples from several DR datasets. This approach has two advantages over other proposed balanced datasets: first, using more than one dataset allows to incorporate variability into the DLN model, which increases the generalization by reducing sensitivity to the image acquisition system; secondly, it uses different real images to complete the grade sets. Other authors have proposed data augmentation to balance the datasets [1,22]. In spite of that, they used a small number of real samples, which will produce low variability in the grade set, specially in the mild DR set.

In our judgement, the results obtained with imbalanced datasets are heavily biased and, as far as we know, we are the first to study the real accuracy obtained by DLN when using a dataset of balanced grade sets by using real images obtained from different publicly available datasets.

Table 4 summarizes the accuracy results for each class obtained from ten state-of-the-art DLNs, trained with 5-Fold cross-validation. These DLNs were trained and tested over the balanced dataset described in Table 2 with 15665 samples for the training set, 6265 samples for the validation set and 9400 samples for the test dataset, equally distributed over all five DR grades.

The experimental results demonstrate that the results obtained with the DL networks do not differ substantially in the overall accuracy, where the VGG16 network shows the highest overall accuracy, but a comparatively low accuracy on grades 2 and 4. The high accuracy for grade 0 (normal retina) detection suggests that we can use these approaches to rapidly make a binary classification, in normal and DR retina. All these networks exhibit poor performance on samples with moderate and proliferative DR, suggesting that these models are weak in learning these two types of samples. Furthermore, swelling and distortion of blood vessels in moderate DR are difficult to identify, while samples of proliferative DR are easily misclassified as moderate or severe DR, namely when there are no severe hemorrhages.

Table 4. Classification results (accuracy) of individual DLN classifiers on the test set for the different DR grading classes considered.

DLN	Grade 0	Grade 1	Grade 2	Grade 3	Grade 4	OA
VGG16	0.991	0.693	0.359	0.619	0.429	0.618
VGG19	0.952	0.803	0.244	0.815	0.227	0.608
ResNet50	0.949	0.771	0.317	0.560	0.334	0.586
ResNet101	0.956	0.753	0.323	0.613	0.256	0.580
Inception-V3	0.960	0.732	0.292	0.703	0.289	0.595
Incep.-ResNet	0.970	0.750	0.262	0.673	0.359	0.603
Xception	0.952	0.697	0.261	0.668	0.323	0.580
DenseNet201	0.960	0.804	0.366	0.568	0.285	0.597
DarkNet53	0.940	0.805	0.452	0.539	0.301	0.607
EfficientNetB0	0.967	0.731	0.234	0.702	0.284	0.584

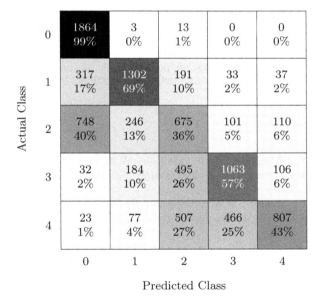

Fig. 4. Confusion matrix of the VGG16 network for the DR grading task.

The confusion matrix in Fig. 4 shows the misclassifications produced by the VGG16 model when applied to a DR grading prediction task. Note that the test set is composed by 9400 samples, equally distributed with 1880 samples for each DR grade. In the confusion matrix, we can see that most of the moderate DR type samples are predicted as normal.

5 Conclusion

Diabetic retinopathy is a complication of diabetes that is mainly caused by the damage of the blood vessels located in the retina. Computer-aided diagnosis approaches are needed to allow an early detection and treatment.

In this paper, we assessed the state-of-the-art deep learning models for DR grading. In our experiments we balanced the DDR dataset using images from the EyePACS, APTOS, Messidor-2 and IDRiD datasets, so that all classes are represented equally. This new balanced dataset aims to reduce biased classification presented in approaches that used imbalanced datasets.

We trained and tested ten individual DLN models, with 5-fold cross-validation. Our results confirm that most of the published approaches that used imbalanced datasets are biased by the cardinality in each grade set, as the overall accuracy benefits the largest grade sets.

In the future, we plan to design a blended framework that combines DR grading from the DLNs and combines their predictions in a final score. This approach has the advantage of training DLNs in different resolutions and increases the robustness by reducing possible over-fitting in individual models.

Acknowledgments. The authors are grateful to the Foundation for Science and Technology (FCT, Portugal) for financial support through national funds FCT/MCTES (PIDDAC) to CeDRI (UIDB/05757/2020 and UIDP/05757/2020) and SusTEC (LA/P/0007/2021).

References

1. Alyoubi, W.L., Abulkhair, M.F., Shalash, W.M.: Diabetic retinopathy fundus image classification and lesions localization system using deep learning. Sensors **21**(11), 3704 (2021)
2. Alyoubi, W.L., Shalash, W.M., Abulkhair, M.F.: Diabetic retinopathy detection through deep learning techniques: a review. Inform. Med. Unlocked **20**, 100377 (2020)
3. Asia Pacific Tele-Ophthalmology Society: Aptos 2019 blindness detection (2019). https://www.kaggle.com/competitions/aptos2019-blindness-detection. Accessed 4 Apr 2022
4. Baker, N., Lu, H., Erlikhman, G., Kellman, P.J.: Local features and global shape information in object classification by deep convolutional neural networks. Vision Res. **172**, 46–61 (2020)
5. Bhatia, K., Arora, S., Tomar, R.: Diagnosis of diabetic retinopathy using machine learning classification algorithm. In: 2016 2nd International Conference on Next Generation Computing Technologies, pp. 347–351 (2016)
6. Bodapati, J.D., et al.: Blended multi-modal deep ConvNet features for diabetic retinopathy severity prediction. Electronics **9**(6), 914 (2020)
7. Chollet, F.: Xception: deep learning with depthwise separable convolutions. In: 2017 IEEE Conference on Computer Vision and Pattern Recognition, pp. 1800–1807 (2017)
8. Dai, L., et al.: A deep learning system for detecting diabetic retinopathy across the disease spectrum. Nat. Commun. **12**(1), 3242 (2021)

9. Decencière, E., et al.: Feedback on a publicly distributed image database: the Messidor database. Image Anal. Stereol. **33**(3), 231–234 (2014)
10. Dekhil, O., Naglah, A., Shaban, M., Ghazal, M., Taher, F., Elbaz, A.: Deep learning based method for computer aided diagnosis of diabetic retinopathy. In: 2019 IEEE International Conference on Imaging Systems and Techniques (IST), pp. 1–4 (2019)
11. Deng, J., Dong, W., Socher, R., Li, L., Li, K., Fei-Fei, L.: Imagenet: a large-scale hierarchical image database. In: 2009 IEEE Conference on Computer Vision and Pattern Recognition, pp. 248–255 (2009)
12. EyePACS: Diabetic retinopathy detection (2015). https://www.kaggle.com/c/diabetic-retinopathy-detection. Accessed 4 Apr 2022
13. Gargeya, R., Leng, T.: Automated identification of diabetic retinopathy using deep learning. Ophthalmology **124**(7), 962–969 (2017)
14. He, K., Zhang, X., Ren, S., Sun, J.: Deep residual learning for image recognition. In: 2016 IEEE Conference on Computer Vision and Pattern Recognition (CVPR), pp. 770–778 (2016)
15. Hu, J., Shen, L., Sun, G.: Squeeze-and-excitation networks. In: Conference on Computer Vision and Pattern Recognition, pp. 7132–7141 (2018)
16. Huang, G., Liu, Z., Van Der Maaten, L., Weinberger, K.Q.: Densely connected convolutional networks. In: IEEE Conference on Computer Vision and Pattern Recognition (CVPR), pp. 2261–2269 (2017)
17. Li, T., Gao, Y., Wang, K., Guo, S., Liu, H., Kang, H.: Diagnostic assessment of deep learning algorithms for diabetic retinopathy screening. Inf. Sci. **501**, 511–522 (2019)
18. Lu, J., Xu, Y., Chen, M., Luo, Y.: A coarse-to-fine fully convolutional neural network for fundus vessel segmentation. Symmetry **10**(11), 607 (2018)
19. Majumder, S., Kehtarnavaz, N.: Multitasking deep learning model for detection of five stages of diabetic retinopathy. IEEE Access **9**, 123220–123230 (2021)
20. Porwal, P., Pachade, S., Kokare, M., et al.: IDRiD: diabetic retinopathy - segmentation and grading challenge. Med. Image Anal. **59**, 101561 (2020)
21. Pratt, H., Coenen, F., Broadbent, D.M., Harding, S.P., Zheng, Y.: Convolutional neural networks for diabetic retinopathy. Procedia Comput. Sci. **90**, 200–205 (2016)
22. Qummar, S., et al.: A deep learning ensemble approach for diabetic retinopathy detection. IEEE Access **7**, 150530–150539 (2019)
23. Redmon, J., Farhadi, A.: YOLOv3: an incremental improvement. arXiv:1804.02767 (2018)
24. Rocha, D.A., Ferreira, F., Peixoto, Z.: Diabetic retinopathy classification using VGG16 neural network. Res. Biomed. Eng. **38**, 761–772 (2022)
25. Simonyan, K., Zisserman, A.: Very deep convolutional networks for large-scale image recognition. In: International Conference on Learning Representations, pp. 1–14 (2015)
26. Szegedy, C., Ioffe, S., Vanhoucke, V., Alemi, A.: Inception-v4, inceptionresnet and the impact of residual connections on learning. In: Proceedings of the Thirty-First AAAI Conference on Artificial Intelligence, pp. 4278–4284 (2017)
27. Szegedy, C., Vanhoucke, V., Ioffe, S., Shlens, J., Wojna, Z.: Rethinking the inception architecture for computer vision. In: 2016 IEEE Conference on Computer Vision and Pattern Recognition (CVPR), pp. 2818–2826 (2016)
28. Tan, M., Le, Q.: EfficientNet: rethinking model scaling for convolutional neural networks. In: Proceedings of the 36th International Conference on Machine Learning, vol. 97, pp. 6105–6114 (2019)
29. Taylor, R., Batey, D.: Handbook of Retinal Screening in Diabetes: Diagnosis and Management, 2nd edn. Wiley-Blackwell, New York (2012)

30. Teo, Z., et al.: Diabetic retinopathy and projection of burden through 2045: systematic review and meta-analysis. Ophthalmology **128**(11), 1580–1591 (2021)
31. Tsiknakis, N., et al.: Deep learning for diabetic retinopathy detection and classification based on fundus images: a review. Comput. Biol. Med. **135**, 104599 (2021)
32. Wan, S., Liang, Y., Zhang, Y.: Deep convolutional neural networks for diabetic retinopathy detection by image classification. Comput. Electr. Eng. **72**, 274–282 (2018)
33. Wilkinson, C., et al.: Proposed international clinical diabetic retinopathy and diabetic macular edema disease severity scales. Ophthalmology **110**(9), 1677–1682 (2003)
34. World Health Organization: World report on vision - Licence: CC BY-NC-SA 3.0 IGO (2019). https://www.who.int/publications/i/item/9789241516570. Accessed 26 Apr 2022
35. Zago, G.T., Andreão, R.V., Dorizzi, B., Teatini Salles, E.O.: Diabetic retinopathy detection using red lesion localization and convolutional neural networks. Comput. Biol. Med. **116**, 103537 (2020)

Attention Mechanism for Classification of Melanomas

Cátia Loureiro[1]([⊠]) [iD], Vítor Filipe[1,2] [iD], and Lio Gonçalves[1,2] [iD]

[1] School of Science and Technology, University of Trás-os-Montes e Alto Douro
(UTAD), Vila Real, Portugal
al67570@utad.eu
[2] INESC Technology and Science (INESC TEC), Porto, Portugal
{vfilipe,lgoncalv}@utad.pt

Abstract. Melanoma is considered the deadliest type of skin cancer and in the last decade, the incidence rate has increased substantially. However, automatic melanoma classification has been widely used to aid the detection of lesions as well as prevent eventual death. Therefore, in this paper we decided to investigate how an attention mechanism combined with a classical backbone network would affect the classification of melanomas. This mechanism is known as triplet attention, a lightweight method that allows to capture cross-domain interactions. This characteristic helps to acquire rich discriminative feature representations. The different experiments demonstrate the effectiveness of the model in five different datasets. The model was evaluated based on sensitivity, specificity, accuracy, and F1-Score. Even though it is a simple method, this attention mechanism shows that its application could be beneficial in classification tasks.

Keywords: Melanoma · Attention mechanism · Classification

1 Introduction

Melanoma is a type of skin lesion considered one of the deadliest types of skin cancer. A skin lesion corresponds to any skin area that has different characteristics from the surrounding skin. Many skin lesions can appear as a result of damage to the skin. Nonetheless, it can also appear as a manifestation of interior disorders, like infections or diabetes. Most skin lesions are benign, though some of them can be malignant, commonly known as skin cancer. The leading cause of skin cancer can be attributed to exposure to ultraviolet radiation, although it can be a combination of genetic and environmental factors [1].

The incidence and deaths of malignant melanoma have increased substantially in the past decade. Between 2008 and 2018 the incidence rates of melanoma rose by 44% and there was an increase of 32% in deaths [2]. As in all cancers, it is always ideal to identify the melanoma in an early stage because it means that it is still contained in the epidermis, and it has not yet had contact with deeper layers therefore it has not reached the blood flow. This implies

A. I. Pereira et al. (Eds.): OL2A 2022, CCIS 1754, pp. 65–77, 2022.
https://doi.org/10.1007/978-3-031-23236-7_5

that it has not metastasized yet, and it can be easily removed by excision [3]. Melanoma presents several subtypes, such as Superficial spreading, Nodular, Lentigo maligna melanoma, and Acral lentiginous melanoma. All of them differ in the incidence, localization, and characteristics that comprise them [4].

Dermoscopy is a non-invasive technique that allows visualization of a pigmented skin lesion *in vivo* right to the starting edge of the reticular dermis. It involves the use of a device similar to an otoscope but with a specific contact lens that creates light that falls on the surface of the skin. This technique utilizes a fluid, for example, oil or water, between the epidermis and the device's glass slide, which makes for light reflection being eliminated, and allows the visualization of the dermoscopic features from the presence of melanin and hemoglobin in the cutaneous layers [5]. Therefore, the main goal of dermoscopy is the differentiation between benign and malignant alterations through a non-invasive technique, particularly through the identification of specific diagnostic patterns related to the dermoscopy structures and colors. In several studies, it has been proven that the use of a dermoscopy increases both specificity and sensitivity when compared to the naked eye. This technique is particularly complex, so it is reserved only for experienced clinicians [3].

Overall, if the cancer is diagnosed at an early stage, the doctors can attribute an appropriate treatment for the patient. The specialists can identify cancer with different techniques, however, there is a need to have an efficient system that can aid in the diagnosis of patients to save lives as quickly as possible. So, Artificial Intelligence has been widely used to aid in the detection of skin lesions and consequently prevent eventual death [6].

Quality, value, and outcome are three words that will always walk side by side with healthcare, and specialists around the globe are looking for ways to deliver on this promise through different technologies. We are in an era where there is a necessity to advance more information to clinicians, so they can make better decisions about treatment and diagnosis. Especially the fact that when we talk about medical images, we are referring to tons of data that can be exhaustive for the human brain to analyze, which can lead to significant errors. That is when Machine Learning has a huge impact on healthcare, as it can process enormous datasets beyond human capability [6].

When referring to skin lesion classification, there is a variety of deep learning methods. However, despite the significant progress, skin cancer classification is still a difficult task. So, inspired by the work [27], this paper studies the effect of triplet attention mechanisms incorporated into a neural network when dealing with the classification of skin lesions. Deep learning networks identify the class by learning the features and nonlinear interactions, with the addition of the triplet attention mechanism it will allow the improvement of the performance by especially focusing on relevant areas of the image. This particular mechanism captures the interaction between channel and spatial domain, helping the capture of rich discriminative feature representations, thereby, increasing the trust in our model.

2   Related Work

In the human brain, attention is characterized by a cognitive process that focuses on one or more things while ignoring others. This principle encouraged the researchers to adapt this feature into neural networks, making attention mechanisms to be one of the most valuable advances in Deep Learning research.

The history of the attention mechanism can be divided into four phases. The first phase begins with the *recurrent attention model* (RAM) [13], which combined the attention mechanism with convolutional neural networks. RAM is built with *recurrent neural network* (RNNs) and *reinforcement learning* (RL), which allows to determine where to pay attention when classifying an image. This method shows to improve image classification results by focusing on the most relevant region of the image while ignoring the irrelevant information.

The second phase is characterized by explicitly predicting discriminatory input features, with works like *spatial transformer networks* (STN) [14] and *deformable convolutional networks* (DCNs) [15]. STN was the method that initiated this phase in which use an explicit procedure to learn the invariance of pictures after rotation, scaling, transformations, and other types of deformation. This method allowed the authors to solve one of the main problems of the *convolutional neural networks* (CNNs) which consists of the lack of robustness when occurred spatial invariance, i.e., poor results when some transformations of the target are made.

At the start of the third phase, Hu et al. proposed the *squeeze-and-excitation network* (SENet) [9] pioneering what is known as channel attention. The main goal was to improve the quality of representations by explicitly predicting the potential key features. Following SENet, a *convolutional block attention module* [10] better known as CBAM was proposed. CBAM joins two important categories of attention mechanism, known as channel and spatial attention, allowing the use of cross-domain relationships of features to tell the network what to focus on and where to focus on. At the same time as CBAM, Park et al. [16] proposed a method that also incorporates channel and spatial domains, known as *bottleneck attention module* (BAM). This module can suppress or emphasize features in both dimensions and allows the improvement of representational power. The dimensional reduction applied to both attentions permits it to be integrated with any convolutional neural network with a tiny computational cost.

Finally, the last phase can be characterized as the self-attention era. This attention mechanism has particular great success in the field of *natural language processing* (NLP), nonetheless, it also shows an enormous potential to be a significant tool in computer vision. They are commonly used in spatial attention mechanisms, which allow capturing global information. Wang et al. [17] were one of the first to introduce self-attention to computer vision and its non-local network, shown to have great success in object detection. However, nowadays, there are several variants of self-attention such as CCNet [18] and HamNet [19]. The development of attention mechanisms has become a necessary technique in computer vision and natural language processing, so it is only natural that these mechanisms were applied in other research domains.

The healthcare domain is always very complex, but the strong need to get better tools that may improve the diagnosis or treatment of patients it's constant run. So, it's only natural that the attention mechanisms were applied in medical applications in the most variety of problems. In 2021, Liang et al. [20] aid the diagnosis of Alzheimer's disease in MRI data by adding an attention mechanism into a backbone network based on ResNet [21]. In the year prior, Jin et al. [22] studied how the combination of a 3D U-Net [23] architecture with residual blocks and an attention module would perform on tumor segmentation by extracting volumes of interest in liver and brain CT images. In summary, there are a ton of applications of attention mechanisms in healthcare domains, including in Covid-19 classification, skin cancer classification, Breast lesion segmentation, Cardiac segmentation, and Retinal disease classification.

In terms of skin cancer classification, CNNs present remarkable success. Many of the current models use transfer learning that is based on pre-trained CNNs like Xception [7], EfficentNetB0 [8], or InceptionV3 [12]. Even though there are a lot of deep learning methods to classify skin cancer, only a few focus on attention mechanisms. However, there are more and more efforts to apply these mechanisms to skin analysis. For example, Datta et al. [24] studied the effectiveness and importance of Soft-Attention integrated with different backbones networks in classifying skin cancer. Also, Yan et al. [25] proposed an attention-based method to aid melanoma recognition in which the attention modules estimate maps that highlight the regions that are more relevant to lesion classification integrated with VGG-16 [26] network. Attention mechanism has been successfully used in various fields of deep learning, and it promises to keep going.

3   Method

3.1   Dataset

The dermoscopic datasets were obtained from ISIC 2019 [29–31] ISIC 2020 [28], PH2 [32], DermeNet NZ [33], and Derm7pt [34]. The ISIC 2020 Dataset contains 33,126 dermoscopic training images from 2,000 patients. It is composed of 16 categories, but for the study, it was divided into 2 categories: "melanoma" and "non-melanoma". One of the main problems encountered is a highly imbalanced dataset where there are 32,542 non-melanoma and 584 melanoma images. As a result, it was necessary to find other datasets that could add more images to the melanoma class. The ISIC 2019 consists of 25,331 dermoscopic training images among 9 diagnostic categories. However, only 4,522 melanoma images were applied. The Pedro Hispano (PH2) dataset contains 200 images in a total of 3 categories as follows: Melanoma, Atypical Nevus, and Common Nevus. Though, only 40 images of melanoma are used for the classification. The DermeNet NZ and Derm7pt datasets utilized 94 and 273 melanoma images, respectively. All the images were resized to 224×224.

The class corresponding to the melanoma images increased from 584 to 5477, which allowed us to significantly reduce the difference between the two classes. However, we still face a very unbalanced database when comparing the 5,477 images with 32,542 non-melanoma images. That said, data augmentation techniques were applied during network training, these transformations include rotation from -15 to $+15$ and randomly horizontal and vertical flips with a probability of 0.5. None of the operations affects the main characteristics of the original image, preserving the relevant proprieties for the automated classification of melanomas. Additionally, these transformations were only applied to the training and validation sets.

The dataset was divided into 70% for training, corresponding to a total of 26614 images between 6834 images of "melanoma" and 22780 images of "non-melanoma". The other 10% fits the validation process where 584 images belong to the "melanoma" class and 3254 belong to the "non-melanoma" class. The last 20% corresponds to the testing process of a total of 7603 images, of which 1095 images of the "melanoma" class and 6508 images of the "non-melanoma" class.

3.2   Triplet Attention

Triplet Attention [27] was created by Misra et al. to address some issues associated with CBAM and BAM. Especially the fact that the channel and spatial attention are computed independently, ignoring relationships between the two domains. So, triplet attention is an intuitive and lightweight attention mechanism that permits the capture of cross-domain interaction, i.e., allows computing both channel and spatial attention in a singular module.

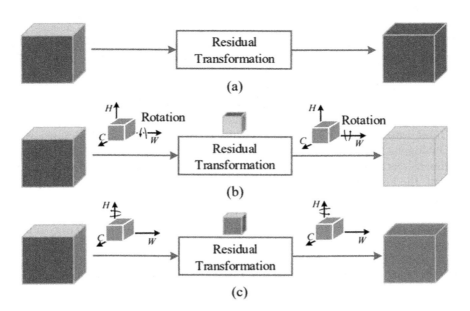

Fig. 1. Illustration of triplet attention with three branches capturing cross-dimension interaction. [27].

Triplet Attention is composed of three parallel branches (Fig. 1), two of which are responsible for computing the attention weights between the channel dimension (C) and spatial dimension (H or W). The remaining branch is responsible for computing simple spatial attention [27]. The top two branches undergo the Z-Pool operator, which basically lowers the zeroth dimension to two by concatenating the average and max-pooled features of the tensor throughout that dimension. The tensor is then passed through a standard convolutional layer and later passed through a sigmoid activation layer. The resulting tensors of the three branches are then collected by simple averaging, obtaining our final tensors. This process can be summarized in the following equation:

$$y = \frac{1}{3}(\overline{\chi_1\omega_1} + \overline{\chi_2\omega_2} + \chi\omega_3) = \frac{1}{3}(\overline{y_1} + \overline{y_2} + y_3),\tag{1}$$

where ω_1, ω_2, and ω_3 represents the cross-domain attention weights. The $\overline{y_1}$ and $\overline{y_2}$ represents the 90° clockwise rotation to maintain the original input shape $\chi \in \mathbb{R}^{C \times H \times W}$.

3.3   Model Setup

A triplet attention block can be easily added to classical backbones networks, due to its simple and lightweight structure. Therefore, it was decided to add this block to an effective neural network known as MobileNetV2 [36]. This network is specially designed for mobile and restricted environments, and when compared to the most common architectures in deep learning, it significantly decreases the number of operations and memory needed while does not affect the accuracy.

The MobileNetV2 architecture is composed of bottleneck residual blocks, and each one contains three convolutional layers: an "expansion" layer, followed by a depthwise convolution layer, and ends in a "projection" layer. The first layer is a 1×1 convolution, and it serves to expand the number of channels in the data before it goes to the next layer, i.e., creates more output channels than input channels. The depthwise convolution layer separates the input image and the filter into distinct channels, and then convolves each input channel with the analogous filter channel. The last layer projects data with a higher number of dimensions into a tensor with a significantly lower number of dimensions. Overall, the bottleneck block reduces the amount of data that flows through the network [37].

One of the new things introduced in this network when compared to its original is the residual connections presented in the bottleneck block. This connection unites the beginning and the end of the block, with the purpose of passing information to deeper layers of the model. Each layer of the block has batch normalization, and the activation function is ReLu6. The output of the projection layer does not have an activation function, which means that our triplet attention layer is going to be introduced after the projection layer. So our model architecture is composed of a fully convolution layer followed by 19 residual bottleneck blocks with the addition of the triplet attention layer at the end of each block [36] (Fig. 2).

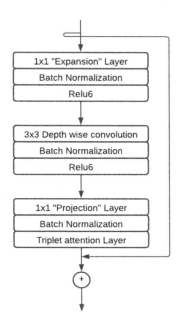

Fig. 2. Illustration of Bottleneck block.

For all the experiments, the training process uses Adam's optimizer [35] with a learning rate of 0.001. This optimizer is known for reaching convergence rapidly, which is why we choose a relatively small number of epochs (30 epochs). As mentioned before, to reduce the class imbalance, we use a series of data augmentation transforms. Also, we decided to use the Transfer Learning technique that consists of utilizing knowledge from a large dataset to finish our task, i.e., we use pretrained weights so that our predictions can make use of representations already learned.

4   Results

Different experiments for skin lesion classification were conducted on different dermoscopic lesions to evaluate the performance of triplet attention when implemented on the MobileNetV2. Our model is binary classifier that distinguish between "melanoma" and "non-melanoma". The classification performance is evaluated using specificity (SPE), sensitivity (SEN), accuracy (ACC) and F1-Score.

In the confusion matrix, true positive (TP) and true negative (TN) represents the number of lesions sample correctly classified as non-melanoma and melanoma, respectively. False positive (FP) represents the number of samples incorrectly classified as non-melanoma and false negative (FN) represents the ratio of samples incorrectly classified as melanoma. ACC describes how the model performs in all classes. The model's ability to identify the TN and TP are measures by the SPE and SEN, respectively. Lastly, F1-Score combines the precision (all positive rates) and recall (true positive ratio) of a classifier and when it is close to 1 means a good performance of the model. An example of a melanoma and non-melanoma lesion can be seen in Figs. 3 and 4.

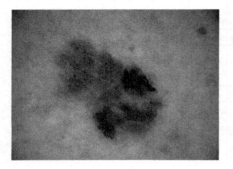
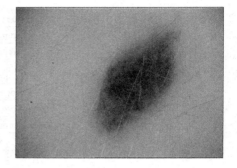

Fig. 3. Example of dermoscopic image of melanoma.

Fig. 4. Example of dermoscopic image of non-melanoma.

Initially, the training of MobileNetV2 with triplet attention was performed on the augmented training set and the progress was monitored on the augmented validation set. The lower loss and higher accuracy of the network on the validation set were selected to evaluate the test set by the network. The results can be seen in Fig. 5, where the model was capable of achieving good performance. However, we observed that it has much more success in classifying "non-melanoma" images (high specificity) than it has when classifying the "melanoma" images (medium sensitivity). One possible reason for this result could be the fact that data transformations were applied to both classes and didn't happen in the down sampling of the most prevalent class. This reason may justify the use of other techniques to achieve better overall results (Fig. 6).

Table 1. Comparisons of our model with MobileNetV2 based on the metrics.

Measure	MobileNetV2 + Triplet Attention	MobileNetV2
Sensitivity	0.9370	**0.9799**
Specificity	**0.9700**	0.9550
Accuracy	**0.9653**	0.9586
F1 Score	**0.8860**	0.0.8720

Comparing the model to MobilenetV2 without triplet attention (Table 1), we observed that the model has better results in all the metrics except for SEN,

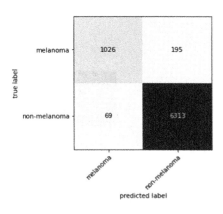 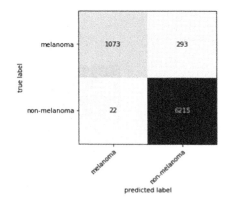

Fig. 5. Confusion matrix of the MobileNetV2 with triplet attention.

Fig. 6. Confusion matrix of the MobileNetV2.

which is 4.29% higher without triplet attention. However, both ACC and F1 score had an improvement of 0.67% and 1.4%, respectively, when using triplet attention (Table 1). Even though the model without triplet attention is capable of having a bit more success when classifying the "melanoma" images, in the overall aspect our model was able to outperform the MobileNetV2.

Table 2. Comparisons of our model with CBAM and BAM module based on the metrics.

Measure	MobileNetV2-Triplet Attention	MobileNetV2-CBAM	MobileNetV2-BAM
Sensitivity	0.9370	0.9242	**0.9799**
Specificity	**0.9700**	0.9551	0.9585
Accuracy	**0.9653**	0.9507	0.9616
F1 Score	**0.8860**	0.8437	0.8802

The evaluation of CBAM and BAM implemented on MobileNetV2 shows that when the channel and spatial attention are computed independently, and it is ignored, the relationship between these two domains can be a down step (Table 2). Triplet attention mechanism outperformed CBAM in all the metrics, with an improvement of 4.23% in the F1-Score. Compared to BAM, triplet attention shows better results in all the metrics except for SEN. Also, triplet attention presents about higher F1-Score than BAM. This shows that even though triplet attention has not had the best results when classifying the "melanoma" class, it has still a better overall result than BAM (Figs. 7 and 8).

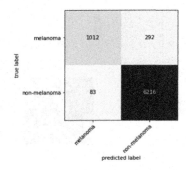

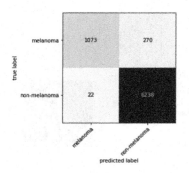

Fig. 7. Confusion matrix of the MobileNetV2 with cbam.

Fig. 8. Confusion matrix of the MobileNetV2 with bam.

5 Discussion and Future Work

According to the results from the different tests, triplet attention combined with MobileNetV2 architecture presents overall better results than MobilenetV2, which proves that the introduction of an attention layer can be beneficial to the classification of skin lesions. Especially when compared to another attention mechanism, because instead of ignoring the relationship between the channel and spatial domains, triplet attention recognizes the importance of cross-domain interactions.

Pre-processing is an essential part of any classification problem as they directly impact the success rate of the study, so data transformation has enormous importance when dealing with such an imbalanced dataset. However, we are talking about different datasets that have different natures and characteristics that directly impact the performance of the model. So, it would be relevant to study in the future time how certain pre-processing techniques, such as color constancy and hair removal, may affect our model.

Overall, triplet attention implemented on MobileNetV2 performed well for skin lesion classification, especially compared to other attention mechanisms. Even though more studies need to be performed, channel and spatial mechanisms can have enormous potential to determinate on how to help models not only to focus on *what to pay attention to* but also on *where to pay attention*.

6 Conclusion

In this paper, we study an attention-based network for melanoma classification with a classical backbone model. The MobileNetV2 with triplet attention was trained in 5 different datasets. With help of some preprocessing techniques such as data augmentation, it was possible to reduce the data imbalance. However, it still is one of the main limitations of this work, as it will normally impact our model performance. Another main limitation is that we only applied the model to a binary classification task. The experimental results show that our model can achieve an overall higher performance than the selected models, even though it needs to do much more experiments to fully take a conclusion.

References

1. Shahana sherin, K. C, Shayini, R.: Classification of skin lesions in digital images for the diagnosis of skin cancer. In: 2020 International Conference on Smart Electronics and Communication (ICOSEC), pp. 162–166. IEEE, India (2020). https://doi.org/10.1109/ICOSEC49089.2020.9215271
2. 2020 Melanoma Skin Cancer Report: Stemming The Global Epidemic. https://www.melanomauk.org.uk/2020-melanoma-skin-cancer-report. Accessed 20 Jul 2022
3. Barata, A.C.F.: Automatic detection of melanomas using dermoscopy images. Technical report, Instituto Superior Tecnico Lisboa (2017)
4. Craythorne, E., Nicholson, P.: Diagnosis and management of skin cancer. Medicine. **51**, 2448–2452 (2021). https://doi.org/10.1016/j.mpmed.2021.04.007
5. Carli, P., et al.: Pattern analysis, not simplified algorithms, is the most reliable method for teaching dermoscopy for melanoma diagnosis to residents in dermatology. Br. J. Dermatol. (2003). https://doi.org/10.1046/j.1365-2133.2003.05023.x
6. Davenport, T., Kalakota, R.: The potential for artificial intelligence in healthcare. Future Hosp. J. **6**, 94–98 (2019). https://doi.org/10.7861/futurehosp.6-2-94
7. Chollet, F.: Xception: deep learning with Depthwise separable convolutions. In: 2017 IEEE Conference on Computer Vision and Pattern Recognition (CVPR), pp. 1800–1807. IEEE, USA (2017). https://doi.org/10.1109/CVPR.2017.195
8. Tan, M., Le,: EfficientNet: Rethinking Model Scaling for Convolutional Neural Networks (2019). https://doi.org/10.48550/arxiv.1905.11946
9. Hu, J., Shen, L., Sun, G., Albanie, S.: Squeeze-and-excitation networks. IEEE Trans. Pattern Anal. Mach. Intell. **42**(8), 2011–2023. (2020). https://doi.org/10.1109/TPAMI.2019.2913372
10. Woo, S., Park, J., Lee, J.-Y., Kweon, I.S.: CBAM: Convolutional block attention module. In: Ferrari, V., Hebert, M., Sminchisescu, C., Weiss, Y. (eds.) ECCV 2018. LNCS, vol. 11211, pp. 3–19. Springer, Cham (2018). https://doi.org/10.1007/978-3-030-01234-2_1
11. Wang, F., et al.: Residual Attention Network for Image Classification (2017). https://doi.org/10.1109/CVPR.2017.683
12. Boonyuen, K., Kaewprapha, P., Weesakul, U., Srivihok, P.: Convolutional neural network inception-v3: a machine learning approach for leveling short-range rainfall forecast model from satellite image. In: Tan, Y., Shi, Y., Niu, B. (eds.) ICSI 2019. LNCS, vol. 11656, pp. 105–115. Springer, Cham (2019). https://doi.org/10.1007/978-3-030-26354-6_10
13. Mnih, V., Heess, N., Graves, A., Kavukcuoglu, K.: Recurrent models of visual attention. In: Proceedings of the 27th International Conference on Neural Information Processing Systems, vol. 2, 2204–2212 (2014)
14. Jaderberg, M., Simonyan, K., Zisserman, A., Kavukcuoglu, K.: Spatial transformer networks. In: Advances in Neural Information Processing Systems, vol. 28 (2015)
15. Dai, J., et al.: Deformable convolutional network. In: IEEE International Conference on Computer Vision (ICCV), pp. 764–773 (2017). https://doi.org/10.1109/ICCV.2017.89

16. Park, J., Woo, S., Lee, J.-Y., Kweon, I.: Bam: Bottleneck attention module (2018)
17. Wang, X., Girshick, R., Gupta, A., He, K.: Non-local neural networks. In: Proceedings of the IEEE Conference on Computer Vision and Pattern Recognition, pp. 7794–7803 (2018). https://doi.org/10.1109/CVPR.2018.00813
18. Huang, Z., Wang, X., Wei, Y., Huang, L., Shi, H., Liu, W.: CCNet: CRISS-cross attention for semantic segmentation. In: Proceedings of the IEEE Transactions on Pattern Analysis and Machine Intelligence, p. 1. (2020). https://doi.org/10.1109/TPAMI.2020.3007032
19. Geng, Z., Guo, M-H., Chen, H., Li, X., Wei, K., Lin, Z.: Is Attention Better Than Matrix Decomposition? (2021)
20. Liang, S., Gu, Y.: Computer-Aided Diagnosis of Alzheimer's Disease through Weak Supervision Deep Learning Framework with Attention Mechanism (2020). https://doi.org/10.3390/s21010220
21. He, K., Zhang, X., Ren, S., Sun, J.: Deep residual learning for image recognition. In: Proceedings of the IEEE Conference on Computer Vision and Pattern Recognition, pp. 770–778 (2016)
22. Jin, Q., Meng, Z., Sun, C., Cui, H., Su, R.: RA-UNet: a hybrid deep attention-aware network to extract liver and tumor in CT scans. Front. Bioeng. Biotechnol. (2020). https://doi.org/10.3389/fbioe.2020.605132
23. Ronneberger, O., Fischer, P., Brox, T.: U-Net: convolutional networks for biomedical image segmentation. In: Navab, N., Hornegger, J., Wells, W.M., Frangi, A.F. (eds.) MICCAI 2015. LNCS, vol. 9351, pp. 234–241. Springer, Cham (2015). https://doi.org/10.1007/978-3-319-24574-4_28
24. Datta, S.K., Shaikh, M.A., Srihari, S.N., Gao, M.: Soft attention improves skin cancer classification performance. In: Reyes, M., et al. (eds.) IMIMIC/TDA4MedicalData -2021. LNCS, vol. 12929, pp. 13–23. Springer, Cham (2021). https://doi.org/10.1007/978-3-030-87444-5_2
25. Yan, Y., Kawahara, J., Hamarneh, G.: Melanoma recognition via visual attention. In: Chung, A.C.S., Gee, J.C., Yushkevich, P.A., Bao, S. (eds.) IPMI 2019. LNCS, vol. 11492, pp. 793–804. Springer, Cham (2019). https://doi.org/10.1007/978-3-030-20351-1_62
26. Simonyan, K., Zisserman, A.: Very Deep Convolutional Networks for Large-Scale Image Recognition (2014). arXiv:1409.1556
27. Misra, D., Nalamada, T., Arasanipalai, A., Hou, Q.: Rotate to attend: convolutional triplet attention module. In: Proceedings of the IEEE Winter Conference on Applications of Computer Vision, pp. 3138–3147 (2020). https://doi.org/10.1109/WACV48630.2021.00318
28. Rotemberg, V., et al.: A patient-centric dataset of images and metadata for identifying melanomas using clinical context. Sci. Data 8, 34 (2021). https://doi.org/10.1038/s41597-021-00815-z
29. Tschandl P., Rosendahl C., Kittler, H.: The HAM10000 dataset, a large collection of multi-source dermatoscopic images of common pigmented skin lesions (2018). https://doi.org/10.1038/sdata.2018.161
30. Codella, N.C.F., et al.: Skin lesion analysis toward melanoma detection: a challenge at the 2017 international symposium on biomedical imaging (ISBI). In: International Skin Imaging Collaboration (ISIC) (2017). https://doi.org/10.1109/ISBI.2018.8363547
31. Combalia, M., et al.: BCN20000: Dermoscopic Lesions in the Wild (2019). arXiv:1908.02288

32. Mendonça, T., Ferreira, P.M., Marques, J., Marcal, A.R.S., Rozeira, J.: PH^2 - A dermoscopic image database for research and benchmarking. In: 35th International Conference of the IEEE Engineering in Medicine and Biology Society, Osaka, Japan (2013)
33. DermNet NZ. All about the skin. https://dermnetnz.org/image-library. Accessed 26 Jun 2022
34. Kawahara, J., Daneshvar, S., Argenziano, G., Hamarneh, G.: Seven-point checklist and skin lesion classification using multitask multimodal neural nets. In: IEEE Journal of Biomedical Health Informatics (IEEE JBHI) special issue on Skin Lesion Image Analysis for Melanoma Detection (2019). https://doi.org/10.1109/JBHI.2018.2824327
35. Kingma, D., Ba, Jimmy.: Adam: a method for stochastic optimization. In: Proceedings of the 3rd International Conference on Learning Representations (ICLR 2015) (2015)
36. Sandler, M., Howard, A., Zhu, M., Zhmoginov, A., Chen, L. C.: MobileNetV2: inverted residuals and linear bottlenecks. In: 2018 IEEE/CVF Conference on Computer Vision and Pattern Recognition, pp. 4510–4520. IEEE, USA (2018). https://doi.org/10.1109/CVPR.2018.00474
37. Indraswari, R., Rokhana, R., Herulambang, W.: Melanoma image classification based on MobileNetV2 network. Proc. Comput. Sci. **197**, 198–207 (2022). https://doi.org/10.1016/j.procs.2021.12.132

Volume Estimation of an Indoor Space with LiDAR Scanner

Jaqueline Bierende[1,2], João Braun[1,3,4,5], Paulo Costa[3,4],
José Lima[1,3,5(✉)], and Ana I. Pereira[1,5]

[1] Research Centre in Digitalization and Intelligent Robotics (CeDRI),
Instituto Politécnico de Bragança, Bragança, Portugal
jaquelinebierende@alunos.utfpr.edu.br, {jbneto,jllima,apereira}@ipb.pt
[2] Universidade Técnológia Federal do Paraná - UTFPR, Curitiba, Brazil
[3] INESC Technology and Science, Porto, Portugal
paco@fe.up.pt
[4] Faculty of Engineering of University of Porto, Porto, Portugal
[5] Laboratório para a Sustentabilidade e Tecnologia em Regiões de Montanha
(SusTEC), Instituto Politécnico de Bragança, Bragança, Portugal

Abstract. Three-dimensional scanning is a task of great importance for
our modern society and has brought significant advances in the precision
of material inventory. These sensors map the material surface continuously, allowing real-time inventory monitoring. Most technologies are
expensive because this process is complex, and even inexpensive ones are
considerate smart investments for the average user. Therefore, this work
presents the simulation of a low-cost time-of-flight based 3D scanning
system that performs the volume estimation of an object-filled indoor
space after a voxelization process. The system consists of a 2D LIDAR
scanner that performs an azimuthal scan of 180° through its rotating
platform and a motor that rotates the platform in angle inclination.

Keywords: LiDAR · Volume estimation · Simulation · 3D scanning ·
Voxelization · Point cloud

1 Introduction

Accurate 3D shape reconstruction and volume estimation are essential in many
applications, for example, the estimation of stockpiles and raw materials. LiDAR
(Light Detection And Ranging) is a laser scanner, also known as laser rangefinder
(LRF), which is an attractive and efficient tool because the sensor remotely
delimits the volume of interest by providing relative distance measurements from
its point of origin.

For LiDAR scanners, the triangulation, phase shift method, and time-of-
flight (ToF) methods are the three common approaches. Triangulation systems
have a restricted range and depth variation but offer higher precision. On the
other, ToF systems have a wide range and depth variation, but lower precision
[10,16]. In the phase shift method case, a signal is sent with a specific frequency.

Next, the phase time difference between the sent and received beams is detected and computed at the receiver [1]. The accuracy of ToF-based systems is mainly determined by the sensor's ability to accurately measure the interval between the laser emission and reception of the reflected signal, which makes it possible to estimate the object's position in space, as such is the case developed in this work.

This accuracy during acquisition can be affected by interference from light, noise, and the angle of incidence of the beam projected on the object being too oblique. Therefore, a controlled environment and a high-quality circuit must be used to perform scans in more complex environments, which generally results in expensive 3D scanning systems [10]. For this reason, a low-cost 3D scanning system that uses a 2D laser scanner with a ToF approach was developed in this work. The objective and scope of this research work are at small environments, such as a deposit, where high performance was not required since there were no windows and it did not need a long reach.

In this work, the scanning is done in two dimensions (2D) with a scan range of 180° and a drive motor that results in several possible combinations between the scan plane and the axis of rotation to obtain a 3D map.

The present work is divided into nine chapters, where in Sect. 2, a bibliographic review is carried out on works developed for volume estimation through a laser scanner. Section 3 describes the hardware parameters used in the software and the LiDAR used. The SimTwo software is presented in Sect. 4, covering the structure created for the simulation and a description of the system architecture. Section 5, 6, and 7 detail data acquisition used in software, data processing, and volume estimation. Section 8 presents the validation of the approach in the software, and finally, Sect. 9 draws conclusion about the results obtained in the tests performed and discusses proposals for future works.

2   State of the Art

Devices integrated for 3D scanning by 2D sensors have been widely used at the low cost of the system because of its inexpensive nature. In environmental modelling, Li et al. [19] uses a high-precision lifting platform and a small laser range sensor. Chou [12], and Surmann [23] developed a 3D mapping system consisting of a mobile platform and a rotating platform consisting of a laser rangefinder. In [18] the viability of the low-cost LiDAR sensor in extracting traces from tree leaves was evaluated.

Level sensors based on the 3D mapping are revolutionizing inventory management, adding the ability to accurately estimate volume without leaving the safety of an office. This technology has been proven in many challenging materials, including food and in the energy and mining industries [2].

Nowadays, there are many devices on the market to detect the level of solids in silos. However, ToF sensors are an advanced non-contact technology that overcomes one of the biggest challenges present in silos, which is the presence of much dust. Another benefit of using a laser is that when inventory monitoring is fully automated, there is no need to climb silos to take measurements, avoiding possible work accidents [13].

The volume of a surface can be quickly calculated using representations such as height grids, voxels, or polygons. The authors in [8], from a laser scanner, created a point cloud that is used to create the 3D surface and, from this, derive the height grid that is used to measure the volume of the payload. However, the related work about voxel-based is mainly used to estimate the volume of trees. For instance, papers [17] and [9] estimated tree's volume by 3D voxel-based modeling using portable scanning LiDAR data.

Laser scanners have also been used successfully to measure the volume of solids. Point clouds are produced in [24] from laser measurements, and then two approaches for 3D surface construction and volume estimation are evaluated. The first method, Meshed Surface, divides the collected points into evenly spaced cells to generate a grid, although separate data requires interpolation. The second approach, called Isolated Points, calculates the volume by dividing the total area scanned by the number of points collected. Due to sampling in obscure locations or when reflectivity is low, the second technique produces erroneous estimates.

The research work of GeoSLAM ZEB-Horizon 3D was used in [2], a mobile scanner within a project to speed up the inventory work significantly. This scanner offers a high surface coverage due to the dense point cloud. The analyzed material in question was minerals that were deposited in storage boxes. This equipment offers software that can be accessed from a single location or throughout the company, facilitating real-time inventory information, generating operational and financial efficiency.

In the mining context, an essential part of the industry's daily operations needs volume estimation as most companies try to take advantage of the latest technology to improve their productivity and maximize profit. With the help of modern point cloud technology, it is possible to estimate volume more scientifically and accurately. In his research, Amaglo [6] searched to use the point cloud and 3D surface model of mass transport to estimate the volume of a stock in the mining field. A volumetric computational method based on point cloud coordinates was formulated in MATLAB software to estimate the volume of inventories using LiDAR data. The point density and filtering algorithm plays a critical role in the volume calculation, which helps to provide a reasonable estimate of the stock.

3 Acquisition System

This section describes the system hardware used to parameterize the SimTwo software, consisting of the LiDAR sensor and drive motor responsible for measuring and collecting data. The motor configured in SimTwo was a direct current motor with a resolution of $1°$ step. The hardware is designed to control the field of view of the scan.

The Neato XV-11 laser scanner, Fig. 1, is a low-cost LRF, small and has low energy consumption. A full rotation provides a measurement range of 360°, with an angular resolution of 1° and a distance range from 0.2 m to 6 m with an error of less than 0.03 m.

Fig. 1. LIDAR model XV-11 [4].

4   Simulation Environment

This section presents the "SimTwo" simulation environment, describing an introduction to its characteristics, the functions of each of the features available found and the elements used to create the scenes.

4.1   Simulation Structure

Developed in *Object Pascal*, SimTwo is a free, open-source software where several types of robots can be modelled: differential, omnidirectional, industrial, and humanoid, among others. It was developed in 2008 and constantly received updates available in [14].

This simulator has the functionality of using specified models of characterized components and the decomposition of a robot in rigid bodies and electric motors, allowing a dynamic realism to the project. SimTwo can develop robots in different programming languages and commercial software such as Matlab and LabVIEW [15].

All the available tools allow the development of a broad diversification of works. Some of the works developed to include the simulation of a quadrotor model and the evaluation of it's dynamics [7], game simulation [22], the validation of a control system of an autonomous vehicle [5] and humanoid robots [20].

SimTwo is a multi-document interface (MDI) application where the windows *"code editor"*, *"spreadsheet"*, *"configuration"*, *"scene editor"* and *"chart"* are under the control of the window *"worldview"*, as shown in the Fig. 2.

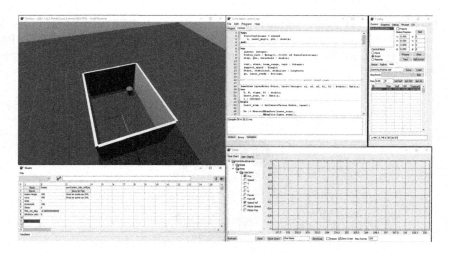

Fig. 2. SimTwo Software. Application windows in clockwise direction from top left: *world view, code editor, configuration, chart,* and *spreadsheet.*

The *"configuration"* window offers control over various parameters of the scene, including the camera position and lighting. External communication via the Serial Port and UDP is possible through the *"I/O"* tab.

The *"code editor"* offers an integrated development environment (IDE) for programming in Pascal language.

In the *"chart"* window, it is possible to plot all the states available of each defined robot in the XML, such as its position and speed. *"Spreadsheet"* is a table that allows you to show the value of any variable in real time and interact with the code editor.

In *"Scene Editor"*, it is possible to create robots, tracks, walls and other entities in the scene. It consists of the main file *"scene.xml"* and other XML files.

4.2   System Architecture

The focus of this work is to simulate a scanning system composed by modelling a real low-cost 2D laser scanner and estimate the volume occupied by objects in a deposit. The work can be defined in three steps for volume estimation:

1) Data collection: the system is going to be simulated in Simtwo simulator, where the data acquisition will be made.
2) Data processing: the collected data's coordinate system is converted from the modified spherical coordinates of the scanning system to cartesian coordinates with the origin being the centre of the LiDAR scanner which is subsequently filtered to remove the walls.
3) Volume estimation: the cloud goes through the voxelization process, allowing the calculation of the volume occupied by the object.

The constructed architecture can be visualized by the diagram in Fig. 3.

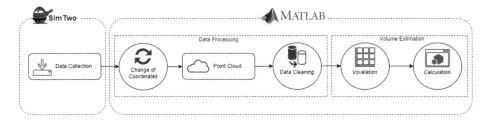

Fig. 3. System architecture.

5   Data Collection

The proposed system consist of a two-dimensional laser scanning subsystem that is actuacted by a motor to achieve 3D acquisition capacity. This system, in real time, distance measurements alongside the orientation of each light beam in the two degrees of freedom of rotation.

When the process starts, the platform, Fig. 4, begins to rotate at a known constant speed. At the same time, the LiDAR device scans the environment, and with each revolution of the 360° platform, the motor increases the inclination angle in a chosen step. In this way, the device will scan new information with each rotation until it reaches 180° in inclination angle. One can note that the step in the inclination angle is a way of regulating the scanning resolution. In the end, a text file (.txt) contains information on distance, azimuth and inclination angle.

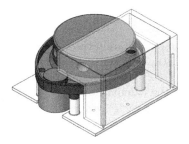

Fig. 4. LiDAR platform.

5.1   Scene Construction

The physical description of each entity is done through XML files. Before starting the construction of the scene, it is essential to remember which entities will be present in the simulation and how they will interact, so it is possible to define what the virtual environment will be like.

It was intended that the scanning system detected the walls and objects located in the centre, creating a text file with the point cloud, to afterwards, the volume estimation algorithm compute the volume.

To characterize the LiDAR sensor in the simulated scene, it was necessary to configure it in the ".xml" file in the scene editor. In this section, it is possible to describe the configuration, such as the beam length, six meters in this case, and the width, five milimeters. The Neato XV-11 laser mathematical model were already modelled in Simtwo, where its parameters were extracted in [11]. Thus, it was used as a basis for this work.

The sensor was configured to have a scan time of 25 ms and a 180° field of view. Moreover, the simulation records 1 sample per degree, totalling 180 samples during a full scan.

6   Data Processing

First, a text file is imported into the MATLAB environment. This file contains the distance from the sensor to the reflecting surface, the azimuth angle, and the inclination angle of each measurement. In other words, the system performs the scans in spherical coordinates for convenience since the architecture of the 3D scanner works in spherical coordinates. However, to perform the calculations and visualization the cartesian coordinate system is better. Thus, this conversion is performed in the point cloud data. Once converted to the cartesian coordinates system, xyz represents the corresponding coordinates in meters of the real system. Soon after, it passes through the wall filtration process, obtaining the point cloud from the interior of the deposit.

6.1   Coordinate Transformation

The system operation is demonstrated in the xyz plane. Two points are observed for the structure characteristic: The sensor position (X_L, Y_L, Z_L) and the point acquired by the scan (X_1, Y_1, Z_1). The system origin is considered at the sensor position S_L (red circle) for the calculation.

The information received in each scan is illustrated in the image with blue colour, as described below:

- φ is the inclination from the plane of the sensor parallel to the xy plane with a range of $[0, \pi]$.
- α is the azimuthal angle measured from the y axis to the projection of R in the xy plane and has a range $[0, \pi]$.
- R is the parameter that represents the distance from the sensor to the object found.

Then, these three variables are used to calculate the transformation of the spherical coordinates to the cartesian coordinates.

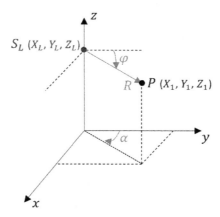

Fig. 5. LiDAR sensor coordinates.

The position P (black circle) in Cartesian coordinates (X_1, Y_1, Z_1) can be defined in terms of the parameters (R, φ, α) with the sensor as the origin, as:

$$x = R\ sen(\varphi)\ cos(\alpha) \qquad y = r\ cos(\varphi) \qquad z = -R\ sen(\varphi)\ sen(\alpha) \qquad (1)$$

This relation can be proved through the variable change theorem in triple integrals available in [21].

The point cloud image is constructed and displayed when the coordinate value calculation is completed. Finally, to emphasize, after the conversion, X, Y, and Z represent the corresponding coordinates in meters of the real-world system.

7 Volume Estimation

7.1 Voxelization

Partitioning squares of equal size primarily characterize this approach in the xy plane to unify all points in that region. Then, the height value of each grid is determined the average height of all points inside each grid, thus obtaining a cube. Thus, with an average height, and standardized width and length, the volume estimation for that specific region is performed.

The resolution of the grid is necessary due to the variation of the density of points of the system. The voxel size must be adequately determined to be large enough to have no unfilled grids and to represent the data properly. Thus, the relation between the points density and the inclination angle, that directly depends on the variation of the motor step, was analyzed. This relation is found by the distance between two beams distanced by the chosen degree of inclination.

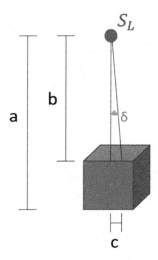

Fig. 6. Grid resolution diagram.

For a better understanding, Fig. 6 presents the chosen proposal with a cube in the middle of the scene.

The letter a characterizes the height of the sensor from the ground, b is the difference between the height of the sensor and the cube, and c corresponds to the minimum value that the grid must have.

The value of c can be calculated by the relation found in Eq. 2 below.

$$c = tg(\delta) \times b \qquad (2)$$

7.2   Volume Calculation

In the end, the total volume deducted in Eq. 3 will be the sum of the individual volume of all the voxels in the xyz plane.

$$V_{TOTAL} = \sum_{j=1}^{M} \sum_{i=1}^{N} x'_{i,j} \cdot y'_{i,j} \cdot z_{i,j} \qquad (3)$$

where M and N is the position of each voxel grid:

- $x'_{i,j}$ represents the width of the grid.
- $y'_{i,j}$ represents the length of the grid.
- $z_{i,j}$ represents the height and is calculated by averaging all points.

8 Results

8.1 Sensor Position

This section contains the results obtained in tests to analyze the best position for the sensor within the scene. For this, two tests were performed in different positions (A, B), as shown in Fig. 7.

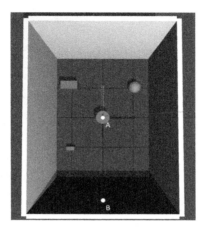

Fig. 7. Test points position.

Figure 8 illustrates the results obtained for each position. The origin of the system is always considered the position of the sensor, so looking at Fig. 8a and Fig. 8b, the origin are at the points A and B with coordinate (0,0,0) in (x,y,z).

When analyzing the three figures, one can notice that the system in the centre obtains a better uniformity in the distribution of the *point cloud*. In contrast, for the position on the wall, the density of points near the sensor is much higher, and as the measurement becomes farther from the sensor, the density decreases, this is due to the scanning format, which generates a pattern, whereas the distance of the sensor increases the group of points is distorted and lose resolution. The difference in the number of points is also noticeable since the cloud formed at position A has 32400 points and at position B 16200 points, which can be justified because when the sensor is on the wall, its inclined range is limited to 90° while the sensor in the centre it up to 180°.

As the position of sensor A presented the best result, the simulations that followed it considered that the sensor would be positioned in A.

8.2 Volume Estimation

The results obtained in three simulations with the sensor located in the centre was analyzed to test the approach illustrated in Fig. 6. The simulation specifications are found in Table 1.

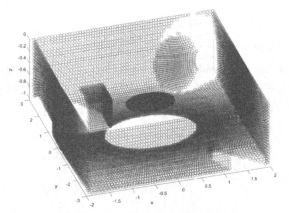

(a) Sensor position in the center.

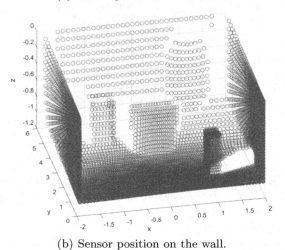

(b) Sensor position on the wall.

Fig. 8. Point cloud obtained in MATLAB software.

Table 1. Specifications for each simulation.

Simulation	Room dimensions (m)	Cube dimensions (m)	a (m)	b (m)	c (m)	Real volume (m³)
1	4 × 3 × 2	0,25 × 0,5 × 0,5	2,0	1,5	0,0261	0,0625
2	4 × 3 × 2	0,25 × 0,125 × 0,25	2,0	1,75	0,0305	0,0078
3	4 × 3 × 2.5	0,25 × 0,5 × 0,5	2,5	2	0,0349	0,0625

The sensor's characteristics implemented in the software were taken from LiDAR Neato XV11, [3] in a review, and modelling was done in SimTwo. A full rotation provides a measurement range of 360° with an angular resolution of 1°. In the simulations, each laser sweep was limited to 180° in angle α. The chosen motor step was 1° in angle φ per scan.

For each simulation, it was necessary to choose a grid that adapts to the density of points in the system.

Table 2 displays the computed grid resolution, the estimated volume calculated by the algorithm, the real volume of the ambient, and the percentage error for each simulation.

Table 2. Simulation results.

Simulation	Resolution grid (m)	Estimated volume (m)	Real volume (m)	Error (%)
1	0,027	0,0623	0,0625	0,32
2	0,0306	0,0084	0,0078	7,69
3	0,035	0,0643	0,0625	2,88

Figure 9 shows the simulated system for the first simulation and Fig. 10 its respective point cloud. By comparing both, it is possible to note that the point cloud represents the simulated system.

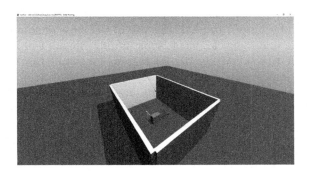

Fig. 9. Simulation 1 - indoor scene with the 3D scanning system in SimTwo simulator.

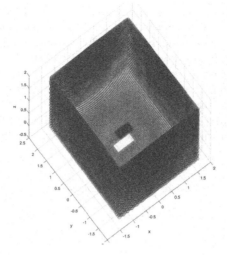

Fig. 10. Point cloud of simulation 1 scene.

9   Conclusion and Future Work

This work proposed a different approach for volume estimation using a low-cost LiDAR sensor, where first, it is verified that the best position for the sensor is in the centre of the environment. Then, the validation of the system from the adaptive grid shows a consistent result because there was a low error with the cube in dimensions closer to the real, and the highest error comes from the cube of simulation two because it has half the size of the cube of simulation 1.

As the work is under development, some improvements will be made in this project, in which the validation of the system for simulations with different objects and positions stands out.

As future work, this procedure will be implemented in a real environment where the 3D scanning system is already being implemented aiming at the application for monitoring the volume of a wharehouse.

Acknowledgements. The authors are grateful to the Foundation for Science and Technology (FCT, Portugal) for financial support through national funds FCT/ MCTES (PIDDAC) to CeDRI (UIDB/05757/2020 and UIDP/05757/2020), SusTEC (LA/P/0007/2021). The project that gave rise to these results received the support of a fellowship from "la Caixa" Foundation (ID 100010434). The fellowship code is LCF/BQ/DI20/11780028.

References

1. Sick sensor intelligence. www.sick.com
2. Volume determination for inventory purposes by means of laser scanning. https://www.laserscanning-europe.com/en/news/volume-determination-inventory-purposes-means-laser-scanning
3. Hacking the neato xv–11 (2015). https://xv11hacking.wikispaces.com/
4. Neato robotics xv–11 tear-down (2015). https://www.sparkfun.com/news/490
5. Abreu, A.D.M.: Autopilot simulator prototype for autonomous driving based on SimTwo (2020)
6. Amaglo, W.Y.: Volume calculation based on lidar data (2021)
7. Amaral, G., Costa, P.: SimTwo as a simulation environment for flight robot dynamics evaluation. U. Porto J. Eng. **1**, 80–88 (2015)
8. Bewley, A., Shekhar, R., Leonard, S., Upcroft, B., Lever, P.: Real-time volume estimation of a dragline payload. In: 2011 IEEE International Conference on Robotics and Automation, pp. 1571–1576. IEEE (2011)
9. Bienert, A., Hess, C., Maas, H., Von Oheimb, G.: A voxel-based technique to estimate the volume of trees from terrestrial laser scanner data. The International Archives of Photogrammetry, Remote Sensing and Spatial Information Sciences (2014)
10. Braun, J., Lima, J., Pereira, A.I., Rocha, C., Costa, P.: Searching the optimal parameters of a 3D scanner through particle swarm optimization. In: Pereira, A.I., et al. (eds.) OL2A 2021. CCIS, vol. 1488, pp. 138–152. Springer, Cham (2021). https://doi.org/10.1007/978-3-030-91885-9_11
11. Campos, D., Santos, J., Gonçalves, J., Costa, P.: Modeling and simulation of a hacked Neato XV-11 laser scanner. In: Robot 2015: Second Iberian Robotics Conference. AISC, vol. 417, pp. 425–436. Springer, Cham (2016). https://doi.org/10.1007/978-3-319-27146-0_33
12. Chou, Y.S., Liu, J.S.: A robotic indoor 3D mapping system using a 2D laser. Int. J. Adv. Robotic Syst. (2012). https://doi.org/10.5772/54655
13. Christensen, J.N.: 3D scanners take volume measurement to a new level (2020)
14. Costa, P.: SimTwo. https://github.com/P33a/SimTwo
15. Costa, P., Gonçalves, J., Lima, J., Malheirosa, P.: SimTwo realistic simulator: a tool for the development and validation of robot software. Theo. Appl. Math. Comput. Sci. **1**(1), 17–33 (2011)
16. Franca, J., Gazziro, M., Ide, A., Saito, J.: A 3D scanning system based on laser triangulation and variable field of view. In: IEEE International Conference on Image Processing 2005, vol. 1, pp. I-425 (2005). https://doi.org/10.1109/ICIP.2005.1529778
17. Hosoi, F., Nakai, Y., Omasa, K.: 3-D voxel-based solid modeling of a broad-leaved tree for accurate volume estimation using portable scanning lidar. ISPRS J. Photogram. Remote Sensing **82**, 41–48 (2013). https://doi.org/10.1016/j.isprsjprs.2013.04.011
18. Karim, P., V., D.A., A., W.K.: Lidarpheno - a low-cost lidar-based 3D scanning system for leaf morphological trait extraction. Front. Plant Sci. 10 (2019)
19. Li, K., Wang, J., Qi, D.: The development and application of an original 3D laser scanning: a precise and nondestructive structural measurements system. Frattura ed Integrità Strutturale (2020). https://doi.org/10.3221/IGF-ESIS.51.28
20. Lima, J.L., Gonçalves, J.A., Costa, P.G., Moreira, A.P.: Humanoid realistic simulator: the servomotor joint modeling (2009)

21. Magalhães, L.T.: Integrais múltiplos (1996)
22. de Domingues e Silva, A.F.: Ferramenta para desenvolvimento de inteligência em jogos simulados em ambiente simtwo (2015)
23. Surmann, H., Nüchter, A., Hertzberg, J.: An autonomous mobile robot with a 3D laser range finder for 3D exploration and digitalization of indoor environments. Robot. Auton. Syst. (2003). https://doi.org/10.1016/j.robot.2003.09.004
24. Zhang, X., Morris, J., Klette, R.: Volume measurement using a laser scanner (2005)

Management of Virtual Environments with Emphasis on Security

André Mendes[1,2,3(✉)] [iD]

[1] Research Centre in Digitalization and Intelligent Robotics (CeDRI),
Instituto Politécnico de Bragança, Campus de Santa Apolónia,
5300-253 Bragança, Portugal
a.chaves@ipb.pt

[2] Laboratório para a Sustentabilidade e Tecnologia em Regiões de Montanha
(SusTEC), Instituto Politécnico de Bragança, Campus de Santa Apolónia,
5300-253 Bragança, Portugal

[3] Department of Systems Engineering and Automatics, Universidade de Vigo,
36.310 Vigo, Spain

Abstract. With the popularity of using virtual environments, it urges important measures that increase its security, as well as maintain a good user experience. A widespread attack is a denial of service which proposes to break the availability of service through a large number of illegitimate requests employing all computing resources of the target and degrading the user experience. In order to be effective in this particular type of attack, usually powerful equipment or a combination of them is required. This article proposes a new approach to this attack through a language-based Erlang application, which uses the processing power of a low-cost device. Its use would open the possibility of effective attacks coming from devices with less processing power, or from IoT devices, but capable of at least degrading the experience of a legitimate user, anonymously.

Keywords: Virtual environments · Attacks of denial of service · Infrastructure · Parallel computing

1 Introduction

The adoption of virtual environments has become more and more common. The emergence of cloud computing has not only enriched the diversity of computing platforms but also promoted the rapid development of big data, the Internet of Things (IoT) and other fields and its use gives organisations greater flexibility for on-demand usage. Cloud computing is defined as a type of parallel and distributed system, consisting of a set of virtualised and interconnected computers, thus enabling its dynamic availability. Three service modes, namely, infrastructure as a service (IaaS), platform as a service (PaaS) and software as a service (SaaS), are provided through cloud computing, allowing enterprises to use resources in accordance with their current needs [8]. Finally, it is presented the

© The Author(s), under exclusive license to Springer Nature Switzerland AG 2022
A. I. Pereira et al. (Eds.): OL2A 2022, CCIS 1754, pp. 93–106, 2022.
https://doi.org/10.1007/978-3-031-23236-7_7

computational resources in a unified way and benchmarked according to the level of service (SLA) [1].

In this way, companies can avoid the need to build and maintain new platforms. Envisioning this growth, technology giants such as Amazon, Google and Microsoft have created and offered proprietary solutions, however, open solutions also exist. Due to the unique advantages of the dynamic, virtual and almost infinite expansion offered by cloud computing, an increasing number of scientific applications and business services are being migrated from traditional computing platforms to cloud computing platforms.

One of the possibilities that virtualisation offers is the reconfiguration of virtualised resources, conferring *levels of elasticity*. That is, resources in a given physical machine can be increased, decreased or migrated to other machines as required by the administrator. For cloud service providers, the use of virtualisation technology enables the integration of scattered and heterogeneous physical resources, which not only improves the utilization and maintenance level of hardware equipment but also mitigates various adverse effects caused by hardware failure [6].

Despite being an excellent solution, virtual environments have some threats that can compromise the operation and credibility of services, for example, loss of data, performance drop, unavailability of the service, in addition to the challenge of maintaining the correct elasticity of the infrastructure.

In order to determine some of the limitations of virtualised environments, this study aims to warn about the use of new technologies demonstrating a new form of denial of service attack, where with the help of parallel computing, it is possible to make unavailable large services through the use of a simple tool.

Therefore, this work aims to collaborate in order to assist in the configuration of virtual environments in a more secure way, to make efficient use of computational resources and, finally, to maintain a more reliable and secure high availability environment.

The paper is organised as follows. Section 2 brings some related works and the 3 section demonstrates the main tool used. Section 4 describes the system model. The results of the overload tests are presented and discussed in Sect. 5, and finally, Sect. 6 concludes the work and lists future works.

2   Related Works

Virtual machine (VM) allocation algorithms can be divided into *static* and *dynamic* strategies [4]. In *static* allocation, a scheduling strategy is generated for VMs according to general task information and resource requirements. In simple terms, a static algorithm provides a solution for the initial placement of VMs over the minimum number of active physical machines (PMs) to maximise the energy efficiency and resource utilization of the data centre. However, such an algorithm does not provide a solution for the reallocation of VMs to new PMs considering dynamic workloads.

In [10] the authors established a mathematical model that considers the mutual influence between VMs to reduce resource contention. Thus, the optimal scheduling of VMs can be calculated under a given amount of energy allocation. In [5], a proposed hierarchical resource management solution that considers the correlations between VMs and the interconnection network topology of these VMs to maximize the overall benefit.

In contrast to static allocation, *dynamic* VM allocation optimises power consumption and cost when migrating existing VMs or forecasting future tasks. During the VM allocation process, new workloads can be accepted by the data centre; as a result, removing some PMs or adding a new PM can make the solution sub-optimal.

Sandpiper [15] is a system that can gather information about the utilisation of PMs and VMs. By finding overloaded PMs, the resource usage of PMs can be handled. Tasks in VMs with a sizeable volume-to-size ratio (VSR) are pushed to VMs with smaller values.

In [16], the authors proposed an approach employing the long-term memory encoder-decoder network (LSTM) with an alertness mechanism. This approach draws the sequential and contextual features of the historical workload data through the encoder-decoder network and integrates the alertness mechanism into the decoder network.

In [9], the authors proposed a VM allocation strategy, which dynamically redistributes VMs based on the actual needs of a single VM, taken as a reference. The proposed solution considers different types of resources and is designed to minimise underuse and overuse in cloud data centres. The experiments highlighted the importance of considering multiple types of resources. However, the above methods do not take into account the communication cost between VMs, which would affect the power consumption in the VM scheduling problem.

In [3], the authors considered the scenario of communication failures that block data transmission. To improve the reliability of data transmission, they improved a Greedy Perimeter Stateless Routing (GPSR) scheme based on perimeter positioning. The work described in [2] proposed a dynamic method of reconfiguration to solve the problem of instability and high resource occupancy of traditional approaches. The LSTM neural network was trained using a web service QoS dataset and service summoner information collected from sensors. The candidate service datasets from the cloud and edge service were used as input and predicted variables.

In [7], several papers present virtual machine migration approaches with advantages such as load balancing, fault tolerance and also energy savings.

None of these works addresses a limitation of virtualised environments, which makes it possible, with the use of parallel computing, to degrade the quality of large services by using a simple tool, based on the Erlang language, that uses the processing power of a low-cost machine, such as an IoT device.

3   Tsung Tool

Tsung is an open-source multi-protocol distributed load testing tool [11]. Currently, the application can be used to stress servers with the following protocols: HTTP, WebDAV, SOAP, PostgreSQL, MySQL, LDAP, MQTT and XMPP.

It has been developed for the purpose of simulating users in order to test the scalability and performance of IP-based client-server-type applications. Moreover, existing protocols can be extended by changing the code and adapting to the new reality.

The choice of using Tsung was mainly based on its capacity to simulate a large number of simultaneous users from a single machine. Also, because of the possibility of distributing the load in a cluster of several client machines in order to simulate hundreds of thousands of virtual users in the same test.

The programming language Erlang [14] was chosen to implement Tsung for being a concurrency-oriented language and for its ability to create real-time, lightweight and massively scalable systems. The tool was created with 3 main features in mind: performance – capable of supporting hundreds of thousands of lightweight processes in a single virtual machine; scalability – with a naturally distributed runtime environment, promoting an idea of process location transparency; and fault tolerance – built to develop robust and fault-tolerant systems, e.g. bad responses received by the server do not interrupt the measurement during test execution.

Besides complete documentation for its use, this application has several features, such as a configuration system based on *XML*, the possibility of creating dynamic sessions with the storage of answers from the server in runtime for later use, monitoring of the Operating System, processing, memory and network traffic through agents in remote servers, the ability to generate realistic traffic and the creation of detailed reports of the tests performed.

To set up the tests, an *XML* file is used with tags that determine all the necessary aspects for its realization. All the scenarios are described between the labels *Tsung* where the registered degree is determined, which stands out: emergency, critical, errors, warnings and debugging. The higher the registered degree, the higher the impact on the test performance.

The first configuration to be done is the determination of the IP address of the client machine and the server to be tested. The server is the entry point to the cluster, in case several servers are added weight is defined for each one (by default it's 1) and each session will choose a server randomly.

Besides, the port number and a protocol type are configured for the server, which may be TCP, UDP, SSL (IPv4 and IPv6) or WebSocket (Listing 1.1).

```
<clients>                                                               1
    <client host="localhost" use_controller_vm="true"/>                 2
</clients>                                                               3
<servers>                                                               4
    <server host="server1" port="80" type="tcp" weight="4"/>            5
    <server host="server2" port="80" type="udp" weight="4"/>            6
</servers>                                                              7
```

Listing 1.1. Server and client configuration.

After that, the progression of the test is defined through phases. Each phase has a duration and the number of users to be created. The test ends when all the users finish their sessions. In the following example (Listing 1.2) there are 3 phases with 2 min duration each. In the first, 2 new users are created every second, in the second 10 new users are created every second and, finally, in the last, 1000 new users are created per second.

```
<load>                                                              1
    <arrivalphase phase="1" duration="2" unit="minute">            2
        <users interarrival="0.001" unit="second"/>                3
    </arrivalphase>                                                 4
    <arrivalphase phase="2" duration="2" unit="minute">            5
        <users interarrival="0.00001" unit="second"/>              6
    </arrivalphase>                                                 7
    <arrivalphase phase="3" duration="2" unit="minute">            8
        <users interarrival="0.000001" unit="second"/>             9
    </arrivalphase>                                                 10
</load>                                                             11
```

Listing 1.2. Configuration of test phases.

Finally, the user sessions are defined where the requests to be executed are described (Listing 1.3). Each session can receive a probability or a weight that is used to determine which session will be chosen for the user to be created. There is the possibility to set an exponentially distributed wait time between requests to better simulate a legitimate request. Another option is to read variables in files and use them at runtime in the created requests.

```
<sessions>                                                         1
    <session name="session-1" probability="50" type="ts_http">     2
        <request>                                                  3
            <http url="/" method="GET" version="1.1"></http> </    4
request>
            <request> <http url="/images/logo.gif" method="GET"    5
version="1.1" if_modified_since="Tue, 14 Jun 2022 02:43:31 GMT">
            </http>                                                6
        </request>                                                 7
        <thinktime value="20" random="true"></thinktime>          8
        <transaction name="req-index">                            9
            <request> <http url="/index.en.html" method="GET"      10
version="1.1" >
            </http> </request>                                     11
            <request><http url="/images/header.gif" method="GET"   12
version="1.1">
            </http> </request>                                     13
        </transaction>                                             14
        <thinktime value="60" random="true"></thinktime>          15
        <request>                                                  16
            <http url="/" method="POST" version="1.1"              17
contents="search=test">
            </http>                                                18
        </request>                                                 19
    </session>                                                     20
        <session name ="next-session" probability="50" type="      21
ts_psql" > . . .
    </session>                                                     22
</sessions>                                                        23
```

Listing 1.3. Configuration of sessions.

In Listing 1.3 there is an example with two sessions, the first with the name "session-1" will occur half the time, because it has a probability of 50%, being of type HTTP. Initially, two GET requests are made, one from the root home page and another from the "logo" image if it was modified after June 14, 2022. After that, a random pause of exponential distribution with an average of 20 s is made and then a transaction named "index_request" is created, which is composed of two GET requests. There is another pause centred in 60 s, and, finally, a POST request passing the value "test" to the parameter *search*. The other session, of type *PostgreSQL*, will occur the other half of the time, and its requests have been omitted.

4   System Model

In order to perform denial of service tests, the following structure was set up: 4 VMs with 4 GB RAM, 4 Core Processor – similar to a Raspberry Pi 4 specs – and 128 GB Storage each, acting as *hosts*; 1 virtual switch with 1 Gbps ports interconnecting these *hosts*.

In one of the hosts, the Xen project hypervisor was installed and created an internal VM with a web server, thus simulating a service provider environment. The other 3 hosts have the Debian Linux operating system installed and were used either to simulate traffic or to perform a denial of service attack.

When creating the environment to perform the tests, the first step was to verify the limits within which the application could work. That is, to verify the level of depletion that the attacker host could support in order to mark the work to be developed. Therefore, as the first tests aimed to monitor and set limits, tests were performed with a high load of generation users.

After that, the web server was stressed with a large number of requests for a long time in order to follow its behaviour. Random times between requests were introduced in order to resemble real requests.

Finally, a traditional attack and the performed attack were compared, highlighting their differences and similarities having as reference *3 factors*: consumed bandwidth, processing load and amount of free memory. With the *overload* of any of these 3, it is possible to generate a denial of service or, at least, the degradation of the user experience, delaying the response time for a legitimate request.

5   Results

Through **first test**, the set of parameters that limit the usage of the attacking machine through maximum user generation, at maximum performance, was sought. The test was divided into 3 phases, where in the initial 30 s, 1.000 users per second were generated; in the following 120 s, 10.000 users per second were generated; and in the last 30 s, 100.000 users per second were generated.

Thus, each user made a connection to the web server and performed an HTTP GET request of the file *index.html*. After receiving any response from the server, the client ceased to exist.

Analyzing the results (Fig. 1), one can observe that after a certain time (approximately 180 s), there was no more generation of users. Besides, it was noticed that the web application stops handling the requests because the growth

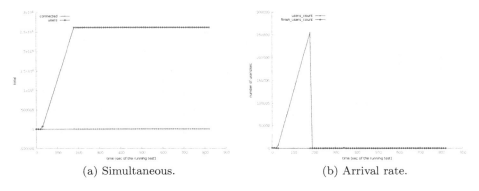

(a) Simultaneous.   (b) Arrival rate.

Fig. 1. Amount of users – 1st Test.

of concurrent users is constant. It can also be verified that the application supported the creation of up to 12.500 users per second, but for values above that there was no response.

Next, the more extensive **second test**, where in the initial 30 min, 100 users per second were generated; in the following 273 min (4,56 h), 1.000 users per second were generated; and, in the last 30 min, 10.000 users per second were generated.

It can be seen that the second phase of the test (after 1.800 s) demands the entire processing load from its beginning until almost 20.000 s (Figs. 2a and 2b). Considering that the second phase lasted until 18.180 s, it is safe to say that the application, under these conditions, has a limit to the creation of 1.000 users per second (Fig. 2c).

The application behaved well when treating 100 users per second in the first phase – until 1.800 s (Fig. 2c). However, in the following phase, there was an instability where, in spite of the first requests having been handled, as more requests arrived, there was a significant overload, maintaining an average of 500 requests per second being served, following this way until the end of the test. This information is confirmed by the processor graphic showing that there was no alteration with the beginning of the third phase, from 8.000 s on (Fig. 2b).

Analyzing the report of this test in Table 1, it could note that from the total of users created, only 8.45 million users were treated, that is, they received as a response the requested page. It is worth pointing out that the average request waiting time was 426 s. Another observation was that the connection with the longest wait was 1.034 s.

After these initial tests to determine the setup parameters of the application, the behaviour of a denial of service (DoS) attack using the *flooding technique* was studied and verified, as it is one of the most common types of DoS.

Traffic flooding occurs in connections using the Transmission Control Protocol (TCP), utilised in services that require reliable data delivery, by exploiting

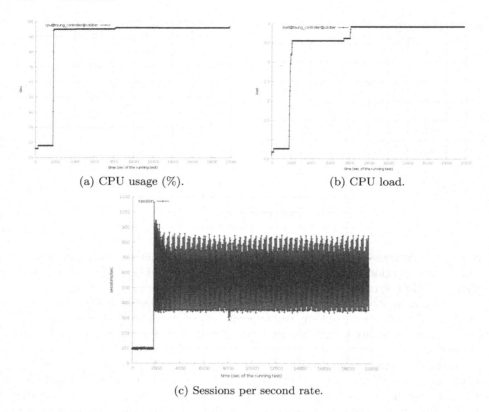

(a) CPU usage (%).   (b) CPU load.

(c) Sessions per second rate.

Fig. 2. 2nd Test.

the connection opening process of this protocol, which begins with the negotiation of certain parameters between the client and the server.

TCP was designed specifically to provide a reliable end-to-end data stream on an untrusted inter-network. An inter-network differs from a single network because its various parts may have completely different topologies, bandwidths, delays, packet sizes, and other parameters [13].

In a standard TCP connection, the client sends a synchronisation packet (SYN) to the server, requesting to open the connection. Upon receipt of the SYN packet, the server processes the connection request and allocates memory to store client information. Next, a synchronisation/confirmation packet (SYN/ACK) is sent as a reply to the client, notifying it that its connection request has been accepted. The client then sends an ACK packet to complete the connection opening. This procedure is known as a *three-way handshake* (Fig. 3c).

The flood attack consists of sending several SYN packets to the target, causing it to reserve a space in memory for the connection it will open. Following the flow, the target returns an SYN/ACK and waits for an ACK to close the connection, but the attacker sends another SYN request forcing the target to

Table 1. Report table – 2nd Test.

Name	Highest rate (users/s)	Average rate (users/s)	Total sessions
Connection	1.034,6	426,8	8.445.969
Page	1.034,6	426,79	8.445.969
Request	1.034.,6	426,79	8.445.969
Session	1.063,4	555,17	10.987.007

reserve another area of memory for a new connection. By performing this action on a large scale the attacker is able to exhaust the target's memory.

To analyze in more detail how each resource is exploited, some parameters related to the target and the attacker machines are set. Let t_a be the time interval between each TCP SYN segment sent by the attacker, t_p be the time required for the target to process a TCP connection request and send a response, and t_m be the time a given memory resource is allocated for a TCP connection.

An *attack of CPU overload* on the target machine can be performed when the attacker can generate segments at a faster rate than the target machine can process them, that is when $t_a < t_p$, as shown in Fig. 3a. In this case, the target machine cannot process connection requests in a timely manner, which causes the request queue to fill up and many of them to be dropped.

Thus, should a legitimate user attempt to access the service under attack, it is very likely that their connection request will be dropped along with the attack traffic. This is because the legitimate user's traffic must compete for the same resource with the numerous segments sent by the attacker.

Importantly, to remain anonymous, the attacker does not need to use your real IP address to carry out the attack. In fact, any IP address can be used as the source address in attack packets. Using forged source addresses does nothing to change the effect suffered by the target machine. However, the response to the connection request does not return to the attacker, but rather to the IP address used in his packets. In this way, the attacker is able not only to deny the target service but also to remain anonymous.

Another resource that can be exploited during TCP SYN segment flood attacks is the target machine's *memory*. When the server receives a request to open a TCP connection, it allocates a small amount of memory to store certain information about the state of the connection, such as the initial sequence numbers, the IP addresses, and the TCP ports used for this connection. Figure 3b illustrates the case where the attacked resource is the memory of the target machine. It is important to note that, even with memory limits controlled by the operating system, denial of service occurs when the memory allocated for connections is exhausted, without the complete exhaustion of the victim's entire memory needed.

Next, a TCP SYN/ACK segment is sent back to the client in order to finalize the three-way agreement. At this point, the TCP connection is said to be half open. The initially reserved resources are then allocated until the connection

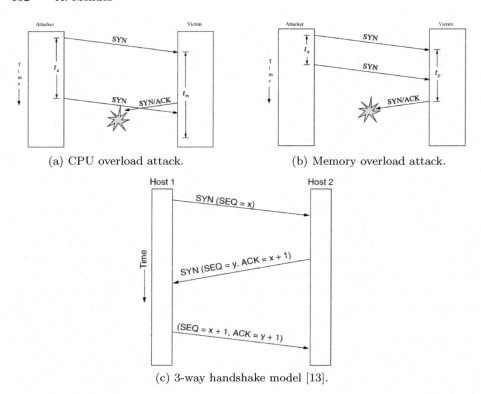

(a) CPU overload attack.   (b) Memory overload attack.

(c) 3-way handshake model [13].

Fig. 3. TCP big picture.

is terminated by conventional means, or until a timer bursts indicating that the expected TCP ACK segment was not received. In this case, the allocated memory is finally freed to be used for future connections.

Note, by definition, that the inequality $t_m > t_p$ is always valid. Thus, *3 possibilities* can happen. The *first* possibility occurs when $t_a < t_p < t_m$, that is, the interval between sending attack packets is less than the victim's processing time. This is the case discussed earlier where the victim's processing is overloaded. It is also worth noting that in addition to processing, the victim's memory is also overloaded. This occurs because the connection requests that the victim manages to fulfil in time, allocate a memory space that is only released when the timer bursts, since packets with forged source addresses are used.

The *second* possibility occurs when $t_p \leq t_a < t_m$. In this case, the victim is able to process requests, but memory spaces are consumed by each new connection and are not freed up in time to service all connections. Therefore, new connections are not accepted due to a lack of memory.

The *final* case occurs when the attacker cannot generate attack packets at a rate sufficient even to overflow memory, i.e., $t_a \geq t_m$. In this case, the victim's resources are not attacked directly and other forms of attacks are required to deny the offered service.

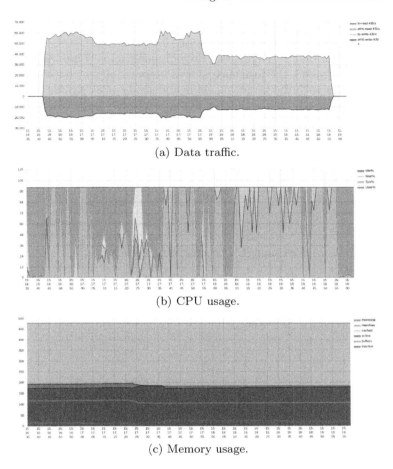

(a) Data traffic.

(b) CPU usage.

(c) Memory usage.

Fig. 4. Flood attack, *Hping3* tool as a reference – 3rd Test.

After that, let's move on to the DoS attack configuration, in which the *Hping3* [12] tool was used with the following configuration:

```
# hping3 -c 1000000 -d 120 -S -w 64 -p 80 --flood <IP>
```

where $-c$ refers to the number of packets to be sent; $-d$ refers to the size of each packet to be sent; $-S$ defines the sending of only SYN packets; $-w$ defines the size of the TCP window; $-p$ defines the TCP port to be attacked; and, $--flood$ parameter that makes the application send the packets as fast as possible, not caring about the response.

Next, the attack on the web server – **third** test – was performed using the *nmon* monitoring tool to collect data, through which large data traffic (sent/received), high processing load and CPU usage could be verified during the whole testing slot. And finally, RAM exhaustion of the target machine (Fig. 4).

These results were employed as a reference to be used in a comparison of the tests performed with the *Tsung* application.

With the intention of verifying the target's behaviour, comparing the attack with Tsung and Hping3, the **fourth test** was prepared in which each user makes a TCP connection with the target machine and sends a 380 kB file, in 3 distinct moments, interspersed with a request of the root web page (*index.html*), the request of another web page with 2 MB and a random amount of time paused modelled by an exponential distribution with the average equal to 4 s (Listing 1.4).

```
<http url="/" method="POST" contents_from_file="<path>/fake_data"    1
/> <http url="/" method="GET"/>
<http url="/" method="POST" contents_from_file="<path>/fake_data"    2
/> <thinktime value="4" random="true"></thinktime>
<http url="/great_tsung.html" method="GET"/>                         3
<http url="/" method="POST" contents_from_file="<path>/fake_data"    4
/>
```

Listing 1.4. DoS attack configuration.

In this fourth test, Fig. 5, in the initial 10 s, 200 users per second were generated; in the following 40 s, 335 users per second were generated; in the next 40 s, approximately 500 users per second were generated; and in the last 20 s, 660 users per second were generated.

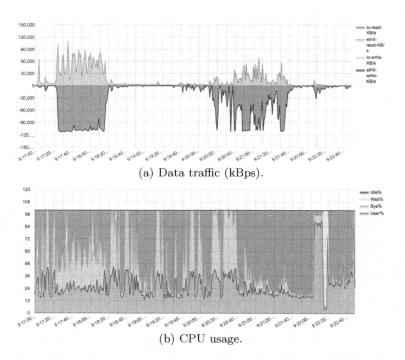

(a) Data traffic (kBps).

(b) CPU usage.

Fig. 5. Flood attack, *Tsung* tool – 4th Test.

It is possible to notice that all the available network bandwidth was occupied by the requests, generating some periods of high processing in the target machine. After all these checks, it was possible to create a test that resembles the flood test with the *Hping3* tool, which, besides occupying all the available bandwidth is capable of generating a high processing power in the chosen target machine.

With an infinite number of possibilities, both the memory, processing and network bandwidth of the target can be exhausted by changing the parameters in the *Tsung* tool, leaving it up to the attacker to configure the behaviour of his attack to approximate that of legitimate requests.

6   Conclusions

The *Tsung* tool has great flexibility in terms of configuration, allowing a high range of ways of use. As it is an application created in Erlang, a concurrency-oriented language, this tool has the characteristic of being light and massively scalable. It was created to be a stress testing tool for other applications, this work explored its use to perform denial of service (DoS) attacks.

As demonstrated, it is possible to perform a massive amount of requests using a piece of a low-cost device (for instance, a Raspberry Pi) in the totality of its processing, consuming in great part the resources of the attacked machine and degrading the experience of the legitimate user, effectively causing the denial of service to a server.

Finally, it was possible to create a large number of users, each performing different types of requests, sending and receiving data from the target. Besides the possibility of making random pauses which can be used to hinder the detection and blocking of requests, besides keeping the connections open for a longer time, approaching legitimate requests.

Acknowledgements. This work has been conducted under the project "BIOMA – Bioeconomy integrated solutions for the mobilization of the Agri-food market" (POCI-01-0247-FEDER-046112), by "BIOMA" Consortium, and financed by the European Regional Development Fund (FEDER), through the Incentive System to Research and Technological Development, within the Portugal2020 Competitiveness and Internationalization Operational Program.

The authors are grateful to the Foundation for Science and Technology (FCT, Portugal) for financial support through national funds FCT/MCTES (PIDDAC) to CeDRI (UIDB/05757/2020 and UIDP/05757/2020) and SusTEC (LA/P/0007/2021).

References

1. Buyya, R., Yeo, C.S., Venugopal, S., Broberg, J., Brandic, I.: Cloud computing and emerging it platforms: vision, hype, and reality for delivering computing as the 5th utility. Futur. Gener. Comput. Syst. **25**(6), 599–616 (2009)
2. Gao, H., Huang, W., Duan, Y.: The cloud-edge-based dynamic reconfiguration to service workflow for mobile ecommerce environments: a QoS prediction perspective. ACM Trans. Internet Technol. (TOIT) **21**(1), 1–23 (2021)

3. Gao, H., Liu, C., Li, Y., Yang, X.: V2VR: reliable hybrid-network-oriented V2V data transmission and routing considering RSUs and connectivity probability. IEEE Trans. Intell. Transp. Syst. **22**(6), 3533–3546 (2020)
4. Greenberg, A., Hamilton, J., Maltz, D.A., Patel, P.: The cost of a cloud: research problems in data center networks (2008)
5. Hwang, I., Pedram, M.: Hierarchical, portfolio theory-based virtual machine consolidation in a compute cloud. IEEE Trans. Serv. Comput. **11**(1), 63–77 (2016)
6. Jain, R., Paul, S.: Network virtualization and software defined networking for cloud computing: a survey. IEEE Commun. Mag. **51**(11), 24–31 (2013)
7. Le, T.: A survey of live virtual machine migration techniques. Computer Sci. Rev. **38**, 100304 (2020)
8. Mell, P., Grance, T., et al.: The nist definition of cloud computing (2011)
9. Mosa, A., Sakellariou, R.: Dynamic virtual machine placement considering CPU and memory resource requirements. In: 2019 IEEE 12th International Conference on Cloud Computing (CLOUD), pp. 196–198. IEEE (2019)
10. Nasim, R., Taheri, J., Kassler, A.J.: Optimizing virtual machine consolidation in virtualized datacenters using resource sensitivity. In: 2016 IEEE International Conference on Cloud Computing Technology and Science (CloudCom), pp. 168–175. IEEE (2016)
11. Niclausse, N.: Tsung documentation (2000)
12. Sanfilippo, S., et al.: Hping-active network security tool (2008)
13. Tanenbaum, A.S., Feamster, N., Wetherall, D.J.: Computer Networks, 6th edn. Pearson Education India (2020)
14. Virding, R., Wikström, C., Williams, M.: Concurrent Programming in ERLANG. Prentice Hall International (UK) Ltd. (1996)
15. Wood, T., Shenoy, P., Venkataramani, A., Yousif, M.: Sandpiper: black-box and gray-box resource management for virtual machines. Comput. Netw. **53**(17), 2923–2938 (2009)
16. Zhu, Y., Zhang, W., Chen, Y., Gao, H.: A novel approach to workload prediction using attention-based lstm encoder-decoder network in cloud environment. EURASIP J. Wirel. Commun. Netw. **2019**(1), 1–18 (2019)

A Rule Based Procedural Content Generation System

Gonçalo Oliveira[1]($\boxtimes$) ⓘ, Lucas Almeida[1]($\boxtimes$), João Paulo Sousa[2]($\boxtimes$) ⓘ,
Bárbara Barroso[2]($\boxtimes$) ⓘ, and Inês Barbedo[1]($\boxtimes$) ⓘ

[1] Instituto Politécnico de Bragança, Campus de Santa Apolónia, 5300-253 Bragança, Portugal
{a42070,a39341}@alunos.ipb.pt, inesb@ipb.pt
[2] Research Centre in Digitalization and Intelligent Robotics (CeDRI), InstitutoPolitécnico de
Bragança, Campus de Santa Apolónia, 5300-253 Bragança, Portugal
{jpaulo,bbarroso}@ipb.pt

Abstract. This paper presents a new method of procedural content generation
(PCG) for natural environments and objects (such as terrain, biomes, river, and
vegetation), with special attention to game design and visual aesthetic. Our solution
allows us to define a set of rules to control the content generation to meet the
requirements of game design and level design teams.

Keywords: Procedural Content Generation · Game Design · Level Design ·
Rules · Algorithm

1 Introduction

Procedural Content Generation (PCG) refers to the practice of generating game content
through an AI-processed procedural generation method [1]. PCG has been used in the
game and cinema industry since the 80s for several different purposes [2]. Some of
the popular motivations are replayability, adaptability, and economics [3][4]. Due to
the amount and diversity of automatically generated content, it is possible to offer more
refreshing gameplay each time the player starts the game providing a different experience
to the players. In a more advanced application, the PCG AI can be sensitive to the player's
skills, and the expected level of difficulty, to adapt the gameplay to their skill level [5].
On the other hand, it is still possible to replace a somewhat time-consuming process in
game development by automating the processes typically addressed by a Human that
are easily performed by AI. For these reasons, the PCG is very often approached by
independent studios that often do not contain the human, technological and sufficient
funds to invest in manpower for these areas of video game design. Thus, with this
approach, it is possible to use algorithms that are easily adaptable to various situations
depending on the circumstances presented during content generation.

In this paper, we propose a novel system that uses biome seeds to create multiple
biomes and populates them densely with specific assets. The research questions of this
paper are the following:

© The Author(s), under exclusive license to Springer Nature Switzerland AG 2022
A. I. Pereira et al. (Eds.): OL2A 2022, CCIS 1754, pp. 107–113, 2022.
https://doi.org/10.1007/978-3-031-23236-7_8

- What are the types of game content that can be generated by PCG?
- What are the studies that address the contributions, difficulties, and challenges that PCG can bring to game development from a game design perspective?
- What technical solutions currently exist? What are its main characteristics, capabilities and limitations?
- Could we propose a new PCG algorithm for natural environments with special attention to game design and visual aesthetic?
- How to describe the new PCG algorithm and its architecture?

The rest of the paper is structured as follows: In section two we provide a literature review about different aspects of PCG generation solutions and the difficulties and challenges of its use in game design and development. In section three we describe the entire process of the design of our solution, identifying the elements to generate and the architecture of the PCG algorithm. Section four gives a conclusion to our research and discusses future work.

2   Literature Review

This section begins with an overview of what kind of content can be generated procedurally, follows several technical methods to generate content, and some specific solutions to help solve our problem are discussed.

In [6], the authors introduced six main classes of game content that can be generated by PCG systems: Game Bits – which are basically the assets of the game, textures, sound, materials, and some simple behaviors. Game Space - the environment in which the game takes place, can be indoor or outdoor maps. Game System - includes more complex environments such as road networks, urban environments, or ecosystems. Game Scenarios - are the scenes organized into levels with events of the game, can be puzzles, levels, or storyboards. Game Design - all the main features that define the design of the game such as rules, goals, and mechanics. Derived Content - content created outside the main gameplay of the game, can be news, leaderboards, or videos.

Several technical approaches can be used to generate content, with different features, capabilities, and tradeoffs for design. In [7] several PCG solutions are identified: Simulation-based - the PCG starts with a template world and a set of operators that can change the world's evolution in a simulation mode. Generation as optimization - it looks for the best combination of components according to a certain evaluation function that determines the desired results to respect as much as possible a value of optimization. Constraint satisfaction - certain design constraints are specified, whereupon a constraints solver will create content that meets these constraints. Constructive generation - implies the generation of content through predefined building blocks which, later, are used in the generation of levels according to the implemented algorithm. It is a type of approach often used in Rogue-Likes. Generation with Grammars - this method consists of specifying rules according to a certain space of defined possibilities which, passing to an interpreter, are processed in the creation of contents. Constructionist selection - although it is debatable whether it should be considered a procedural generation algorithm, in this method the building blocks are selected from a library and used by the PCG to create an environment for the player.

In [8] a study is carried out on how PCG is used in different game genres, for which the algorithms are grouped into three categories: traditional methods, search-based methods, and machine learning methods. Traditional methods - encompass pseudo-random number generators and constructive methods, generative grammars, and others; Search-based - methods that include artificial intelligence and operational search algorithms such as heuristic search, local search, and optimization. Machine learning - includes algorithms that use data to improve performance on a specific task.

However, the difficulties and challenges related to the use of these techniques are the balance of the games itself and making a good construction of levels and content where there are no repetitive or chaotic patterns that can negatively affect the player's gameplay. In [9] is presented a framework for PCG that quantifies the player's experience and the quality of content, based on a computational model, and is able to generate content for different emotional representations. To develop a well-regarded game in terms of design, one must consider the demands required by the type of design that is intended for that same game. It is, therefore, necessary to take into account how the player and the designers will influence the generation of the content and how to pass this information on to the AI, so that it manages the content considering these requirements. [10] Presents a framework for analyzing and discussing the role of PCG in game design and PCG-based design tools. This framework identifies three dynamics that only PCG can provide: replayability offering different surprising content, the possibility to build strategies for the different content on each play and providing different content that supports the replay of mechanisms in different scenarios.

3 Design of PCG Algorithm

The proposed PCG system is designed to be used in an open-world adventure game. In this section, the elements belonging to a natural environment are identified, and then the PCG architecture capable of generating this world is presented.

3.1 Elements Identification

To take a deeper look into our algorithm, we first need to identify all the elements it can generate, Fig. 1 shows exactly that.

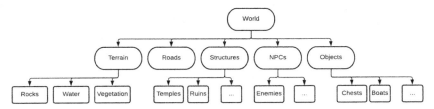

Fig. 1. Identification of the elements that can be included in the Scene.

We divided the elements into three types by granularity. The first with more granularity consists of only one element:

- World - the name World is self-explanatory, we are generating the world where we are placing all the Structures, Objects, NPCs, etc.

The second type of elements are:

- Terrain – is the ground in which the player stands, the terrain varies with height and it's thanks to this variation that we can find lakes, mountains, forests, and all the assets that make these feel like real locations.
- Roads – an offset in hue from the terrain's color allows us to generate roads that the player can follow and explore.
- Structures – our world generation allows us to dictate a set of rules that when met will spawn our structures, these are key points in driving the story forwards while providing elements of exploration for the player.
- NPC's – these spawn when their spawning conditions are met and serve to add enemies for the player to fight.
- Objects – are assets that aren't related to our terrain, these serve to amplify the gameplay experience of the player and allow for better environmental storytelling.

The third type of elements (more granularity), consists of a deconstruction of the key components that make up our second layer, it's where we place all the content you can find inside our main identification elements:

- Under Terrain we have three groups, namely vegetation, rocks, and water, all key components in making sure our terrain generation mimics real-world environments.
- Examples of Structures are temples, ruins, houses, and buildings.
- The only component inside NPC's (non-player characters) is enemies, named this way because they are all hostile mobs.
- Within Objects, we find any type of object that does not belong to the other classes (e.g., chests and boats).

3.2   Architecture/Design/Model

Taking into consideration the aforementioned elements, for a more practical explanation of the process, we can further divide all the elements into distinct layers/groups to understand the phases of content generation (Fig. 2).

The first layer, the input, is when the human designer has an influence on the data being processed by the system. We first start to introduce the assets defined by the assets list provided by the designer. All these assets are inherently required for the level design and given the natural complex subjective properties of this selection, for a more pragmatic approach, this process must be accomplished purely by human input.

The second layer, the configuration, is the intermediate section between both human and AI processes. Here, the designer defines the rules of terrain generation in the form of concrete values. This process allows for a better translation between the more complex designer ideas/rules to a language that the algorithm can properly decipher. Here we evaluate important terrain generation and level design properties such as:

- Height Modifier – One of the three modifiers to be implemented in each biome. The height modifier adjusts the height of the terrain according to the biome in particular (e.g. biomes like swamps tend to have lower heights and valleys tend to be more irregular). The human designer has influence on settings such as height variation, noise map scale, number of passes the algorithm takes, and much more. Here the algorithm will take all these data and work around them using seven different methods that we explain further in the next chapters. Here it's also defined rules for positioning of buildings around the terrain.

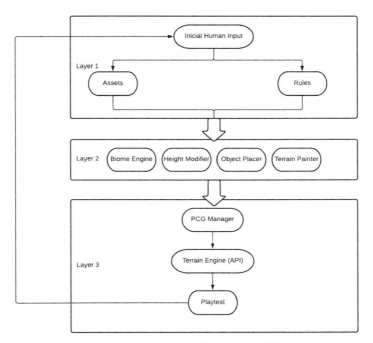

Fig. 2. The architecture of the Seed-based PCG System.

- Biome generation – The biome generation is a crucial part of the system given the fact that we are trying to simulate credible real-world terrain generation. Here, the designer can define settings like decay rate, minimum and maximum intensity and apply modifiers such as textures and height alterations dependent on the biome. After introducing the data, the algorithm takes action by processing all the information provided and carefully spreading each biome property such as textures and other assets throughout the terrain using an ooze-style biome generation method [11] for smoother and more natural transitions between different biomes. This process is better explained in the next chapter of this paper.
- Terrain Painter (Texturization) - The "Terrain Painter", as the name implies, applies textures to the terrain according to rules defined by the designer, to make the game

environment more immersive and natural. This component considers several parameters to apply different textures, such as elevation, biomes, and slope of the terrain. For example, in a situation where the terrain is at a higher height (such as the peak of high mountains), it makes sense for snow to be generated. In the opposite way, when the altitude is close to the water level a sand or grass texture will be applied. In the latter case, the choice of texture to apply will also be influenced by the biome and the slope of the terrain. The first rule will always be the elevation, as the texture generator will choose a texture from a predefined array of textures and apply it to the terrain according to the height, which normally is the y value of the coordinates. Then other parameters will be evaluated for the choice of textures, such as biome or the slope of the terrain.

- Object placer – The object placer is another modifier used in the biome generation configurations. Take into consideration that we identify as "objects": simple and unitary assets with little complexity regarding their shape and number of elements. The aforementioned "buildings" are more complex assets consisting of multiple elements and complex shapes, consequently, requiring more convoluted positioning rules defined by the designer. Here we work with these simple objects by defining rules such as height limits, the density, the number of objects to spawn, defining if the said object can spawn above or in water or even both, the list of assets to spawn, etc. It is important to carefully evaluate certain aspects of object placement to build a more natural and real environment, particularly, where we place them. Rules such as the height limits and verifying if certain objects can go above or under water are crucial to building an immersive terrain. Misplacement of these objects (e.g., trees generally can't go under water and lily pads can't climb up mountains) can immensely compromise the gameplay experience thus being one of the most important aspects of the world generation for better player immersion.

The third layer receives the biome map, the terrain noise map, and the rules defined previously. All these elements are passed to the PCG Manager which will generate the terrain, apply the biomes, and place the objects. The PCG Manager will then control the Terrain Engine, to perform the various necessary transformations such as terrain elevation, texture application, and object placement. The result will be the generation of a natural-looking 3D scenery with features like mountains, lakes, different types of biomes, vegetation, and different objects.

At the end of the generation process, the scenario is included in a prototype that will be playtested by the design team to identify errors and obtain feedback on the players' experience in relation to the generated content and adjust the PCG system. This entire process has a cyclical and iterative nature, where it will be necessary to make the PCG system better to produce a plot according to the requirements of the design team.

4   Conclusions

Procedural Content Generation can significantly reduce the costs and development time of games. However, the systems are often not flexible enough to the requirements defined by the level designer. This paper showed how we approached the design and implementation of a ruled biome-based procedural content generation system, with attention to the requirements of the level design.

We are currently finalizing a vertical slice that uses the architecture presented in Sect. 3.2. It is a 3rd Person Open-World Adventure Game, single player for PC that has as main features: a large, procedurally generated game map; a biome with specific visual characteristics to it. We are also finalizing a playtesting session to get feedback on several aspects of the game (e.g., mechanics, dynamics, and aesthetics) and the procedurally generated 3D open world scenarios.

As future work, we intend to publish the implementation details of the game and the results obtained from the playtesting session.

Acknowledgements. The authors are grateful to the Foundation for Science and Technology (FCT, Portugal) for financial support through national funds FCT/MCTES (PIDDAC) to CeDRI (UIDB/05757/2020 and UIDP/05757/2020) and SusTEC (LA/P/0007/2021).

References

1. Togelius, J., Kastbjerg, E., Schedl, D., Yannakakis, G.N.: What is procedural content generation? mario on the borderline. In: Proceedings of the 2nd International Workshop on Procedural Content Generation in Games, pp. 1–6 Association for Computing Machinery, New York, NY, USA (2011). https://doi.org/10.1145/2000919.2000922
2. Togelius, J., Whitehead, J., Bidarra, R.: Procedural content generation in games (Guest Editorial). Comput. Intell. AI Games IEEE Trans. On. **3**, 169–171 (2011). https://doi.org/10.1109/TCIAIG.2011.2166554
3. Togelius, J., et al.: Procedural content generation: goals, challenges and actionable steps. **6**, 61–75, (2013). https://doi.org/10.4230/DFU.VOL6.12191.61
4. Smith, G., Gan, E., Othenin-Girard, A., Whitehead, J.: PCG-based game design: enabling new play experiences through procedural content generation. In: Proceedings of the 2nd International Workshop on Procedural Content Generation in Games, pp. 1–4 Association for Computing Machinery, New York, NY, USA (2011). https://doi.org/10.1145/2000919.2000926
5. Smith, G., Othenin-Girard, A., Whitehead, J., Wardrip-Fruin, N.: PCG-based game design: creating endless web. In: Proceedings of the International Conference on the Foundations of Digital Games, pp. 188–195 Association for Computing Machinery, New York, NY, USA (2012). https://doi.org/10.1145/2282338.2282375
6. Hendrikx, M., Meijer, S., Van Der Velden, J., Iosup, A.: Procedural content generation for games: a survey. ACM Trans. Multimed. Comput. Commun. Appl. **9**, 1:1–1:22 (2013). https://doi.org/10.1145/2422956.2422957
7. Smith, G.: Procedural content generation - An Overview. (2015)
8. Barriga, N.A.: A short introduction to procedural content generation algorithms for videogames. (2018)
9. Yannakakis, G.N., Togelius, J.: Experience-driven procedural content generation. IEEE Trans. Affect. Comput. **2**, 147–161 (2011). https://doi.org/10.1109/T-AFFC.2011.6
10. Smith, G.: Understanding procedural content generation: a design-centric analysis of the role of PCG in games. In: Conference on Human Factors in Computing Systems - Proceedings (2014). https://doi.org/10.1145/2556288.2557341
11. Scott, P.: Procedural biome generation: ooze-style - PROCJAM tutorials, https://www.procjam.com/tutorials/en/ooze/ . Accessed 23 June 2022

A Hybrid Approach to Operational Planning in Home Health Care

Filipe Alves[1,2,3(✉)] ⓘ, António J. S. T. Duarte[4] ⓘ, Ana Maria A. C. Rocha[3] ⓘ,
Ana I. Pereira[1,2] ⓘ, and Paulo Leitão[1,2] ⓘ

[1] Research Centre in Digitalization and Intelligent Robotics (CeDRI), Instituto
Politécnico de Bragança, Campus de Santa Apolónia, 5300-253 Bragança, Portugal
{filipealves,apereira,pleitao}@ipb.pt
[2] Laboratório para a Sustentabilidade e Tecnologia em Regiões de Montanha
(SusTEC), Instituto Politécnico de Bragança, Campus de Santa Apolónia, 5300-253
Bragança, Portugal
[3] ALGORITMI Center, University of Minho, 4710-057 Braga, Portugal
arocha@dps.uminho.pt
[4] Applied Management Research Unit (UNIAG), Instituto Politécnico de Bragança,
Bragança, Portugal
aduarte@ipb.pt

Abstract. Home health care (HHC) management needs to plan their
operations to synchronize professionals and allocate resources to perform
several HHC services needed by patients. The growing demand for this
type of service dictates the interest of all the stakeholders (professionals
and patients) in finding high-quality daily solutions and logistics. Routing and scheduling are problems of combinatorial nature, extremely complex, and require sophisticated optimization approaches. This work aims
to contribute to cost-efficient decision-making in the general improvement of the service quality. Thus, a mixed integer linear programming
model, a genetic algorithm, and a hybrid approach were used to solve the
operational planning through test instances of different sizes for public
home care providers. Computational results are presented, followed by a
discussion on the advantages and shortcomings, highlighting the strength
of each approach.

Keywords: Home health care · Optimization · MILP · Genetic
algorithm

1 Introduction

The world population is increasingly aging and a decrease in informal care leads
to increasing demand for HHC services [18]. In this context, health institutions

The authors are grateful to the Foundation for Science and Technology (FCT, Portu-
gal) for financial support through national funds FCT/MCTES (PIDDAC) to CeDRI
(UIDB/05757/2020 and UIDP/05757/2020), SusTEC (LA/P/0007/2021) and ALGO-
RITMI Center (UIDB/00319/2020). Filipe Alves thanks the Foundation for Science
and Technology (FCT, Portugal) for supporting its research with the PhD grant
SFRH/BD/143745/2019.

need help to provide these services in order to reduce costs and increase service quality, since it is economically advantageous to keep people at home instead of in health units or hospitals [5,17]. HHC aims to provide medical, paramedical, or social services to patients at their homes. In this sense, and taking Portugal as an example, there has been a steady increase in demand for HHC services, becoming an important topic of public, social and health concern. HHC operations need to plan human and physical resources, such as health professionals (mainly nurses) and vehicles, considering working hours, and operational constraints, among other assumptions. The HHC problem arises when a variety of health care services must be provided in patients' homes in cases of illness or injury, by health professionals from the same geographic area, aiming to optimize the scheduling and routes design, considering time or distance traveled [2]. Also, some problems are characterized by an inherent uncertainty in travel times, care duration, evolution of patients' needs, etc., and a wide variety of workers with different skills and constraints (nurse, auxiliary nurse, social technician, among others). However, these problems present some challenges to optimization, since most of these home visiting services still operate manually and without resorting to computational methods to support the scheduling and routing. Thus, these optimization problems have become increasingly complex and the search for improvements has been gaining impact in recent years [3].

This emerging sector has opened new research avenues in the field of industrial engineering, optimization and operational research (OR). In this sense, it is possible to cite some works that investigated, for example, a proper allocation of resources to each district, complying with various criteria [1], choice and dimensioning of internal resources [12], assignment of the various workers to patients [14], optimization of workers' routes to patients' homes, operational scheduling, and others. In terms of this work, the main focus is on the HHC routing and scheduling, at an operational level. These problems consist in assigning tasks to staff members of the HHC units, planning visiting hours for a set of patients, and designing the routes of visits while respecting regulatory and logistical and operational constraints [6,22]. Other works are more focused on HHC scheduling and routing problems, for example, a comprehensive overview of existing works in the field of routing and scheduling in HHC [5]. In a later work, Cissé et al. [2], analyzed the literature on OR models applied to this topic.

In this sense, mathematical programming techniques, such as deterministic methods including (integer) linear programming, and stochastic or evolutionary approaches are two highly successful streams for optimizing combinatorial problems [4,20]. These types of approaches are frequently applied in many highly important, practical fields, for example, classic vehicle routing problem (VRP), transportation logistics, scheduling, designing efficient communication networks, supply chain and food delivery [9,11,23]. Formulations of HHC problems dealing with real configurations and capturing all the complexity are a challenge for optimization researchers. In the past, optimization techniques have played a fundamental role in the research of scheduling of resources in HHC crew and emergence vehicles routing [17,19,21].

Therefore, the main goal of this work focuses on the solution of a real routing and scheduling problem in HHC in an interior region of Portugal. The strategy is based on two different approaches, evolutionary algorithm and exact method, with a subsequent hybrid approach of the two and respective analyses. Besides that, this work will contribute to the discussion of the two techniques producing a sensitivity analysis in post optimization to the results of different test instances that may result in better decision support on a benchmark of HHC real cases.

The rest of the paper is organized as follows: Sect. 2 describes the problem under study, including problem sets, parameters, and the mathematical model. In Sect. 3 the optimization approaches, which will support the test instances in the Sect. 4, will be presented. The numerical results will be presented and analyzed in Sect. 5. Finally, Sect. 6 rounds up the paper with some conclusions and future work perspectives.

2   Problem Statement

This study deals with the problem that arises from the HHC services, needing to automatically find the optimal operational planning that combines routes design, health professional's scheduling and patients allocation. The goal is to find the best schedule, considering the criteria, resources and constraints presented in the problem, in a reasonable time.

For that, it is important to define the general properties and/or assumptions of the problem, such as the HHC planning process, which includes, geographical area, resource dimension and their different instances, the care workers and patients. Therefore, the number and characterization of health professionals, the number of patients and treatments they need, and patient locations, are considered. This information and data allow the creation of a mathematical model, that represents the time spent on patient visits and travel.

Thus, considering a public Health Unit in Bragança, with a domiciliary team that provides home care to patients requiring different treatments, all the entities involved in the problem were identified.

Consider the following fixed parameters:

- $\bar{P}$ is the set of $np \in \mathbb{N}$ patients that receive home care visits, $\bar{P} = \{p_1, \ldots, p_{np}\}$ and $P = \{1, \ldots, np\}$ is the corresponding index set;
- $\bar{N}$ is the set of $nn \in \mathbb{N}$ nurses that perform home care visits, $\bar{N} = \{v_1, \ldots, v_{nn}\}$ and $N = \{1, \ldots, nn\}$ is the corresponding index set;
- $\bar{L}$ is the set of $nl \in \mathbb{N}$ locations for home care visits, $\bar{L} = \{l_1, \ldots, l_{nl}\}$ and $L = \{1, \ldots, nl\}$ is the corresponding index set;
- $\bar{T}$ is the set of $nt \in \mathbb{N}$ treatments required by patients, $\bar{T} = \{t_1, \ldots, t_{nt}\}$ and $T = \{1, \ldots, nt\}$ is the corresponding index set;
- Q is the vector with treatments duration, $Q \in \mathbb{R}^{nt}$;
- $D_{nl \times nl}$ is the time distance matrix between the nl locations. d_{ij} represents the distance (travel time) from node i to node j.

Taking into account the information regarding these sets and parameters, a mathematical programming problem can be formulated to minimize the travel time spent on visits.

The mathematical model presented is an extension of the Cumulative Routing Problem model (CumVRP) described in [10]. Considering a routing network $G = (L_0, A)$ with nodes $L_0 = \{0, 1, 2, \ldots, nl\}$ (node 0 is the healthcare unit and the others are patient locations) and $A = \{(i, j) : i, j \in L_0, \ i \neq j\}$ is the set of routes. An instance of the problem is defined by the following parameters:

- u_{ik}: equal to 1 if patient $i \in P$ can be attended by nurse $k \in N$ and 0 otherwise;
- MQ: maximum duration of any nurse route (maximum shift duration).

This work proposes a mixed integer flow formulation with two sets of decision variables:

- x_{ijk} – binary variable, 1 if the nurse $k \in N$ goes from $i \in L_0$ to $j \in L_0$ and attends patient that is located in the location j and 0 otherwise;
- y_{ijk} – flow variables, they are used to accumulate the time spent on travel and patient care after each visit.

The cost or the objective function aims to minimize the longest route. A compact mathematical formulation of the proposed model follows. The index $i, j \in L_0$ are associated with the nodes (L_0 set) and $k \in N$ to nurses index.

$$\textbf{Min} \max_{i,k} y_{i0k} \tag{1}$$

$$\textbf{s.t.} \sum_i x_{0ik} = 1, \quad \forall k \in N \tag{2}$$

$$\sum_i x_{i0k} = 1, \quad \forall k \in N \tag{3}$$

$$\sum_i \sum_k x_{ijk} = 1, \quad \forall j \in L \tag{4}$$

$$\sum_j \sum_k x_{ijk} = 1, \quad \forall i \in L \tag{5}$$

$$\sum_i x_{ijk} = \sum_i x_{jik}, \quad \forall j \in L, \ \forall k \in N \tag{6}$$

$$y_{ijk} \leq MQ \cdot x_{jik}, \quad \forall i \in L_0, \ \forall j \in L_0, \ \forall k \in N \tag{7}$$

$$y_{0ik} = x_{0ik} \cdot d_{0i}, \quad \forall i \in L_0, \ \forall k \in N \tag{8}$$

$$\sum_i y_{jik} - \sum_i y_{ijk} = \sum_i x_{jik} (d_{ji} + q_j), \quad \forall j \in L, \ \forall k \in N \tag{9}$$

$$\sum_i x_{ijk} \leq u_{jk}, \quad \forall j \in L_0, \ \forall k \in N \tag{10}$$

$$x_{ijk} \geq 0 \text{ and integer}, \quad \forall i \in L_0, \ \forall j \in L_0, \ \forall k \in N \tag{11}$$

$$y_{ijk} \geq 0, \quad \forall i \in L_0, \ \forall j \in L_0, \ \forall k \in N \tag{12}$$

Equation (1) is the objective function. Equations (2) ensure that all nurses start at the depot, while Eqs. (3) ensure that all nurses arrive at the depot. Equations (4) guarantee that exactly one nurse arrives at any patient node, while Eqs. (5) guarantee that exactly one nurse departs from every patient node. Equations (6) state that the nurse arriving at some patient node must also depart that same node. Equations (7) put an upper bound to the flow in the arcs. Equations (8) initialize the flow in the arc from the depot to the first patient to be equal to the travel time. After that, Eqs. (9) are flow conservation constraints and assure that the flow in each arc accumulates travel and patient care times of all the previous visits in one route. Finally, Eqs. (10) ensure that every patient is visited by a specialized nurse, according to the compatibility coefficients defined before. Equations (11) and (12) define the lower bounds and types of the variables.

If the compatibility matrix between patients and nurses is very restrictive there will be a number of variables whose bound will be set to zero by constraints (10), effectively deleting the variables from the formulation. The number of constraints is in the order of $nl \times nn^2$, most of them being the bounds on the flow variables imposed by constraint set (7).

3   Optimization Approaches for Operational Planning

This section presents the different approaches to deal and support the operational planning for the problem presented in Sect. 2. One approach is based on the mixed integer linear programming model (MILP), where the problem is solved using a deterministic technique. Another approach is the genetic algorithm, where the problem will be solved by a meta-heuristic method. Finally, a hybrid approach will be used, which is based on the combination of the two previous approaches. The main goal is to identify the advantages and the strengths of each approach, individually and/or in combination.

3.1   Mixed Integer Linear Programming Approach

For solving the MILP, the CPLEX and optimization programming language (OPL) were used. The model presented in the Sect. 2 was implemented in OPL and optimized using the CPLEX Solver V12.10.0 with the default optimization parameters. According to the documentation [8], by default, CPLEX Solver employs preprocessing and probing of the model (coefficient reduction, elimination of redundant variables and constraints, etc.) and model strengthening by means of several types of cuts, with the idea of speeding up the solving process. The algorithm was run with the default parameters with the exception of adding stopping criteria of 1 h (3600 s) in the case the optimal solution is not found within that period.

In order to strengthen the model and improve computational results, some extra sets of constraints were added to the formulation. The first one is

$$\sum_i x_{jik} \le u_{jk}, \quad \forall j \in L_0, \ \forall k \in N \tag{13}$$

This constraint mirrors constraint (10) such that only a specialized or compatible nurse is allowed to leave a given location. Of course, this constraint was already implied by constraints (6), but preliminary testing shows their inclusion to improve computational times. We also enforced a lower limit on individual flows in all arcs by means of the following constraints:

$$y_{ijk} \ge x_{jik} \cdot (q_i + d_{ij}), \quad \forall i \in L_0, \ \forall j \in L_0, \ \forall k \in N \tag{14}$$

Similar to the previous set, these constraints are also implied by the flow conservation constraints of the compact model, but they seem to improve computational performance.

Finally, it was imposed a global lower bound (Z_{LB}) on the objective function. This bound is computed with

$$Z_{LB} = \frac{\sum_i q_i + \sum_j \min_{i \ne j} d_{ij} + nl \cdot \min_{i \ne 0} d_{i0}}{nl} \tag{15}$$

The lower bound is just the quotient of the minimum possible time required to complete all visits by the number of vehicles (nurses). The minimum possible time is computed by adding the time for treatments with the minimum time to reach a patient given an unknown location and with the minimum time for the return trip to the central hub for all nurses. This lower bound is not very tight but it seems to improve performance. Although these constraints seem to improve computational performance in preliminary testing, the tests were very limited and further examination of each one is still needed.

3.2 Genetic Algorithm Approach

A Genetic Algorithm (GA) [7] is used to solve the HHC optimization problem (1) to (12) in Sect. 2. GA is inspired by the natural biological evolution, uses a population of individuals and new individuals are generated by applying the genetic operators of crossover and mutation [13]. Genetic algorithms are particularly well suited to solve vehicle scheduling problem that is non-convex with discrete decision variable and couple with the combinatorial nature of the search space [15]. The flexibility of representation of the solutions and genetic operators allows for handling hard constraints.

The GA used in this work is summarized in Algorithm 1. Initially, a population of N_{pop} individuals is randomly generated. Each individual in the population is a vector of decision variables $\mathbf{x}$. Next, for each generation, crossover and mutation operators are applied to generate new solutions. These genetic operators were designed in order to guarantee that new solutions are feasible.

Algorithm 1 : Genetic Algorithm

1: $\mathcal{P}^0 = initialization$: randomly generate a population of N_{pop} individuals.
2: Set iteration counter $k = 0$.
3: **while** stopping criterion is not met **do**
4:     $\mathcal{P}' = crossover(\mathcal{P}^k)$: apply crossover procedure to individuals in population $\mathcal{P}^k$.
5:     $\mathcal{P}'' = mutation(\mathcal{P}^k)$: apply mutation procedure to individuals in population $\mathcal{P}^k$.
6:     $\mathcal{P}^{k+1} = selection(\mathcal{P}^k \cup \mathcal{P}' \cup \mathcal{P}'')$: select the N_{pop} best individuals of $\mathcal{P}^k \cup \mathcal{P}' \cup \mathcal{P}''$.
7:     Set $k = k + 1$.
8: **end while**

The best individuals in the population have a high probability of being selected to generate new ones by crossover and mutation. Therefore, the good features of the individuals tend to be inherited by the offspring. In this manner, the population converges towards better solutions [16]. The iterative procedure terminates after a maximum number of iterations (NI) or a maximum number of function evaluations (NFE).

The model in Sect. 2 and the algorithm presented was implemented and coded in MatLab®. In complex problems belonging to non-deterministic classes, GAs are promising algorithms for searching for fast and good solutions in many applications, areas and domains planning and controlling several operations [15].

In this approach, the scheduling solution can be expressed by the vector $\mathbf{x}$ of dimension $n = 2 \times np$ with the following structure:

$$\mathbf{x} = (\mathbf{w}, \mathbf{z}) = (w_1; ...; w_{np}; z_1; ...; z_{np})$$

where the patient $w_i \in P$ will be visited by the nurse $z_i \in N$, for $i = 1, \ldots, np$. In this structure, $w_i \neq w_j$ for $\forall i \neq j$ with $i, j \in P$. Therefore, for a given $\mathbf{x}$ it is possible to define the nurse's route scheduling by taking into account the order of the components of $\mathbf{x}$.

For a nurse schedule $\mathbf{x}$, the function $d^l(\mathbf{x})$, for $l = 1, .., nn$, gives the total distance (in time) required to perform all visits of the nurse l

$$f(\mathbf{x}) = \max_{l=1,...,nn} d^l(\mathbf{x}) \tag{16}$$

Then, the optimization problem can be defined as:

$$\min_{\mathbf{x} \in \Omega} f(\mathbf{x}) \tag{17}$$

where $\mathbf{x} \in \Omega$ is the decision variable space and $\Omega = \{(\mathbf{w}, \mathbf{z}) : \mathbf{w} \in P^{np}, \mathbf{z} \in V^{np}$ and $w_i \neq w_j$ for all $i \neq j\}$ is the feasible set. For that reason, GA was used to solve the model presented previously.

3.3 Hybrid Approach

Operations research (OR) is often described as a toolbox of methods, from which the most appropriate method for solving any particular problem can be selected. Since all OR methods have different strengths and weaknesses, a hybrid approach (mixing methods) offers the potential to overcome some of the drawbacks of using a single approach. For example, it is expected that working with a MILP model of the identified problem (HHC), it may take a long time to solve to optimality (even for a small case and/or instance).

In this sense, the hybrid approach will be based on the combination of the two previously mentioned approaches (GA and MILP), with the expectation of applying a computational technique that will provide more advantages to detect better solutions for the HHC problem than using the approaches individually. Thus, the idea is to initialize the MILP approach with a feasible solution (quickly obtained) from the GA (feed into the model), also known as "*warm* start". The strategy goes through supply hints to help MILP find an initial solution. The *warm* start comes from the same problem, already solved and with a feasible solution.

4   Test Instances

The HHC service at this Health Unit provides several types of care that can be classified into five different treatments. Clinical data was properly collected and treated following strict anonymity and confidentiality procedures.

The data allowed to combine different types of treatments according to their areas of application and/or performance required by patients, their average time and the different health professionals who perform them (Table 1).

The treatments are thus divided according to their specificity. Thus, Treatment 1 (T.1) refers to curative care (characterized by pressure ulcers, traumatic wounds, and burns, among others) with an average time of 30 min, while Treatment 2 (T.2) refers to Surveillance and Rehabilitation (characterized by evaluations and patient monitoring), with an average duration of 60 min. Treatment 3 (T.3) is Curative and Surveillance care (characterized by wound treatment, frequency and tension monitoring, among other pathology) averaging 75 min, while Treatment 4 (T.4) is only Surveillance care (assess the risk of falls, self-care, dietary, among others) and has average care of around 60 min. Finally, Treatment 5 (T.5) concerns more general health care (characterized by support mourning for example) such as support and monitoring and has an average of 60 min as well. The health unit has a total of 12 health professionals (mostly nurses) assigned to the various days of home visits.

The complete dataset has a total of 40 patients, which can be assigned to a single day or divided over several days of home visits. The same is true for health professionals, who have specific hours of primary health care at home and, therefore, may not always be on the same working day. Thus, the need arose not only to solve the combinatorial problem computationally according to the approaches in HHC planning but also to analyze the sensitivity of different cases/instances (Table 2). Each patient required specific medical assistance consisting of one or more different treatments from the 5 treatments that nurses can perform.

In total, 9 cases will be solved (from different instances) and draw the appropriate conclusions thereof, according to the optimization techniques and generated approaches. From Table 2, it is verified that the routes of nurses allocation

Table 1. Treatments performed by the nurses.

	T.1 (30 min)	T.2 (60 min)	T.3 (75 min)	T.4 (60 min)	T.5 (60 min)
Nurse 1	X			X	
Nurse 2	X	X		X	
Nurse 3	X			X	
Nurse 4	X		X	X	
Nurse 5	X			X	
Nurse 6	X	X		X	X
Nurse 7	X		X	X	
Nurse 8	X			X	
Nurse 9	X			X	
Nurse 10	X			X	
Nurse 11	X			X	
Nurse 12	X			X	

Table 2. List of test instances.

Dataset	Parameters
Case 1	20 patients, 8 nurses, 19 locations
Case 2	20 patients, 10 nurses, 19 locations
Case 3	20 patients, 12 nurses, 19 locations
Case 4	30 patients, 8 nurses, 25 locations
Case 5	30 patients, 10 nurses, 25 locations
Case 6	30 patients, 12 nurses, 25 locations
Case 7	40 patients, 8 nurses, 28 locations
Case 8	40 patients, 10 nurses, 28 locations
Case 9	40 patients, 12 nurses, 28 locations

and scheduling take into account a total of 28 locations, representative of the patients homes in the region under study.

The travel time (in minutes) between the locations is shown in Table 3 (appropriately numbered locations for data protection and used as a time matrix resource), whose diagonal indicates the typical time required to attend to several patients in the same area (e.g., same streets).

The health unit prefers to have average values between locations in the same area (which are not always reached) and assigned these values on the diagonal to make sure they are not exceeded. In this way, each node (e.g., location 1 (first row) and location 1 (first column) are the same location, and so on) identifies a set of origins and destinations between each address or residence. The response is computed using optimization techniques for $M : N$ routes computation.

In this sense, a sensitivity analysis was generated to the uncertainty in the output of a set of different instance sizes. The strategy involves an evaluation of the robustness of the deterministic, stochastic and hybrid approaches, in terms of their behaviors and impacts when subject to different parameters.

5   Numerical Results

In this section it is intended to qualitatively evaluate the flexibility and effectiveness of each of the approaches, taking into account their variability and solutions. The range of values of the numerical results is examined by analyzing how the output value (from all approaches) behaves.

Table 3. Time matrix with sources and targets to list locations.

	1	2	3	4	5	6	7	8	9	10	11	12	13	14	15	16	17	18	19	20	21	22	23	24	25	26	27	28
1	7	32	12	11	10	29	9	30	24	9	18	8	27	13	35	14	27	7	10	24	11	14	26	10	12	12	6	28
2	32	7	33	35	31	31	33	43	41	35	29	29	29	35	27	31	31	33	35	44	35	28	30	33	32	32	32	40
3	12	33	7	12	13	30	10	33	24	6	21	14	29	15	37	9	24	11	7	18	9	17	28	6	7	6	10	25
4	11	35	12	7	11	32	10	35	27	12	24	14	31	19	39	10	25	13	10	24	10	15	30	11	12	11	12	26
5	10	31	13	11	7	27	8	32	28	13	20	11	26	17	34	15	26	11	11	26	11	10	25	13	15	14	10	27
6	29	31	30	32	27	7	30	37	38	32	26	26	16	32	24	28	36	30	32	41	32	25	18	30	29	29	29	37
7	9	33	10	10	8	30	7	33	25	10	21	11	8	15	36	12	26	9	8	23	8	12	26	9	11	11	9	27
8	30	43	33	35	32	37	33	7	28	32	27	28	38	26	46	31	42	28	33	43	7	29	37	32	31	32	29	43
9	24	41	24	27	28	38	25	28	7	26	28	27	36	23	44	22	37	24	25	22	27	28	35	23	22	23	23	38
10	9	35	6	12	13	32	10	32	26	7	23	12	30	14	38	11	25	10	8	20	9	17	29	8	8	8	9	26
11	18	29	21	24	20	26	21	27	28	23	7	16	24	21	32	19	30	19	22	31	23	17	23	20	19	19	18	31
12	8	29	14	14	11	26	11	28	27	12	16	7	25	12	33	17	25	10	12	26	13	10	24	13	15	14	9	26
13	27	29	29	31	26	16	8	38	36	30	24	25	7	30	12	25	34	27	29	38	30	22	13	28	26	27	26	35
14	13	35	15	19	17	32	15	26	23	14	21	12	30	7	38	16	30	11	15	28	16	18	29	17	16	17	11	31
15	35	27	37	39	34	24	36	46	44	38	32	33	12	38	7	33	42	35	37	46	38	30	21	36	34	35	35	43
16	14	31	9	10	15	28	12	31	22	11	19	17	25	16	33	7	21	14	9	20	9	14	25	9	8	9	13	22
17	27	31	24	25	26	36	26	42	37	25	30	25	34	30	42	21	7	28	26	33	25	22	34	25	24	25	27	18
18	7	33	11	13	11	30	9	28	24	10	19	10	27	11	35	14	28	7	10	24	11	15	27	11	13	12	5	29
19	10	35	7	10	11	32	8	33	25	8	22	12	29	15	37	9	26	10	7	19	6	15	29	6	8	8	9	26
20	24	44	18	24	26	41	23	43	22	20	31	26	38	28	46	20	33	24	19	7	22	26	38	18	17	18	23	35
21	11	35	9	10	11	32	8	7	27	9	23	13	30	16	38	9	25	11	6	22	7	13	28	6	8	7	9	25
22	14	28	17	15	10	25	12	29	28	17	17	10	22	18	30	14	22	14	15	26	13	7	23	18	20	19	14	25
23	26	30	28	30	25	18	26	37	35	29	23	24	13	29	21	25	34	27	29	38	28	23	7	28	27	28	27	35
24	10	33	6	11	13	30	9	32	23	8	20	13	28	17	36	9	25	11	6	18	6	18	28	7	6	5	11	24
25	12	32	7	12	15	29	11	31	22	8	19	15	26	16	34	8	24	13	8	17	8	20	27	6	7	7	12	23
26	12	32	6	11	14	29	11	32	23	8	19	14	27	17	35	9	25	12	8	18	7	19	28	5	7	7	12	24
27	6	32	10	12	10	29	9	29	23	9	18	9	26	11	35	13	27	5	9	23	9	14	27	11	12	12	7	28
28	28	40	25	26	27	37	27	43	38	26	31	26	35	31	43	22	18	29	26	35	25	25	35	24	23	24	28	7

5.1   MILP Results

In order to test the proposed MILP formulation, all the datasets in the Table 2 have been solved. The developed OPL model was instantiated with data from the different problems and optimization was run until the optimal solution was found or when a time limit of 1 h (3600 s) was reached. The experiment was carried out using a laptop equipped with an Intel® Core™ i7-10510U CPU with 16 GB of memory. Table 4 summarizes the results.

Table 4. Summary of optimization results for the MILP model.

Case	P	N	R	C	B	Best	LB	Gap	Time
1	20	8	4119	3942	2032	186	186	0.0%	45
2	20	10	4963	4754	2452	186	186	0.0%	58
3	20	12	5807	5566	2872	186	186	0.0%	39
4	30	8	10819	10542	5372	264	210	20.5%	3601
5	30	10	13223	12894	6572	220	169	23.2%	3601
6	30	12	15627	15246	7772	187	148	20.9%	3601
7	40	8	17354	17003	8630	349	285	18.3%	3601
8	40	10	21078	20663	10490	296	229	22.6%	3604
9	40	12	24802	24323	12350	284	284	0.0%	2938

For each case the following information is presented: the number of patients to be treated (P) and the number of vehicles or nurses (N); the number of rows (R), columns (C) and binaries (B) after the resolve and probing as reported by CPLEX, which reflect the effective size of the problem; the objective value for the best solution found (Best), the lower bound (LB), the percentage gap (Gap) between the best solution and the lower bound and the time (in seconds) CPLEX spent to solve the problem. In a case where CPLEX found the optimal solution, the gap is zero (cases 1, 2, 3, and 9).

5.2   GA Results

Following the previous approach, the proposed meta-heuristic (GA) was also applied to the dataset in Table 2.

The experiment was carried out using a laptop equipped with an Intel® Core™ M-5Y71 CPU 1.4 GHz with 8 GB of memory. The numerical results were obtained using the MatLab®. The values of the control parameters used in GA for this problem were tuned after preliminary experiments. A population size of 30 individuals ($N_{pop} = 30$) and a probability rate of 50% for crossover and mutation procedures were used. The stopping criterion was based on the maximum number of iterations defined as 100 ($NI = 100$) or the maximum number of function evaluations of 5000 ($NFE = 5000$). Since GA is a stochastic algorithm, 30 runs were carried out with random initial populations. GA found feasible solutions for all runs in a reasonable time. This study analyses the effect of defined parameters on the output directly and on model performance, thus the analysis is evaluated by comparing the corresponding observations.

Table 5 gives the sensitivity rank of all the parameters for all criteria, starting with criteria on the performance in all runs for each case, such as best or minimal solution (f_{min}), the solution average (f_{avg}), the standard deviation (SD), the number of different best solutions found (N_{min}) and, finally the average time to solve the optimization problem ($Time$), in seconds.

Table 5. Summary of optimization results for the GA meta-heuristic.

Case	f_{min}	f_{avg}	SD	N_{min}	Time
1	233	262	18	2	29.9
2	212	240	17.2	1	31.4
3	188	228	14.4	1	37
4	333	361	16	1	38.4
5	272	324	19.4	1	43.8
6	246	287	21.3	1	48.6
7	425	483	22.8	1	48.7
8	372	430	25.6	2	54.9
9	331	397	22.9	1	57.5

Table 5 presents the results for the different defined criteria that allow to statistically evaluate the balance of the solution outputs. The goal of applying GA is to characterize how the meta-heuristic programming responds to changes in input, with an emphasis on finding the input parameters to which outputs are more or less sensitive to different cases from different instances.

5.3   Discussion

In this section, the results of the two previous approaches are analyzed and compared. In this sense, the illustration of a scheduling example on a Gantt chart, according to the two approaches under study, for the instance of case 2 is shown in Fig. 1. It is possible to see in Fig. 1, the different allocations of patients to their respective nurses and to view the complete routes of home visits, which include travel times, patient treatment times, and consequent return to the point of origin (Health Unit). Both approaches present optimized management of the routes with a good workload balancing between the different entities.

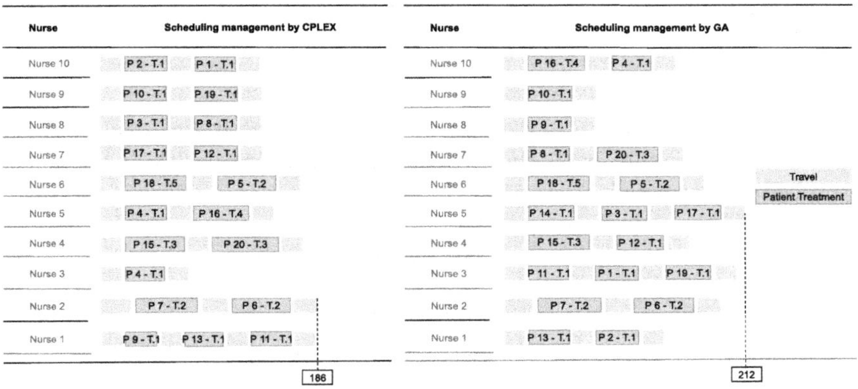

Fig. 1. Example of a scheduling management by the two approaches for case 2.

Regarding the maximum value reached by the two approaches, concerning the total time of home visits, it has a value of 212 min for the GA meta-heuristic and the optimal solution of 186 min for the MILP model by CPLEX. On the other hand, Fig. 2 summarizes Tables 4 and 5.

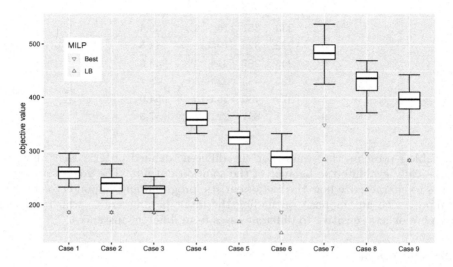

Fig. 2. Objective values for GA and MILP.

Figure 2 compares the results for the GA meta-heuristic (boxplots for the 30 runs of the algorithm) and for the MILP model (best solution and lower bound). It can be seen that the MILP model finds either optimal or better solutions than the GA. However, computational times presented by GA reach solutions more quickly (never exceeding 60 s even in the largest instances), and in some cases with solutions close to the optimum, which makes it possible to support the decision-making in emergency scheduling needs.

5.4   Hybrid Results

In order to further enhance our computational findings, it was also performed a *warm* start procedure with the MILP model combined with GA solutions. The procedure consisted in starting the optimization in CPLEX from an initial solution. The solution provided to CPLEX was the best solution from the GA. Table 6 shows the results from the experiment, where for each case and/or instance the objective values of the starting solution, the best solution, the lower bound, and computation time are presented.

Table 6. *Warm* start computational results in MILP

Case	Start	Best		LB		Time	
1	233	186	(0.0%)	186	(0.0%)	47	(4.4%)
2	212	186	(0.0%)	186	(0.0%)	51	(−12.1%)
3	188	186	(0.0%)	186	(0.0%)	67	(71.8%)
4	333	259	(−1.9%)	210	(0.0%)	3600	(0.0%)
5	272	222	(0.9%)	171	(1.2%)	3601	(0.0%)
6	246	186	(−0.5%)	186	(25.7%)	3565	(−1.0%)
7	425	350	(0.3%)	285	(0.0%)	3600	(0.0%)
8	372	293	(−1.0%)	232	(1.3%)	3600	(−0.1%)
9	331	284	(0.0%)	284	(0.0%)	1294	(−56.0%)

The percentage change relative to the *default* CPLEX start is shown inside the brackets. Figure 3 shows a visualization of the results in terms of boxplots.

The results have high variability and drawing definitive conclusions is difficult with such a small number of instances. The results for the best solution seemed to be about the same. The same applies to the lower bound with the exception of one case (case 6) for which it was possible to close the gap and reach the optimal solution. The computational times show a global decrease of 7.9%, mainly explained by the decrease in one case (case 9).

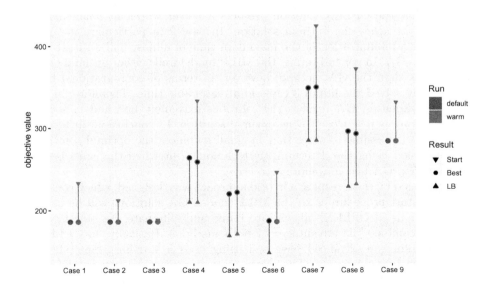

Fig. 3. *Default* and *warm* start comparison for MILP model.

The time taken by the GA meta-heuristic to reach the initial solutions was 390 s (about 6.5 min) and thus the decrease in total time would be only 6%. Taking everything into account, the *warm* start seems to be beneficial for optimizing the computational time and reaching the optimal solutions.

In conclusion, it is important to mention that all solutions were validated (but not yet applied in real context) by the health institution (nurses), which positively reinforces the different strategies used. Furthermore, the different solutions achieved significant savings rates in route optimization when compared to existing planning in the institution (manually scheduling/calendar), in addition to simplifying the planning process with faster response rates.

6   Conclusions and Future Work

In this paper, three optimization approaches, GA, MILP, and a hybrid approach involving the first two have been proposed, formulated, and applied for the coordinated decision-making in HHC services under different test instances based on real cases. This study analyzes and quantifies the impact of one or more variables in the final results to evaluate the robustness of all approaches, reduction of uncertainty, and calibration model for the operational planning to support HHC services. The optimal solution, or the quickest solution, may depend on the needs of the moment, knowing in advance that, with health, great robustness in responses and solutions is always necessary.

According to these principles, and taking into account the numerical results obtained, it was found that the approaches are successful in route allocating and scheduling, reflecting some differences in the solutions for home care visits. It is visible that the CPLEX solution presents a better workload balancing and consequently reaches the optimal solution. In case 2 in particular, the MILP solution has a minimization of the maximum time of almost half an hour when compared to GA. In general terms, the MILP model finds either optimal or better solutions than the GA method, however, in terms of computational times, CPLEX only solved the initial 3 cases in a reasonable time. Therefore, in computational expenses, GA reaches the solutions extremely fast and in some of the test instances it is close to the optimal solution. In conclusion, in terms of screening, it is possible to state that in small instances the optimal solution is easily obtained using the deterministic technique, but when the cases become more complex, GA becomes more attractive.

Encouraged by these results, a hybrid approach was designed, which consisted of a *warm* start procedure with the MILP model. GA solutions will be used as initial solutions in CPLEX, allowing to refine and eliminate the search space, that is, to combine the advantages of both methods. Basically, in CPLEX it means installing an advanced base and using it as a starting point, allowing to prune the branching tree. The *warm* start proved to be beneficial for the performance of MILP solvers, accelerating the resolution of the instances of the HHC problem, thus enhancing the MILP solution.

Some limitations of the work have already been identified, namely the non-inclusion of the priority factor among patients, possible time windows in the attendance and periodic visits, which nowadays are parameters to improve the model of HHC. The natural continuation of this work would be the digitalization of the route definition process, which would involve the creation of an interface that would allow the user to change the problem data (e.g., number and characteristics of patients), as well as the visualization of the routes obtained by the optimization. The accuracy of the model parameters (distances, travel times and treatments) could also be improved through google micro-services. Furthermore, future work will be devoted to extending the approach to different algorithms as well as different methodologies (e.g., multi-agent systems).

References

1. Benzarti, E., Sahin, E., Dallery, Y.: Operations management applied to home care services: analysis of the districting problem. Decis. Support Syst. **55**(2), 587–598 (2013). https://doi.org/10.1016/j.dss.2012.10.015. 1 Analytics and Modeling for Better HealthCare 2. Decision Making in Healthcare
2. Cissé, M., Yalçındağ, S., Kergosien, Y., Şahin, E., Lenté, C., Matta, A.: Or problems related to home health care: a review of relevant routing and scheduling problems. Oper. Res. Health Care **13–14**, 1–22 (2017). https://doi.org/10.1016/j.orhc.2017.06.001
3. Davidson], P.P., Blum, C., Lozano, J.A.: The weighted independent domination problem: integer linear programming models and metaheuristic approaches. Eur. J. Oper. Res. **265**(3), 860–871 (2018). https://doi.org/10.1016/j.ejor.2017.08.044
4. Fathollahi-Fard, A.M., Hajiaghaei-Keshteli, M., Tavakkoli-Moghaddam, R.: The social engineering optimizer (SEO). Eng. Appl. Artif. Intell. **72**, 267–293 (2018). https://doi.org/10.1016/j.engappai.2018.04.009
5. Fikar, C., Hirsch, P.: Home health care routing and scheduling: a review. Comput. Oper. Res. **77**, 86–95 (2017). https://doi.org/10.1016/j.cor.2016.07.019
6. Gutiérrez, E.V., Vidal, C.J.: Home health care logistics management problems: a critical review of models and methods. Revista Facultad de Ingeniería Universidad de Antioquia (68), 160–175 (2013)
7. Holland, J.H., et al.: Adaptation in Natural and Artificial Systems: An Introductory Analysis with Applications to Biology, Control, and Artificial Intelligence. MIT Press (1992)
8. IBM Corporation: IBM ILOG CPLEX Optimization Studio CPLEX User's Manual. IBM Corporation (2019)
9. Kar, A.K.: Bio inspired computing - a review of algorithms and scope of applications. Expert Syst. Appl. **59**, 20–32 (2016). https://doi.org/10.1016/j.eswa.2016.04.018
10. Kara, İ., Kara, B.Y., Yetiş, M.K.: Cumulative vehicle routing problems. In: Caric, T., Gold, H. (eds.) Vehicle Routing Problem, Chap. 6. IntechOpen, Rijeka (2008). https://doi.org/10.5772/5812
11. Knop, D., Kouteckỳ, M., Mnich, M.: Combinatorial n-fold integer programming and applications. Math. Progr., 1–34 (2019)
12. Koeleman, P., Bhulai, S., van Meersbergen, M.: Optimal patient and personnel scheduling policies for care-at-home service facilities. Eur. J. Oper. Res. **219**(3), 557–563 (2012). https://doi.org/10.1016/j.ejor.2011.10.046. Feature Clusters
13. Kramer, O.: Genetic Algorithm Essentials, vol. 679. Springer, Cham (2017). https://doi.org/10.1007/978-3-319-52156-5

14. Lanzarone, E., Matta, A.: A cost assignment policy for home care patients. Flex. Serv. Manuf. J. **24**(4), 465–495 (2012)
15. Lee, C.: A review of applications of genetic algorithms in operations management. Eng. Appl. Artif. Intell. **76**, 1–12 (2018). https://doi.org/10.1016/j.engappai.2018.08.011
16. Metawa, N., Hassan, M.K., Elhoseny, M.: Genetic algorithm based model for optimizing bank lending decisions. Expert Syst. Appl. **80**, 75–82 (2017)
17. Nickel, S., Schröder, M., Steeg, J.: Mid-term and short-term planning support for home health care services. Eur. J. Oper. Res. **219**(3), 574–587 (2012)
18. OECD. Publishing and Organization for Economic Cooperation and Development (OECD) Staff: Health at a glance 2019: OECD Indicators. OECD Publishing (2019). https://doi.org/10.1787/4dd50c09-en
19. Paraskevopoulos, D.C., Laporte, G., Repoussis, P.P., Tarantilis, C.D.: Resource constrained routing and scheduling: review and research prospects. Eur. J. Oper. Res. **263**(3), 737–754 (2017)
20. Raidl, G.R., Puchinger, J.: Combining (integer) linear programming techniques and metaheuristics for combinatorial optimization. In: Blum, C., Aguilera, M.J.B., Roli, A., Sampels, M. (eds.) Hybrid Metaheuristics. SCI, vol. 114, pp. 31–62. Springer, Heidelberg (2008). https://doi.org/10.1007/978-3-540-78295-7_2
21. Rasmussen, M.S., Justesen, T., Dohn, A., Larsen, J.: The home care crew scheduling problem: preference-based visit clustering and temporal dependencies. Eur. J. Oper. Res. **219**(3), 598 – 610 (2012). https://doi.org/10.1016/j.ejor.2011.10.048. Feature Clusters
22. Sahin, E., Matta, A.: A contribution to operations management-related issues and models for home care structures. Int. J. Logist. Res. Appl. **18**(4), 355–385 (2015)
23. Speranza, M.G.: Trends in transportation and logistics. Eur. J. Oper. Res. **264**(3), 830–836 (2018). https://doi.org/10.1016/j.ejor.2016.08.032

Multi VLAN Visualization in Network Management

Aleksandr Ovcharov[1,2], Natalia Efanova[2], and Rui Pedro Lopes[1,3(✉)] 📷

[1] Research Center in Digitalization and Intelligent Robotics (CeDRI), Instituto
Politécnico de Bragança, Bragança, Portugal
`a42648@alunos.ipb.pt, rlopes@ipb.pt`
[2] Kuban State Agrarian University, Krasnodar 350044, Russia
[3] Institute of Electronics and Informatics Engineering of Aveiro (IEETA),
University of Aveiro, Aveiro, Portugal

Abstract. The structure of logical networks in large enterprises can be
complex. Virtual local area networks (VLANs) can include a large number of connections and intermediate devices. Presentation of the network
in the form of a graph diagram simplifies the work of network specialists. We suggest the concept of visualizing a selected VLAN over a physical network diagram. We consider the features of this method using an
implementation of a simple tool for displaying the network status by the
selected criterion.

Keywords: Network management · Network management station ·
Network visualization · SNMP

1 Introduction

The visualization of topologies and network equipment is a part of the network management operation. In this context, the Simple Network Management
Protocol (SNMP) is the most popular and wide implemented framework, covering a large number of equipment (hardware, software and technical knowledge). Regardless of the detailed OSI Management Framework (or shortly the
CMIP/GDMO model) standards [8], the SNMP IETF Management Framework
[5,7,15] soon gained a larger set of followers, maybe due to its simplicity or
ability to be implemented and running in a wide range of devices and platforms.

The use and specification of both SNMP and/or CMIP/GDMO is very low
level, presenting protocols and information structure for the download of network devices parameters (GET) and for the change in operational status (SET).
The network management operation is further complicated with the size of the
network. Large organizations have large local area networks. Many of them use
virtual local area networks (VLANs) in order to realize micro-segmentation of
the network, increase its controllability and reduce the amount of broadcast traffic [2]. However, the topology of VLAN distribution may be complex: VLANs for
video surveillance equipment, Internet of Things (IoT) sensors, and other special
devices can often be distributed across many switches. Supporting a functional

A. I. Pereira et al. (Eds.): OL2A 2022, CCIS 1754, pp. 131–143, 2022.
https://doi.org/10.1007/978-3-031-23236-7_10

and accurate topology requires a visualization tool that presents information more understandable than text or tables. Visualization allows the specialist to quickly understand the output of the program, correlate the desired and available results, quickly find out the problematic element in the structure.

This paper presents and discusses the design and development of a web-based application for the visualization of VLANs in organizations. Is it composed of three main parts, namely, the network management backend, the server and the web graphical user interface.

This document is structured in four sections, starting with this introduction. Section 2 describes the related work, followed by Sect. 3, which describes the architecture and main options. Section 4 describes the final application and Sect. 5 finish with some conclusions and final considerations.

2   Related Work

Communication networks are currently the mainstay of a social and economic model that are an integral part of our way of life. Its importance has grown in recent decades and its role is expected to be increasingly central in this information society.

In social communication, as well as in informal day-to-day conversations, references to devices and technologies that allow access to content and information anywhere and at any time appear with increasing frequency. The Internet continually extends reach beyond the desktop PC to mobile phones, electronic organizers and home devices. This expansion is mainly due to open technologies that support the Internet as well as content based on branded languages, such as HTML/JSON/Javascript and others.

In this context, network management is a task of enormous complexity, whose success or failure has a huge impact on users and depends on the precise knowledge of the operating parameters of the equipment that constitutes it. By equipment we mean not only active and passive material (hardware) but also software, such as operating systems or applications. It is important that this information is as complete and diversified as possible, as it is based on it that decisions are made.

For this reason, each network element is modeled according to the relevant management information to describe its operating status. This information will necessarily have to be accessible to external devices so that they can build a model of how the element works.

The management models are therefore oriented towards retrieving, transporting and changing information, accessed using a virtual database model. The reason for the term "virtual" is that the database does not actually store the operating parameters, obtained through instrumentation operations on the network equipment. According to this architecture, a management model generally consists of one or more entities responsible for instrumentation, commonly known as agents, a communication mechanism and a monitoring and control post where the operating model is created, that is, the management station [12,13] (Fig. 1).

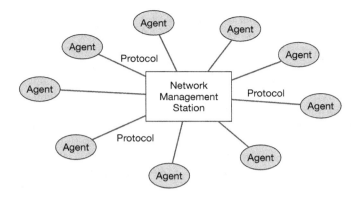

Fig. 1. Network management generic architecture

The management architecture based on SNMP emerged at the end of the 80's as an interim solution aimed essentially at TCP/IP systems. It has survived to the present day through three major evolutions. The first version of the SNMP architecture is described in only three documents, which allows a quick understanding and facilitates the development of management applications [17],?. This simplicity caught the attention of the market, which quickly adopted it for their products.

According to the generic network management model, the SNMP architecture provides an information representation format called SMI (Structure of Management Information) [17]. The functioning of network elements is therefore described in this format, in modules that group related information. Each module is called a MIB (Management Information Base) [16].

The communication protocol associated with the architecture, which gives it its name, consists of a simple protocol that allows the inspection and modification of the management information of a remote network element (agent), as well as the transport of notifications generated by these (traps) [7].

With the increase in the number of users, the need to add more functionality was felt, particularly in terms of protocol and security. Version 2 was relatively successful on the first requirement with the addition of new message types [4]. However, the SNMPv2 security model failed to establish consensual and robust measures, which led to the architecture being often considered unsuitable for configuration operations.

SNMPv3, more recently proposed [6], builds on the protocol defined for version 2 and adds better security mechanisms, particularly in terms of authentication, privacy and access control. Another feature of SNMPv3 is its modularity, which makes it possible to use existing and future protocols in certain functions without the need to update or issue new RFCs for the entire architecture.

According to the previous, the purpose of a network management system is to provide a common framework for remote administration of network devices. Nothing is said (or standardized) in relatio to the visualization of both data and network topology and status. Visualization of a computer network structure is a developed and well-established discipline. Physical and logical diagrams are well suited to present a network view. Most popular monitoring systems support network mapping in a diagram. However, the display of information about VLAN is still a space for experimentation. Basically, the information is provided individually for the device or its interface. Or the visualization tool displays a graph of devices, ports and connections for the selected VLAN. The second option is more obvious, but with its help it is still difficult to imagine the spread of VLAN in the whole set of the organization's network devices.

Krothapalli et al. [10] consider a graphical approach to obtaining information about VLANs. They made a toolkit for displaying VLAN spread as a graph to simplify network troubleshooting operations, that can also be used to detect and diagnose root bridge placements and misconfigurations, such as missing and redundant links. The visualization is performed through an interactive graphical interface, that, in addition to the topology, also presents the effect and impact of various VLAN design changes.

Basu et al. [3] approach the problem of designing and implementing an enterprise wide network monitoring system across 27 countries and more than 10000 buildings. To deal with the massive scale, they used a Kafka cluster with an OpenNMS backend. The system operates mainly on events, by listening for SNMP Traps, and start polling operations when necessary. Moreover, they forward notifications to different user interfaces, such as Microsoft Teams or Slack.

Shidhani et al. [1] support the use of Free and Open Source Software (FOSS) for automated network monitoring tools and, as such, describe the main features and make a comparison between three of the most popular systems, namely Nagios, OpenNMS and Zabbix.

Ljubojević et al. [11] describe the use of the Zenoss Core Software Platform for centralized monitoring. By using scripting and resorting to SNMP, ICMP and syslog, the tools allows to present several visualizations of the status of the network. In a similar approach, Pinzón et al. [14] use SNMP and information processing to monitor several equipment of an electrical power system. They get data from SNMP MIBs and process them to build simple visualizations.

Kontsek et al. [9] make a survey of the most popular tools for monitoring. This is performed in SNMP, Intelligent Platform Management Interface (IPMI), and Windows Management Instrumentation (WMI) and visualized in Zabbix, Nagios, TICK Stack, and Prometheus. The authors conclude that the monitoring platforms are versatile able for dealing with complex environments, such as in Cloud Computing environment.

All of these provide interesting approaches to monitoring and management of networks of several sizes and dimensions. Of the references above, none is able of providing complex visualizations of the physical topology and of VLAN topology. Other commercial tools also existi, such as IBM Tivoli Monitoring. However, sometimes this constitutes a very expensive solution, for simple visualization tasks.

3   NetGlance

The objective of this work, as mentioned above, is the design and development of a network management tool that can provide information about operational parameters as well as display information about VLAN over a logical network diagram using color coding. Additional information about topology elements are displayed as tooltips. Such an approach will make it possible to cover all possible VLAN conditions on devices and connections without overloading the user with a large amount of data. This display method makes it easy to compare VLAN topologies with each other and correlate them with the general network diagram.

NetGlance should display a topology of network devices along with summarized information, which include name, address, and model, as well as the connections between them. The user should be able to add, delete and modify network elements, as well as arranje devices on the screen. Also, zooming and panning should be supported, like geographic online maps.

The current state of network elements should be updates in real-time, using different colors to highlight states. The user can use filters to select different types of information, and specify specific query parameters. Due to the possibility of quick changes, a brief summary of the latest network events should also be presented in textual format.

NetGlance must have the flexibility to support multiple heterogeneous devices, accessible through different network management protocols or even accessible only via ICMP. It should be possible to extend NetGlance with other protocols or even to be able to retrieve device information from a third-party data sources. The state of each device can be represented in 7 different levels: unknown, error, warning, normal and 3 user-defined.

Because of the possibility of the human operator being away from the network management station, there should be also the possibility to send notifications through a messenger app (like Telegram or Signal). To reduce the amount of notifications, these should be parameterized according to their severity.

Figure 2 represents a visual concept. The reach of VLAN N is shown on all supporting devices and connections. Solid lines show the connections where untagged frames are transmitted for this VLAN, and dotted lines are links where this VLAN is allowed as tagged. Unaffected items are grayed out. This visualization is useful for troubleshooting problems with VLAN.

Figure 3 represents an erroneous network configuration. VLAN N does not exist in the database of Switch A, and, therefore its traffic will not be transmitted through it. In addition, the interface of Switch B is not configured to accept frames of this VLAN.

Various visual techniques can be used to display VLAN status on devices and connections, but color changes are recommended on color diagrams. This makes the smallest changes to a diagram view, and is noticeable for the user.

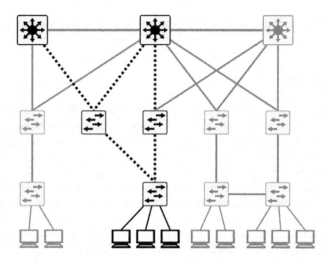

Fig. 2. On a network diagram

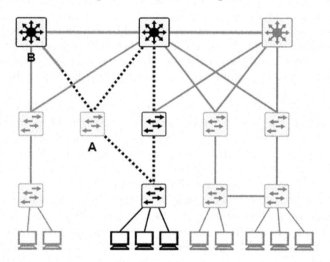

Fig. 3. A misconfigured network

4   Implementation Details

NetGlance, by design, is a Web-based application, composed of two components. One is constantly online, and is the target of the notifications and the responsible for constantly monitoring the network status and devices. The other is responsible for the visualization, and can be accessed anytime, anywhere from a web browser. Both are implemented and deployed as Windows services (Fig. 4).

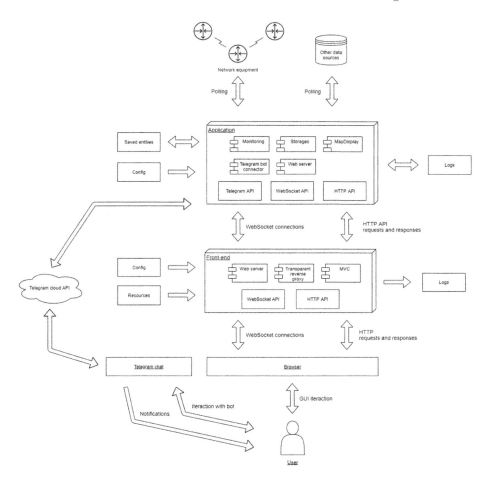

Fig. 4. NetGlance architecture

An example of the interaction is depicted in Fig. 5, highlighting the operation and architecture of NetGlance. In this, the user connects to the frontend through a browser which requests a web page. After authentication, the web page rendered with information retrieved from the backend (Application server). Depending on the operation, the interaction between both components continues, until the user logouts or closes the browser.

The communication between both components is performed through a standard web API (REST/JSON and Web Sockets), which allows the development of

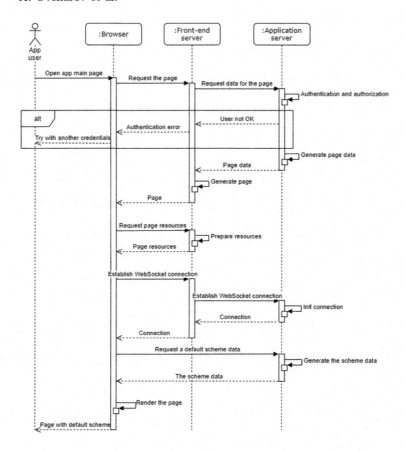

Fig. 5. NetGlance architecture

mobile or desktop application in the future. Moreover, it also paves the way for
multiple monitoring stations for in-band traffic optimization and load balancing,
for example, by placing different components in different hosts.

The backend is constantly online, monitoring and storing the instrumentation
information. It was developed in ASP.NET using .NET Framework and hosted
with Microsoft.Owin. The information it stores is multiple, registering network
topology, receiving events, implementing polling operation for different devices,
and others. If some event or pooling matches some condition, it also notifies
subscribers.

In addition to network operation information, it also logs its internal events,
such as start and stop of operation, changes made by users, authorization procedures, among others. It uses several log levels in a broad set of detail, used
during normal use as well as for debug. The application configuration is stored
in a file, containing polling settings, log level, files location, buffering output
information, for example.

4.1   User Interface

The correct use of the network management station depends heavily on the user interface. If it is not simple, intuitive and extensible there will be no advantages in using the system, so much of the development effort was focused on the user interface.

The user interface should reflect the state of the network and its components, as well as represent the way they are organized. The organization can take many forms and usually follows some logical grouping of topological information. Net-Glance opt for a schematic representation of connections, where lines between various components are visualized (Fig. 6). In addition, the main web page comprises a navigation element, a toolbar, a selector for displayed parameters, and a log of recent events. In the figure, Device "SW_2" stopped responding, so it is highlighted with the "Error" state in red. The connection of "SW_2" with the router is in the "Warning" state.

Monitoring functions are also configured and accessed in a similar maner (Fig. 7). This user interface provides access to several properties, allowing the configuration of pooling threads. These include the access protocol and the active (triggering) code. It also allows selecting the action that should be triggered.

4.2   Use Cases

The use of NetGlance can be further illustrated with some use cases, as follows.

Routine monitoring is a frequent operation. In this, the system administrator evaluates the network in the beginning of the day or in different moments. For that, the main page is opened in a browser, where a network map is displayed along with a predefined set of parameters. By default, the device availability and the link state is represented. The user analyses network topology, paying attention to the colors of the elements and associated labels, if necessary, by holding the cursor over them. He can move or zoom the schematic representation as well as accessing a summary of recent events. Based on all this information, he assesses if further diagnostics are necessary. Using the high visibility of the information, he can determine the location of inaccessible network segments (if any) and make assumptions about the most likely reasons of the failure.

In the event of unexpected failure, the organization's system administrator gets to work before the start of the working day. He receives a messenger notification on his smartphone that two important routers became unavailable 5 min ago, and that the ports on other devices connected to them went down. To better understand the extent of the problem, the administrator activates a VPN connection with the organization's network on the smartphone and opens the web application page. He sees more detailed information about the state of the network in almost real time and has the ability to plan actions to restore the network even before he reaches his office.

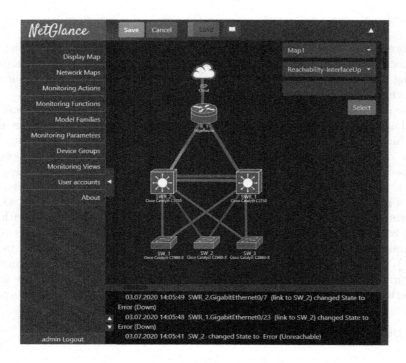

Fig. 6. Example network scheme

Fig. 7. "MonitoringFunction" entity page

If a VLAN topology changes, the administrator needs to quickly forward a VLAN over the network from the distribution router through a series of switches to an end device. He must create the VLAN on those devices where it does not exist, and correctly configure upstream and downstream ports. However, after completing the configuration, the end device cannot communicate with the rest of the network. The administrator opens the web application, indicates the observed parameter type (VLAN) and its number. After 1 period of polling devices (approximately 20 s), he receives the VLAN status on devices (exists or not) and connections (tagged, untagged, absent, not applicable). The administrator saved time on finding a configuration error.

The addition of new devices is a frequent operation. In this use case, several new managed switches were added to the network that are already in use on the network. This model is already in use on the network. They must be added to the monitoring system. The administrator in a few clicks tells the system to add a device. After specifying the connection address and authentication data, the system adds the device to the scheme, automatically receiving information about the name and ports. The device monitoring starts immediately according to the settings for this model and the selected device group. After that, the administrator adds the necessary connections to the device to the scheme, moves the devices for beautiful displaying.

5   Conclusion

NetGlance is a web application for VLAN representation and monitoring. It is modular, separating the network operations from the visualization and business processes, and it is successfully deployed in the KubSAU university network. The use of an easily editable network diagram facilitates its updating, including for temporary network segments. Moreover, it also makes it easier to work with changes in the VLAN topology. Creating an up-to-date and easily updated network management system allowed keeping reliable information about the topology. In this work, a simple and flexible way of grouping devices was used - families of models identical in interaction from the point of view of the program. Since Higher Education Institutions often have a large local network that has developed over time using different generations of network equipment, NetGlance also provides a useful tool, since it can grow and integrate heterogeneous equipment.

The proposed approach is successful and useful. The functionality reduces operation time for VLAN troubleshooting and maintenance works. It also facilitates understanding of the VLAN topology in the network by means of visibility and the use of a common logical network diagram as the basis.

References

1. Al Shidhani, A., Al Maawali, K., Al Abri, D., Bourdoucen, H.: A comparative analysis of open source network monitoring tools. Int. J. Open Sour. Softw. Process. **7**(2), 1–19 (2016). https://doi.org/10.4018/IJOSSP.2016040101. https://services. igi-global.com/resolvedoi/resolve.aspx?doi=10.4018/IJOSSP.2016040101

2. Amaro, J.C.R., Lopes, R.P.: Performance analysis of a wireless MAN. In: IEEE International Symposium on Network Computing and Applications, vol. NCA2001, pp. 358–361. EUA, Cambridge, February 2001

3. Basu, A., Singh, R., Yu, C., Prasad, A., Banerjee, K.: Designing, developing and deploying an enterprise scale network monitoring system. In: 15th Innovations in Software Engineering Conference, Gandhinagar India, pp. 1–5. ACM, February 2022. https://doi.org/10.1145/3511430.3511446. https://dl.acm.org/doi/10.1145/3511430.3511446

4. Case, D.J.D., McCloghrie, K., Rose, D.M.T., Waldbusser, S.: Protocol operations for version 2 of the simple network management protocol (SNMPv2). RFC 1905, January 1996. https://doi.org/10.17487/RFC1905. https://www.rfc-editor.org/info/rfc1905

5. Case, D.J.D., Mundy, R., Partain, D., Stewart, B.: Introduction and applicability statements for internet-standard management framework, December 2002. https://doi.org/10.17487/RFC3410. https://www.rfc-editor.org/info/rfc3410, issue: 3410 Num Pages: 27 Series: Request for Comments Published: RFC 3410

6. Case, D.J.D., Partain, D., Mundy, R., Stewart, B.: Introduction to version 3 of the internet-standard network management framework. RFC 2570, April 1999. https://doi.org/10.17487/RFC2570. https://www.rfc-editor.org/info/rfc2570

7. Fedor, M., Schoffstall, M.L., Davin, J.R., Case, D.J.D.: Simple network management protocol (SNMP), May 1990. https://doi.org/10.17487/RFC1157. https://www.rfc-editor.org/info/rfc1157. issue: 1157 Num Pages: 36 Series: Request for Comments Published: RFC 1157

8. ISO: Information technology — Open Systems Interconnection — Common management information protocol — Part 1: Specification (1993). https://www.iso.org/standard/29698.html

9. Kontsek, M., Moravcik, M., Jurc, J., Sterbak, M.: Survey of the monitoring tools suitable for CC environment. In: 2020 18th International Conference on Emerging eLearning Technologies and Applications (ICETA), Košice, Slovenia, pp. 330–335. IEEE, November 2020. https://doi.org/10.1109/ICETA51985.2020.9379152. https://ieeexplore.ieee.org/document/9379152/

10. Krothapalli, S., Yeo, S.A., Sung, Y.W.E., Rao, S.G.: Virtual MAN: A VLAN management system for enterprise networks. In: SIGCOMM09, Barcelona, Spain (2009)

11. Ljubojevic, M., Bajic, A., Mijic, D.: Centralized monitoring of computer networks using Zenoss open source platform. In: 2018 17th International Symposium INFOTEH-JAHORINA (INFOTEH), pp. 1–5. IEEE, East Sarajevo, March 2018. https://doi.org/10.1109/INFOTEH.2018.8345528. https://ieeexplore.ieee.org/document/8345528/

12. Lopes, R.P., Oliveira, J.L.: A uniform resource identifier scheme for SNMP. In: IEEE Workshop on IP Operations and Management, Dallas, Texas, USA, pp. 85–90 (2002). https://doi.org/10.1109/IPOM.2002.1045761

13. Lopes, R.P., Oliveira, J.L.: Delegation of expressions for distributed SNMP information processing. In: Integrated Network Management VIII, vol. 118, pp. 395–408 (2003)

14. Pinzon, J.D., Osorno, T., Mola, J.A., Valencia, A.: Real-time health condition monitoring of SCADA infrastructure of power transmission systems control centers. In: 2020 IEEE PES Transmission & Distribution Conference and Exhibition - Latin America (T&D LA), Montevideo, Uruguay, pp. 1–6. IEEE, September 2020. https://doi.org/10.1109/TDLA47668.2020.9326135. https://ieeexplore.ieee.org/document/9326135/

15. Presuhn, R.: Version 2 of the Protocol operations for the simple network management protocol (SNMP), December 2002. https://doi.org/10.17487/RFC3416. https://www.rfc-editor.org/info/rfc3416. issue: 3416 Num Pages: 31 Series: Request for Comments Published: RFC 3416

16. Rose, D.M.T., McCloghrie, K.: Management information base for network management of TCP/IP-based internets. RFC 1156, May 1990. https://doi.org/10.17487/RFC1156. https://www.rfc-editor.org/info/rfc1156

17. Rose, D.M.T., McCloghrie, K.: Structure and identification of management information for TCP/IP-based internets. RFC 1155, May 1990. https://doi.org/10.17487/RFC1155. https://www.rfc-editor.org/info/rfc1155

A Review of Dynamic Difficulty Adjustment Methods for Serious Games

Júlio Castro Lopes[1] and Rui Pedro Lopes[1,2]

[1] Research Center in Digitalization and Intelligent Robotics (CeDRI), Instituto Politécnico de Bragança, Bragança, Portugal
{juliolopes,rlopes}@ipb.pt
[2] Institute of Electronics and Informatics Engineering of Aveiro (IEETA), University of Aveiro, Aveiro, Portugal

Abstract. Rehabilitation games can be a novel and effective approach to mental and physical rehabilitation. Since patient's abilities differ, these types of games depend on a variety of levels of difficulty. Furthermore, it is prudent to make continuous adjustments to the difficulty in order to prevent overburdening the patient, whether on emotional or physical level. For this purpose Dynamic Difficulty Adjustment (DDA) can be a very interesting solution, as it allows for the dynamic adaptation of the game based on observed performance and on physiological data of the player. DDA has been used in games for many years as it allows tuning the game to match the player's ideal flow, keeping high levels of motivation and challenge. This paper reviews several DDA approaches used in rehabilitation and entertainment games. We concluded that many studies use Reinforcement Learning (RL) because it requires no pre-training and can adapt the game in real time without prior knowledge.

Keywords: Dynamic difficulty adjustment · Serious games · Rehabilitation · Reinforcement learning

1 Introduction

Games, whether in video or Virtual Reality (VR) format, are usually accomplished through a series of levels of increasing difficulty. When playing games either offline or online, the intuitive approach is to divide them into three difficulty levels [22], commonly labeled as: easy, medium, and hard [32]. This division in three levels can be seen in several applications, such as educational games [27], virtual reality games [9], video games for entertainment purposes [36], and even on gamification systems for educational purposes [18]. Although this division into three levels can be seen as the standard approach, in some cases it can be extended to accommodate more levels or finer degrees of difficulty. The authors in [24] concluded that their game should have more than three levels of difficulty because the player would frequently get stuck on either the lower or higher difficulty.

A. I. Pereira et al. (Eds.): OL2A 2022, CCIS 1754, pp. 144–159, 2022.
https://doi.org/10.1007/978-3-031-23236-7_11

Many games allow the user to select the desired level of difficulty at the beginning of the game, that will be kept until the player decides to change it. When the user is playing a game for the first time, deciding on his/her own can be difficult because they have no idea about the difficulty of each level and do not know the relative level of their skills [22]. Furthermore, requiring players to select difficulty levels on a regular basis may be inconvenient and cause game interruptions. A different approach could be followed through Dynamic Difficulty Adjustment (DDA).

The objective of the work described in this paper is to assess, in the scientific literature, the techniques and algorithms used in video-games to adapt the environment to the player's skills and stress level. It is an ongoing work, within the GreenHealth project [19]. This project, focusing on mental health rehabilitation in people diagnosed on the schizophrenia spectrum, has the main goal of developing and using digital technologies, such as Facial Expressions classification under occlusion by Virtual Reality (VR) goggles [28], Game-Based Learning (GBL), Internet of Things (IoT), Artificial Intelligence (AI), and Advanced Data Analytics (ADA), in the development of innovative rehabilitation techniques, contributing to the promotion of well-being and health in a holistic perspective. The approaches to be developed depend on an adequate and motivating simulation in virtual reality, to increase the impact and success of the rehabilitation procedures.

This paper is structured in four sections, as follows: Sect. 2 describes the methodology used to perform this review, Sect. 3 and Sect. 4 focus on a literature review on game DDA, approaching entertaining games and rehabilitation games respectively; Sect. 5 presents an analysis of the described games in the format of a table; and conclusions are drawn on Sect. 6.

2   Methodology

As mentioned before, the main objective of this literature review is to try to understand the techniques and algorithms for the dynamic adaptation of games in a cognitive rehabilitation scenario. This literature review follows the approach suggested by Materla et al. [20] and by Subhash and Cudney [35]. It is composed of three phases, starting with the planning, followed by the operation (conducting) and dissemination (reporting) phases. The planning phase included both the definition of the bibliography databases and the selection of the query term. The selected databases were Scopus and Web of Knowledge (WoK), since they provide the most relevant and accurate results. The query used the term ("(game OR gaming OR games) AND (adapt OR adapted OR adapts OR adaptation OR readaptation OR adapting) AND (dynamic difficulty adaptation OR dynamic difficulty balancing OR DDA OR dynamic)") for the title, keywords and abstract. The papers were further restricted to the last 13 years, from January 1st, 2009 and December 31st, 2021. Only papers available in the institutional repositories, peer reviewed and written in English were considered. The second phase (conducting) started with the selection of the relevant papers and exclusion of the remaining. Repeated papers and papers without available full-text

PDF were excluded. After these step, a total of 379 papers remained. The process continued with the selection of the most relevant articles, through title and abstract analysis. Non relevant papers were eliminated. Subsequently, the most relevant papers remained, in a total of 12 (Table 1). Note that we have used a wide range of years (from 2009 to 2021), since [17] work, is a well-known and one of the first approaches to solve DDA problems.

3   Dynamic Difficulty Adjustment

When people engage in an activity that is neither boring nor frustrating, they become engrossed in it, allowing them to work for longer periods of time and remain focused on the task. The flow channel is a state of mind whose ideas can be applied to a video game [8]. Following the flow, the idea of using adaptive difficulty mechanisms, is to keep the game's difficulty within a certain range to prevent the player from getting bored if the game is too easy, or frustrated if the game is too difficult. In recent years, there has been a lot of research done on DDA applied to games [39].

DDA aims to adapt the difficulty of the game based on the players' performance, and can be accomplished by considering not only their in-game performance, but also the associated physiological responses. By measuring and integrating physiological data it is possible to map how difficult or easy it is for the player to perform a given task [17]. The study in [34] demonstrated that DDA based on electroencephalography (EEG) signals improved the players' game experience. This statement was backed up by their opinions.

Huber et al. [12] demonstrated the use of experience-driven Procedural Content Generation for DDA in VR exercise games by procedurally generating levels that match the player's current capabilities. Deep Reinforcement Learning (DRL) algorithms were used to adjust the structure of the maze and decide which exercise rooms to include in the maze, in order to match with the player's capabilities. Since most established DRL algorithms share the fact that the required amount of training effort increases with high-dimensional input state spaces, they did not train the algorithm to create mazes from scratch. Instead, they adopted a procedural technique similar to [13]. Because human players require a minimum amount of time to complete each maze, the authors decided not to train the network solely with training data generated by real human players. As a result, they decided to train their network on a user simulation of the difficulty of a given maze. Since the DRL algorithm's goal is to create a maze with the desired difficulty level, the reward is based on the player's difficulty rating (via questionnaire) at the end of each maze. They also took an electrocardiogram (ECG) signal to objectively measure the participants' exertion level during the VR session. They confidently stated that, in addition to traditional in-game parameter adjustment, procedural generation of levels with appropriate difficulty can improve future DDA systems for exergames. However, they also found two drawbacks in their approach: the generated levels took too long to allow for fast adaptation, and the usage of a static user simulation.

Tan et al. [37] proposed two adaptive algorithms that leverage principles of Reinforcement Learning (RL) and evolutionary computing to increase player satisfaction by scaling the game AI difficulty while the game is being played. The proposed algorithms, Adaptive Uni-Chromosome (AUC) and Adaptive Duo-chromosome Controller (ADC), have the advantage of not requiring a training phase, as adaptation occurs during the game session. The controller's behavior-based system can be seen as advantageous due to its scalability, which means that new behavior components, whether complementary or antagonistic, can be easily added or removed from the existing set of behavior components. The adaptive algorithm will automatically select a behavior component combination that is appropriate for its opponent. The AUC controller has the particularity that it can be trained online, which means that the training and adaptation can take place in real time while playing the game. The authors also investigated the effects of varying the learning rate and mutation rate for both algorithms, and they proposed a general rule of thumb for selecting these two parameters. They came to the conclusion that the adaptive controller is only as good as its design, and that it is unable to adapt to a player who exceeds its full potential. As a result, a learning and adaptive game AI would be a natural future extension.

Liu et al. [17], developed an affect-based DDA system for computer games. The game difficulty level is automatically modified in real time as a function of the player's affective state, using physiological data to determine his or her probable anxiety level, which was chosen as the target affective state. The gaming experiences of the participants were reviewed and contrasted when a performance-based DDA mechanism and an affect-based DDA mechanism were used to the same computer game. To the best of the authors' knowledge, this was the first time that the effects of an affect-based DDA on player interaction with a computer game capable of physiology-based affect recognition and real-time difficulty adjustment in a closed-loop way have been explored experimentally. The affect-based DDA improved the overall satisfaction of gaming for the majority of participants, with 77% reporting more challenging gaming experiences. These findings imply that a computer game's ability to recognize a player's affective states and alter game difficulty correspondingly, could improve the gaming experience. Although the affective modeling methodology used in this study could be used to detect the intensity of anxiety, excitement, and frustration at the same time, more sophisticated difficulty adaptation mechanisms would be required to incorporate multiple inferred affective cues and account for other game-playing information of interest, such as the player's performance, personality, and the context and complexity of the game [17]. The authors conducted a preliminary session consisting of six one-hour gaming sessions in order to train their Regression Tree (RT), which was the model used in this work based on their previous research [26]. One of the paper limitations, according to the authors, is the use of physiological sensors by the players, which may be uncomfortable to wear. They emphasized that, as technology advances, these sensors may improved to the point of being imperceptible during the gameplay. Another disadvantage and possibility for future improvement, is to incorporate a method based on RL to perform the adaptation in real time without a previous training process, leading to real time adaptation. This would allow eliminating the need to perform preliminary gaming sessions, to collect training data. The authors' recommendation, on the other hand, was to implement Active Learning (AL). AL and RL are related in that both can reduce the number of labels required for models. Nonetheless, by using AL, you still need to collect data to train the model (although, fewer than the authors' proposal), which should reduce the training time.

Chanel and Lopes [6] built a Tetris game that changes its complexity dynamically, based on an emotional model capable of recognizing anxiety and boredom from raw human physiological data (extracted by electrodermal activity signals). This paper begins by comparing a Linear Discriminant Analysis (LDA) and a Quadratic Discriminant Analysis (QDA), with the combination of Deep Convolutional Neural Network (CNN) and Long Short Term Memory (LSTM). The authors achieved slightly better accuracy and managed to train models capable of identifying the most useful features of the signals and better representation of the problem through intermediary layers. Two types of adaptation methods were investigated: one that uses the model decision directly - absolute (ABS), and the other that compares the previous model output with the current one and then adjusts the difficulty accordingly - relative (REA). The ABS method outperformed the REA method, according to the results. When players stated that they wanted to play on hard or medium difficulty, the ABS model was especially effective at adapting the game difficulty. Based on their previous study [7], the authors only considered two possible emotional states: boredom and anxiety. This can be seen as a disadvantage in studies that require more detailed expressions and emotional states to be analyzed. In order to train the model, the authors collected physiological activity from 20 participants over 6 sessions of 5 min each (10 h of data) while playing Tetris. The authors also mentioned that their adaptation methods only have two outcomes, in direct connection with the emotional states: increase or decrease difficulty. However, a potential third class (maintain difficulty) may be advantageous for ambiguous values outputted by the model. Future enhancements to the proposed models may be obtained if, in addition to physiological data, information from the gameplay was used as input.

Blom et al. [2] published a DDA system based on Facial Expression Analysis (FEA) for predicting in-game difficulty and acting as a modeling mechanism for single player arcade games. Their system performs online adaptation and has the particularity that it is unobtrusive, which means that the user will not feel any discomfort while acquiring facial expression information. They choose to focus on personalising the game space to the individual player with respect to experienced challenge (adapting the game environment, instead of adapting the behaviour of the game characters). This study was divided in two main parts. The first part looks into the connection between in-game difficulty and the emotional condition of the players as expressed through their facial expressions. This was accomplished through the use of classification methods, that allowed the authors to predict the difficulty level of the game being played with good accuracy, by analyzing players' facial features. Based on first part's findings, the second part expands it and introduces FEA as a technique for evaluating player involvement and dynamically changing in-game difficulty. Since player facial expressions are an indicator of current game difficulty, they proposed a FEA-based game personalisation system that aims to improve individual player in-game experience while also maximising player affection levels towards the game itself. To train their model, participants were asked to rate the difficulty of the game on a scale of 1 (very easy) to 7 (very difficult). This value was considered as "perceived difficulty". These values were used in a classification task in which the goal was to predict the difficulty level of the game. The trained model consistently correlated different facial expressions (including head movement) to a specific user challenge level, resulting in smoother in-game adaptations, whereas the same user behavior would result in steep adaptations in the heuristic system. As a result, they concluded that online and unobtrusive game personalisation is possible using only facial expression analysis, and that head pose detection can contribute to an even more effective game adaptation mechanism. They also detected a preference for the personalized system in 18 of 30 tests, while the static system was preferred in only 9 of 30 tests. To improve their work, the authors proposed enriching the training set with observations from more players, regardless of age, gender, or skill level, as well as incorporating more features into their classifier to improve player modeling.

4 DDA on Rehabilitation Games

Game-based rehabilitation can be an effective way to engage patients in therapy and, at the same time, develop innovative rehabilitation challenges. Games can provide a fun and entertaining way to perform rehabilitation, but the real focus is on performing a set of exercises that will aid in patients' rehabilitation process. An adaptive therapeutic game can be very beneficial, since it can change the game behavior based on the patient's results. It can thus adjust the game difficulty dynamically based on the patient's capabilities assessment and motivation, rather than a static user profile. As a result, adaptation can bridge the gap between the patient's health status during the game and the assumed patient profile at the start of the therapy session paradigms [14].

Earlier in 2011, Hocine et al. [11] produced a pre-pilot experiment for a therapeutic serious game, but with abstract information about the DDA technique, intended to reuse it in different games. The proposed technique includes a generic real-time adaptation module that allows each patient's game difficulty to be dynamically adjusted based on his profile and observed performance. To accomplish this, the authors devised a structure known as a matrix of action probabilities, which represents the game's 2D plan. This matrix was constructed by taking into account the presence of a challenge in the game, which required the collection of information about the patient. This stage is known as the assessment, and it results in a matrix with each position $A(i,j)$ representing the patient's success rate. In this, each location $D(i,j)$ holds a probability that an action should be performed at this location by the patient. With this knowledge, the game level must direct game actions toward the locations with the best chances of success. This structure is advantageous because it provides a common interface for all games. This means that the difficulty adaptation module is treated as a black box by the game level, producing a matrix of action probabilities. The DDA module can bridge the gap between the patient's current health status and the profile assumed at the start of the therapy session. Their abstract DDA module was later integrated in Hocine et al. serious game for motor rehabilitation in 2014 [10]. This online adaptation was accomplished by making the following decisions: (i) reduce the difficulty to avoid putting the player in repeated failure situations during the game level; (ii) increase the difficulty when the player has a string of consecutive successes and finds the game to be very easy; and otherwise (iii) maintain momentarily the difficulty [10]. In comparison to the control strategies, DDA increased the number of tasks, number of successful tasks, and total distance. This is a critical factor that allows stroke patients to increase their training volume. The authors also concluded that in future work, the number of subjects and different profiles should be increased.

RL algorithms can be a good approach for dynamically adapting the game while taking patient performance into account at run time. Ávila et al. [29] presented a novel game difficulty adaptation algorithm that efficiently balances the adaptation by conjugating information from the patient's game performance and therapist feedback. A Markov decision process (MDP) was used to define an initial adaptation policy, that was then fed to an RL algorithm, which dynamically updates the adaptation policy by incorporating action rewards (whether negative or positive) from the therapist. The authors have chosen a RL approach because actions are also based on the current state of the system but, unlike the MDP, the decision policy is dynamic and evolves based on given rewards. By monitoring the patient execution, the adaptation policy determines whether to increase or decrease the game level difficulty. The authors have created a modified version of the latter (Q-l+) that computes the action value function by incorporating both the rewards derived from online monitoring of the patient's performance and the rewards set by the therapist as therapy progresses, which they call reward shaping [15]. Because RL policy evolution requires long training periods with initial behavior that is close to erratic, the RL algorithm was seeded with the static policy discovered with the MDP in this game adaptation approach [25]. The learning process is accelerated in this way, and a dynamic optimal policy is always available [29]. This study was limited by therapist guidance because it requires on-line therapist feedback; as an improvement, this system could be updated to an automatic system that does not require any mandatory assistance.

Andrade et al. [1] provided an RL approach to dynamically modeling player capabilities in applications that combine gaming and rehabilitative robotics.

Robots and serious games can be useful rehabilitation tools because they can integrate multiple repetitive movements with only prior programming. In order to adapt the difficulty of the game to player's skill level, the authors have modified the Q-Learning algorithm, with SARSA [33]. The authors made it clear that variables that have a direct effect on game difficulty were chosen to serve as environment states. They used the inverse of the Euclidean distance from the current state to the final state to calculate the immediate reward given at each step interaction (Eq. 1). The reward indicates how far the player has progressed away from the most difficult game level.

$$r = \frac{1}{\sqrt{(v_m - v_i)^2 + (d_n - d_j)^2}} \tag{1}$$

In order to assess the user's performance, the authors take into account not only game scores but also the number of challenges (exercises) the user performs, as measured by its actual movement. It is worth noting that the algorithm chooses the start state at random, so the game could begin at either an easy or challenging level. This study only includes thirty-minute experiments with four players, but the results show that the proposed approach is feasible for modeling user behavior and capturing adaptations and trends for each player based on game difficulty. The authors intend to extend this to clinical subjects in the future, using the obtained map as a guideline for how to make the game easier or harder for each individual player.

Sekhavat et al. [30], presented a customized DDA approach for a rehabilitation game to improve functional arm capabilities, that automatically changes difficulty settings in real-time based on a patient's skills. Since existing RL algorithms are episodic (all objectives are evaluated in the same predefined episodes), the authors decided to modify this idea in order to evaluate a problems' objectives at different times. They needed to find a different approach because DDA requires the history of previous evaluations to evaluate some objectives rather than just the evaluation based on the information at the end of each episode. This opened the need for a Multiple-Periodic Reinforcement Learning (MPRL), which allows for the evaluation of value functions of different goals in separate periods. In the MPRL architecture, the authors stated that some goals may be evaluated more frequently than others. Goals that are evaluated frequently necessitate a shorter history of outcomes, whereas goals that are evaluated infrequently necessitate a longer history of outcomes [30]. When there are direct relationships between goals, it is possible to extract a single objective function by considering the goals all at once. In the case of completely unrelated objectives, on the other hand, reward functions and decision-making policies can be considered separately. The authors used an AUC Controller [37] to demonstrate how game parameters (such as speed, size, and distance) can be changed to meet the objectives. The main advantage of this controller is its ability to train and adapt in real-time while playing the game. The game properties are represented by six real numbers stored in this AUC controller. The controller chromosome simulates the game's difficulty by encoding a set of behaviors that is expected to be difficult enough to earn a score. The chromosome is randomly initialized at the start of the game. They proposed new semantics and procedures for MPRL with two-level probabilistic actions. One of the goals of this study, was also to compare the traditional Multiple-Objective Reinforcement Learning (MORL) with their MPRL. The different between this two definitions of RL is the following: MORL is a significant version of RL that considers many goals for decision-making (all the goals evaluated at the same time), and MPRL is distinguished by its capacity to analyze distinct objectives at different times. They proved that MPRL outperforms traditional MORL in terms of player satisfaction indicators as well as improving the motor control system over time, according to the results of a series of experiments on patients. Their system is limited because it only considers player skill level; learning about his/her play style and individual characteristics would be beneficial. Because MPRL must handle multiple objectives at the same time, the authors did not achieve a high level of accuracy.

Although all of the rehabilitation studies mentioned thus far only take players' performance or their emotional state into account, it can be an effective approach to combine both while playing the game. Pezzera et al. [23] implemented a preliminary version of their home rehabilitation platform on healthy subjects, with the intention of later testing it on patients with multiple sclerosis. Commercial exercise games are not a suitable match for rehabilitation: they may be too risky or difficult to play with, as they typically only offer a few fixed degrees of difficulty, designed for those who are not disabled. For people who have trouble executing specific movements, this may be insufficient. Furthermore, the therapist rarely has access to the raw data collected by the tracking devices, making it impossible to make a quantitative assessment of the patient's performance. Because of these factors, the authors decided to implement DDA in the game, through three independent modules that collaborated to conduct the DDA:

1. an off-line adapter, which computes the patient's ability using data from previous exercises, used as a starting point for determining the appropriate difficulty level;
2. an emotional adapter, based on the outcome of conversations between the patient and an Empathic Virtual Therapist (EVT) [38], where the EVT produces an assessment of the patient's emotional status;
3. an on-line adapter, that adjusts the difficulty level based on the player's score and motion accuracy.

These modules can be used together or separately, but the best results were obtained when combined. To assess the performance of the player, the authors have used the Eq. 2.

$$pi = \alpha FPA(R_h, R_m) + (1 - \alpha)FMA(G_h, G_m) \tag{2}$$

where:

FPA   - Fully Performance Adapter: it only uses the hit rate information and ignores the monitor's value.

FMA   - Fully Monitoring Adapter: from a rehabilitation standpoint, it is safer because it only uses monitor information to adjust the difficulty; even if the patient has a perfect hit rate, the difficulty will not be increased unless the monitors have a good value.

R_h - repetition hit rate.

R_m - repetition monitors activation rate.

G_h - global hit rate.

G_m - global monitors activation rate.

$0 \leqslant \alpha \leqslant 1$ - the therapists will set this parameter based on the patient's recovery.

The authors have implemented two possible algorithms for the FPA and FMA, namely a linear adapter and a fuzzy adapter. When the hit or miss rate exceeds a certain threshold, the linear adapter simply adjusts the difficulty by increasing or decreasing the parameters by a fixed amount. The fuzzy adapter, on the other hand, maps inputs to a fuzzy set and uses fuzzy inference to determine the new level of difficulty. However, patients who do not want to talk with the EVT may choose to ignore the virtual agent because their moods can change throughout the day and not every single player has the patience to answer the virtual agent at each evaluation. Instead of using a virtual agent, this system can be improved by incorporating an automatic mechanism (perhaps based on the emotional state of the players). The authors concluded that incorporating an RGB-D camera to track the patient's body during the game and also to determine the patient's emotional state would be a prudent solution.

Balan et al. [4] presented a VR game for treating acrophobia, based on the concept of real-time automatic adaption of in-game height exposure dependent on the subject's level of fear. To that purpose, they employed physiological signals as input (EEG, Galvanic Skin Response - GSR, and Heart Rate - HR) to forecast the future exposure scenario and estimate the subject's current fear level. The authors have created three modes of expressing fear ratings: the 2-choice scale, the 4-choice scale, and the 11-choice scale. Three fear-level scales were used, with 2, 4, and 11 possible responses (2-choice, 4-choice and 11-choice scale). They used a variety of ML classifiers and DL techniques to determine the current anxiety level and the next exposure scenario, including Support Vector Machine (SVM), k-Nearest Neighbors (kNN), LDA, RF, and four deep neural network architectural models. Two classifiers were used: one to estimate the patient's current fear level (C1) and one to identify the appropriate treatment based on the target fear level (C2). A early experiment in which eight acrophobic individuals were *in vivo* and virtually exposed to various heights yielded the data necessary to train the classifiers. Both a user-dependent and a user-independent modality were employed to calculate the classifiers' accuracy. In the case of the user-independent modality, each classifier was trained using the data of the other individuals. In their experiment the authors concluded that cross-validation scores were a good choice, achieving very high scores for both classifiers, highlighting the kNN and RF techniques. Concerning the physiological signals used as input for the classifiers, the authors concluded that GSR, HR, and EEG values in the beta range were the most important features for fear level classification. The authors hope to develop a VR-based game for treating additional sorts of phobias in the future. Furthermore, they plan to expand the trials and include more people, with their physiological reactions being collected and utilized to train and test the classifiers. Another path they will take is to conduct real-world testing with the 8 acrophobic patients who took part in the current study, exposing them to *in vivo* circumstances and assessing whether their anxiety levels decreased.

Later, the authors expanded their research to include physiological signals as well as patient facial expressions and respiration rate [5]. In this pilot experiment, they proposed a model for automatically adapting exposure scenarios based on the emotional states of the users, which was tested on four acrophobic subjects. This system employs an intelligent virtual therapist who can recognize emotions based on physiological signals, offer encouragement, and adjust exposure levels based on the user's moods.

5   Discussion

This section provides a brief description and comparison of the described papers, in order to draw conclusions about the games described in this paper (Table 1).

It is possible to see that there are studies that only consider the performance of the player, others its emotional state and just few that integrate both into their DDA module. Although the majority of these authors concluded that incorporating players' performance and emotional state rather than just one of them, could be a solution to improve the game.

The studies described before show that it is possible to dynamically change the difficulty of the game using a variety of sensors/data sources. Some of the studies use things as simple as the keyboard, computer, mouse or even a graphics tablet. The majority of these studies only consider the player's performance within the game because it is the only thing they can extract from this type of data source. More complex studies use sensors and cameras, not only to extract the performance of the player in game but also to extract his/her emotional state. Some of the sensors may be considered a limitation since they can be intrusive and uncomfortable to the player. Despite this, as technology advances, sensors become more discrete and efficient [16].

Although there are some existing reviews on DDA systems and methodologies [3,21,31,39], our review is unique in comparison to all of them, making it important to the scientific community. The Table 2, provides a brief overview of

Table 1. Overview of dynamic difficulty adjustment games

Study	Game type	Sensors/Data source	Techniques used	Achievements	Limitations
Huber et al. [12]	Virtual Reality Entertainment Game	Head-Mounted Display (HMD); Electrocardiogram (ECG) sensor attached to patient's upper body	Deep Reinforcement Learning	Generation of levels based on player's skills.	Static user simulation. Generated levels to slow to allow for fast adaptation.
Tan et al. [37]	Entertainment Computer Game	Keyboard; AI algorithm	Reinforcement Learning; Adaptive Uni-Chromosome; Duo-chromosome Controller	Training is not required; adaptation takes place during the game session.	The adaptative controller is only good as its design; unable to adapt if a player exceeds its full potential.
Liu et al. [17]	Entertainment Computer Game	Wearable biofeedback sensors	Machine Learning Classifiers Highlited: Regression Tree	Dynamic difficulty adjustment based on players' affective state.	Uncomfortable sensors. Training time too long.
Chanel et al. [6]	Entertainment Computer Game	Electrodermal Activity (EDA) sensors	Deep Learning Techniques	Dynamic adaptation of the game, based on two possible emotional states.	Module just uses physiological data, nothing related to player's performance.
Blom et al. [2]	Entertainment Computer Game	Computer Camera	Machine Learning Classifiers; Heuristic Algorithm	Dynamic difficulty adjustment based on players' facial expression.	Adaptation based only on players' facial expression. More features could be added.
Hocine et al. [10]	Motor Rehabilitation	Computer Mouse; Graphics tablet	Monte Carlo Tree Search; Reward Based System; Computer Vision Algorithms	The game adapts to each profile in real time.	The number of different subjects and profiles is limited.
Sekhavat [30]	Motor Rehabilitation	Microsoft Kinect	Reinforcement Learning (RL); Multiple-Periodic RL	Automatic Adaptation based on real time patient's skills.	Low accuracy. It only considers players' skill level.
Ávila et al. [29]	Motor Rehabilitation - Virtual Reality Based	Abstract definition of the method; it was unclear how data was received	Reinforcement Learning; Markov Decision Process	Online Adaptation during game.	The therapist needs to be available during game.
Andrade et al. [1]	Motor Rehabilitation	Robotic Device	Reinforcement Learning	Motor Rehabilitation using robotics.	Small sample size. Just four players were included.
Pezzera et al. [23]	Motor Rehabilitation	Microsoft Kinect; Nintendo Wii Balance Board	Fuzzy Logic	Adaptation based not only on players' performance but also on theirs' physiological state.	Physiological state extracted by Virtual Theraphist during game, could be improved with other mechanisms, such as cameras, sensors, etc.
Balan et al. [4]	Mental Rehabilitation - Virtual Reality Based	Acticap Xpress Bundle (EEG data); Shimmers Multi-Sensory (HR and GSR data)	Machine Learning classifiers; Deep Neural Networks	Virtual reality game that dinamically adapts its' difficulty based on patient current level of fear.	Small sample size, possibly leads to overfitting.
Balan et al. [5]	Mental Rehabilitation - Virtual Reality Based	Two HTC Vive Trackers; HMDS; EEG Device	Machine Learning classifiers; Deep Neural Networks	Adaptation based on physiological signals, facial expression and respiration rate.	Small sample size. Discomfort in the head by using sensors.

recent reviews in DDA, proving that our review can fill a gap in the literature by reviewing several DDA rehabilitation games.

The majority of existing DDA studies make use of RL techniques or ideas derived from them (reward based systems). RL algorithms have high expression in the studies, because they do not require pre-training, which means they do not require any prior knowledge to adapt to the abilities of players. The review performed in this paper will serve as a basis for future work within the Green-Health project [19], aiming at filling the gap in the literature on games for mental rehabilitation, with a particular emphasis on patients with schizophrenia.

Table 2. Recent review papers in DDA

Study	Summary
Panagiotis et al. [21]	This is a very complete and recent review. This can be seen as the most similar review to our, however, our paper details several different studies, mainly the ones that focus on rehabilitation purposes.
Sepulveda et al. [31]	Provides an overview of the development of a DDA system in video games. However, instead of detailing concrete DDA approaches, it focuses on the global implementation of a DDA system.
Bontchev et al. [3]	Deals with models for presenting emotions, techniques for measuring behavioral signals, emotion recognition and adaptation mechanisms using affective feedback. It focuses on entertainment games rather than rehabilitation games.
Zohaib et al. [39]	Describes several different methods for performing DDA in games, with an emphasis on providing an overview of various types of methods. This is a more general review that focuses on the classification of DDA approaches.

6   Conclusions

This paper provides an overview of DDA applications in games, with a focus on rehabilitation games. Throughout this review, several techniques to perform DDA, such as fuzzy logic, heuristics, ML, and DL techniques and also RL (the most popular in our review) were described. This was not an extensive review; rather, this paper reviews the studies that have the application context most adequate to cognitive and social rehabilitation of patients, the focus of the project this work is being developed.

It is evident, from the study performed, that a useful rehabilitation game, based on virtual reality simulation, can benefit from a Reinforcement Learning DDA system that use several inputs as basis for decision. It should include the in-game performance, the emotional state (measured through facial expressions, head pose, body pose, physiological data) and even human input, to make adjustments during rehabilitation sessions.

Acknowledgments. This work is funded by the European Regional Development Fund (ERDF) through the Regional Operational Program North 2020, within the scope of Project GreenHealth - Digital strategies in biological assets to improve well-being and promote green health, Norte-01-0145-FEDER-000042.

This work has been supported by FCT - Fundação para a Ciência e Tecnologia within the Project Scope: UIDB/05757/2020.

References

1. Andrade, K.d.O., Fernandes, G., Caurin, G.A., Siqueira, A.A., Romero, R.A., Pereira, R.d.L.: Dynamic player modelling in serious games applied to rehabilitation robotics. In: 2014 Joint Conference on Robotics: SBR-LARS Robotics Symposium and Robocontrol, pp. 211–216, October 2014. https://doi.org/10.1109/SBR. LARS.Robocontrol.2014.41

2. Blom, P.M., Bakkes, S., Spronck, P.: Modeling and adjusting in-game difficulty based on facial expression analysis. Entertain. Comput. **31**, 100307 (2019). https://doi.org/10.1016/j.entcom.2019.100307. https://www.sciencedirect. com/science/article/pii/S1875952119300448

3. Bontchev, B.: Adaptation in affective video games: a literature review. Cybern. Inf. Technol. **16**, 3–34 (2016). https://doi.org/10.1515/cait-2016-0032

4. Bălan, O., Moise, G., Moldoveanu, A., Leordeanu, M., Moldoveanu, F.: An Investigation of various machine and deep learning techniques applied in automatic fear level detection and acrophobia virtual therapy. Sensors **20**(2), 496 (2020). https:// doi.org/10.3390/s20020496. https://www.mdpi.com/1424-8220/20/2/496

5. Bălan, O., Moldoveanu, A., Leordeanu, M.: A machine learning approach to automatic phobia therapy with virtual reality. In: Opris, I., A. Lebedev, M., F. Casanova, M. (eds.) Modern Approaches to Augmentation of Brain Function. CCN, pp. 607–636. Springer, Cham (2021). https://doi.org/10.1007/978-3-030-54564-2_27

6. Chanel, G., Lopes, P.: User evaluation of affective dynamic difficulty adjustment based on physiological deep learning. In: Schmorrow, D.D., Fidopiastis, C.M. (eds.) HCII 2020. LNCS (LNAI), vol. 12196, pp. 3–23. Springer, Cham (2020). https:// doi.org/10.1007/978-3-030-50353-6_1

7. Chanel, G., Rebetez, C., Bétrancourt, M., Pun, T.: Emotion assessment from physiological signals for adaptation of game difficulty. IEEE Trans. Syst. Man Cybern. Part A Syst. Hum. **41**(6), 1052–1063 (2011). https://doi.org/10.1109/TSMCA. 2011.2116000. Conference Name: IEEE Transactions on Systems, Man, and Cybernetics - Part A: Systems and Humans

8. Csikszentmihalyi, M.: Flow: the psychology of optimal experience, January 1990

9. Gabana, D., Tokarchuk, L., Hannon, E., Gunes, H.: Effects of valence and arousal on working memory performance in virtual reality gaming. In: 2017 Seventh International Conference on Affective Computing and Intelligent Interaction (ACII), pp. 36–41, October 2017. ISSN: 2156-8111. https://doi.org/10.1109/ACII.2017. 8273576

10. Hocine, N., Gouaïch, A., Cerri, S.A.: Dynamic difficulty adaptation in serious games for motor rehabilitation. In: Göbel, S., Wiemeyer, J. (eds.) GameDays 2014. LNCS, vol. 8395, pp. 115–128. Springer, Cham (2014). https://doi.org/10.1007/ 978-3-319-05972-3_13

11. Hocine, N., Gouaïch, A., Di Loreto, I., Joab, M.: Motivation based difficulty adaptation for therapeutic games. In: 2011 IEEE 1st International Conference on Serious Games and Applications for Health (SeGAH) (2011). https://ieeexplore.ieee. org/document/6165459/

12. Huber, T., Mertes, S., Rangelova, S., Flutura, S., André, E.: Dynamic difficulty adjustment in virtual reality exergames through experience-driven procedural content generation, August 2021. arXiv:2108.08762 [cs]

13. Khalifa, A., Bontrager, P., Earle, S., Togelius, J.: PCGRL: procedural content generation via reinforcement learning, August 2020. arXiv:2001.09212 [cs, stat]

14. Kuriakose, S., Lahiri, U.: Design of a physiology-sensitive VR-based social communication platform for children with autism. IEEE Trans. Neural Syst. Rehabil. Eng. **25**(8), 1180–1191 (2017). https://doi.org/10.1109/TNSRE.2016.2613879. Conference Name: IEEE Transactions on Neural Systems and Rehabilitation Engineering

15. Laud, A.D.: Theory and application of reward shaping in reinforcement learning. Ph.D., University of Illinois at Urbana-Champaign, USA (2004). aAI3130966

16. Lee, Y.H., Kweon, O.Y., Kim, H., Yoo, J.H., Han, S.G., Oh, J.H.: Recent advances in organic sensors for health self-monitoring systems. J. Mat. Chem. C **6**(32), 8569–8612 (2018). https://doi.org/10.1039/C8TC02230E. https://pubs.rsc.org/en/content/articlelanding/2018/tc/c8tc02230e

17. Liu, C., Agrawal, P., Sarkar, N., Chen, S.: Dynamic difficulty adjustment in computer games through real-time anxiety-based affective feedback. Int. J. Hum. Comput. Interact. **25**(6), 506–529 (2009). https://doi.org/10.1080/10447310902963944. Taylor&Francis_eprint

18. Lopes, R.: An award system for gamification in higher education. In: Conference: 7th International Conference of Education, Research and Innovation, pp. 5563–5573, January 2014

19. Lopes, R.P., et al.: Digital technologies for innovative mental health rehabilitation. Electronics **10**(18), 2260 (2021). https://doi.org/10.3390/electronics10182260, https://www.mdpi.com/2079-9292/10/18/2260

20. Materla, T., Cudney, E.A., Antony, J.: The application of Kano model in the healthcare industry: a systematic literature review. Total Qual. Manag. Bus. Excel. **30**(5–6), 660–681 (2019). https://doi.org/10.1080/14783363.2017.1328980. Routledge_eprint

21. Paraschos, P.D., Koulouriotis, D.E.: Game difficulty adaptation and experience personalization: a literature review. Int. J. Hum. Comput. Interact., 1–22 (2022). https://doi.org/10.1080/10447318.2021.2020008

22. Park, S.y., Sim, H., Lee, W.: Dynamic game difficulty control by using EEG-based emotion recognition. Int. J. Control Autom. (2014). https://doi.org/10.14257/IJCA.2014.7.3.26

23. Pezzera, M., Borghese, N.A.: Dynamic difficulty adjustment in exer-games for rehabilitation: a mixed approach. In: 2020 IEEE 8th International Conference on Serious Games and Applications for Health (SeGAH), pp. 1–7, August 2020. ISSN: 2573-3060. https://doi.org/10.1109/SeGAH49190.2020.9201871

24. Pinto, J.F., Carvalho, H.R., Chambel, G.R.R., Ramiro, J., Goncalves, A.: Adaptive gameplay and difficulty adjustment in a gamified upper-limb rehabilitation. In: 2018 IEEE 6th International Conference on Serious Games and Applications for Health (SeGAH), pp. 1–8, May 2018. ISSN: 2573-3060. https://doi.org/10.1109/SeGAH.2018.8401363

25. Qian, H., Yu, Y.: Derivative-free reinforcement learning: a review. Front. Comput. Sci. **15**(6), 156336 (2021). https://doi.org/10.1007/s11704-020-0241-4. arXiv: 2102.05710

26. Rani, P., Liu, C., Sarkar, N., Vanman, E.: An empirical study of machine learning techniques for affect recognition in human-robot interaction. Pattern Anal. Appl. **9**(1), 58–69 (2006). https://doi.org/10.1007/s10044-006-0025-y. http://link.springer.com/10.1007/s10044-006-0025-y

27. Rello, L., Bayarri, C., Gorriz, A.: What is wrong with this word? Dyseggxia: a game for children with dyslexia. In: Proceedings of the 14th International ACM SIGACCESS Conference on Computers and Accessibility, October 2012. https://doi.org/10.1145/2384916.2384962

28. Rodrigues, A.S.F., Lopes, J.C., Lopes, R.P.: Classification of facial expressions under partial occlusion for VR games. In: Pereira, A.I., et al. (eds.) OL2A 2022. CCIS, vol. 1754, pp. 804–819. Springer, Cham (2022)
29. Ávila-Sansores, S., Orihuela-Espina, F., Enrique-Sucar, L.: Patient tailored virtual rehabilitation. In: Pons, J.L., Torricelli, D., Pajaro, M. (eds.) Converging Clinical and Engineering Research on Neurorehabilitation. BB, vol. 1, pp. 879–883. Springer, Heidelberg (2013). https://doi.org/10.1007/978-3-642-34546-3_143
30. Sekhavat, Y.A.: MPRL: multiple-periodic reinforcement learning for difficulty adjustment in rehabilitation games. In: 2017 IEEE 5th International Conference on Serious Games and Applications for Health (SeGAH), pp. 1–7, April 2017. https://doi.org/10.1109/SeGAH.2017.7939260
31. Sepulveda, G.K., Besoain, F., Barriga, N.A.: Exploring dynamic difficulty adjustment in videogames. In: 2019 IEEE CHILEAN Conference on Electrical, Electronics Engineering, Information and Communication Technologies (CHILECON), pp. 1–6, November 2019. https://doi.org/10.1109/CHILECON47746.2019.8988068
32. Smeddinck, J., Siegel, S., Herrlich, M.: Adaptive difficulty in exergames for Parkinson's disease patients. In: Proceedings of Graphics Interface 2013, GI 2013, pp. 141–148. Canadian Information Processing Society, Canada, May 2013
33. Sprague, N., Ballard, D.: Multiple-goal reinforcement learning with modular Sarsa(0). In: Proceedings of the Eighteenth International Joint Conference on Artificial Intelligence, Jul 2003
34. Stein, A., Yotam, Y., Puzis, R., Shani, G., Taieb-Maimon, M.: EEG-triggered dynamic difficulty adjustment for multiplayer games. Entertain. Comput. **25**, 14–25 (2018). https://doi.org/10.1016/j.entcom.2017.11.003. https://www.sciencedirect.com/science/article/pii/S1875952117301325
35. Subhash, S., Cudney, E.A.: Gamified learning in higher education: a systematic review of the literature. Comput. Hum. Behav. **87**, 192–206 (2018). https://doi.org/10.1016/j.chb.2018.05.028. https://www.sciencedirect.com/science/article/pii/S0747563218302541
36. Sykes, J., Brown, S.: Affective gaming: measuring emotion through the gamepad. In: CHI 2003 Extended Abstracts on Human Factors in Computing Systems, CHI EA 2003, pp. 732–733. Association for Computing Machinery, New York, April 2003. https://doi.org/10.1145/765891.765957
37. Tan, C.H., Tan, K.C., Tay, A.: Dynamic game difficulty scaling using adaptive behavior-based AI. IEEE Trans. Comput. Intell. AI Games **3**(4), 289–301 (2011). https://doi.org/10.1109/TCIAIG.2011.2158434. Conference Name: IEEE Transactions on Computational Intelligence and AI in Games
38. Tironi, A., Mainetti, R., Pezzera, M., Borghese, N.A.: An empathic virtual caregiver for assistance in exer-game-based rehabilitation therapies. In: 2019 IEEE 7th International Conference on Serious Games and Applications for Health (SeGAH), pp. 1–6, August 2019. ISSN: 2573-3060. https://doi.org/10.1109/SeGAH.2019.8882477
39. Zohaib, M.: Dynamic difficulty adjustment (DDA) in computer games: a review. Adv. Hum. Comput. Interact. **2018**, e5681652 (2018). https://doi.org/10.1155/2018/5681652. https://www.hindawi.com/journals/ahci/2018/5681652/

Anxiety Monitoring System: A Preliminary Approach

Diogo Luís[1,2]([⊠]) [iD], Salviano F. P. Soares[1,2][iD], and Gonçalo Carnaz[3][iD]

[1] ECT, Engineering Department, UTAD, 5001-801 Vila Real, Portugal
`diogo.pinto.luis@hotmail.com, salblues@utad.pt`
[2] IEETA, UA Campus, 3810-193 Aveiro, Portugal
[3] DEIS, Polytechnic of Coimbra, ISEC, Coimbra, Portugal
`goncalo.carnaz@isec.pt`

Abstract. Nowadays, there is an increasing number of mental illnesses, especially anxiety, being estimated that 284 million people were living with this disorder, in 2018. This study raises awareness of this mental illness and addresses the challenge of stress/anxiety detection using a supervised machine learning system for classification. We give a focus on the respiratory system and its parameters that correlate with stress/anxiety. The developed work establishes the framework for an anxiety monitoring system using multiple physiological parameters. 5 of the most common algorithms were used for the task and the one achieving the best results was the random forest classifier with 92% accuracy and great values for precision, recall, f1-Score and cohen kappa score. Ultimately, this technology can be applied to self and autonomous stress/anxiety detection purposes or partner with specialists who deal with these problems on a day-to-day basis like psychologists or psychiatrists.

Keywords: Mental health disorders · Breathing · Machine learning · Anxiety

1 Introduction

Mental health disorders are a serious and increasing issue, affecting daily life on a personal and professional level. In 2015, the World Health Organization (WHO, 2017) estimated that 264 million people were living with anxiety disorders, an increase of 14.9% since 2005. Also in 2018, [1] reported that these numbers had increased to 284 million people.

The American Psychiatric Association [2] defined mental health illness as *"a health condition involving changes in emotion, thinking or behavior (or a combination of these)"*. Furthermore, this subject includes an exhaustive list of disorders, such as depression, anxiety, bipolar, eating disorders, and schizophrenia, among others. Anxiety is part of this extensive list of disorders, that require special attention. Therefore, anxiety is defined by an emotional state that interferes with one's mental and physical condition, wielding pressure on multiple systems of our body and exerting influence over our behavior. Although it is normal and inevitable in our lives, it can have a negative impact when not handled in the best way. The Diagnostic and Statistical Manual of Mental Disorders [3] explains how anxiety disorders can be expressed in the form of panic disorder, generalized anxiety disorder (GAD), social anxiety disorder, specific phobia, agoraphobia, separation anxiety disorder, and anxiety disorder due to another medical condition. Experience and observation suggested that people who show stress, anxiety, or panic attack problems present with symptoms characterized by atypical respiratory activity. Sighing can also be seen as affected during these psychological disorders. During these psychiatric crises, breathing was inferred as the most affected factor.

Breathing is an imperative process controlled by the autonomic nervous system (ANS) and various studies have been conducted correlating both the ANS activity and respiratory activity in response to emotions in general, but more specifically, to anxiety, revealing alterations in the breathing process and/or changes in the breathing control [4,5]. Many authors have studied the correlations between breathing patterns and respiratory features regarding anxiety disorders. Some examples of this are [6] that correlated respiratory frequency, tidal volume, and end-tidal PCO2 with anxiety traits from volunteers; [7] associated panic disorder patients (PD) with hyperventilation; [8] hypothesized that patients with PD don't perform diaphragmatic breathing and have a lower vital capacity percentage; [6] studied the patterns of respiration in individuals with induced stress to provoke anticipatory anxiety; [8] investigated the capacity of 28 PD patients to perform diaphragmatic breathing and its effect on vital capacity percentage (%VC), which is the total volume of air that can be displaced from the lungs by maximal expiratory effort; [9,10] suggest a correlation between the anxiety state of an individual and the musculoskeletal system; among many other studies.

The importance of breathing and other parameters to help in the detection of anxiety is referred by various authors. Therefore, there is an increase in the development of computational tools to analyze these parameters to detect anxiety states, at certain moments. Hence, in this paper, we develop a system that allows stress/relaxation (relax) detection using machine learning models. As system input, we defined real-time and offline sources, thus, introducing the ability to follow patients in real-time or analyze the data after events occurred.

The remaining sections of this paper are organized as follows: Sect. 2 a literature review was performed describing the work related to our approach; in Sect. 3, we describe our Anxiety Monitoring System and its steps; Sect. 5 enumerates the limitations and future work; and finally, Sect. 6 describes the conclusions of present work.

2   Literature Review

To support our work, we performed a literature review to analyse related studies of stress/anxiety monitoring systems. In the following paragraphs, the literature review is described and detailed.

[11] proposed the development of a method to monitor psychological stress in real life, detecting it accurately, continuously, and in an unobtrusively way. This application includes 3 machine learning components: a laboratory stress detector, an activity-recognition classifier, and a context-based stress detector. The parameters used in this work are blood volume pulse, heart rate, inter-beat interval, electrodermal activity, and skin temperature. Several algorithms were tested for this task - Majority classifier, J48, Naive Bayes, KNN, SVM, Bagging, Boosting, Random Forest, and Ensemble Selection.

[12] proposed a model using 3 machine learning algorithms, specifically, logistic regression, support vector machine, and naive bayes, to detect mental health stress using electroencephalogram signals. The results showed good potential with 94.6% accuracy for binary stress classification and 83.4% accuracy for multi-level stress classification.

[13] proposed a deep learning model, using a CNN, for evaluating psychological stress levels from breathing patterns, denominated "DeepBreath". The proposed CNN architecture of this work consists of 2 convolutional layers, 2 pooling layers, and one fully connected layer. The participants were given 2 types of cognitive tasks with different difficulty levels, to induce stress. Stress classification was made in a binary classification (no-stress, stress) and a multi-class classification (none, low and high-level). The CNN achieved 84.59% accuracy with binary classification and 56.52% accuracy in multi-class classification.

[14] proposed a model using 5 machine learning algorithms, namely, decision tree, random forest, naive bayes, support vector machine, and k-nearest neighbor to predict occurrences of anxiety, depression, and stress on 5 different levels of severity. According to the authors, the random forest classifier demonstrated to be the best model for the task.

[15] proposed a monitoring system for anxiety disorders by analyzing physiological signals of emotion features. The system denominated "i-RISE" assesses biosignal features like eye-event, activity-related, and heart rate parameters and ambient features like temperature and humidity parameters. With labeled user input, the developed work was validated using a Bayesian network for anxiety detection achieving values of 90% accuracy.

3   Anxiety Monitoring System

This section proposes an Anxiety Monitoring System, built under a pipeline that performs a supervised machine learning classification for stress/anxiety monitoring using multiple physiological parameters. Figure 1 depicts the system with its different steps.

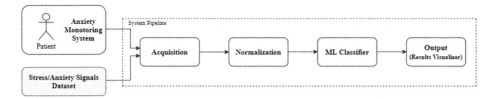

Fig. 1. Anxiety monitoring system pipeline.

The very first step is to search and acquire a useful dataset with relevant variables and annotations of the subject's different mental states. After the data acquisition, it is necessary to normalize the data, or, in other words, it is necessary to process and prepare the data into a format that can be used in the machine learning model. The following step is to adapt and implement a machine learning model and input the already normalized data. The machine learning model classifies these data and outputs the results of the classification, returning it to a visualizer.

3.1   Acquisition Step

This step proposes a stage for data acquisition that consists of an offline acquisition source. More specifically, finding a dataset with relevant physiological variables to assess the states of stress/anxiety of patients that could be used to test/train our classification models.

A major issue in this was regarding annotated datasets that could be used in a context of stress/anxiety state of the patient data, they are few and with limitations. Nevertheless, a dataset was found and considered suitable for our offline acquisition source. The dataset is associated with the paper called *"Non-EEG Dataset for Assessment of Neurological Status"* [16] and available in an open database called "Physionet". The dataset contains data from twenty healthy subjects collected using non-invasive wrist-worn biosensors at the quality of life laboratory at the University of Texas at Dallas. The physiological variables measured consisted of:

- electrodermal activity (EDA);
- temperature;
- heart rate (HR);
- arterial oxygen level (SpO2);
- accelerometer.

The last variable was not considered in the present work due to its context and some lack of information in the literature for being a viable marker for stress/anxiety detection. Figure 2 presents an example of the physiological signals measured from subject 1. For the data collection, the authors used a step procedure divided into seven stages, described below:

1. relaxation moment;
2. walking/jogging exercises to simulate physical stress;
3. relaxation moment;
4. mini-emotional stress phase;
5. math exercises to simulate cognitive stress;
6. relaxation moment;
7. visualization of a clip of a horror movie to simulate emotional stress;
8. relaxation moment

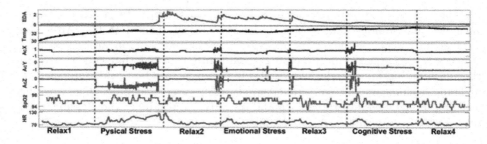

Fig. 2. Measured physiological signals from subject 1, respectively electrodermal activity, temperature, accelerometer, arterial oxygen level, and heart rate [16].

3.2 Normalization Step

The dataset is composed of a set of digital files that grouped physiological signals, divided into two recordings per subject (patient). One record contains information on the accelerometer, temperature, and EDA signals, and the other contains information on the SpO2 and heart rate signals. These recordings are provided in waveform-database format (WFDB). Additionally, one annotation file per subject is given with information on time location and labels of stress transition states.

To develop a machine learning model in the Python programming language, first, a conversion of the WFDB data files into comma-separated value files (CSV) is needed, which is possible through the PhysioBank website. After that, it was necessary to prepare the data. For this, we used pandas, which is a powerful, open-source, data analysis and manipulation tool very useful for this type of work. The CSV files were red in pandas and transformed into dataframes for better management. Next, for each dataframe (20 with the accelerometer, temperature, and EDA signals and another 20 with SpO2 and heart rate signals) unwanted variables were removed, in this case, it was only the accelerometer data. After that, an annotation column with the stress state of the subjects was added. Then, a compilation of the 20 dataframes with temperature, and EDA signals was done and the same for the 20 files with the SpO2 and heart HR signals. Finally, there was a need to reshape the data since the sample intervals for the two file types are different. The temperature and EDA signal dataframe has a sample interval of 0.125 s, while the SpO2 and heart rate signal dataframe has a sample interval of 1 s. Therefore, to concatenate both data frames into another capable of being used in the machine learning model, they should have matching row sizes, which was accomplished by downsampling the temperature and EDA signal data frame by a factor of 8. The final product of all these operations performed on our data culminates on what can be seen in Fig. 3. Since the values of each signal may vary slightly from each other, thus showing a bad distribution, a standard scaler function was used to resize the distribution so that the mean of the values becomes 0.

The script is available for download in github.com/DiogoPL99/Anxiety_ Monitoring_System-_A_Preliminary_Approach/tree/main.

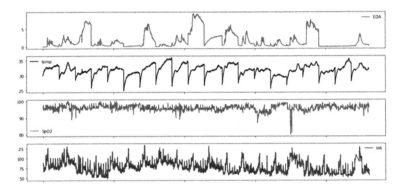

Fig. 3. Processed and compiled physiological signals from 20 subjects, respectively electrodermal activity, temperature, accelerometer, arterial oxygen level, and heart rate.

3.3   Machine Learning Classifier Step

As part of our system, a step was introduced for class prediction given a set of data points, in this study, the stress and relaxation moments of a certain patient. For this step, we implement a classification model that reads the input physiological signals and classifies data as stress and relax labels. To implement this classifier, we evaluate a set of machine learning algorithms, listed below:

– logistic regression;
– decision tree;
– random forest;
– k-nearest neighbor;
– naive bayes.

These are the most known and common algorithms and they were trained and tested using the chosen dataset. However, we established a procedure, described in Fig. 4, that consists of the division of the dataset into two sets: 70% for training, and 30% for testing. The training set has the purpose of generating the classification models, one for each machine learning algorithm and the testing set is used to evaluate the model's performance allied with a few chosen performance metrics.

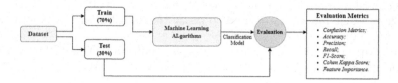

Fig. 4. Procedure to train/test the generated models.

3.4   Output Step

This final step permits the system output, the idea behind this step is to create a simple, but powerful, web-based or application visualizer to present the classifier results over time. This way, it is possible to better analyze the data for either self or autonomous stress/anxiety monitoring, or resort to a specialist like psychologists or psychiatrists to help them in their functions. Figure 5 shows a simplistic line plot visualization of the classification results for the random forest classifier of the first 100 entries.

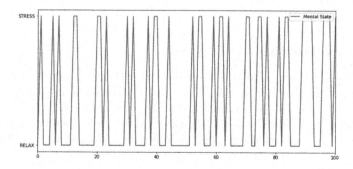

Fig. 5. Random forest classifier results for the first 100 entries.

4   Results and Discussion

After using 70% of the data as training and running the other 30% for testing, the model results for each algorithm used were obtained and crossed for comparison. Figure 6 shows the general schematic of a binary confusion matrix, which is often used to assess machine learning algorithm performances where the true positive (TP) represents the number of instances that the algorithm correctly classified that indicates the presence of a condition or characteristic (presence of stress), true negative (TN) represents the number of instances that the algorithm correctly classified that indicates the absence of a condition or characteristic (absence of stress, or relaxed state), false positive (FP) represents the number of instances that the algorithm classified wrongfully and that indicates the presence of a condition or characteristic, and, lastly, false negative (FN) represent the number of instances that the algorithm classified wrongfully and that indicates the absence of a condition or characteristic. These values on the confusion matrix are needed for the calculations of several metrics, some of them employed as seen below.

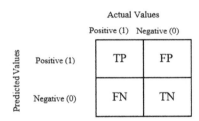

Fig. 6. Overall schematic of a binary confusion matrix.

Table 1 display the confusion matrices results of each algorithm used.

Table 1. Binary confusion matrix tables.

Logistic Regression		Decision Tree		Random Forest	
4273	1824	5568	529	5714	383
2208	3423	1287	4344	495	5136

K-Nearest neighbor		Naive Bayes	
5168	929	4459	1638
888	4743	2462	3169

Table 2 synthesizes the results obtained for each classification model employing different metrics: Accuracy (Acc), Precision (P), Recall (R), F1-Score, and Cohen Kappa Score. Each metrics gives different information:

– Accuracy - gives the percentage of instances predicted correctly by the model;
– Precision - measures how many instances the model classified correctly when predicting a specific label (relax or stress);
– Recall - provides information on how many instances out of all instances with a specific label, the model classified correctly;
– F1-Score - consists of the harmonic mean between the precision and recall metrics;
– Cohen Kappa Score - is a reliability measure, that evaluates how much better your classifier is performing over another one that guesses the class at random, only considering the frequency of each class. It establishes a level of agreement between the 2 classifiers, it's value is given in percentage and can be interpreted this way: value <20% poor agreement, 21–40% indicates fair agreement, 41–60% indicates moderate agreement, 61–80% indicates good agreement and value >80% indicates almost perfect agreement [17].

Table 2. Evaluation measures

Classifier	Classification	Accuracy	Precision	Recall	F1-Score	Cohen Kappa Score
Logistic regression	Relax	0.66	0.66	0.70	68	0.31
https://www.overleaf.com/project/ 629e6e61aac913bf25ea2f7d	Stress		0.65	0.61	63	
Decision Tre	Relax	0.85	0.81	0.91	0.86	0.68
	Stress		0.89	0.77	0.83	
Random Forest	Relax	0.92	0.92	0.94	0.93	0.84
	Stress		0.93	0.91	0.92	
K-Nearest Neighbor	Relax	0.85	0.85	0.85	0.85	0.69
	Stress		0.84	0.84	0.84	
Naive Bayes	Relax	0.65	0.64	0.73	0.69	0.30
	Stress		0.66	0.56	0.61	

Out of all five algorithms used, the one that showed the best results is the classifier that was trained using the *Random Forest* algorithm with an overall accuracy of **92%**, additionally also had the best values for Precision, Recall, and F1-Score both on relax and stress labels, and a Cohen Kappa Score of 84% showing good reliability on the results.

The classifiers trained with *Decision Tree* and *K-Nearest Neighbor* algorithms followed with the best results having 85% accuracies. *Naive Bayes* and *Logistic Regression* algorithms revealed poor results with accuracies under 70% and relatively low Precision, Recall, and F1-Score metrics, also Cohen kappa score evaluates these results as having poor reliability.

The standard procedure is to use 70–80% of the data for training and 20–30% as testing. After a trial-and-error approach, the 70–30% setup presented the best results with an increase of 0.01 accuracy in all five algorithms. In the classifier's parameters, for the *Decision Tree* and *Random Forest* algorithms using a max depth (maximum depth of the tree) parameter value of 10 proved to optimize our results, since setting this value too high might cause over-fitting and setting it too low may increase errors. Also, in the *K-Nearest Neighbor* algorithm, the k value, which represents the number of neighbors, was adjusted to 80, apparently showing the best outcome.

The dataset authors in [16] proposed a classification method using a supervised neural network system and an unsupervised machine learning clustering method called the Gaussian mixture model (GMM). Unlike this work, the classification task was multi-modal, which means the authors classified the data into 4 different categories - relaxation; physical stress; emotional stress, and cognitive stress. The neural network employed consisted of 1 input layer, a hidden layer with 4 neurons, and 4 outputs, one for each class.

From the results, we can infer that the neural network achieved almost perfect results with 98.8% accuracy and values above 98% for sensitivity, specificity, and precision, while the GMM algorithm provided a little poorer result, but still good with accuracy levels of 84.6% and decent sensitivity, specificity, and precision values. When comparing our random forest classifier, the best classifier out of the 5 algorithms used, with these scores we can assume its performance behaved better than GMM's, but was still worse than the neural network system. Keeping in mind that our algorithms are a binary classification (Relax and stress) and these authors are doing multi-modal classification (Relaxed, Physical stress, emotional stress, and cognitive stress)

5 Limitations and Future Work

For future work, in order to improve the proposed work, some paths may be taken. One of them is acquiring data from a real-time acquisition source, using equipment with sensors attached to performs measures of physiological parameters. Making our own measurements instead of using an available dataset, gives us more control and authenticity over the data. Also, build a machine learning model using only parameters from the respiratory system that are relevant to stress/anxiety detection. Some examples of this are the respiratory frequency, end-tidal CO_2 levels, presence of hyperventilation, presence of sighing, vital capacity percentage, rib cage diameter, and electromyography of respiratory muscles of interest such as the diaphragm and external intercostals muscles. It would be interesting and enriching to make a multi-modal classification, focusing on different types of stress/anxiety, like physical, cognitive, and emotional stress. Refining the model, testing different algorithms, and changing its parameters is also always worth considering in order to improve the results.

Our ultimate goal in this work is the application of this technology to self and autonomous stress/anxiety detection purposes or partner it with specialists that deal with these problems on a day-to-day basis like psychologists or psychiatrists.

6   Conclusion

This paper addressed the challenge that emerges from dealing with anxiety as an event detected by a computer system. Thus, this system could help patients and their psychologists or psychiatrists to reduce the impact of anxiety in their day-to-day life. From the literature review, it is unanimous that anxiety disorder is the most common type of mental health disorder. Although there is still much space in this field to learn and improve, many correlations between our body's system and stress/anxiety are already established and well described in the literature.

As mentioned, there is good evidence of interactions between anxiety and the respiratory system more concretely in parameters such as the respiratory frequency, the presence of sighing, hyperventilation, end-tidal CO2 levels, vital capacity percentage, and respiratory muscle activity, emphasizing the diaphragm and the external intercostal muscles.

In this work, we used five of the most common algorithms capable of performing the classification task proposed namely, logistic regression, decision tree, random forest, k-nearest neighbor, and naive bayes algorithms. Developed using a dataset available in a database called "Physionet", this work is focused on the building of a classification model for detecting stress. Data parameters of electrodermal activity, temperature, arterial oxygen levels, and heart rate were taken from 20 subjects and used to train and test the supervised machine learning classification model with a distribution of 70–30%, respectively. Out of the 5 classifiers used the one achieving the best results was the random forest algorithm with an overall accuracy of 92%, which is a pretty good score. Precision, recall, and f1score metrics above 90% for both relax and stress classes and a Cohen kappa score of 84% showing good reliability in these results. The model could successfully classify stress in individuals using these 4 sets of parameters.

References

1. Dattani, S., Ritchie, H., Roser, M.: Mental health. Our World in Data 2018 (2022)
2. American Psychiatric Association. https://www.psychiatry.org. Accessed 08 Mar 2022
3. Edition, F.: Diagnostic and statistical manual of mental disorders. Am. Psychiatric Assoc. **21**, 591–643 (2013)
4. Kop, W.J., Synowski, S.J., Newell, M.E., Schmidt, L.A., Waldstein, S.R., Fox, N.A.: Autonomic nervous system reactivity to positive and negative mood induction: the role of acute psychological responses and frontal electrocortical activity. Biol. Psychol. **86**(3), 230–238 (2011)
5. Kreibig, S.D.: Autonomic nervous system activity in emotion: a review. Biol. Psychol. **84**(3), 394–421 (2010)
6. Masaoka, Y., Homma, I.: The effect of anticipatory anxiety on breathing and metabolism in humans. Respir. Physiol. **128**(2), 171–177 (2001)
7. Tolin, D.F., McGrath, P.B., Hale, L.R., Weiner, D.N., Gueorguieva, R.: A multisite benchmarking trial of capnometry guided respiratory intervention for panic disorder in naturalistic treatment settings. Appl. Psychophysiol. Biofeedback **42**(1), 51–58 (2017)

8. Yamada, T., Inoue, A., Mafune, K., Hiro, H., Nagata, S.: Recovery of percent vital capacity by breathing training in patients with panic disorder and impaired diaphragmatic breathing. Behav. Modif. **41**(5), 665–682 (2017)
9. Schleifer, L.M., Ley, R., Spalding, T.W.: A hyperventilation theory of job stress and musculoskeletal disorders. Am. J. Ind. Med. **41**(5), 420–432 (2002)
10. Ritz, T., Meuret, A. E., Bhaskara, L., Petersen, S.: Respiratory muscle tension as symptom generator in individuals with high anxiety sensitivity. Psychosom. Med. **75**(2), 187–195 (2013)
11. Gjoreski, M., Luštrek, M., Gams, M., Gjoreski, H.: Monitoring stress with a wrist device using context. J. Biomed. Inform. **73**, 159–170 (2017)
12. Subhani, A.R., Mumtaz, W., Saad, M.N.B.M., Kamel, N., Malik, A.S.: Machine learning framework for the detection of mental stress at multiple levels. IEEE Access **5**, 13545–13556 (2017)
13. Cho, Y., Bianchi-Berthouze, N., Julier, S.J.: DeepBreath: deep learning of breathing patterns for automatic stress recognition using low-cost thermal imaging in unconstrained settings. In: 2017 Seventh International Conference on Affective Computing and Intelligent Interaction (ACII), pp. 456–463. IEEE, October 2017
14. Priya, A., Garg, S., Tigga, N.P.: Predicting anxiety, depression and stress in modern life using machine learning algorithms. Procedia Comput. Sci. **167**, 1258–1267 (2020)
15. Sundaravadivel, P., Goyal, V., Tamil, L.: i-RISE: an IoT-based semi-immersive effective monitoring framework for anxiety disorders. In: 2020 IEEE International Conference on Consumer Electronics (ICCE), pp. 1–5. IEEE, January 2020
16. Birjandtalab, J., Cogan, D., Pouyan, M.B., Nourani, M.: A non-EEG biosignals dataset for assessment and visualization of neurological status. In: 2016 IEEE International Workshop on Signal Processing Systems (SiPS), pp. 110–114. IEEE, October 2016
17. Grandini, M., Bagli, E., Visani, G.: Metrics for multi-class classification: an overview. arXiv preprint arXiv:2008.05756 (2020)

Optimization

Optimization

Statistical Analysis of Voice Parameters in Healthy Subjects and with Vocal Pathologies - HNR

Débora Cucubica André[1], Paula Odete Fernandes[2] (iD), and João Paulo Teixeira[1,2(✉)] (iD)

[1] Research Centre in Digitalization and Intelligent Robotics (CeDRI) and Laboratório Para a Sustentabilidade E Tecnologia Em Regiões de Montanha (SusTEC), Instituto Politécnico de Bragança, Campus de Santa Apolónia, 5300-253 Bragança, Portugal
a43858@alunos.ipb.pt, joaopt@ipb.pt
[2] Applied Management Research Unit (UNIAG), Instituto Politécnico de Bragança, 5300-253 Bragança, Portugal
pof@ipb.pt

Abstract. In this article, a statistical analysis of the Harmonic to Noise Ratio (HNR) parameter was performed using the boxplot tool in the SPSS software, using the Cured Database with 901 individuals (707 pathological and 194 control) to create relevant groups, enabling the automatic identification of these dysfunctions. We analyzed whether the HNR parameter for all control and pathological subjects were compared between various voice groups, gender, vowel, and tone, no difference in HNR can be considered between the male and female gender of healthy and pathological voices. Still, there are differences between the vowels and tones of each gender. Trends indicate that this parameter is a good resource for an intelligent diagnostic system, using the vowels /a/ and /u/ in high tones.

Keywords: HNR · Statistical analysis · Cured database · Boxplot · Voice pathologies · Vocal diagnosis

1 Introduction

The diagnosis of speech pathologies is traditionally performed through video laryngoscopy and videostroboscopy exams, which are invasive, uncomfortable for patients, and expensive [1]. An alternative way to diagnose vocal pathologies is using an automatic method based on speech processing techniques. It is a non-invasive method, is fast, and can be a pre-diagnosis of such pathologies [2, 3].

There are two classic approaches in the characterization of vocal pathologies: the acoustic analysis, where features such as fundamental frequency jitter and shimmer are evaluated [4], and the spectral analysis based on noise parameters, where signal-to-noise ratio parameters and the study of the spectral energy of the signal are considered [5].

The harmonic characteristics of the voice can be measured in three parameters, Autocorrelation, NHR (Noise to Harmonic Ratio), and HNR (Harmonic to Noise Ratio), which is the object of study in this article.

A. I. Pereira et al. (Eds.): OL2A 2022, CCIS 1754, pp. 175–186, 2022.
https://doi.org/10.1007/978-3-031-23236-7_13

The HNR measure contains harmonic and noise components information and is sensitive to various periodicities such as jitter and shimmer [6]. This measure is the ratio of the harmonic component's energy and the noise component's energy [7]. It represents the degree of acoustic periodicity expressed in decibels dB.

The harmonic component arises from the vibration of the vocal cords, and the noisy components arise from glottal noise. It reflects the efficiency of the phonation process and characterizes the amount of noise present in the signal spectrum. Its purpose is to determine the degree of dysphonia. The lower the HNR, the more noise there is in the voice [4].

There is a strong relationship between how we perceive voice quality and the HNR. It is a relevant parameter for the identification of speech pathologies because the higher the proportion of noise, the greater the perceived hoarseness, breathing, or roughness, and the lower the HNR. That is, a low HNR indicates a high level of hoarseness, and a high HNR indicates a low level of hoarseness [8].

Laryngeal pathology can lead to poor adduction of the vocal folds, increasing the amount of random noise in vocal production. The problem with vibrating the vocal folds due to growth, paralysis of one or both vocal folds, or another type of laryngeal problem leads to more air escaping during the vibration, creating turbulent noises [9].

This paper aims to perform a statistical analysis using the boxplot tool in the SPSS software using the Cured Database [10] with 9 speech records from different individuals, of which 707 are pathological and 194 control using the HNR parameter.

The HNR measurement was analyzed for all subjects in the database (control and pathological (all pathologies)), comparing different conditions such as vowel, tone, and gender. The objective is to create relevant groups, enabling the automatic identification of these dysfunctions.

2 Methodology

This section presents the database, the pathologies used, present the HNR parameter and the statistical analysis.

2.1 Database

In the development of this paper, the Cured Database was used. This database includes several parameters. In this article, only the HNR was used, extracted from 9 voice registers corresponding to 3 vowels in 3 tones for subjects with 19 pathologies, plus control subjects.

In [10, 11], the Cured Database was built and organized based on the Saarbrucken Voice Database (SVD) [12]. The German database of speech files SVD is available online from the Institute of Phonetics of the University of Saarland. The SVD database comprises voice signals from more than 2000 people with and without pathologies. Each person has the recording of the phonemes /a/, /i/, and /u/ in low, neutral/normal, and high tones, varying between tones, and the German phrase Guten Morgen, Wie Geht es Ihnen? (Good morning, how are you?). The size of the sound files is between 1 and 3 s, recorded with 16 bits resolution and a sampling frequency of 50 kHz [4].

The Cured Database is available in.xls format through the link: http://www.ipb.pt/~joaopt/ and includes several parameters extracted from sounds produced by patients distributed in 19 speech pathologies and one control group. The parameter set of this database consists of jitter, shimmer, HNR, NHR, autocorrelation, and Mel cepstral frequency coefficients (MFCC) extracted from the sound of sustained vowels /a/, /i/ and /u/ in high, low and normal tones and a short phrase in German. The Cured Database has a total number of 901 individuals [10], In this article, the German phrase was not used, and the statistical analysis was performed only with the HNR parameter.

2.2 Pathologies Used in the Database

All pathologies from the Cured Database defined in [10] and [13, 14] were used. In Table 1, the groups studied are presented, each pathological condition was mentioned, and the total size of each sample.

2.3 HNR Parameter

The HNR is a measure that relates the periodic component (corresponding to vocal fold vibration) with the non-periodic component (glottic noise, mainly inter harmonic energy), indicating the efficiency of the phonation process [15].

There is a significant correlation between HNR values and the hoarseness and breathiness parameters [15]. The noisy component is greater the smaller the harmonic components of the issuance. Its value is expressed in dB.

The HNR is, by definition, a logarithmic measure of the ratio of energies associated with the two components, which assumes the integration of spectral power over the audible range of frequencies (see Eq. (1)) [16].

$$HNR = 10 \times \log_{10} \frac{\int_w |H(w)|^2}{\int_w |N(w)|^2} \tag{1}$$

The H(w) corresponds to the harmonic component and N(w) to the noise component.

The logarithmic measure owes its pertinence to the good correlation with the perception of sound intensity (or sound volume). In other words, the HNR attempts to measure the perception of the relationship between the periodic component of a voiced sound and its noise component.

In practice, spectrum calculation is performed using efficient techniques like the FFT. The spectrum is calculated, not as a continuous function but as a sampling of this function, so that, in practice, the integration operator gives a place for the sum (Eq. (2)) [16].

$$HNR = 10 \times \log_{10} \frac{\sum_k |H(w_k)|^2}{\sum_k |N(w_k)|^2} \tag{2}$$

An efficient low complexity algorithm to determine HNR in voiced speech audio files was presented in [17].

Table 1. Groups used for the study.

Group	Sample size male	Sample size female	Total individuals
Control	71	123	194
Vocal Cord Paralysis	67	102	169
Hyper functional dysphonia	32	95	127
Functional Dysphonia	24	51	75
Dysphonia	29	40	69
Spasmodic Dysphonia	22	40	62
Psychogenic Dysphonia	13	38	51
Chronic Laryngitis	25	16	41
Reinke's Edema	5	29	34
Vocal Cords Polyps	17	10	27
Carcinoma of the Vocal Cords	18	1	19
Hypofunctional Dysphonia	8	4	12
Hypopharyngeal Tumor	5	–	5
Laryngeal Tumor	3	1	4
Cyst	1	2	3
Intubation Granuloma	3	–	3
Granuloma	1	1	3
Hypotonic Dysphonia	2	–	2
Fibroma	–	1	1
Laryngeal Dysphonia	1	–	1

2.4 Descriptive Statistical Analysis

Every statistical analysis should start with a good descriptive analysis of the data so that, from graphs and tables, it is possible to know and better understand the data set and decide which inferential analysis should be performed. Although simple, visualizing data from charts is a powerful tool that allows quickly identifying patterns and relationships between variables in the data set. The Boxplot is one of the most valuable graphs in statistical analysis [18].

A Boxplot is a graph in which it is possible to represent the relationship between a quantitative (numerical) variable and a qualitative variable. The Boxplot's vertical axis represents the quantitative variable's values, and the horizontal axis represents the categories of the qualitative variable [19]. In the construction of the Boxplot, some percentiles (median, first, and third quartiles) are used that are little influenced by extreme values.

Initially, the normality test (Kolmogorov-Smirnov) [20] was performed in SPSS. According to Table 2, it was verified that our variable does not have a normal distribution ($p < 0.05$). In this situation, the Boxplot is the ideal statistical analysis because this type of graph must show the central tendency, the dispersion (observations between the first and the third quartile), and data showing extreme values. This set of information is helpful for comparing variables that have wide variability.

Table 2. Normality test result.

	Kolmogorov-Smirnov[a]		
	Statistic	df	Sig.
HNR_dB	.080	8028	$p < .001$

[a]Lilliefors Significance Correction

This article presents a statistical analysis of healthy and pathological voices. The HNR measure was used for all subjects in the Cured Database (control and pathological (all pathologies)), analyzing it by comparing different conditions such as vowel, tone, gender, and pathology. For the gender Analysis of HNR, a comparison was made between the three sustained vowels (/a/, /i/ and /u/) in the three tones (low, neutral, high), and the control and pathological groups were also analyzed. And all these comparisons were made by separating the male gender from the female gender. For the case of the analysis of HNR in vowels, a comparison was made in the three tones (low, neutral, high) in the groups (control and pathological) separating each sustained vowel. For the analysis of the HNR in Tones, a comparison was made for the groups separated by each tone. For the analysis of HNR in Control/Pathological groups, a general comparison of these 2 groups was made across the entire database. And finally, in a more specific way, a comparison was made of the control group with 6 pathologies (in which they have more than 50 individuals), namely: Dysphonia, Functional Dysphonia, Hyperfunctional Dysphonia, Psychogenic Dysphonia, Vocal Cord Paralysis, and Spasmodic Dysphonia.

It should be mentioned that previous to the statistical analysis, the outliers were identified and replaced by limit values (maximum and minimum), as seen in Fig. 1. The interquartile range is given by the difference between the first and third quartiles (IQR = Q3-Q1). The removal of outliers is crucial for this study because some audio files contain speech without any harmonicity resulting in HNR values being extremely low or even extremely high due to error measurements. These extreme values are unrealistic and would distort the analysis of HNR because, generally, there is a relatively low difference between healthy and pathologic voices. The extreme values are also natural but correspond to very low voice quality and are acoustically perceived.

In the different comparisons, statistically significant differences were found, which will be described in the next section.

3   Results and Analysis

A comparison of the HNR parameters is made in the first instance between the female and male genders. The records of the three vowels of the three tones in a total of 9 different records for each individual in the two control and pathological groups were used.

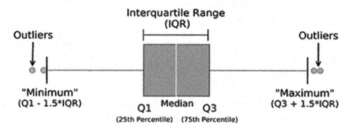

Fig. 1. Boxplot information

The boxplot graphs, the analysis of these graphs is based on [21] in which there are 3 situations. In the 1st, there is no overlap between the boxes, so there is a difference between the groups. In the 2nd, the boxes overlap without their medians, so there is probably a difference between the groups. In the 3rd, the boxes medians overlap, and no distinction can be considered between the groups.

3.1   Gender Comparison

The comparisons in Fig. 2 show a tendency of higher HNR in the vowels /u/ and /i/ compared to the vowel /a/. But, there are no statistically significant differences between vowels /u/ and /i/ in both genders. Nevertheless, vowel /a/ was a statistically significant difference in HNR to vowels /u/ and /i/ in both genders because, according to the graph, the boxes and medians overlap.

Concerning the gender comparison, no statistical difference can be observed between genders in any vowel, tone or control/pathological groups. Despite this, there is a tendency for higher HNR in all cases in female voices.

This is probably because males use a more fluid voice and the basal register, characterized by less glottal closure force, favoring a decrease in harmonics and more glottal noise.

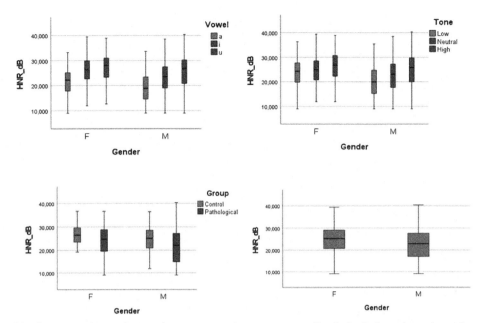

Fig. 2. Comparison of HNR between vowels, tones, control/pathological, and gender using Boxplot

3.2 Vowel and Tone Comparison

Analyzing the comparisons made in the graphs in Fig. 3, a statistically significant lower HNR in vowel /a/than in vowels /i/ and /u/at the three tones can be seen. This was already regarded in the comparison by gender in the previous section. The control group presents a statistically significant higher HNR than the pathological group in vowel /a/, but only a tendency of higher values for the other two vowels. There is no difference between /i/ and /u/ but again /a/ vowel confirms to have lower HNR.

Concerning the tone in Fig. 4, the high tone has higher HNR than the low tone. There is a tendency for HNR to increase along the vowels /a/, /i/ and /u/. There is a tendency for higher HNR in the control group than in the pathological group for the three tones.

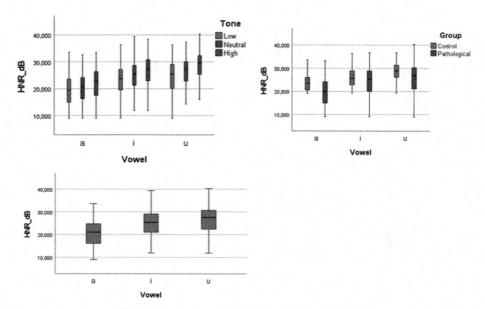

Fig. 3. Comparison of HNR Boxplot for the vowels

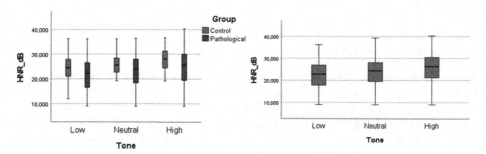

Fig. 4. Comparison of HNR Boxplot for tones

3.3 Control and Pathological Comparison

Analyzing the comparisons presented in Fig. 5, no statistically significant difference between the control and pathological groups can be considered. Still, the control group tends towards higher HNR values.

The previous analysis was done by grouping the subjects of the 19 pathologies. An attempt to separate the analysis for the pathologies with the higher number of subjects resulted in the comparison of 6 pathologies and the control group. This Boxplot shows a statistically significantly lower value of HNR for Vocal Cord Paralysis than the control group. Still, no difference was found for the other pathologies against the control group.

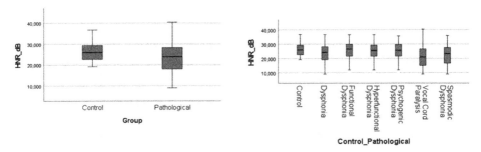

Fig. 5. Comparison of HNR Boxplot for the control-pathological

4 Discussion

Analyzing the results of previous works [22], it can be seen that the following differences were reported in the HNR:

- Higher HNR in High tone than in Neutral and LOW tone.
- Higher HNR in the vowel /u/ than in /i/ and /a/ in the control group.
- Lower HNR in the vowel /a/ than in /u/ and /i/ in dysphonia groups.

Analyzing the results of the work [23], the following can be verified about the HNR:

- There is no difference between gender (although it tends to be slightly greater for females).
- HNR is higher in the High tones (it is in line with the previous work).
- HNR is higher in the vowel /u/ (it agrees with the previous work).

Analyzing the results of the work [21], the following can be verified about the HNR:

- There is a significant difference between the control group and the Laryngeal Tumor pathology.
- There may be a difference between the control group and the pathologies: Reinke's Edema and Carcinoma.
- There is no difference between control and other pathologies.

The present work intends to continue the work started in [21–23]. In [22], the statistical analysis was performed between the control group and 4 speech pathologies only, while in the present work, 19 speech pathologies were included emphasizing the 6 with more than 50 individuals. The current work also verified the differences reported in [22]. Despite the Dysphonia group has not separated by vowels, there was a lower HNR in the vowel /a/ than in /u/ and /i/ in the pathological group.

In the current paper, the research was carried out for healthy and pathological voices. In the article [23], the statistical analysis was performed only for healthy voices. By the work [23], no significant difference was found between genders, only in healthy voices.

This non-difference from HNR is confirmed and extended to pathological voices in current research.

In [21], it was confirmed that there is no difference between the control and the other pathologies. In this article, it was verified. The specific analysis of the Laryngeal Tumor, Reinke's Edema, and Carcinoma pathologies were not performed for the reasons mentioned above. According to the criteria used to select the 6 pathologies, there are differences between the control group and the pathology of Vocal Cord Paralysis.

5 Conclusion

In this article, the Cured Database was used to compare different pathologies with the control group, differences in gender, vowels, and tones for the HNR parameter along healthy and pathological voices.

Concerning the gender comparison, the HNR parameter did not register statistical significance. No difference can be considered between male and female voices, but there is a tendency for higher HNR for female voices.

There are differences between the female vowels /a/ and the male vowel /a/, between the vowels /a/ and /i/ and between the vowels /a/ and /u/. Therefore, the HNR in the vowel /a/ is an interesting parameter for artificial intelligence tools in developing automatic techniques for pre-diagnosis speech pathologies.

Comparing vowels and tones shows a tendency towards higher values of HNR in the high tone for the three vowels. There is a tendency for higher HNR for the control than for the pathological group in the three tones (low, neutral, and high), making them interesting parameters. There are differences between the low and high tones. There is a tendency for higher HNR for the control group than the pathological group along the three vowels.

No statistically significant difference between the control and pathological groups can be considered, but the control group has a tendency for higher HNR values.

There are statistically significant differences between the control group (higher HNR) and Vocal Cord Paralysis pathology.

As future work, already undergone, a similar comparison would be extended to the other parameters, Jitter, Shimmer and Autocorrelation, present in the Cured Database.

Acknowledgments. The authors are grateful to the Foundation for Science and Technology (FCT, Portugal) for financial support through national funds FCT/MCTES (PIDDAC) to CeDRI (UIDB/05757/2020 and UIDP/05757/2020) and SusTEC (LA/P/0007/2021).

References

1. de Almeida, N.C.: Sistema inteligente para diagnóstico de patologias na laringe utilizando máquinas de vetor de suporte. Universidade Federal do Rio Grande do Norte, p. 119 (2010). https://repositorio.ufrn.br/jspui/handle/123456789/15149
2. Cordeiro, H.T.: Reconhecimento de patologias da voz usando técnicas de processamento da fala. Ph.D. thesis, Universidade NOVA de Lisboa, p. 142 (2016). https://run.unl.pt/bitstream/ 10362/19915/1/Cordeiro_2016.pdf

3. Guedes, V., et al.: Transfer learning with audioset to voice pathologies identification in continuous speech. Procedia Comput. Sci. **164**, 662–669 (2019). https://doi.org/10.1016/j.procs.2019.12.233
4. Fernandes, J.F.: Determinação da Autocorrelação, HNR e NHR para Análise Acústica Vocal, p. 84. Master's thesis at the Polytechnic Institute of Bragança (2018)
5. Cordeiro, H.: Parâmetros espectrais de vozes saudáveis e patológicas, no. June, pp. 19–22. Lisbon Polytechnic Institute (2019)
6. Murphy, P.J., Akande, O.O.: Quantification of glottal and voiced speech harmonics-to-noise ratios using cepstral-based estimation. In: Proceedings of 3rd International Conference Non-Linear Speech Processing, no. Nolisp 05, pp. 224–232 (2005)
7. De Sousa, R.J.T.: A New Accurate Method of Harmonic-To-Noise Ratio Extraction, pp. 351–356. School of Engineering, University of Porto (2011). https://doi.org/10.5220/000155290 3510356
8. Franco, D.L.S.: Composição corporal, postura e produção de fala. Universidade de Lisboa (2016)
9. Freitas, S.: Avaliação Acústica e Áudio Percetiva na Caracterização da Voz Humana. Faculdade de Engenharia da Universidade do Porto, p. 251 (2012)
10. Fernandes, J., Silva, L., Teixeira, F., Guedes, V., Santos, J., Teixeira, J.P.: Parameters for vocal acoustic analysis - cured database. Procedia Comput. Sci. **164**, 654–661 (2019). https://doi.org/10.1016/j.procs.2019.12.232
11. Teixeira, J.P., Fernandes, J., Teixeira, F., Fernandes, P.O.: Acoustic analysis of chronic laryngitis statistical analysis of sustained speech parameters. In: BIOSIGNALS 2018 - 11th International Conference on Bio-Inspired Systems and Signal Processing. Proceedings; Part 11th International Joint Conference on Biomedical Engineering Systems and Technologies, BIOSTEC 2018, vol. 4, no. Biostec, pp. 168–175 (2018). https://doi.org/10.5220/000658630 1680175
12. Martínez, D., Lleida, E., Ortega, A., Miguel, A., Villalba, J.: Advances in Speech and Language Technologies for Iberian Languages. Communications in Computer and Information Science, vol. 328, pp. 99–109 (2014). https://doi.org/10.1007/978-3-642-35292-8
13. Passerotti, G.: Doenças Benignas Da Laringe, pp. 1–18 (2005)
14. Guimarães, F.: Patologia da Mucosa das Cordas Vocais. Faculdade de Medicina de Lisboa Universidade de Lisboa, pp. 1–28 (2018)
15. Faria, J.C.F.: Avaliação Complementar da Voz através de Medidas Acústicas de longo Termo em Vozes Disfonicas. Escola Superior De Saúde Politécnico Do Porto (2020)
16. Lopes, J.M.D.S.: Ambiente de análise robusta dos principais parâmetros qualitativos da voz. Faculdade de Engenharia da Universidade do Porto, p. 71 (2008). http://repositorio-aberto.up.pt/bitstream/10216/58997/1/000136648.pdf
17. Fernandes, J., Teixeira, F., Guedes, V., Junior, A., Teixeira, J.P.: Harmonic to noise ratio measurement - selection of window and length. Procedia Comput. Sci. **138**, 280–285 (2018). https://doi.org/10.1016/j.procs.2018.10.040
18. IBM and SPSS: IBM SPSS statistics base 25, p. 341 (2017)
19. Reis, E.A.: Análise Descritiva de Dados. Universidade Federal de Minas Gerais (2002)
20. Miranda, A.: Testes Não Paramétricos, pp. 1–29 (2020)
21. de Oliveira, A.A., Dajer, M.E., Fernandes, P.O., Teixeira, J.P.: Clustering of voice pathologies based on sustained voice parameters. In: BIOSIGNALS 2020 - 13th International Conference on Bio-Inspired Systems and Signal Processing. Proceedings; Part 13th International Joint Conference Biomedical Engineering Systems and Technologies, BIOSTEC 2020, no. Biostec, pp. 280–287 (2020). https://doi.org/10.5220/0009146202800287

22. Teixeira, J.P., Fernandes, P.O.: acoustic analysis of vocal dysphonia. Procedia Comput. Sci. **64**, 466–473 (2015). https://doi.org/10.1016/j.procs.2015.08.544
23. Teixeira, J.P., Fernandes, P.O.: Jitter, Shimmer and HNR classification within gender, tones and vowels in healthy voices. Procedia Technol. **16**, 1228–1237 (2014). https://doi.org/10.1016/j.protcy.2014.10.138

Integrated Feature Selection and Classification Algorithm in the Prediction of Work-Related Accidents in the Retail Sector: A Comparative Study

Inês Sena[1,2,3(✉)] ⓘ, Laires A. Lima[1,2] ⓘ, Felipe G. Silva[1,2] ⓘ,
Ana Cristina Braga[3] ⓘ, Paulo Novais[3] ⓘ, Florbela P. Fernandes[1,2] ⓘ,
Maria F. Pacheco[1,2] ⓘ, Clara B. Vaz[1,2] ⓘ, José Lima[1,2] ⓘ,
and Ana I. Pereira[1,2] ⓘ

[1] Research Center in Digitalization and Intelligent Robotics (CeDRI), Instituto
Politécnico de Bragança, Campus de Santa Apolónia, 5300-253 Bragança, Portugal
{ines.sena,laires.lima,gimenez,fflor,pacheco,clvaz,
jllima,apereira}@ipb.pt
[2] Laboratório para a Sustentabilidade e Tecnologia em Regiões de Montanha
(SusTEC), Instituto Politécnico de Bragança, Campus de Santa Apolónia, 5300-253
Bragança, Portugal
[3] ALGORITMI Centre, University of Minho, 4710-057 Braga, Portugal
acb@dps.uminho.pt, pjon@di.uminho.pt

Abstract. Assessing the different factors that contribute to accidents in
the workplace is essential to ensure the safety and well-being of employees. Given the importance of risk identification in hazard prediction,
this work proposes a comparative study between different feature selection techniques (χ^2 test and Forward Feature Selection) combined with
learning algorithms (Support Vector Machine, Random Forest, and Naive
Bayes), both applied to a database of a leading company in the retail sector, in Portugal. The goal is to conclude which factors of each database
have the most significant impact on the occurrence of accidents. Initial
databases include accident records, ergonomic workplace analysis, hazard
intervention and risk assessment, climate databases, and holiday records.
Each method was evaluated based on its accuracy in the forecast of the
occurrence of the accident. The results showed that the Forward Feature
Selection-Random Forest pair performed better among the assessed combinations, considering the case study database. In addition, data from
accident records and ergonomic workplace analysis have the largest number of features with the most significant predictive impact on accident
prediction. Future studies will be carried out to evaluate factors from
other databases that may have meaningful information for predicting
accidents.

Keywords: Feature selection · Classification algorithms · Accident
prediction

© The Author(s), under exclusive license to Springer Nature Switzerland AG 2022
A. I. Pereira et al. (Eds.): OL2A 2022, CCIS 1754, pp. 187–201, 2022.
https://doi.org/10.1007/978-3-031-23236-7_14

1   Introduction

In 2019, according to Eurostat, in the EU, there were 3.1 million non-fatal accidents, with a higher incidence in the manufacturing industry (18.7% of the total in the EU in 2019), wholesale and retail trade (12.3%), construction (11.8%) and human health and social assistance activities (11.0%). Spain, France, and Portugal were the EU Member States with the highest number of non-fatal accidents per 100 000 employed persons [9].

According to the statistics of accidents at work listed in the Pordata database, in Portugal, the tertiary sector is the primary economic activity sector that contributes to the high number of accidents in the workplace, being the sector of "wholesale and retail, repair of motor vehicles and motorcycles" the main contributor to the number of accidents at work [18].

Occupational accidents and diseases impact operations and costs for companies, workers, and society, decisively affecting the quality of life and the economy. Thus, it is evident the loss of productive capacity, in terms of lost working days, as well as the compensation and pensions to be paid to a large extent by companies. Each non-fatal accident in 2019 in the EU resulted in at least four days of absence from work, which implies a cost between 2.6% and 3.8% of the Gross Domestic Product (GDP) [6].

Then, the health and safety issues in the workplace should be a priority in social and economic policies since security-related concerns are empirically integrated into work performance [1]. The most common indicator of lack of safety in the workplace is the occurrence of accidents [2]. As such, work-related accidents have been the subject of several studies over the years, with the development of theories that try to explain, prevent and reduce them. The most used actions to combat occupational accidents in other sectors are investigating accidents and implementing preventive measures, for example, reducing the excessive workload [5] and providing information and training on Occupational Safety and Health (OSH) to workers [6], among others.

To study hazards, risks, and accidents at work, the other sectors use descriptive statistic tools or tools based on conventional statistical techniques [16], which consist of a historical summary based on detailed information collected about the circumstances of an accident at work. However, there are already different methods of analysis and identification of hazards and risks that help prevent workplace accidents, for example, the ergonomic assessment in the workplace and the hazards identification and risk assessment.

Some studies indicate the ergonomic conditions of a company's workplace as influential factors in the quality of work, stress and physical exhaustion of the employee, and the occurrence of accidents [10,13,14]. Ergonomics, therefore, plays an important role in identifying risks, developing and applying reliable assessment tools, methodologies, and techniques, and defining preventive recommendations to help reduce exposure risks, improve work organization, and design workplaces adequate work [3]. This evaluation is performed by an analyst who checks the postures and movements adopted by an employee performing his/her duties, by calculating different methods, from RULA, REBA, among others.

Bearing this in mind, it is essential to examine the ergonomic conditions in the retail sector due to the high proportion of manual work in handling heavy goods and physiologically unfavorable postures that can trigger future musculoskeletal injuries to employees, which start losses in the sector in terms of money, time and productivity.

Another method for preventing and reducing accidents is the identification of hazards and risk assessment, which investigates situations in the existing activities of an organization that can be harmful to the health and safety of employees.

Risk assessment is the basis for preventing accidents at work and occupational health problems, as it aims to implement the required measures (such as adequate information and training for workers) to improve the health and safety of workers, as well as, in general, contributing to improving the performance of companies [8,22].

However, with the evolution of Artificial Intelligence (AI) techniques, companies must invest in new technologies to improve the safety of employees, and consequently, their productivity and safety. A predictive analytics solution based on AI has already been implemented in several areas, such as the construction industry [19], manufacturing [11], among others, for these purposes, and consequently, in the reduction of injuries in the workplace.

An example of use, is the application of various data-mining techniques to model accident and incident data obtained from interviews carried out shortly after the occurrence of an incident and/or accidents to identify the most important causes for the occurrence of accidents in two companies in the mining and construction sectors, and consequently, develop forecast models that predict them [19]. Another example is the development of a model, through the Random Forest algorithm, to classify and predict the types of work accidents at construction sites using the importance of characteristics and analyzing the relationship between these factors and the types of occupational accidents (OA) [11].

Thus, predictive analytics can analyze different data about the causes of OA and find connecting factors. However, there are few studies aimed at determining the range of factors that give rise to an accident, their interactions, and their influence on the type of accident. Hence, it is challenging to design the kind of well-founded accident prevention policy that is the fundamental objective of safety systems-security management [16].

Taking into account the factors enumerated above, the main objective of the present work is to acquire the features that have the most significant impact on the occurrence of accidents, using different and large databases from a retail company under study. The secondary aim of this research is to compare feature selection methods and classification algorithms for the prediction of workplace accidents. In order to achieve the listed goals, five pre-processed databases (accident records, ergonomic workplace analysis, hazard identification and risk assessment, climate database, and holiday records) will be combined. Thus, two selection methods – χ^2 test and Forward Feature Selection - will be compared and combined with the three selection algorithms prediction - Support Vector

Machine, Random Forest, and Naive Bays – in order to get the relevant features and the selection method-algorithm prediction pair that offer the best accuracy.

The rest of the paper is organised as follows. The methods used during the preparation are reported in Sect. 2. Section 3 presents the database as well as the pre-processing techniques that were used. The methodology that was followed to achieve the listed objectives as set out in Sect. 4. In Sect. 5, the results obtained are presented and discussed. Finally, the study is concluded, and future work is presented in Sect. 6.

2   Methods

To achieve the specified objectives and find the features that obtain the best precision in accident prediction, two methods were selected, and three Machine Learning classification algorithms were established for comparison. The feature selection methods and the prediction algorithms were used and will be described below.

2.1   Feature Selection

A common problem in Machine Learning is determining the relevant features to predict a specific output while maintaining a good model performance. Feature selection is essential because not all variables are equally informative. Selecting an appropriate number of features can directly lead to a better fit, a more efficient and straightforward predictive model, and better knowledge concerning how they interact, which are fundamental factors in the correct interpretation of the problem [4]. Although the use of feature selection techniques implies an additional complexity added to the modeling process, it has the benefits of decreasing processing time and predicting associated responses [4]. In the case of classification problems where the input and output variables are categorical and numerical, it is advisable to use a suitable statistical test to handle the heterogeneity of the data to determine the level of relationship between the variables. This step also simplifies the database, considering the high number of features present in the global database. The most significant features in accident prediction were selected by the χ^2 test and Forward Feature Selection (FFS). These methods were chosen because they have different approaches and for comparison purposes. The output variable adopted was the cause of the accident, divided into 12 categories:

- Physical aggression.
- Hit by object, equipment, or particles.
- Collision (between two or more vehicles).
- Contact with sharp or sharp material agent.
- Object/Environment contact - hot or cold.
- Contact with hazardous substances (gases, vapors, liquids).
- Welding (machines, equipment).

- Blow/Shock against equipment/fixed structure.
- Sting (insects/fish).
- Fall at the same level.
- Fall from height.
- Over-effort.

The χ^2 test enables to test the independence between input and output variables, whether numerical or categorical, based on observed and expected values. The null hypothesis (H_0) of the χ^2 test states that the two variables i and j, in a contingency table, are independent while the alternative hypothesis (H_1) states that these variables are not independent. The χ^2 statistic is calculated according to:

$$Q = \sum_{i=1}^{r} \sum_{j=1}^{c} \frac{(O_{ij} - E_{ij})^2}{E_{ij}} \tag{1}$$

where O_{ij} is termed as the observed frequency, and E_{ij} is termed as the expected frequency for each pair of variables i an j classified in r and c categories, respectively [21]. If H_0 is true, Q follows the χ^2 distribution with $(r-1)(c-1)$ degrees of freedom; and when two variables i and j are independent, the actual and expected values are similar, implying a low Q value and indicating that the hypothesis of independence (H_0) between them is not rejected [21]. For the prediction model, the input variables must be strongly related to the output variable.

Forward Feature Selection (FFS) is an alternative in selecting relevant features, a wrapper method through its implementation of Forward Feature Selection. FFS corresponds to an iterative method that starts with an empty set. In each iteration, the feature that improves the accuracy is added until the addition of a new variable does not improve the performance of the model. In other words, the method is based on the search and definition of subgroups of features that achieve the best accuracy, as illustrated in Fig. 1.

2.2 Predictive Algorithms

Support Vector Machine (SVM) is a supervised Machine Learning algorithm that can be used for both regression and classification challenges, aimed at train and classifying a database. It does not limit data distribution and is mainly used for small samples [21]. SVM aims to find a hyperplane in an n-dimensional space (with n being the number of features) that distinctly classifies the data points, as shown in Fig. 2.

There are infinite possibilities for the hyperplane that separates two groups of data, so the algorithm seeks to find a plane with a maximum margin, which is described by the maximum distance between the points of both groups. The database points can be written as $(\vec{x_i}, y_i), ..., (\vec{x_n}, y_n)$ [17], where the vector $\vec{x_i}$ can be represented by -1 or 1. On the other hand, the hyperplane is described by the Eq. (2) [17]:

$$\vec{w}\vec{x} - b = 0 \tag{2}$$

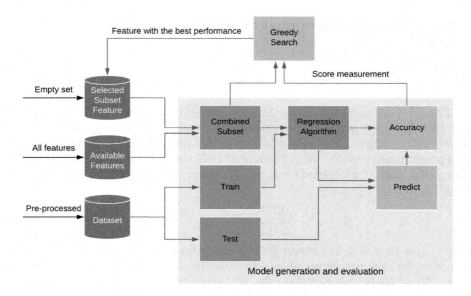

Fig. 1. Functioning of forward feature selection technique. Adapted from [20].

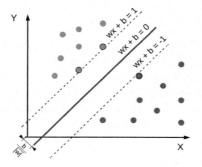

Fig. 2. Support vector machine classifier. Adapted from [17].

The normal vector is represented by $\vec{w}$ while the offset of hyper place along $\vec{w}$ is by $\dfrac{b}{||\vec{w}||}$, more details can be seen in [17]. Maximizing the margin distance allows future data points to be sorted more confidently. Support vectors are data points closest to the hyperplane and influence the position and orientation of the hyperplane. The classifier margin can be maximized using these vectors, and the optimal plane can be drawn.

Random Forest (RF) is composed of Decision Trees formed by a data sample extracted from a training set with replacement, called a bootstrap sample. Of this training sample, one-third of it (out-of-bag sample) is reserved as test data. Once more, a group of random data is injected through feature clustering, adding more diversity to the database and reducing the correlation between the decision trees. The determination of the forecast is based on majority voting, that is, the selection of the most frequent variable. Finally, an out-of-bag sample is used for cross-validation [12]. Figure 3 shows the typical structure of Random Forests.

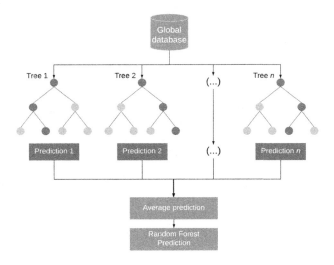

Fig. 3. Random Forest classifier. Adapted from [12].

Random Forest algorithms start with three primary hyperparameters, namely the node size, the number of trees, and the number of features sampled, defined before the training step. From there, the random forest classifier can be used to solve regression or classification problems [12].

Naive Bayes (NB) is a simple probabilistic classifier based on the application of Bayes' theorem [17]:

$$P(A|B) = \frac{P(B|A)P(A)}{P(B)} \tag{3}$$

where A and B are the events (or features), $P(A|B)$ is the probability of A given B is true, $P(B|A)$ is the probability of B given A is true, and $P(A)$ and $P(B)$ are the independent probabilities of A and B.

In basic terms, a Naive Bayes classifier assumes that each feature independently contributes to the probability of the output variable [17]. The conditional probability was calculated considering that the global database has numerical and categorical data. Although Naive Bayes does not account for resource interactions, it is efficient in predicting classification problems. The advantage of the Naive Bayes classifier is that it only requires a small amount of training data to estimate the means and variances of the variables needed for classification. As the independent variables are not specified, only the variances of the variables for each label need to be determined and not the entire covariance matrix [7].

3   Case Study

This section examines and describes how the database was developed and its characteristics. In addition, the pre-processing techniques used to adapt the database to the algorithms' attributes to improve their performance will also be described.

3.1   Database

The database used comprises information from five different databases:

- Accident records – contain information on the general characteristics of the injured employees (age, seniority, etc.), the conditions of the accident (place, time, sector, a task performed at the time of the accident, etc.), the damage caused (severity, type of injury, etc.) and the cause of the accident.
- Ergonomic Workplace Analysis (EWA) – includes the values calculated in an analysis of the postures and movements adopted by employees performing their duties by calculating different methods from RULA, REBA, among others.
- Hazard Identification and Risk Assessment (HIRA) – is composed of risk levels associated with the detail of the micro tasks in each work section.
- Climate database – includes weather data from across the country, since 2019 and 2021 automatically extracted from external sources, more information at [20].
- Holiday records – comprises registration of all national and municipal holidays that occurred between 2019 and 2021 in Portugal, automatically extracted from external sources, see in [15].

Data from accident records, EWA, and HIRA, were collected between 2019 and 2021 from different supermarkets of a company in the retail sector. Thus, the global database was developed through the integration of the five databases mentioned above, resulting in a total of 128 instances or records, totaling 122 input factors and 12 output factors after removing record lines with missing information or out of context. In Fig. 4, the method of association of the five databases can be observed, since they are integrated by the common factors which are the microtask (accident records, EWA, HIRA) and the event date (accident records, climate database, and holiday records).

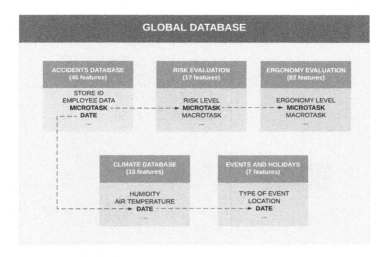

Fig. 4. Methodology adopted for the preliminary integration of simple databases in the formation of the global database.

3.2 Database Pre-processing

The original database was encoded in numerical form since many Machine Learning algorithms do not operate directly on the label data, requiring the input and output variables to be numeric. In other words, categorical data in the global database were converted into a numerical form, more precisely using One Hot Encoding. In this method, each feature is identified with 0 and 1 according to the presence or absence of the feature. This pre-processing step allows the binarization of the categories. Thus, they can be included in the training of the models without assigning weight, as in the case of a simple label encoding.

Then, the global database was normalized in order to increase the learning algorithms' efficiency. Once applied, database normalization ensures that all values are in the range between zero and one.

4 Methodology

The methodology for developing supervised Machine Learning models for accident prediction based on the historical database of a retail company is shown in Fig. 5. A detailed description of each step is discussed.

For the execution of the χ^2 test, the steps adopted were the definition of the null and alternative hypotheses, the creation of a contingency table, the calculation of expected values, calculation of the χ^2 statistic, and acceptance or rejection of the null hypothesis. The significance level considered was 0.10, and the features were selected based on the level of correlation with each target.

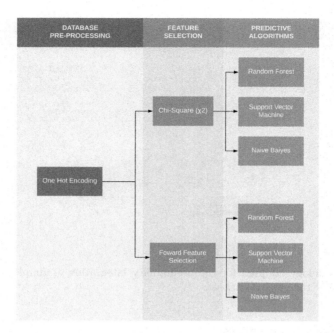

Fig. 5. Methodology for building classification algorithms to predict accidents in the retail sector.

In contrast to the χ^2 test, FFS relies on learning machine methods to select the significant features. Thus, the method becomes more computationally expensive but has better chances of assertiveness. This technique builds feature subgroups with the highest accuracy, which was performed according to the steps in Fig. 1. Since some algorithms (like SVM and NB) are not prepared to predict multiple targets and the database used is composed of 12 different accident causes (targets), the procedure described was carried out for each target (that is, when a target was selected one, the rest were set to zero) to increase the certainty in the selection of features and the performance of the learning algorithms.

The FFS method was executed multiple times for each search algorithm. The FFS feature selection process is usually not deterministic, and the search strategy influences the result. Thus, the repetition of the method sought to identify the most commonly selected features to avoid specific scenarios, atypical subgroups, and overfitting. The FFS method chose up to 10 features for each target. The selection of features and quantities per target was decided according to the average performance obtained by the input features.

The predictive model bias and the average accuracy are the selected features considered to perform the quality analysis of the models generated by learning algorithms using the selected features.

The process was performed with unbalanced data since the global database contains only real data. Strategies to simulate data were not used, so 'false' data did not influence the feature selection process.

Predictive models can present biased predictions created by unbalanced data and still have high accuracy. To optimize accuracy and reduce the number of input features, the FFS can opt for a predictive model which always uses the most dominant label as the final answer. Due to this factor, the metric (4) more sensitive to unbalanced databases was developed considering the percentage of hits of each label.

$$accuracy = \frac{1}{L} \sum_{i=1}^{L} \frac{C(L_i)}{T(L_i)} \tag{4}$$

where L is the number of labels, C is the number of correct predictions of a label L_i, and T is the total number of occurrences of a label L_i.

The metric was used to guide feature choices. The implemented FFS uses the greedy search algorithm as a search strategy, which determines the best feature according to a previously chosen metric. Thus, the models were optimized regarding their quality and not for the total number of hits, seeking the set of features capable of simultaneously creating models with the lowest prediction bias and better accuracy.

5   Results and Discussion

Taking this procedure into account, a better understanding of the results involved the separation into:

- True Positive (TP) – indicates the number of times the model was assertive in the selected target.
- True Negative (TN) – represents the number of times the learning algorithm detected the non-corresponding causes of the accident, that is, the non-occurrence of an accident.
- False Positive (FP) – shows the number of times the model missed the selected target.
- False Negative (FN) – reveals the number of times the model did not identify the accident.
- Final accuracy – shows the overall score for each learning algorithm.

These metrics were calculated because they differentiate assertiveness from precision value. Since the TP and TN metrics enable the identification of the predictive trend about impact, the FP and FN metrics allow identifying the predictive trend about model errors. Table 1 shows the results obtained for each combination tested.

Observing Table 1, it is notable that the FFS selection method obtained greater absolute precision combined with the different classification algorithms, which indicates that by using this selection method, it is possible to get more

Table 1. Results obtained by the adapted confusion matrix and accuracy tests in terms of TP, TN, FP and FN, and final accuracy. The values consider the average calculated based on 1000 executions of the algorithm.

Parameters		Results (% correct answers in 1000 tests)				
Feature selection	Classification algorithm	TP	TN	FP	FN	Final accuracy
χ^2	SVM	0.1233	**0.9967**	**0.0033**	0.0797	0.9239
FFS	SVM	**0.5078**	0.9875	0.0125	**0.0447**	**0.9475**
χ^2	RF	0.2523	**0.9945**	**0.0055**	0.0679	0.9328
FFS	RF	**0.7000**	0.9828	0.0172	**0.0272**	**0.9592**
χ^2	NB	0.5639	0.8407	0.1593	0.0396	0.8176
FFS	NB	**0.7436**	**0.9537**	**0.0463**	**0.0233**	**0.9361**

general hits and maximize the accuracy of less common labels. From all combinations with the FFS, Random Forest had the highest precision value.

Analyzing in more detail this table, it can be noted that the absolute precision of the pairs involving the χ^2 method is also high, however, an imbalance of results between the TP and TN metrics is identified, indicating little predictive assertiveness in the type of target, so the high precision value is not satisfactory for the final objective of the present study.

From these metrics, the FFS-NB pair also seems to be a good solution for accident prediction since it was more assertive in the type of target than the FFS-RF pair and only has a difference of 2.31% of ultimate precision. Through Table 1, it was possible to obtain that the best selection method is the FFS. Table 2 presents the number of features selected from each database in each prediction test with classification algorithms.

Table 2. Number of variables selected from each of the five databases using different combinations of Forward Feature Selection and classification algorithms.

Databases	Classification algorithms combined with FFS		
	Support Vector Machine	Random Forest	Naive Bayes
Accidents records	33	39	39
EWA	25	23	22
Climate database	9	11	10
Holiday records	6	5	5
HIRA	3	3	4
Total	**76**	**81**	**80**

Observing Table 2, it can be mentioned that:

– SVM is the classification algorithm that obtains the smallest number of features, but in terms of precision (see Table 1), it is the one that gets the lowest value of absolute accuracy and assertiveness in the type of target.

– Unanimously, the accident registration and ergonomic workplace analysis
databases have the greatest number of significant features for predicting the
causes of accidents used.

Once again, the difference between RF and NB is minimal, just one feature
differentiating them. Thus, it can be mentioned that using the combination of
FFS-RF and FFS-NB leads to a good prediction of accidents. However, taking
into account what was intended with the present study (identifying the best
features for accident prediction), the FFS-NB pair presents better results since
it obtained a smaller number of features, it was more assertive in accident identification ($>$ TP) and was faster in getting the results than FFS-RF. Although
FFS-RF had a higher total precision, it was less assertive in predicting the accident, which does not fit with what is intended.

6   Conclusions and Future Work

This work presented a comparative study in which some of the standard methods of feature selection (χ^2 and FFS) and learning/classification (SVM, RF, and
NB) were applied to accident prediction. These methods were used to collect five
databases (obtained from a leading retail company in Portugal) and compared
their performance in predicting the causes of accidents. The pre-processing used,
One Hot Encoding, was crucial for the correct functioning of the learning algorithms since it made the training data more expressive and machine-readable
and, consequently, improved the accuracy of the classification algorithms compared to the database without treatment.

Regarding feature selection methods, it was possible to observe that, since
the FFS is a non-deterministic method, it can obtain different output results
at each execution. This obstacle was overcome by repeating the FFS multiple
times. In contrast, χ^2 presents a consistent result and lower computational cost
but ignores the type of learning model in which the data would be used.

Comparing different attribute selection methods combined with prediction
algorithms shows that the FFS-NB pair obtained fewer features, was more
assertive in identifying the accident ($>$ TP), and was faster in getting results
than FFS-RF. However, the FFS-RF presented better performance considering
absolute precision. Thus, considering the study's purpose, the FFS-RF pair is
the most suitable. Nevertheless, both pairs can be considered good options, so it
will be necessary to confirm this information through new tests, like sensitivity
testing and validation.

Taking into account the selection of features, it can be stated that it is
unanimous that the features with the most impact on accident prediction belong
to the databases: accident records and ergonomic workplace analysis.

In summary, the results revealed how an integrated feature selection and
classification algorithm could be a viable tool in identifying the most likely causes
of an accident in the workplace, in addition to the fact that the pre-treatment of
the databases and the choice of algorithms and rating metrics can substantially
influence the rating success.

Further studies include new databases with a potential relationship with the occurrence of accidents, the improvement of the algorithms presented in this work, and the possible testing of new algorithms.

Acknowledgement. The authors are grateful to the Foundation for Science and Technology (FCT, Portugal) for financial support through national funds FCT/MCTES (PIDDAC) to CeDRI (UIDB/05757/2020 and UIDP/05757/2020) and SusTEC (LA/P/0007/2021). This work has been supported by NORTE-01-0247-FEDER-072598 iSafety: Intelligent system for occupational safety and well-being in the retail sector. Inês Sena was supported by FCT PhD grant UI/BD/153348/2022.

References

1. Antão, P., Calderón, M., Puig, M., Michail, A., Wooldridge, C., Darbra, M.R.: Identification of occupational health, safety, security (OHHS) and environmental performance indicators in port areas. Saf. Sci. **85**, 266–275 (2016)
2. Beus, J.M., McCord, A.M., Zohar, D.: Workplace safety: a review and research synthesis. Org. Psychol. Rev. **4**, 352–381 (2016)
3. Capodaglio, E.M.: Occupational risk and prolonged standing work in apparel sales assistants. Int. J. Ind. Ergon. **60**, 53–59 (2017)
4. Cervantes, J., Garcia-Lamont, F., Rodríguez-Mazahua, L., Lopez, A.: A comprehensive survey on support vector machine classification: applications, challenges and trends. Neurocomputing **408**, 189–215 (2020)
5. Cioni, M., Sabioli, M.: A survey on semi-supervised feature selection methods. Work Employ. Soc. **30**, 858–875 (2016)
6. European Commission: Communication from the commission to the European parliament, the council, the European economic and social committee and the committee of the regions (2012). https://www.eea.europa.eu/policy-documents/communication-from-the-commission-to-1. Accessed 20 Jan 2022
7. Dukart, J.: Basic concepts of image classification algorithms applied to study neurodegenerative diseases. Brain Mapp., 641–646 (2015). https://doi.org/10.1016/B978-0-12-397025-1.00072-5
8. Encarnação, J.: Identificação de perigos e avaliação de riscos nas operações de carga e descarga numa empresa de tratamento e valorização de resíduos. Ph.D. thesis, Escola Superior de Tecnologia do Instituto Politécnico de Setúbal (2014)
9. Eurostat Statistic Explained: Accidents at work statistics. https://ec.europa.eu/
10. Garcia-Herrero, S., Mariscal, M.A., Garcia-Rodrigues, J., Ritzel, O.D.: Working conditions, psychological/physical symptoms and occupational accidents. Bayesian network models. Saf. Sci. **50**, 1760–1774 (2012)
11. Kang, K., Ryu, H.: Predicting types of occupational accidents at construction sites in Korea using random forest model. Saf. Sci. **120**, 226–236 (2019)
12. Liaw, A., Wiener, M.: Classification and regression by RandomForest. R News **2** (2002)
13. Loske, D., Klumpp, M., Keil, M., Neukirchen, T.: Logistics work, ergonomics, and social sustainability: empirical musculoskeletal system strain assessment in retail intralogistics. Logistics **5**, 89 (2021)
14. López-García, J.R., Garcia-Herrero, S., Gutiérrez, J.M., Mariscal, M.A.: Psychosocial and ergonomic conditions at work: influence on the probability of a workplace accident. Saf. Sci. **5** (2019)

15. Martins, D.M.D., et al.: Dynamic extraction of holiday data for use in a predictive model for workplace accidents. In: Second Symposium of Applied Science for Young Researchers - SASYR (2022, in Press)
16. Matías, J.M., Rivas, T., Martin, J.E., Taboada, J.: Workplace safety: a review and research synthesis. Int. J. Comput. Math. **85**, 559–578 (2008)
17. Muhammad, L.J., Algehyne, E.A., Usman, S.S., Ahmad, A., Chakraborty, C., Mohammed, I.A.: Supervised machine learning models for prediction of COVID-19 infection using epidemiology dataset. SN Comput. Sci. **2**, 11 (2021)
18. Pordata: Acidentes de trabalho: total e por sector de actividade económica. https://www.pordata.pt
19. Rivas, T., Paz, M., Martin, J.E., Matías, J.M., García, J.F., Taboada, J.: Explaining and predicting workplace accidents using data-mining techniques. Reliab. Eng. Syst. Saf. **96**, 739–747 (2011)
20. Silva, F.G., et al.: External climate data extraction using the forward feature selection method in the context of occupational safety. In: Gervasi, O., Murgante, B., Misra, S., Rocha, A.M.A.C., Garau, C. (eds.) ICCSA 2022. LNCS, vol. 13378, pp. 3–14. Springer, Cham (2022). https://doi.org/10.1007/978-3-031-10562-3_1
21. Trivedi, S.K.: A study on credit scoring modeling with different feature selection and machine learning approaches. Technol. Soc. **63**, 101413 (2020)
22. Wang, Y., Jin, Z., Deng, C., Guo, S., Wang, X., Wang, X.: Establishment of safety structure theory. Saf. Sci. **115**, 265–277 (2019)

Traffic Light Optimization of an Intersection: A Portuguese Case Study

Gonçalo O. Silva(✉)🆔, Ana Maria A. C. Rocha🆔, Gabriela R. Witeck🆔, António Silva🆔, Dalila Durães🆔, and José Machado🆔

Centro ALGORITMI, University of Minho, 4710-057 Gualtar, Braga, Portugal
g.oliveirasilva96@gmail.com, arocha@dps.uminho.pt,
{asilva,dalila.duraes}@algoritmi.uminho.pt, jmac@di.uminho.pt

Abstract. Smart cities aim to rise strategies that reduce issues caused by the urban population growth and fast urbanization. Thus, traffic light optimization emerges as an important option for urban traffic management. The main goal of this study is to improve traffic light management at a specific intersection, in the City of Guimarães (Portugal), where high-intensity traffic and an active pedestrian area were observed, generating traffic queues. To achieve the goals, a simulation-based optimization strategy using the Particle Swarm Optimization combined with the Simulation of Urban Mobility software was used to minimize the average waiting time of the vehicles by determining the optimal value of the traffic light cycle. The computational results showed it is possible to decrease by 78.2% the average value of the waiting time. In conclusion, by better managing the traffic light cycle time, traffic flow without congestion or queues can be achieved.

Keywords: Traffic lights · Particle swarm optimization · Simulation of urban mobility

1 Introduction

Traffic light optimization aims to improve the level of service offered on the roads, by reprogramming the traffic light controllers. Optimizing the transition phase or the shift between the signal timing plans can result in minimal travel time. Apart from the result to minimize the delay, queue length, the number of stops, and preventing congestion, traffic optimization will also have impact on promoting greater safety and comfort for road users, improving the quality of life and the economy, i.e., the excessive fuel consumption of vehicles.

This work has been supported by FCT-Fundação para a Ciência e Tecnologia within the R&D Units Project Scope: UIDB/00319/2020 and the project "Integrated and Innovative Solutions for the well-being of people in complex urban centers" within the Project Scope NORTE-01-0145-FEDER-000086.

A. I. Pereira et al. (Eds.): OL2A 2022, CCIS 1754, pp. 202–214, 2022.
https://doi.org/10.1007/978-3-031-23236-7_15

The goal of smart cities is to provide a possible solution to reduce the issues caused by the urban population growth and fast urbanization. In this environment, pedestrian crossings are one of the most dangerous places in the transport field. Most of the traffic accidents happen there. In urban areas, especially in inner cities, pedestrians crossing the street unquestionably affect the traffic flows [10], which raises the necessity to include pedestrians in the traffic analysis.

Among all the possible strategies already published in the literature, traffic light programming optimization arises as an interesting choice for urban traffic management, since it is an effective, safe, and low-cost solution [3,4,12]. The use of open-source software and simulation guarantees the faithful reproduction of the vehicles in the road system to be optimized.

This article is part of an ongoing research project. The preliminary results obtained in the scope of the project concerning traffic light optimization were promising. They were based on the literature review and some experiments to optimize the waiting time in the one-lane-two-ways traffic light problem, and indicated significant improvements in all aspects considered, in terms of programming languages, simulators, and optimization methods [11,13].

For this second part of the project, a simulation-based optimization strategy for the traffic light challenge is conducted, using offline real data. The main goal is to improve the traffic light management, in the city center of Guimarães (Portugal). The target of this article is a specific intersection of high intensity of traffic and pedestrian activity, that generates traffic queues, especially at certain times of the day and, consequently, originates delays in travel times, increased gas emissions and high economic expenses.

To achieve the goals, it was eligible for this study the Particle Swarm Optimization (PSO) [2,5,8], the Python Programming Language, and the Simulation of Urban Mobility (SUMO) [3,7], that is a portable microscopic road traffic simulation package that offers the possibility to simulate the traffic moving on the road networks. Based on these methodologies, different simulations are performed to define the number of vehicles that cause traffic congestion. Furthermore, the average waiting time is optimized and the obtained results for the traffic light cycle are compared to real data referring to the current cycle time of the traffic lights.

The paper is organized as follows: Sect. 2 describes the case under study, where Sect. 3 defines the data preparation regarding the problem definition in SUMO and Sect. 4 presents the network system configuration. The computational results are presented and analyzed in Sect. 5. Finally, Sect. 6 rounds up the paper with conclusions and future work.

2   Case Study Description

In the context of the project "Integrated and Innovative Solutions for the well-being of people in complex urban centers", the main objective is the study and design of a platform to be used as a decision support system capable of integrating data from different sources. The city of Guimarães is one of the target cities of the project. It was found that traffic in the center of Guimarães could be controlled in order to improve the well-being of people and the environment, reducing stress levels and the emission of gases [1]. These objectives can be achieved through the proper regulation of traffic lights.

In particular, a critical situation was identified in the city center of Guimarães where a lot of traffic was observed, generating traffic queues, especially at certain times of the day. Figure 1 shows the intersection responsible for the congestion of the traffic. This figure was obtained from the Street View feature of Google Maps where the location of each traffic light is displayed.

Fig. 1. Intersection in the city center of Guimarães.

The intersection involves five one-way streets. Av. Conde de Margaride, which leads to a traffic light at the point "A" of Fig. 1, Alameda Dr Alfredo Pimenta together with Av. São Gonçalo leads to a traffic light at the point "B", Rua de Gil Vicente leads to a traffic light at "C". There is a High school located next to point "D", so there is a crosswalk regulated by a traffic light. At the beginning of Rua Paio Galvão there is a crosswalk (point "E"), also regulated by traffic lights, with vehicles coming from directions "A" and "B". This street allows access to the city center.

3   Data Preparation

OpenStreetMap (OSM) is an open source platform formally managed by the OpenStreetMap Foundation that is developed by the contribution of a community of volunteer mappers that constantly update data regarding road network and points of interest all around the globe [9]. The open source traffic simulator SUMO [7] allows to simulate several traffic management topics. Like any other simulation software, it allows the assessment of infrastructure and policy changes before implementation.

In order to obtain the intersection area, presented in Fig. 1, the *Open-StreetMap* website through the OSM Web Wizard was used. OSM Web Wizard its a python script provided by SUMO that allows the selection of any network on the map and automatically converts it into SUMO. Additional parameters can be set in order to also extract vehicle routes, as well as the number of vehicles that will run during the simulation. After the conversion, it was noticed that the SUMO network did not correspond to the real network, namely, the number of lanes, the possible directions of each lane, the priority between different lanes and the traffic light cycle time, as shown in Fig. 2.

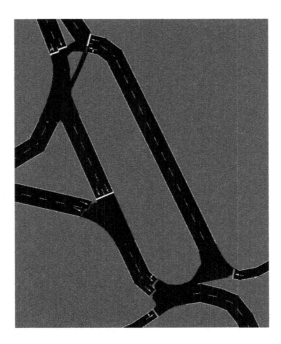

Fig. 2. SUMO network converted from OpenStreetMap: before corrections.

The information about all aspects of the intersection were gathered on-site. Concerning to fix the issues identified data corrections were made. The information regarding the number of lanes, possible directions of each lane and the removal of the option to make a U-turn, were added directly to the OSM platform. Additionally, slight adjustments were made to the positioning of the streets, over the OSM satellite image, to ensure that the streets had the correct length. After the overall correction of the network on OSM, the network files are directly edited, through the graphical network editor provided by SUMO (*netedit*), so that the model resembles reality.

In the network file, the real traffic light cycle was coded based on measurements carried out on-site. Thus, the cycle times of traffic lights at the intersection are shown in Table 1. The five traffic lights operate in a sequential order of 8 stages, which change according to the duration time and color of the traffic light. In the table, the first column, denoted by "Stage", refers to the sequential phase of the traffic lights, and the second column shows the time, in seconds, for each stage and the following columns refer to the traffic light color at each point "A" to "E" of Fig. 1.

Table 1. Current stages of the traffic lights in the network under study.

Stage	Time (s)	Traffic light color				
		A	B	C	D	E
1	20	Green	Red	Red	Green	Green
2	3	Yellow	Red	Red	Green	Green
3	3	Red	Red	Red	Green	Green
4	25	Red	Green	Green	Green	Green
5	3	Red	Yellow	Green	Yellow	Yellow
6	20	Red	Red	Green	Red	Red
7	3	Red	Red	Yellow	Red	Red
8	3	Red	Red	Red	Green	Green

The current fixed cycle, in a total time of 80 s, comprises 8 different stages. At each stage, a distinct set of light colors is present for each traffic light. The cycle starts at Stage 1, where the traffic light at point "A" is green, as well as the traffic lights at points "D" and "E", and proceeds sequentially until Stage 8. After that, the cycle starts again from Stage 1. Note that Stages 2, 5 and 7 refer to stages with fixed times, due to a mandatory yellow light between the transition of the green to red light with the duration of three seconds. Stages 3 and 8 correspond to a red light at the entry points of the intersection ("A", "B" and "C") and a green light on the exit points ("D" and "E") with a duration of three seconds. The purpose of this stage is to prevent the entry of vehicles and, at the same time, clear the intersection.

Using the editor, the crosswalks were added at points "D" and "E", as well as the corresponding traffic lights to stop the vehicles. The priority rules between vehicles were also corrected to be in accordance with the Portuguese road code.

The current network system after making all the corrections above described, can be seen in Fig. 3.

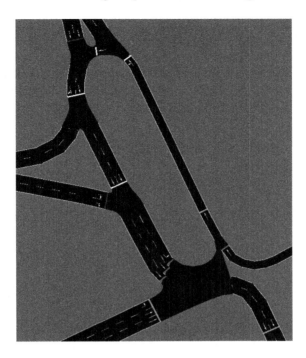

Fig. 3. SUMO network converted from OpenStreetMap: after corrections.

4   Network System Configuration

In order to determine the number of vehicles that congest the system network, a simulation of the real scenario was implemented in SUMO. The simulation involved the setting of some parameters in the OSM Web Wizard, namely the "Through Traffic Factor" and the "Count". The "Through Traffic Factor" defines how many times it is more likely for an edge at the boundary of the simulation area being chosen compared to an edge entirely located inside the simulation area. Thus, in all experiments this parameter value was set to 100 to ensure that each vehicle route starts and ends at the boundary of the system network. The "Count" parameter defines how many vehicles are generated per hour per kilometer. This parameter directly influences the number of vehicles in the system, providing the routes of each vehicle (starting point and final destination), and the time each vehicle enters the simulation.

Hence, several simulations were performed, with different "Count" values to find the number of vehicles that cause congestion in the system, by observing the "Depart Value" (an output value from SUMO) of the vehicles. That is, when the "Depart Value" in one of the cars is greater than zero, it means that there is congestion in the system. Therefore, starting the "Count" value at 10 and increasing it from 10 to 10, simulations were carried out with a duration time of 3600 s seconds of traffic until the "Depart Value" in one of the cars was greater than zero. For each of the simulations, the relationship between the average waiting time and the number of cars in the system was gathered. The waiting time corresponds to the time that each vehicle is stopped due to external factors like traffic lights and queues. Figure 5 shows the evolution of the average waiting time (in seconds) over the increasing number of vehicles in the network system.

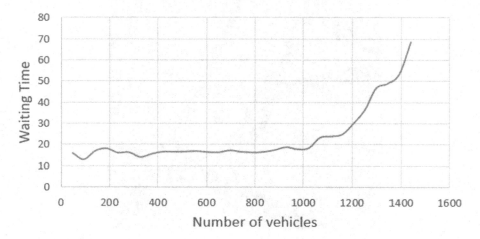

Fig. 4. Evolution of the average waiting time (in seconds) as the number of vehicles in the network system increases.

It can be seen that when the number of vehicles is greater than 1200 the average value of the waiting time increases considerably. When the parameter "Count" was set to 310, corresponding to a number of vehicles of 1440, a congestion on the traffic was verified and the average value of the waiting time was 68.69 s.

Another situation of the current network system was simulated in order to study the impact that crosswalks can have on traffic flow. This version consists of removing the traffic lights from the crosswalks at points "D" and "E". When the network system does not include crosswalks, the color of traffic lights at points "D" and "E" in Table 1 is represented by a green light for all stages. Figure 5 shows the evolution of the average waiting time (in seconds) relatively to the increase in the number of vehicles, when the crosswalks (and corresponding traffic lights) were not included in the network system.

A similar performance of the average waiting time was obtained for a traffic congestion with the same number of vehicles (1440 vehicles), when compared to the results presented in Fig. 4. However, in this version (without configuring crosswalks) the average waiting time reduced to 56.05 s, as expected.

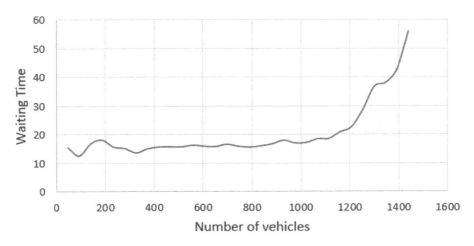

Fig. 5. Evolution of the average waiting time (in seconds) as the number of vehicles in the network system increases, without configuring the crosswalks.

5   Computational Results

5.1   Implementation Details

The strategy herein described intends to optimize the average waiting time of the system with 1440 vehicles, which corresponds to congested traffic, in order to obtain the optimal traffic light cycle times for the network. The simulation-based optimization strategy is developed as a two-step routine: the optimization algorithm and the simulation process. It consists of an interaction between the PSO algorithm, a global optimization algorithm that searches for optimal, or near-optimal, solutions of the traffic light cycle times, and the SUMO software to evaluate the solutions found by the PSO [11]. Figure 6 graphically shows this interaction. Each time PSO finds a traffic light cycle configuration, SUMO proceeds to test it and returns the average waiting time of each vehicle to find new configurations. Each time PSO finds a new traffic light cycle configuration, SUMO proceeds to test it and returns the average waiting time of each vehicle. In this way, after evaluating the solutions, PSO can compute new configurations. This cycle is repeated until the stopping criteria is reached.

In order to use the PSO algorithm, a set of predefined parameters should be set. The parameters that influence the behaviour of each particle, namely the inertia weight, cognitive and social constants were set to 0.729, 1.49445 and 1.49445, respectively, as suggested in [11]. The number of PSO particles was set to 20 and the maximum number of iterations was set to 50. Due to the stochastic nature of the PSO algorithm, 30 independent runs were performed.

Regarding the network system presented in Fig. 3, the python code was updated to embrace the new variables and the new network SUMO file. Some other small changes have also been made to the model before running the

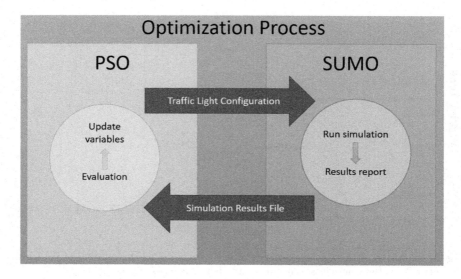

Fig. 6. Interaction between the PSO and SUMO.

simulation-based optimization strategy. According to the Portuguese standards for application on urban streets, the recommended green light phase time for a pedestrian to cross the road (equivalent to the red light phase to stop the vehicles) must be calculated considering a walking velocity of 0.4 m/s [6]. In this case, since each crosswalk is approximately 6 m long, the total time for Stage 6 plus Stage 7 should be 15 s. Furthermore, since Stage 6 and Stage 7 are directly connected to the crosswalk traffic light, as can be seen in Table 1, the minimum duration of Stage 6 should be 12 s. Thus, the bounds of the values on the variables representing the time, in seconds, for the Stages 1, 4 and 6 are [0, 80], [0, 80] and [12, 80], respectively.

The results were obtained using a PC running Windows 10 operating system equipped with AMD Ryzen 7 4800H CPU @ 2.90 GHz, 16 GB RAM.

5.2   Results and Discussion

The simulation-based optimization process obtained, on average, an average waiting time of 15.16 s, with a standard deviation of 0.11. The average execution time was 2119.99 s (about 35 min). The results of the best solution are presented in Table 2, where the first column shows the stage indicating the phase of the traffic lights, and the second column shows the obtained time, in seconds, for each stage. The last columns refer to the traffic light color at each point "A" to "E". The best solution obtained a time of 27.63 s for Stage 1, 22.70 s for Stage 4 and 12 s for Stage 6, with an average value of the waiting time of 14.99 s. Thus there is a reduction of 78.2% against an average waiting time value of 68.69 s in the real scenario (see Sect. 4).

Table 2. Optimized traffic light times for the network under study.

Stage	Time (s)	Traffic light color				
		A	B	C	D	E
1	27.63	Green	Red	Red	Green	Green
2	3	Yellow	Red	Red	Green	Green
3	3	Red	Red	Red	Green	Green
4	22.70	Red	Green	Green	Green	Green
5	3	Red	Yellow	Green	Yellow	Yellow
6	12	Red	Red	Green	Red	Red
7	3	Red	Red	Yellow	Red	Red
8	3	Red	Red	Red	Green	Green

To better analyze the traffic evolution during the simulation, a comparison of the number of vehicles in the system is made between the best optimized run and the real scenario. In Fig. 7, at 1500 s of the simulation, the real scenario starts to accumulate traffic inside the network until 3600 s, the moment where vehicles stop entering the simulation. On the other hand, the optimized scenario ensures an excellent traffic flow that never generates problematic traffic queues.

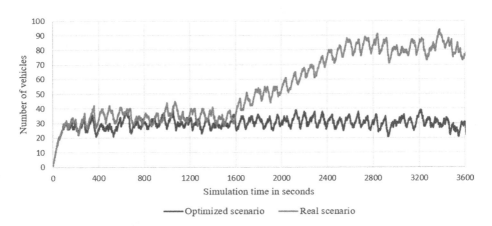

Fig. 7. Number of vehicles in the system along the simulation time of 3600 s, in the optimized scenario and in the real scenario.

In order to analyze the impact that crosswalks can have on traffic flow, the version without configuring the crosswalks was also studied. Note that when the network system does not include crosswalks, the color of traffic lights at points "D" and "E" are green light for all stages.

Among the 30 runs, on average, the average waiting time was 8.02 s with a standard deviation of 0.12. The standard deviation values obtained with and without the configuration of the crosswalks show that the model used can produce consistent results. The running time among the 30 runs took on average 2000.41 s (about 35 min). The best solution obtained the traffic light time of 14.30 s for Stage 1, 9.66 s for Stage 4 and 0 s for Stage 6. Note that when the crosswalks are not included, the Stage 6 should not exist, since it corresponds to the green traffic light at point "C". The best solution for the version without configuring the crosswalks reached an average waiting time of 7.72 s. When comparing this result with the average waiting time at the same situation in the real scenario (average waiting time of 56.05 s) a reduction of 86.2% was observed (see Sect. 4).

Figure 8 shows the number of vehicles in the system along the simulation time of 3600 s. A similar result can be observed, where about 1500 s of the simulation, the real scenario starts to have traffic congestion.

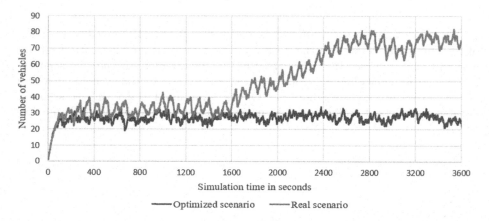

Fig. 8. Number of vehicles in the system along the simulation time of 3600 s, in the optimized scenario and in the real scenario, without configuring the crosswalks.

6   Conclusions

Urban mobility is an emerging challenge that drives contemporary cities towards smart solutions. In this context, traffic light optimization allows an interesting strategy for urban traffic management, while improving the level of service offered on the roads by reprogramming the traffic light controllers. Optimizing the transition phase or the shift between the signal timing plans can result in reduced travel time. Apart from the result of preventing traffic congestion, traffic light optimization will also have the impact of promoting greater safety for road users, and the environment, i.e., reducing the gases and fuel consumption of vehicles.

This research presented a real case study of traffic light simulation-based optimization strategy in the city center of Guimarães (Portugal). A specific intersection of high traffic intensity and pedestrian activity was studied, which generates traffic queues, especially during specific hours of the day. In order to be able to simulate vehicle traffic scenarios in a real way, the data referring to the current cycle time of the traffic lights were collected directly at street level, and methodologies such as PSO, Python, and SUMO were used.

The computational results showed it is possible to reduce the average waiting time from 68.69s (real) to 14.99s, meaning a reduction of 78.2%. In addition, the average waiting time can be decreased from 56.05s to 7.72s, if the traffic lights are removed from the crosswalks - 86.2% of improvement was observed.

When comparing the results of the simulations in the two situations, on average, in the optimized scenario with crosswalks the number of vehicles at each instant is 30, while in the scenario without crosswalks the average number of cars is insignificantly lower. Therefore, it is clear that the crosswalks are not the cause of congested traffic in that area. By better managing the traffic light cycle time, it is possible to obtain a situation where the number of cars in the system remains constant, generating a traffic flow without queue accumulation and without congestion. This confirms that traffic light optimization is an effective, safe, and low-cost management solution. The future work of this project will be based on the Online Traffic Optimization in a city, surrounding a larger area of traffic.

References

1. Balta, M., Özcelik, I.: Traffic signaling optimization for intelligent and green transportation in smart cities. In: 2018 3rd International Conference on Computer Science and Engineering (UBMK), pp. 31–35. IEEE (2018)
2. Chen, Y.R., Chen, K.P., Hsiungy, P.A.: Dynamic traffic light optimization and control system using model-predictive control method. In: 2016 IEEE 19th International Conference on Intelligent Transportation Systems (ITSC), pp. 2366–2371. IEEE (2016)
3. Ferrer, J., López-Ibáñez, M., Alba, E.: Reliable simulation-optimization of traffic lights in a real-world city. Appl. Soft Comput. **78**, 697–711 (2019)
4. Gao, K., Zhang, Y., Sadollah, A., Su, R.: Optimizing urban traffic light scheduling problem using harmony search with ensemble of local search. Appl. Soft Comput. **48**, 359–372 (2016)
5. Goel, S., Bush, S.F., Ravindranathan, K.: Self-organization of traffic lights for minimizing vehicle delay. In: 2014 International Conference on Connected Vehicles and Expo (ICCVE), pp. 931–936. IEEE (2014)
6. Instituto da Mobilidade e dos Transportes: Documento normativo para aplicação a arruamentos urbanos (2021). (in portuguese). https://participa.pt/pt/imt/documento-normativo-para-aplicacao-a-arruamentos-urbanos. Accessed 9 Sept 2022
7. Lopez, P.A., et al.: Microscopic traffic simulation using sumo. In: 2018 21st International Conference on Intelligent Transportation Systems (ITSC), pp. 2575–2582. IEEE (2018)
8. Olayode, I.O., Tartibu, L.K., Okwu, M.O., Severino, A.: Comparative traffic flow prediction of a heuristic ANN model and a hybrid ANN-PSO model in the traffic flow modelling of vehicles at a four-way signalized road intersection. Sustainability **13**(19), 10704 (2021)

9. OpenStreetMap: Copyright and License (2022). https://www.openstreetmap.org/copyright. Accessed 9 Sept 2022

10. Pau, G., Campisi, T., Canale, A., Severino, A., Collotta, M., Tesoriere, G.: Smart pedestrian crossing management at traffic light junctions through a fuzzy-based approach. Future Internet **10**(2), 15 (2018)

11. Silva, G.O., Rocha, A.M.A.C., Witeck, G.R., Silva, A., Durães, D., Machado, J.: On tuning the particle swarm optimization for solving the traffic light problem. In: Gervasi, O., Murgante, B., Misra, S., Rocha, A.M.A.C., Garau, C. (eds.) ICCSA 2022. LNCS, vol. 13378, pp. 68–80. Springer, Cham (2022). https://doi.org/10.1007/978-3-031-10562-3_6

12. Villagra, A., Alba, E., Luque, G.: A better understanding on traffic light scheduling: new cellular gas and new in-depth analysis of solutions. J. Comput. Sci. **41**, 101085 (2020)

13. Witeck, G.R., Rocha, A.M.A.C., Silva, G.O., Silva, A., Durães, D., Machado, J.: A bibliometric review and analysis of traffic lights optimization. In: Gervasi, O., Murgante, B., Misra, S., Rocha, A.M.A.C., Garau, C. (eds.) ICCSA 2022. LNCS, vol. 13378, pp. 43–54. Springer, Cham (2022). https://doi.org/10.1007/978-3-031-10562-3_4

Combined Optimization and Regression Machine Learning for Solar Irradiation and Wind Speed Forecasting

Yahia Amoura[1,4]([✉]) [iD], Santiago Torres[4] [iD], José Lima[1,3] [iD],
and Ana I. Pereira[1,2] [iD]

[1] Research Centre in Digitalization and Intelligent Robotics (CeDRI),
Instituto Politécnico de Bragança, Bragança, Portugal
{yahia,jllima,apereira}@ipb.pt
[2] ALGORITMI Center, University of Minho, Braga, Portugal
[3] INESC TEC - INESC Technology and Science, Porto, Portugal
[4] University of Laguna, Laguna, Spain
storres@ull.edu.es

Abstract. Prediction of solar irradiation and wind speed are essential for enhancing the renewable energy integration into the existing power system grids. However, the deficiencies caused to the network operations provided by their intermittent effects need to be investigated. Regarding reserves management, regulation, scheduling, and dispatching, the intermittency in power output become a challenge for the system operator. This had given the interest of researchers for developing techniques to predict wind speeds and solar irradiation over a large or short-range of temporal and spatial perspectives to accurately deal with the variable power output. Before, several statistical, and even physics, approaches have been applied for prediction. Nowadays, machine learning is widely applied to do it and especially regression models to assess them. Tuning these models is usually done following manual approaches by changing the minimum leaf size of a decision tree, or the box constraint of a support vector machine, for example, that can affect its performance. Instead of performing it manually, this paper proposes to combine optimization methods including the bayesian optimization, grid search, and random search with regression models to extract the best hyper parameters of the model. Finally, the results are compared with the manually tuned models. The Bayesian gives the best results in terms of extracting hyper-parameters by giving more accurate models.

Keywords: Renewable energy · Forecasting · Machine learning · Optimization · Wind speed · Solar irradiation

1 Introduction

With significant population growth followed by rising demand, human energy consumption could become a major concern [1]. The main problem is the rapid

A. I. Pereira et al. (Eds.): OL2A 2022, CCIS 1754, pp. 215–228, 2022.
https://doi.org/10.1007/978-3-031-23236-7_16

increase in electricity consumption, which leads to higher electricity costs as well as environmental pollution, especially when the energy comes from conventional combustion resources [2]. According to a study conducted by the International Energy Agency (IEA), fuel-based electricity production has been estimated to represent more than 64% of total world production, while the remaining 26% would have been shared between renewable resources, in particular only 5% wind and 2% solar [3]. Given their high world potential, this may seem strange, but several reasons have led to a reduction in their use, such as intermittent production, related to the presence of sun or wind, or as for example the solar production has a lower production in winter, while the consumption is higher, this makes their exploitation cost still expensive. For its regeneration, the states consecrated public aids until it becomes a competitive energy [4]. In particular, to be in line with the European Union (EU) objectives for tackling climate change, in the Framework for Action on climate and Energy 2021–2030, the following goals have to be assured: reduce greenhouse gas emissions by at least 40% (compared to 1990 levels), increase the contribution of renewable energy to final energy consumption by at least 32%, and increase energy efficiency by at least 32.5% [5]. Although renewable energy sources are inexhaustible and widely available, their randomness in terms of generation had led to provide innovative ways to get the most out of them. One of the methods is to predict their production allowing us to assess their performance and anticipate preventive actions. This allows, for instance, the size of the back-up systems to be reduced, or to adopt more efficient exploitation approaches. The inquiry of this resources, especially, wind speed and solar irradiation depends on large sizes of data and parameters availability [6]. Nowadays, Supervised Machine Learning (ML) methods are widely provided to achieve an accurate forecast model for wind speed and solar irradiation [7]. a model with inputs and their desired outputs is given to learn a general rule that maps inputs to outputs. These methods need expert intervention and the training data comprising a group of training examples. In supervised learning, each pattern may be a pair that includes an input object and the desired output value. The function of the supervised learning algorithm is intended to analyze the training data and produce an inferred function. As presented in the paper including the first part of this work, regression models are widely used in several types of research related to the prediction of weather parameters including wind speed and solar irradiation. Moreover, to predict wind speed in [16], the authors proposed Regression tree algorithms for the very short time gap. This method included the various types of regression trees in wind speed predictions to check the performances of different regression tree models. In [8] a new forecasting method based on bayesian theory and structure break model was used to predict wind speed parameters, by using prior information to improve the results of the time series model which are predicted as a set of values, different from other models. Gang et al. in [9] proposed Bayesian combination algorithm and NN models for the prediction of wind speed in short term. The work includes the two-step methodology on Bayesian algorithms for wind speed forecasting and it also includes neural network models. Chang et al, in [14] used a hybrid approach of random forest regression and Bayesian model to predict the solar irradiation. In [10] Lauret et al, had described the linear and non-linear statistical techniques auto-regressive (AR) and artificial neural network (ANN), while employing support vector machine (SVM) for predicting solar irradiation. However, employing a hybrid learning techniques combined with optimization methods to develop and optimize the construction of the learning algorithms is used in several works. For instance, in [11] the authors proposed optimized Least Squares Support Vector Machine (LSSVM) optimized by Particle Swarm Optimisation (PSO) algorithm to predict the speed of wind in a short time gap. In that paper, the accuracy rate is tried to improve by combining approaches like Ensemble Empirical Mode Decomposition (EEMD) and Sample Entropy (SE), also the optimization is done by PSO. In [12], an optimized model of wind speed forecasting with the combination of wavelet transform and Support Vector Machines is used. The proposed model includes wavelet transform, Genetic Algorithm (GA), and Support Vector Machines, as well as the consideration of two evolutionary algorithms, and the use of these together overcome the other models. In [13], Zameer et al. employed a hybrid approach based on ANNs and Genetic Algorithm (GA) programming for short-term forecasting of solar irradiation.

The work presented in this paper is a continuation of an already performed approaches for prediction of wind speed and solar irradiation using regression machine learning models. It is proposed in that previous work to investigate further a method to increase the accuracy of tested models. One of the critical point observed were the tuning of the hyper parameters. As a first step, the internal parameters have been tuned manually affecting the performances of the models in certain cases. This paper proposes to combine optimization methods with machine learning to automate the selection of the best hyper parameters values.

This paper is divided into five sections. An overview of solar irradiation and wind speed prediction methods have been presented in Sect. 1. Section 2 presents, analyses and performs a pre-processing of the study data. The approach and use of optimization method to export the best hyper parameters for regression models is explained in Sect. 3. The results of the best optimizable models are presented and explained in Sect. 4. The last section concludes the study and proposes guideline for future works.

2 Data Pre-processing

The weather parameters including the temperature, wind speed, solar irradiation, and relative humidity are presented on Fig. 1. They have been collected using a data monitoring system that can give 15 min range time samples. The system is composed of meteorological sensors in the station of Malviya National Institute of Technology in the Jaipur region in India (Latitude: 26.8622°N, Longitude:75.8156°E). A data set composed of 1922 features was imported from the platform of MNIT Weather Data - Live Feed.

The ranges for each weather parameters are presented on Table 1.

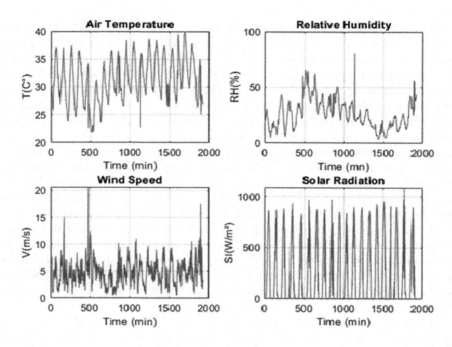

Fig. 1. Weather data

Table 1. Weather data informations.

Parameters	Wind speed (m/s)	Relative humidity (%)	Temperature (C°)	Solar radiation (W/m^2)
Min	0.47	3.41	21.75	0
Max	20.62	80.72	39.97	1089
Average	4.71	26.14	31.39	233.79

2.1 Data Cleaning

Models' precision is highly impacted by the quality of the data employed. It is envisaged to carry out a data-cleaning procedure for improving the quality of the data by filtering it from any error or anomalies including outliers caused by the default in wind speed and solar irradiation measures. Several approaches have been applied in the literature to improve data quality by filtering errors such as the daily clearness index K [15]. In this paper, the inter quartile range (IQR) method is adopted for removing the outliers from wind speed and relative humidity data-set, after plotting the box and whiskers plot and getting the 25 percentile and 75 percentile, Q1, and Q3 respectively, the IQR is calculated considering the difference between Q1 and Q3. The IQR is used to Define the normal data range with a lower limit as $Q1 - 1.5 \times IQR$ and an upper limit as $Q3 + 1.5 \times IQR$. However, any data point outside this range is considered as an outlier and should be removed for further analysis. Figure 2 is showing the data before applying the quarterlies method in Fig. 2a and after Fig. 2b.

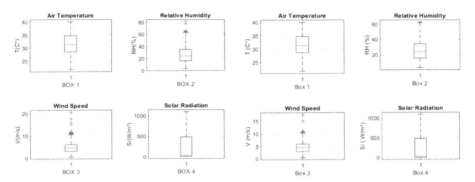

(a) Box and Whiskers plot before data cleaning.

(b) Box and Whiskers plot after data cleaning.

Fig. 2. Data box and Whiskers plots.

Fig 3 and Fig 4 represent the humidity and wind speed data cleaning, before and after removing the outliers using the quartiles method.

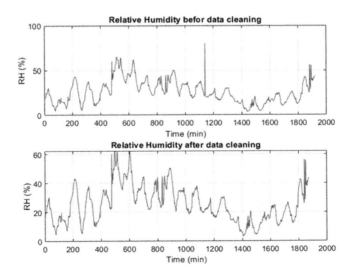

Fig. 3. Humidity data processing

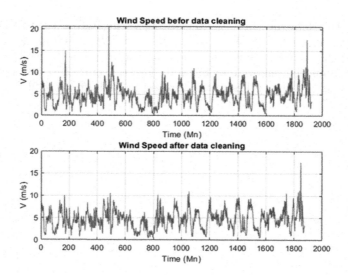

Fig. 4. Wind speed data processing

2.2 Data Correlation

After data analysis, having the relationship of variation between the metro-logical data is important to be used as predictors both for wind speed and solar irradiation, indeed, a correlation matrix will be calculated in this section. The data correlation is characterized by Pearson's correlation coefficients between all pairs of variables in the matrix of time series, including wind speed, solar irradiation, temperature, and relative humidity. The correlation coefficients are plotted on a matrix where the diagonal includes the distribution of a variable as a histogram. Each off-diagonal subplot contains a scatter-plot of a pair of variables with a least-squares reference line, the slope of which is equal to the correlation coefficient. From Fig. 7, a high negative correlation is remarked between the air temperature and relative humidity, physically, the relation between humidity and temperature formula simply says they are inversely proportional. If temperature increases it will lead to a decrease in relative humidity, thus the air will become drier whereas when temperature decreases, the air will become wet means the relative humidity will increase. Since air temperature is directly related to global solar radiation. So, an increase in solar radiation increases the air temperature and this justifies the positive correlation gated between the two items. Because of the solar energy (incoming short-wave radiation), the earth's surface heats up. Air near the ground tends to gain heat from the earth's surface. When air is heated, it expands and starts to rise. Solar energy causes wind due to its effect on air pressure and there is little correlation between them in the data analyzed. No correlation is detected between relative humidity and wind speed.

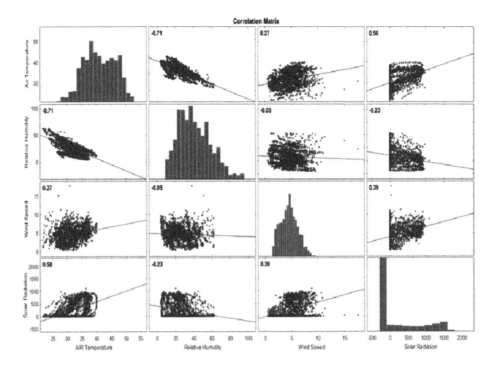

Fig. 5. Data correlation of considered weather parameters.

The calculation of the correlation allowed to determine the parameters used for the prediction of the solar irradiation and the wind speed. However to predict the solar irradiation the predictors used are: time sampling, relative humidity, temperature and wind speed. To forecast the future value of wind speed and as per of research experience made in [7] and actual data correlation, the used predictors were: time, solar irradiation, temperature and previous recorded wind speed.

3   Machine Learning

In the field of Artificial Intelligence, Machine Learning (ML) is widely used in several contexts among them forecasting. ML is composed of two main techniques including supervised and unsupervised learning. Among the approaches used in supervised learning to perform forecasting models is regression methods. Usually, regression models deal with real data mainly to predict continued responses as in the case of this paper regarding wind speed and solar irradiation.

The regression models employed in this paper are regression trees, Gaussian process regression models, support vector machines, and ensembles of regression trees. As explained in Fig. 6, the data are first divided into two sets, one for training and the other for validation. The data preparation phase allows for

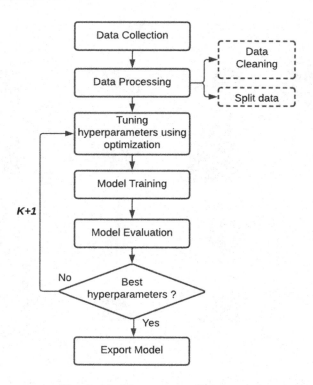

Fig. 6. Model processing flowchart.

reorganizing of the two sets by removing perturbations in the data distribution based on the quartile method.

Once the dataset is ready, it will be used for the model training inputs. A hyperparameter tuning is performed using optimization methods including bayesian, grid Search, and random Search. In general, the goal of optimization is to find a point that minimizes an objective function. In the context of hyperparameter tuning, a point is a set of hyperparameter values, and the objective function is the loss function. In each iteration the training model results are evaluated by the Root Mean Squared Error (RMSE) as shown in Eq. 1.

$$RMSE = \sqrt{\sum_{i=1}^{n} \frac{(V,S)_{predicted} - (V,S)_{measured}}{n}} \tag{1}$$

where, V and S are wind speed and solar irradiation respectively.

If the error results are not sufficient, this will lead to going another step to export the best set hyperparameters for each model as described in Fig. 7.

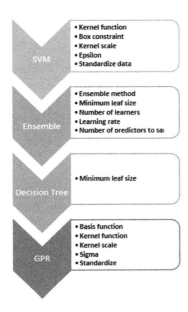

Fig. 7. Optimizable hyperparameters for each model.

4   Results and Discussions

In this paper, the aim is to predict future values of solar irradiation and wind speed from historical data, hence, the model will be implemented with regression techniques from supervised learning. These techniques are implemented in MATLAB, the discussion is divided into three parts, two dedicated to each predicted parameter, and the last part compares the results regarding the manual tuning and tuning by optimization.

4.1   Optimized Models for Solar Irradiation Forecasting

For assessing and improving the regression learning models, tuning the model parameters by optimizing the hyperparameters is used to reduce the RMSE error values. The optimizer models used for hyperparameter tuning are the Bayesian optimization, Grid Search, and Random Search. Table 2 presents the RMSE obtained by tuning the models hyperparameters using the three optimization methods.

The results obtained from all different regression models show that the bayesian method outperforms the two others optimization methods. Bayesian optimization is an approach that uses the bayes theorem to drive the search in order to find the minimum of the objective function. It is an approach that is most useful for objective functions that are noisy as in the case of data presented in this paper. Applied to hyperparameter optimization, Bayesian optimization

Table 2. Optimized model results for solar irradiation prediction (RMSE).

Model	Optimizer			
	Iterations	Bayesian	Grid search	Random search
Optimizable tree	30	51.50	53.70	51.504
Optimizable SVM	30	169.38	250.72	107.82
Optimizable GPR	30	0.09	0.19	0.14
Optimizable ensembles	30	0.65	48.18	36.52

builds a probabilistic model of the function mapping from hyperparameter values to the objective evaluated on a validation set. Bayesian Optimization differs from Random Search and Grid Search in that it improves the search speed using past performances, whereas the other two methods are uniform or independent of past evaluations.

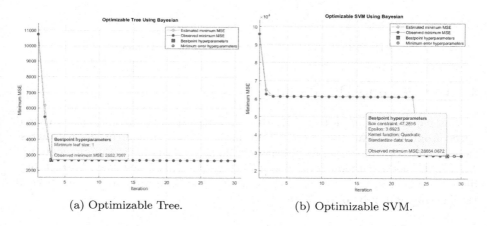

(a) Optimizable Tree.   (b) Optimizable SVM.

Fig. 8. Optimizable models results for solar irradiation forecasting

Fig. 8 and 9 shows the optimization results obtained for the best hyperparameters regarding the four regression models using Bayesian optimization.

The plots are showing the estimated minimum MSE. Each light blue point corresponds to an estimate of the minimum MSE computed by the optimization process when considering all the sets of hyperparameter values tried, including the current iteration. Each dark blue point corresponds to the observed minimum MSE computed by the optimization process. Best point hyperparameters. The red square indicates the iteration that corresponds to the optimized hyperparameters. Minimum error hyperparameters. The yellow point indicates the iteration that corresponds to the hyperparameters that yield the observed minimum MSE.

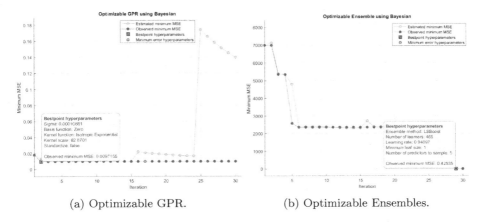

(a) Optimizable GPR.   (b) Optimizable Ensembles.

Fig. 9. Optimizable models results for solar irradiation forecasting.

4.2 Optimizable Models for Wind Speed Forecasting

It was applied the same approach of solar irradiation, to forecast the future values of wind speed four regression methods including, Support Vector Machine (SVM), Gaussian Process Regression, Ensembles, and Regression Tree. The hyperparameters were optimized based on the three optimization methods: Bayesian, Grid Search, and Random Search.

The comparative Table 3 is showing the comparison of the four regression models based on the three optimization methods. The Bayesian outperforms the optimization methods in terms of model improvement.

Table 3. Optimizable model results for wind speed prediction (RMSE).

Model	Optimizer			
	Iterations	Bayesian	Grid search	Random Search
Optimizable tree	30	0.66	0.69	0.68
Optimizable SVM	30	0.19	0.58	0.34
Optimizable GPR	30	0.48	0.79	0.62
Optimizable ensembles	30	0.16	0.73	0.64

Fig. 10 shows the optimization results search for the best hyperparameters regarding the four regression models using Bayesian optimization for wind speed prediction.

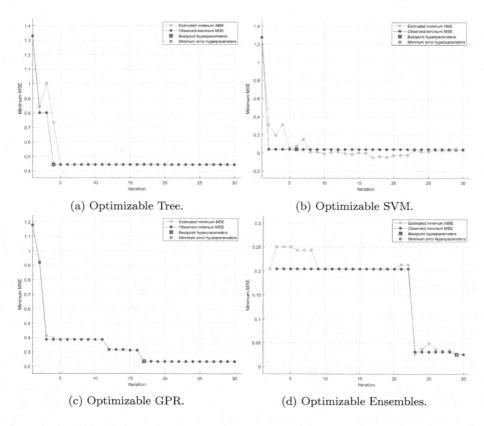

(a) Optimizable Tree.   (b) Optimizable SVM.

(c) Optimizable GPR.   (d) Optimizable Ensembles.

Fig. 10. Optimizable models results for wind speed forecasting.

4.3 Comparison of Manual and Optimized Tuning of Hyperparameters

The Fig. 11 presents the comparison of models in term of accuracy between manually and automated tuned model. The optimization helps to export the best hyper parameters combination. In fact, the accuracy of the models have remarkably been increased.

Automatic Tuning exclude the undifferentiated heavy lifting required to search the hyperparameter space for more accurate models.

This feature allowv saving significant time and effort in training and tuning of machine learning models. In general, Automated hyperparameter tuning of machine learning models can be accomplished using Bayesian optimization. In contrast to random search, Bayesian optimization chooses the next hyperparameters in an informed method to spend more time evaluating promising values.

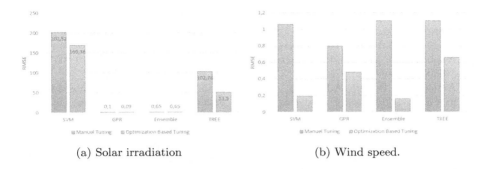

(a) Solar irradiation   (b) Wind speed.

Fig. 11. Manual and optimized tuning comparison.

5   Conclusion and Future Works

In this article, a combined optimization with machine learning has been performed to predict the future values of wind speed and solar irradiation. It is made by performing a tuning of hyper-parameters using optimization methods to build optimized models, four regression models including Regression Tree, Support Vector Machine (SVM), Gaussian Process Regression (GPR) and optimized ensembles, combined with three optimization approaches for each model including, Bayesian, Random Search and Grid Search. The three methods have been compared on a scale of 30 iterations. The Bayesian optimization has shown the best automated hyper-parameter tuning for the four regression models. The results have been compared to the manual tuned models presented in the first part of this work, the optimized models gave a higher accuracy. As a continuation of this work, it is proposed to perform a time series prediction for long term time horizons.

References

1. Akpan, U., Friday, G., Akpan, G.E.: The contribution of energy consumption to climate change: a feasible policy direction. Int. J. Energy Econ. Policy **2**(1), 21–33 (2012). https://doi.org/10.1201/9781003126171-4
2. Shahsavari, A., Akbari, M.: Potential of solar energy in developing countries for reducing energy-related emissions. Renew. Sustain. Energy Rev. **90**, 275–291 (2018). https://doi.org/10.1016/j.rser.2018.03.065
3. Lopez, J.F.A., Granados, A., Gonzalez-Trevizo, A.P., Luna-Leon, M.E., Bojorquez-Morales, A.G.: Energy payback time and greenhouse gas emissions: studying the international energy agency guidelines architecture. J. Cleaner Product. **196**, 1566–1575 (2018). https://doi.org/10.1016/j.jclepro.2018.06.134
4. Engeland, K., Borga, M., Creutin, J.D., François, B., Ramos, M.H., Vidal, J.P.: Space-time variability of climate variables and intermittent renewable electricity production-a review. Renew. Sustain. Energy Rev. **79**, 600–617 (2017). https://doi.org/10.1016/j.rser.2017.05.046

5. Amoura, Y., Ferreira, Â.P., Lima, J., Pereira, A.I.: Optimal sizing of a hybrid energy system based on renewable energy using evolutionary optimization algorithms. In: International Conference on Optimization, Learning Algorithms and Applications, pp. 153–168. Springer, Cham (2021). https://doi.org/10.1007/978-3-030-91885-912

6. Amoura, Y., Pereira, A.I., Lima, J.: Optimization methods for energy management in a microgrid system considering wind uncertainty data. In: Proceedings of International Conference on Communication and Computational Technologies, pp. 117–141. Springer, Singapore (2021). https://doi.org/10.1007/978-981-16-3246-410

7. Amoura, Y., Pereira, A.I., Lima, J.: A short term wind speed forecasting model using artificial neural network and adaptive neuro-fuzzy inference system models. In: International Conference on Sustainable Energy for Smart Cities, pp. 189–204. Springer, Cham, (2021). https://doi.org/10.1007/978-3-030-97027-712

8. Wang, J., Qin, S., Zhou, Q., Jiang, H.: Medium-term wind speeds forecasting utilizing hybrid models for three different sites in Xinjiang, China. Renew. Energy **76**, 91–101 (2015). https://doi.org/10.1016/j.renene.2014.11.011

9. Cadenas, E., Wilfrido, R.: Short term wind speed forecasting in La Venta, Oaxaca, México, using artificial neural networks. Renew. Energy **34**(1), 274–278 (2009). https://doi.org/10.1016/j.renene.2008.03.014

10. Lauret, P., Voyant, C., Soubdhan, T., David, M., Poggi, P.: A benchmarking of machine learning techniques for solar radiation forecasting in an insular context. Solar Energy **112**, 446–457 (2015). https://doi.org/10.1016/j.solener.2014.12.014

11. Yang, L., Wang, L., Zhang, Z.: Generative wind power curve modeling via machine vision: a deep convolutional network method with data-synthesis-informed-training. IEEE Trans. Power Syst. (2022). https://doi.org/10.1109/tpwrs.2022.3172508

12. Liu, D., Niu, D., Wang, H., Fan, L.: Short-term wind speed forecasting using wavelet transform and support vector machines optimized by genetic algorithm. Renew. energy **62**, 592–597 (2014). https://doi.org/10.1016/j.renene.2013.08.011

13. Zameer, A., Arshad, J., Khan, A., Raja, M.A.Z.: Intelligent and robust prediction of short term wind power using genetic programming based ensemble of neural networks. Energy Convers. Manag. **134**, 361–372 (2017). https://doi.org/10.1016/j.enconman.2016.12.032

14. Chang, J.F., Dong, N., Yung, K.L.: An ensemble learning model based on Bayesian model combination for solar energy prediction. J. Renew. Sustain. Energy **11**(4), 043702 (2019). https://doi.org/10.1063/1.5094534

15. Ferkous, K., Chellali, F., Kouzou, A., Bekkar, B.: Wavelet-Gaussian process regression model for forecasting daily solar radiation in the Saharan climate. Clean Energy **5**(2), 316–328 (2021). https://doi.org/10.1093/ce/zkab012

16. Troncoso, A., Salcedo-Sanz, S., Casanova-Mateo, C., Riquelme, J.C., Prieto, L.: Local models-based regression trees for very short-term wind speed prediction. Renew. Energy **81**, 589–598 (2015). https://doi.org/10.1016/j.renene.2015.03.071

An Improved Multi-Threaded Implementation of the MCSFilter Optimization Algorithm

Luís Monteiro[1], José Rufino[1(✉)] (ID), Andrey Romanenko[2] (ID),
and Florbela P. Fernandes[1] (ID)

[1] Research Centre in Digitalization and Intelligent Robotics (CeDRI),
Instituto Politécnico de Bragança, 5300-252 Bragança, Portugal
`a36788@alunos.ipb.pt`, {`rufino,fflor`}`@ipb.pt`
[2] MORE – Laboratório Colaborativo Montanhas de Investigação,
Av. Cidade de Léon 506, 5300-358 Bragança, Portugal
`aromanenko@morecolab.pt`

Abstract. The Multistart Coordinate Search Filter (MCSFilter) is an optimization method suitable to find all minimizers of a nonconvex problem, with any type of constraints. When used in industrial contexts, execution time may be critical, in order to keep production processes within safe and expected bounds. One way to increase performance is through parallelization. In this work, a second parallel version of the MCSFilter method is presented, aiming at faster execution times than a previous parallel implementation. The new solver was tested with a set of fourteen problems, with different characteristics and behavior. The results obtained represent an improvement of the execution times over all previous MCSFilter implementations (sequential and parallel). They also allowed to identify bottlenecks to be lifted in future parallel versions.

Keywords: Optimization · MCSFilter Method · Parallelization

1 Introduction

The main goal of Multilocal Programming is to compute all the minimizers (global and local) of constrained nonlinear optimization problems [9,17], i.e.

$$\min_{x \in \Omega} f(x) \tag{1}$$

where the feasible region is given by $\Omega = \{x \in \mathbb{R}^n : l \le x \le u, \ g_i(x) \le 0, \ i = 1, \cdots, k_1, \ h_j = 0, \ j = 1, \cdots, k_2\}$, l and u are, respectively, the lower and the upper bounds, and g_i and h_j are the constraint functions.

These problems may be simple bound problems, problems with more specific constraints, or even problems with different types of variables. For instance, problems can be nonlinear, nonconvex, with equality (or inequality) constraints and with integer, continuous, or mixed integer variables [1,2,6].

© The Author(s), under exclusive license to Springer Nature Switzerland AG 2022
A. I. Pereira et al. (Eds.): OL2A 2022, CCIS 1754, pp. 229–245, 2022.
https://doi.org/10.1007/978-3-031-23236-7_17

Multilocal programming has a wide range of applications. Particularly, this kind of problems are recurrent in some industrial contexts (e.g., Chemical Engineering related), typically with the aim of obtaining global minimizers. Obtaining these solutions in the shortest amount of time may be of utmost importance, specially if there are time-sensitive industrial processes at play. Efficiently solving these problems can also generate economical savings for companies.

There is a considerable number of techniques and methods to solve those problems. Nevertheless, there are some problem features that should be considered when choosing the solving method. For instance, a large number of problems exists, with practical applications, where the derivatives are not known, or the function is not continuous. In this case, the correct choice of the method to solve the problem is really important [7,11].

The method addressed in this paper is MCSFilter, a derivative-free method able to obtain the minimizers (in particular, the global minimizer) of a non-convex, constrained, nonlinear programming problem. This method is based in a multistart strategy, coupled with a coordinate search filter procedure to treat the constraints. MCSFilter has already shown promising results [1,7], including with real-world applications [3,4,14,16].

MCSFilter has also been implemented in several platforms and languages, starting with a prototype in MATLAB [7] from which a JAVA implementation was derived and used to solve process engineering problems [4]. More recently, a C-based implementation was developed, also with base on the MATLAB code, which proved to be faster than both the MATLAB and JAVA versions [5].

However, all these implementations are sequential, and thus cannot take advantage of the parallel computing capabilities of modern multi-core architectures, which basically became pervasive. Indeed, even industrial-level Systems-on-Chips/embedded systems have already these capabilities in place, and so it becomes imperative to re-architect applications to fully take advantage of them. Having this in mind, a preliminary effort was already undertaken to produce a first parallel version of the C-based MCSFilter implementation [15].

This paper gives continuity to that effort. We present an enhanced parallel version of MCSFilter (ParMCSFilter2) that, like the predecessor (ParMCSFilter1), targets Linux-based multi-core shared memory systems and builds on the Posix Threads programming model. The two versions are compared for a common set of reference problems, with the new version showing a considerable performance improvement, while keeping or improving the amount of minimizers found. In addition, the new version is put to the test with a set of medium/large complexity problems, with the goal of assessing its performance and scalability. This study allowed to identify some bottlenecks to be solved in future work.

The rest of this paper is organized as follows: in Sect. 2, the original MCS-Filter algorithm is briefly revised; in Sect. 3, the parallelization approach is presented; in Sect. 4, the computational experiments conducted and its results are discussed; finally, Sect. 5 concludes and addresses future work.

2   The MCSFilter Optimization Method

The MCSFilter algorithm was originally introduced in [8]. Its main purpose is to find multiple minimizers of nonlinear and nonconvex constrained optimization problems, without the use of derivatives. The approach used involves two complementary tools: the exploration feature relies on a multistart strategy; the exploitation of promising regions is based on the CSFilter algorithm.

The CSFilter procedure combines the coordinate search method with the filter methodology to treat the constraints. Using the coordinate search has the disadvantage of a slow convergence; nevertheless, it is easy to implement and suitable for problems without derivatives [11].

In the original version, the MCSFilter algorithm sequentially calls, inside the multistart part, the local procedure CSFilter. To avoid redundant local procedure calls, the MCSFilter method takes into consideration the regions of attraction of the minimizers already found. Thus, if an initial point, randomly generated, is inside one of those regions, the local procedure may not be called for that point.

The stop condition of MCSFilter is related to the fraction of the unsearched space, meaning that the algorithm stops if the following condition is met:

$$P_{min} = \frac{m(m+1)}{t(t-1)} \leq \epsilon \tag{2}$$

where m is the number of different minimizers found, t is the number of the local procedure calls and $\epsilon \in (0,1]$. Further details can be found in [7,8].

To illustrate the application of this algorithm, the problem P_3 later presented in Sect. 4.1 is used, but only with simple bounds. The representation of the objective function can be seen in Fig. 1, where it is possible to observe the existence of one global minimum and three local minima.

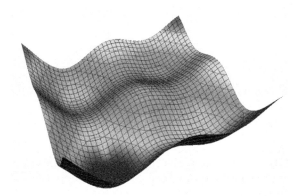

Fig. 1. Representation of the objective function of problem P_3.

Figure 2 shows, step by step, the MCSFilter algorithm when applied to obtain the global and local solutions of the above problem. The red lines represent the

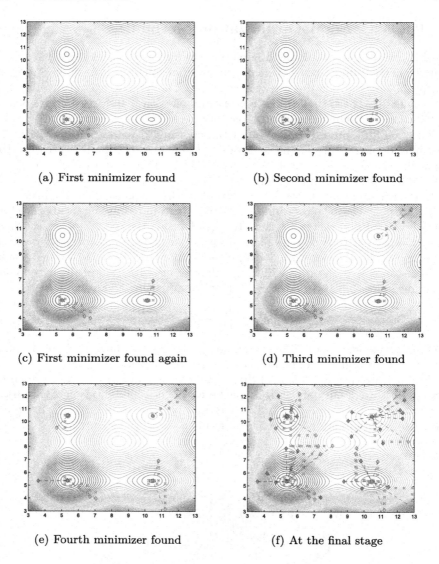

(a) First minimizer found

(b) Second minimizer found

(c) First minimizer found again

(d) Third minimizer found

(e) Fourth minimizer found

(f) At the final stage

Fig. 2. Step by step illustration of MCSFilter [7].

first time the solution was found, the pink lines represent other calls that find minimizers previously obtained, and the blue lines represent calls that weren't executed taking into account the regions of attraction.

3   Parallel Approach

Given the previous description of the MCSFilter algorithm, the easiest path to its parallelization is to have multiple threads working in parallel, with each one conducting successive local searches until it meets the stop condition. This approach is formally represented in Algorithm 1, where the main loop (lines 5 to 30) is executed in parallel by a set of worker threads, spawned by a master thread; then, the master thread basically awaits (line 32) for the workers to finish and consolidates and outputs the findings (line 33). This corresponds to the classical master-workers model, which perfectly fits this use case.

In this approach, the worker threads share some data in order to prevent repeating local searches already performed by others, and to evaluate condition 2 in a consistent way. This means there is a unique set of minimizers found, shared by all threads, and they all must evaluate condition 2 based on glob-ally shared variables representing m and t. These shared resources must be adequately protected during concurrent access, by means of mutual exclusion mechanisms.

The reasoning behind expecting a performance gain from this approach is as follows: multiple local searches in parallel, departing from different random start-ing points, increase the chance of finding minimizers and finding them sooner; moreover, with more searches performed, and potentially more minimizers found, the stop condition 2 will be met sooner and so the overall MCSFilter algorithm will execute faster. It should be noted, however, that the parallel algorithm does not exclude the possibility of the same minimizer being found multiple times by different threads (but even then P_{min} decreases, as t increases).

Both parallel versions discussed in this paper share these general principles. However, the more recent version introduced several optimizations. These dif-ferences are next clarified on the sub-sections dedicated to each version.

3.1   First Version (ParMCSFilter1)

The first parallel version of MCSFilter [15] closely follows Algorithm 1, except for the steps in blue. Its implementation was derived from a first C-based imple-mentation [5] of MCSFilter which, in turn, corresponded to a direct translation of the MATLAB primordial code, with the main focus on the correctness of the implementation and not so much on the code optimization.

As such, the data structure used to store the minimizers found was a dynamic array, that only grew (via `realloc`) one cell at a time, mimicking the MATLAB code; discarding cells was implemented by marking them with a special flag, thus avoiding shrinking the array, but incurring in some waste of memory.

The parallel variant was built on the POSIX Threads programming model, and included the necessary mutual exclusion mechanisms to protect the shared state between the threads (basically, PThreads mutex locks were used).

3.2   Second Version (ParMCSFilter2)

The second parallel version of MCSFilter (ParMCSFilter2) also follows Algorithm 1, but now includes the steps in blue, as well as several other enhance-ments. This version was derived from a new sequential C-based version [12],

Algorithm 1. MCSFilter algorithm – Parallel Version

Require: $M^* = \emptyset$, $k = 1$, $t = 1$, $n_{threads} > 1$;
1: Randomly generate $x \in [l, u]$; compute $B_{\min} = \min_{i=1,\ldots,n}\{u_i - l_i\}$;
2: Compute $m_1 = \mathbf{CSFilter}(x)$, $R_1 = \|x - m_1\|$; Set $r_1 = 1$, $M^* = M^* \cup m_1$;
3: Main thread creates $n_{threads}$ worker threads
4: **if** Current thread = Worker thread **then**
5:     **while** $P_{min} > \epsilon$ **do**
6:         Randomly generate $x \in [l, u]$;
7:         Set $o = \arg\min_{j=1,\ldots,k} d_j \equiv \|x - m_j\|$;
8:         **if** $d_o < R_o$ **then**
9:             **if** $P_{min} \leq \epsilon$ **then** break **endif** // check stop condition
10:            **if** the direction from x to y_o is ascent **then**
11:                Set $prob = 1$;
12:            **else**
13:                Compute $prob = \varrho\,\phi(\frac{d_o}{R_o}, r_o)$;
14:            **end if**
15:        **else**
16:            Set $prob = 1$;
17:        **end if**
18:        **if** $\zeta^{\ddagger} < prob$ **then**
19:            **if** $P_{min} \leq \epsilon$ **then** break **endif** // check stop condition
20:            Compute $m = \mathbf{CSFilter}(x)$; set $t = t + 1$;
21:            **if** $P_{min} \leq \epsilon$ **then** break **endif** // check stop condition
22:            **if** $\|m - m_j\| > \gamma^* B_{\min}$, for all $j = 1, \ldots, k$ **then**
23:                Set $k = k+1$, $m_k = m$, $r_k = 1$, $M^* = M^* \cup m_k$; compute $R_k = \|x - m_k\|$;
24:            **else**
25:                Set $R_l = \max\{R_l, \|x - m_l\|\}$; $r_l = r_l + 1$;
26:            **end if**
27:        **else**
28:            Set $R_o = \max\{R_o, \|x - m_o\|\}$; $r_o = r_o + 1$;
29:        **end if**
30:    **end while**
31: **else**
32:    Main thread waits for all Worker threads to finish
33:    Main thread consolidates and outputs results
34: **end if**

---

that used as reference the JAVA implementation of the MCSFilter method. This JAVA version already included some improvements and refinements at the algorithmic level. Moreover, being much more close to the C syntax than the MATLAB version, its conversion to C was much more straightforward. Also, the main data structure, used to store the minimizers found, was redesigned: it still is based on a growing dynamic array, but the array grows by a chunk of cells at a time, making its use much more efficient, as shown in [12]. The decision to stick with an array as the main data structure is due to it being a cache-friendly data structure. This decision, however, introduced unintended consequences for the performance of the new parallel version, as later found (see Sect. 3.2).

Similarly to the first parallel version, the new implementation was also produced by making use of the POSIX Threads programming model, that targets shared-memory multi-core systems. Besides being derived from a different sequential version, several differences and enhancements deserve to be mentioned.

As already stated, the new version includes the steps in blue from Algorithm 1. These correspond to new evaluations of the stop condition, in addition to the one performed at the head of the main loop (step 5), with the goal of allowing worker threads to end as soon as possible, provided the stop condition is met.

Additionally, several shared resources (e.g., statistical counters, etc.) that were protected by a single mutex lock, in the old version, were unfolded into separate instances, per thread, allowing independent and simultaneous access, without contention. The only downturn was the need for the master thread to sequentially post-process those resources, but the additional time spent in this activity was largely offset by the time spared by the worker threads.

Lastly in order to further improve performance and tackle a bottleneck identified in the access to shared structures, specially to the array of minimizers, all PThreads mutex lock objects were replaced by PThreads read-write locks, allowing full parallel read-access, while enforcing exclusive write access.

Together, all these changes translated in tangible performance gains, as shown in the comparison performed between the two solvers – see next section. However, as often happens when optimizing an application, removing a bottleneck may expose new ones in other areas. During the discussion of the performance evaluation results the bottleneck identified in this new implementation will be detailed and a possible solution to it will be presented.

4   Computational Experiments

This section is devoted to the experimental evaluation of both parallel solvers, with the selected set of benchmark problems. The definition of each problem is given below, along with the experimental evaluation conditions, as well as the obtained results (both numerical and performance-related).

4.1   Benchmark Problems

A total of 14 benchmark problems were chosen from [7,13] (and the references therein). The problems were selected so that different characteristics were addressed: they are multimodal problems with more than one minimizer; they can have just one global minimizer or more than one global minimizer; the dimension of the problems varies between 2 and 310. These are the selected problems:

—Problem (P_1)
dimension: $n = 10$; known global minimum: $f^* = -391.6581$

$$\min f(x) = \frac{1}{2} \sum_{i=1}^{n} x_i^4 - 16x_i^2 + 5x_i$$

$$\text{s.t.} \ -5 \leq x_i \leq 5, i = 1, ..., n$$

—Problem (P_2)

dimension: $n = 2$; known global minimum: $f^* = 0.75$

$$\min f(x) = x_1^2 + (x_2 - 1)^2$$

$$\text{s.t.} \ x_2 - x_1^2 = 0$$

$$-1 \leq x_i \leq 1, i = 1, 2$$

—Problem (P_3)

dimension: $n = 2$; known global minimum: $f^* = -2.4305$

$$\min f(x) = \sum_{i=1}^{n} \sin(x_i) + \sin\left(\frac{2x_i}{3}\right)$$

$$\text{s.t.} \ -2x_1 - 3x_2 + 27 \leq 0$$

$$3 \leq x_i \leq 13, i = 1, 2$$

—Problem (P_4)

dimension: $n = 2$; known global minimum: $f^* = -64.1956$

$$\min f(x) = \frac{1}{2} \sum_{i=1}^{2} x_i^4 - 16x_i^2 + 5x_i$$

$$\text{s.t.} \ (x_1 + 5)^2 + (x_2 - 5)^2 - 100 \leq 0$$

$$-x_1 - x_2 - 3 \leq 0$$

$$-5 \leq x_i \leq 5, i = 1, 2$$

—Problem (P_5)

Problem P_1 with dimension: $n = 14$; known global minimum: $f^* = -548.3261$

—Problem (P_6)

dimension: $n = 300$; known global minimum: $f^* = 0$

$$\min f(x) = \sum_{i=1}^{n-1} \left[x_i^2 + 2x_{i+1}^2 - 0.3\cos(3\pi x_i) - 0.4\cos(4\pi x_{i+1}) + 0.7 \right]$$

$$\text{s.t.} \ -15 \leq x_i \leq 15, i = 1, ..., n$$

—Problem (P_7)

dimension: $n = 5$; known global minimum: $f^* = 0$

$$\min f(x) = \begin{cases} \sum_{i=1}^{n} x_i^6 \left[2 + \sin\left(\frac{1}{x_i}\right) \right] , & \prod_{i=1}^{n} x_i \neq 0 \\ 0 , & \prod_{i=1}^{n} x_I = 0 \end{cases}$$

$$\text{s.t.} \ -1 \le x_i \le 1, i = 1, ..., n$$

—Problem (P_8)

dimension: $n = 5$; known global minimum: $f^* = -1$

$$\min f(x) = -exp\left(-0.5 \sum_{i=1}^{n} x_i^2\right)$$

$$\text{s.t.} \ -1 \le x_i \le 1, i = 1, ..., n$$

—Problem (P_9)

dimension: $n = 50$; known global minimum: $f^* = 1$

$$\min f(x) = \prod_{i=0}^{n-1}\left[1 + (i+1) \sum_{k=1}^{32} \lfloor 2^k x_i \rfloor \, 2^{-k}\right]$$

$$\text{s.t.} \ 0 \le x_i \le 100, i = 1, ..., n$$

—Problem (P_{10})

dimension: $n = 310$; known global minimum: $f^* = 2$

$$\min f(x) = (1 + x_n)^{x_n} \ ; \ x_n = n - \sum_{i=1}^{n-1} x_i$$

$$\text{s.t.} \ 0 \le x_i \le 1, i = 1, ..., n$$

—Problem (P_{11})

dimension: $n = 150$; known global minimum: $f^* = 0$

$$\min f(x) = \sum_{i=1}^{n-1} \left[100(x_i^2 - x_{i+1})^2 + (x_i - 1)^2\right]$$

$$\text{s.t.} \ -5 \le x_i \le 10, i = 1, ..., n$$

—Problem (P_{12})

dimension: $n = 5$; known global minimum: $f^* = 0$

$$\min f(x) = 1 - \cos\left(2\pi \sqrt{\sum_{i=1}^{n} x_i^2}\right) + 0.1 \sqrt{\sum_{i=1}^{n} x_i^2}$$

$$\text{s.t.} \ -100 \le x_i \le 100, i = 1, ..., n$$

—Problem (P_{13})

dimension: $n = 300$; known global minimum: $f^* = 0$

$$\min f(x) = \left(\sum_{i=1}^{n} x_i^2\right)^{\sqrt{\pi}}$$

$$\text{s.t. } -100 \leq x_i \leq 100, i = 1, ..., n$$

—Problem (P_{14})

dimension: $n = 5$; known global minimum: $f^* = 0$

$$\min f(x) = \sum_{i=1}^{n} \left[x_i^2 - 10\cos(2\pi x_i) + 10 \right]$$

$$\text{s.t. } -5.12 \leq x_i \leq 5.12, i = 1, ..., n$$

Problems P_1 to P_4 were already considered in the preliminary evaluation of the old parallel solver [15] (ParMCSFilter1) and are now considered again to allow for a comparison with the new parallel solver (ParMCSFilter2). The 10 newly introduced problems, P_5 to P_{14}, are to be all solved only by the new solver. They are all multidimensional and the definition of the dimension on each one was made to ensure an execution time from a few seconds to up to around 1 min (small, or very small execution times are usually not appropriate for a scalability study). The visualization of some of these problems, with $n = 2$, can be seen in https://www.al-roomi.org/benchmarks, where it is possible to observe the hard problems that were chosen to be solved.

4.2 Experimental Conditions

The problems were evaluated in the same computational system used in previous related works [5, 15] – a virtual machine in the CeDRI cluster with 16 cores from an Intel Xeon W-2195 CPU, 32 GB of RAM, Linux Ubuntu 20.04 Operating System and GNU C Compiler (gcc) version 9.3.0 (optimization level -O2 used).

All problems were solved 100 times, each time with a different random number generator seed per each thread used. Such a number of executions, all with different seeds, prevents any possible biasing in the results. The execution times presented are an average of the 100 executions, ignoring the first one. The benchmark process was fully automated, with the help of BASH scripts.

4.3 Solvers Comparison

In this section, the previous (ParMCSFilter1) [15] and the new (ParMCSFilter2) multithreaded implementations of MCSFilter are compared for problems P_1 to P_4. Again, these problems were selected due to being the same used for the validation of the preliminary ParMCSFilter1 solver [15]. For this comparison, both implementations shared the following common parameters:

- Fraction of the unsearched space (MCSFilter stop condition): $\epsilon = 10^{-1}$ (Eq. 2);
- Newly found minimizers (line 22 of the algorithm): $\gamma^* = 10^{-1}$;
- Local search CSFilter stop condition ($\alpha < \alpha_{min}$): $\alpha_{min} = 10^{-5}$.

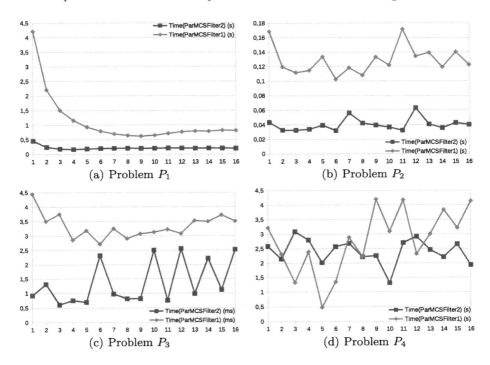

Fig. 3. ParMCSFilter1 vs ParMCSFilter2: execution time for problems P_1–P_4

Table 1. Speedups of the new MCSFilter parallel solver against the old solver.

Threads (n)	1	2	3	4	5	6	7	8	9	10	11	12	13	14	15	16
Prob P_1	**9.3**	**9.3**	8.5	7.3	5.2	4.1	3.5	**3.2**	**3.2**	**3.2**	3.5	3.8	4.0	3.8	4.1	4.2
Prob P_2	**3.9**	3.7	3.4	3.4	3.4	3.2	**2.1**	2.6	3.4	3.3	5.3	**2.1**	3.4	3.3	3.3	3.0
Prob P_3	4.8	2.7	**6.2**	3.8	4.6	**1.2**	3.3	3.6	3.8	**1.2**	4.3	**1.2**	3.6	1.6	3.3	1.4
Prob P_4	1.2	1.1	0.4	0.9	**0.2**	0.5	1.1	1.0	1.9	**2.4**	1.5	0.8	1.2	1.7	1.2	2.1

Figure 3 shows the execution time of both solvers, for the common set of problems, with a different number of threads. All times plotted are measured in seconds, except for problem P_3, for which times are represented in milliseconds.

Except for problem P_4, the performance gains introduced by the new parallel solver are very noticeable. Table 1 shows the speedups involved, corresponding to the ratio Time(ParMCSFilter1)/Time(ParMCSFilter2). These speedups vary, depending on the problem and number of threads. Problem P_1 is the one where the new solver introduces higher speedups (between 3.2 and 9.3), while in problem P_4 it may be marginally faster or visibly slower (speedup of 2.4 vs 0.2).

The execution times exhibit a different evolutionary pattern as the number of threads increase. For problem P_1, that pattern is smooth and matches the expectations. But for the other problems it becomes very irregular. The irregularities for problems P_2, P_3 and P_4 can be explained due to these being problems with equality (P_2) and inequality (P_3 and P_4) constraints in addition to simple bounds. More specifically, for problem P_4 (the one with more extreme variations), due to the complexity introduced by the constraints and the randomness introduced by the algorithm, we observed individual execution times between 0.001157 and 104.779081 s using the old solver, while in the new solver that range was considerably tighter (between 0.000747 and 40.638619 s). It should be noted that for both solvers these times are not directly related to the number of threads used, meaning there could be extremely large or small execution times with any number of threads. With this in mind, for problem P_4, even though the new solver does not translate in a significant performance improvement, the multithreaded behaviour is nevertheless more stable.

It is also fair to say that the optimizations introduced in the code of the new solver make it more efficient to the extent that it became harder to collect additional benefits from parallelization. A significant amount of the execution time in each thread is now spent in the CSFilter local search (line 20 of Algorithm 1), that is intrinsically sequential (non-parallelizable), and in changing the shared set M^* of minimizers (line 23), which can only be done by one thread at a time.

Table 2. Number of minimizers found by each solver vs number of known minimizers.

Problem	Known Mins	Solver	1	2	3	4	5	6	7	8
P_1	1024	Old	884.8	884.5	881.5	880.0	877.1	878.8	878.5	875.3
		New	1002.9	1003.1	998.0	995.2	994.3	997.7	998.5	993.8
P_2	2	Old	4.1	4.2	4.2	4.4	4.3	4.5	4.6	4.8
		New	2.4	2.4	2.3	2.3	2.3	2.3	2.3	2.5
P_3	4	Old	3.9	4.0	3.9	4.1	4.1	4.1	4.1	4.1
		New	3.99	4.0	3.98	4.0	3.99	3.99	4.01	4.0
P_4	5	Old	4.3	4.4	4.5	4.6	4.6	4.7	4.8	4.7
		New	4.8	4.8	4.8	4.7	4.7	4.7	4.8	4.6

(a) Number of threads: $n=1...8$

Problem	Solver	9	10	11	12	13	14	15	16	Average Mins
P_1	Old	875.4	871.2	868.1	873.3	876.1	872.6	873.9	876.2	876.7 (85.6%)
	New	992.4	999.4	998.6	999.1	999.9	999.8	1001.7	1002.0	998.5 (97.5%)
P_2	Old	4.7	4.9	4.9	4.8	5.0	4.9	5.0	4.6	4.6 (230.4%)
	New	2.3	2.4	2.4	2.4	2.6	2.3	2.4	2.5	2.4 (118.4%)
P_3	Old	4.1	4.1	4.1	4.2	4.2	4.1	4.2	4.2	4.1 (102.3%)
	New	4.01	4.0	3.98	4.01	4.01	4.01	3.99	4.0	4.0 (100%)
P_4	Old	4.7	4.9	4.9	4.9	4.9	5.0	4.9	5.0	4.8 (95%)
	New	4.7	4.7	4.6	4.6	4.7	4.5	4.7	4.5	4.7 (93.8%)

(b) Number of threads: $n=9...16$

To finish the comparison between the solvers, Table 2 shows the average number of minimizers found by each one, for each problem, with a different thread number. The table also contains the number of known minimizers (Known Mins) and a global average (Average Mins) of the specific averages of each number of threads; this global average is both presented as an absolute value and also as a relative (%) value against the Known Mins. It can be concluded, for both solvers, that the number of threads used doesn't have a systematic influence on the amount of minimizers found (e.g., that amount may grow or shrink with the number of threads). However, the new solver seems to better avoid overestimating the number of minimizers found (problems P_2 and P_3), while improving (problem P_1) or keeping the same findings as the old solver (problem P_4).

4.4 Performance of the New Solver with Demanding Problems

In this section the performance of the new implementation is assessed when solving problems P_5 to P_{14}. As previously stated, these are multidimensional problems that take some time to solve and so are deemed more appropriate to be handled by a parallel solver, once it should be able to generate more sensible performance gains than with problems that are not so demanding.

Figure 4 and Fig. 5 present the execution time of problems P_5 to P_{14}, with a number of threads ranging from 1 to 16. The results are split in two different charts, to allow a better visualization and reflect the type of evolution (regular/irregular) of execution times as the number of threads used grows.

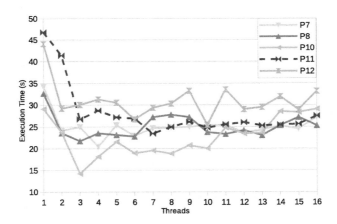

Fig. 4. ParMCSFilter2: execution time for problems P_7, P_8, P_{10}, P_{11}, P_{12}

As may be observed in both figures, the execution time (T_n) decreases with the number of threads used (n), in general up to 3 threads. But further increasing the number of threads does not translate in lower execution times, with very few exceptions (P_7 with 4 threads, P_9 with 5 threads, P_{11} with 7 threads, and P_{12} with 10 threads) that, however, benefit very little from the extra number of threads. These exceptions may be easily identified in Table 3, corresponding to problems with very poor parallel efficiency ($< 50\%$). The table shows the maximum speedups ($S_n = T_1/T_n$) achieved for each problem, and the corresponding

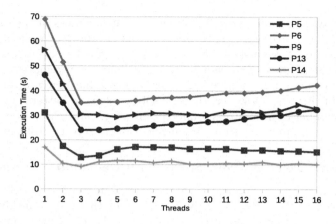

Fig. 5. ParMCSFilter2: execution time for problems P_5, P_6, P_9, P_{13}, P_{14}

number of threads (n) and parallel Efficiency $(E_n = S_n/n)$. Only problems for which the best speedup is reached with 3 threads are able to ensure a parallel efficiency of at least 50%. Moreover, the speedups achieved for these problems are very modest, ranging from 1.5 to 2.4. Clearly, a serious bottleneck is at play.

Table 3. ParMCSFilter2: Best Speedups achieved and respective number of threads.

	P_5	P_6	P_7	P_8	P_9	P_{10}	P_{11}	P_{12}	P_{13}	P_{14}
Number of threads (n)	3	3	4	3	5	3	7	10	3	3
Maximum speedup (S_n)	2.4	1.96	1.67	1.5	1.93	2.05	1.99	1.73	1.92	1.87
Parallel efficiency (E_n)	80%	65%	42%	50%	39%	68%	28%	17%	64%	62%

Through some investigation it was possible to identify the major bottleneck in the new solver, explaining the sudden loss in performance with more than 3 worker threads. The bottleneck derives from the decision brought up in Sect. 3.2, to keep using a growing dynamic array as the main data structure to store the minimizers found (albeit with some modifications). As it was found, the main problem identified with this this approach is the high contention suffered by worker threads when trying to access the shared array, despite replacing the mutex lock of the old solver with a read-write lock in the new one.

There are several reasons for this. Firstly, it's an unsorted array and the algorithm needs to compare every single member with a new minimizer candidate, having to perform a write either once it finds a match or adding it to the end of the array once it's done iterating it. This $O(n)$ search may end up to be very costly, specially for problems with many possible minimizers. Secondly, the competition between threads for read/write access rights to the array becomes more intense as the number of threads grows, which further aggravates the problem.

Thus, even though the local search method is executed in parallel by the worker threads, execution times are strongly penalized by the need for exclusive access to shared data. A possible solution to this problem is to replace the dynamic array by a lock-free sorted data structure, like lock-free Binary Search Trees [10]. Although less cache-friendly, such data structure brings with it at least two benefits which fit our current problems: the binary search represents a much better time complexity compromise $O(log(n))$; it solves (or minimizes) the read/write access contention problem. This will be pursued in future work.

Finally, it was also found that the parallel algorithm may have a limitation regarding the unaccounted redundant searches introduced by the parallelism to local searches, as mentioned in Sect. 3. The reason for this is that there may be multiple threads executing a local search for the same minimizer simultaneously, without before taking advantage of the attraction radius, as it is only updated at the end of each local search. Therefore, as more threads are employed, more redundant searches will occur, resulting in more total time spent processing each local search. A solution for this could be the introduction of a new mechanism in the algorithm to reduce currently unaccounted redundant searches.

5   Conclusions and Future Work

Due to the nature of the local procedure (a pattern search method), the MCS-Filter algorithm may take considerable time to converge to the solution. With this in mind, the original MATLAB implementation was re-coded in JAVA and later in C, with every new implementations showing increased performance over the previous one. In the quest for more performance, parallelization was the next logical step. After a first attempt laid out the foundation of the parallel approach to be taken [15], this paper presented a refinement of the approach, which exhibits better performance than the first parallel solver (that already surpassed all sequential versions), while keeping or improving the number of minimizers found. Moreover, the new parallel solver was shown to solve specially demanding problems in half the time of their sequential execution. And, even though some scalability constraints were found with more than 3 worker threads, the current parallel solver is certainly able to take advantage of low core-count computing systems, like those usually found in industrial-level/embedded systems.

In the future, aiming to overcome the scalability bottlenecks identified, the shared data structure used to store the minimizers will be replaced with a lock-free alternative. It is expected that such change will provide the desirable performance and scalability levels for a parallel multilocal programming solver.

Other possible parallelization approaches will also be investigated, namely based on the domain decomposition of the search space. From a performance perspective, these are usually very promising. However, this would result in the finding of possible minimizers in each sub-domain that could be false positives and would need further validation (their exclusion could be done by checking their compliance with the problem restrictions within the admissible region).

We will also revisit the MCSFilter algorithm in order to assess the possibility of a parallel implementation using many-core co-processors, namely GP-GPUs.

Acknowledgements. This work has been supported by FCT - Fundação para a Ciência e Tecnologia within the Project Scope: UIDB/05757/2020.

References

1. Abhishek, K., Leyffer, S., Linderoth, J.: Filmint: an outer-approximation-based solver for convex mixed-integer nonlinear programs. Inf. J. Comput. **22**, 555–567 (2010)
2. Abramson, M., Audet, C., Chrissis, J., Walston, J.: Mesh adaptive direct search algorithms for mixed variable optimization. Optim. Lett. **3**, 35–47 (2009)
3. Amador, A., Fernandes, F.P., Santos, L.O., Romanenko, A., Rocha, A.M.A.C.: Parameter estimation of the kinetic α-Pinene isomerization model using the MCS-Filter algorithm. In: Gervasi, O., et al. (eds.) ICCSA 2018. LNCS, vol. 10961, pp. 624–636. Springer, Cham (2018). https://doi.org/10.1007/978-3-319-95165-2_44
4. Amador, A., Fernandes, F.P., Santos, L.O., Romanenko, A.: Application of mcs-filter to estimate stiction control valve parameters. AIP Confer. Proc. **1863**(1), 2700051–2700054 (2017)
5. Araújo, L., Pacheco, M.F., Rufino, J., Fernandes, F.P.: Towards a high-performance implementation of the mcsfilter optimization algorithm. In: Pereira, A.I., et al. (eds.) Optimization, Learning Algorithms and Applications, pp. 15–30. Springer International Publishing, Cham (2021)
6. Eronen, V.-P., Westerlund, T., Mäkelä, M.M.: On mixed integer nonsmooth optimization. In: Bagirov, A.M., Gaudioso, M., Karmitsa, N., Mäkelä, M.M., Taheri, S. (eds.) Numerical Nonsmooth Optimization, pp. 549–578. Springer, Cham (2020). https://doi.org/10.1007/978-3-030-34910-3_16
7. Fernandes, F.P.: Programação não linear inteira mista e não convexa sem derivadas. Ph.D. thesis, Univ. of Minho, Braga, Portugal (2014)
8. Fernandes, F.P., Costa, M.F.P., Fernandes, E.M.G.P.: Multilocal programming: a derivative-free filter multistart algorithm. In: Murgante, B., et al. (eds.) ICCSA 2013. LNCS, vol. 7971, pp. 333–346. Springer, Heidelberg (2013). https://doi.org/10.1007/978-3-642-39637-3_27
9. Floudas, C.: Recent advances in global optimization for process synthesis, design and control: enclosure of all solutions. Comput. Chem. Eng. **963**, 963–973 (1999)
10. Howley, S.V., Jones, J.: A non-blocking internal binary search tree. In: Blelloch, G.E., Herlihy, M. (eds.) 24th ACM Symposium on Parallelism in Algorithms and Architectures, SPAA 2012, Pittsburgh, PA, USA, June 25–27, 2012, pp. 161–171. ACM (2012)
11. Kolda, T., Lewis, R., Torczon, V.: Optimization by direct search: new perspectives on some classical and modern methods. SIAM Rev. **45**, 85–482 (2003)
12. Monteiro, L., Rufino, J., Romanenko, A., Fernandes, F.P.: MCSFilter performance: a comparison study, pp. 3–5. Book of Abstracts of SASYR 2022, F. P. Fernandes, P. Morais and P. Pinto (eds.) (2022)
13. Murray, W., Ng, K.M.: Handbook of global optimization. In: Pardalos, P.M., Romeijn, H.E., (eds.) Algorithms for Global Optimization and Discrete Problems based on Methods for Local Optimization, vol. 2, pp. 87–114. (2002)
14. Romanenko, A., Fernandes, F.P., Fernandes, N.C.P.: PID controllers tuning with mcsfilter. In: AIP Conference Proceedings, vol. 2116, p. 220003 (2019)
15. Rufino, J., Araújo, L., Pacheco, M.F., Fernandes, F.P.: A multi-threaded parallel implementation of the mcsfilter optimization algorithm. In: AIP Conference Proceedings. in press (2022)

16. Seiça, J.C., Romanenko, A., Fernandes, F.P., Santos, L.O., Fernandes, N.C.P.: Parameter estimation of a pulp digester model with derivative-free optimization strategies. In: AIP Conference Proceedings, vol. 1863, no. 1, p. 270006 (2017)
17. Yang, X.S.: Optimization Techniques and Applications with Examples. Wiley (2018)

Integer Programming Applied to Wireless Sensor Networks Topology Optimization

Lucas Ferreira Pinheiro⬤, Laura Silva de Assis⬤, and Felipe da Rocha Henriques$^{(\boxtimes)}$⬤

Federal Center of Technological Education of Rio de Janeiro - CEFET/RJ, Rio de Janeiro, Brazil
{lucas.pinheiro,laura.assis,felipe.henriques}@cefet-rj.br

Abstract. Wireless Sensor Networks (WSNs) are systems with great potential for applications in the most diverse areas such as industry, security, public health, and agriculture. In general, for a WSN to achieve high performance, multiple criteria must be considered, such as coverage area, connectivity, and energy consumption. In this work an Integer Programming (IP) model to solve a Sensor Allocation Problem (SAP) is presented. The IP model considers a heterogeneous WSN and deterministic locations to positioning of sensors. The proposed model was validated using the IBM ILOG CPLEX solver. A several computational experiments were performed, and an analysis through small and medium-sized instances of the problem under study are presented and discussed. The proposed model presents good results given the problem premises, constraints and considered objectives, achieving 0.0099% optimality gap for the best scenarios where networks are fully connected and are feasible to implement. Other suboptimal evaluated scenarios with denser distribution of sensor nodes depict about 0.04% of isolated node positioning, spite maintaining overall balance between energy consumption and coverage. Therefore, the proposed model shows promise for achieving practical solutions, i.e., those with implementation feasibility in most considered heterogeneous network scenarios.

Keywords: Sensor allocation · Optimization · Wireless sensor networks · Integer programming

1 Introduction

Wireless Sensor Networks (WSNs) consist of a distribution of several low-cost sensor nodes with limited computing, communication, and energy capacity [2]. Generally, WSN has the objective of autonomously monitoring physical-chemical parameters within a region of interest. The nodes may have different power and transmission range configurations, being able to intercommunicate and pass on the collected data from one point to another, on the network, until reaching a

Supported by organization FAPERJ.

sink where this data is stored and made available for analysis. This type of system proves to be very useful in scenarios where direct human intervention to perform measurements would be impossible or infeasible, in addition to enabling much larger monitoring coverage. There is therefore great potential for applications in areas such as industry [14], security [23], public health [16], agriculture [21] and even militarism [11].

The physical topology of sensor nodes in a region of interest can be organized randomly or deterministic, depending on the type of application. Deterministic positioning of sensors in controllable scenarios is usually preferred, while stochastic distribution is usually applicable to hazardous areas or those that are difficult to access for device recovery. A major advantage of deterministic deployment is the use of a smaller number of nodes to perform the same task [5].

In general, the success of a practical useful implementation of a WSN requires that some criteria are taken in consideration, such as energy efficiency, load balancing, coverage area, communication latency, among others. Considering a deterministic deployment of heterogeneous sensor nodes – with different transmission power configurations – there is a need to manage these criteria in order to obtain the optimal allocation for the devices, i.e., guaranteeing the best network performance as possible [19]. This problem can be named as a Sensor Allocation Problem (SAP) [6].

The present work proposes an Integer Programming (IP) model for a SAP inspired in [5] and [6] where nodes are heterogeneous and a balance between energy consumption, connectivity and network coverage is desired. A study is performed on small and medium-sized instances of the problem using the IBM ILOG CPLEX[1] solver. Computational results show the feasibility of the proposed model for heterogeneous WSNs, with respect to the aforementioned network metrics. The remain of the paper is organized as following. Section 2 presents a summarized literature review on the topic of SAP and highlights the main contributions of this work in relation to existing work. Section 3 exposes a detailed description of the problem under study. The mathematical modeling is discussed in Sect. 4. The results obtained from solving different instances of the proposed problem and its analysis is presented in Sect. 5. Section 6 makes the final considerations and addresses possible developments of this work.

2   Related Work

This section presents a literature review, highlighting works related to the Sensor Allocation Problem. Basically, the main studied methodologies will be cluster in two major classes: *i)* exact (or deterministic) approaches; and *ii)* non-deterministic approaches, which include algorithms based on heuristics, meta-heuristics, with bio-inspired algorithms.

In the context of the first methodologies group, authors of [22] investigated a brute force algorithm for topology optimization of WSNs. A topology composed

---

[1] https://www.ibm.com/br-pt/analytics/cplex-optimizer
   For practical purposes, in the remain of the paper, we will just call it CPLEX.

by clusters is considered in [10], and the optimal location of the cluster-heads is reached by the proposed algorithm. A grid was considered for the computational experiments, and the intensity of radio signal was used as the optimization criterion. Authors pointed up that this brute force based scheme has the disadvantage of computational cost, which could be mitigated by the usage of multi-core processors and accelerators [13].

Sensor nodes of a WSN can perform different tasks: some of them could execute data gathering, others could be relays/router, others could be sink nodes, and others could perform more than one of these tasks. Another distinction can be associated to the transmission range, which leads to higher or lower energy consumption. In this work we define the latter distinction (transmission range) as operational modes. These operational modes can be used to define a heterogeneous sensor network. Following this idea, authors of [4] propose a multi-level optimization framework aiming at reducing the combinatorial complexity. The proposed scheme considers a limited number of relay nodes, communication range, obstacle avoidance and coverage area in the optimization algorithm. Another solution, based on integer linear programming model is implemented to minimize the energy consumption in heterogeneous WSNs in [15]. Work in [9] pushes this further by considering nodes mobility to optimize the coverage area, while maintaining energy constraints.

On another hand, following the second class of approaches, a swarm intelligence heuristic algorithm is used for the optimization procedure in [20], and a survey on nature-inspired optimization algorithms for WSNs is presented in [18]. Authors of [7] investigated optimization methods for bio-inspired networks. In general, these algorithms consider Ant Colony Optimization (ACO) [8], Particle Swarm Optimization (PSO) [17] and Genetic Algorithm (GA) [12].

The problem addressed in this paper is inspired on works [5] and [6]. In [5], the authors applied a Genetic Algorithm methodology in order to optimize node placement for WSNs. Authors implemented the GA in MatLab[2], and the proposed methodology considers distinct operational modes for sensor nodes, based on their transmission range. A grid-based topology was considered for the experiments, and parameters such as energy consumption, connectivity and network density were evaluated. Authors of [6] extends the previous study considering large topologies.

A hybrid algorithm that combines an initial phase that uses Voronoi diagram in order to divide the monitoring field into cells with a second phase that maximizes the coverage area with a GA is proposed in [1]. This approach is evaluated in the context of the Internet of Things, and it outperformed both the Genetic and the Voronoi algorithms. A Genetic algorithm is used in [3] to find optimal sensor allocation applied to a forest fires monitoring system.

In summary, our work can be associated to the first aforementioned class (exact approach), and we can summarize the following contributions regarding to the literature review:

---

[2] https://www.mathworks.com.

- Unlike the work of [5], and intending to extend their analysis, an Integer Programming (IP) model is used to perform the Sensor Allocation Problem, considering a heterogeneous WSN with deterministic positioning of nodes;
- This allows one to find an exact solution for the SAP considering scenarios where nodes are not necessarily evenly distributed in a grid;
- The investigated approach is modeled and implemented in a solver, and evaluated considering instances with distinct sizes and densities.

3   Problem Statement

In this work, we consider a WSN that must be installed on a flat surface of area $H \times W$ for autonomous monitoring of soil parameters. There are n specific positions on the surface that must be monitored whose geographic coordinates are known. It is also known that each node that composes the network can operate with one of three possible operating modes t, where $t \in S = \{X, Y, Z\}$. Each mode represents a different power level – the higher the level, the greater the transmission power and sensing range as well as the energy consumption of the device. Therefore, there is a direct proportionality relationship between these parameters. The available operating modes and their respective power levels (in terms of units) are highlighted in Table 1.

Table 1. Sensor operating modes and power levels.

Operation mode	Power level
X	4
Y	2
Z	1

Thus, it is understood that a sensor in the X operating mode has a transmission and sensing radius on the order of 4 units of distance, while it has the highest energy consumption. Similarly, a sensor in Y mode has transmission and sensing radius of 2 units and average energy consumption, while a sensor in Z mode has radius of 1 unit and minimum energy consumption. It is desired to determine which operating modes to configure at each position of interest on the surface in order to maximize network coverage and communication between nodes, in addition to minimizing system energy consumption with the following constraints:

1. In each monitoring position, a single type of sensor node must be allocated among the three possible ones (X, Y, or Z).
2. At least one X-node, which corresponds to a network sink, must be allocated in the monitoring region.
3. All designated n positions must receive a sensor.

Additionally, the following assumptions are considered:

- Scenarios are considered with n predefined monitoring positions within which, given a position i, for all pairs of positions that include i, at least one pair is at most 4 units of distance apart, i.e., there are no scenarios where the sensor nodes are purposely isolated (that is, not having enough transmission power to reach other nodes).
- Sensor nodes are able to route data collected by other sensor nodes in the network. Thus, for example, a source Z-node can forward data to one or more intermediate Y-nodes or Z-nodes, which will forward this same data to other nodes until reaching the closest possible active destination X-node.
- The X-nodes correspond to network sinks, so they have a greater transmission range, and consequently greater energy consumption. It is essential that all network nodes are able to communicate directly with at least one X-node. If this is not feasible, there must be multiple-hop routes in the network that allow each node to reach at least one X-node.

4   Mathematical Modeling of Sensor Allocation Problem

The SAP in study can be mathematically modeled as a simple, connected and directed graph $G(V, A)$, where V is a set of n nodes and A is a set of m edges. A node $i \in V$ represents a sensor allocation position, that sensor can operate at different power settings. The edge $(i, j) \in A$, with $i \in V$, $j \in V$, and $j \neq i$, represents the possibility of communication between a source node i and a destination node j, i.e., node j is a neighbor of i if and only if, it is within the transmission range of node i. It is intended to determine the operation mode for each sensor node $i \in V$ among three possibilities $t \in S = \{X, Y, Z\}$. Therefore, the set of binary decision variables of the problem can be defined through Eq. (1) where $i \in V$ and $t \in S$.

$$s_i^t = \begin{cases} 1, & \text{if an operating mode } t \text{ is allocated on the } i\text{-th node} \\ 0, & \text{otherwise} \end{cases} \tag{1}$$

After the introduction of the decision variables, and considering the descriptions made in topics 1., 2., and 3., the SAP can be mathematically modeled as a minimization Integer Programming Problem (IPP), represented by Eqs. (2) – (8). The objective function is described as a linear combination between the functions $E(s_i^t)$ and $C(s_i^t)$, which respectively represent the total energy consumption (7) and the network coverage and connectivity (8) according to sensors mode placed in the monitoring region, i.e., in the solution.

$$\min \quad \alpha E(s_i^t) - (1 - \alpha)C(s_i^t) \tag{2}$$

s.t.

$$\sum_{t \in S} s_i^t \leq 1 \qquad \forall\, i \in V \tag{3}$$

$$\sum_{i \in V} s_i^X \geq 1 \tag{4}$$

$$\sum_{i \in V} \sum_{t \in S} s_i^t = n \tag{5}$$

$$s_i^t \in \{0, 1\} \qquad \forall\, i \in V, \quad \forall\, t \in S \tag{6}$$

$$E(s_i^t) = \sum_{i \in V} \frac{4s_i^X + 2s_i^Y + s_i^Z}{n} \tag{7}$$

$$C(s_i^t) = \sum_{i \in V} \left(\frac{s_i^X + s_i^Y + s_i^Z}{n} \right) - \frac{N_{OR}}{n} \tag{8}$$

Constraints in (3) assure that at most one sensor type will be allocated to each monitoring position. Constraint (4) guarantees the existence of at least one sensor of type X in the solution. Constraint (5) determines that the total number of sensor allocations is equal to n, which is the exact number of the monitoring positions of interest. Finally, Constraints presented in (6) defines the decision variables as binary.

Equation (7) describes the energy consumption of the system as the weighted average of each of the allocated active sensor power levels, according to their respective operating modes (Table 1). Equation (8) describes the network coverage and connectivity as the total number of active nodes (of X, Y or Z operation modes) minus the number of nodes that are out of range of sink nodes or possible relays. The expression is normalized by the total number of sensor nodes n. The calculation of the total number of out of range nodes (N_{OR}) is defined by Eq. (9).

$$N_{OR} = N_{OR}^{ZX} + N_{OR}^{ZY} + N_{OR}^{YX} \tag{9}$$

$$N_{OR}^{ZX} = \sum_{i \in N} \max \left(0, (1 - s_i^X - s_i^Y) - \min \left(1, \sum_{j \in N_i^Z} s_j^X \right) \right) \tag{10}$$

$$N_{OR}^{YX} = \sum_{i \in N} \max \left(0, (1 - s_i^X - s_i^Z) - \min \left(1, \sum_{j \in N_i^Y} s_j^X \right) \right) \tag{11}$$

$$N_{OR}^{ZY} = \sum_{i \in N} \max \left(0, (1 - s_i^X - s_i^Y) - \min \left(1, \sum_{j \in N_i^Z} s_j^Y \right) \right) \tag{12}$$

A Z-node or Y-node is defined as out of range of X-nodes if there is not any neighboring X-node to which it can directly forward the traffic. Likewise, a Z-node is defined as out of range of Y-nodes if it has no neighboring Y-nodes to which it can directly forward the traffic. Thus, the Eq. (9) comprises the Eqs. (10), (11) and (12), and represent, respectively: *i)* the number of Z-nodes out of range of X-nodes; *ii)* the number of Y-nodes out of range of X-nodes; and *iii)* the number of Z-nodes out of range of Y-nodes. These definitions are important to satisfy a critical premise of the SAP under study: every Z-node or Y-node must always reach a X-node, even if by multiple hops. That is, the number of out of range sensors (Eq. (9)) must be the minimum as possible in order to maximize network connectivity.

The subsets of nodes $N_i^Z \subset V$, and $N_i^Y \subset V$ correspond to the neighborhoods, considering all n monitoring positions of interest, as long as that in i position is placed a Z-node or Y-node, respectively. Since the geographic coordinates are known for all monitoring positions, the Euclidean distances between each pair of nodes that will be allocated in the network are also known and, therefore, it is feasible to compute the possible neighborhoods of each node i for 1 or 2 distance units (respectively N_i^Z or N_i^Y). A node $j \in V$ is considered a neighbor of a node $i \in V$ if $j \neq i$, and j is within the transmission range corresponding to this node, according to the type of sensor that is placed in i. Each iteration of the sums in Eqs. (10), (11), and (12) presents a binary result, being equal to 1 only if node i is of type Y or Z and if it has at least some j node (of types X or Y) in its neighborhood.

5   Results and Discussion

The next sections evaluate the presented model with 36 different generated network instances for 4 distinct sizes of monitoring area. Each instance represents nodes density and distribution variation. For each network test, 1 of 5 values for α were used, resulting in 180 test scenarios computed. The CPLEX solver and its associated IDE were used in all computational experiments.

5.1   Solver and Model Configuration

The CPLEX solver was used to perform the computational implementation of the IP-SAP under study. The model was run on an AMD Ryzen 5 3500U CPU @ 2.1 GHz with 12 GB RAM.

To understand the behavior of the model, it was decided to initially analyze small and medium-size scenarios consisting of square areas of side $L \in \{10, 15, 20, 25\}$ units of distance. As so the total size of the area is given by $L \times L$ ($H = W = L$). For each scenario, sensor nodes densities from 10% to 90% were considered. The geographic coordinates of each node were predefined randomly, respecting the premise that no node would be placed isolated from others (i.e., more than 4 units of distance apart from any other node).

The solver was set with default configuration considering Mixed Integer Programming problems: balance optimality and feasibility by using dynamic search strategy and relative optimality gap tolerance set to 10^{-4}. A time limit of 20 min was also set to prevent the model from running for too long without obtaining

significant better solutions. This limitation was determined based on total solving time for dense $L = 10$ scenarios, which took a maximum average of 15 min.
The total number of network instances generated were 36 and the model was
run one time for each considered value of $\alpha \in \{0, 0.25, 0.5, 0.75, 1\}$ (see Eq. (2))
adding up 180 numerical results.

5.2 Network and Solution Illustration

For better understanding the proposed model-provided solutions, an illustration of a network instance (Fig. 1a) and of its respective solution (Fig. 1b) are
presented. Figure 1 depicts a solution example for a monitoring field network
of size $L = 10$, with 50% node density and $\alpha = 0.25$, where each position in
the surface of interest is 1 distance unit apart orthogonally. Figure 1a shows the
predetermined monitoring positions for this instance, chosen in a random manner, depicted by nodes in blue, i.e., the network received as input by the model.
Figure 1b shows the optimal solution of operating mode allocation for this network configuration. The transmission ranges for one Z-node and one Y-node are
highlighted, as are the possible minimum paths to a X-node (sink) for all sensor
nodes in this solution.

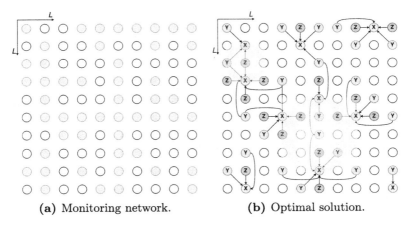

(a) Monitoring network.   (b) Optimal solution.

Fig. 1. An IP-SAP network and solution illustration with $L = 10$ field, 50% node
density, and $\alpha = 0.25$.

Through the analysis of each individual node transmission range (and the
minimum paths to sink) in Fig. 1b, it can be seen that the network is connected,
i.e., all sensors can relay traffic to each other and, mostly important, every node
can reach a X-node with a single hop, which satisfies the premises of the problem.
Considering this value of α and the distribution of nodes, it is understandable
that the number of X-nodes and Y-nodes are higher than needed, as the objective function is prioritizing to maximize connectivity over minimizing energy
consumption.

However, for different values of α in this same scenario of density (50%) and $L = 10$ (Fig. 2), multiple hops may become necessary for the nodes to reach the nearest sink (Fig. 2b). When minimizing energy consumption is priority, the solver ends up adding more Z-nodes which causes the undesirable appearance of isolated sensor nodes (highlighted in red in Fig. 2c). Ultimately, as expected, values of $\alpha = 0$ (Fig. 2a) or $\alpha = 1$ (Fig. 2d) outputs impractical scenarios, where the former only aims to maximize the coverage and connectivity, totally disregarding the energy consumption, and the latter aims only for minimizing the energy consumption.

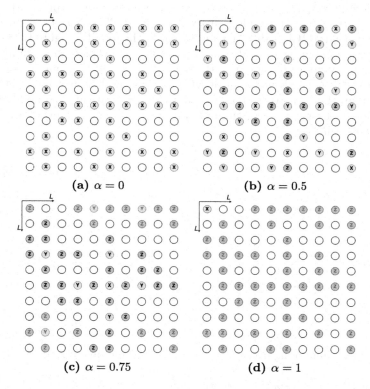

Fig. 2. IP-SAP solutions with $L = 10$ field, 50% node density and varying α. Out of range nodes are highlighted in red (Color figure online).

5.3 Computational Experiments, Results and Discussion

For validating the proposed model, computational experiments were performed by using the CPLEX solver. The experiments aimed to observe if the model was able to output practical and feasible networks with good balance between energy consumption, connectivity and coverage, all within a given execution time limit.

Undesirable or impractical solutions were also collected and analyzed to study possible future improvements to the model. Table 2 lists all setup parameters for the proposed validation experiments and its selected values.

Table 2. Setup parameters for the test scenarios.

Data	Description	Values
α	Linear combination parameter	$\{0, 0.25, 0.5, 0.75, 1\}$
L	Monitoring area size	$\{10, 15, 20, 25\}$
D	Nodes density	$\{0.1, 0.2, 0.3, 0.4, 0.5, 0.6, 0.7, 0.8, 0.9\}$
$time$	Maximum execution time criteria	20 minutes

Given the possible variation of scenarios using the generated networks, the number of associated experiments for this study is $5 \times 4 \times 9$. Consequently, due to the total amount of results obtained, we will show and analyze a small subset of the solutions found below. The full set of results can be found in the public repository of this work[3].

The best results between all considered instances are listed in Table 3. They were obtained by using the following criteria: *i)* instances should present possibility of practical implementation (i.e., no isolated nodes); *ii)* the solver should attain optimal solution within the set time limit; and *iii)* there should be acceptable balance between values of $E(s_i^t)$ and $C(s_i^t)$. These best solutions are depicted in $\mathbb{R}^2$ in Fig. 3.

Table 3. Best results for the IP-SAP under study.

L	α	Number of nodes	Node density (%)	Optimality gap (%)	Objective function	$C(s_i^t)$	$E(s_i^t)$	Isolated nodes	Solving time (s)
10	0.5	90	90	0.0099	0.3889	0.9556	1.7334	0	18.826
15	0.5	180	80	0.0099	0.3916	0.95	1.7334	0	147.535

From Eqs. 7 and 8 it is known that $E(s_i^t) \in (1, 4]$, and also $C(s_i^t) \in [0, 1)$ if and only if $N_{OR} \neq 0$ and there are more active and connected than out of range nodes, which is the case for these best solutions. That being said, it is possible to observe that the energy consumption is less than average of possible range while results maintain good coverage and connectivity between nodes. Despite $\alpha = 0.5$, the objective function presents positive results as $E(s_i^t) > C(s_i^t)$, which is understandable as one can see there are more Y-nodes than needed in the solutions (Fig. 3). In other words, besides admissible levels of energy consumption are achieved, the model can still be improved to obtain even better results.

Regarding network metrics for the two best solutions, it is clear from Fig. 3 that the network is connected and any node is able to reach the nearest sink with

---

[3] Available in https://github.com/LucasPinheiro23/sap-OL2A_2022.

at maximum 2 hops, which directly implies in low network latency. Moreover, X-nodes are nearly evenly distributed in the network and, in normal operation conditions (i.e., without node fault), clusters with an average of 6 nodes converges traffic into each nearest sink, leading to a low sink overhead.

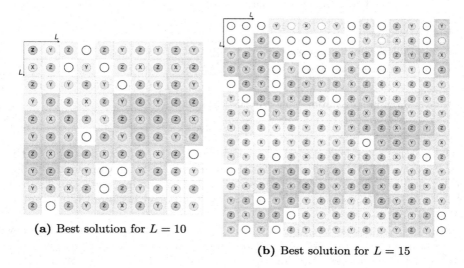

(a) Best solution for $L = 10$

(b) Best solution for $L = 15$

Fig. 3. An example of possible node clusters around each sink in the IP-SAP best solutions.

Figures 4 and 5 summarize the results obtained for the performed scenarios. They depict, respectively, the total solving time and the number of allocated operating modes for different monitoring area sizes, namely $L = \{10, 15, 20, 25\}$.

It can be seen that solving time increases rapidly and directly proportional to the total number of nodes, specially for $\alpha \in \{0.25, 0.50, 0.75\}$ where different levels of balance between $E(s_i^t)$ and $C(s_i^t)$ are considered. The predetermined time limit is reached faster for denser scenarios, resulting in some suboptimal solutions. Despite that, the percentage of isolated nodes (Fig. 6) for denser suboptimal cases are acceptable (near 0.4%) which indicates that no much more solving time may be needed for obtaining better solutions (in terms of $E(s_i^t)$ and $C(s_i^t)$) that represent implementation feasibility even if still suboptimal.

From Fig. 6 it can be also observed that, aside from providing higher solving time, denser scenarios ($\geq 70\%$) provides better probability of obtaining lower percentage of isolated nodes. Therefore, one can conclude that sparser distributions of sensor nodes increases the probability of isolated nodes to appear in the solution. It is important to note however that the sparsity of nodes on the surface were not directly controlled when randomly generating the instances considered in this study.

Moreover, disregarding $\alpha = 0$ and $\alpha = 1$ scenarios (where solving time is lowest due to the simplification of the problem), it is possible to observe that

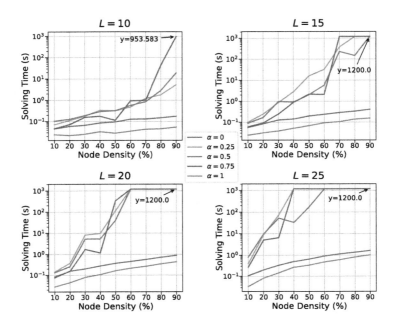

Fig. 4. Solving time for each IP-SAP network size.

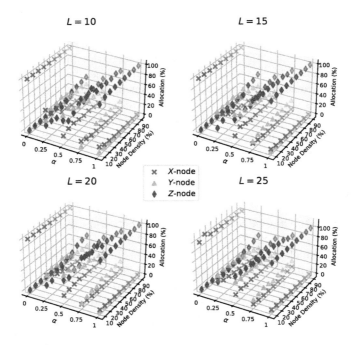

Fig. 5. Percentage of sensor operating mode allocations by node density and α for each network size.

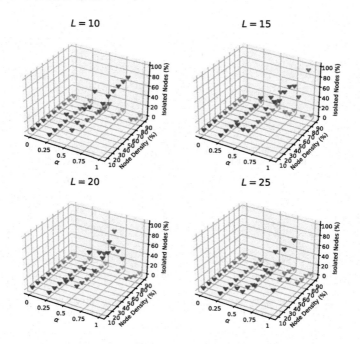

Fig. 6. Percentage of isolated sensor nodes on each network size solution.

the percentage of X-nodes when $\alpha = 0.25$ is very high when compared to other cases, reaching a peak of 50% in the lesser dense scenario. This clarifies why there are no isolated nodes for any node density for this value of α, with the setback of substantially increasing the general energy consumption of the system. On the other hand, cases where $\alpha = 0.75$ shows a great increase in Z-node allocation –80% while maintaining only 1 or 2 X-nodes which reduces energy consumption but generates greater unnecessary latency and sink overhead alongside many undesirable isolated nodes.

6   Conclusion

Through this work, it was possible to study the computational modeling and implementation of a IP-SAP. It was verified that the proposed model is viable for scenarios in which the geographic positions of the heterogeneous sensor nodes are known (e.g., precision agriculture of forest fire monitoring), although best results are obtained for denser sensor node distributions. The model takes as input the number n of desired monitoring positions and its cardinal coordinates, as well as the dimensions of the studied space (H, W). The output shows the exact positioning of each operating mode for each desired monitoring place.

We observed that, for sparser distributions of nodes and for greater α values the results may show up worse, depicting infeasible scenarios with bigger proportion of isolated nodes. Although it was expected that for $\alpha = 0.75$ there would be an increase in Z-nodes and consequent decrease in Y-nodes and X-nodes, these isolated allocations denote that adjusts in the model are needed to maintain connectivity even when energy consumption is being prioritized, which would guarantee better practical results. Besides that, it is concluded that the modeling as presented is sufficient to present good results given selected scenarios with denser distribution of nodes. Modeling traffic and routing between sensors alongside a fine tuning of α may also help improve the proposed model.

It is important to emphasize that, despite the square shape of the surfaces presented in Sect. 5, it is possible to solve the model for any shape of monitoring area in $\mathbb{R}^2$ if the positions of interest coordinates are provided in Cartesian form. For future work, in addition to adjusts in the model, a comprehensive multi-objective study can be considered by aggregating other objective functions (e.g., minimize latency or maximize throughput) as a range of new constraints and premises (e.g., more sensor operation modes, maintaining redundant routes in case of node failure, terrain irregularities, interference, obstacles etc.) to take on more complex challenges which solutions may help practical WSN implementations.

Acknowledgements. The authors are grateful for the financial support provided by the FAPERJ funding agency (Ref.:210.286/2019 - APQ1 2019).

References

1. Abdallah, W., Mnasri, S., Val, T.: Genetic-Voronoi algorithm for coverage of IoT data collection networks. In: 30th International Conference on Computer Theory and Applications, ICCTA 2020 - Proceedings (December), pp. 16–22 (2020). https://doi.org/10.1109/ICCTA52020.2020.9477675
2. Akyildiz, I.F., Su, W., Sankarasubramaniam, Y., Cayirci, E.: Wireless sensor networks: a survey. Comput. Netw. **38**(4), 393–422 (2002)
3. Azevedo, B.F., Brito, T., Lima, J., Pereira, A.I.: Optimum sensors allocation for a forest fires monitoring system. Forests **12**(4), 1–13 (2021). https://doi.org/10.3390/f12040453
4. Balesdent, M., Piet-Lahanier, H.: A multi-level optimization approach for the planning of heterogeneous sensor networks. Adv. Intell. Syst. Comput. **360**(March), 221–233 (2015). https://doi.org/10.1007/978-3-319-18167-7_20
5. Bhondekar, A.P., Vig, R., Singla, M.L., Ghanshyam, C., Kapur, P.: Genetic algorithm based node placement methodology for wireless sensor networks. In: Proceedings of the International MultiConference of Engineers and Computer Scientists I, p. 7 (2009). http://www.iaeng.org/publication/IMECS2009/IMECS2009_pp106-112.pdf
6. De Brito, J.A., Junior, J.R., Henriques, F.R., De Assis, L.S.: Topology control optimization of wireless sensor networks for IoT applications. Proceedings of the 25th Brazillian Symposium on Multimedia and the Web, WebMedia 2019 October, pp. 477–480 (2019). https://doi.org/10.1145/3323503.3361718
7. Dibrita, N.S., Eledlebi, K., Hildmann, H., Culley, L., Isakovic, A.F.: Temporal graphs and temporal network characteristics for bio-inspired networks during optimization. Appl. Sci. (Switzerland) **12**(3), 1041 (2022). https://doi.org/10.3390/app12031315

8. Dorigo, M., Stützle, T.: Ant colony optimization: overview and recent advances. In: Gendreau, M., Potvin, J.-Y. (eds.) Handbook of Metaheuristics. ISORMS, vol. 272, pp. 311–351. Springer, Cham (2019). https://doi.org/10.1007/978-3-319-91086-4_10

9. Elfouly, F.H., Ramadan, R.A., Khedr, A.Y., Azar, A.T., Yadav, K., Abdelhamed, M.A.: Efficient node deployment of large-scale heterogeneous wireless sensor networks. Appl. Sci. (Switz.) **11**(22), 10924 (2021). https://doi.org/10.3390/app112210924

10. Fanian, F., Rafsanjani, M.K.: Cluster-based routing protocols in wireless sensor networks: a survey based on methodology. J. Netw. Comput. Appl. **142**, 111–142 (2019)

11. Ismail, M.N., Shukran, M., Isa, M.R.M., Adib, M., Zakaria, O.: Establishing a soldier wireless sensor network (WSN) communication for military operation monitoring. Int. J. Inform. Commun. Technol. **7**(2), 89–95 (2018)

12. Katoch, S., Chauhan, S.S., Kumar, V.: A review on genetic algorithm: past, present, and future. Multimedia Tools Appl. **80**(5), 8091–8126 (2021)

13. Lopes, A.S.B., Brandalero, M., Beck, A.C.S., Pereira, M.M.: Generating optimized multicore accelerator architectures. In: 2019 IX Brazilian Symposium on Computing Systems Engineering (SBESC), pp. 1–8 (2019). https://doi.org/10.1109/SBESC49506.2019.9046083

14. Majid, M., et al.: Applications of wireless sensor networks and Internet of Things frameworks in the industry revolution 4.0: a systematic literature review. Sensors **22**(6), 2087 (2022)

15. Pinheiro, P.R., Sobreira Neto, Á.M., Aguiar, A.B.: Handing optimization energy consumption in heterogeneous wireless sensor networks. Int. J. Distrib. Sens. Netw. 2013 (2013). https://doi.org/10.1155/2013/328619

16. Saini, J., Dutta, M., Marques, G.: A comprehensive review on indoor air quality monitoring systems for enhanced public health. Sustain. Environ. Res. **30**(1), 1–12 (2020)

17. Sengupta, S., Basak, S., Peters, R.A.: Particle swarm optimization: a survey of historical and recent developments with hybridization perspectives. Mach. Learn. Knowl. Extract. **1**(1), 157–191 (2018)

18. Singh, A., Sharma, S., Singh, J.: Nature-inspired algorithms for wireless sensor networks: a comprehensive survey. Comput. Sci. Rev. **39**, 100342 (2021). https://doi.org/10.1016/j.cosrev.2020.100342

19. Srivastava, A., Mishra, P.K.: A survey on WSN issues with its heuristics and metaheuristics solutions. Wirel. Pers. Commun¿ **121**(1), 745–814 (2021). https://doi.org/10.1007/s11277-021-08659-x

20. Tang, J., Liu, G., Pan, Q.: A review on representative swarm intelligence algorithms for solving optimization problems: applications and trends. IEEE/CAA J. Autom. Sin. **8**(10), 1627–1643 (2021)

21. Thakur, D., Kumar, Y., Kumar, A., Singh, P.K.: Applicability of wireless sensor networks in precision agriculture: a review. Wirel. Pers. Commun. **107**(1), 471–512 (2019)

22. Thike, A.M., Lupin, S., Chakirov, R., Vagapov, Y.: Topology optimisation of wireless sensor networks. In: MATEC Web of Conferences, p. 82 (2016). https://doi.org/10.1051/matecconf/20168201010

23. Xie, H., Yan, Z., Yao, Z., Atiquzzaman, M.: Data collection for security measurement in wireless sensor networks: a survey. IEEE Internet Things J. **6**(2), 2205–2224 (2018)

Two Clustering Methods for Measuring Plantar Temperature Changes in Thermal Images

Vítor Filipe[1,2] 🆔, Pedro Teixeira[1] 🆔, and Ana Teixeira[1,3(✉)] 🆔

[1] University of Trás-Os-Montes E Alto Douro, Quinta de Prados, 5001-801 Vila Real, Portugal
{vfilipe,ateixeir}@utad.pt
[2] INESC TEC - INESC Technology and Science, 4200-465 Porto, Portugal
[3] Mathematics Centre, University of Minho - Pole CMAT – UTAD, Braga, Portugal

Abstract. The development of foot ulcers is associated with the Diabetic Foot (DF), which is a problem detected in patients with Diabetes Mellitus (DM). Several studies demonstrate that thermography is a technique that can be used to identify and monitor the DF problems, thus helping to analyze the possibility of ulcers arising, as tissue inflammation causes temperature variation.

There is great interest in developing methods to detect abnormal plantar temperature changes, since healthy individuals generally show characteristic patterns of plantar temperature variation and that the plantar temperature distribution of DF tissues does not follow a specific pattern, so temperature variations are difficult to measure. In this sequel, a methodology, that uses thermograms to analyze the diversity of thermal changes that exist in the plant of a foot and classifies it as being from an individual with possibility of ulcer arising or not, is presented in this paper. Therefore, the concept of clustering is used to propose binary classifiers with different descriptors, obtained using two clustering algorithms, to predict the risk of ulceration in a foot. Moreover, for each descriptor, a numerical indicator and a classification thresholder are presented. In addition, using a combination of two different descriptors, a hybrid quantitative indicator is presented. A public dataset (containing 90 thermograms of the sole of the foot healthy people and 244 of DM patients) was used to evaluate the performance of the classifiers; using the hybrid quantitative indicator and the k-means clustering, the following metrics were obtained: Accuracy = 80%, AUC = 87% and F-measure = 86%.

Keywords: k-means · Spectral · Features · Classification · Diabetic foot · Thermogram

1 Introduction

The diabetic foot (DF) is one of the main pathologies developed by individuals with diabetes, characterized by foot lesions, infection, ulceration and/or destruction of deep tissues, and its development may even lead to limb amputation [1].

These lesions may be associated with neuropathy or vascular disease [2], and are directly linked to abnormal temperature changes in the sole of the foot; in consequence, a constant temperature monitoring and the identification of typical patterns is of high

© The Author(s), under exclusive license to Springer Nature Switzerland AG 2022
A. I. Pereira et al. (Eds.): OL2A 2022, CCIS 1754, pp. 261–274, 2022.
https://doi.org/10.1007/978-3-031-23236-7_19

importance. In the feet of healthy individuals, it is possible to find a particular spatial temperature pattern, known as butterfly pattern, but, unfortunately, no specific configuration can be detected in DM ones [3–5].

Infrared thermography (IRT) allows to visualize the temperatures of the plant of the foot and to explore the changes that occur [6], thus capturing the interest of several researchers [3–10].

Since the foot does not present a uniform temperature, it is extremely important to analyze the temperature of the foot considering a regional division in order to obtain more detailed information about the temperature variation [11]. Thus, some authors present the analysis of the variation based on the observation of specific points or regions of interest (ROIs). For example, in [12, 13], 33 ROIs (points with the highest probability of ulceration) on both feet were considered for temperature measurement. As one of the main causes of the ulceration in DF is low blood supply, some other researchers used the concept of angiosoma (tissue region blood supplied by a single artery) and divide the sole of the foot into four areas [3–5, 14, 15].

A temperature index calculated using the average of the temperature of some regions, defined using the clustering concept, is proposed in [16]. Unlike other works in which the regions are defined statically, the division of the foot using a clustering method has the advantage of dynamically create the regions that take into account the temperature distribution of each foot. In the present study, the authors continue the work of [17], where the results of [16] were improved using different descriptors and the best performance was obtained with the minimum.

In the present study the authors developed a methodology that uses thermograms to analyze the diversity of thermal changes that exist in the plant of a foot and classifies it as being from an individual with possibility of ulcer arising or not. To this end, different binary classifiers, based on the clustering concept, were developed using both quantitative temperature indexes (computed using statistic measures of the temperature) and classification temperature thresholders.

A clustering method allows close temperature values to be grouped, in this case dividing the foot into different areas (clusters) with similar temperature values [18]. Hence, each one of the regions of the plant of the foot obtained using this technique present similar values of temperature and, thus, permitting to obtain an index that can measure thermal variations.

The k-means and the spectral algorithms were used to obtain the clusters and, for both of them, different indexes, based on the mean, minimum, maximum and range values of the temperature, were obtained. In order to improve the evaluation metrics from the latest descriptors, a hybrid index was proposed. To measure the classifiers' performance, binary experiments were performed using a public data set; the performance metrics Sensitivity, Specificity, Precision, Accuracy, F-measure, and Area Under the Curve were used to assess and validate the proposed classification temperature thresholders.

This paper is organized as follows: In Sect. 2 the proposed method is described. In Sect. 3 the used database is introduced, and the obtained results are presented and analyzed. In Sect. 4 the results are discussed. At last, in Sect. 5 conclusions and future work are addressed.

2   Methodology

The method that was developed has 3 processing phases: temperature clustering, index computation, and classification. More specifically: 1) Using the temperature values, the plant of the foot is divided into regions (5 clusters) using a clustering algorithm; 2) Temperature descriptors are computed for each region, specifically the mean, maximum, minimum and range values, as well as an index that measures the variation of the temperature with respect to a reference value; 3) Results concerning the classification of the individual as healthy or with possibility of ulcer arising are presented, by applying a threshold procedure on the index.

2.1   Clustering

Clustering is an important technique that is used in many areas such as statistics, computer science, biology and social sciences [19]. There are several clustering algorithms, allowing, with this technique, to group data samples into groups based on a certain measure of similarity [20, 21]. The data set is grouped so that similar data points are assembled and different from data points in other groups [18].

Centroid-based, such as k-means [22], are one of the most popular types of clustering algorithms, being graph-based clustering algorithms, like spectral clustering, another popular type [23].

2.2 k-Means Clustering

Because of its speed and computational simplicity when operated on a large data set, k-means clustering is widely used. It is an iterative process, that splits a data set into k groups (clusters) defined by the centroids, by minimizing the sum of the distances of each point of the data set to the cluster centroid, in all the clusters [22]; the number of clusters is previously chosen. The algorithm can be synthetized in the following five steps:

1. Initialize the number of clusters, k, and randomly choose k initial centers (centroid).
2. Compute point-to-cluster-centroid distances of all the elements of the data set to each centroid.
3. Assign each one of the elements of the data set to the cluster with the closest centroid.
4. Compute the average of the elements in each cluster to obtain k new centroid locations.
5. Repeat steps 2 through 4 until the centroids do not change, this means that k-means algorithm converged.

Figure 1. Shows an example of clustering a set of points using the k-means algorithm.

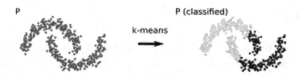

Fig. 1. Clustering example using k-means (adapted from [24])

2.3 Spectral Clustering

Spectral clustering is a graph-based algorithm used to obtain k arbitrarily clusters in a data set. It is especially suitable for non-convex datasets because it does not make any assumptions on the global structure of the data [23].

This algorithm is based on spectral graph theory, for clustering data points in k arbitrarily shaped clusters. It involves constructing a graph, finding its Laplacian matrix (way of representing a similarity graph that models the local neighborhood relationships between data points as an undirected graph), in order to find k eigenvectors to fragment the graph k ways [24]. By default, the algorithm computes the normalized random-walk Laplacian matrix using the method described by Shi-Malik [25], and also supports the (non)normalized Laplacian matrix which uses the Ng-Jordan-Weiss method [26].

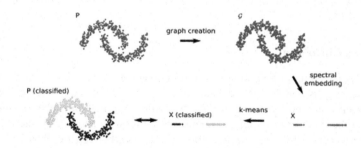

Fig. 2. Clustering example using Spectral Clustering (adapted from [24]).

This algorithm can be synthetized in the following three steps:

1. Create a similarity graph between all the elements of the data set to cluster.
2. Compute the first k eigenvectors of its Laplacian matrix to define a feature vector for each object.
3. Run k-means on these features to separate objects into k classes.

Spectral clustering, unlike k-means and classic algorithms, can group objects belonging to irregular form groups based on connectivity, as shown in Fig. 2 [27].

In this work the image of the foot was divided in five clusters with both algorithms. After that, for each cluster, some descriptors of the temperature are computed, more specifically, the mean, maximum, minimum and range.

2.4   Cluster Temperature Indexes

New indexes, based on the concept of clustering, are proposed to measure the temperature variations in the sole of the foot; they will be called Cluster Temperature Indexes (CTIs) and are computed having as reference the variation of the temperature of each cluster with respect to a reference temperature obtained from the healthy individuals that constitute the control group. Each index was based in a cluster descriptor, specifically in average, maximum, minimum and range values of the temperature.

In each cluster the reference value of the temperature descriptor (average, maximum minimum and range) is computed for the control group.

The index is calculated for each individual as the mean of the absolute value of the differences between the temperatures of the individual (IND) and the correspondent reference values, obtained from the healthy group ($\overline{CTR}$), as is (1), where $\overline{CTR}_i$ is the descriptor reference temperature value of cluster i and IND_i is the value of the temperature of the chosen descriptor (average, maximum, minimum or range) for cluster i for the individual in study

$$CTI = \frac{\sum_{i=1}^{5} |\overline{CTR}_i - IND_i|}{5} \tag{1}$$

Average CTI (ACTI) will be obtained, from (1), when using the mean descriptor; analogously, Maximum CTI (MCTI), the minimum CTI (mCTI) and the range CTI (RCTI) will be obtained when using in (1) the descriptors maximum, minimum and range, respectively. These indexes are used to classify a thermogram as being from an individual with possibility of ulcer arising or not.

2.5   Classification and Performance Evaluation

CTI indexes measure the variations of the temperature values of the sole of the foot between people with DF and healthy ones. Thus, higher CTI values correspond to larger values of temperature variation; therefore, implying higher possibility of ulceration.

During the third stage of the method the thresholding of CTI values is used to classify a thermal photo as belonging to a healthy person or to a diabetic one with the possibility of foot ulceration. The success of this stage relies on the choice of an appropriate threshold value, that will be called Cluster Temperature Threshold (CTT). A CTT is calculated for each descriptor; so, with the average descriptor the Average CTT (ACTT) is obtained, the minimum descriptor gives the minimum CTT (mCTT), the Maximum CTT (MCTT) results from using the maximum descriptor and Range CTT (RCTT) from applying the range descriptor.

With these thresholds and the CTI's, also calculated for each descriptor, a new CTI index, denominated as Hybrid CTI (HCTI), is proposed. This index uses a combination of the indexes mCTI and RCTI, according to (2).

$$HCTI = \frac{mCTI + |mCTT - RCTT| * RCTI}{2} \tag{2}$$

Several performance metrics were calculated during the experiments, like: *Sensitivity* (Se), *Specificity* (Sp), *Precision, Accuracy, F-measure,* and *Area Under the Curve*

(AUC). The correspondent values are obtained from the expressions (3) to (7), where the acronyms TP, FP, TN and FN represent, respectively, the number of cases of *True Positive, False Positive, True Negative* and *False Negative*:

$$Sensitivity = \frac{TP}{TP + FN} \tag{3}$$

$$Specificity = \frac{TN}{FP + TN} \tag{4}$$

$$Precision = \frac{TP}{TP + FP} \tag{5}$$

$$Accuracy = \frac{TP + FN}{TP + TN + FP + FN} \tag{6}$$

$$F_{measure} = \frac{2 * TP}{2 * TP + FP + FN} \tag{7}$$

As the proposed classifiers are used to detect the risk of ulceration, *Sensitivity* and *Specificity* are the most relevant metrics to evaluate the their performance [28]. The optimal value chosen for each CTT was obtained using an approach known as the point closest-to-(0,1) corner in the Receiver Operating Characteristic (ROC) plane. This approach, denominated as ER criteria, uses the point that minimizes the Euclidean distance between the ROC curve and the (0,1) point to define the optimal cut-point, and is obtained using (8) [29].

$$ER = \sqrt{(1 - Se)^2 + (1 - Sp)^2} \tag{8}$$

The AUC is used to summarize the entire location of the ROC curve (a curve that shows the connection between the sensitivity and the 1- specificity), as it is an effective and combined measure of the metrics that describes the inherent validity of diagnostic tests, rather than depending on a specific operating point [30].

3 Results

The public dataset used to evaluate the different classifiers contains 334 individual plantar thermograms (244 of diabetic and 90 of healthy) segmented and vertically adjusted, corresponding to the plant of the left or the right foot of a total of 167 individuals [11]. The computational experiments were carried out using MATLAB.

Now, the results obtained with the two algorithms described in Sect. 2 are presented. Table 1 presents the descriptor values calculated by the two clustering methods. In Subsect. 3.1, the results of the classification with the k-means clustering are described, while in Subsect. 3.2 the results of the classification with the spectral clustering are addressed.

Table 1. Temperature (°C) descriptors per cluster obtained with the two methods.

		Control group		Diabetes mellitus group	
Clustering method		K-means	Spectral	K-means	Spectral
Cluster 1	Avg	23.93	24.08	27.67	27.80
	Min	21.38	21.43	26.19	26.35
	Max	24.71	24.86	28.22	28.34
	Range	3.33	3.43	2.03	2.00
Cluster 2	Avg	25.52	25.61	28.79	28.86
	Min	24.72	24.73	28.24	29.08
	Max	26.05	26.10	29.20	29.24
	Range	1.33	1.37	0.96	1.16
Cluster 3	Avg	26.59	26.63	29.62	29.62
	Min	26.06	26.10	29.21	28.08
	Max	27.10	27.14	30.02	29.98
	Range	1.04	1.03	0.81	0.90
Cluster 4	Avg	27.61	27.54	30.42	30.30
	Min	27.11	27.14	30.02	29.88
	Max	28.25	28.01	30.87	30.62
	Range	1.14	0.87	0.84	0.74
Cluster 5	Avg	28.88	28.75	31.31	31.14
	Min	28.25	27.83	30.87	29.93
	Max	29.80	29.80	32.16	32.16
	Range	1.55	1.97	1.28	2.23
CTI	ACTI	1.23	1.23	3.63	3.62
	mCTI	1.31	1.36	3.90	3.77
	MCTI	1.31	1.21	3.50	3.50
	RCTI	0.44	0.56	0.63	0.85

3.1 k-Means Clustering

In this subsection, the results obtained with the classifiers using the k-means clustering algorithm are presented. After some preliminary experiments, it has been concluded that the division of the foot into five clusters gives the best results, as the metric values improve until five, but from five to six clusters and so one, worse metric values are obtained, as small variations of the temperature between each pair of clusters are verified [16]. The results for healthy people (reference group) and the diabetics are presented in Fig. 3 and Table 1; there, the average values of the temperature per cluster for each descriptor, measured in Celsius degrees (°C), and the CTI average values, are presented.

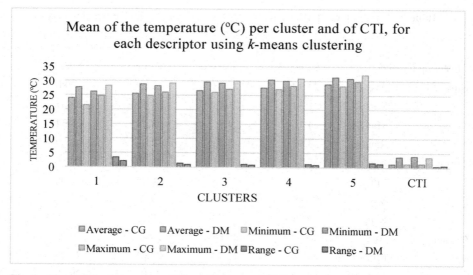

Fig. 3. Mean of the temperature (°C) per cluster and of CTI, for each descriptor using *k*-means

Each CTI indicates the differences in a subject's foot temperature pattern relative to the normal temperature pattern (butterfly pattern). Analyzing Fig. 3, as well as Table 1, and comparing the average temperatures obtained using the descriptors for each cluster, it can be observed that the DM group has higher values than the healthy group, except for the range descriptor that presents similar values. Thus, it can be concluded that higher indexes correspond to higher temperature variations, signaling an increase of the probability of ulceration.

The threshold value used to determine whether a thermogram is either from an individual with risk of ulceration or from a healthy one, will affect the performance of the classification. The ER measure was used to obtain the optimal threshold, in order to balance the metrics sensibility and sensitivity. The values chosen to classify a thermogram as belonging to a healthy person or to a diabetic one with the possibility of foot ulceration are: 1.9 for the average descriptor, 1.84 when using the minimum, 2.22 for the maximum, 0.47 for the range and 1.27 for the hybrid.

From Fig. 4 and Table 1, it can be perceived that similar metric results are obtained with the average and the maximum descriptors, but the last one gives less balanced specificity and sensitivity values. The best results are attained with the minimum descriptor, noticing an increase of 4% in some of the metrics, as F-measure or Accuracy, when compared with the worst results; it is also worth noticing that the value of the metrics increase when the hybrid descriptor is used.

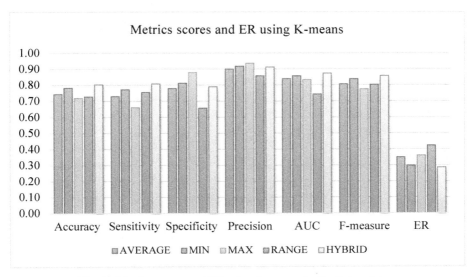

Fig. 4. Metrics scores and ER using k-means, for the 5 descriptors

3.2 Spectral Clustering

In this subsection, the results of the classifiers that use the spectral clustering algorithm are presented. As already mentioned in the previous subsection, these classifiers also use five clusters. Figure 5 illustrates the difference between the control group (reference group) and the DM group; the average values of the temperature per cluster for each descriptor, measured in Celsius degrees, and the CTI average values are presented.

Analyzing Fig. 5 and Table 1, it can be observed that, as previously mentioned, the DM group has higher average temperatures than the control group. Nonetheless, analyzing in particular the amplitude descriptor, it can be seen that, for the first cluster, the amplitude is larger in the control group since this cluster is associated with the toes, which are areas that suffer high variations of the temperature, and can have either very low or very high values of the temperature. Thus, being a descriptor that may bring advantages when combined with other descriptors.

For the spectral clustering, the metrics scores are present in Fig. 6. The values used as the limit to catalogue the individuals as either healthy or DM with the possibility of ulceration, for each descriptor, are: 2.31 for the average descriptor, 1.96 for the minimum, 2.06 for the maximum, 0.6 for the range and 1.47 for the hybrid.

In Fig. 6, it can be observed that the metrics results are similar for all the features, but when comparing the ER value, the minimum is the descriptor that presents the higher values and, like it happens with the k-means approach for the case of the hybrid descriptor, an increase of the metric values can be noticed.

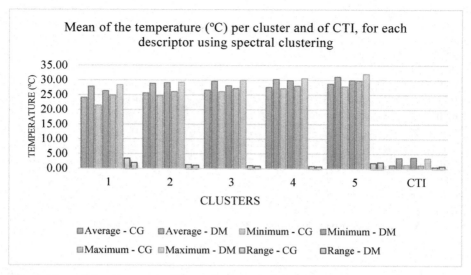

Fig. 5. Mean of the temperature (°C) per cluster and of CTI, for each descriptor using spectral

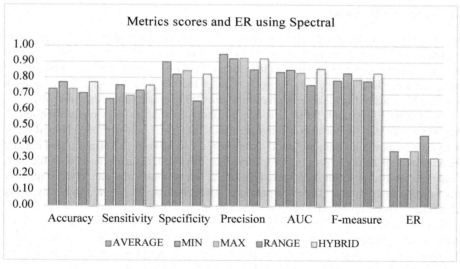

Fig. 6. Metrics scores and ER using Spectral, for the 5 descriptors

4 Discussion

In this work, two different clustering algorithms with five features extraction each, in a total of ten different classifiers, were used to classify foot thermograms. A binary cataloguing technique, that splits the thermograms into binary groups according to the CTI of each feature mentioned in Sect. 2.2 is proposed.

The highest metrics values were obtained with the minimum descriptor for both clustering algorithms. However, when comparing these two classifiers, the best classifier using k-means presents the best metrics results, like ER, F-measure, AUC, Accuracy and also presents a better balance in the sensitivity and specificity, but with smaller differences.

Table 2. Values, per cluster, of CTI and of the temperature (°C) for some foot thermograms of the control and the DM groups in [11].

Subject	Thermal	K-means	HCTIkm	Spectral	HCTISp	Measures	General
CG005			0,51		0,57	Min	22,94
						Max	29,90
						Mean	26,75
						Range	6,95
DM030			1,35		1,31	Min	24,68
						Max	30,12
						Mean	28,25
						Range	5,44
DM010			4,31		4,66	Min	30,26
						Max	35,55
						Mean	34,31
						Range	5,29

To better illustrate the comparison between the used clustering algorithms, three thermograms from the dataset (CG005, DM030, DM010 in [11]) are presented in Table 2. The columns of the table indicate: the identification of the individual (Subject), the thermogram (Thermal), the image obtained after applying the k-means clustering (K-means), the HCTI value with k-means (HCTIkm), the image obtained after applying the spectral clustering (Spectral), the HCTI value with spectral (HCTISp) and the measures of the entire foot (General).

Comparing the performance of the two best classifiers involving each clustering algorithm in different cases, it was noticeable that when the clusters have average temperatures similar to the reference ones (obtained using the feet of the healthy people), small CTI values are obtained and the temperature distribution of the foot approaches the butterfly pattern, typical of non-diabetic subjects (Table 2 (CG005)). It was also observed that when the variations are quite large, up to very high temperatures across the sole of the foot, it will result in very high CTI values, for example (Table 2 (DM010)). In general, in these two cases, both methods accurately classify this type of foot.

In the intermediate thermogram (Table 2 (DM030)), that represents a case where there are small temperature variations and the thermal changes are slightly different from the butterfly pattern, the CTI's are close to the reference CTI values. In these cases, both classifiers have more difficulty finding these small variations, thus affecting their performance, but this is more evident when using spectral clustering. To try to combat this difficulty a hybrid CTI that uses mCTI and RCTI, allowing to increase the classification performance, was proposed. Finally, it can be observed that the algorithm that presents the best results is k-means.

5 Conclusions

A method that uses thermograms of the plant of the foot to help measuring temperature variations and predicts the risk of ulceration is proposed.

The concept of clustering was used to build binary classifiers with different descriptors and using two clustering algorithms. For each descriptor, a temperature index and a cataloguing temperature threshold was calculated; additionally, an optimal threshold value was found by balancing two of the metrics used, sensitivity and specificity.

From the presented results and by comparing the algorithms, it can be noticed that both of them allowed to obtain a global performance similar to others already published, [16, 17] and, in general, when the butterfly pattern can be perceived in the distribution of the temperature of the sole of the foot, or when the hot spots cover the entire plantar area, the performance of the classification are similar. On the other hand, when the temperature variations are small and the thermal variations start to vary slightly from the butterfly pattern, both classifiers have more difficulty finding these small variations, thus affecting their performance (being this behavior more evident in the spectral clustering). To combat this difficulty, a hybrid CTI that uses two of the presented indices was proposed and an increase of the classification performance was obtained.

As the next step, it is intended not only to expand the dataset, to balance the number of photos of healthy and DM individuals, but also to implement and test some other approaches, as well as to create a repository in GITHUB, where the developed code and the thermograms database will be placed.

References

1. Glaudemans, A.W.J.M., Uçkay, I., Lipsky, B.A.: Challenges in diagnosing infection in the diabetic foot. Diabet. Med. **32**, 748–759 (2015). https://doi.org/10.1111/dme.12750
2. Leung, P.: Diabetic foot ulcers - a comprehensive review. Surgeon. **5**, 219–231 (2007). https://doi.org/10.1016/S1479-666X(07)80007-2
3. Hernandez-Contreras, D., Peregrina-Barreto, H., Rangel-Magdaleno, J., Gonzalez-Bernal, J.A., AltamiranoRobles, L.: A quantitative index for classification of plantar thermal changes in the diabetic foot. Infrared Phys. Technol. **81**, 242–249 (2017). https://doi.org/10.1016/j.infrared.2017.01.010
4. Nagase, T., et al.: Variations of plantar thermographic patterns in normal controls and non-ulcer diabetic patients: novel classification using angiosome concept. J. Plast. Reconstr. Aesthet. Surg. **64**, 860–866 (2011). https://doi.org/10.1016/j.bjps.2010.12.003
5. Mori, T., et al.: Morphological pattern classification system for plantar thermography of patients with diabetes. J. Diabetes Sci. Technol. **7**, 1102–1112 (2013). https://doi.org/10.1177/193229681300700502

6. Pereira, C.B., Yu, X., Dahlmanns, S., Blazek, V., Leohardt, S., Teichmann, D.: Infrared thermography. In: Abreude-Souza, M., Remigio-Gamba, H., Pedrini, H. (eds.) Multi-Modality Imaging, pp. 1–30. Springer, Cham (2018). https://doi.org/10.1007/978-3-319-98974-7_1

7. Frykberg, R.G., et al.: Diabetic foot disorders: a clinical practice guideline (2006 revision). J. Foot Ankle Surg. **45**, S1–S66 (2006). https://doi.org/10.1016/S1067-2516(07)60001-5

8. Ring, F.: The Herschel heritage to medical thermography. J. Imaging. **2**, 13 (2016). https://doi.org/10.3390/jimaging2020013

9. Hernandez-Contreras, D., Peregrina-Barreto, H., Rangel-Magdaleno, J., Gonzalez-Bernal, J.: Narrative review: diabetic foot and infrared thermography. Infrared Phys. Technol. **78**, 105–117 (2016). https://doi.org/10.1016/j.infrared.2016.07.013

10. Adam, M., Ng, E.Y.K., Tan, J.H., Heng, M.L., Tong, J.W.K., Acharya, U.R.: Computer aided diagnosis of diabetic foot using infrared thermography: a review. Comput. Biol. Med. **91**, 326–336 (2017). https://doi.org/10.1016/j.compbiomed.2017.10.030

11. Hernandez-Contreras, D.A., Peregrina-Barreto, H., Rangel-Magdaleno, J.D.J., Renero-Carrillo, F.J.: Plantar thermogram database for the study of diabetic foot complications. IEEE Access. **7**, 161296–161307 (2019). https://doi.org/10.1109/ACCESS.2019.2951356

12. Macdonald, A., et al.: Thermal symmetry of healthy feet: a precursor to a thermal study of diabetic feet prior to skin breakdown. Physiol. Meas. **38**, 33–44 (2017). https://doi.org/10.1088/1361-6579/38/1/33

13. Macdonald, A., et al.: Between visit variability of thermal imaging of feet in people attending podiatric clinics with diabetic neuropathy at high risk of developing foot ulcers. Physiol. Measur. **40**, 084004 (2019). https://doi.org/10.1088/1361-6579/ab36d7

14. Peregrina-Barreto, H., et al.: Quantitative estimation of temperature variations in plantar angiosomes: a study case for diabetic foot. Comput. Math. Methods Med. **2014**, 1–15 (2014). https://doi.org/10.1155/2014/585306

15. Peregrina-Barreto, H., Morales-Hernandez, L.A., Rangel-Magdaleno, J.J., Vazquez-Rodriguez, P.D.: Thermal image processing for quantitative determination of temperature variations in plantar angiosomes. In: Conference Record - IEEE Instrumentation and Measurement Technology Conference, pp. 816–820 (2013). https://doi.org/10.1109/I2MTC.2013.6555528

16. Filipe, V., Teixeira, P., Teixeira, A.: A clustering approach for prediction of diabetic foot using thermal images. In: Gervasi, O., et al. (eds.) Computational Science and Its Applications – ICCSA 2020. LNCS, vol. 12251, pp. 620–631. Springer, Cham (2020). https://doi.org/10.1007/978-3-030-58808-3_45

17. Filipe, V., Teixeira, P., Teixeira, A.: Measuring plantar temperature changes in thermal images using basic statistical descriptors. In: Gervasi, O., et al. (eds.) Computational Science and Its Applications – ICCSA 2021. LNCS, vol. 12953, pp. 445–455. Springer, Cham (2021). https://doi.org/10.1007/978-3-030-86976-2_30

18. Omran, M.G.H., Engelbrecht, A.P., Salman, A.: An overview of clustering methods. Intell. Data Anal. **11**, 583–605 (2007). https://doi.org/10.3233/ida-2007-11602

19. Ben Ayed, A., Ben Halima, M., Alimi, A.M.: Adaptive fuzzy exponent cluster ensemble system based feature selection and spectral clustering. In: IEEE International Conference on Fuzzy Systems (2017). https://doi.org/10.1109/FUZZ-IEEE.2017.8015721

20. (PDF) Survey on clustering methods : Towards fuzzy clustering for big data (n.d.). https://www.researchgate.net/publication/280730634_Survey_on_clustering_methods_Towards_fuzzy_clustering_for_big_data. Accessed 24 Mar 2021

21. Berkhin, P.: A survey of clustering data mining techniques. In: Kogan, J., Nicholas, C., Teboulle, M. (eds.) Grouping Multidimensional Data: Recent Advances in Clustering, , pp. 25–71. Springer, Heidelberg (2006). https://doi.org/10.1007/3-540-28349-8_2

22. Dhanachandra, N., Manglem, K., Chanu, Y.J.: Image segmentation using k-means cluster-ing algorithm and subtractive clustering algorithm. Proc. Comput. Sci. **54**, 764–771 (2015). https://doi.org/10.1016/j.procs.2015.06.090

23. Von Luxburg, U.: A tutorial on spectral clustering. Stat. Comput. **17**, 395–416 (2007). https://doi.org/10.1007/s11222-007-9033-z

24. Tremblay, N., Loukas, A.: Approximating spectral clustering via sampling: a review. In: Ros, F., Guillaume, S. (eds.) Sampling Techniques for Supervised or Unsupervised Tasks. USL, pp. 129–183. Springer, Cham (2020). https://doi.org/10.1007/978-3-030-29349-9_5

25. Shi, J., Malik, J.: Normalized cuts and image segmentation. IEEE Trans. Pattern Anal. Mach. Intell. **22**, 888–905 (2000). https://doi.org/10.1109/34.868688

26. Ng, A.Y., Jordan, M.I.: On Spectral Clustering: Analysis and an algorithm (2001)

27. Wang, X., Qian, B., Davidson, I.: On constrained spectral clustering and its applications. Data Min. Knowl. Disc. **28**(1), 1–30 (2012). https://doi.org/10.1007/s10618-012-0291-9

28. Taha, A.A., Hanbury, A.: Metrics for evaluating 3D medical image segmentation: analysis, selection, and tool. BMC Med. Imaging. **15**, 1–28 (2015). https://doi.org/10.1186/s12880-015-0068-x

29. Unal, I.: Defining an optimal cut-point value in ROC analysis: an alternative approach. Comput. Math. Methods Med. **2017**, 3762651 (2017). https://doi.org/10.1155/2017/3762651

30. Hajian-Tilaki, K.: Receiver operating characteristic (ROC) curve analysis for medical diagnostic test evaluation, Caspian. J. Intern. Med. **4**, 627–635 (2013)

A Multi-objective Approach for the Menu Planning Problem: A Brazilian Case Study

Rafaela P. C. Moreira[1](✉), Carolina G. Marcelino[2,3](✉),
Flávio V. C. Martins[1](✉), Elizabeth F. Wanner[1](✉),
Silvia Jimenez-Fernandez[3], and Sancho Salcedo-Sanz[3](✉)

[1] Department of Computing, Federal Center of Technological Education of Minas
Gerais (CEFET-MG), Belo Horizonte, Brazil
`rafapcmor@gmail.com`, {`fcruzeirom,efwanner`}`@decom.cefetmg.br`
[2] Federal University of Rio de Janeiro (UFRJ), Institute of Computing,
Rio de Janeiro, Brazil
`carolina@ic.ufrj.br`
[3] Department of Signal Processing and Communication,
University of Alcalá, Alcalá, Spain
{`silvia.jimenez,sancho.salcedo`}`@uah.es`

Abstract. In this paper, we propose a multi-objective formulation for solving the menu planning problem, in a Brazilian school context. Considering the school category, the student age group, and the school duration time, we propose a formulation of the problem in which the total cost and the nutritional error according to the Brazilian reference are simultaneously minimized. The menus must also meet some qualitative requirements, such as variety and harmony of preparations. We propose a NSGA-II for solving the problem. As a comparison, we use a weighted-sum approach for transforming the multi-objective problem into a mono-objective one and solve it using a generic Genetic Algorithm. Using as test scenario full-time preschool students (4-5 years old), 5-day menus are obtained by both methodologies. The menus are qualitatively and quantitatively assessed applying the Quality Index of Nutritional Food Safety Coordination (IQ COSAN, acronym in Portuguese) and compared to a 5-day menu for a Brazilian school. Results show the methodology is very promising and the obtained menus are adequate.

Keywords: Evolutionary algorithms · Multi-objective optimization · Menu planning problem

1 Introduction

A healthy lifestyle can be achieved by developing lifelong healthy eating habits. According to the Brazilian eating guide [3], a comprehensive concept of healthy eating is as follows: *"Adequate and healthy eating is a fundamental human right that guarantees access to an eating practice appropriate to the biological and social aspects of the individual and which must comply with special dietary needs. It must be referenced by social eating habits, gender, race, and ethnicity; it must be accessible from a physical and financial point of view; it must have a balance between quantity and quality while keeping the concepts of variety, balance, moderation and taste"*.

The school meals are considered as an efficient mechanism to offer, apart from energy, the essential micro-nutrients that, in some situations, are little available in daily eating. Children and students, in general, have problems focusing in school without a balanced diet. School meals are then necessary tools to improve general nutrition and collective health. In 1955, the Brazilian government created the Brazilian School Feeding Programme (PNAE - *Programa Nacional de Alimentação Escolar*). The main goal of PNAE is twofold: (i) to contribute to the growth, development, learning and school performance of students, and (ii) to develop healthy eating habits [4]. The PNAE is one of the most comprehensive school food programs in the world, and by 2019 was responsible for providing daily meals to more than 40 million students offering about 50 million meals a day, totaling more than 10 billion meals a year.

Some of the PNAE basic principles for healthy eating which must be taken into account are: (i) age group; (ii) daily nutritional needs according to the school category (daycare until youth and Adult Education); (iii) school location (urban or indigenous); (iv) school time length (partial or full-time); (v) type of meals (breakfast, lunch, snack and dinner); (vi) variety (e.g. it is not recommended to repeat the same preparations in a given period of time.); (vii) harmony of preparations (e.g. it is not recommended, in the same meal, to have more than one liquid preparation); and, (viii) the maximum amount to be paid for each meal. There are other recommendations such as the daily amount of sugar, salt, calcium, iron, etc. Following the PNAE recommendations, while not exceeding the available budget, it is a hard optimization task. The number of possible combinations among available seasonal fruits, salads and vegetables and types of food preparation is extremely high. It is also necessary to follow PNAE guidelines keeping, in general, a very low budget.

The nutritionist is responsible for that task and, usually, the menu planning requires time. A survey showed that, in 2011, in 20% of Brazilian municipalities, there was a lack of nutritionists responsible for PNAE [8]. Moreover, even in cities with nutritionists, they may not be sufficient for the number of students. Due to the lack of nutritionists and the excessive burden of activities of those professionals, in Brazil, all schools adopt a one-to-four-week cycle for the school meal menu. Some schools create a 5-day menu and repeat it throughout the year. In the best case scenario, four 5-day menus are elaborated and repeated. Aiming to facilitate the nutritionists work and to contribute to the time reduction of menu planning, computational techniques can be seen as useful tools to automatically create healthy menu plans.

The general goals of menu planning are to achieve balanced and economical meals, to comply with the nutritional requirements of the user based on their personal situation (age, gender, height, etc.) while not exceeding the maximum cost allowed. That problem can be seen as a new version of the classic Diet Problem [9], since it combines nutritional and economic objectives with personal requirements. According to [1], the Menu Planning Problem (MPP) focus on obtaining the best combination of items that meet the required objectives and necessary requirements.

Mathematically, the Menu Planning Problem can be reduced to a Multi-objective Knapsack Problem [19], a problem widely known in the literature. Although having an easy problem formulation, it belongs to the NP-Complete class [14]. And such problems are difficult to solve by exact optimization algorithms in a polynomial time [25]. The application of exact algorithms to solve the MPP ensuring optimality may be not viable. However, using heuristics, it is possible to find good solutions in an affordable computational time. Heuristics are inspired by processes that seek a good solution at an acceptable computational cost without, however, being able to guarantee their optimality, as well as guaranteeing how close they are to the optimal solution [23].

In [2], a cross-sectional study with nutritionists from 21 municipalities in Brazil was conducted to analyze the development of school menus. Although the PNAE regulatory guidelines influence the nutritionists' work, the nutritional value of the meal seems to be an incipient criteria. Keeping in mind the relevance of school meals for shaping healthy eating habits and the necessity of providing quality food to students, principally the vulnerable students, meeting the PNAE regulatory guidelines is paramount in Brazil. The MPP presents a high complexity due to the high number of variables and constraints. It can be formulated as a mono- or a multi-objective problem.

In this paper, aiming to meet the daily nutritional needs of the students while reducing the monetary cost, we model the MPP as a bi-objective problem. The total cost of a 5-day menu and the nutritional error (when the guidelines provided by the Brazilian reference [4] are followed) are the two criteria. Subjective properties such as color, variety, and consistency of culinary preparations are defined in a rigorous way and used as constraints for the MPP. The multi-objective MPP is solved via two different approaches: (i) scalarization using the weighted-sum approach and solving it with a mono-objective Genetic Algorithm; and, (ii) the Non-dominated Sorting Genetic Algorithm - NSGA II [10] is applied to solve the multi-objective problem.

The obtained menus have been assessed qualitatively and quantitatively using the Quality Index of Nutritional Food Safety Coordination (IQ COSAN, acronym in Portuguese) [6]. IQ-COSAN is an tool made available by PNAE to assess the school menus. As a comparative analysis, a menu from a school in the southeast part of Brazil is assessed using the same tool. This work is organized as follows. Section 2 presents the related works. Section 3 presents the problem definition. Section 4 describes the applied methodology. Section 5 describes the performed experiments. And, finally, Sect. 6 concludes the work.

2   Related Work

Since 1964, computer-assisted tools have been used to solve the Menu Planning Problem. The work of [1] used Linear Programming (LP) techniques to construct the first menu planner, to find the minimum cost and to follow the daily nutritional needs. Furthermore, it was necessary not only to attend a determined degree of variety but also taking account color and consistency of the food for a given number of days. The proposed algorithm was applied in a hospital and was able to reduce up to 30% of the menu cost. An automatic menu generator, MenuGene, has been developed in 2005. It employs a Genetic Algorithm (GA) aiming to prepare daily and weekly menus for Internet users. More than 150.000 tests have been performed, and the results showed that the method can generate menus that satisfy the nutritional requirements [13]. The authors of [17] formulated a bi-objective diet problem and solved it applying the Linear Scalarization approach using a mono-objective Genetic Algorithm. The objectives were: minimum cost and maximum rating, according to the user's preference.

In [18], the authors presented a modification of the work of [17], solving the original problem in a multi-objective approach by using a multi-objective Genetic Algorithm NSGA-II. The authors also introduced lower and upper limits for the quantity nutritional value. In [24], the authors proposed a multilevel-NSGA-II to solve the menu planning problem for patients in a hospital. The menu was created on an individual basis. In this work, nine objective functions were included: (i) to minimize the cost; (ii) to maximize seasonal quality and functionality; (iii) to minimize the deviations from uniformly distributed aesthetic standards for taste, taking into account; (iv) consistency; (v) color; (vi) temperature; (vii) shape; and (viii) method of preparation. The personal preference of the patient and nutritional requirements were included as constraints. The algorithm was able to find various solutions, meeting the necessary requirements and in a reasonable computational time. The Departments of Nutrition and Computer Science at the University of Sonora in Mexico, in 2007, developed a computer system *PlaDiet*, aiming to calculate individual meals, attending all the nutritional requirements established by a professional. The goal was to minimized the monetary cost while meeting the caloric needs of an individual.

In [11], the authors proposed a non-linear integer programming model to solve the menu problem and solved it using Genetic Algorithms. The program allows to choose the type of meals - lunch, dinner, and intermediates, making available, in seconds, diets for any caloric need within 28 days [11]. Another GA-based tool, GIGISim [7], was developed to make meals for people with diabetes. The approach can comply with the nutritional needs, satisfying the preference of taste, lifestyle and control the blood glucose. In 2012, other software, Pro-Diet [15], is a system that proposes the prescription of menus and diet formulation, to meet the principles of healthy eating, taking into account the colors and meals variety, the combination of flavors the texture and the provision of all nutrients. The software is also based on GA's and can generate menus in seconds, which could, manually, take hours. A model of menu planning for secondary schools in Malaysia using Integer Programming was proposed by Suliad and Ismail [26]. The goal was to maximize the variety of nutrient and to minimize the total cost of the menu. In [27], the authors used the procedure known as *Delete-Reshuffle Algorithm* to delete foods already served, besides being elaborated for seven days.

There are several related works in the literature in which some of them only construct a solution while others try to construct and to optimize those solutions. Some works focus on a particular individual needs while few works deal with collective menus. These previous studies have not assessed the quality of their menus; and despite achieving some core characteristics, such as low price and minor micro and macro-nutrients errors, their menu may not have attended cultural specificities or even qualitative aspects of meals. This work intends to elaborate optimized and collective menus, without collecting personal information, attending to the principles of healthy eating and PNAE, and taking into consideration the monetary cost. We propose a general model to represent the menu. The criteria and constraints are mathematically formulated.

3   Problem Definition

In this Section, we introduce the basic concepts to understand the problem.

Let us suppose we have the following sets:

D: set of days in which $D = \{d_1, d_2, \ldots, d_{max}\}$;
M: set of meals in which
$\quad M = \{breakfast,\ lunch,\ snack\}$;
P: set of preparations in which $P = \{p_1, p_2, \ldots, p_{max}\}$
$\quad \forall m \in M$;
F: set of foods in which $F = \{f_1, f_2, \ldots, f_{max}\}$
$\quad \forall p \in P$;

Our aim is to create a menu for $(|D|)$ days and for each day we have 3 meals. For each meal $m \in M$ we have a different set of preparations P and each preparation $p \in P$ has a specific set of foods F. For each food exists a nutritional table with a set of nutrients, e.g., energy (Kcal), protein (g), carbohydrates (g), lipids (g), fibers (g), minerals: calcium (mg), iron (mg), zinc (mg) and magnesium (mg) [22]. As a test scenario, we consider full-time preschool students (4 to 5 years old) as the age group. Table 1 shows the recommended values for 70% of daily nutritional needs (DNN) for those students. Other references can be found in [5].

Table 1. Reference values for energy, macro and micro nutrients - 70% DNN. CHO refers to carbohydrates, PTN to proteins and LIP to lipids.

Pre-school (4 to 5 years)								
Energy (Kcal)	CHO (g)	PTN (g)	LIP (g)	Fibers (g)	Minerals(mg)			
					Ca	Fe	Mg	Zn
950	154,4	29,7	23,8	17,5	560	7	91	3,5

In our work, a daily menu is composed of tree meals: (i) breakfast; (ii) lunch; and, (iii) snack. Each meal is composed of some preparations and classified according to its type. Breakfast is composed of three preparations: (i) bread or other cereal; (ii) milk or deiry products; and, (iii) fruit. Lunch is composed of seven preparations: (i) rice; (ii) beans; (iii) entree; (iv) side dish; (v) main dish; (vi) dessert: fruit or other; and, (vii) juice. Snack is formed by three preparations: (i) bread or other cereal; (ii) drink (milk or derivatives or juice); and (iii) fruit.

We create a database including preparations from Minas Gerais state document [21]. The database has 82 culinary preparations divided in: 5 preparations of rice; 4 preparations of beans; 13 types of entree; 12 types of side dish; 14 types of main dish; 7 types of fruits; 12 types of dessert; 12 types of juice; 10 types of dairy; and 3 types of bread/other cereal. The values of energy, macro-nutrients, and micro-nutrients of food are obtained using the Brazilian food composition table (TACO, acronym in Portuguese) [22] and Brazilian food composition table from University of Sao Paulo (TBCA-USP, acronym in Portuguese) [12].

The following set of parameters is also defined: c_f represents the cost of food f; v_f is the nutritional value of food f, including all considered nutrients; and n_r is the daily nutritional needs. Two objective functions are modeled. For each one, there is a set of constraints to be meet that are also described here. The first objective function aims at maximizing the nutritional value needed according to the age group. This objective, based on the work proposed by [15], calculates the absolute difference of the sum of the nutrients and the sum of established reference (Eq. (1)):

$$F_1 = \left| \sum_{d \in D} \sum_{m \in M} \sum_{p \in P} \sum_{f \in F} |D| (v_f x_{dm}^{pf} - n_r) \right|. \tag{1}$$

The second objective function aims at minimizing the menu cost. The function calculates the sum of the cost of each meal on the menu (Equation(2)):

$$F_2 = \left| \sum_{d \in D} \sum_{m \in M} \sum_{p \in P} \sum_{f \in F} c_f x_{dm}^{pf} \right|. \tag{2}$$

Promoting healthy and adequate school meals for a given age group is the goal of PNAE. Given this, some constraints are adopted in this work for this principle to be attended: (i) color; (ii) consistency, and (iii) variety. We have also implemented other significant constraints: (i) maximum monetary cost for each meal and for each student, maximum monetary cost; (ii) nutritional error limit. The color, consistency, and variety constraints are related to the nutritional error function (Equation (1)) and, the cost limit constraint is related to the cost function (Eq. (2)).

The constraints of the problem are described below:

– **Color:** A diversified meal in color ensures a balanced and nutrient-rich dietary. For this work four predominant colors have been defined: (i) yellow; (ii) red; (iii) green; and, (iv) brown. The color constraint is verified only for lunch and for the following types of preparations: (i) entree; (ii) side dish; (iii) dessert; and, (iv) drink, as directed by [15]. For guaranteeing the color diversification, the maximum number of repetition of the same color in a given meal should be equal to 2.

- **Consistency:** A good texture transmits confidence in the quality and acceptability of food. For consistency, two categories are considered: (i) liquid/pasty; and, (ii) semi-solid/solid. More than one type of preparations classified as liquid/past in lunch is not permitted. The preparations checked are: (i) beans; (ii) side dish; and, (iii) main dish.

- **Variety:** The food variety is indispensable for all vital nutrients to be supplied. To ensure that meals are varied, we check the number of repeat preparations. We analyze the replicates for: (i) same-day meals; and, (ii) meals on different days. For the same day, in lunch, we check the following preparations: (i) entree; (ii) side dish; (iii) main dish; (iv) dessert; and, (v) drink. Also for the same day, but in breakfast and snack, we check the following preparations: (i) fruit; (ii) drink; and, (iii) cereal. For different days, in lunch, we check the following preparations: (i) entree; (ii) side dish; and, (iii) main dish.

- **Cost Limit:** The Government transfers a value per school day for each student regarding the school time length. Thus, the menu monetary cost has to be less than a predefined value.

- **Nutritional Error Limit:** Each day, each student has nutritional needs according to their age group. The nutritional error constraint assures that no student will have a nutritional need deviating from the ones presented in Table 1.

The problem is classified as a bi-objective minimization problem, and its simplified mathematical formulation is given by:

$$\text{Minimize } F_1 = \left| \sum_{d \in D} \sum_{m \in M} \sum_{p \in P} \sum_{f \in F} v_f x_{dm}^{pf} - n_r |D| \right|$$

$$\text{Minimize } F_2 = \sum_{d \in D} \sum_{m \in M} \sum_{p \in P} \sum_{f \in F} c_f x_{dm}^{pf}$$

$$\text{s.a:} \begin{cases} \text{Color Constraint} \\ \text{Consistency Constraint} \\ \text{Variety Constraint} \\ \text{Cost Limit Constraint} \\ \text{Nutritional Error Limit Constraint} \\ x_{dm}^{pf} \in \{0, 1\}. \end{cases} \tag{3}$$

Figure 1 represents a problem solution representing a 2-day menu. Each menu is defined for some days and for each day we have meals that are composed by preparations. The meals and preparations are represented by lists (Fig. 1-Above-left). In the integer representation (Fig. 1-Above-right), each type of meal receives a number:(i) Breakfast(1), (ii) Lunch(2); and, (iii) Snack(3). The preparations are also represented by numbers and these numbers refer to the position

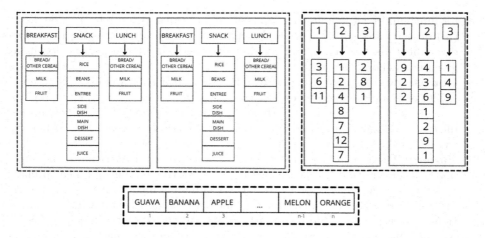

Fig. 1. Representation of a two days menu. Above left: menu representation – above right: integer menu representation below: foods list

of the list according to the type of preparation. Consider the first position of the list 1 that corresponds to breakfast in Fig. 1-Above-right, the number 3 refers to index of a list of fruits with eleven options, according to Fig. 1-Below. In this case, this index represents the papaya.

4   Methodology

In this work, the menu planning problem is characterized as a bi-objective problem, and it is solved via two different methodologies. A priori, the problem is transformed into a mono-objective problem via a weighted-sum approach. The resulting mono-objective problem is then solved via a basic Genetic Algorithm. Subsequently, we use the NSGA-II, to solve the problem in its multi-objective formulation. The weighted-sum approach works appropriately when the functions are convex. When this property can not be verified, only part of the set of the efficient the solution is generated. The mono-objective problem can then be defined by:

$$min_{x \in \mathcal{F}_x} \sum_{i=1}^{q} \lambda_i F_i(x) \tag{4}$$

in which $\sum_{i=1}^{q} \lambda_i = 1, \lambda_i \geq 0$. $\mathcal{F}_x$ represents the feasible set for the problem and q the number of objective functions.

4.1   Genetic Algorithms

In 1960, John Holland defined Genetic algorithms (GAs) [16] as computational methods of search based in mechanism of genetic and natural evolution. This class of algorithm is reaching increasing importance in many fields in optimization. In this algorithm, a set of tentative solution (population) evolves according to probabilistic rules inspired by biological concepts: in each generation, the individuals tend to be better while the evolution process resumes. As the process evolves, better solutions are obtained. From an initial population, selection, crossover and mutation operators are introduced to evolve this population. GA, like any other evolutionary technique, are especially well tuned for solving a wide class of problems due to their ability to explore vast solution spaces and search from a set of solutions rather than from just a single one.

In the multi-objective optimization problems, there is not a solution that is best or global optimum with respect to all objectives. When a problem has multiple objective, it gives rise to a set of non-dominated solutions, *Pareto-optimal set*, in which each objective component of any candidate along the Pareto-front can only be improved by degrading at least one of its other objective components. Since it is not possible to say that one solution in the non-dominated set is better than any other solution, any solution in this set is an acceptable one. In the Multi-objective Genetic Algorithms, some modifications are introduced in the Mono-objective GA, among them the niche technique, that avoids very close solutions, guaranteeing a greater diversity of solutions. Another modification is the concept of dominance wherein one solution is only better than other if it meets, simultaneously, all the objectives. The representation of the solution is given according to Fig. 1. The generation of the initial population and the genetic operators are same for both the mono-objective and the multi-objective algorithms, differentiating only by the fitness function evaluations.

The initial population is randomly created. Depending on the type of meal, random values between zero and the size of the list belonging to that type are generated. For example, since breakfast consists of a snack, a fruit and a drink, we generate three random values according to the size of each list. Each value gives the position in the corresponding list. In this way. the content of that position is included to the breakfast list. In the same way, it happens with other types of meal. The genetic operators, selection, crossover and mutation, are defined as:

- **Selection:** The selection is a tournament selection in which two random individuals are chosen and the one with the best function value is selected.
- **Crossover:** the crossover is performed within each type of meal, according to Fig. 2. Considering the crossover between breakfast and snack, the cutoff point ranges from one to three and, between breakfast and lunch, between one to seven. In this way, new individuals are formed maintaining the genetic trait of its parents.
- **Mutation:** chooses on a random day of the menu, and for each meal of this day, picks randomly a preparation to be modified by another one of the same type (Fig. 3). At each generation, every individual mutates according to a probabilistic mutation rate. For example, one fruit can only be exchanged for another fruit. Thus, in a menu are made 3 exchanges.

In the multi-objective approach, there are two objective functions: the objective function nutritional error (Equation 1) and the objective function cost

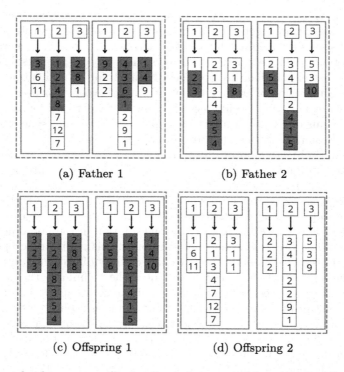

Fig. 2. Example of crossover: offspring 1 gets from parent 1 preparations from the first preparation of each meal to the cut-off points (1, 4 and 2) and the cut-off points to the end of parent 2. Offspring 2 gets preparations from parent 2 of the first preparation of each meal to the cut-off points (1, 4 and 2) and the cut-off points to the end of parent 1.

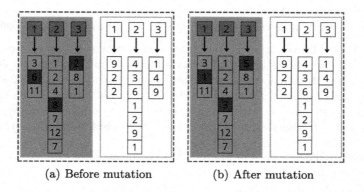

Fig. 3. Example of a mutation that exchanges, in the breakfast, the preparation 6 by 1 of the milk or derivatives; In the lunch, the mutation exchanges the preparation 8 by 3 of the side dish; In the snack meal, exchange the preparation 2 by 5 of the bread/ other cereal on the first day of a 2-day menu.

(Eq. 2). In both cases, we handle the constraints using the well-known penalization approach. Penalty functions are widely employed in many real-world optimization problems (as in [20]). The penalties for color, consistency and variety are incorporated to the nutritional error Two types of penalty are applied: linear and quadratic. The quadratic penalty will be used to differentiate the constraints that, according to us, is more important to be met in determining the menu. The color and consistency constraints are treated with linear penalty and the variety with quadratic penalty. Let α be the sum of all penalties concerning to color, consistency and variety. Thus,

$$\alpha = \sum_{d \in D} \sum_{m \in M} \Phi_{dm}, \tag{5}$$

being Φ_{dm} the penalties on meals m at day d. The penalized F_1 is given by

$$\tilde{F}_1 = F_1 + \alpha. \tag{6}$$

Let β be the penalty, d_{max} the number of days, lc the cost limit established for each meal m. Thus, the penalty is defined as:

$$\beta = (\sum_{m \in M} lc_m \times d_{max}) \times w_m, \tag{7}$$

being $w_m = 1$ if there was cost violation of the meal m and, 0 otherwise. The penalized F_2 is given by
$$\tilde{F}_2 = \mathcal{F}_2 + \beta. \tag{8}$$

The only difference between the mono and multi-objective GAs is related to the fitness function evaluation. In the mono-objective approach, the objective function is defined as to the weighted-sum approach according to Equation (9)

$$fitness(x) = \lambda \tilde{F}_1 + (1 - \lambda)\tilde{F}_2, \tag{9}$$

being $\tilde{F}_1$ the nutritional error and $\tilde{F}_2$ cost.

5   Results and Discussion

The multi-objective optimization is characterized by returning a set of efficient solutions (Pareto set) representing a trade-off between the objective functions and, after that, by allowing the user to choose, among the solutions, the one that best suits him/her. In the mono-objective approach solved via the weighted-sum method, the λ is discretized in the interval [0 1], with a step-size of 0.1. For each λ, the mono-objective GA is executed 30 times. After all runs of the mono-objective GA, the solutions are combined and a non-dominated algorithm is applied to obtain the final non-dominated set of the solutions. In the multi-objective approach, the NSGA-II is also run 30 times. At each run, the non-dominated set is obtained and, after all runs, a combined non-dominated set is obtained. The parameters for both algorithms are: 100 individuals in the population, 1000 iterations, crossover rate equal to 0.8, mutation rate equal to 0.05, three meals in 5 days on the week.

It is worthwhile to notice that the Brazilian government transfers to a munici-pality a certain fixed budget per child/day. Then each municipality complements it. Usually the municipal financial complement is around 65% of the total. Hav-ing that in mind, the daily cost of a menu is limited to R$ 8,00 (breakfast: R$2,00; lunch: R$4,00; snack R$2,00)and the 5-day menu is limited to R$ 40,00. The non-dominated solutions of the mono-objective approach are combined to the non-dominated solutions of NSGA-II. A final combined non-dominated set is then obtained. Fig. 4 shows the final combined non-dominated solutions obtained from both approaches. Observe that using GA, the mono-objective approach found only three non-dominated solutions, two located on one extremity of the Pareto front and one on the other extremity. On the other hand, using the NSGA-II found 60 solutions, a number considerably higher.

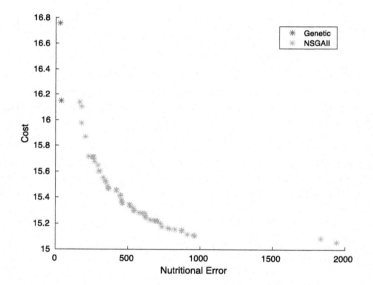

Fig. 4. Combined non-dominated solutions obtained from the mono- and multi-objective approaches.

Three solutions in Fig. 4 are chosen to be further analyzed: (i) a menu pre-senting the lowest nutritional error; (ii) a menu presenting the lowest price; and (iii) a menu located on the central part of the non-dominated front. These solu-tions are assessed using a scheme proposed by PNAE. PNAE aims to standardize the menus, in such a way as to help professionals who work in this area to verify that the menus meet the guidelines of the Program and the pillars of an adequate and healthy diet. PNAE has made available a tool to qualitatively analyze the school menus prepared within the scope of the Program. The Quality Index of

Nutritional Food Safety Coordination (IQ-COSAN, acronym in Portuguese) [6] is an easy-to-use and accessible instrument, developed in Excel, which, through the granting of points, analyzes school menus according to four parameters:

- Presence of six food groups: cereals and tubers; beans; vegetables and greens; fresh fruit; milk and dairy products; meat and eggs;
- Presence of regional foods and socio-biodiversity;
- Weekly diversity of meals offered;
- Absence of foods classified as restricted, prohibited and sweet foods or preparations.

At the end of the assessment, IQ-COSAN adds up the scores for the week and calculates the weekly average. The final score lies within 0-95 points and the menu is classified according to the obtained score: Inadequate (0 to 45.9 points), Needs improvement (46 to 75.9 points) and Adequate (76 to 95 points). Table 2 shows the IQ-COSAN assessment for the menu having the lowest price. The menu is classified as Adequate with a score higher than 92. The menu having the lowest nutritional error and the menu located in the center of the front presented similar tables being classified as Adequate with a score of 93 and 92.5, respectively.

As a comparison, a weekly menu of a city, located in Minas Gerais, in a rich region with a high index of human development, is assessed. This is a situation very contrasting to the majority of the Brazilian municipalities. In general, the menus for full-time preschool students (4 to 5 years old) have the same structure: breakfast, lunch and snack. However, the composition of each meal varies from one municipality to another. Moreover, although this school database includes the preparations from Minas Gerais state document, it is very likely to have other preparations not included in our work. Keeping that in mind, it is not fair to compare this school menu in terms of nutritional error and monetary cost.

Nonetheless, the school menu can be assessed using IQ-COSAN. After the qualitative and quantitative IQ-COSAN assessment, this real school menu is also classified as Adequate. However, the weekly score is 87, less than all menus obtained using our approach. We argue that the MPP is highly influenced by the database. In our case, including preparations used in other Brazilian municipalities, specially the ones located in poor regions, will affect the final output of our approach. It is more likely to obtain a cheaper menu while respecting the PNAE guidelines when database of those impoverished municipalities are used.

6   Conclusions

This work deals with the problem of menu planning for Brazilian schools. The goal is to plan menus in a fast and diversified manner, with low cost, while satisfying the requirements established by the government via the Brazilian School Eating Programme (PNAE) guidelines. The objective functions of the problem are the nutritional error and the cost. The nutritional error is related to the difference of the proposed menu and the reference guidelines. The cost is simply

Table 2. Assessment of the menu having the lowest price

IQCOSAN- QUALITY INDEX OF NUTRITIONAL FOOD SAFETY COORDINATION

COMPONENTS WEEK 1

DAILY ASSESSMENT COMPONENTS	Reference	Day 1	Day 2	Day 3	Day 4	Day 5	Result	Freq.	Obs.
Presence of foods: cereals and tubers	2	2	2	2	2	2	10	5	
Presence of foods: beans	2	2	2	2	2	2	10	5	
Presence of foods: vegetables	2	2	2	2	2	2	10	5	
Presence of fresh fruit	2	2	2	2	2	2	10	5	
Presence of foods: milk and dairy	2	2	2	2	2	2	10	5	
Presence of foods: meat and eggs	2	2	2	2	2	2	10	5	
Absence of restricted foods	2	2	2	2	2	2	10	0	
Absence of sweet foods and preparations	2	2	2	2	2	2	10	0	
SCORE							80		

WEEKLY ASSESSMENT COMPONENTS				Result	Reference
Regional food supply?				2.5	2.5
Food supply from sociobiodiversity?	1 Reference/day or	2 References/day or	3 References/day or		2.5
	20% NND*	30% NND*	70% NND*		
Menu Diversity			36	10	10
Offer of prohibited food					-10
WEEK END SCORE				92.5	

the total cost of the menu. Some constraints are added to the objective functions via penalty terms. For solving the problem, two approaches are used in this work: a mono-objective, in which the bi-objective problem is transformed into a mono-objective one using the weighted-sum approach and solved using a generic GA, and a multi-objective approach, in which the NSGA-II is directly applied to solve the problem. Results show GA and NSGA-II have found feasible solutions for the problem. However, the NSGA-II approach has found a higher number of potential solutions. In all cases, the goals have been achieved and the constraints established by the government have been met. The menus have been qualitatively and quantitatively assessed via IQ-COSAN, a tool made available by PNAE to standardize the menus, and to verify whether the guidelines are being met. Results indicate the proposed approach is very promising and can help the national school food program in Brazil. As future work, new instances using an extended database need to be applied. Effects when the menu is planned for more days (p.e. a 20-day menu) are worth to be analyzed. Other recommendations such as calcium level and sugar intake can also be included in the problem formulation as criteria and/or constraints.

Acknowledgment. This project has received funding from the European Union's Horizon 2020 research and innovation programme under the Marie Skłodowska-Curie grant agreement No 754382. This research has also been partially supported by Comunidad de Madrid, PROMINT-CM project (grant ref: P2018/EMT-4366) and by the project PID2020-115454GB-C21 of the Spanish Ministry of Science and Innovation (MICINN). The authors thank UAH, UFRJ and CEFET-MG for the infrastructure used to conduct this work, and Brazilian research agencies for partially support: CAPES (Finance Code 001), FAPERJ, and CNPq. "The content of this publication does not reflect the official opinion of the European Union. Responsibility for the information and views expressed herein lies entirely with the author(s)."

References

1. Balintfy, J.: Menu planning by computer. Comu. ACM **7**(4), 255–259 (1964)
2. Bianchini, V.U., Martinelli, S., Soares, P., Fabri, R., Cavalli, S.: Criteria adopted for school menu planning within the framework of the Brazilian school feeding program. Revista da Nutrição **33**, 1–13 (2020)
3. Brasil: Guia Alimentar para a população brasileira. Brasil. Ministério da Saúde. Secretaria de Atenção à Saúde. Dep. de Atenção Básica., Brasília, 2 edn. (2014)
4. Brasil: Fundo nacional de desenvolvimento de educação(fnde) pnae: Alimentação escolar (2017). http://www.fnde.gov.br/programas/alimentacao-escolar
5. Brasil: Ministério da educação. fundo nacional de desenvolvimento de educação(fnde) pnae: Alimentação escolar (2017). http://www.fnde.gov.br/programas/alimentacao-escolar
6. Brasil, M.d.E.: Índice de qualidade da coordenação de segurança alimentar nutricional - iq cosan (2022). https://www.fnde.gov.br/index.php/programas/pnae/pnae-area-gestores/ferramentas-de-apoio-ao-nutricionista/item/12142-iq-cosan

7. Bulka, J., Izworski, A., Koleszynska, J., Lis, J., Wochlik., I.: Automatic meal planning using artificial intelligence algorithm in computer aided diabetes therapy. In: 2009 4th International Conference on Autonomous Robots and Agents, pp. 393–397. IEEE (2009)

8. Chaves, L.G., Santana, T., Gabriel, C.: Reflexões sobre a atuação do nutricionista no programa nacional de alimentação escolar no brasil. Ciência e Saúde Coletiva 18, 917–926 (2013)

9. Chvatal, V.: Linear Programming. Series of Books in the Mathematical Sciences, W. H. Freeman (1983)

10. Deb, K.: Multi-Objective Optimization Using Evolutionary Algorithms. Wiley Interscience Series in Systems and Optimization, Wiley (2001)

11. Flores, P., et al.: Pladiet: Un sistema de cómputo para el diseño de dietas individualizas utilizando algoritmos genéticos (2007)

12. (FoRC), F.R.C.: Departamento de alimentos e nutrição experimental. tabela brasileira de composição de alimentos - tbca-usp (2018). http://www.fcf.usp.br/tbca

13. Gaal, B., Vassányi, I., Kozmann, G.: A novel artificial intelligence method for weekly dietary menu planning. Methods Inf. Med. 44(05), 655–664 (2005)

14. Garey, M., Johnson, D.: Computers and Intractability: A Guide to the Theory of NP-Completeness. Series in the Mathematical Sciences, W. H. Freeman (1979)

15. Gomes, F.R.: Pró-dieta: Gerador automático de cardápios personalizados baseado em Algoritmo Genético. Universidade Federal de Uberlândia, Uberlândia, Dissertação de mestrado (2012)

16. Holland, J.H.: Adaptation in Natural and Artificial Systems. Massachusetts, Cambridge (1975)

17. Kahraman, A., Seven, H.A.: Healthy daily meal planner. In: Genetic and Evolutionary Computation Conference - Undergraduate Student Workshop (GECCO 05 UGWS), pp. 25–29 (2005)

18. Kaldirim, E., Kose, Z.: Application of a multi-objetictive genetic algorithm to the modified diet problem. In: Genetic and Evolutionary Computation Coference (GECCO). Seattle, WA, USA. (2006)

19. Kellerer, H., Pferschy, U., Pisinger, D.: Knapsack Problems. Springer (2013)

20. Marcelino, C., et al.: An efficient multi-objective evolutionary approach for solving the operation of multi-reservoir system scheduling in hydro-power plants. Expert Syst. Appl. 185, 115638 (2021). https://doi.org/10.1016/j.eswa.2021.115638

21. de Minas Gerais), G.: Cardápios da alimentação escolar - educação básica (2014). https://www2.educacao.mg.gov.br/images/documentos/

22. NEPA: Núcleo de estudos e pesquisas em alimentação.tabela brasileira de composição de alimentos - taco (2011). http://www.unicamp.br/nepa/taco/tabela.php?ativo=tabela

23. Pearl, J.: Heuristics: Intelligent Search Strategies for Computer Problem Solving. The Addison-Wesley Series in Artificial Intelligence, Addison-Wesley (1984)

24. Seljak, B.K.: Dietary menu planning using an evolutionary method. In: INES-International Conference on Intelligent Engineering Systems, pp. 108–113 (2006)

25. Seljak, B.K.: Comput-based dietary menu planning. J. Food Composit. Anal. 22(5), 414–420 (2009)

26. Sufahani, S., Ismail, Z.: A new menu planning model for Malaysian secondary schools using optimization approach. Appl. Math. Sci. 8(151), 7511–7518 (2014)

27. Sufahani, S.F., Ismail, Z.: Planning a nutritious and healthy menu for Malaysian school children aged 13-18 using delete-reshuffle algorithm in binary integer programming. Appl. Sci¿ 15, 1239–1244 (2015)

Artificial Intelligence

Stock-Pred: The LSTM Prophet of the Stock Market

Thiago Figueiredo Costa$^{(\boxtimes)}$ and André Rodrigues da Cruz

Departamento de Computação, Centro Federal de Educação Tecnológica de Minas
Gerais, Belo Horizonte, MG 30510 -000, Brazil
thiagofigcosta@gmail.com, dacruz@cefetmg.br

Abstract. This paper presents the development process of a LSTM
prophet which predicts stock market prices, based on historical data
and machine learning to identify trends. Predicting prices in the stock
market is a challenging task, surrounded by possible turbulent events
that impact the final result. In this scenario, for the method proposed
here, it is presented (i) the steps to obtain and process the used data
for the applied LSTM network; (ii) the motivations for this implementation; (iii) the details regarding methodology and architecture; (iv) the
neural architecture search technique used to determine the hyperparameters by tuning them through the iRace algorithm, which is responsible
for structuring the network topology in a robust way; and (v) a discussion about quality measures used to compare network settings. Computational experiments in order to analyze the developed tool considered
stock tickers from USA and Brazilian financial markets, in addition to
the foreign exchange market involving BRL–USD. The obtained results
were satisfactory in general, which achieved a high model accuracy, in
relation to price tendency, and a low mean absolute percentage error,
according to price values, with the analyzed test dataset.

Keywords: LSTM · Forecast · Stock market · Neural architecture
search · Irace

1 Introduction

The act of prophesying stock market values is challenging due to the complexity
of the system. The close price of a company share is determined by many factors
explained by fundamental or technical analysis, such as accounting situation,
global or country economy status, the volume of exchanged stocks during the
day, or even issues not directly related to finance which cause speculations [7,21].
This difficulty in estimating prices, the dynamics of the system, the considerable
number of variables that must be analysed and the mutability of the market
represent a risk for investors whom lack an efficient computational tool.

Supported by organization the Brazilian agencies CAPES, CNPq and FAPEMIG.

The dynamic of financial markets presents a sensitivity in relation to intraday fluctuations and previous states. This behavior enables it to be analyzed as a chaotic system [23] with aspects grounded on [17] which affirms that prices of stocks follow random paths. Conversely, the efficient market theory [8] declares that all available historical information of the stock market instantly modifies the final price of a stock.

In this way, the possibility of creating computational models that uses data regarding the financial market to predict its behavior by detecting implicit and explicit trends is considered. These models can either conjecture stock prices or its movement tendency, despite the random behaviour. Other evidences that support this idea is the fact that algorithmic traders have been widely used to improve earnings [14]. Therefore, it is possible to obtain above-average profits with an automated system, since not all agents that operate in the financial market have access to stock market data in an uniform way. Many works in the literature investigated algorithms in order to trade efficiently and those based on machine learning have shown promising results [24].

The goal of this work is to present the creation of a tool to assist investors during decision making, based on Long Short-Term Memory (LSTM) neural networks [3], which predict stock prices in the next days after a time point of reference. The tickers GOOG and AAPL from NASDAQ, IBM and T from NYSE, CSMG3 and ENBR3 from Ibovespa, the Ibovespa index, and exchange rates BRL–USD and BTC–USD were considered. The robust LSTM architecture selection was performed by the tuning algorithm iRace [16] using a composed utility function. A set of measurements was adopted to evaluate the quality of the obtained LSTMs. The model was trained using stock data crawled from Yahoo Finance. The code was developed in Python and is available under the MIT license in the following link https://github.com/thiagofigcosta/stock-pred-v2.

This paper is organized as follows: Sect. 2 presents a literature review about application of forecasting information in stock market using LSTMs. Section 3 provides the methodology applied in this work. Section 4 describes the numerical experiments and the respective results. Section 5 discusses some findings. Finally, Sect. 6 concludes the paper and outlines possible future works.

2   Related Work

Stock market prediction is a challenging task whether it is desired to estimate the direct price of a stock or its trend movement. Many authors have addressed this challenge using different approaches [9]. This work have focused on studies that used neural networks to forecast the price behavior of stock market assets.

The authors in [10] intended to predict the stock movement using 2 ensembles, one with a moderated investor profile and the other with an aggressive profile. The ensembles were made of two Multi-Layer Perceptron (MLP) networks aggregated with an AND gate. A set of 18 tickers of shares and stock indexes was adopted and classified into 2 groups, Brazilian and Not Brazilian.

The results stated that forecasting stocks from a developing country is harder, due to a higher instability of emerging countries.

The work [20] purposed a LSTM classifier to forecast the stock movement. The proposed model was compared with MLP, Random Forest and a Pseudo-Random model. Data with 15 min granularity from 2008 to 2015 was collected for some Brazillian stocks. The features used to feed the network were the Open, Close, Low and High prices, the volume and another 175 market indicators calculated using the TA-lib. The LTSM network was composed by a layer with Tanh activation followed by a dense Sigmoid layer. This network was re-trained every day using the past 10 month data to train, whereas the past one week was used to validate. The results provided the accuracy, precision, recall and F1-Score as output measurements.

The paper [15] also used LSTM networks with 3 layers in order to predict the stock market movement. The authors adopted as features the standard and exponential moving averages and also a set of ratios between intraday prices of a stock. Historical data of the CSI-300 index was gathered to be used in a computational experiment that achieved an accuracy of 0.78. The authors claimed that increasing the amount of layers will improve the accuracy of the model, which is not always true, as illustrated by the results of this work.

The authors in [1] used a normalized dataset containing the close price of S&P500 Index, from 2010 to 2017, to forecast the close price. They selected 80% of the dataset for training and the rest for tests. LSTM networks, with a dense layer as the last layer, were used for short and long term. For the short term networks 10 d of the past were used to predict one day ahead, while the long term they used 30 d to predict a single day. They tested Bidirectional and Stacked LSTM Networks, comparing the results with a simple LSTM and a MLP. The bidirectional LSTM with short term configuration had the best performance in the test scenario.

The ModAugNet proposed in [2] forecasts the close price of market indexes using an ensemble composed of two LSTM networks connected by a dense layer. Both LSTM networks have their own dense layer at the end. ReLU was used as the activation function of the hidden layers. One of the networks serves as a prediction module and the other is a prevention module that aims to prevent overfitting. The used dataset consists of the normalized closing price of the indexes S&P500 and KOSPI200 from 2000 to 2017. The model was trained for 200 epochs, with a batch size of 32, and learning rate of 0.0001. They tested several loss functions, and their final model uses 20 past days to predict the value of one day in the future.

The work [22] predicted the stock market movement of KO, IBM and ORCL, and also of the NASDAQ-100 index, with normalized daily data from 1999 to 2019. Two approaches were used, LSTM and MLP networks. The data initially contained just Open and Close prices, however, the dataset was enriched adding several indicators such as SMA, EMA, MACD, ADX, CCI, RSI, MOM, WILLR, OBV, AD, ADOS and derivative, the features were then filtered using the SelectKBest feature selection algorithm. Two encodings were compared, using a single binary class and 8 binary classes. By using more than one binary class they were able to represent the stock movement and its magnitude. A single binary class, using two past days to predict one day in the feature had the best performance, achieving the F1-Score of 0.984 for IBM stocks.

The authors of [12] classified the daily sentiment of investors regarding Apple Stocks (AAPL) based on comments available at Stocktwits and Yahoo Finance. Using the sentiment analysis and daily historical stock market from 2013 to 2018 they were able use two days of the past to forecast the AAPL price with a MAPE of 1.62%, accuracy of 0.7056, and R^2 of 0.977388. The authors also mention a similar work with accuracy of 0.6415.

3 Methodology

This section serves the purpose of presenting the details, processes and the architecture used to develop the Stock-Pred. This task implements features not only to instantiate a neural network using a set of hyperparameters, train and evaluate it, but also to download the historical data of a given stock, and to enrich and process this data. An additional feature is the integration with optimization algorithms to search for adequate hyperparameters, and with multi-objective non-dominated sorting [5, 25] to compare multiple networks.

3.1 Data

The applied data, as previously mentioned, came from the public API Yahoo Finance. By analyzing the page of historical stock values of a given company in the website, it was observed that the link of the download button of CSV data has query parameters that represents the date range of the stock and the corresponding stock. Based on this finding, we were able to automate the download process of any stock for any available interval, by modifying the query parameters and executing the request. Before saving the downloaded data in the file system, the dataset was filtered to remove rows where there were null values. The data obtained through this endpoint has daily granularity and it contains the features: date, open value of the stock, highest price of the day, lowest price of the day, close value of the stock, adjusted close price, which subtracts dividends and splits, and finally the volume of traded stocks. It is also possible to download data with minute granularity through another endpoint, however training networks with minute granularity is out of the scope of this work.

After the dataset is downloaded, the enrichment process is executed in order to increase the data value by extracting new features, presented in Eq. (1), that encode more information about the problem. The first set are ratios between the available stock prices (Open, Close, Low, High). The other enriched features are the Standard Moving Average (SMA), the Exponential Moving Average (EMA), for a window of size w, and the Log Return (LR) [20]. In the formulas d represents a given day. The smallest d value that can be used in the averages is $w - 1$. The base case of EMA, EMA_{d-1}, is equal to SMA_{d-1}.

$$OC = (Close - Open)/Open$$
$$OH = (High - Open)/Open$$
$$OL = (Low - Open)/Open$$
$$CH = (High - Close)/Close$$
$$CL = (Low - Close)/Close \qquad (1)$$
$$LH = (High - Low)/Low$$
$$SMA_d = \sum_{i=0}^{w-1} Close_{d-i}/w$$
$$EMA_d = (Close_d - EMA_{d-1}) \cdot (2/(w+1)) + EMA_{d-1}$$
$$LR_d = \log(Close_d) - \log(Close_{d-1})$$

For each kind of moving average two values were computed, a fast moving average considering a group of 13 data samples, and a slow moving average that uses 21 data samples. The values of 13 and 21 were chosen because they are respectively the 8th and 9th numbers of the Fibonacci sequence. The dataset was normalized using the min-max normalization technique with a unique scale for each feature, since their amplitudes are completely different. No shuffles were performed in the dataset in order to preserve its sequential order.

Before the training step, the data were prepared and encoded properly. A forecast architecture that predicts the close price of stocks from a given fixed reference day was adopted. The LSTM networks will arrange and use B past data points, in a rolling window which contains the input features. The LSTM output is another window containing the close price of F future data points.

These windows slide in position (reference day) throughout the dataset, with a step of size one, generating the inputs and outputs. The data contained in the first window are the inputs that corresponds to an output which is formed by the data in the second window. The data generated up to the moment in which the second window reaches the end of the dataset can be used for training and testing, because it has labels. Whereas the data formed after this moment and until the first window reaches the end of the dataset can be used only to predict values not yet known.

The processed input and output arrays shall obey the shapes ($\#samples, B,$ $\#features$) and ($\#samples, F$), respectively. It can be observed that labels have a size F in its second dimension, thus for a given F of a network it can have up to F results for the same date. The F results of the inference samples can be arranged in a matrix, where each prediction array which contains the close prices for the next F days in ascending date order is a row. The close prices in which the labels are unknown, i.e. the actual predictions after the last known day d, are contained in and under the line of the secondary diagonal of the matrix. The diagonal itself gives F results for $d+1$, the diagonal below it gives $F-1$ results for $d+2$, and so forth.

From this point, historical data for any asset (shares, currency exchange rates, cryptocurrencies, indexes, etc.) can be downloaded. This data can also be treated and adapted appropriately to be used by the LSTM models. The final dataset is sufficient for training and testing the neural networks, and the illustrated method can serve for other authors to obtain databases as such.

3.2   LSTM

A Long Short-Term Memory, or simply LSTM, is a kind of artificial recurrent neural network architecture with feedback connections that can process and learn from a time series [11]. The state of a cell stores values over arbitrary data series and the gates regulate the flow of information into and out of the cell. Its neurons can be composed of a cell with three gates with activation functions, one for input, another for output and a third for a forget action. An input gate determines what are the relevant information from the data to be added in the cell state. An output gate filters which information from the current cell state goes as a response. A forget gate regulates the information from the previous cell state that should be used to compose the next state.

The LSTM was implemented using the Keras as front-end, and the Tensor Flow as the back-end. Initially, in a stateless LSTM network, the cell memory of the neurons are reset after every batch, which makes the batch size a very significant hyperparameter. The network can also be stateful, at which the memory reset must be implemented by the programmer. It can be after each epoch or a couple of them, for instance.

Besides the regular activation functions that are common in neural networks, there is also the recurrent activation functions that are applied in the gates. Analogously, there is the dropout layer, which can be applied after a layer, and there is also the recurrent dropout, which can be applied between the neuron cycle loops. In Keras there is the "go backwards" option, that reverses the data input array, and there is the "unit forget bias" that adds the value one to the bias of the forget gate at initialization.

LSTM networks takes long periods of time to train. A small dataset was chosen as counter measure, containing data from 01/Jan/2016 to 07/May/2021. Of the total dataset, 70% was destined to training and validation, with 80% of the training dataset being used for actual training and the 20% left for cross validation. For test purposes, the interval ranging is from 07/Jan/2021 to 07/May/2021, which corresponds to 6.2% of the total data. The group of features selected to be used in all experiments of this work is composed by OC, OH, OL, CH, CL, LH, Volume, LR, EMA of 13, EMA of 21 and Close price. Even though more features are present in the dataset, this set was selected to avoid overfitting and to speedup the training process through a small group of features. The features were chosen by a manual feature selection, at which features that encoded similar information as another that was already in the set were avoided. The values of the network gradients were clipped to 0.5, in order to avoid the exploding gradients issue.

For measuring the performance of the models two sets of measurements were defined, model measurements and classification measurements. The model measurements are computed using the raw output of the network, whereas for the classification measurements the network output is converted to a binary signal that represents the stock movement, and then the measurements are calculated. The cosine similarity, Mean Squared Error (MSE), Mean Squared Error (MSE), Mean Absolute Percentage Error (MAPE) and the R^2 were used as model measurements. While for the classification measurements we defined the F1-Score, the Accuracy, the Precision, the Recall, the Area Under the Receiver Operating Characteristic Curve (ROC AUC), and the Accumulated Accuracy Rate (AAR). The AAR is the average of the accuracy of the predictions for the first F days of the test dataset, considering all available results for each day, even the redundant ones. They are compared with the real values of the day. Since the other measurements needs a single value for each day to be calculated, we aggregated the values of the available results using the mean between the first and last available result, ending up with a single predicted price for each day.

The loss function of the neural network was the MSE. Three callbacks were implemented to improve the training performance. An early stop callback, that interrupts the training after a given amount of patience epochs without improvements in the validation loss. A checkpoint callback, that saves the weights of the best model during the training according to the validation loss. This model is then restored after the training. And a learning rate reduce callback, which reduces the learning rate by dividing it by a reduce factor after a given amount of patience epochs without improvements in the validation loss. The hidden states of stateful networks were reset after each epoch. A hyperparameter to decide whether a dense layer with linear activation function must be added to the network or not, was created. When it does not add the dense layer at the end, instead it adds another LSTM layer there. The rest of the hyperparameters were chosen using a Neural Architecture Search (NAS) technique.

3.3   Neural Architecture Search

The NAS aims to select good hyperparameters for the neural network from a search space using an algorithmic optimization instead of manual trial and error. For this work, the iRace heuristic [16] was applied as the tuning procedure. This offline meta-optimizer has been successfully applied to find robust parameter sets for machine learning methods [4,13,18].

The iRace was configured to run a elitist non-deterministic race, with one new elitist instance out of a maximum of two for iteration, using a maximum budget of 777 and parallelism of four. The algorithm was also configured run a maximum of seven iterations, with a μ of five and a confidence level of 0.95. The tuning process solves the noisy and high computational mono-objective problem presented in Eq. (2). It is desired to find the best possible parameter set $\mathbf{p}$ from the search space Π, maximizing the utility function in (3).

$$\max u(\mathbf{p}) \quad s.t. : \mathbf{p} \in \Pi \tag{2}$$

$$u(\mathbf{p}) = \frac{3 \cdot AAR(\mathbf{p}) + F1\_Score(\mathbf{p}) + Accuracy(\mathbf{p})}{5 * MSE(\mathbf{p})} \tag{3}$$

During the hyperparameter search the only stock used was the AT&T (T), which is a dividend aristocrat. This was done to speed up the optimisation process, by avoiding to run this costly operation for many stocks. The search space

Π for the network hyperparameters is presented in Table 1, the ones related with each network layer are contained in Table 2. The values and intervals selected for the search space were based on the literature. The network hyperparameters were restricted to the following constraints: (i) The patience to stop cannot be greater than maximum epochs; (ii) the patience to reduce cannot be greater than maximum number of epochs; and (iii) the batch size must be an even number.

Table 1. Network Hyperparameters Search Space

Hyperparameter	Search space
Backward Samples (B)	[5, 60]
Forward Samples (F)	[7, 14]
Hidden LSTM Layers	[0, 5]
Maximum Epochs	[500, 5000]
Patience to Stop	[1000, 5000]
Patience to Reduce Learning Rate	[0, 1000]
Learning Rate Reduce Factor	[0, 0.2]
Batch size	[0, 128]
Stateful	{True, False}
Optimizer	{SGD, Adam, RMSPro}
Dense layer in output	{True, False}

Table 2. Layer Hyperparameters Search Space

Hyperparameter	Search space
Activation Function	{ReLU, Sigmoid, Tanh, Exponential, Linear}
Recurrent Activation	{ReLU, Sigmoid, Tanh, Exponential, Linear, Hard Sigmoid}
Layer size	[10, 200]
Dropout	[0, 0.3]
Recurrent Dropout	[0, 0.3]
Use bias	{True, False}
Unit forget bias	{True, False}
Go backwards	{True, False}

3.4 Network Evaluation

Eight tickers were picked in order to evaluate the selected neural network architecture models: (i) three North American successful technology companies are Google (GOOG), IBM (IBM) and Apple (AAPL); (ii) two Brazilian companies COPASA (CSMG3.SA) and EDP Energias do Brasil (ENBR3.SA); the

BOVESPA index (BVSP); (iii) the cryptocurrency rate between Bitcoins and Dollars (BTC.USD); and (iv) the exchange rate between Brazilian Reais (BRL) and Dollars (BRL.X). The AT&T (T) stock was used only for iRace.

To compare the performance among different models for the same stock, a non-dominated sorting for multi-objective problems [5,25] was performed, the Pareto front was presented considering the ARR and the MSE as objectives.

4   Experiments and Results

The experiments were executed in a shared server with an Intel Xeon E5-2630 v3 CPU @ 2.40GHz Octa-Core processor, 32 GB of RAM memory and a Nvidia Tesla K40c graphics card. All scenarios and experiments were executed in a single code that adapts itself to the parameters and configurations provided to it. The application was adapted to run in Docker containers to facilitate the deployment process.

The first experiment was the NAS using the iRace to determine a good and robust network hyperparameters using the AT&T stocks. From the iRace results the best set of hyperparameters was selected and labeled it as Subject 1. Two partially optimal results obtained from previous iterations than the Subject 1 iteration were also selected. Those were labeled as Subjects 2 and 3. The subjects of the network hyperparameters are presented in Table 3 alongside with the layer hyperparameters that are contained in Table 4. Since every subject has a single hidden layer, this last table has only three result columns.

Table 3. Best Network Hyperparameters Found

Hyperparameter	Subject 1	Subject 2	Subject 3
Backward Samples	16	31	38
Forward Samples	11	7	10
Hidden LSTM Layers	1	1	1
Maximum Epochs	4889	3183	3002
Patience to Stop	1525	1827	853
Patience to Reduce	539	228	73
Reduce Factor	0.01259	0.05265	0.06082
Batch size	122	46	112
Stateful	False	False	False
Optimizer	RMSProp	Adam	Adam
Dense layer in output	False	False	False

Table 4. Best Layer Hyperparameters Found

Hyperparameter	Sub. 1 - L1	Sub. 2 - L1	Sub. 3 - L1
Activation Function	Sigmoid	Sigmoid	Tanh
Recurrent Activation	Tanh	Tanh	ReLU
Layer size	89	67	164
Dropout	0.03741	0.24864	0.23404
Recurrent Dropout	0.24559	0.15223	0.00155
Use bias	False	True	True
Unit forget bias	True	True	True
Go backwards	True	False	False

The three subjects were then submitted to a test evaluation for the AAPL, BRL.X, BTC.USD, BVSP, CSMG, ENBR, GOOG, and IBM tickers. Following, the resulting measurements were grouped by ticker. The best non-dominating model solutions according for each stock scored one point for the given subject. In the end, the subject with more points was considered the best general model. It is displayed in Fig. 1 an example of a Pareto graph for the BRL.X exchange rate. For this particular scenario two models were part of the non-dominated solutions. According to Table 5, it is observable that the Subject 2 had the best overall performance. The Subject 2 model anatomy can be found in Fig. 2. Table 6 illustrates the measurements obtained by the Subject 2 for the stocks, while Fig. 3 shows the real values accompanied by all predictions made by Subject 2 for F days of IBM stocks. The forecasts were close to the actual close prices. The Fig. 4 shows Subject 2 processed predictions for AAPL, in the image is possible to see that even when the movement is predicted correctly, the scale of the close prices are wrong, the same effect can be seen in the graph of Fig. 5, where the price scale becomes incorrect when forecasts are made for the test dataset, which starts in 2021. Whereas in Fig. 6 the Subject 2 processed predictions for IBM stocks are closer to the actual values in scale and movement.

5   Discussion

The LSTM networks are hard and slow to train and a single wrong hyperparameter can ruin the results. The tuning process with iRace improved the LSTM networks and provided good results. The results shown no need to have more than 2 hidden layers. A huge amount of layers can easily over fit the model, even with a breadth search space. Here, every good solution candidate shown to have just a single hidden LSTM layer and another on the output.

Although the problem of stock market forecasting is challenging, stock market movements can be predicted with success, however there is still a lot to improve. For example, when considering just the stock movement of the forecast, good performances were achieved. The price scale must be improved, the scale was perfect in the training data though, since neural networks learnt from this data.

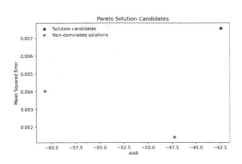

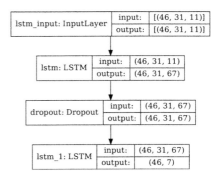

Fig. 1. Pareto graph highlighting the solutions. Subjects 2 (left) and 3 (right).

Fig. 2. Subject 2 model anatomy

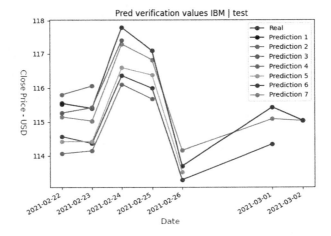

Fig. 3. Real close values and Subject 2 predictions for IBM from 22/Feb/2021 to 02/Mar/2021

Table 5. Points scored by subjects

Stock	Subject 1	Subject 2	Subject 3
IBM		X	
AAPL		X	
CSMG	X	X	X
BRL.X		X	X
BVSP	X		X
BTC.USD	X		
ENBR	X	X	
GOOG		X	
Sum	4	6	3

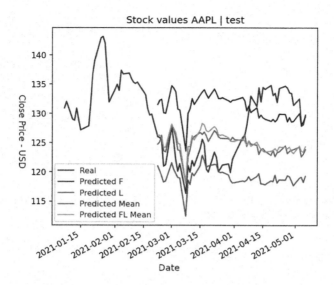

Fig. 4. Real close price and Subject 2 predictions for AAPL in the test dataset

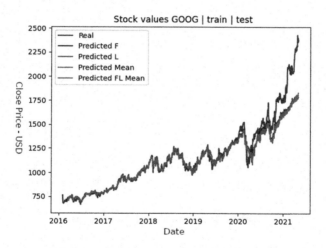

Fig. 5. Real close values and Subject 2 predictions for GOOG in both train and test datasets

The measurements for this problem are tricky. The MSE is not a good measurement to make comparisons between works, because it is scale dependent, i.e. the chosen stock, the test interval, the normalization, the network architecture and features used can cause discrepancies in the measurement value. The same is also true for MAE, therefore many works did not presented results with measurements that enables comparison between them. This, allied with the lack of standardized benchmarks could be the reason why there is so few papers comparing their results.

Table 6. Subject 2 - Measurements

	IBM	AAPL	CSMG3	BRL.X	BVSP	BTC.USD	ENBR3	GOOG
MSE	0.000389	0.004862	0.000684	0.004028	0.000814	0.279191	0.001987	0.030106
MAPE	2.246%	7.645%	4.143%	7.222%	7.397%	52.262%	4.039%	16.671%
Cosine	0.99986	0.99774	0.99968	0.99967	0.99989	0.98747	0.99983	0.99887
R^2	0.913	–	0.817	–	–	–	–	–
F1	0.933	0.735	0.917	0.712	0.928	0.383	0.941	0.615
Acc	0.923	0.750	0.920	0.696	0.920	0.356	0.940	0.519
Prec	0.903	0.818	0.880	0.656	0.962	0.367	0.923	0.571
Recall	0.966	0.667	0.957	0.778	0.896	0.400	0.960	0.667
ROC	0.918	0.753	0.923	0.699	0.924	0.356	0.940	0.492
AAR	91.287%	57.143%	89.285%	35.714%	49.286%	35.714%	42.857%	42.857%

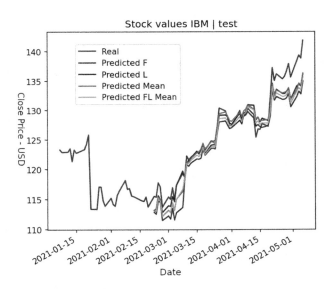

Fig. 6. Real close values and Subject 2 predictions for IBM in the test dataset

The R^2 is a good measurement, because it is based on the point to point distance between the curves, however this measurement is very sensitive, as shown previously due to present a very different curve from the original one [19]. The Cosine similarity is also a good choice, because it considers the angles between the curves, however to compare them, the results must be presented with several decimal places since this measurement is often close to one. Another good measurement is MAPE, because it ignores the scale. However, it is still susceptible to variances due to stock and date chosen. There is also other similar measurements that can be explored, such as Mean Absolute Scaled Error (MASE), Symmetric Mean Absolute Percentage Error (sMAPE), Mean Directional Accuracy (MDA) and Mean Arctangent Absolute Percentage Error (MAAPE). They can overcome weaknesses arising from standard MAPE.

It is also recommended to compute all these measurements externally, directly between the input and output, after retrieving the forecasts from the neural network. In this way Tensorflow will be prevented from mixing the outputs when computing the measurements, since we have F predictions for each sample, some values might be used more than once the measurements. This also eliminates any other effects related to features and avoid the architecture to interfere with the measurements. Considering those concerns, a further work aiming to develop a standardized benchmarks, and discuss good practices in results presentation is recommended, after executing an extensive systematic literature review.

During the experiments, the best individual selected by the iRace algorithm, Subject 1, did not had the best overall performance. There are two hypothesis to explain this behaviour: (i) the NAS was designed for a specific stock, AT&T, therefore the hyperparameters might not be well suited for other stocks; (ii) the NAS had single objective, using a fitness function as a workaround to evaluate the models considering other measurements together. The non-dominated solutions computed later considered a multi-objective treatment with different criteria. The best stock result was IBM stocks, which as AT&T is also a dividend aristocrat. The fact that those stocks belongs to the same group might explain why IBM had better results than the others, supporting the hypothesis (i).

6   Conclusions and Further Works

This work presented the development process of the Stock-Pred, a LSTM model which predicts prices of stock market tickers based on historical data. Here the steps to obtain and process the used data, the motivations for this implementation, the details about the developed methodology and architecture, the neural architecture search via iRace, and a discussion about quality measures used to compare network settings were proposed. Computational experiments, considering stock tickers from USA and Brazilian financial markets and the foreign exchange BRL–USD, indicated satisfactory results with a high model accuracy in relation to quality measures.

An interesting further work can be extended from this one by running a hyperparameter NAS using a multi-objective algorithm [6]. A new NAS optimization can be done for each stock, although more computational budget will be necessary for this particularized specialization.. The search space can be reduced to values near to the Subject 2 hyperparameters, in order to speed up the search process. If the multi-objective NAS present good results, besides being a good feature, it would also be a good replacement for the fitness function, which might have affected results in a negative way due to the MSE measurement. The MSE can mask the results, for example, a network with good F1 Score measurements can be obfuscated by bad MSE measurements. In order to evaluate the performance of the model considering more variables, the non-dominated solutions can also be obtained with more fitness functions.

An algorithmic feature extraction were not performed because deep neural networks does this implicitly, the Stock-Pred wide search space allows this deepness. The problem is that our optimum models were relatively simple, and since they are shallow, their feature extraction capability is reduced. Dense layers could be added in the input, but this would increase the model complexity unnecessarily. A good alternative would be to enrich several more features originated from financial indicators like those used in [20], among others such as derivative, Fibonacci Moving Average and Twitter or news mentions classified by sentiment. Then run an automatic feature extraction to select the best features for the model, or perhaps, extract different sets of features to be tested during the NAS.

Other improvements that worth to be mentioned include implementing profit and trading simulations with the ability to consider transaction costs, clip the gradients with a smaller value in a trade off between result quality and time needed to train, try different dataset intervals including longer ones, test more activation functions in the dense output layer and run more NAS in reduced search spaces to fine tune the hyperparameters. Since it has up to F predictions for a given date, it could connect multiple outputs for a same day in another neural network to obtain a single value per day without simply computing averages. Encoding the network to handle stock movement directly through binary classes could also improve the results. It is possible to predict just the trade movement, or use more classes to predict the movement and its magnitude.

References

1. Althelaya, K.A., El-Alfy, E.S.M., Mohammed, S.: Evaluation of bidirectional LSTM for short-and long-term stock market prediction. In: 9th International Conference on Information and Communication Systems (ICICS), pp. 151–156. IEEE (2018)
2. Baek, Y., Kim, H.Y.: ModAugNet: a new forecasting framework for stock market index value with an overfitting prevention LSTM module and a prediction LSTM module. Expert Syst. Appl. **113**, 457–480 (2018)
3. Bahdanau, D., Cho, K., Bengio, Y.: Neural machine translation by jointly learning to align and translate. arXiv preprint arXiv:1409.0473 (2014)
4. Cramer, S., Kampouridis, M., Freitas, A.A., Alexandridis, A.K.: An extensive evaluation of seven machine learning methods for rainfall prediction in weather derivatives. Expert Syst. Appl. **85**, 169–181 (2017)
5. Deb, K., Mohan, M., Mishra, S.: Evaluating the varepsilon-domination based multi objective evolutionary algorithm for a quick computation of pareto-optimal solutions. Evol. Comput. J. **13**(4), 501–525 (2005)
6. Deb, K., Pratap, A., Agarwal, S., Meyarivan, T.: A fast and elitist multi objective genetic algorithm: NSGA-ii. IEEE Trans. Evol. Comput. **6**(2), 182–197 (2002)
7. Edwards, R.D., Magee, J., Bassetti, W.C.: Technical Analysis of Stock Trends. CRC Press (2018)
8. Fama, E.F.: Efficient capital markets: a review of theory and empirical work. J. Finance **25**(2), 383–417 (1970). http://www.jstor.org/stable/2325486
9. Gandhmal, D.P., Kumar, K.: Systematic analysis and review of stock market prediction techniques. Comput. Sci. Rev. **34**, 100190 (2019)

10. Giacomel, F.d.S.: Um método algorítmico para operações na bolsa de valores baseado em ensembles de redes neurais para modelar e prever os movimentos dos mercados de ações. Tese de mestrado, UFRGS (2016)
11. Hochreiter, S., Schmidhuber, J.: Long short-term memory. Neural Comput. **9**(8), 1735–1780 (1997)
12. Jin, Z., Yang, Y., Liu, Y.: Stock closing price prediction based on sentiment analysis and LSTM. Neural Comput. Appl. **32**(13), 9713–9729 (2020)
13. Kampouridis, M., Otero, F.E.: Evolving trading strategies using directional changes. Expert Syst. Appl. **73**, 145–160 (2017)
14. Kissell, R.: Algorithmic Trading Methods: Applications Using Advanced Statistics, Optimization, and Machine Learning Techniques. Academic Press (2021)
15. Liu, S., Liao, G., Ding, Y.: Stock transaction prediction modeling and analysis based on LSTM. In: 2018 13th IEEE Conference on Industrial Electronics and Applications (ICIEA), pp. 2787–2790. IEEE (2018)
16. López-Ibáñez, M., Dubois-Lacoste, J., Cáceres, L.P., Birattari, M., Stützle, T.: The irace package: iterated racing for automatic algorithm configuration. Oper. Res. Perspect. **3**, 43–58 (2016)
17. Malkiel, B.G.: A random walk down wall street. w. w (1973)
18. Mohamed, I., Otero, F.E.: A multi objective optimization approach for market timing. In: Proceedings of the 2020 Genetic and Evolutionary Computation Conference, pp. 22–30 (2020)
19. Nakagawa, S., Schielzeth, H.: A general and simple method for obtaining R2 from generalized linear mixed-effects models. Methods Ecol. Evol. **4**(2), 133–142 (2013)
20. Nelson, D.M., Pereira, A.C., de Oliveira, R.A.: Stock market's price movement prediction with LSTM neural networks. In: 2017 International Joint Conference on Neural Networks (IJCNN), pp. 1419–1426. IEEE (2017)
21. Palepu, K.G., Healy, P.M., Wright, S., Bradbury, M., Coulton, J.: Business Analysis and Valuation: Using Financial Statements. Cengage AU (2020)
22. Rondel, G., Hilkner, R.: Técnicas de redes neurais para análise e previsão do mercado de ações. Relatório de Graduação, Projeto Final, UNICAMP (2019)
23. Sahni, R.: Analysis of stock market behaviour by applying chaos theory. In: 2018 9th International Conference on Computing, Communication and Networking Technologies (ICCCNT), pp. 1–4. IEEE (2018)
24. Shah, D., Isah, H., Zulkernine, F.: Stock market analysis: a review and taxonomy of prediction techniques. Int. J. Financ. Stud. **7**(2), 26 (2019)
25. Woodruff, M., Herman, J.: pareto.py: a varepsilon-non-domination sorting routine (2013). https://github.com/matthewjwoodruff/pareto.py

Confidence-Based Algorithm Parameter Tuning with Dynamic Resampling

André Rodrigues da Cruz[1]([envelope]) [ID] and Ricardo Hiroshi Caldeira Takahashi[2] [ID]

[1] Centro Federal de Educação Tecnológica de Minas Gerais, Avenue Amazonas, 7675, Nova Gameleira, Belo Horizonte, Minas Gerais, Brazil
dacruz@cefetmg.br
[2] Universidade Federal de Minas Gerais, Avenue Antônio Carlos, 6627, Pampulha, Belo Horizonte, Minas Gerais, Brazil
taka@mat.ufmg.br

Abstract. This work presents an algorithm for tuning the parameters of stochastic search heuristics, the *Robust Parameter Searcher* (RPS). RPS is based on the Nelder-Mead Simplex algorithm and on confidence-based comparison operators. Whilst the latter algorithm is known for its robustness under noise in objective function evaluation, the confidence-based comparison endows the tuning algorithm with additional resilience against the intrinsic stochasticity which exists in the evaluation of performance of stochastic search heuristics. The proposed methodology was used to tune a Differential Evolution strategy for optimizing real-valued functions, with a limited function evaluation budget. In the computational experiments, RPS performed significantly better than other well-known tuning strategies from the literature.

Keywords: Algorithm parameter tuning · Nelder-mead simplex · Evolutionary algorithms · Noisy optimization

1 Introduction

The *parameter tuning* procedure of a search algorithm can be defined as the process of optimization of the parameter vector of that optimization algorithm using a meta-strategy [5]. The systematic parameter tuning is becoming increasingly important in the field of evolutionary computation due to the growing awareness that an evolutionary algorithm may have rather distinct performances for different parameter settings. Therefore, in any practical context, the correct parameter tuning may be essential for reaching a good algorithm performance. Also, a requirement for a fair comparison of a new algorithm with existing ones is that all algorithms under testing should have their parameters correctly tuned. A survey with tuning techniques and applications can be found in [6].

Nelder Mead simplex [15] is a numerical heuristic optimization method which can be applied to nonlinear problems for which derivatives may not be known.

The authors would like to thank the support by the Brazilian agencies CAPES, CNPq and FAPEMIG.

In an m-dimensional parameter space, at each iteration, it maintains a simplex of $m+1$ candidate solutions. This strategy has been successfully applied in noisy problems [11], and it is adapted here to a parameter tuning application.

The tuning procedure proposed in this work, the *Robust Parameter Searcher* (RPS), is based on the Nelder Mead simplex with a dynamic resampling procedure that supports confidence-based comparisons between pairs of solutions, which is based on the Student's t-test [13]. A simplified version of RPS, named as *bounded Nelder Mead* (bNM), which does not employ the confidence-based comparisons, is also examined here as a baseline to allow the study of the specific effect of the introduction of dynamic resampling for confidence-based comparison in RPS.

The proposed methods are compared here with four other: Differential Evolution (DE) [20], Parameter Iterated Local Search (ParamILS) [7], Relevance Estimation Value Callibration (Revac) [14], and Gender-Based Genetic Algorithm (GGA) [1]. They are also compared to a baseline Random Search strategy (RS). Preliminarily, the RPS algorithm parameters were configured via bNM using a set of real-valued functions added with Gaussian noise as objectives. The recommended parameter values for the others were adopted as they can be found in the respective papers.

Using the parameter sets obtained in the former step, the tuner algorithms (bNM, RPS, DE, ParamILS, GGA, Revac, RS) are compared in a set of computational experiments which configure the parameters of a Differential Evolution algorithm [16] for the optimization of functions from IEEE CEC 2014 Competition on Single Objective Real-Parameter Numerical Optimization, in the context of limited budgets of function evaluations. Those experiments reveal that the RPS consistently outperforms the other tuning strategies. This work performed the design and analysis of experiments [13] and applied the nonparametric Quade test [4] to guide the conclusions.

This paper is organized as follows. Section 2 presents a literature review about the parameter tuning strategies and illustrates some applications. Section 3 provides a formal definition of the tuning problem. Section 4 presents the proposed strategies bNM and RPS. Section 5 explains the algorithms employed in comparisons. Section 6 describes the numerical experiments conducted here. Finally, Sect. 7 concludes the paper and outlines possible future works.

2   Literature Review

The simplest parameter tuning procedure is the exhaustive search on a grid of possible values. A sampling method, like Latin-Square, can reduce the need of meta-evaluations in order to reach a result. Furthermore, the lack of a search mechanism refinement leads to a low quality parameter vector. Iterative sampling methods are designed as an improvement of the previous ideas. Model-based methods use a surrogate function to approximate the objective function of the tuning procedure using the available data to predict the parameter vector utility [5].

A combination of the last two techniques produced the sequential model based optimization methods, which allow more refined searches. One example is

Sequential Model-based Algorithm Configuration [8], which supports categorical parameters and multiple instances through a model based on random forest. The advantage of using this model is that it inherently handles the dependencies in the parameter space.

Racing methods, e.g. irace [10], try to find the best parameters from a set with a minimum number of tests. Promising vectors are preferred to be retested instead of the worse ones. Better and robust parameter solutions can be identified with less computational effort than in sampling methods.

Evolutionary Algorithms constitute a family of heuristics which evolve a set of solutions, performing stochastic operations in order to create another set, in the search for the best possible solution. Optimization problems with nonlinearity, interacting variables, multiple local optima, noise, and a lack of analytic properties, can be solved by EAs. Many EAs were developed for the parameter tuning problem [18].

An iterated local search procedure, called ParamILS, and its variation with screening, are found in [7]. This heuristic was applied as a tuner in works like [21] and was used as a baseline for comparison in [2]. Early implementations of Genetic Algorithms for parameter configuration were presented in [12]. A sophisticated Gender-Based Genetic Algorithm, or simply GGA, was developed in [1], whose solutions have age and are separated in two genders, competitive and noncompetitive, with different selection pressure. The paper [14] presented an estimation of distribution algorithm called Relevance Value Calibration, Revac, in which the population approximates the probability density function of the most promising areas of the utility landscape. Revac and its variations successfully tuned many algorithms in the literature [19].

ParamILS, GGA and Revac are the representative tuners to be compared with the proposed ones. Another heuristic to be compared with is a Differential Evolution implementation (DE) [20]. Although its wide range of applications [3], it is not common to use DE in parameter tuning problems.

3   Problem Definition

Let $\mathcal{A}$ denote an evolutionary optimization algorithm, and let $A(\omega)$ denote an instance of $\mathcal{A}$, such that $\omega = (\boldsymbol{\pi}, f, \kappa, \zeta)$ denotes a data structure in which: (i) $\boldsymbol{\pi} = (\pi_1, \pi_2, \ldots, \pi_m) \in \Pi$ is a set with m parameters of A, being $\Pi \subseteq \mathbb{R}^m$ the feasible set within the space of the parameters of A. By convention, all parameters are scaled in such a way that $\Pi = [0, 1]^m$. Any existing discrete parameters (categorical or integer) are assigned real values in the following way. Suppose that there are q possibilities in the search range of a discrete variable. The interval $[0, 1]$ is partitioned in q intervals, $\{[0, 1/q], (1/q, 2/q], \ldots, ((q - 1)/q, 1]\}$. In this way, any $v \in [0, 1]$ will fall in only one interval which represents a possible discrete value; (ii) $f : \mathbb{R}^n \to \mathbb{R}, f \in \mathcal{F}$, is an objective function which is to be minimized. Its optimal solution is $\mathbf{x}^*$ in the feasible set $\mathcal{X}$ within the n-dimensional decision variable search space; (iii) $\kappa \in \mathbb{N}^*$ is the allowed computational cost, measured here in number of evaluated objective functions, in one run of A; and (iv) $\zeta \in \mathbb{N}$ is a seed for the random number generator within the algorithm.

Given a $\omega \in \Omega \subseteq \Pi \times \mathcal{F} \times \mathbb{N}^* \times \mathbb{N}$, the behavior of A becomes determined, so that the algorithm delivers a specific *solution vector* $\tilde{\mathbf{x}} = A(\omega)$, with $\tilde{\mathbf{x}} \in \mathcal{X}$, which is an approximation of the problem optimal solution $\mathbf{x}^*$. Define also the *solution objective* $\tilde{\gamma} = f(\tilde{\mathbf{x}})$. The *tuning problem* is defined as the problem of finding the best parameter vector $\boldsymbol{\pi} \in \Pi$ for a given set of t training objective functions $f :$ $\mathbb{R}^n \rightarrow \mathbb{R} \in \mathcal{F} = \{f_1, f_2, \ldots, f_t\}$, a different seed ζ for each independent run of A and a fixed computational cost κ, in order to minimize a performance measure. Let the solution vector and the solution objective of a single run (each run is indexed by j) of algorithm $A(\omega)$ on the function f_i be denoted by Eq. 1.

$$\tilde{\mathbf{x}}_{i,j}(\boldsymbol{\pi}) = A(\boldsymbol{\pi}, f_i, \zeta_{i,j}, \kappa), \qquad \tilde{\gamma}_{i,j}(\boldsymbol{\pi}) = f_i(\tilde{\mathbf{x}}_{i,j}(\boldsymbol{\pi})) \tag{1}$$

The performance measure uses a statistic $\hat{\gamma}_i = \Gamma(\tilde{\gamma}_{i,1}, \tilde{\gamma}_{i,2}, \ldots, \tilde{\gamma}_{i,e_i})$ from a number e_i of solution objectives $\tilde{\gamma}_{i,j}$ extracted from the runs $A(\boldsymbol{\pi}, f_i, \zeta_{i,j}, \kappa)$, $j \in \{1, 2, \ldots, e_i\}$. Particularly, in this work $\hat{\gamma}_i$ is an averaged value defined in Eq. 2, which is used in the definition of the Mean Best Utility (MBU) function $U(\boldsymbol{\pi})$ (Eq. 3).

$$\hat{\gamma}_i(\boldsymbol{\pi}) = \frac{1}{e_i} \sum_{j=1}^{e_i} \tilde{\gamma}_{i,j}(\boldsymbol{\pi}), \tag{2}$$

$$U(\boldsymbol{\pi}) = \frac{1}{t} \sum_{i=1}^{t} \hat{\gamma}_i(\boldsymbol{\pi}) \tag{3}$$

Note that it is necessary that the functions f_i are scaled properly to obtain a meaningful definition of $U(\boldsymbol{\pi})$. The evaluation of a single value of $U(\boldsymbol{\pi})$ for a given parameter vector $\boldsymbol{\pi}$ requires the algorithm A being executed e_i times for each function f_i, with a different value of $\zeta_{i,j}$ for each algorithm run, and a fixed value of κ for all runs. Such an operation is called a *meta-evaluation*. The simplest case of Eq. 3 occurs when $e_i = 1$ and, therefore, $\hat{\gamma}_i = \tilde{\gamma}_{i,1}$ for all objectives. Equation 4 presents the definition of the *tuning problem*.

$$\min_{\boldsymbol{\pi}} U(\boldsymbol{\pi}) \quad \text{subject to: } \boldsymbol{\pi} \in \Pi = [0, 1]^m \tag{4}$$

A *parameter tuning algorithm* is an algorithm that generates an approximate solution $\tilde{\boldsymbol{\pi}}$ for Problem 4, being allowed to use a budget of μ meta-evaluations.

4   Proposed Algorithm

This section presents the proposed parameter tuning algorithm, the *Robust Parameter Searcher* (RPS), and another called *bounded Nelder Mead Simplex* (bNM) – which corresponds to a canonical implementation of the classical Nelder Mead Simplex algorithm for nonlinear programming [15], modified with a constraint-handling comparison operator. The RPS algorithm is defined as the bNM enhanced with the usage of solution resampling for confidence-based comparisons.

An algorithm which represents both bNM and RPS is presented in Algorithm 1. It operates on a set of $m + 1$ current tentative solutions which constitute a simplex $\mathcal{S} = \{\boldsymbol{\pi}_1, \boldsymbol{\pi}_2, \ldots, \boldsymbol{\pi}_{m+1}\}$ in the $\mathbb{R}^m$ space of the parameters of algorithm $\mathcal{A}$. In Algorithm 1, the vector $\mathbf{u}(\boldsymbol{\pi})$ stores all the meta-evaluations of the cost function $U(\boldsymbol{\pi})$ associated to the parameter vector $\boldsymbol{\pi}$. In the case of bNM algorithm, each parameter vector is meta-evaluated only once, so $\mathbf{u}(\boldsymbol{\pi})$ stores a scalar value. In the case of RPS algorithm, a feasible parameter vector may be meta-evaluated several times, and $\mathbf{u}(\boldsymbol{\pi})$ will store all the results of such meta-evaluations. Let $b(\boldsymbol{\pi})$ denote a feasibility indicator, such that $\boldsymbol{\pi} \in \Pi \Leftrightarrow b(\boldsymbol{\pi}) = 1$ and $\boldsymbol{\pi} \notin \Pi \Leftrightarrow b(\boldsymbol{\pi}) = 0$. For each $i \in \{1, 2, \ldots, m\}$, let $d_i(\boldsymbol{\pi})$ denote the squared deviations from feasibility (Eq. 5). The cost function is defined as in Eq. 6.

$$d_i(\boldsymbol{\pi}) = \begin{cases} \pi_i^2, & \text{if } \pi_i < 0 \\ 0, & \text{if } \pi_i \in [0, 1] \\ (\pi_i - 1)^2, & \text{if } \pi_i > 1 \end{cases} \tag{5}$$

$$u_j(\boldsymbol{\pi}) = b(\boldsymbol{\pi}) \cdot U^j(\boldsymbol{\pi}) + (1 - b(\boldsymbol{\pi})) \cdot \sum_{i=1}^m d_i(\boldsymbol{\pi}) \tag{6}$$

If $\boldsymbol{\pi}$ feasible, then $U^j(\boldsymbol{\pi})$ denotes the j-th meta-evaluation of the MBU function, defined in Eq. 3. Assuming that $U(\boldsymbol{\pi})$ has been meta-evaluated k times, the vector $\mathbf{u}(\boldsymbol{\pi})$ becomes defined in Eq. 7. In the case of an infeasible $\boldsymbol{\pi}$, only one evaluation of (6) is necessary and the expression of $\mathbf{u}(\boldsymbol{\pi})$ becomes reduced to Eq. 8.

$$\mathbf{u}(\boldsymbol{\pi}) = \{u_1(\boldsymbol{\pi}), \ldots, u_k(\boldsymbol{\pi})\} = \{U^1(\boldsymbol{\pi}), \ldots, U^k(\boldsymbol{\pi})\} \tag{7}$$

$$\mathbf{u}(\boldsymbol{\pi}) = \{u_1(\boldsymbol{\pi})\} = \left\{ \sum_{i=1}^m d_i(\boldsymbol{\pi}) \right\} \tag{8}$$

The Algorithm 1 is instantiated either as the bNM algorithm or as the RPS algorithm by choosing the comparison operators used within the algorithm, $\prec_{(*)}$ and $\equiv_{(*)}$, to be the bNM comparison operators ($\prec_{(bnm)}$ and $\equiv_{(bnm)}$) or the RPS comparison operators ($\prec_{(rps)}$ and $\equiv_{(rps)}$). The generic $\prec_{(*)}$ and the $\equiv_{(*)}$ comparison operators, valid both for bNM and for RPS, are defined as:

$$\boldsymbol{\pi}_1 \equiv_{(*)} \boldsymbol{\pi}_2 \Leftrightarrow b(\boldsymbol{\pi}_1) = b(\boldsymbol{\pi}_2) \wedge \mathbf{u}(\boldsymbol{\pi}_1) =_{(*)} \mathbf{u}(\boldsymbol{\pi}_2) \tag{9}$$

$$\boldsymbol{\pi}_1 \prec_{(*)} \boldsymbol{\pi}_2 \Leftrightarrow (b(\boldsymbol{\pi}_1) \wedge \neg b(\boldsymbol{\pi}_2)) \vee (b(\boldsymbol{\pi}_1) = b(\boldsymbol{\pi}_2) \wedge \mathbf{u}(\boldsymbol{\pi}_1) <_{(*)} \mathbf{u}(\boldsymbol{\pi}_2)) \tag{10}$$

In the case of the equality relation (9), $\boldsymbol{\pi}_1$ and $\boldsymbol{\pi}_2$ have the same feasibility condition and the same cost evaluation. The inequality relation (10) is true when $\boldsymbol{\pi}_1$ is feasible and $\boldsymbol{\pi}_2$ is not, or when both have the same feasibility condition and $\boldsymbol{\pi}_1$ has a smaller cost evaluation. As consequences of those definitions, Eq. 11 is defined.

$$\begin{aligned} \boldsymbol{\pi}_1 \not\equiv_{(*)} \boldsymbol{\pi}_2 &\Leftrightarrow \neg(\boldsymbol{\pi}_1 \equiv_{(*)} \boldsymbol{\pi}_2); \\ \boldsymbol{\pi}_1 \preceq_{(*)} \boldsymbol{\pi}_2 &\Leftrightarrow \boldsymbol{\pi}_1 \equiv_{(*)} \boldsymbol{\pi}_2 \vee \boldsymbol{\pi}_1 \prec_{(*)} \boldsymbol{\pi}_2; \\ \boldsymbol{\pi}_1 \succ_{(*)} \boldsymbol{\pi}_2 &\Leftrightarrow \neg(\boldsymbol{\pi}_1 \preceq_{(*)} \boldsymbol{\pi}_2) \\ \boldsymbol{\pi}_1 \succeq_{(*)} \boldsymbol{\pi}_2 &\Leftrightarrow \neg(\boldsymbol{\pi}_1 \prec_{(*)} \boldsymbol{\pi}_2) \end{aligned} \tag{11}$$

The operators $\equiv_{(*)}$, $\prec_{(*)}$ become $\equiv_{(bnm)}$, $\prec_{(bnm)}$ or $\equiv_{(rps)}$, $\prec_{(rps)}$ depending on the operators $=_{(*)}$, $<_{(*)}$ with the form $=_{(bnm)}$, $<_{(bnm)}$ or $=_{(rps)}$, $<_{(rps)}$. The only difference between algorithms bNM and RPS lies in the respective comparison operators $=_{(*)}$, $<_{(*)}$:

bNM Algorithm: The operators $=_{(bnm)}$, $<_{(bnm)}$ are defined as the usual comparison operators $=, <$ that are valid for real numbers.

RPS Algorithm: The operators $=_{(rps)}$, $<_{(rps)}$ are defined as confidence-based comparison operators (Eq. 19), which will rely on the result of the comparison function described in Algorithm 2 in Subsect. 4.1.

Note that the function **SortSimplex**, which is employed in Algorithm 1, uses comparison operators, which means that the corresponding operators, $(\prec_{(bnm)}$ and $\equiv_{(bnm)})$ or $(\prec_{(rps)}$ and $\equiv_{(rps)})$, also should be used inside that function in each case.

Parameters: $\mathcal{D}$
Output: π

1   $\mathcal{S} \leftarrow$ InitializeSimplex($\mathtt{f_p}$)
2   $\mathcal{S} \leftarrow$ SortSimplex($\mathcal{S}$)
3   **repeat**
4     $\mathbf{p}_r \leftarrow$ Reflect($\mathcal{S}, \pi_{m+1}$)
5   **case** $\mathbf{u}(\mathbf{p}_r) \prec_{(*)} \mathbf{u}(\pi_1)$ **do**
6       $\mathbf{p}_e \leftarrow$ Expand($\mathcal{S}, \mathbf{p}_r, \delta_e$)
7   **if** $\mathbf{u}(\mathbf{p}_e) \prec_{(*)} \mathbf{u}(\mathbf{p}_r)$ **then** $\pi_{m+1} \leftarrow \mathbf{p}_e$ **else** $\pi_{m+1} \leftarrow \mathbf{p}_r$
8   **case** $\mathbf{u}(\pi_1) \preceq_{(*)} \mathbf{u}(\mathbf{p}_r) \prec_{(*)} \mathbf{u}(\pi_m)$ **do** $\pi_{m+1} \leftarrow \mathbf{p}_r$;
9   **case** $\mathbf{u}(\pi_m) \preceq_{(*)} \mathbf{u}(\mathbf{p}_r) \prec_{(*)} \mathbf{u}(\pi_{m+1})$ **do**
10       $\mathbf{p}_o \leftarrow$ OutsideContraction($\mathcal{S}, \mathbf{p}_r, \delta_c$)
11   **if** $\mathbf{u}(\mathbf{p}_o) \preceq_{(*)} \mathbf{u}(\mathbf{p}_r)$ **then** $\pi_{m+1} \leftarrow \mathbf{p}_o$
12   **else**
13         $\mathbf{p}_i \leftarrow$ InsideContraction($\mathcal{S}, \mathbf{p}_r, \delta_c$)
14   **if** $\mathbf{u}(\mathbf{p}_i) \preceq_{(*)} \mathbf{u}(\mathbf{p}_r)$ **then** $\pi_{m+1} \leftarrow \mathbf{p}_i$
15   **else**
16           $\pi_{m+1} \leftarrow \mathbf{p}_r$
17           $\mathcal{S} \leftarrow$ ShrinkSimplex($\mathcal{S}, \delta_s$)
18   **end**
19   **end**
20   **case** $\mathbf{u}(\pi_{m+1}) \preceq_{(*)} \mathbf{u}(\mathbf{p}_r)$ **do** $\mathcal{S} \leftarrow$ ShrinkSimplex($\mathcal{S}, \delta_s$)
21     $\mathcal{S} \leftarrow$ SortSimplex($\mathcal{S}$)
22   **if** *meta-evaluation counter* $\leq \mu$ **then**
23   **if** SimplexStagnates($\mathcal{S}$) **then**
24         $\mathcal{S} \leftarrow$ RestartSimplex($\mathcal{S}, \mathtt{f_p}$)
25         $\mathcal{S} \leftarrow$ SortSimplex($\mathcal{S}$)
26   **end**
27   **end**
28 **until** *meta-evaluation counter* $> \mu$
29 $\pi \leftarrow \pi_1$
30 **return** π

Algorithm 1: Template for bNM and RPS procedures.

The bNM algorithm requires the data inputs $\mathcal{D} \leftarrow \{\mathtt{f_p}, \delta_e, \delta_c, \delta_s, \varepsilon, \mu\}$, while the RPS requires $\mathcal{D} \leftarrow \{\mathtt{f_p}, \delta_e, \delta_c, \delta_s, \varepsilon, \mu, \mathtt{e_{max}}, \alpha_c\}$. The meaning of those parameters is: (i) $\mathtt{f_p}$ is the size of the edge of the initial simplex, with $0 < \mathtt{f_p} < 1$; (ii)

δ_e is the expansion coefficient, with $\delta_e > 1$(iii) δ_c is the contraction coefficient, with $0 < \delta_c < 1$; (iv) δ_s is the shrink coefficient, with $0 < \delta_s < 1$; (v) ε is the minimum Euclidean distance between the current best and current worst vertices of the simplex, in order to reinitialize the simplex, with $\varepsilon > 0$; (vi) $\mathsf{e}_{\mathsf{max}}$ is the maximum number of times that a unique vector $\boldsymbol{\pi}$ can be evaluated; and (vii) α_c is the significance of the confidence-based comparisons.

Now, the procedures inside Algorithm 1 are explained. First, assuming that the $m + 1$ solutions within the simplex $\mathcal{S}$ are sorted in ascending order of the cost function $\mathbf{u}(\cdot)$, a parameter vector $\mathbf{p}_c$ of the centroid solution of the first m solutions (excluding the worst solution, which is the $(m + 1)$-th solution) is defined according to Eq. 12.

$$\mathbf{p}_c = \frac{1}{m} \sum_{j=1}^{m} \boldsymbol{\pi}_j \tag{12}$$

This centroid, which does not appear explicitly within Algorithm 1, is employed within other procedures. The operators employed within Algorithm 1 are described as follows.

InitializeSimplex($\mathbf{f_p}$): A regular initial simplex $\mathcal{S}$ with edge size equal to $\mathbf{f_p}$ and random location and orientation is created within the feasible set Π.

SortSimplex($\mathcal{S}$): The $m+1$ solutions within the simplex $\mathcal{S}$ are ascending sorted according to the evaluations of $\mathbf{u}(\cdot)$, with the total order defined by the operator $\preceq_{(*)}$:

$$\mathcal{S} \leftarrow \text{SortSimplex}(\mathcal{S}) \Rightarrow \mathbf{u}(\boldsymbol{\pi}_1) \preceq_{(*)} \mathbf{u}(\boldsymbol{\pi}_2) \preceq_{(*)} \cdots \preceq_{(*)} \mathbf{u}(\boldsymbol{\pi}_{m+1})$$

SimplexStagnates($\mathcal{S}$): It is tested if the distance between the best and the worst parameter vector is less than or equal to the threshold ε:

$$\text{SimplexStagnates}(\mathcal{S}) = \{\|\boldsymbol{\pi}_1 - \boldsymbol{\pi}_{m+1}\| \leq \varepsilon\}$$

If true, this test indicates that the simplex $\mathcal{S}$ has stagnated and it needs to be reinitialized. It is important to note that an adequate value for ε must be considered also to treat discrete parameters in order to avoid the same representation between two distinct configurations considering the m-dimensional real search space.

RestartSimplex($\mathcal{S}$) A regular simplex $\mathcal{S}$ with edge size equal to $(k + 1) \cdot \mathbf{f_p}$ and random orientation is created, with one of its vertices on the former best vertex $\boldsymbol{\pi}_1$. The multiplier k corresponds to the number of times the simplex has been restarted without any change on the position of $\boldsymbol{\pi}_1$ (which corresponds to the current $\mathbf{u}(\boldsymbol{\pi}_1)$ showing no enhancement after k simplex restart operations). This is done to escape from local optima when the current best solution stagnates.

Reflect($\mathcal{S}, \boldsymbol{\pi}_{m+1}$): A reflected solution $\mathbf{p}_r$ is created as a reflection of the worst solution $\boldsymbol{\pi}_{m+1}$ towards the opposite simplex face, according to Eq. 13:

$$\mathbf{p}_r = \mathbf{p}_c + (\mathbf{p}_c - \boldsymbol{\pi}_{m+1}) \tag{13}$$

Expand$(\mathcal{S}, \mathbf{p}_r, \delta_e)$: An expanded solution $\mathbf{p}_e$ is created beyond $\mathbf{p}_r$, being farther than it by a factor $\delta_e > 1$:

$$\mathbf{p}_e = \mathbf{p}_c + \delta_e \cdot (\mathbf{p}_r - \mathbf{p}_c) \tag{14}$$

OutsideContraction$(\mathcal{S}, \mathbf{p}_r, \delta_c)$: An outside contracted solution $\mathbf{p}_o$ is created outside the simplex $\mathcal{S}$, nearer to it than $\mathbf{p}_r$, being nearer by a factor $\delta_c < 1$:

$$\mathbf{p}_o = \mathbf{p}_c + \delta_c \cdot (\mathbf{p}_r - \mathbf{p}_c) \tag{15}$$

InsideContraction$(\mathcal{S}, \mathbf{p}_r, \delta_c)$: An inside contracted solution $\mathbf{p}_i$ is created inside the simplex $\mathcal{S}$, nearer to the centroid $\mathbf{p}_c$ than $\mathbf{p}_r$, being nearer by a factor $\delta_c < 1$:

$$\mathbf{p}_i = \mathbf{p}_c - \delta_c \cdot (\mathbf{p}_r - \mathbf{p}_c) \tag{16}$$

ShrinkSimplex$(\mathcal{S})$: The simplex $\mathcal{S}$ is shrunk by a factor δ_s. The resulting simplex will have the same best vertex $\boldsymbol{\pi}_1$, and the others will approach it by a factor of δ_s:

$$\boldsymbol{\pi}_j = \boldsymbol{\pi}_1 + \delta_s \cdot (\boldsymbol{\pi}_j - \boldsymbol{\pi}_1), \qquad j = 2, \ldots, m+1. \tag{17}$$

4.1   Confidence-Based Comparison

The behavior of the outcomes of a stochastic optimization algorithm with a single real parameter π is illustrated in Fig. 1. For the associated to the parameter values $\{\pi_1, \pi_2, \pi_3, \pi_4\}$, the points A, B, C and D represent the mathematical expectations of objective values $\mathbb{E}(\gamma(\pi_1))$, $\mathbb{E}(\gamma(\pi_2))$, $\mathbb{E}(\gamma(\pi_3))$ and $\mathbb{E}(\gamma(\pi_4))$ and the points E, F, G and H represent an instance of single-run objective values $\tilde{\gamma}(\pi_1)$, $\tilde{\gamma}(\pi_2)$, $\tilde{\gamma}(\pi_3)$ and $\tilde{\gamma}(\pi_4)$.

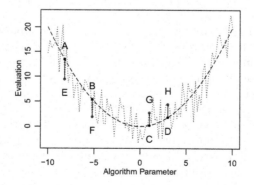

Fig. 1. The abscissa and ordinate represent, respectively, the value of an algorithm parameter π and the corresponding value of the solution objective of the algorithm for that parameter, $\gamma(\pi)$, considering a given objective function. The dashed line represents the curve of mathematical expectation of the solution objective, $\mathbb{E}(\gamma(\pi))$, for the different parameter values, and the dotted line represents the values of $\tilde{\gamma}(\pi)$, the objective values obtained in single-run executions of the algorithm.

It should be noticed that the correct ordering of the expected solution objective values is $\mathbb{E}(\gamma(\pi_1)) > \mathbb{E}(\gamma(\pi_2)) > \mathbb{E}(\gamma(\pi_4)) > \mathbb{E}(\gamma(\pi_3))$. However, the ordering of the estimates of the solution objective values obtained from single-run experiments is $\tilde{\gamma}(\pi_1) > \tilde{\gamma}(\pi_4) > \tilde{\gamma}(\pi_3) > \tilde{\gamma}(\pi_2)$. This inadequacy of single-run estimates for supporting comparisons between candidate parameter vectors motivate the usage of resampling techniques within parameter tuning algorithms. Of course, if a very large sample size were employed, the sample mean would converge to the mathematical expectation. However, in order to control the risk of obtaining a wrong result from a comparison without increasing unnecessarily the number of algorithm runs, a hypothesis test may be executed such that the size of samples is increased only up to the minimum necessary to achieve a predefined confidence level. In this work, the Student's t-test [13] is used for this purpose.

The *Robust Parameter Searcher* (RPS) has the same structure of bNM, as presented in Algorithm 1, with one difference: all comparisons between feasible parameter vectors are performed considering their statistical significance. The hypothesis testing is performed here using a parametric approach, the Student's t-test [13]. This test for two samples, z_1 and z_2, is based on the statistics in Eq. 18. This statistics is used for testing the null hypothesis, which states that the expectations of Z_1 and Z_2, respectively $\bar{Z}_1$ and $\bar{Z}_2$, are identical. The parameters n_1 and n_2 represent the number of observations of samples z_1 and z_2, $\bar{z}_1$ and $\bar{z}_2$ represent the sample mean values and s_1^2 and s_2^2 represent the sample variances. The hypothesis testing is performed under a significance level $\alpha \in [0; 1]$. The value of t_0 is compared with the t-distribution with $n_1 + n_2 + 1$ degrees of freedom. If $|t_0| > t_{\alpha/2, n_1+n_2+1}$, then the null hypothesis is rejected, and it is assumed that the distribution mean values are different.

$$t_0 = \frac{\bar{z}_1 - \bar{z}_2}{\sqrt{\dfrac{(n_1 - 1)s_1^2 + (n_2 - 1)s_2^2}{n_1 + n_2 - 2} \left(\dfrac{1}{n_1} + \dfrac{1}{n_2} \right)}} \tag{18}$$

It should be noticed that Student's t-test assumes that the distributions of Z_1 and Z_2 [13]: (i) are Gaussian; (ii) have identical variances; and (iii) are independent. Although the assumptions (i) and (ii) are not exactly fulfilled in the cases of interest here, there is some evidence that the Student's t-test is still applicable even under some violation of them [17], which provides support to the usage of this hypothesis test in the proposed RPS algorithm.

In RPS algorithm, when a comparison between two solutions is to be performed, if at least one of them is infeasible, the comparison is executed as in the algorithm bNM, and no resampling is needed. However, when two feasible solutions, π_1 and π_2, are to be compared, the solutions may be re-sampled in order to achieve a confidence level on the result of the comparison. In this case, the confidence-based comparison procedure described in Alg. 2 is adopted:

$$R \leftarrow \textbf{ConfidenceCompare}(\pi_a, \pi_b, v) : \begin{cases} 1 : \mathbf{u}(\pi_a) <_{(rps)} \mathbf{u}(\pi_b) \\ 0 : \mathbf{u}(\pi_a) =_{(rps)} \mathbf{u}(\pi_b) \\ -1 : \mathbf{u}(\pi_b) <_{(rps)} \mathbf{u}(\pi_a) \end{cases} \tag{19}$$

In Algorithm 2, the input variables π_a and π_b are feasible parameter vectors, and v represents the total number of solution meta-evaluations executed within the parameter tuning algorithm up to the moment of the function call. There are two global variables, $\mathbf{u}_a$ and $\mathbf{u}_b$, which are vectors that store all meta-evaluations of solutions π_a and π_b, respectively, since the beginning of algorithm RPS (not just in the scope of the current call to Algorithm 2). The parameters α_c, $\mathbf{e}_{max}$ and μ represent, respectively, the significance adopted in the t-test, the maximum number of meta-evaluations allowed to any unique solution π, and the maximum allowed total number of parameter vector meta-evaluations within one run of the RPS algorithm.

In any call of Algorithm 2, a parameter vector π can be meta-evaluated at most $\mathbf{e}$ times. This maximum number of meta-evaluations per unique tentative solution π grows linearly according to the current number of parameter vector meta-evaluations already performed within RPS algorithm, as presented in line 2. Initially, only one meta-evaluation per parameter vector is allowed, and in the end this number becomes $\mathbf{e_{max}}$. This linearly increasing dynamic resampling with confidence comparison can reduce the noise influence during the search. Notice that initially, when the simplex is large, it tends to be possible to recognize differences between the costs of different parameter vectors by samples with a single meta-evaluation per parameter vector, even in the presence of noise. As the simplex becomes smaller, those differences tend to become smaller too, and the noise is likely to become greater than those differences.

```
1  Function ConfidenceCompare(π_a, π_b, v)
      Parameters: α_c, e_max, μ
      Global: u_a, u_b
      Output: R, v
2      e ← ⌈1 + (e_max − 1)(v/μ)⌉
3      [n_a, ū_a, s_a] ← SampleParameters(u_a)
4      [n_b, ū_b, s_b] ← SampleParameters(u_b)
5      H ← tTest(u_a, u_b, α_c)
6      while H = 0 ∧ (n_a < e ∨ n_b < e) do
7          if (n_a < e ∧ s_a > s_b) ∨ (n_b = e) then
8              n_a ← n_a + 1
9              u_a^{n_a} ← MetaEvaluate(π_a)
10         else
11             n_b ← n_b + 1
12             u_b^{n_b} ← MetaEvaluate(π_b)
13         end
14         v ← v + 1
15         H ← tTest(u_a, u_b, α_c)
16     end
17     case ū_a < ū_b do  R ← 1
18     case ū_a = ū_b do  R ← 0
19     case ū_a > ū_b do  R ← −1
20     return R
21 end
```

Algorithm 2: Confidence-based comparison.

Those effects are illustrated in Fig. 1. The comparison $\mathbb{E}(\gamma(\pi_1)) > \mathbb{E}(\gamma(\pi_4))$ tends to be preserved in single-run observations like $\tilde{\gamma}(\pi_1) > \tilde{\gamma}(\pi_4)$ even in the case of unfavorable random deviations from the expectations, as shown in Fig. 1. This is due to the large difference between $\mathbb{E}(\gamma(\pi_1))$ and $\mathbb{E}(\gamma(\pi_4))$, which tends to occur when the points π_1 and π_4 are distant each other. On the other hand, the comparison $\mathbb{E}(\gamma(\pi_2)) > \mathbb{E}(\gamma(\pi_3))$ is more susceptible to be corrupted by noise, as illustrated with $\tilde{\gamma}(\pi_2) < \tilde{\gamma}(\pi_3)$, even for moderate noise sizes, because the difference between $\mathbb{E}(\gamma(\pi_2))$ and $\mathbb{E}(\gamma(\pi_3))$ is small. This tends to occur when π_2 and π_3 are points near each other. This motivates the usage of an increasing number of meta-evaluations in the samples as the search converges to smaller regions.

According to [5], RPS can be classified in taxonomy T_1 as an iterative and multi-stage method, and in relation to taxonomy T_2 the proposed method always performs a fixed number of utility function evaluations in a single execution, applies sharpening in order to statistically differentiate two solutions, and the number of fitness evaluations is fixed for the target algorithm during the tuning phase.

4.2   Parameter Values

The parameter values adopted for bNM are similar to those generally found in literature such that $f_p = 0.10$, $\delta_e = 2.00$, $\delta_c = 0.50$, $\delta_s = 0.50$ and $\varepsilon = 0.10$ [11].

For RPS, once it is not known the interaction with confidence-based comparison operator, a simple tuning procedure was applied using bNM with above parameter values and a pseudo-MBU that uses the objectives Elliptic, Rosenbrock and Rastrigin [9] summed with a Gaussian noise, with zero mean and standard deviation 2, as a composition function. The RPS parameter values were chosen after 10 bNM executions, spending 5000 pseudo-MBU computations in each run. The 10 parameter set candidates returned by bNM were simulated 30 times using the same pseudo-MBU and the one with the smallest sample median, with values $f_p = 0.17$, $\delta_e = 1.40$, $\delta_c = 0.84$, $\delta_s = 0.46$, $\varepsilon = 0.33$, $e_{max} = 4$ and $\alpha_c = 0.78$, was chosen.

5   Selected Algorithms

The Robust Parameter Searcher (RPS) and the bounded Nelder Mead (bNM) are compared to three tuners selected from the literature: ParamILS, GGA, and Revac. They are also compared to a DE implementation and a baseline Random Search strategy, RS. The values of their parameters are set as recommended in the original papers.

The baseline parameterless Random Search, RS, initially creates a random meta-parameter vector. After, these parameters are applied in the algorithm once for each objective and MBU value is returned. Following, this first meta-solution is stored as the best solution. The loop in sequence creates and meta-evaluates new random vectors, and stores the new best ones on each time an enhancement is found. These actions are repeated until the maximum number of meta-evaluations is reached. Finally, the best meta-parameter vector and its meta-evaluation are returned.

The ParamILS has three parameters: $p_i = 0.1$ is the rate of meta-evaluations, in relation to the maximum μ, dedicated to the initial random search; $n_p = 20$ is the total number of perturbations, considering all variables, in the current meta-solution; and $p_r = 0.01$ is the probability of the current meta-solution reinitialization. The real parameters to be tuned are discretized in steps of 0.1 and for the discrete ones a respective set of possible values are provided. More details about this heuristic can be found in [7].

The scheme of GGA has six parameters: $p_i = 30$ is the initial population size; $e_r = 0.1$ is the rate of best parameters in competitive gender selected to mate with solutions in passive (noncompetitive) population; $p_p = 0.9$ is a probability value used inside the crossover operator to assign values from the competitive or passive parent after a labeling process for each variable; $p_m = 0.1$ is the probability of mutation; $v_m = 0.05$ is the variance of the Gaussian distribution used in mutation of real and integer parameters; and $m_a = 3$ is the maximum number of generations (age) a solution can live. The description of GGA is presented in [1].

Revac has four parameters: $p_s = 100$ is the population size; $p_r = 0.01$ is the percent of old metasolutions, in relation to p_s, to be replaced with new ones; $b_c = 0.5$ is the rate of best metasolutions in population, in relation to p_s, to be used in crossover procedure; $m_h = 0.05$ is the mutation distance factor to be used at selecting metasolutions in population in the mutation process. The features of Revac are described in [14].

The DE version [3] used here for parameter tuning has four parameters: $n_p = 50$ is the population size; $f = 0.8$ is the mutation factor; $c_r = 0.9$ is the crossover rate; and $m_s = de/rand/1/bin$ is the mutation strategy. The first step in DE is the creation and meta-evaluation of the parent population with n_p solutions. Inside the evolution loop, a new child population with n_p solutions is created with the mutation strategy designated by m_s using the scaling factor f and the crossover rate c_r. Discrete parameters (integers) are rounded to the closest feasible values. Each child population is meta-evaluated and compared with the respective parent in order to select the best individuals for the next iteration. The best current parameter set is stored and returned in the end.

6   Numerical Experiments

In this section RPS and bNM are compared to three tuners selected from the literature: ParamILS, GGA, and Revac. They are also compared to a baseline Random Search strategy, RS, and a DE implementation. The battery of experiments considers the case of tuning a Differential Evolution strategy to solve real-valued functions. It treats the case in which just one fixed set of parameters must be found in order to be used in the stochastic search heuristics for a relatively large set of different problems. This setting may be interpreted as a tuning intended to be employed by the user as a first attempt when approaching a problem, in situations in which there is little prior information.

Three levels of meta-evaluation budgets were considered for the tuning algorithms in order to observe the quality evolution of the tuned heuristics. Each tuning algorithm was executed 30 times for each one of those budgets. The tuning phase used three different problem instances in order to obtain the target heuristic parameters. The tuner quality was extracted, in all cases, considering samples of the best objective value returned in 10 executions of the tuned target heuristic for each one of the 9 considered test problem instances. Note that in configuration and test phases, different seeds are provided for the algorithms to be tuned.

Within an experiment in a battery represented by a level of meta-evaluation budgets, each one of the 7 parameter tuning algorithms is represented by 270 samples each one (30 parameter tuning algorithm executions × 9 test functions × 10 tuned target heuristic executions per function), according to the previous paragraph. The variables of interest in the experiments are the seven medians $\hat{f}_j$ of the objective function distribution, returned by the tuned target heuristic induced by the parameter vectors which are generated by the parameter tuning algorithm $j \in \{$RS, ParamILS, GGA, Revac, DE, bNM, RPS$\}$. A hypothesis test is performed, with null hypothesis h_0 stating the equality for all pairs $\hat{u}_i = \hat{u}_j$, for different algorithms i and j, against the alternative hypothesis h_1, which states that there exists at least one pair $\{i, j\}$ such that $\hat{u}_i \neq \hat{u}_j$. The confidence level of the test is $\alpha = 0.05$. The nonparametric Quade test with Holm posthoc pairwise comparison is used to decide which parameter tuning algorithm presents the best performance [4].

The battery of experiments aimed the parameter configuration of a Differential Evolution, $\mathcal{A}_{DE}$, in order to solve the benchmark with 9 nonlinear and non-separable objective functions $\mathcal{F} = \{$*Rotated High Conditioned Elliptic, Rotated Bent Cigar, Rotated Discus, Shifted and Rotated Rosenbrock, Shifted and Rotated Ackley, Shifted and Rotated Weierstrass, Shifted and Rotated Griewank, Shifted and Rotated Rastrigin, Shifted and Rotated Schwefel*$\}$, extracted from the *CEC 2014 Competition on Single-Objective Real-Parameter Numerical Optimization* [9]. Those functions are considered in their 10-dimension version with search range $[-100, 100]$ for each decision variable. During the test phase, it is allowed the limit of 1000 objective function evaluations in a single $\mathcal{A}_{DE}$ run.

The tuning phase considered the computational budget μ of 30000, 40000 and 50000 meta-evaluations for each tuner execution. This was planed to observe the tuned algorithm output quality when a greater number of meta-evaluations are carried out. Each individual meta-evaluation applied the limit of $\kappa_{AG} = 500$ objective function evaluations in $\mathcal{A}_{DE}$ considering $\mathcal{F}_T = \{$*Rotated High Conditioned Elliptic, Shifted and Rotated Rosenbrock, Shifted and Rotated Rastrigin*$\} \subset \mathcal{F}$ in order to compute a value of quality criterion MBU.

The $\mathcal{A}_{DE}$ has a structure similar to the DE presented in Sect. 5 with the difference that it is considered the optimization of a real-valued function f inside a search space $\mathcal{X}$ which can be evaluated at most κ times. The six parameters and their possible values are: $\mathbf{n_p} \in \{4, 5, \ldots, 100\}$ the population size; $f \in [0,2]$ the mutation factor; $c_r \in [0.1, 0.9]$ the crossover rate; and $m_s \in \{de/rand/1/bin, de/best/1/bin, de/mean/1/bin, de/rand/1/exp, de/best/1/exp, de/mean/1/exp\}$ the mutation strategy.

For all experiments, the evolution of the sample median of the best objective function values returned by $\mathcal{A}_{DE}$ in relation to all instances in $\mathcal{F}$ is presented by Fig. 2[1]. This figure reveals RPS as the best method with improvement that increases for greater values of allowed meta-evaluations, leaving bNM in second place from 40000 meta-evaluations. It is interesting to note that bNM and DE worsened their performances as the number of allowed meta-evaluations increased. This was possibly due to the effect of the noise inherent in the tuning problem. The other methods remained stable resulting in a final order, from best to worst: RPS, bNM, GGA, ParamILS, Revac, DE and RS. This order only changed, in relation to the first battery of experiments, because the DE worsened the presented quality, being sensible to the alternation of problem.

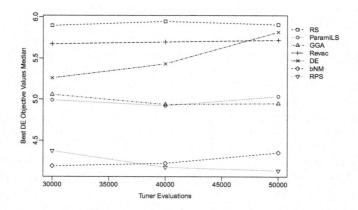

Fig. 2. Evolution of the median of the best objective function values (logarithm) returned by $\mathcal{A}_{DE}$ in all real-valued instances in $\mathcal{F}$ for all computational experiments.

The aforementioned results are statistically corroborated by Quade test in Table 1. Because the distribution of the returned function values were similar, only for the pairs of tuning algorithms GGA–ParamILS and RPS–bNM the test did not recognize a difference in their medians. The rest of paired comparisons detected a significant difference in their median values indicating that the algorithms have distinct efficacy in the scenario considered in the experiment.

---

[1] For an experiment, each sample consists of the best evaluations of objective functions returned in all runs of the tuned DE.

Table 1. General and pairwise p-values returned by Quade test in the real-valued objective functions instances with different meta-evaluations.

(a) $3 \cdot 10^4$ metaevaluations – General p-value: $<10^{-16}$.

	RS	ParamILS	GGA	Revac	DE	bNM
ILS	$<10^{-16}$	–	–	–	–	–
GGA	$<10^{-16}$	0.34	–	–	–	–
RVC	$<10^{-16}$	$<10^{-16}$	$<10^{-16}$	–	–	–
DE	$<10^{-16}$	$6.7e-11$	$1.1e-13$	$<10^{-16}$	–	–
bNM	$<10^{-16}$	$<10^{-16}$	$<10^{-16}$	$<10^{-16}$	$<10^{-16}$	–
RPS	$<10^{-16}$	$<10^{-16}$	$<10^{-16}$	$<10^{-16}$	$<10^{-16}$	$<10^{-16}$

(b) $4 \cdot 10^4$ metaevaluations – General p-value: $<10^{-16}$.

	RS	ParamILS	GGA	Revac	DE	bNM
ILS	$<10^{-16}$	–	–	–	–	–
GGA	$<10^{-16}$	0.0011	–	–	–	–
RVC	$<10^{-16}$	$<10^{-16}$	$<10^{-16}$	–	–	–
DE	$<10^{-16}$	$3.2e-08$	$<10^{-16}$	$<10^{-16}$	–	–
bNM	$<10^{-16}$	$<10^{-16}$	$<10^{-16}$	$<10^{-16}$	$<10^{-16}$	–
RPS	$<10^{-16}$	$<10^{-16}$	$<10^{-16}$	$<10^{-16}$	$<10^{-16}$	0.9133

(c) $5 \cdot 10^4$ metaevaluations – General p-value: $<10^{-16}$.

	RS	ParamILS	GGA	Revac	DE	bNM
ILS	$<10^{-16}$	–	–	–	–	-
GGA	$<10^{-16}$	0.071	–	–	–	–
RVC	$<10^{-16}$	$<10^{-16}$	$<10^{-16}$	–	–	–
DE	$9.3e-10$	$<10^{-16}$	$<10^{-16}$	$<10^{-16}$	–	–
bNM	$<10^{-16}$	$<10^{-16}$	$<10^{-16}$	$<10^{-16}$	$<10^{-16}$	–
RPS	$<10^{-16}$	$<10^{-16}$	$<10^{-16}$	$<10^{-16}$	$<10^{-16}$	$4.7e-10$

The logarithm of the sample median of the best objective value returned by $\mathcal{A}_{DE}$ in each test function, with different variable dimensions, and each budget of meta-evaluations is presented in Table 2. It is shown that RPS and bNM obtained both 11 best results, while ParamILS obtained 3 and Revac obtained 2. The proposed methods led again to the best individual test results.

Table 2. Logarithm of the median of the best objective function values returned by $\mathcal{A}_{GA}$ for each real-valued instance and budget of meta-evaluations.

f	$\mu\ (\times 10^3)$	RS	ParamILS	GGA	Revac	DE	bNM	RPS
Elliptic	30	17.0842	16.6578	16.4287	17.5170	16.8283	**14.9233**	15.9285
	40	16.9554	16.8103	16.4372	17.4801	16.7729	14.9196	**14.7744**
	50	17.1322	16.7952	16.3625	17.5629	17.0256	15.4814	**14.2851**
Bent Cigar	30	21.6004	20.7590	20.5454	21.9075	21.0061	**18.1005**	19.4969
	40	21.5901	20.7549	20.5192	21.8960	21.1487	18.1562	**16.8868**
	50	21.6915	20.6597	20.3865	21.9330	21.7231	18.4351	**17.1026**
Discus	30	9.7599	10.1441	10.0909	10.7086	9.8119	9.3951	**8.9284**
	40	9.8247	10.2363	10.0011	10.5947	9.7581	**9.2872**	9.3067
	50	9.6955	10.1521	9.9595	10.7036	9.9517	9.7293	**9.2386**
Rosenbrock	30	5.8958	4.9839	4.9897	5.6742	5.1851	**4.1572**	4.3138
	40	5.9467	4.9089	4.9007	5.6974	5.3865	4.2164	**3.9692**
	50	5.9079	5.0253	4.9032	5.7203	5.7914	4.3514	**3.9546**
Ackley	30	3.0804	3.0776	3.0768	**3.0706**	3.0711	3.0742	3.0796
	40	3.0803	3.0780	3.0766	**3.0700**	3.0709	3.0740	3.0779
	50	3.0801	3.0775	3.0767	3.0700	3.0710	**3.0694**	3.0774
Weierstrass	30	1.8867	2.0382	2.0399	2.4196	1.9888	**1.6574**	1.7475
	40	1.9141	2.0504	2.0270	2.4132	1.9693	**1.6707**	1.7763
	50	1.8805	2.0416	2.0317	2.4210	1.9627	1.9014	**1.8036**
Griewank	30	4.2017	3.4288	3.1026	3.7692	3.6445	**1.8414**	2.6578
	40	4.1272	3.3128	3.1242	3.6876	3.7746	1.7512	**1.3465**
	50	4.2619	3.3418	3.0894	3.7161	4.0847	2.0565	**1.3743**
Rastrigin	30	3.9678	3.7280	3.7010	4.3477	3.9589	**3.4627**	3.9938
	40	3.9526	3.6701	3.7229	4.3485	3.9519	**3.4834**	3.6378
	50	3.9828	3.7139	3.7429	4.3567	3.8417	**3.4880**	3.5806
Schwefel	30	7.5448	**7.1064**	7.1448	7.4638	7.3728	7.2526	7.5664
	40	7.5561	**7.0560**	7.1131	7.4613	7.3460	7.2577	7.2669
	50	7.5579	**7.0582**	7.1634	7.4689	7.3193	7.1662	7.2600

7   Conclusions and Future Works

This work presented the *Robust Parameter Searcher* (RPS), a tuning method for stochastic optimization algorithms. The RPS is based on the classical Nelder Mead Simplex algorithm for nonlinear programming, which was modified here to include a dynamical resampling procedure which supports confidence-based comparison operators.

Numerical experiments were conducted in order to compare the proposed technique with the parameter tuning methods from literature ParamILS, GGA and Revac, and also with a DE implementation, with a simplified version of RPS which does not employ dynamical resampling (the bNM), and with a baseline Random Search (RS) procedure.

The results showed that RPS algorithm presented significantly better performance than all other algorithms. The good RPS outputs may be attributed to the known ability of the Nelder Mead Simplex to perform searches even in the presence of noise, which is the case of the parameter tuning problem. The comparison between the performances of RPS and bNM suggests that the dynamic resampling procedure proposed here (which is the only difference between RPS and bNM) may be an important component of parameter tuning algorithms – provided that there is a suitable availability of meta-evaluation budget which allows using properly the additional information acquired, as indicated earlier.

For future works, some actions will be investigated: (i) the inclusion of irace [10] in order to represent a screening method to be compared with RPS; (ii) the execution of experiments with low budget of meta-evaluations; (iii) the adoption of a local search based on surrogate models in order to take advantage of the previous utility function evaluations; and (iv) the application of RPS in other classes of problems.

References

1. Ansótegui, C., Sellmann, M., Tierney, K.: A gender-based genetic algorithm for the automatic configuration of algorithms. In: Gent, I.P. (ed.) CP 2009. LNCS, vol. 5732, pp. 142–157. Springer, Heidelberg (2009). https://doi.org/10.1007/978-3-642-04244-7_14
2. Cáceres, L.P., López-Ibáñez, M., Hoos, H., Stützle, T.: An experimental study of adaptive capping in irace. In: Battiti, R., Kvasov, D.E., Sergeyev, Y.D. (eds.) LION 2017. LNCS, vol. 10556, pp. 235–250. Springer, Cham (2017). https://doi.org/10.1007/978-3-319-69404-7_17
3. Das, S., Suganthan, P.N.: Differential evolution: a survey of the state-of-the-art. evolutionary computation. IEEE Trans. **15**(1), 4–31 (2011)
4. Derrac, J., García, S., Molina, D., Herrera, F.: A practical tutorial on the use of nonparametric statistical tests as a methodology for comparing evolutionary and swarm intelligence algorithms. Swarm Evol. Comput. **1**(1), 3–18 (2011)
5. Eiben, A.E., Smit, S.K.: Parameter tuning for configuring and analyzing evolutionary algorithms. Swarm Evol. Comput. **1**(1), 19–31 (2011)
6. Huang, C., Li, Y., Yao, X.: A survey of automatic parameter tuning methods for metaheuristics. IEEE Trans. Evol. Comput. **24**(2), 201–216 (2019)
7. Hutter, F., Hoos, H.H., Leyton-Brown, K.: Automated configuration of mixed integer programming solvers. In: Lodi, A., Milano, M., Toth, P. (eds.) CPAIOR 2010. LNCS, vol. 6140, pp. 186–202. Springer, Heidelberg (2010). https://doi.org/10.1007/978-3-642-13520-0_23
8. Hutter, F., Hoos, H.H., Leyton-Brown, K.: Sequential model-based optimization for general algorithm configuration. In: Coello, C.A.C. (ed.) LION 2011. LNCS, vol. 6683, pp. 507–523. Springer, Heidelberg (2011). https://doi.org/10.1007/978-3-642-25566-3_40
9. Liang, J., Qu, B., Suganthan, P.: Problem definitions and evaluation criteria for the CEC 2014 special session and competition on single objective real-parameter numerical optimization. Zhengzhou University, Computational Intelligence Laboratory, Tech. rep. (2013)

10. López-Ibáñez, M., Dubois-Lacoste, J., Cáceres, L.P., Birattari, M., Stützle, T.: The irace package: iterated racing for automatic algorithm configuration. Oper. Res. Perspect. **3**, 43–58 (2016)

11. Mahmoud, K.: Central force optimization: Nelder-Mead hybrid algorithm for rectangular microstrip antenna design. Electromagnetics **31**(8), 578–592 (2011)

12. Mercer, R.E., Sampson, J.: Adaptive search using a reproductive meta-plan. Kybernetes **7**(3), 215–228 (1978)

13. Montgomery, D.C.: Design and Analysis of Experiments. John Wiley & Sons (2008)

14. Nannen, V., Eiben, A.E.: Relevance estimation and value calibration of evolutionary algorithm parameters. In: IJCAI, vol. 7, pp. 6–12 (2007)

15. Nelder, J.A., Mead, R.: A simplex method for function minimization. Comput. J. **7**(4), 308–313 (1965)

16. Price, K., Storn, R.M., Lampinen, J.A.: Differential Evolution: a Practical Approach to Global Optimization. Springer Science & Business Media (2006)

17. Siegmund, F., Ng, A.H., Deb, K.: A comparative study of dynamic resampling strategies for guided evolutionary multi-objective optimization. In: 2013 IEEE Congress on Evolutionary Computation (CEC), pp. 1826–1835. IEEE (2013)

18. Smit, S.K., Eiben, A.E.: Comparing parameter tuning methods for evolutionary algorithms. In: IEEE Congress on Evolutionary Computation, 2009. CEC 2009, pp. 399–406. IEEE (2009)

19. Smit, S.K., Eiben, A.E.: Beating the world champion evolutionary algorithm via REVAC tuning. In: 2010 IEEE Congress on Evolutionary Computation (CEC), pp. 1–8. IEEE (2010)

20. Storn, R., Price, K.: Differential evolution-a simple and efficient adaptive scheme for global optimization over continuous spaces, vol. 3. ICSI Berkeley (1995)

21. Tanabe, R., Fukunaga, A.: Tuning differential evolution for cheap, medium, and expensive computational budgets. In: 2015 IEEE Congress on Evolutionary Computation (CEC), pp. 2018–2025. IEEE (2015)

Classification of Leftovers from the Stock Cutting Process

Glaucia Maria Bressan[1](✉)[iD], Esdras Battosti da Silva[2][iD],
Matheus Henrique Pimenta-Zanon[3][iD],
and Elisângela Aparecida da Silva Lizzi[1][iD]

[1] Mathematics Department, Universidade Tecnológica Federal do Paraná (UTFPR),
Alberto Carazzai, 1640, Cornélio Procópio, PR 86300-000, Brazil
{glauciabressan,elisangelalizzi}@utfpr.edu.br
[2] Electrical Engineering Department, Universidade Tecnológica Federal do Paraná
(UTFPR), Alberto Carazzai, 1640, Cornélio Procópio, PR 86300-000, Brazil
esdras.2019@alunos.utfpr.edu.br
[3] Computer Science Department, Universidade Tecnológica Federal do Paraná
(UTFPR), Alberto Carazzai, 1640, Cornélio Procópio, PR 86300-000, Brazil

Abstract. The one-dimensional cutting stock problem considers only
one dimension in the cutting process and consists of cutting a set of
objects available in stock to produce the desired items in specified quantities and sizes. Therefore, the cutting process can generate leftovers -
which can be reused in a new demand - or losses, which are discarded. In
this context, the objective of this work is to present a methodology for
generating a numerical data set, considering items demand data and cut
objects, for the problem of classifying leftovers or losses from the cutting
stock process. The paper presents an algorithm to generate such a set and
its evaluation using Machine Learning methods, as Logistic Regression,
Naive Bayes, Decision Trees and Random Forests. These methods are
trained and validated using statistical measures. The provided dataset is
available to be used in supervised training algorithms for classification
tasks. Results show the performance of the Machine Learning methods,
which are evaluated using stratified k-fold cross validation and specific
statistical measures. Since the analysis indicate good performance, we
can also conclude that the generated data set is robust and it can be
used in other classification tasks.

Keywords: Cutting stock problem · Machine learning · Statistical
measures · Classification task

1 Introduction

The cutting stock problem consists of cutting a set of objects available in stock to
produce the desired items in specified quantities and sizes, in order to optimize

Supported by organization Fundação Araucária.

(maximize or minimize) a given objective function [4], as production costs or losses from the cutting process. This problem belongs to an important area of Operational Research to assist in decision making process. For this reason, the study of cutting stock problems has aroused the interest of researchers [1,3,4].

Historically, Gilmore and Gomory [18] were one of the first to address the cutting stock problem, in the 1960s. The authors define the problem as the task of cutting larger objects, available in stock, in order to produce smaller objects (items) to meet a given demand, minimize material loss, or the cost of cut objects. Later, these authors extended and adapted the methods for cutting stock outlined to the specific full-scale paper trim problem [19]. In [20], higher dimensional cutting stock problems are discussed as linear programming problems. Until today, many heuristics have been developed seeking to optimize the cutting stock problem and considering its mathematical and computational aspects [9–11].

The called one-dimensional cutting stock problem, in turns, involves only one dimension in the cutting process, as cutting steel bars, paper rolls and tubes [1,11,12]. Therefore, the cutting process can generate leftovers - which can be reused in a new demand - or losses, which are discarded. In this context, the objective of this work is to develop a numerical data set, considering items demand data and cut objects for loss or leftover classification, from what is left of the cutting process. In order to perform this task, machine learning methods, as logistic regression, Naive-Bayes, decision trees and random forests are trained using pattern recognition algorithms and validated using statistical measures.

In a general definition, [25] describes the Machine Learning methods as the field of study interested in the development of computational algorithms to transform data into intelligent actions. A input data is analyzed and, using pattern recognition algorithms, a model for future actions and classification of new and unknown data is obtained [2,25].

Machine Learning methods consists of 2 phases: the first is the training phase, in which a given model, previously chosen, is adjusted to the input data; the second is the testing phase, in which the performance of the algorithm in classifying a new set of unknown data is analyzed. It is possible to obtain the accuracy of the model and other characteristics of its performance by calculating statistical measures [2,25].

It is important to highlight that, in the literature, some numerical data generators can be found [15,17], which are used to generate instances that are applied to test algorithms and heuristics developed for the cutting stock problem optimization. On the other hand, numerical data sets, containing a large number of instances which are possible to be used in training algorithms and addressing optimization problem variables such as demands, objects and items to be cut, is not easily found in the literature. These data sets are fundamental to be used in supervised training algorithms, that is, with input variables and with the output known, for the classification of the output as loss (discarded) or leftover (which can be reused in a new demand).

In this way, the contribution of this work is to present a methodology for generating a numerical data set for the problem of classifying leftovers from the cutting stock process. The paper presents an algorithm to generate such a set and its evaluation using machine learning algorithms.

2   Methodology

In this section, the methodology used to generate the data set referring to the inputs (object, items, and item demands) and outputs(leftovers or losses) of the optimization problem addressed, is presented, as well as the algorithms of the Machine Learning methods used to the output classification.

The original mathematical formulation of the classical cutting stock problem can be seen in [19]. In this paper, we consider an one-dimensional cutting stock problem, defined in [11], in which the non-used material in the cutting patterns may be used in the future. Then, a heuristic procedure from literature was considered to determine the output, as described below.

2.1   Dataset Generation

Initially, the problem parameters were searched in [27], in order to establish criteria for choosing the categories of variables and for generating data, such as size of items (l_{min}, l_{max}), size of objects (L_{min}, L_{max}) and demand for items (d_{min}, d_{max}). In this way, with the determination of these parameters based on the literature, it is possible to generate a data set close to reality. All the inputs variables are considered as integer. By the definition of the cutting problem, larger objects are cut into smaller items for making products. The partition is defined as a subinterval of the interval (l_{min}, l_{max}), or (L_{min}, L_{max}) or (d_{min}, d_{max}), so that it contains l_{types}, L_{types} or d_{types} subintervals, respectively. The subintervals are equiprobable; then, the means are calculated using the midpoint of the intervals and the standard deviations are calculated considering the Gaussian distribution and the equal distance of the points.

With the parameters established, stochastic pattern data can be generated from probability distributions independent Gaussians, according to the definition of strictly stationary imported from time series studies [21]. The algorithm developed in this work for the dataset generation is described in Algorithms 1 and 2.

A heuristic procedure, known as FFD (*First Fit Decreasing*, which can be seen in [10]), is a greedy heuristic and was considered in this work. This heuristic uses the input variables and determines whether the output corresponding to that set of items is loss or leftover, in the face of a given object. Because of its "greedy" characteristic, this heuristic generates more leftovers than losses, which is interesting, since leftovers can be used in future demands, while losses are discarded. For this reason, FFD greedy method has been chosen. By the other hand, an unbalanced data set is generated, presenting more leftovers than losses as output, which requires specific methods to evaluate its performance, as the stratified k-fold cross validation, in which each k set maintains the same proportion as the original set. The dataset generated in this work presents 350 lines and 19 columns. However, the number of lines of the dataset corresponds to the number of items, which is represented by the parameter n. Then, the user can define it.

Using the Python programming language in a Google Colab environment, using libraries external sources, it was possible to generate a satisfactorily large dataset, so that it could be possible to apply the Machine Learning methods described below. Python language is also used for all the Machine Learning algorithms implementation.

Algorithm 1. Dataset generation

---

1 **Function** Main(l_{min}, l_{max}, l_{types}, L_{min}, L_{max}, L_{types} d_{min}, d_{max}, d_{types}, n_{items}, n_{obj}):

2   Partition $l = [l_{min}, l_{max}]$ into l_{types} parts $\rightarrow [l_1, \ldots, l_{n-1}, l_n]$

3   Partition $L = [L_{min}, L_{max}]$ into L_{types} parts $\rightarrow [L_1, \ldots, L_{n-1}, L_n]$

4   Partition $d = [d_{min}, d_{max}]$ into d_{types} parts $\rightarrow [d_1, \ldots, d_{n-1}, d_n]$

5

6   **For** *each partition of l*

7   Calculate means $Ml_n = \dfrac{l_n + l_{n+1}}{2}$

8   **end**

9   Calculate standard deviation $Sl = \dfrac{l_2 - l_1}{4}$

10   **For** *each partition of L*

11   Calculate means $ML_n = \dfrac{L_n + L_{n+1}}{2}$

12   **end**

13   Calculate standard deviation $SL = \dfrac{L_2 - L_1}{4}$

14   **For** *each partition of d*

15   Calculate means $Md_n = \dfrac{d_n + d_{n+1}}{2}$

16   **end**

17   Calculate standard deviation $Sd = \dfrac{d_2 - d_1}{4}$

18

19     $objs = $ CreateElements(ML_n,SL, L_{min}, L_{max}, L_{types})

20     $items = $ CreateElements(Ml_n,Sl, l_{min}, l_{max}, l_{types})

21     $demands = $ CreateElements(Md_n,Sl, d_{min}, d_{max}, d_{types})

22

23   shuffle *objs*

24   shuffle *items*

25   shuffle *demands*

26

27   **Return** *objs, items, demands*

28 **end**

Algorithm 2. Function CreateElements

---

1 **Function CreateElements**(ϕ_{mean}, ϕ_{sd}, ϕ_{min}, ϕ_{max}, ϕ_{types}):
2   Create an empty *matrix*
3   **For** *each object*
4        $n = 1$
5   **For** *each item*
6   **Repeat**
7              $row \leftarrow$ a random number ϕ_{ran} with Gaussian distribution of mean ϕ_{mean} and standard deviation ϕ_{sd}
8   **until** $\phi_{min} \leq \phi_{ran} \leq \phi_{max}$
9           $n \leftarrow n + 1$
10   **If** $n > \phi_{types}$
11             $n = 1$
12   **end**
13   **end**
14        $matrix \leftarrow row$
15   **end**
16   **Return** *matrix*
17 **end**

2.2 Machine Learning Methods

From a data set generated using parameters from [17,27], statistical methods and a (greedy) heuristic capable of determining the labels of the output, it is possible to apply supervised Machine Learning methods to make predictions. Therefore, supervised methods will determine the output class as leftover or loss, considering a set of items, demands and object. In this work, the following supervised methods were used for the classification task: decision trees, random forests, Naive Bayes and logistic regression.

Decision Tree. Decision tree is a technique very useful in pattern recognition to extract information of a data set. The procedure seeks to create subpartitions in the input data, based on a partition criterion, called recursive partitioning [7]. The objective of the tree procedure is to subdivide the initial problem into smaller problems that will be subdivided recursively so that the distinction between the classes is maximum. Trees can be viewed graphically in hierarchical structures or graphs. Decision tree models can be used in classification tasks (Classification Tree), in order to classify objects or instances in tagged classes. A decision tree consists of a data set, partitioned into groups known as *nodes*. The top node is called *root node*, which is selected using some attribute selection measures. Under the root node are the internal nodes, originating from the division of the data set; they constitute the tree branches. At the end of each branch is the terminal node, designed *leaves*, which represent the most appropriated class for the rule. One rule is composed by each terminal node, plus the

internal nodes that belongs to one specific branch and the root node. The rules
are describe by a IF-THEN model ("IF attribute w is $y1$ AND attribute x is
$y2$ THEN the class is z"). These rules are used to classify unknown data at the
inference process [2,30]. Example of binary decision tree structure can be seen
in Fig. 1.

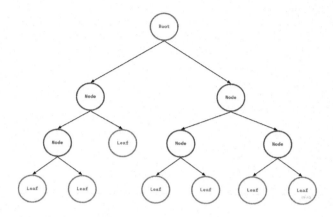

Fig. 1. Example of a binary decision tree structure

Many decision criteria can be adopted, such as impurity, distance and dependence. Consider $p_1, p_2, p_3, \ldots, p_k$ data belong to k different classes in a N node.
The Gini index can be obtained as [2,30]:

$$G(N) = 1 - \sum_{i=1}^{k} p_i^2 \tag{1}$$

The attribute that returns the highest value of the Gini index is the one that
will be chosen as a node. Another choice criterion is the entropy calculation.
Initially, the entropy of the parent node (node before division) is calculated
and the entropy difference between the child nodes (nodes after division) is
calculated. The algorithm uses the *Information Gain*, which is an impurity-based
criteria that uses entropy measure as the impurity measure [29]. The entropy can
be obtained as:

$$g(N) = - \sum_{i=1}^{k} p_i \log (p_i). \tag{2}$$

When calculating the information gains of each attribute, those that performed above average are selected, also applying the gain ratio, a measure that
seeks to solve the problem of attributes with many possible values, generating
high gains but with little usability. Then, it is chosen, among the above-average
attributes, the one with the best gain ratio.

According to [23], the *overfitting* is a problem of quantitative models, which occurs when there are irrelevant components that impair the prediction of the methods. In order to minimize this problem, some pruning methods can be used in order to obtain a greater accuracy in the prediction of the model. These methods can be applied post-pruning (performed after construction of the tree) and pre-pruning (performed during tree construction) [22].

Random Forest. Random Forests method creates several decision trees randomly for the same problem, where each tree influences the final result [8]. The algorithm belongs to the ensemble methods, which combine different models to obtain a single result, making the algorithms more robust and complex, increasing the computational cost, but achieving better results [8].

The main advantage in using ensemble algorithms is the combination of results, since normally, in a non-ensemble method, the model that presents the best results for the dataset is chosen. However, even though it is possible to test different configurations for the chosen model, in the end, only one configuration is chosen. With the use of an ensemble method, all results referring to all tested configurations are used, thus eliminating instability problems.

Let n be classifiers of a dataset $h_1(x), h_2(x), h_3(x), \ldots, h_n(x)$, which maps the features x into a class C. When we combine the classifiers, an ensemble classifier $H(x)$ is obtained, so that the performance is optimized. Therefore, ensemble classifiers aggregate other classifiers in order to obtain generalization, avoiding overfitting [2]. According to [8], a random forest consists of a collection of tree-structured classifiers $\{h(\boldsymbol{x}, \Theta_k), k = 1, \ldots\}$, where $\{\Theta_k\}$ are independent identically distributed random vectors, and each tree votes unitarily for the most popular class in the input $\boldsymbol{x}$. Each decision tree has a unit vote in the classification of a new data and the most voted class is the one that will be assigned to this data. As each tree is built, a random factor is added, increasing the diversity of the classifiers [2,8,14].

Naive Bayes. The Bayesian inference model consists of analyzing conditioned variables in a probabilistic way, that can be done using the Bayes Theorem: suppose $y' = (y_1, ..., y_n)$ is a vector of n observations in which the probability distribution $p(y|\theta)$ depends on the value of k parameters $\theta' = (\theta_1, ..., \theta_k)$. Consider that θ has a probability distribution $p(\theta)$. Therefore, given the observation y, the conditional probability of θ is represented by Bayes Theorem [6], as follows.

$$p(\theta|y) = \frac{p(y|\theta)p(\theta)}{p(y)} \tag{3}$$

The term $p(\theta)$ is the *a priori* distribution of θ, the term $p(\theta|y)$ is the *a posteriori* distribution of θ, given y and $p(y|\theta)$ is the likelihood of θ.

Bayesian networks are probabilistic graphical models that represent knowledge about the data domain. The *a priori* knowledge can be combined with patterns learned from the data. In addition, the user can insert knowledge in some node of the network, which will propagate to other nodes. The models are composed of a directed acyclic graph and a set of probability tables, where the network nodes represent the variables and the arcs represent dependency relationships between the variables.

Bayesian networks can be used as classifiers, calculating the conditional probability of a node, called a class node, given the values of the probabilities of the other nodes, that is, $p(C|V)$, where C represents the analyzed class and V the set of variables that describe the patterns. The Naive Bayes classifier is a particular case of a Bayesian network, in which the domain variables are conditionally independent. The classification is done by applying Bayes' Theorem to calculate the probability of C, given a particular instance of $A_1, A_2, ..., A_n$ and then predicting the class with the highest *a posteriori* probability. Then, the learning process is done inductively, presenting a training dataset and calculating the conditional probability of each attribute A_i, given the class C [16].

Logistic Regression. Logistic regression is a mathematical model that can describe the interaction between independent variables and dichotomous dependent variables, which are those that can have two states (as 0 or 1). It is one of the most popular models for describing binary prediction problems [24]. The logistic model is based on the logistic function, defined as:

$$f(z) = \frac{1}{1 + e^{-z}} \tag{4}$$

Let $X_1, X_2, X_3, \ldots, X_k$ be dichotomous and continuous independent variables. The probability of its value being 1 can be described as:

$$P(D = 1|X_1, X_2, X_3, \ldots, X_k)$$

This model will be defined as logistical if such probability can be described as:

$$P(D = 1|X_1, X_2, X_3, \ldots, X_k) = \frac{1}{1 + e^{-(\alpha + \sum \beta_i X_i)}} \tag{5}$$

Parameters α and β_i are unknown and it will be estimated according to the input data. After that, the model can be used to predict the class of new input data.

2.3   Classifiers Performance Evaluation

Evaluating the performance of the classifiers is a fundamental aspect of machine learning. In this work, Cross-Validation and Confusion Matrix are applied as efficient indicators for assessing the quality of the analysis results.

In k-fold *Cross-Validation*, the data is randomly split into k mutually exclusive subsets of approximately equal size. An inducer is trained and tested k times; each time it is tested on one of the k folds and trained using the remaining $k - 1$ folds. The advantage of this method is that it matters less how the data gets divided. Every data point gets to be in a test set exactly once, and gets to be in a training set $k - 1$ times. The variance of the resulting estimate is reduced as k is increased. Therefore, the basic idea is that some of the data is removed before training begins. Then when training is done, the data that was removed can be used to test the performance of the learned model on "new" data.

In this work, the *stratified k-fold cross validation* is used, since we have unbalanced data. This technique creates k distinct subsets of similar sizes, so that these subsets k have a similar proportion to the original data set X in relation to the instances belonging to each class C_i, which means say that the subset is stratified [2,28]. The $k = 10$ was chosen since it is a common value in the literature and is also consistent with the complexity of the problem studied.

The *Confusion Matrix* is used as an indication of the properties of a classification rule. It contains the number of elements that have been correctly or incorrectly classified for each class. The main diagonal presents the number of observations that have been correctly classified for each class. The off-diagonal elements present the number of observations that have been incorrectly classified [2].

The Confusion Matrix $M(C_i, C_j)$, for $i, j = 1, ..., k$, classes provides an effective measure of the classification model performance, since it shows the number of elements correctly classified and predict, for each class. Let T be a set of examples and h the hypothesis. The Confusion Matrix of h is given by:

$$M(C_i, C_j) = \sum_{\forall (x,y) \in T : y = c_i} \| h(x) = C_j \|$$

where C_i is the true class and the C_j is the predict class.

According to [5,13] the accuracy fails when evaluating the performance of a classifier in unbalanced sets, having a bias towards the most present instances in the set. Therefore, [26] introduced the *Matthews Correlational Coefficient* (MCC), which is a consistent evaluation for unbalanced datasets. The coefficient varies between $[-1, 1]$ and evaluates how much better the performance of the classifier used is compared to a purely random classification.

Since the dataset is unbalanced, *F1-score* and the *Area Under the Curve (AUC) of the Receiver Operator Characteristic (ROC)* curve are also presented. F1-score is a classification error metric used to evaluate the classification algorithms, which considers not only the number of prediction errors, but also the type of errors. Mostly, F1-score is useful in evaluating the prediction for binary classification of data and it uses the precision and the recall to be calculated. AUC-ROC indicates how well the Machine Learning binary classifiers are performing. It is the measure of the ability of a classifier to distinguish between classes. The closer to 1 the value of F1-score and AUC-ROC, the better the performance of the classifiers at distinguishing between output classes.

3 Results and Discussion

Based on the classifiers described above and considering their characteristics and algorithms, the cross-validation was executed with the strategy of stratified k-folds, with $k = 10$. The results from the algorithms are presented in the Table 1.

Table 1. Results from stratified 10-folds for each classifier

Classifiers	Class	Precision	Recall	F1-Score	Accuracy	AUC ROC	MCC
Logistic regression	Loss	0.8571	0.9000	0.8571	0.9143	0.9340	0.7980
	Leftover	0.9583	0.9615	0.9388			
Naive-Bayes	Loss	0.5882	0.9999	0.7407	0.8000	0.9800	0.6508
	Leftover	0.9999	0.7308	0.8444			
Decision tree	Loss	0.8571	0.9999	0.9091	0.9429	0.9760	0.8756
	Leftover	0.9999	0.9600	0.9583			
Random forest	Loss	0.9999	0.9000	0.9474	0.9714	0.9920	0.9303
	Leftover	0.9615	0.9999	0.9804			

Performance metrics must be analyzed in a joint and structured way, therefore, it is important to highlight that the evaluation of the accuracy through the global accuracy and the coefficients of agreement, provides results with a higher degree of confidentiality among the studied discrimination criteria. From Table 1 we can observe that there were optimal levels of accuracy for the Random Forest, Decision Tree and Logistic Regression methods, citing them in descending order (0.9714; 0.9429 and 0.9143, respectively). The Naive Bayes method obtained a good accuracy, around 0.8000, which is considered a good accuracy. Observing the F1-score and the AUC-ROC, as the values are close to 1, we can conclude that the binary classifiers are performing well, i.e., the classifiers are distinguishing the two output classes.

Analyzing the statistical measures of Random Forest and Decision Tree methods, we can notice that the numerical values are very close. Knowing the computational complexity of Random Forests in relation to Decision Trees [2, 22, 25], since Random Forests combine several trees, we can say that Decision Trees achieve the same performance descriptors requiring less computational effort. In this way, the usability of decision trees is considered in some cases, since this method presented excellent values with emphasis on specificity (recall); that is, classify as "loss" the instances that really are "loss".

The MCC is a robust evaluation for unbalanced datasets. The coefficient is a more reliable statistical rate which produces a high score only if the prediction obtained good results, especially on unbalanced datasets [13]. The Decision Tree and Random Forest methods presented the highest MCC. When the precision, recall and F1 Score measures are analyzed, the highest values are found in the "leftover" class in the Logistic Regression method, compared to the "loss" class. The lowest precision occurred in the "loss" class in the Naive Bayes method and the highest values are presented in Decision Trees and Random Forests for both the "loss" and the "leftover" classes.

The analyzes of the ROC curves for each one of the folds provide an overview of the methods behavior over the course of the considered subsets. The variation between the values obtained from the folds for all methods is permissive. Decision Trees have the largest variation when compared to the other methods; Random Forests have the smallest variation and the largest average value obtained, proving to be consistent. Regarding the area under the curve, when the ROC curve is evaluated, the Random Forests, Naive Bayes and Decision Trees methods presented indicators greater than 0.95. Logistic Regression presented a value of 0.9340.

The confusion matrices that presented the best accuracy and the highest MCC, considering the stratified 10-fold cross validation, are presented in Table 2, for each classifier.

Table 2. Confusion matrix of (a) logistic regression, (b) Naive-Bayes, (c) decision tree and (d) random forest

(a) Logistic Regression			(b) Naive-Bayes		
	Loss	Leftover		Loss	Leftover
Loss	9	1	Loss	10	0
Leftover	2	23	Leftover	7	18

(c) Decision Tree			(d) Random Forest		
	Loss	Leftover		Loss	Leftover
Loss	10	0	Loss	9	1
Leftover	2	23	Leftover	0	25

Analyzing the confusion matrices illustrated in Table 2 for the test data, after and optimizing the classifiers in the training data, it is possible to observe that the classifiers present good classification, as all of them managed to divide the classes satisfactorily, even with the sample unbalanced that favors the leftover class. This fact can be proved by observing that the main diagonal of the matrices exhibit the highest values.

The Naive Bayes algorithm has obtained biased estimates for the leftover class and is more likely to assign outputs for this class. For this reason, focusing only on precision to choose the best classifiers is not a good strategy, as mentioned in the results of Table 1.

Figures 2, 3, 4 and 5 illustrates the AUC ROC curves graphics for each classifier using the stratified k-fold cross validation, showing good discrimination between the output classes (loss or leftover) in terms of the methods used. The ROC Curve associated with the proposed models measures the prediction capacity, therefore, it helps in the visualization and classification of the model's discrimination based on the predictive performance. These graphs are two-dimensional, that is, they consider the relationship between the rate of true positives in the model and the rate of false positives predicted. So, the more to the left of the upper corner of the graph the model is profiled, the better the classification performance between the outputs (loss and leftover) in this study.

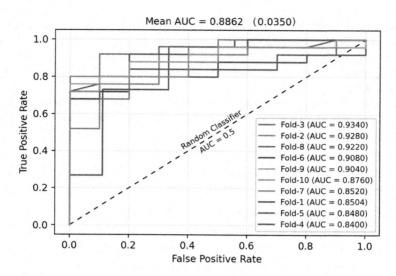

Fig. 2. AUC ROC for logistic regression

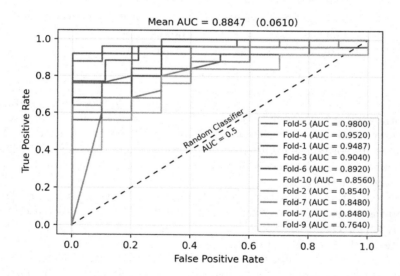

Fig. 3. AUC ROC for Naive-Bayes

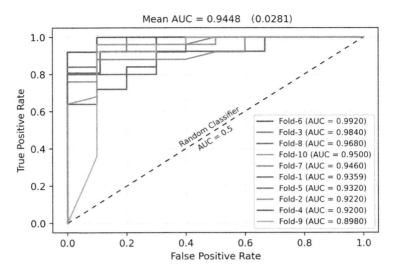

Fig. 4. AUC ROC for random forest

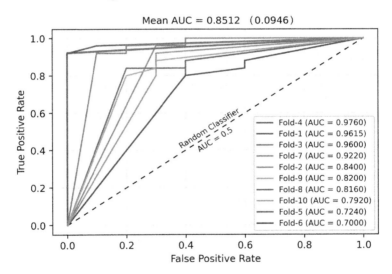

Fig. 5. AUC ROC for decision tree

4   Conclusion

In this work, a numerical data set is generated in order to be used in supervised training algorithms for classification task. This dataset addresses the cutting stock problem, which consists of a classical and well known optimization problem. The provided dataset considers numerical values of demands, objects and items to be cut as input variables and, as output variables, loss (to be discarded) or leftover (which can be reused in a new demand), which come from the stock cutting process.

The greedy heuristic FFD [10] was considered to generate the outputs of the dataset. This greedy heuristic generates more leftovers than losses, which is particularly interesting, since leftovers can be used in future demands. On the other hand, an unbalanced dataset is obtained, which requires specific statistical measures to analyze the performances. Since the results and the analysis indicate good performance, we can also conclude that the generated data set is robust and it can be used in other classification tasks.

The research developed in this work and the obtained results contribute to the Optimization, Operational Research and Artificial Intelligence research areas. The generated numerical dataset and the source code, as well as all the materials for the complete replication of this work, have been available at https://github.com/ximiraxelo/leftoverproblem. Therefore, another contribution of this work is to provide a dataset for use by the scientific community.

As future works, we can indicate the use of different heuristics to generate the outputs (loss or leftovers), in order to evaluate the performance of different heuristics to generate the outputs and also to evaluate the performance of the Machine Learning algorithms to classify different balanced or unbalanced datasets.

References

1. Abuabara, A., Morabito, R.: Cutting optimization of structural tubes to build agricultural light aircrafts. Ann. Oper. Res. **169**(1), 149–165 (2009)
2. Aggarwal, C.C. (ed.): Data Classification: Algorithms and Applications. Chapman & Hall/CRC Data Mining and Knowledge Discovery Series, vol. 35. CRC Press/Chapman & Hall, Boca Raton (2014)
3. Arbib, C., Marinelli, F., Rossi, F., Di Iorio, F.: Cutting and reuse: an application from automobile component manufacturing. Oper. Res. **50**(6), 923–934 (2002)
4. Arenales, M.N., Cherri, A.C., Do Nascimento, D.N., Vianna, A.: A new mathematical model for the cutting stock/leftover problem. Pesquisa Operacional **35**, 509–522 (2015)
5. Boughorbel, S., Jarray, F., El-Anbari, M.: Optimal classifier for imbalanced data using Matthews Correlation Coefficient metric. PLoS ONE **12**(6), e0177678 (2017)
6. Box, G.E., Tiao, G.C.: Bayesian Inference in Statistical Analysis, vol. 40. Wiley, Hoboken (2011)
7. Bramer, M.: Principles of Data Mining. Undergraduate Topics in Computer Science, 3rd edn. Springer, London (2016). https://doi.org/10.1007/978-1-4471-7307-6
8. Breiman, L.: Random forests. Mach. Learn. **45**(1), 5–32 (2001)
9. Campello, B., Ghidini, C., Ayres, A., Oliveira, W.: A residual recombination heuristic for one-dimensional cutting stock problems. TOP **30**(1), 194–220 (2022)
10. Cerqueira, G.R.L., Aguiar, S.S., Marques, M.: Modified Greedy Heuristic for the one-dimensional cutting stock problem. J. Comb. Optim. **42**(3), 657–674 (2021). https://doi.org/10.1007/s10878-021-00695-4
11. Cherri, A.C., Arenales, M.N., Yanasse, H.H.: The usable leftover one-dimensional cutting stock problem-a priority-in-use heuristic. Int. Trans. Oper. Res. **20**(2), 189–199 (2013)

12. Cherri, A.C., Arenales, M.N., Yanasse, H.H., Poldi, K.C., Vianna, A.C.G.: The one-dimensional cutting stock problem with usable leftovers-a survey. Eur. J. Oper. Res. **236**(2), 395–402 (2014)
13. Chicco, D., Jurman, G.: The advantages of the Matthews correlation coefficient (MCC) over F1 score and accuracy in binary classification evaluation. BMC Genom. **21**(1), 1–13 (2020)
14. Fawagreh, K., Gaber, M.M., Elyan, E.: Random forests: from early developments to recent advancements. Syst. Sci. Control Eng. **2**(1), 602–609 (2014)
15. Foerster, H., Wascher, G.: Pattern reduction in one-dimensional cutting stock problems. Int. J. Prod. Res. **38**(7), 1657–1676 (2000)
16. Friedman, N., Geiger, D., Goldszmidt, M.: Bayesian network classifiers. Mach. Learn. **29**(2), 131–163 (1997)
17. Gau, T., Wäscher, G.: CUTGEN1: A problem generator for the standard one-dimensional cutting stock problem. Eur. J. Oper. Res. **84**(3), 572–579 (1995)
18. Gilmore, P.C., Gomory, R.E.: A linear programming approach to the cutting-stock problem. Oper. Res. **9**(6), 849–859 (1961)
19. Gilmore, P.C., Gomory, R.E.: A linear programming approach to the cutting stock problem-Part II. Oper. Res. **11**(6), 863–888 (1963)
20. Gilmore, P.C., Gomory, R.E.: Multistage cutting stock problems of two and more dimensions. Oper. Res. **13**(1), 94–120 (1965)
21. Hamilton, J.D.: Time Series Analysis. Princeton University Press, Princeton (2020)
22. Han, J., Kamber, M., Pei, J.: Classification: basic concepts. In: Data Mining, pp. 327–391 (2012)
23. Hawkins, D.M.: The problem of overfitting. J. Chem. Inf. Comput. Sci. **44**(1), 1–12 (2004)
24. Hosmer, D.W., Lemeshow, S., Sturdivant, R.X.: Applied Logistic Regression. Wiley Series in Probability and Statistics, vol. 398, 3rd edn. Wiley, Hoboken (2013)
25. Lantz, B.: Machine Learning with R: Learn How to Use R to Apply Powerful Machine Learning Methods and Gain an Insight into Real-World Applications. Packt Publishing Ltd., Birmingham (2013)
26. Matthews, B.: Comparison of the predicted and observed secondary structure of T4 phage lysozyme. Biochimica et Biophysica Acta (BBA) Protein Struct. **405**(2), 442–451 (1975)
27. do Prado Marques, F., Arenales, M.N.: The constrained compartmentalised knapsack problem. Comput. Oper. Res. **34**(7), 2109–2129 (2007)
28. Purushotham, S., Tripathy, B.K.: Evaluation of classifier models using stratified tenfold cross validation techniques. In: Krishna, P.V., Babu, M.R., Ariwa, E. (eds.) ObCom 2011. CCIS, vol. 270, pp. 680–690. Springer, Heidelberg (2012). https://doi.org/10.1007/978-3-642-29216-3_74
29. Quilan, J.R.: Decision trees and multi-valued attributes, pp. 305–318. Oxford University Press Inc., Oxford (1988)
30. Rokach, L., Maimon, O.: Data Mining with Decision Trees: Theory and Applications. Series in Machine Perception and Artificial Intelligence, vol. 69. World Scientific, Singapore; Hackensack (2008)

Active GA Accelerated by Simulated Annealing to Solve SPP in Packet Networks

Daniel S. Fonseca[1]([✉]), Elizabeth F. Wanner[1]([✉]), Carolina G. Marcelino[2,3]([✉]),
Gabriel P. Silva[2]([✉]), Silvia Jimenez-Fernandez[3]([✉]),
and Sancho Salcedo-Sanz[3]([✉])

[1] Department of Computing, Federal Center of Technological Education of Minas
Gerais (CEFET-MG), Belo Horizonte, Brazil
daniel0547@gmail.com, efwanner@decom.cefetmg.br
[2] Institute of Computing, Federal University of Rio de Janeiro (UFRJ),
Rio de Janeiro, Brazil
{carolina,gabriel}@ic.ufrj.br
[3] Department of Signal Processing and Communication, University of Alcalá (UAH),
Alcalá de Henares, Spain
{silvia.jimenez,sancho.salcedo}@uah.es

Abstract. This paper presents two approaches to deal with the shortest
path problem (SPP) solution for routing network packets in an optimized
way. The first one uses Simulated Annealing (SA), and the second one is
a novel hybridization of the Genetic Algorithm with Dijkstra mutation
accelerated by the SA (SGA). Also, two different case scenario configurations, each with 144 nodes, are employed to assess these two proposals,
and the total time spent to fill out the routing tables, referring to the
transmission of a packet from the initial to the destiny nodes, is measured. A statistical comparison is applied to identify differences among
the algorithm's solutions. Experiments and simulations have shown that
the SGA presented competitive results compared to standard SA and
can solve the problem with fast convergence, which makes us conclude
that it can operate efficiently in actual computer networks.

Keywords: Optimization · Evolutionary algorithms · Shortest path
problem

1 Introduction

On Internet, routing is the process by which computers receive and deliver packets of information. The Internet uses a routing model named *hop-by-hop*. In this
model, each computer or router examines the packet's destination address, executes a routing algorithm to determine the next hop, and delivers it to the next
router or computer, where the process will be again performed. Efficient routing
algorithms can use diverse techniques to find an adequate route path for packet
transmission [1].

A. I. Pereira et al. (Eds.): OL2A 2022, CCIS 1754, pp. 342–356, 2022.
https://doi.org/10.1007/978-3-031-23236-7_24

Routing tables and protocols are necessary to achieve the expected results of the transmission process. Network members' addresses are the most relevant information in the routing tables. Besides the contents of the routing table, a protocol also defines the best routes for delivering packets. As an assessment of the quality of service, some performance metrics inherent to the network's communication, such as the number of hops, delays, and transmission costs of a given packet, are also considered [2,3].

1.1 Related Works

The use of software agents for network routing produces better results than conventional approaches, as shown by many studies [4,5]. These algorithms have proven to be viable candidates for solving problems of dynamic and unpredictable nature, such as routing in large networks. It is mainly due to the continuous active search for non-local information that agents allow. Network routing is the mechanism chosen to send packets from any source to a destination in the network. Lopez and Heisterkamp [6] proposed a solution using the Simulated Annealing (SA) algorithm with hierarchical Q-routing, producing a dynamic routing protocol. In a 6×6 grid topology, this approach efficiently provided the route tables in a short time.

Flying Ad-hoc Networks are a special type of wireless network that, in general, has been using optimization algorithms to establish efficient and dynamic routes. Following Q-routing ideas, Rovira-Sugranes et al. [7] concluded that SA adapts to the network dynamicity without requiring manual re-initialization at transition points. SA showed to be an alternative routing algorithm in wireless sensor networks lifetime [8] and flying-software defined networks [9]. Raj and Rahimunnisa [10] proposed a hybrid approach coupling the Genetic Algorithm (GA) and SA to solve the routing packages in wireless Ad-hoc networks. Sundar and Kathirvel [11] proposed a delivered mechanism over variable length density using the SA in mobile ad-hoc network. The efficiency of coupled GA and SA was verified by Prasad and Rayanki [12] when applied to computer network routing.

Hamed [13] proposed a genetic version of an algorithm to find the k-shortest paths in a network. Zhang et al. [14] applied GA in a small simulation to improve the quality of service in computer networks, reporting effective results. A multicast routing algorithm, also using genetic algorithms, was proposed using an approach with both bandwidth and delay constraints [15]. Recently, some works used GA with many goals: to minimize the construction of network routing tables [16], to provide an energy-efficiency network protocol [17], and to improve the efficiency in routing packets [18,19]. GA was successfully used for routing Internet of Things (IoT) networks [20]. A new network protocol based on GA was proposed in [21]. Results showed that the time to construct network routes was reduced in 12.74%. Energy consumption should be considered as one of the foremost vital limitations in autonomous systems, and to provide a solution for that Bhardwaj and El-Ocla [16] proposed a multipath routing protocol based on GA.

This work objective is to solve the shortest path in computer networks. To achieve this goal, we propose a genetic algorithm with a new mutation scheme inspired by Dijkstra's algorithm [22] – the Genetic Algorithm with Dijkstra mutation (GA). To accelerate the search space, we couple GA with an SA mechanism. To the best of our knowledge, this is the first time that a mixed approach between GA and Dijkstra algorithms is reported. To validate our proposal, we conduct an experimental simulation comparing the results obtained by the three evaluated algorithms. Specifically, in our simulation, we adopt an experimental scenario, using a topology with 144 interconnected routers, differentiating the approach taken in other related works, which used a maximum of 30 routers. In our perspective, the size of the 144-node network is well-suited for the simulated experiments.

This work is organized as follows: Sect. 2 describes the shortest path problem and presents the optimization modeling proposed. Section 3 describes the standard Simulated Annealing and addresses the coupled approaches. Section 4 explains the simulation methodology adopted. The experiments carried out and the data analysis are presented in Sect. 5. Finally, Sect. 6 concludes the report and presents future perspectives.

2   Problem Description

The shortest path problem can be described as finding the shortest path that satisfies a given condition. In this work, we propose a mixed meta-heuristic to solve this problem, always keeping in mind the real characteristics of the Internet. This heuristic is based on the analogy of finding the shortest path between two nodes in a computer network. So, meta-heuristics is an emerging idea able to solve this type of problem. This approach differs from the algorithms reported in the internet protocols literature.

Usually, conventional methods compare all the possibilities to find the best solution. This mechanism is time-consuming, increasing the delay for a network with a large number of nodes and edges. In this context, computer networks can be described as a weighted directed graph $G = (N, E)$, in which N indicates the set of nodes and E indicates the set of links connecting the nodes. $|N|$ and $|E|$ denote the number of nodes and links in the network, respectively [23].

2.1   Shortest Path Optimization Modeling

In this work we propose an optimization model to solve the shortest path problem, having the previous graph notation to computer networks in mind. In graph theory, the minimal path problem is characterized by finding a path between two nodes such that the sum of weights of its edges is minimum. In this way, an objective function of the optimization problem can be defined by Eq. (1),

$$dist(v, i) = \min_{(u,v)\epsilon E} \{dist(u, i - 1) + \ell(u, v)\} \tag{1}$$

in which, for each vertex v and each integer $i \leq k$, $dist(v, i)$ is the shortest path from source vertex s to v using i edges, $dist(u, i - 1)$ is the shortest path from source vertex s to u using $i - 1$ edges, and $\ell(u, v)$ is the distance between u and v.

In our optimization model, all the paths are valid as their bandwidth availability is checked before finding out their delay factor,

$$AveragePacketDelay = \frac{Delay}{number\ of\ links} \tag{2}$$

in which,

$$Delay = \sum_{i=1}^{n} \frac{BandwidthAvailable_i}{DataSize}.$$

Fitness is calculated through Total Cost Time, in seconds (s):

$$Fit = min \sum_{i=1}^{n} (AveragePacketDelay + TimeRoute). \tag{3}$$

The optimal path selection is mainly based on the AveragePacketDelay term and in the TimeRoute spent at each link where the route walks. If there are two or more paths with the same fitness value, the algorithm will choose the one with fewer hops.

3   Meta-heuristics Addressed

A meta-heuristic can be defined as a high-level problem-independent set of guidelines and strategies to design heuristic optimization algorithms [24]. Meta-heuristics can combine several mechanisms as diversity, memory, multiple populations, and self-adaptive schemes [25]. This work addresses two distinct meta-heuristics: a proposed Genetic Algorithm with Dijkstra mutation (GA), and the standard Simulated Annealing (SA) [26] to solve the shortest path problem in computer networks with comparative performance analysis.

3.1   The Proposed Genetic Algorithm with Dijkstra Mutation

Genetic algorithms (GA) are search meta-heuristics utilized to find approximate solutions to general optimization problems. GA is based on evolutionary biology with genetic heritage, mutation, natural selection, and breeding [27]. GA is implemented as a computer simulation in which a given population of abstract representations of solutions is selected in the search for better solutions.

The evolution process usually starts with a randomly generated set of solutions and occurs throughout generations. As generation passes by, the fitness of each solution in that generation is evaluated. Generally, the operators in GA are crossover, mutation, selection, and elitism. The new population is used as an input to the next iteration of the algorithm. The evolutionary loop is executed

Algorithm 1. Genetic algorithm pseudo-code

```
 1  begin
 2  │    Initialize current population;
 3  │    Evaluate the fitness of each individual;
 4  │    Store the individual with highest fitness;
 6  │    while Stop criteria is not met do
 8  │    │    for  0 to population size do
 9  │    │    │    Select to individuals to breed;
10  │    │    │    Apply crossover to the individuals;
11  │    │    │    Apply mutation to the children if necessary;
12  │    │    │    Save the children for the next generation;
13  │    │    │    Evaluated children fitness;
14  │    │    end
15  │    │    Current generation replaced by next generation;
16  │    │    Evaluate mean fitness;
18  │    │    if Any fitness in the population > best fitness then
19  │    │    │    Erase previously stored best individual;
20  │    │    │    Store new best individual;
21  │    │    end
22  │    end
23  end
```

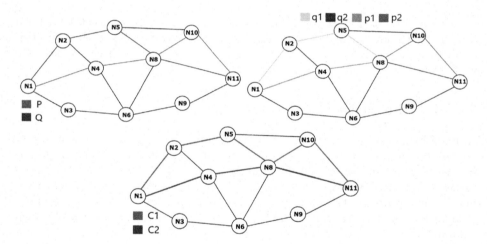

Fig. 1. Let P[N1-N4-N8-N10-N11] and Q[N1-N2-N5-N8-N11]. Choice a partition point to cut P and Q in p1[N1-N4-N8], p2[N8-N10-N11], q1[N1-N2-N5-N8], q2[N8-N11]. The new offspring C1[N1-N2-N5-N8-N10-N11] and C2[N1-N4-N8-N11] will be generated.

until one or more solutions meet the expected result by the implemented objective function. Algorithm 1 presents a pseudo-code for the Genetic Algorithm.

To solve the specific minimal path problem, in which the individual is a route vector that contains nodes, the mutation and crossover operators are explained as follows. In our GA implementation, the mutation operator has a Dijkstra structure to provide an improvement in the GA cycle. We are proposing a merged approach that uses the best characteristics of both algorithms. Figure 1 and 2 show the crossover and mutation operators, respectively.

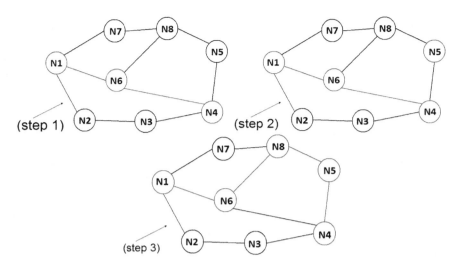

Fig. 2. Given the route N1-N6-N4, in the mutation process, its randomized that the node N5 will be added between N6 and N4, thus the route from N6 to N5 (by N8) and N5 to N4 must be calculated to construct a valid route.

CROSSOVER

1. Given two routes parents P and Q with a common node:
2. Separate the route P in p1 and p2, from the start to the common node and from the common node to the destination respectively;
3. Separate the route Q in q1 and q2, from the start to the common node and from the common node to the destination respectively;
4. Generate 1st offspring (C1) with combination of p1 and q2;
5. Generate 2nd offspring (C2) with combination of q1 and p2.

MUTATION

1. Select a random position in the route;
2. Insert a random node in this position;
3. Calculate the route from the previous node to the new inserted node using Dijkstra [22] and insert it in the route.

3.2 Standard Simulated Annealing

Simulated annealing is a well-studied local search meta-heuristic applied to a large variety of optimization problems. The key feature of this algorithm is that it provides a mechanism to escape local optima by allowing hill-climbing moves that worsen the objective function value in search of global optima.

The name comes from an analogy to the process of physical annealing with solids, in which a crystalline solid is heated and then allowed to cool very slowly until it achieves its most regular possible crystal lattice configuration and thus is free of crystal defects. Simulated annealing establishes the connection between this type of thermodynamic behavior and the search for global minima for a discrete optimization problem.

At each iteration of a simulated annealing algorithm, the values for two solutions (the current solution and a newly selected solution) are compared. Improving solutions are always accepted, while a fraction of non-improving solutions are accepted in the hope of escaping local optima in search of global optima. The probability of accepting non-improving solutions depends on a temperature parameter, which is reduced with each iteration of the algorithm [26]. Algorithm refSAPC presents a pseudo-code for the Simulated Annealing.

Algorithm 2. Simulated annealing pseudo-code

```
 1  begin
 2  |   Select an initial solution ω;
 3  |   Select an initial temperature T;
 4  |   Select the temperature reduction factor, α;
 5  |   Select a repetition schedule, Mₖ;
 6  |   Select a maximum number of iterations, maxᵢₜ;
 7  |   k = 0;
 8  |   t = T;
10  |   while k < maxᵢₜ do
12  |   |   for m = 0 to Mₖ do
13  |   |   |   Generate a solution ω';
14  |   |   |   Calculate Δ_{ω,ω'} = f(ω') − f(ω);
16  |   |   |   if Δ_{ω,ω'} <= 0 then
17  |   |   |   |   ω = ω';
18  |   |   |   end
20  |   |   |   if Δ_{ω,ω'} > 0 then
21  |   |   |   |   ω = ω' with probability exp(−Δ_{ω,ω'}/t);
22  |   |   |   end
23  |   |   end
24  |   |   t = α × t;
25  |   |   k = k + 1;
26  |   end
27  end
```

In the present work, to generate a new solution ω', the mutation operator from the genetic algorithm is applied in the previous solution ω.

3.3   Active Genetic Algorithm Accelerated by Simulated Annealing

In this work, we also propose a method to combine the advantages of each of the previously presented algorithms. The GA should take longer times to run due to its populational nature, while the SA should be able to find a local optimum faster.

Given this hypothesis, we propose a method to use the results obtained quickly in the first iterations of the simulated annealing as the initial population for the genetic algorithm, allowing it to converge faster. We call this method Active Genetic Algorithm Accelerated by Simulated Annealing – SGA.

In this method, the simulated annealing is applied to a portion of the individuals in the initial population of the genetic algorithm, thus allowing the genetic algorithm to start with improved solutions probably closer to the optimal solution. The SGA also implements a new stop criterion: the algorithm terminates when all individuals converge to the same result, thus allowing the algorithm to execute fewer generations.

4 Methodology and Simulation

The methodology used to validate the efficiency of each meta-heuristic is based on a framework made to simulate routing algorithms in computer networks. Thus, we use the Simulator for Network Algorithms (SinalGo) in this work. SinalGo is a computer network simulation framework developed to test and validate routing algorithms, which has been built with a focus on algorithm verification, abstracting the different layers in a computer network environment. It offers a simple interface to control packet transmission between network nodes, which allows an accurate approximation from the actual operational network hardware.

Figure 3 shows an example of SinalGo execution, which simulates a network with 144 nodes. Figure 3(a) means a grid network topology as in [6], but twice in size. In order to build a more realistic experiment, we propose the construction of a totally randomized topology. Figure 3(b) shows the proposed network used as an experiment. This topology is inherently more difficult for routing algorithms, in general, to construct routes.

Both meta-heuristics addressed in this work have been implemented inside SinalGo using JAVA language. In this framework, each network node emulates

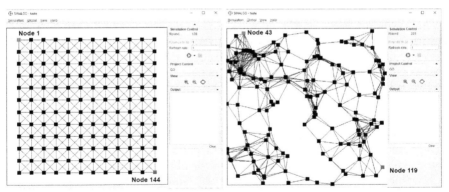

(a) Grid network. In witch the origin and destination nodes are 1 and 144, respectively marked in blue and red.

(b) Fully randomized network. In witch the origin and destination nodes are 43 and 119, respectively marked in blue and red.

Fig. 3. Two distinct network typologies simulation with 144 nodes.

a generic router that can run the previously presented algorithms and thus provide routing service. A comparison among the execution times has been carried out in this work. Moreover, three different network configurations are tested to bring the simulation to a real-world problem. That comparison allows us to derive plausible conclusions about the efficiency of each algorithm in a set of environment configurations.

5   Experiments and Results

Each algorithm was executed 30 times for each one of the two environment configurations with 144 nodes each (see Fig. (3) in Sect. 4). Each configuration represents distinct network structures, the first is a 12×12 grid representation, and the second one represents a totally random network. After each execution, the network is deconstructed and rebuilt, erasing all nodes and connections. This procedure avoids any interference due to the forwarding of routing information from one simulation to another. Before each algorithm execution, a time frame of two hundred events is executed in the network for convergence agents (SA) and network recognition (all methods).

The first step of the three presented algorithms is the discovery phase, which follows a decentralized routing model, with no central element that knows all the network's structure, just those who know their immediate neighbors. In this phase, each node recognizes its neighbors and informs each neighbor of the others. With this data, each node has the information of whatever nodes are reachable through each of its neighbors. Specifically for GA approaches, the crossover operator receives two possible routes, searches for a common node between them, and divides them at this point by generating two new individuals from the combination of the four resulting parts of the division.

The mutation operator receives an individual and searches throughout its length for possible shorter paths between distant nodes, reducing the route's cost and avoiding loops on the network. Initial delay values for each edge in the network is defined as 5 s (it's an input necessary to SinalGo). The same delay values are used in all the simulations performed in this work. This range of values is based on the proportion between each edge's transmission and delay times in a network found in the literature [28]. The algorithms have been implemented in JAVA programming language in the SinalGo environment. Table 1 shows the empirical initialization parameters used in all optimization algorithms.

Each algorithm is applied to two distinct network scenarios, where message delivery and delay times, and total time results are accounted for. Statistical inference techniques are applied to analyze the obtained results. Techniques used are boxplot graphics and t-test student [29] (since the result's samples satisfy the normality assumptions). Boxplot is a graphical method to expose numeric data groups through its quartiles. A quartile is a point among the three points that divides a group of data into four sets with the same amount of elements, one-fourth of the total number of data elements.

The first quartile (Q1) is defined as the median number between the smallest number and the group median (disregarding outliers). The second quartile (Q2)

Table 1. Optimization parameter for the algorithms

Genetic algorithm		Simulates annealing	
Population size	30	Initial temperature T	1000.0
Crossover rate	0.9	Temperature reduction factor α	0.9
Mutation rate	0.02	Repetition schedule M_k	4
Number of generations	30	Maximum number of iterations max_{it}	100

is defined as the median, finally, the third quartile is defined as the median between the group median and the highest values (disregarding outliers) [29]. To perform the comparisons, inference tests, searching to identify the difference between the meta-heuristics used here, are applied. The response variable is the total routing time of the minimal path or, in other words, it is the sum of the time spent to fill out the routing tables of the nodes on the minimum path found.

5.1 Grid Network Topology – Simulation Results

Here we are evaluating the algorithms performance in solving the grid network topology, the 12×12 grid with 144 nodes – shown in the Fig. 3(a)). In a visual analysis of the samples of the algorithms, Fig. 4 shows the boxplot for this network. It is possible to notice that SA shows a small time to execute and find a route, as can be seen in Fig. 4(a) when compared to GA. This behavior happens because the SA builds and improves only one solution. At the same time, the GA has to manage and improve a population of solutions, allowing it to enhance those solutions further. When we analyze the total time (Fig. 4(b)) to construct a route and send a packet between origin and destination, it's noticeable that the GA finds and sends packets in a shorter average time.

Moreover, we see that the boxes in Fig. 4(b) do not overlap. This statistically indicates that the null hypothesis of equality of means is refuted. To guarantee this result, a t-student test was performed. The result indicated that with a p-value of 8E-08 the means of the algorithm are statistically different. Since SA builds a solution quickly, but has the disadvantage that it is slower to build routes when compared to GA, we decided to make a coupling between GA and SA (the SGA version). When evaluating time, it is observed that the SGA systematically stops before the GA once there is a stagnation of the final population (Fig. 4(c)). In addition, the average times obtained by the SGA were lower than the GA. This fact indicates that with adjustments to the algorithm parameters, the SGA tends to get better times (Fig. 4(c, d)).

5.2 Fully Randomized Network Topology – Simulation Results

This test case aims to demonstrate the algorithms' behavior on a reduced-scale worldwide network composed of small intra-AS computer networks. This topology can facilitate communication, the sharing of information, and much more

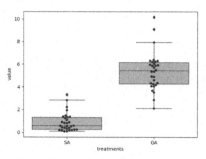

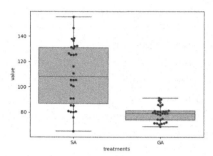

(a) Time for each algorithm execute and find a route.

(b) **Time for each algorithm execute, find a route and send a packet between origin and destination.**

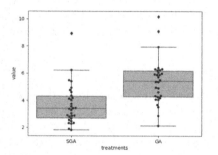

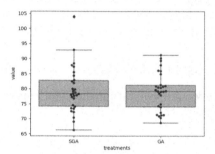

(c) Time for each algorithm execute and find a route.

(d) **Time for each algorithm execute, find a route and send a packet between origin and destination.**

Fig. 4. Grid network topology: boxplot analysis of results

between devices from around the world through connected routers. In this experiment, we are simulating a totally randomization network, composed of 144 network nodes (which exemplify routers). This network is shown in Fig. 3(b). We can observe that, in this more complex network, the results showed a similar behavior to the grid network. Figure 5(a) shows that SA needs less time in the execution and construction phase of an optimized route.

Note that here, the time is almost double compared to the grid network scenario. This is because the nodes are more dispersed and, in some cases, clustered. However, in the packet sending phase, it can be noted that GA has a slightly shorter time, as shown in Fig. 5(b). The boxes do not overlap, which indicates that the hypothesis of equality of means can also be refuted. A student t-test confirmed this statement, since the p-value found was 7E-04.

A non-overlapping boxes can be noted among the boxes in Fig. 5(c, d). Here the observed times indicate that the SGA finds an optimized route slightly faster than the GA (see the line that marks the median value in Fig. 5(c)). This is due

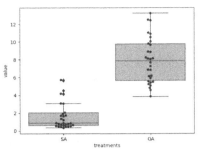

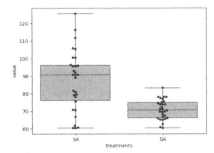

(a) Time for each algorithm execute and find a route.

(b) **Time for each algorithm execute, find** a route and send a packet between origin and destination.

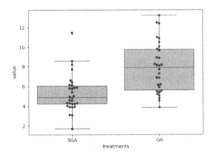

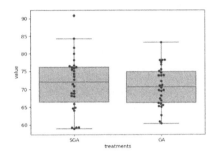

(c) Time for each algorithm execute and find a route.

(d) **Time for each algorithm execute, find** a route and send a packet between origin and destination.

Fig. 5. Fully randomized network topology

to the stagnation of the final population. However, no statistically significant difference was observed between the GA and SGA approaches. As future work we indicate a study of parameter setting for the coupled SGA technique. Possibly by adjusting the algorithm, the estimated time for building a route and sending packets from source to destination tends to be shorter.

6   Conclusion

The efficiency, simplicity, and robustness that link-state algorithms have performed over the last decades corroborate the use of these routing algorithms for IP packet traffic in backbone networks. This work has addressed the use of meta-heuristics to solve the problem of the minimal path in packet networks: the Genetic Algorithm with Dijkstra mutation, the Simulated Annealing technique, and coupled algorithm version based on the first two mentioned, using a new simple simulation model approach. These meta-heuristics were compared using two distinct case scenarios with 144 nodes in the network. The experiments indicated that SGA showed competitive results in the presented cases when compared to standard ones. This fact can be justified by the search acceleration in the optimization space done by the SA over the GA proposed. Another advantage is the use of the proposed mutation in GA, which employs the Dijkstra algorithm (link-state one) during the optimization process. The idea of conceiving and developing algorithms based on the evolutionary mixed link-state algorithms proved very plausible based on the data collected. This proposal of new mixed-algorithms can be a solution applicable to the actual demand in the context of processing packets in simulations of small intra-AS computer networks. In this work, we compared three metaheuristics in the framework SinalGo which proved to be a potent simulation tool. For future outlook, we highlight the experimentation with other goals, such as implementing different technics in SinalGo for comparison, maximizing the quality of service, minimizing weights in link-state routing algorithms, and experimenting with a multi-objective approach.

Acknowledgment. This project has received funding from the European Union's Horizon 2020 research and innovation programme under the Marie Skłodowska-Curie grant agreement No 754382. This research has also been partially supported by Comunidad de Madrid, PROMINT-CM project (grant ref: P2018/EMT-4366) and by the project PID2020-115454GB-C21 of the Spanish Ministry of Science and Innovation (MICINN). The authors thank UAH, UFRJ and CEFET-MG for the infrastructure, and Brazilian research agencies for partially support: CAPES (Finance Code 001), FAPERJ, FAPEMIG, and National Council for Scientific and Technological Development - CNPq. "The content of this publication does not reflect the official opinion of the European Union. Responsibility for the information and views expressed herein lies entirely with the author(s)."

References

1. Fazli, F., Mansubbassiri, M.: V-RPL: an effective routing algorithm for low power and lossy networks using multi-criteria decision-making techniques. Ad Hoc Netw. **132**, 102868 (2022)
2. Yao, Y., Cao, Q., Vasilakos, A.V.: EDAL: an energy-efficient, delay-aware, and lifetime-balancing data collection protocol for heterogeneous wireless sensor networks. IEEE/ACM Trans. Netw. **23**, 810–823 (2015)
3. Anwar, N., Deng, H.: Ant colony optimization based multicast routing algorithm for mobile ad hoc networks. IEEE Adva. Wirel. Opti. Commun. (RTUWO) **1**, 62–67 (2015)
4. Yadav, Rajiv, Indu, S.., Gupta, Daya: Review of evolutionary algorithms for energy efficient and secure wireless sensor networks. In: Khanna, Kavita, Estrela, Vania Vieira, Rodrigues, Joel José Puga Coelho. (eds.) Cyber Security and Digital Forensics. LNDECT, vol. 73, pp. 597–608. Springer, Singapore (2022). https://doi.org/10.1007/978-981-16-3961-6_49
5. Rovira-Sugranes, A., Razi, A., Afghah, F., Chakareski, J.: A review of AI-enabled routing protocols for UAV networks: trends, challenges, and future outlook. Ad Hoc Netw. **130**, 102790 (2022)

6. Lopez, A., Heisterkamp, D.R.: Simulated annealing based hierarchical Q-routing: a dynamic routing protocol. In: 2011 Eighth International Conference on Information Technology: New Generations, pp. 791–796 (2011)
7. Rovira-Sugranes, A., Afghah, F., Qu, J., Razi, A.: Fully-echoed Q-routing with simulated annealing inference for flying adhoc networks. IEEE Trans. Netw. Sci. Eng. **8**(3), 2223–2234 (2021)
8. Wang, H., Li, K., Pedrycz, W.: A routing algorithm based on simulated annealing algorithm for maximising wireless sensor networks lifetime with a sink node. Int. J. Bio-Inspir. Comput. **15**(4), 264–275 (2020)
9. Zhao, L., Saldin, A., Hu, J., Fu, L., Shi, J., Guan, Y.: A novel simulated annealing based routing algorithm in F-SDNs. In: IEEE INFOCOM 2020 - IEEE Conference on Computer Communications Workshops (INFOCOM WKSHPS), pp. 1202–1207 (2020)
10. Raj, J.S., Rahimunnisa, K.: Hybridized genetic-simulated annealing algorithm for performance optimization in wireless ad-hoc network. J. Soft Comput. Paradig. **1**(3), 1–13 (2019)
11. Sundar, R., Kathirvel, A.: Aggressively delivered mechanism over variable length density using a simulated annealing algorithm in mobile ad hoc network. Trans. Emerg. Telecommun. Technol. **31**(12), e3863 (2020)
12. Prasad, A.Y., Rayanki, B.: A generic algorithmic protocol approaches to improve network life time and energy efficient using combined genetic algorithm with simulated annealing in manet. Int. J. Intell. Unmanned Syst. **8**(3), 23–42 (2020)
13. Hamed, A.: A genetic algorithm for finding the k shortest paths in a network. Egypt. Inform. J. **11**, 75–79 (2010)
14. Zhang, L., Cai, L., Li, M., Wang, F.: A method for least-cost QoS multicast routing based on genetic simulated annealing algorithm. Comput. Commun. **32**, 105–110 (2009)
15. Younes, A.: Multicast routing with bandwidth and delay constraints based on genetic algorithms. Egypt. Inform. J. **312**, 107–114 (2011)
16. Bhardwaj, A., El-Ocla, H.: Multipath routing protocol using genetic algorithm in mobile ad hoc networks. IEEE Access **8**, 177534–177548 (2020)
17. Wang, C., Liu, X., Hu, H., Han, Y., Yao, M.: Energy-efficient and load-balanced clustering routing protocol for wireless sensor networks using a chaotic genetic algorithm. IEEE Access **8**, 158082–158096 (2020)
18. Muruganantham, N., El-Ocla, H.: Routing using genetic algorithm in a wireless sensor network. Wirel. Pers. Commun. **111**, 2703–2732 (2020)
19. Singh, M., Amin, S., Choudhary, A.: Genetic algorithm based sink mobility for energy efficient data routing in wireless sensor networks. AEU Int. J. Electron. Commun. **131**, 1–10 (2020)
20. Heidari, E., Movaghar, A., Motameni, H., Barzegar, B.: A novel approach for clustering and routing in WSN using genetic algorithm and equilibrium optimizer. Int. J. Commun. Syst., e5148 (2022)
21. Chu-hang, L., Xiao-li, W., You-jia, H., Huang-shui, H., Sha-sha, W.: An improved genetic algorithm based annulus-sector clustering routing protocol for wireless sensor networks. Wirel. Pers. Commun **123**, 3623–3644 (2022)
22. Dijkstra, E.W.: A note on two problems in connexion with graphs. Numer. Math. **1**, 269–271 (1959)
23. Chen, H., Sun, B.: Multicast routing optimization algorithm with bandwidth and delay constraints based on GA. J. Commun. Comput. **2**, 63–67 (2005)

24. Sorensen, K., Glover, F.W.: Metaheuristics. In: Gass, S.I., Fu, M.C. (eds.) Encyclopedia of Operations Research and Management Science, vol. 1, pp. 960–970. Springer, Boston (2013). https://doi.org/10.1007/978-1-4419-1153-7_1167

25. Stockt, S., Engelbrecht, A.: Analysis of selection hyper-heuristics for population-based meta-heuristics in real-valued dynamic optimization. Swarm Evol. Comput. **43**, 127–146 (2018)

26. Nikolaev, A., Jacobson, S.: Simulated annealing. In: Gendreau, M., Potvin, J.Y. (eds.) Handbook of Metaheuristics, pp. 1–39. Springer, Boston (2010). https://doi.org/10.1007/978-1-4419-1665-5_1

27. Goldberg, D.E.: The compact genetic algorithm. IEEE Trans. Evol. Comput. **3**, 287–297 (1999)

28. Kumar, R., Kumar, M.: Exploring genetic algorithm for shortest path optimization in data networks. Global J. Comput. Sci. Technol. **10**, 1–5 (2010)

29. Montgomery, D., Runger, G.: Applied statistics and probability for engineers. LTC (2009)

Long-Term Person Reidentification: Challenges and Outlook

Anderson Manhães[1] , Gabriel Matos[1] , Douglas O. Cardoso[2] ,
Milena F. Pinto[1] , Jeferson Colares[1], Paulo Leitão[4] , Diego Brandão[1,3] ,
and Diego Haddad[1(✉)]

[1] Celso Suckow da Fonseca Federal Center of Technological Education,
Rio de Janeiro, Brazil
{anderson.manhaes,jeferson.paula}@aluno.cefet-rj.br,
{gabriel.araujo,milena.pinto,diego.brandao,diego.haddad}@cefet-rj.br
[2] Smart Cities Research Center, Polytechnic Institute of Tomar, Tomar, Portugal
douglas.cardoso@ipt.pt
[3] Research Centre in Digitalization and Intelligent Robotics,
Polytechnic Institute of Bragança, Bragança, Portugal
[4] Research Center in Digitalization and Intelligent Robotics (CeDRI),
Instituto Politécnico de Bragança, Campus de Santa Apolónia,
5300-253 Bragança, Portugal
pleitao@ipb.pt

Abstract. Person reidentification, i.e., retrieving a person of interest
across several non-overlapping cameras, is a task that is far from trivial.
Despite its great commercial value and wide range of applications (e.g.,
surveillance, intelligent environments, forensics, service robotics, marketing), it remains unsolved, even when the individuals do not change
clothes during the recognition period. This paper provides an outlook
on long-term person reidentification, an emerging research topic regarding when consecutive acquisitions of an individual can be found apart
for days or even months, making such a task even more challenging. A
long-term reidentification system using face recognition is presented to
emphasize current techniques' limitations.

Keywords: Long-term person ReID · Deep learning · Computer
vision · Multimodal retrieval

1 Introduction

The reidentification of people consists in using images of different individuals
taken by multiple cameras with non-overlapping fields of view, such as those used
for video surveillance, to infer whether the people in these images are the same or
not [1]. It is a complex problem given that images compared by different cameras
often show large differences in lighting, capture angle, optical characteristics of
the lenses used, partial occlusion, self-occlusion, confusing backgrounds, and
other complicating factors. The reidentification was listed, in a recent report by

A. I. Pereira et al. (Eds.): OL2A 2022, CCIS 1754, pp. 357–372, 2022.
https://doi.org/10.1007/978-3-031-23236-7_25

Institute for Scientific Information (which belongs to the same conglomerate as Clarivate Analytics and Web of Science) as a "frontier of science" [45].

Long-term reidentification (ReID-LP), which is the focus of this paper, is characterized by the occurrence of an interval between image captures that is longer than that which characterizes short-term ReID [18]. It is an interval of no specific duration (although it is commonly longer than a day) in which the observed person may have changed clothes or accessories, or undergone through other changes in appearance: for example, the adoption of a new haircut or beard. Another important example, in the context of a pandemic such as COVID-19, is a breathing mask. Longer intervals between image captures pose an additional challenge, as clothing colors and textures are widely used features for reidentification but are not as effective as for shorter intervals [56].

From a computational point of view and in a nutshell, the ReID problem consists of comparing the image of a given person with images of other people stored in a gallery. In this comparison, a score is assigned to each person in the gallery. This score corresponds to the degree of the associativity of the query image with the people whose images were known *a priori*. The identification of the person in the query image becomes the association to the individual with the highest score or the indication of the k best placed in the score ranking. This process is widely used in multi-class classification problems [8, 17].

This paper presents an overview of this rich research topic, highlighting the challenges and prospects. Each of the remaining sections contributes to this end, which is briefly described below. Section 2 provides more details about the challenge at hand and the strategies considered to be state of the art for addressing it. A review of the most important datasets used by the scientific community in this context is provided in Sect. 3. Section 4 indicates seminal works in the area, being suggested starting points for the following contributions to be developed. Section 5 deals specifically with the use of facial data in people reidentification, which puts into perspective the relevance of this type of feature for this task. Finally, Sect. 6 presents some final considerations.

2   The Long-Term Reidentification Problem

Although the topic of people reidentification has been attracting more and more attention, there are few papers dealing specifically with the topic of long-term ReID, possibly due to the very difficult nature of the problem. At the same time, reidentifying people is a typical task in computer vision, which is intended to make sense of images obtained from cameras. The long-term reidentification does not belong necessarily to this area. After all, the features best suited for this task may be more related to the biometrics area, which may use other types of sensors to capture them. In general, reidentification techniques can be categorized between those that focus on representation (i.e., obtaining features that best distinguish people in images) [15]; on learning distance metrics and developing new algorithms to compare a reference image with those in a gallery [25, 26, 29]; or those that address both at the same time [30].

Even in surveys long-term reidentification is still barely mentioned [4,25,39, 51]. Despite this, it is possible to find some works that look for solutions that can be applied to solving this problem using computer vision and specialized devices: for example, previously [34] it was used low-cost 3D cameras to obtain depth data which were used to create a three-dimensional representation of the gait of individuals. Although the tests aimed to reidentify people in the short term, the technique used seems promising for long-term ReID, since it focuses on features maintained over long periods. Several other works have explored using RGB-D cameras, which capture color and depth in reidentifying people, but this technology has been most successful when applied to identifying actions in videos [7,16,18,35].

A recent paper [57] addressed long-term reidentification by learning a hybrid representation of features through a network called SpTSkM, which incorporates a spatio-temporal flow and another one related to skeleton motion. While the later operates on 3D skeletons normalized through convolutional graph networks, the former operates directly on sequences of images, aiming at learning identity patterns related to the geometric structure of the body and its motion.

A distributed person reidentification framework was introduced in the literature [33], which incorporates the information brought by the network topology and the structure of the environment. This information can be exploited to improve the reidentification process. In this case, the trajectories of the various individuals in the area under monitoring generate different degrees of correlation between pairs of cameras. The different degrees of correlation can be used to improve the accuracy of ReID techniques. Although the article does not specifically address long-term ReID, the strategy is extensible to this setting.

3 Datasets

One of the main barriers to research on long-term ReID is the lack of proper datasets. Some of the few existing datasets have a minimal amount of labeled examples. To be useful for long-term ReID training, the dataset must contain images captured on various occasions so that individuals are wearing different clothes and accessories, and possibly even different haircuts and beard styles. In a past work [3] researchers chose to create a synthetic dataset for training, the SOMAset, and the developed model obtained expressive performance when tested with other popular datasets. Another original way around this problem was adopted previously [14], so that it was selected from a popular dataset only the images of people wearing all-black clothing. In this way, the neural network was forced to find discriminating features of each individual that did not include the colors of the clothes. This approach is very similar to using silhouettes and gait energy images, which carry no color information, to feed to the learning model.

Obtaining a solution for long-term ReID is facilitated by incorporating specific datasets for this task. Several datasets available for training and evaluating person ReID models. For our purposes, which are to re-identify people in images generated by different cameras at different times, it must contain:

- video sequences, taken by multiple cameras;
- multiple clothing per individual;
- same individuals filmed on multiple occasions.

Among the main public domain datasets for ReID, those that best satisfy such conditions are those described in Table 1. Since we do not intend to exhaust all datasets with the desired characteristics here, those not available for research have been excluded. Such unavailability may occur for various reasons: for example, the restriction can be due to confidentiality reasons [41].

Table 1. Main datasets for ReID of people in the public domain, with the respective quantities of people (P), sequences (S), and cameras (C), as well as the availability of data of the same individuals in more than one outfit (R) or in different occasions (O).

Dataset	P	S	C	R	O
PRID2011 [19]	200	400	2	No	No
iLIDS-VID [50]	300	600	2	No	No
Airport [25]	9651	N.A.	6	No	No
RPIField [59]	112	6577	12	No	No
TUM GAID [21]	305	3370	1	Yes	Yes

The dataset PRID2011 [19] is composed of images of individuals performing a trajectory filmed by two different static surveillance cameras, A and B. It observes significant camera characteristics, viewpoints, backgrounds, and lighting changes. About 385 people appear in the footage from Camera A and 749 people in the footage from Camera B. The first 200 people appear in both cameras. The dataset can be used in two versions: in the multi-shot version, a collection of images is taken while the individual executes a given trajectory, and the amount of images depends on the path executed and the speed of the individual, with the minimum amount of images per view being five images; on the other hand, in the single-shot version, only one image per individual is randomly selected and provided. The dimensions in pixels of all images are 128×64. Some examples of these are shown in Fig. 1.

A seminal paper [50] presented the dataset iLIDS-VID, which has similar features to PRID2011. It consists of images of 300 individuals taken by two cameras with different viewpoints. In this case, no individuals appear in only one of the views. However, it is also possible to notice changes in camera characteristics, background, illumination, blurred background, and occlusions. iLIDS-VID also features the multi-shot and single-shot versions. The multi-shot version presents a sequence of images of a person as they develop a trajectory in the camera's vision field. By observing each individual's trajectory and speed, the sequences vary in size from 23 to 193 images, with a rounded average size of 73. The single-shot version contains only one image per individual per view, randomly selected

Fig. 1. Examples of the multi-shot set of the dataset PRID2011. Each row contains a different view of the same individual

Fig. 2. Examples of the multi-shot set of the dataset iLIDS-VID. Each row contains a different view of the same individual

from the corresponding sequence. Once again, the dimensions in pixels of all images are 128 × 64. Some examples of these are shown in Fig. 2 as well.

The dataset Airport [25] was acquired through 6 cameras covering a central security checkpoint. Each camera has a resolution of 768 × 432 pixels at 30 fps. The bounding boxes on people were automatically generated employing the Aggregated Channel Features (ACF) [10] people detector, together with the Feature from Accelerated Segment Test (Fast) [37] corner detector and the Kanade-Lucas Tomasi (KLT) [32,43,48] tracker to track people. It generated 39,902 images from 9,651 people, an average of 3.13 images per person. It is worth noting that 1,382 people appear on at least two cameras. At Airport, the size of the images extracted from the bouding boxes is variable, ranging from 130 × 54 to 403 × 166 pixels. As with the other datasets, Airport also exhibits great variation in the background, lighting, pose, and occlusions. Examples from this dataset appear in Fig. 3.

Fig. 3. Examples of the dataset Airport

Past research introduced RPIField [59], a multi-shot dataset acquired with the aid of 12 synchronized surveillance cameras with 1440×1080 pixels resolution, situated on six poles spread in an outdoor area at the campus of the Rensselaer Polytechnic Institute. Therefore it is possible to observe a background containing mostly grass (green). Since each post is a control point, 112 unique paths were established, passing through these 6 points. Each of 112 individuals was responsible for executing one of these paths. The dataset also contains images of distractors or unknown pedestrians. The dataset contains 601,582 images of 3,996 distractors and 112 known actors that reappear 802 times. All these images were organized into 6,577 sequences. The bounding box of each image was automatically generated with the help of ACF. A proprietary heuristic was adopted to track the bounding boxes of the same individual. Each new box is compared to the boxes found in the previous 90 frames. The one with the largest Intersection over Union (IoU) was grouped and associated with the same individual. A new label is created if the largest IoU is less than 0.4. Trajectory errors and false positives were manually corrected. Figure 4 displays some of these images.

The dataset TUM GAID [21] was acquired with a Microsoft Kinect. Therefore, it contains some modalities: *i*) RGB image sequences with resolution 640 × 480 pixels at 30 fps; *ii*) depth sequences with resolution 640 × 480 pixels at 30 fps; *iii*) 4-channel audio sampled with 24 bits at 16 kHz. In addition, the dataset also contains RGB and depth sequences with people tracked and cropped. The sequences consist of a person walking in a corridor near the same wall. Therefore they all have the same background. The recordings were made in two sections, separated by months. The first contains 176 individuals, and the second contains 161. A subset of 32 individuals participated in both sections, so the set contains 305 individuals. The 3370 sequences have the following variations: *i*) normal walking (individuals normally walk three times to the right and three times to the left); *ii*) individuals wear a backpack, walking once to the right and once to the left; *iii*) individuals cover their shoes, walking once to the right and once to the left. Of the datasets described, this is the only one that

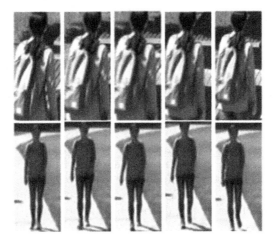

Fig. 4. Examples of the dataset RPIField of the same individual. Each row contains an image from a different camera.

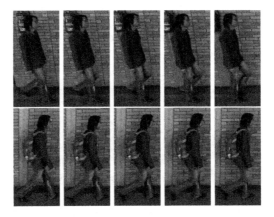

Fig. 5. Examples of the dataset TUM GAID. Each line contains a different appearance of the same individual with change of accessory

features controlled variations in clothing. Examples of this collection are shown in Fig. 5.

4   Related Works

4.1   Face Recognition

Taking advantage of the fact that the human face contains rich biometric information [53], face recognition consists of comparing an input image containing a face with other images of faces stored in a gallery and identifying which images in the gallery correspond to the same individual as the input image [31]. In general, the process is divided into three steps: face detection and extraction, feature extraction and recognition (classification). Generally, recognition compares the extracted features with a previously obtained reference [24]. The face recognition technique has attracted considerable attention in the computer vision community due to the increasing demand for biometric applications [38], particularly for avoiding the violation of traditional security systems such as passwords [36].

Detection. Before the face recognition activity can be performed, it is necessary to locate the position of the face in the image. In other words, a bounding box must be constructed that delimits the image region where the face to be recognized is supposed to be located. An example of a bounding box is shown in Fig. 6. The area of the image defined by the bounding box is then stored for further processing; the rest of the image is usually discarded. Such bounding is known as face detection [54]. Several neural network models specialize in detecting different types of objects, animals, and plants. In the specific case of face detection, the most widely spread model, for its computational efficiency and performance, is known as "Viola-Jones" [49]. This model, as well as most of its similar ones, is quite efficient in detecting faces in frontal position. However, for this work, the detection model must detect faces at various angles; in other words, it must be pose-invariant.

Fig. 6. Example of delimiting the image area containing the face using a bounding box.

Alignment. After detecting and storing the face, an alignment processing of the face is performed. Alignment can significantly improve the efficiency of many automatic video processing systems, including those for person re-identification [2]. Since many feature extraction methods are not pose invariant, alignment can help obtain more clustered features in the attribute space making identification easier. In alignment, the image of a face is moved and deformed to fit a reference pose (usually frontal) [60]. This alignment often demands detecting key points or fiducial points (landmark-points). Figure 6 contains examples of such key points, which can be the eyes, corners of the eyebrows, mouth, and nose tip, among others. This alignment is one of the most researched topics in computer vision in the last few decades [20]. Initially, the alignment techniques were based on pictorial structures (e.g., eye center detection using Gaussian filters). Later, more sophisticated extensions are capable of modeling significant changes in appearance. Finally, there was a convergence toward the adoption of cascaded regression methods [20] and convolutional neural networks [44].

It is interesting to note that, being sighted on different days, the individual under analysis may be nearer or farther from the camera. For this reason, during processing, when the areas of the images containing the detected faces are resized to the standard input size of the network, this will result in images with different resolutions representing the same individual. Thus, the ability to detect and recognize faces in images with multiple resolutions (multi-resolution) is very relevant for the overall good performance of the model.

Feature Extraction. In the feature extraction step, a machine learning algorithm learns which photo features are the most relevant for identifying the person [46]. During recognition, the extraction of features consists of mapping the pattern of interest from the pixel domain into another space, of possibly different dimensions, in which classification is more straightforward than other operations. A neural network for image classification can be trained with a sufficient amount of samples and, from these, learn to automatically extract the relevant features to recognize objects or animals with high accuracy, as demonstrated in [27].

It was observed that the initial layers of a neural network, after training, become feature extractors [28], which means that using these networks for image recognition can dispense with the need to manually develop these extractors through *a priori* knowledge. Besides being easier to implement, automatic feature extraction with neural networks is not infrequently more efficient than manual methods [42].

Classification. Classification is the final step in the face recognition process, where the comparison with the images in the gallery takes place, which is recognition proper. The topic of person reidentification not infrequently (though not only) refers to face recognition since a person's face is a non-volatile feature. However, for the application proposed in this work, it is necessary to take into account that the images are obtained using ordinary surveillance cameras, and for this reason, we have:

- Images of faces obtained from ordinary surveillance cameras, usually positioned at a distance, in non-controlled conditions (in the wild);
- Face images with low sharpness and in a reduced size;
- Great variance in lighting conditions and image capture angle;
- Long interval between two image captures, to the point that the person to be recognized has changed appearance or aged.

At first glance, the face recognition technology does not appear well suited to this type of application, as scenarios without acquisition control are challenging [22,52]. Furthermore, perspective changes are one of the main factors reducing the performance of face recognition algorithms [58]. However, studies show that images as small as 30 pixels can be used to obtain various biometric information about the analyzed individual, such as gender, age, or ethnicity [6]. Therefore, this paper advocates face recognition as an auxiliary technique for long-term person recognition while respecting its limitations. One of these limitations is that most image recognition techniques are optimized for faces present in images and not in videos. When videos are used, blurring and loss of focus problems can occur. Furthermore, a significant part of the work, when contemplating some variation (such as pose or illumination) to which faces may be subjected, focuses on a particular variation and assumes the absence of the others in a "divide and conquer" strategy that hampers the design of a robust and generic classifier [12].

As mentioned earlier, using a convolutional neural network for face recognition eliminates the need to manually develop the feature extractors since the initial layers of the network will learn to perform this task during the training stage. However, for this very reason, the final performance of the network depends on the database used for its training. A data set with slight variation will not be sufficient for a neural net to generalize well. It is therefore critical to train the net using a good data set or even train it using more than one dataset.

In the context of this paper, where we will be using neural networks in the process, the model used for face detection must be trained on a dataset that contains images of people captured from multiple angles. We want the network to acquire sufficient generalization ability to be later employed in long-term person recognition.

4.2 Long-Term Person Recognition

While short-term recognition is extensively researched, the challenge becomes even more significant due to the variations in person characteristics over an interval of time when it comes to recognition over a long-term interval. Among such variations are clothing (as described in [23]), accessories such as backpacks, bags, hats, and caps, and changing features such as wearing a beard, mustache, or short or long hair.

In order to address long-term person recognition, the work [23] was found, which looks at the challenge of variation in each person's attire and presents a new dataset called Celebrities-reID. In that dataset, each person never repeats the same outfit on different occasions. In [18] anthropometric biometrics is used to improve feature selection based on a statistical analysis of body measurements in a large-scale database. They also introduced a new anthropometric signature. The work [56] describes the hypothesis that people have consistent motion patterns under distraction-free walking conditions. They are based on natural motion cues from videos called Fine motion encoding (FITD), and in [7], 3D camera information was used to capture biometric cues such as face and body length to improve long-term reidentification. The following section describes how face recognition can be used for reidentification purposes.

5   Long Term Identification Using Faces

5.1   Face Detection

In the proposed solution, the first processing step consists of detecting in each frame of each sequence the region where the individual's face is located. In this step, the proposed system will build bounding boxes to delimit the region of interest. Although this is the most widely adopted procedure in the literature, some alternative methods are sometimes used, such as stripes that span the entire horizontal dimension [5] and the adoption of a regular grid, from which color and texture features is extracted from overlapping blocks [26]. However, such techniques also require segmentation procedures for obtaining a mask that separates the individual's region from the background region [47]. The segmentation procedure can use spatial and temporal information to obtain robust performance, in the case of video signals [13].

To perform the procedure of determining the bounding boxes, the MTCNN neural network model [55], pre-trained with the dataset VGGFace2, is used. This model can analyze the dataset images and detect people's faces, even if they are not looking directly at the camera.

The MTCNN can not only locate the parts of the image that contain faces, but it can also obtain the position of specific face landmarks (facial landmarks), for example, eyes, nose tip, and corners of the mouth. The structure of the MTCNN is composed of 3 networks: P-Net, R-Net, and O-Net. The first one processes the entire image and proposes several candidate kiibounding boxes quickly. The second one refines the output of the previous network, discarding the proposed bounding boxes that do not contain faces. Finally, the third network refines the result and determines the position of the final bounding boxes and the facial landmarks.

No additional training or modification was performed to fit the MTCNN model to the scope of this work. Still, it is expected to obtain a good generalization capability thanks to the many examples available in VGGFace2.

With the coordinates obtained by MTCNN, the part of the original image containing the face of the person is cut out so that the expected output of this module is a new image containing only the face of the person. A new file is created for each original image provided with the segmented face, according to Fig. 7.

5.2   Face Feature Extraction

The detection component has the sole objective of obtaining the part of the original image that contains the face. This second component has more complex assignments since the neural network model used in this step needs to receive the faces' images and learn the characteristics that allow it to differentiate one individual from another. At this stage, the goal is to have the neural network intuitively learn a metric that brings together faces with the same label, i.e.,

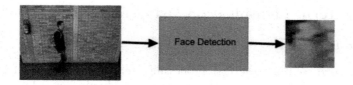

Fig. 7. Example input and output of the face detection module.

belonging to the same person, and pushes away those belonging to different individuals.

It is necessary to train the models as a classifier for face recognition to evaluate their ability to extract relevant features. Given an image of a face, the model needs to probabilistically evaluate whether that face corresponds to one of the people previously stored in a gallery. The accuracy of this classification determines the quality of the model. To use the model in the desired application, the layers of the neural network used to make this classification are removed so that it works as an extractor of features. The dataset used is a crucially important element for the project's success, as it must contain enough samples of each feature that the neural network needs to learn to distinguish. For example, for long-term ReID, the dataset needs to contain samples of the same person wearing different clothes.

Once trained, this neural network model, already without the classification layer, will receive as input the image of a person's face and produce a vector containing features that individualize it. This vector is used later as input for the long-term task of re-identifying people. In other words, we have an extractor and encoder (encoder) of facial features.

The convolutional neural network model selected to perform the activities described above was FaceNet [40], pre-trained with the VGGFace2 [9] dataset. The number of classes in the last fully connected layer of the model was modified to reflect the 305 classes in the dataset TUM GAID. The fully connected layer was retrained using the dataset TUM GAID.

According to the Inception architecture, the FaceNet model implements a Resnet residual network with parallel convolution layers. For this work, a Resnet-50 was used, adapted from [11]. The training of the last FaceNet layer took place over 20 epochs, with partial accuracies measured at each epoch, shown in Fig. 8.

After obtaining satisfactory classification results, the adapted model was used as a features extractor to produce vectors representing each of the identities in the dataset. In summary, this step of the proposed model receives the various faces extracted from each of the frames in the dataset TUM GAID and generates, for each face, a corresponding 512-byte vector. At the end of the whole process, the accuracy achieved in the test set was 96.66%, in rank-1. This result should not be seen with excessive optimism since the database was obtained in a very controlled way, which unfortunately does not occur in practice.

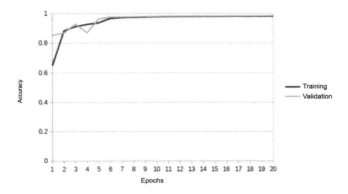

Fig. 8. Data from training the FaceNet network for face recognition on the TUM GAID dataset. On the horizontal axis, the epochs. On the vertical axis, the accuracy (rank-1).

6   Final Remarks

Presenting an overview of long-term re-identification is a non-trivial task since it is a problem whose solution is far from what is currently obtained by state-of-the-art. Given the practical potential of this type of task, this paper presents some techniques and databases about it. The results obtained through a system based purely on facial recognition were presented as a proof of concept to illustrate the limitations faced by designers of such a solution. From this survey, it is possible to list some future work considered promising: the creation of new data sets for ReID-LP, meeting the various specific requirements of these; better use of data fusion techniques, leading to combinations such as facial and walking characteristics (gait), thus providing greater accuracy and robustness of solutions to the problem considered.

Acknowledgements. This work has been financially supported by national grant from the FCT (Fundação para a Ciência e a Tecnologia), under the project UIDB/05567/2020. Diego Haddad would like to thank the Brazillian organization National Council for Scientific and Technological Development (CNPq) for its financial support.

References

1. Baabou, S., et al.: A study of person re-identification system. Am. J. Eng. Rese. (AJER) **7**, 210–218 (2018)
2. Bansal, A., et al.: The do's and don'ts for CNN-based face verification. In: Proceedings of IEEE International Conference on Computer Vision Workshops (2017)
3. Barbosa, I.B., et al.: Looking beyond appearances: synthetic training data for deep CNNs in re-identification. Comput. Vis. Image Understand. **167**, 50–62 (2018)
4. Bedagkar-Gala, A., Shah, S.K.: A survey of approaches and trends in person re-identification. Image Vis. Comput. **32**, 270–286 (2014)

5. Bird, N.D., et al.: Detection of loitering individuals in public transportation areas. IEEE Trans. Intell. Transp. Syst. **6**, 167–177 (2005)
6. Bobeldyk, D., Ross, A.: Predicting soft biometric attributes from 30 pixels: a case study in NIR ocular images. In: IEEE Winter Applications of Computer Vision Workshops (2019)
7. Bondi, E., Pala, P., Seidenari, L., Berretti, S., Del Bimbo, A.: Long term person re-identification from depth cameras using facial and skeleton data. In: Wannous, H., Pala, P., Daoudi, M., Flórez-Revuelta, F. (eds.) UHA3DS 2016. LNCS, vol. 10188, pp. 29–41. Springer, Cham (2018). https://doi.org/10.1007/978-3-319-91863-1_3
8. Bucak, S.S., et al.: Efficient multi-label ranking for multi-class learning: Application to object recognition. In: IEEE International Conference on Computer Vision (2009)
9. Cao, Q., et al.: VGGFace2: a dataset for recognising faces across pose and age. In: Proceedings of 13th IEEE International Conference on Automatic Face and Gesture Recognition (2018)
10. Dollár, P., et al.: Fast feature pyramids for object detection. IEEE Trans. Pattern Anal. Mach. Intell. **36**, 1532–1545 (2014)
11. Esler, T.: Face recognition using PyTorch (2020)
12. Geng, X., et al.: Individual stable space: an approach to face recognition under uncontrolled conditions. IEEE Trans. Neural Netw. **19**, 1354–1368 (2008)
13. Gheissari, N., et al.: Person reidentification using spatiotemporal appearance. In: IEEE Computer Society Conference on Computer Vision and Pattern Recognition (2006)
14. Gou, M., et al.: Person re-identification in appearance impaired scenarios. In: Proceedings of the British Machine Vision Conference 2016 (2016)
15. Gray, D., Tao, H.: Viewpoint invariant pedestrian recognition with an ensemble of localized features. In: Forsyth, D., Torr, P., Zisserman, A. (eds.) ECCV 2008. LNCS, vol. 5302, pp. 262–275. Springer, Heidelberg (2008). https://doi.org/10.1007/978-3-540-88682-2_21
16. Han, F., et al.: Space-time representation of people based on 3D skeletal data: a review. Comput. Vis. Image Underst. **158**, 85–105 (2017)
17. Har-Peled, S., et al.: Constraint classification for multiclass classification and ranking. In: Advances in Neural Information Processing Systems (2002)
18. Hasan, M., Babaguchi, N.: Long-term people reidentification using anthropometric signature. In: IEEE 8th International Conference on Biometrics Theory, Applications and Systems (BTAS) (2016)
19. Hirzer, M., Beleznai, C., Roth, P.M., Bischof, H.: Person re-identification by descriptive and discriminative classification. In: Heyden, A., Kahl, F. (eds.) SCIA 2011. LNCS, vol. 6688, pp. 91–102. Springer, Heidelberg (2011). https://doi.org/10.1007/978-3-642-21227-7_9
20. Hoang, V.T., et al.: 3-D facial landmarks detection for intelligent video systems. IEEE Trans. Ind. Inform. **17**, 578–586 (2021)
21. Hofmann, M., et al.: The TUM Gait from Audio, Image and Depth (GAID) database: multimodal recognition of subjects and traits. J. Vis. Commun. Image Represent. **25**, 195–206 (2014)
22. Hu, C.H., et al.: Face illumination recovery for the deep learning feature under severe illumination variations. Pattern Recogn. **111**, 107724 (2021)
23. Huang, Y., et al.: Celebrities-ReID: a benchmark for clothes variation in long-term person re-identification. In: Proceedings of the International Joint Conference on Neural Networks (2019)

24. Jayaraman, U., et al.: Recent development in face recognition. Neurocomputing **408**, 231–245 (2020)
25. Karanam, S.: A systematic evaluation and benchmark for person re-identification: features, metrics, and datasets. IEEE Trans. Pattern Anal. Mach. Intell. **41**, 523–536 (2019)
26. Köstinger, M., et al.: Large scale metric learning from equivalence constraints. In: IEEE Conference on Computer Vision and Pattern Recognition (2012)
27. Krizhevsky, A., et al.: ImageNet classification with deep convolutional neural networks. In: Advances in Neural Information Processing Systems (2012)
28. LeCun, Y., Bengio, Y.: Convolutional networks for images, speech, and time-series. In: Handbook of Brain Theory and Neural Networks (1998)
29. Li, W., Wang, X.: Locally Aligned Feature Transforms across Views. In: IEEE Conference on Computer Vision and Pattern Recognition (2013)
30. Liu, Z., et al.: Person reidentification by joint local distance metric and feature transformation. IEEE Trans. Neural Netw. Learn. Syst. **30**, 2999–3009 (2019)
31. Lu, J., et al.: Learning compact binary face descriptor for face recognition. IEEE Trans. Pattern Anal. Mach. Intell. **37**, 2041–2056 (2015)
32. Lucas, B.D., Kanade, T.: An iterative image registration technique with an application to stereo vision. In: Proceedings of the 7th International Joint Conference on Artificial Intelligence (1981)
33. Martinel, N., et al.: Person reidentification in a distributed camera network framework. IEEE Trans. Cybern. **47**, 3530–3541 (2017)
34. Munaro, M., et al.: 3D reconstruction of freely moving persons for re-identification with a depth sensor. In: 2014 IEEE International Conference on Robotics and Automation (ICRA) (2014)
35. Pala, P., et al.: Enhanced skeleton and face 3D data for person re-identification from depth cameras. Comput. Graph. **79**, 69–80 (2019)
36. Plichoski, G.F., et al.: A face recognition framework based on a pool of techniques and differential evolution. Inf. Sci. **543**, 219–224 (2021)
37. Rosten, E., Drummond, T.: Machine learning for high-speed corner detection. In: Leonardis, A., Bischof, H., Pinz, A. (eds.) ECCV 2006. LNCS, vol. 3951, pp. 430–443. Springer, Heidelberg (2006). https://doi.org/10.1007/11744023_34
38. Sang, X., et al.: Nonconvex regularizer and latent pattern based robust regression for face recognition. Inf. Sci. **547**, 384–403 (2021)
39. Satta, R.: Appearance descriptors for person re-identification: a comprehensive review. arXIv (2013)
40. Schroff, F., et al.: FaceNet: a unified embedding for face recognition and clustering. In: IEEE Conference on Computer Vision and Pattern Recognition (2015)
41. Schumann, A., Monari, E.: A soft-biometrics dataset for person tracking and re-identification. 11th IEEE International Conference on Advanced Video and Signal-Based Surveillance (2014)
42. Seide, F., et al.: Feature engineering in Context-Dependent Deep Neural Networks for conversational speech transcription. In: IEEE Workshop on Automatic Speech Recognition and Understanding (2011)
43. Shi, J., Tomasi, C.: Good features to track. In: IEEE Conference on Computer Vision and Pattern Recognition (1994)
44. Sun, Y., et al.: Deep convolutional network cascade for facial point detection. In: Proceedings of the IEEE Computer Society Conference on Computer Vision and Pattern Recognition (2013)
45. Szomszor, M., et al.: Identifying research fronts in the web of science: from metrics to meaning. Technical report, Institute for Scientific Information (2020)

46. Taghipour-Gorjikolaie, M., et al.: Deep adaptive feature enrichment. Expert Syst. Appl. **162**, 113780 (2020)
47. Tao, D., et al.: Person reidentification by minimum classification error-based KISS metric learning. IEEE Trans. Cybern. **45**, 242–252 (2015)
48. Tomasi, C., Kanade, T.: Detection and tracking of point features. Technical report, International Journal of Computer Vision (1991)
49. Viola, P., Jones, M.J.: Robust real-time face detection. Int. J. Comput. Vis. **57**, 137–154 (2004)
50. Wang, T., et al.: Person re-identification by video ranking (2014)
51. Wu, D., et al.: Deep learning-based methods for person re-identification: a comprehensive review. Neurocomputing **337**, 354–371 (2019)
52. Wu, F., et al.: Spectrum-aware discriminative deep feature learning for multi-spectral face recognition. Pattern Recogn. **111**, 107632 (2021)
53. Yan, H., Song, C.: Multi-scale deep relational reasoning for facial kinship verification. Pattern Recogn. **110**, 107541 (2021)
54. Zafeiriou, S., et al.: A survey on face detection in the wild: past, present and future. Comput. Vis. Image Underst. **138**, 1–24 (2015)
55. Zhang, K., et al.: Joint face detection and alignment using multitask cascaded convolutional networks. IEEE Signal Process. Lett. **23**, 1499–1503 (2016)
56. Zhang, P., et al.: Long-term person re-identification using true motion from videos. In: IEEE Winter Conference on Applications of Computer Vision (2018)
57. Zhang, P., et al.: Learning spatial-temporal representations over walking tracklet for long-term person re-identification in the wild. IEEE Trans. Multimed. **23**, 3562–3576 (2020)
58. Zhang, Z., et al.: Semi-supervised face frontalization in the wild. IEEE Trans. Inf. Forensics Secur. **16**, 909–922 (2021)
59. Zheng, M., et al.: RPIfield: a new dataset for temporally evaluating person re-identification (2018)
60. Zhu, X., et al.: face alignment in full pose range: a 3D total solution. CoRR (2018)

Sentiment Analysis Applied to IBOVESPA Prediction

Yngwi Guimarães Vieira Souza[1], Luís Tarrataca[1]([⊠]),
Douglas O. Cardoso[2], and Laura Silva de Assis[1]

[1] Celso Suckow da Fonseca Federal Center of Technological Education,
Rio de Janeiro, RJ, Brazil
yngwi.guimaraes@aluno.cefet-rj.br,
{luis.tarrataca,laura.assis}@cefet-rj.br
[2] Smart Cities Research Center, Polytechnic Institute of Tomar, Tomar, Portugal
douglas.cardoso@ipt.pt

Abstract. Social media is increasingly being used as a source of news,
a trend which has resulted in large amounts of data. This work presents
an evaluation strategy for assessing the impact that social media has
on the Bovespa Index (IBovespa), the benchmark index of the Brazilian
stock market. A total of 105000 tweets were collected from the twitter
profile of "G1 Economia", one of the main Brazilian finance portals. This
data was processed using sentiment analysis methods which were then
incorporated into the development of an artificial neural network whose
objective was to predict the IBovespa. A hyperparameter optimization
study is also presented. The experimental results show that of the 1279
topologies studied, 82.4% exhibited better performance when using sentiment analysis in conjunction with historical data, against the baseline
of using only the latter. Curiously, even though the average performance
was higher, the absolute best result was obtained without the use of NLP
techniques. In the context of the method developed and the data used,
it appears that approaches using sentiment analysis alongside historical
records may be more effective than using only one or the other.

Keywords: Artificial Neural Networks · Sentiment analysis · Stock
market · VADER

1 Introduction

Artificial Neural Networks (ANN) have a wide range of applications in economy,
business, industry and science. One such potential application is the use of ANN
to predict market behavior [12]. Due to the complex nature of the stock market
it is difficult to model an ANN capable of making accurate predictions. This
difficulty may be due to the absence of features that adequately describe stock
market evolution but can also be attributed to the non-linear essence of the
market [31]. ANNs are trained on data sets correlating a set of input data to the
corresponding outputs. Therefore, the quality of the prediction is dependent on
that of the training set.

A. I. Pereira et al. (Eds.): OL2A 2022, CCIS 1754, pp. 373–388, 2022.
https://doi.org/10.1007/978-3-031-23236-7_26

Typically, news and opinions that directly relate with the economic scenario of a corporation or country have an impact on the psychological attitude of investors towards a market. Market sentiment is therefore influenced by how investors process such news. Fortunately, the proliferation of economic online news channels in social networks has resulted in a large and rich dataset that is constantly being updated [20]. Such a dataset is ideally suited for training ANNs. This work assesses how market sentiment can be incorporated into ANNs through sentiment analysis (SA) using this data.

In order to do so, the following methodology is used: an ANN model is built using standard features that correlate strongly with stock markets, *e.g.,* price of gold, oil and exchange rates. This result is then expanded by using a SA method capable of mapping the sentiment of a text as either positive or negative. This method can then be fed with economic texts collected via online news channels to try to characterize market sentiment at a specific point in time. This metric can then be used with the original set of economic features to predict the IBovespa. The ANN model chosen is the Long Short-Term Memory (LSTM) that has a recurrent neural network architecture and can be applied to time series forecasting. The method chosen for natural language processing (NLP) was VADER (**V**alence **A**ware **D**ictionary and s**E**ntiment **R**easoner) [10], a tool capable of performing SA through well defined rules using a dictionary of words.

The main contributions of this work are the following: *(i)* adaptation of VADER to the Portuguese language; *(ii)* ANN development using different topologies for assessing their respective prediction accuracy; *(iii)* development of a SA strategy for economic news; and *(iv)* incorporation of the SA feature in the development of ANNs and performance evaluation. The remaining sections of this work are organized as follows: Sect. 2 presents the basic concepts of ANN and SA; Sect. 3 describes the related works; Sects. 4 and 5 detail the VADER adjustment process as well as the dataset creation process; Sect. 6 details the results obtained; Sect. 7 presents the conclusions of this work.

2   Contextualization

This section provides a brief description of the concepts and tools employed in the development of this research. It aims at laying the ground for a proper understanding of the proposed methodology and results obtained. In this regard, Sect. 2.1 concerns Neural Networks (NN) while Sect. 2.2 covers SA.

2.1   Artificial Neural Networks

ANNs are biologically inspired computational systems that mimic the neural networks that can be found in animal brains [4]. They are the result of a cross-disciplinary approach involving neuroscience, mathematics and artificial intelligence [27]. ANNs represent an intelligent model that learns by example during a training stage. This knowledge can then be used for making future predictions or classifications [1]. The networks employed loosely mimic the neurons found in brains. These neurons can process the information provided and transmit their results to other neurons. Typically, the neurons and the respective interconnecting edges have weights that are adjusted during training. When a neuron is processing multiple inputs it may be possible that the output signal will only be produced if the aggregate signal crosses a threshold [18].

The LSTM is a Recurrent Neural Network (RNN) architecture that incorporates order dependence in its specification and is therefore used when predicting sequences. The ability of the model to remember values in arbitrary intervals is used to classify, process and predict time series with time intervals of unknown duration [8]. LSTMs were developed from the analysis of error flow in existing RNNs. This examination concluded that the backward propagation of errors decays exponentially [7]. An LSTM layer consists of a set of memory blocks connected in a recurrent manner. Each one contains one or more memory cells recurrently connected and three multiplicative units that provide continuous equivalents to the operations of recording (input gate), reading (output gate) and reset (forget gate) for the cells. The interactions between the neural network and the cells are performed exclusively through the cell gates [7]. LSTM networks are constituted by the following elements:

- **Forget Gate:** Removes information in the state of the cell that is no longer useful. Two inputs: x_t (input x in instant t) and h_{t-1} (output of the previous cell) are provided to the gate and multiplied by weight matrices. This is followed by the addition of a bias. The result is fed to an activation function that outputs a binary result. If the function evaluates to 0 then the information is forgotten, otherwise, the information is kept for future use;
- **Input Gate:** Adds useful information to the state of the cell. First, the information is provided to a sigmoid function responsible for filtering the values (in a similar manner to the forget gate) using the inputs h_{t-1} and x_t. In addition, a vector containing all possible values of h_{t-1} and x_t is transformed using the tanh (tangent) function. The outputs of the previous two stages are multiplied to obtain the useful information.
- **Output Gate:** Responsible for the task of extracting useful information from the current state cell. First, a vector is constructed using the tanh function in the cell. This is then fed to the sigmoid function that filters the values to be remembered by using the inputs h_{t-1} and x_t. The vector values and the regulated ones are multiplied and represent the output which can then be provided as input to another cell.

2.2   Sentiment Analysis

SA is used to refer to the automatic processing of opinions, sentiments and subjectivity in texts [16] and is an active research field in the area of NLP. The extraction of sentiments from a text can be performed in different levels, namely:

- **Document Level Analysis:** Assuming that each document expresses the opinions about a single entity this technique performs the evaluation of the overall sentiment in a specific document;

- **Sentence Level Analysis:** Determines the overall opinion polarity (positive or negative) expressed within each sentence;
- **Aspect Level Analysis:** Performs a deeper appreciation than the previous levels by contemplating polarity (negative or positive) and subjected to the perspective of an opinion.

SA can be performed through dictionary-based approaches and machine learning (ML) methods. The former is usually more practical and versatile since it does not require a training set whilst the latter tends to present better results. In this work, we opted to employ the dictionary-based tool VADER. Dictionary-based approaches explore a sentiment lexical that is constructed from a set of documents. The objective of this dictionary is to index the largest number of words that carry some opinion. In contrast, ML approaches require that text is properly classified with a sentiment so that these methods can learn to classify future instances as either positive, negative or neutral [35]. The main resources employed are: *(i)* words, *(ii)* bigrams; *(iii)* trigrams; *(iv)* grammatical class; and *(v)* polarity [30]. Some possible approaches that use ML techniques to perform classification are Support Vector Machine (SVM) and Naive Bayes (NB) classifiers [9]. More recently, deep learning methods have also been developed since they are able to outperform NB techniques [25] but require significantly larger datasets and computational resources [32].

3   Related Work

Stock market forecast is a highly active research field due to the potential financial gains to be had. Not surprisingly, the question of whether or not it is possible to accurately predict market trends using ML attracts significant attention [19]. The Efficient-market hypothesis (EMH) argues that stock prices reflect all available information at any given point in time. As a result of the EMH it is difficult to predict asset returns since any potential public information that would result in a profit would be quickly factored in the price of an asset. However, some works state that it is possible to predict market prices to some level [3].

In [24] a method is presented for performing SA using word dictionaries to process *tweets* applied to the financial market. The authors use a probabilistic analysis to assess how the words in a dictionary represent positive or negative sentiments. The work presents an investment simulation using the develop model that is able to reach 70% accuracy and that was able to achieve a 3.53% profit over the initial investment during 25 simulation days. A study of the relationship between *Apple* stock price and texts obtained from *Twitter* was presented in [6]. The results show a correlation coefficient of 0.7955 between the score of the *tweets* and stock market price variation. A method for SA obtained by combining SentiWordNet and the NB algorithm was described in [13]. The authors collected the texts of *Twitter* users which were then processed and used by SVM to predict the behavior of a stock market.

The work described in [3] applies SA to *Twitter* users by making use of the OpinionFinder software. This application performs NLP through a word dictionary and is capable of determining the polarity and intensity of each word within a sentence. The work made use of ANNs and reported an 87.6% accuracy when predicting the Dow Jones index. In [34] an approach was developed for integrating SA of social media alongside NB. The authors were able to achieve a decrease of 16% of average error when compared against the results obtained without using SA.

In [21] a ML method using SVMs was presented for performing SA as well as stock market prediction. The results obtained were able to deliver a 9.83% accuracy increase when compared against models that did not employ SA during the training stages. The work described in [28] uses ANN and SVMs to improve the accuracy of stock market price prediction models by making use of SA of social media. The authors applied the developed techniques to predict the Dow Jones and obtained ambiguous results. Namely, the best performing method employed SVM alongside SA to obtain a prediction accuracy of 64.10%. However, this result does not improve significantly on the one the authors obtained when using an SVM without SA, respectively, 62.03%.

In [23] a NLP processing method using ANNs was utilized that was capable of classifying a sentence in three different ways: *i)* positive; *ii)* negative; or *iii)* neutral. The authors employed a dataset consisting of Brazilian online news sources, namely: G1, Estadão e Folha de São Paulo. The authors were able to correctly define the sentiment of a sentence with 86.5% accuracy. The work described in [33] aimed at predicting the S&P500 by using a solution based on different ML methods. The approach using a Convolutional Neural Network (CNN) presented the best result for SA whilst the approach using an ANN was able to achieve better stock market patterns.

A Multi Layer Perceptron alongside SA was used in [22] to predict the stock market of Ghana. The tests performed employed data collected from the Ghana stock exchange between 2010 and 2019 alongside texts obtained from Twitter, Google trends, forums and digital newspapers. The approach was able to obtain an average 73.9% accuracy. The work described in [17] attempted to understand the impact on stock markets caused by high magnitude events using SA. The work considered four companies from different countries. The authors collected 11.42 million *tweets* which were then processed using a lexical method and used for training a CNN. The results obtained showed that by employing SA there was a decrease in the average error of the predictions.

In [14] a method was developed based on ML and SA using lexical analysis of four different dictionaries to predict the Hong Kong stock exchange. In [29] the authors measured speech intensity through lexical analysis and employed it to better understand the relationship between social media and stock market. The work concludes that SA can be used to assess the opinion of a group of persons and has an impact on stock prices. A hybrid approach using CNNs and SA was presented in [11] with the objective of predicting the Xangai stock exchange.

The work detailed in [5] employs opinion mining to improve accuracy prediction of stock market models from several countries. The authors made use of a total of 6.48 million *tweets* of the *Xueqiu* social network, which is used by investors in the Chinese financial market. This data was then used for SA [36]. The authors applied a SVM to model and predict stock prices.

4   Sentiment Analysis Adaptation

VADER was chosen given its ability to perceive not only the polarity but also the intensity of sentiments. In addition, it also has higher classification accuracy when compared with other tools [10]. VADER was developed for the English language. Consequently, it was necessary to adapt it to Portuguese given that IBovespa is a Brazilian index and is therefore more susceptible to news in this language. This meant adapting VADER whilst maintaining its structural essence. Overall, the majority of changes consisted in translating English words of the VADER dictionary to Portuguese using *Google Translator* API. Some minor adaptations due to structural differences in grammar were also performed.

After concluding the translation process, it was necessary to assess the performance of the adapted version of VADER. In order to do so we employed 50 economy-related articles that were randomly chosen from a set consisting of 2000 articles obtained from G1 news website [26]. This test considered the text body, title and subtitle of each article. VADER was asked to classify these articles, and its predictions were compared to those of a human agent. The results matched in 78% of the articles. Table 1 brings some examples of these results. The full set of results are publicly available in the project repository.[1]

Table 1. Prediction examples of the Portuguese-adapted version of VADER.

Article title	VADER score	Human assessment
Sanitation improves, but half of Brazilians still have no sewage in the country	−0.7062	Negative
New labor law: termination no longer needs union approval	0.9389	Positive
S&P lowers credit score of Brazil	0.9816	Negative
Market breaks 20-week sequence of falling GDP forecast and projects lower inflation	−0.7783	Positive

5   Data Acquisition

When dealing with supervised ML methods it is important to choose a set of features that presents a strong correlation with the output variable [15]. As an initial approach we chose to employ a set of features that, typically, correlate strongly

---

[1] https://gitlab.com/yngwi/SA_IBOVESPA_Prediction.

with the IBovespa, namely: *(i)* gold; *(ii)* oil; *(iii)* real and dollar exchange rate; *(iv)* Dow Jones; *(v)* Nasdaq; and *(vi)* S&P 500. Each entry of our dataset describes the closing values of these items for a specific day. The data collected encompasses the time period from 4/17/2013 to 2/11/2014.

Figure 1 shows the correlation matrix (generated using the Pearson method [2]) between all the features. As it is possible see, most of the features chosen present high correlation with the IBovespa.

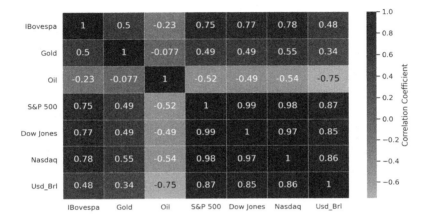

Fig. 1. Correlation matrix for the dataset.

We developed a web scraper for obtaining the news dataset. We opted to use news articles from Twitter given that many news channels have verified accounts in the platform. The web scraper works by performing an advanced query in Twitter and stores in *.csv* format the *tweets* returned. This approach allowed for the creation of a dataset consisting of 105000 *tweets* from the economy specific profile of G1, respectively, "G1 Economia" (in English, G1 Economy).

The adapted VADER method was then employed to perform SA to each *tweet* and classify it as either positive or negative. For each trading day (9:00 to 17:00), the original dataset of features was combined with the SA of the tweets that were in compatible time windows. This enabled the definition of a new feature to represent market sentimental state. The new feature values are obtained through a simple average of the sum of SA values of the day. The historical plot for the SA feature is presented in Fig. 2.

It was also tested an alternative to expressing market sentimental state in a single feature. This second approach adds two features that describe the positive sentiment and the negative sentiment for a specific day. These features are composed, respectively, by: *(i)* the sum of the values that are larger than zero;

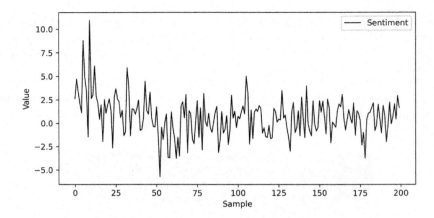

Fig. 2. Sentiment plot.

and *(ii)* the sum of the values that are smaller than zero. The historical plot for the positive and negative sentiment features are presented in Fig. 3.

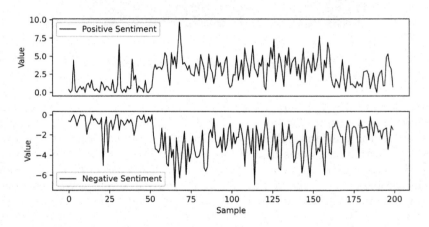

Fig. 3. Positive and negative sentiments plot.

6   Experimental Results

This section presents the results obtained for a diverse number of experiments using the set of hyperparameters described in Table 2. The values employed were the result of an exploratory analysis performed in order to gain a comprehension of the prediction ability of the model.

Table 2. Hyperparameters utilized and their respective values.

Hyperparameter	Description	Value
B_s	Batch size	1024
shuffle	Shuffle input data	No
N_t	Proportion of dataset used for training	80%
N_v	Proportion of dataset used for tests	20%
$L_{\max}$	Maximum number of neurons	256
P_s	Past time series steps used to produce input pattern	1
SP_s	Past time SA steps used to produce input pattern	1
T_s	Number of predictions to be made from an input pattern	1
L_s	Maximum number of hidden layers	5
E_t	Training error	$[0, 1]$
E_v	Validation error	$[0, 1]$
E_s	Number of epochs for training	500

The next sections presented results for the following experiments: *(i)* a topology exploratory analysis; and *(ii)* an assessment of the number of main components employed. These results can be found, respectively, in Sect. 6.1 and Sect. 6.2. The results concerning the use of SA are described in Sect. 6.3.

6.1   Exploratory Analysis of Topologies

These experiments were performed in order to determine which NN topology produced the best results. Accordingly, we opted to test these by varying the maximum number of layers and neurons. In the subsequent text we opted to represent each topology as a sequence of numbers $\{a_1, a_2, \cdots, a_m\}, \forall\ i \in [1, l_s]$ describing the number of neurons in each layer. Tables 3 and 4 present, respectively, the set of values for each parameter tested and the top 10 results.

6.2   Principal Components Analysis

This section aims to assess how the number of principal components impacts prediction accuracy. Accordingly, the 30 topologies that exhibited the smallest E_v's were then tested against different numbers of principal components. Namely, for each topology we trained an ANN with different numbers of principal components, $C_s = \{1, 2, 3, 4, 5, 6\}$. Table 5 presents the best results obtained for the topologies considered. The best performing topology was $(256, 128, 128, 32, 16)$ that used 6 principal components and was able to achieve $E_v = 2.5831\%$.

Table 3. Parameters used in exploratory of the topology analysis.

Parameter	Description	Value
l_s	Number of layers	$\{1, 2, 3, 4, 5\}$
N_{max}	Maximum number of neurons	256
N_v	Step increase in the number of neurons	2^p
p	Power index	$\{1, 2, 3, 4, 5, 6, 7, 8\}$
C_s	Number of principal components	$\{1, 2, 3, 4, 5, 6\}$
E_t	Training error	$[0, 1]$
E_v	Validation error	$[0, 1]$
E_s	Number of training epochs	500

Table 4. 10 best results of topology analysis.

Index	Topology	E_v	E_t
1	128, 64, 32, 4, 4	2.986%	2.258%
2	128, 128	3.027%	2.105%
3	256, 64, 16	3.027%	2.298%
4	256, 64, 32, 32, 32	3.059%	2.343%
5	128, 64, 16, 16, 16	3.063%	2.085%
6	128, 128, 128, 32, 8	3.108%	2.007%
7	128, 128, 128, 64, 4	3.109%	2.256%
8	256, 32	3.208%	1.998%
9	256, 256, 128	3.255%	3.221%
10	256, 64, 32, 8, 4	3.272%	2.621%

6.3   Sentiment Analysis Approach

This section presents the experiments that result from adding the SA strategy described in Sect. 5. The first experiment consisted in considering the original dataset consisting of 2000 articles from G1. Namely, the texts from G1 for each day of the dataset were analyzed using SA and incorporated as a new feature into the original dataset. Table 6 shows the training results for the best topologies for three different strategies, namely: *(i)* without using SA; *(ii)* with a single overall SA feature; and *(iii)* when positive and negative SA features are employed.

The results presented in Table 6 did not lead to conclusive observations, although, this was to be expected given the small size of the dataset employed (2000 articles). As such, we opted to perform a similar analysis but this time using the 105000 *tweets* from "G1 Economy". Table 7 shows the training results for the best topologies for three different strategies, namely: *(i)* without using SA; *(ii)* with a single overall SA feature; and *(iii)* when positive and negative SA features are employed.

Table 5. 10 best results of C_s analysis.

Index	Topology	E_v	E_t	C_s
1	32, 32, 32, 32, 8	3.9335%	3.9186%	2
2	32, 32, 32, 32, 16	4.0057%	3.9292%	2
3	256, 256, 4, 4, 2	3.2855%	3.2091%	3
4	64, 32, 4, 4, 4	3.4233%	3.4531%	3
5	256, 256, 256, 64, 32	2.8519%	2.856%	4
6	32, 32	3.1184%	3.0928%	4
7	256, 256, 128, 32	2.7873%	2.6994%	5
8	64, 32, 16, 16, 2	2.9027%	2.7293%	5
9	**256, 128, 128, 32, 16**	**2.5831%**	**2.4897%**	**6**
10	256, 256, 64, 2, 2	2.6071%	2.4916%	6

Table 6. Training results when using SA from G1 texts.

Topology	C_s	Mean average error %		
		Without SA	Overall SA	+/− SA
256, 128, 128, 32, 16	6	**2.14%**	**2.62%**	**2.32%**
256, 256, 128, 32	5	2.42%	2.69%	2.49%
256, 256, 256, 64, 32	4	2.57%	2.98%	2.64%

Table 7. Training results using SA from "G1 Economy" *tweets*.

Topology	C_s	Mean average error %		
		Without SA	Overall SA	+/− SA
256, 128, 128, 32, 16	6	2.48%	**2.41%**	2.50%
256, 256, 64, 2, 2	6	2.56%	2.49%	**2.38%**
64, 32, 16, 16	6	2.94%	**2.35%**	2.81%
256, 256, 256, 64, 32	6	2.45%	2.24%	**2.22%**
64, 32, 16, 16, 2	6	2.87%	2.75%	**2.44%**
256, 256, 4, 4, 4	6	2.49%	**2.40%**	15.75%

In addition, besides the *tweets* from "G1 Economy", an additional 25000 *tweets* from the "O Globo Economia" portal were collected. Table 8 shows the corresponding training results for the best topologies for three different strategies, namely: *(i)* without using SA; *(ii)* with a single overall SA feature; and *(iii)* when positive and negative SA features are employed.

The overall conclusions of the experiments performed can be found in Table 9 which shows the top three results obtained for each approach. From the data presented it is possible to observe that the approach without SA exhibits the best results in absolute values.

Table 8. Training results using SA from "O Globo Economia" *tweets*.

Topology	C_s	Mean Average Error %		
		Without SA	Overall SA	+/− SA
256, 128, 128, 32, 16	6	2.49%	2.71%	**2.21%**
256, 256, 64, 2, 2	6	2.26%	2.27%	**2.04%**
64, 32, 16, 16	6	3.04%	2.69%	**2.47%**
256, 256, 256, 64, 32	6	2.16%	2.21%	**2.03%**
64, 32, 16, 16, 2	6	2.85%	2.83%	**2.64%**
256, 256, 4, 4, 4	6	2.39%	**2.25%**	16.96%

Table 9. Top three results for each approach.

Topology	Approach	E_t	E_v
256, 256, 256	Without SA	1.851%	1.948%
256, 256, 256, 128, 128	Without SA	1.791%	2.004%
256, 256, 256, 256, 64	Without SA	1.848%	2.005%
256, 256, 256, 256, 2	Overall SA	1.904%	2.014%
256, 128, 128, 128, 64	Overall SA	1.816%	2.023%
256, 128, 128, 64	Overall SA	1.734%	2.023%
256, 256, 128, 128	+/− SA	1.624%	1.952%
256, 256, 256, 256, 32	+/− SA	1.780%	2.002%
256, 256, 256, 128, 64	+/− SA	1.762%	2.015%

However, for most topologies, the approach that incorporates the positive and negative features outperforms the approach without SA. This behavior can be seen in Table 10 that describes how each approach fared against the others, namely: the first two columns indicate the approaches being compared, with the third column describing the percentage improvement. The last three columns characterize the minimum, maximum and average difference between the approaches being compared. For instance, the first line of Table 10 compares the approach without SA against the one that employs the overall SA strategy. In this specific case, 33, 46% of the topologies analyzed without SA showcased better performance than the ones with the overall SA feature. This means that the method employing the overall SA technique exhibited better performance in 100%–33,46% = 66,54% of the topologies considered. The same line states that: *(i)* the best E_v value of the approach without SA was just 0.08% better than the best value obtained from using the overall SA strategy; *(ii)* the minimum E_v value was 1.12% worse; and *(ii)* on average, not using SA resulted in a penalty of 0.86%

Overall, the main conclusion that can be derived from Table 10 is that the approaches using SA outperformed the baseline for the majority of the topologies considered. The best result achieved was when the +/− SA approach was

Table 10. Comparison results between the different approaches.

Approach 1	Approach 2	Topologies Improved	Winning approach	Differences (E_v)		
				Max.	Min.	Avg.
Without SA	Overall SA	33.46%	Overall SA	0.08%	−1.12%	−0.86%
Without SA	+/− SA	17.59%	+/− SA	0.07%	−2.22%	−1.73%
Overall SA	Without SA	66.30%	Overall SA	1.12%	−0.08%	0.86%
Overall SA	+/− SA	24.94%	+/− SA	0.01%	−1.13%	−0.88%
+/− SA	Without SA	82.40%	+/− SA	2.22%	−0.07%	1.73%
+/− SA	Overall SA	74.98%	+/− SA	1.13%	−0.01%	0.88%

compared against the baseline which resulted in 82, 40% of the topologies having better performance.

The previous set of experiment employed $SP_s = 0$ to convert the time series. The next set of experiments (Table 11) describe the results obtained for $SP_s = [0, 1, 2, 3]$. In addition, E_s was altered to 20000 epochs. Overall, the results obtained indicate that the approaches without SA showcased the best absolute values.

Table 11. Top three results for each SP_s value, ordered by SP_s and E_v.

Topology	E_v	E_t	SP_s
256, 256, 256, 128, 128,	1.784%	1.124%	0
256, 256, 256, 128,	1.796%	1.316%	0
256, 256, 256, 256, 32,	1.801%	1.162%	0
256, 256, 128, 128, 128,	1.831%	1.291%	1
256, 256, 256, 64,	1.900%	1.211%	1
256, 256, 256, 256, 128,	1.920%	1.363%	1
256, 256, 256, 128, 128,	1.784%	1.124%	2
256, 256, 256, 128,	1.796%	1.316%	2
128, 128, 128, 128,	1.801%	1.162%	2
256, 256, 256, 256, 64,	2.042%	1.264%	3
256, 256, 128, 128, 128,	2.088%	1.287%	3
256, 128, 128, 128, 64,	2.137%	1.635%	3
256, 256, 128, 128, 128,	1.463%	1.079%	Without SA
256, 128, 128, 128,	1.570%	1.135%	Without SA
256, 256, 128, 128, 64,	1.578%	1.225%	Without SA

7   Conclusion

This work assessed the impact of features resulting from sentiment analysis of news text excerpts in Portuguese on Brazilian stock market forecasting. Such features were produced by a version of the VADER tool whose dictionary was translated from English to Portuguese, enabling its use for a language which differs from the one it originally targeted. Among all considered ANN-based predictors, over 82% had a superior performance when such features integrated the input compared to their counterparts which considered only conventional economic indicators. In spite of such fact, it is interesting to notice that the best performance overall ($E_v = 1.948\%$) was obtained by one whose input did not include such features, while the second best did ($E_v = 1.952\%$).

As a future work, it could be interesting to limit the dictionary to economy-related terms: this could avoid misinterpretations resulting from taking into account words which could be considered neutral in this specific context. Another possible continuation would be the employment or even the development of a tool similar to VADER but with Portuguese as its original target language, since such specialized version would probably produce better results than the adapted version used.

Acknowledgements. This work has been financially supported by national grant from the FCT (Fundação para a Ciência e a Tecnologia), under the project UIDB/05567/2020.

References

1. Barreto, J.M.: Introdução às redes neurais artificiais, pp. 5–10. V Escola Regional de Informática. Sociedade Brasileira de Computaçao, Regional Sul, Santa Maria, Florianópolis, Maringá pp (2002)
2. Benesty, J., Chen, J., Huang, Y., Cohen, I.: Pearson correlation coefficient. In: Noise Reduction in Speech Processing. vol. 2. Springer, Berlin, pp. 1–4 (2009). https://doi.org/10.1007/978-3-642-00296-0_5
3. Bollen, J., Mao, H., Zeng, X.: Twitter mood predicts the stock market. J. Comput. Sci. **2**(1), 1–8 (2011)
4. Conway, C.M.: How does the brain learn environmental structure? Ten core principles for understanding the neurocognitive mechanisms of statistical learning. Neurosci. Biobehav. Rev. **112**, 279–299 (2020)
5. Derakhshan, A., Beigy, H.: Sentiment analysis on stock social media for stock price movement prediction. Eng. Appl. Artif. Intell. **85**, 569–578 (2019)
6. Dey, S.K.: Stock market prediction using twitter mood. Int. J. Sci. Eng. Res. **5**(5), 44–47 (2014)
7. Graves, A., Schmidhuber, J.: Framewise phoneme classification with bidirectional LSTM networks. In: Proceedings. 2005 IEEE International Joint Conference on Neural Networks, 2005, vol. 4, pp. 2047–2052 (2005)
8. Graves, A., et al.: A novel connectionist system for unconstrained handwriting recognition. IEEE Trans. Pattern Anal. Mach. Intell. **31**(5), 855–868 (2009)
9. Hasan, A., Moin, S., Karim, A., Shamshirband, S.: Machine learning-based sentiment analysis for twitter accounts. Math. Comput. Appl. **23**(1), 11 (2018)

10. Hutto, C., Gilbert, E.: Vader: A parsimonious rule-based model for sentiment analysis of social media text. In: Proceedings of the International AAAI Conference on Web and Social Media, vol. 8 (2014)

11. Jing, N., Wu, Z., Wang, H.: A hybrid model integrating deep learning with investor sentiment analysis for stock price prediction. Expert Syst. Appl. **178**, 115019 (2021)

12. JingTao, Y., Chew Lim, T.: Guidelines for financial prediction with artificial neural networks. Int. J. Comput. Appl. **135**(8), 28–32 (2009)

13. Li, J., Meesad, P.: Combining sentiment analysis with socialization bias in social networks for stock market trend prediction. Int. J. Comput. Intell. Appl. **15**(01), 1650003 (2016)

14. Li, X., Wu, P., Wang, W.: Incorporating stock prices and news sentiments for stock market prediction: a case of Hong Kong. Information Processing & Management **57**(5), 102212 (2020)

15. Lippmann, R.: An introduction to computing with neural nets. IEEE ASSP Mag. **4**(2), 4–22 (1987)

16. Liu, B.: Sentiment analysis and opinion mining. Synth. Lect. Hum. Lang. Technol. **5**(1), 1–167 (2012)

17. Maqsood, H., et al.: A local and global event sentiment based efficient stock exchange forecasting using deep learning. Int. J. Inf. Manage. **50**, 432–451 (2020)

18. McCulloch, W.S., Pitts, W.: A logical calculus of the ideas immanent in nervous activity. Bull. Math. Biophys. **5**(4), 115–133 (1943)

19. Nabipour, M., Nayyeri, P., Jabani, H., Mosavi, A., Salwana, E., et al.: Deep learning for stock market prediction. Entropy **22**(8), 840 (2020)

20. Nguyen, T.H., Shirai, K.: Topic modeling based sentiment analysis on social media for stock market prediction. In: Proceedings of the 53rd Annual Meeting of the Association for Computational Linguistics and the 7th International Joint Conference on Natural Language Processing (Volume 1: Long Papers), pp. 1354–1364 (2015)

21. Nguyen, T.H., Shirai, K., Velcin, J.: Sentiment analysis on social media for stock movement prediction. Expert Syst. Appl. **42**(24), 9603–9611 (2015)

22. Nti, I.K., Adekoya, A.F., Weyori, B.A.: Predicting stock market price movement using sentiment analysis: evidence from Ghana. Appl. Comput. Syst. **25**(1), 33–42 (2020)

23. de Oliveira Carosia, A.E., Coelho, G.P., da Silva, A.E.A.: Investment strategies applied to the Brazilian stock market: a methodology based on sentiment analysis with deep learning. Expert Syst. Appl. **184**, 115470 (2021)

24. Pagolu, V.S., Reddy, K.N., Panda, G., Majhi, B.: Sentiment analysis of twitter data for predicting stock market movements. In: 2016 International Conference on Signal Processing, Communication, Power and Embedded System (SCOPES), pp. 1345–1350. IEEE (2016)

25. Paredes-Valverde, M.A., Colomo-Palacios, R., Salas-Zárate, M.d.P., Valencia-García, R.: Sentiment analysis in Spanish for improvement of products and services: a deep learning approach. Sci. Program. **2017** (2017)

26. e Participações S.A., G.C.: G1 - o portal de notícias da globo (2000). http://g1.globo.com/

27. Pehlevan, C., Chklovskii, D.B.: Neuroscience-inspired online unsupervised learning algorithms: artificial neural networks. IEEE Signal Process. Mag. **36**(6), 88–96 (2019)

28. Porshnev, A., Redkin, I., Shevchenko, A.: Machine learning in prediction of stock market indicators based on historical data and data from twitter sentiment analy-

sis. In: 2013 IEEE 13th International Conference on Data Mining Workshops, pp. 440–444. IEEE (2013)

29. Reed, M.: A study of social network effects on the stock market. J. Behav. Financ. **17**(4), 342–351 (2016)

30. Sindhu, C., ChandraKala, S.: A survey on opinion mining and sentiment polarity classification. Knowl. Based Syst. **89**, 14–46 (2013)

31. Soni, S.: Applications of ANNs in stock market prediction: a survey. Int. J. Comput. Sci. Eng. Technol. **2**(3), 71–83 (2011)

32. Tang, D., Qin, B., Liu, T.: Document modeling with gated recurrent neural network for sentiment classification. In: Proceedings of the 2015 Conference on Empirical Methods in Natural Language Processing. pp. 1422–1432 (2015)

33. Vargas, M.R., De Lima, B.S., Evsukoff, A.G.: Deep learning for stock market prediction from financial news articles. In: 2017 IEEE International Conference on Computational Intelligence and Virtual Environments for Measurement Systems and Applications (CIVEMSA), pp. 60–65. IEEE (2017)

34. Zhang, G., Xu, L., Xue, Y.: Model and forecast stock market behavior integrating investor sentiment analysis and transaction data. Clust. Comput. **20**(1), 789–803 (2017). https://doi.org/10.1007/s10586-017-0803-x

35. Zhang, Q., Wang, B., Wu, L., Huang, X.: Fdu at trec 2007: Opinion retrieval of blog track. In: TREC, pp. 500–274. Citeseer (2007)

36. Zhang, X., Shi, J., Wang, D., Fang, B.: Exploiting investors social network for stock prediction in china's market. J. Comput. Sci. **28**, 294–303 (2018)

F0, LPC, and MFCC Analysis
for Emotion Recognition Based on Speech

Felipe L. Teixeira[1,2]([envelope]) [iD], João Paulo Teixeira[2,3]([envelope]) [iD],
Salviano F. P. Soares[1,4][iD], and J. L. Pio Abreu[5,6][iD]

[1] School of Sciences and Technology-Engineering Departament (UTAD),
5000-801 Vila Real, Portugal
felipe.lage@ipb.pt, salblues@utad.pt
[2] Research Centre in Digitalization and Intelligent Robotics (CEDRI) and
Laboratório para a Sustentabilidade e Tecnologia em Regiões de Montanha (SusTEC)
- Instituto Politécnico de Bragança, 5300-253 Bragança, Portugal
joaopt@ipb.pt
[3] Applied Management Research Unit (UNIAG), Instituto Politécnico de Bragança,
5300-253 Bragança, Portugal
[4] Institute of Electronics and Informatics Engineering of Aveiro (IEETA),
3810-193 Aveiro, Portugal
[5] Hospital da Universidade de Coimbra, 3004-561 Coimbra, Portugal
pioabreu@icloud.com
[6] Faculdade de Medicina da Universidade de Coimbra (FMUC),
3000-548 Coimbra, Portugal

Abstract. In this work, research was done to understand what is needed
to build a database to recognise emotions through speech. Some features
that can highlight a good success rate for emotion recognition through
speech were investigated. Also studied were some characteristics (symptoms) that can be associated with a specific emotional state. On the
other hand, we also studied some features that can be used to identify
some emotional states. A System Emotion Recognition (SER) was built
with SVM, and the binary analysis was compared with a multi-category
analysis. The binary analysis achieved an accuracy of 87.5% and the
multi-class 42.6%. The parameters Fundamental Frequency-F0, Linear
Predictive Coefficients (LPC), and Mel Frequency Cepstral Coeficients
(MFCC) were used. The modest accuracy of this work was achieved using
only F0, LPC and MFCC features.

Keywords: Emotional state · Speech · SVM

1 Introduction

Since the 1960's, several emotion models have been proposed. There are two main
categories: the discrete emotion theory and the dimensional emotion theory. The
discrete emotion theory states that emotions are divided into discrete categories
and are biologically fixed. These are universal to all humans and many animals.

© The Author(s), under exclusive license to Springer Nature Switzerland AG 2022
A. I. Pereira et al. (Eds.): OL2A 2022, CCIS 1754, pp. 389–404, 2022.
https://doi.org/10.1007/978-3-031-23236-7_27

The basic examples are anger, disgust, fear, happiness, sadness, and surprise. The dimensional emotion theory states that emotions are a combination of one or more psychological dimensions [1]. It is difficult to understand human emotions quantitatively, yet understanding them is fundamental to human social interactions. The best way to analyse them is through the assessment of facial expressions or speech. Speech is a complex signal that has information about the message (what is said), the speaker (who said it), the language, and the emotions [2].

The emotional state is an important condition for ensuring a good lifestyle and can be influenced by social relations, physical conditions, or health status. Various sources of information like facial expression, brain signals (EEG) and speech can be used to identify the emotion of a person. Always, the analysis of two (or more) of these sources is called *"Multi-modal Emotion Recognition"* [3]. There is six basic types of emotions: anger, happiness/joy, disgust, surprise, fear, sadness and a neutral emotional state, the others are derived from these [4]. Knowing that the methods based on speech or vital signals can just appropriately separate active emotions with high arousal from passive ones with low arousal, precise separation of emotions with the same arousal using voice or vital signals is impossible [5].

The speech features (acoustic) for emotion recognition are almost similar in all languages, so the same classification model can be used across languages. However, this is not true for linguistic features [3]. There are multiple functional paralanguages embodying the same emotion [6].

A recognition emotion system in speech has the objective of identifying the human emotional state via speech analysis [7] in the least possible time [8]. These systems were made because speech can be misleading and it may not be easy for humans to correctly interpret the emotional state of the speaker [2]. Speech Emotion Recognition (SER) is used in several applications and could be helpful in psychological treatments. Modern speech-based systems are designed primarily using neutral speech [3]. The biggest challenge of SER is to find a set of features in speech that can have specific information about each emotional state [4], so it is important to note that speech emotion-related analysis needs a good emotion corpus [9].

Although the study journey of SER is three decades long, the results are not yet good enough for an application in natural environments. The explanation for this is that a speech signal contains lexical content (what has been spoken), the speaker emotions, and language. If the SER has to recognise particular information in speech, then ideally the effect of other information should be nullified [3].

The cause of this problem is the mismatch between speaker, text, language, and "environment" (culture). The variation in recording environments is another mismatch and can be created by different types of noise, compression data, and distance variation between speaker and microphone [3]. Alternatively, some authors, such as [6] was mentioning that functional paralanguage features (i.e., laughter, crying, and sighing) jointly with speech features include considerable emotional information that can be promissory.

Some works, such as [9] created a new database with the goal of analysing the influence of a speaker's culture and age on emotion expression, and [6] created a speech emotion database with emotional paralanguages (EPSED).

Generally, a SER is divided into three parts: features, models, and testing. Inside the feature part, there is preprocessing, feature extraction, and feature selection. The preprocessing step is used to denoise the speech and to find salient segments [3].

The SER system employs a variety of techniques for extracting features from speech signals [2] and occasionally combines different sets of features, which is a commonly used skill to improve SER prediction [4].

The feature selection methods simplify classification algorithm tasks by avoiding dimensionality and overfitting issues, improving SER performance, and reducing time and computational memory [4].

It is intended that the SER application has a natural interaction with the computer instead of applying traditional input devices [10] and can be employed as a diagnostic tool for therapists [7].

In this paper, we intend to understand what it is important to construct our corpora emotion database, in addition to constructing our SER system. To the best of our knowledge, the European Portuguese emotion speech corpus is not available in the public domain, but we used a public database (in another language) in this work [11].

We did a binary and multi-classification with SVM implementation to try to predict the emotional state with analysis of three feature sets: F0, LPC, and MFCC. The features set was extracted from Emo-DB.

This work has been developed in the context of the GreenHealth Project[1] [12], where we intend to detect schizophrenia through speech.

This paper consists of six chapters, where the first is the introduction, where a theoretical approach is made to the subject studied. Chapter two talks about the state of the art. Chapter three discusses the theory of speech parameters and databases for the study of emotional states. Chapter four deals with the methodology implemented in the course of the work, and Chapter five presents the results obtained and, finally, the conclusion and future work to be carried out.

2   State of Art

With technological advances, the interface between man and machine will be most significantly improved if the machines can recognise the emotional state of the user [10].

In recurrent days, the research is focused on finding powerful combinations of classifiers that advance the classification efficiency in real-life applications. There

---

[1] GreenHealth project "Digital strategies based on biological assets to improve well-being and promote green health" - NORTE-01-0145-FEDER-000042.

is the possibility to use many machine learning tool for classify, such as Markov Model (HMM), Gaussian Mixture Model (GMM) or Artificial Neural Networks (ANN) for other neurological diseases like Alzheimer [13–16], or using transfer learning methodologies for speech pathologies classification [17,18]. However it is important to know that classify emotional state is a multi-categories classification problem [2]. It is possible identify the emotional state with many biological signals, for example [19]use the ECG signal for recognise about valence and arousal and obtained recognition accuracy rate between 76,8% 78,3% but we focused on works developed with speech signals.

To do these types of studies, it is important to have access to a good database. The small sample size can be the study's limitation [20].

In [21], a deep study was conducted, and 64 emotional speech databases were acquired between 1986 and 2005, the authors of [22] used the previous 64 emotions speech databases and added 24 databases for their research.

The most interesting features are the fundamental frequency (F0) and formants, the short-term energy, the MFCC's, the cross-section areas, the Teager energy operator-based features, jitter, shimmer and HNR [11,21,23].

Different classification rates can be found using SVM, for example in the work developed by [2] they recognised 7 emotions using pitch and prosody features and obtained recognition rate of 81%, the same authors find a recognition rate of 94,2% to recognised 4 emotions. In [4] was obtained a classification accuracy between 69% and 86%, classifiyng the pitch, formants and MFCC. [10] study 2 databases to compare arousal and valence level thus obtained recognition rates between 85% and 95% to arousal, and between 72% and 86% to valence (the same author was done the same study with HMM but the obtained results were lower). [24] was studied 32 works developed with same goal and 19 of them used a SVM with pitch, MFCC or LPC, but this author used a MLP and obtained 85,1% of accuracy.

On other hand, with SVM, [25–27] used a prosodic features, and [28] used spectral features. [27] used too a Voice Quality and Teo-Based Features. The developed system by [26] gives 66% classification accuracy only using energy and pitch features.

According to [10] the recognition performance using local prosodic features is better compared to the performance of global prosodic features, and experimental results obtained in [29] demonstrate that there is a significant improvement in the performance of spontaneous speech emotion recognition.

Features extraction is the most important step in Pattern Recognition Systems. [30] show a new feature extraction method, that can be implement in real-time with gender and speaker independent SER, was done the test with three different database and obtained an accuracy between 86% and 96,3%. Other work that introduce news in this field was developed by [31], where was implemented the Whale-Imperialist Optimization algorithm (Whale-IpCA), thus they obtained 99,9% of precision.

3   Speech Signal and Databases

Sentiment analysis of speech signals focuses on identifying the emotional or physical state of a person by analysing their voice [1].

The speech signal is the most natural method of communication between people. For access to emotional content, in the extraction moment, are applied signal processing techniques. However, some authors use a set of predefined features, such as [4] Gammatone Cepstral Coefficients (GTCC) or software (openSMILE) for feature extraction. Feature selection or feature transformation techniques lika Principal Component Analysis (PCA) are used for have the best input features of a classifier system [32]. The transformation techniques consist of doing a remapping of the original features set and changing them into new features sets with different axis (in general, these techniques are applied without selection techniques). The feature selection techniques can be classified into supervised, unsupervised, semi-supervised and divided into five categories: filter, wrapper, embedded, hybrid and ensemble (for more information see: [4,32]).

3.1   Databases

The databases used in this type of work can be of many types: physiological and multimodal physiological databases, textual, video, image, and audio databases. In this work we focused on audio databases. According to how emotional speech is generated, the databases (of emotional speech) are categorised into three groups [9]: **Acted, Evoked, Natural**. Audio databases usually contain natural or acted emotional speech data, but a large portion of acted speech data contains unlabeled data (it is unsuitable for research purposes) [1,3].

The **acted database** is most commonly used and is collected from experienced professional artists. These databases contain high-quality audio and avoid recording problems such as microphone distance, codec-effect, or noise. Its pros are: All desired emotions are available; Standardised and predefined speaker and text and easy to compare with existing works. Its cons are: Large cost in database construction; there is a lack of context in the utterances; Read-out emotions; absence of natural emotions.

The **evoked database** are collected by generating an emotional situation. In this database, the speaker converses with an anchor, who generates various contextual states to produce induced emotions that are reflected in the speaker's speech. However, this database doesn't produce all categories of emotions, and the context is artificial. Its pros are: Close to natural and context is present, and its cons are: context is artificial; all emotions may not be present; unbalanced data.

The **natural database** are naturally expressed and useful for real-word emotion modeling. For collecting these databases, there are many ways, such as patient-doctor conversations, public place recordings, call centre conversations, or cockpit recordings. However, these may not contain all emotions. Its pros are: real emotions; such databases are abundant in nature; low cost in database construction and contextual information is present. Its cons are: data unbalanced with respect to emotions and utterance lengths; all emotions may not be present; ethical issues in using a database; presence of background noise; overlapping of multiple emotions in an utterance and utterances themselves.

In this work, we used an acted database, the Berlin Database of Emotional Speech (Emo-db), and it has samples of 10 speakers, each recording at a sample frequency of 16 KHz with a resolution of 16 bits in mono. The database contains 10 subjects (5 females), with an average age of 29.7 years. The emotional states "anger" has 127 samples, "boredom" has 81, "disgust" has 49, "anxiety/fear" has 69, "happiness" has 71, "sadness" has 62, and "neutral" has 79 samples.

3.2   Features

There are various physiological features that can be used to detect an emotional state. Some examples are cited in [1] such as features made in electromyogram, electroencephalogram, blood volume pulse, respiratory volume, skin temperature, heart rate or respiration pattern.

Speech is another rich source of features for detecting the emotional state. It is important to know that the labelled emotion is not present in the total utterance. For this reason, preprocessing is required to find the salient segments that are specific to the corresponding emotion. Another reason is to remove background noise in the speech signal [3]. After choosing a database, the next step is to find efficient features that can be discriminant of emotions.

The extraction of features generates a large amount of data and can thus provoke over-fitting, so we need more time during the training process. This problem is generally solved by reducing the dimensionality of extracted features. The speech features can be categorised as continuous, voice quality, spectral, and non-linear Teager Energy Operator (TEO) features (Fig. 1) [4,7]. On the other hand, some authors do a different classification. For example, in [10], the features may be categorised into two categories: acoustic and linguistic features. The Low-Level Descriptors (LLD) and duration-related features are highlighted within the acoustic categorical.

Duration features are related to segment distribution of voiced or unvoiced and include features such as chunk length (measured in seconds) and the zero-crossing rate (to roughly decode speaking rate). For pause detection (and associated features), it is necessary to apply a voice activity detector algorithm. Thus, pauses are considered to be the proportion of non-speech detected.

The linguistic features can analyse grammatical alteration and have different ways that can interpret them, such as keyword spotting, rule-based modeling, semantic trees, latent semantic analysis, transformation-based learning, world-knowledge-modeling, key-phrase spotting [10].

3.3   Acoustic Features in Speech Emotions

It is important to understand that any emotional state has unique characteristics. Many of these characteristics are "shown" in the sympathetic and parasympathetic nervous systems via arousal level, heart rate, blood pressure, and, in

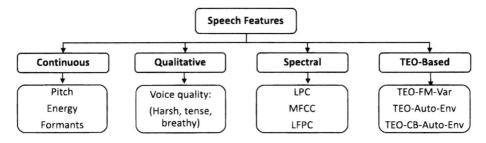

Fig. 1. Features of classification according to: [7]

some cases, the mouth stays dry and the muscles react instinctively. However, it is important to mention that speech emotion recognition is very challenging because it is not clear which speech features are most powerful in distinguishing between emotions, there may be more than one perceived emotion in the same utterance, and emotional state depends on each speaker, culture, and environment [7].

This will be reflected in the speech, resulting in a quick or slow speech, high or low intensity, and with much or little energy in determined frequencies, depending on the emotional state and provoked effects.

The citation of [10] affirms the mentioned above:

"When one is in a state of anger, fear or joy, the sympathetic nervous system is aroused, the heart rate and blood pressure increase, the mouth becomes dry and there are occasional muscle tremors... When one is bored or sad, the parasympathetic nervous system is aroused, the heart rate and blood pressure decrease and salivation increases, which results in slow, low-pitched speech with little high-frequency energy."

Emotional state has unique characteristics in speech. In Table 1 (author source), it is possible to see the typical characteristics of speech that indicate a determinate emotional state. For possible emotion identification, prosody features such pitch, and voice quality may have important information [2]. On the other hand, some important features for emotional recognition are Linear Predictive Coefficients (LPC), Line Spectral Frequencies (LSF), and Linear Prediction Cepstral Coefficients (LPCC) [23]. According to [2], the emotional state of "disgust" is more difficult to identify. This can be justified as it is a slightly complex emotion that is difficult for a human to identify (to label) correctly. In Table 2 (author source), we can see some promissory features that have proved direct interference in some emotional states.

According to our knowledge, the speech features most commonly used to identify the emotional state are: raw time signal, formants, pitch, energy, MFCC, speech intensity, speaking rate. Actually, some quality voice features were used, such as HNR, jitter, and shimmer [33,34]. The duration features generally used are: the number of voiced and unvoiced regions; the number of voiced and unvoiced frames; the longest voiced and unvoiced region; ratio of number of voiced vs. unvoiced frames; ratio of number of voiced vs. unvoiced regions; ratio of number of voiced vs. total number of frames; ratio of number of voiced vs. total number of regions, jitter, and tremor [10].

In this work we focused in three features:

Pitch (Fundamental Frequency (F0)): Corresponds to the number of cycles that the mucous of the vocal folds oscillates in one second [35]. The typical values for men 120 Hz 210 Hz for women, with acoustic characteristics [36] and usually varying with time in speech [37], but these values can change with age or physical conditions [38].

Linear Predictive Coding (LPC) Coefficients: is a method that results in a number of coefficients that can be transformed into the envelope of the spectrum of the input frame. As a spectrum is suitable for determining the harmonic content, so are the LPC-coefficients [39].

Mel-Frequency Cepstral Coefficients (MFCCs): Calculated through the frequency spectrum of small windows of the speech signal, which is obtained by the Fast Fourier Transform (FFT) of the signal. In order to obtain an approximation of the perception of the human auditory system to the frequencies of sound, the frequency spectrum is subjected to a bank of triangular filters, equally spaced in the Mel frequency scale. Through the discrete co-sine transform applied to the output of the filters, the coefficients of the Mel Frequency are determined [40].

Table 1. Emotional state with correspondence characteristics

Emotional state	Characteristics
Anger	High Pitch; High Energy; High variation in intensity; In the men the speech rate is lower than in women;
Disgust	Low mean Pitch; Low Intensity; In the men the speech rate is lower than in women;
Fear	High Pitch; High Intensity; The speech rate is faster than in emotional state "Disgust"
Happiness/Joy	High mean Pitch; High Intensity; High Speech rate; Few syllables (the last one is usually accented)
Sadness	Low mean Intensity; Low mean Pitch;
Neutral	Slow speaking speed;

3.4 How to Create a Database to Study Emotional State

There are some speech databases that can be employed in applications for a wide range of domains. One of the restrictions in speech databases is the number of available voices. To assure, in emotion recognition, the coverage of the most common sequences in a given language, the inventory must contain a considerable number of speech recordings (from 3 to 10 h or more). It is important to choose carefully the contents that can provide a good coverage of the phonetics and intonation of the selected language [41]. The duration recording session needs a large number of recording sessions and a strict recording procedure to assure

Table 2. Features that can identify some emotional states

Features	Description
Pitch	Allows to separate "fear" of "joy"; In "sadness" show similar characteristics to "neutral".
Speech Rate	In "sad" the speech speed of mans is more quickly than when they are angry
Arousal (and valence dimensions)	can be used to identify basics emotional states
Pitch (related features)	Can identify emotional state with high level of ativation (high arousal- Anger and Happiness)
MFCC + Pitch	Can identify emotional states with high arousal level (anger, fear, joy) of emotional state with low level (sadness).
Formants	Good recognition rate for Anger; Standard desviation more high in female voices (15%); Have a significant diferences between "neutral" and others emotional states (with vowels analyzing);
Pitch + MFCC + Formants	Good recognition rate in general for all emotional states.

the uniformity of the database [42]. To create a speech database it is important to take several factors into account:

Creation of Recording Prompts: There are various approaches (for example, speech about specific domains, reading a specific text, or describing images);

Speaker Selection: Generally, the speaker selection is based on the results of recording test sessions or all speakers that have conditional status on the initial stage (the critical participation features are based on features such as age, gender, culture, or language).

Recording Setup: In addition to the basic equipment (computers, microphones, mixing desks, etc.), some recording rooms contain mirrors or video cameras to help the speaker maintain the recommended distance from the microphone [41].

Quality Control: The control of the recordings is done in two stages. The first is conducted during the recording session and the second by the analysis of the recordings performed after the session [41].

In the emotion recording samples, it is important to have defined the set of emotions that we want to record. Generally, all emotion databases have the set of emotions known as "the Big Six": sadness, happiness, anger, fear, surprise, and disgust [42]. Appropriate size begins with one hour of recordings [42], and it is important to note recording language, number and gender of speakers, label emotions, and type of kind (simulated, natural, or elicited) [21].

4   Methodology

We used the Berlin Database of Emotional Speech (Emo-DB) described in Sect. 3.1. In this work, we used the Support Vector Machine (SVM) to classify the emotional state and implemented the leave-one-out method (see Sect. 4.1). Our working model is made up of seven SVMs, each of which is responsible for distinguishing between two categories. Table 3 shows a description of each SVM as well as all subjects used.

The features used consist of Pitch or Fundamental Frequency (F0), Linear Predictive Coeficients (LPC), and Mel Frequency Coeficients Cepstral (MFCC's-13) and were used in their combination to try to find the best solution for identifying emotional state. In a more advanced step, we apply a SVM capable of classifying between multiple classes (different from the traditional SVM that only does binary classification).

In this work, five measures are used to evaluate the system. All the measures were calculated according to the following equations:

$$Accuracy(Acc) = (TP + TN)/N \tag{1}$$

$$Precision(P) = TP/(TP + FP) \tag{2}$$

$$Sensibility(S) = TP/(TP + FN) \tag{3}$$

$$Specificity(Sp) = TN/(FP + TN) \tag{4}$$

$$F1score(F1) = 2 * (P * S)/(P + S) \tag{5}$$

where N is the number total of samples, TP True Positives, TN True Negatives, FP False Positives, and FN are False Negatives. As the classes to be classified are too unbalanced, the precision values are meaningless, only F1.

Table 3. Number of subjects used in each category

SVM	Description (categorie vs. all)	Subject number (categorie/all)
1	Neutral vs. Others	79/456
2	Anger vs. Others	127/408
3	Anxiety vs. Others	69/466
4	Boredom vs. Others	81/454
5	Disgust vs. Others	46/489
6	Happiness vs. Others	71/464
7	Sadness vs. Others	62/473

4.1   Cross Validation "Leave-One-Out"

The lack of features can make the model generalisation difficult because there may not be sufficient features to create a training and test set. This problem can be resolved by applying cross validation techniques. One possibility is cross validation in k-folds. This method consists of testing all subjects and performing as many training sessions as subjects exist in the sample size. In N session of training, N–1 subjects were used to train and the remaining were used to test.

At the end, all subjects were tested and never used in the training process. This methodology is a time-consuming process but allows using a larger number of subjects to train and to test [43].

5   Results

The obtained results may be compromised because of two factors: unbalanced database that have more instances in a category than another one, or the existence of many similar features between categories that can be used to induce error in the classification tool.

In Tables 4a–4d, it is possible to see the obtained results with the features F0, LPC, MFCC and set of all features, correspondingly. The graphic in Fig. 2 shows the comparison of the accuracy obtained in the 7 svm's implemented with the different parameter sets.

To identify the "neutral" emotional state, the highest accuracy rate obtained was 81.1% with the use of the LPC (Table 4b)). To identify the "Anger", "anxiety", "boredom" and "hapiness" emotional states, the most promising was the total set (3 parameters) with an accuracy of 68%, 78,5%, 82% and 77.2% correspondingly (Table 4d)). For "disgust", the accuracy rate was similar in all parameters with 79.8% (Table 4a, 4b and 4d), and for "sadness" it was 87.5% with the F0 analysis (Table 4a). However, there are similar results with the others set of features.

With the analysis of Fig. 2, it can be seen that the identification of the category "anger" (SVM 2), regardless of the parameters analysed, presents an accuracy rate much lower than the remaining emotions. For the emotions "anxiety" and "boredom", the classification is better using the all set of features.

For a multiple classifier, the Table 5 show the obtained results. We applied the same methodology that in binary classification (analysed the same set of features and leave-one-out). The difference is that in multi-classification, each emotional state was labelled with a different categorical name, and the main goal in this task is to identify what emotional state the tested subject is in. Thus, the SVM function is to predict, according to the features of the tested subject, what its emotional state is.

For a multi-category classification, the most promising feature set in this work was the LPC which achieved an accuracy rate of 42.6%, precision of 59.1%, sensitivity of 60.5%, specificity of 59.1%, and F1 of 59.8% (Table 5). The F0 features produces the lowest values.

Figure 3 shows the confusion matrix obtained in the multi-category classification with the analysis of all parameters, where 'A' corresponds to the emotion "anxiety/fear", E-"disgust", F-"happiness", L-"boredom", N-"neutral", T-"sadness" and W-"anger". In the main diagonal are the samples that were correctly identified.

Table 4. Metrics obtained with:

(a) F0

SVM	Acc (%)	P(%)	S(%)	Sp(%)	F1 (%)
Neutral	80	32,5	32,9	88,2	32,7
Anger	66,5	32,7	38,6	75,3	35,4
Anxiety	74,8	19,4	30,4	81,3	23,7
Boredom	80	37	45,7	86,1	40,9
Disgust	**79,8**	5,7	8,7	86,5	6,9
Happiness	76,6	20,6	26,8	84,3	23,3
Sadness	**87,5**	45,9	45,2	93	45,5

(b) LPC

Acc (%)	P(%)	S(%)	Sp(%)	F1 (%)
81.1	29.6	20.3	91.7	24
66	32.3	39.4	74.3	35,5
75	20.2	31.9	81.3	24.7
80.2	37.4	45.7	86.3	41.1
79.8	5.7	8.7	86.5	6.9
76.8	20.2	25.4	84.7	22.5
87.3	45	43.6	93	44.3

(c) MFCC

SVM	Acc(%)	P(%)	S(%)	Sp(%)	F1 (%)
Neutral	80.9	34.3	31.7	89.5	32.9
Anger	66.4	32.9	40.2	74.5	36.2
Anxiety	75	19.6	30.4	81.6	23.8
Boredom	80.2	37.6	46.7	86.1	41.7
Disgust	79.6	5.6	8.7	86.3	6.8
Happiness	77	20.5	25.4	84.9	22.7
Sadness	87.1	44.3	43.6	92.8	43.9

(d) F0+LPC+MFCC

Acc(%)	P(%)	S(%)	Sp(%)	F1 (%)
80,6	34,9	36,7	88,2	35,8
68	35,5	42,5	76	38,7
78,5	23,3	29	85,8	25,8
82	41,6	45,7	88,6	43,5
79,8	5,7	8,7	86,5	6,9
77,2	22	28,2	84,7	24,7
87,3	44,6	40,3	93,4	42,4

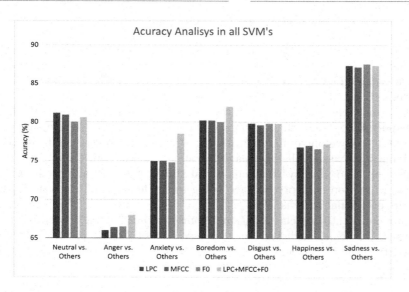

Fig. 2. Accuracy comparation between features sets and SVM's

Table 5. Metrics obtained for multi-classification.

	F0	LPC	MFCC	ALL
Acc (%)	34,2	**42,6**	39,3	35,1
P(%)	49,2	**59,1**	57,1	50,8
S(%)	52,9	**60,5**	55,7	53,3
Sp(%)	49,2	**59,1**	57,1	50,8
F1(%)	51,0	**59,8**	56,4	52,0

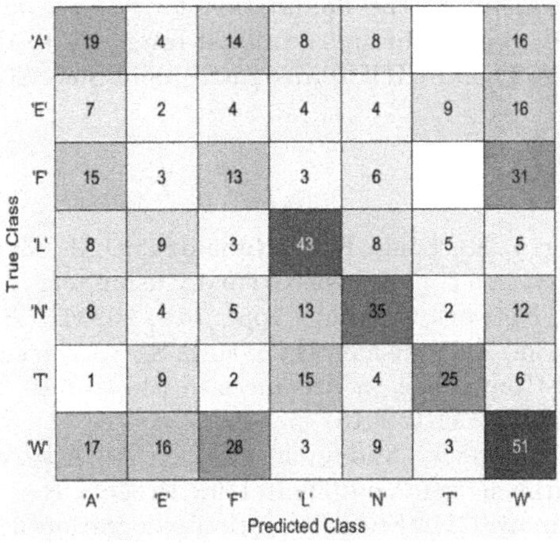

Fig. 3. Confusion matrix of multi-classification with set of all features

6   Conclusions and Future Work

In this work, SVM was used and two types of classification were implemented: binary and multi-classification. In binary classification, we separated one emotional state from another, and SVM had a function to identify if the test subject done part of the identified emotional state or another one. We did seven binary classifications (one for each emotional state).

In multi-classification, we analysed all emotional states in the same SVM, with the goal of identifying the emotional state of the test subject (among several possibilities). For binary classifications, we reached a maximum accuracy of 87.5% with F0 analysis to discriminate "sadness" from the remaining emotional states. For multi-category classification, the results were lower, but LPC presented the best measures achieved. Despite applying the leave-one-out method, the results could be improved if the categories had a more balanced sample size.

In future work, we intend to detect the emotional state in a database that we are building in a natural context based on free speech and on the reading of a short excerpt. In future work, we intend to use prosodic and quality speech (previously mentioned in 3) features extracted in speech segments instead of considering all utterances as unique segment. We intend to implement different classification models to try to improve the success rate obtained.

Acknowledgements. This work has the support of Research Centre in Digitalization and Intelligent Robotics (CEDRI), Instituto Politécnico de Bragança (IPB), School of Sciences and Technology-Engineering Department (UTAD). This project is supported by the European Regional Development Fund (ERDF) through the Regional Operational Program North 2020, within the scope of Project GreenHealth - Digital strategies in biological assets to improve well-being and promote green health, Norte -01-0 145-FEDER-000042.

The authors are grateful to the Foundation for Science and Technology (FCT, Portugal) for financial support through national funds FCT/MCTES (PIDDAC) to CeDRI (UIDB/05757/2020 and UIDP/05757/2020) and SusTEC (LA/P/0007/ 2021).

References

1. Shoumy, N.J., Ang, L.M., Seng, K.P., Rahaman, D.M., Zia, T.: Multimodal big data affective analytics: a comprehensive survey using text, audio, visual and physiological signals. J. Network Comput. Appl. **149**, 102447 (2020)
2. Lalitha, S., Madhavan, A., Bhushan, B., Saketh, S.: Speech emotion recognition. In: 2014 International Conference on Advances in Electronics, Computers and Communications, vol. 7, pp. 7–10 (2015)
3. Shah Fahad, M., Ranjan, A., Yadav, J., Deepak, A.: A survey of speech emotion recognition in natural environment. Digital Sig. Process. Rev. J. **110**, 102951 (2021)
4. Bandela, S.R., Kumar, T.K.: Speech emotion recognition using unsupervised feature selection algorithms. Radioengineering **29**, 353–364 (2020)
5. Imani, M., Montazer, G.A.: A survey of emotion recognition methods with emphasis on E-Learning environments. J. Network Comput. Appl. **147**, 102423 (2019)
6. Mao, Q.R., Zhao, X.L., Huang, Z.W., Zhan, Y.Z.: Speaker-independent speech emotion recognition by fusion of functional and accompanying paralanguage features. J. Zhejiang Univ. Sci. C **14**, 573–582 (2013)
7. El Ayadi, M., Kamel, M.S., Karray, F.: Survey on speech emotion recognition: features, classification schemes, and databases. Pattern Recogn. **44**(3), 572–587 (2011)
8. Malova, I.S., Tikhomirova, D.V.: Recognition of emotions in verbal messages based on neural networks. Procedia Comput. Sci. **190**, 560–563 (2021)
9. Vasuki, P., Sambavi, B., Joe, V.: Construction and evaluation of tamil speech emotion corpus. Natl. Acad. Sci. Let. **43**, 533–536 (2020)
10. Ramakrishnan, S., El Emary, I.M.: Speech emotion recognition approaches in human computer interaction. Telecommun. Syst. **52**(3), 1467–1478 (2013)
11. Nunes, A., Coimbra, R.L., Teixeira, A.: Voice quality of european portuguese emotional speech. In: Pardo, T.A.S., Branco, A., Klautau, A., Vieira, R., de Lima, V.S. (eds.) PROPOR 2010. LNCS (LNAI), vol. 6001, pp. 142–151. Springer, Heidelberg (2010). https://doi.org/10.1007/978-3-642-12320-7_19
12. Lopes, R.P., et al.: Digital Technologies for Innovative Mental Health Rehabilitation, pp. 1–15 (2021)
13. Khalil, R.A., Jones, E., Babar, M.I., Jan, T., Zafar, M.H., Alhussain, T.: Speech emotion recognition using deep learning techniques: a review. IEEE Access **7**, 117327–117345 (2019)

14. Rodrigues, P.M., Teixeira, J.P.: Alzheimer's disease recognition with artificial neural networks, pp. 112–119 (2013)
15. Rodrigues, P.M., Teixeira, J.P.: Classification of electroencephalogram signals using artificial neural networks. In: Proceedings - 2010 3rd International Conference on Biomedical Engineering and Informatics, BMEI 2010, vol. 2, pp. 808–812 (2010)
16. Rodrigues, P., Teixeira, J.: Artificial neural networks in the discrimination of alzheimer's disease. In: Cruz-Cunha, M.M., Varajão, J., Powell, P., Martinho, R. (eds.) CENTERIS 2011. CCIS, vol. 221, pp. 272–281. Springer, Heidelberg (2011). https://doi.org/10.1007/978-3-642-24352-3_29
17. Guedes, V., Junior, A., Fernandes, J., Teixeira, F., Teixeira, J.: Long short term memory on chronic laryngitis classification. In: Procedia Computer Science, vol. 138 (2018)
18. Guedes, V., et al.: Transfer learning with audioset to voice pathologies identification in continuous speech. Procedia Comput. Sci. **164**, 662–669 (2019)
19. Panahi, F., Rashidi, S., Sheikhani, A.: Application of fractional Fourier transform in feature extraction from ELECTROCARDIOGRAM and GALVANIC SKIN RESPONSE for emotion recognition. Biomed. Signal Process. Control **69**, 102863 (2021)
20. Pestana-Santos, A., Loureiro, L., Santos, V., Carvalho, I.: Patients with schizophrenia assessing psychiatrists' communication skills. Psych. Res. **269**, 13–20 (2018)
21. Ververidis, D., Kotropoulos, C.: Emotional speech recognition: resources, features, and methods. Speech Commun. **48**, 1162–1181 (2006)
22. Akçay, M.B., Oğuz, K.: Speech emotion recognition: emotional models, databases, features, preprocessing methods, supporting modalities, and classifiers. Speech Commun. **116**, 56–76 (2020)
23. Pribil, J., Pribilova, A., Matousek, J.: Comparison of formant features of male and female emotional speech in czech and slovak. Elektronika ir Elektrotechnika **19**(8), 83–88 (2013)
24. Prasanth, S., Roshni Thanka, M., Bijolin Edwin, E., Nagaraj, V.: Speech emotion recognition based on machine learning tactics and algorithms. Mater. Today Proc. (2021)
25. Rao, K.S., Koolagudi, S.G., Vempada, R.R.: Emotion recognition from speech using global and local prosodic features. Int. J. Speech Technol. **16**, 143–160 (2013)
26. Shen, P., Changjun, Z., Chen, X.: Automatic speech emotion recognition using support vector machine. In: Proceedings of 2011 International Conference on Electronic and Mechanical Engineering and Information Technology, EMEIT 2011, vol. 2, pp. 621–625 (2011)
27. Low, L.S.A., Maddage, N.C., Lech, M., Sheeber, L.B., Allen, N.B.: Detection of clinical depression in adolescents' speech during family interactions. IEEE Trans. Biomed. Eng. **58**, 574–586 (2011)
28. Bitouk, D., Verma, R., Nenkova, A.: Class-level spectral features for emotion recognition. Speech Commun. **52**(7), 613–625 (2010)
29. Chakraborty, R., Pandharipande, M., Kopparapu, S.K.: Knowledge-based framework for intelligent emotion recognition in spontaneous speech. Procedia Comput. Sci. **96**, 587–596 (2016)
30. Abdulmohsin, H.A. Abdul Wahab, H.B., Abdul Hossen, A.M.J.: A new proposed statistical feature extraction method in speech emotion recognition. Comput. Electric. Eng. **93**, 107172 (2021)

31. Mannepalli, K., Sastry, P.N., Suman, M.: Emotion recognition in speech signals using optimization based multi-SVNN classifier. J. King Saud Univ. Comput. Inform. Sci. **34**(2), 384–397 (2022)
32. Silva, L., Bispo, B., Teixeira, J.P.: Features selection algorithms for classification of voice signals. Procedia Comput. Sci. **181**, 948–956 (2021)
33. Fernandes, J., Teixeira, F., Guedes, V., Junior, A., Teixeira, J.P.: Harmonic to noise ratio measurement - selection of window and length. Procedia Comput. Sci. **138**, 280–285 (2018)
34. Teixeira, J.P., Gonçalves, A.: Algorithm for jitter and shimmer measurement in pathologic voices. Procedia Comput. Sci. **100**, 271–279 (2016)
35. Bohadana, S.C.: Vibração das pregas vocais pré e pós aproximação cricotireóidea: estudo experimental em laringes humanas por videoquimografia (2001)
36. Demircan, S., Örnek, H.K.: Comparison of the effects of mel coefficients and spectrogram images via deep learning in emotion classification. Traitement du Signal **37**(1), 51–57 (2020)
37. Dong, B.: Characterizing resonant component in speech: a different view of tracking fundamental frequency. Mech. Syst. Sign. Process. **88**, 318–333 (2017)
38. Netto, W.F., Traunmuller, H., Eriksson, A.: A extensão da frequência fundamental da voz na fala de homens e mulheres adultos (2009)
39. Struwe, K.: Voiced-unvoiced classification of speech using a neural network trained with LPC coefficients. In: Proceedings - 2017 International Conference on Control, Artificial Intelligence, Robotics and Optimization, ICCAIRO 2017, pp. 56–59 (2017)
40. Fernandes, J., Silva, L., Teixeira, F., Guedes, V., Santos, J., Teixeira, J.P.: Parameters for vocal acoustic analysis - cured database. Procedia Comput. Sci. **164**, 654–661 (2019)
41. Oliveira, L.C., Paulo, S., Figueira, L., Mendes, C., Nunes, A., Godinho, J.: Methodologies for designing and recording speech databases for corpus based synthesis," Proceedings of the 6th International Conference on Language Resources and Evaluation, LREC 2008, pp. 2921–2925 (2008)
42. Saratxaga, I., Navas, E., Hernáez, I., Luengo, I.: Designing and recording an emotional speech database for corpus based synthesis in Basque. Proceedings of the 5th International Conference on Language Resources and Evaluation, LREC 2006, pp. 2126–2129 (2006)
43. Teixeira, F.L., Teixeira, J.P.: Deep-learning in identification of vocal pathologies. In: BIOSIGNALS 2020–13th International Conference on Bio-Inspired Systems and Signal Processing, Proceedings; Part of 13th International Joint Conference on Biomedical Engineering Systems and Technologies, BIOSTEC 2020, vol. 4, no. Biostec 2020, pp. 288–295 (2020)

Solanum lycopersicum - Fusarium oxysporum Fo47 Interaction Study Using ML Classifiers in Transcriptomic Data

Vânia Rodrigues[1]([✉]) [iD] and Sérgio Deusdado[2] [iD]

[1] USAL - Universidad de Salamanca, 37008 Salamanca, Spain
vania.rodrigues@usal.es
[2] CIMO - Centro de Investigação de Montanha, Instituto Politécnico de Bragança,
5301-855 Bragança, Portugal
sergiod@ipb.pt

Abstract. *Fusarium oxysporum* Fo47 is a pervasive endophyte that can colonize plant roots, initiating an interaction that can provide phytosanitary defenses. The response triggered by this non-pathogenic fungus is not well understood. To elucidate the *Solanum lycopersicum - Fusarium oxysporum* Fo47 interaction, machine learning methods were used to identify the informative genes (IGs) using publicly available transcriptomic data. The assembled dataset revealed 244 significantly differentially expressed genes (DEGs). The experimental work with machine learning classifiers achieved significant identification of these DEGs. Multilayer Perceptron (MLP) classifiers and Kernel Logistic Regression metalearners (meta-KLR) parameterization was optimized, achieving MLP-b and meta-KLR-b near optimal performance. Afterwards, these classifiers were used as attribute evaluators identifying two sets (A,B) of highest-rated genes, 393 (set A) by MLP-b and 317 (set B) by meta-KLR-b. Regarding the percent of significantly differentially expressed genes found by the classifiers compared to the total 244 DEGs, the set A presented 92.2%, while the set B presented 84.8%. Considering B⊂A, the IGs identified by MLP-b (set A) were used in the subsequent analysis. Among this 393 IGs, 379 were identified as *Solanum lycopersicum* genes, 1 as *Escherichia coli* protein (Hygromycin-B 4-O-kinase), 1 as *Saccharomyces cerevisiae* protein (galactose-responsive transcription factor GAL4) and 12 were unidentified. Then, a functional enrichment analysis of the *Solanum lycopersicum* IGs showed 283 biological processes and 20 biological pathways involved in the *Solanum lycopersicum* - Fo47 interaction.

Keywords: Machine learning · Informative genes · Tomato - *Fusarium oxysporum* 47 interaction

1 Introduction

The non-pathogenic *Fusarium oxysporum* Fo47 is a biological control agent. Its efficiency against pathogenic Fusarium strains has been demonstrated in several plant species [1–5]. The mechanisms triggered in plants treated with this beneficial fungus Fo47 are not well understood. In tomato roots, Fo47 is a good candidate for priming the defense responses [6]. The endophyte-mediated resistance conferred by the Fo47 against Fusarium wilt disease in tomato is independent of ethylene, jasmonic acid and salicylic acid [7]. This implies that this induced resistance-response is distinct from the classical Induced Systemic Resistance (ISR) response. Veloso and Díaz study [8] suggests that Fo45 is not able to protect tomato wild type cv Pearson against Verticillium dahlia but, intriguingly, it was able to protect the ethylene-insensitive tomato mutant Never-ripe. To understand the biological mechanism trigged in tomato-Fo47 interaction, machine learning (ML) methods on transcriptomic data can be used to provide novel insights. ML is widely used in biological data, including plants transcriptomic data, but the research field in Plant-Endophytic microorganisms interaction is very incipient.

In this paper, we have employed ML classifiers to identify informative genes (IGs) involved in Tomato-Fo47 interaction. Primarily, multicollinearity tests were performed on the datasets (Sect. 2.1) to validate the samples assigned to each group. Then, Multilayer Perceptron (MLP) and Kernel Logistic Regression metalearners (meta-KLR) were used for classification and those that obtained the better results were used to identify IGs. Multilayer Perceptron is based on an artificial neural network where the mapping between inputs and output is non-linear [9]. KLR model is based on probabilistic assignment of data that generates a fit model by minimizing the negative log-likelihood with a quadratic penalty using the Broyden-Fletcher-Goldfard-Shanno (BFGS) optimization [10]. For each KLR metalearner, chi-squared statistic was applied as attribute evaluator. Afterwards, the identification of the biological processes and the biological pathways of highest-rated *Solanum lycopersicum* genes were researched to understand their functions and interactions.

2   Materials and Methods

2.1   Dataset Collection

The original datasets were obtained from GEO/NCBI database with GSE49432 reference accession. Composed by 10209 attributes and 6 samples, they gather the expression profiles of tomato wild-type cv. Pearson line analysed 48 h after treatment with Fo47 [8].

2.2   Experimental Procedures

Aiming to validate the datasets integrity, Uniform Manifold Approximation and Projection (UMAP) was applied on the original datasets, removing the samples classification, to visualize how the samples are correlated. Then, multicollinearity tests [11] were performed to co-validate results. After sample groups classification confirmation, correctly assigned to treated and control, the datasets were preprocessed and normalized to [−1,1], composing the final assembled dataset. Then,

MLP classifiers and KLR metalearners were executed using different parameterization (see Sect. 2.3). Accuracy, mean absolute error, precision, recall, f-measure, and area under precision-recall curve [12], were used for performance evaluation. These experiments ran 10 times several schemes using leave-one-out cross-validation (LOOCV) testing with Paired T-Tester (corrected). Then, the classifier with the best performance evaluation was used to identify the informative attributes (genes), being important to add that the other tested classifiers corroborate the same attributes but in less number. To do this, applying the best outcome of our experimental work, the classifier was used for estimating the accuracy and root mean squared error (RMSE) of attributes combinations subsets with 4 folds, using 3-fold CV. If the standard deviation of the means exceeded 0.01, the attributes combinations were repeated, otherwise, the ranks were obtained according to the evaluation.

The experimental work was based on WEKA, version 3.9.5, a datamining workbench publicly accessible at: www.cs.waikato.ac.nz/ml/weka/.

Using g:Profiler [13], a functional enrichment analysis by GO terms of biological processes was performed to provide biological gene annotations of highest-rated *Solanum lycopersicum* genes. Subsequently, a Kyoto Encyclopedia of Genes and Genomes (KEGG) analysis was performed to understand their functions and interactions.

Limma precision weights (vooma function) and quantile normalization were applied to the sample groups to obtain significantly differentially expressed genes with adjusted p-value < 0.05 (Benjamini & Hochberg false discovery rate).

2.3   Parameters Tunning

A grid search approach was used to optimize the parameters of MLP classifiers and KLR metalearners. The parameters optimized for MLP classifiers were learning rate (LR) and hidden layers (HL), with momentum set to 0.2. LR was tested between 0.2 and 0.9, while tunning HL = 1, and for the same range of LR tunning HL = 2. After performing grid search, two MLP classifiers emerged as the best performers, MLP-a (LR = 0.3, HL = 1) and MLP-b (LR = 0.3, HL = 2). In KLR metalearners, chi-squared attribute evaluator was used to reduce dimensionality. The parameter λ was adjusted in two iterations to, respectively, 0.01 and 0.001, both using a linear kernel function with the reduction of the number of attributes to 7191, chosen after several tests. These two iterations configured two instances of the meta-KLR classifier, respectively meta-KLR-a and meta-KLR-b. All grid searches were executed using LOOCV.

3   Results and Discussion

3.1   Datasets Analysis

According to UMAP analysis, presented in Fig. 1, the samples GSM1199191, GSM1199195 and GSM1199193 are correlated. It is also verified a relation involving GSM1199190, GSM1199192 and GSM1199194 samples. These results suggest that the sample groups should be defined according to this sets. Comparing these results with the sample group shown in the GEO/NCBI database, we verified that the sample groups are differently assigned, control samples are GSM1199190, GSM1199191, and GSM1199192, and treated samples are GSM1199193, GSM1199194, GSM1199195. According to our analysis, it is probable that GSM1199191 and GSM1199194 were misassigned.

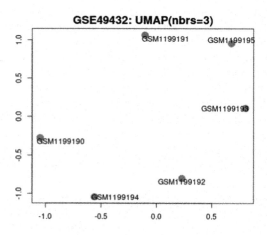

Fig. 1. UMAP applied without sample group selection. Nbrs=3 is the number of nearest neighbors used in the calculation.

To corroborate this assumption, multicollinearity tests were performed, determining the parameters of coefficient of determination, variance inflation factor (VIF) and condition index (CI), presented in Table 1. The coefficient of determination of all samples are very strong, ranging from 0.951 to 0.99. These results were expected, since the samples are from the same organism and data type (gene expression). The VIF identifies the correlation strength among the samples and increases with correlations proliferation among them. The function GSM1199194 = f(GSM1199190, GSM1199192) presents VIF = 104.025, the highest, and the function GSM1199195 = f(GSM1199191,GSM1199193) presents VIF = 77.749, indicating the higher multicollinearity among these samples ((GSM1199194, GSM1199190, GSM1199192) and (GSM1199195, GSM1199191, GSM1199193)). Furthermore, CI of both control and treated samples, proposed using UMAP, are higher than their corresponding groups. It is important to mention that these datasets can also be obtained from .cel files, and having processing them using the Transcriptomic Analysis Console tool, we strengthen the samples misassignment assumption. Therefore, in this study the treated samples were assigned to GSM1199191, GSM1199193 and GSM1199195 datasets, and the control samples were assigned to GSM1199190, GSM1199192 and GSM1199194 datasets.

Table 1. Multicollinearity tests results.

	Function	R^2	VIF	CI
Control samples	GSM1199190 = f(GSM1199191,GSM1199192)	0.979	48.369	
	GSM1199191 = f(GSM1199190,GSM1199192)	0.976	42.068	15.400
	GSM1199192 = f(GSM1199190,GSM1199191)	0.951	20.61	
Control samples	GSM1199190 = f(GSM1199192,GSM1199194)	0.978	46.267	
proposed using UMAP	GSM1199192 = f(GSM1199190,GSM1199194)	0.978	44.914	**21.544**
	GSM1199194 = f(GSM1199190,GSM1199192)	0.990	**104.025**	
Treated samples	GSM1199193 = f(GSM1199194,GSM1199195)	0.973	36.392	
	GSM1199194 = f(GSM1199193,GSM1199195)	0.967	29.882	15.393
	GSM1199195 = f(GSM1199194,GSM1199193)	0.981	52.811	
Treated samples	GSM1199193 = f(GSM1199191,GSM1199195)	0.972	35.053	
proposed using UMAP	GSM1199191 = f(GSM1199193,GSM1199195)	0.976	41.52	**18.64**
	GSM1199195 = f(GSM1199191,GSM1199193)	0.987	**77.749**	

R^2- coefficient of determination; VIF-Variance Inflation Factor; CI-Condition Index.

3.2 Classifiers Results

The experimental work was carried out with the classifiers parameterization described in the previous section. The results of the performance evaluation of meta-KLR with 7191 attributes and MLP are present in Table 2.

Table 2. Meta-KLR and MLP classifiers performance evaluation using LOOCV.

Metrics	Meta-KLR-a	Meta-KLR-b	MLP-a	MLP-b
ACC	83.33 (37.58)	100	98.33 (12.91)	100
k	0.83 (0.38)	1	0.98 (0.13)	1
MAE	0.15 (0.29)	0.09 (0.19)	0.11 (0.12)	0.13 (0.13)
PREC	1	1	1	1
REC	0.67 (0.48)	1	0.97 (0.18)	1

Meta-KLR-b and MLP-b achieved the best results in performance evaluation, followed by MLP-a and then meta-KLR-a. Due to the better results of meta-KLR-b and MLP-b, those were used as attribute evaluators, evaluating the worth of an attribute by estimation of the accuracy and root mean squared error of attributes combinations subsets with 4 folds, using 3-fold CV. Next, the attributes were ranked according to the average merit (Fig. 2). Emerged from the results, with score 1, two sets (A, B) of highest-rated genes, 393 (set A) by MLP-b and 317 (set B) by meta-KLR-b.

Knowing that 244 significantly differentially expressed genes (DEGs) with adjusted p-value < 0.05 threshold are present in the assembled dataset, from the set A there are 225 (92.2%) DEGs, 137 up-regulated and 88 down-regulated.

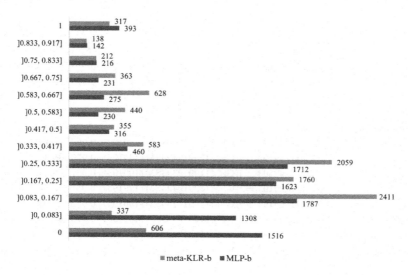

Fig. 2. Number of attributes and respective average merit obtained from meta-KLR-b and MLP-b.

From the set B, there are 207 (84.8%) DEGs, 120 up-regulated and 87 down-regulated. It is important to underline that the machine learning approach does not take DEG information into account.

Concomitantly, set A and set B were compared (data not shown), verifying that B⊂A, therefore, MLP-b identified 76 different IGs.

Consequently, the set A, with higher percentage of differential expression was chosen for further studies. Among the 393 IGs present in the set A, 379 were identified as *Solanum lycopersicum* genes, 1 as *Escherichia coli* protein, Hygromycin-B 4-O-kinase ($\log_2$FC = 2.98E-01, adjusted p-value = 2.55E-01), 1 as *Saccharomyces cerevisiae* protein, galactose-responsive transcription factor GAL4 ($\log_2$FC = -4.20E-01, adjusted p-value = 1.21E-01) and 12 attributes were unidentified.

3.3   Functional Enrichment Analysis

To the best of our knowledge, g: Profiler is the reference web server for functional enrichment analysis that presents information of the Gene Ontology and the biological pathways involved in *Solanum lycopersicum*. From the 379 attributes of set A, 97 were not included in the g: Profiler survey (4 were discarded due to ambiguous query and 93 were not found). The outcome showed that 154 of the 282 *Solanum lycopersicum* genes included in the survey were classified into 283 GO terms of biological processes, and 37 genes were classified into 20 pathways from KEGG, as shown in Table 6.

Biological Processes of the Tomato-*Fusarium oxysporum* Fo47 Interaction. The biological processes with more genes identified were: cellular process (132), metabolic process (111), primary metabolic process (98), cellular metabolic process (97), organic substance metabolic process (91), macromolecule metabolic process (67) and nitrogen compound metabolic process (66).

The expression profiles of tomato cv Pearson analysed 48h after treatment with Fo47 also showed the participation of four genes involved in defense response to fungus (Table 3). Among them, only the gene 1-aminocyclopropane-1-carboxylate oxidase was significantly differentially expressed.

Table 3. Informative genes involved in defense response of tomato to Fo47.

Probe ID	Gene description	$\log_2$FC	adj.pvalue
LES.122.1.S1_AT	Chitinase (CHI3)	0.36	2.80E-01
LES.5259.1.S1_AT	Protein EMSY-LIKE 3	0.296	3.51E-01
LESAFFX.57999.1.S1_AT	Plant UBX domain-containing protein 2	−0.362	2.46E-01
LES.132.1.S1_AT	1-aminocyclopropane-1-carboxylate oxidase	1.44	1.11E-03

Besides the response to fungus genes, were also identified five ethylene related genes (Table 4). Among them, three are significantly differentially expressed. Two up-regulated genes (1-aminocyclopropane-1-carboxylate oxidase and 1-aminocyclopropane-1-carboxylate synthase 2), and one down-regulated gene (ethylene response factor A.2). The biological process of basipetal auxin transport was also identified through up-regulated of the LOC101260574 gene (LESAFFX.24397.1.S1_AT), with $\log_2$FC equal to 2.19. In *Arabidopsis thaliana*, basipetal auxin transport is required for gravitropism in roots [14]. This gene is also involved in seed germination and seedling development.

Table 4. Informative genes involved in ethylene response and ethylene metabolic process.

Probe ID	Gene description	$\log_2$FC	adj.pvalue
LESAFFX.44837.1.S1_AT	Probable E3 ubiquitin-protein ligase XBOS32	−0.372	7.27E-02
LES.132.1.S1_AT	1-aminocyclopropane-1-carboxylate oxidase	1.44	1.11E-03
LES.3662.1.S1_AT	1-aminocyclopropane-1-carboxylate synthase 2	1.11	1.27E-03
LES.4140.1.S1_AT	Ethylene response factor A.2	−1.58	3.73E-04
LES.3575.1.S1_AT	Pti5	0.224	4.50E-01

The pathogenesis-related leaf protein 6 PR1b1 gene (Les.3408.1.S1_at) was also identified with $\log_2$FC equal to 2.28 (adjusted p-value = 1.25E-03). According to Tomato Functional Genomics Database (TFGD), this gene is involved in defense response to fungus and in response to biotic stimulus. TSI-1 protein TSI-1 gene (Les.3583.1.A1_at) shows $\log_2$FC equal to 1.58 (adjusted p-value = 2.41E-03) and it is also involved in response to biotic stimulus. Another pathogenic-related gene identified was the pathogenesis-related protein P4 gene (Les.4693.1.S1_at) that shows $\log_2$FC equal to 1.72 (adjusted p-value = 4.34E-03). Protein EIN3-like2 EIL2 gene (Les.3471.1.S1_at) shows the $\log_2$FC equal to −1.74 (adjusted p-value = 3.73E-04). Through the KEGG, this gene is named ethylene - insensitive protein 3. The MAP kinase phosphatase MKP1 gene (Les.3699.1.A1_at) shows $\log_2$FC equal to 1.54 (adjusted p-value = 5.11E-03). Auxin-responsive protein IAA19 gene (Les.3701.1.A1_at) shows $\log_2$FC equal to −1.65 (adjusted p-value = 5.35E-04). A recent study [15] did the comparison of sun, ovate, fs8.1 and auxin application on tomato fruit shape and gene expression. Ripening regulated protein DDTFR8 gene (Les.3726.1.S1_at) shows $\log_2$FC equal to −1.8 (adjusted p-value = 2.93E-04). According to Uniprot, it is involved in chaperone - mediated protein complex assembly and the protein folding both inferred from biological aspect of ancestor [16]. Proteinase inhibitor ARPI gene (Les.3756.1.S1_a_at) shows $\log_2$FC equal to 1.57 (adjusted p-value = 1.53E-03). This gene is an auxin-inducible proteinase inhibitor [17]. OVATE family protein OVATE gene (Les.3819.1.S1_at) presents $\log_2$FC equal to 1.27 (adjusted p-value = 3.73E-04). This gene is associated with fruit shape in tomato [15, 18, 19]. Universal stress protein USP gene (Les.4233.2.A1_at) shows $\log_2$FC equal to 1.66 (adjusted p-value = 4.85E-04). Annexin-interacting SpUSP plays important roles in the drought tolerance of tomato by influencing ABA-induced stomatal movement, increasing photosynthesis, and alleviating oxidative stress [20]. Xyloglucan endotransglucosylase-hydrolase XTH3 gene (Les.4353.1.S1_at) shows $\log_2$FC equal to −1.76 (adjusted p-value = 2.38E-03). According to Uniprot, this gene cleaves and religates xyloglucan polymers, an essential constituent of the primary cell wall, and thereby participates in cell wall construction of growing tissues. Ripening regulated protein DDTFR19 gene (Les.439.1.S1_at) shows $\log_2$FC equal to 1.74 (adjusted p-value = 2.39E-04). Type 2 metallothionein MT4 gene (Les.4426.1.A1_s_at) presents $\log_2$FC equal to 1.62 (adjusted p-value = 4.58E-03). According to Uniprot, metallothioneins have a high content of cysteine residues that bind various heavy metals. G-box binding protein GBF4 gene (Les.57.1.S1_at) shows $\log_2$FC equal to 1.36 (adjusted p-value = 2.93E-01). Root-knot nematode resistance protein Mi-1.2 gene (Les.74.1.S1_at) shows $\log_2$FC equal to 1.77 (adjusted p-value = 3.71E-03). According to Uniprot, it is involved in defense response. MAR-binding filament-like protein 1 MFP1 gene (Les.98.1.S1_at) presents $\log_2$FC equal to −1.63 (adjusted p-value = 2.45E-04). According to TFGD, it is involved in oxidation reduction. Extensin-like protein Dif54 gene (Les.99.1.S1_at) shows $\log_2$FC equal to −1.92 (adjusted p-value = 1.10E-03). It codes a hydroxyproline-rich glycoprotein that is thought to form crosslinked protein networks in the plant cell wall [21].

Nitrogen compound transport was also involved in tomato-Fo47 interaction, through LOC101267903 gene (LES.1152.1.S1_AT) which shows $\log_2$FC equal to −3.4 (adjusted p-value = 7.70E-04), and AP-3 complex subunit sigma-like gene (LESAFFX.41234.1.S1_AT) with $\log_2$FC equal to −0.23 (adjusted p-value = 3.95E-01). Pentose-phosphate shunt, non-oxidative branch is another biological process presents through LOC101260137 gene (LESAFFX.57367.1.S1_AT).

There is a strong association of the non-oxidative pentose phosphate pathway with photosynthesis metabolism [22]. Pyridoxal phosphate metabolic process is also involved in their interaction through LOC101257782 gene (LES.2517.1.A1-AT). Probable pyridoxal 5'-phosphate synthase subunit PDX1 gene in *Arabidopsis thaliana* was reported as essential for vitamin B6 biosynthesis, development, and stress tolerance [23]. Purine ribonucleoside monophosphate metabolic process is involved through LOC101252648 gene (LESAFFX.61709.1.S1_AT). There were also 13 identified genes involved in response to hormone (Table 5).

Table 5. Informative genes involved in response to hormone.

Probe ID	Gene description	log_2FC	adj.pvalue
LES.602.1.A1_AT	Auxin response factor 8a	1.18	3.29E-03
LESAFFX.1251.1.S1_AT	Auxin-responsive protein SAUR50-like	1.07	7.59E-03
LESAFFX.3253.1.S1_AT	Abscisic acid 8'-hydroxylase CYP707A2	1.32	2.16E-03
LESAFFX.30900.1.S1_AT	Calcium-dependent protein kinase 32-like	1.33	8.04E-04
LESAFFX.59895.1.S1_AT	Copper transporter 5	2.06	3.73E-04
LES.132.1.S1_AT	1-aminocyclopropane-1-carboxylate oxidase	1.44	1.11E-03
LES.2313.1.A1_AT	Auxin response factor 3	1.6	3.73E-04
LESAFFX.44837.1.S1_AT	Probable E3 ubiquitin-protein ligase XBOS32	−0.372	7.27E-02
LES.4140.1.S1_AT	Ethylene response factor A.2	−1.58	3.73E-04
LESAFFX.3059.1.S1_AT	AP2/ERF domain-containing protein	−1.93	1.35E-03
LES.3575.1.S1_AT	Pti5	0.224	4.50E-01
LES.3551.1.S1_AT	Ethylene-responsive transcriptional coactivator	−0.404	1.97E-01
LESAFFX.71330.1.S1_AT	Gibberellin 3-beta-dioxygenase 1-like	−0.295	2.19E-01

The informative genes identified are also involved in post-embryonic root development and in lateral root development, through guanine nucleotide-binding protein subunit gamma 1 gene (LESAFFX.24397.1.S1_AT), with log_2FC equal to 2.19 (adjusted p-value = 2.93E-04), and by probable E3 ubiquitin-protein ligase XBOS32 gene (Table 5).

Biological Pathways of Tomato-*Fusarium oxysporum* Fo47 Interaction. According to KEGG analysis, twenty pathways were involved in tomato-Fo47 interaction. They are presented in Table 6. Among them, the metabolic pathways and the biosynthesis of secondary metabolites contains the higher number of genes assigned, 25 and 20 genes, respectively. These pathways have an important role in plant development and growth [24–27].

Biosynthesis of cofactors pathway was identified through six genes, porphobilinogen deaminase, chloroplastic gene (LES.1929.1.A1_AT, log_2FC = − 0.223, adjusted p-value = 3.08E-01), probable pyridoxal 5'-phosphate synthase subunit PDX1 gene (LES.2517.1.A1_AT, log_2FC = 1.35, adjusted p-value = 5.66E-04), myo-inositol monophosphatase 2 IMP2 gene (LES.3600.1.S1_AT, log_2FC = –0.243, adjusted p-value = 2.94E-01), enoyl-[acyl-carrier-protein]

Table 6. Biological pathways from KEGG for the survey of 282 tomato genes.

Biological pathway	KEGG-id	adj.pvalue	Number of genes
KEGG root term	00000	1.34E-08	37
Biosynthesis of secondary metabolites	01110	1.73E-05	20
Metabolic pathways	01100	1.73E-05	25
Biosynthesis of cofactors	01240	6.23E-04	6
Cysteine and methionine metabolism	00270	9.69E-03	2
Ribosome	03010	1.98E-02	4
Endocytosis	04144	2.30E-02	1
Pentose and glucuronate interconversions	00040	2.78E-02	2
Vitamin B6 metabolism	00750	3.95E-02	1
Valine, leucine and isoleucine degradation	00280	4.39E-02	1
Alanine, aspartate and glutamate metabolism	00250	4.39E-02	1
Pentose phosphate pathway	00030	4.39E-02	1
Porphyrin metabolism	00860	4.39E-02	2
Ascorbate and aldarate metabolism	00053	4.39E-02	2
Selenocompound metabolism	00450	4.72E-02	1
Flavonoid biosynthesis	00941	4.72E-02	2
Carbon fixation in photosynthetic organisms	00710	4.72E-02	1
One carbon pool by folate	00670	4.72E-02	1
Glycine, serine and threonine metabolism	00260	4.72E-02	1
Biotin metabolism	00780	4.74E-02	1

reductase [NADH] 2, chloroplastic gene with probe ID LES.507.2.A1_AT (log_2FC = 1.77, adjusted p-value = 5.00E-04), GDP-L-galactose phosphorylase gene (LES.5408.1.S1_AT, log_2FC = −1.62E-01, adjusted p-value = 7.28E-01), and bifunctional riboflavin kinase/FMN phosphatase gene with probe ID LES.4736.1.S1_AT (log_2FC = 2.67E-01, adjusted p-value = 4.59E-01).

Cysteine and methionine metabolism pathway was involved through both up-regulated of 1-aminocyclopropane-1-carboxylate oxidase EFE gene with probe ID LES.132.1.S1_AT (log_2FC = 1.44, adjusted p-value = 1.11E-03) and 1-aminocyclopropane-1-carboxylate synthase 2 ACS2 gene (LES.3662.1.S1_AT, log_2FC = 1.11, adjusted p-value = 1.27E-03).

Ribosome pathway was involved through four genes. 50S ribosomal protein L11 gene with probe ID LESAFFX.64546.1.S1_AT (log_2FC = −1.23E-01, adjusted p-value = 8.19E-01), 50S ribosomal protein L4, chloroplastic gene with probe ID LES.2522.1.S1_AT (log_2FC = 2.08, adjusted p-value = 1.43E-03), 60S ribosomal protein L27-3 gene with probe ID LES.2744.1.S1_AT (log_2FC = 1.99, adjusted p-value = 4.46E-03) and 60S acidic ribosomal protein P2-2 gene with probe ID LES.2728.1.A1_AT (log_2FC = 1.38, adjusted p-value = 2.87E-03).

Endocytosis pathway was assigned through the down-regulated of AP-2 complex subunit mu gene, probe ID LES.1152.1.S1_AT ($log_2FC = -3.4$, adjusted p-value = 7.70E-04). Porphyrin metabolism pathway was identified through porphobilinogen deaminase, chloroplastic gene with probe ID LES.1929.1.A1_AT ($log_2FC = -0.223$, adjusted p-value = 3.08E-01), and magnesium-chelatase subunit ChlH, chloroplastic gene with probe ID LES.3322.1.S1_AT ($log_2FC = 1.61$, adjusted p-value = 1.18E-03).

Pentose and glucuronate interconversions pathway was involved through both up-regulated of polygalacturonase-2a PG2 gene, probe ID LES.4463.1.S1_S_AT ($log_2FC = 1.73$, adjusted p-value = 9.66E-04) and pectinesterase 1-like gene with probe ID LES.1917.1.A1_AT ($log_2FC = 1.72$, adjusted p-value = 2.45E-04).

Vitamin B6 metabolism pathway was involved through up-regulated of probable pyridoxal 5'-phosphate synthase subunit PDX1 gene, LES.2517.1.A1_AT ($log_2FC = 1.35$, adjusted p-value = 5.66E-04).

One carbon pool by folate pathway was involved through up-regulated of phosphoribosylglycinamide formyltransferase, chloroplastic gene with probe ID LESAFFX.61709.1.S1_AT ($log_2FC = 1.23$, adjusted p-value = 6.85E-04).

Probable ribose-5-phosphate isomerase 2 gene, LESAFFX.57367.1.S1_AT ($log_2FC = -0.168$, adjusted p-value = 6.11E-01) is involved in both pentose phosphate pathway and in carbon fixation in photosynthetic organisms pathway.

Selenocompound metabolism pathway was involved through up-regulated of thioredoxin reductase 2 gene with probe ID LES.660.1.A1_AT ($log_2FC = 2.14$, adjusted p-value = 2.39E-04).

Flavonoid biosynthesis pathway was involved through hydroxycinnamoyl CoA quinate transferase gene with probe ID LES.4472.1.S1_AT ($log_2FC = -2.15E-01$, adjusted p-value = 3.77E-01) and LES.3218.1.S1_AT ($log_2FC = -4.59E-01$, adjusted p-value = 1.16E-01)

Valine, leucine and isoleucine degradation pathway, alanine, aspartate and glutamate metabolism pathway and glycine, serine and threonine metabolism pathway were involved through alanine–glyoxylate aminotransferase 2 homolog 2, mitochondrial gene with probe ID LES.5309.1.S1_AT ($log_2FC = -1.97E-01$, adjusted p-value = 5.96E-01).

Ascorbate and aldarate metabolism pathway was involved through GDP-L-galactose phosphorylase gene with probe ID LES.5408.1.S1_AT ($log_2FC = -1.62E-01$, adjusted p-value = 7.28E-01) and myo-inositol monophosphatase 2 IMP2 gene, LES.3600.1.S1_AT ($log_2FC = -0.243$, adjusted p-value = 2.94E-01).

Biotin metabolism pathway was involved through enoyl-[acyl-carrier-protein] reductase [NADH] 2, chloroplastic gene (LES.507.2.A1_AT, $log_2FC = 1.77$, adjusted p-value = 5.00E-04).

4 Conclusion

The assembled dataset revealed 244 significantly differentially expressed genes (DEGs). Further analysis using ML methods was conducted to study IGs present in the plant-endophyte interaction. Meta-KLR-b and MLP-b achieved near optimal performance evaluation in classifying transcriptomic data from *Fusarium oxysporum* Fo47 inoculated in *Solanum lycopersicum* root tissue. From the 244 DEGs initially detected, meta-KLR-b identified 84.8%, while MLP-b identified 92.2%. Meta-KLR-b showed 317 IGs, whereas MLP-b discovered the same and 76 additional IGs. Among the 393 IGs identified by MLP-b, 379 are assigned to *Solanum lycopersicum* genes, 1 to *Escherichia coli* protein (Hygromycin-B 4-O-kinase), 1 to *Saccharomyces cerevisiae* protein (galactose-responsive transcription factor GAL4) and 12 attributes were unidentified. There were 283 biological processes identified involved in this interaction. The higher number of genes were assigned to cellular process (132), metabolic process (111), primary metabolic process (98), cellular metabolic process (97), organic substance metabolic process (91), macromolecule metabolic process (67) and nitrogen compound metabolic process (66). Twenty biological pathways have been identified where most of the genes were assigned to metabolomic pathways and the biosynthesis of secondary metabolites, following the biosynthesis of cofactors, ribosome, cysteine and methionine metabolism, pentose and glucuronate interconversions, ascorbarte and aldarate metabolism, flavonoid biosynthesis, endocytosis, vitamin B6 metabolism, valine, leucine and isoleucine degradation, alanine, aspartate and glutamate metabolism, pentose phosphate pathway, selenocompound metabolism, carbon fixation in photosynthetic organisms, one carbon pool by folate, glycine, serine and threonine metabolism and biotin metabolism.

To our knowledge, this is the first analysis of tomato-Fo47 root tissue interaction using machine learning approach. This work not only identified the informative genes of the plant-fungus interaction but also revealed the microorganisms that played a role at the time of biological samples extraction.

References

1. Alabouvette, C., Olivain, C., Migheli, Q., Steinberg, C.: Microbiological control of soil-borne phytopathogenic fungi with special emphasis on wilt-inducing Fusarium oxysporum. New Phytol. **184**, 529–544 (2009). https://doi.org/10.1111/j.1469-8137.2009.03014.x
2. de Lamo, F.J., Spijkers, S.B., Takken, F.L.W.: Protection to tomato wilt disease conferred by the nonpathogen fusarium oxysporum Fo47 is more effective than that conferred by avirulent strains. phytopathology®, vol. 111, pp. 253–257 (2021). https://doi.org/10.1094/PHYTO-04-20-0133-R
3. Fravel, D., Olivain, C., Alabouvette, C.: Fusarium oxysporum and its biocontrol. New Phytol. **157**, 493–502 (2003). https://doi.org/10.1046/j.1469-8137.2003.00700.x
4. Veloso, J., Díaz, J.: Fusarium oxysporum Fo47 confers protection to pepper plants against Verticillium dahliae and Phytophthora capsici, and induces the expression of defence genes: Fo47 protection of pepper through defence induction. Plant Pathol. **61**, 281–288 (2012). https://doi.org/10.1111/j.1365-3059.2011.02516.x
5. Zhang, J., Chen, J., Jia, R., Ma, Q., Zong, Z., Wang, Y.: Suppression of plant wilt diseases by nonpathogenic Fusarium oxysporum Fo47 combined with actinomycete strains. Biocontrol Sci. Technol. **28**, 562–573 (2018). https://doi.org/10.1080/09583157.2018.1468996

6. Aimé, S., Alabouvette, C., Steinberg, C., Olivain, C.: The endophytic strain fusarium oxysporum Fo47: a good candidate for priming the defense responses in tomato roots. Mol. Plant-Microbe Interact. **26**, 918–926 (2013). https://doi.org/10.1094/MPMI-12-12-0290-R

7. Constantin, M.E., de Lamo, F.J., Vlieger, B.V., Rep, M., Takken, F.L.W.: Endophyte-mediated resistance in tomato to fusarium oxysporum is independent of ET, JA, and SA. Front. Plant Sci. **10**, 979 (2019). https://doi.org/10.3389/fpls.2019.00979

8. Veloso, J., Díaz, J.: The non-pathogenic fusarium oxysporum Fo47 induces distinct responses in two closely related solanaceae plants against the pathogen verticillium dahliae. J. Fungi **7**, 344. https://doi.org/10.3390/jof7050344

9. Witten, I.H., Frank, E., Hall, M.A., Pal, C.J.: Data Mining: Practical Machine Learning Tools and Techniques, 4nd edn. Morgan Kaufmann series in data management systems. Morgan Kaufman, Amsterdam; Boston, MA (2016)

10. Smith, B., Wang, S., Wong, A., Zhou, X.: A penalized likelihood approach to parameter estimation with integral reliability constraints. Entropy **17**, 4040–4063 (2015) https://doi.org/10.3390/e17064040

11. Kim, J.H.: Multicollinearity and misleading statistical results. Korean J. Anesthesiol. **72**, 558–569 (2019). https://doi.org/10.4097/kja.19087

12. Tharwat, A.: Classification assessment methods. Appl. Comput. Inform. (2018). https://doi.org/10.1016/j.aci.2018.08.003

13. Raudvere, U., et al.: g:Profiler: a web server for functional enrichment analysis and conversions of gene lists (2019 update). Nucleic Acids Res. **47**, W191–W198 (2019). https://doi.org/10.1093/nar/gkz369

14. Rashotte, A.M., Brady, S.R., Reed, R.C., Ante, S.J., Muday, G.K.: Basipetal auxin transport is required for gravitropism in roots of arabidopsis. Plant Physiol. **122**, 481–490 (2000). https://doi.org/10.1104/pp.122.2.481

15. Wang, Y., Clevenger, J.P., Illa-Berenguer, E., Meulia, T., van der Knaap, E., Sun, L.: A comparison of sun, ovate, fs8.1 and auxin application on tomato fruit shape and gene expression. Plant Cell Physiol. 60, 1067–1081 (2019). https://doi.org/10.1093/pcp/pcz024

16. Gaudet, P., Livstone, M.S., Lewis, S.E., Thomas, P.D.: Phylogenetic-based propagation of functional annotations within the Gene Ontology consortium. Brief. Bioinform. **12**, 449–462 (2011). https://doi.org/10.1093/bib/bbr042

17. Young, R.J., Scheuring, C.F., Harris-Haller, L., Taylor, B.H.: An auxin-inducible proteinase inhibitor gene from tomato. Plant Physiol. **104**, 811–812 (1994). https://doi.org/10.1104/pp.104.2.811

18. Liu, J., Van Eck, J., Cong, B., Tanksley, S.D.: A new class of regulatory genes underlying the cause of pear-shaped tomato fruit. Proc. Natl. Acad. Sci. **99**, 13302–13306 (2002). https://doi.org/10.1073/pnas.162485999

19. Tanksley, S.D.: The genetic, developmental, and molecular bases of fruit size and shape variation in tomato. Plant Cell Online **16**, S181–S189 (2004). https://doi.org/10.1105/tpc.018119

20. Loukehaich, R., Wang, T., Ouyang, B., Ziaf, K., Li, H., Zhang, J., Lu, Y., Ye, Z.: SpUSP, an annexin-interacting universal stress protein, enhances drought tolerance in tomato. J. Exp. Bot. **63**, 5593–5606 (2012). https://doi.org/10.1093/jxb/ers220

21. Veloso, J., Díaz, J.: The non-pathogenic fusarium oxysporum Fo47 induces distinct responses in two closely related solanaceae plants against the pathogen verticillium dahliae. J. Fungi **7**, 344 (2021). https://doi.org/10.3390/jof7050344

22. Sharkey, T.D.: Pentose phosphate pathway reactions in photosynthesizing cells. Cells **10**, 1547 (2021). https://doi.org/10.3390/cells10061547

23. Titiz, O., et al.: PDX1 is essential for vitamin B6 biosynthesis, development and stress tolerance in Arabidopsis. Plant J. **48**, 933–946 (2006). https://doi.org/10.1111/j.1365-313X.2006.02928.x

24. Lewinsohn, E., et al.: Enhanced levels of the aroma and flavor compound S-linalool by metabolic engineering of the terpenoid pathway in tomato fruits. Plant Physiol. **127**, 1256–1265 (2001)

25. Li, Y., et al.: MicroTom metabolic network: rewiring tomato metabolic regulatory network throughout the growth cycle. Mol. Plant **13**, 1203–1218 (2020). https://doi.org/10.1016/j.molp.2020.06.005

26. Xu, H., Lybrand, D., Bennewitz, S., Tissier, A., Last, R.L., Pichersky, E.: Production of trans-chrysanthemic acid, the monoterpene acid moiety of natural pyrethrin insecticides, in tomato fruit. Metab. Eng. **47**, 271–278 (2018). https://doi.org/10.1016/j.ymben.2018.04.004

27. Zhu, G., et al.: Rewiring of the fruit metabolome in tomato breeding. Cell **172**, 249-261.e12 (2018). https://doi.org/10.1016/j.cell.2017.12.019

Smart Data Driven System
for Pathological Voices Classification

Joana Fernandes[1]($\boxtimes$) , Arnaldo Candido Junior[2] , Diamantino Freitas[3] ,
and João Paulo Teixeira[4]

[1] Research Centre in Digitaization and Intelligent Robotics (CeDRI),
Instituto Politecnico de Braganca (IPB), Braganca 5300, Portugal, Faculdade de
Engenharia da Universidade do Porto (FEUP), Porto 4200-465, Portugal
joana.fernandes@ipb.pt
[2] São Paulo State University, Institute of Biosciences, Language and Physical
Sciences, São José do Rio Preto, SP, Brazil
arnaldo.candido@unesp.br
[3] Faculdade de Engenharia da Universidade do Porto (FEUP),
Porto 4200-465, Portugal
dfreitas@fe.up.pt
[4] Research Centre in Digitaization and Intelligent Robotics (CeDRI),
Applied Management Research Unit (UNIAG) and Laboratório para a
Sustentabilidade e Tecnologia em Regiões de Montanha (SusTEC),
Instituto Politecnico de Braganca (IPB), Braganca 5300, Portugal
joaopt@ipb.pt

Abstract. Classifying and recognizing voice pathologies non-invasively
using acoustic analysis saves patient and specialist time and can improve
the accuracy of assessments. In this work, we intend to understand which
models provide better accuracy rates in the distinction between healthy
and pathological, to later be implemented in a system for the detection
of vocal pathologies. 194 control subjects and 350 pathological subjects
distributed across 17 pathologies were used. Each subject has 3 vowels in 3 tones, which is equivalent to 9 sound files per subject. For each
sound file, 13 parameters were extracted (jitta, jitter, Rap, PPQ5, ShdB,
Shim, APQ3, APQ5, F0, HNR, autocorrelation, Shannon entropy and
logarithmic entropy). For the classification between healthy and pathological, several classifiers were used (Decision Trees, Discriminant Analysis, Logistic Regression Classifiers, Naive Bayes Classifiers, Support Vector Machines, Nearest Neighbor Classifiers, Ensemble Classifiers, Neural
Network Classifiers) with various models. For each patient, 118 parameters were used (13 acoustic parameters * 9 sound files per subject, plus
the subject's gender). As pre-processing of the input matrix data, the
Outliers treatment was used using the quartile method, then the data
were normalized and, finally, Principal Component Analysis (PCA) was
applied in order to reduce the dimension. As the best model, the Wide
Neural Network was obtained, with an accuracy of 98% and AUC of 0.99.

Keywords: Speech pathologies · Machine learning · Speech features ·
Principal component analysis · Vocal acoustic analysis

© The Author(s), under exclusive license to Springer Nature Switzerland AG 2022
A. I. Pereira et al. (Eds.): OL2A 2022, CCIS 1754, pp. 419–426, 2022.
https://doi.org/10.1007/978-3-031-23236-7_29

1   Introduction

Vocal pathologies interfere with vocal quality, altering the phonation process. These pathologies affect about 10% of the population [1] and exist in different stages of evolution and severity. Harmful habits lead to a drastic increase in these pathologies [2].

For the detection of pathologies associated with the voice, there are a several exams, which can be perfomed, but they are uncomfortable and invasive for patients, as well as time intensive.

The auditory acoustic analysis intends, in a non-invasive way, to quantify and characterize the voice sound, but it is not objective and will depend on the experience of the physician who performs the evaluation [3]. The development of automatic techniques for acoustic analysis saves time for the patient and gives support to the specialist to improve the accuracy of assessments [4].

Therefore, this article aims to understand which models provide better accuracy rates in the distinction between healthy and pathological.

This article is organized as follows: Sect. 2 describes the state of the art. Section 3 describes the database, the speech parameters and the feature extraction process. Section 4 presents the results obtained for the different classifier models. Finally, Sect. 5 presents the discussion and final conclusions.

2   State of the Art

The automatic recognition of voices with pathologies, using speech processing tools, has shown significant results. Most of the published works classify the sign as having the pathology or not, or by the classification of a specific pathology. Reid et al. 2022 [5], Zhang et al. 2021 [6] and Castellana et al. 2018 [7] are examples where the classification between healthy and pathological voice is made.

Recognition voice pathologies intends to identify the specific pathology that affects the patient's voice. However, this area has few contributions and the group of different pathologies is limited. These results do not allow these systems to be used in clinical evaluations, requiring a deeper investigation with different pathologies.

Ankışhan, 2018 [8] and Rabeh, et al., 2018 [9] obtained an accuracy of 100% in the classification between pathological and healthy and Chen and Chen 2022 [10] obtained an accuracy of 99.4%. Hammami, et al., 2020 [12] obtained an accuracy of 99.26% in the classification between pathological and healthy, however, when distinguishing between hyperfunctional dysphonia and recurrent paralysis, the accuracy is 90.32%. Ali, et al., 2018 [13] for the classification between pathological and healthy obtained an accuracy of 99.72%, however, to distinguish between polyp, keratosis, vocal cord paralysis, nodules and spasmodic dysphonia obtained accuracies of 97.54%, 99.08%, 96.75%, 98.65%, 95.83%, 95.83% and 99.13%. The classification of pathologies in the proposed system is binary in nature. Mojaly, et al., 2014 [14] in the binary classification between healthy and pathological obtained an accuracy of 99.98% with a standard deviation of 0.0263. For the multiclass classification (nodules, vocal cord polyps and keratosis), the accuracy was 99.85% with a standard deviation of 0.1657.

Published works demonstrate that it is possible to classify between healthy and pathological speech with a high degree of accuracy. However, these works use only a few pathologies and do not extend to a wider group of pathologies.

In studies that seek to classify different pathologies, they usually use a very small group of pathologies and with lower accuracy.

3   Materials and Method

This section describes the database, the speech parameters and the feature extraction process.

3.1   Database

The German Saarbrucken Voice Database (SVD) was used. This database is available online by the Institute of Phonetics at the University of Saarland [15]. The database consists of voice signals of more than 2000 subjects with several diseases and controls/healthy subjects. Each person has the recording of phonemes /a/, /i/ and /u/ in the low, normal and high tones, swipe along tones, and the German phrase "Guten Morgen, wie geht es Ihnen?". The size of the sound files is between 1 and 3 s and have a sampling frequency of 50 kHz.

For the analysis, 194 control subjects and 350 pathological subjects distributed across 17 pathologies were used. In the description of the curated database by Fernandes et al. 2019 [16], the total number of subjects is 901. However, since some sound files had some noise, these were excluded. Dysphonia was also excluded, as it is not a pathology, but a voice disorder, therefore, as a pathology, Hyperfunctional Dysphonia (89 subjects), Vocal Cord Paralysis (74), Functional Dysphonia (51), Psychogenic Dysphonia (31), Spasmodic Dysphonia (24), Chronic Laryngitis (23), Vocal Cord Polyp (14), Reinke's Edema (14), Hypofunctional Dysphonia (9), Carcinoma of Vocal Cord (7), Hypopharyngeal Tumor (4), Cyst (3), Granuloma (2), Hypotonic Dysphonia (2), Laryngeal Tumor (1), Intubation Granuloma (1), Fibroma (1).

3.2   Speech Parameters

This section describes the set of features extracted from each sound file.

Jitter is defined as the glottal variation between the vibration cycles of the vocal cords. Subjects who have difficulty controlling the vocal cords usually have higher jitter values [16,17]. The measures to be used of jitter will be Absolute Jitter (jitta), Relative Jitter (jitter), Relative Average Perturbation Jitter (RAP) and Five-point Period Perturbation Quotients Jitter (PPQ5).

Shimmer is defined as the variation in magnitude over the glottal periods. Higher shimmer values may be caused by reduced glottal resistance and injuries, leading to variations in glottal magnitude [16,17]. The shimmer measures to be used are Absolute Shimmer (ShdB), Relative Shimmer (shim), Three-point Amplitude Perturbation Quotient Shimmer (APQ3) and Five-point Amplitude Perturbation Quotient Shimmer (APQ5)

Fundamental Frequency (F0) in a speech signal, the vibration frequency of the vocal cords is considered to correspond to the fundamental frequency [18]. The F0 is determined using the Autocorrelation method with a frame window length of 100 ms and considering a minimum F0 50 Hz.

Harmonic to Noise Ratio (HNR) allows measuring the relationship between the harmonic and noise components of a speech signal, where the periodicity of the signal is provided, quantifying the relationship between the harmonic part and noise. The HNR value of a signal can vary as there are different configurations of the vocal tract, providing different amplitudes for the harmonics [19–21].

Autocorrelation measures the similar parts of the speech signal, repeated throughout the signal. The more similar repetitions there are along the signal, the greater the autocorrelation value [16,22].

Entropy it considers the amount of energy present in a complex system, as it allows quantitative assessment of the degree of randomness and uncertainty of a given data sequence. Entropy analysis makes it possible to accurately assess the nonlinear behavior characteristic of speech signals [23].

3.3   Feature Extraction Process

Each subject has 9 sound files per subject. For each sound file, 13 parameters were extracted (jitta, jitter, RAP, PPQ5, ShdB, Shim, APQ3, APQ5, F0, HNR, autocorrelation, Shannon entropy and logarithmic entropy), making 117 parameters per subject and the subject's sex was added. The input matrix is composed of 118 lines x N subjects.

Considering the work by Silva et al. 2019 [24], where an improvement of up to 13% points was obtained, the data of the input matrix were pre-processed using the treatment of Outliers by the quartile method. This process aims to identify outliers and change their value by a threshold value determined according to the method used.

Then the data were normalized using the resizing method between $[-1, 1]$.

To reduce the dimension, Principal Component Analysis (PCA) was used. This technique uses mathematical concepts such as standard deviation, covariance of eigenvalues and eigenvectors. Starting from the covariance matrix, eigenvectors and eigenvalues are calculated, being necessary to decide the quantity of principal components. Then it is only necessary to calculate the accumulated percentage of the eigenvalues. Therefore, the first eigenvectors that will correspond to 90% or 95% of the accumulated percentage will be selected, meaning that 90% or 95% of the data are explained in the first eigenvectors. Finally, the fitted data are multiplied by the inverse of the selected eigenvector matrix [25]. This analysis was applied to the 118 parameters, with a variance of 95%, resulting in 21 new features.

4   Results and Discussion

In Table 1, it is possible to observe the results for the various classifiers used. For all classifiers, the cross-validation technique was applied, with cross-validation of 10 times.

Subjects were grouped into two groups, one group with control subjects and a second group with all subjects with some pathology. Therefore, the model is a binary classification process.

Table 1. Results of the various techniques used to classify.

Classifier	Model type	Accuracy (%)
Decision Tree	Fine Tree	88.1
	Medium Tree	88.1
	Coarse Tree	89.5
Discriminant Analysis	Linear Discriminant	96.1
	Quadratic Discriminant	94.3
Logistic Regression	Logistic Regression	96.5
Naive Bayes	Gaussian Naive Bayes	85.3
	Kernel Naive Bayes	86.8
Support Vector Machines (SVM)	Linear SVM	96.5
	Quadratic SVM	96.9
	Cubic SVM	97.2
	Fine Gaussian	92.1
	Medium Gaussian SVM	95.2
	Coarse Gaussian	64.9
Nearest Neighbor (KNN)	Fine KNN	89.7
	Medium KNN	84.9
	Coarse KNN	65.8
	Cosine KNN	91.7
	Cubic KNN	84.2
	Weighted KNN	84.2
Ensemble	Boosted Trees	87.1
	Bagged Trees	93.4
	Subspace Discriminant	96.1
	Subspace KNN	96.7
	RUSBoosted Trees	92.1
Neural Network	Narrow Neural Network	97.8
	Medium Neural Network	97.4
	Wide Neural Network	**98.0**
	Bilayered Neural Network	96.7
	Trilayered Neural Network	97.4

Analyzing the results presented in Table 1, it is possible to perceive that the best results are obtained with the Wide Neural Network, where an accuracy of 98% was obtained to distinguish between healthy and pathological subjects. For healthy individuals, in 194 cases it classified 7 incorrectly, and for pathological individuals in 350 it classified 4 incorrectly. However, it is possible to verify the good performance of this network, since it obtained an AUC of 0.99. This model has 100 node in the hidden layer and the activation function used was ReLU. Taking into account the state of the art these results are similar to what already exists, however these results are obtained taking into account more pathologies.

Teixeira et al., 2017 [26] presented hit rates of 100% to distinguish between female subjects and 90% for males, in the distinction between healthy and pathological, however they only used dysphonia as a pathology. Zakariah et al. 2022 [11] in the classification between healthy and pathological obtained an accuracy of 77.49%, as pathologies used Dysphonia, chronic laryngitis, dysody, functional dysphonia, vocal cord cordectomy and leukoplakia. Comparing these two studies with the results obtained, it is possible to perceive that the obtained ones are better, as they obtain a higher rate and consider more pathologies. If the results are compared with the state of the art, these results are similar to what already exists, however, these results are obtained taking into account more pathologies.

5   Conclusion

The objective of this work is to try to find a simple Artificial Intelligence model, which requires little computational load, and which achieves good accuracy rates in the distinction between healthy and pathological subjects, to later be implemented in a system for the detection of vocal pathologies. This system in a first experimental phase will be placed in hospitals and will allow to collect voices of subjects giving an indication if the subject is healthy or pathological. A second phase aims to distinguish the various pathologies.

Taking into account the state of the art, it is possible to see that there are several works where this topic is addressed and with high accuracy rates, however these works usually have few pathologies, even those that do not identify pathologies. In this work, 17 pathologies were considered, thus, 194 control subjects and 350 pathological subjects were used.

For each subject there are 9 sound files, which correspond to 3 vowels, and each vowel has 3 tones. For each sound file, 13 parameters were extracted, giving a total of 117 input features per subject, to which the subject's gender was also added. The input matrix is then composed of 118 lines x N number of subjects.

As pre-processing of the input matrix data, the Outliers treatment was used, where the quartile method was used. Then the data were normalized between $[-1,1]$ and finally the Principal Component Analysis technique was applied in order to reduce the size of the data.

For the classification between healthy and pathological, several classifiers with different models were used. As the best model, the Wide Neural Network was obtained, with an accuracy of 98% and AUC of 0.99. This result is within the best values described in the state of the art.

As future work, we intend to identify the pathology and the degree of severity. However, there are certain difficulties as there are many pathologies with similar symptoms and voice characteristics. The database is still limited in size for the vast majority of pathologies, so an extension process of the database is already underway.

Acknowledgments. The work was supported by the Foundation for Science and Technology UIDB/05757/2020, UIDP/05757/2020 and 2021.04729.BD and by SusTEC LA/P/0007/2021.

References

1. Martins, R.H.G., Santana, M.F., Tavares, E.L.M.: Vocal cysts: clinical, endoscopic, and surgical aspects. J. Voice **25**(1), 107–110 (2011). https://doi.org/10.1016/J.JVOICE.2009.06.008
2. Godino-Llorente, J.I., Gomez-Vilda, P., Blanco-Velasco, M.: Dimensionality reduction of a pathological voice quality assessment system based on gaussian mixture models and short-term cepstral parameters. IEEE Trans. Biomed. Eng. **53**(10), 1943–1953 (2006). https://doi.org/10.1109/TBME.2006.871883
3. Fonseca, E.S., Guido, R.C., Junior, S.B., Dezani, H., Gati, R.R., Mosconi Pereira, D.C.: Acoustic investigation of speech pathologies based on the discriminative paraconsistent machine (DPM). Biomed. Signal Process. Control. **55**, 101615 (2020). https://doi.org/10.1016/J.BSPC.2019.101615
4. Hegde, S., Shetty, S., Rai, S., Dodderi, T.: A survey on machine learning approaches for automatic detection of voice disorders. J. Voice **33**(6), 947.e11-947.e33 (2019). https://doi.org/10.1016/J.JVOICE.2018.07.014
5. Reid, J., Parmar, P., Lund, T., Aalto, D.K., Jeffery, C.C.: Development of a machine-learning based voice disorder screening tool. Am. J. Otolaryngol. **43**(2), 103327 (2022). https://doi.org/10.1016/J.AMJOTO.2021.103327
6. Zhang, X.-J., Zhu, X.-C., Wu, D., Xiao, Z.-Z., Tao, Z., Zhao, H.-M.: Nonlinear features of bark wavelet sub-band filtering for pathological voice recognition. Eng. Lett. **29**(1), 49–60 (2021)
7. Castellana, A., Carullo, A., Corbellini, S., Astolfi, A.: Discriminating pathological voice from healthy voice using cepstral peak prominence smoothed distribution in sustained vowel. IEEE Trans. Instrum. Meas. **67**(3), 646–654 (2018). https://doi.org/10.1109/TIM.2017.2781958
8. Ankışhan, H.: A new approach for detection of pathological voice disorders with reduced parameters. Electrica **18**(1), 60–71 (2018)
9. Hamdi, R., Hajji, S., Cherif, A.: Voice pathology recognition and classification using noise related features. Int. J. Adv. Comput. Sci. Appl. **9**(11), 82–87 (2018). https://doi.org/10.14569/IJACSA.2018.091112
10. Chen, L., Chen, J.: Deep neural network for automatic classification of pathological voice signals. J. Voice **36**(2), 288.e15-288.e24 (2022). https://doi.org/10.1016/J.JVOICE.2020.05.029
11. Zakariah, M., Ajmi Alotaibi, Y., Guo, Y., Tran-Trung, K., Mamun Elahi, M.: An Analytical Study of Speech Pathology Detection Based on MFCC and Deep Neural Networks (2022). https://doi.org/10.1155/2022/7814952
12. Hammami, I., Salhi, L., Labidi, S.: Voice pathologies classification and detection using EMD-DWT analysis based on higher order statistic features. IRBM **41**(3), 161–171 (2020). https://doi.org/10.1016/J.IRBM.2019.11.004

13. Ali, Z., Hossain, M.S., Muhammad, G., Sangaiah, A.K.: An intelligent healthcare system for detection and classification to discriminate vocal fold disorders. Futur. Gener. Comput. Syst. **85**, 19–28 (2018). https://doi.org/10.1016/J.FUTURE.2018. 02.021

14. Al Mojaly, M., Muhammad, G., Alsulaiman, M.: Detection and Classification of Voice Pathology Using Feature Selection (2014). https://doi.org/10.1109/ AICCSA.2014.7073250

15. Pützer, M., Barry, W.J.: Saarbruecken Voice Database: Institute of Phonetics at the University of Saarland (2007). http://www.stimmdatenbank.coli.uni-saarland. de. Accessed 05 Nov 2021

16. Fernandes, J., Silva, L., Teixeira, F., Guedes, V., Santos, J., Teixeira, J.P.: Parameters for vocal acoustic analysis - cured database. Procedia Comput. Sci. **164**, 654–661 (2019). https://doi.org/10.1016/J.PROCS.2019.12.232

17. Teixeira, J.P., Gonçalves, A.: Algorithm for jitter and shimmer measurement in pathologic voices. Procedia Comput. Sci. **100**, 271–279 (2016). https://doi.org/10. 1016/J.PROCS.2016.09.155

18. Hamdi, R., Hajji, S., Cherif, A., Processing, S.: Recognition of pathological voices by human factor cepstral coefficients (HFCC). J. Comput. Sci. (2020). https://doi. org/10.3844/jcssp.2020.1085.1099

19. Fernandes, J., Teixeira, F., Guedes, V., Junior, A., Teixeira, J.P.: Harmonic to noise ratio measurement - selection of window and length. Procedia Comput. Sci. **138**, 280–285 (2018). https://doi.org/10.1016/J.PROCS.2018.10.040

20. Teixeira, J.P., Fernandes, P.O.: Acoustic analysis of vocal dysphonia. Procedia Comput. Sci. **64**, 466–473 (2015). https://doi.org/10.1016/J.PROCS.2015.08.544

21. Teixeira, J.P., Fernandes, J., Teixeira, F., Fernandes, P.O.: Acoustic analysis of chronic laryngitis statistical analysis of sustained speech parameters. In: BIOSIGNALS 2018–11th International Conference on Bio-Inspired Systems and Signal Processing, Proceedings; Part of 11th International Joint Conference on Biomedical Engineering Systems and Technologies, BIOSTEC 2018, vol. 4, pp. 168–175 (2018). https://doi.org/10.5220/0006586301680175

22. Boersma, P.: Stemmen meten met Praat. Stem-, Spraak- en Taalpathologie **12**(4), 237–251 (2004)

23. Araújo, T., Teixeira, J.P., Rodrigues, P.M.: Smart-Data-Driven System for Alzheimer Disease Detection through Electroencephalographic Signals (2022). https://doi.org/10.3390/bioengineering9040141

24. Silva, L., et al.: Outliers treatment to improve the recognition of voice pathologies. Procedia Comput. Sci. **164**, 678–685 (2019). https://doi.org/10.1016/J.PROCS. 2019.12.235

25. Teixeira, J.P., Alves, N., Fernandes, P.O.: Vocal acoustic analysis: ANN versos SVM in classification of dysphonic voices and vocal cords paralysis. Int. J. E-Health Med. Commun. **11**, 37–51 (2020)https://doi.org/10.4018/IJEHMC.2020010103

26. Teixeira, J.P., Fernandes, P.O., Alves, N.: Vocal acoustic analysis - classification of dysphonic voices with artificial neural networks. Procedia Comput. Sci. **121**, 19–26 (2017). https://doi.org/10.1016/J.PROCS.2017.11.004

Gene Expression Analysis of *Solanum lycopersicum* - *Bacillus megaterium* Interaction to Identify Informative Genes Using Machine Learning Classifiers

Vânia Rodrigues[1]([✉])[ID] and Sérgio Deusdado[2][ID]

[1] USAL - Universidad de Salamanca, 37008 Salamanca, Spain
vania.rodrigues@usal.es
[2] CIMO - Centro de Investigação de Montanha, Instituto Politécnico de Bragança,
5301-855 Bragança, Portugal
sergiod@ipb.pt

Abstract. There has been a growing interest in identifying specific plant growth-promoting rhizobacteria that confer health, growth, and protective benefits to plant host. Understanding the mechanisms of this association as well as the differences that determine the different outcomes can be exploited to optimize beneficial interactions. To this end, we developed a classifier capable of predicting the presence of *Bacillus megaterium* inoculated in tomato root tissue and identify potential informative genes related to their interaction. Two machine learning models, Kernel Logistic Regression and Multilayer Perceptron were studied. From the 4 Multilayer Perceptron classifiers tested (MLP-a, MLP-b, MLP-c and MLP-d) with different parameters, MLP-a and MLP-c achieved near optimal performance considering all the relevant metrics. Then, these classifiers were used as attribute evaluators to identify two sets of informative genes (IGs). MLP-a showed 216 highest-rated attributes. Among these IGs, 173 were identified as *Solanum lycopersicum* genes, 37 were assigned to 5 *Bacillus subtilis* protein, 4 were assigned to 1 *Escherichia coli* protein and 2 were unidentified. On the other hand, MLP-c showed the same highest-rated attributes adding 27 new attributes. Based on the results of MLP-a and MLP-c, considering the identified tomato IGs, a functional enrichment analysis was developed showing nine and eight biological pathways, respectively. Furthermore, the same IGs were used to compose biological networks from *Arabidopsis thaliana* orthologous genes. The biological networks identified for the first set were co-expression, shared protein domains, predicted interaction and co-localization. The second set presented the same networks adding physical interaction.

Keywords: Machine learning · Informative genes · Tomato - *Bacillus megaterium* interaction

© The Author(s), under exclusive license to Springer Nature Switzerland AG 2022
A. I. Pereira et al. (Eds.): OL2A 2022, CCIS 1754, pp. 427–441, 2022.
https://doi.org/10.1007/978-3-031-23236-7_30

1   Introduction

Plant growth-promoting rhizobacteria (PGPR) are soil bacteria that colonize the roots of plants following inoculation onto seed, positively affecting plant physiology and development [1]. *Solanum lycopersicum* (tomato) is the most important horticultural crop around the world, and the second most consumed vegetable after potato [2]. *Bacillus megaterium* strain is known to be a plant-growth promoting bacteria [3]. A recent study shows that *Bacillus megaterium* promoted growth in mature wild type tomato [4]. Understanding the mechanisms involved in the link among specific microbes, the ecosystem properties, and the plant under study, is an ongoing challenge due to the complexity of the different biological systems. To assist this challenge, integration of advances in DNA/RNA sequencing technology with machine learning can yield relevant information.

Machine learning (ML) methods are widely used in several research fields, including climate change, human health, clinical decision-making, plant science [5], and in the field of microbiology [6]. Regarding the understanding of the interactions between microorganisms and the surrounding environment, research is still incipient. ML addresses the analysis of large amounts of data by discovering relationships between the target output and the input attributes, and it is mostly used for prediction and classification tasks. The analysis of metagenomic microbial bring several difficulties [7]. Data is typically high dimensional with a small number of samples collected in each study. Furthermore, sequencing results are noisy and yield sparse datasets [8]. This kind of dimensionality has critical importance to conduct feasible and pilot work, however it can lead to biased ML performance estimates. ML validation process should be designed to help avoid optimistic performance estimates. Commonly, the higher the ratio of attributes to samples sizes the more likely that a ML model will fit the noise in the data instead of the underlying pattern [9]. One way to overcome bias-variance tradeoff is to ensure that the training data is diverse and represents all possible groups or outcomes.

The aim of this study is to develop a machine learning model capable of predicting the presence of *Bacillus megaterium* inoculated in tomato root tissue and able to identify the informative genes (IGs) related to their interaction under well-watered conditions. Additionaly, the choosen ML classifier can also be used to identify microorganisms that have the same molecular mechanisms as *Bacillus megaterium* and, therefore, be useful to identify plant growth-promoting microorganisms. Kernel Logistic Regression (KLR) and Multilayer Perceptron (MLP) were applyied for classification and those that obtained better results in their performance evaluation were used to identify IGs. KLR model is a statistical classifier [10] that generates a fit model by minimizing the negative log-likelihood with a quadratic penalty using the Broyden-Fletcher-Goldfard-Shanno (BFGS) optimization [11]. Multilayer Perceptron is based on an artificial neural network where the mapping between inputs and output is non-linear [12]. Moreover, biological pathways were determined, and biological networks were constructed based on the corresponding *Arabidopsis thaliana* orthologous genes from heterogeneous data sources. The resulting biological networks might comprise physical interactions, co-expression, predicted interactions, shared protein domains, genetic interaction, and co-localization.

2   Materials and Methods

2.1   Dataset Collection

The original datasets were obtained from GEO/NCBI database with reference accession: GSE106317. The used dataset was achieved selecting the appropriate data for this work, specifically three replicates of root tomato wild-type cv. Pearson line non-inoculated under well-watered conditions (GSM2835866, GSM2835867, GSM2835868), and three replicates of *Bacillus megaterium* inoculated root tomato wild-type cv. Pearson line under well-watered conditions (GSM2835869, GSM2835870, GSM2835871).

2.2   Experimental Procedures

The original datasets from GEO/NCBI database were log2 GC-RMA signals. Before applying the machine learning models, the inverse signals were obtained to achieve a more approximate behavior of the relative genes expression, and then they were normalized to [−1,1] on the assembled dataset. Then, KLR and MLP were executed using different parameterization (see Sect. 2.3). Accuracy, mean absolute error, precision, recall, f-measure, and area under precision-recall curve were used for performance evaluation. These experiments ran 10 times several schemes using 3-fold cross-validation and leave-one-out cross-validation (LOOCV) testing with Paired T-Tester (corrected). Then, the classifier with the best performance evaluation was used to identify the informative attributes (genes). To do this, applying the best outcome of our experimental work, the classifier was used for estimating the accuracy and root mean squared error (RMSE) of attributes combinations subsets with 4 folds, using 3-fold CV. If the standard deviation of the means exceeded 0.01, the attributes combinations were repeated, otherwise, the ranks were obtained according to the evaluation.

The experimental work was based on WEKA, version 3.9.5, a datamining workbench publicly accessible at: www.cs.waikato.ac.nz/ml/weka/.

The performance assessment was based on accuracy (1), kappa coefficient (2) using the guidelines outlined by Landis et.al. [13], where strength of the k is interpreted in the flowing manner: 0.01–0.20 slight; 0.21–0.40 fair, 0.41–0.60 moderate, 0.61–0.80 substantial, 0.81–1.00 almost perfect, mean absolute error (3), precision (4), recall (5), f-measure (6), and area under precision-recall (PR) curve [14].

$$ACC = \frac{TP + TN}{TP + FP + FN + TN} \tag{1}$$

$$k = \frac{Observed\ accuracy - Expected\ accuracy}{1 - Expected\ accuracy} \tag{2}$$

$$MAE = \frac{\sum_{i=1}^{n} |predicted_i - actual_i|}{1 - Expected\ accuracy} \tag{3}$$

$$PREC = \frac{TP}{TP + FP} \tag{4}$$

$$REC = \frac{TP}{TP + FN} \tag{5}$$

$$f - measure = \frac{2 * PREC * REC}{PREC + REC} \tag{6}$$

Tomato Functional Genomics Database (TFGD) [15] was used to identify the gene ID of the probe ID from Affymetrix genome array. Subsequently, protein sequences from *Solanum lycopersicum* were aligned using NCBI BLAST [16] BLASTP against *Arabidopsis thaliana* setting nonredundant protein sequences database using default parameters. At the same time, using g:Profiler [17], functional enrichment analysis of biological pathways by Kyoto Encyclopedia of Gene and Genomes (KEGG) analysis was performed to understand their functions and interactions. Resorting to GeneMANIA Cytoscape [18], the corresponding genes of the protein found by BLASTP with higher hit values: query coverage ≥ 90 %, percent identity >80 % and e-value ≤ 0 were used to construct inherent biological networks. Moreover, biological interpretation for highest-rated genes set were also based on literature. These set of experiments were conducted on a computer with an Intel Core i7-5500U CPU 2.40 GHz processor, with 8.00 GB RAM.

2.3 Parameters Tunning

A grid search approach was applyied to optimize the parameters of KLR and MLP classifiers. In KLR, different penalty parameter λ were conjugated with different types of kernel functions. After performing grid search for KLR, the parameter λ was adjusted in two iterations to, respectively, 0.01 and 0.001, both using a linear kernel function, resulting in KLR-a and KLR-b classifiers. In MLP the neural network was trained with backpropagation. It is the learning mechanism that allows the MLP to iteratively adjust the weights in the network, with the goal of minimizing the cost function. The parameters optimized were learning rate (LR) and hidden layers (HL) with momentum set to 0.2. LR was tested between 0.2 and 0.9, tunning HL = 1, and for the same range of LR tunning HL = 2. After performing grid search, 4 MLP classifiers were obtained with best performance, MLP-a (LR = 0.3, HL = 1), MLP-b (LR = 0.5, HL = 1), MLP-c (LR = 0.3, HL = 2) and MLP-d (LR = 0.5, HL = 2). All grid searches were executed using LOOCV.

3 Results and Discussion

From the conducted experimental work with the classifiers parameterization described in Sect. 2.3, we present the performance evaluation of KLR and MLP in Table 1 and Table 2, respectively. Resorting the performance assessment described in Sect. 2.2, KLR obtained good results in its performance evaluation, although presenting significant standard deviation (Table 1), due to the small number of samples. Setting the penalty parameter λ to 0.01 or 0.001 produced the same performance results.

Table 1. KLR performance evaluation using LOOCV.

Metrics	KLR-a (Std. dev.)	KLR-b (Std. dev.)
ACC	83.33 (37.58)	83.33 (37.58)
k	0.83 (0.38)	0.83 (0.38)
MAE	0.13 (0.22)	0.12 (0.23)
PREC	1	1
REC	0.67 (0.48)	0.67 (0.48)
f-measure	1	1
AUPR	1	1

* KLR-a: Kernel Logistic Regression: $\lambda = 0.01$,
KLR-b: Kernel Logistic Regression: $\lambda = 0.001$.

Considering the small size of the analysed dataset in terms of the number of samples, we expected to improve performance results using MLP. Accordingly, the results presented in Table 2 show that MLP-a and MLP-c achieved the best results for their performance evaluations with accuracy of 100%, followed by MLP-b (98.33% ± 12.91) and then MLP-d (91.67% ± 27.87). The mean absolute errors are small for all classifiers. Precision, recall, f-measure, and area under precision-recall curve achieved optimal results.

Table 2. MLP performance evaluation using LOOCV.

Metrics	MLP-a (Std.dev.)	MLP-b (Std.dev.)	MLP-c (Std.dev.)	MLP-d (Std.dev.)
ACC	100	98.33 (12.91)	100	91.67 (27.87)
k	1	0.98 (0.13)	1	0.92 (0.28)
MAE	0.11 (0.08)	0.11 (0.15)	0.12 (0.09)	0.15 (0.15)
PREC	1	1	1	1
REC	1	0.97 (0.18)	1	1
f-measure	1	1	1	1
AUPR	1	1	1	1

* MLP-a: Multilayer Perceptron (LR = 0.3, HL = 1), MLP-b: Multilayer Perceptron (LR = 0.5, HL = 1), MLP-c: Multilayer Perceptron (LR = 0.3, HL = 2), MLP-d: Multilayer Perceptron (LR = 0.5, HL = 2).

Due to the superior results of MLP-a and MLP-c performance, they were afterwards used as attribute evaluators, evaluating the worth of an attribute by estimation of the accuracy and root mean squared error of subsets of attributes combinations with 4 folds, using 3-fold CV. Subsequently, the attributes were ranked according to the average merit (Fig. 1).

Gathering MLP into 13 genes groups, the five highest scores of MLP-a (Fig. 1.a) are: 216 genes with score 1, 157 genes with score 0.917 ± 0.118, 229 genes with score 0.833 ± 0.118, 175 genes with score 0.75 ± 0.240 and 224 genes with score 0.667 ± 0.236. MLP-c (Fig. 1.b) presents 243 genes with score 1, 151 genes with score 0.917 ± 0.118, 229 genes with score 0.833 ± 0.118, 174 genes with score 0.75 ± 0.240 and 242 genes with score 0.667 ± 0.236.

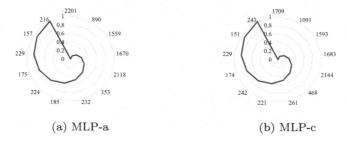

(a) MLP-a   (b) MLP-c

Fig. 1. Number of attributes with its average merit obtained from (a) MLP-a and (b) MLP-c as attribute evaluators.

The gene IDs of the 216 attributes identified with score 1 were searched in Tomato Functional Genomics Database (TFGD) and in Gene/NCBI database. From those, 173 are assigned to *Solanum lycopersicum* genes. There were also identified 4 probes IDs that are assigned to 1 protein of *Escherichia coli* (biotin synthetase) and 37 probes IDs that are assigned to 5 protein of *Bacillus sub-tilis*, (polyA polymerase, threonine synthase, lysA, GTPase ObgE and anthranilate phosphoribosyltransferase). MLP-a and MLP-c identified the same IGs, but MLP-c contains 26 suplementary tomato genes and 1 new attribute assigned to *Oenothera berteroana*, corresponding to NADH-ubiquinone oxidoreductase chain 1 protein.

In oder to add consistency to these results, we also identified IGs through the KLR classifiers (data not shown) and verified that all were identical. KLR-a identified 138 IGs and KLR-b identified 157. We believe that this consistency in the identified IGs, reinforces the correct identification of the tomato-bacillus gene interaction.

3.1   Literature Information of Highest Score Attributes

MLP-a algorithm identified 216 informative genes of the tomato-bacillus inter-action. All these genes are included in the results obtained from MLP-c (243). The probe ID LesAffx.17169.1.A1_at corresponds to the K(+) efflux antiporter

2, chloroplastic gene. According to Tomato Functional Genomics Database (TFGD), it is involved in potassium ion transport, cation and ion transport and metabolic process, and in potassium:proton antiporter activity [19]. Transcription factor ALC gene (Les.1064.1.S1_at) also identified, controls a petal fusion and fruit development in tomato [20]. ATP-citrate synthase alpha chain protein 2 gene was also identified (Les.2817.1.S1_at). It is involved in diverses processes such as acetyl-CoA biosynthetic process, cellular carbohydrate metabolic process, coenzyme A metabolic process and ATP catabolic process. Glutathione peroxidase gene (GPXle-2) was identified (Les.1911.1.S1_at). Recent evidence suggests that plant glutathione peroxidases does not only protect cells from stress induced oxidative damage, but they can be implicated in plant growth and development [21]. According to TFGD, SPY gene (LES.3463.1.S1_AT) is involved in several biological process such as regulation of oxygen and reactive oxygen species metabolic process, gibberellic acid mediated signaling, flower development, multicellular organismal development and cytokinin mediated signaling. Calcium load-activated calcium channel gene (LES.3036.2.S1_AT) was also identified. It is an essential macronutrient in plants. Several studies have been conducted revealing critical roles of calcium transport systems such as in intracellular signaling, elongation growth, cytoskeleton regulation, biotic and abiotic stress responses, programmed cell death and gravity sensing [22]. According to Uniprot, it is related to the calcium-selective channel required to prevent calcium stores from overfilling, having as biological processes the cellular calcium ion homeostasis and endoplasmic reticulum calcium ion homeostasis. Eukaryotic translation initiation factor iso4E gene (LES.5785.1.S1_AT) is involved in RNA 7-methylguanosine cap binding and in translation initiation factor activity [19]. According to Uniprot, 3-hydroxy-3-methylglutaryl-coenzyme A reductase 1 gene (HMGR) with probe ID of LES.4372.1.S1_AT, catalyzes the synthesis of mevalonate. The specific precursor of all isoprenoid compounds present in plants. GAGA-binding transcriptional activator gene (BBR/BPC1), with probe ID of LES.1304.2.S1_AT, is a transcriptional regulator that specifically binds to GA-rich elements (GAGA-repeats) present in regulatory sequences of genes involved in developmental processes. It is involved in response to ethylene [19]. Glutamate decarboxylase gene (LES.249.1.S1_AT) is involved in GABA biosynthesis. The mechanism of GABA accumulation and catabolism in tomato fruits during fruit development was described in [23]. 3-ketoacyl-CoA synthase 11-like gene (LES.4040.1.S1_AT) is involved in the pathway fatty acid biosynthesis, which is part of Lipid metabolism. Pectin acetylesterase 9 (LES.4754.1.S1_AT) is involved in cell wall organization. UDP-galactose: myo-inositol galactosyltransferase (GolS-1) gene (LES.3696.1.S1_AT) is involved in galactose metabolic process and response to stress. Galactinol is formed from UDP-Gal and myo-inositol by the action of GALACTINOL SYNTHASE (GOLS, EC 2.4.1.123), which is putatively the committed enzyme step in the raffinose family oligosaccharides (RFOs) biosynthetic pathway. RFOs have been implicated in mitigating the effects of environmental stresses on plants [24]. A recent study suggests that COP1-interacting protein 7 gene (Les.2219.1.A1_at) regulates plant growth and development in response to light at the post-translational level [25]. According to Uniprot, selenoprotein family protein gene (LesAffx.11886.1.S1_at) is involved in oxidoreductase activity. Indole-3-glycerol phosphate synthase, chloroplastic gene (LesAffx.28368.2.S1_at) is involved in tryptophan biosynthetic process. This gene is a branchpoint of indole-3-acetic acid biosynthesis from the tryptophan biosynthetic pathway in *Arabidopsis thaliana*. Where this phytohormone plays a vital role in plant growth and development as a regulator of several biological processes [26]. According to KEGG, malate dehydrogenase gene (Les.3378.1.S1_at) is involved citrate cycle (TCA cycle), cysteine and methionine metabolism, carbon fixation in photosynthetic organisms, biosynthesis of secondary metabolites, pyruvate metabolism and glyoxylate and dicarboxylate metabolism. According to Uniprot, calreticulin gene (Les.3416.1.S1_at) is involved in calcium ion binding, carbohydrate binding and unfolded protein binding. Lutescent 2 gene (Les.5228.1.A1_at) is involved in several biological processes such as response to ethylene stimulus, response to light stimulus, thylakoid membrane organization and chloroplast organization. A study that performed cloning of the lutescent 2 gene has identified a link between chloroplast development and as-yet-unidentified factors that influence the onset of fruit ripening [27]. Ethylene-inducible CTR1-like protein kinase (CTR1) gene (Les.31.1.S1_s_at) is involved in various biological process such as ethylene mediated signaling pathway, actin cytoskeleton organization, protein amino acid phosphorylation, sugar mediated signaling, gibberellin biosynthetic process, regulation of timing of transition from vegetative to reproductive phase, chemotaxis, and phagocytosis.

In addition to the genes mentioned above, the following genes were identified by MLP-c. According to Uniprot, Zinc finger CCCH domain-containing protein 24 gene (LES.5364.1.A1_AT) is involved in the regulation of nitrogen, macromolecule and primary compound metabolic processes. Zinc-finger proteins, a superfamily of proteins with a typical structural domain that coordinates a zinc ion and binds nucleic acids, participate in the regulation of growth, development, and stress adaptation in plants [28]. Protein XAP5 CIRCADIAN TIMEKEEPER gene (LES.4898.1.S1_AT) was identified as a novel gene with pleiotropic effects on plant growth and development and acts downstream of a major transcriptional regulator in an organ-specific manner, playing an environment-dependent role in the regulation of plant growth [29]. According to Uniprot, plant UBX domain-containing protein 4-like gene (LesAffx.67661.2.S1_at) is involved in proteasome-mediated ubiquitin-dependent protein catabolic process, nuclear membrane reassembly, membrane fusion, Golgi organization and autophagosome assembly. Histone 1 gene (LES.4839.1.A1_AT) is involved in nucleosome assembly. SWR1-complex protein 4 gene (Les.5247.1.S1_at) is involved DNA repair, green leaf volatile biosynthetic process, histone exchange and negative regulation of transcription by RNA polymerase II. Probable xyloglucan endotransglucosylase/hydrolase (SlXTH15) gene with prob ID (LesAffx.24799.1.S1_at) catalyzes xyloglucan endohydrolysis (XEH) and/or endotransglycosylation (XET). Cleaves and religates xyloglucan polymers, an essential constituent of the primary cell wall, and thereby participates in cell wall construction of growing tissues. Glucose-induced degradation protein 4 homolog gene (LES.4927.1.A1_AT) is involved in negative regulation of gluconeogenesis, proteasome - mediated ubiquitin-dependent protein catabolic process, protein catabolic process in the vacuole and protein targeting to vacuole [19]. Universal stress protein PHOS32 gene (LesAffx.2998.1.S1_at) was also identified in the network of tomato-bacillus interaction. A recent study suggests that universal stress protein (AtUSP) *Arabidopsis thaliana* gene plays a role in cell expansion, and controls plant growth and development [30]. CBL-interacting serine/threonine-protein kinase 23 gene (LESAFFX.344.13.A1_AT) is involved in signal transduction. A recent study indicates that CBL-interacting protein kinase NtCIPK23 positively regulates seed germination and early seedling development in tobacco [31]. The activity of defective in cullin neddylation 1 (DCN1)-like protein 4 gene (LesAffx.25914.1.S1_at) is required for pollen development transitions and embryogenesis, and for pollen tube growth in tobacco [32]. According to Uniprot, MLO gene (LesAffx.64.1.S1_at) is involved in defense response and in response to biotic stimulus. F-box/kelch - repeat protein At1g23390 gene (LesAffx.20391.1.S1_at) is involved in proteasome-mediated ubiquitin-dependent protein catabolic process. The protein from cyclin-dependent kinases regulatory subunit 1 gene (Les.2589.1.S1_at) binds to the catalytic subunit of the cyclin dependent kinases and it is essential for their biological function. N6-adenosine-methyltransferase MT-A70-like gene (Les.5243.1.S1_at) is involved in mRNA methylation. Calmodulin 3 gene is involved in calcium ion binding. A recent study reported that calmodulin had broad expression patterns in abiotic stress conditions and with hormone treatments, in different tissues of stress-tolerant wild tomato species, *Solanum pennellii* [33]. CaM gene interacts with a wide range of downstream target molecules that mediate diverse cell process [34]. According to TFGD, vicilin-like seed storage protein At2g28490 (Les.5168.1.S1_at) is involved xenobiotic metabolic process, defense response to fungus and defense response to bacterium. ATP synthase subunit d, mitochondrial gene (Les.3141.1.S1_at) is involved in ion transport, ATP synthesis coupled proton transport, proton transport and in response to salt stress.

There are IGs identified as *Bacillus subtilis subsp. subtilis str. 168* proteins, namely threonine synthase, GTPase obgE, lysA, polyA polymerase and anthranilate phosphoribosyltransferase involved in tryptophan biosynthesis [19]. Another identified bacteria was *Escherichia coli* through biotin synthetase protein. Biotin synthase is a member of the 'radical SAM' (S-adenosylmethionine) family, which converts DTB (dethiobiotin) into biotin [35].

3.2   Biological Pathways of Tomato - Bacillus Interaction

To the best of our knowledge, g:Profiler is the reference web server for functional enrichment analysis that presents information of the biological pathways involved in tomato. It is imperative to refer that g:Profiler results are constantly updated, and the order of the IGs identified affects the outcomes. From 173 tomato IGs identified by MLP-a, 140 are reported in g: Profiler and 4 were not included in the survey due to ambiguous query. The outcomes showed 38 genes sorted into

9 pathways by KEGG, as shown in the Table 3. From 199 tomato IGs identified by MLP-c, 157 are reported in g:Profiler and 4 were not included in the survey due to ambiguous query. The outcomes showed 42 genes sorted into 8 pathways by KEGG, as shown in the Table 4. The results of the biological pathways are similar, adding aminoacyl-tRNA biosynthesis to the set of IGs identified by MLP-a.

Table 3. Biological pathways from KEGG for the survey of 140 tomato genes.

Biological pathway	KEGG-id	Adjusted-p-value	Number of genes
Ribosome	03010	2.41E-13	14
KEGG root term	00000	4.58E-12	38
Metabolic pathways	01100	4.62E-03	14
Biosynthesis of secondary metabolites	01110	6.30E-03	10
One carbon pool by folate	00670	2.69E-02	1
Other types of O-glycan biosynthesis	00514	2.80E-02	1
Aminoacyl-tRNA biosynthesis	00970	3.69E-02	1
Biosynthesis of amino acids	01230	3.86E-02	3
D-Amino acid metabolism	00470	3.95E-02	1

Ribosome has a regulatory role in plant development [36]. Plant secondary metabolites play a significant role in plant adaptation to various environmental constraints that influence plant growth [37]. One carbon pool by folate pathway is involved in tomato-bacillus interaction. Folates are absolutely essential for plant development [38]. A recent study indicates that plants seem to have adopted different D-Amino acids as nitrogen source, building blocks, or signaling molecules. The number and diversity of D-Amino acids functions indicate their relevance for the plants's physiology [39].

Table 4. Biological pathways from KEGG for the survey of 157 tomato genes.

Biological pathway	KEGG-id	Adjusted-p-value	Number of genes
Ribosome	03010	6.01E-17	17
KEGG root term	00000	3.46E-13	42
Metabolic pathways	01100	4.13E-03	15
Biosynthesis of secondary metabolites	01110	1.38E-02	10
Other types of O-glycan biosynthesis	00514	1.68E-02	1
One carbon pool by folate	00670	3.80E-02	1
Biosynthesis of amino acids	01230	3.80E-02	3
D-Amino acid metabolism	00470	4.80E-02	1

3.3 Biological Networks Analysis

In order to identify possible biological networks, *Arabidopsis thaliana* orthologous genes of tomato were searched for both IGs identified by MLP-a and MLP-c. For the 173 tomato IGs (MLP-a) were identified 35 orthologous genes. Applying GO biological process based as network weighting, the outcomes showed four interaction networks: co-expression data (38.94%), predicted interactions (16.20%), shared protein domains (3.67%) and co-localization data (0.33%), producing a total of 1525 links, as shown in Fig. 2. For the 199 tomato IGs (MLP-c) were identified 40 orthologous genes. The outcomes showed five interaction networks: physical interaction (39.03%), co-expression data (38.94%), predicted interactions (16.20%), shared protein domains (3.67%) and co-localization data (0.33%), producing a total of 2167 links, as shown in Fig. 3.

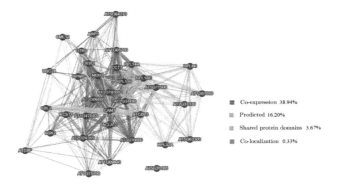

Fig. 2. Gene interaction networks of the 35 *Arabidopsis thaliana* orthologous genes in GeneMANIA.

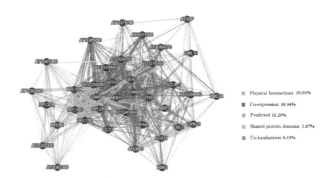

Fig. 3. Gene interaction networks of the 40 *Arabidopsis thaliana* orthologous genes in GeneMANIA.

According to the informative genes identified, the bacteria is *Bacillus subtilis*. We assume that being *Bacillus subtilis* a well-studied bacterium, used as a model organism and because it has homologous genes, the probe ID for bacillus was appointed to *Bacillus subtilis*.

4   Conclusion

Considering the typology and dimensionality of the analysed dataset, MLP-a and MLP-c classifiers achieved near optimal performance evaluation to predict *Bacillus megaterium* in tomato root tissue. Applying these classifiers as attribute evaluators, both predicted the same informative genes, even if MLP-c identified additional 27 new attributes. The IGs identified by MLP-a were 173 tomato genes, 5 bacillus proteins, 1 *Escherichia coli* protein and 2 unknowns. The IGs identified by MLP-c were 199 tomato genes, 5 bacillus proteins, 1 *Escherichia coli* protein, 1 *Oenothera berteroana* protein and 2 unknowns.

Functional enrichment analysis of IGs identified by MLP-c showed eight biological pathways (ribosome, KEGG root term, metabolic pathways, other types of O-glycan biosynthesis, biosynthesis of amino acids, biosynthesis of secondary metabolites, one carbon pool by folate and D-Amino acid metabolism), presenting MLP-a one more biological pathway, namely, aminoacyl-tRNA biosynthesis. Furthermore, the biological pathways involved in tomato genes identified are known for their important role in plant development and growth.

The biological networks obtained by application of *Arabidopsis thaliana* orthologous genes showed 38.94 % of co-expression, 16.20 % of predicted interaction, 3.67 % of shared protein domains and 0.33 % of co-localization data, for the 35 *Arabidopsis thaliana* orthologous genes of the tomato IG obtained by MLP-a, producing a total of 1525 links. Physical interaction (39.03%), co-expression data (38.94%), predicted interactions (16.20%), shared protein domains (3.67%) and co-localization data (0.33%), were identified for the 40 *Arabidopsis thaliana* orthologous genes of the tomato IGs obtained by MLP-c, producing a total of 2167 links.

To our knowledge, this is the first analysis of *Solanum lycopersicum - Bacillus megaterium* root tissue interaction using machine learning approach. Our results provide new insight to understand the mechanisms underlying the tomato-PGPR interaction.

References

1. Vejan, P., Abdullah, R., Khadiran, T., Ismail, S., Nasrulhaq Boyce, A.: Role of plant growth promoting rhizobacteria in agricultural sustainability-a review. Molecules **21**, 573 (2016). https://doi.org/10.3390/molecules21050573
2. Schwarz, D., Rouphael, Y., Colla, G., Venema, J.H.: Grafting as a tool to improve tolerance of vegetables to abiotic stresses: thermal stress, water stress and organic pollutants. Sci. Hortic. **127**, 162–171 (2010). https://doi.org/10.1016/j.scienta.2010.09.016

3. Marulanda-Aguirre, A., Azcón, R., Ruiz-Lozano, J.M., Aroca, R.: Differential effects of a bacillus megaterium strain on lactuca sativa plant growth depending on the origin of the arbuscular mycorrhizal fungus coinoculated: physiologic and biochemical traits. J. Plant Growth Regul. **27**, 10–18 (2008). https://doi.org/10.1007/s00344-007-9024-5

4. Ibort, P., et al.: Tomato ethylene sensitivity determines interaction with plant growth-promoting bacteria. Ann. Bot. **120**, 101–122 (2017). https://doi.org/10.1093/aob/mcx052

5. van Dijk, A.D.J., Kootstra, G., Kruijer, W., de Ridder, D.: Machine learning in plant science and plant breeding. iScience **24**, 101890 (2021) https://doi.org/10.1016/j.isci.2020.101890

6. Taş, N., de Jong, A.E., Li, Y., Trubl, G., Xue, Y., Dove, N.C.: Metagenomic tools in microbial ecology research. Curr. Opin. Biotechnol. **67**, 184–191 (2021) https://doi.org/10.1016/j.copbio.2021.01.019

7. Peiffer-Smadja, N., et al.: Machine learning in the clinical microbiology laboratory: has the time come for routine practice? Clin. Microbiol. Infect. **26**, 1300–1309 (2020) https://doi.org/10.1016/j.cmi.2020.02.006

8. Landis, J.R., Koch, G.G.: The measurement of observer agreement for categorical data. Int. Biom. Soc. **33**, 159–174 (1977)

9. Raudys, S.J., Jain, A.K.: Small sample size effects in statistical pattern recognition: recommendations for practitioners. IEEE Trans. Pattern Anal. Mach. Intell. **13**, 252–264 (1991). https://doi.org/10.1109/34.75512

10. Wahba, G., Gu, C., Wang, Y., Chappell, R.: Soft classification, a.k.a. risk estimation, via penalized log likelihood and smoothing spline analysis of variance. In: Computational Learning Theory and Natural Learning Systems, pp. 133–162 (1995)

11. Smith, B., Wang, S., Wong, A., Zhou, X.: A penalized likelihood approach to parameter estimation with integral reliability constraints. Entropy **17**, 4040–4063 (2015). https://doi.org/10.3390/e17064040

12. Witten, I.H., Frank, E., Hall, M.A., Pal, C.J.: Data Mining: Practical Machine Learning Tools and Techniques, 4nd edn. Morgan Kaufmann series in data management systems. Morgan Kaufman, Amsterdam; Boston, MA (2016)

13. Li, H.: Microbiome, metagenomics, and high-dimensional compositional data analysis. Annu. Rev. Stat. Its Appl. **2**, 73–94 (2015). https://doi.org/10.1146/annurev-statistics-010814-020351

14. Tharwat, A.: Classification assessment methods. Appl. Comput. Inform (2018). https://doi.org/10.1016/j.aci.2018.08.003

15. Fei, Z., et al.: Tomato Functional Genomics Database: a comprehensive resource and analysis package for tomato functional genomics. Nucleic Acids Res. **39**, D1156–D1163 (2011). https://doi.org/10.1093/nar/gkq991

16. Altschul, S.F., Gish, W., Miller, W., Myers, E.W., Lipman, D.J.: Basic local alignment search tool. J. Mol. Biol. **215**, 403–410 (1990). https://doi.org/10.1016/S0022-2836(05)80360-2

17. Raudvere, U., et al.: g:Profiler: a web server for functional enrichment analysis and conversions of gene lists (2019 update). Nucleic Acids Res. **47**, W191–W198 (2019). https://doi.org/10.1093/nar/gkz369

18. Montojo, J., et al.: GeneMANIA Cytoscape plugin: fast gene function predictions on the desktop. Bioinformatics **26**, 2927–2928 (2010). https://doi.org/10.1093/bioinformatics/btq562

19. Gaudet, P., Livstone, M.S., Lewis, S.E., Thomas, P.D.: Phylogenetic-based propagation of functional annotations within the Gene Ontology consortium. Brief. Bioinform. **12**, 449–462 (2011). https://doi.org/10.1093/bib/bbr042

20. Ortiz-Ramírez, C.I., Giraldo, M.A., Ferrándiz, C., Pabón-Mora, N.: Expression and function of the BHLH genes ALCATRAZ and SPATULA in selected Solanaceae species. Plant J. **99**, 686–702 (2019). https://doi.org/10.1111/tpj.14352

21. Bela, K., Horváth, E., Gallé, Á., Szabados, L., Tari, I., Csiszár, J.: Plant glutathione peroxidases: emerging role of the antioxidant enzymes in plant development and stress responses. J. Plant Physiol. **176**, 192–201 (2015). https://doi.org/10.1016/j.jplph.2014.12.014

22. Demidchik, V., Shabala, S., Isayenkov, S., Cuin, T.A., Pottosin, I.: Calcium transport across plant membranes: mechanisms and functions. New Phytol. **220**, 49–69 (2018). https://doi.org/10.1111/nph.15266

23. Akihiro, T., et al.: Biochemical mechanism on GABA accumulation during fruit development in tomato. Plant Cell Physiol. **49**, 1378–1389 (2008). https://doi.org/10.1093/pcp/pcn113

24. Downie, B., et al.: Expression of a GALACTINOL SYNTHASE gene in tomato seeds is up-regulated before maturation desiccation and again after imbibition whenever radicle protrusion is prevented. Plant Physiol. **131**, 1347–1359 (2003). https://doi.org/10.1104/pp.016386

25. Kim, J.Y., Song, J.T., Seo, S.: COP1 regulates plant growth and development in response to light at the post-translational level. J. Exp. Bot. **68**, 4737–4748 (2017). https://doi.org/10.1093/jxb/erx312

26. Ouyang, J., Shao, X., Li, J.: Indole-3-glycerol phosphate, a branchpoint of indole-3-acetic acid biosynthesis from the tryptophan biosynthetic pathway in Arabidopsis thaliana. Plant J. **24**, 327–334 (2000). https://doi.org/10.1046/j.1365-313x.2000.00883.x

27. Barry, C.S., et al.: Altered chloroplast development and delayed fruit ripening caused by mutations in a zinc metalloprotease at the lutescent2 locus of tomato. Plant Physiol. **159**, 1086–1098 (2012). https://doi.org/10.1104/pp.112.197483

28. Han, G., Qiao, Z., Li, Y., Wang, C., Wang, B.: The roles of CCCH zinc-finger proteins in plant abiotic stress tolerance. Int. J. Mol. Sci. **22**, 8327 (2021). https://doi.org/10.3390/ijms22158327

29. Martin-Tryon, E.L., Harmer, S.L.: XAP5 CIRCADIAN TIMEKEEPER coordinates light signals for proper timing of photomorphogenesis and the circadian clock in arabidopsis. Plant Cell **20**, 1244–1259 (2008). https://doi.org/10.1105/tpc.107.056655

30. Lee, E.S., et al.: Universal Stress Protein (USP) enhances plant growth and development by promoting cell expansion. J. Plant Biol. **65**, 231–239 (2022). https://doi.org/10.1007/s12374-022-09348-3

31. Shi, S., et al.: The CBL-interacting protein kinase NtCIPK23 positively regulates seed germination and early seedling development in tobacco (Nicotiana tabacum L.). Plants **10**, 323 (2021). https://doi.org/10.3390/plants10020323

32. Hosp, J., et al.: A tobacco homolog of DCN1 is involved in pollen development and embryogenesis. Plant Cell Rep. **33**, 1187–1202 (2014). https://doi.org/10.1007/s00299-014-1609-4

33. Shi, J., Du, X.: Identification, characterization and expression analysis of calmodulin and calmodulin-like proteins in Solanum pennellii. Sci. Rep. **10**, 7474 (2020). https://doi.org/10.1038/s41598-020-64178-y

34. Bergey, D.R., Kandel, R., Tyree, B.K., Dutt, M., Dhekney, S.A.: The role of calmodulin and related proteins in plant cell function: an ever-thickening plot. Springer Sci. Rev. (2014). https://doi.org/10.1007/s40362-014-0025-z

35. Lotierzo, M., Tse Sum Bui, B., Florentin, D., Escalettes, F., Marquet, A.: Biotin synthase mechanism: an overview. Biochem. Soc. Trans. **33**, 820–823 (2005). https://doi.org/10.1042/BST0330820

36. Byrne, M.E.: A role for the ribosome in development. Trends Plant Sci. **14**, 512–519 (2009). https://doi.org/10.1016/j.tplants.2009.06.009

37. Bhattacharya, A.: High-temperature stress and metabolism of secondary metabolites in plants. In: Effect of High Temperature on Crop Productivity and Metabolism of Macro Molecules, pp. 391–484. Elsevier (2019). https://doi.org/10.1016/B978-0-12-817562-0.00005-7

38. Gorelova, V., Ambach, L., Rébeillé, F., Stove, C., Van Der Straeten, D.: Folates in Plants: Research Advances and Progress in Crop Biofortification. Front. Chem. **5** (2017). https://doi.org/10.3389/fchem.2017.00021

39. Kolukisaoglu, Ü.: d-amino acids in plants: sources, metabolism, and functions. Int. J. Mol. Sci. **21**, 5421 (2020). https://doi.org/10.3390/ijms21155421

A Kernel Clustering Algorithm Based on Diameters

M. Fernanda P. Costa[1](✉) [ID], Ana Maria A. C. Rocha[2] [ID],
and Edite M. G. P. Fernandes[2] [ID]

[1] Centre of Mathematics, University of Minho, Campus de Gualtar, 4710-057 Braga,
Portugal
mfc@math.uminho.pt
[2] ALGORITMI Center, University of Minho, Campus de Gualtar,
4710-057 Braga, Portugal
{arocha,emgpf}@dps.uminho.pt

Abstract. This paper analyzes an iterative kernel partitioning clustering algorithm that dynamically merges, removes and adds clusters using
some characteristics, like the radii and diameters of the clusters, and
distance between centers. The clustering is carried out in feature space
in terms of a kernel function so that non-linearly separable clusters are
identified. The preliminary experiments with seven datasets show that
the proposed algorithm is able to successfully converge to the expected
clustering. It is also shown that the algorithm performance is sensitive
to the parameter σ of the Gaussian kernel.

Keywords: Partitioning clustering · Kernel function · Cluster
diameter and radius

1 Introduction

Clustering is an unsupervised machine learning task and consists of grouping a
set of data points in a way that similarity of the elements in a group – also called
cluster – is maximized, whereas similarity of elements in two different groups, is
minimized [1,2]. Applications of clustering are very common in areas like data
mining, bioinformatics, pattern recognition and image processing [3].

The partitioning and hierarchical clustering are the most popular. The well-
known K-means clustering is a partitioning type clustering [4] that subdivides
the dataset into K clusters, where K is specified *a priori*, and uses the centroid
(mean) of the data points belonging to a cluster as the representative point of
that cluster. Partitioning and hierarchical clustering are suitable to find convex
clusters since they work well when clusters are compact and separated. However,
they inaccurately identify clusters when non-convex clusters and noise points are

This work has been supported by FCT – Fundação para a Ciência e Tecnologia
within the R&D Units Project Scope: UIDB/00319/2020, UIDB/00013/2020 and
UIDP/00013/2020 of CMAT-UM.

A. I. Pereira et al. (Eds.): OL2A 2022, CCIS 1754, pp. 442–456, 2022.
https://doi.org/10.1007/978-3-031-23236-7_31

present. When a partitioning clustering algorithm cannot identify clusters that are non-linearly separable in the input space, the use of a kernel function solves the problem [5]. The goal is to use an appropriate nonlinear function that maps the points in the input space to points in some higher-dimensional feature space, known as the kernel space. Then, the kernel clustering method can partition the data points that are linearly separable in the new space [2].

Unlike K-means and pure hierarchical clustering, the partitioning clustering algorithm of this study is able to iteratively adjust the number of clusters. The algorithm may merge, remove and add clusters depending on some pre-defined conditions. During the initialization of the algorithm, a number of clusters is required to start the points assigning process, although this number is updated whenever clusters are merged, removed or split. The kernel clustering algorithm uses a distance-based methodology, a Gaussian kernel function to carry out the clustering in the feature space, and concepts like the cluster diameter, and the cluster radius, to select a cluster to be split, and to be merged, respectively. Thus, the algorithm proceeds as follows. First, at each iteration, the algorithm identifies the pair of clusters that may be merged and checks if a cluster center may be deleted, and consequently the cluster is removed. Second, it identifies the cluster that may be split according to conditions that involve the size of the two clusters with closest centers. Finally, each point in the dataset is assigned to the closest mean in feature space, resulting in a new clustering.

The paper is organized as follows. Section 2 briefly describes the ideas of a cluster analysis and Sect. 3 presents the details of the new kernel clustering diameter-based algorithm. In Sect. 4, the results of clustering seven sets of data points with two attributes are shown. Finally, Sect. 5 contains the conclusions of this work.

2   Cluster Analysis

Let a set of n data points (or vectors) of dimension a, the so-called attributes, be given. These points can be represented by a data matrix $\mathbf{X}$ with n vectors/points of dimension a. Each element $X_{i,j}$ corresponds to the jth attribute of the ith point [6]. Thus, given $\mathbf{X}$, a partitioning clustering algorithm tries to find a partition $\mathcal{C} = \{C_1, C_2, \ldots, C_K\}$ of K clusters (or groups), in a way that similarity of the points in the same cluster is maximum and points from different clusters differ as much as possible. In hard clustering, it is required that the partition satisfies three conditions:

1. each cluster should have at least one point, i.e., $|C_k| \neq 0$, $k = 1, \ldots, K$;
2. a point should not belong to two different clusters, i.e., $C_k \bigcap C_l = \emptyset$, for $k, l = 1, \ldots, K$, $k \neq l$;
3. each point should belong to a cluster, i.e., $\sum_{k=1}^{K} |C_k| = n$;

where $|C_k|$ is the number of points in cluster C_k. Since there are several ways to partition the points and maintain these properties, a fitness function should be provided to evaluate the adequacy of the partitioning. Thus, the goal in the clustering problem is to find an optimal partition, $\mathcal{C}^*$, that gives the optimal (or near-optimal) adequacy, when compared to all the other feasible solutions.

3   Kernel Clustering Diameter-Based Algorithm

To partition data points into clusters, the distance-based clustering algorithms are the most popular, and are used in a large variety of applications [7]. In this section, a clustering approach that uses the distance between specific points and a kernel function is described.

The algorithm uses the kernel trick to carry out the clustering in feature space in terms of the Gaussian kernel function. Although the algorithm starts by defining a set of K clusters, it has mechanisms to try to find the optimal (or near-optimal) clustering by merging and removing clusters, and adding (splitting an existing cluster) based on some characteristics of the current clusters. In particular, the largest distance between points in a cluster (diameter), the smallest distance between cluster points, and the largest distance between the points in a cluster and the center point (radius), are considered. It is termed Kernel Clustering Diameter-based algorithm (KCDbased algorithm).

At the initial step, a number K of clusters must be provided and the corresponding centers $m_1, m_2, \ldots, m_K$ are randomly selected from the set of data points $\mathbf{X}$. Then, at each iteration, the KCDbased algorithm merges two featured clusters, removes a rather small cluster, adds a new cluster by splitting a specific cluster, according to some conditions, and ends up by assigning the dataset points to the existent clusters.

Next, the details of each procedure are presented.

After a set of points being randomly selected from $\mathbf{X}$, to define the initial cluster centers $m_k, k = 1, \ldots, K$ (given K), each point X_i ($i = 1, \ldots, n$) is assigned to a cluster. To find which cluster to assign the point X_i, the simplest idea is to find the closest distance from X_i to the m_k, $k = 1, \ldots, K$.

In a kernel function context, the details to compute the distance from a point X_i to the centers m_k, $k = 1, \ldots, K$ follow. Let the cluster centers in the feature space be given as $m_k^{\phi}, k = 1, \ldots, K$ where

$$m_k^{\phi} = \frac{1}{|C_k|} \sum_{X_i \in C_k} \phi(X_i), \tag{1}$$

and ϕ is an appropriate nonlinear function that maps the points in the input space to points in the higher-dimensional feature space [5]. In this space, the distance of a point $\phi(X_i)$ to the mean m_k^{ϕ} is defined as

$$\|\phi(X_i) - m_k^{\phi}\|^2 = \|\phi(X_i)\|^2 - 2\phi(X_i)^T m_k^{\phi} + \|m_k^{\phi}\|^2$$

and consequently, using (1) and the kernel function $\mathbf{K}(\cdot, \cdot) = \phi(\cdot)^T \phi(\cdot)$:

$$\|\phi(X_i) - m_k^{\phi}\|^2 = \mathbf{K}(X_i, X_i) - \frac{2}{|C_k|} \sum_{X_j \in C_k} \mathbf{K}(X_j, X_i) + \frac{1}{|C_k|^2} \sum_{X_j \in C_k} \sum_{X_l \in C_k} \mathbf{K}(X_j, X_l). \tag{2}$$

Algorithm 1 presents the details of the KCDbased algorithm.

Algorithm 1. KCDbased Algorithm

Require: n (number of dataset points), $X_i, i = 1, \ldots, n$ (points of the dataset); $It_{\max}$
1: Set initial K and $N_{\min}$; Set $It = 1$
2: Randomly select a set of K points from the dataset $\mathbf{X}$ to initialize the K cluster centers m_k, $k = 1, \ldots, K$
3: Assign each point $X_i \in \mathbf{X}$ to the cluster based on the closest center, using Algorithm 2, to define K clusters $\mathcal{C}_K = \{C_1, \ldots, C_K\}$
4: **repeat**
5:     Compute the distance between the two closest cluster centers, $D_{\min}$, using (7) and identify the indices k_i and k_j of the centers
6:     Compute the largest distance of each center $m_{k_i}^\phi$ (resp. $m_{k_j}^\phi$) to the points in cluster C_{k_i} (resp. C_{k_j}), r_{k_i} (resp. r_{k_j})
7:     Compute the average distance of each center $m_{k_i}^\phi$ (resp. $m_{k_j}^\phi$) to the points in cluster C_{k_i} (resp. C_{k_j}), $\bar{r}_{k_i}$ (resp. $\bar{r}_{k_j}$)
8:     Merge the 2 clusters with closest cluster centers (based on $D_{\min}, r_{k_i}, r_{k_j}, \bar{r}_{k_i}$ and $\bar{r}_{k_j}$) and remove the cluster with fewer points (based on $N_{\min}$), using Algorithm 3
9:     **for** $k = 1$ to K **do**
10:        Compute distances $d_{j,l} = \|\phi(X_j) - \phi(X_l)\|^2$ for all $X_j, X_l \in C_k$ using (6)
11:        Identify diameter $D_1^k = \max d_{j,l}$ and the minimum distance $D_0^k = \min d_{j,l}$
12:    **end for**
13:    Identify the cluster C_{k_i}, where the index $k_i = \arg\max_k(D_1^k - D_0^k)$, and the points $X_{i_1}, X_{i_2} \in C_{k_i}$ corresponding to $D_1^{k_i}$
14:    Split the cluster C_{k_i} using Algorithm 4
15:    Assign points to the cluster with closest center, using Algorithm 2
16:    Set $It = It + 1$
17: **until** $It > It_{\max}$ OR number of points in clusters has not changed for two consecutive iterations
18: **return** K^* and $\mathcal{C}^* = \{C_1^*, \ldots, C_K^*\}$.

3.1   Assign Points to Clusters

To assign point X_i to the closest cluster center, the following condition is set:

$$X_i \in C_{k_i} \text{ such that } k_i = \arg\min_{k=1,\ldots,K} \left(\|\phi(X_i) - m_k^\phi\|^2 \right) \\ = \arg\min_{k=1,\ldots,K} \left(SqN_k - 2Avg_{i,k} \right) \tag{3}$$

where the SqN_k (squared norm of cluster means) for each $k = 1, \ldots, K$ is given by:

$$SqN_k = \frac{1}{|C_k|^2} \sum_{X_j \in C_k} \sum_{X_l \in C_k} \mathbf{K}(X_j, X_l), \tag{4}$$

and the average kernel value for X_i and C_k, $Avg_{i,k}$ ($i = 1, \ldots, n$ and $k = 1, \ldots, K$), is

$$Avg_{i,k} = \frac{1}{|C_k|} \sum_{X_j \in C_k} \mathbf{K}(X_j, X_i). \tag{5}$$

We note that in the last expression of (3), the term $\mathbf{K}(X_i, X_i)$ has not been included because it is the same for all the clusters.

Subsequently, the distance of a point $\phi(X_j)$ to another point $\phi(X_l)$ of the dataset in feature space, can be computed as

$$d_{j,l} = \|\phi(X_j) - \phi(X_l)\|^2 = \|\phi(X_j)\|^2 - 2\phi(X_j)^T\phi(X_l) + \|\phi(X_l)\|^2 \qquad (6)$$
$$= \mathbf{K}(X_j, X_j) - 2\mathbf{K}(X_j, X_l) + \mathbf{K}(X_l, X_l).$$

The Algorithm 2 contains the steps required to the process of assigning points to clusters.

Algorithm 2. Assign points to clusters

Require: $K, n, X_i, i = 1, \ldots, n, C_k, k = 1, \ldots, K$
 1: **for** $k = 1$ to K **do**
 2:     Compute squared norm of cluster means SqN_k using (4)
 3: **end for**
 4: **for all** X_i, $i = 1, \ldots, n$ **do**
 5:     **for all** C_k, $k = 1$ to K **do**
 6:         Compute average kernel value $Avg_{i,k}$ using (5)
 7:     **end for**
 8: **end for**
 9: Set $C_k = \emptyset, k = 1, \ldots, K$
10: **for** $i = 1$ to n **do**
11:     **for** $k = 1$ to K **do**
12:         Compute $d_{i,k} = SqN_k - 2Avg_{i,k}$
13:     **end for**
14:     Assign point X_i to cluster C_{k_i} by identifying the index $k_i = \arg\min_{k=1,\ldots,K} d_{i,k}$
15: **end for**
16: **for** $k = 1$ to K **do**
17:     **if** $|C_k| = 0$ **then**
18:         Remove C_k
19:     **end if**
20: **end for**
21: Update K
22: **return** $C_k, k = 1, \ldots, K$

3.2   Merge Two Clusters

The two clusters with the closest centers are merged if the distance between their centers satisfies some conditions based on their radii. Let the radius of a cluster be defined by the largest distance from its center to the points of the cluster, r_k, $k = 1, \ldots, K$. The average of all the distances from the center to the points of a cluster is denoted averaged radius and is represented by $\bar{r}_k$. The two clusters with the closest centers may be merged if the distance between their centers, $D_{\min}$, is not greater than the sum of their radii and at the same time less than the average of their averaged radii multiplied by a positive factor ≥ 1, where $D_{\min}$ is computed using

$$
\begin{aligned}
D_{\min} &= \min_{i=1,\ldots,K, j>i} \left(\|m_i^\phi - m_j^\phi\|^2 \right) \\
&= \min_{i=1,\ldots,K, j>i} \left(\|m_i^\phi\|^2 - 2\bar{m}_{i,j} + \|m_j^\phi\|^2 \right) \\
&= \min_{i=1,\ldots,K, j>i} \mathbf{K}(m_i^\phi, m_i^\phi) - 2\bar{m}_{i,j} + \mathbf{K}(m_j^\phi, m_j^\phi),
\end{aligned}
\tag{7}
$$

and $\bar{m}_{i,j}$, the average kernel value for C_i and C_j, is given by

$$
\bar{m}_{i,j} = \frac{1}{|C_i||C_j|} \sum_{i=1,\ldots,k} \sum_{j>i} \mathbf{K}(m_i^\phi, m_j^\phi).
$$

See details of the merge and remove clusters algorithm in Algorithm 3.

Algorithm 3. Merge and remove clusters

Require: n, K, C_{k_i}, C_{k_j}, $D_{\min}$, $\bar{r}_{k_i}$, $\bar{r}_{k_j}$, r_{k_i}, r_{k_j}, $N_{\min}$

1: **if** $D_{\min} \leq (r_{k_i} + r_{k_j})$ AND $D_{\min} < \dfrac{\bar{r}_{k_i} + \bar{r}_{k_j}}{2} \dfrac{n}{|C_{k_i}| + |C_{k_j}|}$ **then**

2:    Include points of C_{k_i} into cluster C_{k_j} and remove C_{k_i}

3:    Update K and $|C_{k_j}|$; set $N_0 = |C_{k_j}|$ and $N_1 = 0$

4: **else**

5:    Set $N_0 = |C_{k_j}|$ and $N_1 = |C_{k_i}|$

6: **end if**

7: Identify the index k_l such that $|C_{k_l}| = \min_k |C_k|$

8: **if** $|C_{k_l}| < N_{\min}$ **then**

9:    Define all points in C_{k_l} as 'noise/outlier'

10:    Remove C_{k_l}

11:    Update K

12: **end if**

13: **return** C_k, $k = 1,\ldots,K$, N_0, N_1.

3.3 Split a Cluster

Based on the diameter of a cluster, defined as the largest distance between points in that cluster, and on the minimum distance between points of the cluster, the algorithm may split the cluster into two clusters. Let D_1 be the diameter of a cluster and D_0 be the minimum distance between points of the cluster. The candidate cluster to be split has the largest difference $D_1 - D_0$. We choose to split that cluster if its diameter exceeds the (previously identified) smallest distance between centers and if its size (number of points in that cluster) exceeds the size of the cluster when two clusters are merged or the size of the largest cluster previously identified for the merging process. Algorithm 4 describes the main steps of the splitting process.

Algorithm 4. Split a cluster

Require: $K, k_i, C_{k_i}, D_1^{k_i}, X_{i_1}, X_{i_2} \in C_{k_i}, D_{\min}, N_0, N_1$
1: **if** $D_1^{k_i} > D_{\min}$ AND $|C_{k_i}| > \max(N_0, N_1)$ **then**
2:     Assign points $X_i \in C_{k_i}$ to the new clusters with the selected centers X_{i_1} and X_{i_2} to define clusters C_{K+1} and C_{K+2}
3: **end if**
4: Set $C_{k_i} \leftarrow C_{K+2}; K \leftarrow K+1$
5: **return** C_{k_i} and C_K

---

4   Computational Results

In this section, some preliminary results are shown. Seven datasets of points with two attributes are used to test the algorithm.

The Algorithm 1 is coded in MATLAB®. Its performance depends on the parameter of the Gaussian kernel, σ, where for U and V vectors,

$$\mathbf{K}(U, V) = \exp(-\gamma\|U - V\|_2^2) \text{ and } \gamma = (2\sigma^2)^{-1}.$$

Note that this kernel value $\mathbf{K}$ is inversely related to the distance between the two vectors. In practice, different values for σ are usually set by trial and error. Other parameters that have not much influence in the algorithm performance are initial $K = \max\{v, \min\{2, \lceil 0.005n \rceil\}\}$, where v is a positive integer in $[2, 6]$, $N_{\min} = \max\{5, \lceil 0.01n \rceil\}$ and $It_{\max} = 10$. The algorithm is assumed to converge when the cluster points do not change for two consecutive iterations.

The clustering obtained in this study is compared with those obtained by two well-known partitioning algorithms, DBSCAN and K-means. DBSCAN is a density-based clustering algorithm that is designed to discover clusters and noise in data [8]. Noise points are outliers that do not belong to any cluster. There are two parameters that must be provided before the algorithm stars, ϵ and *MinPts*. A point is assigned to a cluster if it satisfies the condition that its ϵ neighborhood contains at least a minimum number of neighbors, *MinPts*. The distance metric used to measure the similarity between observations is the Euclidean distance (default). K-means is an iterative partitioning algorithm that assigns the n data points to one of K clusters, where K must be provided at the beginning of the algorithm [9]. Each cluster is represented by the centroid and the clustering aims to minimize the sum of squared distances of the points to the centroids. The default distance metric for the minimization is the Euclidean distance. The maximum number of iterations, *MaxIter* is also provided to the algorithm.

The first two datasets of points are available in the internet. The others are randomly generated datasets. In Figs. 1, 2, 3, 4, 5, 6 and 7 below, the results obtained for Problems 1–7 are depicted.

Problem 1. 'mydata'. 300 data points and two attributes:
available at https://yarpiz.com/64/ypml101-evolutionary-clustering [10].

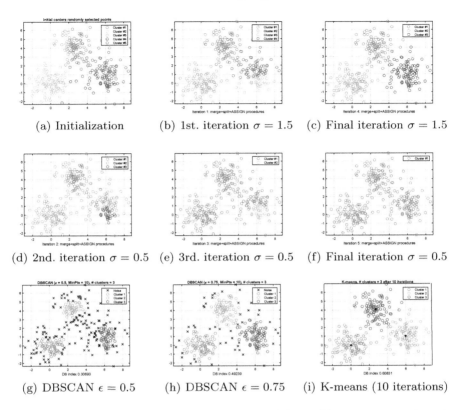

(a) Initialization   (b) 1st. iteration $\sigma = 1.5$ (c) Final iteration $\sigma = 1.5$

(d) 2nd. iteration $\sigma = 0.5$ (e) 3rd. iteration $\sigma = 0.5$ (f) Final iteration $\sigma = 0.5$

(g) DBSCAN $\epsilon = 0.5$ (h) DBSCAN $\epsilon = 0.75$ (i) K-means (10 iterations)

Fig. 1. Clustering process of Problem 1. Plots (a), (b) and (c) are from our algorithm with $\sigma = 1.5$ in the Gaussian kernel, (d), (e) and (f) are from our algorithm with $\sigma = 0.5$, (g) and (h) come from DBSCAN, and (i) is from K-means.

Algorithm 1 was tested with Problem 1 starting with 5 clusters (see Fig. 1). Plot (a) shows the initial clustering with the 5 clusters. Plots (b) and (c) show the obtained well succeeded clustering (1st. iteration and 4th. iteration respectively) using $\sigma = 1.5$ in the Gaussian kernel. However, when $\sigma = 0.5$ is used, the iterative process starts with the clustering shown in plot (a) - the initialization - and converges to one cluster (see plots (d), (e) and (f)). Plots (g) and (h) show the DBSCAN clustering when the parameter ϵ is set to 0.5 and 0.75, respectively, with $MinPts = 10$ (for best clusterings) and both clustering identify 3 groups, but with plenty of noise points. Finally, plot (i) shows the K-means successful clustering when $K = 3$ is provided.

Problem 2. 'mydataDBSCAN'. 1000 data points and two attributes: available at https://yarpiz.com/255/ypml110-dbscan-clustering [11].

With Problem 2, the two values (1.5 and 0.5) of σ were tested, and the results are depicted in Fig. 2. Starting with 4 clusters, plots (b) and (c) show a

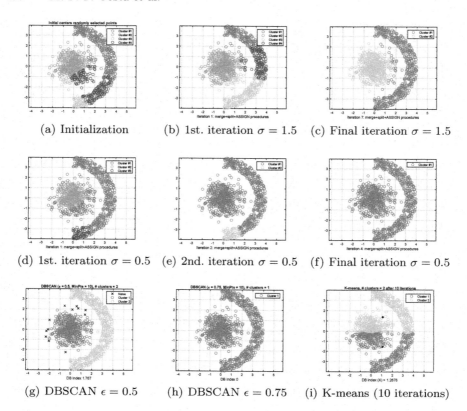

(a) Initialization   (b) 1st. iteration $\sigma = 1.5$ (c) Final iteration $\sigma = 1.5$

(d) 1st. iteration $\sigma = 0.5$ (e) 2nd. iteration $\sigma = 0.5$ (f) Final iteration $\sigma = 0.5$

(g) DBSCAN $\epsilon = 0.5$ (h) DBSCAN $\epsilon = 0.75$ (i) K-means (10 iterations)

Fig. 2. Clustering process of Problem 2. Plots (a), (b) and (c) are from our algorithm with $\sigma = 1.5$ in the Gaussian kernel, (d), (e) and (f) are from our algorithm with $\sigma = 0.5$, (g) and (h) come from DBSCAN, and (i) is from K-means.

successful clustering of Algorithm 1, while plots (d), (e) and (f) (starting with the same 4 clusters) display an unsuccessful clustering. Plots (g) and (h), with $\epsilon = 0.5$ and $\epsilon = 0.75$ respectively (with $MinPts = 10$), show a successful and an unsuccessful clustering of DBSCAN. As expected, K-means clustering (with provided $K = 2$) is unable to identify non-linearly separable clusters.

Problem 3. 400 data points with two attributes: (Four clusters with generated points using multivariate Normal distributions with equal variances.)

```
Sigma = [0.5 0.05; 0.05 0.5];  f1 = mvnrnd([0.5 0],Sigma,100);
f2 = mvnrnd([0.5 0.5],Sigma,100); f3 = mvnrnd([0.5 1],Sigma,100);
f4 = mvnrnd([0.5 1.5],Sigma,100); X = [f1;f2;f3;f4];
```

When solving Problem 3, and using both $\sigma = 1.5$ and $\sigma = 0.5$, the performance of the KCDbased algorithm, shown in Fig. 3, is similar to the two previous examples. When $\sigma = 1.5$, and starting from the initial clustering (shown in plot (a)), the algorithm is able to identify 4 clusters (plots (b) and (c)). The 4 clusters

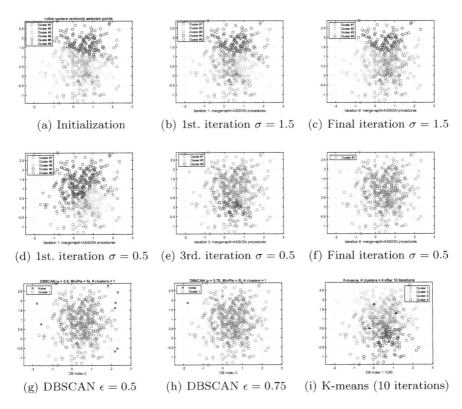

(a) Initialization   (b) 1st. iteration $\sigma = 1.5$ (c) Final iteration $\sigma = 1.5$

(d) 1st. iteration $\sigma = 0.5$ (e) 3rd. iteration $\sigma = 0.5$ (f) Final iteration $\sigma = 0.5$

(g) DBSCAN $\epsilon = 0.5$ (h) DBSCAN $\epsilon = 0.75$ (i) K-means (10 iterations)

Fig. 3. Clustering process of Problem 3. Plots (a), (b) and (c) are from our algorithm with $\sigma = 1.5$ in the Gaussian kernel, (d), (e) and (f) are from our algorithm with $\sigma = 0.5$, (g) and (h) come from DBSCAN, and (i) is from K-means.

are not identified by DBSCAN when ϵ is set to 0.5 and 0.75, using $MinPts = 5$. The same is true when $MinPts = 10$ is used. Setting $K = 4$, K-means identifies 4 linearly separable clusters.

Problem 4. 300 data points with two attributes: (Three clusters with generated points using Uniform distributions.)

```
f1 = randn(100,2)*0.75+ones(100,2); f2 = randn(100,2)*0.5-ones(100,2);
f3 = randn(100,2)*0.75; X = [f1;f2;f3];
```

To cluster the dataset in Problem 4, $\sigma = 1.5$ and $\sigma = 0.5$ are also used (see Fig. 4). The performance of the KCDbased algorithm is similar to the previous examples. We note that DBSCAN identifies one cluster with $\epsilon = 0.5$ and $MinPts = 10$, and only for $\epsilon = 0.25$ is able to identify more than one cluster but with plenty of noise points (see plots (g) and (h)). K-means converges by linearly separating 3 clusters (plot (i)).

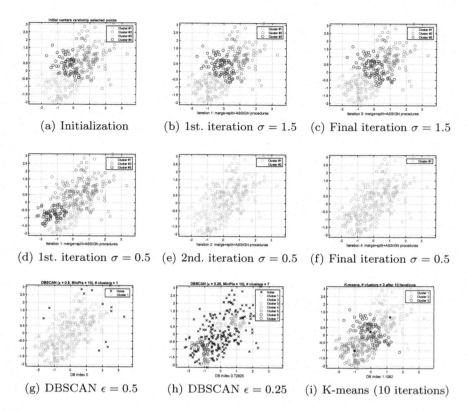

(a) Initialization   (b) 1st. iteration $\sigma = 1.5$ (c) Final iteration $\sigma = 1.5$

(d) 1st. iteration $\sigma = 0.5$ (e) 2nd. iteration $\sigma = 0.5$ (f) Final iteration $\sigma = 0.5$

(g) DBSCAN $\epsilon = 0.5$ (h) DBSCAN $\epsilon = 0.25$ (i) K-means (10 iterations)

Fig. 4. Clustering process of Problem 4. Plots (a), (b) and (c) are from our algorithm with $\sigma = 1.5$ in the Gaussian kernel, (d), (e) and (f) are from our algorithm with $\sigma = 0.5$, (g) and (h) come from DBSCAN, and (i) is from K-means.

Problem 5. 300 data points with two attributes: (Two clusters with generated points using multivariate Normal distributions.)

```
mu1 = [1 2]; sigma1 = [3 .2; .2 2]; mu2 = [-1 -2]; sigma2 = [2 0; 0 1];
f1 = mvnrnd(mu1,sigma1,200); f2 = mvnrnd(mu2,sigma2,100); X = [f1;f2];
```

To cluster the set of points in Problem 5, $\sigma = 1.5$ and $\sigma = 0.5$ are also used. The initial clustering (plot(a)), based on 4 clusters, is the same for both experiments. The performance of the KCDbased algorithm is similar to the previous examples, as shown in Fig. 5. With the DBSCAN, $MinPts$ is set to 10 to show the best clustering found (plot (g) for $\epsilon = 0.5$ and plot (h) for $\epsilon = 0.75$). K-means linearly separates 2 clusters (plot (i)).

Problem 6. 200 data points and two attributes: (Two clusters with generated points giving two moons, distorted with some added noises.)

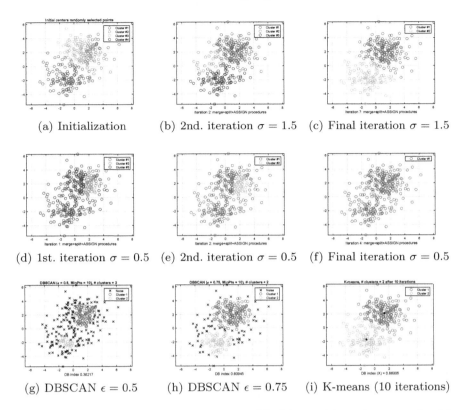

(a) Initialization   (b) 2nd. iteration $\sigma = 1.5$ (c) Final iteration $\sigma = 1.5$

(d) 1st. iteration $\sigma = 0.5$ (e) 2nd. iteration $\sigma = 0.5$ (f) Final iteration $\sigma = 0.5$

(g) DBSCAN $\epsilon = 0.5$ (h) DBSCAN $\epsilon = 0.75$ (i) K-means (10 iterations)

Fig. 5. Clustering process of Problem 5. Plots (a), (b) and (c) are from our algorithm with $\sigma = 1.5$ in the Gaussian kernel, (d), (e) and (f) are from our algorithm with $\sigma = 0.5$, (g) and (h) come from DBSCAN, and (i) is from K-means.

```
for i=1:100
    f1(i) = (-1+2*(i-1)/99, sqrt(1-(-1+2*(i-1)/99)^2)+unifrnd(-0.1,0.1));
    f2(i) = (-2+4*(i-1)/99, -sqrt(4-(-2+4*(i-1)/99)^2)+unifrnd(-0.1,0.1));
end
X = [f1;f2];
```

The data points in Problem 6 constitute 2 non-convex clusters. The clustering obtained by the Algorithm 1 when $\sigma = 0.75$ successfully identifies the 2 clusters (plots (a), (b) and (c)) of Fig. 6. However, when $\sigma = 1.5$, there is a point that is not assigned to the corresponding cluster when the algorithm stops (see plots (d), (e) and (f)). DBSCAN successfully identifies the 2 clusters (setting $MinPts$ to 5), although for $\epsilon = 0.5$ defines 2 noise points (see plots (g) and (h)). The K-means clustering (plot (i)), with provided $K = 2$, identifies 2 clusters as if they were linearly separable.

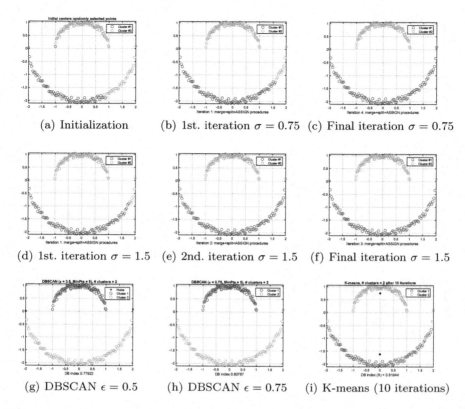

(a) Initialization   (b) 1st. iteration $\sigma = 0.75$ (c) Final iteration $\sigma = 0.75$

(d) 1st. iteration $\sigma = 1.5$ (e) 2nd. iteration $\sigma = 1.5$ (f) Final iteration $\sigma = 1.5$

(g) DBSCAN $\epsilon = 0.5$ (h) DBSCAN $\epsilon = 0.75$ (i) K-means (10 iterations)

Fig. 6. Clustering process of Problem 6. Plots (a), (b) and (c) are from our algorithm with $\sigma = 0.75$ in the Gaussian kernel, (d), (e) and (f) are from our algorithm with $\sigma = 1.5$, (g) and (h) come from DBSCAN, and (i) is from K-means.

Problem 7. 150 data points and two attributes: (Three clusters with two spherically shaped clusters inside 3/4 of a perturbed circle.)

```
for i=1:50
  f1(i) = (0.4+1.1*sin(2*pi*(30+5*(i-1))/360),
           0.8*cos(2*pi*(30+5*(i-1))/360)+unifrnd(-0.025,0.025));
end
Sigma = [0.01 0; 0 0.01]; mu1 = [0 0]; mu2 = [0.8 0];
f2 = mvnrnd(mu1,Sigma,50); f3 = mvnrnd(mu2,Sigma,50); X = [f1;f2;f3];
```

The data points in Problem 7 define non-linearly separable clusters. A successful clustering is obtained by the KCDbased algorithm with a small value of σ (0.35), starting with an initial clustering of 5 groups, as shown in plots (a), (b) and (c) of Fig. 7. When σ is set to a larger value (1.5), the clustering process evolves very slowly and the algorithm stops with still 5 clusters - plots (d), (e) and (f). DBSCAN successfully identifies the 3 clusters when ϵ is set to 0.25 (plot (h)), but converges to just one cluster when $\epsilon = 0.5$ (plot (g)). The *MinPts* was

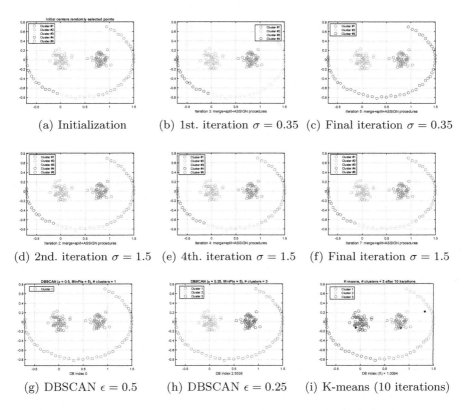

(a) Initialization   (b) 1st. iteration $\sigma = 0.35$ (c) Final iteration $\sigma = 0.35$

(d) 2nd. iteration $\sigma = 1.5$ (e) 4th. iteration $\sigma = 1.5$ (f) Final iteration $\sigma = 1.5$

(g) DBSCAN $\epsilon = 0.5$ (h) DBSCAN $\epsilon = 0.25$ (i) K-means (10 iterations)

Fig. 7. Clustering process of Problem 7. Plots (a), (b) and (c) are from our algorithm with $\sigma = 0.35$ in the Gaussian kernel, (d), (e) and (f) are from our algorithm with $\sigma = 1.5$, (g) and (h) come from DBSCAN, and (i) is from K-means.

set to 5 so that the successful clustering in plot (h) is obtained. As expected, K-means (setting $K = 3$) converges to 3 clusters assuming that they are linearly separable.

5   Conclusions

A kernel-based partitioning clustering algorithm is presented to address the issue related to the identification of non-linearly separable clusters. The Kernel Clustering Diameter-based algorithm iteratively merges clusters, based on the radii and average radii of the two clusters with the closest centers, and removes a cluster that has a very small number of points. The algorithm is also able to split a cluster that has the largest difference between its diameter and the smallest distance between its cluster points. To activate the splitting process, the cluster diameter and the number of points in the cluster have to satisfy some conditions.

In the kernel sense, assigning points to clusters involves minimizing the sum of the squared distances of the points to the centers in the feature/kernel space.

The Gaussian kernel is used to compute the squared distances of the points to the centers, between centers, and between points of a cluster.

The experiments with seven datasets show that the performance of the KCD-based algorithm is sensitive to the value of the parameter σ, in the Gaussian kernel. A large value gives a successful clustering for datasets with clusters not well separated, and a small value is better when the points in the dataset form well separated clusters. Furthermore, larger values of σ imply larger Gaussian kernel values.

The experiments with this algorithm will be extended to higher dimensional datasets. Furthermore, as the iterations proceed, the smallest distance between points of two clusters will be used to identify well separated clusters and select an adequate value for the parameter σ.

Acknowledgments. The authors wish to thank the three anonymous referees for their comments and suggestions to improve the paper.

References

1. Xu, D., Tian, Y.: A comprehensive survey of clustering algorithms. Ann. Data Sci. **2**(2), 165–193 (2015)
2. Mohammed, J.Z., Meira Jr., W.: Data Mining and Machine Learning: Fundamental Concepts and Algorithms, 2nd edn. Cambridge University Press (2020)
3. Greenlaw, R., Kantabutra, S.: Survey of clustering: algorithms and applications. Int. J. Inf. Retr. Res. **3**(2), 29 (2013)
4. MacQueen, J.B.: Some methods for classification and analysis of multivariate observations. In: Le Cam, L.M., Neyman, J. (eds.) Proceedings of the fifth Berkeley Symposium on Mathematical Statistics and Probability, vol. 1, pp. 281–297. University of California Press (1967)
5. Schölkopf, B., Smola, A., Müller, K.R.: Nonlinear component analysis as a kernel eigenvalue problem. Neural Comput. **10**, 1299–1319 (1998)
6. Jain, A.K., Murty, M.N., Flynn, P.J.: Data clustering: a review. ACM Comput. Surv. **31**(3), 264–323 (1999)
7. Xu, R., Wunsch, D., II.: Survey of clustering algorithms. IEEE Trans. Neural Netw. **16**(3), 645–678 (2005)
8. Ester, M., Kriegel, H.-P., Sander, J., Xiaowei, X.: A density-based algorithm for discovering clusters in large spatial databases with noise. In: Proceedings of the Second International Conference on Knowledge Discovery in Databases and Data Mining, pp. 226–231. AAAI Press, Portland, OR (1996)
9. Lloyd, S.P.: Least squares quantization in PCM. IEEE Trans. Inf. Theory **28**, 129–137 (1982)
10. Heris, M.K.: Evolutionary Data Clustering in MATLAB, Yarpiz (2015). https://yarpiz.com/64/ypml101-evolutionary-clustering
11. Heris, M.K.: DBSCAN Clustering in MATLAB, Yarpiz, (2015). https://yarpiz.com/255/ypml110-dbscan-clustering

Forecasting Omicron Variant of Covid-19 with ANN Model in European Countries – Number of Cases, Deaths, and ICU Patients

Kathleen Carvalho[1,2]([✉]) [ID], Luis Paulo Reis[2] [ID], and João Paulo Teixeira[1,3] [ID]

[1] Research Centre in Digitalization and Intelligent Robotics (CeDRI), Instituto Politecnico de Braganca, 5300-253 Bragança, Portugal
carvalho.kath@gmail.com, joaopt@ipb.pt
[2] Faculdade de Engenharia da, Universidade do Porto, Porto, Portugal
preis@fe.up.pt
[3] Laboratório Para a Sustentabilidade e Tecnologia em Regiões de Montanha (SusTEC),
Instituto Politécnico de Bragança, Campus de Santa Apolónia, 5300-253 Bragança, Portugal

Abstract. Accurate predictions of time series are increasingly required to support judgments in a variety of decisions. Several predictive models are available to support these predictions, depending on how each field offers a data variety with varied behavior. The use of artificial neural networks (ANN) at the beginning of the COVID-19 pandemic was significant since the tool may offer forecasting data for various conditions and hence assist in governing critical choices. In this context, this paper describes a system for predicting the daily number of cases, fatalities, and Intensive Care Unit (ICU) patients for the next 28 days in five European countries: Portugal, the United Kingdom, France, Italy, and Germany. The database selection is based on comparable mitigation processes to analyze the impact of safety procedure flexibilization with the most recent numbers of COVID-19. Additionally, it is intended to check the algorithm's adaptability to different variants throughout time. The network's input data has been normalized to account for the size of the countries in the study and smoothed by seven days. The mean absolute error (MAE) was employed as a comparing criterion of two datasets, one with data from the beginning of the pandemic and another with data from the last year, since all variables (cases, deaths, and ICU patients) may be tendentious in percentage analysis. The best architecture produced a general MAE prediction for the 28 days ahead of 256,53 daily cases, 0,59 daily deaths, and 1,63 ICU patients, all numbers normalized by million people.

Keywords: Artificial Neural Network · Forecasting · COVID-19 · Mitigation procedures · COVID-19 Variants

1 Introduction

Since the beginning of the Coronavirus outbreak, the world has seen a significant impact on people's lives, including a strong influence on the economy, society, and most notably,

A. I. Pereira et al. (Eds.): OL2A 2022, CCIS 1754, pp. 457–469, 2022.
https://doi.org/10.1007/978-3-031-23236-7_32

public system procedures. The virus spreading control proved to be more difficult than envisaged, requiring governing bodies to make complex judgments in mitigation processes while balancing needs and economic considerations. During the pandemic, health professionals labor around the clock to meet vaccine and medication needs, and many individuals look for the best ways to reduce the impact on people's lives [1–6].

The rising demand for precise and variable data opened the way for predictive mathematical models. Nowadays, prediction numbers assist the governor, even individuals, in leading many types of events and scenarios, such as road traffic, climatic fluctuations, or even some branches of the financial market. In this context, with the increased necessity of accurate prediction methods, the use of artificial neural networks (ANN) finds your field to assist governmental, business, and health decisions [7–11].

Furthermore, studies demonstrating the success of mitigation techniques helped not only in governmental choices but also encouraged the general public to follow crucial rules, such as wearing masks and vaccinating themselves and their children. Moreover, ANN has been broadcasted as a method for time-series predictions since the tool allows the modeling and forecasting of several types of data.

Specifically, for the COVID-19 number, some authors have already used time-series forecasting to predict coronavirus spread data. Borghi et al. [12] trained a multilayer perceptron network (MLP) using data from thirty nations, utilizing the past 20 days of new cases and deaths and the total number of cases and deaths to predict the total number of cases and deaths for the next six days. Some studies, such as Wieczorek et al. [13], used a deep architecture with the NAdam training model to forecast fourteen days for several countries and regions of the accumulative number of cases. Using three different analyses, Tamang et al. [14] proposed a method to predict the cumulative number of cases for ten days in India, the United States, France, and the United Kingdom. Oliveira et al. [15] used an MLP to predict seven days forward for Brazil, Portugal and the United States of America.

Whereas the approach described in this work forecasts data for twenty-eight days for the daily number of new cases, deaths, and ICU patients, and it incorporates information regarding mask use and vaccination status in each country in order to verify the forecasting adaptation of network to different virus variants and flexibilization of mitigation procedures.

Following this introduction, the work is divided into a section of materials and methods describing the network architecture and the proposed methodology. The results section analyzed the influence of different variants and the vaccination campaign on the number of new cases and deaths, respectively. Also, in the third section, a discussion about the use of a complete and a reduced dataset is proposed. Lastly, a conclusion is shown in section four.

2   Materials and Methods

The proposed methodology intends to predict the number of daily new cases, deaths with COVID-19, and ICU patients of COVID-19, for 28 days ahead to compare the results with the network architecture presented by [16]. The main goal is to verify the algorithm's capacity to adapt to new variants scenarios and the flexibilization of mitigation procedures.

For the time-series analyses, it was necessary to normalize the dataset per million people and smooth it by seven days. Therefore, the study is not influenced by the country size and the variation of data reporting during the week, respectively. Moreover, for comparison purposes, two datasets were used, one with a complete dataset, including data from the beginning of the pandemic until nowadays, and another with data from last year only.

The network architecture used data from the last 21 days to predict a range of days ahead by a week, i.e., from n to n + 6, n + 7 to n + 13, n + 14 to n + 20, n + 21 to n + 28, as the model presented by Carvalho et al., 2021 [16]. With this approach, the network training understands the trend better without accumulating errors for each interaction, as could happen with a recursive process.

Furthermore, to evaluate the efficacy of mitigation procedures in the predicted data, considering the mandatory use of face masks and the new scenario with the flexibilization of the procedures. The lockdown information could not be considered an input feature in both analyses since the procedures were different for each country and sometimes different for each region, even for European Union countries.

2.1   Data Collection Source

To build the database used in this work, quantitative and qualitative data were used. The quantitative data consists of the number of daily new cases, deaths, ICU patients, and percentage of the population fully vaccinated (first two doses), and the qualitative data consists of the mitigation procedure for the mandatory use of masks. The analyzed period consists of the beginning of the pandemic, more precisely January 25th of 2020, and May 06th of 2022, for Portugal, the United Kingdom, Germany, Italy, and France.

In order to compose the used database, two main sources were employed, the websites Worldometer [17] and Our World in Data [18], both references to distinctive media, such as The New York Times, The Guardian, BBC, and prestigious universities, as Harvard, Cambridge and Oxford. These platforms combine data of each country and present it in the same place, with the advantage of Our World in data to provide the percentage of variants since May 2020 [19–23].

A binary approach was used to classify the mandatory use of masks, being 1 to obligatory use and 0 to not demanded. The information about the mitigation procedure was collected on the website Masks4All, and the updates about the flexibilization came from the website of the Ministry of Health of each country under analysis [24–26].

2.2   Data Processing

The country's population is one of the main variables that influence the absolute number of new cases, deaths, and ICU patients. Thus, it was necessary to normalize this number. The normalization process consisted of converting the absolute values into numbers per million people to standardize the rates and not influence the quantitative analysis.

Moreover, the percentage of vaccinated people considers the complete dose, without the reinforced shots, and considers the data from the previous day (n-1). Also, the mandatory use of masks is considered on the previous day (n-1). Since these variables are related only to the last day and are in percentage and binary values, they do not require normalization.

The network architecture comprises 70 input nodes. Five nodes are for a binary codification of each country, 63 nodes are used for the quantitative data about 21 days before (n-21 to n-1) for the number of cases, deaths and ICU, and the last 2 input nodes receive the qualitative data about the use of masks and percentage of vaccinated of the previous day (n-1).

As one of the purposes of this work is to analyze the algorithm adaptation with two different datasets, the following procedures were used in the completed dataset and the database for one year only. That way, the data were combined and randomly divided into 75% for training and 25% for validation, not considering the last 28 days that were separated for the test, since it is a consecutive period and the most recent, to evaluate the prediction performance without influence in the training stage.

The second dataset, from May 06th of 2021, to May 06th of 2022, was considered to verify the ANN accuracy without training with infection behavior and mortality rates of old variants data.

In the training stage, the ANN learns the time series behavior, adjusting the synaptic weights, using only the training data in a sequence of iterations. The validation dataset is used at each iteration to stop the training when the performance stops increasing. This process avoids the ANN overfitting the training database, which would risk losing generalization capacity.

2.3 N Approach Methodology

The proposed methodology uses one ANN for each variable, daily new cases, deaths, and ICU patients, and provides the prediction numbers per week for four weeks. This approach has the main advantage of not accumulating errors during the forecasting processing, as could happen in a recursive procedure. In Fig. 1, the three main steps of the model, data collection, processing, and the prediction process, are shown.

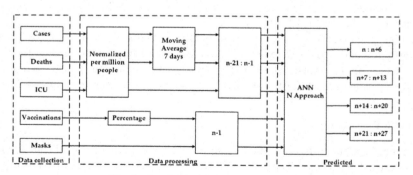

Fig. 1. Prediction diagram. Source: [16]

As presented in the schematic, the ANN has four outputs, one for each predicted week, completing almost a month. The forecasted period of 2022 represents the following vectors:

- First node (n: n + 6): April 09th to April 15th
- Second node (n + 7: n + 13): April 16th to April 22nd
- Third node (n + 14: n + 20): April 23th to April 29th
- Fourth node (n + 21: n + 27): April 30th to May 06th

This methodology uses three prediction networks, one for each variable (cases, deaths, and ICU patients), all with one hidden layer. A different number of neurons in the hidden layer was experimented. The training algorithm was the Levenberg-Marquardt [27]. The final architecture is referred to in Table 1 for each prediction network.

Table 1. Final ANN topology. HL: hidden layer; OL: output layer

Prediction network	HL n° of neurons	HL function	OL function
Cases	4	Elliot	Linear
Deaths	18	Elliot	Linear
ICU patients	15	Elliot	Linear

2.4 Error Measurement

To compare the prediction using the total database, the one-year database, and the errors presented by the source paper [16], the chosen method to measure the errors was the mean absolute error (MAE), Eq. (1), since the analyzed data has some peculiarities that can influence the analyses, such as the size of daily data normalized per million people

$$MAE = \frac{1}{N} \sum_{i=1}^{n} |Real_i - Predicted_i| \tag{1}$$

where N is the total size of the samples under analysis.

The predictions of daily new cases, death, and IUC patients correspond to the period of 4 weeks, as follows:

- Next week: April 09th to April 15th, 2022
- Two weeks ahead: April 16th to April 22nd, 2022
- Three weeks ahead: April 23rd to April 29th, 2022
- Four weeks ahead: April 30th to May 06th, 2022
- Next month: April 09th to May 06th, 2022.

3   Results

The selection of countries that comprise the database considers similar mitigation procedures, as justified by European Union decisions. As illustrated in Fig. 2, the different approaches of each country follow similar behavior of infection waves.

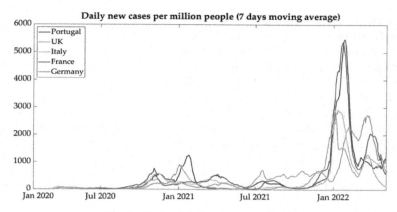

Fig. 2. Updated daily new cases (2022)

As previously described in the methodology section, the networks' inputs are made up of a database normalized per million people and smoothed with a seven-day moving average. The moving average was required due to the high variance during the week. Typically, the registration of new cases was deficient over the weekend, followed by a high registration on Mondays.

Equivalent mitigation procedures and the percentage of variants could produce a hypothesis about the similarity of the curves. Analyzing the rate of Omicron variant in Portugal, Italy, and France on January 10th of 2022 (two weeks before the peak of the fifth wave), Fig. 3, it is possible to note the similarities of the curve behavior in Fig. 2, as an example of the range of days between the beginning and end of the fifth wave.

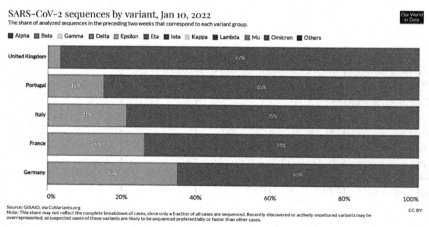

Fig. 3. Variants percentage, January 10th. Source: [18]

On the other hand, Germany's new cases curve, shown in Fig. 2, displays a delay until the peak of the fifth wave, which might be explained by the lower percentage of Omicron, Fig. 3, when compared to others.

Another substantive aspect was the high drop in mortality numbers following the beginning of vaccination, as seen in Fig. 4, at least the first dosage, indicating vaccine effectiveness against death by Covid-19. It is critical to highlight that even with a significant rise in the number of new cases, mortality remains at an average of 5 deaths per million persons across all nations studied.

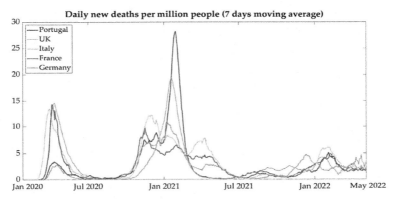

Fig. 4. Daily new deaths.

3.1 Prediction Model

The selected method is the same as the N approach presented by Carvalho, 2021 [16], in that it takes daily inputs of cases, deaths, ICU patients, vaccinations, and the use of mandatory masks and is employed one network for each output. However, the main goal of this work is to evaluate network adaptation to the behavior of the new Omicron variant of the SarsCov-2 virus data, to test a reduced database, and, most importantly, to examine predictions after the release of some restrictions like the mandatory use of face masks.

The proposed approach forecasts daily new cases, deaths, and ICU patients per week, using the vectors: n: n + 6, n + 7: n + 13, and successively until to cover four weeks.

The following sections compare the plots, considering the complete dataset and one-year dataset, comparing Portugal and UK results. Carvalho et al. (2021) analyzed these two countries together since both had a similar behavior of infections and deaths at the beginning of the pandemic, which was associated with the variants alpha B1.1.7, and analogous mitigation procedure. Now, to compare the algorithm adaptation to the same countries, they will be analyzed together.

3.2 Analyses of New Predictions

Comparing Figs. 5 and 6 Predicted cases–Portugal and UK–One-year database, it is possible to verify that the ANN adapted well to the new scenario with flexibilization of the use of masks and new variants. In Fig. 5, it is possible to note that the data follows the real curve behavior, with an emphasis on the UK curve for the entire test period, which has an almost ideal prediction, even in the fourth week.

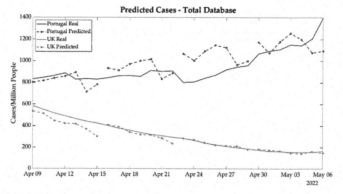

Fig. 5. Predicted cases - Portugal-UK – Total database.

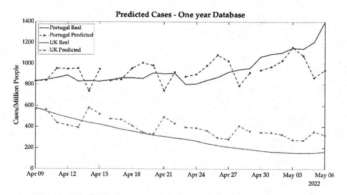

Fig. 6. Predicted cases - Portugal-UK – One-year database

Furthermore, as shown in Figs. 7 and 8, it is possible to observe that the algorithm had a better performance trained with the total dataset in the UK numbers since the predictions follow better the real curve behavior in the first two weeks, whereas for Portugal the numbers follow well the trend.

It is important to highlight that the death forecasts have a decimal value, which is impossible in real life, but with the moving average used before the data is fed into the network, consequently, the ANN provides a decimal output.

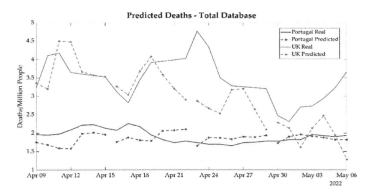

Fig. 7. Predicted deaths - Portugal-UK - Total database.

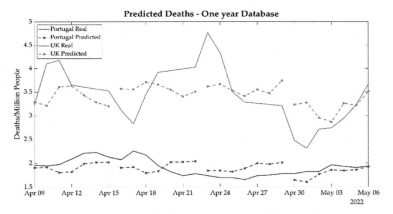

Fig. 8. Predicted deaths - Portugal-UK – One-year database.

The ICU patients' predictions (Figs. 9 and 10) are more challenging for the network to estimate, because Portugal's data have been reported weekly since March 10th, 2022. As a result, by the end of the second week, Portugal's forecasted data curve had a discrete behavior. Meanwhile, in a daily database, as in the UK instance, the forecast was well acceptable for the first two weeks but lost the trend in the last two weeks.

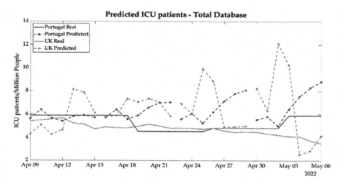

Fig. 9. Predicted ICU patients - Portugal-UK – Total database.

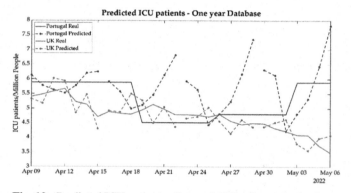

Fig. 10. Predicted ICU patients - Portugal-UK – One-year database.

3.3 Comparison of Two Forecasting Databases

The results of completed and one-year datasets were compared for the five countries under analysis to three parameters: cases, deaths, and ICU patients. The MAE numbers account for each country's weekly prediction and average value, as given in Table 2.

Analyzing the weekly MAE of all countries reveals that the error increases with the distance of the outputs from the real data, implying that the fourth week has the highest inaccuracy in virtually all data.

Moreover, the absolute error in the cases is on a scale of more than a thousand daily new cases per million individuals for France, which might impact a percentage error analysis.

Concerning the number of new cases, the predictions made by a complete and one-year datasets are analyzed for five countries. It is important to highlight that the number of infections had a considerable increase, as seen in Fig. 2. Consequently, the new analysis presents a higher value in absolute error. However, considering the average percentage error for all five countries, it is possible to note an improvement in the predictions, considering four weeks together (n: n + 27).

On the other hand, for the predictions of the deaths, with the one-year dataset, the absolute error was satisfactory, being lower than 1 for all countries and in the four weeks under analysis.

The ICU patients analysis also improved outputs, even with Portugal's situation of weekly report data.

Table 2. Mean absolute error comparative analyses

Total database (2022)				One-year database (2022)		
	Cases	Deaths	ICU	Cases	Deaths	ICU
Portugal n:n + 6	49,29	0,29	0,22	71,07	0,15	0,25
Portugal n + 7:n + 13	82,79	0,30	1,00	71,88	0,25	0,96
Portugal n + 14:n + 20	178,76	0,15	0,64	118,02	0,19	1,00
Portugal n + 21:n + 27	113,37	0,08	0,83	171,30	0,09	1,07
Portugal n:n + 27	106,05	0,21	0,67	108,07	0,17	0,82
France n:n + 6	38,31	0,23	0,81	28,83	0,09	0,34
France n + 7:n + 13	620,09	0,63	1,74	360,98	0,11	0,73
France n + 14:n + 20	1084,83	1,85	3,57	344,88	0,08	3,21
France n + 21:n + 27	1481,50	3,23	6,39	331,42	0,30	7,67
France n:n + 27	806,18	1,48	3,13	266,53	0,15	2,99
Italy n:n + 6	16,41	0,06	0,19	52,68	0,07	0,13
Italy n + 7:n + 13	98,51	0,12	0,19	52,32	0,21	0,68
Italy n + 14:n + 20	136,47	0,20	0,20	137,26	0,33	0,74
Italy n + 21:n + 27	270,37	0,27	1,51	131,62	0,40	1,03
Italy n:n + 27	130,44	0,16	0,52	93,47	0,26	0,64
UK n:n + 6	66,59	0,32	3,06	71,10	0,33	0,31
UK n + 7:n + 13	20,74	0,53	3,09	80,18	0,42	0,32
UK n + 14:n + 20	4,78	0,92	1,73	125,71	0,43	0,21
UK n + 21:n + 27	9,50	0,89	1,05	159,21	0,37	0,34
UK n: n + 27	25,40	0,64	2,23	109,05	0,40	0,30
Germany n:n + 6	83,79	0,12	1,52	111,37	0,18	0,84
Germany n + 7:n + 13	142,83	0,34	1,63	170,23	0,49	1,21
Germany n + 14:n + 20	304,96	0,19	0,91	144,39	0,90	2,29
Germany n + 21:n + 27	326,71	1,21	2,26	367,81	0,53	3,96
Germany n: n + 27	214,57	0,46	1,58	198,45	0,52	2,07
Total n:n + 6	50,88	0,21	1,16	67,01	0,17	0,37
Total n + 7:n + 13	192,99	0,38	1,53	147,12	0,30	0,78
Total n + 14:n + 20	341,96	0,66	1,41	174,05	0,39	1,49
Total n + 21:n + 27	440,29	1,13	2,41	232,27	0,34	2,81
Total n:n + 27	256,53	0,59	1,63	155,11	0,30	1,36

4 Conclusions

This work provides an investigation of the adaption of an ANN that forecasts COVID-19 data, specifically the daily new cases, deaths, and ICU patients, to a new pandemic scenario, with the flexibilization of the use of face masks. Furthermore, it analyzed the use of a reduced dataset containing just data from the previous year and the efficiency of vaccination in reducing death rates.

Examining the five countries' COVID-19 waves revealed a link between the behavior of curves in each country with a comparable number of Delta and Omicron variations at the beginning of 2022. Aside from that, it is essential to note that even at the high peak of new cases, death rates were lower compared to the first peaks.

The network outputs were determined with two datasets, a completed one (since the beginning of the pandemic) and one with one-year data. Both datasets offer good predictions for the following 28 days.

Furthermore, for all nations, it seems the ANN could produce satisfactory predictions, even when the circumstance changed regarding the mandatory use of masks and the percentage of distinct virus variants.

Acknowledgments. The authors are grateful to the Foundation for Science and Technology (FCT, Portugal) for financial support through national funds FCT/MCTES (PIDDAC) to CeDRI (UIDB/05757/2020 and UIDP/05757/2020) and SusTEC (LA/P/0007/2021).

References

1. Dairi, A., Harrou, F., Zeroual, A., Hittawe, M.M., Sun, Y.: Comparative study of machine learning methods for COVID-19 transmission forecasting. J. Biomed. Inform. **118**, 103791 (2021). https://doi.org/10.1016/j.jbi.2021.103791. (WE - Science Citation Index Expanded (SCI-EXPANDED))
2. Elsheikh, A.H., Saba, A.I., Panchal, H., Shanmugan, S., Alsaleh, N.A., Ahmadein, M.: Artificial intelligence for forecasting the prevalence of COVID-19 pandemic: an overview. In: HEALTHCARE, vol. 9, no. 12 (2021). https://doi.org/10.3390/healthcare9121614. (WE - Science Citation Index Expanded (SCI-EXPANDED). WE - Social Science Citation Index (SSCI))
3. Farooq, J., Bazaz, M.A.: A deep learning algorithm for modeling and forecasting of COVID-19 in five worst affected states of India. ALEXANDRIA Eng. J. **60**(1), 587–596 (2021). https://doi.org/10.1016/j.aej.2020.09.037WE-ScienceCitationIndexExpanded(SCI-EXPANDED)
4. Zagrouba, R., et al.: Modelling and simulation of COVID-19 outbreak prediction using supervised machine learning. C. Mater. Contin. **66**(3), 2397–2407 (2021). https://doi.org/10.32604/cmc.2021.014042WE-ScienceCitationIndexExpanded(SCI-EXPANDED)
5. Gallagher, J.: Covid vaccine update: those that work - and the others on the way. BBC (2021)
6. Krstic, K., Westerman, R., Chattu, V.K., Ekkert, N.V., Jakovljevic, M.: Corona- triggered global macroeconomic crisis of the early 2020s. Int. J. Environ. Res. Public Health **17**(24), 1–9 (2020). https://doi.org/10.3390/ijerph17249404
7. Siami-Namini, S., Tavakoli, N., Siami Namin, A.: A comparison of ARIMA and LSTM in forecasting time series. In: Proceedings of 17th IEEE International Conference on Machine Learning Application ICMLA 2018, pp. 1394–1401 (2019). https://doi.org/10.1109/ICMLA.2018.00227

8. Chung, C.F.: A generalized fractionally integrated autoregressive moving average process. J. Time Ser. Anal. **17**, 111–140 (1996). https://doi.org/10.1111/j.1467-9892.1996.tb00268.x

9. Jain, A., Kumar, A.M.: Hybrid neural network models for hydrologic time series forecasting. Appl. Soft Comput. J. **7**(2), 585–592 (2007). https://doi.org/10.1016/j.asoc.2006.03.002

10. Jatobá, M., Santos, J., Gutierriz, I., Moscon, D., Fernandes. P.O., Teixeira, J.P.: Evolution of artificial intelligence research in human resources. Proc. Comput. Sci. Elsevier. **164**, 137–142 (2019). https://doi.org/10.1016/j.procs.2019.12.165

11. Guedes, V., et al.: Transfer learning with audioset to voice pathologies identification in continuous speech. Proc. Comput. Sci. Elsevier. **164**, 662–669 (2019). https://doi.org/10.1016/j.procs.2019.12.233

12. Borghi, P.H., Zakordonets, O., Teixeira, J.P.: A COVID-19 time series forecasting model based on MLP ANN. Proc. Comput. Sci. **181**(2021), 940–947 (2021). https://doi.org/10.1016/j.procs.2021.01.250

13. Wieczorek, M., Siłka, J., Wózniak, M.: Neural network powered COVID-19 spread forecasting model. Chaos Solit. Fractals. **140**, 110203 (2020). https://doi.org/10.1016/j.chaos.2020.110203

14. Tamang, S.K., Singh, P.D., Datta, B.: Forecasting of Covid-19 cases based on prediction using artificial neural network curve fitting technique. Glob. J. Environ. Sci. Manag. **6**, 53–64 (2020). https://doi.org/10.22034/GJESM.2019.06.SI.06

15. Oliveira, L.S., Gruetzmacher, S.B., Teixeira, J.P.: COVID-19 time series prediction. Proc. Comput. Sci. **181**, 973–980 (2021). https://doi.org/10.1016/j.procs.2021.01.254

16. Carvalho, K., Vicente, J.P., Jakovljevic, M., Teixeira, J.P.R.: Analysis and forecasting incidence, intensive care unit admissions, and projected mortality attributable to COVID-19 in Portugal, the UK, Germany, Italy, and France. Predictions for 4 weeks ahead. Bioengineering. **8**(6), 84 (2021). https://doi.org/10.3390/bioengineering8060084

17. Worldometer, "COVID-19 Coronavirus Pandemic. https://www.worldometers.info/coronavirus/

18. Coronavirus Pandemic (COVID-19). Our World in Data. https://ourworldindata.org/

19. Covid-19 - Direção-Geral da Saúde. https://covid19.min-saude.pt/

20. Data.gouv.fr. https://www.data.gouv.fr/fr/

21. Italian Department of Civil Protection. https://github.com/pcm-dpc/COVID-19

22. Department of Health and Social Care: 30 million people in UK receive first dose of coronavirus (COVID-19) vaccine. Dep. Heal. Soc. Care (2021). https://www.gov.uk/government/news/30-million-people-in-uk-receive-first-dose-of-coronavirus-covid-19-vaccine

23. Achternbosch, Y., et al.: Alle Corona-Fälle in den Landkreisen, Bundesländern und weltweit (2021)

24. Germany Federal Ministry of Health: Current information for travellers (2022). https://www.zusammengegencorona.de/en/current-information-for-travellers/

25. Portuguesa, R.: Máscaras passam a ser obrigatórias e, apenas três casos (2022). https://www.portugal.gov.pt/pt/gc23/comunicacao/noticia?i=mascaras-passam-a-ser-%0Aobrigatorias-em-apenas-tres-casos%0A

26. Française, R.: End of vaccination pass and indoor mask (2022). https://www.service-public.fr/particuliers/actualites/A15543?lang=en

27. Marquardt, D.W.: An algorithm for least-squares estimation of nonlinear parameters. J. Soc. Ind. Appl. Math. **11**(2), 431–441 (1963). https://doi.org/10.1137/0111030

Anomaly Detection Using Smart Shirt and Machine Learning: A Systematic Review

E. C. Nunes[1]([✉]) [iD], José Barbosa[1,3] [iD], Paulo Alves[2] [iD], Tiago Franco[2] [iD],
and Alfredo Silva[4]

[1] Mountains of Research Collaborative Laboratory, 5300-358 Bragança, Portugal
{enunes,jbarbosa}@morecolab.pt
[2] Research Centre in Digitalization and Intelligent Robotics,
Polytechnic Institute of Bragança, Bragança, Portugal
{palves,tiagofranco}@ipb.pt
[3] Centre for Robotics in Industry and Intelligent Systems (CRIIS)-INESC TEC,
4200-465 Porto, Portugal
[4] INOVA+, 4450-309 Porto, Portugal
alfredo.silva@inova.business

Abstract. In recent years, the popularity and use of Artificial Intelligence (AI) and significant investments in the Internet of Medical Things (IoMT) will be common for products such as smart socks, smart pants, and smart shirts. These products are known as Smart Textile or E-textile, which can monitor and collect signals our body emits. These signals allow it to extract anomalous components using Machine Learning (ML) techniques that play an essential role in this area. This study presents a Systematic Literature Review (SLR) on Anomaly Detection using ML techniques in Smart Shirt. The objectives of the SLR are: (i) identify machine learning techniques for anomaly detection in the smart shirt; (ii) identify the datasets used to train the ML algorithm; (iii) identify smart shirts or devices for acquiring vital signs; (iv) identify the performance metrics for evaluating the ML model; (v) types of ML being applied. The SLR selected eleven primary studies published between January/2017-May/2022. The results showed that six anomalies were identified, with the Fall anomaly being the most cited. The Support Vector Machines (SVM) algorithm is the most used. Most of the primary studies used public or private datasets. The Hexoskin smart shirt was most cited. The most used metric performance was Accuracy. Almost all primary studies presented a result above 90%, and all primary studies used the Supervisioned type of ML.

Keywords: Machine learning · Anomaly detection · Smart shirt · Smart textile · Systematic review

1 Introduction

Population ageing is poised to become one of the most significant social transformations of the 21st century. The number and proportion of people aged 60

A. I. Pereira et al. (Eds.): OL2A 2022, CCIS 1754, pp. 470–485, 2022.
https://doi.org/10.1007/978-3-031-23236-7_33

and older are increasing. According to the World Health Organization (WHO), the number of people aged 60 and over was 1 billion. This number is increasing to 1.4 billion by 2030 and 2.1 billion by 2050 [41]. This significant change in the global population requires adaptations in all sectors, such as Transportation, Housing, Urban Planning, and Health Care.

Nowadays, the internet is so essential in our lives that it is considered an utility. With this facility of access to the internet, many internet-connected devices are being used in our lives, such as smart TV, home appliances, smartwatch, home security systems, and medical devices. This emergence of connected devices is often referred to as the Internet of Things (IoT). An extension of the IoT is the Internet of Medical Things (IoMT), which aims to improve the quality and accessibility of healthcare services using a collection of medical devices and applications that connect to health IT systems. Any internet-connected devices connected to healthcare IT systems are categorized as IoMT devices. The most common are wearable devices such as smartwatches, smart clothing, and other wireless devices (glucose meter, blood pressure monitor, smart oximeter) [13].

The rapid evolution and implementation of emerging technologies such as Artificial Intelligence (AI) in IoMT are expected to make healthcare services more efficient and thus drive market demand. As a result, according to [8] the size of the Global IoMT Market is expected to grow from \$60.83 billion in 2019 to \$260.75 billion by 2027, delivering at a Compound Annual Growth Rate (CAGR) of 19.8% through 2027. In parallel with the IoMT market, the smart textile market is growing [2,20]. Smart textiles, also known as e-textiles, are clothes that contain integrated actuators that can connect to a device using Wi-Fi or Bluetooth. There are several fashion categories in the smart textile market, including smart socks [34], smart pants [39], and smart shirts [14] where physiological information can be monitored.

A smart shirt is a type of smart textile that can monitor human activities [1,9] and detect anomalies [6,12] through sensors such as accelerometers, gyroscopes, magnetometers, electrocardiograms (ECG), skin temperature, and oxygen saturation (SpO2) [10]. With all this data available to analyze, it is possible to identify anomalies using Machine Learning (ML) techniques which can bring significant benefits to users, especially the elderly [32].

The main objective of this study is to present a Systematic Literature Review (SLR) to verify the state of the art in the detection of anomalies in smart shirts using machine learning techniques. It is understood as an anomaly something unusual in the vital signs of the person wearing a smart shirt. For example, it can be an imminent fall, non-standard heartbeat, fever, oxygen saturation far below average, and another anomaly that a specialist can set.

To the best of our knowledge, there are few studies about machine learning for anomaly detection in smart shirts, which was the main reason for this SLR. The primary studies were read thoughtfully and selected based on the methodology of Kitchenham and Charters [16] concerning the objectives that are: (i) identify machine learning techniques for anomaly detection in the smart shirt; (ii) identify the datasets used to train the ML algorithm; (iii) identify smart shirts or devices for acquiring vital signs; (iv) identify the performance metrics for evaluating the ML model; (v) types of ML being applied. The remainder of this study is divided into five sections: Sect. 1 provides the main theoretical background. Section 2 describes the methodology used in this SLR. Section 3 lists the results answering this SLR's questions. Finally, Sect. 5 contains the conclusion.

2   Theoretical Background

This section gives an overview of the three main research fields related to this article, namely Smart Textile, Machine Learning, and Anomaly Detection.

2.1   Smart Textile

In the 1980s, Steve Mann was one of the first researchers to develop smart textile, also called the e-textile, at the Massachusetts Institute of Technology (MIT). This was one of the first attempts to connect hardware to clothing. E-textiles can be classified into three main areas: smart clothing, electrical engineering (wearable electronics), and information science (wearable computers) [15,35].

Smart textile is defined as a product composed of fibres, yarns, filaments, and yarns that integrate electronic components such as sensors, circuits, and communication systems that are powered by some internal or external power supply [17,18]. These communication systems usually use Bluetooth technology, which allows the connectivity of the textile to other smart devices so that it can visualize and analyze data in real-time [17].

Smart textile integrates a high level of intelligence and is recognized in three subgroups [15,18,36]. **Passive Smart Textiles**: only able to sense the environment or the user using textile sensors. **Active Smart Textiles**: reactive sensing to stimuli from the environment, which means integrating an actuator function and a sensing device. **Very Smart Textile**: able to sense, react and adapt their behavior regarding the ambient conditions.

A review study [17] showed that smart shirts contain several sensors for measuring physiological signals such as ECG, electromyography (EMG), skin temperature, blood oxygen saturation, and respiratory rate. These physiological signals can be used in applications such as healthcare, medicine, transportation and auto use, fashion and entertainment, trackers, and military services [7].

2.2   Machine Learning

The field of ML has received several formal definitions in the literature. Samuel defines machine learning as "the field of study that provides computers with the ability to learn, without being explicitly programmed" [33]. For Mohri et al., ML can be broadly defined as computational methods using experience to make predictions, experience (usually in the form of electronic data) referring to past information available for learning [23]. Mitchell, on the other hand, provides a small formalism in his definition, "a computer program is said to learn from experience (E), with respect to some class of tasks (T) and performance measure (P), if its performance on tasks in (T), as measured by (P), improves with experience (E)" [22]. From these definitions, it can summarize that ML is the science of making computers learn and act like humans, improving their learning over time autonomously by feeding them data and information in the form of observations and interactions from the real world.

Learning is the process of acquiring knowledge. Unlike us, computers do not learn by reasoning but learn from computer algorithms. Learning is the process of acquiring knowledge. Unlike us, computers do not learn by reasoning but learn from computer algorithms. ML algorithms are organized into taxonomy, based on the desired outcome of the algorithm. Common algorithm type includes [4, 28, 31]: Supervised Learning, Unsupervised Learning, Semi-Supervised Learning, and Reinforcement Learning.

2.3 Anomaly Detection

Anomaly detection is a process of identifying unusual patterns that do not conform to expected behaviour, and these unusual patterns are generally referred to as anomalies and outliers [3]. This topic of anomaly detection has been used in several fields of study, such as data breaches, identity theft, manufacturing, networking, video surveillance, and medicine [3].

An important aspect is a proper understanding of the nature of anomalies in the development of anomaly detection methods. Anomalies are classified into three categories [3, 25, 26]: **Point Anomalies**: A data point-based anomaly is an instance of data that is considered an anomaly for the rest of the data, this type of anomaly is the simplest, and it is usually the focus of most research on anomaly detection. **Contextual Anomalies**: Context-based anomaly is an instance of data that is considered an anomaly if a particular context is verified. The instance is an anomaly, but it is not an anomaly in another context. **Collective Anomalies**: This category defines that a set of data instances are anomalous in relation to the entire dataset.

The use of ML-based anomaly detection is increasingly used, and this technique is used to build a model that distinguishes between normal and abnormal classes. The anomaly techniques can be divided into three categories based on the data function [3, 25]. **Supervised Anomaly Detection** requires all instances of the dataset to be labelled "normal" and "anomalous". This technique is basically a type of task that uses binary classification. **Semi-Supervised Anomaly Detection**: requires only instances considered "normal" to be labelled in a dataset. In this technique, the model will only predict normal instances. **Unsupervised Anomaly Detection**: does not require instances to be labelled. In these techniques, the model will try to predict which instances are "normal" or "abnormal".

3   Research Method

In this study, a Systematic Literature Review (SLR) was conducted using the methodology of Kitchenham and Charters [16]. This study was developed considering the three phases: planning, execution, and analysis of results. In the planning phase, a protocol is defined specifying research questions, keywords, inclusion and exclusion criteria for primary studies, and other topics of interest. In the execution phase, the literature search is conducted following with defined protocol, and in this stage that the inclusion and exclusion of primary studies are carried out. Finally, data extraction is done in the results analysis phase, and the results are compared.

3.1 Research Questions

This SLR intends to summarize, clarify and examine the ML techniques and implementations applied in anomaly detection in smart shirts from January 2017 through May 2022 inclusive. Table 1 presents four research questions (RQs) are raised for this purpose.

Table 1. Research questions.

RQ#	Research questions	Motivation
RQ_1	What anomalies were identified in smart shirt?	Identify which anomaly the primary study tries to detect.
RQ_2	Which ML techniques have been used for anomaly detection in smart shirts?	Aims to identify the ML techniques commonly being used in anomaly detection in smart shirts
RQ_3	What kind of empirical validation for anomaly detection in smart shirts is used in the ML techniques found in RQ1?	Assess the empirical evidence obtained
$RQ_{3.1}$	Which datasets are used?	Identify datasets reported to be appropriate
$RQ_{3.2}$	Which devices are used for data acquisition?	Identify devices being used
$RQ_{3.3}$	Which performance measures are used?	Identify the performance of the ML techniques
RQ_4	What is the overall performance of the ML techniques for anomaly detection in smart shirts?	Analyze the results from the performance metric
RQ_5	What types of ML algorithms are being applied in anomaly detection in smart shirts?	Specify which ML types have been used

3.2 Search Strategy

The search terms and synonyms were formed according to related studies using machine learning, anomaly detection, and smart textile. All these terms and synonyms were included in the Search Query (SQ), which is presented as follows:

*query_01: ("Smart Shirt" **OR** "Smart Clothing" **OR** "Smart Clothes" **OR** "Smart Cloth" **OR** "Smart Textiles" **OR** "Smart Textile" **OR** "e-textile" **OR** "Clothing Tech" **OR** "Wearable Smart Textile" **OR** "e-clothes" **OR** "clothing tech")*

*query_02: ("Anomaly Detection" **OR** "Anomalous Detection" **OR** "Abnormal Detection" **OR** "Outlier Detection" **OR** "Machine Learning" **OR** "Artificial Intelligence" **OR** "Expert System" **OR** "Intelligence System" **OR** "Supervised Anomaly Detection" **OR** "Semi-Supervised Anomaly Detection" **OR** "Unsupervised Anomaly Detection")*

$$SQ: \quad query\_01 \; \textbf{AND} \; query\_02$$

After identifying the search terms, important digital portals were selected. The following six electronic databases were used to search the primary studies:

- **ACM Digital Library**: https://dl.acm.org/
- **Scopus**: http://www.scopus.com
- **Google Scholar**: https://scholar.google.com/
- **PubMed**: https://pubmed.ncbi.nlm.nih.gov/
- **Web of Science**: https://www.webofknowledge.com/
- **ScienceDirect**: https://www.sciencedirect.com/

3.3   Study Selection

The whole process of filtering and searching the primary studies is illustrated in Fig. 1. Searches were carried out in the digital databases using the SQ described in Sect. 3.2, where studies in the determined interval (IC_1) were selected. This first step has collected 522 studies, of which 206 from ScienceDirect, 94 from ACM Digital Library, 94 from Scopus, 57 from Google Scholar, 49 from Web of Science, and 22 from PubMed.

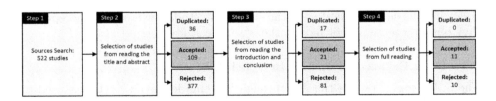

Fig. 1. Selection process of primary studies.

The inclusion (IC) and exclusion (EC) criteria summarized in Table 2 were applied to select the studies in steps two, three, and four. In the second step, the title and abstract of all selected studies were read, where there were 36 duplicate studies, 377 rejected studies, and 109 accepted studies. In the third step, the introduction and conclusion of the studies accepted in the previous step were read, where there were 17 duplicate studies, 81 rejected studies, and 21 accepted studies. In the fourth step, the studies accepted in the previous step were read in their entirety, where there were no duplicated studies, 10 rejected studies, and finally, 11 accepted studies.

Table 2. Inclusion and exclusion criteria.

Inclusion	Criteria
IC_1	Studies published in the range January/2017 - May/2022
IC_2	Studies written in English
IC_3	Studies use ML techniques for anomaly detect in smart textile
IC_4	Studies primary
Exclusion	Criteria
EC_1	Studies with no clear publication information
EC_2	Studies that do not use smart textile
EC_3	Studies that do not use ML techniques for anomaly detection
EC_4	Studies that do not use techniques ML in smart textile
EC_5	Studies that are not written in English
EC_6	Studies that do not provide the full paper
EC_7	Studies that do not present the abstract
EC_8	Studies in which year of publication is before 2017
EC_9	Books, letters, notes, and patents are not included in the review

3.4   Quality Assessment Rules

The Quality Assessment Rules (QARs) are fundamental to ensure and assess the quality of the primary studies and are performed in the final step to define which studies will be added for review. Inspired by the study [25], 10 QARs were assigned (Table 3) where each QAR can be assigned a score from 1 to 10. Following the same method as in the study [25], studies will only be accepted if they obtain a score of 5 or more, otherwise, the study is rejected.

3.5   Data Extraction and Data Synthesis

The StArt tool (State of the Art through Systematic Review) [11] was used to support the SLR process, mainly in data extraction and data synthesis. During the data extraction step, within the StArt tool, it was possible to summarize the primary studies such as author name, study title, publication details, devices used in the smart shirt, dataset, evaluation metrics, and machine learning and anomaly techniques. In summary, the goal of synthesizing data is to accumulate and combine facts and figures from the selected primary studies to reformulate answers and address the research questions [40]. Visualization techniques such as line graphs, bar graphs, and box plots were used to answer those questions. Tables were also used to summarize and present the results of this SLR.

Table 3. Quality assessment questions.

Q#	Quality questions
QAR_1	Are the study objectives clearly recognized?
QAR_2	Are the anomaly detection techniques well defined and deliberated?
QAR_3	Is the specific application of anomaly detection clearly defined?
QAR_4	Does the paper cover practical experiments using the proposed technique?
QAR_5	Are the experiments well designed and justifiable?
QAR_6	Are the experiments applied on sufficient datasets?
QAR_7	Are estimation accuracy criteria reported?
QAR_8	Is the proposed estimation method compared with other methods?
QAR_9	Are the techniques of analyzing the outcomes suitable?
QAR_{10}	Overall, does the study enrich the academic community or industry?

4   Results and Discussions

This section presents the results obtained from selected primary studies. First, an overview of the selected works is presented and then the results for each research question in this SLR.

4.1   Description of Primary Studies

After following all the steps of the SLR, Table 4 shows all the accepted primary studies. In total, 11 were considered for meta-analysis. Various graphs and tables are normally used for meta-analysis, but as in this study, there were few primary studies accepted. It is possible to see in Table 4 information about the primary studies, such as the assignment of an ID to each study, title, year of publication, type, and its respective reference.

A1: Feng *et al.* [12] propose an architecture called SR-ScatNet to detect abnormal ECG signals in smart shirts. The authors used the MIT-BIH Arrhythmia Database to validate the proposed architecture, where it obtained 98% accuracy for abnormal signals.

A2: The focus of the study by Abid *et al.* [1] is to investigate Human Activity Recognition (HAR) using a smart shirt. The study detects 10 types of activities, and one of them is fall detection which is an important anomaly in a smart shirt. The experiment involved 44 persons, and they used tree ML techniques (see Table 5) for HAR.

A3: The study by Petz *et al.* [27] describes the development of a smart shirt for recording upper body movement and shows that it is possible to perform posture recognition. Results show the potential of the smart shirt for applications in the field of occupational safety.

A4: Lanata *et al.* [19] propose a sensor suite with a smart shirt for physiological work risk levels. The combination of the wireless sensor and smart fabric allows for worker risk assessment. This study focuses on the description of the sensors and proposes a k-nearest neighbours (KNN) algorithm for risk assessment and detection.

Table 4. Selected primary studies.

ID	Title	Year	Type	Refs.
A1	"SR-ScatNet Algorithm for On-device ECG Time Series Anomaly Detection"	2021	Conf.	[12]
A2	"Physical Activity Recognition Based on a Parallel Approach for an Ensemble of Machine Learning and Deep Learning Classifiers."	2021	Jour.	[1]
A3	"Sensor Shirt as Universal Platform for Real-Time Monitoring of Posture and Movements for Occupational Health and Ergonomics"	2021	Jour.	[27]
A4	"A New Smart-Fabric based Body Area Sensor Network for Work Risk Assessment"	2020	Conf.	[19]
A5	"Violent Activity Recognition by E-textile Sensors based on Machine Learning Methods"	2020	Jour.	[29]
A6	"Smart Healthcare Framework for Ambient Assisted Living using IoMT and Big Data Analytics Techniques"	2019	Jour.	[38]
A7	"Application of Hierarchical Temporal Memory to Anomaly Detection of Vital Signs for Ambient Assisted Living"	2019	Thes.	[6]
A8	"An Investigation of Different Machine Learning Approaches for Epileptic Seizure Detection"	2019	Conf.	[30]
A9	"Physical Activity Classification using a Smart Textile"	2018	Conf.	[9]
A10	"Fall Detection System for Elderly People using IoT and Big Data"	2018	Jour.	[42]
A11	"Context Aware Adaptable approach for Fall Detection bases on Smart Textile"	2017	Jour.	[21]

A5: Randhawa *et al.* [29] study aims to recognize if a person is being physically attacked through sensors installed in a smart shirt. The study analyzed the best sensor positions and applied several ML techniques (see Table 5) to recognize physical aggressions where these aggressions can be considered anomalies.

A6: Syed *et al.* [38] propose a healthcare framework to monitor the physical activities of the elderly using IoMT and ML algorithms. In total, it is proposed to recognize 12 types of activities, and one of the activities to recognize is the elderly's fall, which can be considered an anomaly.

A7: The study is a PhD thesis by Bastaki [6] where it presents the development of a framework for vital sign anomaly detection for an Ambient Assisted Living (AAL) health monitoring scenario. This study created its own dataset and used three ML techniques.

A8: Resque *et al.* [30] investigate the performance of five ML algorithms in terms of accuracy for Epileptic Seizure Detection. The study concluded that the ML techniques had good accuracy for identifying epileptic seizures from EEG, which can also be considered an anomaly in smart shirts.

A9: The aim of the study by Cherif *et al.* [9] is to develop a human activity classification system using a smart shirt. The study used ML techniques. One of the activities is falling, which can be considered an anomaly.

A10: Yacchirema *et al.* [42] built a framework for fall detection in the elderly. If the system detects a fall, an alert is issued, and the system automatically sends it to the groups responsible for providing care to the elderly. The resulting study found high success rates in fall detection in terms of accuracy, precision, and gain.

A11: The study Mezghani *et al.* [21] presents a novel fall detection system using smart textile and ML techniques. The system classifies falls based on their respective orientations among 11 classes. The results showed that the system is 98% accurate for fall detection.

4.2   RQ1: What Anomalies Were Identified in Smart Shirt?

The anomalies of the primary studies were identified and are shown in Table 5. The most frequent anomaly is the fall present in five studies. A fall is an unintentional displacement of the body to a lower level than the initial position, with the inability to correct it promptly caused by multifactorial circumstances. Fall-related injuries may be fatal or non-fatal.

Primary study A1 addresses the anomaly related to cardiac arrhythmia. Cardiac arrhythmia is characterized by a lack of rhythm in a heartbeat. Tachycardias is when the rhythm is fast, and bradycardias are when the rhythm is too slow, both of which can worsen and lead to heart complications. The study A3 addresses posture recognition where it can be considered an anomaly because postural diseases are caused by poor posture [27]. The A5 study presents a smart shirt to detect violent attacks or aggression. The study A7 uses a set of vital signs for monitoring and detecting anomalies in patients. The detection of epilepsy is addressed in study A8, considered also an anomaly that can issue an alert if the patient is in a crisis. Moreover, finally, the A4 study is the development of a smart shirt to detect risk at work.

4.3   RQ2: Which ML Techniques Have Been Used for Anomaly Detection in Smart Shirts?

Table 5 presents the ML techniques used in each primary study. The analyzed ML techniques frequently used were Support Vector Machines (SVM) with seven or 63% of the studies and K-Nearest Neighbors (KNN) with six or 54% of the selected studies.

The Naive Bayes (NB) technique was used in three or 23% of the studies, the Decision Trees (DT) technique was used in two or 18% of the studies, Linear Discriminant Analysis (LDA) technique was used in two or 18% of the studies, and Convolutional Neural Network (CNN) technique was used in two or 18% of the studies.

Table 5. Summary of each study where the anomaly, device, ML techniques, dataset, performance metrics and result were identified.

ID	Anomaly	Device	Sensor data	ML techniques	Dataset	Performance metric	Result
A1	Cardiac Arrhythmia	Smart Shirt Prototype	ECG	KNN, SVM CNN	MIT-BIH Arrhythmia [24]	Accuracy	98.30%
A2	Fall	Hexoskin Smart Shirt	Accelerometer	SVM, CNN LDA	Own Dataset	Precision, Recall F1-Score	87%–97%
A3	Posture	Smart Shirt Prototype	IMU	LSTM	Own Dataset	Accuracy	≥80%
A4	Undefined	Smart Shirt Prototype	Respiration Sensor, ECG, IMU, Sweat Sensor	KNN	Own Dataset	-	-
A5	Violent Attack	Smart Shirt Prototype	Pressure Sensor, Accelerometer Stretch Sensor	SVM, KNN NB, DT	Human Motion [43]	Accuracy	93%–97.60%
A6	Fall	Wearable	IMU, ECG	NB	MHEALTH [5]	Accuracy, Precision, Recall	96.38%–97%
A7	Vital Signs	Wearable	Heart Rate, Respiratory Rate, Arterial Blood Pressure	HTM, KNN SVM	MIMIC-III [44] Precision	F1-Score, Recall, Precision	27%–90%
A8	Epilepsy	Wearable	ECG	SVM, RF NB, NN, KNN	EEG UCI [45]	Accuracy	90.01%–97.31%
A9	Fall	Hexoskin Smart Shirt	Respiratory Activity, Cardic Activity, Blood Pressure Rate	KNN, SVM	Own Dataset	Accuracy	95.40%–96.37%
A10	Fall	Wearable	IMU	DT	SisFall [37]	Accuracy, Precision, Recall	91.67%–93.75%
A11	Fall	Hexoskin Smart Shirt	Acceleration	SVM	Own Dataset	Accuracy, Sensitivity, Specificity	97.60%–98%

The following techniques were the least used being used in only one or 9% of the selected primary studies: Long Short Term Memory (LSTM), Principal Component Analysis (PCA), Hierarchical Temporal Memory (HTM), Random Forest (RF), and Neural Network (NN).

4.4   RQ3: What Kind of Empirical Validation for Anomaly Detection in Smart Shirts Is Found Using the ML Techniques Found in RQ1?

This section aims to identify the datasets, the devices for data acquisition, and the performance measures used in the selected primary studies.

RQ3.1: Which Datasets Are Used? Data is an essential component of any ML technique. The dataset can be used to train an ML algorithm that aims to find predictable patterns from the entire dataset. In total, 11 datasets were identified, which are shown in the Table 5. Each primary study used only a dataset, where five studies created and used their own dataset, and six studies used public and private datasets.

RQ3.2: Which Devices Are Used for Data Acquisition? Sensors capture data from the world around us, and these sensors are integrated into devices so that data can be displayed, analyzed and stored. Using a smart shirt, it is possible to capture vital signs and measure the body's inertia. Table 5 shows the type of smart textile and the sensors used in the selected primary studies.

In this SLR, seven smart shirts were identified, and only one (Hexoskin) is being sold commercially. The rest are proposals or prototypes. The remaining were classified as wearables, but with one exception, it is wearables that are located in the human's chest.

RQ3.3: Which Performance Metrics Are Used? When implementing an ML technique, the developer must ask himself how good the technique is for anomaly detection. All ML techniques need a metric to evaluate performance. Thus, in total, seven metrics were identified in the primary studies, which are shown in Table 5.

Some studies (A1, A2, A3, A5, A6, and A10) contained the confusion matrix to illustrate the performance of the ML technique. The most used performance metric is Accuracy, followed closely by the Precision and Recall measures. Specificity and F1-Score are other commonly used metrics. The Kappa metric is less used cited in a primary study. The primary study A4 did not mention any metric performance, but as it uses KNN as ML techniques, it can use the metrics shown in Table 5.

4.5   RQ4: What is the Overall Performance of the ML Techniques for Anomaly Detection in Smart Shirts?

Table 5 shows main results. Most techniques are classic ML algorithms that do not require significant computational power. Almost all algorithms present satisfactory results in their respective studies.

Primary study A4 did not mention the result because the main objective was to show the development of the smart shirt. After that, according to the authors, they will do a study focusing on machine learning techniques. The primary study A3 did not present an exact value, and it only showed that according to the tests, it obtained an accuracy greater than 80%.

4.6   RQ5: What Types of ML Algorithms Are Being Applied in Anomaly Detection in Smart Shirts?

The purpose of this question is to identify the type of ML and anomaly detection for each selected primary study. All selected primary studies are of the supervised type, which is that all studies have classification or multiclassification problems.

5   Conclusion

This paper presents a systematic literature review in order to identify machine learning techniques for anomaly detection in smart shirts. First, the theoretical background of smart textile, machine learning and anomaly detection was described. Second, the adopted research method was described following a systematic series of steps analyzing the quality of the primary studies. In total, eleven primary studies (January/2017 - May/2021) were selected for analysis. And finally, the results, which are the answers to the research questions of the systematic review, are presented.

From the selected primary studies, six different anomalies were identified, which are: fall, cardiac arrhythmia, posture, violent attack, vital signs and epilepsy, with the fall anomaly being the most frequent being cited in five primary studies. Therefore, it is possible to define a set of anomalies to be detected in smart shirts.

About the machine learning techniques for anomaly detection in smart shirts, eleven different techniques were identified: SVM, KNN, NB, DT, LDA, CNN, LSTM, PCA, HTM, RF, and NN, with the SVM technique being the most frequent in seven primary studies.

For the machine learning algorithm training, five primary studies created their dataset and six primary studies used public or private datasets, with each study using a dataset. In general, no dataset was cited more than once.

Evaluating the performance of the machine learning algorithm is a fundamental process. Five different metrics were identified. The accuracy of the performance metric was the most cited metric in eight primary studies. Overall, almost all primary studies showed high ($\geq$90%) and good accuracy values on their respective problems. It was also observed that the primary studies used the confusion matrix to validate and show the performance of the machine learning algorithm.

Finally, seven primary studies used or built a smart shirt regarding data acquisition devices, and four studies used a wearable simulating a smart shirt. A smart shirt can contain one or more sensors, and the accelerometer sensor was the most cited since most studies involve fall detection.

This study aims to analyse state of the art in anomaly detections in smart shirts bringing contributions and directions for future research. Furthermore, it is hoped with future work to implement an intelligent system of anomaly detection in smart shirts based on the results of this analysis.

Acknowledgment. This work has been supported by Nanomateriais aplicados na reabilitação muscular de IDosos com recurso à Inteligência Artificial (46985).

References

1. Abid, M., et al.: Physical activity recognition based on a parallel approach for an ensemble of machine learning and deep learning classifiers. Sensors **21**, 4713 (2021)
2. E-textiles and smart clothing market surpass $15,018.9 mn by 2028 carg 32.3% says acumen research and consulting. https://bit.ly/3oxQ4jv. Accessed 7 Feb 2022
3. Alla, S., Adari, S.K.: Beginning Anomaly Detection Using Python-Based Deep Learning. Apress, Berkeley (2019). https://doi.org/10.1007/978-1-4842-5177-5
4. Ayodele, T.: Types of machine learning algorithms. New Adv. Mach. Learn. **3**, 19–48 (2010)
5. Banos, O., et al.: mHealthDroid: a novel framework for agile development of mobile health applications. In: International Workshop on Ambient Assisted Living, pp. 91–98 (2014)
6. Bastaki, B.: Application of hierarchical temporal memory to anomaly detection of vital signs for ambient assisted living. Staffordshire University (2019)
7. Bhatia, S., Chopra, S., Pandey, J., Yadav, N.: Smart shirt a new dimension towards wearable. Int. J. Eng. Adv. Technol. **9**, 177–182 (2020)
8. BioSpace, IoT in healthcare market to reach USD 260.75 billion by 2027-reports and data. https://tinyurl.com/29yjp3k6. Accessed 4 Feb 2022
9. Cherif, N., Ouakrim, Y., Benazza-Benyahia, A., Mezghani, N.: Physical activity classification using a smart textile. In: 2018 IEEE Life Sciences Conference (LSC), pp. 175–178 (2018)
10. Deep, S., Zheng, X., Karmakar, C., Yu, D., Hamey, L., Jin, J.: A survey on anomalous behavior detection for elderly care using dense-sensing networks. IEEE Commun. Surv. Tutor. **22**, 352–370 (2019)
11. Fabbri, S., Silva, C., Hernandes, E., Octaviano, F., Di Thommazo, A., Belgamo, A.: Improvements in the StArt tool to better support the systematic review process. In: Proceedings of the 20th International Conference on Evaluation and Assessment in Software Engineering, pp. 1–5 (2016)
12. Feng, H., Chen, P., Hou, J.: SR-ScatNet algorithm for on-device ECG time series anomaly detection. In: SoutheastCon 2021, pp. 1–5 (2021)
13. Gupta, D., Kayode, O., Bhatt, S., Gupta, M., Tosun, A.: Hierarchical Federated Learning based Anomaly Detection using Digital Twins for Smart Healthcare. arXiv Preprint arXiv:2111.12241 (2021)

14. Hexoskin Homepage. https://www.hexoskin.com/. Accessed 07 Feb 2022
15. Kan, C., Lam, Y.: Future trend in wearable electronics in the textile industry. Appl. Sci. **11**, 3914 (2021)
16. Keele, S., et al.: Guidelines for performing systematic literature reviews in software engineering. Technical report, ver. 2.3 EBSE Technical report. EBSE (2007)
17. Khundaqji, H., Hing, W., Furness, J., Climstein, M.: Smart shirts for monitoring physiological parameters: scoping review. JMIR MHealth UHealth **8**, e18092 (2020)
18. Kubicek, J., et al.: Recent trends, construction and applications of smart textiles and clothing for monitoring of health activity: a comprehensive multidisciplinary review. IEEE Rev. Biomed. Eng. (2020)
19. Lanata, A., et al.: A new smart-fabric based body area sensor network for work risk assessment. In: 2020 IEEE International Workshop on Metrology for Industry 4.0 & IoT, pp. 187–190 (2020)
20. Smart clothing market by textile type, product type (upper wear, lower wear, innerwear, and others), end-user industry (military and defense, sports and fitness, fashion and entertainment, healthcare), and geography - global forecast to 2024. https://www.marketsandmarkets.com/Market-Reports/smart-clothing-market-56415040.html. Accessed 07 Feb 2022
21. Mezghani, N., Ouakrim, Y., Islam, M., Yared, R., Abdulrazak, B.: Context aware adaptable approach for fall detection bases on smart textile. In: 2017 IEEE EMBS International Conference on Biomedical & Health Informatics (BHI), pp. 473–476 (2017)
22. Mitchell, T.: Machine Learning, 1st edn. McGraw-Hill Inc., New York (1997)
23. Mohri, M., Rostamizadeh, A., Talwalkar, A.: Foundations of Machine Learning. MIT Press, Cambridge (2018)
24. Moody, G., Mark, R.: The impact of the MIT-BIH arrhythmia database. IEEE Eng. Med. Biol. Mag. **20**, 45–50 (2001)
25. Nassif, A., Talib, M., Nasir, Q., Dakalbab, F.: Machine learning for anomaly detection: a systematic review. IEEE Access **9**, 78658–78700 (2021)
26. Pecht, M., Kang, M.: Machine Learning: Anomaly Detection. Wiley-IEEE Press, Hoboken (2019)
27. Petz, P., Eibensteiner, F., Langer, J.: Sensor shirt as universal platform for real-time monitoring of posture and movements for occupational health and ergonomics. Procedia Comput. Sci. **180**, 200–207 (2021)
28. Portugal, I., Alencar, P., Cowan, D.: The use of machine learning algorithms in recommender systems: a systematic review. Expert Syst. Appl. **97**, 205–227 (2018)
29. Randhawa, P., Shanthagiri, V., Kumar, A.: Violent activity recognition by E-textile sensors based on machine learning methods. J. Intell. Fuzzy Syst. **39**, 8115–8123 (2020)
30. Resque, P., Barros, A., Rosário, D., Cerqueira, E.: An investigation of different machine learning approaches for epileptic seizure detection. In: 2019 15th International Wireless Communications & Mobile Computing Conference (IWCMC), pp. 301–306 (2019)
31. Russell, S.: Artificial Intelligence a Modern Approach. Pearson Education Inc., London (2010)
32. Šabić, E., Keeley, D., Henderson, B., Nannemann, S.: Healthcare and anomaly detection: using machine learning to predict anomalies in heart rate data. AI Soc. **36**, 149–158 (2021)
33. Samuel, A.: Some studies in machine learning using the game of checkers. II-recent progress. Comput. Games I 366–400 (1988)

34. Sensoria Fitness Homepage. https://www.sensoriafitness.com/smartsocks/. Accessed 07 Feb 2022
35. Singha, K., Kumar, J., Pandit, P.: Recent advancements in wearable & smart textiles: an overview. Mater. Today: Proc. **16**, 1518–1523 (2019)
36. Stoppa, M., Chiolerio, A.: Wearable electronics and smart textiles: a critical review. Sensors **14**, 11957–11992 (2014)
37. Sucerquia, A., López, J., Vargas-Bonilla, J.: SisFall: a fall and movement dataset. Sensors **17**, 198 (2017)
38. Syed, L., Jabeen, S., Manimala, S., Alsaeedi, A.: Smart healthcare framework for ambient assisted living using IoMT and big data analytics techniques. Futur. Gener. Comput. Syst. **101**, 136–151 (2019)
39. Wearablex Homepage. https://www.wearablex.com/pages/how-it-works_v0. Accessed 07 Feb 2022
40. Wen, J., Li, S., Lin, Z., Hu, Y., Huang, C.: Systematic literature review of machine learning based software development effort estimation models. Inf. Softw. Technol. **54**, 41–59 (2012)
41. Ageing and health. https://www.who.int/news-room/fact-sheets/detail/ageing-and-health. Accessed 04 Feb 2022
42. Yacchirema, D., Puga, J., Palau, C., Esteve, M.: Fall detection system for elderly people using IoT and big data. Procedia Comput. Sci. **130**, 603–610 (2018)
43. Kuehne, H., Jhuang, H., Garrote, E., Poggio, T., Serre, T.: HMDB: a large video database for human motion recognition. In: Proceedings of the International Conference on Computer Vision (ICCV) (2011)
44. Johnson, A., Pollard, T., Mark, R.: MIMIC-III Clinical Database (version 1.4). PhysioNet (2016). https://doi.org/10.13026/C2XW26
45. Sykacek, P., Roberts, S.: Adaptive classification by variational Kalman filtering. In: Advances in Neural Information Processing Systems, vol. 15 (2002)

Decision Making System to Support the Cost of Ordered Products in the Budget Stage

Lucas Henrique Matte[1,2] and Clara Bento Vaz[1,2,3]

[1] Research Centre in Digitalization and Intelligent Robotics (CeDRI),
Instituto Politécnico de Bragança (IPB), Campus Santa Apolónia,
5300-253 Bragança, Portugal
a49139@alunos.ipb.pt, clvaz@ipb.pt
[2] Laboratório para a Sustentabilidade e Tecnologia em Regiões de Montanha
(SusTEC), Instituto Politécnico de Bragança, Campus de Santa Apolónia,
5300-253 Bragança, Portugal
[3] Centre for Management and Industrial Engineering (CEGI/INESC TEC), Porto,
Portugal

Abstract. This work aims to identify the critical production costs, related to raw materials and labor, of ordered inflatable-based products without standardization in order to develop a quantitative model to predict these costs accurately in the early project stage, within the budget step. In order to achieve this goal, it was necessary to understand the production processes and the raw materials, as well as to study the principal theoretical aspects related to cost estimating techniques and methods, cost estimating models, model selection, and validation. Therefore, it is intended to develop a multiple linear regression model, applied to historical quantitative data, to estimate each critical variable concerning the quantity of the main raw material and the labor times for critical processes. Six models were analyzed, in which two models are identified for each critical variable such as the linear meters value of the main raw material used in the product, the main raw material cut time involved in the product and the sew time required by the product. The models were evaluated, selected, and validated, defining the best model for each critical variable. The model parameters were obtained using a train dataset and, afterwards, the results of the selected models were validated using a test dataset. The obtained results, through the proposed methodology, were evaluated and proved to be reliable for use in the early stage of product development within the budget step.

Keywords: Product budgeting · Production costs · Cost estimation · Multiple linear regression

1 Introduction

With globalization, an increasingly competitive market emerges in which companies must seek ways to produce with lower costs and to increase their business

A. I. Pereira et al. (Eds.): OL2A 2022, CCIS 1754, pp. 486–501, 2022.
https://doi.org/10.1007/978-3-031-23236-7_34

productivity [1]. Rapid challenges and changes are common in the business environment but they require from the companies to plan carefully their business, in order to respond in short time to the market. This planning is critical in industries that do not work with standardization in their products, processing them according to the design ordered by each customer [2]. When talking about the inclusion of a new product in the market, the budget is the first step that a customer wants before approving a specific product ordered as the sale price is normally unchangeable after this stage. Thus, it is essential that the realized budget approaches to the product real value plus the company margin, maximizing the profit and avoiding possible losses. A good budgeting process should accurately reflect the costs of raw materials, cost of direct labor and factory overhead costs. This requires that a company should estimate the production costs before the activities start indeed [3], which depend on the effective planning of the operations required to achieve the desired product design. After the production of the ordered product, its real cost should be approximately equal to the value of the budget estimated at the project stage, since it has already been presented to the customer, in order to minimize its deviation. If the real product cost is higher than its previous budget estimated, it implies a decrease in the sales margin, allowing the possibility of losing money or less competitiveness due to changes in the selling values to customers. This budget stage must be carried out as quickly and accurately as possible, that is in this context that the problem involved in this study fits. The objective of this paper is to propose a decision making system to support the budget stage of ordered products to minimize the deviation between the real product cost and its previous budget estimated, taking into account the product characteristics and the processes where they are processed and the difficulties in the current budgeting method in order to bring an ideal solution to this specific problem. Thus, a methodology based on Multiple linear regression was proposed to estimate the critical cost components of ordered inflatable-based products, in a really specific industry in the textile sector, which is the novel contribution of this work.

In order to achieve this goal, the literature review is accomplished to study the principal theoretical aspects related to cost estimating techniques, methods and models in the next section. Besides, it was necessary to understand the most relevant features of the production processes and raw materials to identify the critical cost components which are described in Sect. 3. Afterwards, in Sect. 4, the multiple linear regression model to predict each critical cost component is evaluated in the training set and validated in the testing set. Finally, Sect. 5 concludes the paper and presents further research work.

2   Literature Review

This section aims to review some studies that refer to concepts and methods used as pillars in solving the described problem, helping to estimate the costs involved in the production of products in the budgeting phase. Some topics such as cost estimation, cost-generating characteristics in products, and some methods for determining costs in products are presented.

2.1   Cost Estimation

In the products cost determination, the calculation of the production costs and the selling price of a product are usually involved which require to estimate the costs of research and development, design, manufacturing, marketing, logistics, and customer service [4]. In addition, cost estimation requires to find the costs related to a set of activities before they are performed [5].

The potential customer demands a price proposal as soon as possible, sometimes even unconcerned with factors such as the dimension of customization, the nature of the data required, and the complexity of the design. In this way, more accurate budget process becomes a point of great focus for operational strategies and a fundamental point for the decisions made by the organization for the production of new products in the initial stages of development [6].

2.2   Cost-Generating Characteristics in Products

According to the analysis of [7] concerning the product development process and its decision making, it can be concluded that the costs during the development are caused by the geometry, the raw material (RM) used, the production processes, and the production planning, as described hereafter.

The geometry determines the amount of material and the production processes that will be needed. Geometry includes shape, dimensions, and tolerances. In the present case under study, the shape directly influences the contour of the seams needed in the product, inducing a direct increase in labor expenses due to the increase in production time and the amount of RM due to the determined dimensions.

The RM costs correspond to all materials consumed and involved during manufacturing a product, which will undergo transformation operations and constitute the finished product [8].

Production processes are required to transform raw materials into a component or include the assembly of components. Resources (e.g. operators, tools, machines) are needed to develop this productive activity. For each production process, there is a time of labor or machine involved, this time generates a cost of production, which is involved in the cost of the product. In the case under study, sewing is one of the productive process in manufacturing products. Therefore, the sewing time is one of the variables that generates cost in the product, being dependent on its dimension, since this influences the sewing time, generating cost to the final product.

In production planning, decisions are made about the use of production resources to satisfy the demand forecast over a certain horizon at a reasonable cost [9]. Thus, the operations should be strategically allocated [5] to minimize losses related to internal transport, resulting in optimizing the process and reducing unnecessary costs. This is a very relevant point, since manufacturing a product with an erroneously planned production process can lead to increased production times, directly related to the labor costs involved, thus making the product more expensive compared to a one well-organized and developed process.

2.3   Budgeting Methods

According to [6], the Product Cost Estimation (PCE) techniques are classified into qualitative and quantitative approaches based on similar features and data types.

Qualitative budgeting techniques are based on a comparative analysis of a new product with products that have already been previously manufactured to identify similarities. The use of rule-based systems as well as decision trees can help to generate reliable estimates based on the manufacturing data and a design database. Qualitative techniques can be classified into intuitive or analogical [10]. Intuitive ones are based on the use of practical knowledge (know-how) which can be defined in the form of rules, decision diagrams, such as a database, to support the end user to improve/optimize the decision-making process and prepare the budget for new products based on previous information. Analogical techniques use similarity criteria based on historical cost data for products with have already defined costs, but with limited information, such as regression analysis models with qualitative, binary (dummy) variables and neural networks (back propagation methods) [6]. The qualitative method is generally favorable for making cost estimates in the early stages of design, using historical data without requiring very detailed information, such as geometric data or process planning results [6].

Quantitative techniques are based on a detailed analysis of a specific product, its components and singularities, and production processes. Although these methods generate more accurate results, they are normally used only in the final stages of development due to the requirement for more detailed product information [6]. Quantitative techniques can be categorized into parametric and analytical [10]. Parametric models are derived by applying statistical methodologies and expressing the cost as a function of its determinant variables, considered independent. This model can be effective in situations where parameters, sometimes known as cost factors, can be easily identified. These models are generally used to quantify the unit cost of such a product. The analytical approach requires decomposing the product into several elementary units (product divided into components), separating the operations and activities for each of these units, which represent different resources consumed during the production cycle, and expressing the cost as a sum of all these units [6]. One way to estimate costs through quantitative methods is also to use the regression method. It is possible to use this method by creating a database, with the information of the existing products related to the calculation of the components for each operation, separating between the different processes and defining the costs for each one separately, concerning labor. This approach reflects the allocation of costs based on the activities required to obtain the product, according to the Activity-Based Costing (ABC) method [11]. Likewise, the regression method can be used to estimate the amount of raw material, creating a database with the calculation of raw material costs for existing products.

2.4   Regression Models for Costs

The application of different cost estimation tools showed that professionals in this area use regression method to design their cost analysis models [12].

In [13], the Multiple linear regression (MLR) was used to obtain cost functions for different types of resources (pumps, pipes, tanks) connected to water supply systems, based on their hydraulic and physical characteristics. In this work, a five-step methodology was used which includes the construction of a database and characterization of resources, current calculation of cost values, definition of key parameters and establishment of the cost function, specification of the model and finally the testing and validation of the proposed model using 20% of randomly selected data.

In [14], a cost estimation model for machines used in underground mining, loading, transport, and unloading was presented, using the simple linear regression model, in which the independent variable was the bucket capacity (given in cubic meters). In the MLR model, independent variables included bucket capacity, total machine width, total height and horsepower. The MLR was conducted in three steps, firstly with the aid of software, a correlation between the independent variables was calculated, then only the variables with significant correlations were selected and used as independent variables in the MLR models. In the last step, the cost relationships were established as functions of the initial variables, which were bucket capacity, total machine width, total height and power. After analyzing the different approaches, the authors concluded that the MLR model could be a useful tool for cost estimates in the budget and initial phase of the project and in the detailed project feasibility studies.

These cost functions obtained in the MLR models generate prior knowledge of the product costs for the company and can be used in choosing the design of new products and in managing the production of the existing products [10].

3   Data and Models

The main objective is to develop a decision making system to support the calculation of the most critical cost components involved in new products, in the budget project stage. In this section, the case study and the data are introduced as well as the MLR method.

3.1   Data

The company under study works in a really specific industry in the textile sector by production of inflatable-based products, such as advertising products, decorative products and agricultural tarpaulins, in which cutting and sewing processes are required. These products were classified into three distinct families, with similar production processes and raw materials. Family 1 (F1) comprises advertising-related products, such as tents, totems, and flags, family 2 (F2) includes inflatable decorative products, and family 3 (F3) is made up of agricultural tarpaulins which can be ordered with different features. Canvas, nets, and fabrics are used as the main raw material for the production of these ordered products. These raw materials are received in rolls, which have a width and a length that can be measured in linear meters value (LMV). Thus, each product uses a certain LMV, that is, a certain roll length. In the case of new products, totally different from the existing ones, it is hard to estimate the LMV and the labor times involved.

Analyzing the RM costs, it is noted that the canvas, fabrics, and nets are the ones that most contribute to the cost of each product in the families F2 and F3. The RM cost contributes to 81%, on average, in case of the products in family F2 and it is, on average, approximately equal to 87% for the products in family F3. For the products in family F1, the contribution is smaller, but it is also quite considerable, around 45%, on average, of the product raw material cost. Concerning the costs related to labor, calculated using the ABC method, it is noted that the activity that most contributes to the product labor cost is the sewing, as it is a more time-consuming activity due to its characteristics and complexity, with 61% of contribution on average to the product labor cost in F1, 58% in F2 and 51% in F3. Like sewing, cutting is also a critical activity for some products, which have more complex geometry, with curves and asymmetrical shapes. In this case, for the products in F2, the cutting time is relatively high, contributing 22% to the product labor cost, on average.

Based on the described product costs, it is possible to conclude that the most critical cost components in the products are the LMV of canvas, fabric, and nets for the raw material cost, and the cutting time (T_c) and sewing time (T_s) for the labor cost. Therefore, it is intended to develop a multiple linear regression model, applied to an historical quantitative data, to estimate each critical cost components, LMV, T_c and T_s, which are considered the dependent variables.

To estimate each dependent variable, it is necessary to consider independent variables that should be available in the initial stage of the project by the company. Thus, these data should be easily obtained and are taken manually, with the aid of SolidWorks software, analyzing in individually way the project of the products. The selected variables were the raw material area (a) used in the product project, the product weight (w), the product approximate volume (V), the total perimeter (P) of all parts that make up the product and the average height of the product (h). These data correspond to the independent variables for the development of each MLR model.

Once the critical variables were identified, a database was created for each one of them, resulting in three databases. The database for the LMV was created considering the actual LMV used in the existing products and the aforementioned independent variables, resulting in 83 observations concerning the 6 variables. To estimate the T_c, the cutting database considered the times spent cutting the canvas, nets, and fabrics, as well as the five independent variables, resulting in 67 observations for the 6 variables. Finally, to estimate the T_s, the sewing database considered the actual sewing times used to obtain the product and the same independent variables were considered, resulting in 67 observations for the

6 variables. Note that, the cutting and sewing databases resulted in an equal dimension but considered different data.

3.2   Multiple Linear Regression Model

The Multiple linear regression (MLR) is used to model the relationship between a dependent variable (y) and multiple independents (x_i) variables. Although, this model is limited to expressing a linear function, it benefits from a well-developed mathematical framework that produces point estimates and confidence intervals for the regression coefficients [15].

A Multiple linear regression model is used to estimate each critical cost components, LMV, T_c and T_s, which are considered the dependent variables. In general, a MLR model with k independent variables is defined by the equation (1).

$$Y = \beta_0 + \beta_1 x_1 + \beta_2 x_2 + \ldots + \beta_k x_k + \varepsilon \tag{1}$$

Where Y is the dependent variable estimated by the model, β_0 is the y-intercept, $\beta_1, \beta_2, \ldots, \beta_k$ are the regression coefficients, $x_1, x_2, \ldots, x_k$ are the independent variables of the system, and ε are the residual errors.

Regression coefficients represent the mean change for each of the independent variables for a unit of change in the dependent variable, when all the remaining independent variables are held constant. That is, they represent how much each independent variable impacts the predicted value. In the case under study, the independent variables, $x_1, x_2, \ldots, x_k$, are quantitative characteristics of the products defined by the raw material area (a) used in the product project, the product weight (w), the product approximate volume (V), the total perimeter (P) of all parts that make up the product and the average height of the product (h).

4   Results and Discussion

The first step in analyzing the MLR model is to check whether the assumptions are satisfied, which are the linear relationship between the dependent and the independent variables, the independence of the residuals, the normality of the residuals, the homoscedasticity and the absence of multicollinearity, which means that the variables x_i are independent of each other. After this step, the equation that best describes the data is obtained, followed by the validation of the equation, analyzing the accuracy of the model. Each MLR model was implemented in R software.

To visualize how the regression model behaves with data never seen before by the model, it is necessary to make the separation between the training dataset and the test dataset. The training dataset is used to create the model, estimate the coefficients and analyze them, while the test dataset is used to validate it, as it includes new data for the model. For this study, training data comprised 80% of the total database, and consequently, 20% of these were used for testing. Initially, to obtain this separation, the data is randomized in order to guarantee a coherent distribution among the data. After randomization, it is possible to multiply the database by the corresponding percentages, 80%, and 20%, to obtain the training and test datasets, respectively. The size of the training and test datasets for each critical variable can be viewed in the Table 1.

Table 1. Number of observations in the training and test databases to estimate each critical variable.

MLR Model to estimate	Training dataset (80%)	Test dataset (20%)
LMV	66	17
T_c	53	14
T_s	53	14

4.1   Obtaining the MLR Models

Firstly, two models were developed, using the training database, for each critical variable. One model considers all independent variables $(a, w, V, P,$ and $h)$ and the intercept, while the other model considers the same independent variables, but disregards the intercept. The model without the intercept implies that the regression line starts at the point $x = 0$ and $y = 0$. This model was considered for analysis because it is expected that if all independent variables are zero, the dependent variables LMV, the T_c, and the T_s must be also zero.

Secondly, the variables selection in the regression model should include all particular variables that add independent information and avoid multicollinearity and excessive overlap [15].

For developing the regression model for each critical variable to be estimated, it is necessary to select the variables that are statistically significant for the model. In this sense, the method adopted was backward elimination [16], which starts with the model in which all variables are included, removing a single variable at each step if it is not statistically significant for the model based on the t-test. The null hypothesis (H_0) of the t-test states that the regression coefficient is equal to zero, while the alternative hypothesis (H_1) states that the regression coefficient is different from zero. If the p-value is less than 0.05 (significance level adopted), H_0 is rejected (in this case the variable remains in the model), otherwise, H_0 is not rejected (in this case the variable is removed from the model). After the execution of the backward elimination method, the most significant independent variables are kept in the models.

An important assumption of the MLR is the absence of multicollinearity, that is, a very high correlation between the independent selected variables, which generates an impact on the estimation of coefficients, generating redundancies and erroneous coefficients [17]. The multicollinearity can be measured by the calculation of the variance inflation factor (VIF), which precisely evaluates the correlation between the independent variables in a regression model. When the VIF exceeds a threshold of 10 which is a sign of a serious multicollinearity problem [18], it is necessary to solve it by eliminating one or more variables from the analysis [19]. Thus, after verifying the VIF values, it was possible to obtain two models for the LMV, (2) and (3), two models for the cutting time, (4) and (5), and two models for the sewing time, (6) and (7). The six models had only statistically significant variables and no multicollinearity.

$$\widehat{LMV_1} = b_0 + b_1 a + b_2 w + b_3 V + b_4 P + b_5 h \tag{2}$$

$$\widehat{LMV_2} = b_1 w + b_2 V + b_3 h \tag{3}$$

$$\widehat{T_{c1}} = b_0 + b_1 a + b_2 P + b_3 h \tag{4}$$

$$\widehat{T_{c2}} = b_1 V + b_2 P + b_3 h \tag{5}$$

$$\widehat{T_{s1}} = b_0 + b_1 a + b_2 V + b_3 h \tag{6}$$

$$\widehat{T_{s2}} = b_1 m + b_2 V + b_3 h \tag{7}$$

where $\widehat{LMV}$ is the estimated linear meters value, $\widehat{T_c}$ is the estimated cutting time, $\widehat{T_s}$ is the estimated sewing time, and b_k, $k = 0, \ldots, 5$ are the estimation of coefficients related to β_k, $k = 0, \ldots, 5$.

Then, the evaluations of the assumptions related to the residuals of the MLR models were made, namely homoscedasticity, normality of residuals, and independence of residuals. The Table 2 shows which models met these assumptions, by indicating "Yes" if each model met the assumption and by "No", otherwise. Only a single model for estimating LMV (2) and T_c (4) met all the assumptions, being considered to perform the estimates.

Table 2. Assumptions checking related to the residuals of the MLR models.

Model	Homoscedasticity	Normality of residuals	Independence of residuals
(2)	Yes	Yes	Yes
(3)	No	No	Yes
(4)	Yes	Yes	Yes
(5)	No	No	Yes
(6)	Yes	Yes	Yes
(7)	Yes	Yes	Yes

For estimating T_s, both regression models met the assumptions related to residuals, requiring a deeper analysis. Since these two models met all the assumptions and presented a very high adjusted R^2, a more in-depth comparison was made between the models, using the Akaike Information Criteria (AIC) [20] to select the model that best represents the data. The AIC estimates the quality of each model and can be used to compare regression models with different parameters [21]. The AIC predicts the relative amount of information lost for a given model, and the less information a model has to lose, the higher is its quality [22]. Thus, the best model should have a lower AIC value. The AIC value obtained was 199.4 for the model (6) and 213.6 for the model (7). Thus, it is possible to conclude that the model (6) has a higher quality in the adjustment, according to the AIC value.

4.2 Validation

Validation is an essential step in the MLR methodology, as it is necessary to verify, for this case study, whether the estimates obtained with the models make sense for strategic and decision-making purposes. Validation can be done by dividing the database into training and test data, and verifying how the model behaves in predicting the values of the test data [23]. Thus, the validation was performed using test data that the model did not use to be parameterized. These data are composed of the test database previously created for each variable, which encompasses 20% of the total observations of the database, obtained randomly and considering products from the three different families presented in the study.

Applying the MLR model defined for each case, predictions were made for the critical variables of the different products. Using the model predictions, the following error measures are calculated: Mean Absolute Error (MAE), which represents the arithmetic mean of the absolute errors, and the Mean Squared Error (MSE), defined as the mean squared error and the root mean square error (RMSE) [24]. These errors were calculated for the test and training dataset, shown in Table 3.

Table 3. Error measures calculation using test and train dataset for each model.

Model	Dataset	MAE	MSE	RMSE
(2)	Test	5.462	46.196	6.797
	Train	3.493	20.691	4.549
(4)	Test	0.241	0.122	0.349
	Train	0.354	0.221	0.470
(6)	Test	1.546	3.485	1.867
	Train	1.147	2.087	1.445

It is expected that the error measures for the test dataset will be slight higher than for the training dataset, as it was not used to build the models. It is observed that the models (2) and (6) present better results in the test dataset than the model (4), due to the fact that models (2) and (6) fit better to the data. Although, all models present reduced values of MAE, MSE, and RMS which generate a very small impact in terms of cost variation.

Additionally, the MLR models to estimate the three critical variables were presented to the company to obtain its feedback. Since the company is fully aware of its products, production processes, and raw materials, its evaluation about the models is the main tool to verify if the estimated results make sense and are useful. Results were analyzed for each case and verified for all product families. The feedback obtained showed that the results of the MLR models made sense for the company in estimating the amount of raw material used, the cutting and sewing times, corresponding to a very good estimates for the initial stages of the project. In this way, the estimates obtained could be used to calculate the three main critical costs involved in the product within the initial stage of the budget delivered to the customer. Hereafter the results of the selected MLR models are presented.

4.3   Results of the MLR Models

The results obtained for the models (2), (4) and (6) to estimate the LMV, T_c and T_S, respectively, are shown in the Tables 4, 5 and 6.

The independent variables along with the intercept are presented in the first column of these tables while the regression coefficient estimate for each independent variable and the intercept value are shown in the second column. The third column shows the standard error for each coefficient while the fourth column presents the test statistic, which is the ratio between the coefficient estimate and its standard error. As the selection of variables has already been performed, it is verified that the p-values for the independent variables are lower than 0.05 in all models.

The last two rows of the tables show some statistical information, in terms of R^2 and adjusted R^2 which characterize the quality of the regression model in terms of data fitting [23, 25]. Note that R^2 represents the percentage of variation in the dependent variable explained by the linear model. Additionally, the adjusted R^2 coefficient should be included to correct the R^2 value taking into account the number of predictors used in the model.

Concerning the model (2), all variables are statistically significant, except the intercept. According to [26], the intercept is maintained even with a p-value above the limit, in this case, it is not influential because it has a very low value. This model has a residual standard error (RSE) of 4.711. The model presents the value of R^2 equal to 0.9565 while the corrected R^2 value is equal to 0.9528, very close to 1, meaning that the model fits the data very well.

In the model (4) to estimate T_c, it is verified that all independent variables are statistically significant for the model (p-value< 0.05). The adjusted R^2 value indicates that the linear model explains 79% of the variation of the dependent variable, being a very relevant score.

Table 4. Results for the model of Eq. (2).

Variable	Coefficients	Standard error	t-value	p-value
Intercept	-1.75941	1.28062	-1.374	0.17459
a	0.2446	0.050077	4.817	1.03E-05
w	0.62836	0.07739	8.12	3.06E-11
V	0.29114	0.03495	8.33	1.34E-11
P	-0.02959	0.01036	-2.856	0.00588
h	2.56415	0.38602	6.642	1.02E-08
	RSE	4.711	in 60 df	
	R^2	0.9565	adjusted R^2	0.9528

Table 5. Results for the model of Eq. (4).

Variable	Coefficients	Standard error	t-value	p-value
Intercept	-0.350196	0.133626	-2.621	0.011652
a	0.019721	0.003287	6	2.34E-07
P	0.00418	0.001095	3.819	0.000378
h	-0.091292	0.043923	-2.078	0.042928
	RSE	0.4888	in 49 df	
	R^2	0.8031	adjusted R^2	0.7911

Regarding the results of the model (6) to estimate T_s, it can be seen that all p-values are less than 0.05, which imply rejecting the null hypothesis, taking into account the alternative hypothesis, that the coefficients of the independent variables are statistically significant. The adjusted R^2 value indicates that the linear model explains 85% of the variation of the dependent variable, being a high score.

Table 6. Results for the model of Eq. (6).

Variable	Coefficients	Standard error	t-value	p-value
Intercept	2.313278	0.432582	5.348	2.33E-06
a	0.074298	0.013403	5.543	1.17E-06
V	0.028768	0.009866	2.916	0.00534
h	-0.285469	0.127299	-2.243	0.02949
	RSE	1.502	in 49 df	
	R^2	0.8573	adjusted R^2	0.8485

4.4 Final Models

After the previous steps, the MLR models are defined for each variable to be estimated. The estimation of the LMV will be made from the model (2), the estimation of the T_c will be carried out from the model (4) and the estimation of the T_s will be made from the model (6).

$$\widehat{LMV} = -1.75941 + 0.2446a + 0.62836w + 0.29114V - 0.02959P + 2.56415h \quad (8)$$

$$\widehat{T_c} = -0.350196 + 0.019721a + 0.00418P - 0.091292h \quad (9)$$

$$\widehat{T_s} = 2.313278 + 0.074298a + 0.028768V - 0.285469h \quad (10)$$

It can be concluded that for each square meter of raw material area, the LMV increases, on average, 0.245 (t-value = 4.817 ; p-value < 0.01), the T_c increases, on average, 0.0197 (t-value = 6; p-value < 0.01) and T_s increases, on average, by 0.0743 (t-value = 5.543; p-value < 0.01). For each kilogram of raw material weight, the LMV increases, on average, by 0.628 (t-value = 8.12; p-value < 0.01). For each cubic meter of product volume, the LMV increases, on average, by 0.291 (t-value = 8.33; p-value < 0.01) and the T_s increases, on average, by 0.0288 (t-value = 2.916; p-value < 0.01). For each meter of perimeter of the product parts, the LMV decreases, on average, by 0.0296 (t-value = -2.856; p-value < 0.01) and the T_c increases, on average, by 0.00418 (t-value = 3.819; p-value < 0.01). And finally, for each meter of average height of the product, the LMV increases, on average, 2.56 (t-value = 6.642; p-value < 0.01), the T_c decreases, on average, 0.0913 (t-value = -2.078; p- value < 0.05) and T_s decreases on average by 0.285 (t-value = -2.243; p-value < 0.05).

4.5   Critical Costs Calculation

After presenting the final models, it is now possible to use them to estimate the variables and calculate their respective costs. Table 7 shows the cost calculation, with the real (y) and estimated ($\hat{y}$) variables, for one of the products that was presented in the test dataset of the three models.

Table 7. Critical costs calculation for a product of family F1.

	Critical variables			Unit cost			Cost of critical variables		
	LMV [ml]	T_c [h]	T_s [h]	LMV	Cutting	Sewing	LMV	Cutting	Sewing
y	30.3	1.0	7.4	3€/ml	10€/h	6€/h	89.5€	10€	44.3€
$\hat{y}$	43.2	0.98	6.8				128€	9.8€	40.6€

The costs were calculated by multiplying the values of the estimated and real critical variables by their unit cost. After these calculations, it is possible to visualize the difference between the estimated cost and the real one. Thus, the cost for the estimated LMV was 38.5€ more than the real value. The cost of labor related to the cutting time was 0.2€ less than the real value while the cost of sewing labor was 3.7€ less than the real value.

An Excel based tool was created to support the company as this software is familiar and simple to handle. The tool integrates the MLR models (8), (9) and (10) which allow estimating the critical variables of the product cost. The only steps that the company must carry out are to define the independent variables of the system (input variables), collected in the 3D design of the product, and to introduce the unit costs concerning the LMV and the cutting and sewing time processes. In this way, estimates of critical variables and their respective costs will be obtained. Confidence intervals will also be available, in case the company deems it necessary to make adjustments to the calculations.

5   Conclusion

The proposed problem was the development of a decision support system in the budget stage of ordered products in order to estimate the critical costs. The identification of the most critical costs was the most difficult, in the embryonic stage of this study. As a way of demonstrating the functioning of the decision support system, the case study included the results and validation for examples of new products, which were presented to the company.

Three models based on MLR were developed, using a training dataset, to estimate the critical variables of the cost of the product, that is, the LMV and the time of labor spent in cutting and sewing operations to calculate the respective costs in the budget stage of the project. The validation of these estimates was done using a test dataset, in which the models performed well, evaluated by the company. Additionally, the comparison of the values returned by the models with the real values of LMV and labor times spent reinforces that the models should be used in the initial stages of the project, enabling a more accurate budget. The proposed decision support system enables to test alternatives of different designs, changing formats, dimensions in order to reduce the amount of raw material used and the processing time involved in the product since it allows to compare costs and selects the most profitable alternative design for a given product.

The definition of a methodology to calculate and estimate the critical production costs of ordered products of a really specific industry in the textile sector is the novel contribution of this paper. Future works may improve this methodology with an enrichment of the database, to encompass all the product families produced by the company, even the most complex ones that are made up of inflatables for fun and sports competitions. Another way to further optimize the work is to develop a programming application to generate a more integrated tool between the database, the regression model, and the graphical user interface.

Acknowledgement. This work has been supported by Foundation for Science and Technology (FCT, Portugal) for financial support through national funds FCT/MCTES (PIDDAC) to CeDRI (UIDB/05757/2020 and UIDP/05757/2020) and SusTEC (LA/P/0007/2021).

References

1. Maciel, D.B., Rocha, J.S., Almeida, S.: A importância dos custos e da formação do preço básico do produto na tomada de decisões em micros, pequenas e médias empresas: um estudo de caso numa indústria de confecções em Sanharó-PE. Anais do Congresso Brasileiro de Custos-ABC (2005)
2. Colina, E., Peña, M., Morocho, V., Siguenza-Guzman, L.: Mathematical modeling to standardize times in assembly processes: application to four case studies. J. Indus. Eng. Manag. **14**(2), 294–310 (2021)
3. Mandolini, M., Campi, F., Favi, C., Cicconi, P., Germani, M., Raffaeli, R.: Parametric cost modelling for investment casting. In: Roucoules, L., Paredes, M., Eynard, B., Morer Camo, P., Rizzi, C. (eds.) JCM 2020. LNME, pp. 386–392. Springer, Cham (2021). https://doi.org/10.1007/978-3-030-70566-4_61
4. Park, J.H., Seo, K.K., Wallace, D., Lee, K.I.: Approximate product life cycle costing method for the conceptual product design. CIRP Ann. **51**(1), 421–424 (2002)
5. Weustink, I.F., Ten Brinke, E., Streppel, A.H., Kals, H.J.J.: A generic framework for cost estimation and cost control in product design. J. Mater. Process. Technol. **103**(1), 141–148 (2000)
6. Niazi, A., Dai, J.S., Balabani, S., Seneviratne, L.: Product cost estimation: technique classification and methodology review. J. Manuf. Sci. **128**, 563–575 (2006)
7. Ullman, D.G.: The Mechanical Design Process: Part 1. McGraw-Hill, New York (2010)
8. Pires, P.M.: Controlo e gestão de produção: o caso da Nestlé Portugal, SA (Doctoral dissertation) (2017)
9. Gelders, L.F., Van Wassenhove, L.N.: Production planning: a review. Eur. J. Oper. Res. **7**(2), 101–110 (1981)
10. Ben-Arieh, D., Qian, L.: Activity-based cost management for design and development stage. Int. J. Prod. Econ. **83**(2), 169–183 (2003)
11. Cooper, R., Kaplan, R.: Profit priorities from activity-based costing. Harvard Bus. Rev. **69**, 130–135 (1991)
12. Smith, A., Mason, A.K.: Cost estimation predictive modeling: regression versus neural network. Eng. Econ. **42**(2), 137–161 (1997)
13. Marchionni, V., Cabral, M., Amado, C., Covas, D.: Estimating water supply infrastructure cost using regression techniques. J. Water Resour. Plann. Manage. **142**(4), 1–9 (2016)
14. Sayadi, A.R., Lashgari, A., Paraszczak, J.J.: Hard-rock LHD cost estimation using single and multiple regressions based on principal component analysis. Tunn. Undergr. Space Technol. **27**(1), 133–141 (2012)
15. Marill, K.A.: Advanced statistics: linear regression, part II: multiple linear regression. Acad. Emerg. Med. **11**(1), 94–102 (2004)
16. Hocking, R.R.: A Biometrics invited paper. The analysis and selection of variables in linear regression. Biometrics **32**, 1–49 (1976)
17. Farrar, D.E., Glauber, R.R.: Multicollinearity in regression analysis: the problem revisited. Rev. Econ. Stat. **49**(1), 92 (1967)
18. Paul, R.K.: Multicollinearity: causes, effects and remedies. IASRI **1**(1), 58–65 (2006)
19. O'Brien, R.M.: A caution regarding rules of thumb for variance inflation factors. Qual. Quant. **41**(5), 673–690 (2007)
20. Profillidis, V. A., Botzoris, G. N.: Modeling of Transport Demand: Analyzing, Calculating, and Forecasting Transport Demand. Elsevier, Amsterdam (2018)

21. Scott, A.J., Hosmer, D.W., Lemeshow, S.: Applied logistic regression. Biometrics **47**(4), 1–20 (1991)
22. McElreath, R.: Statistical Rethinking: A Bayesian Course with Examples in R and Stan, 2nd edn. CRC Press, Boca Raton (2020)
23. Lilja, D.J.: Linear Regression Using R: An Introduction to Data Modeling, 1st edn. University of Minnesota Libraries Publishing, Minnesota (2016)
24. Hyndman, R.J., Koehler, A.B.: Another look at measures of forecast accuracy. Int. J. Forecast. **22**(4), 679–688 (2006)
25. Amoozad-Khalili, M., Rostamian, R., Esmaeilpour-Troujeni, M., Kosari-Moghaddam, A.: Economic modeling of mechanized and semi-mechanized rain-fed wheat production systems using multiple linear regression model. Inf. Proces. Agric. **7**(1), 30–40 (2020)
26. Batista, J.: Análise de Regressão Aplicada. ESALQ - USP 265 (2004)

Optimization in Control Systems Design

Analysis of Topological Characteristics Impacting the Allocation of Controllers in an SD-WAN Network

Vicente Padrenuestro[3] and André Mendes[1,2,3(✉)]

[1] Research Centre in Digitalization and Intelligent Robotics (CeDRI), Instituto Politécnico de Bragança, Campus de Santa Apolónia, 5300-253 Bragança, Portugal
a.chaves@ipb.pt
[2] Laboratório para a Sustentabilidade e Tecnologia em Regiões de Montanha (SusTEC), Instituto Politécnico de Bragança, Campus de Santa Apolónia, 5300-253 Bragança, Portugal
[3] Department of Systems Engineering and Automatics, Universidade de Vigo, 36.310 Pontevedra, Spain

Abstract. Finding a viable and optimal solution to the Software-Defined Networks (SDN) controller allocation problem in an open SDN network is a challenging task. In this context, this work was developed to expose a network's real characteristics, which may impact the choice of positioning an SDN controller. Furthermore, the experiments with the Pareto-based Optimal Controller-placement (POCO) tool and with the ONOS and Floodlight controllers are shown, which served as a comparison to assist in decision-making regarding the best positioning of the controller within the network. In summary, the results showed that not only the static aspects of the network should be considered, but also the dynamic characteristics and aspects related to the model and the purpose for which the controllers are used, factors that can impact the positioning.

Keywords: SDN · Controller placement problem · OpenFlow Controllers

1 Introduction

In recent years, since open Software-Defined Networks (SDN) emerge, using a protocol like OpenFlow to control the behaviour of virtual and physical switches at the data plane level, has gained a lot of attention and is earning more strength with the current scenarios. Thus, flexibility, programmability and scalability are some of the benefits brought by SDN compared to traditional network infrastructure.

In this sense, an important issue during the implementation of an SDN is the controller positioning in the network, i.e., deciding where to position an overview of the network, which allows managing resources in a simple and effective way, considering the use of programmable capacity to obtain efficient responses, with minimal latency between the nodes and the controller, reaching the maximum throughput between them.

The first approach on the subject was made in the work [4], followed by other researchers who added different issues in their observations. However, most of the research in the SDN area about the controller placement problem (*Controller Placement Problem*, CPP) focuses most of its efforts on the analysis of networks considering only their static characteristics data [5], such as considering geographical distances and latencies related to these distances.

Moreover, the network characteristics and the individual load caused by different nodes connected to a controller are still little considered in detail. Also quantifying how many controllers are needed, so that there is not a limiting point, and which controllers have the best performance according to the placement position in each scenario, are important issues in order to minimise the cost of network overlay and ensure good performance.

Given this, the main contributions of this work are in investigating, in a comparative way, which topological characteristics can impact the positioning of controllers in real SD-WAN networks, through a study on the use of the exhaustive method implemented by the POCO (Pareto-based Optimal COntroller) tool [5], which consists of, in a summarised way, calculating the geographical distances in relation to all $\mathcal{P}$ positions of topology, to connect the k controllers in a network containing n nodes.

Thus, the results defined by the POCO tool are compared in the case study of the *Ipê network*, of RNP (Brazilian National Network for Education and Research), considering its natural characteristics and also the analysis of ONOS and Floodlight controllers in a virtualised environment.

As a result, it is shown that in the studies about the controllers positioning, only the considerations about geographical distances and latencies defined by the POCO tool are not enough, therefore, the tests proved that the latency characteristics together with the bandwidth and traffic information, are also important factors in the positioning definition, in addition, the tests also showed that the aspects related to the model and the use of the controllers are important.

After this brief introduction, with thoughts on the theoretical background and motivation, the paper is organized as follows. Section 2 provides the related works, basic concepts and problems encountered when dealing with the placement controller problem. A methodology used and applied tools are presented in Sect. 3. Simulation and results are presented and discussed in Sect. 4, and finally, Sect. 5 concludes the paper and lists future works.

2   Related Work

Several studies have been carried out aiming to address the problem of controller positioning, other studies have worked towards comparing SDN controllers in an isolated way, focusing only on the controller performance. However, few studies have helped in decision-making to select a controller with the best performance, taking into account its proper position within a network with real characteristics.

The controller positioning problem in SDN architecture was first introduced by [4], where optimisation was performed in relation to the latency of the nodes up to the designated controller. In this paper, the author cites that for WANs, the best positioning depends, among other metrics, on latency.

In the field of the positioning problem, [4] shows the network performance by varying the position of controllers in the network. Finding the location and number of controllers that will be needed is a challenging task in a network architecture like SD-WAN.

In [6], POCO (*Pareto-based Optimal COntroller placement*) [5], a framework for finding the optimal controller placement so that the connectivity between the switches and the controller is maximized taking into account the capacity of the controller, is presented. First, the authors propose a brute-force algorithm, but it is valid only for small networks. Then, the authors propose heuristics to solve the controller placement problem in large networks. To this end, they use an algorithm based on *Pareto Simulated Annealing* [2]. In this work, the authors focus on maximising network resilience, where they considered the placement of controllers in a dynamic SDN network, in which there are latency variations between controllers and their switches. However, they do not consider the placement of controllers taking into consideration the dynamic network allocation.

The positioning needs to be chosen carefully. The *framework* POCO, has the ability to handle small and medium-size topologies, which provides the solution in seconds. However, for large-scale networks, the exhaustive evaluation needs a considerable amount of computational effort and memory usage. It is in this context that the search for a computational solution closer to real environments becomes necessary.

The work described in [9] performs a comparative analysis in terms of traffic capacity. The central objective of the work is to present an analysis of two controllers named Pox and Ryu respectively, in terms of traffic handling capacity. The Mininet emulator was used to emulate the environment of SDN controllers and thus monitor traffic performance. However, the work did not consider the real network characteristics, such as link capacity and occupancy.

As for the comparison of controllers, the work done by [11], one of the first comparative studies of SDN controllers, considered a limited number of controllers (NOX, NOX-MT, Beacon and Maestro) focusing only on controller performance. With the advancement of technologies, such controllers are already considered outdated.

The work described in [1] makes a qualitative comparison between two open-source SDN controllers, OpenDaylight and Open Network Operation System (ONOS). The study focuses on the Northbound interface of these devices.

More recent research, such as the one conducted by [8], studies and evaluates the performance of some popular open-source controllers such as ONOS, Ryu, Floodlight and OpenDaylight in terms of only latency as a metric, using an OpenFlow *benchmarking* tool called *Cbench*. In the paper by [3], a *survey* is presented with an in-depth survey of the SDN controller placement problem, which extensively classifies existing work from various perspectives.

The work described in [10] performs a qualitative evaluation of open source SDN controllers (MUL, Beacon, Maestro, ONOS, Ryu, OpenDaylight, Floodlight, NOX, IRIS, Libfluid-based and POX). The metrics evaluated are latency and throughput performed over a variable number of switches. The results obtained suggest that MUL and Libfluid-based have the best throughput performance while Maestro showed the best latency performance.

In this work, ONOS and Floodlight controllers will be compared and evaluated in two placement scenarios in an SD-WAN network, according to the methodology that will be presented in the next section.

3 Metodology

In this section, we show the base tool used, named POCO [5], an exhaustive method to compute the optimal placement of controllers, implemented in Matlab and available as open-source software, but considering the geographical distance and static latencies, only. Also, we used the Mininet [7] as an SDN emulator for performance analysis and to compare the impact of placement ONOS and Floodlight controllers in the operation of OpenFlow enabled networks. Figure 1, shows the RNP topology used in POCO's graphical interface.

The entire testing environment was configured on a virtual machine (VM), created with the Ubuntu 16.04.05 LTS operating system, containing the default kernel version 4.4.0-87-generic, 8 GB RAM, 8 processors and internal storage space of 30 GB. This VM was configured on a desktop with Windows 10 Home - 64 bits, Intel Core i7-9700 processor and 16 GB of RAM.

We choose the Ipê network, from RNP, which is the first Internet access network in Brazil and integrates more than 800 education and research institutions

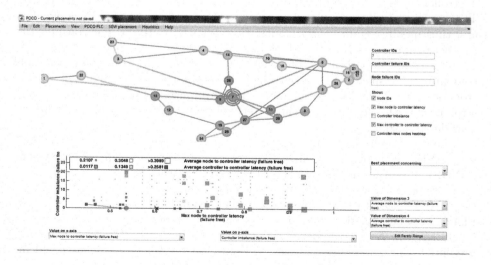

Fig. 1. Graphic interface of POCO.

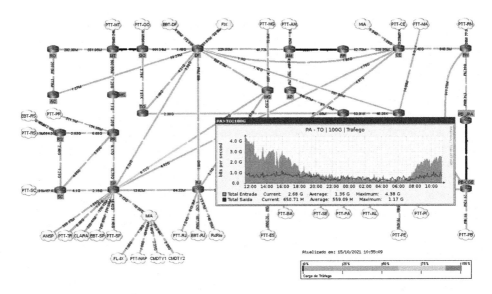

Fig. 2. RNP connections and traffic panorama.

in the country, with 28 nodes positioned in all states of the country territory for the experiments. All information used in the experiments regarding the connections between the links, bandwidth and incoming and outgoing traffic between the nodes were collected from the RNP's real topology traffic panorama, available on the institution's website, as a snapshot shown in Fig. 2.

Initially, a study of the main functionalities of the POCO tool for defining the controller positioning in an SD-WAN network was carried out. Besides that, ONOS and Floodlight controllers were also compared, which were evaluated in 2 placement scenarios, where in the first scenario only the geographical distances and latencies were considered (without link occupancy) and in the second scenario, link occupancy was considered. Then, all 28 possible positions for the controller in RNP's topology were evaluated, and these positions were defined as (i) optimal position and (ii) worst position. The optimal position is that where latency between nodes and controllers is minimised.

Thus, the placement positions indicated by Mininet were compared with the results from the exhaustive method tool – the POCO tool –, which only considers scenario 1 (without traffic). These comparisons considered not only static metrics such as the geographical distances between network nodes but also quantitative measures, such as data transfer, *jitter* and packet loss according to the scenarios.

4   Results

With the entire test environment configured, the tests were performed within Mininet, integrating the controllers in scenarios without traffic (scenario 1) and with traffic (scenario 2). Then, for each of the 28 RNP topology nodes, we use the *fping* command to obtain the latency data from the controller to the destination place in all the other nodes each time. Data gathered has a confidence interval of 95%. Results are shown with the controller positions – over these RNP topology nodes – on the x-axis.

To perform the tests in scenario 2, that considered network traffic (link occupation), the *iPerf* tool was used for measurements, considering the capacities of the links and the real traffic values extracted from the RNP's topology traffic panorama. After that, the test was also performed with the *fping*, in the same way as in the scenario without traffic.

This way, the results of the tests with the controllers in scenario 1 (without traffic), considering the best and worst position defined for the controller, were compared with the results obtained by the calculations of the POCO tool. Thus, these results could confirm the positions established by the POCO tool or show new ones, considering other factors such as the link capacity. The tests in scenario 2 (with traffic) showed the importance of considering metrics such as link capacity, data transfer capacity, *jitter* and packet loss, besides only the geographical distance between nodes.

For the execution of the tests with the POCO tool, the RNP's topology data was gathered during 3 different courses (November 2020, March 2021 and July 2021) after some changes were observed in the topology, for example, some links ceased or their capacities were extended, or other new links were established, creating, in fact, 3 different topologies according to these courses.

4.1   POCO

As the first results, it was calculated the placement positions defined by the POCO tool for the 3 topologies mentioned. For this, the fault-free scenario was considered, with only one controller (k = 1). In these results, it is possible to notice that the values of the average latencies are identical or very close for the same positions of the tested topologies. Therefore, it can be noticed that the results were maintained with the exhaustive method used by the POCO tool for the latencies calculations based only on the geographical distances. Thus, it can be concluded that even with the changes in the topologies links, not in the geographical positions of the nodes, the results did not show significant changes, that is, the distances and latencies were maintained, as shown in Fig. 3

Then, for the 3 topologies tested, position 7 (DF) was defined as the best position, with the lowest average latency, and position 1 (AC) as the worst position, with the highest latency. The position definitions are represented by larger circles in Fig. 4a and Fig. 4b.

In Fig. 4a, it is also possible to notice that the node defined with the lowest latency (7-DF), is also the most centralized node in the topology, therefore, the one with the shortest distance between two points, considering only the geographical distances between the nodes with established links. Also, it is verified that node 7 (DF), has a good amount of redundant links, which facilitates the connection with the other nodes of the network. From another perspective, the

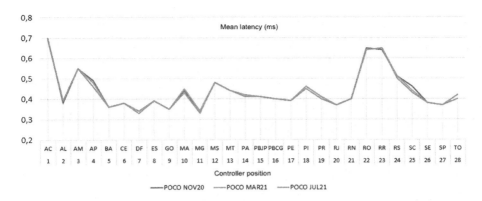

Fig. 3. Classification of positions – POCO.

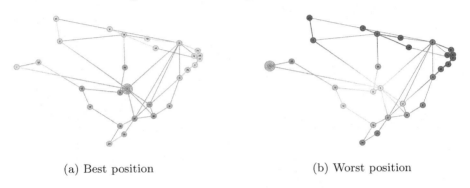

(a) Best position   (b) Worst position

Fig. 4. POCO.

reason for node 1 (AC) to have been defined as the worst position can be justified by its geographical position being the most distant in relation to the other nodes of the topology. Thus, it becomes another indication that the geographical distance between the nodes has enough weight in the decisions through the POCO tool, which may not be sufficient for the decision of the controller positioning in a real environment.

4.2 Controllers' Classification

After the classification of the positions by the POCO tool, the topologies were also tested in Mininet using the ONOS and Floodlight controllers, considering the 2 proposed scenarios. Also, tests were performed considering critical performance metrics, such as *jitter* and data loss.

Finally, the results of the scenarios were compared, thus realizing the impacts of such metrics on the SDN controller placement.

Scenario 1 – No Link Occupancy – We show the comparisons of the latency metric between the POCO tool and the controllers in the scenario without traffic. For a matter of space, only the results of the November 2020 topology will be discussed.

First, the tests with the ONOS and Floodlight controllers performed without occupation of the links (scenario 1), showed that both controllers considered position 28 (TO) as the best position, contrary to the choice calculated by the POCO tool, which defined the position 7 (DF) as the best position, shown in Fig. 4a. In the definition of the worst position, the test results considered position 22 (RO), whereas the POCO tool considered position 1 (AC), as in Fig. 4b. These positions are identified by the markers in the curve of Fig. 5.

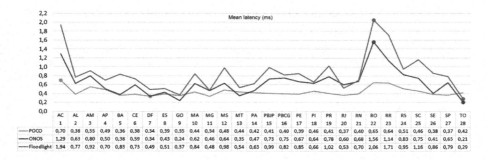

Fig. 5. Topology RNP Nov/20 – no link occupancy (scenario 1).

	AC	AL	AM	AP	BA	CE	DF	ES	GO	MA	MG	MS	MT	PA	PBJP	PBCG	PE	PI	PR	RJ	RN	RO	RR	RS	SC	SE	SP	TO
	1	2	3	4	5	6	7	8	9	10	11	12	13	14	15	16	17	18	19	20	21	22	23	24	25	26	27	28
POCO	0,70	0,38	0,55	0,49	0,36	0,38	0,34	0,39	0,35	0,44	0,34	0,48	0,44	0,42	0,41	0,40	0,39	0,46	0,41	0,37	0,40	0,65	0,64	0,51	0,46	0,38	0,37	0,42
ONOS	1,29	0,63	0,80	0,50	0,38	0,59	0,34	0,43	0,24	0,62	0,46	0,64	0,35	0,47	0,73	0,75	0,67	0,64	0,78	0,60	0,68	1,56	1,14	0,83	0,75	0,41	0,65	0,21
Floodlight	1,94	0,77	0,92	0,70	0,83	0,73	0,49	0,51	0,37	0,84	0,48	0,98	0,54	0,63	0,99	0,82	0,85	0,66	1,02	0,53	0,70	2,06	1,71	0,95	1,16	0,86	0,79	0,29

So, it can be observed that with the inclusion of the controllers in the network other parameters were considered, besides the distances, such as for example, the processing of the controllers and the processes of network discovery and definition of the best paths. This way, in the scenario without traffic, the positions defined as the lowest and highest latency contradicted the POCO definitions. However, in a more careful analysis, position 28 (TO), defined as the best position in the tests with both controllers, in spite of also being a central position, may not be the most advantageous in a real scenario, with several types of applications and traffic, where it depends on several other factors. An indication of the disadvantage of this position could be the small number of redundant links (TO-GO; TO-PA), which may generate a bottleneck in the network.

Another fact observed in the tests was that the ONOS controller presented better performance compared to Floodlight regarding latency, shown in Fig. 6. In this graph, it is possible to see that the results with ONOS showed lower average latency in most of the tested positions, which means that this controller had the best use in the processing demanded by each received flow in the scenario without traffic.

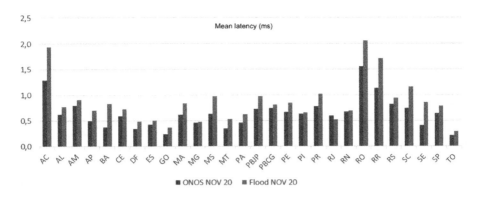

Fig. 6. Comparison of latency metric in scenario 1.

Scenario 2 – With Link Occupancy – In this scenario, the experiments were developed considering the traffic parameters of a real network that can significantly impact the placement of the SDN controller. Therefore, in this case, the results could not be directly compared with the placement defined by the POCO tool, because the tool does not consider the dynamic parameters characteristic of real networks. However, in the graphics presented in the results the definitions of the POCO tool calculations were included, just to demonstrate the differences and the importance of the considerations of the tested characteristics.

Initially, the experiments were performed with the November 2020 topology, with the occupancy of the links. The tests with the ONOS controller presented position 9 (GO) as the position with the lowest average latency and position 23 (RR) with the highest latency. Therefore, comparing these results to the tests with the same topology in a scenario without traffic, where positions 28 (TO) and 22 (RO) were defined, respectively, as the best and worst positions, one can notice that the definitions of the positions were changed, that is, in a scenario with traffic and an active controller in the network other factors were considered, such as, for example, packet traffic, *jitter* and data loss, besides the processing performed by the controller for the treatment of packet flows.

Furthermore, tests were performed with the Floodlight controller in the same topology, which also presented different results from the tests performed with the same controller in the scenario without traffic. In the first scenario, without traffic, Floodlight tests also defined positions 28 (TO) and 22 (RO) as the best and worst positions. In the scenario with traffic, position 9 (GO) was defined as the best position, which coincided with the definition of the test with ONOS in the same scenario, and position 18 (PI) as the worst position. Figure 7 shows the markers with the positions defined in the presented tests and the average latencies for comparison of the other positions.

Figure 7 also shows that the result for the definition of the best position (9-GO) in the tests with the two controllers was very close to the result of the position defined by the POCO tool (7-DF), however, if the position defined in the tests with the controllers in the POCO tool is simulated, that is, if the

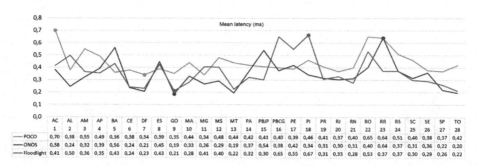

Fig. 7. Topology RNP Nov/20 – with link occupancy (scenario 2).

controller position is changed from position 7 (DF) to 9 (GO), other paths will be established, considering only the distances between the nodes.

As confirmation, the Table 1 brings the example of the comparison between two paths with the same origin and destination, having as origin node 9 (GO) and destination node 1 (AC). In this example, also observed in Fig. 8a, it is shown that the path with the smallest number of jumps (9-7-1) is the most distant, and for this reason, it was not chosen in the simulation with the tool, which defined the path with the greatest number of jumps (9-13-22-1), but with the smallest geographical distance. So, if the definition of the POCO tool is followed for the calculation of the best position, perhaps a path with the smallest number of hops between two points is not considered for the positioning of the controller, a fact that may not be true in a real network, where other factors must be considered, such as, for example, the routing protocol. For comparison, Fig. 8b shows the setting calculated by the POCO tool for the best position.

Table 1. Comparison of paths and distances.

Ways and distances								
Source	Dest.	Jump 1	Dist (Km)	Jump 2	Dist (Km)	Jump 3	Dist (Km)	Total jumps	Total dist.
9	1	(9,13)	764,35	(13,22)	946,38	(22,1)	437,81	3	2,148,54
9	1	(9,7)	161,40	(7,1)	2.234,77	–	–	2	2.396.17

Thus, these results also highlight the importance of considering other metrics, besides distances and latencies, for SDN controller positioning decision-making.

Finally, in this scenario, similar to the previous scenario, the ONOS controller also showed better overall performance with reference to average latencies, shown in Fig. 9.

Comparisons Between Scenarios 1 and 2. The scenario without traffic presented higher latency compared to the scenario with traffic. This fact can be justified by the network discovery and best path processes, besides the treatment

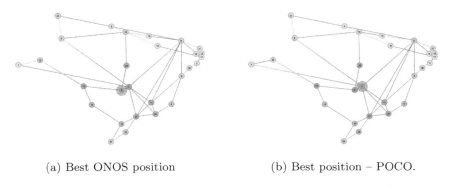

(a) Best ONOS position   (b) Best position – POCO.

Fig. 8. POCO.

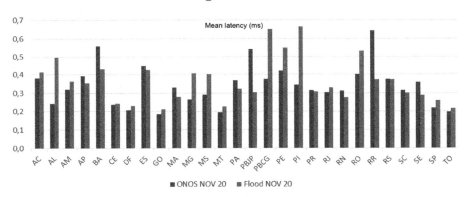

Fig. 9. Comparison of latencies in scenario 2.

of packet flows by the controllers, which caused this difference in the tests with the two scenarios. In other words, the way the controllers store data in RAM, in the *buffer* and in the *cache*, and also the processing demanded by each received flow makes the controllers have different performance. Therefore, these factors can also reduce the responsiveness of the controller and tend to degrade its performance.

In this sense, when a triggered flow is received by an OpenFlow switch and the destination is not found in its flow table, the switch forwards the first packet of the flow to the controller. Then, the controller after receiving the packet defines the forwarding rule to be used for the flow and forwards a message to the switch, which from then on will forward the next packets in the flow direction. Thus, it is expected that the first packet of each generated flow presents a higher latency (RTT – *Round-Trip Time*) compared to subsequent packets.

This fact occurred in the tests with both scenarios, however, in the scenario with traffic the network discovery and best-paths processes started with the first packets transmitted with the *iPerf* in the traffic generation phase between node pairs, that is, before the tests with the *fping*, unlike the scenario without traffic, that the network discovery and best-paths processes happened together with the latency test with the *fping* when firing the first flow, therefore, in this scenario the resulting latency was higher. Figure 10 shows the difference in testing with the ONOS controller in the November 2020 topology.

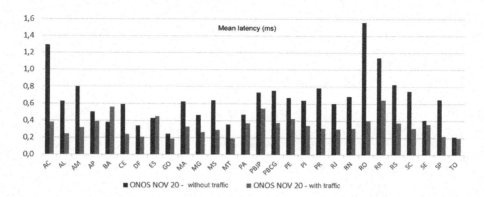

Fig. 10. ONOS – comparison of latencies in scenarios 1 and 2.

Furthermore, it was observed that the ONOS controller in the scenario with traffic did not show higher latencies in the first packets of the test flows with *fping* since, after the start of the traffic transfer with *iPerf* between the pairs of directly connected nodes, the controller maintained a connection to each Open-Flow switch and thus did not change the latency of the first packets of the test with *fping* and the switches were able to send and receive packets as long as there was space in the controller buffers.

The same tests were performed including the Floodlight controller in the surveyed topology. Then, in the same way, as occurred in the tests with ONOS, the tests in the scenario without traffic showed higher average latency than in the tests in the scenario with traffic. Figure 11, shows this difference.

Finally, with reference to the first packets of the generated flows, it is possible to conclude that comparing the two controllers in the tests with the scenario without traffic, the ONOS controller presented a worse performance in the process of calculating the best path, which generated higher latencies in the transmission of the first packets. However, it outperformed the Floodlight controller in the scenario with traffic, where it stabilised the connection with the network nodes after the generation of traffic for the occupation of links and did not generate delay in the first packets of the tests with *fping*.

Critical Performance Metrics. In this section, other tests are presented considering some critical metrics that can impact the positioning and also in controller operation.

The information displayed was obtained through the generation of network traffic using the *iPerf* tool, in the same way as performed in the tests with

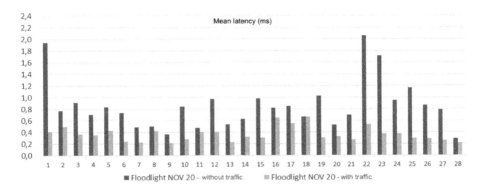

Fig. 11. Floodlight – comparison of latencies in scenarios 1 and 2.

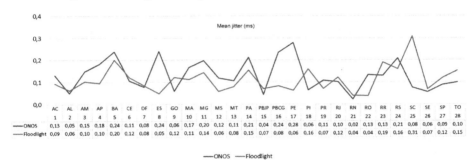

Fig. 12. ONOS x Floodlight – *jitter* metric.

scenario 2, described in Fig. 12. This traffic was generated for a total time of 60 sec, and after that, the generated information was analysed and compared, as will be presented in the next Sections.

Jitter. Briefly, *jitter* is the variation in latency, i.e. this metric can be defined as the measure of variation or "fluctuation" in the time it takes for a data packet to go to a destination and back.

Figure 12 shows that the ONOS controller had a slight disadvantage in the isolated comparison of the metric *jitter* with the Floodlight controller, as it presented a higher variation of the total delay, considering all the tested positions. Therefore, other factors should also be analysed.

Packet Loss. These experiments were run on fault-free scenarios, so only packet transfer losses were considered, and no failures on the links or devices were simulated.

Figure 13 shows the comparison between controllers on the measured packet loss. The results show that the ONOS controller had a lower average packet loss than the loss tested with the Floodlight controller.

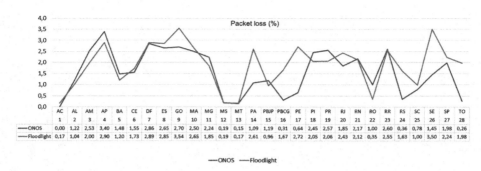

Fig. 13. ONOS x floodlight – packet loss metric.

In summary, in the comparison between the 2 controllers, the Floodlight controller showed less variation of the delay (*jitter*), however, higher packet loss.

Therefore, with the same amount of packets transferred in the two tests with the controllers, the fact that ONOS presented lower packet loss, can be justified by the better treatment given to the flow received in the controller, which is linked to its storage capacity. On the other hand, Floodlight presented lower *jitter*, which evidences the low storage of data in RAM, in the *buffer* and in the *cache*, however, this can cause higher data loss and can reduce the response capacity of the controller.

Thus, it is also noted that in addition to the metrics of distances, latencies and considerations of network traffic, it is also important to identify traffic priorities and decide which will be the most appropriate controller for this purpose.

5   Conclusions and Future Work

This work presented an analysis of the use of the POCO tool and simulation to shedding light on the problem of controller placement in SDN. In this context, it was described the implementation performed in the *framework* POCO that, in general, presented reliable results considering a static network topology, however, the dynamic characteristics of the network can impact significantly the choice of the controller placement. Also, it is possible to observe that the choice of a particular type of controller should be thought of in accordance with the desired purpose because its characteristics can also impact the placement position choice.

Also, considering the real characteristics of the tested topologies, the ONOS controller presented better results in both test scenarios (with and without traffic), regarding the latency parameter. In these results, both controllers diverged from the definitions and positions uncovered by using the POCO tool.

Finally, it is worth emphasising that efficient controller positioning tries to improve the performance of metrics such as latency, traffic priorities, loss and so on. However, the study for the controller positioning problem can still comprise several different solutions. Therefore, it is expected to extend the study to the development and improvement of tools for controller positioning based on performance measures of real networks, and that these tools can analyze the controller positioning problem in the presence of data traffic.

Acknowledgements. This work has been conducted under the project "BIOMA – Bioeconomy integrated solutions for the mobilization of the Agri-food market" (POCI-01-0247-FEDER-046112), by "BIOMA" Consortium, and financed by the European Regional Development Fund (FEDER), through the Incentive System to Research and Technological Development, within the Portugal2020 Competitiveness and Internationalization Operational Program.

The authors are grateful to the Foundation for Science and Technology (FCT, Portugal) for financial support through national funds FCT/MCTES (PIDDAC) to CeDRI (UIDB/05757/2020 and UIDP/05757/2020) and SusTEC (LA/P/0007/2021).

References

1. Bondkovskii, A., Keeney, J., van der Meer, S., Weber, S.: Qualitative comparison of open-source SDN controllers. In: NOMS 2016–2016 IEEE/IFIP Network Operations and Management Symposium, pp. 889–894. IEEE (2016)
2. Czyżżak, P., Jaszkiewicz, A.: Pareto simulated annealing-a metaheuristic technique for multiple-objective combinatorial optimization. J. Multi-Criteria Dec. Anal. **7**(1), 34–47 (1998)
3. Das, T., Sridharan, V., Gurusamy, M.: A survey on controller placement in SDN. IEEE Commun. Surv. Tutorials **22**(1), 472–503 (2019)
4. Heller, B., Sherwood, R., McKeown, N.: The controller placement problem. ACM SIGCOMM Comput. Commun. Rev. **42**(4), 473–478 (2012)
5. Hock, D., Gebert, S., Hartmann, M., Zinner, T., Tran-Gia, P.: Poco-framework for pareto-optimal resilient controller placement in sdn-based core networks. In: 2014 IEEE Network Operations and Management Symposium (NOMS), pp. 1–2. IEEE (2014)
6. Lange, S., et al.: Heuristic approaches to the controller placement problem in large scale SDN networks. IEEE Trans. Network Serv. Manage. **12**(1), 4–17 (2015)
7. Lantz, B., Heller, B., McKeown, N.: A network in a laptop: rapid prototyping for software-defined networks. In: Proceedings of the 9th ACM SIGCOMM Workshop on Hot Topics in Networks, pp. 1–6 (2010)
8. Mamushiane, L., Lysko, A., Dlamini, S.: A comparative evaluation of the performance of popular SDN controllers. In: 2018 Wireless Days (WD), pp. 54–59. IEEE (2018)
9. Rastogi, A., Bais, A.: Comparative analysis of software defined networking (SDN) controllers-in terms of traffic handling capabilities. In: 2016 19th International Multi-Topic Conference (INMIC), pp. 1–6. IEEE (2016)
10. Salman, O., Elhajj, I.H., Kayssi, A., Chehab, A.: SDN controllers: a comparative study. In: 2016 18th Mediterranean Electrotechnical Conference (MELECON), pp. 1–6. IEEE (2016)
11. Tootoonchian, A., Gorbunov, S., Ganjali, Y., Casado, M., Sherwood, R.: On controller performance in software-defined networks. In: 2nd {USENIX} Workshop on Hot Topics in Management of Internet, Cloud, and Enterprise Networks and Services (Hot-ICE 12), pp. 1–6 (2012)

A Hybrid Approach GABC-LS to Solve mTSP

Sílvia de Castro Pereira[1,3(✉)] ⬭, E. J. Solteiro Pires[1,2] ⬭,
and P. B. de Moura Oliveira[1,2] ⬭

[1] Universidade de Trás-os-Montes e Alto Douro, Vila Real, Portugal
silvia.pereira@ipb.pt
[2] INESC TEC - INESC Technology and Science, Porto, Portugal
[3] Instituto Politécnico de Bragança, Campus de Santa Apolónia,
5300-253 Bragança, Portugal

Abstract. The Multiple Traveling Salesman Problem (mTSP) is an interesting combinatorial optimization problem due to its numerous real-life applications. It is a problem where m salesmen visit a set of n cities so that each city is visited once. The primary purpose is to minimize the total distance traveled by all salesmen. This paper presents a hybrid approach called GABC-LS that combines an evolutionary algorithm with the swarm intelligence optimization ideas and a local search method. The proposed approach was tested on three instances and produced some better results than the best-known solutions reported in the literature.

Keywords: Multiple traveling salesman problem · Genetic algorithm · Artificial Bee Colony · Local search

1 Introduction

The Travel Salesman Problem (TSP) is one of the well-known studied problems in operations research and IA can be applied to solve many problems in many domains like routing and scheduling [2], collection of materials in a depot [19], printed circuit board drilling [4], construction of DNA sequences [1], transportation and delivery [12], WSN data collection and network connectivity [25], search and rescue [26] and precision agriculture [6]. Some problems require additional salesman (more than one) to be solved, so in those cases, mTSP is applied. In general, mTSP can be defined as a given number of n edges that will be visited by m salesmen only once, and the total cost (distance) of visiting all edges is minimized. The mTSP has many variants: the different characteristics of the salesmen, the depot, the city, the problem constraints and objectives [5]. This study focused on the variant single-depot where all salesmen start and return to the same node (Fig. 1).

A. I. Pereira et al. (Eds.): OL2A 2022, CCIS 1754, pp. 520–532, 2022.
https://doi.org/10.1007/978-3-031-23236-7_36

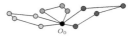

Fig. 1. Example of a mTSP solution

2 Literature Review

The techniques used to solve mTSP can be classified into exact, heuristic, and meta-heuristic algorithms. For small-scale problems, the exact methods analyze the solutions (paths) and then select the optimal solution. Over the years, many exact algorithms have been proposed and studied for solving mTSP. One of these algorithms is the brute-force that is one of the fundamental search algorithms. The way brute-force works is to try, one by one, the existing possibilities until all possibilities have been tried, then compare the results obtained and choose the smallest one [24]. However, this method is less efficient, even impossible for a large set of cities within acceptable computational times. One way to get around the complexity of the problem is to solve a relaxation of the same, not considering the restrictions [2]. This relaxation, known as assignment relaxation, can be solved in polynomial time. Another usual approach is the Branch and Bound algorithm which divides the problem into smaller problems to obtain the optimal solution. The algorithm uses relaxations of the initial problem to obtain a lower bound (LB) and admissible solutions of the problem initial to get an upper bound (UB). This approach can solve the mTSP problem more efficiently because it does not evaluate all possibilities [16].

When the problem size increases, its resolution becomes impossible using exact methods, so heuristics are used to find a solution in a reasonable time. A heuristic is a method created to solve a complex problem. Some well-known heuristics used to solve mTSP are k-opt [17], minimum spanning tree [13], Lin-Kernighan [10], Tabu-Search [3], and Simulated Annealing [18]. The importance of heuristic methods comes from the good average performance of these methods when applied to the handling problems (usually NP-hard) for which they are not known efficient methods that provide guarantees.

The research results in recent decades on the heuristics' performance and, in particular, on the characteristics that lead to the success of such methods led to the creation of generic strategies called meta-heuristics. The meta-heuristics can be classified into different types according to the approach used. Genetic algorithm (GA) is an evolutionary meta-heuristic based on the similarity between the process of finding optimal solutions and the theory of evolution of species by Charles Darwin [8]. In GA, each population element is called a chromosome, encoding a solution in the form of a sequence of symbols: a gene. A GA must also define a function that measures the fitness of each individual. The population is altered through two main operators: mutation, which modifies one of an individual's genes and has a low probability of occurring, and the crossover, which builds a new individual using only the genetic information of two other randomly selected individuals.

Another evolutionary algorithm is the Ant Colony Optimization (ACO), based on the behavior used by ant colonies to trace routes between the anthill and the sources of food. The main aspect of this behavior is a substance - called pheromone - which is secreted by ants during their travels, in order to indicate promising paths to other ants. The basic idea of this meta-heuristic is to use artificial ants, represented by concurrent processes, that trace paths in a graph whose vertices represent components of the solution.

Finally, the Particle Swarm Optimization (PSO) meta-heuristic is based on the behavior of swarms, such as birds in flocks. Algorithmically, a set of particles that traverse the search space presents random behavior concerning the individuality and sociability. The particle individuality is related to the emphasis given, in its movements, to the best solution already found by itself, while its sociability reflects the degree of importance to the best solution already found by your neighbors.

A hybrid algorithm is proposed in this work, combining GA and ABC. Then, to improve the finals results, a 2-opt and a move1 algorithm is applied. This approach is tested in multiple traveling instances. The remainder of this paper is organized as follows. Section 3 defines the mTSP problem and its formulation. Section 4 the genetic, artificial bee colony, 2-opt and move1-within algorithms are explained in more detail. Next, Sect. 5 presents the proposed algorithm. Computational results are presented in Sect. 6, followed by conclusions in Sect. 7.

3   Multiple Traveling Salesman Problem

The original definition of mTSP consists in a set of cities, m salesmen, a unique depot and a function called objective function. The goal is finding a set of tours for m salesmen who start in a city and return to the same city (depot). All cities are visited only once by a unique salesman. Because mTSP has been applied to different application domains, this gave rise to new variants of this optimization problem [5]. Some of those variants are mentioned below:

- Single depot/Multiple depot;
- Fixed depot/Mobile depot;
- Closed path/Open path;
- Standard mTSP/Colored mTSP;
- Single objective/Multi-objective.

According to the objective function, two main formulations of mTSP generally exist, which are [23]:

- MinSum mTSP: in this mTSP variant, the objective function consists in minimizing the sum of all salesmen tour costs.
- MinMax mTSP: in this variant, the objective function consists in minimizing the longest tour cost (such as in terms of distance or time) among all salesmen tours.

3.1   Problem Definition

Usually, the problem can be described as: there is a set of n number of cities and m number of salesmen. For the single-depot variant, each salesman is placed in the same city (depot), starts and takes a tour route, and returns to the starting city. Each tour route has a distance (cost) associated. c_{ij} is the cost associated with travelling from city i to city j. Each tour route should have no common cities. The aim of this problem is to minimize the total traveling cost.

4   Description of Algorithms

The proposed approach combines GA and ABC algorithms to create a first solution that will be improved by one of two methods that optimize the solutions at the path level: the 2-opt and the move1-within.

4.1   The Genetic Algorithm

Proposed by J.H. Holland in 1992, the well-known Genetic Algorithm is a meta-heuristic inspired by biological evolution [15]. The essential elements of GA are chromosome representation, fitness selection, and biological-inspired operators [11]. GA starts with some candidates solutions, called initial population, encoded in some form of a string. Then a function called fitness is used to evaluate each solution performance. The initial population is then selected to contribute to the population of next generation. The selection operator allows choosing some chromosomes for reproduction based on a probability defined on GA's initialization parameters. Furthermore, the crossover operator is applied to produce new children for the next generation by combining two parents chromosomes. Figure 2 illustrates this operation.

Fig. 2. Crossover with one point

Finally, the mutation operator is applied and randomly flips individual values of chromosomes with a usually very low probability. Figure 3 shows a swap performed between city 2 and 4.

Fig. 3. Swap mutation

4.2   Artificial Bee Colony

In 2005, Dervis Karaboga proposed the Artificial Bee Colony algorithm (ABC) to solve optimization problems inspired by the intelligent behavior of bees in the search for food sources. This algorithm is based on a model composed of food sources, whose positions represent the possible solutions to the problem, and bees (explorers, workers, and followers) represent the search agents for the optimal solution. In this algorithm, it is necessary to adjust some parameters, such as:

- The size of the bee colony;
- The maximum number of cycles;
- The number of project variables;
- The limit that allows bees to abandon or not a food source.

The main goal of this algorithm is for bees to be able to discover the food sources with the greatest amount of nectar and, among these, be able to discover the one that has the maximum amount, simulating local and global optimal solutions, respectively, so this algorithm clearly comprises a hybrid technique combining local and global demand. Initially, the population is created equally between worker and non-worker bees. The positions of food sources are randomly generated in a multidimensional search space using the formula:

$$x_{i,j} = x_{\min,j} + \text{random}(0,1)(x_{\max,j} - x_{\min,j}) \qquad (1)$$

where $i = 1, 2..., TP/2; j = 1, 2, ..., Q$. The function random(0,1) generates random values between 0 and 1. TP represents the population size and Q the number of project variables.

Explorer bees are, in this algorithm, responsible for the search and totally random discovery of new food sources. They perform this task without any influence from other hive mates. On the other hand, the workers, after observing the *waggle dance*, choose those that they consider being the best sources of food, memorizing their positions and sharing this information with the follower bees, which depending on their experience and the amount of nectar presented by the workers, decide which source they will exploit. Each worker then chooses a food source x_i to be exploited, generating a candidate solution according to the formula:

$$v_{i,j} = x_{i,j} + \phi_{i,j}(x_{i,j} - x_{k,j}) \qquad (2)$$

with $k \in \{1, 2..., TP/2\}; j \in \{1, 2, ..., Q\}; k \neq i$; and $\phi_{i,j}$ represent a random number between -1 e 1. The bees iteratively seek to improve the solutions found, moving towards abandoning the worst solutions. They evaluate the quality of the solution found based on the fit_i value given by:

$$fit_i = \begin{cases} 1/(1 + f_i), & fi \geq 0 \\ 1 + |f_i|, & fi < 0 \end{cases} \qquad (3)$$

where f_i represents the objective function. The probability of a bee being recruited to exploit a better source is given by the formula:

$$p_i = \frac{fit_i}{\sum_{n=1}^{TP} fit_n} \tag{4}$$

After all the bees have been distributed among the food sources, these sources have to be tested, verifying if the number of cycles is greater than a given limit defined during the initial parametrization. If this situation happens, the exploration of the food source is abandoned, and the bee becomes an explorer with the mission of discovering new sources, according to the equation:

$$v_{i,j} = x_{i,j} + \phi_{i,j}(x_{i,j} - x_{k,j}) \tag{5}$$

4.3   The 2-Opt Algorithm

2-Opt is an algorithm from the local search family. Local search methodologies like the 2-opt heuristic can be used to solve hard combinatorial optimization problems and produce good quality solutions for a large set of problems [20]. Initially proposed by Croes [7] for solving TSP standards, it is used to improve the founded solutions by removing two nonadjacent arcs from a tour and adding two new arcs while the tour structure is maintained.

4.4   The Move1-Within Algorithm

The Move1-within operator is a local search that consists of, per path, removing an edge and inserting it into the best position within the path. The best position corresponds to the path's position such that the edge insertion in this location produces the greatest reduction in the solution's value.

5   The Proposed Approach

In this section, the new approach GABC-LS is described. There are three essential steps: first, define the instance and salesmen used; second, define the GA control parameters and last, define the ABC control parameters. Then apply two methods of local search and choice the best value found. To use GA, it's necessary to find a method to represent a chromosome. For the mTSP, three representation methods are used: the one chromosome method [22], the two chromosomes method [14], and the two-part chromosome method [9]. GABC-LS used the one chromosome method. An example of our chromosome for $n = 9$ and $m = 3$ is shown in Fig. 4.

The chromosome length represents the problem instance number of cities. The values inside the array are generated using the nearest neighbor algorithm and represent the number of salesmen used. In the nearest neighbor algorithm, the salesman starts at a random city and repeatedly visits the nearest city until all have been visited. The chromosome in Fig. 4 represents one tour for each

TSP | 0 | 1 | 1 | 1 | 1 | 0 | 0 | 2 | 2 | 1 |
City: *0   1   2   3   4   5   6   7   8*

Fig. 4. Chromosome representation

of the three salesmen $T = \{0,1,2\}$. That means the first salesman visits the cities $\{0,4,5\}$, the second salesman $\{1,2,3,8\}$, and the third visits the cities $\{6,7\}$. After representing the initial population of GA, a tournament selection technique was applied, where chromosomes are probabilistically copied to the next generation. Next, the one-point crossover technique is applied to generate new offspring chromosomes, and finally, the mutation operator is applied with a very low fixed probability.

To evaluate each solution created in each GA iteration, the objective function (6) is called. In this function, S_j is a set of $|S_j|$ arcs travelled by the salesman j. I.e., to evaluate the fitness of a chromosome, the GABC-LS executes an ABC algorithm for each salesman generating a solution with path and distance. Next, a local search 2-opt and a move1-within method are applied sequentially to improve the solutions for each city's path. Finally, all salesman path distances are summed.

$$f = \sum_{k=1}^{m} \sum_{j=1}^{|S_j|} (1/m) * c_j, \qquad j \in S_j \qquad (6)$$

The flowchart of the evaluation phase is shown in Fig. 5.

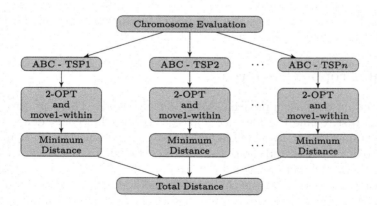

Fig. 5. Flowchart of evaluation phase for a problem with n salesmen

6   Computational Results

This new approach was simulated using Google Colaboratory, or Colab for short, which allows anybody to write and execute arbitrary python code through the browser and in an AMD Ryzen 7 with 16GB. In the experiments, all test cases were chosen from mTSP instances, which are a set of files that includes the exact location of each city by a pair of coordinates (x, y). The number of salesmen used in simulations is 3, 5, and 10.

6.1   Parameter Settings

The algorithm's performance depends on the appropriate selection the values of its parameters. GA and ABC used some parameters necessary to be defined before the execution started. First, the initial point (depot) for mTSP instances was chosen. For this purpose, the first point of the file was not chosen as the starting point. Thus, the alternative was to choose the point closest to the mid-point of the set of points (cities). For instance, with 51 cities, the initial depot was $(32, 39)$ and for 100 cities $(1819, 814)$. The selected parameters for GA are listed in Table 1 and for ABC in Table 2.

Table 1. Parameters for GA

Parameters	Values
Population size	17
Crossover probability	95%
Mutation probability	5%
Termination criterion	30000
Number of runs	30

Table 2. Parameters for ABC

Parameters	Values
Swarm size	50
Worker percent	60%
Explorer percent	40%
Follower percent	50%
Forager limit	300

The global test results obtained with the proposed algorithm are presented in Table 3. The first column indicates the number of cities n, in the second the number of salesmen m. The following columns are the best-known solutions found in the literature. All table values are found in [21]. All the presented results are rounded to the nearest integer.

Table 3. GABC-LS results and comparison with other algorithms

n	m	GA	GGA	GA2PC	TCX	ACO	NMACO	GABC-LS
51	3	460	924	543	492	449	447	**445**
	5	499	882	586	519	481	**473**	474
	10	669	1001	723	670	592	583	**563**
100	3	22959	79347	26653	26130	22241	**22051**	23332
	5	24559	70871	30408	28612	23901	**23678**	25006
	10	33136	89778	31227	30988	27981	**27643**	27930

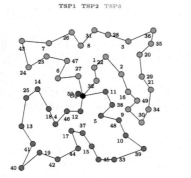

TSP1 TSP2 TSP3

Fig. 6. Tour for 3mTSP51

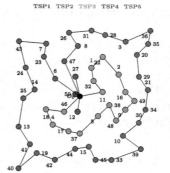

Fig. 7. Tour for 5mTSP51

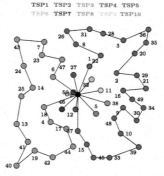

Fig. 8. Tour for 10mTSP51

Figures 6, 7, and 8 show the tours for 3, 5, and 10 travelers in 51 cities. For this small-scale problem, this approach obtains better results for 3 and 10 travelers and a similar result for five salesmen.

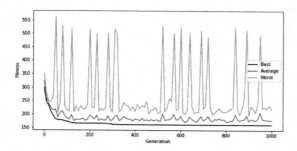

Fig. 9. Evolution of 3mTSP51 in 1000 generations

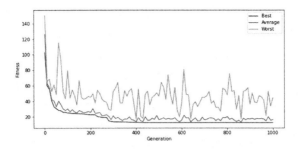

Fig. 10. Evolution of 5mTSP51 in 1000 generations

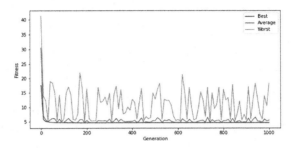

Fig. 11. Evolution of 10mTSP51 in 1000 generations

Figures 9, 10, and 11 show the evolution of objective function value for 3, 5, and 10 travelers in 51 cities, in the first 1000 generations. As would be expected using meta-heuristics, the fitness value drops very quickly in the first iterations of the algorithm. A lower fitness value will imply a lower total distance traveled. A zoom of only 1000 iterations was performed given the difficulties of interpreting the behavior of the algorithm for the total number of iterations, in a graph with those dimensions. In the case of the instance with 100 cities, Tables 4, 5, and 6 show the routes of each salesman for 100mTSP instance.

Table 4. Tour for 3mTSP100

TSP	Tour for 3TSP
1	0 →54→90→0
2	0→16→63→84→18→81→25→20→9→10→21→47→12→28→56→94→26
	→86→55→91→48 →2→99→30→35→60→44→92→4→70→39 →72→15→0
3	0→68→83→41→24→27→87→78→13→1→50→34→80→38→65→52→46
	→8→23→42→88 →11→89→17→93→32→96→97→49→69→22 →58→29→36
	→66→74→7→73→61→75→79→71 →57→31→77→98→45→33→67→14→64
	→85→95→59→6→40→82→3→5→19→51→37→62→53→43→76→0

Table 5. Tour for 5mTSP100

TSP	Tour for 5TSP
1	0→90→76→43→63→59→6→40→82→3 →5→62→37→19→51→35→30 →99→2→48 →91→55→86→26→94→56→20→25→81→64 →14→67→33→45 →98→77→31→57→71→79 →75→61→73→7→74→66→36→29→58→22 →42 →23→11→17→89→88→69→49→97→96 →32→93→50→1→80→34→38→65 →8→52 →46→68→0
2	0→84→18→47→12→28→21→10→9→53 →60→44→92→4→70→39→72 →41→78→13 →87→27→24→83→15→0
3	0→85→95→0
4	0→16→0
5	0→54→0

Table 6. Tour for 10mTSP100

TSP	Tour for 10TSP
1	0→63→59→84→18→25→20→10→55→91→48 →2→99→30→35→51→19 →37→62→60→92 →70→72→83→41→24→27→87→78→13→1 →50→93→32 →96→17→89→88→42→23→73 →61→75→79→77→64→85→95→0
2	0→4→44→53→5→3→82→40→6→9 →26→86→94→56→21→28→12 →47→81→14 →67→33→45→98→31→57→71→7→74→66 →36→29→58→22 →69→49→97→11→34→80 →38→65→8→52→46→0
3	0→68→0
4	0→43→0
5	0→39→0
6	0→15→0
7	0→76→0
8	0→16→0
9	0→90→0
10	0→54→0

7   Conclusion

This work proposed a hybrid method to solve multiple traveling salesman problem with a minsum objective and a single depot. To achieve this purpose, a combination of different algorithms was used: GA, ABC, 2-Opt, and move1-within. This approach was tested on two benchmark TSPLIB instances - mTSP51 and mTSP100 with 3, 5, and 10 travelers. The results confirmed that for one-third of the cases studied, the hybrid algorithm produces better results than the ones from the literature. It can also be seen that for ten salesmen and one hundred cities, the results are quite promising. In future work, we will further improve this approach and continue to study the hybrid techniques to solve some other large-scale multiple TSP problems.

Acknowledgments. This work is financed by National Funds through the Portuguese funding agency, FCT – Fundação para a Ciência e a Tecnologia, within project UIDB/50014/2020.

References

1. Agarwala, R., Applegate, D., Maglott, D., Schuler, G.S.A.: A fast and scalable radiation hybrid map construction and integration strategy. Genome Res. **10**, 350–364 (2000)
2. Angel, R.D., Caudle, W., Noonan, R., Whinson, A.: Computer assisted school bus scheduling. Manag. Sci. **10**, 279–288 (1972)
3. Basu, S.: Tabu search implementation on traveling salesman problem and its variations: a literature survey. Am. J. Oper. Res. **2**(2) (2012)
4. Calado, F., Ladeira, A.: Traveling salesman problem: a comparative approach by using artificial intelligence techniques. Centro Universitário de Belo Horizonte, Belo Horizonte, MG (2011)
5. Cheikhrouhou, O., Khoufi, I.: A comprehensive survey on the multiple traveling salesman problem: applications, approaches and taxonomy. Comput. Sci. Rev. **40**, 100369 (2021)
6. Conesa-Muñoz, J., Pajares, G., Ribeiro, A.: Mix-opt: a new route operator for optimal coverage path planning for a fleet in an agricultural environment. Expert Syst. Appl. **54**, 364–378 (2016)
7. Croes, G.A.: A method for solving traveling-salesman problems. Oper. Res. **6**(6), 791–812 (1958)
8. Darwin, C.: On the origin of species by means of natural selection, or the preservation of favoured races in the struggle for life, 6th edn. John Murray, London (1859). http://www.gutenberg.org/etext/1228
9. Falkenauer, E.: Genetic Algorithms and Grouping Problems. Wiley, New York (1992)
10. Karapetyan, D., Gutin, G.: Lin-kernighan heuristic adaptations for the generalized traveling salesman problem. Eur. J. Oper. Res. **208**(3), 221–232 (2010)
11. Katoch, S., Chauhan, S.S., Kumar, V.: A review on genetic algorithm: past, present, and future. Multimedia Tools Appl. **80**(5), 8091–8126 (2020). https://doi.org/10.1007/s11042-020-10139-6
12. Kitjacharoenchai, P., Ventresca, M., Moshref-Javadi, M., Lee, S., Tanchoco, J., Brunese, P.: Multiple traveling salesman problem with drones: mathematical model and heuristic approach. Comput. Ind. Eng. **129**, 14–30 (2019). https://doi.org/10.1016/j.cie.2019.01.020
13. Malik, W., Rathinam, S., Darbha, S.: An approximation algorithm for a symmetric generalized multiple depot, multiple travelling salesman problem. Oper. Res. Lett. **35**(6), 747–753 (2007)
14. Malmborg, C.: A genetic algorithm for service level based vehicle scheduling. Eur. J. Oper. Res. **93**(1), 121–134 (1996)
15. Michalewicz, Z., Schoenauer, M.: Evolutionary algorithms for constrained parameter optimization problems. Evol. Comput. **4**(1), 1–32 (1996)
16. Morrison, D.R., Jacobson, S.H., Sauppe, J.J., Sewell, E.C.: Branch-and-bound algorithms: a survey of recent advances in searching, branching, and pruning. Discret. Optim. **19**, 79–102 (2016). https://doi.org/10.1016/j.disopt.2016.01.005
17. Potvin, J., Lapalme, G., Rousseau, J.: A generalized k-opt exchange procedure for the MTSP. Inf. Syst. Oper. Res. **27**(4), 474–481 (1989)

18. Rahbari, M., Jahed, A.: A hybrid simulated annealing algorithm for travelling salesman problem with three neighbor generation structures. In: 10th International Conference of Iranian Operations Research Society (ICIORS 2017) (2017)
19. Ratliff, H., Rosenthal, A.: Order-picking in a rectangular warehouse: a solvable case for the traveling salesman problem. Georgia Institute of Technology, PDRC Report Series, PDRC Report Series No. 81-10 (1981)
20. Reeves, C.: Modern Heuristic Techniques for Combinatorial Problems. Mcgraw-Hill transfer from Blackwell Scientific (1993)
21. Soylu, B.: A general variable neighborhood search heuristic for multiple traveling salesmen problem. Comput. Ind. Eng. **90**, 390–401 (2015). https://doi.org/10.1016/j.cie.2015.10.010
22. Tang, L., Liu, J., Rong, A., Yang, Z.: A multiple traveling salesman problem model for hot rolling scheduling in Shangai Baoshan iron & steel complex. Eur. J. Oper. Res. **124**, 267–282 (2000)
23. Trigui, S., Cheikhrouhou, O., Koubaa, A., Zarrad, A., Youssef, H.: An analytical hierarchy process-based approach to solve the multi-objective multiple traveling salesman problem. Intel. Serv. Robot. **11**(4), 355–369 (2018). https://doi.org/10.1007/s11370-018-0259-8
24. Violina, S.: Analysis of brute force and branch & bound algorithms to solve the traveling salesperson problem (TSP). Turkish J. Comput. Math. Educ. **12**(8), 1226–1229 (2021)
25. Wichmann, A., Korkmaz, T.: Smooth path construction and adjustment for multiple mobile sinks in wireless sensor networks. Comput. Commun. **72**, 93–106 (2015)
26. Zhao, W., Meng, Q., Chung, P.: A heuristic distributed task allocation method for multivehicle multitask problems and its application to search and rescue scenario. IEEE Trans. Cybern. **46**(4), 902–915 (2015)

On the Complexity of a Linear Programming Predictor-Corrector Algorithm Using the Two Norm Neighborhood

Ana Teixeira[1,2] and R. Almeida[1,2(✉)]

[1] Mathematics Centre, University of Minho - Pole CMAT - UTAD, Braga, Portugal
[2] Department of Mathematics, University of Trás-os-Montes e Alto Douro, 5000-801
Vila Real, Portugal
{ateixeir,ralmeida}@utad.pt

Abstract. In this work the complexity of a feasible variant of a Linear Programming Predictor-Corrector algorithm specialized for transportation and assignment problems is explored. A $O(n|\log(\epsilon)|)$ iteration complexity was achieved by proving that the step size computed by the studied algorithm is bounded at each iteration by $\frac{\theta(4-3\theta)(1-\theta)^2}{n}$, where $\theta \in [0,1[$. Therefore, allowing to conclude that the analyzed Predictor-Corrector algorithm that uses the 2-norm neighborhood has polynomial iteration complexity and is Q-linearly convergent.

Keywords: Feasible predictor-corrector algorithm · Transportation and assignment problems · Polynomial complexity

1 Introduction

Interior Point Methods emerged from a paper due to Karmarkar [6] in 1984, where he presented a method for solving Linear Programming problems with polynomial convergence, what was considered quite a theoretical improvement when compared with the simplex method developed by Dantzig in the late 1940's [4]. As the name indicates, the method moves through the interior of the feasible solution of the problem in order to reach the optimal solution; that procedure contrasts with the simplex method that pursues the same goal by moving, in each iteration, from an extreme point to an adjacent extreme point. Primal-dual and predictor-corrector algorithms are considered the most useful algorithms within the interior point methods. The main difference between these two type of methods is in the way used to obtain the next iterate; the primal-dual methods do it in one step, computing one search direction, while predictor-corrector methods do it in two stages, first a predictor direction is obtained and, then, a corrector direction is computed. Due to its high efficiency, the predictor-corrector methods have been implemented in several optimization packages. Most of these implementations use versions of the predictor-corrector algorithm presented by Mehrotra in 1989 [8]. This algorithm had great success and is one of the most implemented and studied, for e.g., [1,2,7,9–11,14–17].

In [3] a feasible predictor-corrector variant of Mehrotra's algorithm special-ized for transportation and assignment problems is proposed. In this variant: 1) the predictor direction is calculated as in the primal-dual methods; 2) the one-sided ∞-norm neighborhood is used, and 3) no line search is needed to obtain a duality measure that is used in both directions. In [2] the authors not only prove the polynomial complexity and the superlinear convergence of this algorithm, but they also present the state of the art on this topic.

In this work a feasible variant of the algorithm presented in [3] that uses the 2-norm neighborhood is analyzed, in order to understand if a future imple-mentation of this algorithm and application to transportation and assignment problems would also be supported by its theoretical efficiency. It was possible to prove that this variant has polynomial complexity and, thus, is Q-linearly convergent, by obtaining a complexity bound of $O(n|\log(\epsilon)|)$.

This paper is organized as follows: In Sect. 2 the methodology is described, and some notation and concepts are presented. In Sect. 3 some technical results, as well as the main results are introduced and proved. Finally, conclusions and future work ideas are presented in Sect. 4.

2   Methodology

In order to prove the polynomial complexity of the variant of the algorithm pre-sented in [3] with the 2-norm neighborhood we need to introduce some concepts and notation, as well as to develop some technical results. In this section, we will introduce those concepts and notation, that will be used throughout the paper.

Let us consider the standard primal-dual pair of Linear Programming (LP) problems in the matrix form

$$\text{(P)} \min_{x} c^T x \qquad \text{(D)} \max_{u,v} b^T u$$
$$\text{s.t. } Ax = b \qquad \text{s.t. } A^T u + v = c$$
$$x \geqslant 0 \qquad \qquad v \geqslant 0$$

with $A \in M_{m \times n}(\mathbb{R})$, $c, x, v \in \mathbb{R}^n$ and $b, u \in \mathbb{R}^m$, where $\mathbb{R}^n$ and $M_{m \times n}(\mathbb{R})$ represent, respectively, the set of the real vectors with dimension n and the set of the real $m \times n$ matrices.

The set of the strictly feasible solutions of this primal-dual pair of LP prob-lems can be written as

$$\mathcal{F}^\circ = \left\{ (x, u, v) \in \mathbb{R}^n \times \mathbb{R}^m \times \mathbb{R}^n : (x, v) > (0, 0), \ Ax = b, \ A^T u + v = c \right\}.$$

The directions used by the algorithm developed by Bastos and Paixão [3] have their origins in Newton's method and can be obtained by using, at the k-th iteration, the system

$$\begin{cases} A\triangle Xe & = 0 \\ A^T\triangle Ue + \triangle Ve & = 0 \\ V^k\triangle Xe + X^k\triangle Ve = \mu^k e - X^k V^k e + \Lambda \end{cases} \tag{1}$$

with $\Lambda = 0$ for the predictor direction, $(\triangle x^a, \triangle u^a, \triangle v^a)$ and $\Lambda = -\triangle X^a \triangle V^a e$ for the corrector direction $(\triangle x, \triangle u, \triangle v)$.

Concerning the system in (1), the matrices $X^k = diag\left(x^k\right)$, $V^k = diag\left(v^k\right)$, $\triangle X = diag\left(\triangle x\right)$, $\triangle U = diag\left(\triangle u\right)$, $\triangle V = diag\left(\triangle v\right)$, $\triangle X^a = diag\left(\triangle x^a\right)$, $\triangle U^a = diag\left(\triangle u^a\right)$ and $\triangle V^a = diag\left(\triangle v^a\right)$ are diagonal matrices obtained by using the elements of the correspondent vectors in the diagonal, the vector e has all the components equal to one and

$$\mu^k = \frac{c^T x^k - b^T u^k}{\beta(n)}, \quad \text{with} \quad \beta(n) = \begin{cases} n^2, & n \leqslant 5000 \\ n\sqrt{n}, & n > 5000 \end{cases} \tag{2}$$

represents the duality measure.

For simplicity of notation, we omit the iteration index of the triples that represent the predictor and the corrector directions.

As previously mentioned, here we will analyze the complexity of a feasible variant of the predictor-corrector algorithm developed by Bastos and Paixão [3] that uses the 2-norm neighborhood, defined by

$$\mathcal{N}_2(\theta) = \left\{ (x^k, u^k, v^k) \in \mathcal{F}^\circ : \|XVe - \mu e\| \leqslant \theta\mu \right\}, \tag{3}$$

where $\theta \in [0, 1[$.

Algorithm 1 summarizes the procedure used by the variant of the method developed by [3].

In this paper we consider $\lambda_k = \min\{\alpha_p^k, \alpha_d^k\}$, as well as the following index sets, concerning the components of the predictor direction,

$$\mathcal{I}_+ = \{i \in \mathcal{I} : \triangle x_i^a \triangle v_i^a > 0\}, \qquad \mathcal{I}_- = \{i \in \mathcal{I} : \triangle x_i^a \triangle v_i^a < 0\}.$$

As previously said, some technical results are needed to prove the polynomial complexity of Algorithm 1. These results, as well as the main ones, are presented and proved in the next section.

3   Complexity Analysis

Lemma 1 is one of the technical results needed to prove that Algorithm 1 has polynomial complexity. This result allows us to obtain an upper bound for the non linear term involving the predictor direction used by Algorithm 1, while

Algorithm 1.

Require: $\theta \in [0, 1[$, $(x^0, u^0, v^0) \in \mathcal{N}_2(\theta)$ defined in (3), $\epsilon > 0$;

Set $k = 0$;

while $(x^k)^T v^k \geq \epsilon$ **do**

   (a) Compute (2) to obtain μ_k;

   (b) Solve (1) with $\Lambda = 0$ to obtain the predictor direction $(\triangle x^a, \triangle u^a, \triangle v^a)$;

   (c) Solve (1) with $\Lambda = -\triangle X^a \triangle V^a e$ to obtain the corrector direction $(\triangle x, \triangle u, \triangle v)$;

   (d) Compute

$$(\alpha_p^k, \alpha_d^k) = \max_{(\alpha_1, \alpha_2) > (0,0)} \left\{ (\alpha_1, \alpha_2) : (x^k + \alpha_1 \triangle x, u^k + \alpha_2 \triangle u, v^k + \alpha_2 \triangle v) \in \mathcal{N}_2(\theta) \right\},$$

   in order to obtain the primal and dual step sizes, α_p^k and α_d^k respectively;

   (e) Actualize the iterate by calculating

$$x^{k+1} = x^k + 0.9995 \alpha_p^k \triangle x,$$

$$(u^{k+1}, v^{k+1}) = (u^k, v^k) + 0.9995 \alpha_d^k (\triangle u, \triangle v);$$

   (f) Set $k = k + 1$;

   end while

Ensure: The optimal solution $(x^{k-1}, u^{k-1}, v^{k-1})$ is obtained.

Proposition 1 gives us an upper bound for a norm involving the non linear term of the corrector direction of Algorithm 1. Lemmas 2, 3 and 4 are results previously published, that we include in order to make this paper self contained.

Lemma 1. Let $(\triangle x^a, \triangle u^a, \triangle v^a)$ be the predictor direction of Algorithm 1. Then, for all $i \in \mathcal{I}_+$,

$$\triangle x_i^a \triangle v_i^a \leq \frac{1}{4} \frac{(\mu^k)^2}{x_i^k v_i^k}.$$

Proof. Using the third condition of (1) with $\Lambda = 0$, we have

$$\frac{\triangle x_i^a}{x_i^k} + \frac{\triangle v_i^a}{v_i^k} = \frac{\mu^k}{x_i^k v_i^k} - 1. \tag{4}$$

Since

$$0 \leq \left(\frac{\triangle x_i^a}{x_i^k} - \frac{\triangle v_i^a}{v_i^k} \right)^2 = \left(\frac{\triangle x_i^a}{x_i^k} \right)^2 + \left(\frac{\triangle v_i^a}{v_i^k} \right)^2 - 2 \frac{\triangle x_i^a \triangle v_i^a}{x_i^k v_i^k},$$

then

$$\left(\frac{\triangle x_i^a}{x_i^k} \right)^2 + \left(\frac{\triangle v_i^a}{v_i^k} \right)^2 \geq 2 \frac{\triangle x_i^a \triangle v_i^a}{x_i^k v_i^k}. \tag{5}$$

Therefore, using

$$\left(\frac{\triangle x_i^a}{x_i^k} + \frac{\triangle v_i^a}{v_i^k} \right)^2 = \left(\frac{\triangle x_i^a}{x_i^k} \right)^2 + \left(\frac{\triangle v_i^a}{v_i^k} \right)^2 + 2 \frac{\triangle x_i^a \triangle v_i^a}{x_i^k v_i^k},$$

equality (4) and inequality (5), we have

$$\frac{\triangle x_i^a \triangle v_i^a}{x_i^k v_i^k} \leq \frac{1}{4} \left(\frac{\mu^k}{x_i^k v_i^k} - 1 \right)^2$$

$$\leq \frac{1}{4} \left(\frac{\mu^k}{x_i^k v_i^k} \right)^2.$$

Now, we observe that the previous result is fundamental to the proofs of Proposition 1 and Theorem 1 and, also, that, in the sequel of the paper, we will consider that the predictor direction of Algorithm 1 satisfies the condition $\triangle x^{a^T} \triangle v^a \geq 0$.

In order to prove Proposition 1 we also need the following result (herein called Lemma 2), transcribed from [13, Lemma 5.3 (p.88)] and that presents a upper bound estimate for $\|UVe\|$.

Lemma 2. *[13, Lemma 5.3 (p.88)]. Let u and v be any two vectors in $\mathbb{R}^n$ with $u^T v \geq 0$. Then,*

$$\|UVe\| \leq 2^{-\frac{3}{2}} \|u + v\|^2,$$

where $U = diag\,(u_1, \ldots, u_n)$ and $V = diag\,(v_1, \ldots, v_n)$.

The next result presents an upper bound estimate for $\|\triangle V \triangle X e\|$ in terms of the duality measure.

Proposition 1. *Let $(x^k, u^k, v^k) \in \mathcal{N}_2(\theta)$ be the current iterate of Algorithm 1 and $(\triangle x, \triangle u, \triangle v)$ be the corrector direction of Algorithm 1. Then,*

$$\|\triangle V \triangle X e\| \leq A(\theta)\,\mu^k,$$

for $\triangle x^{a^T} \triangle v^a \geq 0$, and $A(\theta) = \dfrac{n}{16(1 - \theta)^3}.$

Proof. In order to prove this result we start by multiplying the third equation of (1) with $\Lambda = -\triangle X^a \triangle V^a e$ by $\left(X^k V^k\right)^{-\frac{1}{2}}$, obtaining

$$\left(X^k\right)^{-\frac{1}{2}} \left(V^k\right)^{\frac{1}{2}} \triangle x + \left(V^k\right)^{-\frac{1}{2}} \left(X^k\right)^{\frac{1}{2}} \triangle v = \tag{6}$$
$$= \left(X^k V^k\right)^{-\frac{1}{2}} \left(\mu^k e - \triangle X^a \triangle V^a e - X^k V^k e\right).$$

Taking the first term of (6) and

$$D = \left(V^k\right)^{-\frac{1}{2}} \left(X^k\right)^{\frac{1}{2}},$$

we have

$$\left(X^k\right)^{-\frac{1}{2}} \left(V^k\right)^{\frac{1}{2}} \triangle x + \left(V^k\right)^{-\frac{1}{2}} \left(X^k\right)^{\frac{1}{2}} \triangle v = D^{-1} \triangle x + D \triangle v.$$

Let us denote

$$w_1 = D^{-1} \triangle x, \quad w_2 = D \triangle v, \quad W_1 = \mathrm{diag}(w_1), \quad W_2 = \mathrm{diag}(w_2).$$

Using Lemma 2, follows

$$\|W_1 W_2 e\| = \|\triangle V \triangle X e\|$$

$$\leqslant 2^{-\frac{3}{2}} \|w_1 + w_2\|^2$$

$$= 2^{-\frac{3}{2}} \left\| \left(X^k V^k\right)^{-\frac{1}{2}} \left(\mu^k e - \triangle X^a \triangle V^a e - X^k V^k e\right) \right\|^2$$

$$\leqslant 2^{-\frac{3}{2}} \left(\left\| \left(X^k V^k\right)^{-\frac{1}{2}} \left(\mu^k e - X^k V^k e\right) \right\| + \left\| \left(-X^k V^k\right)^{-\frac{1}{2}} \triangle X^a \triangle V^a e \right\| \right)^2$$

$$\leqslant 2^{-\frac{3}{2}} \left(\left(\sum_{i \in \mathcal{I}} \frac{1}{x_i^k v_i^k} \right)^{\frac{1}{2}} \left\| X^k V^k e - \mu^k e \right\| + \left(\sum_{i \in \mathcal{I}} \frac{(\triangle x_i^a \triangle v_i^a)^2}{x_i^k v_i^k} \right)^{\frac{1}{2}} \right)^2.$$

Since $(x^k, u^k, v^k) \in \mathcal{N}_2(\theta)$, then $\left\| X^k V^k e - \mu^k e \right\| \leqslant \theta \mu^k$. Additionally, using Lemma 1, we get

$$\|W_1 W_2 e\| = \|\triangle V \triangle X e\|$$

$$\leqslant 2^{-\frac{3}{2}} \left(\theta \mu^k \left(\sum_{i \in \mathcal{I}} \frac{1}{x_i^k v_i^k} \right)^{\frac{1}{2}} + \frac{(\mu^k)^2}{4} \left(\sum_{i \in \mathcal{I}} \frac{1}{(x_i^k v_i^k)^3} \right)^{\frac{1}{2}} \right)^2.$$

Taking $\min_i \{x_i^k v_i^k\} \geqslant (1 - \theta)\mu^k$, we have

$$\|W_1 W_2 e\| = \|\triangle V \triangle X e\|$$

$$\leqslant 2^{-\frac{3}{2}} \left(\theta \mu^k \left(\sum_{i \in \mathcal{I}} \frac{1}{x_i^k v_i^k} \right)^{\frac{1}{2}} + \frac{(\mu^k)^2}{4} \left(\sum_{i \in \mathcal{I}} \frac{1}{(x_i^k v_i^k)^3} \right)^{\frac{1}{2}} \right)^2$$

$$\leqslant 2^{-\frac{3}{2}} \left(\theta \left(\frac{n\mu^k}{1-\theta} \right)^{\frac{1}{2}} + \frac{(\mu^k)^{\frac{1}{2}}}{4} \left(\frac{n}{(1-\theta)^3} \right)^{\frac{1}{2}} \right)^2$$

$$\leqslant 2^{-\frac{3}{2}} \frac{n}{16(1-\theta)^3} \left(4\theta(1-\theta) + 1 \right)^2 \mu^k$$

$$\leqslant \frac{n}{32(1-\theta)^3} \left(4\theta - 4\theta^2 + 1 \right)^2 \mu^k.$$

Since $0 \leqslant \theta < 1$ and the function $f(\theta) = 4\theta - 4\theta^2 + 1$ has a minimum at $\theta = \frac{1}{2}$, then

$$1 \leqslant (4\theta - 4\theta^2 + 1)^2 \leqslant 4.$$

Therefore,

$$\|W_1 W_2 e\| \leqslant \frac{n}{32(1-\theta)^3} \left(4\theta - 4\theta^2 + 1 \right)^2 \mu^k$$

$$\leqslant \frac{n}{16(1-\theta)^3} \mu^k.$$

The next result, proved in [12], relates the duality measure of the next iterate of Algorithm 1 with the duality measure of its current iterate.

Lemma 3. *Consider μ_k defined in (2). Then,*

$$\mu^{k+1} = \left(1 - \delta_k(\lambda_k) \right) \mu^k$$

where

$$\delta_k(\lambda_k) = \lambda_k \left(1 - \frac{n}{\beta(n)} + \frac{\triangle v^{aT} \triangle x^a}{v^{kT} x^k} \right).$$

The previous results allows us to obtain an upper bound for the steplength taken by Algorithm 1, as shown in the following theorem.

Theorem 1. *Consider that the current iterate of Algorithm 1, (x^k, u^k, v^k), is in $\mathcal{N}_2(\theta)$. Suppose that $(\triangle x^a, \triangle u^a, \triangle v^a)$ is the solution of (1) with $\Lambda = 0$ satisfying $\triangle x^{aT} \triangle v^a \geqslant 0$ and that $(\triangle x, \triangle u, \triangle v)$ is the solution of (1) with $\Lambda = -\triangle X^a \triangle V^a e$. Then, the maximum step size, λ_k, that keeps the next iterate of Algorithm 1, $(x^{k+1}, u^{k+1}, v^{k+1})$, in $\mathcal{N}_2(\theta)$, satisfies*

$$\lambda_k \leqslant \frac{\theta(4 - 3\theta)(1 - \theta)^2}{n}, \qquad k \geqslant 0, \quad n \geqslant 2.$$

Proof. We aim to find the maximum steplength $\lambda_k \geqslant 0$ that guarantees that $(x^{k+1}, u^{k+1}, v^{k+1}) \in \mathcal{N}_2(\theta)$.

Consider $i \in \mathcal{I}_+$ (we observe that $\mathcal{I}_+ \neq \emptyset$, because $\triangle x^{aT} \triangle v^a \geqslant 0$). Thus,

$$x_i^{k+1} v_i^{k+1} = x_i^k v_i^k + \lambda_k \left(\mu^k - x_i^k v_i^k - \triangle x_i^a \triangle v_i^a \right) + \lambda_k^2 \triangle x_i \triangle v_i$$

$$= (1 - \lambda_k) x_i^k v_i^k + \lambda_k \mu^k - \lambda_k \triangle x_i^a \triangle v_i^a + \lambda_k^2 \triangle x_i \triangle v_i.$$

To maintain the next iterate of Algorithm 1, $(x^{k+1}, u^{k+1}, v^{k+1})$, in $\mathcal{N}_2(\theta)$, we consider $x_i^{k+1} v_i^{k+1} - \mu^{k+1}$ and using Lemma 3, we get

$$x_i^{k+1} v_i^{k+1} - \mu^{k+1} = x_i^k v_i^k (1 - \lambda_k) + \lambda_k \mu^k - \lambda_k \triangle x_i^a \triangle v_i^a + \lambda_k^2 \triangle x_i \triangle v_i$$

$$- \mu^k \left(1 - \lambda_k \left(1 - \frac{n}{\beta(n)} + \frac{\triangle v^{aT} \triangle x^a}{v^{kT} x^k} \right) \right)$$

$$= (x_i^k v_i^k - \mu^k)(1 - \lambda_k) - \lambda_k \triangle x_i^a \triangle v_i^a + \lambda_k^2 \triangle x_i \triangle v_i$$

$$+ \mu^k \lambda_k \left(1 + \frac{\triangle v^{aT} \triangle x^a}{v^{kT} x^k} - \frac{n}{\beta(n)} \right)$$

$$= (x_i^k v_i^k - \mu^k) \left(1 - \lambda_k \left(1 + \frac{\triangle x_i^a \triangle v_i^a}{x_i^k v_i^k - \mu^k} - \lambda_k \frac{\triangle x_i \triangle v_i}{x_i^k v_i^k - \mu^k} \right.\right.$$

$$\left.\left. - \frac{\mu^k}{x_i^k v_i^k - \mu^k} \left(1 + \frac{\triangle v^{aT} \triangle x^a}{v^{kT} x^k} - \frac{n}{\beta(n)} \right) \right) \right).$$

Therefore, in order to obtain the maximum step size, λ_k, that keeps the next iterate of Algorithm 1, $(x^{k+1}, u^{k+1}, v^{k+1})$, in $\mathcal{N}_2(\theta)$, we consider

$$1 + \frac{\triangle x_i^a \triangle v_i^a}{x_i^k v_i^k - \mu^k} - \lambda_k \frac{\triangle x_i \triangle v_i}{x_i^k v_i^k - \mu^k} - \frac{\mu^k}{x_i^k v_i^k - \mu^k} \left(1 + \frac{\triangle v^{aT} \triangle x^a}{v^{kT} x^k} - \frac{n}{\beta(n)} \right) \geqslant$$

$$\geqslant 1 + \frac{\triangle v^{aT} \triangle x^a}{v^{kT} x^k} - \frac{n}{\beta(n)}$$

which is equivalent to

$$\triangle x_i^a \triangle v_i^a - \lambda_k \triangle x_i \triangle v_i - \mu^k \geqslant (x_i^k v_i^k) \left(\frac{\triangle v^{aT} \triangle x^a}{v^{kT} x^k} - \frac{n}{\beta(n)} \right)$$

and, consequently, we obtain

$$\triangle x_i^a \triangle v_i^a + (x_i^k v_i^k) \left(-\frac{\triangle v^{aT} \triangle x^a}{v^{kT} x^k} + \frac{n}{\beta(n)} \right) - \mu^k \geqslant \lambda_k \triangle x_i \triangle v_i.$$

Due to $\dfrac{\triangle v^{aT} \triangle x^a}{v^{kT} x^k} \geqslant 0$ and $\left(-\dfrac{\triangle v^{aT} \triangle x^a}{v^{kT} x^k} + \dfrac{n}{\beta(n)} \right) \leqslant 1$, we have

$$\triangle x_i^a \triangle v_i^a + x_i^k v_i^k - \mu^k \geqslant \lambda_k \triangle x_i \triangle v_i. \tag{7}$$

Furthermore, by Lemma 1 and $\min_i \{x_i^k v_i^k\} \geqslant (1-\theta)\mu^k$, we get

$$\triangle x_i^a \triangle v_i^a \leqslant \frac{1}{4} \frac{\left(\mu^k - x_i^k v_i^k \right)^2}{x_i^k v_i^k}$$

$$\leqslant \frac{\left(\mu^k - x_i^k v_i^k \right)^2}{4(1-\theta)\mu^k}.$$

Substituting in (7) and as $x_i^k v_i^k - \mu^k > 0$, we obtain

$$\frac{\left(\mu^k - x_i^k v_i^k \right)^2}{4(1-\theta)\mu^k} + (x_i^k v_i^k - \mu^k) \geqslant \lambda_k \triangle x_i \triangle v_i.$$

Using $(x_i^k v_i^k - \mu^k)^2 \leqslant \|X^k V^k e - \mu^k e\|^2 \leqslant (\theta\mu^k)^2$ as well as $x_i^k v_i^k - \mu^k \leqslant \theta\mu^k$, we get

$$\frac{\theta^2}{4(1-\theta)} \mu^k + \theta\mu^k \geqslant \lambda_k \triangle x_i \triangle v_i.$$

From Proposition 1, we have

$$\triangle x_i \triangle v_i \leqslant \|\triangle V \triangle X e\|$$

$$\leqslant \frac{n}{16(1-\theta)^3} \mu^k.$$

Thus,

$$\lambda_k \triangle x_i \triangle v_i \leqslant \frac{n}{16(1-\theta)^3} \, \mu^k \lambda_k$$

$$\leqslant \frac{\theta(4-3\theta)}{4(1-\theta)} \mu^k.$$

Therefore, obtaining

$$\lambda_k \leqslant \frac{\theta(4-3\theta)(1-\theta)^2}{n}, \qquad k \geqslant 0, \quad n \geqslant 2.$$

Theorem 3.2 of [13, p. 61] (that we transcribe and rename as Lemma 4) is needed to prove Theorem 2, which allows us to conclude that Algorithm 1 has polynomial complexity, by indicating an upper bound for the number of iterations in which this algorithm stops.

Lemma 4. *[13, Theorem 3.2 (p.61)] Let $\epsilon \in \,]0,1[$ be given. Suppose that our algorithm for solving the Karush-Kuhn-Tucker conditions associated with the standard primal-dual pair of Linear Programming problems generates a sequence of iterates that satisfies*

$$\mu^{k+1} \leqslant \left(1 - \frac{\delta}{n^\omega}\right)\mu^k, \qquad k = 0, 1, \dots$$

for some positive constants δ and ω. Suppose too that the starting point (x^0, u^0, v^0) satisfies

$$\mu^0 \leqslant \frac{1}{\epsilon^\kappa}$$

for some positive constant κ. Then there exists an index K with

$$K = O\left(n^\omega \,|\log(\epsilon)|\right)$$

such that

$$\mu^k \leqslant \epsilon \qquad for \ all \ \kappa \geqslant K.$$

The next result establishes an upper bound for the number of iterations in which Algorithm 1 stops, therefore allowing us to conclude that this feasible version of the algorithm developed by Bastos and Paixão that uses the 2-norm neighborhood is Q-linear convergent.

Theorem 2. *Let $\epsilon \in \,]0,1[$ and $\triangle x^{a\,T} \triangle v^a \geqslant 0$. Algorithm 1 stops after at most $O(n|\log(\epsilon)|)$ iterations with a solution for which $x^T v \leqslant \epsilon$.*

Proof. Considering the definition of μ^k presented in (2) and using Lemma 3, we have

$$\mu^{k+1} = \left(1 - \delta_k(\lambda_k)\right)\mu^k,$$

where

$$\delta_k(\lambda_k) = \lambda_k \left(1 - \frac{n}{\beta(n)} + \frac{\triangle v^{aT}\triangle x^a}{v^{kT}x^k}\right).$$

In order to obtain an upper bound for μ^{k+1} we need to determine an lower bound for $\delta_k(\lambda_k)$. Since $\triangle x^{aT}\triangle v^a \geqslant 0$, then

$$\delta_k(\lambda_k) \geqslant \lambda_k \left(1 - \frac{n}{\beta(n)}\right).$$

Furthermore, since $n\sqrt{n} \leqslant \beta(n) \leqslant n^2$, we have

$$\delta_k(\lambda_k) \geqslant \lambda_k \left(1 - \frac{1}{\sqrt{n}}\right).$$

Using Theorem 1, for $n \geqslant 2$ and

$$\lambda_k = \frac{\theta(4 - 3\theta)(1 - \theta)^2}{n},$$

we obtain

$$\mu^{k+1} \leqslant \left(1 - \lambda_k \left(1 - \frac{1}{\sqrt{n}}\right)\right)\mu^k$$

$$\leqslant \left(1 - \frac{\theta(4 - 3\theta)(1 - \theta)^2}{n}\right)\mu^k.$$

Finally, applying Lemma 4 we complete the proof.

We end this section by synthesizing the path taken to obtain our final result. Lemma 1, that gives us an upper bound estimation for a quantity involving the non linear term of the predictor direction of Algorithm 1, jointly with Lemma 2 [13, Lemma 5.3 (p.88)] allow us to get an upper bound for a norm involving the non linear term of the corrector direction of Algorithm 1, as stated in Proposition 1. Then, Lemma 3, that relates the duality gaps of two consecutive iterates, together with Lemma 1 and Proposition 1 allow us to obtain an upper bound to the step length taken by Algorithm 1, as can be seen in Theorem 1. Finally, we use this theorem combined with Lemma 4 [13, Theorem 3.2 (p.61)] to achieve an upper bound for the number of iterations in which Algorithm 1 stops (presented in Theorem 2), thus proving its polynomial complexity.

4   Conclusions

Most researchers use the numerical performance of an algorithm as its measure of efficiency, because, most of the times, the worst-case complexity bounds obtained for interior-point algorithms are too conservative or too far from average cases. Nonetheless, the worst-case complexity of interior-point algorithms has been studied by several authors (for example, [2,5,7,9–11,14–18]), as it is considered that an algorithm with a polynomial complexity bound is likely to be more reliable than one that do not satisfies this condition. With this in mind, in this work, we proved that, at each iteration, the step size computed by the analyzed algorithm is bounded by $\frac{\theta(4-3\theta)(1-\theta)^2}{n}$, where $\theta \in [0,1[$, and, consequently, obtaining an $O(n|\log(\epsilon)|)$ iteration complexity bound for the feasible version of the algorithm developed by Bastos and Paixão in [3] that uses the 2-norm neighborhood; thus, proving its polynomial iteration complexity and, therefore, its Q-linear convergence.

Although it may be possible to improve the current results, they show that it could be worth to implement the feasible version of the algorithm developed by Bastos and Paixão that uses the 2-norm neighborhood and, also, analyze the results of its from its application to transportation and assignment class of problems.

Concerning future work, among other things, we intend to strengthen the presented results, study the convergence results of this algorithm and proceed with its implementation.

Acknowledgements. The research was partially financed by the Portuguese Funds through FCT (Fundação para a Ciência e a Tecnologia), within the Projects UIDB/00013/2020 and UIDP/00013/2020.

References

1. Al-Jeiroudi, G., Gondzio, J.: Convergence analysis of the inexact infeasible interior-point method for linear optimization. J. Optim. Theory Appl. **141**, 231–247 (2009)
2. Almeida, R., Teixeira, A.: On the convergence of a predictor-corrector variant algorithm. TOP **23**(2), 401–418 (2015)
3. Bastos, F., Paixão, J.: Interior-point approaches to the transportation and assignment problems on microcomputers. Investigação Operacional **13**(1), 3–15 (1993)
4. Dantzig, G.B.: Linear programming, in problems for the numerical analysis of the future. In: Proceedings of the Symposium on Modern Calculating Machinery and Numerical Methods. Appl. Math. **15**, 18–21 (1951)
5. Güler, O., Ye, Y.: Convergence behavior of interior-point algorithms. Math. Program. **60**, 215–228 (1993)
6. Karmarkar, N.K.: A new polinomial-time algorithm for linear programming. Combinatorica **4**, 373–395 (1984)
7. Korzak, J.: Convergence analysis of inexact infeasible-interior-point algorithms for solving linear programming problems. SIAM J. Optim. **11**(1), 133–148 (2000)
8. Mehrotra, S.: On the implementation of a primal-dual interior point method. SIAM J. Optim. **2**, 575–601 (1992)

9. Mizuno, S.: Polynomiality of infeasible interior-point algorithms for linear programming. Math. Program. **67**, 109–119 (1994)
10. Potra, F.: A quadratically convergent predictor-corrector method for solving linear programs from infeasible starting points. Math. Program. **67**, 383–406 (1994)
11. Salahi, M., Peng, J., Terlaky, T.: On mehrotra-type predictor-corrector algorithms. SIAM J. Optim. **18**(4), 1377–1397 (2007)
12. Teixeira, A.P., Almeida, R.: A study of the complexity of an infeasible predictor-corrector variant of Mehrotra algorithm. In: Murgante, B., et al. (eds.) ICCSA 2014. LNCS, vol. 8580, pp. 253–266. Springer, Cham (2014). https://doi.org/10.1007/978-3-319-09129-7_19
13. Wright, S.J.: Primal-Dual Interior-Point Methods. SIAM, Philadelphia (1997)
14. Wright, S., Zhang, Y.: A superquadratic infeasible interior point method for linear complementarity problems. Math. Program. **73**, 269–289 (1996)
15. Zhang, Y.: On the convergence of a class of infeasible interior-point methods for the horizontal linear complementarity problem. SIAM J. Optim. **4**(1), 208–227 (1994)
16. Zhang, Y., Zhang, D.: On polynomiality of the Mehrotra-type predictor-corrector interior-point algorithms. Math. Program. **68**, 303–318 (1995)
17. Zhang, Z., Zhang, Y.: A Mehrotra-type predictor-corrector algorithm with polynomiality and Q-subquadratic convergence. Ann. Oper. Res. **62**, 131–150 (1996)
18. Zhang, Y., Tapia, R.A., Dennis, J.E.: On the superlinear and quadratic convergence of primal-dual interior point linear programming algorithms. SIAM J. Optim. **2**, 304–324 (1992)

Modelling and Control of a Retrofitted Oven for SMD Reflow

Rafael Luis Yanase de Rezende[1] and João Paulo Coelho[1,2]([⊠])

[1] Polytechnic Institute of Bragança, Campus de Santa Apolónia,
5300-253 Bragança, Portugal
jpcoelho@ipb.pt

[2] Research Center for Digitization and Intelligent Robotics (CeDRI), Polytechnic
Institute of Bragança, Campus de Santa Apolónia, 5300-253 Bragança, Portugal

Abstract. This paper deals with the modelling and control of an oven for reflowing electronic surface-mounted devices. The modelling is done taking into account that the system has a second-order dynamic behaviour whose parameters were obtained through a genetic algorithm. It is also shown that this system exhibits a high pure time-delay which makes the design of the control system very difficult. In particular, the performance of a PI controller is evaluated with respect to tracking two different types of reference signals. It is observed that the performance of such a controller is severely affected by the huge inertia of the system. In order to mitigate this effect, tests were performed with a different architecture known as the Smith predictor. It is concluded that, although with differences, neither the PI controller nor the Smith allows the tracking of the typical reference in a reflow process.

Keywords: Controller design · Dead-time processes · SMD reflow · System modelling

1 Introduction

When talking about printed circuit board (PCB) design, there are two types of electronic components to consider: those whose connecting leads are soldered to the circuit on the opposite face of the PCB where the component body is located and the others that are soldered on the same layer where the circuit lays. The former are called through-hole components and the latter, are surface mount devices (SMD).

Until recently, through-hole-type electronic components were the basis of most PCB circuits. However, the need to reduce the equipment dimensions has led, gradually, to the use of SMDs. This paradigm shift meant that, at the moment, many manufacturers do not even offer through-hole packaging alternatives to their components. Discrete SMD components, such as resistors, inductors and capacitors, have nowadays a fraction of the dimension of their earlier equivalent counterpart. Moreover, actual state-of-the-art high-density integrated circuits, such as microprocessors, digital signal processors or graphical processing units are only available in leadless circuits packages such as bullet-grid array (BGA). Indeed, it is safe to say that most components used in mass-produced small electronics, such as laptops or smartphones, come in SMD packages.

Being able to create electronic circuits using SMD devices is not an exclusive competence of companies that aim at large-scale production. Even at the prototyping level, it is essential to be able to manipulate this type of component. On one hand, due to design constraints and, on the other, because some components are only available with SMD packaging.

Being able to manipulate such a class of components, even at the prototyping level, requires suitable equipment able to handle tasks such as SMD component soldering. It is worth noticing that, those machines are rather expensive when viewed in the high-school education context.

Since there is an increasing trend regarding the integration of SMD components in the prototypes being developed at the Polytechnic Institute of Bragança, and in order to both keep the costs down and seize the opportunity to apply mechatronics and control systems design concepts, an SMD reflow oven was built by repurposing an off-the-shelf recycled electric kitchen oven. In this framework, this paper describes the steps carried out during the retrofitting process which include the development of measurement and actuation loops, system modelling and digital controller design. Regarding the latter, different algorithms have been implemented and tested leading to a set of results which are presented in Sect. 4.1. The design constraints and the reflow oven electronic and structural components will be presented in Sect. 2. Section 3 will be devoted to obtaining a mathematical model that will be used, during Sect. 4 to design, using a systematic approach, the closed-loop controller. A curve fitting approach using genetic algorithms (GAs) was carried out in order to best approximate the simulated step response to the measured one. Finally, the main conclusions and further work directions will be provided in the last section.

2   Material and Methods

Retrofitting old electric ovens for SMD reflow is not a new proposal and has already been documented in both scientific and technical literature or websites. Examples of custom-made SMD reflow ovens can be found at [2,12,17] just to refer to a few. However, the solution described in this article is singular in many aspects when compared with the ones commonly found. Particularly in the methodology used to design the oven's controller which resorts to a mathematical model derived from empirical data. Details regarding this methodology will be presented in the following sections. At the moment, both the design criteria and operating conditions that the oven must exhibit will be presented.

Reflow oven soldering is a common technology for soldering PCBs populated with SMD components. However, in order to get the required results regarding electrical and mechanical properties, the soldering must be carried out by reflowing the PCB with a temperature profile that depends on the characteristics of the solder paste used. For example, Fig. 1 presents the temperature that should be followed if a lead-free soldering paste is to be used.

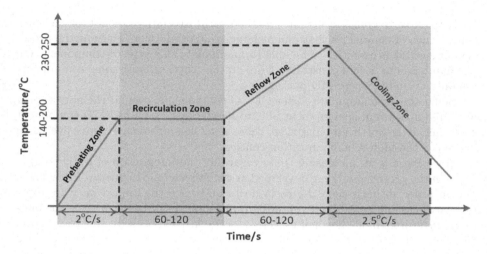

Fig. 1. Typical temperature profile for reflowing a lead-free solder paste.

In this temperature contour, four different zones can be identified. During the preheat zone, the oven temperature is raised from ambient temperature up to the temperature required for the recirculation phase. The temperature increase rate must not be too steep in order to prevent PCB's thermal stress or too flat that solvent volatilising is not promoted enough. As a rule of thumb, gradients between 1 °C to 4 °C per second should be considered at this stage. After the preheating interval, follows the recirculation zone. The aim of this stage is to provide enough time such that the temperature of the larger component, with more thermal mass, reaches the temperature of the smaller component. Moreover, a time interval between one minute and one minute and a half is required to ensure that the soldering flux existing in the soldering paste, required to remove the oxides from the component pads, is completely volatilised. After the recirculating stage, the oven enters the reflow zone where the air temperature reaches the melting point of the powder in the solder paste. Finally, during the cooling zone, the air temperature is to be reduced as fast as possible. Typical gradients for this stage are between −3 °C to −10 °C per second.

In the project described in this paper, this temperature profile will be attained through the closed-loop feedback control strategy illustrated in Fig. 2. At the head of this architecture lays the reflow oven. In this case, a 30 litres off-the-shelf domestic electric oven was recycled and repurposed. The leftmost image presented in Fig. 3 shows the overall shape of this appliance and, at the centre of the same figure, the oven is shown completely stripped. Moreover, since the oven's top heating element was damaged, it was replaced by a coil shape resistance as can be seen from the rightmost image of Fig. 3. This device was fitted right above the PCB support grill in order to reduce the time taken for the heat generated by this element to reach the surface of the PCB.

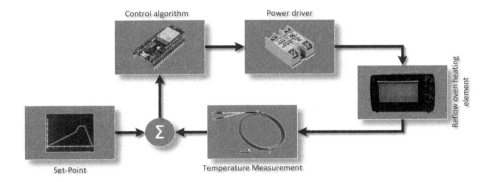

Fig. 2. Overall architecture of the reflow oven closed-loop control strategy.

Besides this added element, the oven has two 32 Ω heating resistances placed below the grill and connected in series. The total heating power of both the top and bottom resistances adds up to 1600 W. This configuration allows reaching a maximum temperature, at the central plane of the oven, of around 240 °C which is more than enough for SMD reflow.

It is worth noticing that, besides two heating elements, the oven is equipped with an air recirculating fan positioned on the lateral right-hand side. At the current stage of the project, this actuator does not represent an additional degree of freedom for the system. Instead, the fan is just activated at full speed during the time required for the full reflow cycle.

Fig. 3. At the left, overall shape of the recycled oven. The central image show the oven completely stripped. At the right, the retrofitted heating element.

Additional structural and operational changes to the oven are being evaluated such as the inclusion of thermal padding or the addition of an automatic system to open the door for faster temperature reduction. But those changes are ongoing improvements and will not be considered in this paper.

Temperature measurement plays a fundamental role in the control system's performance. The sensor and signal conditioning dynamics must be negligible when compared to the thermal inertia of the oven. Moreover, it must exhibit a measurement range that is compatible with the application. For this reason, a K-Type thermocouple was selected as the front-end of the measurement system. The measurement range spans from -200 °C to 1200 °C which is well within the oven's dynamic temperature limits. This sensor provides an accuracy of ± 2.2 °C and exhibits a time constant in the neighbourhood of 3 s. Since, as will be shown in the next section, the oven's time constant is around 8 min, the sensor bandwidth is well above the one presented by the system. In this reference frame, the dynamics imposed by the sensor is negligible and can be disregarded for controller design purposes.

The thermocouple signal conditioning is handled by the MAX6675 integrated circuit manufactured by the Maxim Integrated company. This device performs cold-junction compensation and provides the temperature, in a 12-bit digital format, through an SPI communication protocol.

It is worth highlighting that the target temperature, the one that should follow the solder paste recommended temperature profile, is the one at the PCB's surface. Usually, knowing the exact value of the temperature at that surface is not possible using direct measurement strategies. For this reason, statistical models and other methods such as machine-learning approaches are usually used to predict the PCB's surface temperature [1, 7]. In this work, since only batches of one board are considered, this question was tackled by building the movable bracket presented in the left-hand image of Fig. 4. This bracket aims to support the thermocouple measurement junction as near as possible to the PCB's surface.

The average power delivered to the heating elements is provided by a 40 A solid-state relay. The control signal applied to this relay is pulse width modulated (PWM) with an 8-bit resolution. This signal is generated by a digital controller embedded in a 32-bit microcontroller. The microcontroller, a generic ESP32 manufactured by Espressif, handles both the mathematics associated with the digital controller and the user interface. Regarding the latter, a 1.8"LCD TFT display provides, graphically, both the oven's temperature and set-point. This display was mounted over a custom-designed bracket which was then 3D printed using PLA filament. The shape of this bracket is presented in the central image of Fig. 4.

The oven operating conditions, for example, the selection of set-point profiles or fine-tuning the corner temperatures, can be parameterised through a menu presented in this display. The user can navigate along this menu by means of a rotary encoder as presented in the rightmost image of Fig. 4.

Fig. 4. At the left, the thermocouple bracket and at the centre, the LCD support. The knobs and their functions are presented at the rightmost image.

In the following section, the dynamic model of the retrofitted oven will be presented. This model will play an important role in simulation and control system design.

3   System Modelling

The internal thermal behaviour of a reflow oven requires a very complex 3D temperature flow model. This kind of approach has been followed by several authors in order to be able to estimate the instantaneous temperature at a given point of the PCB aiming to reduce the soldering failures and improve their electrical and mechanical properties [4, 6, 8, 14].

In this work, the non-homogeneous nature of the temperature inside the reflow oven will be neglected since the temperature sensor is very near the PCB. Moreover, since the size of the PCBs to be reflow have small dimensions, the temperature is considered constant within that area.

Moreover, due to the fact that many phenomena, such as radiation, convection and conduction, takes place inside the oven, a first-principles model of the reflow oven was not considered. Instead, a more empirical system identification approach was carried out by fitting data to a set of parametric continuous-time models. In particular, the open-loop step response was measured and then, using a genetic algorithm, two different models were fitted to the data. In the next section, the results from the open-loop step response will be provided.

3.1   Measured System Step Response

There are several methods to excite a system in order to perform system identification. Using pseudo-random binary sequences as the driving signal is one such example. However, in this work, a simple step type input (equivalent to a 100% duty cycle PWM signal) is applied to the power driver and the thermocouple temperature is recorded. For the trials carried out, a sampling period of 200 ms was considered suitable and more than enough to fully capture the temperature dynamics. Indeed, as will be seen later, the slow dynamics of the oven can lead to a further reduction in the sampling frequency.

Figure 5 show the obtained results for the first half hour. It is worth noticing that, at a temperature around 100 °C, the estimated temperature gradient is around 0.4 °C per second which is incompatible with the temperature gradients indicated during the previous section. This limitation is due to the actuator's heating power which should be increased in order to handle higher gradient temperatures. However, for this paper, we will relax such conditions and consider a set-point with a temperature slew rate of 0.2 °C per second.

As can be seen, an overdamped type response with near one minute of dead-time and a time-constant (measured at 63% of the steady state value) near seven minutes. This information can be used to derive the parameters of a first-order transfer function with a pure-time delay with the generic form:

$$H(s) = K \frac{e^{-s\tau}}{as + 1} \tag{1}$$

where K is the DC gain, τ denotes the dead-time and a the time-constant.

However, even if the measured parameters are in the neighbourhood of the expected result, this approach requires a process of trial and error to fit the data to the model. That is, the three degrees of freedom of the model must be tuned in order to reduce the modelling error. For this reason, a different approach was carried out where the model parameters are found by an iterative procedure driven by an evolutionary algorithm. Details regarding this method are provided in the section that follows.

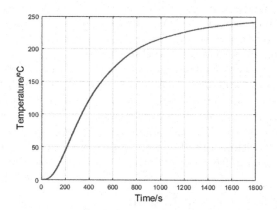

Fig. 5. Open-loop step response of the retrofitted reflow oven. For convenience, the data origin was offset by an amount equal to the ambient temperature.

3.2   Genetic Algorithm Based Modelling

Evolutionary algorithms are stochastic-based computer programs capable of performing optimisation tasks through the process of perfecting a set of solutions by means of naturally inspired principles and processes. Among the high number of evolutionary optimisation strategies, genetic algorithms (GAs) are among the most popular. They owe their name to the fact that they use simplified models of biological processes based on the mechanisms of natural selection. Those algorithms were first proposed by Holland [5], and applied in search problems by Goldberg [3]. Details regarding the conceptual and operational features of this class of algorithms are outside the scope of the present work. However, the reader can refer to the seminal book of John Holland or many other more modern book titles such as [16].

The system identification procedure, based on the use of GAs, begins by establishing the individual's phenotype. In the current work, the phenotype regards the model's degrees-of-freedom which, in a first trial, will be just the gain, pole location and dead-time value represented in (1). In the second set of trials, one additional pole and a zero are included in the model in order to improve data fitting capability.

The use of genetic algorithms requires the definition of some parameters. In the set of trials presented in the following two subsections, a population size of 100 individuals is considered. Moreover, a tournament-type crossover with 80% probability is selected with a Gaussian mutation scheme. Elitism is implemented and decision variables domain constraints are imposed since instability or non-minimum phase behaviours shouldn't be allowed

3.3   First-Order Transfer Function

For this set of trials, the optimisation problem can be stated as a quadratic programming problem subject to linear constraints with the form:

$$
\begin{aligned}
\min_{K,a,\tau} \quad & J \\
\text{s.t.} \quad & 0.5 \leq K \leq 1.5 \\
& 100 \leq a \leq 1000 \\
& 10 \leq \tau \leq 180
\end{aligned}
\tag{2}
$$

where the objective function J regards the set-point accuracy computed by:

$$
J \triangleq \int_{T_{sim}} \left(Temp(t) - \hat{Temp}(t) \right)^2 dt
\tag{3}
$$

where T_{sim} denotes the simulation time, $Temp(t)$ is the measured oven temperature at time instant t and $\hat{Temp}(t)$ is the estimated temperature computed by the model.

Due to the convexity and low dimensionality of the problem, the GA converged systematically, after less than 100 generations, to the solution $K = 0.962 \,°C/\%$, $a = 421.8$ s and $\tau = 108.7$ s.

The root-mean square (RMS) modelling error for this approximation, computed using (4), has led to a value of 2.96 °C.

$$E_{RMS} = \sqrt{\frac{J}{T_{sim}}} \tag{4}$$

In the left-hand side of Fig. 6, the typical convergence plots and, in the right-hand, the comparison between the measured and simulated step response using the first-order model.

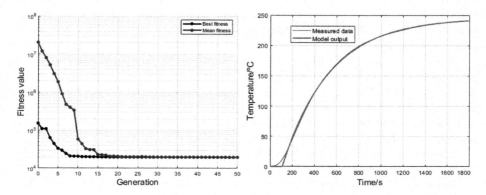

Fig. 6. The left image present typical convergence plots from running the GA algorithm over the first-order model. In the right, a comparison between the measured and simulated system step response.

The main drawback of this model is its inability to closely match the system response within the first three minutes. For this reason, a second-order model was test-fitted leading to the results presented in the next subsection.

3.4   Second-Order Transfer Function

In the previous section, a GA was used to derive the parameters of a first-order plus pure time-delay transfer function. Since there were dynamics unable to be described by this model, this section presents the results regarding the use of a second-order transfer function such as the one presented in (5).

$$H(s) = K \frac{e^{-s\tau}}{(as)^2 + 2abs + 1} \tag{5}$$

Following a procedure similar to that carried out earlier, the coefficients K, a, b and τ will be the decision variables in a quadratic minimisation problem where $0 \leq \tau \leq 80$, $0 < a \leq 300$, $0 < b \leq 600$ and $0.5 \leq K \leq 1.5$.

After a large number of trials, it was found that the solution that led to the smallest error was $K = 2.45$ °C/%, $a = 158.7$ s, $b = 1.48$ s and $\tau = 55.4$ s.

In this condition, the RMS error attained by using this set of parameters was around 1.18 °C.

The genetic algorithm's convergence plot, in conjunction with the model's accuracy, is shown in Fig. 7.

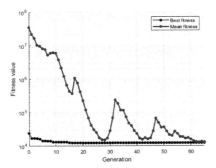 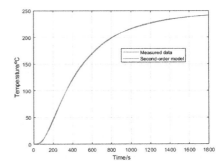

Fig. 7. The left plot shows the algorithm convergence associated with the second-order transfer function and, in the right, the model accuracy.

The final model is presented in (3).

$$H(s) = 2.45 \frac{e^{-55.4s}}{25190s^2 + 469.5s + 1} \tag{6}$$

At this point, the model is considered to be sufficiently accurate to capture the most important dynamics of the oven's thermal behaviour. Using this model, it is possible to design, in a more systematic way, a controller aiming at both set-point tracking accuracy and disturbances rejection. The use of simple on-off control techniques has already been tested and proved to be unsuited due to large oscillations along the set-point profile [13]. For this reason, other control strategies were tested and documented in the following section.

4   Digital Controller Design

Choosing the right control strategy has a large impact on any system's closed-loop performance. If the system is linear and time-invariant, a proportional, integral and derivative (PID) controller will lead, frequently, to acceptable results. This is why this control paradigm is ubiquitous and can be found in most industrial and automotive contexts. This class of controllers have three gains that must be adjusted in order for the system to attain a given closed-loop behaviour. However, there is not a single way to do that. If the system is not critical and allows performing field tests, heuristics based on step response or trial and error methods can be used. On the other hand, more systematic ways can be employed if mathematical models of the system are available.

Within this paper's framework, the use of PID for temperature control has already been addressed. For example, [11], uses a PID control algorithm where the gains are determined using Ziegler- Nichols method. This heuristic method resorts to the reaction step response curve in order to define the controller gains. However, despite its simplicity, with this method is not possible to tune the controller for a given dynamic response. For this reason, a more systematic approach using the Bode plot's reshaping method will be employed in this paper.

In particular, a proportional plus integral controller will be designed taking into consideration the following criteria: zero steady-state error to a step input, less than 5% of overshoot and the maximum bandwidth possible.

First, the phase and gain margins are computed by plotting the Bode diagram of $\frac{H(s)}{s}$ where $H(s)$ is defined in (3) and s is the Laplace complex frequency. From the left-hand side plot of Fig. 8 it is possible to conclude that the system is unstable and both the phase margins must be increased. According to the design constraints, a phase margin of 75 °(or more) must be attained and a gain margin higher than 15 dB.

By adding a zero at $\omega = 0.0025$ rad/s and adjusting the gain for a crossover frequency equal to the zero's frequency leads to the following PI controller transfer function:

$$K(s) = 8.04 \times 10^{-4}\frac{400s + 1}{s} \tag{7}$$

which, as can be seen from the right-hand plot of Fig. 8, meet the above defined design conditions.

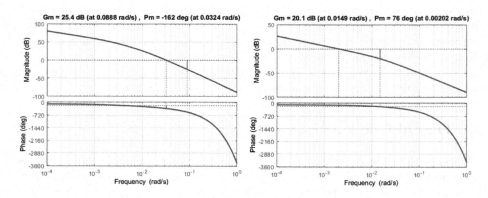

Fig. 8. Gain and phase margins. In the left, for $\frac{H(s)}{s}$ and on the right for $K(s)H(s)$.

This transfer function, after being discretized using the bilinear transform with $T_s = 200$ ms, leads to:

$$K(z) = \frac{0.32932z - 0.32916}{z - 1} \qquad (8)$$

The closed-loop simulation for a step input signal with amplitude equal to 220 °C, and the respective control signal, is presented in Fig. 9.

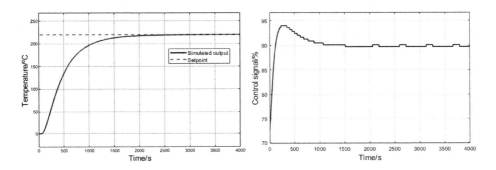

Fig. 9. Closed-loop step response and control signal.

As can be seen, simulation results are aligned with the design constraints. The question at the moment is how robust is the controller regarding eventual mismatches between the model and the true system. To answer this question, the digital control law was embedded in the microcontroller and the dynamic response was tested to both step and piece-wise linear set-points.

Figure 10 show the results regarding the step input response and Fig. 11 the response to the reflow temperature profile presented in Fig. 1. In the left-hand plot of each figure, the set-point tracking accuracy is shown and on the right-hand side, the control signal.

There are two main conclusions to derive from the obtained results. The first is that there is a close match between the simulated and the measured closed-loop signals which further validates the model's accuracy. The second is that the set-point accuracy regarding the ability to follow the reflow temperature soldering profile is not acceptable. On one hand, the peak temperature is not enough to fully melt the soldering paste and, on the other, the recirculation region is not clearly defined. This inability to closely follow the reference signal is mainly due to the system's high dead time. Hence, any controller architecture devised to control the reflow oven must be able to compensate for this effect. One such control structure, which is ubiquitous in the literature when talking about large dead-time processes is the Smith predictor.

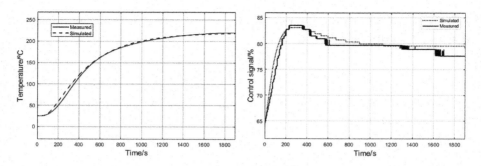

Fig. 10. Comparison between the measured and simulated closed-loop system response: at the left, the oven temperature and at the right the control signal.

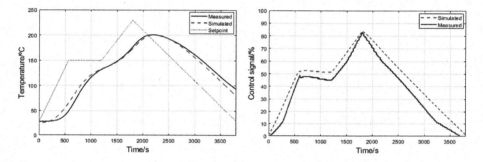

Fig. 11. Comparison between the measured and simulated closed-loop system response: at the left, the oven temperature and at the right the control signal.

4.1   The Smith Predictor

The Smith predictor is a widely known method usually associated with closed-loop control in the context of large time-delay systems [9,10]. The reasoning behind this approach is to use a delay-free model of the process in order to predict the effect of the current control action on the actual process. In this way, this methodology seeks to remove the dead-time effects such that the controller will perform as if there were no time delay present. The general Smith predictor controller architecture, in the context of digital control systems, is presented in Fig. 12.

In this figure, $G_p(z)$ is the system's digital model by removing the effect of the dead-time and n in z^{-n} regards the number of sample periods equivalent to the system's pure time delay. One of the major differences regarding the implementation of such a strategy, when compared to a simple bang-bang or PI/PID controller, is the necessity to include a nominal system model. In this work, the discrete-time system model was obtained from its continuous-time counterpart by considering a sampling period of 0.2 s and through the bilinear

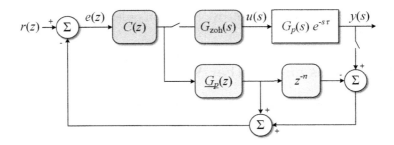

Fig. 12. The Smith predictor controller architecture.

transformation. The derived model has the following appearance:

$$H(z) = z^{-277} \frac{a_1 + a_2 z^{-1} + a_3 z^{-2}}{1 + b_1 z^{-1} + b_2 z^{-2}} \tag{9}$$

where $a_1 = 9.71 \times 10^{-7}$, $a_2 = 1.94 \times 10^{-6}$, $a_3 = 9.708 \times 10^{-7}$, $b_1 = -1.996$ and $b_2 = 0.9963$.

The obtained results are presented in Fig. 13 where both the set-point accuracy and control signal can be viewed.

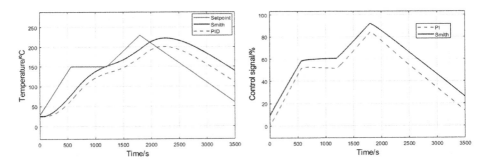

Fig. 13. Comparison between the Smith predictor and PI closed-loop system response: at the left, the oven temperature and at the right the control signal.

As can be seen, the Smith predictor is able to attain a higher temperature but the overall least squares error regarding the set-point tracking has increased when compared to the PI controller. Indeed, the RMS set-point error regarding the PI controller was equal to 49 °C while the Smith predictor led to 78 °C. Despite the slight increase in performance regarding the peek temperature accuracy, the Smith predictor performance is still unacceptable. As a matter of fact, and for this case, we believe that the Smith predictor has not improved the closed-loop response when compared with the PI controller. The obtained results are in line with the claim put forward in [15]. For this reason, ongoing research is now focusing on the use o model predictive control in order to mitigate the effect of the large system inertia.

5   Conclusions and Further Work

This paper presents the details regarding the process of retrofitting an off-the-shelf domestic oven into an SMD reflow device. Contrary to what happens with ovens used in cooking, where the set-point is almost always kept constant throughout the entire cooking process, in reflow ovens the set-point is changed more dynamically in order to guarantee the temperatures and times associated with the different phases required by the solder paste. For this reason, a controller must be designed so that the system is able to follow a reference signal with sections involving different velocities. In this paper, we have tackled this problem by considering a PI controller whose parameters were obtained through a system model. This model was obtained by a system identification procedure involving the use of GAs.

Experimental results have shown that the measured closed-loop control system has a behaviour that closely matches the one obtained from simulation which validates the model quality. Moreover, the obtained results suggest that the closed-loop system is able to attain a small steady-state error for constant reference inputs. However, when considering the reflow set-point pattern, the system was unable to perform well in the ramp segments. This is essentially due to the large system's time delay which prevents the controller to attain the required performance for first-order reference inputs. This issue can be perceived in both custom-made solutions, such as the ones found in many online resources, or low-end commercial products.

It was also demonstrated that using a Smith predictor architecture does not alleviate those symptoms and that a different methodology must be employed.

In this context, ongoing research is devoted to both hardware improvements and testing different control strategies. In relation to the first, the power of the actuators will be increased and heat exchange will be promoted by including a convection fan. Regarding the latter, feed-forward control will be tested in conjunction with PID feedback. An embedded model predictive control strategy will also be tested hoping that this methodology will lead to better set-point accuracy.

References

1. Azimi, N., Attarzadeh, S.: Heat transfer modeling and reflow oven soldering temperature curve optimization of printed circuit board reflow soldering (2022)
2. Burke, T.: The poor man's solder reflow oven [hands on]. IEEE Spectrum **49**, 26–27 (2012). https://doi.org/10.1109/MSPEC.2012.6172801
3. Goldberg, D.E.: Genetic Algorithms in Search, Optimization and Machine Learning. Addison-Wesley, Reading (1989)

4. Gonzalez, J., Tavarez, A.: Modeling the thermal behavior of solder paste inside reflow ovens. J. Electron. Packag. **125**, 335 (2003). https://doi.org/10.1115/1.1569955

5. Holland, J.H.: Adaptation in Natural and Artificial Systems. University of Michigan Press, Ann Arbor (1975)

6. Illés, B., Harsanyi, G.: Heating characteristics of convection reflow ovens. Appl. Therm. Eng. **29**, 2166–2171 (2009). https://doi.org/10.1016/j.applthermaleng.2008.10.014

7. Li, Y., He, J., Won, D., Yoon, S.W.: Non-contact reflow oven thermal profile prediction based on artificial neural network. IEEE Trans. Compon. Packag. Manuf. Technol **11**(12), 2229–2237 (2021). https://doi.org/10.1109/TCPMT.2021.3120310

8. Ma, G., Huang, X., Liu, S.: Heat transfer modeling and oven temperature curve optimization of integrated circuit board reflow soldering. IEEE Access **9**, 141876–141889 (2021). https://doi.org/10.1109/ACCESS.2021.3120496

9. Normey-Rico, J.E., Camacho, E.F.: Control of Dead-time Processes. Springer, London (2007). https://doi.org/10.1007/978-1-84628-829-6

10. O'dwyer, A.: Handbook of PI and PID Controller Tuning Rules. World Scientific, Singapore (2009)

11. Pambudi, A., Hariadi, F., Arsyad, M.: Development of low-cost reflow oven for SMT assembly, pp. 51–56 (2017). https://doi.org/10.1109/ISESD.2017.8253304

12. Pawlowski, P., Dabrowski, A., Grenz, M., Bladowski, M.: Reflow oven for heating and soldering SMD and BGA components, pp. 324–329 (2018). https://doi.org/10.23919/MIXDES.2018.8436841

13. Rezende, R., Paulo Coelho, J.: Bang-bang temperature controller for a custom-made SMD reflow oven. In: SASYR Symposium of Applied Science for Young Researchers (2020)

14. Rosu, B., Reyes-Turcu, P., Simion-Zanescu, D.: Thermal management system for reflow oven, pp. 306–309 (2003). https://doi.org/10.1109/ISSE.2003.1260538

15. Sigurd Skogestad, C.G.: Should we forget the smith predictor? IFAC-PapersOnLine **51**(4), 769–774 (2018). https://doi.org/10.1016/j.ifacol.2018.06.203. https://www.sciencedirect.com/science/article/pii/S2405896318305007. 3rd IFAC Conference on Advances in Proportional-Integral-Derivative Control PID 2018

16. Sivanandam, S.N., Deepa, S.N.: Introduction to Genetic Algorithms. Springer, Heidelberg (2008). https://doi.org/10.1007/978-3-540-73190-0

17. Vulcaman: DIY reflow oven. https://www.instructables.com/DIY-REFLOW-OVEN/

Measurements with the Internet of Things

Investigation of the Partial Discharges in the High Voltage Measurement Transformers

Gediminas Daukšys[(✉)] [iD]

Kaunas University of Applied Engineering Sciences, Kaunas, Lithuania
gediminas.dauksys@edu.ktk.lt

Abstract. It is well known the use of on-line partial discharge (PD) measurements as an indicator of stator winding insulation condition. The scheduled PD measurements could be used as a test to evaluate the quality of the equipment. The test results could help to diagnose the insulation problems, call for corresponding action before failure occurs. High voltage transformers are one of the most important elements in an electric power system. Each one of them is affected by various external factors: overvoltage, partial discharge (PD), overheating, vibrations etc., which are created by the strong electric field, thermal effect, humidity, impurities, factory defects, dissolved water and gas in oil type transformer's insulation. These and other factors caused by the environment, reduces the device's exploitation period. This work reviews different contact and non-contact methods, used to evaluate the condition of transformers, by measuring the level of PDs. The selected method of non-contact measurement of electromagnetic waves radiation was used to evaluate voltage transformers status. The experiment was performed at 110 kV substation. Authors discusses efficiency of the selected method to evaluate the voltage transformers insulation condition.

1 Introduction

Partial Discharge (PD) is an electrical discharge that does not completely bridge the space between two conducting electrodes. It occurs across a portion of the insulation between two conducting electrodes. PD activity can initiate under normal working conditions in high voltage equipment where the insulation condition has deteriorated with age, has been aged prematurely by thermal or electrical over-stressing or due to improper installation [1]. Partial Discharge is low energy electrical activity that can have very serious implications. Although each discharge is small, they are a very localized and can happen many times every second. Over time this can cause damage such that the insulation becomes so weak that it fails. Partial discharge is generally accepted as an important cause of long term degradation and eventual failure of electrical insulation [1,2]. The point of the PD appearance usually is in the weakest place of insulation (for example - dewy insulation or contaminated with impurities). PD can also occur along the boundary between different insulating materials.

A. I. Pereira et al. (Eds.): OL2A 2022, CCIS 1754, pp. 565–574, 2022.
https://doi.org/10.1007/978-3-031-23236-7_39

Insulation of high voltage transformers could change its properties due to various factors: vibrations, high temperatures, heating and cooling cycles, operating voltage, over voltages, pulse and dynamic loading [4,5]. The outdoor factors (such as: moisture, chemical compounds, various types of radiations, impurities) also can make influence to the deterioration of insulation [6,7]. Life time and stability of equipments insulation depends on intensity and duration of thermal, electrical and mechanical stresses [8].

Deterioration of transformer insulation is one of the main reasons of failures. Over the past several years, a number of practical methods are created for measuring the PD activity in the high voltage insulation of transformer windings. One of the most important factors which influence the insulation's life time is temperature. Due to high temperatures, processes of thermal-oxidative in high voltage insulation destruction take quicker action. That can usually cause the decrease of mechanical strength; reduce of elasticity and damage of fleet components, what can be the reason for the formation of gas filled cavities in high voltage insulation [1,13].

The objective of this work is to assess transformers status of 110 kV substations, using the non-contact measurements of electromagnetic waves radiation.

Please note that the first paragraph of a section or subsection is not indented. The first paragraphs that follows a table, figure, equation etc. does not have an indent, either.

Subsequent paragraphs, however, are indented.

2   Scheme of Investigation

The electromagnetic energy measurement method is based on the measurement of the current, which is induced during phenomena of partial discharge and flows through the grounding conductor, using the current transformer [6]. Two key devices are used in this approach: PD signal recording device and a device for data analysis. This approach enables to record PD signal by connecting measurement devices (voltage transformer and current transformer) directly to the object under investigation (power transformer, cable, etc.) [4]. A typical scheme of equipment connection for electrical partial discharge measurement is shown in Fig. 1.

With this approach, recording of partial discharge can be performed without stopping the operation of the power transformer. Therefore, it allows online evaluation of the present condition of the power transformer. Afterwards, the acquired information is analysed and the time-dependent deviations of the PD parameters are observed to evaluate the condition of the device insulation [4].

Even the electrical method of partial discharge measurement is very accurate, it has several disadvantages. The main disadvantage is the sensitivity of the measuring device to the ambient electromagnetic noises [6]. High voltage and power equipment (power transformers, cables, insulators and etc.) emit electromagnetic noises in narrow and wide spectral bands, which can affect the recorded data. In some cases, it is difficult to distinguish between the presence of PD and

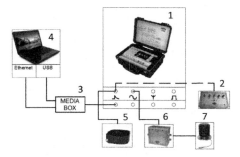

Fig. 1. Electrical partial discharge measurement set-up: 1 – PD equipment for data processing; 2 – PD calibrator; 3 – device for connecting PD measuring equipment to personal computer systems; 4 – PC with data processing software; 5 – sensor for coupling out HF PD signals; 6 –measurement data splitting box; 7 – PD decoupler [10].

ambient electromagnetic noise due to very short signal duration of PD impulse. In such a case, recorded data should not be used for evaluation of the equipment insulation condition [4].

3 Application of the UHF Method for Registration of the Electromagnetic Waves Radiation of High-Voltage Transformers

In order to investigate applicability of UHF method on-site (in real substations) the DFA300 Doble Lemke device is used for the measurements of electromagnetic waves radiation. This device is intended for detection of insulation or mechanical defects in gas-insulated substations or in open-source substations. The DFA300 registers radio frequency interference (RFI) of radiated electromagnetic waves due to PD from 50 to 1000 MHz MHz and acoustic emission (AE) from 10 to 300 kHz [11,12].

3.1 Measurement Principle

Using the DFA300 measuring device, 110 kV substations equipped with high voltage Pfiffner manufacturer voltage (EJOF 123) transformers were subjected to a condition analysis study. The object under investigation is presented in Fig. 2.

Measurement principle:

1. A plan for the installation of the substation's measuring equipment is drawn up;
2. A baseline background spectrum analysis near the substation is conducted, more than 20 m away from the high power components;

Fig. 2. The object under investigation: voltage transformers

3. A baseline background spectrum is captured on the DFA300 to allow instant evaluation of the component condition;
4. A spectrum analysis of received electromagnetic wave signals of each investigated component is performed, which is compared to the baseline background;
5. Doble Lemke recommends a range of 600 to 900 MHz of the spectrum to be analysed for detection of partial discharge;
6. If spectral mismatches are detected within the specified frequency range, additional analysis of the component under investigation is performed by recording radiation intensities during the wave period, recording level values with alternating phase and level measurements;
7. Device failures are identified.

During the measurements, the background spectrum within the range from 50 to 1000 MHz, more than 20 m away from the nearest interfering component, was scanned. At the points shown in Fig. 3, the measurement was repeated in order to compare with the background spectrum. Measurements close to the component under investigation were made at a distance of 1–1.5 m, depending on the height of the component installation. Measuring results in these measuring points were considered to be affected by other transformers as little as possible. Spectral analysis of each component was performed twice.

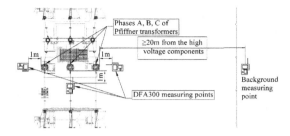

Fig. 3. Partial discharge measurement plan

The results of the stored spectrum were further analysed using MATLAB software. The spectral analysis values recorded for each subject were compared with the baseline background. The results are plotted, showing the spectral analyses together (background and component) and providing a differential graph that subtracts the spectral analysis values of the background from the spectral values of the component. The differential graphs of each phase transformer are compared to determine which phase transformer is most affected by insulation degradation. Examples of graphs are provided in Chapter IV of this article.

3.2   Advantages of the Selected Measurement Method

Using DFA300 measurements are performed under real operating conditions. Components under investigation are connected to power grid. The power grid system does not suffer from extra line loads as the particular component does not need to be disconnected.

The measuring device provides various tools for monitoring and assessing the condition of the object being measured, such as:

- "Spectrum analyser": during this measuring mode, the device registers radiation of electromagnetic waves at different frequencies in the range of 50 to 1000 MHz MHz;
- "Time resolved": during this measuring mode, the device synchronizes with the frequency of the power grid via the wireless synchronization adapter. In this way, the distribution of electromagnetic wave intensity over the corresponding period is recorded at the selected fixed frequency. This type of measurement can accurately represent the type of fault existing in component under investigation;
- "Level versus Phase": these measurements detect a periodic distribution of peak-wave magnitudes at a given fixed frequency. When the measuring device is synchronized with the main frequency of the power grid, selecting the number of different peaks per measurement (1000, 2000, 5000) shows the pattern of peak distribution. According to this regularity, it is possible to characterize the defect;

- "Level meter": it records the intensity level of electromagnetic wave at a certain fixed frequency. This measurement can be used to estimate which high voltage component emits electromagnetic waves of higher intensity than nearby ones (thus determining which particular component requires additional analysis) or which component is already defected.

The measuring device is mobile, user friendly and convenient for daily measurements by visiting a couple of different substations.

3.3   Disadvantages of the Selected Measurement Method

During the measurements, the environmental impact on the measuring device operating characteristics was encountered. Depending on the humidity of the air, the accuracy of the measurements changes. In the morning, when the humidity level of the environment was relatively high, the device was not able to perform registration of distribution of the peak values of emitted electromagnetic waves intensity versus phase at fixed frequency value ("Level versus Phase" mode measurement). By the middle of the day when the air humidity had dispersed, the measurements were performed again smoothly.

The registered spectrum values of emitted electromagnetic waves (background or particular high voltage component) during the spectrum analysis had a significant error from about 4% to 9%. This error is calculated by comparing the results of two consecutive measurements of the same component.

The intensity values of emitted electromagnetic waves registered during the period at selected frequency cannot be stored in a time interval for later analysis. The only way to save data is to stop the measurement and capture the current image. The disadvantage of this is that during the recording period, an anomaly is not always recorded which could identify a malfunction of component under analysis. This causes additional difficulty during analysis of the measurement results.

Different measurement times were estimated during measurement of the level of electromagnetic wave during measuring mode "Level versus Phase". As a result, during investigation of high voltage components, for some components it was accumulated 1000 peak values during a few seconds and for others during a few minutes. Therefore, it is not possible to determine total duration of time when recording a measurement.

The device does not have the ability to compare the results of certain measurements. For this reason, additional measurements are required when analysing the recorded data using a mathematical model and in case of doubt concerning the measured results.

4   Results

During analysis of each phase transformer data, the baseline background spectrum and particular phase transformer spectrum (Fig. 4), the difference between

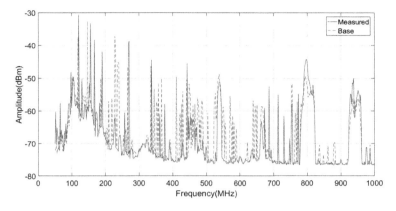

Fig. 4. Baseline background and B phase spectra of transformer "ІТ-Т101".

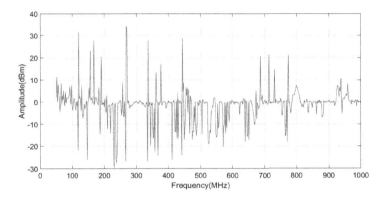

Fig. 5. Difference between "ІТ-Т101" B phase spectrum and baseline background spectrum.

these spectra (Fig. 5), and a comparative graph of the difference between all phase transformers (Fig. 6) were provided. The data below is from one of the 110 kV substations voltage transformer "ІТ-Т101" (mark - EOF 123).

According to the recommendations of Doble Lemke, the manufacturer of the DFA300 instrument, partial discharge signals are analysed in the 600–900 MHz range where maximum spectral divergence are determined [11]. Based on this assumption, an anomaly is detected in the frequency range of 780–820 MHz - the intensity of electromagnetic wave is higher than the background in the whole spectrum. This effect, although small, is attributed to PD. Based on the information provided in Fig. 6 for the comparison of the difference of all three phase spectra with the baseline background spectrum, it can be stated that the phase B voltage transformer possesses the highest PD level and phase A has the lowest PD level.

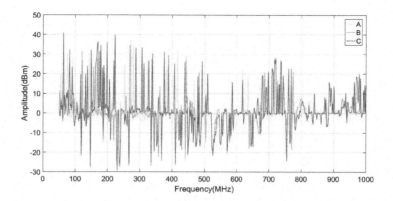

Fig. 6. Comparison of the differences of all of the three phase spectra of the "ĮT-T101" with the baseline background spectrum

These measurements were made on 2019.04.19. In May, an accident occurred in one of the 110 kV substations - a phase B voltage transformer "ĮT-T101" exploded. Prior to the accident, parameters of power grid did not exceed normal mode limits.

On July 26, 2019, additional measurements were carried out with the replacement of the new B phase voltage transformer "ĮT-T101" (mark - EOF 123). The comparison of the differences between the three phase (A, B and C) spectra of the replaced "ĮT-T101" with the baseline background spectrum is shown in Fig. 7. The comparative spectra of the first and second measurement in absolute values for the B phase voltage transformer of "ĮT-T101" are shown in Fig. 8.

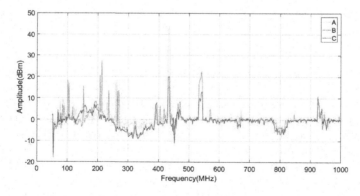

Fig. 7. Comparison of the differences of all of the three phase spectra of the replaced "ĮT-T101" with the baseline background spectrum after the B phase accident.

According to the information in Fig. 8, a similar anomaly of spectral differences for B phase is observed in the frequency range 780–820 MHz as before

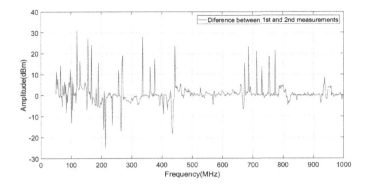

Fig. 8. Comparative analysis of the absolute values of spectra of the first measurements (defected "ĮT-T101", before the replacement) and second measurements (after the replacement of "ĮT-T101") of B phase voltage transformer.

the accident of the transformer. Therefore, such difference could be used as reliable parameter for estimation condition that level of PD is increased and the transformer is under the risk to be affected by failure.

Comparing the spectra in Fig. 7 and 8, it can be concluded that during the second measurement the substation was much less loaded. For this reason, it is possible to see the difference in Fig. 9 within 780–820 MHz. When analysing the comparative graph (Fig. 8), it can be stated that phase B of the replaced transformer "ĮT-T101" is no longer different from other phases (A and C).

This comparative method of background and high voltage component spectra differences is based on the accuracy of the results recorded. If the results are false, frequencies of the possible PD may not be determined, which may result in an incorrect estimation of the insulation condition of component under investigation.

5 Conclusions

1. The spectrum of emitted electromagnetic waves and registered by DFA300 device is with 4%–9% error tolerance, therefore during unfavourable conditions the frequency needed for detection of partial discharges could be undetermined.
2. This work reviews different contact and non-contact methods, used to evaluate the condition of operating transformers which are not disconnected from the electrical grid, by measuring the level of PDs. The selected non-contact UHF measurement method of electromagnetic waves radiation was used to evaluate voltage transformers status. The experimental investigations were performed at 110 kV substation.
3. It makes the most sense to perform condition evaluation of the component when the substation has the highest power load.

4. During measurements performed in one of the 110 kV substations could have helped to evade the failure, however, the registered differences between phase spectrums within frequency range of 780–820 MHz were quite small to identify the presence of the high level of "IT-T101" B phase failure. However, such comparative difference we have detected shows that level of PD is increased and the transformer is under the risk to be affected by failure.

5. A broader parameter capture is needed, involving the combination of electro-magnetic and vibrodiagnostic partial discharge measurement methods (if it is allowed by the measuring device's type), additionally considering the systems voltage, frequency, current and other surrounding factors such as temperature and humidity.

References

1. CIGRE WG A2.37, Transformer Reliability Survey (2015)
2. CIGRE WG A2.18: Life management techniques for power transformer. Brochure 227, Paris (2003)
3. Akiyoshi, D.F., et al.: Evaluation of Low Cost Piezoelectric Sensors for the Iden-tification of Partial Discharges Evolution. Proceedings 2019/4/36
4. Soomro, I.A., Ramdon, M.N.: Study on different techniques of partial discharge detection in power transformers winding: simulation between paper and EPOXY resin using UHF method. Int. J. Concept. Electr. Electron. Eng. 2(1), 57 (2014)
5. Rao, R., Li Z., Song, H., Chen, Y., Li, D.: A New Kind of Transformer Oil State Detection Method based on Multi-frequency Detection Technique and Multivariate Statistics (2016)
6. Yaacob, M., Alsaedi, M., Rashed, J., Dakhil A., Atyah S.: Review on partial dis-charge detection techniques related to high voltage power equipment using different sensors. Photonic Sensors 4, 325–337 (2014)
7. Kumar, A.S., Gupta R.P., Udayakumar, K., Venkatasami, A.: Online partial dis-charge detection and location techniques for condition monitoring of power trans-formers: a review. In: 2008 International Conference on Condition Monitoring and Diagnosis, Beijing, pp. 927–931 (2008)
8. Kozioł, M., Nagi, Ł, Kunicki, M., Urbaniec, I.: Radiation in the optical and UHF range emitted by partial discharges. Energies 12, 22 (2019)
9. Oda M., Fuchigami, Y., Sawabe, Y.: Development of diagnostic technologies for electrical facilities and portable instruments utilizing these techniques. JFE Tech-nical Report, 153–160 (2016)
10. Gudzius, S., Jonaitis, A., Miliune, R., Morkvenas, A., Valatka, P., Malazinskas, V.: Investigation of influence of short duration overvoltage disturbances on partial discharge characteristics. In: 2017 IEEE 58th International Scientific Conference on Power and Electrical Engineering of Riga Technical University (RTUCON), Riga, pp. 1–5 (2017)
11. DFA300 Dielectric Fault Analyzer User Guide, Doble Engineering Company, USA, Rev. 1 (2013)
12. DFA300 Training course, Doble Engineering Company (2015)
13. Farahani, M., Borsi, H., Gockenbach, E., Kaufhold, M.: Partial discharge and dissipation factor behavior of model insulating systems for high voltage rotating machines under different stresses. IEEE Electr. Insul. Mag. 21(5), 5–19 (2005)

Smart Systems for Monitoring Buildings - An IoT Application

Rebeca B. Kalbermatter[1,2,3,6](✉) , Thadeu Brito[2,3,4,5](✉) ,
João Braun[2,3,4,5](✉) , Ana I. Pereira[2,3](✉) , Ângela P. Ferreira[2,3](✉) ,
António Valente[5,6](✉) , and José Lima[2,3,5](✉)

[1] Federal University of Technology – Parana (UTFPR), Curitiba, Brazil
[2] Research Centre in Digitalization and Intelligent Robotics (CeDRI),
Instituto Politécnico de Bragança, Campus de Santa Apolónia,
5300-253 Bragança, Portugal
{kalbermatter,brito,jbneto,apereira,apf,jllima}@ipb.pt
[3] Laboratório para a Sustentabilidade e Tecnologia em Regiões de Montanha
(SusTEC), Instituto Politécnico de Bragança, Campus de Santa Apolónia, 5300-253
Bragança, Portugal
[4] Faculdade de Engenharia, Universidade do Porto, Porto, Portugal
[5] INESC Technology and Science, Porto, Portugal
[6] Universidade de Trás-os-Montes e Alto Douro, Vila Real, Portugal
avalente@utad.pt

Abstract. Life in society has initiated a search for comfort and security
in social centers. This search generated revolutions within the knowledge
about the technologies involved, making the environments automated
and integrated. Along with this increase, ecological concerns have also
arisen, which have been involved since the design of intelligent buildings,
remaining through the years of their use. Based on these two pillars, the
present study aims to monitor three central systems inside the apartments of the Apolo Building (Bragança city, Portugal). The electrical
energy consumption, water flow, and waste disposal systems are integrated through a single database. The data is sent remotely via WiFi
through the microcontroller. For better visualization and analytics of the
data, a web application is also developed, which allows for real-time monitoring. The obtained results demonstrate to the consumer his behavior
regarding household expenses. The idea of showing the consumer their
expenditure is to create an ecological awareness. Through the data collected and the environmental alternatives found, it is possible to observe
whether there was a behavior change when receiving this data, either in
the short or long term.

Keywords: Internet of Things · Intelligent buildings · Wireless sensor
network

A. I. Pereira et al. (Eds.): OL2A 2022, CCIS 1754, pp. 575–588, 2022.
https://doi.org/10.1007/978-3-031-23236-7_40

1   Introduction

As life in society advanced, the need to create spaces that brought more comfort and safety became a priority [1]. To centralize social spaces, of either economic activities or residences, buildings were created to become the center of activities.

The first centralized control equipment appeared primarily in-room acclimatization equipment. With the greater dissemination of microcontroller processes, there was a high expansion in the control processes, which allowed the supervision and control of more developed equipment in larger quantities. But it was in the 80s, with the increase of the necessities to improve workplaces, bringing more comfort and safety to the environment, telecommunications services, and flexibility of workplaces that contributed to the emergence of the three pillars for the intelligent building system, these being: automation, telecommunications, and computing systems [1].

The term "smart" generated confusion in the designation of intelligent buildings because it induced people to have unreasonable expectations for these constructions. Due to the economic reality and the unfamiliarity of the users with new technologies, these expectations were frustrated, reducing the number of specialists, proliferation of brands and equipment, and appearing, in a way, a negative association to the term [1].

Although the presented work does not intend to classify or determine terms related to the field of intelligent buildings, a brief history related to the theme will be discussed in Sect. 2. The work focuses on collecting data regarding the systems of electric energy consumption, waste disposal, and water flow per apartment to create a database for developing future consumer awareness applications.

The remainder of the paper is organized as follows: following the introduction are the works related to the present development in Sect. 2. Next, Sect. 3 presents the description of the systems involved and the communication and data storage. Section 4 demonstrates the prototypes' developments and results. And finally, Sect. 5 concludes the results and points to possible future work.

2   Related Work

This section is dedicated to making a brief summary of the main works related to the systems that will be used in this project. Initially, in order to contextualize it, studies about the definition of smart buildings were also discussed.

2.1   Definition of Smart Building

The search for a definition of the smart building has always been accompanied by polemic. According to research conducted by Wigginton and Harris [2], there are more than 30 definitions of intelligent when related to buildings. In order to centralize, support, and promote issues related to intelligent buildings, the Intelligent Building Institute (IBI) organization was created in 1986 in the United States of America. This institution defined a concept restricted to the branch of the enterprise, being an intelligent building defined by [2]:

A building that provides a productive and cost-effective environment through optimization of its four basic elements - structure, systems, services, and management - and the interrelationship between them. Intelligent buildings help business owners, property managers and occupants to realize their goals in the areas of cost, comfort, convenience, safety, long-term flexibility and marketability.

In contrast to this definition, the UK-based European Intelligent Building Group defines it as [2]:

One that creates an environment which maximizes the effectiveness of the building's occupants, while at the same time enabling efficient management of resources with minimum life-time costs of hardware and facilities.

According to [3], the need to search for an exact definition for intelligent building s critical when "new building will not be optimally designed to meet the next century". Some more recent publications, such as by Yang and Peng [4], have added to the concept of intelligent building the "learning ability" and "performance adjustment from its occupancy and the environment".

The research developed by Wong et al. [5] sought to conduct a comprehensive review of the concepts and definitions of intelligent building, taking on some important directions for research related to intelligent building investment.

It is worth mentioning that it is explicit that an intelligent building will be the one with more integration between systems and not necessarily the one that is more automated. The integrated systems may be related to building infrastructure, automation of systems and integrated control, and management and maintenance of the whole system. In [6], it is pointed out that since there is no correct definition for intelligent building, the most sense, in her view, would be to classify buildings gradually according to "degrees" of intelligence, where:

A determined building as having basic intelligence (25% automation of the systems), moderate intelligence (50% automation of the systems), or sophisticated intelligence (over 80% automation of the systems).

2.2 Monitoring Systems

In [7], the main systems to be monitored for the human comfort standard are listed. They are generally classified within temperature, luminosity, and hearing to air quality (i.e., CO_2 level). Based on this, in [8], a system for monitoring the parameters of luminosity, temperature, relative humidity, and air quality was developed to ensure a service, according to them "intelligent, safe, and comfortable to live".

Thus, to obtain increasingly efficient buildings, the principal goal of automation was to make the processes involved efficient [9]. Specifically, energy efficiency is a concern when associated with smart buildings due to the costs and ecological care [10]. According to the Journal of the European Union [11], buildings account for 40% of total electricity consumption. This worry runs through all stages, from the building's design, construction, and usage. The optimization of electricity use must be monitored and goes through process control, applying improvements continuously at the points that lag behind.

The monitoring of energy consumption can be done through Hall Effect type sensors. These sensors can measure both DC and AC without the need for intervention between the monitoring circuit and the power circuit to be monitored. Hall Effect is the principle whereby a magnetic field passes perpendicularly through a rectangular conductor with current flow. As a result, electrons are deflected towards the ends of the conductor, generating a voltage known as Hall Voltage, the output voltage of which is proportional to the magnetic field in which the sensor is exposed [12].

Water efficiency has also become important as part of the ecological process surrounding intelligent buildings. According to World Water Development Report (WWRD), the immediate concern is its availability and management of it [13].

The work developed by Teixeira [14] aimed to develop a system that allows the certification and labeling of water efficiency, providing the consumer with knowledge about it. With the application of water efficiency measures to his case study, there was a 63.9% reduction in water consumption.

With the Internet of Things (IoT) technology, the waste management system has evolved in developing smart cities with Smart Waste Management (SWM), covering everything from monitoring the containers to planning the route taken to collect them. The work developed by Cerchecci et al. [15] proposes optimizing waste management by monitoring the capacity of dumpsters. The system uses LoRaWAN [16], and the measurement is made by an ultrasonic sensor, which is coupled to a Raspberry Pi board that sends the data to a central analysis. In real-time, the waste collection route is planned according to the quantities of waste garbage cans. It was observed that with these techniques applied, there was a reduction of 18% in the collection time, and the waste policies were optimized in the long term.

In [17], a temperature and humidity monitoring system was developed using low-cost sensors and ZigBee communication. The system can communicate with the smartphone by an Android application through a Raspberry Pi-based host and the STM32L100RCT7 microcontroller, with a power consumption of only 0.5W.

2.3   Internet of Things

The implementations of the monitoring systems were based on IoT technology. The term, which appeared in 1999 disseminated by researcher Kevin Ashton, with which the technology of integration between inanimate objects became known, allowing communication, transmission, and execution of various functions [18]. The root of this term is directly linked to the developed study of RFID (Radio Frequency Identification) technology. In [19], we see that IoT is not derived from technologies but uses them to fulfill functionality.

According to Debasis and Jaydip [20], the IoT system is a network of physical objects and virtual devices that can communicate with each other. Thus, it is possible to highlight that the IoT is responsible for generating multidisciplinary connectivity between professionals working on the system project, whether in hardware or software, allowing the construction of a quality and safety system [21]. For Ma [22], the increasing evolution and growing complexity involved in IoT technology bring challenges such as heterogeneity, device availability, exorbitant amounts of data, and security and privacy.

2.4   Wireless Sensors Network

In [23] Wireless Sensors Network (WSN) is defined as a self-configured network capable of monitoring physical or environmental conditions through sensors that have a centralized database where data can be observed and analyzed. The system can consist of thousands of sensors, where sensor nodes can communicate via radio signal [24,25]. According to [26], the WSN is divided into a hardware part, composed of a low-power embedded processor, memory, sensor with ADC units, radio transceiver, location finding system, and power supply, and another part for software, composed of operation system microcode, sensor drivers, communication processors, communication drivers, and data-processing mini-applications. Thus, one can characterize the WSN as a system consisting of sensing, computing, and communication between devices at a single network node. This centralization allows the measurement, data storage, and control of the systems involved.

In [27], a software application capable of communicating with a raw hardware system consisting of Magnetic Target Switch (MTS) sensors plugged into Processor and Radio Modules (MPR) is proposed. The TinyOS application developed "to support the concurrency-intensive operations required by networked sensors with minimal hardware requirements". In [28], WSN was used as a solution for energy management, with the data being visualized through a web application, which also allowed control of the devices involved in the system.

3   System Description

The proposed system in this work integrates three main sensors that transmit data via WiFi through the ESP32 microcontroller to a database in InfluxDB. The sensors are used for monitoring water flow, and waste discard (YF-B2, and load cell, respectively). Additionally, an IoTaWatt is applied to monitor electric energy consumption. For better comparisons between the data collected in the mentioned systems above, sensors were also added to monitor the local temperature and humidity, DHT11. The system architecture can be simplified as shown in Fig. 1. Each sensor's choice focuses on monitoring the basic usage of a regular apartment. This way, it is expected to find a correlation between each parameter. The used sensors are described throughout this section.

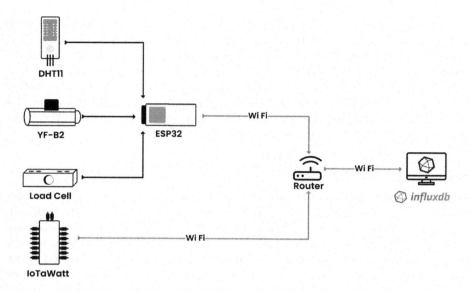

Fig. 1. Simplified System Architecture.

Energy System. Based on the operation of the Hall Effect, equipment from the company IoTaWatt [29] was installed in the system to be monitored. This equipment has a wall transformer that converts the local voltage to a standard reference voltage, allowing the line voltage and frequency to be determined. The transformer is capable of reading up to 14 different circuits with passive clamp-type sensors, i.e., it is not necessary to interrupt the cables to insert the sensors. Data storage can be done locally or remotely. The device also has its web server, where it is possible to monitor the system in real-time and remotely. For the case study in question, the configuration performed in the equipment allowed data to be sent directly to the project's database. Figure 2 shows the communication interface and the equipment already allocated for the testing phase.

The choice of measuring this parameter is to make hypotheses of energy consumption with external factors. For example, does temperature increase/decrease affect energy consumption? If yes, then by how much? And how can be this discerned if it was caused by an increase of people or temperature in the apartment?

Water System. The flow rate monitoring system will consist of a YF-B2 sensor [30]. This sensor is composed of a copper metal body, water rotor, and Hall effect sensor. As the speed at which the water passes through the rotor varies, the Hall sensor sends out pulse signals corresponding to the flow. To convert these signals, These signals are read by the ESP32 microcontroller and converted to the flow rate in liters per minute.

The YF-B2's small size makes it easy to install, making it possible to install it in $\frac{1}{2}$" pipes. Its operating voltage ranges from 5-15V, and the maximum

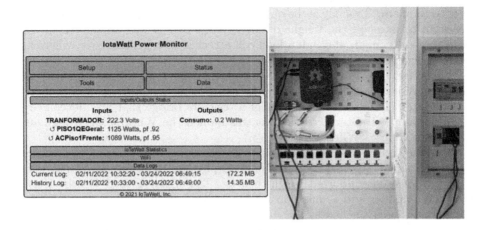

Fig. 2. IoTaWatt's communication interface in the test phase.

operating current is 15 mA. The flow rate reading is 1–25 L/min, with a liquid temperature capability up to 120°C. It is worth noting that the external operating temperature of the sensor is limited to 0–80°C. As the building where the system is being developed already has the hydraulic part finished, it is necessary to have the sensor installed by a professional. At the time of this publication, this installation was not possible, and for this technical reason, the approach to this sensor will not be the focus of the work presented here. The electronic connection between the sensor and the microcontroller is shown in Fig. 3.

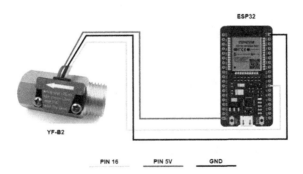

Fig. 3. Eletronic connection YF-B2 sensor.

As with the other systems, the purpose of measuring the flow rate is to create relationships between environmental data and consumption, such as the difference in water consumption in different seasons, hence different temperatures of the year, and show how these variables are related.

Waste System. To analyze the quantities of garbage discarded in the residence, a system to measure the weight of the garbage drums was implemented. This measurement is made through a load cell attached to a generic base, where any waste basket can be placed on it.

The types of load cells can be characterized by their output signal (pneumatic, electrical or hydraulic) or by the principle of weight detection (bending, tension, etc.). Its operation consists of a resistors bridge that was developed in 1833 by Samuel Hunter Christie, but was named the Wheatstone Bridge after its diffuser Charles Wheatstone.

The load cell used in this work acts by changing the electrical resistance of the signal as the applied weight generates physical deformation on the plate, with a maximum supported weight of 5 kg. The signal is read via the HX711 load cell amplifier and acquisition module, which sends the data to the ESP32 microcontroller.

For this system, the purpose of measuring waste disposal goes beyond having weight data. It is necessary to evaluate the relationship between the waste disposed and, for example, the increase in temperature or energy consumption. The goal of this study is to create these relationships between the monitored consumption and to analyze the behavior patterns with the changes associated with temperature, humidity, season, visits to the apartment, and other changes.

Temperature and Humidity Monitoring. The DHT11 sensor was also added to the system, which allows the monitoring of local humidity and temperature, allowing a more comparative analysis between the state of the environment and the expenses generated. As mentioned in the previous topics, the purpose of monitoring these systems is to create relationships between the data. The choice to measure the local temperature and humidity becomes of crucial importance since it is one of the factors that can cause the most changes in the consumption generated. This sensor has a low cost and it is easy to install, with an operating voltage of 3–5.5 V, which allows it to be used directly in the ESP32. This type of sensor is already factory calibrated and is capable of having readings of 20–80% humidity and temperatures between 0–50 °C, with an error of 5% and ± 2 °C, respectively.

Communication and Database Description. The ESP32 [31] is an embedded system board, produced by Espressiff System. By having a low cost, integrating WiFi and Bluetooth systems on the same embedded board, the ESP32 is commonly used in IoT projects. The microcontroller's operating range is 2.2V to 3.6V, and power consumption is around 0.3W. The source code was integrated into the ESP32 board, which is a bridge between acquiring the data from the sensors and sending it via iFi to the database.

For a better analysis and comparison of the obtained data, an important feature in data collection is the date and time tag. Thus, the Time Series Database (TSDB), offers an optimization when used in time series, as the present case. This type of database was created so that the user could have the freedom to create, update, manipulate and organize time series more efficiently, allowing the visualization of long-term changes [32].

InfluxDB [33] is a database developed by InfluxData, which allows to create a TSDB database. According to DB-Engines Ranking [14,34], InfluxDB ranks first among Time Series models. The [34] is an independent site that ranks databases according to search engine popularity and frequency of technical discussions.

For the project, the web application Grafana [35] was also used, which allows better visualization of the data with the creation of several interactive dashboards. This application also allows updates of the visualized data automatically and even in real-time. Figure 4 allows the visualization of one of the charts generated to monitor the data obtained from the test apartment. It is possible to see that the graph for the water flow is null, because, as mentioned in Sect. 3, this sensor could not be installed at the time of this publication and will be discussed as future work. However, the database and the Grafana are already configured to receive the data.

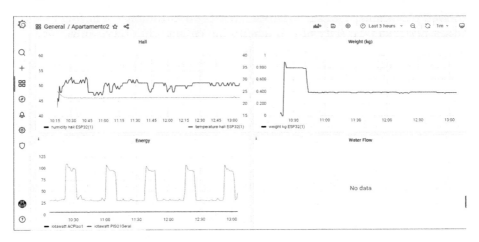

Fig. 4. Grafana Monitorization.

4   Development and Results

The study developed was installed in the Apolo Building, in Bragança, Portugal. Although the building was under construction, most of the structure was already finished, so it was necessary to find a solution that had minimal intervention in the construction. A pilot apartment was chosen to serve as a test since the building cannot be inhabited yet. The implementation done in this project pursued low-cost solutions, as can be seen in Table 1. The values were based on Portuguese stores of electronic components for the sensors and microcontroller and the IoTaWatt site for its equipment.

First of all, IoTaWatt is already installed initially with two sensors, one to capture the overall consumption of the apartment and the other specifically for

Table 1. Project cost.

Component	Cost (€)
ESP32	6,50
DHT11 Sensor	4,50
YF-B2	7,40
Load Cell + HX711 Module	11,40
IoTaWatt (Module + 5 sensors)	201,50

air conditioning consumption. In the future, it will be used to monitor more specifically the apartment's consumption, such as consumption from the power supply of the induction stove, or consumption only with the lights. This specification of consumption can be done through the electric panel. Initially, was installed the Shelly EM equipment, from the company Shelly. This meter, despite working very similarly to the IoTaWatt, has the disadvantage of having modules with a maximum capacity of two monitoring circuits. In other words, for measurements in larger quantities, which was planned, more equipment from Shelly would be needed. The idea was then replaced by the IoTaWatt equipment, which as mentioned earlier, allows the reading of up to 14 different circuits.

From Fig. 4, the data obtained through IoTaWatt allows us to observe some peaks in overall electricity consumption. As mentioned earlier, this test apartment has no residents yet, which allows us to conclude that these peaks are from the refrigerator, the only equipment turned on uninterruptedly. Also, by observing the graph, it is possible to validate the functioning of the garbage system. A 3D prototype was developed for this system, which can be visualized in Fig. 5. A button was also attached to the system that allows the tare of the scale to be reset when the garbage can changes.

It is important to mention that the systems that are integrated inside the apartment, namely the DHT11 and load cell sensors, are connected to the same ESP32, which is located inside the apartment. The water flow sensor, on the other hand, which is located at the entrance to the building, is connected to

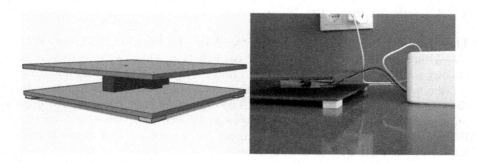

Fig. 5. 3D prototype and weighing balance system.

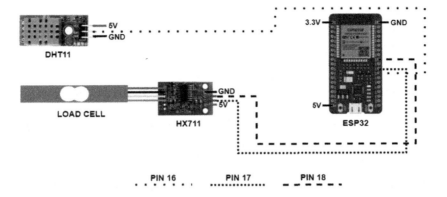

Fig. 6. Diagram between sensors and microcontroller.

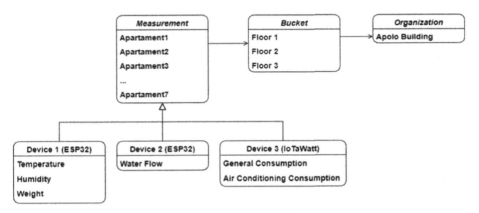

Fig. 7. Architecture of InfluxDB.

another ESP32, where in the future all flow sensors of all the apartments will be connected. And as mentioned earlier, the IoTaWatt has an integrated microcontroller, so its communication is direct via WiFi, without the need for a connection to the apartment's ESP32. Figure 6 shows the connection between the sensors and the ESP32.

The database was divided between floor and apartment tags, with the floor being "bucket" and apartments, "measurements", in order to optimize for a future machine learning implementation. The simplified system architecture is shown in Fig. 7. In summary, the database was divided between floors and apartments, to allow better machine learning applications in the future through these filters.

5   Conclusion and Future Work

The integration of systems via IoT allows centralizing all the information obtained in the building. As mentioned earlier, the idea of making the building intelligent aims to promote not only the automation of it, such as doors with electronic locks, remote on/off function for lights, but to integrate all the systems involved.

This paper presented a low-cost solution using open-source tools to integrate metering systems in buildings. The data obtained allow performing a diagnostic analysis of the consumption. Although the data collected is not real, since the building is not inhabited yet, it allowed the prototype development and its validation. As some of the hardware is still under development, it has not been shown completely. After the complete data acquisition prototype has been installed and developed, better data analysis will be possible. We presented the current results only to demonstrate the operation of the designed system and list the intended next steps for this project. Among them is the application of machine learning, in order to create relationships between the consumption and the resident's behavior. In the future, a printed circuit board is being developed that will allow the addition of various sensors that may be desirable to monitor other parameters of the apartment, for example, light intensity, air quality or sound noise.

As future work, is worth mentioning create an specific application to make the data collected and processed available to the resident. The main objective of the project is not to control the behavior of the resident, but to monitor the data collected, with the consent of the same and show viable alternatives that bring ecological solutions to the expenses generated. The application can be either via smartphone or tablet, or even displayed on the interactive screen inside the apartment. Through data analytics it will be possible to observe whether there will be short- and long-term changes through the information presented to the resident. There can also be integration of the other systems already present in the building, such as monitoring the air conditioning operation cycle, opening the entrance door, among other systems.

Acknowledgment. The authors are grateful to the Foundation for Science and Technology (FCT, Portugal) for financial support through national funds FCT/MCTES (PIDDAC) to CeDRI (UIDB/05757/2020 and UIDP/05757/2020) and SusTEC (LA/P/0007/2021). Thadeu Brito was supported by FCT PhD grant SFRH/BD/08598 /2020 and João Braun received the support of a fellowship from "la Caixa" Foundation (ID 100010434) with code LCF/BQ/DI20/11780028.

References

1. de Pádua, I.P.: Caracterização de Edifícios Inteligentes - Um caso exemplo. Master's thesis, Pontifícia Universidade Católica de Minas Gerais, Brazil (2006)
2. Wigginton, M., Harris, J.: Intelligent Skins. Routledge, London (2013)

3. So, A.T., Wong, A.C., et al.: A new definition of intelligent buildings for Asia. Facilities. **17**, 485–491 (1999)
4. Yang, J., Peng, H.: Decision support to the application of intelligent building technologies. Renew. Energy **22**(1–3), 67–77 (2001)
5. Wong, J.K., Li, H., Wang, S.: Intelligent building research: a review. Autom. Constr. **14**(1), 143–159 (2005)
6. Braga, L.C.: Estudo de aspectos de eficiência energética de edificações com uma abordagem de automação predial. Master's thesis, Universidade Federal de Minas Gerais, Brasil (2007)
7. Fincher, W., Boduch, M.: Standards of human comfort: relative and absolute. University of Texas, Austin, USA, pp. 02–04 (2009)
8. Al-Kuwari, M., Ramadan, A., Ismael, Y., Al-Sughair, L., Gastli, A., Benammar, M.: Smart-home automation using IoT-based sensing and monitoring platform. In: 2018 IEEE 12th International Conference on Compatibility, Power Electronics and Power Engineering (CPE-POWERENG 2018), pp. 1–6 (2018). https://doi.org/10. 1109/CPE.2018.8372548
9. Sauter, T., Soucek, S., Kastner, W., Dietrich, D.: The evolution of factory and building automation. IEEE Ind. Electron. Mag. **5**(3), 35–48 (2011). https://doi. org/10.1109/MIE.2011.942175
10. Martins, R.W.D.: Otimização preditiva de operação energética de edifícios inteligentes. Ph.D. thesis, Universidade do Porto (2016)
11. Union, E.: Energy efficient buildings. https://energy.ec.europa.eu/topics/energy-efficiency/energy-efficient-buildings_en. Accessed 15 Jan 2022
12. Smith, G.M.: Como medir a corrente usando sensores e transdutores de corrente (2021), https://dewesoft.com/br/aquisicao-de-dados/como-medir-corrente-usando-sensores-de-corrente. Accessed 4 May 2022
13. Connor, R.: The United Nations world water development report 2015: water for a sustainable world, vol. 1. UNESCO publishing (2015)
14. Teixeira, R.M.M.: Uso Sustentável da Água: Avaliação de benefícios adotando eficiência hídrica em edifícios. Master's thesis, Universidade de Coimbra, Portugal (2015)
15. Cerchecci, M., Luti, F., Mecocci, A., Parrino, S., Peruzzi, G., Pozzebon, A.: A low power IoT sensor node architecture for waste management within smart cities context. Sensors. **18**(4), 1282 (2018). https://doi.org/10.3390/s18041282, https:// www.mdpi.com/1424-8220/18/4/1282
16. Semtech: LoRaWAN® Standart. https://www.semtech.com/lora/lorawan-standard. Accessed 4 May 2022
17. Adiono, T., Fathany, M.Y., Fuada, S., Purwanda, I.G., Anindya, S.F.: A portable node of humidity and temperature sensor for indoor environment monitoring. In: 2018 3rd International Conference on Intelligent Green Building and Smart Grid (IGBSG), pp. 1–5 (2018). https://doi.org/10.1109/IGBSG.2018.8393575
18. Ashton, K., et al.: That 'internet of things thing. RFID J. **22**(7), 97–114 (2009)
19. Faccioni Filho, M.: Internet das coisas. Unisul Virtual (2016)
20. Bandyopadhyay, D., Sen, J.: Internet of things: applications and challenges in technology and standardization. Wirel. Pers. Commun. **58**(1), 49–69 (2011)
21. Mascarenhas, A.P.R.M., et al.: Desenvolvimento de produtos iot. Braz. J. Dev. **7**(1), 4711–4724 (2021)
22. Ma, H.D.: Internet of things: objectives and scientific challenges. J. Comput. Sci. Technol. **26**(6), 919–924 (2011)
23. Matin, M.A., Islam, M.: Overview of wireless sensor network. Wirel. Sensor Netw. Technol. Protoc. **1**(3), 1–25 (2012)

24. Brito, T., Pereira, A.I., Lima, J., Valente, A.: Wireless sensor network for ignitions detection: an IoT approach. Electronics **9**(6), 893 (2020). https://doi.org/10.3390/electronics9060893

25. Brito, T., et al.: Optimizing data transmission in a wireless sensor network based on LoRaWAN protocol. In: Pereira, A.I., et al. (eds.) OL2A 2021. CCIS, vol. 1488, pp. 281–293. Springer, Cham (2021). https://doi.org/10.1007/978-3-030-91885-9_20

26. Nack, F.: An overview on wireless sensor networks. Institute of Computer Science (ICS), Freie Universität Berlin, vol. 6 (2010)

27. Rajaravivarma, V., Yang, Y., Yang, T.: An overview of wireless sensor network and applications. In: Proceedings of the 35th Southeastern Symposium on System Theory 2003, pp. 432–436 (2003). https://doi.org/10.1109/SSST.2003.1194607

28. Grindvoll, H., Vermesan, O., Crosbie, T., Bahr, R., Dawood, N., Revel, G.M.: A wireless sensor network for intelligent building energy management based on multi communication standards-a case study. J. Inf. Technol. Constr. **17**, 43–61 (2012)

29. IoTaWatt: The best kept energy monitoring secret. https://iotawatt.com/. Accessed 25 Aug 2022

30. SEEED: https://media.digikey.com/pdf/DataSheets/SeeedTechnology/114991172_Web.pdf. Accessed 6 May 2022

31. Espressif: Esp32-wroom-3d datasheet. https://www.espressif.com/. Accessed 4 May 2022

32. Giacobbe, M., Chaouch, C., Scarpa, M., Puliafito, A.: An implementation of InfluxDB for Monitoring and analytics in distributed IoT environments. In: Bouhlel, M.S., Rovetta, S. (eds.) SETIT 2018. SIST, vol. 146, pp. 155–162. Springer, Cham (2020). https://doi.org/10.1007/978-3-030-21005-2_15

33. Data, I.: Open source time series database. https://www.influxdata.com/. Accessed 6 May 2022

34. DB-Engines: Db-engines ranking of time series DBMs. https://db-engines.com/en/ranking/time+series+dbms. Accessed 6 May 2022

35. Labs, G.: The open observability platform. https://grafana.com/. Accessed 6 May 2022

Map Coverage of LoRaWAN Signal's Employing GPS from Mobile Devices

Thadeu Brito[1,2,3]($\boxtimes$) (ID), João Mendes[1]($\boxtimes$) (ID), Matheus Zorawski[1] (ID),
Beatriz Flamia Azevedo[1,4]($\boxtimes$) (ID), Ala Khalifeh[5]($\boxtimes$) (ID), Florbela P. Fernandes[1] (ID),
Ana I. Pereira[1,4]($\boxtimes$) (ID), José Lima[1,3]($\boxtimes$) (ID), and Paulo Costa[2,3]($\boxtimes$) (ID)

[1] Research Centre in Digitalization and Intelligent Robotics (CeDRI),
Instituto Politécnico de Bragança, Campus de Santa Apolónia,
5300-253 Bragança, Portugal
{brito,joao.cmendes,matheuszorawski,beatrizflamia,
fflor,apereira,jllima}@ipb.pt
[2] Faculty of Engineering of University of Porto, Porto, Portugal
paco@fe.up.pt
[3] INESC TEC - INESC Technology and Science, Porto, Portugal
[4] Algoritmi Research Centre, University of Minho, Guimarães, Portugal
[5] German Jordanian University, Amman, Jordan
ala.khalifeh@gju.edu.jo

Abstract. Forests are remote areas with uneven terrain, so it is costly to map the range of signals that enable the implementation of systems based on wireless and long-distance communication. Even so, the interest in Internet of Things (IoT) functionalities for forest monitoring systems has increasingly attracted the attention of several researchers. This work demonstrates the development of a platform that uses the GPS technology of mobile devices to map the signals of a LoRaWAN Gateway. Therefore, the proposed system is based on concatenating two messages to optimize the LoRaWAN transmission using the Global Position System (GPS) data from a mobile device. With the proposed approach, it is possible to guarantee the data transmission when finding the ideal places to fix nodes regarding the coverage of LoRaWAN because the Gateway bandwidth will not be fulfilled. The tests indicate that different changes in the relief and large bodies drastically affect the signal provided by the Gateway. This work demonstrates that mapping the Gateway's signal is essential to attach modules in the forest, agriculture zones, or even smart cities.

Keywords: Internet of Things · Map coverage · LoRaWAN · GPS tracking · Signal quality

1 Introduction

Protecting forests is an emerging issue worldwide, given the enormous importance of these ecosystems to the planet. The possibilities and challenges in developing a robust surveillance system are several. Portugal has the highest incidence of wildfires in the Mediterranean region [1]. Recent studies point out that, in the case of forest fires in Portugal, plans for macro-scale actions are already more than consolidated. These plans demonstrate that it is possible to mitigate fire damage considerably. However, according to [2], there is a perspective that only these macro plans are still insufficient to solve this problem. Therefore, there is a need for a thorough study of innovative technologies with the potential to intensify fire fighting or even create new plans on a micro-scale. In this sense, the new features inserted in Forest 4.0 can digitize regions to help combat teams in decision-making.

The project Forest Alert Monitoring System (SAFe) comes with the proposal to develop innovative technologies to allow efficient forest monitoring based on Internet of Things (IoT) technologies. For any IoT application, the study of device position and data transmission is essential to guarantee system efficiency [3–6]. Forests are generally remote, abandoned/unmanaged areas, hard to protect due to their characteristic of large dimensions, irregular lands, trees, animals, and other obstacles that can interfere the signal quality and, consequently, compromise the integrity and transfer of crucial information that guarantee the correct functioning of the system.

As the forest is remote areas with irregular lands, it becomes even more challenging to map the range of signals that implement systems based on wireless and long-distance communication. However, the interest in IoT functionalities for forest monitoring systems has increased the attention of several researchers. Motivated by the popularization of technologies such as LoRaWAN and Global Positioning System (GPS), many researchers are concentrating on overcoming the difficulty in providing signal and communication guarantees between IoT devices. The use of Long Range Communication (LoRa) and GPS can be seen in [7], in which a forest monitoring system through flame sensors modules is presented. The system can predict and detect forest fire through a sensor (Flame Sensor Module YL-38) and send an alert message to the fire authorities. In this case, the Global System for Mobile (GSM) technology is used to give an alert signal through a cell phone, and the integration between the LoRa transmitter and the GPS systems allows the recognition of the fire location precisely. Another proposal of the LoRa module with GPS integration to forest fire monitoring system is shown in [8]. The system uses LoRa with a GPS hat module integrated into Raspberry Pi 3 to transmit and receive data using radio frequency communication. A set of flame sensor modules is used to detect fire, and through the system integration (sensor, LoRA, and GPS), it is possible to know the fire location, taking the coordinates data from the GPS.

Developing a platform that uses GPS technology from mobile devices to map the signals of a LoRaWAN Gateway can optimize the mapping. In this sense, the platform would use the mobile internet network (3G, 4G, or 5G) to inform the values of the coordinates (latitude and longitude). This process would prevent data from being transmitted via LoRaWAN, as they are data with many decimal places (e.g., 41.796289, −6.767479). Therefore, to not waste LoRaWAN transmission during mapping, the proposed system is based on the concatenation of two messages: a message from a mobile device's GPS and another from a device with communication-based on LoRaWAN. The proposed approach is expected to guarantee data transmission by finding the ideal locations to fix the nodes concerning LoRaWAN coverage. At the same time, it is keeping the Gateway bandwidth not fully occupied.

The rest of the paper is organized as follows. After the introduction, section 2 presents the related work. In section 3, the system architecture is addressed, and the focus of this paper is highlighted. Section 4 presents the mapping used to identify the LoRaWAN coverage area, and section 5 stresses the results of the proposed application. Section 6 concludes the paper and points to future work.

2   Related Work

The performance of any IoT-based system is intrinsically related to positioning issues. Since these systems depend on remote connection, it is essential to guarantee signal transmission and reception quality. Besides, in some IoT applications, such as forest monitoring systems, it is crucial to know the real device's position since this location will guide the fire-fighting actions. GPS has been widely used in IoT applications, however, the GPS technology is relatively expensive and has high power consumption, becoming unappropriated for long-range and low-power IoT devices [9]. Communication technology that has increased more and more popularity in the IoT domain, especially for long distances communication, is the Low Power Wide Area Network (LPWAN), with a particular highlight on LoRa technology, which is a physical layer that enables the long-range communication link [10] with low power consumption [11]. The LoRaWAN uses the LoRa spectrum modulation method in a communication protocol and system architecture for the network designed to support a large part of the billions of devices associated with the IoT [10].

Signal modulation in the LoRa architecture is carried out using the Chirp Spread Spectrum and is broadcast in unlicensed Industrial, Scientific, and Medical (ISM) frequency bands, which can minimize the cost of its use [12]. This frequency range is available according to the place of use, and in Europe, the frequency range available is between 863 MHz to 870 MHz [13]. In addition to the restrictions made, the frequency to be used is still necessary to obey a set of constraints like the transmission power +14 dBm, Duty-cycle < 1% and a Bandwidth of 125 kHz [14,15]. Another parameter that directly affects this modulation's distance and transmission quality is the relationship between the bit rate and the chip rate, and the Spreading Factor (SF). The SF can assume values from 7 to 12, and the higher the assumed value, the more the Signal-to-Noise Ratio (SNR), also increasing the sensitivity and the range of the packet, however, it also increases the transmission airtime [16].

Considering these restrictions in the article [17], the authors propose a new approach based on cloud-centric systems for automatically creating coverage maps in complex scenarios. To elaborate on this system, the authors use Laird's Sentrius RG186 gateway. The Microchip RN2483 is connected to a notebook to provide the GPS coordinates since the microchip does not have this capability as an end device. The used configurations were divided into three topics, better transmission confidence, wider range both with an SF of 12, and faster data rate with an SF of 7. The presented results in this paper solidify the need to carry out network mapping, demonstrating that the area coverage can be very uneven, with multiple barriers between end nodes and gateways hindering successful communications.

As the forest usually is large and remote, the LPWAN is the optimum solution for IoT device development. Although there are other LPWAN technologies such as SigFox, LTE, Random Phase Multiple Access (RPMA) and 5G that can be used in remote areas. The low-cost LoRa nodes and gateways led to the increment of its attraction, mainly in the area with difficult access. Additionally, compared to SigFox, the closest technology, LoRa can reach a higher Data Transfer Rate [11]. Once the LoRa signal can cover a wide area, it is essential to analyze the quality of the signal power available in the sender device's position and the receiver's position. The Received Signal Strength Indication (RSSI) receives signal power in milliwatts and is measured in dBm. This value can be used to measure how well a receiver can "hear" a signal from a sender [18]. Another critical parameter to be measured is the SNR, which describes the relationship between the received power signal and the noise floor power level [19].

3   System Architecture

The map coverage of the LoRaWAN signal is of great importance for systems that require a guarantee that they will be receiving the data at the LoRa gateways, thus being of greater or lesser importance according to which system will be applied. One of the LoRa network problems is to provide coverage in certain areas, as previously mentioned, in addition to the fact that there is no tool to map the network coverage points. This section will deal with which system this work aims to use and its respective architecture for tracking the LoRa signals.

3.1   SAFe

The SAFe project intends to integrate some tools that can work collaboratively and form the architecture of the system, illustrated in Fig. 1. The region that SAFe project intends to monitor is represented by Ⓐ. A set of wireless sensor modules, represented by Ⓑ will be allocated on strategy points to collect data. The Gateway is represented by Ⓒ, with an internet connection represented by Ⓓ. The Gateway will receive the data from each sensor module by radio frequency communication, and then forward the data through a 4G/LTE link (or by Ethernet where available) represented by Ⓔ to a server represented by Ⓕ. The received data by the server will be processed on the control center Ⓖ, that computes the data and sends alerts for hazardous situations or forest fire ignitions to the surveillance agent in the region. The received data will also be stored and processed by artificial intelligence procedures to correlate data from sensor modules with external data represented by ⒣; such as satellite image, local scale real-time fire hazard indexes, availability fuel content and weather data.

In general, the system proposed by SAFe can be divided into 4 main elements: I - the monitoring region, which involves the study of regions with a potential risk of forest fires, II - the set of sensor modules, where the sensor technical specification is considered and also the sensor positioning, III - the communication system in which the technologies that make it possible to receive and send data are defined, and finally the element IV - the control center, where the data are stored, processed and the decision are taken.

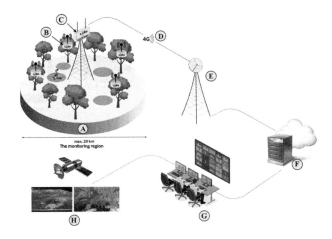

Fig. 1. Illustration of SAFe system architecture [5,6].

Due to the complexity in the description and development of each one of these elements, this work will focus only on the study of the communication system, expressly, the study of the signal range provided by the Gateway. For this, it is necessary to map the region where the sensors may be installed, ensuring data transmission.

3.2   Overview LoRa Tracker

The LoRa mapping system presented here results from a combination of several free software programs, resulting in a graphical presentation of the coverage relative to a given LoRaWAN Gateway. The entire system was implemented using the programming tool Node-RED. It was necessary to import the location data and the data from the test module. Since this is a mapping system and considering that the test module is not equipped with GPS, it is necessary to use a mobile device equipped with these functions allied to the LoRa module. Therefore, localization software must be used to obtain the locations with a specific time interval, thus enabling the configuration simultaneously with the data from the module.

For this purpose, the OwnTracks application was used; this is a free and open-source application that allows the location of mobile devices, ensuring various options for the time interval between locations. Once the exact location is obtained, it is also necessary to ensure the transmission of the module data to be able to interconnect the data and perform reliable coverage. In this way, The Things Network (TTN) application is used; this global community aims to build an open-source and decentralized LoRaWAN network. The following Fig. 2 shows the system's operation.

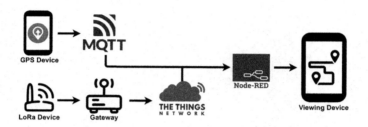

Fig. 2. System architecture for acquiring the map coverage.

As it can be seen, there are two sources of data import, the OwnTracks software for importing the location data and the TTN platform that guarantees data acquisition regarding the modules. Implementing the OwnTracks software in the system depends on the Message Queuing Telemetry Transport (MQTT) protocol, which will send the data from the software to the Node-RED program using mobile internet. The data obtained through the TTN platform will be further divided, taking into account its signal strength and its SNR, resulting in different colors depending on the power and the associated SNR.

The system is configured to allow multiple measurements on different hours or days, saving all data individually, thus allowing the user to choose whether to access the database in its entirety or only on a particular day. Next, the system's operation will be presented in more detail, from data acquisition to the map presented to the user.

4   Mapping

The literature demonstrates several types of tracking signals' transmission based on LoRaWAN technology, and most studies point to the use of a GPS shield inserted into nodes that perform the communication. Thus, this GPS shield will send the coordinates together with the LoRaWAN signal; that is, when there is some data transmission, the module sends the GPS location incorporated into the payload. When performing this tracking process, the user will consume a large amount of LoRaWAN's duty cycle (an example of fair use policy can be seen in [20]). After all, one of the variables that influence the accuracy of this tracking is the number of bytes used by the decimal places of coordinates. In other words, the user consumes a significant amount of bytes to transmit the floating points of the GPS location. This excessive consumption of the duty cycle leads to a high transmission interval during the tracking process (amount of sampling of transmitted signals); consequently, the identification of the transmission point can be affected. For example, if a device is installed on a truck with a 3-minute transmission interval, it may be that the truck is too fast to track at some points. In this case, by optimizing the sending of the location to increase the amount of sampling, the truck does not need to reduce its speed.

Considering the problem of excessive consumption of bytes when employing a GPS shield to perform the tracking of LoRaWAN signals, an alternative was sought to monitor the gateways transmission used in the SAFe project [3–6]. Therefore, the work's purpose is to use two devices to create the signal map coverage. Thus, one device is in charge of transmitting the data via LoRaWAN, and another device is responsible for informing the GPS coordinate using MQTT. In this sense, the flowchart shown in Fig. 3 summarizes the union of the data from these two devices. This process occurs in the system's first part, identified as Data Acquisition and Storage. On the other hand, the second part is named Monitoring and Updating of Data; in this step, the data stored in the previous process is read and published in a dashboard.

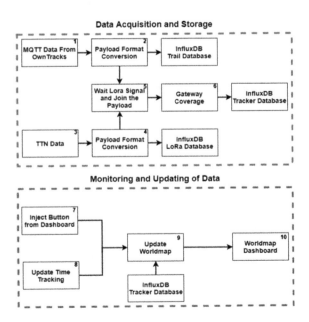

Fig. 3. Flowchart of all processes connected during the map coverage.

The first device is namely the node that transmits data via LoRaWAN; for this approach, a node adapted from [4,5] was used. As it is only necessary to obtain the LoRaWAN transmission at a certain point, this node has been adapted to send only the battery levels. Thus, during the creation of the map coverage, the proposed approach consumes 2 bytes of payload transmission. The second device, responsible for sending the GPS location is a Galaxy Tab A7 tablet model $SM-T505$ from the manufacturer Samsung. It was chosen for bearing: Android operating system (compatible system to install OwnTracks) and having access to the internet via WiFi and 4G LTE (these networks can be used to receive GPS locations through MQTT). Note that any other device could replace the second device with internet access and support for the OwnTracks application.

As previously mentioned, the system is developed to work on the Node-RED platform. In this platform, to generate the map coverage, all data (GPS location and LoRaWANs' transmission) are acquired, stored with the support of InfluxDB, and viewed through the Node-RED dashboard. Therefore, all data concerning location, module data, and the conjunction of these two are saved in different databases. The `Monitoring and Updating Data` is done using a world map implemented in Node-RED, the plugin `Worldmap`, where all the acquired data is placed, resulting in a map that combines not only the validated data according to signal strength and SNR but also the GPS data where there is no coverage. This way, it will be possible to elaborate a more specific coverage map facilitating the implementation of any system that uses LoRaWAN transmission. Figure 3 exemplifies the `Flow` implemented in Node-RED, starting with the description of the first part (`Data Acquisition and Storage`):

- **MQTT Data from OwnTracks** ①: the coordinate's values informed by the mobile device are received via MQTT using 4G LTE communication from GPS tablet.
- **Payload Format Conversion - GPS** ②: a function is applied to select only the values necessary to perform the work. They are Accuracy, Altitude, Latitude and Longitude. Then, these values are saved in the `Trail` database created in InfluxDB.
- **TTN Data** ③: the values of the LoRaWAN transmission produced by the node are received, indicating that at a certain point, there is coverage of the signal provided by the Gateway.
- **Payload Format Conversion - LoRaWAN** ④: a function is dedicated that guarantees the correct acquisition of the payload for a given Gateway (named by TTN as `gtw_id`). In other words, verify if the transmission was performed by the Gateway in focus, then the data will be saved in the `LoRa` database created in InfluxDB. These data are Airtime, Channel, Frequency, Gateway Altitude, Gateway Latitude, Gateway Longitude, Payload, RSSI and SNR.
- **Wait LoRa Signal and Join the Payloads** ⑤: Buffer the last message provided by the tablet's GPS until a TTN message appears. Then, these two messages are grouped and checked if the values are different from null.

– **Gateway coverage ⑥**: saves the final message in the `Tracker` database created in InfluxDB and executes the information available to the Worldmap dashboard.

After the acquisition of all data and its storage, it is always necessary to maintain the coverage map updated. For this purpose, the second part `Monitoring and Updating of Data` is dedicated (Fig. 3):

– **Inject Button from Dashboard ⑦**: Button for updating map when the user wants to see if there are new changes.
– **Update time tracking ⑧**: time interval in loop mode that performs the map update automatically.
– **Update Worldmap ⑨**: this function will access all the messages stored in `Tracker` database to search for the information that generates the LoRaWAN coverage map.
– **Worldmap dashboard ⑩**: Receives a data stream with the information each time the node has communicated with its respective coordinate provided by the mobile device. It indicates a colored line according to the signal strength and the entire trail made by the GPS.

The code implemented in Node-RED to perform all the steps detailed above can be seen in Fig. 4.

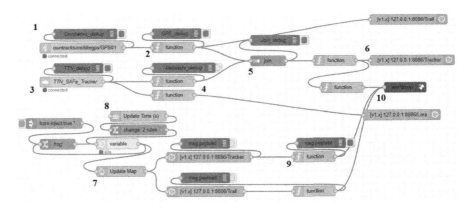

Fig. 4. Flow implemented for concatenating messages of MQTT and LoRaWAN and providing the coverage mapping in dashboard view mode.

5   Results

As mentioned before, a module based on SAFe project [4,5] was used with some adaptations and a tablet Tab A7 Galaxy model SM-T505. In this sense, it is possible to validate whether the platform developed in this work can perform the coverage map of the LoRaWAN network of the SAFe project. With these two devices, it is expected that the LoRaWAN network coverage mapping is identified through the adapted module's communication and the sending of messages of the Tablet's GPS location. These two devices should always be as close as possible to each other so that the mapping has better accuracy when both send the information.

The mapping will be focused on analyzing the quality of the LoRaWAN signal provided by the Gateway RAK 7249 installed on the roof of the *Escola Superior de Tecnologia e Gestão de Bragança* (ESTiG) - Polytechnic Institute of Bragança (IPB). Therefore, only the data obtained by this one will be accounted for in generating the map, ignoring others in the area. This Gateway contains the default settings for 16 channels; that is, the two concentrators are enabled and configured to operate between 863 MHz to870 MHz. As previously mentioned, the node used in this test is only configured to send the battery level information. This configuration was chosen only to optimize the sending of messages during the test; in other words, not to occupy the Gateway's duty cycle too much and increase the sending time interval. Therefore, the time interval for this node is 30 seconds. On the other hand, the tablet has the OwnTracks settings recommended by default, except for the location sending interval. This interval is set to send the current coordinates every 100 meters or every 30 seconds. Before starting the test, it was verified that all databases were empty, as shown in Fig. 5. Then, a button to refresh the map by request is created, and a possibility to set an automatic time to update the map.

Fig. 5. Map Layout in Node-RED dashboard.

The first test was carried out around the Gateway RAK 7249, which implies the two devices were carried by a person walking approximately 500 meters away from the Gateway. Figure 6 demonstrates the result obtained in this LoRaWAN signal coverage map, where it is possible to see the person's trail represented with a human symbol. A blue line was designed according to the signal strength when there was a simultaneous combination between the two communication signals (GPS location and LoRaWAN signal).

Fig. 6. The first test - walking close to the Gateway.

The blue coloration was established according to Table 1, where nine levels of sizes and blue colors range from −85 dB to −125 dB (RSSI). These values are obtained through LoRaWAN communication, as the TTN service informs communication quality data and the message payload. Each blue line is created with a Euclidean equation from the position of the Gateway to the two devices, and the pixel size gives its thickness in the Worldmap.

Table 1. Opacity and weight according to the RSSI signal.

RSSI [dBm]	Weight [px]	Blue opacity
-85	20	0,9
-90	18	0,8
-95	16	0,7
-100	14	0,6
-105	12	0,5
-110	10	0,4
-115	8	0,3
-120	6	0,2
-125	4	0,1

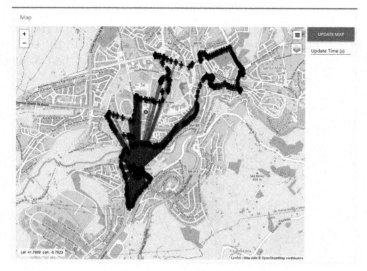

Fig. 7. The second test - walking near the downtown buildings.

Another test was performed to determine the coverage of the LoRaWAN signal, named the second test. Figure 7 demonstrates the LoRaWAN signal coverage map in this test far away, almost 2000 meters from Gateway, where it is possible to notice that some points of the trail did not have LoRaWAN coverage (the regions where there is no blue line with the human symbol).

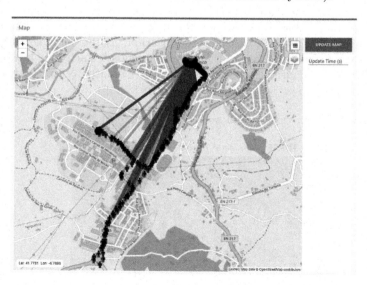

Fig. 8. The third test - walking on the outskirts of the city.

The third test was dedicated to the outskirts areas of the city to identify how the signal coverage behaves in regions with less construction density. The furthest point of the track was approximately 2200 meters in a straight line with the Gateway. It is possible to notice through Fig. 8 that there are more blue lines than in the previous test.

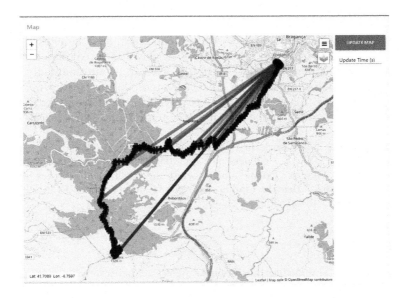

Fig. 9. The fourth test - verifying signals in rural zones.

The last test was conducted in rural areas close to the city center, so a car was used to perform the trail. The furthest point registered was approximately 11000 meters in a straight line from the Gateway. As Fig. 9 shows, there was good quality communication compared with the previous measurements. In this case, the terrain relief contributed to the transmission between the module and the Gateway since the area is 1320 meters altitude (from the sea).

After completing all tests, it is clear that some regions in the city center of Bragança have low or even no connectivity with the Gateway (as shown in Fig. 7). On the other hand, other peripheral regions to the city center have good coverage (Fig. 8). According to the manufacturer, factors such as the ground relief, the density of buildings and trees, and even the positioning of the Gateway can influence the signal quality. Therefore, three zones were chosen around the city of Bragança to test the developed platform with the static LoRaWAN Gateway (any positioning of the Gateway was modified to improve the transmission signal during the tests). This choice was based on this work's main objective: to develop the map coverage platform without excessively consuming the bandwidth of the LoRaWAN Gateway.

6   Conclusions and Future Work

IoT applications are increasing daily, but one of the most critical requirements is communication, sometimes remote and wireless transmission. This paper presented a GPS-based system to map the coverage of the LoRaWAN signal. In fact, it combines the localization information with the LoRa signal strength allowing to identify the lack of signal zones. It is a tool mainly developed to plan the installation of fire detection modules developed in the SAFe project. Although, the proposed approach can be used in different areas, such as agriculture and animal tracking, among others. Results are beneficial in a real experiment validation since the modules' installation coordinates can be automatically affected, and to optimize managing the fire detection areas. Future work direction can be pointed out using this developed tool to optimize the Gateway positioning in other projects depending on the terrain and environment characteristics.

Acknowledgment. This work has been supported by Fundação La Caixa and FCT - Fundação para a Ciência e Tecnologia within the Project Scope: UIDB/5757/2020. Thadeu Brito is supported by FCT PhD Grant Reference SFRH/BD/08598/2020. Beatriz Flamia Azevedo is supported by FCT PhD Grant Reference SFRH/BD/07427/2021.

References

1. Hernández, L.: The Mediterranean burns: WWF's Mediterrenean proposal for the prevention of rural fires. WWF (2019)
2. Sistemas de videovigilância de prevenção de incêndios a partir de 2017 com apoio po seur. https://poseur.portugal2020.pt/media/4140/plano_nacional_defesa_floresta_contra_incendios.pdf. Accessed 15 May 2021
3. Azevedo, B.F., Brito, T., Lima, J., Pereira, A.I.: Optimum sensors allocation for a forest fires monitoring system. Forests. **12**(4), 453 (2021). https://doi.org/10.3390/f12040453, https://www.mdpi.com/1999-4907/12/4/453
4. Brito, T., Azevedo, B.F., Valente, A., Pereira, A.I., Lima, J., Costa, P.: Environment Monitoring Modules with Fire Detection Capability Based on IoT Methodology. In: Paiva, S., Lopes, S.I., Zitouni, R., Gupta, N., Lopes, S.F., Yonezawa, T. (eds.) SmartCity360∘ 2020. LNICST, vol. 372, pp. 211–227. Springer, Cham (2021). https://doi.org/10.1007/978-3-030-76063-2_16
5. Brito, T., Pereira, A.I., Lima, J., Valente, A.: Wireless sensor network for ignitions detection: an IoT approach. Electronics **9**, 1–16 (2020)
6. Brito, T., Pereira, A.I., Lima, J., Castro, J.P., Valente, A.: Optimal sensors positioning to detect forest fire ignitions. In: Proceedings of the 9th International Conference on Operations Research and Enterprise Systems, pp. 411–418 (2020)
7. Anitha, P., Deepa, V.S., Sobana, D.K.: An automatic forest fire detection using Lora wireless mesh topology. Int. Res. J. Eng. Technol. (IRJET). 3173–3177 (2020)
8. Sasmita, E.S., Rosmiati, M., Rizal, M.F.: Integrating forest fire detection with wireless sensor network based on long range radio. In: 2018 International Conference on Control, Electronics, Renewable Energy and Communications (ICCEREC), pp. 222–225 (2018). https://doi.org/10.1109/ICCEREC.2018.8711991

9. Choi, W., Chang, Y.S., Jung, Y., Song, J.: Low-power Lora signal-based out-door positioning using fingerprint algorithm. ISPRS Int. J. Geo-Inf. **7**(11), 440 (2018). https://doi.org/10.3390/ijgi7110440, https://www.mdpi.com/2220-9964/7/11/440

10. Alliance, L.: A technical overview of LoRa and LoRaWAN. https://lora-alliance.org/resource_hub/what-is-lorawan. Accessed 15 May 2021

11. Sendra, S., García, L., Lloret, J., Bosch, I., Vega-Rodríguez, R.: Lorawan network for fire monitoring in rural environments. Electronics. **9**(3), 513 (2020). https://doi.org/10.3390/electronics9030531

12. Augustin, A., Yi, J., Clausen, T., Townsley, W.M.: A study of LoRa: Long range & amp; low power networks for the internet of things. Sensors. **16**(9), 1466 (2016). https://doi.org/10.3390/s16091466, https://www.mdpi.com/1424-8220/16/9/1466

13. Lauridsen, M., Vejlgaard, B., Kovacs, I.Z., Nguyen, H., Mogensen, P.: Interference measurements in the European 868 MHZ ISM band with focus on LoRa and SigFox. In: 2017 IEEE Wireless Communications and Networking Conference (WCNC), pp. 1–6 (2017). https://doi.org/10.1109/WCNC.2017.7925650

14. Sanchez-Iborra, R., Sanchez-Gomez, J., Ballesta-Viñas, J., Cano, M.D., Skarmeta, A.F.: Performance evaluation of LoRa considering scenario conditions. Sensors. **18**(3), 772 (2018). https://doi.org/10.3390/s18030772, https://www.mdpi.com/1424-8220/18/3/772

15. Carlsson, A., Kuzminykh, I., Franksson, R., Liljegren, A.: Measuring a LoRa network: performance, possibilities and limitations. In: Galinina, O., Andreev, S., Balandin, S., Koucheryavy, Y. (eds.) NEW2AN/ruSMART -2018. LNCS, vol. 11118, pp. 116–128. Springer, Cham (2018). https://doi.org/10.1007/978-3-030-01168-0_11

16. Yim, D., et al.: An experimental LoRa performance evaluation in tree farm. In: 2018 IEEE sensors applications Symposium (SAS), pp. 1–6, March 2018. https://doi.org/10.1109/SAS.2018.8336764

17. Alves, H.B.M., et al.: Introducing a survey methodology for assessing LoRaWAN coverage in smart campus scenarios. In: 2020 IEEE International Workshop on Metrology for Industry 4.0 IoT, pp. 708–712 (2020). https://doi.org/10.1109/MetroInd4.0IoT48571.2020.9138300

18. LoRa: LoRaWAN documentation. https://lora.readthedocs.io/en/latest/#rssi. Accessed 15 May 2021

19. Carlsson, A., Kuzminykh, I., Franksson, R., Liljegren, A.: Measuring a LoRa network: performance, possibilities and limitations. In: Galinina, O., Andreev, S., Balandin, S., Koucheryavy, Y. (eds.) NEW2AN/ruSMART -2018. LNCS, vol. 11118, pp. 116–128. Springer, Cham (2018). https://doi.org/10.1007/978-3-030-01168-0_11

20. Brito, T., et al.: Optimizing data transmission in a wireless sensor network based on LoRaWAN protocol. In: Pereira, A.I., et al. (eds.) OL2A 2021. CCIS, vol. 1488, pp. 281–293. Springer, Cham (2021). https://doi.org/10.1007/978-3-030-91885-9_20

Node Assembly for Waste Level Measurement: Embrace the Smart City

Adriano S. Silva[1,2,3,4,5(✉)] iD, Thadeu Brito[1,3] iD, Jose L. Diaz de Tuesta[2,5,6] iD,
José Lima[1,3] iD, Ana I. Pereira[1,3] iD, Adrián M. T. Silva[3,4] iD,
and Helder T. Gomes[2,3] iD

[1] Research Centre in Digitalization and Intelligent Robotics (CeDRI),
Instituto Politécnico de Bragança, 5300-253 Bragança, Portugal
{adriano.santossilva,brito,jlima,apereira}@ipb.pt
[2] Centro de Investigação de Montanha (CIMO), Instituto Politécnico de Bragança,
5300-253 Bragança, Portugal
{jl.diazdetuesta,htgomes}@ipb.pt
[3] Laboratório para a Sustentabilidade e Tecnologia em Regiões de Montanha
(SusTEC), Instituto Politécnico de Bragança, 5300-253 Bragança, Portugal
[4] Laboratory of Separation and Reaction Engineering – Laboratory of Catalysis and
Materials (LSRE-LCM), Faculty of Engineering, University of Porto, Porto, Portugal
adrian@fe.up.pt
[5] ALiCE - Associate Laboratory in Chemical Engineering, Faculty of Engineering,
University of Porto, Porto, Portugal
[6] Department of Chemical and Environmental Technology, ESCET,
Rey Juan Carlos University, Madrid, Spain

Abstract. Municipal Solid Waste Management Systems (MSWMS)
worldwide are currently facing pressure due to the rapid growth of the
population in cities. One of the biggest challenges in this system is the
inefficient expenditure of time and fuel in waste collection. In this regard,
cities/municipalities in charge of MSWMS could take advantage of information and communication technologies to improve the overall quality of
their infrastructure. One particular strategy that has been explored and
is showing interesting results is using a Wireless Sensors Network (WSN)
to monitor waste levels in real-time and help decision-making regarding
the need for collection. The WSN is equipped with sensing devices that
should be carefully chosen considering the real scenario in which they
will work. Therefore, in this work, three sets of sensors were studied to
evaluate which is the best to be used in the future WSN assembled in
Bragança, Portugal. Sets tested were HC-SR04 (S1), HC-SR04 + DHT11
(S2), and US-100 (S3). Tests considered for this work were air temperature and several distances. In the first, the performance of each set to
measure a fixed target (metal and plastic box) was evaluated under different temperatures (1.7–37 °C). From these results, two best sets were
further used to assess distance measurement at a fixed temperature. This
test revealed low absolute errors measuring the distances of interest in
this work, ranging from 0.18% to 1.27%.

Keywords: Smart City · Waste management · Ultrasonic sensor · Wireless Sensors Network

1   Introduction

Within the emergence of the 21st century, Information and Communication Technologies (ICT) became a tool that can help modern society to achieve sustainable living spaces [1]. Such tool plays an important role in the measurement, storage, and processing of data from systems to improve services, life quality, and profits (in companies) [2]. One of the driving agents for the required paradigm shift on how our data are treated is the growing population in cities, that demands smarter solutions to provide well-being for citizens [3]. In this regard, the integration of innovative technologies in city environments represents one of the biggest challenges of the last decades [4]. The integration of physical structures in a city with smart devices to support decision making overcome in a new concept of city: Smart City (SC) or City 2.0 [5].

Cities equipped with smart gadgets enables integrated operations of systems digitally connected in the city infrastructure in different sectors (*e.g.*, healthcare, energy infrastructure, transportation, and mobility systems) [6]. Different communication technologies are employed for this purpose, such as real-time data collection infrastructures and data analytic platforms to process data and make decisions with real-time accuracy [7]. Cities with this architecture works as living organisms, with computing resources, sensing infrastructure, and data analytic exchanging information to enable synchronized operations. The integration of the systems described before is also known as Internet of Things (IoT), another concept that has been introduced worldwide in cities to upgrade city's infrastructure [8]. One of the sectors that can benefit from IoT technologies is the Municipal Solid Waste Management System (MSWMS).

MSWMS is a complex system that covers activities and actions related to managing the waste, since its conception to the proper disposal. In urban areas, the tasks includes collect the waste from dumpsters, carry the waste to recycling centers or transfer stations, and then to the final destination (*e.g.* landfills, incinerators, or stakeholders) [9]. The activity that consumes most resources is generally the waste collection, that is carried out traditionally in most cities worldwide, with drivers making decision of which sites should be visited or even with pre-scheduled routes. This approach often lead to inefficient expenditure of resources since the truck can travel longer distances to collect insignificant amounts of waste, or even take too long to collect overfilled dumpsters [10]. In this scenario, the adoption of technological solutions could optimize the waste collection and bring benefits for both companies and citizens. Among solutions, the utilization of a Wireless Sensors Network (WSN) to collect real-time data regarding waste level and use this information for route planning [11]. In this strategy, one important task is the choice of sensing devices to be used.

In this work, the initial strategy adopted to assemble the future nodes on the WSN will be studied. The main goal was to settle what is the best set of sensors for the particular implementation of sensors in dumpsters for selective collection of waste in the city of Bragança, located in the Northeast region of Portugal. The region face temperature oscillations throughout the year, from −4 °C in a cold winter to 37 °C during summer. In this case, ignoring weather conditions could hinder waste level measurement. The sets of sensors considered here were HC-SR04 (S1), HC-SR04 + DHT11 (S2), and US-100 (S3). HC-SR04 and US-100 are ultrasonic sensors widely used in diverse range of applications, such as waste level measurement, and DHT11 is a sensor for temperature and humidity measurement. Distance measurements data were collected in serial communication, using Arduino Uno microcontroller and PuTTY software, an open-source tool. Sets were chosen to evaluate if considering temperature would improve precision on measurements and to evaluate cost-efficiency in distance measurement considering temperature.

The rest of the paper is organized as follows: Sect. 2 brings the related literature and real data regarding MSW generation in Europe; Sect. 3 presents the methodology employed; Sect. 4 summarizes the results; and finally, Sect. 5 shows the main findings of the present study and future work.

2 Related Literature and Technical Information

The most relevant literature for this study was found searching in Scopus and Web of Science databases for works with "ultrasonic sensor" and "waste management" as keywords in the last 5 years. Documents obtained within this search were analyzed in the opensource tool ScientoPy [12] to understand what the literature is currently covering. Figure 1 illustrates the evolution of the most relevant keywords in this field.

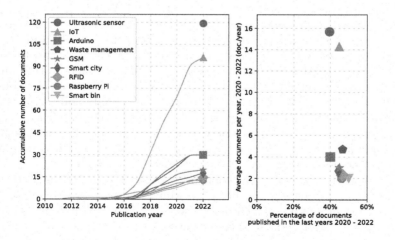

Fig. 1. Evolution of 10 most used keywords.

The result shows the relevance of the study in recent years, with the increase of number of studies using the keywords since 2016. For this study the keywords IoT, waste management, SC, and Arduino are of particular interest and will be briefly reviewed. Before reviewing the literature, some data regarding MSW will be shown to reinforce the relevance of this topic.

2.1 Municipal Solid Waste: European and Portuguese Panorama

Total European waste generation in 2018 was 2377 million tonnes, an average of 5.2 tonnes per EU inhabitant. In the same year, only 37.9% were recycled, and surprisingly 38.5% were disposed in landfills. Waste generation in 2018 according to the different economic activities and households is shown in Fig. 2 for EU countries (average) and Portugal. In the EU, the most significant share of generated wastes is related to construction, followed by mining and quarrying, and manufacturing. In Portugal the order is different, with other economic activities (agriculture, forestry, and fishing; services; energy) presenting the highest share, followed by households and manufacturing [13].

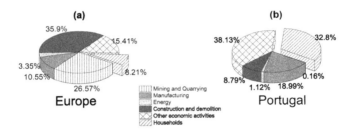

Fig. 2. Waste generation per economic activity in (a) Europe and (b) Portugal.

MSW represents an average of 7–10% of the total waste generation in EU countries, being one of the most complexes to manage due to their complex matrix since undifferentiated waste consists of organic and inorganic fractions of different nature [14]. On the other hand, in Portugal this type of waste has a high share of the total waste generated (*ca.* 33%). The waste generated in cities presents a complex composition, with high public visibility and a direct impact on human health. Data for MSW generation showed that each European citizen was responsible for an average of 505 kg of municipal waste in 2020. MSW generated by European citizens had an increase of 8.2% compared to the first record in 1995. In this scenario, Portugal is one of the countries with the highest increase in waste generation, with 45.7% more urban waste generated compared to the first record.

2.2 Municipal Solid Waste Management Systems in Smart Cities

The concept and idea of SC are now arriving at MSWMS in most recent years, with the increase in the acknowledgment of policymakers regarding the need to improve the way MSW is managed [15]. In this regard, most works consider the utilization of improved decision-making using real-time measurements with numerous types of sensors. For now, most of the work is being developed by scholars that are still trying to find the best combination of hardware, middleware, and software to provide the best efficiency. However, some cities have already taken the lead and implemented smart services on their MSWMS, such as Shangai (China) and Brisbane (Australia) [10].

Solving the MSWS problem may require different approaches for some cities. However, the WSN technique can potentially contribute to the communication solution in most cities. WSN is a technique that has been used and researched in recent years to monitor remote locations (with small infrastructure resources) or even in urban areas (commonly with more infrastructure). A set of strategically placed nodes can define the basis of a good WSN [16]. Depending on the approach, these nodes support sensors that can be used to collect data and send it through an IoT system [17].

The utilization of WSNs to collect real-time information is one particular approach that has shown promising results. Works in this strand often use the data from the cloud to apply optimization algorithms and find the shortest path to collect the waste. The physical system is designed toward the specific operation of the region of interest, assembling the system to sense specific parameters. Despite each system with its own considerations, distance measurement, load, temperature and humidity are often chosen as relevant data for route optimization [15,18].

2.3 Arduino

Microcontrollers have diverse uses in offices, homes, and research environments [19]. In brief, microcontrollers are single-board computers that have both software and hardware, and their use is generally towards the control of one dedicated task in the device [20]. In this regard, Arduino is an open-source electronics platform that is the first option for anyone working with interactive software and hardware projects due to the cost-efficient performance that this platform offers [21].

The big community built around Arduino projects, moderate inexpensive board costs, and easy implementation has motivated students, teachers, and developers to use this technology in their projects [22]. Arduino boards are equipped with a microcontroller, such as Atmel ATmega328p or ATmega168, which are responsible for the development of projects and prototypes. The code uploading of Arduino boards can be done in Arduino IDE, considered a good choice for individuals with some knowledge in C and simplified C++ programming languages. Arduino currently exists in many variants, such as the Arduino Uno, Arduino Mega, Arduino Leonardo, and Arduino Due.

Many fields have already found benefits in using Arduino platform, such as remote sensing, hardware communication, mining, and system design [23]. Among the applications in remote sensing, some studies are using Arduino for the optimization of decision-making in waste collection systems. Aguila *et al.*, for example, assembled a smart bin able to send an alert to the staff responsible for waste collection when a certain condition was reached inside the bin. In this example, the authors used ultrasonic sensors on the cover of the bin to measure waste level and a balance to check the weight of waste. The whole system was controlled with the aid of an Arduino UNO [24]. Kumar *et al.* used a similar approach, with the ultrasonic sensor measuring waste level to inform the staff once the bin is filled. In this work, Arduino UNO was also used to control the system. Once the dustbin is emptied, the operator confirms the task with the aid of an RFID tag [25]. Several other works [26,27] are devoted to show approaches of prototypes for this application, most of them using a similar strategy with one or another modification according to specific cases of the problem perspective.

2.4 Ultrasonic Sensor

Ultrasonic sensors, or sonar, are devices able to detect presence of objects within a given range and field of view. These devices works based on the principle of transmitting high-frequency sound wave at objects and measuring the reflected echo off of the target. The sensors are able to convert alternating current into ultrasound and the other way around. Some devices in this class uses separate sensors to transmit and receive; others are able to combine both functions in only one sensor. The system determined distances based on Time of Flight (ToF) measurements, considering the propagation speed of the sonic wave in the medium. Several studies uses this type of sensor for measuring waste level in dumpsters [18,28].

One of the most common models used in different projects is the HC-SR04 [18,25]. This model is equipped with an ultrasonic transmitter and receiver, and has four pins: Ground, VCC, Trig, and Echo. The ultrasonic signal is propagated by a wave directed at an angle of about 30°, and the most effective measuring angle is 15°. The sensor returns the time that the signal takes to travel back, and post calculations are necessary to transform this information into distance. The reading is not affected by sunlight or colors, but material and surface shape have influence [29].

Another sensor available on market at relative low price is the US-100. This sensor has one advantage compared to HC-SR04, which is the serial UART mode operation that allows adjusting the speed of sound according to the room temperature during measurement. Furthermore, the sensor can operate in pulse width mode by removing the jumper on the back, but in this mode is not possible to use temperature information for more precise distance measurements. In solid waste management system, no work using this sensor was found. In fact, literature on this device had to be searched outside the database used in previous sections, and most of the works found were dealing with robotic applications [28].

3   Methodology

Due to the *modus operandi* of the company ascribed to MSW management in the city of Bragança, dumpsters are made of metal on the face that is in touch with the ground and all the rest is made of hard plastic. This design was chosen by the company because in this way they can collect the waste by pulling the dumpster with the aid of a winch and open the bottom, that works as a floodgate. In future works, the idea is to place the each node of the WSN on top of the dumpster, so the system can measure waste level and communicate to the cloud real-time information, used to optimize collection routes. Positioning the measurement set in this spot will not be a problem in the future once the dumpsters design does not allow citizens to interact with the structure (*i.e.* there is no way to leave it open or damage structures on the inside). To arrive at this stage, tests with different sets of sensors was considered necessary. Thus, the sets used in this work were HC-SR04 (S1), HC-SR04 coupled with DHT11 (S2), and US-100 (S3). All systems were controlled by Arduino UNO. More information regarding description of components can be found in [22, 30–32] for HC-SR04, DHT11, US-100, and Arduino UNO, respectively.

Hard plastic and metal were used as targets to measure distances and evaluate the performance of each set. In brief, the temperature test consisted in evaluating the performance of each set when measuring distances inside a container with controlled temperature oscillation through time. In distance test, the sets were evaluated for measuring distances ranging from 185 cm to 5 cm, with intervals of 10 cm. The maximum value was chosen because it represents the height of dumpsters in which the sensors will be positioned in the future. The whole procedure is illustrated in Fig. 3, and will be explained in more detail on the next sections.

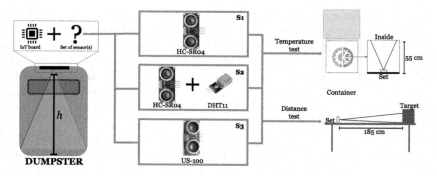

Fig. 3. Representation of the tests performed.

3.1   Sets Assembly

Both ultrasonic sensors used in this work did not return the distance from measurement directly. On the other hand, it is possible to determine the distance given an obstacle by triggering the sensor and then measuring the echo time from a pulse width output (this process occurs individually in each sensor). In this context, it is expected that the physical air environment could sometimes disturb the wave sent by each sensor. The sensor US-100 (S3) has an integrated system to compensate the external temperature. Despite HC-SR04 (S1) does not account for temperature during operation, the set was also assembled with temperature measurement using DHT11 for future comparison. The difference between sets 1 and 2 is the equation used to calculate distance, one considering the average speed of sound (S1) and the other regarding the sapped calculated based on temperature (S2).

Libraries used to control the sensors were NewPing.h for HC-SR04, DHT.h for DHT11, and `SoftwareSerial.h` for US-100. S1 and S2 codes were written using the function 'sonar.ping_median' that returns the average time of n measurements, default being 5. The equations used to calculate distance in each program are below.

$$D_{S1} = \frac{\Delta t/2}{\overline{V_s}} \tag{1}$$

$$D_{S2} = \frac{\Delta t/2}{V_s} \wedge V_s = 331.4 + 0.606 * T \tag{2}$$

$$D_{S3} = MSB * 256 + LSB \tag{3}$$

Δt is the time that wave takes to travel back to the sensor, $\overline{V_s}$ is the average speed of sound (343 m/s), V_s is the speed of sound calculated based on temperature T registered by DHT11 (°C), MSB and LSB are the bytes carried to answer the request 0×55 for US-100. Temperature measurements using US-100 are returned upon request 0×50. The equation that correlates speed of sound with temperature used in S2 was taken from the literature [33]. The results are obtained in meters for D_{S1} and D_{S2}, and in millimeters for D_{S3}.

3.2 Temperature Test

The goal of this test was to determine the influence of temperatures for measuring distances. It was already shown in the literature that speed of sound has dependence on the temperature of the medium in which the wave sound is propagated. Using real dumpsters for temperature evaluation is infeasible due to the difficulties to obtain the desired temperature inside. For this reason, each set was positioned inside a container with changeable temperature (a refrigerator in this case) to evaluate if distance measurement would be affected by temperature oscillation. The sets were placed exactly on the middle of the platform, positioned 55.1 cm from the top of the container. This distance was chosen based on theoretical calculations of wave propagation that were performed considering real dumpster dimensions and field of view of sonars. In this setup, equal distance was assessed during the test.

Once the set was positioned inside the container and temperature was stable, which happened around 1.7 °C, the refrigerator was turned off and the interior was exposed to the medium, so temperature could raise to room temperature. Since the moment the refrigerator was turned off, PuTTY software was already recording measured distances and temperature. When temperature reached room temperature and stabilized, a heater was placed inside the container to reach temperature around 37 °C. At last, the heater was removed from the container and the refrigerator was turned on when temperature reached room temperature, to cool down to 1.7 °C again and close the cycle of analysis. The first part of the test was named heating step, and second one is the cooling step. All tests were performed in triplicate to ensure data reliability, and the results gathered were post-processed in Python package Pandas, to determine average distance, error, and precision of each set with the aid of Numpy package.

3.3   Distance Measurements

Tests for measuring targets made of plastic and metal were performed using a large table as surface. Sets and table were adjusted to ensure that optimum conditions for measurements, and the system was assembled on top of a measuring tape placed on top of the table to compare measured values with real distances.

Once the physical system was assembled, measurements were collected for distances starting in 185 cm and going to 5 cm moving the target with intervals of 10 cm for each set. Data collection for each distance was done using software PuTTY to store results in a `.csv` file, and each collection run took about 70 s of measurement. The experiments of distance measurement were repeated 3 times for each distance to ensure data reliability. All data collected were post-processed in Python package Pandas. The number of signals was set the same for all distances measured for the same set and target, to ensure fair evaluation of performance.

4   Results

In this section, the results obtained for measurements using different sets in the tests will be presented and discussed. The discussion will be focused towards the performance of each set, considering the particular application that one of them will be used in the future of this study: measure waste level inside real dumpsters.

4.1   Temperature Test

The temperature inside the refrigerator stabilized in 1.7 °C, that was the lowest temperature used in this study. The highest temperature achieved with the aid of the heated was 37 °C. Thus, temperature range in which distance measurement was studied for the sets is 1.7–37 °C, which covers great part of temperatures faced during one year for the city of Bragança, where the future system will be assembled [34]. The main goal of this test is to evaluate the effect of temperature in measurement of waste levels in cities that have high temperature differences throughout the year. The result of distance measurement during heating and cooling down are represented in Fig. 4.

Distances measured using each set have average errors of 9.76, 3.37 and 2.84% for S1, S2, S3 in heating and 10.24, 1.46, and 5.03% for S1, S2, S3 in cooling. The

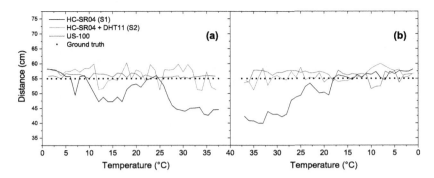

Fig. 4. Distance measurement results for different sets in (a) heating and (b) cooling.

errors were calculated based on the average distance measured in a determined temperature compared to the ground truth (determined with measuring tape). As can be seen on the graph and errors, set S1 that is considering the utilization of HC-SR04 only has higher errors in measurements compared to sets 2 and 3. Gathering the results obtained for cooling and heating steps in temperature test reveals that errors are 10, 2.41, and 3.93% for S1, S2 and S3 set. Differences in distance measurement were already expected even before the experiment since studies have already proven the dependence on the speed of sound according to temperature. However, errors were above theoretical error expected, probably due to other errors coming from real operations (*e.g.* sensors parts may face problems in cold or hot conditions).

The result obtained show how temperature could interfere in distance measurement, with S1 measurements showing a strong influence on temperature. The Eq. 2, that correlates speed of sound with temperature, shows that these parameters are directly proportional. This is also observed in distance measurement with S1, since in lower temperatures measured distance was higher than real distance (sound was moving slower), and in high temperature distance measured was lower (sound was moving faster). On the other hand, S2 was able to measure with low errors the distance in both heating and cooling test since takes into consideration temperature to calculate the speed of sound. For instance, the weather in the model region approached in this work (Bragança, Portugal) is characterized as Csb (Warm-summer Mediterranean climate) according to Köppen Climate Classification (KCC). Regions that have Csb weather are characterized by a cold and rainy winter and fall, and a mild, hot summer and spring [35]. In other words, the temperature throughout the year probably has significant differences depending on the month/season, which could lead to wrong waste level measurements if ignored when choosing a proper distance measurement set.

Using the highest (or lowest) temperature record for each month, it is possible to analyze a possible error in measurement of waste levels in real scenario. In this regard, here the highest temperature for each month was found using temperature history during 2020 measured by weather station 85750 in Bragança.

The highest temperature was chosen having in mind that waste collection task is performed during day, a period in which higher temperatures are more likely to be registered. In a hypothetical scenario in which these sets are measuring waste level, the real errors associated to each set are shown in Fig. 5, along with highest temperature found for each month during 2020. Errors were determined considering real measurements for the temperatures of interest and the real distance, 55.1 cm in this case.

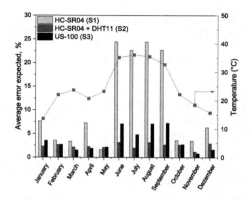

Fig. 5. Errors in measurement according to highest temperature per month in 2020.

In most months, higher error was obtained considering S1 as measurement set. Higher errors were observed for summer months, which is related to the reduced precision of all sets working at temperatures higher than room temperature. The graph confirms the infeasibility of using only HC-SR04 for waste measurement, since higher errors could be faced during the season that is known for higher generation of waste due to tourism, one important economic sector in Europe during summer.

4.2   Distance Test

Temperature test showed that at least one strategy has to be considered to take into account temperature in distance measurement, for this particular application. Accordingly, distance test was carried out using sets S2 and S3. The errors obtained for the average measurements in plastic and metal are shown in Fig. 6. All experiments were performed at room temperature, that was about 23 °C.

Errors for measurement with S2 range from 0.26 to 2.53% (1.01% average) for metal and 0.14 to 2.83% (1.27% average) for plastic. Using S3, errors range from 0 to 1.13% (0.18% average) for metal and 0.25 to 2.85% (0.91% average) for plastic. The result demonstrates that errors are higher for low distances in all situations. Errors obtained for measurements in range 5 cm to 25 cm can be neglected in this work considering the future application, because it represents a range out

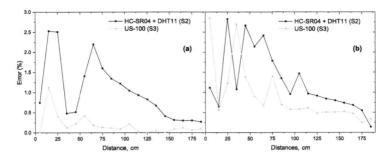

Fig. 6. Errors for distance measurement using targets made of (a) metal and (b) plastic.

of the interest considering the dumpsters design where measurements will be done in the future. The distance between opening in which waste is deposited to the top of the dumpster is around 26 cm, so in practice distances lower than this cannot be considered for measurements once this would mean dumpster overfilling. For this reason, the offset distance that should be considered is higher than 25 cm, meaning that sensor will be calibrated to consider 25 cm as lowest distance measured (full dumpster).

4.3   Cost-efficiency Analysis

The implementation of solutions for real case scenarios does not depend solely on the quality of the solution, but also the costs. For this reason, balance cost and efficiency is essential when developing/assessing new strategies. In this study, the main cost associated to measurement set are the sensors. To proceed with this evaluation, average accuracy in distance measurement using sets S2 and S3 were assessed along with average price of components. The average price was determined upon search in 5 different European commercial websites, resulting in an average price of 4.16 € for S2 (2.68 € for HC-SR04 and 1.42 € for DHT11), and 6.98 € for S3. Figure 7 illustrates the result obtained with cost efficiency analysis, as cost per accuracy of each set. Arduino UNO price was not considered for this analysis because it is a common item in both sets.

Differences between measurements for metal and plastic were below 1% as shown in previous section. Thereby, the difference between cost efficiency in distance measurement considering different materials was not significant. The result observed in this section shows that S2 is the most cost efficient set for measuring distances for this application. Furthermore, searching for prices of components revealed another important characteristic to be considered: the availability. In most cases, few unities of US-100 sensor was available to purchase, while HC-SR04 had higher number of unities available for immediate delivery.

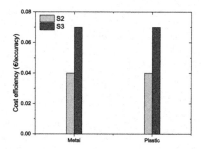

Fig. 7. Cost efficiency of each set in distance measurements.

5   Conclusions and Future Work

The evaluation of different options of sensors to be used in the future node of a WSN was performed in this work. The evaluation included tests with temperature oscillation since model region faces different temperatures throughout the year. Furthermore, best sets were used to determine distance measurement performance considering the real distance range they might be used to measure in the future. At last, average prices of the 2 best sets were used along with distance measurement results to analyze cost efficiency of both approaches.

Temperature test revealed that ignoring temperature in distance measurement can lead to errors of about 10%. As a result of this finding, S1 was not evaluated in distance test since its usage in the future application was already ruled out. Distance measurement result revealed that S3 has the best performance, which is not surprising considering US-100 has higher precision than HC-SR04. However, the cost efficiency showed that the good result obtained with US-100 does not compensate efficiency in comparison with S2. In other words, the best set for the particular application evaluated in this work is the set comprised of HC-SR04 ultrasonic sensor and DHT11 sensor for temperature and humidity measurement. This result can be extrapolated for any other application considering ultrasonic sensors as devices for distance measurement in environments that might experience temperature oscillation as well.

For the future work, experiments accounting for humidity in air could be performed, as this parameter also have influence on the speed of sound. This additional experience would not require any other component in S2 for example, once DHT11 is also capable of measuring relative humidity. Furthermore, a safety system could be designed to send an alert if the dumpster is on fire, which can happen in paper waste dumpsters for example. This system would only require a proper set of data previously recorded by the DHT11 sensor for a condition in which the dumpster is on fire (dataset for training alert models, for example).

Acknowledgements. This work has been supported by FCT - Fundação para a Ciência e Tecnologia within the R&D Units Project Scope: UIDB/05757/2020, UIDB/00690/2020, LA/P/0045/2020, UIDB/50020/2020, and UIDP/50020/2020. Adriano Silva was supported by FCT-MIT Portugal PhD grant SFRH/BD/151

346/2021, and Thadeu Brito was supported by FCT PhD grant SFRH/BD/08598 /2020. Jose L. Diaz de Tuesta acknowledges the finantial support through the program of Atraccion de Talento of Atraccion al Talento of the Comunidad de Madrid (Spain) for the individual research grant 2020-T2/AMB-19836.

References

1. Borthakur, A., Singh, P.: 9 - mapping the emergence of research activities on e-waste: a scientometric analysis and an in-depth review. In: Prasad, M.N.V., Vithanage, M., Borthakur, A. (eds.) Handbook of Electronic Waste Management, pp. 191–206. Butterworth-Heinemann (2020). https://doi.org/10.1016/B978-0-12-817030-4.00017-6

2. Dey, K., Fries, R., Ahmed, S.: Future of transportation cyber-physical systems - smart cities/regions. In: Deka, L., Chowdhury, M. (eds.) Transportation Cyber-Physical Systems, pp. 267–307. Elsevier (2018). https://doi.org/10.1016/B978-0-12-814295-0.00011-3

3. Esmaeilian, B., Wang, B., Lewis, K., Duarte, F., Ratti, C., Behdad, S.: The future of waste management in smart and sustainable cities: a review and concept paper. Waste Manage. **81**, 177–195 (2018). https://doi.org/10.1016/j.wasman.2018.09.047

4. Sepasgozar, S.M., Hawken, S., Sargolzaei, S., Foroozanfa, M.: Implementing citizen centric technology in developing smart cities: a model for predicting the acceptance of urban technologies. Technol. Forecast. Soc. Change **142**, 105–116 (2019). https://doi.org/10.1016/j.techfore.2018.09.012

5. Bibri, S.E., Krogstie, J.: Smart sustainable cities of the future: an extensive interdisciplinary literature review. Sustain. Cities Soc. **31**, 183–212 (2017). https://doi.org/10.1016/j.scs.2017.02.016

6. Nirde, K., Mulay, P.S., Chaskar, U.M.: IoT based solid waste management system for smart city. In: 2017 International Conference on Intelligent Computing and Control Systems (ICICCS), pp. 666–669 (2017). https://doi.org/10.1109/ICCONS.2017.8250546

7. Deka, L., Khan, S.M., Chowdhury, M., Ayres, N.: Transportation cyber-physical system and its importance for future mobility. In: Deka, L., Chowdhury, M. (eds.) Transportation Cyber-Physical Systems, pp. 1–20. Elsevier (2018). https://doi.org/10.1016/B978-0-12-814295-0.00001-0

8. Kiran, D.: Chapter 35 - internet of things. In: Production Planning and Control, pp. 495–513. Butterworth-Heinemann (2019). https://doi.org/10.1016/B978-0-12-818364-9.00035-4

9. Tolaymat, T., El Badawy, A., Sequeira, R., Genaidy, A.: A system-of-systems approach as a broad and integrated paradigm for sustainable engineered nanomaterials. Sci. Total Environ. **511**, 595–607 (2015). https://doi.org/10.1016/j.scitotenv.2014.09.029

10. Lu, X., Pu, X., Han, X.: Sustainable smart waste classification and collection system: a bi-objective modeling and optimization approach. J. Clean. Product. **276**, 124183 (2020). https://doi.org/10.1016/j.jclepro.2020.124183

11. Akinyemi, L.A., Makanjuola, T., Shoewu, O., Folorunso, C.O.: Smart city and vehicle pollution monitoring using wireless network system. Urban Design - ITS (2018). https://doi.org/10.31058/j.ud.2018.12005

12. Ruiz-Rosero, J., Ramirez-Gonzalez, G., Viveros-Delgado, J.: Software survey: ScientoPy, a scientometric tool for topics trend analysis in scientific publications. Scientometrics **121**(2), 1165–1188 (2019). https://doi.org/10.1007/s11192-019-03213-w
13. Municipal waste statistics - european commission. https://ec.europa.eu/eurostat/statistics-explained/index.php?title=Municipal_waste_statistics. Accessed 25 May 2022
14. Tsai, F.M., Bui, T.D., Tseng, M.L., Lim, M.K., Hu, J.: Municipal solid waste management in a circular economy: a data-driven bibliometric analysis. J. Clean. Product. **275**, 124132 (2020). https://doi.org/10.1016/j.jclepro.2020.124132
15. Memon, S.K., Shaikh, F.K., Mahoto, N.A., Memon, A.A.: IoT based smart garbage monitoring & collection system using wemos & ultrasonic sensors. In: 2019 2nd International Conference on Computing, Mathematics and Engineering Technologies (iCoMET), pp. 1–6. IEEE (2019). https://doi.org/10.1109/ICOMET.2019.8673526
16. Brito, T., Pereira, A.I., Lima, J., Valente, A.: Wireless sensor network for ignitions detection: an IoT approach. Electronics **9**(6), 893 (2020). https://doi.org/10.3390/electronics9060893
17. Brito, T., et al.: Optimizing data transmission in a wireless sensor network based on LoRaWAN protocol. In: Pereira, A.I., et al. (eds.) OL2A 2021. CCIS, vol. 1488, pp. 281–293. Springer, Cham (2021). https://doi.org/10.1007/978-3-030-91885-9_20
18. Misra, D., Das, G., Chakrabortty, T., Das, D.: An IoT-based waste management system monitored by cloud. J. Material Cycles Waste Manage. **20**(3), 1574–1582 (2018). https://doi.org/10.1007/s10163-018-0720-y
19. Rafiquzzaman, M.: Microcontroller Theory and Applications with the PIC18F. Wiley (2018)
20. Güven, Y., Coşgun, E., Kocaoğlu, S., Gezici, H., Yılmazlar, E.: Understanding the concept of microcontroller based systems to choose the best hardware for applications. Int. J. Eng. Sci. (2017). https://hdl.handle.net/20.500.11857/1024
21. El-Abd, M.: A review of embedded systems education in the arduino age: lessons learned and future directions. Int. J. Eng. Pedagogy (2017). https://doi.org/10.3991/ijep.v7i2.6845
22. Arduino UNO datasheet. http://store-usa.arduino.cc/products/arduino-uno-rev3. Accessed 25 May 2022
23. Kondaveeti, H.K., Kumaravelu, N.K., Vanambathina, S.D., Mathe, S.E., Vappangi, S.: A systematic literature review on prototyping with arduino: applications, challenges, advantages, and limitations. Comput. Sci. Rev. **40**, 100364 (2021). https://doi.org/10.1016/j.cosrev.2021.100364
24. Aguila, J., Dimayuga, H., Pineda, K., Magwili, G.: Development of smart waste bin with integrated volume and weight sensor. In: 2019 IEEE 11th International Conference on Humanoid, Nanotechnology, Information Technology, Communication and Control, Environment, and Management (HNICEM), pp. 1–5. IEEE (2019). https://doi.org/10.1109/HNICEM48295.2019.9072885
25. Kumar, N.S., Vuayalakshmi, B., Prarthana, R.J., Shankar, A.: IoT based smart garbage alert system using arduino uno. In: 2016 IEEE region 10 conference (TENCON), pp. 1028–1034. IEEE (2016). https://doi.org/10.1109/TENCON.2016.7848162
26. Talukder, S., Sakib, M.I.I., Talukder, Z.R., Das, U., Saha, A., Bayev, N.S.N.: Usensewer: Ultrasonic sensor and gsm-arduino based automated sewerage manage-

ment. In: 2017 International Conference on Current Trends in Computer, Electrical, Electronics and Communication (CTCEEC), pp. 12–17. IEEE (2017). https://doi.org/10.1109/CTCEEC.2017.8455169

27. Fei, T.P., et al.: SWM: Smart waste management for green environment. In: 2017 6th ICT International Student Project Conference (ICT-ISPC), pp. 1–5. IEEE (2017). https://doi.org/10.1109/ICT-ISPC.2017.8075303

28. Haq, F.A., Dewantara, B.S.B., Marta, B.S.: Room mapping using ultrasonic range sensor on the atracbot (autonomous trash can robot): a simulation approach. In: 2020 International Electronics Symposium (IES), pp. 265–270. IEEE (2020). https://doi.org/10.1109/IES50839.2020.9231734

29. Zhmud, V., Kondratiev, N., Kuznetsov, K., Trubin, V., Dimitrov, L.: Application of ultrasonic sensor for measuring distances in robotics. In: Journal of Physics: Conference Series, vol. 1015, p. 032189. IOP Publishing (2018). https://doi.org/10.1088/1742-6596/1015/3/032189

30. HC-SR04 datasheet. https://www.alldatasheet.com/datasheet-pdf/pdf/1132203/ETC2/HC-SR04.html. Accessed 28 May 2022

31. DHT11 datasheet. https://www.alldatasheet.com/datasheet-pdf/pdf/1132088/ETC2/DHT11.html. Accessed 28 May 2022

32. US-100 datasheet. https://www.alldatasheet.com/datasheet-pdf/pdf/1283987/ETC1/US-100.html. Accessed 28 May 2022

33. Cramer, O.: The variation of the specific heat ratio and the speed of sound in air with temperature, pressure, humidity, and co2 concentration. J. Acoust. Soc. America **93**(5), 2510–2516 (1993). https://doi.org/10.1121/1.405827

34. Instituto Português do Mar e da Atmosfera. https://www.ipma.pt/pt/index.html. Accessed 25 May 2022

35. Vieira, S., et al.: Atmospheric features and risk of ST-elevation myocardial infarction in porto (portugal): a temperate mediterranean (csb) city. Revista Portuguesa de Cardiologia **41**(1), 51–58 (2022). https://doi.org/10.1016/j.repc.2020.11.015

Trends in Engineering Education

Data Analysis Techniques Applied to the MathE Database

Beatriz Flamia Azevedo[1,2,5](✉)(iD), Sofia F. Romanenko[1,4](iD),
Maria de Fatima Pacheco[1,3,5](iD), Florbela P. Fernandes[1,5](iD),
and Ana I. Pereira[1,2,5](iD)

[1] Research Centre in Digitalization and Intelligent Robotics (CeDRI),
Instituto Politécnico de Bragança, 5300-252 Bragança, Portugal
{beatrizflamia,sofia.romanenko,pacheco,fflor,apereira}@ipb.pt
[2] Algoritmi Research Centre, University of Minho, 4800-058 Guimarães, Portugal
[3] Center for Research & Development in Mathematics and Applications CIDMA,
University of Aveiro, Aveiro, Portugal
[4] University of Coimbra, Coimbra, Portugal
[5] Laboratório para a Sustentabilidade e Tecnologia em Regiões de Montanha
(SusTEC), Instituto Politécnico de Bragança, 5300-253 Bragança, Portugal

Abstract. MathE is an international online platform that aims to provide a resource for in-class support as well as an alternative instrument to teach and study mathematics. This work focuses on the investigations of the students' behavior when answering the training questions available in the platform. In order to draw conclusions about the value of the platform, the ways in which the students use it and what are the most wanted mathematical topics, thus deepening the knowledge about the difficulties faced by the users and finding how to make the platform more efficient, the data collected since the it was launched (3 years ago) is analyzed through the use of data mining and machine learning techniques. In a first moment, a general analysis was performed in order to identify the students' behavior as well as the topics that require reorganization; it was followed by a second iteration, according to the students' country of origin, in order to identify the existence of differences in the behavior of students from distinct countries. The results point out that the advanced level of the platform's questions is not adequate and that the questions should be reorganized in order to ensure a more consistent support for the students' learning process. Besides, with this analysis it was possible to identify the topics that require more attention through the addition of more questions. Furthermore, it was not possible to identify significant disparities in the students behavior in what concerns the students' country of origin.

This work has been supported by FCT Fundação para a Ciência e Tecnologia within the R&D Units Project Scope FCT/MCTES (PIDDAC) to CeDRI (UIDB/05757/2020 and UIDP/05757/2020) and SusTEC (LA/P/0007/2021); Erasmus Plus KA2 within the project 2021-1-PT01-KA220-HED-000023288; Beatriz Flamia Azevedo is supported by FCT Grant Reference SFRH/BD/07427/2021.

A. I. Pereira et al. (Eds.): OL2A 2022, CCIS 1754, pp. 623–639, 2022.
https://doi.org/10.1007/978-3-031-23236-7_43

Keywords: E-learning platforms · Mathematics · Active learning ·
Education technologies · Data analysis

1   Introduction

All actors in the educational process are aware of the need to improve the quality
of lectures and intensify research on innovations that contribute to better engage
students and lower failure rates in the discipline. Due to its cumulative nature,
courses that rely on a strong mathematical core present enormous challenges
both to professors and students: in mathematics, students learn that through
adequate reasoning and relying on proper assumptions, they can arrive at results
that are fully trustable and applicable in a wide variety of scientific and real-
life contexts. Guiding the students to the appropriate degree of attainment,
comprehension, and autonomy has long been one of the significant challenges for
professors, including at the higher-education level. Poor performance, especially
in introductory courses, is a massive concern that college mathematics lecturers
face [10, 11].

Although lecturing, in an exposition-centered approach, has been the traditional way of teaching, there is theoretical evidence of the need for students to
be more active in constructing their understanding [2, 9, 14, 19].

Active learning methodologies, grounded in the constructivist theory of
teaching and learning that holds that humans learn by actively using new information and experiences and that reality is shaped by the experiences of the
learner, can be a meaningful contribution to boosting the students' engagement.
Some of the main features of the constructivist teaching practice, such as the
encouragement of the students' autonomy, initiative, and dialogue among their
peers and with the professors, promote a sense of personal agency since the students have control of their learning and, to some extent, to their assessment
[5, 7, 12, 18].

Students retain much more if they are challenged to reflect on and do more
than just passively receive information. Active learning interventions can include
approaches as diverse as workshops, group problem-solving and team quizzes,
worksheets or tutorials completed throughout the class, use of personal response
systems ("clickers") displaying a graph with the responses (there are many
online applications for this purpose, such as https://www.polleverywhere.com),
moments of individual thinking alternating with small group activities, all subject to immediate feed-back, are all powerful techniques for helping students work
through and understand and solve a problem and are among the evidence-based
best practice in active learning, and lead to greater learning [6, 17]. Cooperative
learning is a component of active learning that is worth highlighting: it refers to
work developed by the students, organized into teams, in order to produce an
outcome of some sort: a laboratory or project report, the design of a product
or a process or, within the context of learning mathematics, the solutions to a
set of problems. The dynamics of cooperative learning should encourage face-to-
face interaction, interdependence, individual accountability, appropriate use of
interpersonal skills, and several moments of self-assessment of team performance

and dynamics. Extensive research has shown that, when compared to traditional pedagogical models, cooperative learning – when it is implemented adequately – leads to greater learning and development of communication and teamwork skills, such as leadership, project management, and conflict resolution. Furthermore, the characteristics described before, go in the same direction as the 4th goal of the Sustainable Development Goals (SDGs), it is quality education, that intends to ensure inclusive and equitable quality education for all and promote lifelong learning [8].

The MathE online teaching platform is in line with the described scenario: it provides educational resources for students and lecturers, covering the traditional mathematics contents of higher-education courses. By registering on the platform, the users' have access to a wide variety of educational resources such as videos, solved exercises, podcasts, or pdf files, as well as questions that allow the students to undertake self-assessment tests and the professors to perform evaluation. MathE also provides the users with a forum where the students can share questions and challenges, teaching each other and, therefore, being active agents in the construction of new skills and knowledge. Professors and researchers also benefit from the existence of their forum in the platform where there is in-depth peer-to-peer interaction for the exchange of expertise and knowledge [13].

The platform aims to offer a dynamic and engaging tool to teach and learn mathematics, relying on interactive digital technologies that enable customized study. The goal of this research is to analyze the data collected on the MathE platform, over the 3 years, the platform has been online. So, the aims consist of investigating the topics available on the platform that need to be restructured in terms of questions level and also analyzing the students' performance according to the countries they belong to. This information will be combined with the conclusion of previous works [3,4], in which [3] had investigated the profiles of different groups of students exclusively in the Linear Algebra topic, and [4] analyzed the optimum way to reorganize the resources available on the platform into different levels of difficulty. The information acquired in this work will complement the conclusions obtained in both papers. It will help the platform developers to trace the future path to provide intelligence for the MathE platform since it is expected that shortly the MathE will be able to make use of intelligent mechanisms, based on optimization algorithms and machine learning, to make autonomous decisions, tailored according to the needs of each user.

The rest of this paper is organized as follows. In Sect. 2, the collaborative educational platform MathE is briefly described. Section 3 presents the methodology adopted. Section 4, describes the data collected throughout the time that the platform is online, that are analyze in this paper. The results and discussion obtained based on the data analyze is presented in Sect. 5. Finally, the conclusion and consequently the direction of future works are presented in Sect. 6.

2   The MathE Platform

The development of Information and Communication Technologies (ICT) facilitates access to education and made the learning process more accessible, effective. Promoting an e-learning method requires different types of resources, in particular digital and technological resources. MathE is an e-learning platform focused on the mathematical contents of higher education courses. On the platform, any student or professor, has free access to a collection of questions, videos, and other pedagogical materials related to mathematics at higher education level. MathE was developed and implemented by a consortium of seven institutional partners from five European countries: Polytechnic Institute of Bragança (Portugal), the Limerick Institute of Technology (Ireland), the University of Genova, Pixel (Italy), Kaunas University of Technology (Lithuania), Technical University of Iasi (Romania) and EuroED (Romania). Each partner institution has built a solid community of professors in the corresponding countries that has been actively collaborating and responding to the project's challenges.

The MathE platform comprises three main sections: the *Student's Assessment* section is subdivided into two subsections: *Self Need Assessment* (SNA) and *Student Final Assessment* (SFA); the students can self-evaluate their knowledge using the subsection SNA whereas, on the other hand, under SFA, the professors can organize online tests about selected topics in this subsection. On the *MathE library*, the users can access a collection of videos and additional resources about the topics covered by the platform. Finally, the *Community of Practice* provides a free forum where users can create and share their experience, knowledge and information: the students are invited to discuss related issues and challenges in the Students' Community, and the professors can build a solid network of learning and teaching practices in the Lecturers' Community.

Moreover, MathE also offers a YouTube channel where all the videos of the platform are available. There are two types of videos (both available in the platform and in the MathE YouTube channel): the ones that were selected from the internet by the MathE experts (all linked with the MathE platform) and others exclusively produced by the MathE consortium according to the platform's needs (provided on the MathE platform and MathE YouTube Channel).

The MathE platform is currently being used by a significant number of users: there are enrolled 1171 students of 15 nationalities – Portuguese, Brazilian, Turkish, Tunisian, Greek, German, Kazakh, Italian, Russian, Lithuanian, Irish, Spanish, Slovenian, Dutch and Romanian. There are also 99 professors from 12 countries and 49 higher education institutions registered. It is important to emphasize that, besides the users signed up in the MathE portal, there are users from countries like India, Philippines and Egypt, taking into account the information obtained from the YouTube channel. Figure 1 illustrates the MathE presence around the world, that is, the countries where the MathE has, at least, one person enrolled – either a professor or a student.

Currently the platform has 1841 questions, covering the fifteen most classical mathematical topics addressed in graduation courses. The questions available are divided into two levels of difficulty (basic and advanced) – this categorization

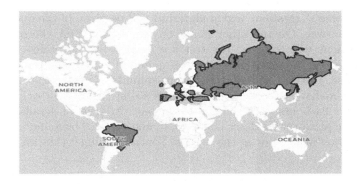

Fig. 1. MathE around the world

is done by a professor registered on the platform, both for the SNA and SFA sections. Table 1 describes the number of questions available in each topic at each section, SNA and SFA.

Table 1. MathE available questions according to topics and sections

Topics	SNA questions	SFA questions	Total questions
1. Linear Algebra	211	101	312
2. Fund. Mathematics	327	43	370
3. Graph Theory	49	21	70
4. Differentiation	144	52	196
5. Integration	127	63	190
6. Analytic Geometry	40	20	60
7. Complex Numbers	41	20	61
8. Dif. Equations	41	20	61
9. Statistic	41	21	62
10. R. F. Single Var.	52	20	72
11. Probability	46	27	73
12. Optimization	96	37	133
13. R. F. Several Var.	58	22	80
14. Set Theory	40	19	59
15. Num. Methods	42	0	42
Total	**486**	**1355**	**1841**

It is essential to clarify that each time a student selects a topic and a question difficulty level to answer on SNA, a set of seven multiple-choice questions is randomly generated from an assessment platform database. After submitting the test for evaluation, the students will immediately receive feedback on their scores and some suggestions (extra material) will be given in the questions with the wrong answer. On the other hand, on the section SFA the quantity and which questions will compose the test are defined by the professor, who will schedule a test on the platform system composed by questions from an exclusive SFA database. In this case, after a student submits the test for evaluation, the professor immediately receives the student's score; the student only has access to their score 24 hours after the end of the test. Additional details about each section of the platform are described in [3, 4], and can also be found in its website (mathe.pixel-online.org) or at the MathE Youtube channel (MathE Channel).

3   Methodology

The methodology adopted in this paper consists in the application of strategies of data mining and machine learning to assess the data collected under the MathE platform. Using statistic tools, the data is analyzed with regard to student's hit probability for each performed topic. In this way, it is possible to identify the topic that requests more attention according to the student's difficulties to answer the available questions. Thereafter, the data is evaluated in compliance to the country of origin of the student, in order to search for different students' profiles according to their nationalities.

After that, the *k-means clustering algorithm* is used to identify the similarities and dissimilarities in the students' behavior, per country. Among the unsupervised methods, clustering techniques can be considered the most popular for grouping a set of elements with similarities in the same group and dissimilarities in other groups [15], an approach that is appropriate for exploring relationships between data and detecting the underlying structures.

The k-means partitioning clustering algorithm is one of the most well-known clustering algorithms. It consists of trying to separate samples into groups of equal variance, minimizing a criterion known as the inertia or within-cluster sum-of-squares (WSS) [1]. As k-means is not an automatic clustering algorithm, it requires the definition of the initial parameter k, that represents the number of clusters division. The value of k can be specified by different techniques, but in this work the *Silhouette method* [16], which is a similarity measurement, is adopted. Once this value is established, the k-means algorithm divides a set of X samples $X_1, X_2, ..., X_m$ into k disjoint clusters C_k, each described by the mean of the samples in the cluster, μ_i, also denoted as cluster "centroids". In this way, the k-means algorithm aims to choose centroids that minimize the inertia, or within-cluster sum-of-squares criterion, presented in Eq. (1) [1].

$$WSS = \sum_{i=0}^{m} \min ||X_j - A_i||^2, \text{ in which } \mu_i \in C_k \tag{1}$$

From these centers, a clustering is defined, grouping data points according to the center to which each point is assigned. The k-means clustering algorithm and the Silhouette algorithm exist in the MatLab® library and they were applied in the research that this work describes.

4   Description of the MathE Data

MathE is an international platform and, currently there are 1171 students enrolled and 99 professors and researchers from 15 different nationalities. Table 2 describes this information with more detail; it is possible to observe that the countries with more users under the profile of student are Portugal, Lithuania and Italy.

Table 2. MathE users distribution according to their countries

Country	Students	Professors	Institutions
Portugal	646	33	18
Lithuania	231	21	11
Italy	171	13	3
Ireland	63	12	2
Romania	50	10	2
Slovenia	4	1	1
Tunisia	2	0	1
Spain	1	3	3
Netherlands	1	2	1
Turkey	1	1	1
Russia	1	1	1
Germany	0	0	1
Greece	0	0	1
Kazakhstan	0	1	1
Brazil	0	1	2
Total	**1171**	**99**	**49**

The data collected for analysis in this work considers information of 6927 answers distributed among the 15 topics of Table 1. These answers were provided by 284 students that uses the SNA section, since the platform' launch, in 2019. It is important to highlight that the questions and the topics are constantly being added to the platform, then, naturally some topics have more questions answered than others. Table 3 describes the MathE collected data.

In this table Fund. Mathematics, Dif. Equation, R. F. Single Var. and, R. F. Several, Var, means respectively Fundamentals of Mathematics, Differential Equation, Real Function of Single Variable, and Real Function of Several Variables. The data is fully characterized by the topic and the two levels of difficulty – basic and advanced. The *Topics* column describes all the MathE topics available on the platform. Moreover, in both levels (middle block and right block) the *Std* column shows the number of students that answered questions on that topic; the number of correct answers and incorrect answers is described in the columns

Table 3. MathE collected data

Topics	Basic level				Advanced level			
	Std	CA	IA	TQ	Std	CA	IA	TQ
1. Linear Algebra	135	1353	1624	2977	56	363	428	791
2. Fund. Mathematic	45	332	364	696	3	33	32	65
3. Graph Teory	5	13	14	27	2	16	5	21
4. Differentiation	49	180	357	537	3	15	10	25
5. Integration	13	45	52	97	2	4	3	7
6. Analytic Geometry	23	139	143	282	6	17	33	50
7. Complex Numbers	29	78	173	251	22	130	105	235
8. Dif. Equations	11	50	42	92	0	0	0	0
9. Statistic	57	152	174	326	0	0	0	0
10. R. F. Single Var.	8	28	39	67	0	0	7	7
11. Probability	11	27	50	77	3	11	5	16
12. Optimization	3	4	21	25	0	0	0	0
13. R. F. Several Var.	3	5	13	18	0	0	0	0
14. Set Theory	3	22	13	35	0	0	0	0
15. Num. Methods	8	97	106	203	0	0	0	0
Total	–	**2525**	**3185**	**5710**	–	**589**	**628**	**1217**

CA and IA, respectively. Finally, the columns TQ present the total number of questions answered at each level (by topic), which corresponds to the sum of all correct and incorrect answers of that difficulty level.

5 Data Analysis

In this section, the analysis of the data previously described is presented, which aims to investigate the students' behavior on the MathE Platform since it has been online. First of all, it is essential to clarify that, as mentioned above, there are 1171 students enrolled on the platform, of which 284 use the SNA section; the others students use other resources of the platform such as videos and/or peda-gogical materials or, even, the community of Practice. These 284 students belong to 8 countries: Portugal, Lithuania, Italy, Ireland, Romania, Russia, Spain, and Slovenia. Considering the information these students provided, a global analysis of the data set is done after a complementary analysis by countries.

5.1 General Database Analysis

Initially, the global performance of the students on the platform was analyzed, that is, the data of students who used the platform to answer the questions available in the topics of the Student Need Assessment section (SNA). From

Table 3, it is possible to see that the number of basic questions answered (5710 in total) represents 82% of the total questions answered on the platform against 1217 advanced questions answered. So, it is clear that the students prefer to utilize the basic questions more than the advanced ones. In terms of the type of answer, in general, the number of incorrect answers is higher than the correct ones, 3185 incorrect answers in the basic level (56%) and 628 (51, 6%) in the advanced one.

Comparing the data presented in Table 1, which describes the number of questions available, and Table 3 that presents the number of questions answered by the students, it is possible to note that the topics most required by students are those with the great variety of questions available. It can be justified because the contents of the MathE platform are constantly updated, with additional questions on each topic. So, in Table 3, Linear Algebra is the most used topic, followed by Fundamentals of Mathematics, Differentiation, and Complex Number, with more than 450 answers in terms of total answers.

Therefore, to investigate the distribution of the hit obtained in each topic, the individual hit probability per topic is calculated for each student. The graphic results of this evaluation are presented in terms question level Basic (Fig. 2 – 275 students) in which it is intend to compare the probability of questions correctly answered on the 15 topics available on the MathE Platform.

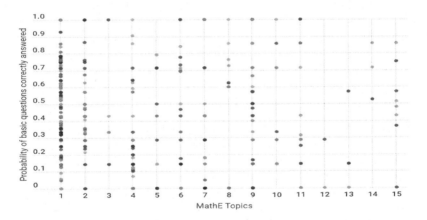

Fig. 2. Probability of correct answers per topic for all student who answered basic questions

As it is possible to see, in some topics the students distribution is almost homogeneous over the interval [0, 1], which means there are both students with excellent performance (close to 1), and students with poor performance (close to 0), as well as students with average performance. These characteristics can be found in topics 1, 2, 4, and 9, which are the topics with more presence of students, which is denoted by the colorful points.

Nonetheless, in some topics, it is possible to observe the presence of gaps in the performance interval, which can also be associated with the low number of students that use the topic, but some peculiarities can be observed that lead us to meaningful observations. The topic 5 (Integration) is used by 13 students, only 2 have a performance greater than 0.5, whereas in the topic 7 (Complex Numbers), which 29 students use, only 1 student has a performance between the interval]0.5, 1[. The absence of students in these topics may indicate the lack of easier questions. On the other hand, in the topic 8 (Differential Equation), in which there are 10 students enrolled, there is no student with a performance in the interval]0, 0.6[, which indicates that is mandatory more complex questions in the basic level of this topic. Finally, on the topic 15 (Numerical Methods), the majority of students have a performance between]0.35, 0.6[, which indicates the necessity of questions with more variability in terms of difficulties.

Although all the questions belong to a basic level, some are more basic than others, while others have a more difficult degree, the questions are not all at the same level. The variability in difficulty within a given level is expected, and it is important to maintain this, considering that there are students with different needs enrolled on the platform. But some topics are not meeting this expectation, which calls for a better distribution of the questions in more levels of difficulty, as already indicated in [4]. Such observations are fundamental for the level of difficulty of the future questions that will be inserted in the topics; mainly, the topics 5 and 7 need easier questions, and the topic 8 requires more complex questions. In contrast, the topic 15 needs both of them.

Considering the few questions answered and also the few students practicing advanced questions, it is not possible to have consistent conclusions about the topics and the advanced level of the questions' difficulty.

5.2   Students Assessment per Country

As previously mentioned, in the SNA section, there are students from 7 countries, so in this section, the students' performance according to the countries is surveyed. Table 4 describes the data through countries in terms of the number of students per country that answered basic and advanced questions; and also in terms of the type of the answer (correct and incorrect) in both difficulty levels (basic and advanced). Finally, at the last column the sum of all questions answered is presented.

As can be seen, most students using the SNA are from Portugal, Lithuania, and Italy. These three countries have at least one institution on the platform's developer team, contributing to greater platform dissemination. Table 2 shows that the three countries have the most registered students, professors, and institutions on the platform. Besides, it is worth mentioning that Portuguese students correspond to practically half of the students enrolled in the platform 646 (out of 1171). Concerning the SNA section, Portuguese students are more than 60% of the total students, it is 174 out of 284.

Thus, to analyze the students' performance by country, the probability of correct answers for the questions by country was obtained and is shown in Table 5.

Table 4. Students performance (per country)

Country	Number of students			Basic answers		Advanced answers		Total
	Basic	Advanced	Total	Correct	Incorrect	Correct	Incorrect	
Portugal	168	60	174	1529	1879	366	402	4176
Lithuania	53	11	55	486	634	113	148	1381
Italy	35	7	35	333	446	48	28	855
Ireland	12	3	13	100	138	30	19	287
Romania	3	1	3	18	14	17	11	60
Russia	1	1	1	30	54	11	17	112
Spain	1	0	1	12	16	0	0	28
Slovenia	2	1	2	17	4	4	3	28
Total	275	84	284	2525	3185	589	628	6927

Thus, the columns *Basic Questions* and *Advanced Questions* correspond to the hit average of the students in the basic and advanced levels, respectively. Furthermore, the last column, *All Questions* is the hit probability considering both levels.

Table 5. Students hit average probability (per country)

Country	Basic questions	Advanced questions	All questions
Portugal	0.45	0.48	**0.45**
Lithuania	0.43	0.43	**0.43**
Italy	0.43	0.63	**0.45**
Ireland	0.42	0.61	**0.45**
Romania	0.56	0.61	**0.58**
Russia	0.36	0.39	**0.37**
Spain	0.43	0.00	**0.43**
Slovenia	0.81	0.57	**0.75**

From Table 5, it can be seen that the hit average for the advanced questions is almost always more significant than the probability of correct answers for the basic questions, and the opposite was expected, since in the basic questions, the students make many mistakes, so a low hit probability was expected at the advanced questions. This observation may indicate that the questions are not adequately organized on the platform since the basic questions have a degree of difficulty higher than expected and the advanced ones are not as complex as wished. Thus, for the best use of it, this issue is one of the urgent points to be reviewed for platform improvement.

The OECD Programme for International Student Assessment (PISA) examines what students know about mathematics, and according to this ranking, the countries and their mean classification are: Slovenia (509), Ireland (500), Portugal (492), Russia (488), Italy (487), Lithuania and Spain (481) and Romania (430) [11]. Since there is not an expressive number of students in all countries, it is not easy to establish a highly reliable comparison. Thus, in order to consider only countries with more than 30 students (Portugal, Lithuania, and Italy), it is noted that the average of both in PISA is close, with Portugal in 28th position, Italy in 31st and Lithuania in 34th [11]. Thus, it was already expected that the student's performance would be similar, as can be seen in the averages of correct answers in Table 5, mainly by the last column, which considers all the questions answered by the students of that country.

5.3   Portuguese, Lithuanian and Italian Students Assessment on Basic Questions

As already mentioned, there is a small number of students per country, so it is not feasible to assess the profile of students from the 8 countries. Therefore, this section will only consider data from Portuguese, Lithuanian, and Italian students, as there are more than 30 students in each group. Moreover, the number of advanced answers is few representative when compared to the basic answers. Therefore, only basic answers are considered in this section.

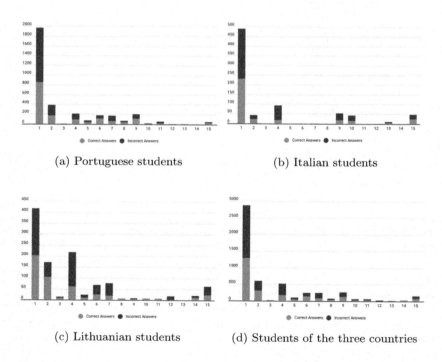

(a) Portuguese students   (b) Italian students

(c) Lithuanian students   (d) Students of the three countries

Fig. 3. Students' assessment on basic questions for each topic (per country)

As shown in Fig. 3, students from the three countries predominantly answer topic 1 - Linear Algebra. This one is widespread in practically all higher education courses, regardless of the country. This may be the main reason for such a significant number of answers.

In respect to Portuguese students, in Fig. 3a, it is possible to verify that they pay extreme attention to topic 1 (Linear Algebra) reaching approximately 2000 responses, while all other topics have less than 210 responses (with the exception of topic 2 - Fundamentals of Mathematics). In addition to the already presented justification of Algebra Linear being present in several courses, the fact that the other topics are less used may be related to the encouragement given by the professors during the classes. Similar behavior is found in Italian students, Fig. 3b, in this case, while Algebra Linear collects almost 500 responses, the other topics have less than 100. On the other hand, in Lithuania, Fig. 3c this pattern is less expressive, and although with a smaller amount of answers than in other countries, the topics 2 – Fundamentals of Mathematics, 4 – Differentiation, 6 – Analytic Geometry, 7 – Complex Numbers and 15 – Numerical Methods, are also being significantly explored by the students in relation to the other topics used by the Lithuanian students.

The data collected presented on Fig. 3 is interesting and worthy to be explored in future works. If one can perceive strengths that lead students to have a preference for Linear Algebra, it will be possible to export this characteristics to others, thus captivating students to use the platform constantly and intensively in other topics too.

Finally, to identify the similarities and dissimilarities in the students' behavior, a clustering analysis was performed and the results are shown in Fig. 4.

Regarding the Portuguese students, in Fig. 4a, the algorithm grouped the students into 3 clusters. Thence, in cluster 1 (red), there are the students that answered fewer questions in relation to the other clusters, as it is the cluster with the highest population density. These students answer a maximum of 50 questions, which is represented by the sum of the x and y coordinates. Thus, the cluster 1 represents students who use less the platform, with mean equal to 12 answered and the students have an average performance in relation to the others. On the other hand, the cluster 2 (blue), are the students who answered more basic questions correctly. All students of this cluster answered at least 30 basic questions correctly and more than 18 incorrectly, while the majority answered less than 40 incorrectly. Furthermore, the average of answers is 78, so on cluster 2, students who use the platform more often and have to perform better than other students. Finally, in cluster 3 (green), there are students who also use the platform a lot, an average equal to 55 but do not perform well since they have a high error rate and a low rate of success in basic questions.

In the case of Italian students, Fig. 4b there are also 3 clusters, but with different behavior from Portuguese students. In the case of cluster 1 (red) of Italians, we have students who answer a few questions (mean equal to 2 and maximum of 17 question), and most of the answers are incorrect. In cluster 2 (blue), there are the students who answered the largest number of questions,

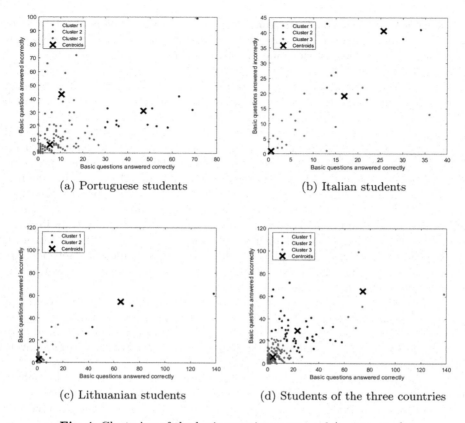

(a) Portuguese students

(b) Italian students

(c) Lithuanian students

(d) Students of the three countries

Fig. 4. Clustering of the basic questions answered (per country)

with mean of answers equal to 66, but the number of incorrect answers is much higher in relation to the number of correct answers. Finally, in cluster 3 (green), we have students with average performance, in this case the number of correct answers and errors is more balanced than the others, and these students answer an average of 36 questions.

For the Lithuania, Fig. 4c there are 2 clusters. Students are heavily concentrated in cluster 1 (red), responding to a few questions (means of answer equal to 5) with more incorrect than correct answers. Furthermore, in cluster 2 (blue), we have the students who answer the most questions (means equal to 133); however, this is a small group composed of 4 students, and although the performance is slightly higher than the students in cluster 1, it is still not excellent, considering the number of errors.

Finally, in Fig. 4d, there are the students from the 3 countries, cluster 1 are the students who answer fewer questions and with a low rate of correct answers; cluster 2, students who answer more questions than those in cluster 1 and less than those in cluster 3, but still with an intermediate performance. Moreover, in cluster 3, the students who answer more questions are represented by a small number of students.

6 Conclusions

The MathE platform is an online educational system that aims to help students who struggle to learn college mathematics, as well as students who want to deepen their knowledge of a multitude of mathematical topics, at their own pace. The platform currently provides a set a diversified questions, videos and pedagogical resources for the higher educational level. The question are randomly generated, independently of the profile of the users (there is only the possibility to choose topic, subtopic and level of difficulty), but it is expected that in the near future the platform will be able to make use of intelligent mechanisms, based on optimization algorithms and machine learning, to make autonomous decisions, able to direct the questions in a customized way, according to the students profile and needs.

The research [3,4] aimed to investigate the difficulties and potentialities of the platform, as well as the characteristics that could be used to make the platform more efficient. Thus, the approach presented in this paper seeked to evaluate the adequate level of difficulty of the questions in the topics that are available on the platform, based on the students' hit probability at the SNA section. In addition, it was also evaluated whether the country of origin is a relevant variable in the students' performance. Thus, the information collected through this research will serve as a guide to make the choice of optimal strategies to improve the performance of the platform.

From the results obtained in this work, together with the others already carried out [3,4], it is evident the need to reorganize the questions in more levels of difficulty. However, the results of this analysis will be fundamental for defining the type of questions that each topic needs. In addition, currently the assignment of a question to a certain level is done by a collaborating professor, so this division is subject to partiality and subjectivity, and may vary from person to person. Thus, finding a way to assign the questions to their respective difficulty level autonomously, through an intelligent system, is one of the possible ways to improve the organization of questions on the platform. This is also a way to keep students constantly active on the platform, as more engaged the students are in the platform uses, more questions they performs.

Finally, in relation to the analysis by countries, from the data analyzed so far, it is not possible to conclude whether students from a particular country perform better than from other countries (due, for example, to the quality of education in the country in question or other factors). In general, countries among the ones that have more than 30 students enrolled in the platform, show very similar outcomes in questions of both levels of difficulty. Thus, with the data that is currently have available, the country of origin does not appear as a determining variable in the customization of questions for students, in a future version of the platform.

References

1. Arthur, D., Vassilvitskii, S.: K-means++: the advantages of careful seeding. In: Proceedings of the Eighteenth Annual ACM-SIAM Symposium on Discrete Algorithms, pp. 1027–1035. SODA 2007, Society for Industrial and Applied Mathematics, USA (2007)
2. Ausubel, D.: The Acquisition and Retention of Knowledge: A Cognitive View. SPRINGER-SCIENCE+BUSINESS MEDIA, B.V (2000)
3. Azevedo, B.F., Rocha, A.M.A.C., Fernandes, F.P., Pacheco, M.F., Pereira, A.I.: Evaluating student behaviour on the mathe platform - clustering algorithms approaches. In: (In press) Book of 16th Learning and Intelligent Optimization Conference - LION 2022, pp. XX-XX. Milos - Greece (2022)
4. Azevedo, B.F., Amoura, Y., Rocha, A.M.A.C., Fernandes, F.P., Pacheco, M.F., Pereira, A.I.: Analyzing the mathe platform through clustering algorithms. In: Gervasi, O., Murgante, B., Misra, S., Rocha, A.M.A.C., Garau, C. (eds.) Computational Science and Its Applications - ICCSA 2022 Workshops. LNCS, vol. 13378, pp. 201–218. Springer, Cham (2022). https://doi.org/10.1007/978-3-031-10562-3_15
5. Bransford, J., Brown, A.L., Cocking, R.R.: How people learn: brain, mind, experience, and school (2000). http://www.nap.edu/books/0309070368/html. Accessed June 2022
6. McKeachie, W.J.: Teaching Tips: Strategies, Research, and Theory for College and University Teachers. Houghton Mifflin, Boston, MA (2002)
7. MCLeod, S.A.: Constructivism as a theory for teaching and learning (2019). www.simplypsychology.org/constructivism.html. Accessed June 2022
8. Nation, U.: Sustainable development goals (2020). www.un.org/sustainabledevelopment/education/. accessed August 2022
9. Novak, J.D., Gowin, D.B.: Learning How to Learn. Cambridge University Press (1984)
10. OECD: The future of education and skills - education 2030 (2018). https://www.oecd.org/education/2030/E2030%20Position%20Pape%20(05.04.2018).pdf. Accessed June 2022
11. OECD: PISA 2018 Results, Vol. I. OECD Publishing (2019)
12. Oliver, K.: Methods for developing constructivist learning on the web. Educ. Technol. **40**, 5–18 (2000)
13. Pacheco, M.F., Pereira, A.I., Fernandes, F.: Mathe - improve mathematical skills in higher education. In: Proceedings of the 2019 8th International Conference on Educational and Information Technology (ICET2019), pp. 173–176. United Kingdom (2019)
14. Piaget, J., Claparède, E.: The Language and Thought of the Child. Routledge (1959)
15. Rokach, L., Maimon, O.: Clustering methods. In: Maimon, O. and Rokach, L. (eds). Clustering Methods Data Mining and Knowledge Discovery Handbook, Springer, Boston (2005). https://doi.org/10.1007/0-387-25465-X_15

16. Rousseeuw, P.J.: Silhouettes: a graphical aid to the interpretation and validation of cluster analysis. J. Comput. Appl. Math. **20**, 53–65 (1987)
17. Trujillo, G., Tanner, K.: Considering the role of affect in learning: Monitoring students' self-efficacy, sense of belonging, and science identity. CBE life Sci. Educ. **13**, 6–15 (03 2014)
18. Vygotsky, L.S.: Mind in Society: The Development of Higher Psychological Processes. Harvard University Press (1978)
19. Vygotsky, L.S.: Thought and Language. MIT Press (1986)

Evolution of Soft Skills for Engineering Education in the Digital Era

Leonardo Breno Pessoa da Silva(iD), Bernardo Perota Barreto,
Fernanda Tavares Treinta(iD), Luis Mauricio Martins de Resende(iD),
Rui Tadashi Yoshino(iD), and Joseane Pontes$^{(\boxtimes)}$(iD)

Federal University of Technology - Parana (UTFPR), Ponta Grossa, PR, Brazil
{leonardos.1995,bernardobarreto}@alunos.utfpr.edu.br,
{fernandatreinta,lmresende,ruiyoshino,joseane}@utfpr.edu.br

Abstract. The challenges of the 4th Industrial Revolution and of an imminent 5th Industrial Revolution promote changes in the labor market, requiring more directed qualification and reskilling for the workforce and the training of hard skills and, in this period, mainly soft skills. To this end, it is necessary to understand how education has evolved over time, leading to Education 5.0, important for the training of, for example, Engineering professionals, being a necessary professional for the digital transformation to occur. Therefore, this paper aims to present the evolution toward Education 5.0 and the development of soft skills in engineering education. As a method, a Systematic Literature Review was used, by means of the PRISMA methodology, to survey pertinent literature. The bibliographic portfolio was analyzed through content analysis with the help of the tool QSR NVIVO version 10. The analyzed content allowed us to verify the advent of industrial revolutions until Industry 5.0, how education has evolved over time until the Education 5.0 and what are the main soft skills developed. This research can help universities, graduating students, teachers, and professionals to qualification and reskilling themselves according to the needs of Industry 4.0 and 5.0.

Keywords: Industry 4.0 · Industry 5.0 · Digital Era · Education 5.0 · Soft skills

1 Introduction

In the face of digitalization and robotics, the evolutionary stage known as Industry 4.0 is being experienced [1], with the goal of establishing an interconnected, intelligent, and self-regulating industrial value creation [2]. Industry 4.0 has a great opportunity for job enrichment, as the environment has become more autonomous and with better opportunities for self-development [4]. As such, workers will possess more initiative, because in the industrial environment of

---

Supported by organization x.

the future, work is expected to be more related to strategic decisions and problem solving, and autonomous learning efforts should be encouraged [5].

Some studies present evolution towards Industry 5.0, where manufacturing should be human-centring, putting the well-being of workers at the center of production processes [6, 9]. In this evolutionary stage of the industry, a type of co-working between human and machines becomes evident [9], in which people will concentrate on tasks related to creativity and machines on the other activities of the industry, with the capacity for immediate change, reducing risks of accidents to the worker and increasing the efficiency of the system [10].

The industrial revolutions have caused changes beyond production systems, reverberating in changes in society. Technological advancement must prioritize the development of human resources, which involves developing the skills that will be needed now and in the future, [13]. Industry 4.0 will be known for its multidisciplinary [20], requiring leaders to encourage and invest in workforce skills to increase the learning curve [7, 8].

This has required an evolution in education and how institutions train the future workforce to meet the challenges of digital transformation. The current education models started to adapt to train and retrain the workforce. According to a Deloitte Company [15] survey, education systems around the world were the primary trainers of young people for the workforce. The Education Commission [17] predicts that by 2030 more than half of the world's nearly 2 billion young people will not have the skills or qualifications needed to participate in the emerging global workforce. Deloitte Company [16] in another survey states that just under 33% of workers are prepared for the digital changes, especially remote work.

With education, the workforce can be trained and reskilling, so human resources need to update their skills according to the demand of organizations [18], developing lifelong learning and meeting the SDGs (Sustainable Development Goals) 4 proposed by the United Nations Member States that talks about Quality Education. With this, the idea of developing manpower for Industry 4.0 and clearly explaining its principles, from solutions to real cases, developed programs for training people focused on Industry 4.0 [14, 19]. To adapt educational institutions to the requirements of Industry 4.0 and 5.0, training programs are important initiatives. The training programs are an opportunity for undergraduate students to incorporate formal knowledge and experience into their university education [11, 12], developing hard and soft skills [22].

For example, the MEI-U, an innovative teaching method for Industry 4.0, from the university-industry partnership for solving real cases [19]. With the importance of soft skills for Industry 4.0 - [18, 20], being a characteristic that differentiates people from machines - [8], the methodology allows students to develop soft skills such as creativity, leadership, and problem solving through the challenges they solve. In the study of [22], 90% to 95% of the students who investigated the study mentioned that teamwork and communication were the soft skills most developed and used during participation in subjects of the MEI-U methodology.

Among these perspectives, it is necessary to understand how education has evolved and what skills were developed in each era, especially when talking about the next stage of Industry 5.0 and the importance of the engineering profession. Therefore, the article aims to answer the following Research Question (RQ): "What is the importance of the advance to Education 5.0 in the development of soft skills?"

Therefore, this paper aims to present the evolution toward Education 5.0 and the development of soft skills in engineering education. To this end, a systematic review of literature was conducted to survey the literature that characterizes Industry 4.0 and 5.0 (Digital Era), searching for references to the evolutionary stages of education until reaching Education 5.0 and which soft skills are required by the market.

2   Materials and Methods

To determine how education has advanced over time, especially how the industrial revolutions have interfered with this process, a Systematic Literature Review was conducted to gather pertinent literature on the topic. This method helps to analyze relevant evidence and find relevant literature in a clear, systematic, and transparent way, with all its steps documented [23].

For this study the PRISMA (Preferred Reporting Items For Systematic Reviews And Meta Analyses) method was used [21]. This method aims to help authors improve the construction of systematic literature reviews, which was adopted. This method addresses questions that have not yet been answered by individual studies, identifying research questions and theories [21]. This methodology is illustrated by the application of three phases, namely, identification, screening, and inclusion. These steps are necessary to bring the article portfolio closer to the objective of this study and are widely used in different research fields.

The search started with a combination of keywords representing the research group related to "Industry 4.0 and 5.0" and "Education and Skill". Due to the variety of terms that can translate the search group, the Boolean index "AND" was used to connect the search group and "OR" to return synonyms or alternative terms on the same search group. The initial data entry was represented by a database search according to the filters used. The research was carried out in 2021, without a temporal cut-off. The research protocol used is described in Table 1.

In the identification step, from the application of the protocol described in Table 1. The initial portfolio had 5340 paper, from the search in the selected databases. Mendeley was used as a reference manager to organize references, remove duplicates, and read titles and abstracts. From the initial search base, 2508 files considered duplicates in the search and eligible for the next step were removed.

In the Screening step, the papers were considered for reading the title and abstract to verify adherence to the objective to be achieved by this paper. Thus,

Table 1. Research protocol

Search term (Title, Abstract or Keywords)	Group 1 (Industry 4.0 and 5.0)
	- ("Industry 4.0" OR "Industrie 4.0" OR "Fourth Industrial Revolution" OR "4th Industrial Revolution" OR "Smart Industry" OR "Smart Manufacturing" OR "Smart Factory" OR "Industry 5.0")
	Group 2 (Education and Skill)
	- ("Education" OR "Learning" OR "Training" OR "Skill" OR "Competence")
Search strategy	AND among groups
Database	Scopus (2871 documents), Science Direct (967 Documents), Web of Science (1502 documents)
Publication type	Research Paper and Review Paper (Considering classification of the database)
Language	English
Search period	Not specific

2,552 papers were excluded from the title reading and another 130 papers were excluded from the abstract reading. Thus, 50 papers were eligible for the inclusion stage.

In the last step, included, the idea is to verify studies that present the evolution of education in the context of Industry 4.0 and 5.0, presenting an evolutionary panorama. Among this, it is also necessary to identify some key skills for the evolutionary eras of education, from 1.0 to 5.0. Therefore, as a result of this step, a final portfolio of papers is to be submitted for content analysis. Among the 50 papers included, only 40 papers were eligible. Figure 1 presents the information flow of PRISMA, showing the amount of inclusion and exclusion of each step.

The portfolio of papers was analyzed using Content Analysis. This approach allows the construction of models, generation of theories, interpretation, conceptualization, and establishment of relationships [24]. This type of analysis allows, in a systematic way, the description of messages and attitudes linked to the context of the information, as well as the understanding of the meanings and relationships that are established beyond what was properly said [25].

From the analyzed portfolio, a word cloud was built with the keywords used by the articles. The size of the words is represented by the number of mentions of the articles in the final portfolio. From Fig. 2, we verify the adherence to the portfolio with the main words being Industry 4.0, Engineering Education and Students.

Engineering education was not used as a keyword in the searches, but it stands out in the papers from the Systematic Literature Review, being a

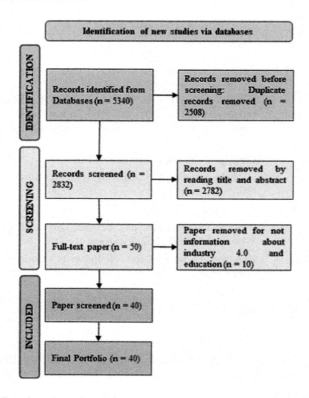

Fig. 1. Results of applying PRISMA to the systematic literature review

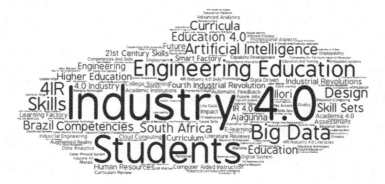

Fig. 2. Keywords cloud

highlight in the word cloud. This is due to the fact that it is one of the important areas for the new evolutionary stage, being essential for the conception and use of digital technologies and with a greater concern for the feared Industry 4.0 and 5.0.

3 Industry 4.0 and 5.0

Technological innovations are considered key drivers for sustainable economic development and productivity growth [27,28]. The world is experiencing the 4th Industrial Revolution marked by connectivity and the use of digital technologies, creating a digital value chain. Industry 4.0 is linked to an incremental adaptation of work systems, as in the three previous revolutions, and on the set of new technologies and forms of application with a degree of technical maturity and systemic effect [5].

The First Industrial Revolution is marked by the exchange of agrarian economy for the economy, in general, industrial, with mechanical production facilities, the introduction of steam power and hydraulics [29]. The Second Industrial Revolution is characterized by the division of labor and the introduction of electricity, favoring mass production and the assembly line [26].

The Third Industrial Revolution begins the so-called Digital Revolution, presenting principles of automated production utilizing electronic and information process technologies [29]. With the introduction of the Cyber-physical Systems for monitoring and decision making, the Fourth Industrial Revolution begins, providing machine autonomy and process monitoring and decision making [30]. The evolutionary stage of the Industrial Revolutions is shown in Fig. 3.

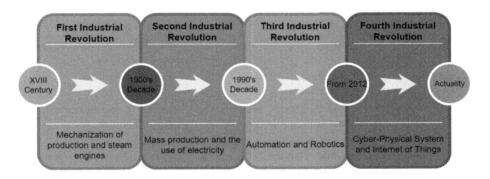

Fig. 3. Evolution of industrial revolution

The concept of Industry 4.0 is defined as an interconnected process of machines, people, and products, service-oriented and related to the application of digital technologies [31,32]. This new phase has a particularity linked to machine autonomy, generating a large amount of data that underpin decision making [5]. As a consequence, the market and the job profiles will adapt to the application of digital technologies, being architects, developers, and engineers [3,33], categories related to job profiles connected to the development and application of digital technologies.

As with previous revolutions, Industry 4.0 will not only influence the manufacturing industry, but will also interfere in the social, educational, and economic sectors [5], which will reflect on the work environment. Because of this interference, the Society 5.0, or Creative Society, the initiative has emerged, enabling social issues to be solved with the help of digital technologies [34].

Society 5.0 originates from a consolidation of Industry 4.0 [35]. From this, it is characterized as a society developed by transformations guided by scientific and technological innovation, creating cooperation values, data standardization plans, systems architecture models and human development [36].

In this context, Industry 5.0 emerges, giving a start to the Fifth Industrial Revolution, with people-centered manufacturing and significant impacts in areas such as medicine, civil society, and business models [6,10]. Industry 5.0 is characterized by closer collaboration between man and machine, unlike Industry 4.0, which focuses on integrated connecting devices [9].

Industry 5.0 restructures human tasks in ways that benefit workers. The use of the potential of the human brain for creativity and an intelligent system to increase efficiency to benefit the workforce [36]. From this, there is the enhancement of the cognitive skills of employees, providing value-added tasks at work alongside an autonomous workforce, i.e. collaborative robots (co-bots) that will be perceptive and informed of human intent and desire [?]. Thus, Table 2 presents this evolutionary stage from Industry 4.0 to 5.0.

Table 2. Industry 4.0 and Industry 5.0

	Industry 4.0	Industry 5.0
Theme	Smart Manufacturing	Human-Robot Collaborative and Bioeconomy
Motivation	Flexibility and Mass Customization	Smart Society and Sustainable
Energy source	Electric Power, Fossil Fuels and Renewable Sources	Electricity and Renewable Energy Sources
Involved technologies	Internet of Things, Big Data, Cloud, Robotic	Artificial Intelligence, Human-Robot Collaborative, Cognitive CPS

To ensure the sustainability and resilience of systems, Industry 5.0 points to the centrality of human [50]. With advances in technology such as Artificial Intelligence, better system performance is achieved when technologies and people work together, as a collaborative intelligence, ensuring co-evolution [6].

4   Evolution of Education Towards the Digital Era

The need for change in educational approaches has been recognized by industry and academia [37]. Studies point to the changes in education as industry evolves. In this regard, one can divide education into eras, similar to the eras of industrial revolutions, as presented in Fig. 4.

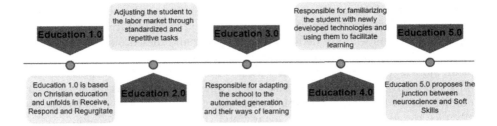

Fig. 4. Evolution of education

Education 1.0 is influenced by Christianity, which held the knowledge and how it was transmitted. When education evolves to 2.0 and 3.0, the industry begins to massively influence education, meeting the demands of industry and learning processes [43,44]. Education in the last 100 years, especially in engineering, has changed the relationship between theory and practice for project development, with an emphasis on technology [38], programming and IT.

Education 4.0 features the use of Industry 4.0 technologies playing an important role [40]. These enabling technologies are essential for knowledge to be passed on to the future workforce, creating a framework for advanced manufacturing education [37,40]. This education system aims to bring new and experienced employees up to speed with the innovative proposals of Industry 4.0, creating a sustainable environment that will accelerate its adoption in manufacturing [39].

There are two factors of great relevance for education related to industrial automation and digitization. The main factor is the importance played by Industry 4.0 technologies in the construction and implementation of curricula, to consider the improvement of investigative skills and problem-solving [39,42]. As a second factor, it is the role of learning factories, in the context of the Fourth Industrial Revolution, in assisting in the development of creative, collaborative, communicative, innovative professionals with familiarity with the industrial digital environment and a sense of criticality [45].

Therefore, Education 4.0 is the educational system that aims to train the new workforce and qualify or retrain them, creating a sustainable environment that will accelerate the adoption of smart manufacturing [39,42], creating a system to organize and analyze large amounts of data. Education 4.0 also considers the use of digital technologies, such as virtual reality, to facilitate the learning process and familiarize the workforce with the Industry 4.0 environment, algorithms and your applications [37,40] from historical data and real-time adaptation [41]. In it, it considers learning theory to teach technology to future workforce.

Integração de dados históricos e em tempo real em nível de componente e sistema, permitindo a adaptação da análise em tempo real e algoritmos de supervisão baseados em regras após a implantação;

With the concern for the centralization of people in the productive system and about the evolution to Society and Industry 5.0, Education 5.0 [37] emerges.

This new stage seeks to offer necessary competencies to the new professionals inserted in this context. Despite being a recent area of research, it is possible to find researchers who are dedicated to studying and disseminating the theme. Education 5.0 should combine the benefits of well-established and validated education models, inspired by and in the past to build the future, incorporating radically innovative aspects and relying on advanced technologies, as a necessary complement to transform education more effectively and efficiently to successfully face the global challenges of society and the environment [37,46].

Actions are needed that enable lifelong learning and transdisciplinarity for education [37,46]. Specific to engineering education, technological advances require changes in the workforce, needing to be more flexible and adaptable [37]. Education 5.0 is based on innovation and industrialization, done to align knowledge generated through research and development to industrial needs based on the principle of human-centered [47].

Important ethical questions continue to arise, since technologies are constantly present in people's lives, raising issues with privacy, and questions related to social prejudices, gender, and race [46]. Consequently, to form a new generation of professionals, capable of leading and guiding the next technological advances and their application in a more just and sustainable world, a reformulation of education is urgent [46].

In the midst of this, each era has demanded the development of different skills [48], mainly that meet the changes brought about by the industrial revolutions. The acquisition of skills goes beyond purely theoretical knowledge, it also includes the ability to apply knowledge to solve practical problems [49]. Therefore, Fig. 5 presents a summary of the eras of the evolution of education aligned to the industrial revolutions.

The transition from Industry 4.0 to 5.0 (Digital Era) requires changes in important skills for the development of work. While in the 4.0 Era the focus was on digitally transforming the industry, focusing on skills such as learning algorithms, digital literacy and Critical Thinking [18], the 5.0 Era is known for the increased interaction with co-bots. The centrality of the design of Industry 5.0 demands new skills from people, promoting a fusion of technology, communication, and leadership [51].

Thus, there is a trend towards developing human resources capable of using digital technologies. Furthermore, digital technologies help in the education process, with the development of educational testbeds focused on the development of soft skills and the necessary hard skills, instigating the present and future workforce in reskilling and upskilling according to the challenges of Industry 4.0 and transition to Industry 5.0 [18].

The engineers of the next generation need a wide range of knowledge in different technologies, methods, and methodologies [37]. In addition, discussions about sustainability and the scope of the SDGs need to be part of the curricula of the engineers of the future. In addition, the engineers of the future need a high degree of hard skills, such as programming and digital tools, as well as soft

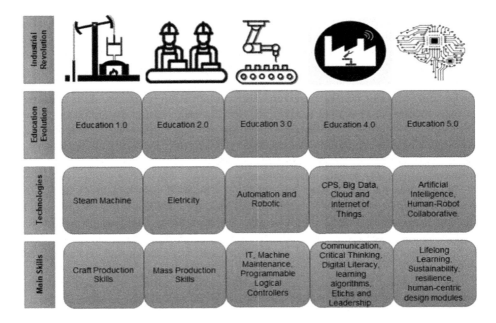

Fig. 5. Industry and education evolution

skills like communication and critical thinking [52]. This balance allows for a job profile that is highly investigative and competent to manage resources.

Thus, there are some challenges to achieving Education in the digital age. Universities need to search for new ways of teaching and partnerships to enhance the training of workforce 4.0. However, the bureaucratic processes and the rigid mentality of top management create obstacles in the search for innovation and potential partnerships with the industry.

The protagonist of training programs needs to shift from the teacher to the students to enhance the formation of soft skills and hard skills. The workforce needs to understand the challenges to overcome, seek qualifications, and leverage the skills required by the industry. Moreover, the industry, increasingly demanding in the training of workers, through partnerships with universities can assist in the qualification of the future workforce, presenting the required requirements and bringing the market closer to the university.

5   Conclusion

Industrial revolutions bring about changes in both industry and society's way of life. From the 1st to the middle of the 5th Industrial Revolution, the labor market needs to adapt to develop the necessary skills for the workforce. These transformations require Education to evolve according to society's needs in keeping up with the digital transformation and teaching how to use technology.

Education is responsible for developing teaching methodologies that help train and retrain the workforce. For workers to be prepared for the challenges arising from the Industrial Revolutions, education needs to work at a faster pace, to prepare people for the demands of technological evolution.

Furthermore, the technologies arising from Industry 4.0 and 5.0 can be used in the learning process, generating connectivity, innovation practices, skills training, and the formation of digital natives. To do this, educational organizations need to be open to change and form partnerships with government institutions and industry. These partnerships are necessary to identify the skill that needs to be trained, promote synergy between the institutions, and use real cases from the industry to promote learning and training.

This paper presented how education has evolved and how it is linked to workforce training for Industry 4.0 and 5.0. Moreover, from the articles surveyed, one can see a trend toward Engineering Education as an essential profession for digital transformation and technology development. Therefore, there is a need to develop soft skills for people to develop their work tasks and use as digital technologies.

As a proposal for future study, it is suggested mapping the skills that will be important for the transition from Industry 4.0 to 5.0, is necessary to adapt training programs to develop these new skills with new learning methods, and your applications.

References

1. Baygin, M., Yetis, H., Karakose, M., Akin, E.: An effect analysis of industry 4.0 to higher education. In: 2016 15th International Conference on Information Technology Based Higher Education and Training (ITHET), pp. 1–4. IEEE. (2016). https://doi.org/10.1109/ITHET.2016.7760744
2. Liao, Y., Deschamps, F., Loures, E.D.F.R., Ramos, L.F.P.: Past, present and future of Industry 4.0-a systematic literature review and research agenda proposal. Int. J. Product. Res. **55**(12), 3609–3629 (2017). https://doi.org/10.1080/00207543.2017.1308576
3. Pontes, J., et al.: Relationship between trends, job profiles, skills and training programs in the factory of the future. In: 2021 22nd IEEE International Conference on Industrial Technology (ICIT), vol. 1, pp. 1240–1245. IEEE (2021). https://doi.org/10.1109/ICIT46573.2021.9453584
4. Kaasinen, E., et al.: Empowering and engaging industrial workers with Operator 4.0 solutions. Comput. Indust. Eng. **139**, 105678 (2020). https://doi.org/10.1016/j.cie.2019.01.052
5. Bongomin, O., Gilibrays Ocen, G., Oyondi Nganyi, E., Musinguzi, A., Omara, T.: Exponential disruptive technologies and the required skills of industry 4.0. J. Eng. (2020). https://doi.org/10.1155/2020/4280156
6. Lu, Y., et al.: Outlook on human-centric manufacturing towards Industry 5.0. J. Manufact. Syst. **62**, 612–627 (2022). https://doi.org/10.1016/j.jmsy.2022.02.001
7. Cortellazzo, L., Bruni, E., Zampieri, R.: The role of leadership in a digitalized world: a review. Front. Psychol. **1938** (2019). https://doi.org/10.3389/fpsyg.2019.01938

8. Fareri, S., Fantoni, G., Chiarello, F., Coli, E., Binda, A.: Estimating Industry 4.0 impact on job profiles and skills using text mining. Comput. Indust. **118**, 103222 (2020). https://doi.org/10.1016/j.compind.2020.103222

9. Demir, K.A., Döven, G., Sezen, B.: Industry 5.0 and human-robot co-working. Procedia Comput. Sci. **158**, 688–695 (2019). https://doi.org/10.1016/j.procs.2019.09.104

10. Özdemir, V., Hekim, N.: Birth of industry 5.0: making sense of big data with artificial intelligence,"the internet of things" and next-generation technology policy. Omics J. Integrat. Biol. **22**(1), 65–76 (2018). https://doi.org/10.1089/omi.2017.0194

11. Pillai, S., Khan, M.H., Ibrahim, I.S., Raphael, S.: Enhancing employability through industrial training in the Malaysian context. High. Educ. **63**(2), 187–204 (2012). https://doi.org/10.1007/s10734-011-9430-2

12. Renganathan, S., Karim, Z.A.B.A., Li, C.S.: Students' perception of industrial internship programme. Education + Training (2012). https://doi.org/10.1108/00400911211210288

13. Schallock, B., Rybski, C., Jochem, R., Kohl, H.: Learning Factory for Industry 4.0 to provide future skills beyond technical training. Procedia Manufact. **23**, 27–32 (2018). https://doi.org/10.1016/j.promfg.2018.03.156

14. Kliment, M., Pekarcikova, M., Trebuna, P., Trebuna, M.: Application of TestBed 4.0 technology within the implementation of Industry 4.0 in teaching methods of industrial engineering as well as industrial practice. Sustainability **13**(16), 8963 (2021). https://doi.org/10.3390/su13168963

15. Delloite Company: Preparing tomorrow's workforce for the Fourth Industrial Revolution For business: a framework for action (2018). https://www2.deloitte.com/content/dam/Deloitte/global/Documents/About-Deloitte/gx-preparing-tomorrow-workforce-for-4IR.pdf. Accessed 9 Apr 2022

16. Delloite Company: Workforce Ecosystems: Managing the Future of Work (2021). https://deloitte.wsj.com/articles/workforce-ecosystems-managing-the-future-of-work-01626894129. Accessed 9 Apr 2022

17. Education Commission: What is the International Finance Facility for Education? (2017). https://educationcommission.org/international-finance-facility-education/. Accessed 9 Apr 2022

18. da Silva, L.B.P., et al.: Human Resources Management 4.0: literature review and trends. Comput. Indust. Eng. 108111 (2022) https://doi.org/10.1016/j.cie.2022.108111

19. Yoshino, R.T., Pinto, M.M.A., Pontes, J., Treinta, F.T., Justo, J.F., Santos, M.M.: Educational Test Bed 4.0: a teaching tool for Industry 4.0. Eur. J. Eng. Educ. **45**(6), 1002–1023 (2020) https://doi.org/10.1080/03043797.2020.1832966

20. Jerman, A., Pejic Bach, M., Aleksic, A.: Transformation towards smart factory system: examining new job profiles and competencies. Syst. Res. Behav. Sci. **37**(2), 388–402 (2020). https://doi.org/10.1002/sres.2657

21. Page, M.J., et al.: The PRISMA 2020 statement: an updated guideline for reporting systematic reviews. Int. J. Surg. **88**, 105906 (2021). https://doi.org/10.1016/j.ijsu.2021.105906

22. da Silva, L.B.P., Barreto, B.P., Pontes, J., Treinta, F.T., de Resende, L.M.M., Yoshino, R.T.: Evaluation of soft skills through educational testbed 4.0. In: Pereira, A.I., et al. (eds.) OL2A 2021. CCIS, vol. 1488, pp. 678–690. Springer, Cham (2021). https://doi.org/10.1007/978-3-030-91885-9_51

23. Kitchenham, B.: Procedures for performing systematic reviews. Keele, UK, Keele University **33**(2004), 1–26 (2004)

24. Bringer, J.D., Johnston, L.H., Brackenridge, C.H.: Maximizing transparency in a doctoral thesis1: the complexities of writing about the use of QSR* NVIVO within a grounded theory study. Qual. Res. **4**(2), 247–265 (2004). https://doi.org/10.1177/1468794104044434

25. Cavalcante, R.B., Calixto, P., Pinheiro, M.M.K.: Análise de conteúdo: considerações gerais, relações com a pergunta de pesquisa, possibilidades e limitações do método. Informação & sociedade: estudos **24**(1) (2014)

26. Hermann, M., Pentek, T., Otto, B.: Design principles for industrie 4.0 scenarios. In: 2016 49th Hawaii International Conference on System Sciences (HICSS), pp. 3928–3937. IEEE (2016). https://doi.org/10.1109/HICSS.2016.488

27. Ibarra, D., Ganzarain, J., Igartua, J.I.: Business model innovation through Industry 4.0: a review. Procedia Manufa. **22**, 4–10. (2018). https://doi.org/10.1016/j.promfg.2018.03.002

28. Stock, T., Seliger, G.: Opportunities of sustainable manufacturing in industry 4.0. Procedia CIRP **40**, 536–541 (2016). https://doi.org/10.1016/j.procir.2016.01.129

29. Kagermann, H., Wahlster, W., Helbig, J.: Securing the future of German manufacturing industry: recommendations for implementing the strategic initiative INDUSTRIE 4.0. Final report of the Industrie, **4**(0) (2013)

30. Sumer, B.: Impact of Industry 4.0 on occupations and employment in Turkey. Eur. Sci. J. **14**(10), 1–17 (2018). https://doi.org/10.19044/esj.2018.v14n10p1

31. Lu, Y.: Industry 4.0: a survey on technologies, applications and open research issues. J. Indust. Inform. Integrat. **6**, 1–10 (2017). https://doi.org/10.1016/j.jii.2017.04.005

32. Sung, T.K.: Industry 4.0: a Korea perspective. Technol. Forecast. Soc. Change **132**, 40–45 (2018). https://doi.org/10.1016/j.techfore.2017.11.005

33. Sakurada, L., Geraldes, C.A., Fernandes, F.P., Pontes, J., Leitão, P.: Analysis of new job profiles for the factory of the future. In: Borangiu, T., Trentesaux, D., Leitão, P., Cardin, O., Lamouri, S. (eds.) SOHOMA 2020. SCI, vol. 952, pp. 262–273. Springer, Cham (2021). https://doi.org/10.1007/978-3-030-69373-2_18

34. Fujii, T., Guo, T., Kamoshida, A.: A consideration of service strategy of japanese electric manufacturers to realize super smart society (SOCIETY 5.0). In: Uden, L., Hadzima, B., Ting, I.-H. (eds.) KMO 2018. CCIS, vol. 877, pp. 634–645. Springer, Cham (2018). https://doi.org/10.1007/978-3-319-95204-8_53

35. Gladden, M.E.: Who will be the members of Society 5.0? Towards an anthropology of technologically posthumanized future societies. Soc. Sci. **8**(5), 148 (2019). https://doi.org/10.3390/socsci8050148

36. Hayashi, H., Sasajima, H., Takayanagi, Y., Kanamaru, H.: International standardization for smarter society in the field of measurement, control and automation. In: 2017 56th Annual Conference of the Society of Instrument and Control Engineers of Japan (SICE), pp. 263–266. IEEE (2017). https://doi.org/10.23919/SICE.2017.8105723

37. Broo, D.G., Kaynak, O., Sait, S.M.: Rethinking engineering education at the age of industry 5.0. J. Indust. Inform. Integrat. **25**, 100311 (2022). https://doi.org/10.1016/j.jii.2021.100311

38. Froyd, J.E., Wankat, P.C., Smith, K.A.: Five major shifts in 100 years of engineering education. Proceedings of the IEEE, 100(Special Centennial Issue), pp. 1344–1360 (2012). https://doi.org/10.1109/JPROC.2012.2190167

39. García, J.L., & de los Ríos, I.: Model to develop skills in accounting students for a 4.0 industry and 2030 agenda: from an international perspective. Sustainability **13**(17), 9699 (2021). https://doi.org/10.3390/su13179699

40. Mourtzis, D., Vlachou, E., Dimitrakopoulos, G., Zogopoulos, V.: Cyber-physical systems and education 4.0-the teaching factory 4.0 concept. Procedia Manufact. **23**, 129–134 (2018). https://doi.org/10.1016/j.promfg.2018.04.005

41. Peres, R.S., Rocha, A.D., Leitao, P., Barata, J.: IDARTS-towards intelligent data analysis and real-time supervision for industry 4.0. Comput. Indust. **101**, 138–146 (2018). https://doi.org/10.1016/j.compind.2018.07.004

42. Mourtzis, D., Vasilakopoulos, A., Zervas, E., Boli, N.: Manufacturing system design using simulation in metal industry towards education 4.0. Procedia Manufact. **31**, 155–161 (2019). https://doi.org/10.1016/j.promfg.2019.03.024

43. Lengel, J.G.: Education 3.0: Seven Steps to Better Schools. Teachers College Press (2013)

44. Fava, R.: Educação 3.0: como ensinar estudantes com culturas tão diferentes. São Paulo: Editora Tanta Tinta (2012)

45. Sackey, S.M., Bester, A.: Industrial engineering curriculum in Industry 4.0 in a South African context. South African J. Indust. Eng. **27**(4), 101–114 (2016). https://doi.org/10.7166/27-4-1579

46. Lantada, A.D.: Engineering education 5.0: continuously evolving engineering education. Int. J. Eng. Educ. **36**(6), 1814–1832 (2020)

47. Togo, M., Gandidzanwa, C.P.: The role of Education 5.0 in accelerating the implementation of SDGs and challenges encountered at the University of Zimbabwe. Int. J. Sustain. High. Educ. (2021). https://doi.org/10.1108/IJSHE-05-2020-0158

48. Tan, S.Y., Al-Jumeily, D., Mustafina, J., Hussain, A., Broderick, A., Forsyth, H.: Rethinking our education to face the new industry era. In: Proceedings of EDULEARN 18 Conference 2nd-4th July 2018, pp. 65–66. (2018)

49. Maheso, N., Mpofu, K., Ramatsetse, B.: A Learning Factory concept for skills enhancement in rail car manufacturing industries. Procedia Manufact. **31**, 187–193 (2019). https://doi.org/10.1016/j.promfg.2019.03.030

50. Wang, L.: A futuristic perspective on human-centric assembly. J. Manufact. Syst. **62**, 199–201 (2022). https://doi.org/10.1016/j.jmsy.2021.11.001

51. Maddikunta, P.K.R., et al.: Industry 5.0: a survey on enabling technologies and potential applications. J. Indust. Inform. Integrat. **26**, 100257 (2022). https://doi.org/10.1016/j.jii.2021.100257

52. Maisiri, W., Darwish, H., Van Dyk, L.: An investigation of industry 4.0 skills requirements. South African J. Indust. Eng. **30**(3), 90–105. (2019)

Communication in Educational Robots: From Coordination to IoT Systems

José Cascalho[1,2(✉)] [iD], Armando Mendes[1,2] [iD], Francisco Pedro[2,3] [iD],
Alberto Ramos[2,4], Paulo Medeiros[1,2] [iD], and Matthias Funk[1,2] [iD]

[1] FCT - Universidade dos Açores, Ponta Delgada, Portugal
[2] GRIA - LIACC, Ponta Delgada, Portugal
jose.mv.cascalho@uac.pt
[3] Escola Básica Integrada de Rabo de Peixe, Ponta Delgada, Portugal
[4] APRODAZ, Ponta Delgada, Portugal
http://gria.uac.pt

Abstract. Educational robotics is nowadays used in various learning
environments, adopting different learning goals depending on the application context (*e.g.* collaborative *vs.* competitive activities). The digital
transformation and Industry 4.0 with the use of an increasing number of
sensors, and the use of smart devices, have been demanding environments
where robots communicate and collaborate. This paper discusses the use
of multi-robotic educational environments, trying to identify some scenarios where more than one robot is used in collaborative environments
and what impact it has in the learning activities. In a teacher training
course ranging from primary to secondary and to vocational teachers, a
low-cost robot with Wi-Fi capabilities was used to test simple challenges
for coordination using an MQTT protocol. A simple questionnaire was
developed to record teachers' opinions about this experience. In the end,
we argue that activities of this type, using a mixture of IoT and robotics
can foster students imagination and opens up the possibility of creating
tasks in important areas of knowledge linked to IoT and robotics.

Keywords: Educational robotics · IoT · MQTT protocol

1 Introduction

The literature on educational robotics for K-12 usually considers the environment
where only a single user-robot is used. The robot is programmed and tested in a
specific laboratory environment or competition tracks. Communication between
robots is not usually considered a tool to coordinate robots' behaviours, although
it is a long practice in the industry and also in some competition environments
such as in open robotics competitive settings [16].

Recent advances in robotics technology have made it feasible to assign complex tasks to a large number of low-cost robots [22]. The robots as an ensemble
are generally considered a multi-robot system (MRS), which can be used in

A. I. Pereira et al. (Eds.): OL2A 2022, CCIS 1754, pp. 654–666, 2022.
https://doi.org/10.1007/978-3-031-23236-7_45

many applications where a single robot is not efficient or feasible. Concerning real applications, MRS are used for various applications domains such as military, agriculture, smart home, disaster relief, etc. Some authors refer to these systems as Intelligent Cyber-Physical Systems (CPSs) [7,13]. For these authors, one of the components of a CPSs is the robots as autonomous entities that perceive the external environment, make intelligent decisions and trigger physical actions.

On the other hand, an MRS environment is usually associated with cloud robotics (CR). In this kind of system, robots communicate with a server, collecting and sending data to the cloud (or to an *edge*) belonging to the robotic cloud system. In MRS, robots are not isolated artefacts. The concept of robotics eco-systems extends the idea of MRS. Robots not only interact with the environment and humans but also with other robots and devices, opening the door to the integration of robots in an Internet of Things (IoT) environment (see [20] for a description of a cloud robotics eco-system and its complexity associated).

In this paper, we present the first steps toward a MRS environment in the context of educational robotics and where discuss the possible connection to CPSs and the Internet of the Thing (IoT). So, in the following section, we discuss the concept of multi-robotic systems and how it applies to educational scenarios. Then we briefly introduce how communication can be used to promote coordination between robots in Educational Robotics. Then, we present the context of the experience where low-cost robots were used in a teacher training activity where participants built a robot and used Message Queuing Telemetry Transport (MQTT) protocol in a publish-subscriber communication interaction. Finally, we present the results of a survey of teachers' views about using coordination among robots and sensors as a possible subject to be considered in a robotic activity in a classroom, discussing the implications of considering the IoT in robotics activities.

2   Contextualizing the Multirobotics Systems

Some authors when referring to MRS, identify the main concerns with its implementation which are communication between devices, centralisation of control and scalability [11]. The Internet of Things (IoT) architecture generally helps to address these issues by providing scalable and efficient communication systems, *etc.*.

The convergence between IoT and robotics systems has been identified in [19], associated with the paradigms of network robot systems, robot ecologies or cloud robotics. The authors consider the IoT as a distributed robotics system enabler. They point out nine different areas where the interconnection to IoT can improve robotics abilities, from basic abilities (*e.g.* perception and motion) to higher decision abilities (*e.g.* interaction and autonomy).

In the Fig. 1 the frontier between IoT and Robotics is coined *Internet of robotic things*. Sensor data from a variety of sources are fused, processed using

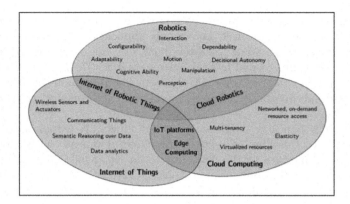

Fig. 1. MRS and its relation to IoT and Cloud Robotics. [19].

local and distributed intelligence and used to control and manipulate objects in the physical world, joining both concepts of robotics and IoT. Several authors argue that the interaction between these two research areas can improve robotic abilities and already have a real impact in robotics [17,19]. On the other hand, cloud robotics uses cloud computing to retrieve and extend the capacity for processing data. But also, in the MRS context, it supports the interaction of different robots.

Naturally, using multi-robotic systems implies additional efforts that are not easy for the youngest. However, we argue that in controlled environments, it is possible to set up interesting experiments that open up the possibility of addressing the concept of IoT and discussing subjects like how to coordinate different robots, what is cooperation in a MSR, or how vital communication security is in robotic systems.

3   Communication and Coordination in Educational Robotics

Communication and coordination are already part of the robotic systems. With the increasing use of intelligent sensors, it is natural to use concepts such as connectivity and collaborative sensing in school projects. In [21] a muti-robotic laboratory in an environment with Wi-Fi connection, software for developing IoT applications are used to support experiments for students in secondary school with communication between drones and robot to support collaborative sensing. A MRS is implemented where agents cooperate to achieve a goal in a program inspired by the Beaver Works Summer Institute (BWSI) ideas of the Massachusetts Institute of Technology and driven by the purpose of providing high school students with access to the learning of Industry 4.0 concepts and technologies. In [15], a multi-robotics platform is used to implement coordination in a platooning algorithm with open software and low-cost components. The platform is a train-like setup, where robots move along a rail, each measuring their speed and distance to their immediate predecessor and capable of communicating relevant data to each other, enabling cooperative control schemes. Other authors argue that the multi-robotics platforms can be used to promote the study of cyber-physical systems (CPS). For example, in [12] an experiment with three omnidirectional robots uses the Message Queuing Telemetry Transport (MQTT) protocol to communicate between them. These robots aim to move to a specific vertex of a polygon, and it is through communication and some planning that they achieve this goal. The same authors argue that using a CPS platform contributes to learning the mechanics, electronics and communication fields.

In the context of open robotics, some competition environments demands communication between robots and coordination.

We can find a paradigmatic use of coordination in soccer robotics in context of the Robocup initiative [6]. As in real soccer games, robots have to coordinate their plays, change tactics, and adapt to the opponent. In particular, these capabilities should be achieved in Robocup by robots that act autonomously by [8]:

- Collecting sensor observations;
- Maintaining a representation of the state of the game;
- Reasoning and planning their actions individually and collectively.

Concerning challenges in Open Robotics which use multi-robotics and promote IoT and CPS, environments are still limited. We analysed the recent challenges from the Portuguese Robotics Open competition. Tables 1 and 2 enumerates the use of communication in the different challenges, where the symbol '$\sqrt{}$' means that the competition demands the use of the robotic features identified in the first column of the table. The mark '?' means that, in the competition, it can be used or it is used in a particular stage of the competition. Finally, the symbol '–' means that the robotic feature is useless for fulfilling challenge goals.

Columns in Table 1 depict the different junior challenges: *Robot@Factory Lite* (Fl), *onStage* (St), *Junior Soccer* (Js), *Freebots* (Fb), *First Challenger* (Fc) and *Rescue* (Rc) challenges. Only *Js* implies coordination to fulfil the goals. In *St*, where robots must coordinate with humans, this coordination can be achieved through interaction with humans and not autonomously. In *Fl*, teams have the option to have more than one robot executing the challenge at the same time. So it can be assumed that there could be coordination and, eventually, cooperation. *Fb* is a challenge where teams are free to build their robot without a pre-defined use, so it is impossible to anticipate its features.

Table 2 shows features for senior competitions. They are the *Dragster* (Dg), *Industrial Robotics Manipulators* (Rm), *Robot@Factory 4.0* (F4), *Robot@Factory Lite* (Fl), *Freebots* (Fb) and *Autonomous Drive* (Ad). We found the possible use of coordination and cooperation only for *Fl*, *Fb*, *F4* and *Rm*. For the first two, *Fl* and *Fb*, by the same reasons explained for junior competition, with *F4* being a more complex version of *Fl*. For the latter, because, according to the rules,

Table 1. Identifying coordination and cooperation in 2022 Portuguese Robotics Open junior challenges.

Robotic Features	Fl	St	Js	Fb	Fc	Rc
Communication to fulfil goals (Wi-Fi, Bluetooth, etc.)	?	√	√	?	–	–
Coordination to fulfil goals	?	?	√	?	–	–
Cooperation to fulfil goals	?	?	?	?	–	–
Using IoT or CPS environments	–	–	–	?	–	–

Table 2. Identifying coordination and cooperation in 2022 Portuguese Robotics Open senior challenges.

Robotic features	Dg	Rm	F4	Fl	Fb	Ad
Communication to fulfil goals (Wi-Fi or Bluetooth)	–	?	?	?	?	–
Coordination to fulfil goals	–	?	?	?	?	–
Cooperation to fulfil goals	–	?	?	?	?	–
Using IoT or CPS environments	–	–	–	–	?	–

there is one specific part of the challenge using the cooperation between robots and humans.

For both junior and senior competitions, explicitly coordination and cooperation are just present in particular scenarios. For some challenges, coordination and cooperation are intrinsic goals. However, none considers the use of IoT explicitly or the concept of CPS. This could change if learning goal targets shift to concepts related to Industry 4.0 and digitalization [18, 21].Other Portuguese competition activities follow the same paradigm towards robotics like Botolympics and Roboparty (*e.g.* https://botolympics.pt/ and https://www.roboparty.org).

4   Experiments in Simple Robot Coordination

The coordination experiments were done in a teacher training event for 8 participants. A robot was assembled and then tested using the train track from First Challenge's Portuguese Robotics Open competition. It had the following goals:

- To acquire basic knowledge about robotics and, in particular, how educational robotics can be used in school classes.
- To learn how to program an *Arduino* type micro-controller and understand its basic functionality (*e.g.* power, digital, pulse wide modulation and analog ports).
- To learn about some basic challenges in educational robotics and how to coordinate the behaviour of robots using the publish-subscribe communication protocol.

In the following subsections, we present the robot used and the communication protocol and then describe experiments in detail.

4.1   A Low-Cost Robot for Educational Proposes

The robots used in experiments are differential driving robots with two low-cost micro DC motors driven by a dual H-Bridge l298N motor driver IC, with an ultrasonic sensor, an infrared sensor and colour sensor. It was opted to use a micro-controller *ESP32 DevKit* instead of Arduino because it has embedded the Wi-Fi board [10].

The Table 3 lists the hardware components of the robot used in the experiment. It is equipped with two *DFRobot 6V micro DC motors* controlled by a *L298* driver. Each motor has a *1:48 gearbox*. Finally, it operates in a voltage range from 2.7 V to 10.8 V and has built-in protection against reverse voltage, under-voltage, over-current and over-temperature.

Table 3. Components of the low cost robot

Component	Azoresbot
Microcontroller	ESP32 DevKit
Motor Driver	L298N
Ultrasonic Sensor	HC-SR04
Infrared line sensor	3xTCRT5000
colour Sensor	TCS3200
Motor	2x Micro DC Motor 6V
Power	2x Li-Ion MR18650 Battery

The colour sensor was not used since the only goals of the robots were following a line and avoiding obstacles. A 3D printer produced the robot structure elements. The software and 3D-printing source files can be found in [1] and [2].

4.2   Publish/Subscribe Communication Protocol

Message Queuing Telemetry Transport (MQTT) technology is a light communication protocol that implements a publish/subscribe (P/S) model [5].

A MQTT client publishes messages of a certain set of address/topic in an MQTT broker. Then, other clients that have subscribed to those topics will receive the messages. The MQTT broker can support thousands of clients and provides several layers of security to offer the privacy of all data, and so it is ideal to be used in the context of IoT paradigm [14].

In the implementation, the MQTT broker chosen was the Mosquitto, a lightweight open source broker suitable for use on all devices from low-power single board computers to full servers [3]. To test the communication, we implemented the MQTT-Explorer [4], a simple MQTT client with a friendly interaction. The *PubSubClient library* available for the Arduino Framework is also applied in the ESP32 controller. This software allowed us to test the P/S model by defining

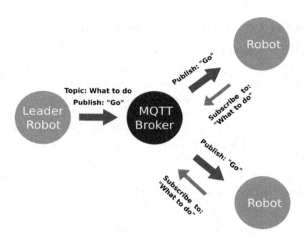

Fig. 2. The MQTT broker schemata with the example of topics and messages exchanged between robots.

types of message (*e.g.* topics) and understand how the protocol allows the communication between a publishing and a subscribing agent.

Figure 2 shows the schema for the communication between a leader who publishes the topic *What to do* and clients that subscribe to the topic to receive the leader's message. This type of interaction tested the coordination of behaviours between the robots.

```
66   // Setup MQTT Client
67   void setupMQTT()
68   {
69     mqttClient.setServer(mqttServer, mqttPort);
70     // set the callback function
71     mqttClient.setCallback(callback);
72   }
73
74
75   void setup() {
76     MotorControl.attachMotors(17,18,26,27);
77     Serial.begin(115200);
78
79     Serial.println();
80
81     connectToWiFi();
82     setupMQTT();
83   }
```

Fig. 3. The *setup()* code for a client robot using the Arduino code structure.

The code used in the robots is very simple and follows the C++'s Arduino code structure or *Arduino Sketch* [9], with the *setup()* and *loop()* functions and a callback function that is triggered every time the robot receives a message from the broker. Each robot has a simple alternative command to execute the actions sent by the leader (see Fig. 3) with the callback function changing the "state" of the robot (Figs. 4 and 5).

```
45   // Receive message from topic (subscribe)
46   void callback(char *topic, byte *message, unsigned int length)
47   {
48     String messageTemp =""; //
49     for (int i = 0; i < length; i++) //
50     {
51       messageTemp += (char)message[i];
52     }
53     if (String(topic)== "What to do"){
54       if(messageTemp == "stop"){
55         state = 1;
56       }
57       if(messageTemp == "right"){
58         state = 2;
59       }
60       if(messageTemp == "left"){
61         state = 3;
62       }
63     }
64   }
65
```

Fig. 4. The callback function triggered every time a message is sent from broker.

```
104   void loop() {
105     if (!mqttClient.connected())
106       reconnect();
107     mqttClient.loop();
108     if(state == 1){
109       MotorControl.motorStop(0);
110       MotorControl.motorStop(1);
111     }
112     if(state == 2){
113       MotorControl.motorForward(1,50);
114       MotorControl.motorReverse(0,50);
115     }
116     if(state == 3){
117       MotorControl.motorForward(0,50);
118       MotorControl.motorReverse(1,50);
119     }
120   }
```

Fig. 5. The actions of the robot depending on the messages received.

4.3   Description of the Experiments

During the course, two experiments were tested, using Wi-Fi communication with MQTT protocol. The first one tested the synchronization between three robots using a simple start and stop command. All the robots start to turn around if the leader asks them to start or stop otherwise. Figure 6 shows three robots, two subscribing to the leader's message. The interaction showed that it is possible to coordinate between the robots with starting and stopping behaviour well coordinated.

Fig. 6. Turning around robots commanded by a leader.

The second experiment aimed to control a convoy of robots in the First Challenger track with a leader at the front sending messages to stop when an obstacle arises. Figure 7 shows the three robots in a convoy that stops after an obstacle arises.

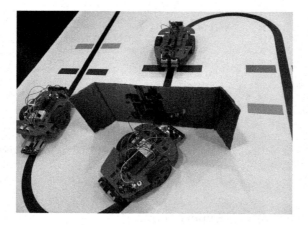

Fig. 7. Convoy stopped by an obstacle.

These two experiments showed that it is easy to implement simple contexts of interaction between robots using communication among several machines (*i.e.* the publish/subscribe protocol).

In a final questionnaire related to the concept of IoT and robotics and how to use them in classes, six responses were obtained. The survey had three open, and one closed question about the level of education respondents teach.

In this last question, we had a good variability of answers with respondents at every teaching level, as seen in Fig. 8. This is relevant to the variability of viewpoints over the theme of communication in robotics. Naturally, such a small sample can not be representative of a region or even a school, but having answers for all levels gives us a broader picture.

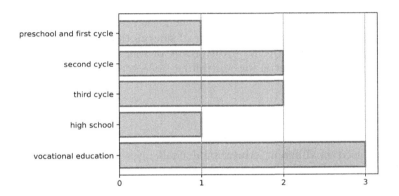

Fig. 8. Number of respondents by educational level.

The first open question on the relevance of the existence of communications during robot operation for educational activities was unanimous. All respondents strongly agree with the need for IoT-like technologies in educative robotics. Furthermore, they all mention the possibilities that communication with the robots opens for teaching by controlling a robot or a group of robots in real time. One of the answers adds the notion of improved interactivity between the human and the machine and considers it relevant that the kids also understand how IoT works.

The second open question builds on the IoT concept. It states that the IoT allows communication with equipment that contains sensors and the use of this information to make decisions in real time and asks about the relevance of exploring these concepts in a school activity. The answers range from "I need to think better about how this technology can be used" to suggesting interactive scenarios where the connection between IoT and robotics can be especially relevant. Some examples explained include monitoring climate parameters for problem resolution and decision-making. Other examples include measuring temperature or humidity for monitoring a chemical reaction. Intelligent systems that respond to changing environments were also suggested, like an intelligent camera for insect observation that is motion activated.

The last question in the questionnaire asked about using IoT technologies in the classroom. Again, the variability of answers is wide. Several answers mention that they could use several automatic responses to sensor values and the programming side of the problem is also of interest in a classroom. Others consider that the response to sensor values can be translated into robots' actions. One of the answers alert for the increased complexity for very small kids, but with imagination is always possible to design scenarios engaging even for small children in two main dimensions: collaborative work and acting on the information feedback. One of the answers was very concrete in designing a situation where a group of students controlled a robot for a specific path designed by a different group. Other respondents see more activities linked to remote labs, like controlling experiences from home, noting that thematic areas like physics, chemistry, and biology already have a large number of sensors that can be used in all sorts of remote experiences with the involvement of real time controlled robots. It also notes the great potential for controlling biological cultures and mechanized agriculture.

5 Discussion

MRSs are used in different educational challenges. The best known are the robotic soccer challenges. In these scenarios, the communication between robots is used to coordinate their position and behaviour. Notwithstanding, with the digitalisation process and the increasing number of sensors deployed, it is natural to expect robots to interact with smart devices in different places, creating an Internet of Robotic Things [19]. Moreover, cooperation to achieve goals in robotics is a challenge that could be more explored in educational contexts. In these contexts, it is natural to consider the IoT systems as these systems provide distributed information related to other robots and objects or features in a specific environment.

The two experiments using P/S protocol tested the communication in two simple scenarios usually used in open robotics competitions. We argue that it is possible to extend these experiments where the following features could be added:

- Create challenges where cooperative behaviours are necessary to achieve goals (*e.g.* carrying objects in different contexts using a different type of robots [21]).
- Propose challenges where the number of robots used to solve those challenges could be a team's option, balancing issues related to communication, coordination complexity and the amount of time to fulfil the goal.
- Propose scenarios where a smart set of fixed sensors could send/receive data to/from robots in an MRS environment that could constrain the robots' behaviours to achieve their own goals.

6   Conclusions

Educational robotics is nowadays used in various learning environments, adopting different learning goals depending on the application context (*e.g.* collaborative *vs.* competitive activities). The digital transformation and Industry 4.0 with the increasing use of sensors and smart devices have been demanding environments where robots communicate and collaborate. In this paper, we present simple experiments where a P/S MQTT protocol was used to test robot behaviour coordination in a teacher training course context.

We demonstrate in simple experiments that extending MRS scenarios with the interaction between robots and other sensors can create new challenges in educational robotics. For example, they might foster the understanding of the importance of communication and allow to explore other dimensions of robotics, such as using cooperation to achieve a goal. These new scenarios extend the usual and more straightforward scenarios where robots act individually. So, this paper is an initial contribution to what we expect to have a future impact concerning the use of technologies crossing with other areas of learning in schools.

Acknowledgements. This work has been supported by DRCT - Direção Regional de Ciência e Tecnologia, Governo dos Açores, under the project M3.4.B/PRO.ROBÓTICA/001/2021.

References

1. https://github.com/Robotics-and-AI-Group-of-UAc/AzoresBotV2
2. https://github.com/Robotics-and-AI-Group-of-UAc/Ants
3. Eclipse Mosquitto an all-round MQTT client that provides a structured topic overview. https://mosquitto.org/. Accessed 22 Feb 2012
4. MQTT - Explorer an open source MQTT broker. http://mqtt-explorer.com/. Accessed 22 Feb 2012
5. MQTT the standard for IoT messaging. https://mqtt.org/. Accessed 22 Feb 2012
6. Robocup. https://www.robocup.org/. Accessed 22 Feb 2012
7. Afrin, M., Jin, J., Rahman, A., Rahman, A., Wan, J., Hossain, E.: Resource allocation and service provisioning in multi-agent cloud robotics: a comprehensive survey. IEEE Commun. Surv. Tutorials **23**(2), 842–870 (2021). https://doi.org/10.1109/COMST.2021.3061435
8. Antonioni, E., Suriani, V., Riccio, F., Nardi, D.: Game strategies for physical robot soccer players: a survey. IEEE Trans. Games **13**(4), 342–357 (2021). https://doi.org/10.1109/TG.2021.3075065
9. Arduino: Arduino doc pages. https://docs.arduino.cc/learn/. Accessed 22 Feb 2012
10. Cascalho, J., Pedro, F., Mendes, A., Funk, M., Ramos, A., Novo, P.: Azoresbot v2: a new robot for learning robotics and science at schools. In: 2021 IEEE International Conference on Autonomous Robot Systems and Competitions (ICARSC), pp. 62–67 (2021). https://doi.org/10.1109/ICARSC52212.2021.9429815
11. Efraín, G.B.D., del Carmen, V.C.A., Fernando, E.C.L., Cesar, L.M.D.: Implementation of an IoT architecture based on MQTT for a multi-robot system. In: 2018 IEEE Third Ecuador Technical Chapters Meeting (ETCM), pp. 1–6 (2018). https://doi.org/10.1109/ETCM.2018.8580321

12. Escobar, L., Moyano, C., Aguirre, G., Guerra, G., Allauca, L., Loza, D.: Multi-robot platform with features of cyber-physical systems for education applications. In: 2020 IEEE ANDESCON, pp. 1–6 (2020). https://doi.org/10.1109/ANDESCON50619.2020.9272030

13. Klötzer, C., Weißenborn, J., Pflaum, A.: The evolution of cyber-physical systems as a driving force behind digital transformation. In: 2017 IEEE 19th Conference on Business Informatics (CBI), vol. 02, pp. 5–14 (2017). https://doi.org/10.1109/CBI.2017.8

14. Mukhandi, M., Portugal, D., Pereira, S., Couceiro, M.S.: A novel solution for securing robot communications based on the MQTT protocol and ROS. In: 2019 IEEE/SICE International Symposium on System Integration (SII), pp. 608–613 (2019). https://doi.org/10.1109/SII.2019.8700390

15. Peters, A., Vargas, F., Garrido, C., Andrade, C., Villenas, F.: Pl-toon: a low-cost experimental platform for teaching and research on decentralized cooperative control. Sensors **21**, 2072 (2021). https://doi.org/10.3390/s21062072

16. Ribeiro, A., Lopes, G.: Learning robotics: a review. Current Robot. Rep. **1**, 1–11 (2020)

17. Romeo, L., Petitti, A., Marani, R., Milella, A.: Internet of robotic things in smart domains: applications and challenges. Sensors **20**(12) (2020). https://doi.org/10.3390/s20123355

18. Salkin, C., Oner, M., Ustundag, A., Cevikcan, E.: A Conceptual Framework for Industry 4.0, pp. 3–23. Springer, Cham (2018). https://doi.org/10.1007/978-3-319-57870-5_1

19. Simoens, P., Dragone, M., Saffiotti, A.: The internet of robotic things: a review of concept, added value and applications. Int. J. Adv. Robot. Syst. **15**(1), 1729881418759424 (2018). https://doi.org/10.1177/1729881418759424

20. Siriweera, A., Naruse, K.: Survey on cloud robotics architecture and model-driven reference architecture for decentralized multicloud heterogeneous-robotics platform. IEEE Access **9**, 40521–40539 (2021). https://doi.org/10.1109/ACCESS.2021.3064192

21. Verner, I.M., Cuperman, D., Reitman, M.: Exploring robot connectivity and collaborative sensing in a high-school enrichment program. Robotics **10**(1) (2021). https://doi.org/10.3390/robotics10010013, https://www.mdpi.com/2218-6581/10/1/13

22. Sahni, Y., Cao, J., Jiang, S.: Middleware for multi-robot systems. In: Ammari, H.M. (ed.) Mission-Oriented Sensor Networks and Systems: Art and Science. SSDC, vol. 164, pp. 633–673. Springer, Cham (2019). https://doi.org/10.1007/978-3-319-92384-0_18

Educational Testbed in the Context of Industry 4.0 and 5.0: Literature Review

Mateus Henrique Ferreira Iensen⬤, Leonardo Breno Pessoa da Silva⬤, and Joseane Pontes(✉)⬤

Federal University of Technology - Parana (UTFPR), Ponta Grossa PR, Brazil
{mateusiensen,leonardos.1995}@alunos.utfpr.edu.br, joseane@utfpr.edu.br

Abstract. The transformations caused by the Industrial Revolutions, over time have transformed the job profiles, causing changes in the way to qualification and the workforce. With the advent of Industry 4.0 and the next evolutionary stage known as Industry 5.0, institutions promoting qualification need to incorporate new educational models to qualification and re-qualification people. Educational testbeds are known as a virtual environment, where it is possible to integrate digital tools for the development of teaching, but it is necessary to understand what characteristics encompass an educational testbed to guide future research. Thus, the objective of this paper is to identify the characteristics and thematic areas of research of educational testbeds in the context of industry 4.0 and 5.0. As methodology, a Systematic Literature Review was used, based on the PRISMA method, identifying 47 papers pertinent to the theme. The research results point out 8 main characteristics of an educational testbed, its connection between university and industry and the 5 main subject areas that encompass the concept. The paper seeks to collaborate with engineering education and the formation of skills that meet the needs of the 4.0 and 5.0 job market.

Keywords: Educational testbed · Industry 4.0 · Industry 5.0 · Workforce · Technologies · Skills

1 Introduction

The term Industry 4.0 has become increasingly popular over the past decade. Considered as the new digital revolution [1], Industry 4.0 brings a scenario of development and integration of various technologies, such as Cyber-physical systems, big data [2], virtual reality, augmented reality, internet of things, 3D printing, drones, among other things [4]. The integration of these concepts in production systems constitutes this new production model. The concept of Industry 5.0 brings an accentuation of the human dimension in industry, referring to the collaboration between people and intelligent production systems and, therefore, goes beyond the production of goods and services for profit. [5].

Supported by organization x.

With production systems increasingly incorporating technologies into their routines, it is essential that there are qualified professionals capable of sustaining the new needs of the industry [6]. Training is a key factor in preparing professionals for the job market, and it is necessary to understand which skills, whether soft or hard, are relevant for the Industry 4.0 scenario [3,23].

Universities and their engineering departments play a crucial role in training professionals capable of meeting the needs of industry. Therefore, it is necessary to ensure that the knowledge and skills development of current students and future professionals who will drive the Fourth Industrial Revolution [29]. It is not new to discuss the importance of reformulating the traditional education model. An essential part of preparing for Industry 4.0 is adapting higher education to the requirements of this new reality, in particular engineering education [7]. Some active learning strategies have been incorporated into teaching methodologies in order to improve students' competitiveness in different professional fields [31].

From this, the concepts of education 4.0 and 5.0 begin to emerge. The 4.0 education model considers the exploitation of technologies to drive learning processes and prepare new education methods for future involvement in factories [8]. Education 5.0, on the other hand, uses technologies to develop a more human education focusing on the students' soft skills [9]. Industry 4.0 and 5.0 form the digital era industry, just as the characteristics of education 4.0 and 5.0 form the concept of digital era education. These models bring into their teaching approach concepts such as learning factories, living labs, serious games, self factories, among other things, that have long been targets of research. With this, a new concept is gaining space in this context, the educational testbeds. Testbeds are considered to be environments for testing and developing solutions for real industry challenges [20]. Through university-industry partnerships, these environments demonstrate a great educational potential in the training of the 4.0 and 5.0 workforce [22], bridging industry and educational testbed.

Educational testbeds have been cited in academia and in the market. Research by ABDI (2017) points to savings of up to 73 billion reais per year from the adoption and concepts of Industry 4.0 in the Brazilian production matrix. The impact of investments in 5G solutions alone can reduce costs and increase business productivity, reaching 590 billion reais per year [33].This highlights the importance of studies and investments in this area. In Brazil, investments have been made from Edital 01/2018 - ABDI/Ministério da economia "Fábricas do Futuro" (Factories of the Future), 3 million reais distributed among 10 projects prepared by companies and educational institutions to carry out testbeds aligned with the themes of the Brazilian government strategy for Industry 4.0.

Having this in mind, this paper aims to identify the characteristics and thematic areas of research of educational testbeds in the context of industry 4.0 and 5.0 from a systematic literature review. It is expected from the survey of these characteristics to understand the concept of educational testbed, since it is not yet evident in the literature. From this, it is expected to disseminate this concept aiming to contribute to engineering education and the formation of skills for the 4.0 and 5.0 job market.

This paper is organized in the following format. Section 2 presents the methodology used, reporting the steps for searching and analyzing the article portfolio by means of a Systematic Literature Review and Content Analysis. Section 3 presents the results achieved, subdivided into sections presenting the main concepts of Industry 4.0 and 5.0 and Education 4.0 and 5.0. The next subsection of results reports on Educational Testbeds. Finally, Sect. 4 presents the final considerations about this study.

2   Methodology

To conduct this study, it was necessary to identify literature pertinent to the research topic, papers that help characterize the Educational Testbed focused on the context of Industry 4.0 and 5.0. As a research method, we used the protocol described by the PRISMA (Preferred Reporting Items for Systematic Reviews and Meta-Analyses) methodology, updated by the [17]. Systematic Reviews play a critical role by presenting a synthesis of the state of knowledge on a given theme, and can support or evaluate theories on how a phenomenon occurs [17].

Initially, the search protocol used was aligned, seeking to select keywords that represent the research theme. As research groups were defined the group that represents Industry 4.0 and 5.0, the group defined by Learning, and the group defined by Educational Testbed. The Table 1 shows the described protocol.

Table 1. Research protocol

Direction	Protocol
Search term (Title, Abstract or Keywords)	**Group 1 (Industry 4.0 and 5.0)**: ("industry 4.0" OR "industrie 4.0" OR "Fourth Industrial Revolution" OR "4th Industrial Revolution" OR "industry 5.0" OR "industrie 5.0" OR "Fifth Industrial Revolution" OR "5th Industrial Revolution" OR "Smart Industry" OR "Smart Manufacturing" OR "Smart Factory") **Group 2 (Learning and Teaching Methods)**: ("teaching" OR "teaching platform" OR "teaching method" OR "learning" OR "learning platform" OR "learning method" OR "education" OR "educational platform" OR "education method") **Group 3 (Educational Testbed)**: ("testbed" OR "test-bed" OR "test bed")
Search strategy	AND among groups
Database	Scopus (3159 documents), Web of Science (3067 documents) and Outhers sources (2 documents)
Publication type	Research Paper, Review Paper and Conference Paper
Language	English
Search period	2011–2022

For this work we used the Web of Science and Scopus databases, selected due to their relevance in publications related to the Industry 4.0 and 5.0 theme [18]. Furthermore, due to the amount of keywords collected, the Booleans were used. The Boolean "OR" represents the synonyms in the same groups and the Boolean "AND" the connector between the groups, thus increasing the probability of searching for documents relevant to the topic.

With the protocol described, the PRISMA steps were applied. Identification talks about the application of the protocol in the databases. To help in this phase, the software Mendeley Desktop was used, as a tool for organizing and managing references. With the files downloaded from the database, it was possible to identify duplicates and organize the filtering process.

The next step consists of screening, which is the step that consists of applying filters. First, articles were excluded by reading the titles, abstracts, and finally reading the complete article. The readings consisted in searching for studies that helped to define the educational testbed concept, its benefits, technologies and teaching methodologies used in manpower training programs for Industry 4.0 and 5.0.

Finally, the Included step, consists of describing the portfolio of papers identified from the databases along with the articles identified from other sources. By applying these steps, the Fig. 1 presents the information flow of the method, showing the inclusion and exclusion amounts for each step described.

Thus, after the application of the steps proposed by the PRISMA methodology, the final portfolio is composed of 47 articles, being 29 research articles and 18 congress articles. These articles were considered relevant to the theme of educational testbed for workforce training oriented to Industry 4.0 and 5.0, and were submitted to content analysis.

Content analysis is an approach used to construct knowledge and generate theories from qualitative data [16]. This type of analysis allows you to interpret, conceptualize and synthesize already structured research knowledge, allowing you to identify research gaps.

To assist this analysis, NVIVO© 10 software was used, being one of the most used software for content analysis [19]. Many studies make use of Qualitative Data Analyses Software (QDSA) as a tool to support qualitative research, facilitating and speeding up the process, ensuring greater transparency, rigor and traceability of the studies used [19].

First, the 47 articles were exported in pdf format to the tool and organized in order to facilitate their traceability. Some commands of the software allowed us to know the portfolio of articles we were working on, such as the automatic coding (to automatically identify themes addressed by the articles) and the frequency of words. These tools were used to guide the study and verify the adherence of the articles to the research theme.

The next step is related to the reading of the sources and the manual coding performed by the researcher. For this, it was necessary to know about the theme researched by the authors allowing the construction of nodes and subnodes in relation to the research objective proposed by this article. For example, the

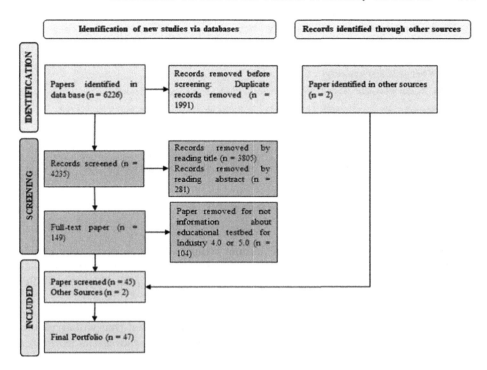

Fig. 1. Results of applying PRISMA to the systematic literature review.

Fig. 2 presents the node of the main technologies involved to the testbeds aimed at education. By reading the article, it is possible to verify text excerpts that present a discussion about the analyzed theme. This excerpt was coded into the existing node, as shown in the Fig. 2.

The coding process is dynamic and interactive, where new nodes are created and/or regrouped according to the needs of the study and to each new discovery from the reading of the articles. Thus, the defined themes were addressed in the results section of this study.

3   Results

3.1   Industry 4.0 and 5.0 and Education 4.0 and 5.0

Industry 4.0 can be defined as a set of enabling technologies of wide application possibility that increase the efficiency of a factory, composed of a set of technologies such as: Internet of Things, Big Data, cloud manufacturing, robotics, artificial intelligence and additive manufacturing [24]. The rise of Industry 4.0 brought several benefits to manufacturing, but it did not consider human resources as a priority, which resulted in unemployment. Thus, the search for skilled professionals is one of the main challenges of Industry 4.0. However, Industry 5.0 is being studied to solve issues like this [32].

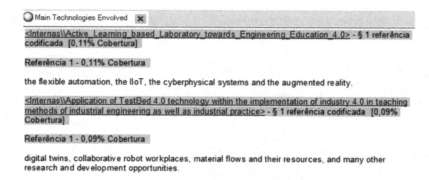

Fig. 2. Main technologies envolved node example

Industry 5.0 is centered on the human being, seeking a good relationship between man and machine, exalting in man the creativity, customization and critical analysis, and in the machine the repetitive work [32]. However, skilled labor remains a challenge in this transition from Industry 4.0 to 5.0.

From this, Education 4.0 comes with the goal of training the new workforce, qualifying or retraining it, creating a sustainable environment that will accelerate the adoption of intelligent manufacturing [8], digitally upgrading the workforce. Education 5.0 integrates the human sphere with technology, stimulating not only the development of solutions that solve industry challenges, but also social and economic issues through the development of appropriate soft skills. [32]. Current curricula are not really preparing students for the new industry reality. Thus, it is necessary to have workforce training programs for Industry 4.0 for both new and old forms of work, developing the required skills [16]. The Fig. 3 presents an overview of the transition from Industry 4.0 to 5.0 and from Education 4.0 to 5.0.

Figure 3 summarizes the concept of industry in the digital era, integrating the concept of industry 4.0 and 5.0 where industry becomes intelligent as a function of emerging technologies (4.0) and people have grater welfare and quality of life, and sustainability also benefits as a function of intelligent process and technologies. Similarly, the integration between education 4.0 and 5.0 provides the concept of education for the digital era. In education 4.0 there is the teaching of smart technologies to students, facilitating their learning and also teaching them to practice them in the labor market. In education 5.0, technologies are used to enhance the students social economic skills. Thus, the way to apply digital era education to the market where the digital era industry demands new skills becomes a challenge, where the educational testbed may become an option to help minimize this challenge, from its disruptive and relevant characteristics, witch will be presented in the next section.

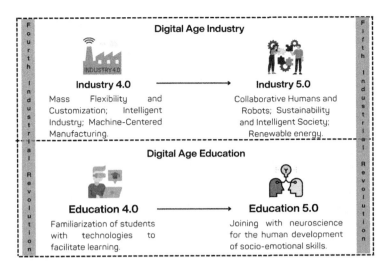

Fig. 3. Industry and education transitions

It is then necessary to teach students to work on complex problems and not only to design and build, but to think long-term and make big decisions, as in the case of transportation projects for large cities already expecting their growth in the next 50 years [21]. Engineers need human skills to consider innovative solutions that serve both industry and society. These skills should include probing, feeling, and analyzing. In addition, key skills required for a 4.0 professional include continuous improvement, teamwork, creativity, problem-solving skills, holistic thinking, and the ability to learn quickly, among others [22].

3.2   Educational Testbeds

A testbed can be understood as an interconnected and adaptable environment in which you can research, develop, test and evaluate solutions to a problem [20]. Testbeds are used in industry as a means of evaluation for proposed solutions, without changes being made directly on the production lines, thus avoiding waste of resources, time, and the environment. This environment can be seen as an experimental work place with technologies that allow to verify the result of innovative ideas in a virtual environment in connection with real production, helping in the design of new facilities and optimization of existing ones [27].

Testbeds bring important benefits when it comes to industry decision making. With testbeds, these decisions can be made without affecting the process already underway. As a result, production is not interrupted to test possibilities for improvement or new applications, and if the test is not effective, time and resources are saved. [27]. In addition, this test environment, which can include real and virtual entities, has the potential to generate a large amount of data that, when transformed into graphical visualizations or interactive dashboards, provide relevant and timely information to decision makers. From this, it is possible to have a holistic view of the processes, working with this data in order to test possibilities of changes that configure the best solutions [20].

From these definitions, it can be seen that a testbed is not intended for educational purposes, nor is the concept new to the industry, but the term is gaining prominence in the academic world, proving to be an ally in the development of skills in the context of Industry 4.0 and 5.0. Testbeds can be of various types, but in this paper we will focus on educational testbeds. Besides the concepts, the literature presents some examples, such as the ones that will be seen below.

Knowing the labor needs of the industry, a new teaching method was developed at the Federal Technological University of Paraná (Brazil) called Educational Testbed 4.0 [22], which aims to make university-industry partnerships in order to bring benefits for both. The project was developed as one of the projects awarded by the Edital 01/2018 - ABDI/Ministério da economia "Fábricas do Futuro" (Factories of the Future). The method has as its principle the exchange of knowledge, where the industry brings real problems for students to solve, allowing the possibility of learning both through practice and through the experiences of industry professionals. [28]. In this way, learning is student-centered, they work in teams and are encouraged to develop both technical and soft skills. The case study conducted by [23] to evaluate the development of soft skills through the Educational Test Bed 4.0 method of [22] came to the conclusion that the main skills developed in the students were creativity, teamwork, and communication.

Also in Brazil, the Technological Park of São José dos Campos developed the Virtual Testbed Platform that integrates technologies such as sensors, 3D printers, and industrial33 machining machines, which enable the formulation of a database that can be accessed by startups, information technology and communication companies, industries from various sectors, universities, and educational institutions. Through the database it is possible to validate products, test scientific theories, do proofs of concept, and other tests with the data. One of the project's objectives is to enable the training and preparation of skilled labor for the Industry 4.0 context.

A testbed was also developed at the CEITEC institute in cooperation with the Faculty of Electrical and Communication Engineering at Brno University of Technology [25]. The testbed is part of a project aimed at combining additive and subtractive technology, demonstrating a flexible manufacturing process, cooperation with other testbeds, and other functions. The testbed includes milling machines, industrial manipulators, robots, and other technologies, and is used to demonstrate Industry 4.0 highlights to students at Brno University and also at the Czech University in Prague, to prepare professionals familiar with new era digital technologies.

In Slovakia the first testbed focused on Industry 4.0 processes was developed, located at the Technical University in Košice. The testbed was created to help small and medium-sized companies make strategic decisions in the area of production process innovation and its real impacts. The location of the testbed is strategic, as being in a university environment allows students to also learn about its possibilities directly in the teaching process, developing skills consistent with the needs of industry [27].

Through the testbeds presented, it is possible to identify certain similar characteristics. First, it is possible to identify that the testbeds strongly involve the industry in their concepts, involving important technologies that help the industry in decision making from proofs of concept. By being a test environment, this platform brings the human being closer to technology, opening doors for research, allowing integration with education systems, such as universities, for example. Once the educational sphere becomes part of the testbed, skills development becomes a possibility, adding value to the industry and to education. The Fig. 4 presents a summary of the main characteristics of an educational testbed identified in the examples presented.

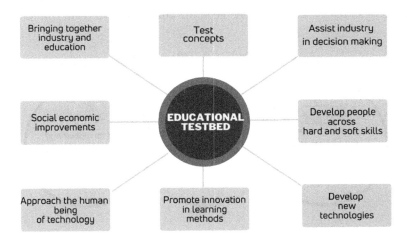

Fig. 4. Educational testbed characteristics

From an educational testbed, the benefits of a testbed become shared between industry and education. It is known that since Industry 4.0, the gap between education and industry has been widening. Manufacturing has been vastly developed while education and workforce preparation has not kept up [32]. An educational testbed is an assertive strategy in this respect, because besides fulfilling its basic role of testing concepts and assisting the industry in decision making, it can also bring human beings closer to the new 4.0 technologies in an adjustable and reliable test environment. With this, the new (and also future) soft and hard skills required by the new industry context can be developed, promoting innovation in learning methods and bringing important social and economic improvements.

Indeed there have been changes in the job market as soon as 4.0 technologies have gained space in the industrial context. If the workforce does not adapt to this new reality, problems such as unemployment and lack of human capital in many areas of industry are inevitable. In this way, universities play a crucial role in training the workforce to meet the needs of industry [29].

It is fundamental that universities incorporate in their educational models creative innovation, practical problem solving, and adding value to society [30]. By investing in a challenging, collaborative and iterative learning environment (such as that of an educational testbed), the student is able to integrate with real and relevant information that genuinely prepares them for the challenges of the Industry 4.0 reality [31].

Thus, educational testbeds can be understood as the link that unites the needs of the industry, especially for manpower 4.0, and the need of educational institutions, especially higher education, to foster this skilled workforce for this new reality, responding the main objective of industry 5.0. That's why the dissemination of this term in research like this that encourages more collaboration between university and industry are so relevant. The Fig. 5 illustrates a testbed in the educational context as a learning and workforce training environment for the needs of Industry 4.0 due to the need for universities to train this workforce.

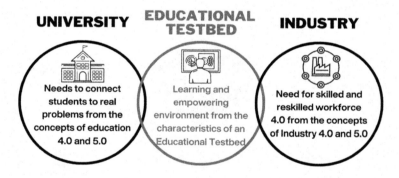

Fig. 5. Industry university link

To conclude the analysis, the Table 2 brings a summary of the main thematic areas related to educational testbeds, the key words linked to the themes and also the main related authors.

The first area listed is "workforce 4.0", because the testbeds are an answer to the need for qualified and re-qualified labor for the industry needs. The main keywords related to workforce within a testbed environment were "Workplace on University", "Training Programs", "Opportunity", "Interactive Space" and "Hands-on experience". The second area is the main technologies linked to the testbeds, which are: "Iot", "Digital Twins", "Cyber-physical Systems", "3D printing" and "Industrial Manipulators".

Table 2. Main thematic areas

Main thematic areas	Key words related	Main research topics	Main authors
Workorce 4.0	Workplace on University Training Programs Opportunity Interactive Space Hands-on experience	In the researchs it is possible to understand why the implementation of the testbeds on university ground is important to prepare as many students as possible, who will be invaluable people on the job market in the future.	[6, 23, 27]
Main Tecnologies	Iot Digital Twins Cyber-physical Systems 3D printing Industrial Manipulators	The authors presents the main technologies that are been used such as industry but also in the proof of concepts environments to train people for the future job market.	[4, 14, 15, 27, 29]
Main Methodologies Applied in Educational Testbeds	Challenge-Based Learning Explorative Learning Flipped Classroom Project-Based-Learning	In the quest to find the best methodologies that develop the students, the main methodologies that show important results in the development and confidence of the students when they arrive in the industry are presented.	[12, 13, 22, 27]
Advantage for Industry	Efficiency New Technologies Problem solving Satisfactory Results Solution of Real Problems	The studies presents the identification of possible problems that companies are facing, and how university-industry integration shows gains in solving real problems in various areas.	[12, 20, 22, 27, 31]
Advantage for students and Skills Development	Experience Communication Creativity Critical ability Flexibility Intellectual Defense of Solutions Interpreting Relevant Data Leadership Motivation Team Work	The studies present how university-industry integration through educational testbeds prepares more motivated, skilled, and valued professionals in the 4.0 market. Projects are listed that develop the necessary skills and competencies in students.	[12, 22, 27, 31]

The third thematic area identified are the main teaching methodologies applied in educational testbeds, considered the most pertinent to the development of skills. The methodologies identified are: "Challenge-Based Learning", "Explorative Learning", "Flipped Classroom' and "Project-Based-Learning". The fourth area is the main advantages for industry when presenting their challenges and real problems in an educational testbed. The advantages listed were: "Efficiency", "New Technologies", "Problem solving", "Satisfactory Results", "Solution of Real Problems". Last are the advantages to students and the skills developed by them in an educational testbed. The main advantages and skills identified are: "Experience", "Communication", "Creativity", "Critical ability", "Flexibility", "Intellectual Defense of Solutions", "Interpreting Relevant Data", "Leadership", "Motivation" and "Team Work".

The main research topics help us to link how educational testbeds have been implemented and what results they have generated. The need for an adequate workforce is the point that stimulates the emergence of adequate teaching methodologies to develop the necessary skills. These methodologies can and should include the main technologies used in the new digital era, because it is through the expertise in integrating technologies with education that qualified and re-qualified professionals will be trained. The advantages for students and industry are evident, showing how efficient the university-industry integration is for both atmospheres, solving real problems, one of them being the unqualified workforce itself, besides collaborating with the formation of professionals with adequate skills for the digital era. It is worth noting the great opportunity to develop skills in terms of programming, algorithms and data analysis, as these test environments are capable of generating data that can be converted into simulations, dashboards and programming systems, enabling students to use digital tools that help industry in decision making.

Despite presenting important advantages, the implementation of educational testbeds for students and for industry can also bring challenges, especially in terms of the bureaucracies that involve the university-industry relationship. Access to technology can also be a challenging process for higher education institutions, since this technology develops rapidly and keeping it up to date in an educational environment is not cheap. Inserting students in a real industrial environment also depends on an adequate, safe, and accessible management model.

Even with the challenges encountered, it is undeniable that new education models need to be implemented to form an adequate workforce. Like any breaking cycle, redesigning an educational model is not an easy task, but it should not be put aside. The need for people with adequate skills for the future represents not only economic gains, but also social and cultural gains. An educational testbed represents one answer to a massive need in terms of skills, employability, labor quality and social development for the digital era. From this study, we hope to contribute to the knowledge surrounding this term, strengthening the university-industry relationship in order to train professionals prepared for the future of society and industry.

4   Conclusion

Industry 4.0 and 5.0 characterize the digital industry in the digital era, which demands a new job market and new professions focused on hard and soft skills. Thus, education for the digital era needs to find ways to teach and train the new workforce. In this sense, this study aimed to present the main characteristics and thematic areas about educational testbed in the context of Industry 4.0 and 5.0. To meet the proposed objective, it was necessary to conduct a systematic literature review to map the main works in relation to the theme. To assist in the literature review, PRISMA was used as a method to identify the relevant papers, then NVIVO software was used to analyze the papers. With this, it was concluded that the objective proposed by the study was achieved.

The analysis took into consideration a final portfolio of 47 papers pertinent to the theme. From this, the gap between education and the needs of Industry 4.0 and 5.0 can be presented. It is a fact that there is a gap between these two spheres of society, and universities and industries need to work in partnership to reduce the impacts of this gap. Educational testbeds come as an answer to this problem. The study presents 8 characteristics that validate the potential of training skilled labor for Industry 4.0 from an educational testbed, bringing benefits to education and industry, as follows: test concepts; assist industry in decision making; develop people across hard and soft skills; develop new technologies; promote innovation in learning methods; approach the human being of technology; social economic improvements; bringing together industry and education. Thus, an educational testbed can be considered the link between university and industry in the digital era.

The contribution of this research is to survey the characteristics involved in educational testbeds in order to determine what is actually part of this educational environment, it also contributes to the identification of thematic areas of research. In the literature, there is a gap regarding the details of what makes up an educational testbed. From the 8 characteristics presented and 5 thematic areas related to educational testbeds presented in this paper, it is expected that future researches will have a better theoretical basis to develop these educational environments, being able to categorize what would or would not be an educational testbed and encourage the use of the term in the literature and in the practice of education 4.0 and 5.0 for the development of workforce for industry 4.0 and 5.0.

As a limitation of this paper, one can cite the fact that it covers few studies involving Industry 5.0, since it is still an initial theme of studies and is of interest to researchers for future works. Thus, as a proposal, we suggest identifying possible transformations for educational testbeds based on the concepts of Industry 5.0. Another proposal is to further deepen the theme by comparing the educational testbed with other forms of proof of concept, such as learning factories, for example. It was identified that in certain studies, the term "learning factory" is used as a synonym for educational testbed, demonstrating both are proofs of concept and have similar characteristics. Even so, a study comparing the advantages and characteristics of both could present pertinent results.

References

1. Ilkovičová, Ĺ., Ilkovič, J.: Industry 4.0 in architecture education. World Trans. Eng. Technol. Educ. Slovak **19**(3), 331–336 (2021)
2. Madsen, O., Møller, C.: The AAU smart production laboratory for teaching and research in emerging digital manufacturing technologies. Procedia Manufact. **9**, 106–112 (2017). https://doi.org/10.1016/j.promfg.2017.04.036
3. Pontes, J., et al.: Relationship between trends, job profiles, skills and training programs in the factory of the future. In: 2021 22nd IEEE International Conference on Industrial Technology (ICIT), vol. 1, pp. 1240–1245. IEEE (2021). https://doi.org/10.1109/ICIT46573.2021.9453584
4. Hernandez-de-Menendez, M., Escobar Díaz, C., Morales-Menendez, R.: Technologies for the future of learning: state of the art. Int. J. Interact. Design Manufact. **14**(2), 683–695 (2019). https://doi.org/10.1007/s12008-019-00640-0
5. Sułkowski, Ł., Kolasińska-Morawska, K., Seliga, R., Morawski, P.: Smart learning technologization in the Economy 5.0-The Polish perspective. Appl. Sci. **11**(11), 5261 (2021). https://doi.org/10.3390/app11115261
6. Kuttolamadom, M., Wang, J., Griffith, D., Greer, C.: Educating the workforce in cyber and smart manufacturing for Industry 4.0. In: ASEE Annual Conference Exposition Proceedings (2020). https://doi.org/10.18260/1-2-34491
7. Coşkun, S., Kayıkcı, Y., Gençay, E.: Adapting engineering education to industry 4.0 vision. Technologies **7**(1), 10 (2019). https://doi.org/10.3390/technologies7010010
8. Mourtzis, D., Boli, N., Dimitrakopoulos, G., Zygomalas, S., Koutoupes, A.: Enabling Small Medium Enterprises (SMEs) to improve their potential through the Teaching Factory paradigm. Procedia Manufact. **23**, 183–188 (2018). https://doi.org/10.1016/j.promfg.2018.04.014
9. Lantada, A.D.: Engineering education 5.0: continuously evolving engineering education. Int. J. Eng. Educ. **36**(6), 1814–1832. (2020)
10. Muzira, D.R., Bondai, B.M.: Perception of educators towards the adoption of education 5.0: a case of a state university in Zimbabwe. East African J. Educ. Soc. Sci. **1**(2), 43–53 (2020). https://doi.org/10.46606/eajess2020v01i02.0020
11. Broo, D.G., Kaynak, O., Sait, S.M.: Rethinking engineering education at the age of industry 5.0. J. Indust. Inform. Integrat. **25**, 100311 (2022). https://doi.org/10.1016/j.jii.2021.100311
12. Sánchez, J., Mallorquí, A., Briones, A., Zaballos, A., Corral, G.: An integral pedagogical strategy for teaching and learning IoT cybersecurity. Sensors **20**(14), 3970 (2020)
13. Ilori, M.O., Ajagunna, I.: Re-imagining the future of education in the era of the fourth industrial revolution. Worldwide Hospitality and Tourism Themes (2020). https://doi.org/10.1108/WHATT-10-2019-0066
14. Kemény, Z., et al.: Complementary research and education opportunities-a comparison of learning factory facilities and methodologies at TU Wien and MTA SZTAKI. Procedia CIRP **54**, 47–52 (2016). https://doi.org/10.1016/j.procir.2016.05.064
15. Tihinen, M., Pikkarainen, A., Joutsenvaara, J.: Digital manufacturing challenges education-SmartLab concept as a concrete example in tackling these challenges. Future Internet **13**(8), 192 (2021)
16. da Silva, L.B.P., et al.: Human Resources Management 4.0: literature review and trends. Comput. Indust. Eng. 108111 (2022). https://doi.org/10.1016/j.cie.2022.108111

17. Page, M.J., et al.: The PRISMA 2020 statement: an updated guideline for reporting systematic reviews. Int. J. Surg. **88**, 105906 (2021). https://doi.org/10.1016/j.ijsu.2021.105906

18. de Paula Ferreira, W., Armellini, F., De Santa-Eulalia, L.A.: Simulation in industry 4.0: a state-of-the-art review. Comput. Indust. Eng. **149**, 106868 (2020). https://doi.org/10.1016/j.cie.2020.106868

19. Woods, M., Paulus, T., Atkins, D.P., Macklin, R.: Advancing qualitative research using qualitative data analysis software (QDAS)? Reviewing potential versus practice in published studies using ATLAS. ti and NVivo, 1994–2013. Soc. Sci. Comput. Rev. **34**(5), 597–617 (2016). https://doi.org/10.1177/0894439315596311

20. Damgrave, R.G.J., Lutters, E.: Synthetic prototype environment for industry 4.0 testbeds. Procedia CIRP **91**, 516–521 (2020). https://doi.org/10.1016/j.procir.2020.02.208

21. Hadgraft, R.G., Kolmos, A.: Emerging learning environments in engineering education. Austral. J. Eng. Educ. **25**(1), 3–16 (2020). https://doi.org/10.1080/22054952.2020.1713522

22. Yoshino, R.T., Pinto, M.M.A., Pontes, J., Treinta, F.T., Justo, J.F., Santos, M.M.: Educational Test Bed 4.0: a teaching tool for Industry 4.0. Eur. J. Eng. Educ. **45**(6), 1002–1023 (2020). https://doi.org/10.1080/03043797.2020.1832966

23. da Silva, L.B.Pe., Barreto, B.P., Pontes, J., Treinta, F.T., de Resende, L.M.M., Yoshino, R.T.: Evaluation of soft skills through educational testbed 4.0. In: Pereira, A.I., et al. (eds.) OL2A 2021. CCIS, vol. 1488, pp. 678–690. Springer, Cham (2021). https://doi.org/10.1007/978-3-030-91885-9_51

24. Martinelli, A., Mina, A., Moggi, M. The enabling technologies of industry 4.0: examining the seeds of the fourth industrial revolution. Indust. Corporate Change **30**(1), 161–188 (2021). https://doi.org/10.1093/icc/dtaa060

25. Zalud, L., Burian, F., Kalvodova, P.: Industry 4.0 testbed at brno university of technology. In: Mazal, J. (ed.) MESAS 2018. LNCS, vol. 11472, pp. 147–157. Springer, Cham (2019). https://doi.org/10.1007/978-3-030-14984-0_13

26. Lin, W.D., Low, M.Y.H.: An integrated engineering education alignment model towards Industry 4.0.In: Proceedings of the International Conference on Industrial Engineering and Operations Management, pp. 1204–1213 (2021)

27. Kliment, M., Pekarcikova, M., Trebuna, P., Trebuna, M.: Application of TestBed 4.0 technology within the implementation of Industry 4.0 in teaching methods of industrial engineering as well as industrial practice. Sustainability **13**(16), 8963 (2021). https://doi.org/10.3390/su13168963

28. Salvador, R., et al.: Challenges and opportunities for problem-based learning in higher education: Lessons from a cross-program industry 4.0 case. Industry and Higher Education (2022). https://doi.org/10.1177/09504222221100343

29. Prieto, M.D., Sobrino, Á. F., Soto, L.R., Romero, D., Biosca, P.F., Martínez, L.R.: Active learning based laboratory towards engineering education 4.0. In: 2019 24th IEEE International Conference on Emerging Technologies and Factory Automation (ETFA), pp. 776–783. IEEE (2019). https://doi.org/10.1109/ETFA.2019.8869509

30. Vu, T.L.A.: Building CDIO approach training programmes against challenges of industrial revolution 4.0 for engineering and technology development. Int. J. Eng, **11**(7), 1129–1148 (2018)

31. López, H.A., Ponce, P., Molina, A., Ramírez-Montoya, M.S., Lopez-Caudana, E.: Design framework based on TEC21 educational model and Education 4.0 implemented in a Capstone Project: A case study of an electric vehicle suspension system. Sustainability **13**(11), 5768 (2021). https://doi.org/10.3390/su13115768

32. Maddikunta, P.K.R., et al.: Industry 5.0: a survey on enabling technologies and potential applications. J. Indust. Inform. Integrat. **26**, 100257 (2022). https://doi.org/10.1016/j.jii.2021.100257

33. ABDI: Agência Brasileira de Desenvolvimento Industrial. Indústria 4.0 pode economizar R$ 73 bilhões ao ano para o Brasil, https://www.abdi.com.br/postagem/industria-4-0-pode-economizar-r-73-bilhoes-ao-ano-para-o-brasil. Accessed 12 May 2022

Advances and Optimization
in Cyber-Physical Systems

Adaptive Environment System to Manage Comfort Preferences and Conflicts

Pedro Filipe Oliveira[1]($\boxtimes$)(iD), Paulo Novais[1](iD), and Paulo Matos[2](iD)

[1] Departamento de Informática, Centro Algoritmi/Universidade do Minho, Braga, Portugal
poliveira@ipb.pt, pjon@di.uminho.pt
[2] Research Centre in Digitalization and Intelligent Robotics (CeDRI), Instituto Politécnico de Bragança, Bragança, Portugal
pmatos@ipb.pt

Abstract. Managing comfort preferences conflicts of the different users and locals on an Internet of Things (IoT) adaptive system is a actual problem. This paper, proposes a protocol and hierarchical rules to develop a multi-agent system to achieve an Adaptive Environment System that supports interaction between persons and physical spaces, where spaces smartly adapt to their preferences in a transparent way. And also a set of security customization's to secure the actuators and users on space, that has been developed using a multi agent system architecture with different features to achieve a solution that supports the proposed objectives. Supported by a base architecture to achieve the full system implementation.

Keywords: Adaptive-system · AmI · Multi-agent · IoT · Conflicts

1 Introduction

Artificial Intelligence field continues with an exponential growth rate, and multi-agent systems have been used to solve several situations, related to Ambient Intelligence [5]. Ambient Intelligence (AMI), is an ubiquitous, electronic and intelligent environment, recognized by different technologies/systems interconnection, in order to carry out different daily tasks in a transparent and autonomous way for the user [5].

Thus, multi-agent systems are made up of autonomous agents present in the environment and who have the ability to make decisions derived from interpreted stimulus and connection with other agents, to achieve common goals [15].

Currently there are different languages and platforms for this type of systems development, namely *3APL, Jack, Jade/Jadex, Jason*, among others [4]. *3APL, Jadex* and *Jason* use agents with cognitive reasoning models as an alternative to more traditional reactive models.

A. I. Pereira et al. (Eds.): OL2A 2022, CCIS 1754, pp. 685–700, 2022.
https://doi.org/10.1007/978-3-031-23236-7_47

With a focus on Belief-Desire-Intention (BDI) cognitive model, which allows the creation of intelligent agents capable of making decisions based on beliefs and perceptions, desires and intentions that the agent may have at a given moment.

Jason is a framework for Multi Agent System (MAS) development, which has an interpreter for the *Java* developed *AgentSpeak* language, which implements BDI model previously mentioned. There is also an extension for *Jason*, called *ARGO*, this being a customized architecture that allows programming of cognitive agents using controllers (taking advantage of sensors and actuators).

There are already different literature works that present solutions for integrating MAS with AMI, and specifically with Smart Homes, using *Jade* [3,6], which is reactive, and using *Jason* with *JaCaMo* [1,7,8].

Projects that use *Jason* as development language are mainly simulated and there are no literature works on physical integration with real environments or hardware to meet ubiquitous computing that use *Jason* as MAS.

ARGO is an architecture that aims to facilitate ubiquitous MAS programming using *Jason*, regardless of the chosen field.

This work propose an autonomous Smart Home model controlled by cognitive agents using *Jason* and *ARGO* and to manage physical devices, since *ARGO* agents allow communication with different controllers (Arduino, Raspberry).

For this, the work has a prototype of a house with six divisions, each with lighting, and a heating system.

To evaluate the MAS development and prototype, a series of performance tests were designed to be performed considering parameters such as the number of agents and controllers, the agents speed of reasoning, moment of the environment perception and information filtering, in order to explore different implementation strategies about the system.

The main expected contribution of this work is the possibility of applying MAS to ubiquitous prototypes using the *Jason* framework and *ARGO* architecture applied to intelligent environments.

As in any environment where different users are present, there will be a native conflict of interest regarding the most diverse issues. Also in this case of developing an intelligent environment adaptable to the comfort preferences of each user, this problem will be present. It is well known that in everyday life, we deal with people with different comfort preferences, both in terms of temperature or humidity values, as well in terms of musical or video tastes, etc. This is more critical, as these values interfere with people's well-being, or even their health, namely in terms of allergies, diseases, etc.

In this project, a protocol was created, which allows to resolve as much as possible this type of conflicts, thus trying to reach a optimum preference value, which satisfies as much as possible the majority of users present in the environment. This work resulted in the complete specification of an architecture that supports the solution found, to solve the presented problem. It will now be implemented, tested and validated using real case studies, so as to gather statistical information to assess its effectiveness and performance in the context of application.

2   Materials and Methods

Figure 1, shows the scenario of an environment around which the present work was developed. It can be seen the user, that through its different devices (smartphone, wearable, and other compatible) communicates with the system, and for that different technologies can be used (WIFI Direct, Near Field Communication (NFC), Bluetooth Low Energy (BLE)). After, the system performs communication with the Cloud, to validate the information. And then the system will perform the management of the different components in the environment (climatization systems, security systems, other smart systems).

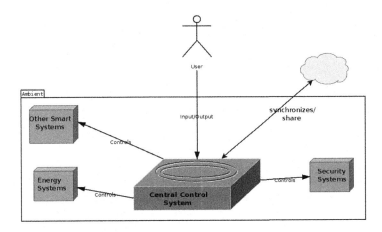

Fig. 1. Overall scenario

This scenario, represents an environment (at a given location and at a given time). As mentioned above, for a proper solution that fits all users, it is necessary to consider the user mobility. This implies considering time and space dimensions [9].

As such, for a better overall scenario understanding in the user's daily life, Fig. 2 contextualizes the temporal and space dimensions present in this problem, where we can see that each overall scenarios it will occur at different locations, and at different time, during the user quotidian. It can be seen that different user locations, combined with time context, naturally results in an environment with different characteristics. This kind of global scenario is also addressed in this project [10].

2.1   Assumptions

To optimize the predictions of the solution proposed, an architecture for a multi-agent system was defined. The roles that each agent should represent, as well

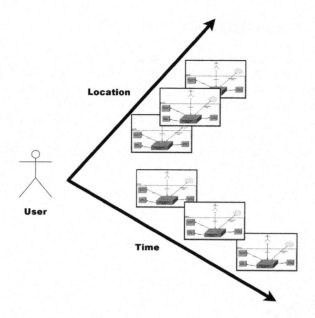

Fig. 2. Contextualization of time/space dimensions

the negotiation process to be taken, and the different scenarios in which this negotiation should take place and the way it should be processed were specified.

For the project development, two phases are defined as follows:

– Hardware (local systems) installation;
– Multi-agent system development;

Firstly, the entire physical structure must be prepared, where the local devices (Raspberry) equipped with the network technologies previously identified, so that they can detect the users present in the space.

The comfort preferences of each user present in the environment is sent to the agent every time an *ARGO* agent performs his reasoning cycle (by calling the *getPercepts* method, which must exist in all controllers that need to send perceptions to agents).

Thus, the MAS must be programmed independently from the hardware, taking into account only the actions that must be performed to achieve the ideal comfort values for the space in question, and then these values are sent to the actuators. The actuators connection was not considered in this work, implying that it is automatic and without any constraint for the user.

A prototype was thus implemented in a house, taking into account all the MAS architecture and the comfort actuators present in it.

For this purpose, a *Raspberry* is used per division, in this case three on the ground floor (living room/kitchen, office, bedroom) and three on the first floor (one at each environment).

Regarding the actuators, these divisions have a hydraulic radiant floor heating system heated by a heat pump, and a home automation system that controls the luminosity intensity in the different rooms. Figure 3 and 4 illustrates where the six different local systems (*Raspberry's*) are placed in each of the floors.

Fig. 3. Ground floor   **Fig. 4.** First floor

Viewing in more detail, a 3D model was designed, where the operation of the system for a specific space can be visualized, like can be seen in Fig. 5. Explaining the model, we can see different people present in the space, as well as the local system present in it, the arrows illustrate the autonomous communication process between the users' peripherals (smartphones) and the local system and the one with the central server (Cloud), which will allow to have the information for each of the agents to work and to reach the values of comfort preferences to use in the actuators.

This work proposes an autonomous Smart Home model, controlled through cognitive agents, which get the final information to be applied by actuators.

For do that, a six divisions house was prototyped with different comfort features, namely temperature, luminosity, audio and video. The considered parameters for performance evaluation are as follows:

- Number of agents used;
- Agent speed reasoning;
- Information filtering;
- Environment perception time;

2.2 Framework Jason

This section presents the technologies used in this project for the development of the entire MAS applied to AMI.

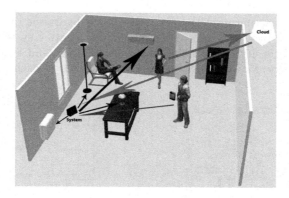

Fig. 5. Example of the system in a environment

Jason is a framework with its own language for the development of cognitive MAS, and using the customized architecture of ARGO agents it is possible to bridge the gap between MAS, actuators and sensors present in the real world.

Figure 6 exemplifies the use case diagram, explaining this diagram, we can verify the functioning of the different agents. Namely the information received by them, and how the negotiation process is carried out, those involved in it, and how the final result of the negotiation is passed to the actuator.

Initially, we can verify, the agent that represents the local system receives its information, namely the security information (maximum values of temperature, gases, and others). For each user present at the local, there will be an agent who represents him, it will receive information about the user preferences from the central system.

The negotiation process will then be made up of the local system agent and each of the users agents present at the local. The negotiation result will then be passed on to the different actuators present in the local.

Jason is a framework with an agent-oriented programming language, has an *AgentSpeak* Java interpreter for the development of intelligent cognitive agents using BDI.

The BDI consists of three basic constructions: beliefs, desires and intentions. Beliefs are information taken as truths for the agent, which can be internal, acquired through the relationship with other agents or through the perceptions observed in the environment. Desires represent an agent's motivation to achieve a certain objective and intentions are the actions that the agent has committed to perform.

AgentSpeak is a programming language focused on the agent approach, which is based on principles of the BDI architecture.

In addition to these concepts, the Procedural Reasoning System allows the agent to build a real-time reasoning system for performing complex tasks. Jason's agents have a reasoning cycle based on events that are generated from

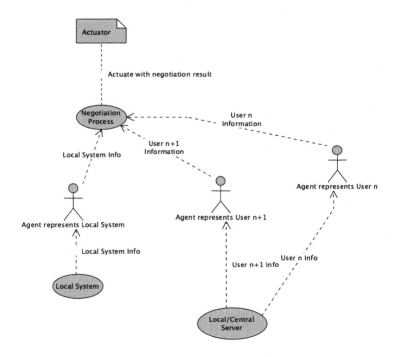

Fig. 6. AmI system - use case agent diagram

capturing perceptions of the environment, messages exchanged with other agents and through their own conclusions based on their reasoning.

These events can be triggered by triggers that lead to the execution of plans (available in specific libraries) composed of several actions. Jason's agents are programmed based on the definition of objectives, intentions, beliefs, plans and actions internal to the agent and actions performed in the environment. A MAS in Jason does not traditionally have an interface for capturing perceptions directly from the real world using sensors. The ARGO custom architecture is used for this, Jason uses a simulated environment.

3 Results

3.1 Multi-agent System Architecture

ARGO is a customized Jason agent architecture to enable the programming of robotic and ubiquitous agents using different prototyping platforms.

ARGO allows cognitive agents and a real environment (using controllers) intermediation through *Javino* middleware, which communicates with hardware (sensors and actuators). In addition, use of BDI on robotic platforms can generate bottlenecks in perceptions processing and, consequently, unwanted execution delays, this extension also has a perception filtering mechanism at run time [14].

A MAS using *Jason* and *ARGO* can be made up of traditional *Jason* and *ARGO* agents that work simultaneously. *Jason* agents can carry out plans and actions only at software level and communicate with other agents in the system (including *ARGO* agents).

On the other hand a *ARGO* agent, is a traditional agent with additional characteristics, such as, for instance, the ability to communicate with the physical environment, perceive and modify it, and also filter the perceived information.

Figure 7 represent the different layers architecture separation, to easily identify the purpose of each, and agents containing it.

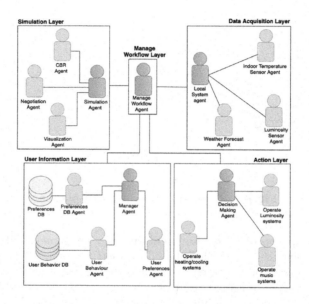

Fig. 7. Multi-agent system architecture

The layers description is as follows:

- **Data acquisition layer**, will import necessary information for the agents operation, namely information of interior and exterior temperature and light sensors.
- **User layer**, this layer has an agent that will represent each user and his preferences that must be used in the negotiation process.
- **Local System layer,** here each local system will be represented by an agent, which contains all necessary information to this location, either the referred to user preferences, or local/users security (maximum/minimum temperature, safety values for CO_2, etc.).
- **Simulation layer**, in this layer will be the negotiation between different agents involved, namely conflicts management between different users and

local systems. After the negotiation process ends we will have as result the values to be applied at the environment.
- **Action layer**, after the simulation layer process execution, the values to be applied are obtained. These are used in this layer and sent to actuators that will apply them in the different automation systems and actuators present at the environment.

There will be one principal agent who will represent local system, namely each individual environment, where it was a need to ensure individualized comfort conditions, such as a room in a house, or a office in a building. This agent will take into account any directives that may exist for this environment, such as lower or upper limits to different comfort conditions, or also safety parameters that may be critical for a given space. This agent will have a obviously prevalence relative to others, since it will be the dominant for a given environment.

With users respect, each one in the space, will also be represented by an agent, this will receive user preferences from main system, for the place where it is, as well for the time in which it is. Also in this situation there will be a prioritization that identifies which user will have environment supremacy, so it also has an increase in the negotiation process.

In decision-making process, all users agents and agents representing the environment will be taken into account. With the different priorities that each of them has, and with this information will begin the negotiation process.

3.2 Multi-agent System Schema

The Multi-agent that supports the system was developed using JADE [2], and implements five different roles types to agents:

- **Environment Agent**, provide information on the environment status. A new Environment Agent is created for each environment that is introduced into the system.
- **Sensor Agent(s)**, responsible for retrieve information of different conditions on the environment, namely temperature, brightness, and others depending of each environment conditions.
- **Preference Agent**, keeps track of the preferences card.
- **User Agent(s)**, responsible for the negotiation process. Each user agent is associated with a single user present in the environment.
- **Negotiation manager Agent**, created in each environment in order to manage the negotiation process between different User Agents.

At Fig. 8, is summarized the developed schema.

3.3 Conflicts Management

At Fig. 7 is represented the different architecture layers, the agent that represents the local system receives its information, namely security information (maximum

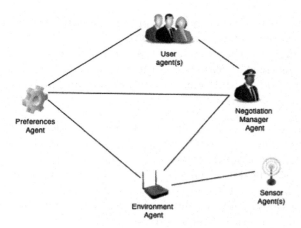

Fig. 8. Multi-agent system schema

values of temperature, gases, and others). Also for each user present at the local, there will be an agent who represents him, it will receive information about the user preferences from the central system, that will be used for the negotiation process.

The negotiation process will then be made up of the local system agent and each of the users agents present at the local. The negotiation result will then be passed to the different actuators present in the local.

During this project, the environments focuses will be on domestic/family, professional environments (workplaces) and public spaces, where a large number of persons are usually present.

One of the rules used for conflict resolution was the preferences hierarchy. Starting with family contexts, it was taken into account maximize adult elements (parents) preference value over the children, in a ratio of 1 to 0.75. Another hierarchy is the space preference value if it exists, in this case a proportion of 1.5 will be used. These cases may exist in spaces where there is some conditioning, such as Kitchens/Wc, or other spaces that have some type of conditioning.

The proportions described and used for the rules are detailed in Table 1.

At professional context, proportion values are also defined in a hierarchical way, and in this context the professional hierarchy of space will be used, as well space preference value if it exists. The proportions described are detailed in Table 2.

Regarding public/social spaces, the predominant value will obviously be the space value with a proportion of 2, and each user will have a 0.15 proportion, because in these spaces is natural that there are little values variation, derived by high people movement. The proportions described are detailed in Table 3. The equation used to achieve the optimum preference value to the different spaces is the following:

$$prefValue = \frac{\sum_{user=1}^{n} uP * uHP + (sP * sProp)}{\sum_{user=1}^{n} uHP + sProp} \quad (1)$$

In Eq. 1, is depicted the equation for calculate the preference value to apply in the actuators present at the space. In this equation we have:

- n - number of users present in space;
- uP - each user preference for the space;
- uHP - each user hierarchy proportion;
- sP - space preference;
- sProp - space proportion;

This equation uses the different users preferences and respective hierarchy proportions for each user, and sums the total, with space preference value multiplied by respective space proportion. These total, will be divided by the total sum of hierarchy proportions of all users in the space, summed with space proportions.

Table 1. Home space

Type	Proportion
Adult	1
Child	0,75
Visitor	1
Space	1,5

Table 2. Work space

Type	Proportion
Hierarchy_1	(100-1)
Hierarchy_2	(100-2)
Hierarchy_n	(100-n)
Space	150

Table 3. Public/social space

Type	Proportion
User_1	0,15
User_2	0,15
User_n	0,15
Space	2

Different constraints exist for each system, at Fig. 9 is detailed a example of constraints table that for each agent enters in the negotiation process.

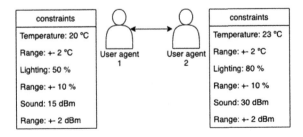

Fig. 9. Two agents constraints table

4   Base Architecture

Figure 10, shows the base architecture developed. Explaining this architecture, first it can be seen one user that enter at the environment with his smartphone, a local system is present at the environment. In an autonomous way the smartphone communicates with Local System for this process different technologies can be used (Wi-Fi Direct, NFC, BLE), and transmits User ID to the Local System, this Local System validates the User ID in the cloud, and after a correct match the respective preference's card is retrieved by Local System.

With that information Local System start the negotiation process, as is in the schema at Fig. 8, when the negotiation is concluded, Local System has the final parameters to apply in the different actuators systems that are present at the environment like energy, security, multimedia, and other smart systems.

Continuing Fig. 10 explanation, a second user enters the environment, the same process of user validation and retrieve of preferences card is done, and the negotiation process, and possible conflict management is done at Local System. Finalized the negotiation process, new result parameters will be achieved and in the same way the parameters will be sent to different actuators.

This process it will occurs as many times, as new users arrive at the environment, and in that way the environment always have best comfort conditions to match all users preferences that are on the environment at a determined time.

The entire framework/architecture was developed in order to be easily scalable, dynamically, and with no need to change. In this sense, at the users level, the increase of these is carried out in a transparent way through the application installation on their device and initial configuration of their comfort preferences, from that moment, it will be automatically integrated into the system.

Regarding performance, after verification it was also clearly achieved, as the application present in local systems (Raspberry's), and which controls all user entries in different locations, easily allows the insertion of information, achieving hundreds of records per second.

The multi-agent solution performance, as it is critical and clearly lacks more computational power, will always be performed on the application server, and the results will be immediately communicated to each local system, so that they can be applied to each of the actuators present in the space. In this way, whenever it is necessary to increase performance for the multi-agent system solution processing, it will also be possible and quick to scale the servers.

5   Multi-agent System - Validation and Statistical Analysis

To measure satisfaction, with the comfort preferences applied by a given local system, the following table of criteria was defined in order to identify when the conditions applied by the result of the multi-agent system satisfy the different users present in the space. Considering different actuators inertia as mentioned

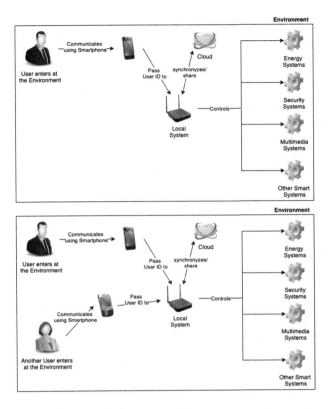

Fig. 10. Base architecture

above, the preferences calculation to be applied at a given moment will always be carried out for periods of thirty minutes.

In this way, to validate user satisfaction we need to consider the manually change of the preferences at the space, after each automatic application by the system. As well the difference between the applied and manual value requested by the user for that period, as it is known that, the more uncomfortable the space is for any preference or in several, greater will be the adjustment differential will be performed in the manual change.

If there is any change, if there are no manual changes, full satisfaction will be considered (100%).

Table 4, defines the percentage values that will be used to calculate the satisfaction, for each manual adjustment (higher or lower) of one change rate, the 100% of satisfaction will be discounted by the percentage value defined for each preference. To arrive at this value, the Eq. 2 was used, for each of the preferences used at the system.

$$Insatisfaction = \frac{mProp * cR}{(maxV - minV)} \tag{2}$$

In Eq. 2, is depicted the equation for calculate the insatisfaction percentage, that will be discounted to the user satisfaction for each preference. In this equation we have:

- mProp - metric Proportion;
- cR - change range;
- maxV - maximum preference value;
- minV - minimum preference value;

For the metric proportion we use 200, for the other values, we use the values for each preference, that are present at Table 4.

Table 4. Satisfaction metrics

Preference/constrain	Min. value	Max. value	Change range	Insatisfaction (%)
Lighting	0	90	±5	11,11%
Temperature	15	28	±0.5	7,69%
Luminance	0	40	±2	10%
Brightness	0	100	±2	4%
Relative Humidity	20	80	±5	16.66%
Sound	0	30	±1	6,66%

Thus, all manual changes made during the testing phase were analyzed, and the satisfaction metric was calculated, by period of time/place.

The average satisfaction was also measured, for the different periods: morning (8am–1pm), afternoon (1pm–7pm) and night (7pm–12pm), associated with each type of space (home, work, leisure.

Also regarding energy savings, and knowing that it is currently a factor that is not, and cannot be, neglected by any individual user, as well any business entity. Considering the increase in costs with different types of energy, as well the ecological footprint that its production represents.

The savings metric in this field was also calculated, always considering the purpose of this solution would not have this as prime factor, but indeed the maximum comfort of the user.

But knowing from the start that with all the introduced automatism's (detection of users present at the site, adjustment to minimum reference values in empty spaces, etc.) solutions that implement pre-programmed fixed adjustments and which most of the time don't include any automatism, or users forget to program that adjustments.

Such as simply allowing to detect absence periods, for example in the workspace, such as vacation, holidays or others. In this way, savings are expected to be significant.

To check exact values, the annual global consumption will be verified for each space, and compared with the same annual global consumption, after applying the solution. It is foreseeable that there will obviously an adjustment period for the multi-agent system, which is expected to automatically adjust and improve its efficiency over time, namely considering the different seasons.

However, in the first year, we will be able to get an idea of the savings values, and it is expected that they will increase slightly over time until the solution is stable, and if the routines and users of the space remain constants.

6   Discussion and Conclusions

This work resulted in the complete specification of an architecture that supports the solution found, to solve the presented problem. The agent system model is fully developed. At this stage the agent layer was fully developed, implemented, and is now in a testing phase at the testing environment developed for this project. Now It will be tested and validated using real case studies, so as to gather statistical information to assess its effectiveness and performance in the context of application.

With this, the specification of constraints for all specifications of proposed preferences for this work was achieved. In this way the safety of users and actuators present in space is achieved.

Also the total development of an architecture and respective cognitive model for a Smart Home was achieved, using an MAS with BDI agents, developed using Jason and ARGO.

The main objective of this project was to verify the potential that this type of architecture has for the development of ubiquitous MAS using low cost ($\sim$30€) hardware, such as Raspberry's.

For future work, the results of the testing phase, will be analyzed and evaluated and with that results improve this project and support other works in this field.

This paper aims to give continuity and finalize the doctoral project presented in other conferences [9–13].

Acknowledgements. This work has been supported by FCT - Fundação para a Ciência e Tecnologia within the R&D Units Project Scope: UIDB/00319/2020.

References

1. Andrade, J.P.B., Oliveira, M., Gonçalves, E.J.T., Maia, M.E.F.: Uma abordagem com sistemas multiagentes para controle autônomo de casas inteligentes. In: XIII Encontro Nacional de Inteligência Artificial e Computacional (ENIAC) (2016)
2. Bellifemine, F., Poggi, A., Rimassa, G.: Developing multi-agent systems with JADE. In: Castelfranchi, C., Lespérance, Y. (eds.) ATAL 2000. LNCS (LNAI), vol. 1986, pp. 89–103. Springer, Heidelberg (2001). https://doi.org/10.1007/3-540-44631-1_7
3. Benta, K.I., Hoszu, A., Văcariu, L., Creţ, O.: Agent based smart house platform with affective control. In: Proceedings of the 2009 Euro American Conference on Telematics and Information Systems: New Opportunities to Increase Digital Citizenship, pp. 1–7 (2009)

4. Bordini, R.H., Hübner, J.F., Wooldridge, M.: Programming Multi-agent Systems in AgentSpeak Using Jason, vol. 8. Wiley, Chichester (2007)
5. Chaouche, A.-C., El Fallah Seghrouchni, A., Ilié, J.-M., Saïdouni, D.E.: A higher-order agent model with contextual planning management for ambient systems. In: Kowalczyk, R., Nguyen, N.T. (eds.) Transactions on Computational Collective Intelligence XVI. LNCS, vol. 8780, pp. 146–169. Springer, Heidelberg (2014). https://doi.org/10.1007/978-3-662-44871-7_6
6. Kazanavicius, E., Kazanavicius, V., Ostaseviciute, L.: Agent-based framework for embedded systems development in smart environments. In: Proceedings of the 15th International Conference on Information and Software Technologies IT, pp. 194–200 (2009)
7. Martins, R., Meneguzzi, F.: A smart home model to demand side management. In: Workshop on Collaborative Online Organizations (COOS 2013) @ AAMAS (2013)
8. Martins, R., Meneguzzi, F.: A smart home model using JaCaMo framework. In: 2014 12th IEEE International Conference on Industrial Informatics (INDIN), pp. 94–99. IEEE (2014)
9. Oliveira, P., Matos, P., Novais, P.: Behaviour analysis in smart spaces. In: 2016 Intl IEEE Conferences on Ubiquitous Intelligence and Computing, Advanced and Trusted Computing, Scalable Computing and Communications, Cloud and Big Data Computing, Internet of People, and Smart World Congress (UIC/ATC/ScalCom/CBDCom/IoP/SmartWorld), pp. 880–887. IEEE (2016)
10. Oliveira, P., Novais, P., Matos, P.: Challenges in smart spaces: aware of users, preferences, behaviours and habits. In: De la Prieta, F., et al. (eds.) PAAMS 2017. AISC, vol. 619, pp. 268–271. Springer, Cham (2018). https://doi.org/10.1007/978-3-319-61578-3_34
11. Oliveira, P., Pedrosa, T., Novais, P., Matos, P.: Towards to secure an IoT adaptive environment system. In: Rodríguez, S., et al. (eds.) DCAI 2018. AISC, vol. 801, pp. 349–352. Springer, Cham (2019). https://doi.org/10.1007/978-3-319-99608-0_43
12. Oliveira, P.F., Novais, P., Matos, P.: A multi-agent system to manage users and spaces in a adaptive environment system. In: De La Prieta, F., et al. (eds.) PAAMS 2019. CCIS, vol. 1047, pp. 330–333. Springer, Cham (2019). https://doi.org/10.1007/978-3-030-24299-2_31
13. Oliveira, P.F., Novais, P., Matos, P.: Using Jason framework to develop a multi-agent system to manage users and spaces in an adaptive environment system. In: Novais, P., Vercelli, G., Larriba-Pey, J.L., Herrera, F., Chamoso, P. (eds.) ISAmI 2020. AISC, vol. 1239, pp. 137–145. Springer, Cham (2021). https://doi.org/10.1007/978-3-030-58356-9_14
14. Stabile, M.F., Sichman, J.S.: Evaluating perception filters in BDI Jason agents. In: 2015 Brazilian Conference on Intelligent Systems (BRACIS), pp. 116–121. IEEE (2015)
15. Wooldridge, M.: An Introduction to Multiagent Systems. Wiley, Chichester (2009)

Asynchronous and Distributed Multi-agent Systems: An Approach Using Actor Model

Felipe D. Reis[1]([✉]), Tales B. Nascimento[1]([✉]), Carolina G. Marcelino[2,3]([✉]),
Elizabeth F. Wanner[1]([✉]), Henrique E. Borges[1]([✉]),
and Sancho Salcedo-Sanz[3]([✉])

[1] Department of Computing, Federal Center of Technological Education of Minas
Gerais (CEFET-MG), Belo Horizonte, Brazil
{felipeduarte,tales,henrique,}@lsi.cefetmg.br, efwanner@cefetmg.br
[2] Institute of Computing, Federal University of Rio de Janeiro (UFRJ),
Rio de Janeiro, Brazil
carolina@ic.ufrj.br
[3] Department of Signal Processing and Communication, University of Alcalá,
Alcalá de Henares, Spain
sancho.salcedo@uah.es

Abstract. Agent-based and individual-based modeling have been widely
used to simulate ecological systems. The historical architectures designed
to artificial life simulation, namely LIDA and MicroPsy, rely into classical concurrence mechanisms based on threads, shared memory and locks.
Although these mechanisms seem to work fine for many multi-agent systems (MAS), notably for those requiring synchronous communication
between agents, they present severe restrictions in case of complex asynchronous MAS. In this work, we explore an alternative approach to handle concurrency in distributed asynchronous MAS: the actor model. An
actor is a concurrent entity capable of sending, receiving and handling
asynchronous messages, and creating new actors. Within this paradigm,
there are no shared memory and, hence, no data race conditions. We introduce L2L (a short for: Learn to Live, Live to Learn) architecture, a biological inspired distributed non-deterministic MAS simulation framework,
in which the autonomous agents (creatures) are endowed with a functional and minimal nervous system model enabling them to learn from its
own experiences and interactions with the two-dimensional world, populated with creatures and nutrients. Both creatures and nutrients are
encapsulated in actors. The system as a whole performs as a discrete non-
deterministic dynamical system, as well as the creatures themselves. The
scalability of this actor-based framework is evaluated showing the system
scales up and out − many processes per processor node and in a computer
cluster. A second experiment is realized to validate the architecture, consisting of an open-ended foraging simulation with both one or many creatures and hundreds of nutrients. Results from this specific actor-based version are compared to those from a classical concurrency version of the same
architecture, showing they are equivalent, despite the fact that the former
version scales a lot better. Moreover, results show that exploration of the
world is unbiased, leading us to conjecture that our system follows ergodic

© The Author(s), under exclusive license to Springer Nature Switzerland AG 2022
A. I. Pereira et al. (Eds.): OL2A 2022, CCIS 1754, pp. 701–713, 2022.
https://doi.org/10.1007/978-3-031-23236-7_48

hypothesis. We argue that the actor-based model proves to be very promising to modeling of asynchronous complex MAS.

Keywords: Distributed MAS · Complex agents · Situated cognition

1   Introduction

It is well known that simulating ecological systems in an individual-based (IB) or an agent-based (AB) perspective, is more intuitive and faithful to reality instead of pure mathematical approaches [1]. Furthermore, the complexity of those systems is naturally handled with AB models (ABM) [2]. Although the ABM is consolidated in literature, there is no general technique to handle the continued growth of complexity of multi-agent systems (MAS) [2].

Despite the fact IB and AB modeling are not equivalent in concept, both have been used to understand the complexities of ecological management. Bousquet & Le Page [3] show many concepts based on ecosystems modeling and point out the possibility of rich hierarchy simulation to understand natural phenomena from different perspectives. However, there is no mention concerning technological difficulties related to this kind of simulation.

In the field of cognitive science, the ABM has been used to simulate and investigate the possibilities of various mind and brain theories. As an example, the LIDA architecture is based on Global Workspace Theory [4]. It specifies for the agents a cycle of sensing, processing sensor signals and decision making that occurs in parallel and asynchronously, while respecting the order of component stimulation to maintain the cognitive process coherence.

In the model MicroPsi - a multi-agent cognitive framework based on the Psy theory [5,6] - the agent is composed of several components, including sensors and modulators which interacts with the environment, and a motivation set defined by the needs of the agent (*i.e.*, energy, hunger, thirst). These needs trigger the internal cognitive process of the agent and modulate its behavior. There is also a component that coordinate the allocation of the resources to internal components during execution.

Modeling natural phenomena has to take into account the simultaneity of various events. In real cases, the agent and the environment interacts through a stimulation process simultaneously [7]. From this perspective, the actor model is a powerful technique to design this kind of interaction. In the actor model, "computation is conceived as distributed in space where computational devices communicate asynchronously and the entire computation is not in any well-defined state" [8]. Following this definition, actor model helps to design and implement systems in which the events must happen asynchronously and simultaneously. Furthermore, as the computation is defined as distributed, this approach gives the model the ability to scale over many machines, without changing the fundamental implementation decision.

Given that the actor model is very congruent with the need in agent-based modeling systems (ABMS), its usage now is widespread over the literature. *Angiani et al.* [9] presents a framework based on actors to simulate agent-based modeled systems. The authors claim that the actor model of computation has affinity with designing ABMS since both are grounded on reactive behaviour, isolating its internal state from the outside world and communicating through message exchange. The framework is distributed and can be executed in a cluster. A prof of concept is presented for study crowd-behaviour in a building evacuation scenario. Another framework designed for ABMS is AgentScriptCC [10], a domain-specific language for designing rule-based agents. The language is translated to an execution environment that is based on Akka actor framework. According to the authors, defining the agent via actor model results in a more fine-grained architecture and the execution of agent- oriented program is enhanced, both in scalability and performance perspectives.

Other architectures that take advantages of the actor computational model, *e.g.* the distributed-first and asynchronous-first perspectives, can be found in the literature. Leon [11] creates a .NET framework based on multi-agent systems inspired by actor model. A new framework for the analysis of financial networks is proposed by Crafa [12]. The approach uses agent-based to actor-based reactive systems. Results indicates that the systemic effect of initially defaulting the banks of some country with price shock parameter is approximately the same that is obtained by shocking all the European system. In [13] agent-systems based on actors are proposed to optimize the resources in IoT systems. Actor modelling can also be used to improve optimization algorithms, as ant colony optimization [14] and multi-objective in a hierarchical approach [15]. In addition, multi-agent system can be applied to reinforcement learning models [16,17].

Given that the actor model has been shown to be useful for constructing distributed and efficient MAS, we propose here a new architecture called L2L (Live to learn, learn to live) for simulating artificial creatures. This simulator, a biologically inspired MAS, is a new implementation of a former version previously described by [18]. The later could only be executed in one machine with a narrow limit on the number of agents, thus preventing ecosystems simulations. The current implementation specifies each creature and nutrients as actors, which interact through message passing. The results shows a remarkable enhancement in system scalability, allowing further simulations and involving hundreds of complex creatures in a computer cluster.

The organization of this paper is as follows: the L2L architecture is presented together with the actor model in Sect. 2. Experimental results are discussed in Sect. 3. The, Sect. 4 concludes the work.

2   Proposed Model

2.1   L2L Architecture

L2L is a biologically inspired architecture of embodied and embedded cognition that has been used to study foraging and action selection [18]. The architecture consists of a two-dimensional surface of a toroidal world, which is populated by artificial creatures (active components) and nutrients (passive components). Both of them interact asynchronously exchanging stimuli. The nutrients have different nourishing values and the creature does not have *a priori* knowledge about those values neither the food distribution around the world.

The creature is endowed with a basic nervous, emotional and sensory-motor systems, and various internal "organs" that interact asynchronously with each other. This interaction represents the biological nervous and hormonal stimulation and is implemented via threads and shared memory. The access to shared memory is controlled by locks, and is implemented by all threads.

The creature internal state is modulated, but not determined, by the external stimuli received through the sensory system. The whole system operates in a non-deterministic dynamics through time and space. It is expected that the behaviour of adaptation, and thus the establishment of food preferences, emerges from the inner emotional-cognitive process. However, it is not the focus of this paper to describe that process (for more details see [18]).

The intrinsic model's complexity combined with implementations of decision about concurrency (use of shared memory, threads and locks) have made a single creature computationally heavy, limited to two creatures by computer core. Increasing this number causes the creature behavior becoming incoherent in the sense that, behavioral dynamics loose congruence with inner nervous system dynamics. This upper bound severely limits the studies involving ecological simulations, e.g. socio-genesis, semiotics, population dynamics, etc. Aiming to use more machines to run a large number of creatures in one simulation, it is necessary to decouple them from the shared memory. The chosen alternative to achieve this goal relies on the actor model.

2.2   The Actor Model

An actor is a mathematical concept of a universal primitive of digital computation [8]. The actor is an entity capable of sending messages, receiving and handling messages, as well as creating new actors. The actor model is by conception concurrent, and all the communications are asynchronously done through exchange, *i.e.*, there is no shared memory and hence no data race conditions. The messages in the actor model are decoupled from the sender and delivered by the system on a best efforts basis [19]. There are no guarantees as to the ordering of messages, so, the system must be carefully prepared to handle the incoming messages no matter their order.

There are many implementations of the actor model, *e.g.*, Erlang - a programming language which its concurrency mechanism works asynchronously as actors [20], and Quasar[1] library that runs over Java Virtual Machine (JVM). The Akka toolkit[2] is one of these, and we chose it because it best fit the technologies we already used. It does not respects all of the theoretical description from above due to technological constraints and practical factors. Since Akka runs on a JVM and is a library, it cannot strictly guarantee data separation from the actors. Also, the toolkit implements message ordering between pairs of actors. All actions taken by

---

[1] http://docs.paralleluniverse.co/quasar/.
[2] http://akka.io/.

an Akka actor are in response to some received message, whether sent by itself or by another actor, i.e. the system is reactive. Yet, it does not guarantee message delivery between two computers.

The advantage of using the actor model is that it provides a higher level of abstraction when compared with the classical concurrent model. Due to the fact that there are no data race conditions, the model scales up, using efficiently the available resources in one machine. Also, the toolkit we used provides an implementation that works with multiple machines, enabling scaling out. In the new implementation, the actor model is used to simulate a two-dimensional world which is composed of artificial creatures and nutrients. Either creatures and components are encapsulated in actors and they exchange stimuli with each other. The creatures' and nutrients' implementations are kept as proposed by *Campos et al.* [18], being just the communication between them implemented using the actor model. There is an underling control structure responsible for managing the simulations and replenish the nutrients, if necessary. This structure is shown in Fig. 1.

As said previously, the creature is an actor, and it encapsulates its nervous systems and its other subsystems. Those creature components still use threads as the concurrence model and must run in the same machine. For managing those creatures, there is a holder actor that creates and keeps track of them, and a repository actor that delegates which holder will receive the next creation order. The nutrient repository and holder are analogous to its creature counterparts. The simulation manager is an actor responsible to create, start and stop a given simulation, *i.e.*, given how many creatures and nutrients are populating the world, it asks the repositories to create them and wait for the ready response. When everything is configured, it send messages to start the simulation.

For the control messages (those exchanged by control actors), we implement a synchronous protocol. It increases the reliability of message delivery with a penalty on the overall performance. A miscommunication between this kind of actors would result in simulation failure. Since this kind of communication is not prevailing, the performance cost is acceptable. The creature and nutrient actors communicate with the collision detector actor using a fire-forget (best effort) method, that is faster than the synchronous method. Since these actors produce the statistics for the simulation, some message loss is tolerable.

3   Experimental Results

We propose two experiments to validate the present model and evaluate its scalability. The experiments have been performed in a small computer cluster, composed of eight slave machines and a master connect through a Gigabit Ethernet network. The cluster machines have 3 Intel i5-3470 processors, 32 GB dual channel DDR3 RAM. In those simulations, a number of artificial creatures has been created, without any kind of *a priori* knowledge about the world, in a virtual world filled with different kind of nutrients. In both experiments the nutrient density has been maintained constant during the executions, *i.e.*, if a nutrient is eaten, another one of the same type is promptly created in an aleatory position (uniform distribution).

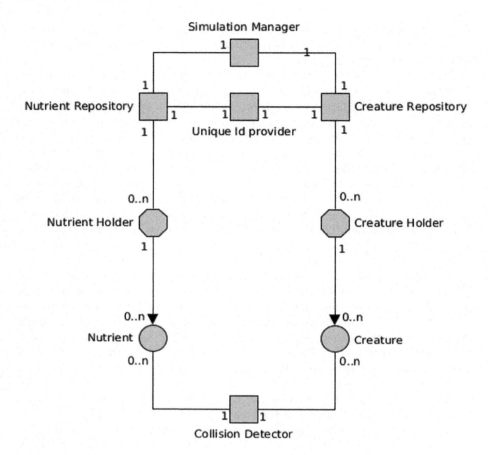

Fig. 1. Block diagram for the implemented model. All but the Creature and Nutrient are control actors. Each simulation must have at least one of each type of actor, and at most one actor represented by a square. The communication between the Creature and Nutrient actors with the Collision detector are fire-forget. The other communications have a acknowledge mechanism

3.1   Model Scalability

For evaluating the scalability of the implementation using the actor model, we measure the average number of exchanged external stimuli between actors as a function of computer nodes running, while keeping the ratio of creatures per machine constant. We start with 10 creatures and 90 nutrients, using one machine for the creatures and another one for the rest of the system. A simulation comprises 30 runs for each configuration, and each run is interrupted after 300 s, as our purpose is to evaluate only the system scalability. It is worth noticing, however, that L2L is designed for open-ended simulations (see Fig. 2).

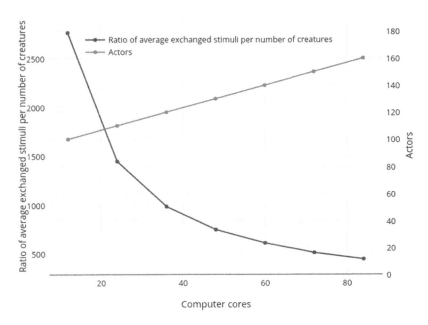

Fig. 2. Average of exchanged stimuli over number of creatures versus number of computer cores. Each computer node possesses 12 cores. The experiment shown that it is possible to increase the number of actors by adding more computer cores in the simulation. This doesn't cause a degradation in the chosen performance indicator (ratio of exchanged stimuli per creature). In fact, this PI tends to a constant, showing that the number of creatures grows faster than the average of exchanged stimuli.

Figure 2 shows, in the left axis, the ratio of average of exchanged stimuli over number of creature, as well as the total number of actors in the right axis. By increasing both the number of computers and creatures, the ratio curve tends to a constant, which means that the number of creatures grows faster than the average exchanged stimuli. This is the expected behavior because the nutrient density in the world does not change and all the creatures operate in the same manner, thus exchanging approximately the same amount of stimuli.

3.2   Model Validity

A experiment has been designed to compare the version using actor model and the former version, based on threads and shared memory, and to verify the correctness of the first. It consists of a simple open-ended (the simulation finish when the creature dies) foraging simulation with one creature and ninety nutrients. It has been repeated 50 times for both versions of architecture. Three measures are collected during the experiment: the creature position updates, the hunger deprivation, and the behavioural efficiency over time. The system has a spacial dynamics. Figure 3 shows the superimposed path covered by 30 creatures in both implementations. It can be seen the creatures tend to cover all space. Simulations with more creatures show an increased covered area and indicate that the system as a whole seems to be ergodic [21]. It also shows that the creatures are not skewed in just one direction.

Hunger deprivation is the difference between the metabolic consumption of a creature and its energetic income from nutrients, measured in arbitrary units [18]. The metabolism is constant, thus the hunger deprivation grows at a constant rate. It reduces when the creature eats, with intensity equivalent to nutrient energetic value. When the deprivation reaches 7, the creature dies. Figure 4 shows the hunger deprivation of a typical creature, (*i.e.*, a creature whose lifetime is close to the mean lifetime of all creatures) of both implementations.

Behavioral efficiency is a function of the hunger deprivation that determines the speed and the opening of the creature's vision field, thus changing its ability to find food. It has been modeled according to Yerkes-Dodson law [22] and differs between simple and complex tasks efficiency. A simple task is the one made by a creature when sensing only one nutrient while the complex task happens when there are more than one in the sensitive field.

Figure 5 shows the temporal mean of behavioral efficiency for both implementations. The creature behavior is similar in both versions, which means the creatures of the new implementation retains a coherent behavior. In the Fig. 5a, there is a shrinkage on time axis, caused by changes made on the system to implement the actor model, which can be corrected by tuning the creature metabolic rate. In either Fig. 5a and 5b, the majority of the creatures is dead from 0.15 h on, and the results are no longer statistically valid, due to the sampling error.

Looking into the 30 superimposed tracing of both akka and no-akka implementations in Fig. 3, both experiments explore evenly the artificial world space. The akka version looks more dense, and this is given by the fact that we are running more agents in this experiment. If we look inside the indicators' average over time, arousal in Fig. 4 and behavioural efficiency in Fig. 5, we can see the curves exhibit strictly the same shape. Both the experiments have, for either simple and complex tasks, a period of reaching the maximum efficiency, a small period of stability for complex task and then its decay, while the efficiency for complex task continues growing. This is also in accordance with the results shown in the original where L2L is presented [18].

Given that functionally both implementations are similar, the main difference between the original architecture and the version presented in this paper is that, in the last one is possible to execute many creatures in the same simulation, and scale that with the number of machines in the cluster. In the first version of L2L, this was not possible due to the limitations the concurrency model based on shared memory imposes on the communication between the simulation entities. The main shared resource was the environmental shared pool where creatures and nutrients communicate. Removing this single point of communication, enabling direct communication between creatures and the environment

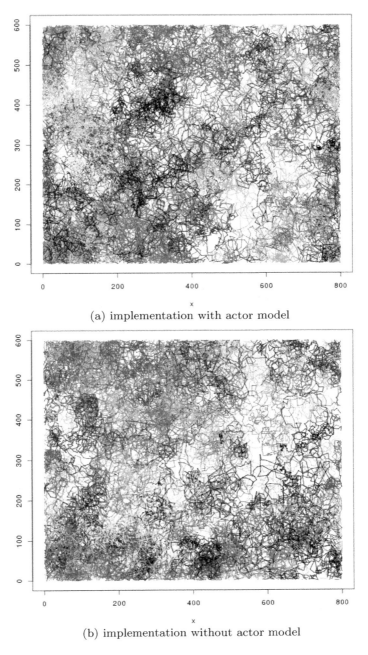

(a) implementation with actor model

(b) implementation without actor model

Fig. 3. Two dimensional plot of superimposed world exploration by 30 independent creatures. The x and y axis are Cartesian coordinates. a) in an actor-based implementation b) in a classical implementation (using threads and shared memory)

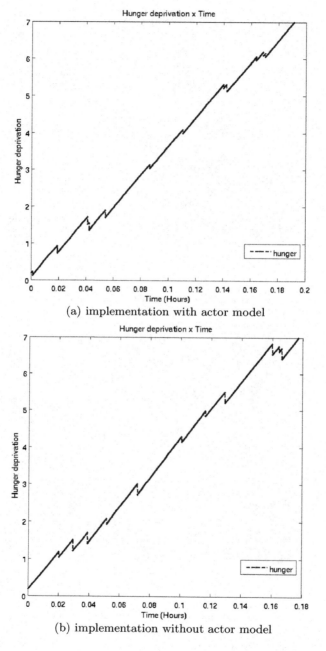

(a) implementation with actor model

(b) implementation without actor model

Fig. 4. Hunger deprivation a typical creature of both implementations.

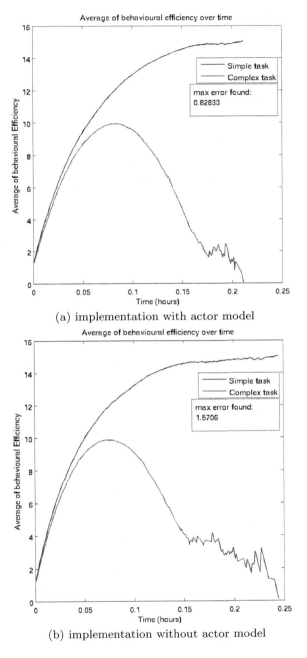

(a) implementation with actor model

(b) implementation without actor model

Fig. 5. Behavioral efficiency of creatures in both implementations.

enabled us to run many-creature simulations without performance degradation. We consider this the main contribution of this work. Future work is to enable direct communication between the internal creature components, so we expect to improve more the performance and be able to implement new structures that could show more fine social behaviors such as reproduction.

4   Conclusion

The L2L architecture was used as a foraging simulator, and while there are many more simulators of this kind, L2L has a non-deterministic spatially-explicit and temporal dynamics. Also, the system appeared to be ergodic, a point which needs further investigation. It was built having in mind the perspective of simulating population dynamics. However, the scalability problems we faced made it infeasible. Nonetheless, using the actor model, we were able to scale out the architecture to multiple machines, clustered or not, and reopen new research possibilities, including ecological simulations. A work in this direction is currently being done. Finally, the toolkit we have adopted fits well enough our purposes as our system model is asynchronous and fault tolerant. Actor-based approach may not be appropriate to all MAS, mainly those not presenting these traits. Albeit other nontraditional implementations of actor model may be useful in such scenarios.

Acknowledgment. This project has received funding from the European Union's Horizon 2020 research and innovation programme under the Marie Skłodowska-Curie grant agreement No 754382. This research has also been partially supported by Comunidad de Madrid, PROMINT-CM project (grant ref: P2018/EMT-4366) and by the project PID2020-115454GB-C21 of the Spanish Ministry of Science and Innovation (MICINN). The authors thank UAH, UFRJ and CEFET-MG for the infrastructure, and Brazilian research agencies for partially support: CAPES (Finance Code 001), FAPERJ, FAPEMIG and National Council for Scientific and Technological Development - CNPq. "The content of this publication does not reflect the official opinion of the European Union. Responsibility for the information and views expressed herein lies entirely with the author(s)."

References

1. Beecham, J.A., Farnsworth, K.D.: Animal foraging from an individual perspective: an object orientated model. Ecol. Model. **113**, 141–156 (1998)
2. An, L.: Modeling human decisions in coupled human and natural systems: review of agent-based models. Ecol. Model. **229**, 25–36 (2012)
3. Bousquet, F., Le Page, C.: Multi-agent simulations and ecosystem management: a review. Ecol. Model. **176**(3), 313–332 (2004)
4. Friedlander, D., Franklinb. S.: LIDA and a theory of mind. In: Proceedings of the first AGI Conference on Artificial General Intelligence, vol. 171, p. 137. IOS Press (2008)

5. Bach, J.: The MicroPsi agent architecture. In: Proceedings of ICCM-5, International Conference on Cognitive Modeling, Bamberg, Germany, pp. 15–20. Citeseer (2003)

6. Bach, J.: MicroPsi 2: the next generation of the MicroPsi framework. In: Bach, J., Goertzel, B., Iklé, M. (eds.) AGI 2012. LNCS (LNAI), vol. 7716, pp. 11–20. Springer, Heidelberg (2012). https://doi.org/10.1007/978-3-642-35506-6_2

7. Maturana, H.R.: Everything is said by an observer. In: Thompson, W.I. (ed.) Gaia: A Way of Knowing. Political Implications of the New Biology, pp. 11–36 (1987)

8. Hewitt, C. , Zenil, H.: What is computation? Actor model versus Turing's model. In: A Computable Universe: Understanding and Exploring Nature as Computation, pp. 159–185 (2013)

9. Angiani, G., Fornacciari, P., Lombardo, G., Poggi, A., Tomaiuolo, M.: Actors based agent modelling and simulation. In: Bajo, J., et al. (eds.) PAAMS 2018. CCIS, vol. 887, pp. 443–455. Springer, Cham (2018). https://doi.org/10.1007/978-3-319-94779-2_38

10. Parizi, M., Sileno, G., van Engers, T., Klous, S.: Run, agent, run! Architecture and benchmarking of actor-based agents. In: Proceedings of the 10th ACM SIGPLAN International Workshop on Programming Based on Actors, Agents, and Decentralized Control, pp. 11–20 (2020)

11. Leon, F.: ActressMAS, a. NET multi-agent framework inspired by the actor model. Mathematics **10**(3), 382 (2022)

12. Crafa, S.: From agent-based modeling to actor-based reactive systems in the analysis of financial networks. J. Econ. Interact. Coord. **16**(3), 649–673 (2021). https://doi.org/10.1007/s11403-021-00323-8

13. Nguyen, H., Do, T., Rotter, C.: Optimizing the resource usage of actor-based systems. J. Netw. Comput. Appl. **190**, 103143 (2021)

14. Starzec, M., Starzec, G., Byrski, A., Turek, W.: Distributed ant colony optimization based on actor model. Parallel Comput. **90**, 102573 (2019)

15. Idzik, M., Byrski, A., Turek, W., Kisiel-Dorohinicki, M.: Asynchronous actor-based approach to multiobjective hierarchical strategy. In: Krzhizhanovskaya, V.V., et al. (eds.) ICCS 2020. LNCS, vol. 12139, pp. 172–185. Springer, Cham (2020). https://doi.org/10.1007/978-3-030-50420-5_13

16. Cao, D., Hu, W., Zhao, J., Huang, Q., Chen, Z., Blaabjerg, F.: A multi-agent deep reinforcement learning based voltage regulation using coordinated PV inverters. IEEE Trans. Power Syst. **35**(5), 4120–4123 (2020)

17. Li, J., Yu, T., Zhang, X.: Coordinated load frequency control of multi-area integrated energy system using multi-agent deep reinforcement learning. Appl. Energy **306**, 117900 (2022)

18. Campos, L., Dickman, R., Graeff, F., Borges, H.: A concurrent, minimalist model for an embodied nervous system. In: International Brazilian Meeting on Cognitive Science (2015)

19. Hewitt, C.: Actor model of computation: scalable robust information systems. arXiv preprint arXiv:1008.1459 (2010)

20. Armstrong, J.: Programming Erlang: software for a concurrent world. Pragmatic Bookshelf (2007)

21. Cornfeld, I.P., Fomin, S.V., Sinai, Y.G.: Ergodic Theory, vol. 245. Springer, New York (2012)

22. Yerkes, R.M., Dodson, J.D.: The relation of strength of stimulus to rapidity of habit-formation. J. Comp. Neurol. Psychol. **18**(5), 459–482 (1908)

Stock Management Improvement in a Nursing Ward Using Lean Approach and Mathematical Modelling

Javier Rocha[1], Caroline Dominguez[1,2] , and Adelaide Cerveira[1,3(✉)]

[1] School of Science and Technology, University of Trás-os-Montes and Alto Douro, 5000-801 Vila Real, Portugal
{carold,cerveira}@utad.pt
[2] CETRAD-Center of Interdisciplinary Development Studies, Vila Real, Portugal
[3] INESC-TEC, UTAD's Pole, Vila Real, Portugal

Abstract. Reducing the costs associated with health care services is on the agenda, if possible, improving their quality. The Lean management approach has proven to provide good results in creating value and reducing waste. This paper is based on an exploratory case study in the logistic operations of a Northern Portuguese hospital, focusing on the delivery plans of products needed between the central warehouse and the internal medicine ward. Using PDCA improvement cycles and other lean tools, this study analyzed the actual delivery system, identified inefficiencies, and proposed and evaluated some solutions. The aim was to address different types of waste, such as the time the ward head nurse spent to launch orders and perform the reception/arrangement of the products or the excess of products leaving the central warehouse. Although a daily delivery with a fixed stock level seems to be a good delivery system for a large group of products, the recorded or possible failures have led us to devise an optimization model to improve the deliveries. The preliminary results suggest that a weekly plan with a daily delivery of products (to be repeated every week) is even more optimal, not only because it relieves the head nurse of logistical tasks but also because it takes into account the units of products per package.

Although this model can be generalized to other nursing wards, some limitations are addressed, namely its non (daily) standardization, leading to some complexity in its handling by the logistic central warehouse operators.

Keywords: Hospital logistics · Optimization · Waste · Lean management · Delivery plans

1 Introduction

Reducing the costs associated with health care services is on the agenda, maintaining and improving their quality. Therefore, it is important to perform changes

A. I. Pereira et al. (Eds.): OL2A 2022, CCIS 1754, pp. 714–728, 2022.
https://doi.org/10.1007/978-3-031-23236-7_49

to increase quality at lower costs. It is now well known that the Lean management approach [18] has been used with good results, not only in industries where it originated from (Toyota), but also in services, including the health services [15]. Moreover, the Lean principles and tools are increasingly used in hospitals, as presented in [6,7,11], due to the need for flexible methodologies to optimize healthcare systems. In [10], Lean tools are applied on a regular basis to the entire process flow of healthcare delivery systems. Based on the Just in Time concept, which means delivering the right quantity at the right time in the correct place, lean management seeks to create value and reduce waste in constant cycles of improvement, usually known as PDCA [12] through a set of tools which help 1) identify the steps in the operations' flow where value is (can be) created, and waste reduced, 2) plan for improvement, 3) implement the planned improvement measures, 4) check and adjust. One of the areas where hospital managers want to optimize operations is logistics, aiming to reduce costs, improve service quality, and make processes more efficient. In their state-of-the-art literature on material logistics management in hospitals, [16] indicate four focus domains: supply and procurement, inventory management, distribution and scheduling and supply chain management. In those four domains, it is always possible to detect and reduce the 8 main wastes that the lean management literature refers to: Overproduction (excess of production), Waiting (time wasted when people or machines are not working), Transportation (carrying from one place to another), Over processing (everything that the final customer is not willing to pay for), Defects (all the products/services that do not fulfill the specifications), Motion (all the movements done during an operation where no value is added), Stocks or Inventory (classic waste that is present in most organizations), People (non involvement of people in solutions).

In healthcare services, the main goal of efficient stock management is to ensure that the correct product/medicine is delivered in time to the patient without having costs of overstock or shortage. Usually, inventory means stacked money which requires more resources to be handled, such as the area needed for storage purposes (sometimes scarce in hospitals) and the teams needed to manage products. As stated in [17], stocks can overtake 25% of the value generated during the year. However, there are main reasons not to eliminate stocks, such as: production and consumption times usually do not coincide, stocks constitute leverage of external and internal disturbances (e.g. in the supply chain), the possibility of obtaining quantity discounts or ordering the economic purchase. For all these reasons, stock management is a crucial part of all institutions, including hospitals. Together with lot sizing and delivery plans of materials, stock management has been studied, and "best" models searched for. In order to know which are the best options to ensure the lower cost and better service quality with stocks, some hospitals are already considering making use of optimization models which allow managers to make the best choice based on parameters that they set or that are limited. In [2], a multi-item inventory distribution problem is proposed, motivated by a practical case study occurring in the logistic operations of a hospital which considers a single warehouse supplying several nursing wards. The goal is to determine a weekly distribution plan of medical products, ensuring a balanced workload for working teams and the satisfaction of all the required constraints (inventory capacities, safety stock levels, vehicle capacities, etc.) that minimize the total number of visits to locations. In [13], several applications of Operations Research in the domain of Healthcare are presented. They include, among others, healthcare planning aspects, such as demand forecasting, location planning issues and capacity planning. In addition, management and logistics health problems, such as patient and resource scheduling and healthcare practices with treatment planning and preventive care, are included. From the point of view of inventory management, complex problems combining inventory management and distribution decisions have received increased attention in the last years [1,3,4].

The most known models for materials delivery and distribution having consequences on stock management, are the daily, once a week, and biweekly models. This article studies the effect of some lean and optimization tools in the analysis of the current material delivery process from the central warehouse to an advanced warehouse (ward) of a Northern Portuguese hospital and studies the results of an improved optimization model, not only at the level of stocks and delivery efficiency but also at freeing resources (in this case head nurses). In order to achieve these goals, a study case of the internal medicine service will be used as a pilot, where a "waste hunt" will be launched to analyze the possibility of reducing, adjusting/improving the stocks that are being delivered and an improved model will be proposed and analyzed in order to make some recommendations.

2   Material and Methods: PDCA Cycle

A study case of the internal medicine service will be the basis of this study, focusing on the lot sizing and delivery plans from the central warehouse to the advanced warehouse of this service. The Plan Do Check Act tool was used to perform this study, [5]. In this section, only the Plan and Do phases will be presented. This will allow us to describe the current situation, set the objectives and indicate what was done to achieve the objectives.

2.1   Plan Phase

In the Plan phase it was important to clearly define the problem, analyze the context, identify the possible root causes and set the objectives. *Gemba* walks with the logistic team members were made in order to better understand their problems and concerns, having helped to characterize and describe the current situation (pre improvement situation) regarding the delivery systems in place: daily and weekly deliveries (once or twice), see Fig. 1.

Regarding the different systems of delivery being used in the hospital we can clearly notice that (Fig. 1):

- In the once a week or biweekly deliveries more stakeholders are involved, namely nurses occupied doing stock management (instead of taking care of

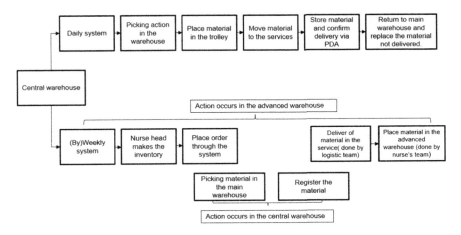

Fig. 1. Current situation of the delivery systems in the hospital.

the patients). In these system, only the quantities needed are moved from the main warehouse to the advanced ones.

– In the daily system, a fixed quantity of materials is accommodated in the transportation equipment (trolley). Since the quantity to be actually left/delivered in the advanced warehouses is decided according to the consumption of the day before, sometimes the operator returns to the central warehouse with a lot of products "not needed", leading to waste of transportation, of movement, of production excess and stocks.

Observing the situation, documents and operators of the central warehouse, it was possible to see that the products delivered to the advanced warehouses were divided in three different categories according to Pareto's principle of classification [14]: A, B and C. All the advanced warehouses had the daily and a weekly or/and bi-weekly systems working, or the 3 systems together. In this case, the advanced warehouse of the internal medicine service had the daily and bi-weekly systems functioning. As part of the Plan phase, a brainstorming session with all the stakeholders involved in the service was performed, in order to find the root causes of the excess of materials being transported, in the daily delivery system, from the central warehouse (Fig. 2). The Ishikawa's lean tool was used for that purpose [9], taking into account the known 6M dimensions that can impact a problem (Man/ Measurement/ Method/ Machine/ Material/ Environment).

The available data related to the deliveries of type A products were analyzed (daily and weekly deliveries included). The main goal was to find out the consumption behaviour of those products compared with the products actually delivered. The chart presented in Fig. 3 shows the monthly consumption behaviour and delivered quantities for a specific product between January and

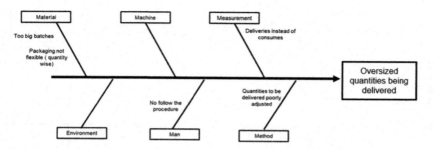

Fig. 2. Ishikawa root causes for the oversized delivered quantities.

October. It turned out that the quantity leaving the central warehouse for delivery was higher than what was consumed. This is a common situation within the products analysed. Furthermore, in this figure the proposed adjusted quantities obtained in Sect. 2.2 is presented.

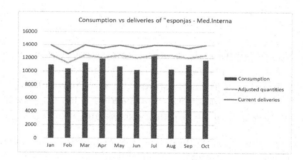

Fig. 3. Comparison between consumption and deliveries for "esponjas" (sponjes).

Based on the general current situation two main objectives were defined in this Plan Phase:

Objective 1 - Adjust the quantities of the 6 type A products being delivered in the daily system in order to reduce in 5% the difference between consumption and deliveries.

Objective 2 - Analyze and optimize the delivery plan for all 26 type A products in order to release the nurses from logistical activities performed (stock inventorying and ordering in the bi-weekly delivery system).

2.2   Do Phase

In the Do phase of the PDCA, after the previous phase gave us a clear vision of what was going on in terms of these materials in the advanced warehouses, and the goals set, it was necessary to forecast the demand in the service for these products and propose an adjustment.

For **Objective 1**, as a first step and in order to easily estimate the demand, we calculated the confidence interval at the 98% level for the average demand, based on the available sample, and we proposed the upper limit, denoted by CI, for the demand. In a second step, another method of demand forecast was used (the Simple Smoothing Method (SES)). To the forecasted quantities, a safety stock was added to ensure 98% of service level [8].

For **Objective 2**, in the Do phase, three steps were performed:

- *First step*: Analyze the possibility of extending to the remaining 20 type A products the delivery in the daily system instead of their current biweekly delivery. The products under biweekly deliveries were categorized into A, B and C, according to their price and consumption. This resulted in a list of 20 products to be considered. The data were collected and analyzed for the 3 previous years. Regarding the bi-weekly deliveries, the raw data were provided monthly. Therefore some adjustments were made, dividing the monthly quantity by the days of the month resulting in an estimation of the daily consumption. This method had a limitation consisting in the assumption that the consumption was equal every day of the month. Considering the average daily consumption during 3 years, the demands of these products were forecasted using the simple exponential smoothing method (SES) and the safety stock was considered to ensure 98% of service level [8].
- *Second step*: Compare the costs corresponding to the proposed daily deliveries (picking, transport and overstock cost) with those generated by a simulated weekly and biweekly deliveries based on the forecasted demand.
- *Third step*: Optimize the number of deliveries of each of the 26 type A products during the week, considering the second step's results. The goal is to obtain a weekly delivery plan based on three restrictions:
  - There is no obligation to have daily and fixed deliveries of the same product.
  - Ensure a certain regularity in deliveries so that there are no work peaks, requiring that the amount (number of items) of material delivered in a period has to be between 80% and 120% of the total amount of deliveries in the previous period.
  - The ward and car capacities, in volume, are also considered so that no deliveries require that employees go twice to the central warehouse.

In the following, the optimization model is presented.

Optimization Model. This section presents a MILP model to determine the optimal weekly delivery plan for supplies in the internal medicine service. Based on the demand values obtained using the simple exponential smoothing method, the weekly delivery plan consists of creating a delivery structure that optimizes the quantities in stock and meets the expected demand.

The used notation is described in the following.

Consider the sets $T = \{1, \ldots, 5\}$, and $P = \{1, \ldots, 26\}$, representing the set of time periods, corresponding to a week, and the set of products to deliver, respectively.

For each product $j \in P$: d_j represents the daily demand; k_j represents the number of items per box; c_j is the cost of a box; v_j is the volume of each box. Let CAP be the capacity of the transportation trolley. Furthermore, it has been considered that the labour cost of one employee per minute is $cm = 0.08$ € and the picking time per box/item is $tp = 0.067$ minutes and the transition time in picking per box/item is $tt = 0.3$ minutes.

We define the following decision variables:

- binary variables z_i^t take value 1 if there is a delivery of item $i \in P$ at time period $t \in T$, and 0 otherwise;
- integer variables y_i^t representing the number of boxes of item $i \in P$ delivered at time period $t \in T$.

The objective function minimizes the total cost including the purchase cost, the picking and reposition time of central warehouse operators' costs, and the storage cost, which is assumed to be 20% of the material cost. It is stated as follows.

$$minimize\ Z = \sum_{i \in P} \sum_{t \in T} \left(c_i y_i^t + 2 \cdot \left(tp \cdot y_i^t + tt \cdot z_i^t\right) \cdot cm + 0.2 \cdot c_i y_i^t\right) \tag{1}$$

The set of constraints are given by:

$$z_i^t \leq y_i^t \leq \left(7 \cdot \frac{d_i}{k_i} + 1\right) z_i^t, \qquad i \in P, t \in T \tag{2}$$

$$\sum_{\ell=1}^{t} k_i y_i^\ell \geq t \cdot d_i, \quad i \in P, t \in \{1, \ldots, 4\} \tag{3}$$

$$\sum_{t \in T} k_i y_i^t \geq 7 \cdot d_i, \qquad i \in P \tag{4}$$

$$0.8 \cdot \sum_{i \in P} y_i^t \leq \sum_{i \in P} y_i^{t+1} \leq 1.2 \cdot \sum_{i \in P} y_i^t \cdot t, \qquad t \in \{1, 2, 3\} \tag{5}$$

$$2.4 \cdot \sum_{i \in P} y_i^4 \leq \sum_{i \in P} y_i^5 \leq 3.6 \cdot \sum_{i \in P} y_i^4 \tag{6}$$

$$\sum_{t \in T} y_i^t = k \tag{7}$$

$$\sum_{t \in T} k_i y_i^t \leq 7 \cdot d_i + k_i - 0.1, \qquad i \in P \tag{8}$$

$$\sum_{p \in P} y_i^t \cdot v(i) \leq CAP \qquad t \in T \tag{9}$$

$$y_i^t \in Z_0^+, z_i^t \in \{0, 1\}, i \in P, t \in T. \tag{10}$$

Constraints (2) relate variables z and y, assuring that $z_i^t = 1$ if there are deliveries of product i at period t, otherwise it is 0. Constraints (3) and (4) assure that the demand in the internal medicine service must be met, imposing that the total quantity delivered by each day must be sufficient to meet the demand of each day. Constraints (5) and (6) state regularity in deliveries throughout the week, in terms of quantity, *i.e.*, the quantity delivered in period $t + 1$ should always be between 80 to 120% of the quantity delivered in period t. Constraint (6) is the particular case of Friday, where the material distribution is for 3 days (Friday, Saturday and Sunday).

Constraint (7) allows to restrict the number of deliveries of each item, by imposing that each item is delivered k times during the week.

Constraints (9) assure that the transportation capacity is not exceed. Constraints (10) are the variable domain constraints.

The model was constructed using FICO Xpress Mosel (Version 4.8.0) and then it was solved using the interfaces provided by these packages to the Optimizer.

3 Checking Results

As part of the PDCA cycle, after the implementation of the actions (Do phase), it is time to check the results.

For **Objective 1** (adjustment of the quantities for the 6 type A products delivered daily): During 21 days the internal medicine service was supplied with the adjusted quantities and new data were collected (shortage occurrences). These shortages were compared with the ones that would appear if the service was supplied with the existing pre-defined current quantities.

Table 1 presents the occurrence of stock shortage with the actual system, "SActual", and the stock Shortage with the adjusted proposed system, "SProposed", in number of days and in percentage,.

Results allow to conclude that the adjusted quantities were not the most accurate to improve the delivery system, since the occurrences of stock shortages increased.

After the analysis of these results, a brainstorming was made in order to understand what were the main reasons for this output:

1. In the implementation test, the service flow was higher than expected, according to the medical team's perception.
2. Short test time.
3. Connection failures in the registration of the deliveries with the PDA system.
4. A potential limitation of the statistical analysis performed based only on the confidence interval for the average deliveries independently of the time date of their observation (far away past or recent).

Table 1. Occurrences of products' shortage in the current delivery *versus* proposed one, in days and percentage.

Products	SActual		SProposed	
	(days)	(%)	(days)	(%)
Product1	0	0.0	3	14.3
Product2	0	0.0	8	38.1
Product3	0	0.0	1	4.8
Product4	1	4.8	8	38.1
Product5	0	0.0	11	52.4
Product6	1	4.8	7	33.3

Having in mind what could have happened wrong in the first trial we decided to initiate a Do sub-phase, to tackle the potential statistical limitation in the demand forecast. For that, we used the Simple Exponential Smoothing method (SES), choosing the smoothing parameter by minimizing the sum of the squared errors. This method was chosen because it is suitable for forecasting data with no clear trend or seasonal pattern [8].

By the SES method, the predicted value at instant $t + k$ using the observed data until instant t, $\hat{x}_{t+k|t}$, is given by:

$$\hat{x}_{t+1|t} = \alpha x_t + (1 - \alpha)\hat{x}_{t|t-1}, \quad \text{for } t \geq 1 \tag{11}$$

and

$$\hat{x}_{1|0} = x_1, \tag{12}$$

where $x_1, x_2, \ldots, x_n$ is the observed sample and α is the smoothing parameter, with $0 \leq \alpha \leq 1$.

– If α is chosen close to 1, we get $\hat{x}_{t+1|t} \approx x_t$ there is a weakly significant smoothing.
– If α is chosen close to 0 comes $\hat{x}_{t+1|t} \approx \hat{x}_{t|t-1}$ there is a locally intense smoothing, assigning little significance to the recent observation.

The smoothing parameter α is chosen in order to minimize the sum of the squared errors, SSE, *i.e.* minimizing

$$SSE = \frac{\sum_{t=2}^{n}(x_t - \hat{x}_{t|t-1})^2}{n - 1} \tag{13}$$

being n the sample size.

In Table 2 the stipulated current daily delivered quantities, "Stip. Daily", the proposed delivery quantities using the upper limit of confidence interval "CI", and the proposed delivery quantities using the SES method, "$\hat{x}$", and the optimal smoothing parameter, "α", are presented.

Analyzing this table, we can see that the values suggested with the SES method are different than the ones obtained by CI, some of them even lower

Table 2. Daily delivery quantities: current stipulated values; CI proposed values; SES forecast demand and optimal smoothing parameter.

Products	Stip. daily	CI	SES method	
			α	$\hat{x}$
Product 1	450	400	0.033	367
Product 2	600	500	0.174	387
Product 3	1000	800	0.141	955
Product 4	1000	800	0.163	887
Product 5	200	175	0.113	163
Product 6	200	175	0.096	175

than the initial ones, which would lead to shortages. The differences between the two proposed values, by CI and by SES, are due to the fact that in the SES, depending on the smoothing parameter, the recent past is more important in the forecast than the distant past, whereas using CI all the observations have the same importance. Since it makes more sense to not consider all observations with the same weight, we adopted the demand values obtained by using the SES method. Furthermore, we added a safety stock to ensure a 98% of service level. This safety stock was calculated based on the following formula:

$$SS = z \cdot \sigma, \tag{14}$$

where z is the percentile of a normal distribution and σ the standard deviation.

The results obtained are presented in Table 3 where "Std." is the standard deviation, "SS" is the safety stock, $\hat{x}$ is the SES forecasted demand, "Cur. Deliv." is the current daily delivery from central warehouse.

Table 3. Daily delivery quantities: stipulated values; SES forecasted demand, $\hat{x}$, with safety stock.

Product	Std.	SS	$\hat{x}$ + SS	Cur. deliv.
Product 1	16	30	397	450
Product 2	84	164	551	600
Product 3	128	253	1208	1000
Product 4	190	373	1260	1000
Product 5	23	44	207	200
Product 6	16	30	205	200

The differences in the values between the current stipulated daily delivery quantities and the forecasted ones with safety stock were presented to the nurses, in order to validate the proposed ones. In fact, the nurses mentioned that the products with suggested quantities increase by the forecast are those with more known shortages in the current situation. We considered these results as more satisfactory on one side, but not so satisfactory because some products' quantities are higher than the current ones. Unfortunately, these new values were not able to be tested.

Second Objective: Analyze and Optimize the Delivery Plan for the Remaining 26 Type A Products. The first step of the Do phase for this objective resulted in the forecasted daily demand (with the SES method) for the 20 type A products which were in the bi-weekly delivery system (Table 4). Additionally, the quantity of each product by package is indicated, which allows us to calculate the overstock and its costs.

Table 4. Daily demand of the remaining 20 products type A using the SES method with safety stock and generated overstock due to quantity of products per box.

Prod.	$\hat{x}$	Std.	SS	$\hat{x}+$SS	Qty/pack	Overstock (units)	Overstock cost (€)	Total cost (€)
P1	861	131	257	1118	200	82	0.1722	2.52
P2	132	86	170	302	200	98	0.3332	1.36
P3	236	64	126	362	1000	638	6.5714	10.3
P4	132	34	67	199	100	1	0.027	5.4
P5	66	27	55	121	100	79	0.7031	1.78
P6	125	36	70	195	100	5	0.0425	1.7
P7	115	20	39	154	100	46	0.7406	3.22
P8	91	16	31	122	100	78	1.5132	3.88
P9	78	12	23	101	100	99	2.9106	5.88
P10	91	14	28	119	80	41	1.886	7.36
P11	104	11	21	125	200	75	11.145	29.72
P12	23	4	8	31	50	19	6.8362	17.99
P13	181	27	53	234	800	566	22.923	32.4
P14	7	3	5	12	50	38	1.4478	1.905
P15	14	5	9	23	100	77	10.01	13
P16	136	23	44	180	200	20	0.972	9.72
P17	32	5	10	42	100	58	3.132	5.4
P18	38	8	15	53	100	47	4.465	9.5
P19	124	22	42	166	100	34	0.7446	4.38
P20	112	26	51	163	100	37	0.814	4.4
					Total	14966	541.7258	1202.705

In the second step of the Do phase for this second objective, using the forecasted daily demand, three delivery scenarios with different periodicity, daily, bi-weekly and weekly, were evaluated in terms of the overstock generated (units and cost), and the correspondent used transport capacity for the deliveries of the 20 products type A (Table 5).

Table 5. Overstock (quantities and cost values), % of used transport capacity and total costs/week, for 1, 2 and 7 deliveries/week

System type	Excess/week (unit)	Excess/week €	Used trolley capacity (%)	Total cost/week (€)
Daily deliveries	15099	549	11%	1202.72
Bi-weekly deliveries	3856	134.47	28%	714.50
Once a week deliveries	1392	60.65	45%	614.79

Results show that the cost with overstock decreases as the time between deliveries increases. However, other factors need to be considered, such as the volume capacity of the transportation equipment (trolley) and of the advanced warehouse. Regarding the volume capacity of this advanced warehouse, there is no space limitation.

Table 6. Optimal delivery weekly plan minimizing the total cost.

Prod.	Monday	Tuesday	Wednesday	Thursday	Friday	Excess (units)	Excess cost (€)	Delivery cost (€)
P1	16	0	8	8	24	0	0	32.76
P2	5	5	5	6	14	0	0	368.9
P3	16	0	1	5	17	50	1.21	94.38
P4	12	54	0	0	18	0	0	203.28
P5	12	12	15	15	30	0	0	203.28
Pr	1	1	1	4	0	0	0	389.2
P7	6	6	5	6	17	174	0.3654	16.8
P8	4	0	7	0	0	86	0.2924	7.48
P9	2	0	0	1	0	466	4.7998	30.9
P10	2	6	0	0	6	7	0.189	37.8
P11	2	1	6	0	0	53	0.4702	80 154
P12	4	0	2	2	6	35	0.2924	11.9
P13	2	2	7	0	0	22	0.3542	17.71
P14	2	1	2	0	4	46	0.8924	17.46
P15	2	1	5	0	0	93	2.7343	235 208
P16	2	1	8	0	0	47	2.162	40.48
P17	1	1	1	0	2	125	18.5778	148 622
P18	2	0	0	3	0	33	11.8743	8 995 675
P19	1	0	0	2	0	762	30.861	97.2
P20	1	0	1	0	0	16	0.609536	38 096
P21	1	0	0	0	1	39	5.0708	26 004
P22	1	1	1	4	0	140	6.7971	679 714
P23	1	0	2	0	0	6	0.3242	162 084
P24	1	1	0	2	0	22	2.09	38
P25	2	3	0	2	5	38	0.8322	26.28
P26	5	0	0	2	5	59	1.298	26.4
TOTAL	106	96	77	62	149		92.1	2044.32

To evaluate the remaining free capacity of the transportation tool during the daily system, we calculated the current volume being used and the complete capacity of the transport tool, taking into account the packages' dimensions. Only 32% of the volume was available to transport more material, which is a limitation to apply the weekly plan. However, there was still room to apply the bi-weekly option where the cost with material in excess is lower than in the daily option.

The third step of the Do phase was then to use the mathematical optimization model (1)–(10) in order to find the best delivery plans, taking into account the limitations and the objective of minimizing the total costs (including purchase costs of products, the cost of picking and reposition time of central warehouse operators, storage cost). In Table 6 the results obtained minimizing the total costs are presented.

Analyzing the results, we can conclude that there are some type A products that shouldn't be delivered every day. Only product 1 has daily delivery. Furthermore, on Fridays the deliveries are higher in order to fulfill the demand of the weekend. Also it is visible that the packaging with more units generates more waste with overstock. With all the model restrictions and these results, there is always a saving of head nurse time in the ward because the task of inventorying and ordering products is no longer needed, and the costs are related to the logistic team of the central warehouse.

4   Conclusions and Limitations

The main goal of this study was to propose optimized quantities of type A products to be delivered to the internal medicine advanced warehouse because the delivery plans are currently oversized and/or require time from the nursing team to manage stocks (instead of delivering healthcare). A PDCA methodology was used. After analyzing the current situation and describing the two delivery plans (daily and bi-weekly), we set the goals. First, we tried to adjust the quantities of type A products (of Pareto) being delivered on a daily basis using two statistical methods (6 products). The first method was based on the confidence interval at 98% level for the average demand. A trial was performed implementing the quantities proposed by this method, and shortages data were collected. In the current daily delivery plan, quantities are fixed, and there is no need for the nurses' stock management intervention. However, the analyzed results were not satisfying since shortages were registered. The second method used was the Simple Exponential Smoothing which allowed us to forecast new quantities to which the safety stocks were added. Unfortunately, no concrete trial for this solution was possible to perform. However, the perception of the nurses' team was that products with the larger quantities proposed by this method corresponded to the ones with more current shortages, which is positive.

In order to relieve the nurses' team from managing stocks related to the biweekly delivery, we studied the possibility of extending the number of products (from the biweekly system) to be delivered in the daily system, using the

Simple Exponential Smoothing adding to the forecasted quantities a safety stock. Calculating the costs of this solution and comparing them with the forecasted ones of the biweekly and weekly deliveries, it was clear that the daily delivery system was not the best option. Indeed the best was the weekly delivery plan. However, due to the capacity of the transportation trolley, the biweekly plan would be the best.

These results led us to find a mathematical model that would optimize the deliveries with the best compromise that would best satisfy the demand with the minimization of all costs (picking time, storage, acquisition, overstock) involved in the deliveries. The mathematical model resulted in a weekly delivery plan for each product, indicating its optimized quantities to be delivered each day of the week, having a total cost similar to the previous biweekly proposal. The limitation of this solution in comparison with the biweekly proposal is its complexity (different quantities of each product every day), meaning that the operators' tasks in the main warehouse will not be standard because the quantities of the same product differ from day to day. On the other hand, in the biweekly forecasted system, the quantities would be standard in every delivery.

This study case adds to the literature on lean and optimization management in hospitals, shedding light on the results of the different methods of forecasting products' deliveries from the central warehouse to the wards. Using some lean tools to identify the current situation, set goals and perform some improvement cycles was helpful since it resulted in a mathematical model of a delivery plan which minimizes all costs. Although this model can be generalized, it is important to know its limitations, namely a higher level of complexity due to a non-standardized delivery throughout the week.

References

1. Agra, A., Cerveira, A., Requejo, C.: A branch-and-cut algorithm for a multi-item inventory distribution problem. In: Machine Learning, Optimization, and Big Data, pp. 144–158, August 2016. https://doi.org/10.1007/978-3-319-51469-7_12
2. Agra, A., Cerveira, A., Requejo, C.: Logistic operations in a hospital: a multi-item inventory distribution problem with heterogeneous fleet. In: Barbosa-Povoa, A.P., Jenzer, H., de Miranda, J.L. (eds.) Pharmaceutical Supply Chains - Medicines Shortages. LNL, pp. 215–227. Springer, Cham (2019). https://doi.org/10.1007/978-3-030-15398-4_16
3. Bijvank, M., Vis, I.: Inventory control for point-of-use locations in hospitals. J. Oper. Res. Soc. **63**, 497–510 (2012). https://doi.org/10.1057/jors.2011.52
4. Burdett, R., Kozan, E.: An integrated approach for scheduling health care activities in a hospital. Eur. J. Oper. Res. **264** (2017). https://doi.org/10.1016/j.ejor.2017.06.051
5. Deming, W.E.: Out of the crisis. Massachusetts Institute of Technology Center for Advanced Engineering Study (1986)
6. Graban, M., Toussaint, J.: Lean Hospitals: Improving Quality, Patient Safety, and Employee Engagement. Productivity Press, New York (2018)

7. Groene, O., Botje, D., Sunol, R., López, M., Wagner, C.: A systematic review of instruments that assess the implementation of hospital quality management systems. Int. J. Qual. Health Care J. Int. Soc. Qual. Health Care/ISQua **25** (2013). https://doi.org/10.1093/intqhc/mzt058

8. Hyndman, R., Athanasopoulos, G.: Forecasting: Principles and Practice, 2nd edn. OTexts, Melbourne (2018)

9. Best, M., Neuhauser, D.J.: Kaoru Ishikawa: from fishbones to world peace. Qual. Saf. Health Care **17**(2), 150–152 (2008). https://doi.org/10.1136/qshc.2007.025692

10. Matt, D., Arcidiacono, G., Rauch, E.: Applying lean to healthcare delivery processes - a case-based research. Int. J. Adv. Sci. Eng. Inf. Technol. **8**, 123 (2018). https://doi.org/10.18517/ijaseit.8.1.4965

11. Mitchell, A., Taylor, I., Baker, M.: Making Hospitals Work. Lean Enterprise Academy Limited, Goodrich (2009)

12. Moen, R., Norman, C.: Evolution of the PDCA cycle, January 2009

13. Rais, A., Viana, A.: Operations research in healthcare: a survey. Int. Trans. Oper. Res. **18** (2010). https://doi.org/10.1111/j.1475-3995.2010.00767.x

14. Sanders, R.: The pareto principle: its use and abuse. J. Serv. Mark. **1**(2), 37–40 (1987)

15. Scoville, R., Little, K.: Comparing lean and quality improvement. IHI White Paper, pp. 1–30 (2014)

16. Volland, J., Fügener, A., Schoenfelder, J., Brunner, J.: Material logistics in hospitals: a literature review. Omega **69** (2016). https://doi.org/10.1016/j.omega.2016.08.004

17. Wilson, L.: How To Implement Lean Manufacturing. McGraw-Hill Education, New York (2010)

18. Womack, J., Jones, D., Roos, D.: The Machine That Changed the World: The Story of Lean Production, Toyota's Secret Weapon in the Global Car Wars That Is Now Revolutionizing World Industry. Free Press, New York (1990)

Monitoring Electrical and Operational Parameters of a Stamping Machine for Failure Prediction

Pedro Pecora[1]([⊠])(ID), Fernando Feijoo Garcia[2](ID), Victória Melo[1](ID),
Paulo Leitão[1](ID), and Umberto Pellegri[3]

[1] Research Center in Digitalization and Intelligent Robotics (CeDRI), Instituto
Politécnico de Bragança, Campus de Santa Apolónia, 5300-253 Bragança, Portugal
{pedropecora,victoria,pleitao}@ipb.pt
[2] Universidad de Burgos, C. Don Juan de Austria, s/n, 09001 Burgos, Spain
ffeijoo@ubu.es
[3] Catraport Lda, Zona Industrial de Mós, Lote n.° 1, 5300-692 Mós, Bragança,
Portugal
u.pellegri@p-cautomotive.pt

Abstract. Given the industrial environment, the production efficiency
is the ultimate goal to achieve a high standard. Any deviation from the
standard can be costly, e.g., a malfunction of a machine in an assembly
line tends to have a major setback in the overall factory efficiency. The
data value brought by the advent of Industry 4.0 re-shaped the way
that processes and machines are managed, being possible to analyse the
collected data in real-time to identify and prevent machine malfunctions.
In this work, a monitoring and prediction system was developed on a cold
stamping machine focusing on its electrical and operational parameters,
based on the Digital Twin approach. The proposed system ranges from
data collection to visualization, condition monitoring and prediction. The
collected data is visualized via dashboards created to provide insights
of the machine status, alongside with visual alerts related to the early
detection of trends and outliers in the machine's operation. The analysis
of the current intensity is carried out aiming to predict failures and warn
the maintenance team about possible future disturbances in the machine
condition.

Keywords: Condition monitoring · Digital Twin · IoT

1 Introduction

The digital transformation occurring in the context of Industry 4.0 [11] stimulates the emergence of new concepts and technologies, reshaping the manufacturing world. One of the main foundations for this transformation is the

Supported by FCT - Fundação para a Ciência e Tecnologia within the Project Scope
UIDB/05757/2020.

A. I. Pereira et al. (Eds.): OL2A 2022, CCIS 1754, pp. 729–743, 2022.
https://doi.org/10.1007/978-3-031-23236-7_50

adoption of cyber-physical components, which are represented by intelligent and connected assets and products that are part of a dynamic ecosystem. The integration of these components forms the Cyber-Physical Systems (CPS), that are complex engineering systems that integrates physical, computation/ networking, and communication processes [13], which can improve the resource productivity and efficiency, the production systems' performance, responsiveness and reconfigurability, can efficiently manage the complexity and uncertainty and enable more flexible models of work organization [4,16].

Industrial manufacturing environments are considered dynamic and chaotic. Therefore, the implementation of maintenance systems becomes the key to ensure production efficiency, since the occurrence of unexpected disturbances can cause system performance degradation and, consequently, loss of productivity and business opportunities, critical factors in terms of competitiveness [2]. In terms of maintenance decisions, machine diagnostics can be performed after a failure has occurred, being a reactive approach that cannot prevent downtime and associated costs. Although, a shift in maintenance strategy from traditional fail-and-fix (diagnostics) to a predict-and-prevent approach (prognostics) is required, performing the maintenance in a proactive manner to reduce its costs and ensure the greatest feasible machine uptime [14]. Therefore, one of the important tasks in the performance of industrial machines is the monitoring of their health condition, in order to identify their performance and to early determine failures and/or the need to optimize their operating parameters. Traditionally, this condition monitoring uses techniques that are very targeted, case by case, to the particularities and requirements of the machine in question.

Given the idea of condition monitoring, predictive maintenance (PdM) proactively plans maintenance tasks based on a system's current and predicted future condition. With the advent of new technologies, such as the Industrial Internet of Things (IIoT) or Cloud Computing, and the continuing decline of costs for necessary hardware, PdM is becoming more attractive for the whole production sector [6]. However, PdM still relies in the expertise of technicians for a correct interpretation of the data [9]. Moreover, the increasing quantity of available data increases the complexity of treatment and interpretation [23]. Each sensor, e.g., pressure, temperature, vibration, and electrical current, provides new dimensions to be analyzed. Artificial Intelligence (AI) is applied in this context, with time series data series automatically being classified in different categories corresponding to healthy, degradation and critical stages, or used to calculate healthy metrics, e.g., Time-to-Failure or Remaining Useful Life (RUL) [15]. Machine Learning algorithms are suitable to deal with multivariate problems. As an example, Susto et al. [21] applied a multiple classifier approach based on Support Vector Machine and k-Nearest Neighbors classifiers to define the PdM policy in semiconductor manufacturing process with data from 31 sensors. Lu et al. [17] proposed a clustering diagnostic method for bearings using features extracted from the vibration signal. Juez-Gil et al. [10] proposed a method to early detect multi-faults in induction motors based on Principal Component Analysis and multilabel decision trees using voltages, stator currents, rotational speed and vibrations. Carvalho *et al.* [3] provides a review on ML techniques and their application to PdM.

The adoption of emerging digital techniques in the context of Industry 4.0 allows leveraging the development of new solutions based on the collection of data from heterogeneous sources through the use of, e.g., sensor networks and IoT technologies. These sources can be combined with AI techniques for further analysis, aiming to make this data available for data-driven systems enabling, e.g., monitoring, diagnosis, prediction and optimization [18].

The Digital Twin concept is being largely adopted to enable the condition monitoring for manufacturing resources. According to [20], a Digital Twin is a digital copy of a physical object or system, that is connected and shares functional and/or operational data, enabling the collected data to be later analyzed to allow the optimization and improvement of the physical object. In this sense, this data is collected by machines' controllers and external sensors and used for the synchronous adjustment of digital models and their simulation, allowing the monitoring and prediction of the condition and status of the machines as a result from the simulation of physics-based models, without the use of invasive techniques commonly used in predictive maintenance solutions [1]. The use of the Digital Twin concept will significantly contribute to the development of Industry 4.0 compliant solutions, allowing the use of a virtual machine model that is aligned with real-time data and the integration of various emerging digital technologies for its operation, such as IoT, AI, and cloud computing. However, the implementation of the Digital Twin solution faces many difficulties in industrial environment. Mainly due to the shop floor constrains and the parameters to be analyzed, including also the need to ensure the security of this data to guarantee the integrity of the company's private data privacy [5].

Having this in mind, the objective of this paper is to develop a condition monitoring and prediction system that uses IoT, AI and cloud technologies, taking advantage of the fusion of operational and electrical data encapsulated in the Digital Twin concept. The designed condition monitoring system was deployed in an industrial metal stamping press, with the achieved preliminary experimental results contributing for the improvement of the system efficiency.

The rest of the paper is organized as follows: Sect. 2 describes the case study and introduces the Digital Twin based condition monitoring system architecture. Section 3 presents the deployment of the Digital Twin based condition monitoring for the industrial case study and Sect. 4 describes the implementation of a Recurrent Neural Network (RNN) algorithm to forecast the current intensity that will allow to predict failures in the machine. Finally, Sect. 5 rounds up the paper with the conclusion and points out some future work.

2 Digital Twin Condition Monitoring System Architecture

This chapter describes the designed condition monitoring and prediction system architecture for the industrial case study using the digital twin concept.

2.1   Description of the Case Study

The case study considered in this work considers an industrial metal cold stamping machine, hosted in the Catraport factory plant, illustrated in Fig. 1, that stamps metal parts to make complex shapes, applying up to 600 tons of force and operating in a range of 1 to 60 strikes per minute. As the machine has various stamping dies, the process can vary in the number of stamping steps it takes to make a final piece, and also in the pressure of each strike, among other variables.

Fig. 1. Metal cold stamping machine used as industrial case study.

This type of machine is supplied with a metal coil to be pressed through a feeding system, composed by an steel roll placed at one end point and a transfer system responsible for unrolling the steel sheet, which moves with each stroke. These systems operate synchronously through the use of a PLC (Programmable Logic Controller) alongside with motor controllers that are responsible of controlling all the three phases of the stamping machine. The machine is equipped with some loggers to collect the warnings and errors generated during its operation, accessible through excel spreadsheets, but operational and electrical data is not automatically available to support the condition monitoring and the failure prediction.

2.2   System Architecture

The architecture of the proposed condition monitoring and prediction system is illustrated in Fig. 2, and takes advantage of the analysis of the collected real-time data, to identify abnormalities and failures in advance, as well as to perform diagnosis and optimization in the machine operation. This architecture is based on the use of the Digital Twin concept, that brings the capability to digitize an asset as a virtual model that is fed with the real-time data to perform condition monitoring and failure prediction. The Digital Twin is complemented with the use of several digital technologies, namely IoT and AI, that will support the collection, transmission, storing and visualization of data and their posterior analysis to extract value and knowledge.

As seen in Fig. 2, the physical asset comprises a set of sensors to acquire the operational and electrical data, namely vibration, current intensity, power and power factor. This data is made available to the Digital Twin hosted in the cloud by using IoT communication protocols, e.g., publish-subscribe and request-response, allowing the scalable and loosely coupled design of condition monitoring solutions.

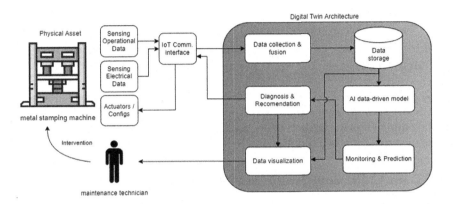

Fig. 2. Digital Twin based condition monitoring system architecture.

The *data collection and fusion* module is responsible for gathering the machine's electrical and operational data via a IoT communication protocol. The collected data is cleaned, aggregated and stored in a database for posterior analysis. Since heterogeneous data sources are considered, this module also includes data fusion tasks, particularly focusing multi-temporal and multi-spacial fusion. Key aspects to be considered in the data collection are related to the scale and frequency of the data acquisition as well as the clock synchronization to ensure the harmonization in the time stamps of different data sources.

The *data visualization* module allows the visualization of the collected data in an user interface through dashboards that makes use of time series graphs, gauges and icons to show the evolution of some parameters along the time, as well as some Key Performance Indicators (KPIs), illustrated through the use of statistical measures, like the average and the standard deviation. The dashboard must be designed to be illustrative and simple to be understood, and yet provide useful information regarding to the machine operation.

The *monitoring and prediction* module is responsible for the identification of anomalies and performance degradation, by applying abnormalities detection algorithms in the collected data and the early detection of possible failures, by applying trend detection and machine learning algorithms, that correlate the different machine parameters to forecast future occurrences. This task should consider the analysis of the streaming data.

The *diagnosis and recommendation* module is responsible to perform a diagnosis of the monitored data, as mentioned above, and make recommendations to improve and optimize the system performance. This recommendation can be simple alerts to the users, suggestions of the machine operation configuration or the need for maintenance interventions to the technicians, or even automatic change of the operation configuration in the machine. The information resulting from this module is also made available in the interface designed for the user to facilitate the understanding of the system's operation and support the necessary decision-making actions.

3   Deployment of the Digital Twin Based Condition Monitoring

The digital twin based condition monitoring and prediction system architecture described in the previous section is applied to the industrial case study, which special emphasis is in the data collection, visualization and monitoring to support the early prediction of failures.

3.1   Data Collection, Fusion and Storage

In the case study, data is collected from different data sources, focusing some operational and electrical parameters. The operational data, namely the vibration of the machine in the X, Y and Z axis, is collected with a frequency of 5 samples per second by a LSM303 compass that has a 3-axis accelerometer with 16-bit data output, supporting ±16 g acceleration. This sensor is connected to an ESP8266 microcontroller through the Inter-Integrated Circuit (I^2C) protocol. The electrical data, namely voltage, current intensity and power-related data, is collected each 5 s using an IoTWatt device [8]. The installation of these devices is shown in Fig. 3.

These sensing modules constitute IoT nodes capable of acquiring and transmitting the collected data over Wi-Fi, following a JSON format, and publishing them onto a time-series driven database directly, using the HTTP protocol. In this work, the InfluxDB database was used, taking advantage of its high-performance time series engine [7] and its easy integration with data visualization platforms, such as Grafana. The collected data is published through the Influx's API service, being used a virtual machine running Ubuntu 20.04.4, with 16GB of RAM and AMD EPYC 7351 16-core processor to serve as an anchor point to the published data. It is important to point out that this is a private cloud, which ensure data security and privacy. Table 1 summarizes some collected electrical and operational parameters that are stored in the database (note that α represents the different measured electrical phases).

Data related to warning and machine breakdowns, such as lack of oil in the strike chamber, micro-stops, step adjustment, and tool change is also collected

Fig. 3. IoT devices installed in the stamping machine. On the left, the IoTaWatt, and on the right, the ESP8266 including the LSM303 sensor.

using Excel files. This data is manually cleaned and fused, since each work order creates a new process order, containing more than only stops.

Table 1. Stored electrical and operational data

Parameter	Description
Curr_phaseα	Current intensity measured in the α phase [A]
PF_phaseα	Power factor measured in the α phase
Power_phaseα	Power measured in the α phase [W]
Frequency	Frequency of the reference power supply [Hz]
Voltage	Voltage of the reference power supply [V]
Accel_X	Vibration in the X axis [m/s^2]
Accel_Y	Vibration in the Y axis [m/s^2]
Accel_Z	Vibration in the Z axis [m/s^2]

The aggregated stored data becomes available for visualization, monitoring and prediction, through the other digital twin modules.

3.2 Visualization and Monitoring

The data visualization is performed by using the Grafana software platform, a web-server tool that is installed in the same virtual machine, allowing the easy communication between the database and the web-server. Aiming to develop an user-friendly and easy-to-understand interface, the dashboard displays some important electrical and operational parameters, as well as some alerts related to the system operation, KPIs, being illustrated in Fig. 4.

The left part of the dashboard is designed to illustrate the evolution of the power, current and power factor for the three phases over time. The middle part

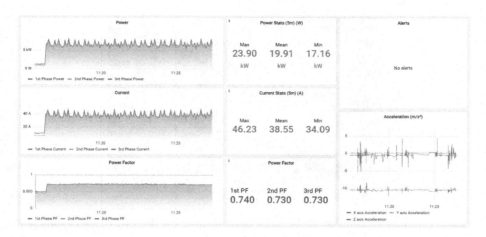

Fig. 4. Dashboard for visualization of the collected parameters.

shows the KPIs for these electrical parameters, namely the minimum, average, and maximum values, with a moving window that considers a predefined amount of last collected data, in this case 5 min. On the top right of the dashboard, an alert panel is presented, where the detected alerts regarding the monitoring can be shown. Lastly, on the bottom right the acceleration measurements are presented using time series graphs for the three axis.

A color scheme is used to highlight the particularities of the data, giving the user a better understanding of the values. For this purpose, the illustrated values regarding the electrical parameters are color-coded. Similar dashboards were deployed to illustrate the vibration data and the machine's stops/warnings.

Aiming to monitor the health condition of the stamping machine to support its correct operation and also to detect abnormal situations, preferably in advance, the collected data is analyzed in real-time. For this purpose, alerts are generated to warn risk situations related to the functioning of the stamping machine, e.g., in case of peaks in the current or power, or excessive vibration in one axis. These alerts are generated by applying Nelson rules [19], which is a process control method that use the mean value and the standard deviation to determine if a measured variable is out of control or presents a trend that shows that the variable is near to be out of control. In the deployed system, Rules 1, 3, 4 and 6, illustrated in Fig. 5, are implemented.

Briefly, rule 1 is used to detect an outlier in the operation of the stamping machine and is triggered when a value of the variable being analyzed is greater, or lower than 3σ from the mean. Rule 3 allows identifying a continuous growth trend in values of the measured variable, i.e. six successive increasing values in a row, allowing to detect in advance possible failures. Rule 4 uses fourteen or more values in a row, to pinpoint a variance that is not more a standard noise. It disregards their position relative to mean, checking only if they alternate in direction, increasing and then decreasing. Rule 6 identifies a tendency of the machine to be slightly out of control during the stamping process, by checking four successive values that are more than 1σ both above or below from the mean.

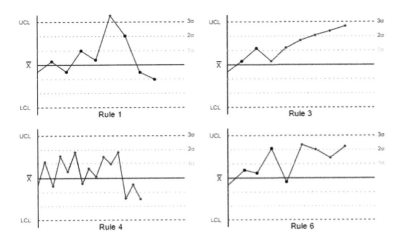

Fig. 5. Implemented Nelson rules, with red dots representing values that may trigger the rule (adapted from [19]). (Color figure online)

These rules were applied for the variables of current and vibration in all three axis, according to their mean and standard deviation values considering the normal operation. The monitoring of the vibration in Z axis is illustrated in Fig. 6. The distinct red and green areas show the corrected threshold for Rule 1 to be fired, and the red circles are examples of when the rule is fired. The generated alerts appear on the dashboard as notes, showing which measure is near to be out-of-control and also triggering emails that are sent to the maintenance department, notifying the type and time of problem that has occurred.

Upon analyzing the electrical data, the power factor value stood out as being a low number. A more in-depth analysis showed that the power factor value for every phase was below the legally desired value of 0.96 (since 2010, Portugal actively penalizes industries with a power factor lower than 0.96). A further study about this problem was triggered and a cost-effective solution was proposed, based on the implementation of a capacitor bank, to correct this lag between the measured power factor value and the desired value.

4   Prediction of Failures

Besides the monitoring, the developed system was also able to predict the failures that occurs in the machine operation.

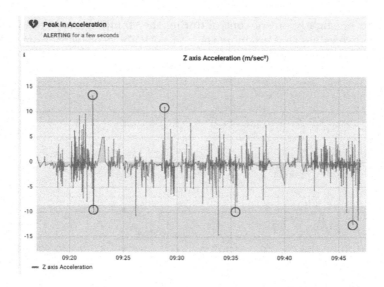

Fig. 6. Monitoring Z vibration and alerts triggered by the implemented rules. (Color figure online)

4.1 Clustering Technique Applied to Oil Alarms

A first evaluation of the press machine operation was performed to analyse possible failures due to the high pressure in the oil. Interruptions due to high oil pressure alarm, which prevents further damage in mechanical parts due to over-stress, occurred 12 times during the one month data collection period. The feasibility of prediction of this alarm has been studied using the electric data obtained from the data collection and fusion module.

The data has been divided into 12 series corresponding to the data collected between oil alarms and subjected to summary statistics, such as mean, standard deviation, skewness, and kurtosis that are illustrated in Table 2, which can provide aggregated information of the time series [17,21,22]. They have been calculated using a 30 samples (2.5 min) sliding window over the phase 1 current. Three series have been discarded because they were too short for the sliding window.

Table 2. Summary of statistical features: mean (F1), standard deviation (F2), skewness (F3) and kurtosis (F4).

$$F_1 = \bar{x} = \frac{1}{n}\left(\sum_{i=1}^{n} x_i\right) \quad F_2 = \sigma = \sqrt{\frac{\sum_{i=1}^{n}(x_i - \bar{x})^2}{n-1}}$$

$$F_3 = \frac{\sum_{i=1}^{n}(x_i - \bar{x})^3}{(n-1)\sigma^3} \quad F_4 = \frac{\sum_{i=1}^{n}(x_i - \bar{x})^4}{(n-1)\sigma^4}$$

Figure 7 shows the results of plotting the complete set of features for one case of failure. The data have been divided in 3 categories: values corresponding to 10 min prior to the failure are classified as 3, values between 60 min and 10 min before the failure are classified as 2, and the values from the starting of the process to 60 min before the failure are classified as 1. In addition to the classification, the points were colored for an easier understanding: points over 60 min are designed a gray color, points between 60 and 10 min are colored as yellow, and points below 10 min are colored as red.

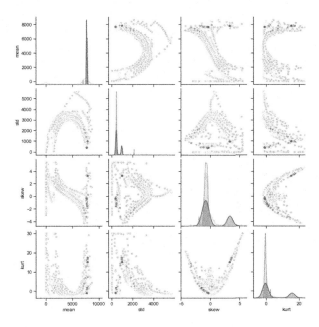

Fig. 7. Relationship between features for one failure type (oil alarm). (Color figure online)

Upon plotting the statistical features, it was desirable to find a potential cluster of values near-failure. However, it can be observed that for each correlation, the red and yellow points are disperse and with many gray dots in the vicinity, not allowing an accurate prediction. In the other hand, this analysis unveiled a new view point of the data, where the analysis of the physical data should be used along to analyze possible correlations, using vibration data and additional features in time and frequency domains.

4.2   Forecasting the Current Intensity

As stated before, due to overlapping points between near-failure conditions and normal working conditions, it is hard to create a classification algorithm. However, the proposed approach considers a ML algorithm to predict the current intensity, since it is one of the parameters being monitored by the Nelson rules, aiming to predict of anomalies, such as spikes or trends, to provide early triggers to the maintenance team to work quickly and mitigate the failure occurrence.

The chosen ML algorithm is the Convolutional Neural Network (CNN) Bi-directional-LSTM (Bi-LSTM), named EECP-CBL. The CNN part extracts the key information over the desired variables, and the Bi-LSTM part analyzes the data by forward and back propagation to make the predictions. The network's inputs are the current intensity, power factor and power for each phase.

The LSTM's layout is based in the layout presented in [12], consisting of a CNN to conglomerate the input variables. Two Bi-LSTM layers are considered, consisting of 64 units each. The output is composed of two standard densely connected layers, the last one, with the number of units equals to the number of samples to predict, an illustration of this layout is presented in Fig. 8. The compiled model have the Adaptive Moment Estimation (Adam) function as the optimizer, and the mean squared error as the loss function.

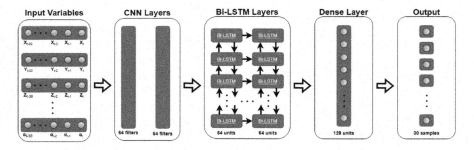

Fig. 8. The proposed network layout. Adapted from [12].

The cleaned data consists of 43,845 points, sampled every 20 s over the span of a month. The data points were splited in 80% for training, and 20% for tests. During all the tests, the amount of timesteps for the forecasted data and previous data is the same, i.e. for a forecast of 3 min, 3 min of previous data is used.

For means of comparison, Table 3 compares some common metrics such as the Root Mean Square Error (RMSE), Mean Absolute Error (MAE) and Mean Absolute Percentage Error (MAPE) on the test data. These metrics are widely used as a way to check the generalization capabilities of the trained network. As a ground truth to check the model's performance, the model predicted 20 s (1 sample), 3 min (9 samples) and 5 min (15 samples) ahead, against the autoregressive integrated moving average (ARIMA) model, with an order of p = 8, d = 0 and q = 2, that corresponds to the autoregressive, the differentiative, in case of a data with trends, and the moving average components.

The achieved results show that the EECP-CBL network performed better than the ARIMA model for a single step ahead, and upon further testing, the EECP-CBL out scales the ARIMA, since ARIMA tends to converge to the mean

Table 3. Comparison between the proposed EECP-CBL and ARIMA model

Model	Forecasted steps	RMSE [A]	MAE [A]	MAPE [%]
EECP-CBL	1	5.40	2.83	39.62
	9	11.30	8.48	26.64
	15	8.30	6.83	40.45
ARIMA	1	11.93	11.93	97.95
	9	13.53	13.41	49.31
	15	13.83	13.76	76.38

of the data, and the proposed model learned from the train data, being a more generalized model for the problem. A live-data application of the model is illustrated on Fig. 9, where the yellow line is the forecast intensity and the green line the real intensity. It is possible to visualize that, although the prediction is not as accurate, the model was able to successfully generalize the high peaks in the current intensity, therefore being able to generate an alert to the technician as intended.

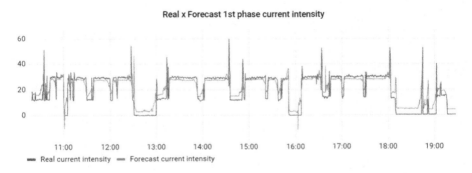

Fig. 9. Real and forecast current intensity comparison. (Color figure online)

Note that the trained model was implemented in the monitoring and prediction system, gathering live data from the data storage module as part of the Digital Twin, as its inputs. For each forecast value, the Nelson Rules were applied allowing to trigger alerts to the maintenance team.

5   Conclusions

The condition monitoring, as part of the predictive maintenance of industrial machines, is currently a critical issue aiming to increase the system performance. The use of emergent digital technologies under the scope of Industry 4.0, e.g., IoT, AI, and Digital Twin, can contribute to develop more efficient systems.

This paper describes the implementation of a Digital Twin approach developed for monitoring electrical and operational parameters of an industrial cold stamp machine. This approach allows extracting information from the collected data to supervise machine's condition operation and to detect anomalies and performance degradation in advance, supporting the diagnosis, prediction and optimization of the machine's operation. For the visualization of the system's data, a user interface was created, displaying the system data, statistical information and the alerts generated through the implementation of control rules.

The monitoring of the system is carried out via Nelson Rules, that can detect samples out of control, trends, and uncommon oscillations while the machine is working. Aiming to foresee potential dangers, The prediction of failures was performed by using the EECP-CBL algorithm to forecast the value of the current intensity 5 min ahead, which allows the maintenance team to react aiming to mitigate the possible occurrence of such failure.

The application of ML techniques in industrial environments faces multiple difficulties due to the peculiarities of this environment. While most of the works consider data sets obtained in a laboratory, with controlled conditions, in this case the capture of data had to cope with the noise and daily movements of a factory, which makes more difficult to obtain steady data. Future work will be devoted to implement more powerful ML algorithms to identify more complex correlations among the collected data in the industrial case study, as well as to implement the diagnosis and recommendation module using also ML algorithms.

References

1. Aivaliotis, P., Georgoulias, K., Chryssolouris, G.: The use of Digital Twin for predictive maintenance in manufacturing. Int. J. Comput. Integr. Manuf. **32**(11), 1067–1080 (2019). https://doi.org/10.1080/0951192X.2019.1686173
2. Alves, F., et al.: Deployment of a smart and predictive maintenance system in an industrial case study. In: Proceeding of the 29th IEEE International Symposium on Industrial Electronics (ISIE 2020), pp. 493–498 (2020)
3. Carvalho, T., Soares, F., Vita, R., Francisco, R., Basto, J., Alcalá, S.: A systematic literature review of machine learning methods applied to predictive maintenance. Comput. Ind. Eng. **137**, 106024 (2019)
4. Germany Trade & Invest (GTAI): INDUSTRIE 4.0 - Smart Manufacturing for the Future (2014)
5. Hearn, M., Rix, S.: Cybersecurity considerations for Digital Twin implementations. IIC J. Innov., 107–113 (2019)
6. Hesabi, H., Nourelfath, M., Hajji, A.: A deep learning predictive model for selective maintenance optimization. Reliab. Eng. Syst. Saf. **219**, 108191 (2022)
7. InfluxDB: Influxdb: Open source time series database. https://www.influxdata.com. Accessed 27 Apr 2022
8. IoTaWatt: IoTaWatt - Open WiFi Electricity Monitor. https://iotawatt.com/. Accessed 26 Apr 2022
9. Jardine, A., Lin, D., Banjevic, D.: A review on machinery diagnostics and prognostics implementing condition-based maintenance. Mech. Syst. Signal Process. **20**(7), 1483–1510 (2006)

10. Juez-Gil, M., et al.: Early and extremely early multi-label fault diagnosis in induction motors. ISA Trans. **106**, 367–381 (2020)
11. Kagermann, H., Wahlster, W., Helbig, J.: Recommendations for implementing the strategic initiative INDUSTRIE 4.0. Final report of the Industrie 4.0 WG (2013)
12. Le, T., Vo, M.T., Vo, B., Hwang, E., Rho, S., Baik, S.W.: Improving electric energy consumption prediction using CNN and Bi-LSTM. App. Sci. **9**(20), 4237 (2019)
13. Lee, J.: Smart factory systems. Informatik-Spektrum **38**(3), 230–235 (2015)
14. Lee, J., Wu, F., Zhao, W., Ghaffari, M., Liao, L., Siegel, D.: Prognostics and health management design for rotary machinery systems—reviews, methodology and applications. Mech. Syst. Signal Process. **42**(1–2), 314–334 (2014)
15. Lei, Y., Li, N., Guo, L., Li, N., Yan, T., Lin, J.: Machinery health prognostics: a systematic review from data acquisition to RUL prediction. Mech. Syst. Signal Process. **104**, 799–834 (2018)
16. Leitão, P., Barbosa, J., Funchal, G., Melo, V.: Self-organized cyber-physical conveyor system using multi-agent systems. Int. J. Artif. Intell. **18**(2), 171–185 (2020)
17. Lu, Y., Xie, R., Liang, S.Y.: CEEMD-assisted bearing degradation assessment using tight clustering. Int. J. Adv. Manuf. Technol. **104**(1), 1259–1267 (2019)
18. Melo, V., Funchal, G., Queiroz, J., Leitão, P.: A fuzzy logic approach for self-managing energy efficiency in IoT nodes. In: Camarinha-Matos, L.M., Heijenk, G., Katkoori, S., Strous, L. (eds.) IFIPIoT 2021. IFIP AICT, vol. 641, pp. 237–251. Springer, Cham (2022). https://doi.org/10.1007/978-3-030-96466-5_15
19. Nelson, L.S.: The Shewhart Control Chart-Tests for Special Causes. J. Qual. Technol. **16**(4), 237–239 (1984)
20. Pires, F., Melo, V., Almeida, J., Leitão, P.: Digital Twin experiments focusing virtualisation, connectivity and real-time monitoring. In: Proceedings of IEEE Conference on Industrial Cyberphysical Systems (ICPS 2020), vol. 1, pp. 309–314 (2020)
21. Susto, G.A., Schirru, A., Pampuri, S., McLoone, S., Beghi, A.: Machine learning for predictive maintenance: a multiple classifier approach. IEEE Trans. Ind. Inf. **11**(3), 812–820 (2015)
22. Worden, K., Staszewski, W.J., Hensman, J.J.: Natural computing for mechanical systems research: a tutorial overview. Mech. Syst. Signal Process. **25**, 4–111 (2011)
23. Wuest, T., Weimer, D., Irgens, C., Thoben, K.D.: Machine learning in manufacturing: advantages, challenges, and applications. Prod. Manuf. Res. **4**(1), 23–45 (2016)

Computer Vision Based on Learning Algorithms

Super-Resolution Face Recognition: An Approach Using Generative Adversarial Networks and Joint-Learn

Rafael Augusto de Oliveira[1]([✉]), Michel Hanzen Scheeren[2],
Pedro João Soares Rodrigues[1], Arnaldo Candido Junior[3],
and Pedro Luiz de Paula Filho[2]

[1] Instituto Politécnico de Bragança, Bragança, Portugal
olirafa@protonmail.com
[2] Universidade Tecnológica Federal do Paraná, Paraná, Brazil
michelscheeren@alunos.utfpr.edu.br
[3] Universidade Estadual Paulista, São Paulo, Brazil
arnaldo.candido@unesp.br

Abstract. Face Recognition is a challenging task present in different applications and systems. An existing challenge is to recognize faces when imaging conditions are adverse, for example when images come from low-quality cameras or when the subject and the camera are far apart, thus impacting the accuracy of these recognizing systems. Super-Resolution techniques can be used to improve both image resolution and quality, hopefully improving the accuracy of the face recognition task. Among these techniques, the actual state-of-the-art uses Generative Adversarial Networks. One promising option is to train Super-Resolution and Face Recognition as one single network, conducting the network to learn super resolution features that will improve its capability when recognizing faces. In the present work, we trained a super resolution face recognition model using a jointly-learn approach, combining a generative network for super resolution and a ResNet50 for Face Recognition. The model was trained with a discriminator network, following the generative adversarial training. The images generated by the network were convincing, but we could not converge the face recognition model. We hope that our contributions could help future works on this topic. Code is publicly available at https://github.com/OliRafa/SRFR-GAN.

Keywords: Super-resolution · Face Recognition · Generative Adversarial Networks · Machine learning

1 Introduction

Face Recognition (FR) is present in several tasks, such as face filters in social media, authentication/unlocking for smartphone and other devices, building

Supported by Universidade Tecnológica Federal do Paraná and Instituto Politécnico de Bragança.

access liberation, and missing person recognition. It is performed by extracting characteristics (or biometrics) from faces and can be used, for example, to identify people in photos or videos.

There are challenges for FR, such as the resolution of cameras already installed in facilities, the distance between the camera and the subject (which causes low-resolution sub-images), and possible artifacts on image capture. In order to capture images with better resolutions, the change of cameras would be required, as well as changes in the infrastructure around the cameras, since new captured image need more storage and network traffic, resulting in additional costs.

In order to improve this system, Super-Resolution (SR) techniques could be used to enhance resolution of images and their quality. SR is a method to reconstruct high-quality images derived from one or more low-quality ones, aiming on reducing existing image degradations [18], and providing FR system better images for feature extraction. This method can be applied to FR in order to reduce costs and improve accuracy. Among existing SR techniques, the ones that use Deep Learning are the most promising, and has the best results to date, more specifically the ones using Generative Adversarial Networks (GANs), which are considered the state-of-the-art.

For FR on low quality images, one promising technique is to train both SR and FR networks at the same time, using what is called a Joint-Learn approach, as suggested by [3]. The main objective of this study is to evaluate whether Face Recognition could be enhanced by Generative Super-Resolution trained in Joint-Learn.

2   Related Work

Some works shown that low resolution images reduces accuracy of FR networks by a significant amount. [13] demonstrated that the recognition rate of a 200×220 px image downsampled more than 90% (20×22 px or less) dropped significantly. [6,14] tested the performance of Principal Component Analysis (PCA) and Elastic Bunch Graph Matching varying the pixel distance between the eyes using the values 111, 56, 28, 14, and 7 px. They observed that the performance dropped while the distance between eyes were reduced.

[9] proposed three strategies to mitigate this problem: (i) reducing the images on database to a compatible resolution to the input ones; (ii) applying SR to the input image, augmenting its resolution to match the resolution of images on the database; (iii) applying SR and biometrics extraction simultaneously.

[20] utilized SR to improve object detection on satellite images. The two methods utilized were Very Deep Super Resolution (VDSR) [11] and Random-Forest Super-Resolution, created by the authors to compare a simple and light method to a state-of-the-art convolutional network. The approach was used together with the detection methods YOLT and SSD from the framework SIM-RDWN. Using the dataset xView, the detection accuracy improved between 13% and 36%.

Using SR on faces, [19] used a SRCNN (Super-Resolution Convolutional Neural Network) [5] to augment face images, extracting them from high resolution images using Haar Cascade, and reducing its size from 60×60 px to 15×15 px. Next, the images were presented to a FR network, using HMMs (Hidden Markov Models) and SVD (Singular Value Decomposition) algorithms. They utilized datasets Essex, HP, FERET, and iCV-F (the last one created by the authors) and they obtained an improvement up until 46.96% on FR accuracy compared to recognizing those faces directly on low resolution images.

In [23], the authors tried four different Convolutional Neural Networks (CNNs), testing them on UCSS dataset, achieving results of 59.03% on the best model.

The most used method to train SR networks is to use low resolution images artificially reduced from high resolution images. The SR FR systems, as showed by [3], have better accuracy on those artificially low resolution images compared to natively low resolution ones. Another problem the authors found is that when a FR network is used with a SR network on native low resolution datasets the FR had worse accuracy in all cases, possibly because the SR network was adding noise and artifacts on the super-resolved images. This implies that, when used as a separate network, SR isn't helping to better recognize faces, but instead it is degrading its performance, contradicting the second strategy proposed by [9].

Based on the exposed problems, [3] proposed the network Complement Super-Resolution and face Identity (CSRI), which is a model composed by a SR and a FR network trained together, which is called Joint-Learn. The idea behind this approach is that the network would learn the most important features on SR that would help on recognizing faces. This model has two branches, there is, two parallel convolutional layers. The first branch is used to train the model from scratch, having artificial low resolution images as its input. The second branch is used on the fine-tuning stage, having only native low resolution images as input. Both branches connect into a VDSR [11] network which outputs a super-resolved image to the CenterFace [25] network, where the face is recognized. This system was trained on the CelebA dataset, fine-tuned on the TinyFace dataset (which was created by the authors on the same paper) and tested on TinyFace and MegaFace2 datasets (the former had its resolution artificially reduced). Using this approach, the authors improved the accuracy of the Rank-1 recognition by 12.7% on the dataset TinyFace in comparison with the best model (44.8% vs 32.1%).

On the SR side, the first attempt to apply GANs to this problem was made by [12] with their network SRGAN. In their work, they presented a new loss function to reduce the blur on images outputted using Mean Squared Error-based functions, leading to perceptually better images, with richer textures. With these improvements their network became state-of-the-art.

In order to improve this architecture, [22] introduced the concept of Residual-in-Residual Dense Block (RRDB) to the Generative network, improving accuracy and reducing training time. The authors called this network Enhanced Super-Resolution Generative Adversarial Network (ESRGAN). In their paper, the authors discovered that batch normalization layers were introducing artifacts on images, because the mean and standard deviations of the training images are a lot different from the test dataset, in consequence reducing the network generalization. By removing these layers, the authors reduced training complexity and memory cost. Another modification was the addition of skip connections between convolutional layers in the residual blocks to prevent instabilities during training. In the discriminative network, the authors used the concept of Relativistic Average Generative Adversarial Network (RaGAN), where the network tries to predict the probability of a real image being more realistic than the super-resolved images. By introducing those concepts, the authors won the first place in the PIRM2018-SR Challenge [1], and the network became state-of-the-art.

3   Proposed Approach

Our proposed approach was to combine the findings from [3] with the network made by [22], to see whether this powerful Super-Resolution network, trained together with the Face Recognition network using the joint-learn approach, could improve even further the accuracy on recognizing faces in low resolution.

Therefore, we designed the network architecture with the following principles. First, the network should be an aggregation of a SR and a FR, trained using joint-learn. Second, the network should be trained using the GAN framework. Third, the SR part of the network should be a generator. Fourth, the FR part of the network should be a CNN. As prerequisites, the discriminator should discriminate SR images generated by the network and real ones, and should be trained apart of the network, that is, should have its own gradients. Finally, the network should have two branches, one for artificial low resolution images, and the other one for the native ones.

With those principles in mind, we developed the Super-Resolution Face Recognition - Generative Adversarial Network (SRFR-GAN). Its architecture can be visualized on Fig. 1.

This network has, on the SR part, a generator as designed by [22], with 23 RRDBs. Each RRDB is composed by 3 residual dense blocks, which are blocks with 5 convolution layers containing 32 filters each, 3×3 kernels, 1×1 strides, and padding 1. Each convolutional output is concatenated with the previous ones and the residuals. At the end of each residual dense block and RRDB its outputs are multiplied by a β parameter and have the residual added to this value.

After each RRDB we have a convolution, followed by two layers of upsampling and convolution. At the end of this architecture we have two convolutions, which generates the SR image, with a resolution of 112×112 px. Every convolution on this part follows the settings presented before. As showed by [22], we are not using any batch normalization layer on this part of the network, but some tests were made regarding this and will be discussed in Sect. 4. On every layer of our architecture we tested the use of Mish activating function [16]. The authors claim an improvement on generalization and accuracy of the network.

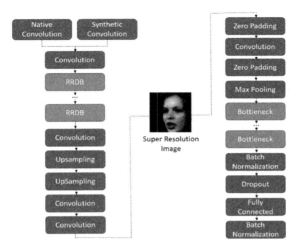

Fig. 1. SRFR-GAN network architecture

For recognizing faces we used a ResNet 50 [8], having on the inputs a zero padding layer of 3×3, followed by a convolution layer of 64 filters, 7×7 kernel, and stride 2. In sequence, we have another zero padding layer of 1×1, a 3×3 max pooling layer with stride 2, and after that bottleneck layers. After the bottleneck layers, we have a batch normalization with momentum of 0.9, followed by a dropout with rate of 0.4, a dense layer which reflect the size of the embeddings vector and, finally, one last batch normalization layer. We used embeddings of size 512, as suggested on literature [4,15,25].

The input of our architecture is composed by two convolutional layers in parallel, both with 3×3 kernel, 1×1 stride and 62 filters. Each layer is trained using only synthetic or native low resolution images. Using this approach, the synthetic convolution will help to train the native convolution, not only making this layer trainable (as ground truth images does not exist for native low resolution) but also causing this layer to become specialized on discovering the relevant features only existing in this image type.

Both this convolutional inputs are connected to the SR part of the architecture, generating as the first output, the super-resolved images. The FR part receives this image and generates the second output, the embeddings. For training, these embeddings are the input of a dense layer, which will output the corresponding class, and this information will be used in the loss function. Also, those SR images are sent to the discriminator along with the ground-truth images, which results will be part of the loss function too.

3.1 Loss Functions

For training such architecture, we build a loss function $L_{SRFR-GAN}$ based on the findings from [3,22], which is described on Eq. 1:

$$L_{SRFR-GAN} = (L_{FR}^{SYN} + \eta L_{FR}^{NAT}) + \lambda L_{SR} \tag{1}$$

where L_{FR}^{SYN} and L_{FR}^{NAT} are loss functions from FR applied on synthetic (SYN) and natural (NAT) images, respectively. We assume that L_{FR}^{SYN} has constant weight, and η and λ are scalars to weight L_{FR}^{NAT} and L_{SR}, respectively.

For facial recognition losses, we tested two possibilities, ArcLoss (Eq. 2) [4] and Cross-Entropy (Eq. 3) applied on the Softmax function σ (Eq. 4). In Eqs. 2–4, W and b are the weights and biases from the model, x represents an input layer, y represents a layer output. P and Q are statistical distributions. Additionally, θ determines the ArcLoss angle and m its additive margin. Finally, N is the number of examples in batch and n the number of output neurons.

$$\Phi = -\frac{1}{N} \sum_{i=1}^{N} \log \frac{e^{s \cos(\theta_{y_i} + m)}}{e^{s \cos(\theta_{y_i} + m)} + \sum_{j=1, j \neq y_i}^{N} e^{s \cos(\theta_j)}} \tag{2}$$

$$H(P, Q) = \mathbb{E}_{x \sim P}[-\log(Q(x))] \tag{3}$$

$$\sigma(y_i) = \frac{e^{W_{y_i}^T x_i + b_{y_i}}}{\sum_{j=1}^{n} e^{W_j^T x_i + b_j}} \tag{4}$$

On L_{SR}, we follow the proposed by [12, 22], as described on Eq. 5. This equations sums L_{percep}, which is a distance metric based on the outputs of the last convolution layer before activations of a pre-trained Vgg19 [21], L_G^{Ra}, which is a standard RaGAN loss function, and a L1 distance between the generated image and its ground truth counterpart. The factors α, β e γ are scalars to adjust training for the three parameters, and is the only change from original equation.

$$L_{SR} = L_G = \alpha L_{percep} + \beta L_G^{Ra} + \gamma L_1,$$

$$L_{percep} = \frac{1}{W_{i,j} H_{i,j}} \sum_{x=1}^{W_{i,j}} \sum_{y=1}^{H_{i,j}} (\phi_{i,j}(I^{HR})_{x,y}$$

$$- \phi_{i,j}(G_{\theta_G}(I^{LR}))_{x,y})^2 \tag{5}$$

$$L_G^{Ra} = -\mathbb{E}_{x_r}[\log(1 - D_{Ra}(x_r, x_f))]$$

$$- \mathbb{E}_{x_f}[\log(D_{Ra}(x_f, x_r))]$$

$$L_1 = \mathbb{E}_{x_i} \| G(x_i) - x_r \|_1$$

where x_r is the real image, x_f is the super-resolved image. I^{HR} is the high resolution image (same as x_r), while I^{LR} is the low resolution image. $\Phi_{i,j}$ represent a feature map for layer i before convolution j for the pretrained VGG19. W and

H are the width and height of the feature map. D_{R_a} is a discriminator network. Finally G_{θ_G} represents the application of the generator network.

The loss function for the discriminator is the same proposed by [22], which is described in Eq. 6.

$$L_D^{Ra} = - \mathbb{E}_{x_r}[\log(D_{Ra}(x_r, x_f))]$$
$$- \mathbb{E}_{x_f}[\log(1 - D_{Ra}(x_f, x_r))] \qquad (6)$$
$$D_{Ra}(x_r, x_f) = \sigma(C(x_r) - \mathbb{E}_{x_f}[C(x_f)])$$

where σ is the Sigmoid function, and $C(\cdot)$ is the non-transformed Discriminator output.

4   Experiments & Results

In order to train our model, we chose four datasets: CASIA-WebFace [26]; Labeled Faces in The Wild (LFW) [10]; TinyFaces [22]; and VggFace2 [2]. Both CASIA-WebFace and VggFace2 were selected for training from scratch. TinyFaces was selected for fine-tuning the model, as its a native low resolution dataset, with 169.403 images, divided into 15.975 labeled images of 5.139 subjects and 153.428 non-labeled images, varying from 6×6 to 32×32 pixels. LFW was selected for validation, using the face verification task. This task aims to, given a pair of face images, predict whether those images belongs to the *same person* or *different people* using a metric of distance (in this case L_2 distance) and a threshold.

4.1   Accuracy Metrics

For SR images we chose Peak Signal-to-Noise Ratio (PSNR), which is based on Mean Squared Error and captures the ratio between the magnitude of a signal and the magnitude of the noise.

For FR task we chose the following metrics: Accuracy, Area Under Curve (AUC), False Alarm Ratio (FAR), Equal Error Rate (EER) and Validation Rate.

As the LFW dataset is tested with different thresholds, both Accuracy and Validation Rate are presented as a Mean of those values along with the Standard Deviation.

4.2   Preprocessing

For the preprocessing phase, we detected the faces on images, aligned them, and reduced its resolution to build the synthetic low resolution versions of those datasets. In the face detection, we used the network MTCNN[1] [27] implemented[2] on TensorFlow, and this was chosen because of being a standard on literature [4,15,25]. For the images that contained more than one face, we used a metric of distance from the center of the bounding box in relation of the center of the image, and we selected the closest bounding box to the center.

After detecting the faces, we aligned them using 5 facial points given by the network (two eyes, nose, and two corners of the mouth) and cropped the region of interest in 112×112 px. This was used as ground truth for training the SR. Using the ground truths, we reduced its resolution 4 times, transforming them into 28×28 px images, using bicubic interpolation. To address the problem of having the same person in both training and validation sets[3], we filtered those classes from training datasets.

Before training, we flipped all images as a way of augmenting the data, and we normalized the values of each pixel by subtracting 127.5 and dividing it by 128, so each pixel value would be between $(-1, 1)$, as suggested on the literature [4,15,25].

4.3 Training

The training process occurs in two phases. In the first phase, we trained the network with synthetic low resolution images only, in order to make the network learn how to map a low resolution image into a high resolution one. In the second phase, both low resolution types of image would be presented, to perform the fine-tuning and make the network learn the intrinsic features of a natural low resolution image.

All trainings were done using mixed-precision[4] technique, in order to reduce the memory footprint of the network and release more space for greater batches. Using this, we could train with a batch size of 32, 16 images per GPU.

On our first tests we used the NovoGrad optimizer [7] to improve performance and generalization, and VggFace2 as our training dataset. We tested the proposal of [22] about Batch Normalization (BN) layers and degradation of super-resolved images into our proposed architecture. For that we trained two models in parallel, one using batch normalization layers on the FR part of the architecture and the other model without the layers.

For the first batch of trainings we fixed $\lambda = 0.001$, $\eta = 1$, $\alpha = 0.100$, $\beta = 1.000$, $\gamma = 0.100$, scale $= 64$, and margin $= 0.5$. This values were determined in preliminary experiments. The others hyperparameters can be seen on Table 1.

As can be seen on Fig. 2, the model learned the format and contours of a face to some degree, but the images had a lot of artifacts. On recognizing faces, the model did not learn at all how to distinguish between different subjects, as can be seen on Table 2.

---

[1] https://kpzhang93.github.io/MTCNN_face_detection_alignment/.

[2] https://github.com/ipazc/mtcnn.

[3] https://github.com/happynear/FaceDatasets.

[4] https://www.tensorflow.org/guide/mixed_precision.

Table 1. Hyperparameters used in training with NovoGrad and ArcLoss

ID	LR	β_1	β_2	Weight decay	BN
01	0.001	0.9	0.999	0	Yes
02	0.001	0.9	0.999	0	No
03	0.004	0.9	0.9	0.005	Yes
04	0.004	0.9	0.9	0.005	No
05	0.001	0.4	0.999	0.005	Yes
06	0.001	0.4	0.999	0.005	No

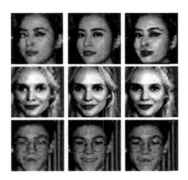

Fig. 2. Examples of images from training using NovoGrad and ArcLoss. On the left, the low resolution input; on the center, the ground truth image; On the right, the super-resolved image generated by the model.

Table 2. Accuracy of the training with NovoGrad and ArcLoss, tested on LFW dataset. Missing ids are from experiments that did not converge and were omitted.

ID	Mean acc.	AUC	EER	FAR	Validation rate
02	50.01 ± 0.025	0.500	0.500	1.000	1.000 ± 0
04	50.01 ± 0.025	0.500	0.500	1.000	1.000 ± 0
06	50.01 ± 0.025	0.500	0.500	1.000	1.000 ± 0

After the nonconvergence of the model and some analysis of the loss function graphs, we decided to simplify the loss function on the FR part, trying to facilitate the convergence of the model. For that, we swapped the ArcLoss function for the Cross-Entropy function, fixed weight decay = 0.002 and $\beta_2 = 0.25$, were β_1 and β_2 are parameters used by the optimizer based on prelimary experiments. The variable hyperparameters can be seen on Table 3.

On training number 09 to 12 we swapped the upsampling layers from UpSampling2D followed by Conv2D to Conv2DTranspose. The UpSampling2D layer does the image stretching by using some interpolation algorithm, in this case using nearest neighbours which, in practice, duplicates every row and column of

Table 3. Variable hyperparameters used in training with NovoGrad and Cross Entropy. Null lines on iterations represents trainings that were interrupted by errors and were ignored. In all cases, Learning Rate (LR) Decay Steps is equal to 1000.

ID	LR	β_1	λ	η	α	β	γ	BN	Iterations
07	0.007	0.9	0.001	1	0.100	1.000	0.100	Yes	18k
08	0.007	0.9	0.001	1	0.100	1.000	0.100	No	56k
09	0.007	0.9	0.001	1	0.100	1.000	0.100	Yes	50k
10	0.007	0.9	0.001	1	0.100	1.000	0.100	No	54k
11	0.007	0.9	0.1	1	0.001	0.050	0.010	Yes	–
12	0.007	0.9	0.1	1	0.001	0.050	0.010	No	40k
13	0.007	0.5	0.1	0.1	0.001	0.050	0.010	Yes	12k
14	0.007	0.5	0.1	0.1	0.001	0.050	0.010	No	9k
15	0.002	0.5	0.1	0.1	0.001	0.050	0.010	Yes	–
16	0.002	0.5	0.1	0.1	0.001	0.050	0.010	No	16k

the image. On the other hand, Conv2DTranspose stretches the image by doing the transposed operation of a convolution. We tested those two layers as a way of improving the perceptual quality of images, but the change brought more artifacts, as black pixels surrounded by noise. Possibly, after longer trainings with a better fine-tuning, using Conv2DTranspose could lead to better results on image quality, but this did not applied to our tests with few iterations/epochs.

The results for this batch of trainings, as can be seen on Fig. 3 and Table 4, shows that the network still didn't converge for the FR task, with the exception of training number 11 which had accuracy above random.

Fig. 3. Examples of images from validation on LFW dataset of models trained using NovoGrad and Cross Entropy. On the left, the low resolution input; on the center, the ground truth image; On the right, the super-resolved image generated by the model.

After this series of nonconvergence, we decided to use an bayesian optimizer [17] to help finding the best hyperparameters for training. The accuracy of the network in recognizing faces is optimized by the function, and the searched hyperparameters are: LR (Learning Rate); LR Decay Steps; β_1; Face Recognition

Table 4. Accuracy of the training with NovoGrad and ArcLoss, tested on LFW dataset. Missing ids are from experiments that did not converge and were omitted.

ID	Mean acc.	AUC	EER	FAR	Validation rate
07	50.16 ± 0.952	0.504	0.497	0	0 ± 0
08	50.01 ± 0.025	0.500	0.500	1.000	1.000 ± 0
09	50.01 ± 0.025	0.500	0.500	1.000	1.000 ± 0
11	51.07 ± 3.270	0.510	0.491	0.587	$0.608 \pm 0{,}032$
13	50.01 ± 0.025	0.500	0.500	1.000	1.000 ± 0
14	50.01 ± 0.025	0.500	0.500	1.000	1.000 ± 0
16	50.01 ± 0.025	0.500	0.500	1.000	1.000 ± 0

Weight λ; Super-Resolution Weight η; Perceptual Weight α; Generator Weight β; and Weight γ.

We then fixed $\beta_2 = 0.999$, and the hyperparameters found by the optimizer can be seen on Table 5.

Table 5. Hyperparameters found by the bayesian optimizer on training with NovoGrad and Cross-Entropy, using dataset VggFace2.

ID	LR	LR decay	β_1	λ	η	α	β	γ	BN	Iters.	Mean acc.
17	0.00354	$1.52 \cdot 10^3$	0.724	0.202	0.506	0.00136	0.021	0.0103	Yes	$20k$	0
18	0.00164	$1.58 \cdot 10^3$	0.659	0.32	0.437	0.00944	0.0132	0.0116	Yes	$20k$	0
19	0.00398	$4.56 \cdot 10^3$	0.779	0.945	0.127	0.0012	0.0114	0.0417	Yes	$20k$	0
20	0.00468	$4.12 \cdot 10^3$	0.799	0.135	0.128	0.00579	0.0428	0.0181	Yes	$20k$	0
21	0.00333	$2.79 \cdot 10^3$	0.52	0.182	0.682	0.00146	0.0232	0.0772	Yes	$20k$	0
22	0.00501	$3.13 \cdot 10^3$	0.558	0.155	0.5	0.00972	0.052	0.0389	Yes	$20k$	0
23	0.0049	$2.44 \cdot 10^3$	0.503	0.402	0.725	0.00148	0.0486	0.0587	Yes	$20k$	0
24	0.00297	$2.62 \cdot 10^3$	0.646	0.381	0.707	0.00332	0.0145	0.0569	No	$3.5k$	0
25	0.00627	$4.53 \cdot 10^3$	0.813	0.493	0.857	0.00199	0.0158	0.0686	No	$20k$	0
26	0.00287	$2.66 \cdot 10^3$	0.514	1	0.103	0.00292	0.0609	0.0132	No	$20k$	0
27	0.00221	$1.27 \cdot 10^3$	0.536	0.114	0.341	0.00733	0.012	0.0239	No	$20k$	0
28	0.00404	$1.92 \cdot 10^3$	0.86	0.239	0.14	0.00132	0.0264	0.0584	No	$20k$	0
29	0.00251	$4.2 \cdot 10^3$	0.515	0.106	0.353	0.00794	0.0405	0.0218	No	$20k$	0
30	0.0022	$2.5 \cdot 10^3$	0.853	0.12	0.961	0.00456	0.017	0.015	No	$20k$	0

As can be seen by the accuracy, the model still did not converge. We then changed the dataset, using this time CASIA-WebFace. As this dataset is smaller than VggFace2 the training should take less time, which could speed up the process of hyperparameter tuning. The hyperparameters found for this batch of trainings can be seen on Table 6.

After another batch of trainings without convergence, we chose to split the networks in two, first training the Super-Resolution, after that training the Face

Table 6. Hyperparameters found by the bayesian optimizer on training with NovoGrad and Cross Entropy, using CASIA-WebFace dataset.

ID	LR	LR decay	β_1	λ	η	α	β	γ	BN	Iters.	Mean acc.
31	0.00354	$1.52 \cdot 10^3$	0.724	0.202	0.506	0.00136	0.021	0.0103	Yes	$20k$	0
32	0.00164	$1.58 \cdot 10^3$	0.659	0.32	0.437	0.00944	0.0132	0.0116	Yes	$20k$	0
33	0.00468	$4.12 \cdot 10^3$	0.799	0.135	0.128	0.00579	0.0428	0.0181	Yes	$20k$	0
34	0.00333	$2.79 \cdot 10^3$	0.52	0.182	0.682	0.00146	0.0232	0.0772	Yes	$20k$	0
35	0.00501	$3.13 \cdot 10^3$	0.558	0.155	0.5	0.00972	0.052	0.0389	Yes	$20k$	0
36	0.0049	$2.44 \cdot 10^3$	0.503	0.402	0.725	0.00148	0.0486	0.0587	Yes	$20k$	0
37	0.0024	$2.6 \cdot 10^3$	0.722	0.722	0.707	0.00192	0.0656	0.049	No	$25k$	0

Recognition, and, finally, perform the fine-tuning in Joint-Learn. This approach was applied due to the necessity of identifying where the convergence problem originated. We then decided to revert the architectures changes, resulting in networks closer to what was proposed by the original authors on both networks.

With that in mind, we removed the weight decay from the hyperparameters to be searched by the bayesian optimizer and swapped the NovoGrad optimizer in favor of Adam with weight decay decoupled. We started training using the same hyperparameters of [22] in first iteration of the optimizer. All hyperparameters can be seen on Table 7.

Table 7. Hyperparameters found by the bayesian optimizer on training the SR network with Adam optimizer using weight decay decoupled, and CASIA-WebFace dataset. β_1 corresponds to the parameter of Adam optimizer.

ID	LR	β_1	α	β	γ	Iterations
38	0.0002	0.9	1	0.005	0.01	$62k$
39	0.00349	0.811	0.0146	0.0336	0.0717	$47k$
40	0.0002	0.9	0.0146	0.005	0.01	$34k$
41	0.0002	0.9	0.0146	0.005	0.02	$50k$
42	0.00252	0.9	0.0392	0.00506	0.0571	$22k$
43	0.00300	0.9	0.0400	0.00500	0.0580	$33k$

The network converged relatively fast, with convincing results and few artifacts, as can be seen on Fig. 4.

After that, we started training the FR part, using again Adam with weight decay decoupled. We fixed ArcLoss Scale and ArcLoss Angular Margin to 64 and 0.5, as proposed by [4], and β_2 as 0.999. The others hyperparameters were found by the bayesian optimizer and can be seen on Table 8.

After the nonconvergence, we tried switching the optimizer to a Stochastic Gradient Descent (SGD) with weight decay decoupled, to use the same optimizer as the original paper. Besides that, we used the same hyperparameters as the

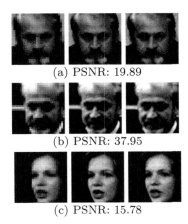

(a) PSNR: 19.89

(b) PSNR: 37.95

(c) PSNR: 15.78

Fig. 4. Examples of generated images from validation on LFW dataset. On the left, the low resolution input; on the center, the ground truth image; On the right, the super-resolved image generated by the model.

Table 8. Hyperparameters found by the bayesian optimizer on training the FR network with Adam optimizer using weight decay decoupled, and CASIA-WebFace dataset.

ID	LR	β_1	Weight decay	Iterations	Accuracy
44	0.0002	0.9	0.0005	$74k$	0.5
45	0.000925	0.79	0.000758	$74k$	0.5
46	0.00485	0.608	0.000333	$74k$	0.5
47	0.00177	0.573	0.0009	$74k$	0.5

original work. The hyperparameters found by the bayesian optimizer for this batch of trainings and the results can be seen on Table 9.

As the models continued to produce random guesses, we decided to implement the LR decay as proposed by [4], for the CASIA-WebFace dataset, dividing

Table 9. Hyperparameters found by the bayesian optimizer on training the FR network with SGD optimizer using weight decay decoupled, and CASIA-WebFace dataset.

ID	LR	Momentum	Weight decay	Iterations	Accuracy
48	0.1	0.9	0.0005	$74k$	0.5
49	0.00282	0.654	0.000253	$74k$	0.5
50	0.0028	0.757	0.000753	$74k$	0.5
51	0.98	0.504	0.000394	$74k$	0.5
52	0.0282	0.756	0.000371	$74k$	0.5
53	0.026	0.583	0.000323	$74k$	0.5
54	0.015	0.675	0.000104	$74k$	0.5
55	0.0467	0.801	0.000547	$74k$	0.5

the LR by 10 on iterations $20k$ and $28k$. The hyperparameters and results for this batch of trainings can be seen on Table 10.

Table 10. Hyperparameters found by the bayesian optimizer on training the FR network with SGD optimizer using weight decay decoupled, LR decay, over the CASIA-WebFace dataset.

ID	LR	Momentum	Weight decay	Iterations	Accuracy
56	0.1	0.9	0.0005	$74k$	0.5
57	0.00692	0.73	0.000785	$74k$	0.5
58	0.00522	0.729	0.000216	$74k$	0.5
59	0.997	0.605	0.000129	$74k$	0.5

Even with the same hyperparameters and training architecture as [4], and because of time restrictions, we could not make the FR network converge. The ArcLoss proved to be very unstable during training.

5   Conclusion

One of the most challenging obstacles for the Face Recognition is to recognize faces on low resolution images. The use of Super-Resolution algorithms seems to be promising to improve image quality and accuracy on recognizing faces. Additionaly, as GAN networks are becoming state-of-the-art in SR, it may enable new research possibilities FR and attempt to mitigate the exposed problem.

The main objective of this work was to verify the impact of SR on the FR task. Unfortunately, we could not attest that Facial Recognition was improved by Super-Resolution. During this work that SR GANs were able to achieve satisfactory results on improving resolution and quality of face images, given their initial conditions, and the training is efficient. We also observed, for the tested FR networks, that the Softmax-based loss functions tested are difficult to train, demanding very precise hyperparameters so that they do not add instabilities during training.

As we could not make the FR network converge, we could not reach some of the objectives presented before. As a consequence, we could not compare the proposed network with other state-of-the-art networks in low resolution face recognition. We cannot conclude that the Joint-Learn training architecture, nor the deepness of the proposed network, were the causes of nonconvergence, since it did not converge even when trained alone with the hyperparameters proposed in the original work.

For the Batch Normalization layers, as the network did not converge, we cannot conclude if those layers affected the results for SR, but they brought more stability during training. Some experiments for future work include:

– Modify the architecture for the FR part: we have used ResNet50 in our architecture but other networks can be tested too in the search of convergence, such as ResNet101 and ResNet152, or even a completely different network;
– Change the loss function for the FR part: as we find ArcLoss to be unstable for training we propose to test with other functions based on Softmax, such as Center Loss [25] or SphereFace Loss [15]. Another possibility is to use a loss function based on triplet loss [24] which, despite not having the best results currently and consuming more memory during training, these functions were well tested over time and are considered a solid choice for the problem;
– Add more layers of Batch Normalization and Dropout: as Batch Normalization and Dropout layers perform regularization, having more of those layers maybe can help the network to converge, even at the cost of having less perceptual quality on super-resolved images. So, we propose having more of these layers on the architecture to test if this helps the network to converge.

In order to facilitate reproducibility of the experiments, all codes are available on a public repository on GitHub[5].

References

1. Blau, Y., Mechrez, R., Timofte, R., Michaeli, T., Zelnik-Manor, L.: The 2018 PIRM challenge on perceptual image super-resolution (2019)
2. Cao, Q., Shen, L., Xie, W., Parkhi, O.M., Zisserman, A.: VGGFace2: a dataset for recognising faces across pose and age (2018)
3. Cheng, Z., Zhu, X., Gong, S.: Low-resolution face recognition. CoRR abs/1811.08965 (2018)
4. Deng, J., Guo, J., Zafeiriou, S.: ArcFace: additive angular margin loss for deep face recognition. CoRR abs/1801.07698 (2018). https://arxiv.org/abs/1801.07698
5. Dong, C., Loy, C.C., He, K., Tang, X.: Image super-resolution using deep convolutional networks. CoRR abs/1501.00092 (2015). https://arxiv.org/abs/1501.00092
6. Fookes, C., Lin, F., Chandran, V., Sridharan, S.: Evaluation of image resolution and super-resolution on face recognition performance. J. Vis. Commun. Image Represent. **23**(1), 75–93 (2012). https://doi.org/10.1016/j.jvcir.2011.06.004. https://www.sciencedirect.com/science/article/pii/S1047320311000721
7. Ginsburg, B., et al.: Stochastic gradient methods with layer-wise adaptive moments for training of deep networks (2020)
8. He, K., Zhang, X., Ren, S., Sun, J.: Deep residual learning for image recognition (2015)
9. Hennings-Yeomans, P.H., Baker, S., Kumar, B.V.: Simultaneous super-resolution and feature extraction for recognition of low-resolution faces. In: 2008 IEEE Conference on Computer Vision and Pattern Recognition. IEEE, June 2008. https://doi.org/10.1109/cvpr.2008.4587810
10. Huang, G.B., Ramesh, M., Berg, T., Learned-Miller, E.: Labeled faces in the wild: a database for studying face recognition in unconstrained environments. Technical report 07-49, University of Massachusetts, Amherst, October 2007

---

[5] https://github.com/OliRafa/SRFR-GAN.

11. Kim, J., Lee, J.K., Lee, K.M.: Accurate image super-resolution using very deep convolutional networks. CoRR abs/1511.04587 (2015). https://arxiv.org/abs/1511.04587

12. Ledig, C., et al: Photo-realistic single image super-resolution using a generative adversarial network (2017)

13. Lemieux, A., Parizeau, M.: Experiments on eigenfaces robustness. In: Object Recognition Supported by User Interaction for Service Robots. IEEE Computer Society (2002). https://doi.org/10.1109/icpr.2002.1044743

14. Lin, F.C.H.: Super-resolution image processing with application to face recognition. Ph.D. thesis, Queensland University of Technology (2008). https://eprints.qut.edu.au/16703/

15. Liu, W., Wen, Y., Yu, Z., Li, M., Raj, B., Song, L.: SphereFace: deep hypersphere embedding for face recognition (2018)

16. Misra, D.: Mish: a self regularized non-monotonic neural activation function. arXiv preprint arXiv:1908.08681 (2019)

17. Močkus, J.: On Bayesian methods for seeking the extremum. In: Marchuk, G.I. (ed.) Optimization Techniques 1974. LNCS, vol. 27, pp. 400–404. Springer, Heidelberg (1975). https://doi.org/10.1007/3-540-07165-2_55

18. Nguyen, K., Fookes, C., Sridharan, S., Tistarelli, M., Nixon, M.: Super-resolution for biometrics: a comprehensive survey. Pattern Recogn. **78**, 23–42 (2018). https://doi.org/10.1016/j.patcog.2018.01.002

19. Rasti, P., Uiboupin, T., Escalera, S., Anbarjafari, G.: Convolutional neural network super resolution for face recognition in surveillance monitoring. In: Perales, F.J.J., Kittler, J. (eds.) AMDO 2016. LNCS, vol. 9756, pp. 175–184. Springer, Cham (2016). https://doi.org/10.1007/978-3-319-41778-3_18

20. Shermeyer, J., Etten, A.V.: The effects of super-resolution on object detection performance in satellite imagery. CoRR abs/1812.04098 (2018). https://arxiv.org/abs/1812.04098

21. Simonyan, K., Zisserman, A.: Very deep convolutional networks for large-scale image recognition (2015)

22. Wang, X., et al.: ESRGAN: enhanced super-resolution generative adversarial networks (2018)

23. Wang, Z., Chang, S., Yang, Y., Liu, D., Huang, T.S.: Studying very low resolution recognition using deep networks. CoRR abs/1601.04153 (2016). https://arxiv.org/abs/1601.04153

24. Weinberger, K.Q., Saul, L.K.: Distance metric learning for large margin nearest neighbor classification. J. Mach. Learn. Res. **10**(2), 207–244 (2009)

25. Wen, Y., Zhang, K., Li, Z., Qiao, Yu.: A discriminative feature learning approach for deep face recognition. In: Leibe, B., Matas, J., Sebe, N., Welling, M. (eds.) ECCV 2016. LNCS, vol. 9911, pp. 499–515. Springer, Cham (2016). https://doi.org/10.1007/978-3-319-46478-7_31

26. Yi, D., Lei, Z., Liao, S., Li, S.Z.: Learning face representation from scratch (2014)

27. Zhang, K., Zhang, Z., Li, Z., Qiao, Y.: Joint face detection and alignment using multitask cascaded convolutional networks. IEEE Signal Process. Lett. **23**(10), 1499–1503 (2016). https://doi.org/10.1109/LSP.2016.2603342

Image Processing of Petri Dishes for Counting Microorganisms

Marcela Marques Barbosa[1], Everton Schneider dos Santos[1]([✉]),
João Paulo Teixeira[2], Saraspathy Naidoo Terroso Gama de Mendonca[1],
Arnaldo Candido Junior[1], and Pedro Luiz de Paula Filho[1]

[1] Federal University of Technology - Paraná, Avenida Brasil, Medianeira,
Paraná 4232, Brazil
{marcelabarbosa,everton.2019}@alunos.utfpr.edu.br,
{naidoo,arnaldoc,pedrol}@utfpr.edu.br
[2] Polytechnic Institute of Bragança (IPB), Bragança, Portugal
joaopt@ipb.pt
http://www.utfpr.edu.br/campus/medianeira
https://www.ipb.pt/

Abstract. For a food to be considered functional it is necessary to prove that it has microorganisms in its composition. In order to determine the presence of microorganisms in a food, laboratory analyzes can be carried out using of Petri dishes, which must pass through an incubation period, to then manually count the number of bacterial colonies that are present in each board. Therefore, the objective of this work was to develop a software to perform the automated counting of colonies contained in Petri plates and to validate the efficiency of the tool through comparisons with the results of a manual count. For this, an algorithm was developed based on digital image processing techniques capable of identifying the Petri dish within the image and counting the number of colonies present on each plate. As a result, a global correlation of 0.948 was observed in relation to the manual count, and in an individual analysis, a correlation of 0.8134 was obtained. Thus, it can be concluded that counts of microorganisms can be performed automatically and reliably with the developed software.

Keywords: Petri counting · Digital image processing

1 Introduction

Pasteurisation, the process that eliminates undesirable microorganisms from food, is assigned/attributed to the French physician Luiz Paster, for the pioneering study, in 1837. Since then, the study of Microbiology has grown a lot and today the microorganisms can be classified as: spoilage, which cause harmful chemical changes (changes in color, odor, taste, texture and appearance of the food); pathogenic, which represent risk to the health of man and animals (contamination of precarious hygiene conditions of cultivation, preparation and/or handling); beneficial to health, which often are added intentionally to food so they can modify original characteristics on novel foods (fermented foods) [4].

Bacteria may be added intentionally to food during processing, through inoculation (adding a known amount of microorganisms, under favorable conditions for growth of each species). Each food has a specific legislation that calls for the minimum and maximum acceptable amount of microorganisms. For the realization of the estimate of this concentration, it is necessary to count it. This, in most cases, is performed by naked eye analysts of Microbiology. This practice is not always getting accurate results due to a number of factors, which may compromise the quality of the final product [2].

In view of this problem, it is important the use of more precise techniques for the count of microorganisms, reducing interfering and count related errors. Through digital processing of images it is possible to define a two-dimensional function $f(x, y)$, being x and y coordinates of a spatial plan, where the values f for each pair (x, y) assume finite and discrete values (pixels). Image processing is capable of performing tasks that would be difficult using only human vision [5].

That way, this work presents a tool that, through standardized images and techniques of segmentation and processing of images, is capable of performing counting of colonies of bacteria in Petri dish in an automated manner.

2   Related Work

Mukherjee et al. [7] used imaging techniques to perform counting of bacteria on Petri dishes, and obtained results similar to counting by humans. Differentiation of the image pixels was performed in three groups: colony, background and grid. The grid is maintained in order to make a later comparison with the manual count.

The images used by Mukherjee et al. [7] were captured with constant zoom and later a pre-processing was performed, in which the average of eight images were used to attenuate reflection effects of the images. Later, they evaluated the differences in the mean value of each pixel to increase the contrast between the pixels of the bottom colonies and also the grid. The images were passed through a threshold and a transformation by distance, where the image was subdivided into quadrants of 3 × 3. Thus, the quadrants became 0 (background) or 1 (colonies).

For counting Colony Forming Units (CFUs), Osowsky et al. [8] developed a compact, low cost and efficient prototype for areas greater than 0.8 mm^2. The study was based on the development of a lighting system using red led in order to avoid overheating, which can lead to an acceleration of the development of the colonies, the standardization of the images with contrast enhancement. The algorithm used by the authors to perform the counting of the colonies was divided in five steps: (a) the calculation of the average for 20 images to reduce the noise; (b) the identification of the region of interest, using logical AND with a reference mask; (c) the removal of the gray level and consequently the increase of the contrast using the algorithm of background subtraction; (d) the use of a gray level threshold equal to twelve; and (e) the application of a recursive algorithm in order to count the colonies of bacteria. Osowsky et al. [8] observed that regions near the edge are lost in the operation of logical ANDs, which also occurs after background subtraction, and it is impossible to select the entire area of the Petri dish. Due to the processing performed on the images, the Automatic Colony Count System was limited to colonies larger than 0.8 mm^2, however, according to the authors, this can not be considered a limiting factor, because colonies smaller than this do not even develop.

Marotz et al. [6] studied an adaptation to spatial recognition for the detection of object centers using the average of local maximums based on images with resolution of 1200×1200 pixels and 300 dpi[1]. The algorithm was able to recognize microcolonies of five area pixels, or 0.4 mm, but they cite three difficulties obtained during the work, such as increasing the number of colonies during the process, the microcolonies and the contamination of plates reused and not sterilized completely. Due to these factors, Marotz et al. [6] started pre-processing with a low-pass filter, in order to eliminate extreme values, followed by detection of the edges of the plates through the sharp change of pixel intensity, given a set threshold. In this case, the thresholding process was instrumental at identifying the background as no single value could be defined for all images. The authors used a low-pass filter to adjust the value of this threshold for each image.

For the recognition of the colonies, Marotz et al. [6] traced eight lines with a distance of $45°$ from the pixels, where the intensity is maximum and the uniformity of the rays was verified, forming a circular figure to its asymmetry. According to Marotz et al. [6] this method allowed the recognition of colonies, even when a high degree of occlusion occurred, having sufficient accuracy and detection performance the authors considered acceptable. The best result was obtained using sixteen lines. In this study, values very close to those obtained by manual counting were achieved, proving to be reliable.

The use of a low cost system for counting and classifying colonies on Petri dishes was studied by Chen and Zhang [3]. The process was started from a pre-processing that distinguishes between colored and grayscale images. In the second step, targeting, it was assumed that the image is subdivided into three groups: bottom (lowest level); plate (medium level); and colonies (highest level). After the identification of the colonies, the authors evaluated their morphology in order to verify if there is any grouping that might impair the accuracy of the colonies count. The classification was made through the shape and color. In this way, it was possible that the user included different morphology colonies, not identified in the previous step, due to differences between colonies.

To analyze the characteristics of the colonies Chen and Zhang [3] used the classifier Support Vector Machine (SVM), which identifies two classes, colonies or rest. In a comparison with manual counting, very close values could be observed for colored images, showing that the developed software was capable of counting

---

[1] Quantity of pixels per inch.

the colonies automatically, besides being able to differentiate colonies of different species with little human interversion and with low cost.

Alves et al. [1] developed an automatic CFU counting system. For this, the authors sub-divided their work into five stages: image acquisition, pre-processing, processing, post-processing, and finally, analysis and result generation. A wooden box was developed for image acquisition in which 20 W light bulbs were packed frontally to the Petri dish, as Osowsky et al. [8] proposed. Through this system, the uniformity of illumination was maintained, preventing the formation of distortions in image histograms, that would make the image thresholding unfeasible, compromising subsequent steps.

Alves et al. [1] used the Otsu statistical method to determine the threshold value, although it is possible to use the image histogram. After dividing the image into two classes by means of threshold, a Laplacian filter was applied to detect the borders of bacteria, so that it could be applied to the Hough transform, which would identify points of peaks (which indicate the center of the bacterium). In the study, the Backmapping technique was applied to reduce the false peaks produced by the Hough transform. As results, correlation coefficients between 0.98% and 0.99% were obtained with manual analysis, making it possible to quantify CFU in Petri dishes by automatic counting.

3   Materials and Methods

3.1   Acquisition of Images

A controlled environment was created to maintain the images quality. During the process of image acquisition the lighting was controlled and the camera was kept in a fixed position. This environment was made using a Polyvinyl Chloride tube with a diameter of 200 mm. The camera was kept at the top and the Petri plates, separated by a height of 40 cm, at the bottom. The tube had a ribbon of LEDs affixed in its interior positioned at a height of 4 cm.

The tube allowed the accommodation of a 90 × 15 mm Petri dish. This also allowed the laboratory analyst to execute the exchanging between plates without difficulties.

A Nikon camera model Coolpix L820 was used to acquire the images. This camera was also equiped with a Sixteen-megapixel Complementary Metal Oxide Semiconductor (CMOS) sensor coupled with NIKKOR fixed objective lens with 30x optical zoom; 4.0–120.0 mm. The camera was set to focus on auto mode during image capture.

3.2   Samples

The sample unit was composed of Petri dishes containing colonies of the Lactobacillus plantarum microorganism grown in MRS agar medium for 48 h at 37 °C. Overall, 45 duplicate plates were produced, resulting in 90 unique plates. Plates from a duplicated pair have in common the dilution and analysis time-step. Next, plating was repeated, this time with the bacterium cultured in MRS agar medium, totaling 180 images on two bases.

4 Proposed Algorithm

In the developed software, it is possible to select a folder containing the images to be processed. When a folder is chosen, a list containing the names of all image files is loaded and the first image is automatically displayed. The algorithm is executed when the user clicks on the image name, using the values indicated in controls. After that, the selected image is updated based on the achieved results.

4.1 Image Processing

The images were segmented into three distinct parts: the plate region; the possible bacteria CFUs and possible contaminants.

In order to determine the location of the Petri dish within the image, a range of colors based on the HLS color system was computed. In the resulting image, the mathematical morphology operation closing is applied with a cross-sectional element of size 5×5 and 3 repetitions. Then the edges of the resulting image are highlighted through a morphological gradient, with a cross-structural element of size 3×3, with the highlighted edges applied to the algorithm proposed by [9] to find the contours of the image. Figure 1 shows a diagram of all image processing steps performed by the software. After this phase, the software executes the stage of identification of possible contaminants (Fig. 2). In this step, the contaminants are separated from the image background using the TopHat mathematical morphology. A median filter sequence was used to remove the remaining contaminants, CFUs and borders. After that, a binarization was applied followed by opening and dilation morphological operations. The final result is an image containing only the contaminants.

The process ends with the segmentation of the CFU (Fig. 3). The input image is transformed in gray level image and a TopHat operation is used. After binarization, a median filter is applied to the image. For each identified object, a validation is executed based on the contour area proportion in relation to its minimum enclosing rectangle. The objects where this relation is close to zero are discarded. Some bacteria are lost during this process. To retrieve them, a skeletonization algorithm is executed in all discarded elements. If more than one element is identified, these are incorporated as a CFU.

For each remaining object, the algorithm checks whether it is contained in any of the contours identified as a fungus, in which case the object is rejected.

4.2 Validation

Manual counting was performed by a laboratory professional and compared with the automated counting, considering the average logs of each dilution, forming a single average for each time-step. Using this mean, absolute and percentage errors were calculated, as well as the correlation between the means by Pearson's correlation (Eq. 1). A comparison was also made among the absolute count of each plate and its respective replica of the manual and automatic counting. From

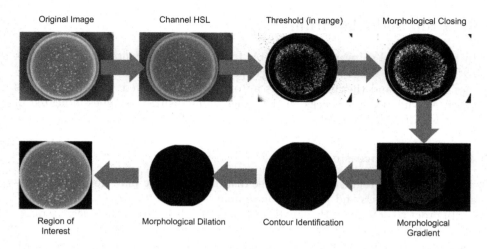

Fig. 1. The described steps for identifying the Petri dish within the image.

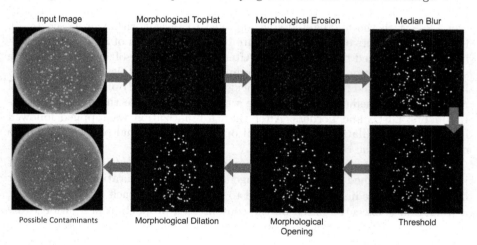

Fig. 2. The implementation of the described steps for identifying possible contaminants inside the Petri dish.

this comparison, the absolute, percentage, quadratic and correlation errors were calculated.

$$r = \frac{1}{n-1} \sum \left(\frac{x_i - \bar{X}}{Sx} \right) \left(\frac{y_i - \bar{Y}}{Sy} \right) \tag{1}$$

In Eq. 1, r represents the Pearson correlation coefficient, n is the number of elements, x and y are the observed variables, $\bar{X}$ and $\bar{Y}$ are the averages of the observed variables and S_x and S_y are the standard deviation of the observed variables.

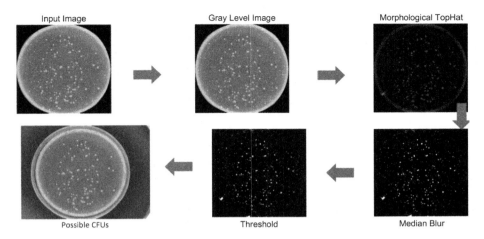

Fig. 3. The execution of the steps described for identification of the probable CFUs contained in the Petri dish.

5 Experimental Result

In total, 180 images were used in 16 time-steps during experiments. Each time-step contains three dilutions with the values 10^{-7}, 10^{-8} e 10^{-9}, in duplicated. Each duplicate has two images. The counting of a plate is given by the mean of the two images of each plate.

The bacteria CFUs counting aims to calculate the R^2 (determination coefficient). This value is going to determine the amount of microorganisms that are going to be added to the food, in this case yogurt. The estimation of bacteria strain concentration is made with the development of a concentration curve correlating the absorbance measure (Optical Density – O.D.) with the bacteria concentration logarithm. This value is achieved with the colony counting by plate in depth. Based on this data, an equation is created to calculate the bacteria concentration in the environment and the broth culture volume needed to obtain the intended number of CFUs in the yogurt. The equation fitting to the data is evaluated based on the R^2 analysis.

Figure 4 shows the comparison between the manual counting growth and automatic counting growth. This value is correlated to the logarithm of the bacterium growth $(log(UFC.mL^{-1}))$ and the time-step, in hours, of each plate. It can be observed that the manual and automatic counts are similar but do not fully match. Despite that, the manual and automatic counting follow the same growth characteristics. It is worth noting that after the time-step 14 h, the manual counting becomes "uncountable" because of the number of bacteria present in the Petri plate. The automatic counting, however, is still predicted.

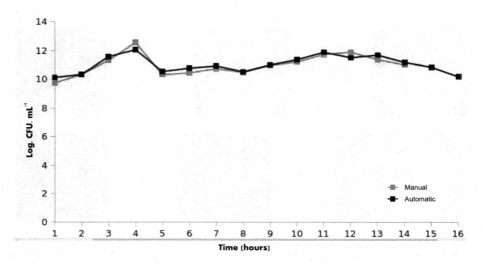

Fig. 4. Comparison between manual and automatic counts

From a total of 180 images, in 173 (95.77%) it was possible to identify the plates. In 8 images, or 4.23% of the total, some kind of partial loss in the edges of the plate were obtained. In these cases, the image contained both the Petri dish and its lid, which generated reflections and small distortions on the Petri dish region.

Figure 5 illustrates some results. CFUs were highlighted in red and the possible contaminants were flagged in purple. Analyzing Fig. 5b, a considerable number of false positives were found for CFUs in areas where contaminants might be present. This was expected due to the high saturation intensity in this region and the difficulty to distinguish between the bacteria CFU and the Petri dish reflection.

The developed software is capable to count a set of plates. The individual count is stored and, after this step, a table is shown containing counting results. It's also possible to export the results for data analysis.

Comparing the methods, there is good similarity, both methods followed the same growth characteristics. Comparing the software counting to the manual counting, an R^2 of 0.9734 was obtained (Fig. 6a) and the automatic counting obtained an R^2 of 0.9876 (Fig. 6b).

Table 1 shows the result of the logarithm of the average between dilutions 10^{-7}, 10^{-8} and 10^{-9} of manual and automatic counts. Their respective absolute and quadratic errors, ordered by descending quadratic error, are also reported. It is possible to note that the first five instances present quadratic errors above the mean. These points coincide with the points of highest divergence in Fig. 4.

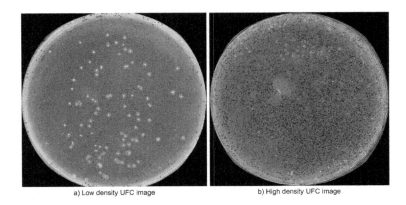

a) Low density UFC image   b) High density UFC image

Fig. 5. Resulting images.

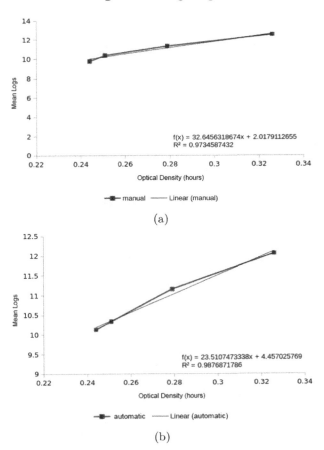

Fig. 6. Figures (a) represent the R^2 graph of the Manual count and (b) represent the R^2 chart for Automatic counting.

Table 1. Absolute and quadratic error logs in relation to counts of automatic bacteria CFUs

Time (h)	Manual counting (CFUs)	Automatic counting (CFUs)	Absolute error	Quadratic error
T3	12.5651	12.0620	0.5031	0.25310
T11	11.8974	11.5124	0.3849	0.14817
T0	9.7486	10.1296	0.3810	0.14517
T5	10.4484	10.7758	0.3274	0.10717
T12	11.3775	11.6957	0.3183	0.10129
T2	11.3226	11.5869	0.2642	0.06982
T4	10.3166	10.5380	0.2214	0.04904
T6	10.7373	10.9311	0.1938	0.03755
T13	11.0137	11.1817	0.1680	0.02821
T9	11.2144	11.3718	0.1573	0.02475
T10	11.7424	11.8956	0.1532	0.02347
T7	10.4900	10.5230	0.0331	0.00109
T8	10.9819	11.0091	0.0272	0.00074
T1	10.3455	10.3383	0.0072	0.00005

A correlation calculation was performed using the Pearson method, and a value of 0.9486 was obtained, demonstrating the existence of a strong correlation between manual counting and automatic counting.

Table 2 shows the absolute mean, quadratic mean and standard deviation errors for each mean. This table shows that the standard deviation of the automatic count was smaller than the manual count, indicating a greater uniformity of the automatic count.

Table 2. Statistical summary of the logarithm of the means obtained in Table 1

	Averages	Standard deviation
Manual counting	11.0144	0.7437
Automatic counting	11.1108	0.6020
Absolute error	0.2243	0.1481
Quadratic error	0.0707	0.0731

The load mean analysis shows different results when compared to the individual analysis, when only plates with a quadratic error above the mean (discrepant) are taken into account. Table 3 shows the discrepant plates, taking into consideration a squared error above the mean. Standouts from this analysis include plates at time-step 7 with 10^{-8} dilution with percentage error greater than 120%, time-step 11 and dilution 10^{-9} with more than 500%, time-step 6 and dilution 10^{-7} with approximately 190%. Time-steps 3 and 12 with dilutions 10^{-9} and 10^{-8} with absolute errors 3,442 and 5,785, respectively, are also standouts since they also have superior error values when compared with other plates.

Table 3. Summary of the manual count comparison with respect to automatic count

Time (h)	Replica.	Dilution.	Manual counting	Automatic counting	Absolute error	Percent error	Quadratic error
T7	2	10^{-8}	2130	952	1178	123.74%	1387684
T7	1	10^{-8}	600	1795	1195	66.57%	1428025
T11	2	10^{-9}	1478	221	1257	568.78%	1580049
T13	2	10^{-8}	1415	2675	1260	47.10%	1587600
T9	2	10^{-7}	2623	3929	1306	33.24%	1705636
T10	2	10^{-8}	1749	3067	1318	42.97%	1737124
T10	2	10^{-9}	1049	2449	1400	57.17%	1960000
T2	1	10^{-8}	3546	5010	1464	29.22%	2143296
T6	1	10^{-7}	2465	841	1624	193.10%	2637376
T9	1	10^{-8}	1717	3377	1660	49.16%	2755600
T3	2	10^{-9}	4405	6070	1665	27.43%	2772225
T11	1	10^{-7}	1017	2996	1979	66.05%	3916441
T2	1	10^{-7}	4118	6511	2393	36.75%	5726449
T3	1	10^{-9}	2942	6384	3442	53.92%	11847364
T12	2	10^{-8}	2385	8170	5785	70.81%	33466225

Observing the plate with time-step T7, dilution 10^{-8} (replica 2), the manual counting showed 2,130 bacteria CFUs and the automatic counting showed 952 bacteria CFUs. The visual analysis of the corresponding resulting image, showed in the Fig. 7, presents the automatic counting, which identified almost all bacteria CFUs, with only some false positives on the plate border. This could indicate that some error might have occurred during the manual counting.

Table 4 shows the Table 3 global means. A positive correlation, using Pearson calculation, of 0.8134% was achieved. This time-step, the manual counting standard deviation was small, contrasting with the results from Table 2.

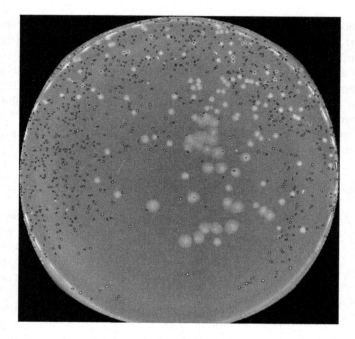

Fig. 7. Automatic detection of time-step T7, dilution 10^{-8}, with 952 CFUs in total.

Table 4. Mean of errors per plate

	Averages	Standard deviation
Manual counting	1259.9254	1195.3828
Automatic counting	1690.0448	1741.2812
Absolute error	658.5077	906.9502
Quadratic error	1115.3088	4357033.2404

6   Conclusion

In this work, digital processing techniques, such as image pre-processing and noise minimization algorithms, were studied to be applied in the counting of bacterial CFUs.

It was possible to define the standardization in the acquisition of the images that formed the base. The software developed showed itself to be faster and with a similar precision tending to be more efficient than the manual count. The approach using only image processing techniques centered on saturation and brightness proved to be viable. Automatic counting had a strong correlation compared to manual counting.

According to Pearson's correlation, a value of 0.9486 was achieved with an average absolute error of 0.2243. However, it must be taken into account that the results were achieved with a small image dataset. Further tests with more data are needed to verify whether the results remain satisfactory.

In this way, it is concluded that the desired objectives were initially achieved. Suggestions for future work include the use Deep Learning to count and classify the CFUs.

Acknowledgements. The authors are grateful to the Foundation for Science and Technology (FCT, Portugal) for financial support through national funds FCT/MCTES (PIDDAC) to CeDRI (UIDB/05757/2020 and UIDP/05757/2020) and SusTEC (LA/P/0007 /2021).

References

1. Alves, G.M.: Método fundamentado em processamento digital de imagens para contagem automática de unidades formadoras de colônias (2006)
2. Binns, N.: Probióticos, prebióticos e a microbiota intestinal. Ilsieurope concise (2014)
3. Chen, W.B., Zhang, C.: Bacteria colony enumeration and classification for clonogenic assay. In: 2008 Tenth IEEE International Symposium on Multimedia, pp. 487–488. IEEE (2008)
4. Franco, B.D.G.d.M., Landgraf, M.: Microbiologia dos alimentos. In: Microbiologia dos alimentos, pp. 182–182 (2003)
5. Gonzalez, R., Woods, R.: Digital Image Processing, 3rd edn., Saddle River (2008)
6. Marotz, J., Lübbert, C., Eisenbeiß, W.: Effective object recognition for automated counting of colonies in petri dishes (automated colony counting). Comput. Methods Program. Biomed. **66**(2), 183–198 (2001). https://doi.org/10.1016/S0169-2607(00)00128-0
7. Mukherjee, D.P., Pal, A., Sarma, S., Majumder, D.: Bacterial colony counting using distance transform. Int. J. Bio-Med. Comput. **38**(2), 131–140 (1995). https://doi.org/10.1016/0020-7101(94)01043-Z. https://www.sciencedirect.com/science/article/pii/002071019401043Z
8. Osowsky, J., Gamba, H.R.: Sistema automático para contagem de colônias em placas de petri. Revista Brasileira de Engenharia Biomédica **17**(3), 131–139 (2001)
9. Suzuki, S., be, K.: Topological structural analysis of digitized binary images by border following. Comput. Vis. Graph. Image Process. **30**(1), 32–46 (1985). https://doi.org/10.1016/0734-189X(85)90016-7. https://www.sciencedirect.com/science/article/pii/0734189X85900167

Caenorhabditis Elegans Detection Using YOLOv5 and Faster R-CNN Networks

Ernesto Jesús Rico-Guardiola[ID], Pablo E. Layana-Castro[ID],
Antonio García-Garví[ID], and Antonio-José Sánchez-Salmerón[✉][ID]

Instituto de Automática e Informática Industrial, Universitat Politècnica
de València, Valencia, Spain
asanchez@isa.upv.es

Abstract. The detection of *Caenorhabditis elegans* (*C. elegans*) is a
complex problem due to the variety of poses they can adopt, the aggregations and the problems of dirt accumulation on the plates. Artificial
neural networks have achieved great results in detection tasks in recent
years.

In this article, two detection network architectures have been compared: YOLOv5s and Faster R-CNN. Accuracy and computational cost
have been used as comparison criteria. The results show that both models perform similar in terms of accuracy but the smaller version of the
YOLOv5 network (YOLOv5s) is able to obtain better results in computational cost.

Keywords: *C. elegans* · Detection network · YOLOv5 · Faster R-CNN

1 Introduction

The nematode *Caenorhabditis elegans* (*C. elegans*) has been used as an important animal model for many years [2]. In advanced ages, just like humans, they
present some pathologies, physical deterioration, mobility loss, etc. It has a short
life (approximately 3 weeks) and a length of 1 mm, which makes it easy to handle
and grow. They can be stored in large quantities and small spaces (Petri dishes)
[15]. These characteristics allow large-scale assays to be performed economically
and make this nematode an ideal model for research into neurodegenerative
diseases and the development of new drugs.

Despite these advantages, handling and observation of these nematodes are
costly and require qualified technicians. For this reason, computer vision techniques allow these processes to be automated, increasing productivity and precision in the development of assays.

The detection of *C. elegans* is the first task in automatic image processing
applications such as monitoring, tracking [9–12], lifespan [6,18] and healthspan
[4,7,13]. To date, many methods perform segmentation pre-processing and
search for worm characteristics in order to filter worms (object of interest) from
non-worms (noise), which takes an additional computational cost.

A. I. Pereira et al. (Eds.): OL2A 2022, CCIS 1754, pp. 776–787, 2022.
https://doi.org/10.1007/978-3-031-23236-7_53

In recent years, image processing methods based on artificial neural networks have gained much popularity in these *C. elegans* applications, as they have great advantages compared to traditional computer vision methods based on feature extraction (using segmentation, edge detection, textures). Feature extraction is a costly process as it requires experience and trial and error to select the optimal ones. In addition, it is difficult to adjust the parameters of the image processing algorithms to work on different images.

Detection methods based on artificial neural networks have achieved great results, outperforming classical methods. The main detection methods based on deep learning can be classified into two groups: one-stage methods (YOLO, SSD, RetinaNet) and two-stage methods (Faster R-CNN, RFCN, Mask R-CNN).

These are some of the latest studies that show the advantages of artificial neural networks in the detection of *C. elegans*:

- [1] implement Faster R-CNN object detection models for detection and location of *C. elegans* in different conditions. This study demonstrates some of the advantages of Faster R-CNN algorithm to identify, count and track behaviors in comparison to traditional methods in terms of speed and flexibility. These traditional image processing methods, such as background subtraction or using morphological features, are more sensitive to changes in the environmental conditions due to complex experimental setups, resulting in low accuracy to detect objects of interest.
- [5] present a low-cost system including a DIY microscope to capture low-resolution images. They use the framework Mask R-CNN to detect, locate and classify *C. elegans* with high accuracy, rather than traditional methods such as human counting and analyzing high-resolution microscope images, which result in longer times and lower efficiency. They also generate a great number of masks by a preprocessing method that includes visual inspection, since the Mask R-CNN algorithm needs them as an input.

In summary, the main goals of this study are:

- Analyze the use of detection methods based on artificial neural networks for the detection of *C. elegans* in low resolution images.
- Compare two of the most widely used object detection architectures (YOLO [21] and Faster R-CNN [22]) in terms of accuracy and computational cost.

2   Materials and Method

2.1   *C. elegans* Strains and Culture Conditions

The *C. elegans* that were used to perform detection assays had the following features: strains N2, Bristol (wild-type) and CB1370, *daf*-2 (e1370). They were provided by the Caenorhabditis Genetics Centre at the University of Minnesota.

All worms were age-synchronized and pipetted onto Nematode Growth Medium (NGM) in 55 mm Petri plates, where the temperature was kept at 20 °C.

The worms were fed with strain OP50 of *Escherichia coli*, seeded in the middle of the plate to avoid occluded wall zones, as *C. elegans* tend to stay on the lawn. To reduce fungal contamination, fungizone was added to the plates [23], and FUdR (0.2 mM) was added to the plates to decrease the probability of reproduction.

In the laboratory, the operator had to follow a specific methodology to obtain the images: (1) Extract the plates from the incubator to put them in the acquisition system; (2) Examine the lid, before initiating the capture, to check there is no condensation and wipe it if detected; (3) Capture a sequence of 30 images per plate at 1 fps and return the plates to the incubator. This method was designed to prevent condensation in the cover.

2.2 Image Capture Method

Images were captured using the monitoring system developed in [19], that uses the active backlight illumination method proposed in [20]. Active backlighting technique has been shown to be effective for low-resolution *C. elegans* applications for both the mentioned [20] and [17] capture systems. The monitoring system is based on an RGB Raspberry Pi camera v1.3 (OmniVision OV5647, with a resolution of 2592 × 1944 pixels, a pixel size of 1.4 × 1.4 µm, a view field of 53.50º × 41.41°, optical size of 1/4", and focal ratio of 2.9) placed in front of the lighting system (a 7" Raspberry Pi display 800 × 480 at a resolution at 60 fps, 24 bit RGB colour) and the inspected plate in between both devices. A Raspberry Pi 3 was used as a processor to control lighting. The distance between the camera and the Petri plate was sufficient to enable a complete picture of the Petri plate, and the camera lens was focused at this distance (about 77 mm). The system captured images of 1944 × 1944 pixels at a frequency 1 Hz. A graphic of the capture system is shown in Fig. 1.

The code, components and the guidelines to build the monitoring system and the assembly description can be found in the repository https://github.com/JCPuchalt/SiViS.

2.3 Dataset Generation and Labeling

The dataset is composed of 1901 images captured from 106 test plates with the SiViS system [20]. Each plate contains between 10 and 15 nematodes. These images were manually labeled by marking the bounding boxes of each nematode.

The dataset was divided into three subsets using the following proportions: 70% for training, 10% for validation and 20% for test. Number of images and labels in each subset are shown Table 1.

2.4 Detection Method

In this article it was decided to test with the best-known detection methods based on artificial neural networks: YOLOv5 and Faster R-CNN.

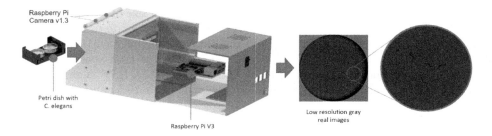

Fig. 1. Image capture system. Location of the Petri dishes, as well as the other components of the image acquisition system.

Table 1. Number of images and labels in each subset.

	Images	Labels
Train	1330	14004
Val	190	1993
Test	381	3920

Faster RCNN is an architecture proposed in [22]. It consists of three parts: (1) a convolutional neural network that extracts the image features; (2) a Region Proposal Network (RPN) in charge of obtaining the candidate bounding boxes and (3) a network in charge of performing the classification and regression of the bounding box coordinates.

YOLOv5 is an object detection algorithm created by Glenn Jocher in 2020. Considering previous models of the YOLO series, YOLOv5 offers higher accuracy, faster calculated speed and smaller size. Among the YOLOv5 models, YOLOv5s works the fastest, although the average precision is the lowest. The YOLOv5 network consists in three main parts: Backbone, Neck and Head. Backbone gathers and produces picture characteristics on various image granularities when the image is supplied. The picture characteristics are then stitched and transmitted to the prediction layer by Neck, where the image features are predicted by Head to generate bounding boxes and predicted categories [3].

2.5 Training and Evaluation Method

The networks were implemented and trained using the Pytorch deep learning framework [16] on a computer Gigabyte Technology Z390 AORUS PRO machine, Intel(R) Core (TM) i9-9900KF CPU @ 3.60 GHz x16 with 32 GB of RAM, and NVIDIA GeForce RTX 2080 Ti graphics card with 4352 Cuda cores, Ubuntu 19.04 64bits operating system.

Faster R-CNN. In this work the Faster R-CNN model architecture was used with a ResNet-50-FPN backbone pre-trained with COCO dataset [14] (Fig. 2).

The network was trained for 150 epochs with a batch size of 6 samples using the implementation of https://pytorch.org/tutorials/intermediate/torchvision_tutorial.html. A Reduce Learning Rate on Plateau scheduler with a patience of 3 epochs and a factor of 0.1 was used. The optimizer used was SGD with momentum 0.9 and weight decay 0.0005. Vertical flip (0.5), HSV augmentation (hue = 0.015, saturation = 0.7, value = 0.4), image scale (0.5) and translation (0.1) were used as data augmentation techniques.

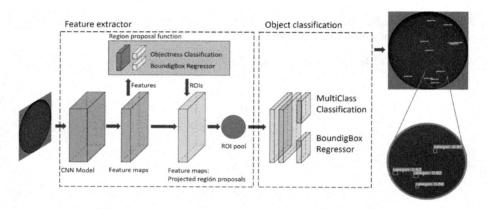

Fig. 2. Image pipeline through Fast R-CNN architecture. The blocks of the Fast R-CNN architecture were made using the PlotNeuralNet tool [8].

YOLOv5. To train YOLOv5 we used the implementation of (https://github.com/ultralytics/yolov5) in its YOLOv5s version, which is the smallest and fastest (Fig. 3).

We used the weights pretrained on the COCO dataset. It was trained with a batch size of 6 samples for 150 epochs using the SGD optimizer with momentum 0.937 and weight decay 0.0005. LambdaLR Learning Rate scheduler was used with the configuration proposed in the original implementation and other data augmentations, such as Vertical flip (0.5), HSV augmentation (hue = 0.015, saturation = 0.7, value = 0.4), image scale (0.5) and translation (0.1) were used.

The YOLOv5 model needed an image size multiple of 32 and, consequently, this model resized automatically the images to 1952 pixels. To make both algorithms work in the same image conditions, the images were resized with the same scale factor for Faster R-CNN model. Before this, in this model's dataloader, a function to crop and resize the images was implemented, since Faster R-CNN model needed an image size between 800 and 1333 pixels.

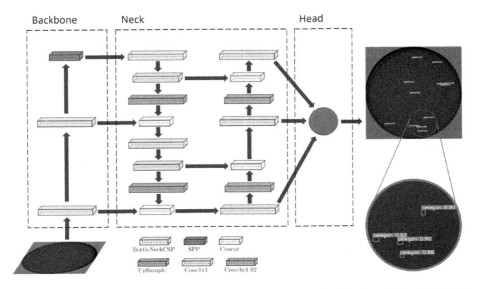

Fig. 3. Image pipeline through YOLOv5 architecture. The blocks of the YOLOv5 architecture were made using the PlotNeuralNet tool [8].

2.6 Evaluation Methods (Metrics)

To compare YOLOv5 and Faster R-CNN it is necessary to use some metrics that can be applied to both models, so the comparison is fair and adequate. The main metrics that will be used are computational cost and mean Average Precision (mAP), which is obtained from other metrics, precision and recall.

To decide whether a prediction is correct, the IoU is used, which measures the degree of overlap between the real box delimiting the object and the one predicted by the network. If the IoU value exceeds a threshold, it is considered True Positive (TP), otherwise it is considered False Positive (FP). If the network does not find an object, it is considered False Negative (FN).

Precision: It represents the relation between the correct detections and all the detections made by the model (Eq 1).

$$Precision = \frac{TP}{TP + FP} \tag{1}$$

Recall: It shows the ability of the model to make correct detections out of all ground true bounding boxes (Eq 2).

$$Recall = \frac{TP}{TP + FN} \tag{2}$$

Average Precision (AP): It is calculated as the area under the precision-recall curve, thus summarizing the information of the curve in one parameter (Eq 3).

$$AP = \int_0^1 P(R)dR \tag{3}$$

Mean Average Precision (mAP): This is obtained calculating the mean of APs over all IoU tresholds. In this case, the range of IoU tresholds used is [0.5; 0.95] (Eq. 4).

$$mAP = \frac{1}{N} \sum AP(n) \tag{4}$$

where N is the total number of IoU thresholds and AP(n) is the average precision for each IoU threshold value.

Computational Cost: It measures the amount of resources a neural network uses in a process, which determines the amount of time the process lasts. In this case, time per prediction will be measured to compare the computational costs in inference, which allows to determine how both models would work for possible real-time applications. For this reason, this metric will be measured in seconds.

3   Experimental Results

This section presents the results obtained after training with the YOLOv5s and Faster R-CNN networks. The results were obtained with the best trained models in the three subsets (train, validation, test, Table 2, 3, 4 respectively).

Table 2. Train results.

Model	Parameters	mAP@0.5	mAP@[0.5–0.95]
YOLOv5s	7.5M	0.961	0.762
Faster R-CNN	41.3M	0.983	0.759

Table 3. Eval results.

Model	mAP@0.5	mAP@[0.5–0.95]
YOLOv5s	0.957	0.776
Faster R-CNN	0.947	0.705

In Figs. 4, 5, 6 we can find examples of true positives, false positives and false negatives respectively obtained when predicting with the models.

Table 4. Test results

Model	Time/prediction (ms)	mAP@0.5	mAP@[0.5–0.95]
YOLOv5s	6.03	0.932	0.806
Faster R-CNN	43.25	0.944	0.691

Fig. 4. Example of true positives obtained by applying the detection models. The model predictions are shown in red and the labels in green. (Color figure online)

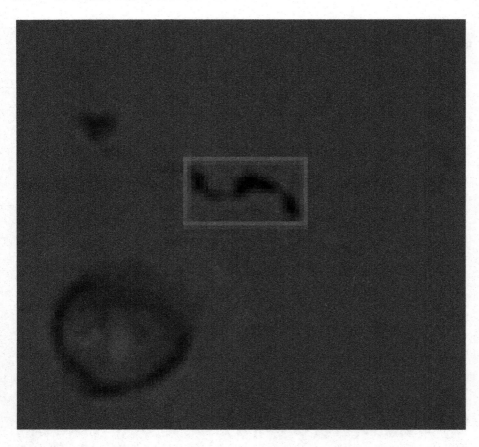

Fig. 5. Example of false positives due to dirt of the plate. The model predictions are shown in red and the labels in green. (Color figure online)

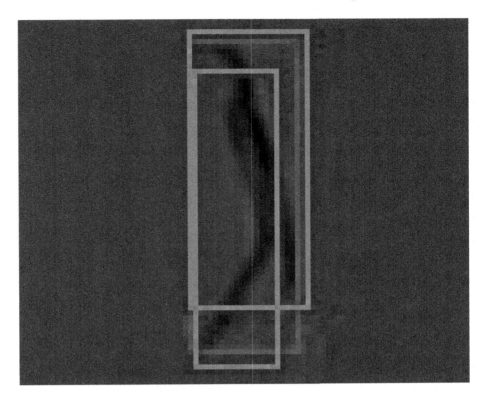

Fig. 6. Example of false negatives due to worm aggregations. The model predictions are shown in red and the labels in green. (Color figure online)

4   Discussion

The experiments carried out in this study have shown that, as expected, due to the greater number of parameters of the Faster R-CNN model used (backbone resnet50) with respect to YOLOv5s, the computational cost is higher, as reflected in the inference times of both models. Generally, in *C. elegans* image acquisition, the images are captured at a frequency 1 Hz, maximum 15 Hz, due to the low speed of movement of the nematodes. It has thus been shown that both detection techniques could be used for real-time monitoring of *C. elegans*. This would be useful for healthspan assays in which the movements of the nematodes are analysed.

In terms of network performance, the results of the experiments show that they perform similarly, achieving a mAP value of around 93–94% for an IoU treshold of 0.5. As explained in section *2.6 Evaluation methods (Metrics)*, this metric is quite representative, as it considers precision and recall values. The YOLOv5s model obtains a better mAP result for IoU treshold [0.5–0.95].

5   Conclusion and Future Work

Finally, it can be concluded that the YOLOv5s model performs better in this application of *C. elegans* detection, as it achieves similar accuracy results to those obtained with Faster R-CNN (accuracy values of 93.2% and 94.4% respectively for our dataset) but in less time and, consequently, with a lower computational cost.

As future work, the available dataset could be labelled by obtaining the nematode masks. With this new dataset, a Mask R-CNN network could be trained, which would have the advantage over YOLO of obtaining a segmentation. Another option to avoid the cost of labelling would be to use synthetic images to train the network.

Acknowledgment. This study was supported by the Plan Nacional de I+D with Project RTI2018-094312-B-I00, FPI Predoctoral contract PRE2019-088214, Ministerio de Universidades (Spain) under grantFPU20/02639 and by European FEDER funds. ADM Nutrition, Biopolis SL, and Archer Daniels Midland provided support in the supply of *C. elegans*.

References

1. Bates, K., Le, K.N., Lu, H.: Deep learning for robust and flexible tracking in behavioral studies for C. elegans. PLOS Comput. Biol. **18**(4), e1009942 (2022)
2. Biron, D., Haspel, G. (eds.): C. elegans. MMB, vol. 1327. Humana Press, Totowa (2015). https://doi.org/10.1007/978-1-4939-2842-2
3. Chen, Z., et al.: Plant disease recognition model based on improved YOLOv5. Agronomy **12**(2), 365 (2022)
4. Di Rosa, G., et al.: Healthspan enhancement by olive polyphenols in C. elegans wild type and Parkinson's models. Int. J. Mol. Sci. **21**(11) (2020). https://doi.org/10.3390/ijms21113893
5. Fudickar, S., Nustede, E.J., Dreyer, E., Bornhorst, J.: Mask R-CNN based C. elegans detection with a DIY microscope. Biosensors **11**(8), 257 (2021)
6. García Garví, A., Puchalt, J.C., Layana Castro, P.E., Navarro Moya, F., Sánchez-Salmerón, A.J.: Towards lifespan automation for Caenorhabditis elegans based on deep learning: analysing convolutional and recurrent neural networks for dead or live classification. Sensors **21**(14) (2021). https://doi.org/10.3390/s21144943
7. Hahm, J.H., et al.: C. elegans maximum velocity correlates with healthspan and is maintained in worms with an insulin receptor mutation. Nat. Commun. **6**(1), 1–7 (2015). https://doi.org/10.1038/ncomms9919
8. Iqbal, H.: Harisiqbal88/plotneuralnet v1.0.0 (2018). code https://github.com/HarisIqbal88/PlotNeuralNet
9. Javer, A., et al.: An open-source platform for analyzing and sharing worm-behavior data. Nat. Methods **15** (2018). https://doi.org/10.1038/s41592-018-0112-1
10. Koopman, M., et al.: Assessing motor-related phenotypes of Caenorhabditis elegans with the wide field-of-view nematode tracking platform. Nat. Protoc. **15**, 1–36 (2020). https://doi.org/10.1038/s41596-020-0321-9
11. Layana Castro, P.E., Puchalt, J.C., García Garví, A., Sánchez-Salmerón, A.J.: Caenorhabditis elegans multi-tracker based on a modified skeleton algorithm. Sensors **21**(16) (2021). https://doi.org/10.3390/s21165622

12. Layana Castro, P.E., Puchalt, J.C., Sánchez-Salmerón, A.J.: Improving skeleton algorithm for helping Caenorhabditis elegans trackers. Sci. Rep. **10**(1), 22247 (2020). https://doi.org/10.1038/s41598-020-79430-8

13. Le, K.N., Zhan, M., Cho, Y., Wan, J., Patel, D.S., Lu, H.: An automated platform to monitor long-term behavior and healthspan in Caenorhabditis elegans under precise environmental control. Commun. Biol. **3**(1), 1–13 (2020). https://doi.org/10.1038/s42003-020-1013-2

14. Lin, T.-Y., et al.: Microsoft COCO: common objects in context. In: Fleet, D., Pajdla, T., Schiele, B., Tuytelaars, T. (eds.) ECCV 2014. LNCS, vol. 8693, pp. 740–755. Springer, Cham (2014). https://doi.org/10.1007/978-3-319-10602-1_48

15. Olsen, A., Gill, M.S. (eds.): Ageing: Lessons from C. elegans. HAL. Springer, Cham (2017). https://doi.org/10.1007/978-3-319-44703-2

16. Paszke, A., et al.: PyTorch: an imperative style, high-performance deep learning library. In: Advances in Neural Information Processing Systems 32 (2019)

17. Puchalt, J.C., Gonzalez-Rojo, J.F., Gómez-Escribano, A.P., Vázquez-Manrique, R.P., Sánchez-Salmerón, A.J.: Multiview motion tracking based on a cartesian robot to monitor Caenorhabditis elegans in standard petri dishes. Sci. Rep. **12**(1), 1–11 (2022). https://doi.org/10.1038/s41598-022-05823-6

18. Puchalt, J.C., Layana Castro, P.E., Sánchez-Salmerón, A.J.: Reducing results variance in lifespan machines: an analysis of the influence of vibrotaxis on wild-type Caenorhabditis elegans for the death criterion. Sensors **20**(21) (2020). https://doi.org/10.3390/s20215981

19. Puchalt, J.C., Sánchez-Salmerón, A.J., Eugenio, I., Llopis, S., Martínez, R., Martorell, P.: Small flexible automated system for monitoring Caenorhabditis elegans lifespan based on active vision and image processing techniques. Sci. Rep. **11** (2021). https://doi.org/10.1038/s41598-021-91898-6

20. Puchalt, J.C., Sánchez-Salmerón, A.J., Martorell Guerola, P., Genovés Martínez, S.: Active backlight for automating visual monitoring: an analysis of a lighting control technique for Caenorhabditis elegans cultured on standard petri plates. PLoS ONE **14**(4), 1–18 (2019). https://doi.org/10.1371/journal.pone.0215548

21. Redmon, J., Divvala, S., Girshick, R., Farhadi, A.: You only look once: unified, real-time object detection. In: Proceedings of the IEEE Conference on Computer Vision and Pattern Recognition, pp. 779–788 (2016)

22. Ren, S., He, K., Girshick, R., Sun, J.: Faster R-CNN: towards real-time object detection with region proposal networks. In: Advances in Neural Information Processing Systems 28 (2015)

23. Stiernagle, T.: Maintenance of C. elegans. WormBook. The C. elegans research community. WormBook (2006)

Object Detection for Indoor Localization System

João Braun[1,2,3]([⊠]) [iD], João Mendes[1,3] [iD], Ana I. Pereira[1] [iD], José Lima[1,2,3] [iD], and Paulo Costa[2] [iD]

[1] Research Centre in Digitalization and Intelligent Robotics (CeDRI), Instituto Politécnico de Bragança, Campus de Santa Apolónia, 5300-253 Bragança, Portugal
{jbneto,joao.cmendes,apereira,jllima}@ipb.pt
[2] INESC TEC - INESC Technology and Science, Faculty of Engineering of University of Porto, Porto, Portugal
paco@fe.up.pt
[3] Laboratório para a Sustentabilidade e Tecnologia em Regiões de Montanha (SusTEC), Instituto Politécnico de Bragança, Campus de Santa Apolónia, 5300-253 Bragança, Portugal

Abstract. The urge for robust and reliable localization systems for autonomous mobile robots (AMR) is increasing since the demand for these automated systems is rising in service, industry, and other areas of the economy. The localization of AMRs is one of the crucial challenges, and several approaches exist to solve this. The most well-known localization systems are based on LiDAR data due to their reliability, accuracy, and robustness. One standard method is to match the reference map information with the actual readings from LiDAR or camera sensors, allowing localization to be performed. However, this approach has difficulties handling anything that does not belong to the original map since it affects the matching algorithm's performance. Therefore, they should be considered outliers. In this paper, a deep learning-based object detection algorithm is not only used for detection but also to classify them as outliers from the localization's perspective. This is an innovative approach to improve the localization results in a real mobile platform. Results are encouraging, and the proposed methodology is being tested in a real robot.

Keywords: Object detection · Convolutional neural networks · Deep learning · Autonomous mobile robot · Indoor positioning · Indoor localization

1 Introduction

Mobile robot applications in industry and service areas are increasing daily. These autonomous applications require certain characteristics from the robots, and one of the most crucial ones is the localization. That is, developing a localization system so that the robot can "answer" the question "where am I?" repeatedly in static and dynamic environments. For this reason, there are several different approaches to handling this problem. These approaches, albeit different,

A. I. Pereira et al. (Eds.): OL2A 2022, CCIS 1754, pp. 788–803, 2022.
https://doi.org/10.1007/978-3-031-23236-7_54

utilize several sensors, sensor fusion algorithms, and localization techniques to maximize the "belief" that the robot is where the estimation was made, i.e., to mitigate the estimation error. One simple example, considered a broad classification for localization systems in mobile robotics, is indoor and outdoor environments. Different sensors can be employed depending on the classification, such as the GPS that would not work in indoor applications yet is highly effective in outdoor applications [1]. Also, with the advance in technology, these systems have become more trustworthy and feasible to implement. Therefore, the use of autonomous mobile robots is increasing in different areas of our society. For indoor localization purposes, which is the scope of this research work, LiDAR is a choice that is usually selected due to its reliability. Its output data should be interpreted and processed with an algorithm to obtain the correct robot's pose. In this reasoning, there are different approaches such as Perfect match (PM) [2], Iterative Closest Point (ICP) [3], and Normal Distributions Transform (NDT) [4]. Although different, these approaches, in their essence, work similarly by matching the map information with the actual readings from 2D or 3D sensors, i.e., minimizing the matching error or loss function between the two. However, what happens if objects that were previously positioned somewhere when the reference map was built are then moved to different places during the robot's operation? In addition, there is also the situation that objects or personnel that do not belong to the map can be present during the robot's execution. The matching error will increase in such situations, decreasing the localization's performance. Therefore, these objects and personnel can be considered outliers from the localization's perspective. Using artificial intelligence (AI), it would be hypothetically possible to ignore them. An object detection system based on computer vision, for instance, can be an extra input to the localization algorithm since it can classify the objects as movable, immovable, permanent, temporary, and so on.

Moreover, it can decide if these objects belong to the pre-built map of the environment. Besides, it could even update the reference map if it identifies that a particular object was moved (a chair in an office, for instance) after a certain number of detections in a different position from the original one. Therefore, object detection is not only an area of knowledge that is of interest to computer vision and machine learning researchers but also to researchers of other areas of expertise that can use such tools in engineering applications. Thus, this paper describes an object detection system that semantically characterizes the obstacles and map discrepancies from imagery data to compare with the map data coming from the 2D LiDAR and analyze if it is possible to identify the outliers in it. YOLOv4 was used as the AI for object detection in real-time. The described system is implemented on an actual mobile robot prototype that was the base of the experiments. The remaining paper is organized as follows: after a brief introduction, Sect. 2 will detail the state of the art regarding object detection based on deep learning and its applications in the localization of mobile robots. The methodology applied is described in Sect. 3. The results of the tests applied to validate the prel iminary proposal are addressed in Sect. 4. Section 5 describes the conclusion and future work intended for this project.

2   State of the Art

The state of the art of object detection with deep learning is pervasive, and several review papers address it [5–7]. According to [8], in the context of mobile robotics, deep learning is the field of science that engages in training extensive neural networks using complex functions to change raw high-dimensional data from a multi-modal state to another that a robotic system can understand. In addition, one can conclude that real-time processing speed is the utmost concern for object identification in mobile robotics, alongside accuracy. Therefore, one type of layer that is necessary its mentioning for its extreme importance in image processing is the convolutional layer. In contrast to traditional layers (which are fully connected), those apply the same weights and are locally connected, significantly reducing the final number of weights in the neural network [7]. Thus, these layers are expected to stand out in image processing applications [8]. One can better understand the importance of this type of layer by considering the scenario of images, which are typically composed of hundreds of thousands to millions of pixels that requires processing [8].

The state of the art of object detection can be separated into two periods, namely before and after the introduction of deep learning for object detection in 2013, where AlexNet served as the watershed between traditional and CNNs-based methods [6]. Figure 1 illustrates a classification diagram of object detection algorithms.

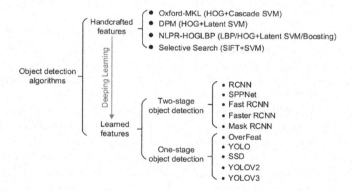

Fig. 1. Classification of object detection algorithms [6].

For a complete story and milestone review of the state of the art of object detection, the reader is referred to [6]. That said, before 2013, there were works such as [9–11]. The authors of the first-mentioned work proposed a novel machine learning approach for object detection capable of rapidly processing images.

They proposed three key contributions, and their approach runs at 15 frames per second. The authors of the second work showed that Histograms of Oriented Gradient (HOG) descriptors outperformed existing feature sets for human detection. They studied the influence of each phase of the computation on performance. Finally, the third work introduced a general framework that trains Latent Support Vector Machines (LSVMs), which is employed in their system that is based on multiscale deformable models [11].

After the introduction of convolutional neural networks (CNNs), the approaches for object detection can be divided into two categories, two-stage and one-stage [6]. According to [12], two-stage detectors are typically more accurate, and single-shot detectors are normally faster. In addition, for two-stage detectors, the first stage is usually used to generate proposals that are classified during the second stage [12]. According to [6], the papers that are considered milestones for two-stage detectors are displayed in Fig. 2.

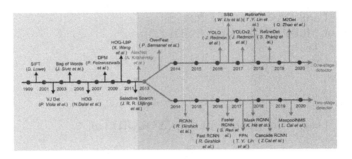

Fig. 2. Milestones of object detection evolution [6].

In this reasoning, the list below displays them with some more added to it to update for 2021:

– Region-based Convolutional Neural Networks (R-CNN) [13].
– Fast R-CNN [14].
– Faster R-CNN [15].
– Feature Pyramid Networks (FPN) [16].
– Mask R-CNN [17].
– Cascade R-CNN [18].
– Maxpool Non-maximum Suppression (MaxpoolNMS) [19].
– Granulated Region-based Convolutional Neural Networks (G-RCNN) [20].

According to [12], R-CNN popularized the two-stage approach. The algorithm works by generating category-independent region proposals using Selective Search, in which their features are extracted using a large CNN. Finally, they are classified using a set of linear SVMs. Fast R-CNN extended R-CNN by using a convolutional implementation of the sliding window approach to classify the regions [12]. Faster R-CNN improved Fast R-CNN by employing a CNN to propose regions instead of selective search [12]. The authors from [16] proposed the architecture entitled Feature Pyramid Networks, which implements feature pyramids in the Faster R-CNN system. They stated that they achieved state-of-the-art single-model results surpassing the ones at that time. Mask R-CNN expands Faster R-CNN by adding a branch for predicting an object mask in parallel with the existing branch for bounding box recognition [17]. Cascade R-CNN [18] addressed problems regarding the trade-off of low and high intersection over union (IoU) threshold. MaxpoolNMS was proposed in [19] to eliminate the bottlenecks in two-stage detectors, achieving a 20 times faster speed than Gree-dyNMS. Finally, by incorporating the concept of granulation in a deep CNN, G-RCNN improves Fast R-CNN and Faster R-CNN [20].

Regarding one-stage object detection algorithms, the most important ones, with more added to the list, according to [6] are:

- OverFeat [21].
- You Only Look Once (YOLO) [22].
- Single Shot MultiBox Detector (SSD) [23].
- RetinaNet [24].
- RefineDet [25].
- M2Det [26].
- YOLOv3 [27].
- YOLOv4 [28].
- You Only Learn One Representation (YOLOR) [29].

Authors from [21] proposed Overfeat architecture, which integrated object classification and location into one network architecture [6]. YOLO introduced a new approach to object detection in 2016. In contrast to previous works that use classifiers to perform detection, YOLO frames the object detection as a regression problem to spatially separated bounding boxes and associated class probabilities [22]. In other words, the algorithm can predict bounding boxes and class probabilities from full images in one stage. According to the authors, their architecture is extremely fast, reaching 45 FPS on a Titan X. In addition, a smaller version, called Fast YOLO, reaches 155 FPS while still achieving double mean average precision (mAP) of other real-time detectors [22]. In addition, the authors admit that even though their approach makes more localization errors, their approach is less likely to predict false positives. Moreover, it is possible to see that their approach outperforms other detection methods, such as R-CNN, in certain situations [22].

In comparison, SSD utilizes convolutional layers instead of fully connected layers that YOLO uses [12]. RetinaNet addressed the class imbalance problem that dense detectors had by reshaping the standard cross-entropy loss [24]. RefineDet, a single-shot detector with better accuracy than two-stage detectors and that maintains the efficiency of single-shot approaches, was proposed by [25]. Authors in [26] proposed a multi-level FPN to construct more effective pyramids for object detection. Finally, some improvements were made in YOLO over the years [27–29]. According to the authors, YOLOv3 achieves a similar mAP as SSD three times faster. Finally, YOLOv4, compared with YOLOv3, achieved an improvement of 10% in the average precision and 12% in FPS.

2.1 Applications of Object Detection in Mobile Robots

The usage of object detection in autonomous mobile robots is not abundant, and even among the ones reported, they are not solely used for localization. The detection system can also be used in other processes of the AMRs, navigation, for instance. In this way, some of the research works found in the literature that used object detection in mobile robots are stated in this subsection.

A localization system was validated in a challenging indoor environment using objects from images. Their system used an object detector that relied on heatmaps, and a particle filter [30]. In addition, authors in [31] used an Internet of Things approach to develop a localization system for mobile robots using CNNs for feature extraction of the images. Their system uses a topological mapping methodology to explore the environment. Moreover, an object detection system and mapping for service robots was developed in [32]. Their robot autonomously navigates in a domestic environment whilst performing simultaneous localization and mapping (SLAM). Also, the robot detects predefined objects and integrates them into the generated map by estimating their position. In [33], authors proposed two object detection methods: contour detection and a descriptor-based technique. They are combined to overcome their respective limitations for semantic navigation. Finally, authors in [34] proposed a scene recognition system using common indoor objects such as furniture and doors. In other words, they presented a generative probabilistic hierarchical model that utilizes object category classifiers to associate low-level features to objects and contextual relations to associate these objects to scenes.

3 Methodology

The idea behind the AI embedded in the localization system is to use an object detection algorithm to identify the objects that an RGB camera will capture. In this way, the AI will analyze if these objects are helpful for localization at a given time. The preliminary approach is better described in the flowchart in Fig. 3.

The flowchart describes one control cycle of the AI approach, which would be a part of the general control cycle of the localization system. Following the illustration, it is possible to see that the data from the sensors and the robot are inserted into the object detection algorithm, which will identify and perform decisions about the detected objects. Therefore, an RGB camera is crucial to this approach because the other sensors provide too little information about the objects. Even more, if they are, in fact, objects that belong to the environment but were moved from their original place, the AI could remap them, in the robot's internal map, to their new location after a specific criterion is met. In this

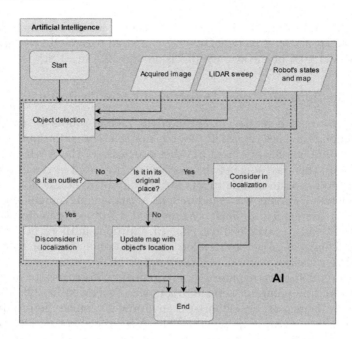

Fig. 3. Flowchart of one control cycle of the AI approach.

reasoning, one can note that the AI will depend heavily on the object detection algorithm. This is not a problem since, as already described in Sect. 2, there are state-of-the-art detection algorithms with good accuracy and speed. The database used to train the CNNs' frameworks might need to be adapted for each work scenario for optimization purposes. In this reasoning, to better understand the preliminary's AI proposal, some examples following the flowchart of Fig. 3 will be described.

Consider the hypothetical situation where a mobile robot, equipped with several sensors, performs its localization using a map-matching algorithm. In this scenario, an employee enters the robot's operation area, affecting the robot's localization since it is an outlier. In this way, by using computer vision with AI, the robot would discern not to consider the data from the sensors that came from the employee's location. Therefore, improving the localization's performance midst of dynamic outliers.

Moreover, it would theoretically work with static outliers as well. Imagine the situation where an object's position, which belongs to the work environment, was switched. In this case, the robot would see and identify the object, ignoring it for localization. Even more, the robot could remap this object to its new position in the robot's reference map since it could assume that the object (a chair, for instance) was left in that position.

This proposed work can be tested for validation in numerous possible scenarios and domains since the demand and usage of autonomous mobile robots are increasing rapidly. Some examples are offices, shopping centres, industries, and hospitals. The localization system's design can change depending on the environment in which it will be applied since there are several types of sensors and sensor fusion techniques. All of them have advantages and disadvantages that also depend on the environment. Still, it is possible to sketch a general architecture for the system that can be later adapted for the selected case study. In this reasoning, Fig. 4 describes the general architecture of the localization system.

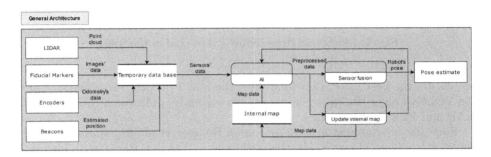

Fig. 4. Data flow diagram of the general architecture for the localization system.

Following Fig. 4, one can note that proprioceptive and exteroceptive sensors' data will be stored in a temporary database to address the synchronization problem between the sensors. Afterwards, they will be sent to the AI's process block. Soon after, the AI will preprocess the data, which will be used in the sensor fusion algorithm's block. This block will generate the robot's pose estimate that will be used for its localization and to update the robot's internal map for future reference in combination with the newer preprocessed data. In other words, the previous internal map, pose estimate, and preprocessed data will be used in the AI's process block for future iterations.

3.1 Robot Architecture

The AMR used in the tests is a differential-drive mobile platform that uses two 17HS16-2004S1 stepper motors for actuation, one Raspberry Pi 3B for the high-level control of the robot, a 12V lead battery, and an Arduino Uno for the low-level control of the robot. Regarding the sensors, it has one Raspberry Pi Camera V2 and one Hokuyo URG-04LX-UG01 LiDAR sensor. Figure 5 displays the AMR.

3.2 YOLO

Given the high processing speed requirement of the proposed approach, a single-stage detection algorithm was used. In other words, although the latter does

Fig. 5. Differential-drive mobile robot used in the tests.

not ensure the best mAP, they guarantee the best FPS processing speed. Thus, the YOLOv4 algorithm was selected for the system's application, considering its mAP and FPS characteristics.

Since its development in 2015 by Joseph Redmon et al. [22], this single-stage detector has been improved. In this first version, the raw frame is divided into S x S grid cells of equal dimensions, each responsible for identifying if a given object's centre is inside. These cells can also predict several bounding boxes composed of five distinct values, namely the box's centre coordinates, height, width, and confidence. These are "evaluated" through the Intersection over Union approach (IOU), where less accurate bounding boxes are eliminated. In addition, the structure based on Googlenet has 24 convolutional layers followed by two fully connected layers, changing the inception module by using a 1×1 reduction layer followed by 3×3 convolutional layers. Finally, this detector uses the sum of squares to calculate the loss.

In the second version, published in 2017 in [35], the authors presented the so-called YOLO9000 or YOLOv2, a system capable of detecting more than 9000 distinct objects. In this version, all fully convolutional layers of YOLOv1 were removed, leaving 19 convolutional layers and five max-pooling layers. In addition to the adjustment of the structure, several other improvements were made. The first, and the most notorious for introducing batch standardization, was high-resolution classifiers that allowed the increase in training input to a resolution of 448×448 pixels compared to the 224×224 pixels of YOLOv1. The second contribution was the addition of anchor boxes. The utilization of the k-means model to cluster grids for artefacts was the third. The fourth was the fine-grained approach to improve the distinction of small objects. Finally, the fifth was the multi-scale training that allowed the prediction of the results for different resolutions, reaching 90 FPS speeds in low image resolution and 78.6 mAP when high-resolution images are used.

The third version of YOLO [27], presented in 2018, continued to value the speed, ensuring the same accuracy as SSD [23] but three times faster. To achieve this, the authors made some adjustments that, according to them, were no more than "We mostly took good ideas from other people". In this reasoning, the authors presented a system with a different cost function concerning bounding boxes, now using logistics regression. Also, the class forecast was improved by replacing the SoftMax function with logistics classifiers. Classification Loss is also measured in a new form using Sigmoid Cross-center for each number. Moreover, the feature extractor was exchanged using a Darknet-53 instead of the Darknet-19 used in the previous version to improve the classifier's accuracy. The result of these adaptations is an improvement in object identification and detection, especially in objects of small dimensions.

Two years later, in 2020, came the fourth version, the YOLOV4 [28]. It was announced as "Optimal Speed and Accuracy of Object Detection", designed for parallel computing and production systems. The authors stated that training and testing this algorithm is available to anyone with a conventional GPU since the training process has been adjusted by replacing the traditional mini-batches with a smaller mini-batch. The resource extractor was also changed, using the CSPDarkNet-53 instead of the conventional DarkNet-53. Additionally, another modification was the replacement of YOLOv3's FPN (Feature Pyramid Network) with the use of spatial Pyramid Pooling (SPP) and Path Aggregation Network (PAN). These and other modifications that were not mentioned ensured an improvement of 10% of mAP and 12% of FPS compared to YOLOv3.

After the evolution presented, in 2021, a new version of this detector, the YOLOv5, emerged. However, our focus will be on the fourth version of the detector, considering the good results (mAP/FPS) it achieves in some cases with its own dataset [36,37]. In addition to the original versions, there are also adaptations with fewer trainable layers for proper operation in embedded systems and mobile applications [38]. Thus, allowing the presented work to be applied on other platforms. In this way, in this first phase, YOLOv4 was implemented on a computer with the following specifications:

- CPU: Intel®Core^{TM} i7-10875H.
- GPU: NVIDIA®GeForce RTX^{TM} 3060 Laptop GPU 6 GB GDDR6.
- RAM: 32 GB DDR4.
- Storage: 1 TB NVMe SSD.

In this first application of the system, all the image processing was performed on the specified computer, using the Raspberry Pi 3B present in the robot only for its control. All the default definitions of the framework were used, and the pre-trained weights were derived from the MS Coco Dataset [39]. Images from the Raspberry Pi Camera V2, installed on the robot, were used to evaluate its operation, serving as the work's first iteration to test the software's applicability. In the future, all processing will be done on the robot itself using a microcomputer, such as a Raspberry Pi 4B, Jetson Nano or a Jetson Xavier NX.

3.3 LiDAR

The technical characteristics of the laser rangefinder used in this research work are presented in Table 1.

Table 1. Hokuyo URG-04-LX-UG01 technical specifications [40].

Attribute	Value
Range	5.6 [m]
Accuracy	from 60 to 1000 [mm]: ±30 [mm] from 1000 to 4095 [mm]: 3% of the measure distance
Scan window	240º
Angular resolution	0.36º
Frequency	10 [Hz]

A software was developed to take advantage of the information that the laser rangefinder provides by reading the data that comes from the sensor and interpreting it graphically. Figure 6 displays the software's main features.

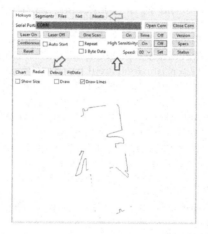

Fig. 6. Software that communicates with the Hokuyo LiDAR and interprets its data.

As one can see in the illustration, the software has several primary tabs pointed by the green arrow. It can also communicate and process the data that comes from Neato XV11 LiDAR. Moreover, there is also support to record the data in ".lasd" files, send it over the internet by UDP protocol, and configure a filter for the raw data. In the Hokuyo tab, several configuration options are pointed by the blue arrow, where the most important are the "Serial Port" and the "High Sensitivity" options. The former is responsible for opening the communication with the sensor, and the latter is responsible for turning on a high-sensitivity filter for the raw data. There are two plots to see the LiDAR sweeps in each iteration, and they can be accessed in the tabs indicated by the red arrow. The first type is a chart of the distances from the sensor's $[-\pi, \pi]$

angle range. The second one is a radial plot from the sensor's perspective, i.e., the centre of the sensor is the origin of the plot.

4   Prototype Validation

In this initial phase of the project, the results obtained only serve to validate the functioning of all the systems involved in this approach. In this way, it is possible to divide them into two distinct parts, the results of object classification and the results obtained through the LiDAR sensor.

Two tests were carried out to validate the system's functioning. The tests used mobile and fixed objects easily found in any work office that can be easily moved from their original position. Hence, they can be considered as outliers from the localization's perspective. Initially, only static objects were used, and in the second test, a person was also positioned in the image. After selecting the two scenarios, the robot was placed in the environment, and the test data were collected.

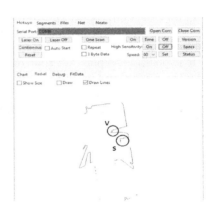

Fig. 7. YOLOv4 results from the first test.

Fig. 8. LiDAR results from the first test.

The first test is displayed in Figs. 7 and 8. The former shows a frame from the camera where the YOLOv4 detects and classifies what each object is. In the same reasoning, the latter shows a horizontal LiDAR sweep of the environment from the robot's perspective. In this radial plot, it is possible to identify the regions of points that correspond to these classified objects: their composition and relative position to the robot. The region representing the vase is indicated by the circle labelled V and the suitcase by the circle labelled S.

Afterwards, another "obstacle" was considered in the test scenario as shown in Fig. 10. In this case, a volunteer was asked to appear on the scene to observe the system's behaviour. The identification of the volunteer is more complicated because of the human body's non-homogenous form. Nevertheless, the system's behaviour was encouraging, with the volunteer being detected in both systems.

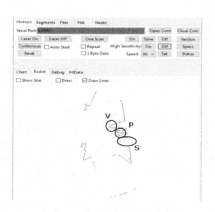

Fig. 9. YOLOv4 results from the second test.

Fig. 10. LiDAR results from the second test.

As shown in Fig. 10, LiDAR demonstrates the relative distance and composition at which the obstacles are located, where the vase is indicated by V, the person by P, and the suitcase by S. Moreover, the YOLOv4 algorithm detects the volunteer's presence with 64% confidence (Fig. 9) despite only the person's inferior body part being visible.

It is possible to perceive that by detecting the objects as outliers and associating their position and dimension with the localization system sensor's data, it will be possible to design an AI to process the erroneous data. With this information associated with the localization system's sensor data, LiDAR data, in this case, the AI would be possible to take action since it would have semantic information about the objects from around the robot.

5   Conclusion and Future Work

This paper presented an approach for a possible improvement of localization systems that relies on map-matching algorithms. The latter is a standard method for processing 2D or 3D data from LiDAR or cameras from a localization perspective. In the proposed approach, 2D LiDAR data is gathered and processed into a radial plot with a high-sensitivity filter. Moreover, an RGB camera is used to stream frames to the YOLOv4 object detection algorithm, which detects and classifies the objects in an office scenario. Thus, a mobile robot platform was prepared and used as a test bed. The validation consisted of two tests with objects easily found in an office environment. In this reasoning, the robot was positioned in front of a vase and a suitcase during the first test. During the second, besides the previous objects, a person walked in front of the robot. The results showed that it is possible to hypothetically improve a localization system for AMRs based on map-matching methods using an object detector and classifier. Future work aims to develop a localization system that relies on a map-matching algorithm with an AI that detects and removes the part of the data from the exteroceptive sensors of the map-matching algorithm that corresponds to the outliers. This way, it will be possible to validate if this approach improves the localization performance. Moreover, it is planned to develop an AI that will decide what the detected objects mean from a localization perspective, taking action based on it. In this reasoning, the pose estimation of the detected objects and their respective association with LiDAR's data will be addressed.

Acknowledgment. The authors are grateful to the Foundation for Science and Technology (FCT, Portugal) for financial support through national funds FCT/MCTES (PIDDAC) to CeDRI (UIDB/05757/2020 and UIDP/05757/2020) and SusTEC (LA/P/0007/2021). The project that gave rise to these results received the support of a fellowship from "la Caixa" Foundation (ID 100010434). The fellowship code is LCF/BQ/DI20/11780028.

References

1. Siegwart, R., Nourbakhsh, I.R., Scaramuzza, D.: Introduction to Autonomous Mobile Robots. MIT Press, Cambridge (2011)
2. Lauer, M., Lange, S., Riedmiller, M.: Calculating the perfect match: an efficient and accurate approach for robot self-localization. In: Bredenfeld, A., Jacoff, A., Noda, I., Takahashi, Y. (eds.) RoboCup 2005. LNCS (LNAI), vol. 4020, pp. 142–153. Springer, Heidelberg (2006). https://doi.org/10.1007/11780519_13
3. Besl, P.J., McKay, N.D.: Method for registration of 3-D shapes. In: Sensor Fusion IV: Control Paradigms and Data Structures, vol. 1611, pp. 586–606. Spie (1992)
4. Biber, P., Straßer, W.: The normal distributions transform: a new approach to laser scan matching. In: Proceedings 2003 IEEE/RSJ International Conference on Intelligent Robots and Systems (IROS 2003)(Cat. No. 03CH37453), vol. 3, pp. 2743–2748. IEEE (2003)
5. Zhao, Z.-Q., Zheng, P., Shou-tao, X., Xindong, W.: Object detection with deep learning: a review. IEEE Trans. Neural Netw. Learn. Syst. **30**(11), 3212–3232 (2019)
6. Xiao, Y., et al.: A review of object detection based on deep learning. Multimedia Tools Appl., 23729–23791 (2020). https://doi.org/10.1007/s11042-020-08976-6
7. Zhiqiang, W., Jun, L.: A review of object detection based on convolutional neural network. In: 2017 36th Chinese Control Conference (CCC), pp. 11104–11109. IEEE (2017)
8. Shabbir, J., Anwer, T.: A survey of deep learning techniques for mobile robot applications. arXiv preprint arXiv:1803.07608 (2018)
9. Viola, P., Jones, M.: Rapid object detection using a boosted cascade of simple features. In: Proceedings of the 2001 IEEE Computer Society Conference on Computer Vision and Pattern Recognition. CVPR 2001, vol. 1, pp. I–I (2001)
10. Dalal, N., Triggs, B.: Histograms of oriented gradients for human detection. In: 2005 IEEE Computer Society Conference on Computer Vision and Pattern Recognition (CVPR 2005), vol. 1, pp. 886–893. IEEE (2005)
11. Felzenszwalb, P., McAllester, D., Ramanan, D.: A discriminatively trained, multiscale, deformable part model. In: 2008 IEEE Conference on Computer Vision and Pattern Recognition, pp. 1–8 (2008)

12. Rajaratnam, S.: Development of a real-time vision framework for autonomous mobile robots in human-centered environments. Master's thesis, University of Toronto, Canada (2019)
13. Girshick, R., Donahue, J., Darrell, T., Malik, J.: Rich feature hierarchies for accurate object detection and semantic segmentation. In: Proceedings of the IEEE Conference on Computer Vision and Pattern Recognition, pp. 580–587 (2014)
14. Girshick, R.: Fast R-CNN. In: Proceedings of the IEEE International Conference on Computer Vision, pp. 1440–1448 (2015)
15. Ren, S., He, K., Girshick, R., Sun, J.: Faster R-CNN: towards real-time object detection with region proposal networks. In: Advances in Neural Information Processing Systems, vol. 28, pp. 91–99 (2015)
16. Lin, T.-Y., Dollár, P., Girshick, R., He, K., Hariharan, B., Belongie, S.: Feature pyramid networks for object detection. In: Proceedings of the IEEE Conference on Computer Vision and Pattern Recognition, pp. 2117–2125 (2017)
17. He, K., Gkioxari, G., Dollár, P., Girshick, R.: Mask R-CNN. In: Proceedings of the IEEE International Conference on Computer Vision, pp. 2961–2969 (2017)
18. Cai, Z., Vasconcelos, N.: Cascade R-CNN: delving into high quality object detection. In: Proceedings of the IEEE Conference on Computer Vision and Pattern Recognition, pp. 6154–6162 (2018)
19. Cai, L., et al.: MaxpoolNMS: getting rid of NMS bottlenecks in two-stage object detectors. In: Proceedings of the IEEE/CVF Conference on Computer Vision and Pattern Recognition, pp. 9356–9364 (2019)
20. Pramanik, A., Pal, S.K., Maiti, J., Mitra, P.: Granulated RCNN and multi-class deep sort for multi-object detection and tracking. IEEE Trans. Emerg. Topics Comput. Intell. **6**, 171–181(2021)
21. Sermanet, P., Eigen, D., Zhang, X., Mathieu, M., Fergus, R., LeCun, Y.: OverFeat: integrated recognition, localization and detection using convolutional networks. arXiv preprint arXiv:1312.6229 (2013)
22. Redmon, J., Divvala, S., Girshick, R., Farhadi, A.: You only look once: unified, real-time object detection. In: Proceedings of the IEEE Conference on Computer Vision and Pattern Recognition, pp. 779–788 (2016)
23. Liu, W.: SSD: single shot multibox detector. In: Leibe, B., Matas, J., Sebe, N., Welling, M. (eds.) ECCV 2016. LNCS, vol. 9905, pp. 21–37. Springer, Cham (2016). https://doi.org/10.1007/978-3-319-46448-0_2
24. Lin, T.-Y., Goyal, P., Girshick, R., He, K., Dollár, P.: Focal loss for dense object detection. In: Proceedings of the IEEE International Conference on Computer Vision, pp. 2980–2988 (2017)
25. Zhang, S., Wen, L., Bian, X., Lei, Z., Li, S.Z.: Single-shot refinement neural network for object detection. In: Proceedings of the IEEE Conference on Computer Vision and Pattern Recognition (CVPR), June 2018
26. Zhao, Q., et al.: M2Det: a single-shot object detector based on multi-level feature pyramid network. In: Proceedings of the AAAI Conference on Artificial Intelligence, vol. 33, pp. 9259–9266 (2019)
27. Redmon, J., Farhadi, A.: YOLOv3: an incremental improvement. arXiv preprint arXiv:1804.02767 (2018)
28. Bochkovskiy, A., Wang, C.-Y., Liao, H.-Y.M.: YOLOv4: optimal speed and accuracy of object detection. arXiv preprint arXiv:2004.10934 (2020)
29. Wang, C.-Y., Yeh, I.-H., Liao, H.-Y.M.: You only learn one representation: unified network for multiple tasks. arXiv preprint arXiv:2105.04206 (2021)

30. Anati, R., Scaramuzza, D., Derpanis, K.G., Daniilidis, K.: Robot localization using soft object detection. In: 2012 IEEE International Conference on Robotics and Automation, pp. 4992–4999. IEEE (2012)
31. Dourado, C.M.J.M., et al.: A new approach for mobile robot localization based on an online IoT system. Future Gener. Comput. Syst. **100**, 859–881 (2019). Already included
32. Ekvall, S., Kragic, D., Jensfelt, P.: Object detection and mapping for service robot tasks. Robotica **25**(2), 175–187 (2007)
33. Astua, C., Barber, R., Crespo, J., Jardon, A.: Object detection techniques applied on mobile robot semantic navigation. Sensors **14**, 6734–6757 (2014)
34. Espinace, P., Kollar, T., Roy, N., Soto, A.: Indoor scene recognition by a mobile robot through adaptive object detection. Robot. Auton. Syst. **61**, 932–947 (2013)
35. Redmon, J., Farhadi, A.: Yolo9000: better, faster, stronger. In: Proceedings of the IEEE Conference on Computer Vision and Pattern Recognition, pp. 7263–7271 (2017)
36. Asad, M.H., Khaliq, S., Yousaf, M.H., Ullah, M.O., Ahmad, A.: A real-time and AI-on-the-edge perspective. In: Advances in Civil Engineering, Pothole Detection Using Deep Learning (2022)
37. Nepal, U., Eslamiat, H.: Comparing YOLOv3, YOLOv4 and YOLOv5 for autonomous landing spot detection in faulty UAVs. Sensors **22**(2), 464 (2022)
38. Jiang, Z., Zhao, L., Li, S., Jia, Y.: Real-time object detection method for embedded devices. In: Computer Vision and Pattern Recognition (2020)
39. Lin, T.-Y., et al.: Microsoft COCO: common objects in context. In: Fleet, D., Pajdla, T., Schiele, B., Tuytelaars, T. (eds.) ECCV 2014. LNCS, vol. 8693, pp. 740–755. Springer, Cham (2014). https://doi.org/10.1007/978-3-319-10602-1_48
40. Génération Robots: Hokuyo URG-04-LX-UG01 laser range finder. Accessed 30 Aug 2022

Classification of Facial Expressions Under Partial Occlusion for VR Games

Ana Sofia Figueiredo Rodrigues[1], Júlio Castro Lopes[1] (iD),
Rui Pedro Lopes[1,2](✉) (iD), and Luís F. Teixeira[3] (iD)

[1] Research Center in Digitalization and Intelligent Robotics (CeDRI),
Instituto Politécnico de Bragança, Bragança, Portugal
`a41737@alunos.ipb.pt`, {`juliolopes,rlopes`}`@ipb.pt`
[2] Institute of Electronics and Informatics Engineering of Aveiro (IEETA),
University of Aveiro, Aveiro, Portugal
[3] INESC TEC, Faculdade de Engenharia da Universidade do Porto, Porto, Portugal
`luisft@fe.up.pt`

Abstract. Facial expressions are one of the most common way to externalize our emotions. However, the same emotion can have different effects on the same person and has different effects on different people. Based on this, we developed a system capable of detecting the facial expressions of a person in real-time, occluding the eyes (simulating the use of virtual reality glasses). To estimate the position of the eyes, in order to occlude them, Multi-task Cascade Convolutional Neural Networks (MTCNN) were used. A residual network, a VGG, and the combination of both models, were used to perform the classification of 7 different types of facial expressions (Angry, Disgust, Fear, Happy, Sad, Surprise, Neutral), classifying the occluded and non-occluded dataset. The combination of both models, achieved an accuracy of 64.9% for the occlusion dataset and 62.8% for no occlusion, using the FER-2013 dataset. The primary goal of this work was to evaluate the influence of occlusion, and the results show that the majority of the classification is done with the mouth and chin. Nevertheless, the results were far from the state-of-the-art, which is expect to be improved, mainly by adjusting the MTCNN.

Keywords: Facial expression recognition · Emotions · ResNet · VGG · MTCNN · Virtual reality

1 Introduction

Facial expression recognition is playing an increasingly critical role in several areas and applications. Beyond verbalization, non-verbal cues, such as facial emotions, play a vital role, providing clues in understanding and inferring the hidden emotional state of individuals. In fact, facial expressions are the most common way to externalize emotions and one of the most important means of communication in interpersonal relationships.

Humans have evolved to easily read the other people's facial expressions. Often these are expressed automatically without the transmitter even realizing

A. I. Pereira et al. (Eds.): OL2A 2022, CCIS 1754, pp. 804–819, 2022.
https://doi.org/10.1007/978-3-031-23236-7_55

that he is executing them [29]. Based on these signals, we adjust our behaviour and make choices according to our perception of the emotional state of the other person. In other words, the interaction may be conditioned by the mutual interpretation of the emotional state, derived from reading the other's facial expression (and complemented with body language, voice tone, and others).

Extending this possibility to computers, the automatic identification of human facial expressions introduces several benefits. It has the potential to develop better and more useful human-computer interaction, provide visually impaired with haptic clues regarding the expression of others [24], monitor the motivation of students in the classroom [25], among many other applications. Although difficult, it is constantly evolving with several proposed solutions by the scientific community [35].

The work described in this paper aims to investigate and evaluate Machine Learning (ML) algorithms to infer human emotional state through the classification of facial expressions. Specifically, two tasks are explored: face detection and expression recognition. The main objective of this work is to develop a system capable of evaluating humans facial expression in real-time and, eventually, use this information to assess the emotional state while playing a virtual reality game.

This work is developed within the GreenHealth project [17]. This project addresses the use of digital technologies, namely Virtual Reality (VR), Game-based Learning (GBL), Internet of Things (IoT), Artificial Intelligence (AI), and Advanced Data Analytics (ADA), in the development of innovative rehabilitation techniques, contributing to the promotion of well-being and health in a holistic perspective, focusing, mainly on mental health rehabilitation in people diagnosed on the schizophrenia spectrum. Together with patient's body posture analysis, physiological data (e.g. patient's heart rate), and performance in the game, facial expression recognition enables to automatically adapt the game to the individual characteristics of the player. Since the player is wearing VR goggles, the classification of expressions has to be performed with part of the face hidden, which introduces further challenges. The purpose of this paper is to study the impact of occlusion in the classification of facial expressions for the dynamic adaptation of the difficulty level in cognitive rehabiliation serious games [16].

The paper is organized as follows: Sect. 2 presents the related work, and Sect. 3 discusses the methodology behind this study. Section 4 describes the results, and Sect. 5 rounds up the paper with the conclusions, particularly analyzing the challenges associated to the facial expressions classification.

2   Related Work

Over the centuries there have been several attempts to organize emotions into several categories. Cicero [20], held that they should be divided into four categories: fear (*metus*), pain (*aegritudo*), lust (*libido*) and pleasure (*laetiti*). Darwin and Prodger [21], for example, have used twenty-two categories, including anxiety, joy, love, devotion, anger, helplessness, surprise, fear, among others.

More recently, Plutchik have introduced the wheel of emotions, with 8 primary dimensions of emotion, namely joy, trust, fear, surprise, sadness, disgust, anger, anticipation [8].

The sole analysis of facial expressions is not enough to assess a person's sentiment. However, 55% of information is communicated by facial expressions, 38% by other gestures and signals (such as voice and sound) and 7% by spoken language [19]. Based on this, facial expression recognition account as an important factor for human sentiment recognition. With constantly improving of the computing power, jointly with the development of big data processing technology and algorithms, the automatic classification of facial expressions have been growing in accuracy and interest.

Devries et al. [7], demonstrated that a system trained to reason about facial geometry while recognizing expressions outperforms one trained solely to recognize expressions. Since facial landmark prediction has many publicly implementations available, the authors decided to use Zhu and Ramanan's facial landmark detector, which uses coordinates for 68 reference points per face. All of these points are used to outline facial features like the mouth, nose, eyes, and eyebrows. The authors simplified the problem by focusing on the most expressive features of humans facial expression: the eyebrows and mouth (rough reference points). Each of the positions of the left brow, right brow, and mouth were represented by a binary mask image.

The authors have used a Convolutional Neural Network (CNN) that was based on the winning architecture of the 2013 International Conference on Machine Learning (ICML) Facial Expression Recognition Competition [28]. They opted for a CNN with 3 convolutional layers fully connected, each with a ReLU activation function and max pooling. The network's output consisted of three binary output maps (one for each of the reference locations), and it was thus in charge of modeling the location and shape of each of its features. Two datasets were used in their work: ICML Dataset [10] and Toronto Face Database (TFD) [26]. The ICML consists of 28709 48 × 48 training images, each with 7 labels and 7177 test images. Since the images were taken from a wild environment, the faces have different orientations and are not always facing forward. In this dataset, the authors evaluated 2 different techniques: CNN with 3 convolutional layers fully connected and a Multi-task CNN. The TFD is also made up of 48 × 48 images and 7 labels, however, all faces are looking directly at the camera. It contains 4178 images, 70% of the images were used for training, 10% for validation, and 20% for testing. The authors used the same evaluation techniques applied in ICML dataset.

Baltrusaitis et al. [3] use the OpenFace facial behavior analyses pipeline, which includes the following algorithms: facial landmark detection, head pose tracking, eye gaze and facial Action Units (AUs). For the facial landmark detection and tracking, the authors have used the Conditional Local Neural Fields (CLNF), with 2 main components: Point Distribution Model (PDM) and patch experts. The PDM was been trained in 2 datasets, the Labeled Face Parts in the Wild (LFPW) and Helen. The CLNF patch experts was been trained in 3 datasets, including the ones used in the PDM and also the Multi-Pie dataset [11].

In order to estimate the head pose, information about the position of the head (translation and orientation) was extracted, as well as the detection of facial landmarks. This information was obtained thanks to the CLNF, which internally uses a 3D facial landmark representation and projects it to the image using orthographic camera projection. To train their model the authors have used the Mpiigaze [34] dataset.

Regarding the eye gaze estimation, CLNF and PDM were also used, since they allow detecting reference points of the eye region, such as the eyelids, iris and pupil. The PDM was trained with the Syntheseyes [30] dataset. The information obtained by the CLNF was used to compute the eye gaze vector individually for each eye (lightning is fired from the camera's source through the center of the pupil in the image plan, and its intersection is computed to determine the pupil's location in 3D camera coordinates).

Finally Openface predicts AU presence using a linear Support Vector Machine (SVM) kernel and AU intensity using a linear Support Vector Regression (SVR) kernel.

Loizou [15] proposed and evaluated a system for analyzing automated speech signals and images for seven different human emotions: normal, happy, sad, dislike, fear, anger, and surprise. Voice and image recordings of more than 70000 people aged twenty to seventy-four years old were organized. The authors have used multi-classification models to select the features that identify the seven emotions through an SVM with a 10-fold validation, using a Gaussian Radial Basis Function (RBF) with $c = 1$ and $\gamma = 0.01$. Statistically, a Correct Classification (CC) score of 93% was obtained.

Mindlink-Eumpy [14], an open-source toolbox, was designed to detect emotions by integrating information from Electrocardiogram (EEG) and facial expressions. First, a set of tools was used to automatically collect physiological data, which was then used to analyze user facial expressions and EEG data. Regarding the analysis of user's facial expression, they used a multitask CNN pre-trained with the FER2013 dataset [10].

On the surface, the idea of using a pre-trained CNN, is to transfer the labeled data or knowledge from some domains (previously performed tasks - Source Tasks), to help the ML algorithm to perform better in the domain of interest. Regarding the EEG analysis, MindLink-Eumpy [14] uses two different algorithms: SVM and Long Short-Term Memory Network (LSTM). In the decision-level fusion, Weight enumerator and Adaboost techniques were applied to combine the predictions of the CNN and the SVM. The authors have achieved an accuracy of 71% for SVM and 78.56% for the LSTM.

Almeida and Rodrigues [2], developed a system capable of capturing real-time images and alerting the user if there are any signs of stress. The system was divided into several modules, such as:

1. Real-time image capture, via computer camera, sending the images to the next module.
2. Determining the user's face position by the Haar-like feature. The image is further readjusted and normalize.

3. After properly training the classification model, the model will be able to classify each face and return a list of seven classification probabilities, one for each facial expression.
4. The facial expression most likely to be embedded in this module determines whether or not the person is under stress.

The authors have used a CNN previously trained (transfer learning), that was applied using two different techniques: Global Average Pooling (GAP) and Convolution Layer. The classification took into account seven emotions (as in [15]). The authors used two multi-classification models, using them to predict facial expressions and binary classification to classify images with stress/non-stress. They achieved an accuracy of 92% in the best model (VGG16 [27]).

In [5], Bartlett et al. developed a real-time face recognition system that can recognize faces in a video sequence and encode each frame with one of the seven corresponding emotions. All the recognized faces were converted into images of the same size, using Gabor energy filters and were later analyzed by Adaboost, which encodes facial expressions in 7 dimensions (corresponding to 7 emotions). The system was trained and tested with an SVM in the DFAT-504 dataset [13], which is constituted by 100 university students between the ages of 18 and 30: 65% were female, 15% African American, and 3% Asian or Latino. To validate their approach the authors combined a SVM with Adaboost and named it as Adasvm, which produced an accuracy of 93.3%. By themselves, Adaboost achieved an accuracy of 90.1% and SVM 89%, so both were used simultaneously.

Considering situations where the face is partially hidden, mainly the eyes, Cheng et al. [6] used the following approach:

1. Images containing faces are segmented from human images of the same size;
2. The result obtained in the first step is then used to normalize and transform the images into figures of Gabor magnitude through multi-scale and multi-orientation of the Gabor filters. Through these filters the low-level image characteristics of facial figures are reinforced, such as the edges, peaks, contours of crests, eyes, nose and mouth, which are considered to be the main components of the face;
3. The Gabor characteristics are extracted to form a 2D matrix, and the sampling completed downwards to slightly reduce the dimension;
4. The samples are divided into mini-batches and the weights are updated to speed up the pre-training of each Restricted Boltzmann Machine (RBM), which is a bipartite structure with a visible layer and a hidden layer;
5. According to the dimension of the features, set the size of each layer from three layers network (in general);
6. Generate weights and adjust them by fine-tuning;
7. The deep structure training process is divided into two stages: pre-tuning, which treats the data labelled as unmarked for unsupervised training to provide each weight from the lower layer to the top, and fine-tuning which is a simple process of gradient descent under supervision;
8. The test is carried out in number 6 until convergence.

In addition to the Gabor filter, the authors also used other methods that use this filter to compare with the proposed method: Local Gabor Binary Pattern Histogram Sequence (LGBHPS), modified LGBPHS, with the K-Nearest Neighbors (K-NN) Classification method respectively. The authors used the Japanese Female Facial Expression (JAFFE) dataset [9], which consists of 213 images of 10 different individuals with seven different facial expressions: happiness, anger, sadness, fear, surprise, disgust and neutral. Considering that this dataset is not available with natural partial occlusion facial images, the authors simulated the occlusion by overlay graphic masks in the images of this dataset.

The resulting images are divided into 2 parts: 143 images for training and 70 images for testing (images containing occlusion of the eyes, mouth, upper and lower parts of the face). They obtained an accuracy of 85.71% with no occlusion, 82.86% with occlusion of the eyes, 77.14% with oclusion of the upper part of the face and 82.86% with oclusion of the lower part of the face.

Houshmand and Mefraz [12] focused essentially on facial expression identification in the presence of a severe occlusion while the subject is utilizing a head-mounted display in a Virtual Reality (VR) environment. Since display measurements are known, the authors were able to replicate occlusion caused by these headsets using face detection applied to grayscale images using a modification to the conventional Histogram of Oriented Gradients (HOG) and Linear SVM-based approach for object detection. The authors estimated 68 reference coordinates that map the face anatomy on the iBUG 300-W dataset [23]. Because the dataset contains images with varying sizes, the distance between the two temporal bones of the temporal landmarks was used as the reference length, and the polygonal occlusion patch was generated using the midpoint of the line that passes through the center points of the eye as the VR headset's central coordinate.

The authors have evaluated the effectiveness of two different architectures: VGG and ResNet. They chose three datasets that cover different scales of face images and contain images with momentary occlusions to test these two architectures, namely FER+ [4], RAF-DB and Affectnet. The authors have defined a rescale factor of 224 * 224 at the input of the CNNs, which meant that all images used for training, testing, and validation were rescaled for the same measurements and normalized using min-max normalization. The training procedure was carried out by optimizing the multinomial logistic regression objective, which employs mini-batch gradient descent based on momentum back propagation. To regularize the train phase in the ResNet, a max-norm kernel restriction was added. The best result obtained by the authors was 79.98% of accuracy in the ResNet model with transfer learning in the FER+ dataset.

Cornejo et al. [22] have structured their approach in 5-steps. First, preprocessing on all images. This includes the automatic detection of the facial fiducial point, and then the coordinates of the eyes are extracted, the image is rotated, and the image is aligned. Still at this stage, facial expression regions are cut through an appropriate bounding rectangle, RGB images are converted to grayscale, and then randomly generated rectangles are applied over various regions of the face, such as the left lower eye, right eye, both eyes, right lower side, or lower side. Next, occluded facial expression is reconstructed with the Dual Algorithm based on the principles of the Robust Principal Component Analysis (RPCA) where the Contrast-Limit Adaptive Histogram Equalization (CLAHE) is subsequently applied to reconstructed facial regions, to increase image contrast levels (Fig. 1). Third, a set of facial expression characteristics were extracted through 3 strategies: Weber Local Descriptor (WLD) - applied over the entire facial expression image for extraction of textural features, Local Binary Patterns (LBP) - applied over the entire image to extract histograms of LBP and HOG - applied to the entire image, to extract the HOG features. Fourth, reduction of dimensionality of the characteristics extracted in the previous step, and the resulting descriptor is transferred in a lower dimensional space through PCA and LDA, applied sequentially. Finally, occluded facial expressions are recognized through K-NN and SVM classifiers.

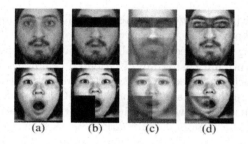

Fig. 1. (a) Cropped images without occlusions from MUG dataset [1] and Jaffe dataset [9]; (b) faces with occlusive areas; (c) reconstructed faces via RPCA; (d) filling the occluded facial regions from (c). [22]

The authors have tested the proposed method on three datasets: the Cohn-Kanade (CK+) [18], JAFFE [9] and Facial MUG Expression [1] and obtained results of 91.01% accuracy in CK+ dataset with K-NN, 92.86% in JAFFE dataset with SVM and 90.1% in MUG with K-NN, in occluded images.

The work described in this paper builds on these, to study the impact of occlusion caused by VR goggles in the identification of facial expressions.

3   Methodology

According to the previous section, the followed approach in this work is based on an CNN ensemble, composed of a ResNet-18 and a VGG19 (Fig. 2) [32]. The weights were initialized with the imagenet weights for both ResNet-18 and VGG19, with xavier for the final fully connected layer.

The same architecture was used in both the scenarios: without occlusion and with occlusion. The chosen dataset was FER2013, composed of 28709 48 × 48

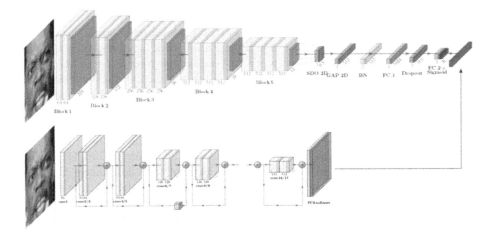

Fig. 2. Ensemble between ResNet-18 and VGG19, with a Fully Connected Layer as output.

grayscale images for training and 3589 for testing, with seven categories (0 = Angry, 1 = Disgust, 2 = Fear, 3 = Happy, 4 = Sad, 5 = Surprise, 6 = Neutral). Since the ResNet-18 and VGG19 expect 224 × 224 RGB images in the input, it was necessary to scale the images up and replicate a single channel image to the remaining two (Fig. 3).

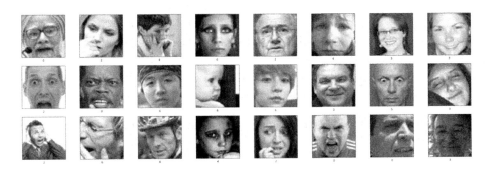

Fig. 3. Sample of the FER2013 dataset.

To simulate the presence of VR goggles, it was necessary to hide the upper part of the face, namely, the eyes. Considering that the face can assume different tilt and yaw positions, the relative position of the eyes change, so the algorithm to calculate the goggles position should contemplate this. For that, it was necessary to obtain location of the face as well as facial landmarks, composed of the position of the eyes, nose and mouth. For that, Multi-task Cascade Convolutional Neural

Networks (MTCNN) was used [31,33]. It consists essentially of 3 parts: i) a network of proposals (P-NET) that foresees potential face positions and their bounding boxes. This process results in a large number of facial detections, many of which are false; ii) a refined network (R-Net) which makes use of the result from step i), thereby refining the result to eliminate most false detection and limiting aggregates; and iii) a network similar to the one used in step ii), called O-Net, further refines the forecasts and adds facials forecasts to the implementation of MTCNN.

With the position of the eyes, the algorithm starts by calculating the middle point between the eyes, and the distance between them (Algorithm 1). It continues by estimating the width and height of the goggles as 20% larger than the distance between the eyes and 150% the distance between the eye line and the nose. The tilt angle is also calculated and, with these, the rectangle is drawn in gray on top of the *sample* image. When the landmarks is empty, meaning that the facial features could not be found, the goggles are not drawn (Fig. 4).

Algorithm 1. Occlusion algorithm.

1: **procedure** MAKEGOGGLES(sample, landmarks)
2:     $left\_eye\_x, left\_eye\_y \leftarrow landmarks[0][0], landmarks[0][5]$
3:     $right\_eye\_x, right\_eye\_y \leftarrow landmarks[0][1], landmarks[0][6]$
4:     $nose\_x, nose\_y \leftarrow landmarks[0][2], landmarks[0][7]$
5:     $middle\_x, middle\_y \leftarrow \frac{right\_eye\_x + left\_eye\_x}{2}, \frac{right\_eye\_y + left\_eye\_y}{2}$
6:     $goggles\_width = 2.2 * \sqrt{(right_e ye_y - left_e ye_y)^2 + (right_e ye_x - left_e ye_x)^2}$
7:     $goggles\_height = 1.5 * \sqrt{(middle_e yes_y - nose_y)^2 + (middle_e yes_x - nose_x)^2}$
8:     $rectangle = (0, 0, goggles\_width, goggles\_height)$
9:     $middle\_rectangle\_x, middle\_rectangle\_y = \frac{goggles_width}{2}, \frac{goggles_height}{2}$
10:    $angle = \frac{right_e ye_y - left_e ye_y}{right_e ye_x - left_e ye_x} * \frac{180}{\pi}$
11:    $rectangle = rectangle.rotate(-angle, (middle_r ectangle_x, middle_r ectangle_y))$
12:    $final_s ize = rectangle.size$
13:    $sample.paste(rectangle, \frac{middle_e yes_x - final_s ize[0]}{2}, \frac{middle_e yes_y - final_s ize[1]}{2})$

The accuracy of the classification was measured through the confusion matrix and accuracy of each class.

4   Results

Two identical versions of the classification network were trained for 50 epocs with the mini batch of 64 on a AMD Ryzen Threadripper 3970X 32-Core Processor with an NVIDIA GeForce RTX 3090 with 64 GB RAM. The same training and validation datasets were used in both situations, although on the second all the examples were changed to introduce an occlusion over the eyes.

The training process happened in three steps: i) training of the ResNet18; ii) training of the VGG19; iii) training of the full assembly. Both CNNs were

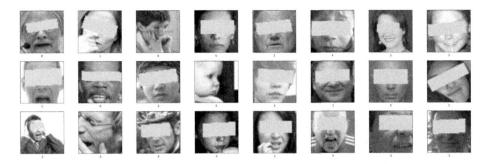

Fig. 4. Sample of the FER2013 dataset with the occlusion algorithm.

initialized with the pretrained ImageNet-1K weights, although all the parameters were allowed to change (Fig. 5). There is a slight better result with the no occlusion dataset, as expected.

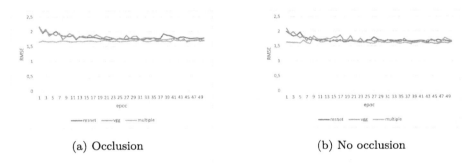

(a) Occlusion   (b) No occlusion

Fig. 5. Evolution of RMSE during training

The accuracy also improves with the epochs (Fig. 6). In the occlusion dataset (Fig. 6a) the highest accuracy is obtained with the multiple model (consisting on the combination of both models). However, in the no occlusion situation (Fig. 6b) it is the lowest. Looking at the progress during the epochs, it seems that the increase in the number of epochs would achieve better accuracy.

To illustrate the classification capacity of the three models in predicting the seven facial expressions in the FER-2013 dataset, confusion matrices were built comparing the situation between occlusion and no occlusion datasets (Figs. 7, 8 and 9).

The classes are not balanced so, intra-class normalization was also performed (Table 1). The impact of occlusion of the eyes is, apparently, marginal. The highest accuracy in both situations (occlusions and no occlusion) is in the class 'neutral', immediately followed by 'happy' in the occlusion and 'sad'/'surprise' for the no occlusion. The lowest accuracy was in the classes 'disgust' and 'fear',

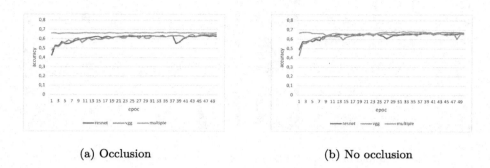

(a) Occlusion   (b) No occlusion

Fig. 6. Evolution of the accuracy during training

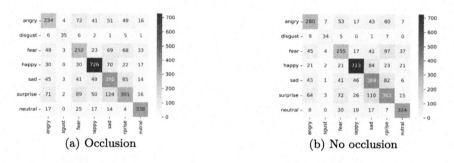

(a) Occlusion   (b) No occlusion

Fig. 7. Confusion matrix for the ResNet18

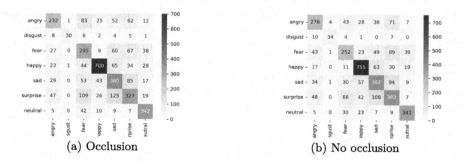

(a) Occlusion   (b) No occlusion

Fig. 8. Confusion matrix for the VGG19

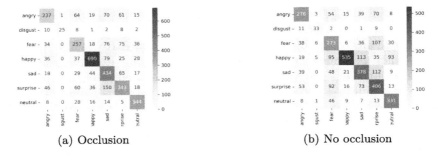

(a) Occlusion   (b) No occlusion

Fig. 9. Confusion matrix for the combined model

respectively. According to the previous confusion matrices, the 'disgust' class is often misclassified as 'angry' or 'surprise'.

Table 1. Accuracy per class

	(a) Occlusion			(b) No occlusion		
Class	ResNet18	VGG19	Combined	ResNet18	VGG19	Combined
angry	0,501	0,497	0,508	0,6	0,591	0,595
disgust	0,625	0,536	0,446	0,607	0,607	0,589
fear	0,508	0,595	0,518	0,514	0,508	0,55
happy	0,811	0,782	0,771	0,808	0,844	0,598
sad	0,61	0,626	0,715	0,639	0,629	0,623
surprise	0,461	0,501	0,525	0,556	0,585	0,623
neutral	0,814	0,824	0,829	0,805	0,822	0,798
F1-score	0,627	0,645	0,649	0,663	0,673	0,628

The overall accuracy of the combined model was 61.6% for the occlusion and 62.5% for the no occlusion, which is far from the state of the art result. Nevertheless, the purpose of this work was to assess the impact of occlusion and the results confirm that most of the classification is performed with the mouth and chin.

5 Conclusions

In this paper, a residual network (ResNet), a VGG and the combination of both models, were used to predict facial expressions in real-time, occluding part of the face (eyes and the upper part of the nose). The model achieved an accuracy of 64.9% for the occlusion dataset and 62.8% no occlusion, using the FER-2013 dataset. As this dataset only contains frontal images of the face, the correct evaluation of facial expression is not performed if the individual's face is not located in a position other than the frontal, and it also does not perform the correct classification of people wearing glasses or other accessories. Similarly, it was also observed that the MTCNN does not correctly locate the face in real-time, that is, any other object is often identified as a face. It was also found that with a small movement made in real-time (such as, for example, the upward movement of the muscles of the cheek and the sides or edges of the lips to form a smile that indicates, to the human eye, that the person is happy), the model is not very robust in its classification. That means that it should classify this movement as 'Happy', instead of classifying it as 'Neutral', 'Angry' and 'Sad', only in a small fraction of the time, it is classified correctly as 'Happy'. For the above-mentioned situations, it is proposed to study other datasets as well as other classifiers that allow evaluating facial expressions, the adjustment of the MTCNN to enable correct face detection and the addition of more MTCNN tools to be also able to locate the eyes and lips.

Acknowledgment. This work is funded by the European Regional Development Fund (ERDF) through the Regional Operational Program North 2020, within the scope of Project GreenHealth - Digital strategies in biological assets to improve well-being and promote green health, Norte-01-0145-FEDER-000042. This work has been supported by FCT - Fundação para a Ciência e Tecnologia within the Project Scope: UIDB/05757/2020.

References

1. Aifanti, N., Papachristou, C., Delopoulos, A.: The MUG facial expression database. In: 11th International Workshop on Image Analysis for Multimedia Interactive Services WIAMIS 10, pp. 1–4. IEEE (2010)
2. Almeida, J., Rodrigues, F.: Facial expression recognition system for stress detection with deep learning. In: Proceedings of the 23rd International Conference on Enterprise Information Systems, pp. 256–263. SCITEPRESS - Science and Technology Publications, Online Streaming, – Select a Country – (2021). https://doi.org/10.5220/0010474202560263. https://www.scitepress.org/DigitalLibrary/Link.aspx?doi=10.5220/0010474202560263
3. Baltrusaitis, T., Robinson, P., Morency, L.P.: OpenFace: an open source facial behavior analysis toolkit. In: 2016 IEEE Winter Conference on Applications of Computer Vision (WACV), Lake Placid, NY, USA, pp. 1–10. IEEE, March 2016. https://doi.org/10.1109/WACV.2016.7477553. https://ieeexplore.ieee.org/document/7477553/
4. Barsoum, E., Zhang, C., Ferrer, C.C., Zhang, Z.: Training deep networks for facial expression recognition with crowd-sourced label distribution. In: Proceedings of the 18th ACM International Conference on Multimodal Interaction, Tokyo, Japan, pp. 279–283. ACM, October 2016. https://doi.org/10.1145/2993148.2993165. https://dl.acm.org/doi/10.1145/2993148.2993165
5. Bartlett, M., Littlewort, G., Lainscsek, C., Fasel, I., Movellan, J.: Machine learning methods for fully automatic recognition of facial expressions and facial actions. In: 2004 IEEE International Conference on Systems, Man and Cybernetics (IEEE Cat. No. 04CH37583), The Hague, Netherlands, vol. 1, pp. 592–597. IEEE (2004). https://doi.org/10.1109/ICSMC.2004.1398364. https://ieeexplore.ieee.org/document/1398364/

6. Cheng, Y., Jiang, B., Jia, K.: A deep structure for facial expression recognition under partial occlusion. In: 2014 Tenth International Conference on Intelligent Information Hiding and Multimedia Signal Processing, pp. 211–214 (2014). https://doi.org/10.1109/IIH-MSP.2014.59

7. Devries, T., Biswaranjan, K., Taylor, G.W.: Multi-task Learning of Facial Landmarks and Expression. In: 2014 Canadian Conference on Computer and Robot Vision, Montreal, QC, Canada, pp. 98–103. IEEE, May 2014. https://doi.org/10.1109/CRV.2014.21. https://ieeexplore.ieee.org/document/6816830/

8. Donaldson, M.: Plutchik's wheel of emotions-2017. Update (2017)

9. Cheng, F., Yu, J., Xiong, H.: Facial expression recognition in JAFFE dataset based on gaussian process classification. IEEE Trans. Neural Netw. 21(10), 1685–1690 (2010)

10. Goodfellow, I.J., et al.: Challenges in representation learning: a report on three machine learning contests. Neural Netw. 64, 59–63 (2015)

11. Gross, R., Matthews, I., Cohn, J., Kanade, T., Baker, S.: Multi-PIE. Image Vis. Comput. 28(5), 807–813 (2010)

12. Houshmand, B., Mefraz Khan, N.: Facial expression recognition under partial occlusion from virtual reality headsets based on transfer learning. In: 2020 IEEE Sixth International Conference on Multimedia Big Data (BigMM), New Delhi, India, pp. 70–75. IEEE, September 2020. https://doi.org/10.1109/BigMM50055.2020.00020. https://ieeexplore.ieee.org/document/9232653/

13. Kanade, T., Cohn, J., Tian, Y.: Comprehensive database for facial expression analysis. In: Proceedings Fourth IEEE International Conference on Automatic Face and Gesture Recognition (Cat. No. PR00580), pp. 46–53. IEEE Comput. Soc, Grenoble, France (2000). https://doi.org/10.1109/AFGR.2000.840611. https://ieeexplore.ieee.org/document/840611/

14. Li, R., et al.: MindLink-Eumpy: an open-source Python toolbox for multimodal emotion recognition. Front. Hum. Neurosci. 15, 621493 (2021)

15. Loizou, C.P.: An automated integrated speech and face imageanalysis system for the identification of human emotions. Speech Commun. 130, 15–26 (2021)

16. Lopes, J.C., Lopes, R.P.: A review of dynamic difficulty adjustment methods for serious games. In: Pereira, A.I., et al. (eds.) OL2A 2022, CCIS 1754, pp. xx–yy (2022)

17. Lopes, R.P., et al.: Digital technologies for innovative mental health rehabilitation. Electronics 10(18) (2021). https://doi.org/10.3390/electronics10182260. https://www.mdpi.com/2079-9292/10/18/2260

18. Lucey, P., Cohn, J.F., Kanade, T., Saragih, J., Ambadar, Z., Matthews, I.: The extended Cohn-Kanade dataset (CK+): a complete dataset for action unit and emotion-specified expression. In: 2010 IEEE Computer Society Conference on Computer Vision and Pattern Recognition-Workshops, pp. 94–101. IEEE (2010)

19. Mehrabian, A.: Communication without words. In: Mortensen, C.D. (ed.) Communication Theory, Routledge, 2 edn., pp. 193–200, September 2017. https://doi.org/10.4324/9781315080918-15. https://www.taylorfrancis.com/books/9781351527538/chapters/10.4324/9781315080918-15

20. Poria, S., Majumder, N., Mihalcea, R., Hovy, E.: Emotion recognition in conversation: research challenges, datasets, and recent advances. IEEE Access 7, 100943–100953 (2019)

21. Prodger, P.: Darwin's Camera: Art and Photography in the Theory of Evolution. Oxford University Press, Oxford (2009)

22. Ramirez Cornejo, J.Y., Pedrini, H.: Emotion recognition from occluded facial expressions using weber local descriptor. In: 2018 25th International Conference on Systems, Signals and Image Processing (IWSSIP), Maribor, Slovenia, pp. 1–5. IEEE, June 2018. https://doi.org/10.1109/IWSSIP.2018.8439631. https://ieeexplore.ieee.org/document/8439631/

23. Sagonas, C., Tzimiropoulos, G., Zafeiriou, S., Pantic, M.: 300 faces in-the-wild challenge: the first facial landmark localization challenge. In: 2013 IEEE International Conference on Computer Vision Workshops, Sydney, Australia, pp. 397–403. IEEE, December 2013. https://doi.org/10.1109/ICCVW.2013.59. https://ieeexplore.ieee.org/document/6755925/

24. Saurav, S., Saini, A., Saini, R., Singh, S.: Deep learning inspired intelligent embedded system for haptic rendering of facial emotions to the blind. Neural Comput. Appl. **34**(6), 4595–4623 (2022). https://doi.org/10.1007/s00521-021-06613-3. https://www.scopus.com/inward/record.uri?eid=2-s2.0-85117830803&doi=10.1007%2fs00521-021-06613-3&partnerID=40&md5=ff31d4bd7bc4190b4483b813b2837a34, publisher: Springer Science and Business Media Deutschland GmbH

25. Singh, S., Gupta, A., Pavithr, R.S.: Automatic classroom monitoring system using facial expression recognition. In: Sanyal, G., Travieso-González, C.M., Awasthi, S., Pinto, C.M.A., Purushothama, B.R. (eds.) International Conference on Artificial Intelligence and Sustainable Engineering. LNEE, vol. 836, pp. 151–165. Springer, Singapore (2022). https://doi.org/10.1007/978-981-16-8542-2_12. https://www.scopus.com/inward/record.uri?eid=2-s2.0-85130262593&doi=10.1007%2f978-981-16-8542-2_12&partnerID=40&md5=3d727b02a4b6cbca64032f67f9156366. ISBN: 9789811685415

26. Susskind, J.M., Anderson, A.K., Hinton, G.E.: The Toronto face database. Department of Computer Science, University of Toronto, Toronto, ON, Canada, Technical report 3 (2010)

27. Tammina, S.: Transfer learning using VGG-16 with deep convolutional neural network for classifying images. Int. J. Sci. Res. Publ. (IJSRP) **9**(10), 9420 (2019). https://doi.org/10.29322/IJSRP.9.10.2019.p9420. https://www.ijsrp.org/research-paper-1019.php?rp=P949194

28. Tang, Y.: Deep learning using linear support vector machines, February 2015. arXiv:1306.0239 [cs, stat]

29. Viana, I.: Comunicação não verbal e expressões faciais das emoções básicas. Revista de Letras **13**(II), 165–181 (2014)

30. Wood, E., Baltruaitis, T., Zhang, X., Sugano, Y., Robinson, P., Bulling, A.: Rendering of eyes for eye-shape registration and gaze estimation. In: 2015 IEEE International Conference on Computer Vision (ICCV), Santiago, Chile, pp. 3756–3764. IEEE, December 2015. https://doi.org/10.1109/ICCV.2015.428. https://ieeexplore.ieee.org/document/7410785/

31. Xiang, J., Zhu, G.: Joint face detection and facial expression recognition with MTCNN. In: 2017 4th International Conference on Information Science and Control Engineering (ICISCE), pp. 424–427 (2017). https://doi.org/10.1109/ICISCE.2017.95

32. Yu, Z., Zhang, C.: Image based static facial expression recognition with multiple deep network learning. In: Proceedings of the 2015 ACM on International Conference on Multimodal Interaction, Seattle, Washington, USA, pp. 435–442. ACM, November 2015. https://doi.org/10.1145/2818346.2830595. https://dl.acm.org/doi/10.1145/2818346.2830595

33. Zhang, K., Zhang, Z., Li, Z., Qiao, Y.: Joint face detection and alignment using multitask cascaded convolutional networks. IEEE Signal Process. Lett. **23**(10), 1499–1503 (2016)
34. Zhang, X., Sugano, Y., Fritz, M., Bulling, A.: Appearance-based gaze estimation in the wild. In: 2015 IEEE Conference on Computer Vision and Pattern Recognition (CVPR), Boston, MA, USA, pp. 4511–4520. IEEE, June 2015. https://doi.org/10.1109/CVPR.2015.7299081. https://ieeexplore.ieee.org/document/7299081/
35. Zhao, X., Zhang, S.: A review on facial expression recognition: feature extraction and classification. IETE Techn. Rev. **33**(5), 505–517 (2016)

Machine Learning to Identify Olive-Tree Cultivars

João Mendes[1,3,6(✉)] ⓘ, José Lima[1,2,6] ⓘ, Lino Costa[3] ⓘ, Nuno Rodrigues[4,6] ⓘ,
Diego Brandão[5] ⓘ, Paulo Leitão[1,6] ⓘ, and Ana I. Pereira[1,3,6] ⓘ

[1] Research Centre in Digitalization and Intelligent Robotics (CeDRI), Instituto
Politécnico de Bragança, 5300-253 Bragança, Portugal
{joao.cmendes,jllima,pleitao,apereira}@ipb.pt
[2] INESC TEC - INESC Technology and Science, Porto, Portugal
[3] ALGORITMI Center, University of Minho, 4710-057 Braga, Portugal
lac@dps.uminho.pt
[4] Centro de Investigação de Montanha (CIMO), Instituto Politécnico de Bragança,
5300-253 Bragança, Portugal
nunorodrigues@ipb.pt
[5] Celso Suckow da Fonseca Federal Center of Technological Education, Rio de
Janeiro, Brazil
diego.brandao@cefet-rj.br
[6] Laboratório para a Sustentabilidade e Tecnologia em Regiões de Montanha
(SusTEC), Instituto Politécnico de Bragança, Campus de Santa Apolónia, 5300-253
Bragança, Portugal

Abstract. The identification of olive-tree cultivars is a lengthy and
expensive process, therefore, the proposed work presents a new strategy for identifying different cultivars of olive trees using their leaf and
machine learning algorithms. In this initial case, four autochthonous
cultivars of the Trás-os-Montes region in Portugal are identified
(Cobrançosa, Madural, Negrinha e Verdeal). With the use of this type
of algorithm, it is expected to replace the previous techniques, saving
time and resources for farmers. Three different machine learning algorithms (Decision Tree, SVM, Random Forest) were also compared and
the results show an overall accuracy rate of the best algorithm (Random
Forest) of approximately 93%.

Keywords: Machine learning · Identification · Leaf · Cultivars ·
Varieties

1 Introduction

Some researchers estimate that people have consumed olive oil and olives for
6000 years, making the olive tree one of the first fruit trees to be domesticated
[14]. However, its origin is not subject to consensus. It is considered acceptable
to say that the olive tree is native to the entire Mediterranean basin with its
origin in Asia Minor, where it is highly abundant and grows in dense forests [1].

A. I. Pereira et al. (Eds.): OL2A 2022, CCIS 1754, pp. 820–835, 2022.
https://doi.org/10.1007/978-3-031-23236-7_56

Since its domestication, olive cultivation has expanded worldwide, being cultivated in dozens of countries on all continents except for Antarctica. Its production is mainly used (90%) for the production of olive oil, with the rest being processed as table olives. All of the countries where they are cultivated, it is possible to highlight 23 countries [14] that are responsible for about 85% of all world olive production. According to the International Olive Council (IOC), of these most representative countries, it is estimated that there are about 139 domesticated cultivars. This number grows significantly if we also consider wild species, making a total of more than 2,000 different cultivars [13].

Olive production is still a developing process despite thousands of years of domestication, breaking production records practically every year. In addition to the production records, the economic valuation also increased, reaching 1.23 billion dollars in world trade transactions in 2020. Portugal is an active part of this process, being responsible for about 6.9% of this value, highlighting as third-ranked among the countries that export the Most [2].

Olive growing is the main activity in Portugal, contributing economically, socially, and environmentally to the country. Looking at data from the National Statistics Institute (INE) for 2019 [22], there are 361,483 hectares of olive groves in the country, on around 118,450 farms, with a particular focus on inland regions, with Alentejo, Trás-os-Montes, Beira Interior, Ribatejo and Oeste being the central producing regions. According to provisional data from the INE [23], the year 2021 was another year of records, with a production of 2.25 million hectoliters of olive oil being expected. Within these dimensions and similarly to the other fruit trees, the olive tree also has different cultivars, each one being more adapted to specific climatic and geographical conditions. The use of different cultivars for the production of olive oil makes it possible to ensure a more harmonious composition of the oil from an organoleptic point of view since each one of them has unique chemical and physical characteristics [19,31]. In addition to the taste, different cultivars also allow to improve the season or date of harvest by selecting types with different maturation periods.

Formerly it was enough to crush the olives and make olive oil. Consumers are showing more and more interest in the composition of the products they buy, olive oil being no exception. There is a need for the farmer's knowledge because there is a great variety of olives. He/She must be able to distinguish the lots and know how to specify the type of cultivars present. This identification makes it possible to add value to the product compared to others. This process can be facilitated in recent olive groves that the producer has already planted. However, it may cause some difficulties in the case of olive groves with some age and where there is no certainty of the cultivars present. In such cases, it is necessary to use identification techniques.

The most of the techniques applied for the identification of cultivars use genetic analysis [5–7,15]. These techniques have a high index of reliability. However, they involve time-consuming and expensive processes requiring laboratory analysis, preventing identification on the farm itself. According to research carried out in recent years, other identification techniques have been observed, using artificial vision. These have encouraging hit rates, as suggested by the authors [8,30,39]. On the other hand, these techniques always use the tree's fruit (olives and seeds) to perform the classification. Thus, they are restricted to a specific time of the year when producers are busy harvesting the fruit. In most cases, it is not possible to have the time necessary for them to assist in the identification process.

Analyzing the problems that arise from the techniques presented above, the focus of this work is to ensure an innovative form of identification, on-site, with minimal impact on the tree and that can be carried out at any season of the year. In this way and analyzing what is being done in other crops, the presented solution involves using machine learning algorithms to identify the leaves of the tree. This solution solves practically all the problems shown above and guarantees an instant classification without having to resort to specialized technicians. It is possible to do it any time of the year since the olive tree is a permanent leaf tree. We also guarantee that the impact on the tree is null as it is not necessary to take samples to ensure identification.

This implementation becomes easier considering the advances in the area of artificial intelligence algorithms. Following the hardware developments, this type of algorithm has proven to be highly qualified for solving this type of task, being applied to various species such as pistachios [20], grapes [28], apples [27], among others and other examples [18,26].

In this way, it is the purpose of this work to analyze various types of machine learning algorithms, comparing them to each other, in order to understand which one presents better results for the intended classification. To this end, a survey of related works are carried out, composed not only of the most used methods for the identification of cultivars but also which are the most used machine learning algorithms for image classification, which will be presented in Sect. 2. Then, in the Sect. 3, the proposed methodology will be discussed. In the Sect. 4, the main results and their analysis will be presented, and finally, the Sect. 5 will address the conclusion and main future works.

2   Related Works

A literature review was conducted on the various identification techniques applied to identify olive variety. For this purpose, two databases were used (Scopus and Web of Science), where two terms, "Olive identification cultivars" or "Olive variety identification", were searched. The search resulted in 921 and 536 documents in the WOS and Scopus databases. After their collection, the R software was used, combined with the Bibliometrix tool [4], where trends and main groupings of keywords were analyzed.

This first research resulted in several keywords indicating that most of the published articles use genetic identification techniques, microsatellites [37], simple-sequence repeats (SSRs) markers [10], and mainly random amplified polymorphic DNA (RAPDS) [16] and single nucleotide polymorphisms (SNPs) [35]. This type of technique achieves high rates of effectiveness, however, as this is not the focus of the article, a second research was carried out in which the term "learning" was added to the terms previously used. This second iteration resulted in an article that fits the theme, in the article [36], the authors present a method of identifying olive tree cultivars using deep learning algorithms and ISSR markers. They use a dataset with 800 training and 200 test images to train a convolutional neural network. As a result, they have an overall accuracy of 89.57% across four different leaf cultivars.

With no more published articles identified in this area, it was necessary to carry out a new search, leaving aside the term "olive" and adding "Leaf". By searching the words "identification cultivars learning leaf" or "variety identification learning leaf" within this group, it was possible to verify the existence of some articles that use tree leaves and artificial intelligence algorithms to identify cultivars, as is the case of Liu, et al., who present in their paper [27] a new method for classifying apple cultivars. In this study, a TensorFlow model was developed capable of identifying fourteen distinct apple cultivars with an overall accuracy of 97.11%. The authors of the article used a self-built dataset with 12,435 images.

Similarly, the authors of the article [38] developed a system based on convolutional neural network to identify twelve distinct bean cultivars belonging to three species. The results obtained were divided into three different classes, evaluated by classifying species (level I) with an accuracy of 95.86%, cultivars from the same species (level II) with 91.37%, and cultivars from different species (level III) with 86.87%.

Another example is the grapevine leaves, presented in the article [32] using the six most representative cultivars of that region with 240 images for training and 60 for testing (using data-augmentation techniques). The authors present a model of Deep Convolutional Neural Network, based on the transfer learning technique with a VGG16 structure, in which the structure was modified, adding the global average pooling layer, dense layers, a batch normalization layer, and a dropout layer. The results obtained by the authors are pretty encouraging, achieving accuracy in recognizing and grouping different cultivars of grapevine with an average classification of over 99%

As can be seen, the application of artificial intelligence algorithms in agriculture and, more specifically in identifying both cultivars and species is still a recent process and development. Thus, the number of published articles is still restricted to some species and specific algorithms. There is, therefore, the possibility of exploring the behavior in other species and other types of algorithms to improve identification efficiencies, thus making this type of process increasingly reliable.

3   Method and Materials

As the main objective of this work is to develop an artificial intelligence system capable of identifying the different cultivars of olive trees present in the region, there is a set of steps to be taken and implemented, thus ensuring the correct functioning of the system. Therefore, this section was divided into subsections: Dataset, Classification Models, Evaluation Metrics, and Methodology.

3.1   Dataset

Machine learning (ML) systems work similarly to humans, learning from experience. However, in the case of ML, this experience is controlled, with the programmer responsible for all of it. The experience we talk about here is nothing more than the dataset made available to the algorithms for their training and testing, on which all the success or failure of the application will depend. It is a consensus in the literature that the performance presented by the machine learning algorithms is entirely dependent on the dataset that is used [24]. In this way, and since it is an innovative approach to the problem in question, it was necessary to create a sufficiently large dataset of images to ensure the operation of supervised classification algorithms.

The process of creating the dataset consists of several stages. The initial phase is collecting leaves, prepared in partnership with certified technical personnel in the area, in monovarietal olive groves, to be sure of the cultivars collected.

This collection process followed all seasons of the year, analyzing all times of growth and recession of leaves and other factors that impact their development, such as water or nutrient stress, thus ensuring correct identification, regardless of the phase and conditions of the tree. In this way, samples were collected from several olive groves in the district of Bragança, in the most random way possible, leaves from the inside and outside of the canopy, leaves of the year and older leaves, with an average of 20–25 leaves per tree being collected.

After collecting the leaves, it is necessary to digitize them. This process was carried out with the help of a digital camera with a resolution of 2610×4640 pixels. All samples were photographed in RGB type and JPG format. The background image was white to facilitate their treatment and application in the algorithms.

After digitizing the samples, their pre-processing was realized. Depending on the sample size, some processes were carried out. The first step was the cutting of the images. This was done autonomously, using threshold and find contour techniques to identify the shape of the leaf and then cut it out. For this purpose, the image was changed to gray format, and the adaptive gaussian-weighted [11] threshold method was used. After this transformation, the OpenCV library was used to find the image contour using the findContours function. It allows identifying the sheet's shape that will define the area to be cut. After obtaining the area size to be cropped, it was applied to the original image (RGB). The last step of the pre-processing was to resize the images to a resolution of 299×299 pixels to facilitate the algorithms' processing.

Once the pre-processing was completed, the result obtained was a dataset with approximately 1500 images of the region's four most representative categories (Fig. 1). A balance was also made between the categories, ensuring that they all had the same number of images.

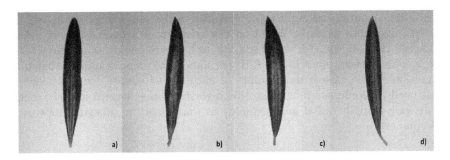

Fig. 1. Dataset cultivars: a) Cobrançosa; b) Madural; c) Negrinha; d) Verdeal

3.2   Classification Models

The identification of olive tree cultivars is a typical classification problem. In this type of problem, the main objective is to predict the category of an unobserved data based on the algorithm's input data. Three supervised classification algorithms [25] will be compared for the intended effect in this case.

The choice of these algorithms was based on a bibliographic research process, the articles presented in the Scopus and WOS databases were gathered, in the time interval from 2018 to 2022 that had the terms "Machine learning classification comparison" or "Machine learning classification leaf". This resulted in a universe of 6096 articles, which were later analyzed with the bibliometrix software. After the analysis, the most used author keywords were used to choose the algorithms and it was concluded that the most used algorithms are the Support vector machine (SVM), and Random Forest (RF). Aside from these, the Decision Tree algorithm (CART) was also selected due to its straightforward interpretation, easily identifying which variables have the most significant influence on the classification of images. In addition to this advantage, it is a method that does not require a long training process and, therefore, can save a lot of modeling time [40].

Decision Tree. Decision trees are one of several supervised machine learning methods, introduced in 1986 by JR Quinlan [34]. It is obtained by recursively partitioning the data space and fitting a simple prediction model within each partition. As a result, the partitioning can be graphically represented as a decision tree, which can be used for classification and regression. Classification trees are designed for dependent variables that take on a finite number of unordered values, with prediction error measured in terms of the cost of misclassification [29].

Support Vector Machine. Originally proposed to build a linear classifier, the support vector machine (SVM) algorithm was developed by Vapnik in 1963 [21]. Used as a supervised machine learning algorithm, SVM can be applied to linear and non-linear data, making it quite versatile in the range of possible uses. The way this algorithm works is based on the creation of a decision limit between two classes that allows later the prediction of labels of one or more characteristic vectors. This decision limit is called Hyperplane, and its positioning is calculated in function of the closest data points of each of the classes (support vectors). When used in nonlinear functions, this algorithm uses several kernel functions (linear, polynomial, radial and sigmoid) to maximize the margins between the Hyperplanes [3].

Random Forest. The Random Forest (RF) algorithms are the most recent of those chosen for this comparison, published for the first time in 2001 in the article by Leo Breiman [12]. This type of algorithms has a field of applications similar to the previous ones, being able to be used both in regression or in classification problems [9]. Its operation follows a simple but very effective concept, the wisdom of crowds, i.e., the combination of several decision trees (not correlated with each other) operated as a committee, will always produce better results than any of the individual constituents. The constitution of RF models is composed of several decision trees, each one of which is trained on a sample of the original training data, and searches only on a randomly selected subset of the input variables to determine a split. To elaborate the final classification, each of the trees casts a unit vote of the obtained class, and, finally, the classifier's output is determined by the majority of the votes of the trees [17].

3.3   Evaluation Metrics

Since this is a classification problem, all the used metrics will be based on the confusion matrix generated for each algorithm, so it is essential to define all its constituents. Based on the predefined constitution for any type of binary problem, in this case too, the confusion matrix will be composed of True Positives (Predicted Positive and truly Positive), True Negatives (Predicted Negative and truly Negative), False Positives (Predicted Positive but truly Negative) and False Negatives (Predicted Negative but truly Positive). However, in this specific case, we will have a confusion matrix depending on the olive tree categories, which will resemble as presented in Table 1.

Table 1. Confusion matrix example.

		Predict label			
		Cobrançosa (c)	Madural (m)	Negrinha (n)	Verdeal (v)
True label	Cobrançosa (c)	N_{cc}	N_{cm}	N_{cn}	N_{cv}
	Madural (m)	N_{mc}	N_{mm}	N_{mn}	N_{mv}
	Negrinha (n)	N_{nc}	N_{nm}	N_{nn}	N_{nv}
	Verdeal (v)	N_{vc}	N_{vm}	N_{vn}	N_{vv}

As possible to seen in Table 1, the arrangement is a little different from the traditional True Positives/True Negatives, being necessary to add some values to arrive at some categories, such as:

- Cobrançosa True Positives (TP) = N_{cc}
- Cobrançosa False Positive (FP) = $N_{mc} + N_{nc} + N_{vc}$
- Cobrançosa True Negative (TN) = $N_{mm} + N_{mn} + N_{mv} + N_{nm} + N_{nn} + N_{nv} + N_{vm} + N_{vn} + N_{vv}$
- Cobrançosa False Negative (FN) = $N_{cm} + N_{cn} + N_{cv}$

Where N_{cc} represents the number of predicted Cobrançosa that are actually Cobrançosa and so on. Once the confusion matrix is explained, all the other metrics that will be based on that with very simplified calculations, as follows:

Accuracy. The accuracy is the most used metric in this type of problem, its formula describes the number of correct predictions as a function of all predictions made and can be calculated as (Eq. 1):

$$Accuracy = \frac{TP + TN}{TP + FP + TN + FN} \tag{1}$$

Precision. The precision is used to measure positive patterns that are correctly predicted from the total predicted patterns in a positive class and is calculated using (Eq. 2):

$$Precision(p) = \frac{TP}{TP + FP} \tag{2}$$

Recall. The recall (Eq. 3) is used to measure the fraction of True Positives that were correctly classified:

$$Recall(r) = \frac{TP}{TP + TN} \tag{3}$$

F-score. The traditional F-score (or F1) is the harmonic mean of precision and recall and is defined by (Eq. 4):

$$F - score = \frac{2 * Precision(p) * Recall(r)}{Precision(p) + Recall(r)} \tag{4}$$

3.4 Methodology

All the algorithms presented in this work were tested, trained, and implemented on a computer equipped with an Intel(R) Core(TM) i7-10875H processor, with a RAM DDR4 32 GB memory and Python version 3.8.12 using the machine learning library scikit-learn [33]. The methodology used is shown in Fig. 2.

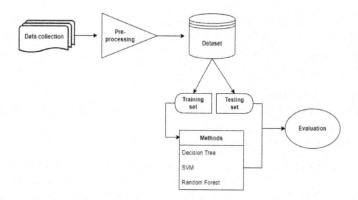

Fig. 2. Proposed system methodology

```
{'C': 0.1,
 'break_ties': False,
 'cache_size': 200,
 'class_weight': None,
 'coef0': 0.0,
 'decision_function_shape': 'ovr',
 'degree': 3,
 'gamma': 0.001,
 'kernel': 'poly',
 'max_iter': -1,
 'probability': False,
 'random_state': None,
 'shrinking': True,
 'tol': 0.001,
 'verbose': False}
```

```
{'ccp_alpha': 0.0,
 'class_weight': None,
 'criterion': 'gini',
 'max_depth': None,
 'max_features': None,
 'max_leaf_nodes': None,
 'min_impurity_decrease': 0.0,
 'min_samples_leaf': 1,
 'min_samples_split': 2,
 'min_weight_fraction_leaf': 0.0,
 'random_state': 0,
 'splitter': 'best'}
```

```
{'bootstrap': True,
 'ccp_alpha': 0.0,
 'class_weight': None,
 'criterion': 'gini',
 'max_depth': None,
 'max_features': 'auto',
 'max_leaf_nodes': None,
 'max_samples': None,
 'min_impurity_decrease': 0.0,
 'min_samples_leaf': 1,
 'min_samples_split': 2,
 'min_weight_fraction_leaf': 0.0,
 'n_estimators': 100,
 'n_jobs': None,
 'oob_score': False,
 'random_state': 0,
 'verbose': 0,
 'warm_start': False}
```

Fig. 3. SVM best hyper-parameters.

Fig. 4. Decision tree best hyper-parameters.

Fig. 5. Random Forest best hyper-parameters.

After collecting and pre-processing the dataset, the training and test sets were divided. Here, it was stipulated *a priori* to use 90% of the dataset data for training and the remaining 10% for testing the algorithms. This division was done randomly using the split function of the library used. In this way, cross-validation of 5 times was applied to each of the algorithms either in the training stage or in the test stage.

The algorithm training process was an adapted process where some adjustments were made to improve its performance. This adjustment was made with the GridSearchCV function that allows to study the behavior of the fitting function according to the hyperparameters used, and in this way optimize their behavior. The first algorithm to be tested was the SVM, where the parameters of "C" (Regularization parameter), Gamma (kernel coefficient), and even the kernel to be used were tested, since it is a non-linear problem. After the evaluation with the GridSearchCV function and with a five times Cross-validation, the following combination of hyper-parameters was obtained in Fig. 3.

Observing Fig. 3, it is possible to verify that from all the used combinations, the one that produced the best results was C = 0.1, Gamma = 0.001, and kernel = "poly", with the remaining hyperparameters with default values. The exact process was carried out for the remaining DT (Fig. 4) and RF (Fig. 5) algorithms. In these cases, the hyperparameters that were tested were the minimum number of samples needed to split an internal node (min samples split), the minimum number of samples required to be at a leaf node (min samples leaf) and the maximum depth of the tree (max depth). Adding one more in the case of RF, the number of trees in the "forest" (n estimators), obtaining ideal values similar to those adopted by default in the respective algorithms.

4   Results and Discussion

After the optimization of the algorithms parameters was completed, their training was carried out by adopting the respective best parameters values. Once the training process was completed, they were then evaluated in the test set with the metrics chosen in Subsect. 3.3. To ensure that the algorithm generalizes correctly and can identify the leaves regardless of their position, color, or dimensions, the test set was randomly divided, and five-time cross-validation was used. The results obtained are presented in the following subsections:

4.1   Decision Tree

The training of this specific algorithm with the training dataset (1224 images) took approximately 17.414 s. Predicting the ratings in the test set (136 images) took about 1.281 s. The confusion matrix is presented in Table 2 was obtained through the average of the five tests performed.

Table 2. Decision tree confusion matrix.

		Predict label			
		Cobrançosa	Madural	Negrinha	Verdeal
True Label	Cobrançosa	22	4	2	6
	Madural	5	26	1	2
	Negrinha	4	2	27	1
	Verdeal	4	2	1	27

As seen from Table 2, the most problematic category is Cobrançosa, with only 22 hits in the set of 34 possible while the remaining categories have a similar rate of hits between them. For better understanding the behavior of the algorithm in the classification, the other metrics were applied, noting that here the results are the averages of the five iterations performed (Table 3).

Analyzing the data in Table 3, it is possible to see that the behavior of the metrics is similar for all categories, being the species Negrinha the one that

Table 3. Decision tree metrics.

	Precision	Recall	F-score	Accuracy
Cobrançosa	0.66	0.65	0.65	
Madural	0.78	0.78	0.78	0.75
Negrinha	0.86	0.80	0.83	
Verdeal	0.74	0.78	0.76	

allows a better identification. The species Cobrançosa as it had already been perceptible in the confusion matrix is the species that cause the most identification difficulties in this algorithm. Observing the accuracy as a whole, it is noticeable that the Decision Tree still has some limitations in classifying of the four categories.

4.2 SVM

The training of the SVM algorithm took approximately 64.329 s, 3.5 times more than the Decision Tree when compared to the time required to make the test set predictions. The SVM also needs more time, using approximately 8.479 s, about 6.5 times more than the competitor. The confusion matrix resulting from the predictions of the SVM method is presented in Table 4.

Table 4. SVM confusion matrix.

		Predict label			
		Cobrançosa	Madural	Negrinha	Verdeal
True label	Cobrançosa	25	4	1	4
	Madural	4	28	0	2
	Negrinha	2	1	30	1
	Verdeal	5	1	1	27

In agreement with the previous results, the SVM algorithm also has some difficulties in identifying the Cobrançosa category, which is the one with the fewest hits, but already with an improvement of 3 images. Looking at the remaining categories, there is an improvement, albeit slight, in all categories, reaching the point of identifying 30 out of 34 possible examples in category Negrinha. The results of the remaining evaluation metrics are presented in Table 5.

As observed in the confusion matrix, from Table 5, it is possible to verify an increase in the performance of the SVM algorithm when compared to the Decision Tree. Variety Negrinha continues to be the most easily identifiable, achieving a harmonic average (F-score) of 0.9. When analyzing the accuracy of the SVM algorithm, it was noticed that despite the difficulty in identifying the first variety, there was a significant improvement compared to the previous method, with an increase of 0.06.

Table 5. SVM metrics.

	Precision	Recall	F-score	Accuracy
Cobrançosa	0.71	0.75	0.73	
Madural	0.84	0.83	0.84	0.81
Negrinha	0.92	0.88	0.90	
Verdeal	0.80	0.78	0.79	

4.3 Random Forest

The latest algorithm to be tested, Random Forest, took approximately 104.493 s to perform its training, six times more when compared to the Decision Tree. To perform the test set classifications, this algorithm took about 1.318 s, roughly the same time as the Decision Tree method. The results obtained by this latest algorithm are presented in the following confusion matrix Table 6.

Table 6. Random Forest confusion matrix.

		Predict label			
		Cobrançosa	Madural	Negrinha	Verdeal
True label	Cobrançosa	30	1	0	3
	Madural	1	33	0	0
	Negrinha	1	0	33	0
	Verdeal	3	0	0	31

Observing the values in Table 6, it is possible to verify that the Random Forest algorithm has a higher hit rate than its competitors, achieving 33 out of 34 hits in two categories. Looking deeper, Table 7 summarizes the remaining evaluation metrics presented below.

Table 7. Random Forest metrics.

	Precision	Recall	F-score	Accuracy
Cobrançosa	0.87	0.88	0.88	
Madural	0.98	0.95	0.97	0.93
Negrinha	0.97	0.98	0.97	
Verdeal	0.91	0.90	0.90	

After analyzing Table 7, it is possible to verify a significant improvement in the system's overall accuracy. Despite continuing to be the most difficult to identify, the Cobrançosa variety presented an F-score of 0.88, that represents an improvement of 0.15 compared to the SVM algorithm.

In short, after analyzing the results obtained, mainly confusion matrices, we can confirm that there are several mistakes in the identification of cultivars. This failure is undoubtedly linked to the problem's difficulty, emphasizing once again that the visible differences in the leaves are very tenuous, making its identification very complex. In general, it is possible to classify the category Cobrançosa as the most challenging and most susceptible to errors. On the other hand, category Negrinha was the one that showed the highest hit rate in all algorithms.

Regarding the comparison of the algorithms, the method with higher observed accuracy, according to the used metrics, despite having a training time much higher than its competitors, the Random Forest algorithm guaranteed an overall accuracy of 93%, making the identification of olive tree species very reliable.

5   Conclusion and Future Works

The traditional methods of identifying the different cultivars of olive trees resort to genetic analysis. Such processes require time for execution and high associated costs. These factors make species identification a complicated process for farmers who need to do so. With the approach explored here, it is possible to make an identification on the spot, in real-time, and without associated costs. It is undoubtedly an added value for all producers who want to differentiate their oils. In addition to the producers, this approach is also an asset for tourism, giving tourists the ability to understand what type of olive grove they visit and what kind of oil will result from it.

As it was possible to verify throughout the article, there are currently no published articles that use only the image of the leaves to identify the olive tree cultivars. Thus, it becomes difficult to evaluate the effectiveness of the system when compared to other approaches. Observing the leaves of the different types, the difficulty in finding their differences is remarkable. However, analyzing the results obtained through the application of the three algorithms, it became clear that at least one of them can make this identification, not guaranteeing the efficiency rate of genetic methods; however, with an accuracy of 93%, which gives us the motivation to continue in this direction.

In this way, as main future works, it is intended to explore the classification algorithms in depth, approaching the aspect of deep learning. In addition to optimizing the classification model, web and smart devices interfaces will be developed giving the producers the possibility of testing in the field.

Acknowledgement. This work was carried out under the Project "OleaChain: Competências para a sustentabilidade e inovação da cadeia de valor do olival tradicional no Norte Interior de Portugal" (NORTE-06-3559-FSE-000188), an operation to hire highly qualified human resources, funded by NORTE 2020 through the European Social Fund (ESF). The authors are grateful to the Foundation for Science and Technology (FCT, Portugal) for financial support through national funds FCT/MCTES (PIDDAC) to CeDRI (UIDB/05757/2020 and UIDP/05757/2020) and SusTEC (LA/P/0007/2021).

References

1. International olive oil. https://www.internationaloliveoil.org/olive-world/olive-tree/. Accessed 07 June 2022
2. The observatory of economic complexity. https://oec.world/en/profile/hs/olive-oil-fractions-refined-not-chemically-modifie. Accessed 10 May 2022
3. Ahmad, I., Basheri, M., Iqbal, M.J., Rahim, A.: Performance comparison of support vector machine, random forest, and extreme learning machine for intrusion detection. IEEE Access **6**, 33789–33795 (2018)
4. Aria, M., Cuccurullo, C.: Bibliometrix: an R-tool for comprehensive science mapping analysis. J. Informetr. **11**(4), 959–975 (2017)
5. Bautista, R., Crespillo, R., Cánovas, F.M., Gonzalo Claros, M.: Identification of olive-tree cultivars with scar markers. Euphytica **129**(1), 33–41 (2003)
6. Besnard, G., Baradat, P., Bervillé, A.: Olive cultivar identification using nuclear RAPDs and mitochondrial RFLPs. In: International Symposium on Molecular Markers for Characterizing Genotypes and Identifying Cultivars in Horticulture, vol. 546. pp. 317–324 (2000)
7. Besnard, G., Breton, C., Baradat, P., Khadari, B., Bervillé, A.: Cultivar identification in olive based on RAPD markers. J. Am. Soc. Hortic. Sci. **126**(6), 668–675 (2001)
8. Beyaz, A., Özkaya, M.T., İçen, D.: Identification of some Spanish olive cultivars using image processing techniques. Scientia Horticulturae **225**, 286–292 (2017)
9. Biau, G., Scornet, E.: A random forest guided tour. TEST **25**(2), 197–227 (2016). https://doi.org/10.1007/s11749-016-0481-7
10. Bracci, T., Sebastiani, L., Busconi, M., Fogher, C., Belaj, A., Trujillo, I.: SSR markers reveal the uniqueness of olive cultivars from the Italian region of Liguria. Scientia Horticulturae **122**(2), 209–215 (2009)
11. Bradski, G.: The OpenCV library. Dr. Dobb's J. Softw. Tools (2000)
12. Breiman, L.: Random forests. Mach. Learn. **45**(1), 5–32 (2001)
13. Breton, C., Terral, J.F., Pinatel, C., Médail, F., Bonhomme, F., Bervillé, A.: The origins of the domestication of the olive tree. Comptes Rendus Biologies **332**(12), 1059–1064 (2009)
14. International Olive Oil Council: World catalogue of olive varieties. International Olive Oil Council, 2000, Madrid, Spain (2000)
15. Ergulen, E., Ozkaya, M., Ulger, S., Ozilbey, N.: Identification of some Turkish olive cultivars by using RAPD-PCR technique. In: IV International Symposium on Olive Growing, vol. 586, pp. 91–95 (2000)
16. Fabbri, A., Hormaza, J., Polito, V.: Random amplified polymorphic DNA analysis of olive (Olea europaea L.) cultivars. J. Am. Soc. Hortic. Sci. **120**(3), 538–542 (1995)
17. Gislason, P.O., Benediktsson, J.A., Sveinsson, J.R.: Random forests for land cover classification. Pattern Recognit. Lett. **27**(4), 294–300 (2006)
18. Grinblat, G.L., Uzal, L.C., Larese, M.G., Granitto, P.M.: Deep learning for plant identification using vein morphological patterns. Comput. Electron. Agric. **127**, 418–424 (2016)
19. Guinda, A., Lanzón, A., Albi, T.: Differences in hydrocarbons of virgin olive oils obtained from several olive varieties. J. Agric. Food Chem. **44**(7), 1723–1726 (1996)
20. Heidary-Sharifabad, A., Zarchi, M.S., Emadi, S., Zarei, G.: An efficient deep learning model for cultivar identification of a pistachio tree. Br. Food J. (2021)

21. Huang, S., Cai, N., Pacheco, P.P., Narrandes, S., Wang, Y., Xu, W.: Applications of support vector machine (SVM) learning in cancer genomics. Cancer Genomics Proteomics **15**(1), 41–51 (2018)
22. INE: Instituto nacional de estatística, estatísticas agrícolas de base. https://www.ine.pt/xportal/xmain?xpid=INE&xpgid=ine_base_dados. Accessed 11 May 2022
23. INE: Instituto nacional de estatística, previsões agrícolas. https://www.ine.pt/xportal/xmain?xpid=INE&xpgid=ine_destaques&DESTAQUESdest_boui=526211517&DESTAQUESmodo=2. Accessed 11 May 2022
24. Jain, A., et al.: Overview and importance of data quality for machine learning tasks. In: Proceedings of the 26th ACM SIGKDD International Conference on Knowledge Discovery & Data Mining, pp. 3561–3562 (2020)
25. Kotsiantis, S.B., Zaharakis, I., Pintelas, P., et al.: Supervised machine learning: a review of classification techniques. Emerg. Artif. Intell. Appl. Comput. Eng. **160**(1), 3–24 (2007)
26. Larese, M.G., Granitto, P.M.: Hybrid consensus learning for legume species and cultivars classification. In: Agapito, L., Bronstein, M.M., Rother, C. (eds.) ECCV 2014. LNCS, vol. 8928, pp. 201–214. Springer, Cham (2015). https://doi.org/10.1007/978-3-319-16220-1_15
27. Liu, C., Han, J., Chen, B., Mao, J., Xue, Z., Li, S.: A novel identification method for apple (Malus domestica Borkh.) cultivars based on a deep convolutional neural network with leaf image input. Symmetry **12**(2), 217 (2020)
28. Liu, Y., et al.: Development of a mobile application for identification of grapevine (Vitis vinifera L.) cultivars via deep learning. Int. J. Agric. Biol. Eng. **14**(5), 172–179 (2021)
29. Loh, W.Y.: Classification and regression trees. Wiley Interdiscip. Rev. Data Min. Knowl. Discov. **1**(1), 14–23 (2011)
30. Martínez, S.S., Gila, D.M., Beyaz, A., Ortega, J.G., García, J.G.: A computer vision approach based on endocarp features for the identification of olive cultivars. Comput. Electron. Agric. **154**, 341–346 (2018)
31. Montaño, A., Sánchez, A., Casado, F., De Castro, A., Rejano, L.: Chemical profile of industrially fermented green olives of different varieties. Food Chem. **82**(2), 297–302 (2003)
32. Nasiri, A., Taheri-Garavand, A., Fanourakis, D., Zhang, Y.D., Nikoloudakis, N.: Automated grapevine cultivar identification via leaf imaging and deep convolutional neural networks: a proof-of-concept study employing primary Iranian varieties. Plants **10**(8), 1628 (2021)
33. Pedregosa, F., et al.: Scikit-learn: machine learning in Python. J. Mach. Learn. Res. **12**, 2825–2830 (2011)
34. Quinlan, J.R.: Induction of decision trees. Mach. Learn. **1**(1), 81–106 (1986)
35. Reale, S., et al.: SNP-based markers for discriminating olive (Olea europaea L.) cultivars. Genome **49**(9), 1193–1205 (2006)
36. Sesli, M., Yegenoğlu, E., Altıntaa, V.: Determination of olive cultivars by deep learning and ISSR markers. J. Environ. Biol. **41**(2), 426–431 (2020)
37. Shahriari, M., Omrani, A., Falahati-Anbaran, M., Ghareyazei, B., Nankali, A.: Identification of Iranian olive cultivars by using RAPD and microsatellite markers. In: V International Symposium on Olive Growing, vol. 791, pp. 109–115 (2004)
38. Tavakoli, H., Alirezazadeh, P., Hedayatipour, A., Nasib, A.B., Landwehr, N.: Leaf image-based classification of some common bean cultivars using discriminative convolutional neural networks. Comput. Electron. Agric. **181**, 105935 (2021)

39. Vanloot, P., Bertrand, D., Pinatel, C., Artaud, J., Dupuy, N.: Artificial vision and chemometrics analyses of olive stones for varietal identification of five French cultivars. Comput. Electron. Agric. **102**, 98–105 (2014)
40. Zhao, Y., Zhang, Y.: Comparison of decision tree methods for finding active objects. Adv. Space Res. **41**(12), 1955–1959 (2008)

Author Index

Printed in the United States
by Baker & Taylor Publisher Services